CRITICAL SURVEY OF

Long Fiction

Fourth Edition

CRITICAL SURVEY OF

Long Fiction

Fourth Edition

Volume 9

Gore Vidal—Émile Zola

Topical Essays

Editor

Carl Rollyson

Baruch College, City University of New York

SALEM PRESS

Pasadena, California   Hackensack, New Jersey

Editor in Chief: Dawn P. Dawson

Editorial Director: Christina J. Moose
Development Editor: Tracy Irons-Georges
Project Editor: Judy Selhorst
Manuscript Editor: Desiree Dreeuws
Acquisitions Editor: Mark Rehn
Editorial Assistant: Brett S. Weisberg
Research Supervisor: Jeffry Jensen
Research Assistant: Keli Trousdale
Production Editor: Joyce I. Buchea
Design and Graphics: James Hutson
Layout: William Zimmerman
Photo Editor: Cynthia Breslin Beres

Cover photo: Eudora Welty (©Ulf Andersen/Getty Images)

Some of the essays in this work, which have been updated, originally appeared in the following Salem Press publications: *Critical Survey of Long Fiction, English Language Series* (1983), *Critical Survey of Long Fiction, Foreign Language Series* (1984), *Critical Survey of Long Fiction, Supplement* (1987), *Critical Survey of Long Fiction, English Language Series, Revised Edition* (1991; preceding volumes edited by Frank N. Magill), *Critical Survey of Long Fiction, Second Revised Edition* (2000; edited by Carl Rollyson).

∞ The paper used in these volumes conforms to the American National Standard for Permanence of Paper for Printed Library Materials, Z39.48-1992 (R1997).

Library of Congress Cataloging-in-Publication Data

Critical survey of long fiction / editor, Carl Rollyson. — 4th ed.
p. cm.
Includes bibliographical references and index.
ISBN 978-1-58765-535-7 (set : alk. paper) — ISBN 978-1-58765-536-4 (vol. 1 : alk. paper) — ISBN 978-1-58765-537-1 (vol. 2 : alk. paper) — ISBN 978-1-58765-538-8 (vol. 3 : alk. paper) — ISBN 978-1-58765-539-5 (vol. 4 : alk. paper) — ISBN 978-1-58765-540-1 (vol. 5 : alk. paper) — ISBN 978-1-58765-541-8 (vol. 6 : alk. paper) — ISBN 978-1-58765-542-5 (vol. 7 : alk. paper) — ISBN 978-1-58765-543-2 (vol. 8 : alk. paper) — ISBN 978-1-58765-544-9 (vol. 9 : alk. paper) — ISBN 978-1-58765-545-6 (vol. 10 : alk. paper)
1. Fiction—History and criticism. 2. Fiction—Bio-bibliography—Dictionaries. 3. Authors—Biography—Dictionaries. I. Rollyson, Carl E. (Carl Edmund)
PN3451.C75 2010
809.3—dc22

2009044410

First Printing

PRINTED IN CANADA

CONTENTS

COMPLETE LIST OF CONTENTS

Volume 1

Volume 2

Volume 3

Volume 4

Volume 5

Volume 6

Volume 7

Volume 8

Volume 9

Volume 10

PRONUNCIATION KEY

Foreign and unusual or ambiguous English-language names of profiled authors may be unfamiliar to some users of the *Critical Survey of Long Fiction*. To help readers pronounce such names correctly, phonetic spellings using the character symbols listed below appear in parentheses immediately after the first mention of the author's name in the narrative text. Stressed syllables are indicated in capital letters, and syllables are separated by hyphens.

VOWEL SOUNDS

Symbol	*Spelled (Pronounced)*
a	answer (AN-suhr), laugh (laf), sample (SAM-puhl), that (that)
ah	father (FAH-thur), hospital (HAHS-pih-tuhl)
aw	awful (AW-fuhl), caught (kawt)
ay	blaze (blayz), fade (fayd), waiter (WAYT-ur), weigh (way)
eh	bed (behd), head (hehd), said (sehd)
ee	believe (bee-LEEV), cedar (SEE-dur), leader (LEED-ur), liter (LEE-tur)
ew	boot (bewt), lose (lewz)
i	buy (bi), height (hit), lie (li), surprise (sur-PRIZ)
ih	bitter (BIH-tur), pill (pihl)
o	cotton (KO-tuhn), hot (hot)
oh	below (bee-LOH), coat (koht), note (noht), wholesome (HOHL-suhm)
oo	good (good), look (look)
ow	couch (kowch), how (how)
oy	boy (boy), coin (koyn)
uh	about (uh-BOWT), butter (BUH-tuhr), enough (ee-NUHF), other (UH-thur)

CONSONANT SOUNDS

Symbol	*Spelled (Pronounced)*
ch	beach (beech), chimp (chihmp)
g	beg (behg), disguise (dihs-GIZ), get (geht)
j	digit (DIH-juht), edge (ehj), jet (jeht)
k	cat (kat), kitten (KIH-tuhn), hex (hehks)
s	cellar (SEHL-ur), save (sayv), scent (sehnt)
sh	champagne (sham-PAYN), issue (IH-shew), shop (shop)
ur	birth (burth), disturb (dihs-TURB), earth (urth), letter (LEH-tur)
y	useful (YEWS-fuhl), young (yuhng)
z	business (BIHZ-nehs), zest (zehst)
zh	vision (VIH-zhuhn)

CRITICAL SURVEY OF

Long Fiction

Fourth Edition

GORE VIDAL

Born: West Point, New York; October 3, 1925
Also known as: Eugene Luther Vidal; Edgar Box

PRINCIPAL LONG FICTION

Williwaw, 1946
In a Yellow Wood, 1947
The City and the Pillar, 1948 (revised 1965)
The Season of Comfort, 1949
A Search for the King: A Twelfth Century Legend, 1950
Dark Green, Bright Red, 1950
Death in the Fifth Position, 1952 (as Edgar Box)
The Judgment of Paris, 1952 (revised 1965)
Death Before Bedtime, 1953 (as Box)
Death Likes It Hot, 1954 (as Box)
Messiah, 1954 (revised 1965)
Julian, 1964
Washington, D.C., 1967
Myra Breckinridge, 1968
Two Sisters: A Memoir in the Form of a Novel, 1970
Burr, 1973
Myron, 1974
1876, 1976
Kalki, 1978
Creation, 1981
Duluth, 1983
Lincoln, 1984
Empire, 1987
Hollywood: A Novel of America in the 1920's, 1990
Live from Golgotha, 1992
The Smithsonian Institution, 1998
The Golden Age, 2000

OTHER LITERARY FORMS

Gore Vidal (vuh-DAHL) has written short stories as well as novels, and he is known as a master essayist, having regularly published collections of essays. Vidal also wrote and adapted plays for the small screen during the so-called golden age of television, and he wrote screenplays during the last days of the Hollywood studio system.

ACHIEVEMENTS

Gore Vidal is considered a leading American literary figure. While primarily a novelist, he has mastered almost every genre, except poetry. He has won success in films, in television, and on Broadway. Many readers consider him a better essayist than novelist, though Vidal emphatically rejects that judgment.

While many of his contemporaries have focused their writings on mundane details of everyday life, Vidal has continued to write the novel of ideas. He has maintained his focus on the largest questions: What is the nature of Western civilization? What flaws have prevented the United States from achieving its democratic promise? How does a free individual live an intellectually fulfilling and ethically proper life in a corrupt society? These concerns are reflected not only in his writing but also in his political activities, including a bid for the U.S. Senate in 1982. Vidal won a National Book Award in 1993 for his collection of essays *United States: Essays, 1952-1992*, and his books are routinely included in "best" lists and course syllabi.

BIOGRAPHY

Gore Vidal was born Eugene Luther Vidal on October 3, 1925, at West Point, where his father, Eugene Vidal, taught aeronautics at the military academy. His father helped to establish civil aviation in the United States and later became the director of air commerce in Franklin D. Roosevelt's presidential administration. His mother, Nina, was a beautiful socialite, the daughter of Thomas P. Gore, the powerful U.S. senator from Oklahoma, and soon after Vidal's birth, the family moved to Senator Gore's mansion in Washington, D.C. He began using the name Gore Vidal when he was fourteen years old.

One of the most learned of contemporary writers, Vidal never went to college. His education began at the home of Senator Gore: The senator, who was blind, used his grandson as a reader and in return gave him free run of his huge library. In 1935, Nina and Eugene Vidal were divorced, and Nina married Hugh D. Auchincloss, a member of a prominent family of bankers and lawyers. Gore Vidal then moved with his mother to the Auchincloss estate on the Potomac River in Virginia, where his education included rubbing shoulders with the nation's political, economic, and journalistic elite.

Vidal was brought up removed from real life, he has stated, protected from such unpleasant realities as the effects of the Great Depression. He joined other patrician sons at St. Albans School, after which he toured Europe in 1939, then spent one year at Los Alamos School in New Mexico before finishing his formal education with three years at Phillips Exeter Academy in New Hampshire.

In 1943, Vidal joined the U.S. Army and served on a transport ship in the Aleutian Islands. His military service gave him subject matter and time to write his first novel, *Williwaw*. He finished his second book, *In a Yellow Wood*, before he left the Army. In 1946, he went to work as an editor for E. P. Dutton and soon published *The City and the Pillar*. Good critical and popular response brought him recognition as one of the nation's best young authors. He used Guatemala as his home base from 1947 to 1949 and then bought an old estate, Edgewater, on the Hudson River in New York. He wrote five more novels before he was thirty years old.

Meanwhile, a controversy engulfed Vidal and shifted his life and career. *The City and the Pillar* deals with homosexuality, and because of this, the literary establishment removed him from its list of "approved" writers and critics largely ignored his next few novels. To earn money in the 1950's, Vidal wrote mysteries under the name Edgar Box and wrote scripts for the major live television dramatic series. He also became a successful screenwriter, with such films as *The Catered Affair* (1956) and *Suddenly Last Summer* (1959, with Tennessee Williams). In addition, he wrote plays. He achieved major Broadway successes with *Visit to a Small Planet: A Comedy Akin to a Vaudeville* (pr. 1957) and *The Best Man: A Play About Politics* (pr., pb. 1960).

Gore Vidal. (Jane Bown)

Vidal has called these his years of "piracy," aimed at gaining enough financial security to allow him to return to his first love, novels. His years in Hollywood and on Broadway established Vidal's public reputation for sophisticated wit and intelligence. He ran for Congress in 1960, supported by such famous friends as Eleanor Roosevelt, Joanne Woodward, and Paul Newman. Although he was defeated, he ran better in his district than did the Democratic presidential candidate, John F. Kennedy. Vidal shared a stepfather with Jacqueline Kennedy and had become friends with the Kennedy family; this connection pulled him further into public affairs. In 1964, Vidal published *Julian*, his first novel in ten years. It was a major critical and public success. Many best sellers followed, including *Myra Breckinridge*, *Burr*, *Creation*, and *Lincoln*.

Conflicts over civil rights, the Vietnam War, and the Watergate scandal made the 1960's and 1970's one of the most tumultuous periods in

American political history. Vidal's essays, published in major journals, established his reputation as an astute and hard-hitting social critic. His acid-tongued social commentary brought him to many television talk shows, where he made many friends and enemies. He had spectacular public feuds with members of the Kennedy family and with such fellow celebrities and authors as William F. Buckley, Jr., Norman Mailer, and Truman Capote. In 1968, Vidal was a cofounder of the New Party, and in 1970-1972 he was cochair of the People's Party. In 1982, he ran for the U.S. Senate in California and, out of a field of eleven in the Democratic primary, came in second, behind Governor Jerry Brown.

The range and breadth of Vidal's interests showed in *United States*, a thousand-page collection of his essays that won the National Book Award for 1993. Here one finds literary discussions ranging from readings of Henry James and William Dean Howells to attacks on those of his contemporaries (John Barth, Thomas Pynchon) whom he calls "the academic hacks," novelists writing only for an audience of literature professors. He also attacks what he calls the "heterosexual dictatorship" and the increasingly grandiose and imperial self-image of the United States.

Palimpsest: A Memoir (1995) is a book that Vidal said he had sworn never to write, a personal memoir. In it he reveals his family background and tells of his struggles with establishments literary and political, concluding with his view of his quarrel with the Kennedy family. In a lyrical passage, he writes of the great love of his teenage years, a classmate named Jimmie Trimble, who died in World War II. In the 1990's, Vidal added a new aspect to his public persona by appearing as a character actor in several films, including *Bob Roberts* (1992), *With Honors* (1994), *The Shadow Conspiracy* (1997), and *Gattaca* (1997).

In 1998 Vidal became embroiled in further public debate as a member of the committee that selected the Modern Library's one hundred best twentieth century English-language novels. One of many controversial aspects of the list was the absence of those writers he called academic hacks. Vidal insisted that his role was only to make recommendations and that he bore no responsibility for the final selections.

In *Point to Point Navigation: A Memoir, 1964 to 2006* (2006), Vidal updates *Palimpsest*. In this work he bids farewell to Howard Auster, his companion of fifty-three years, who died in 2003. Following Auster's death, Vidal moved from his Italian villa to the Hollywood Hills of Los Angeles, where, he says, he is graciously edging toward the door marked Exit.

Analysis

In an age and country that have little room for the traditional man of letters, Gore Vidal has established that role for himself by the force of his writing and intelligence and by his public prominence. He is a classicist in writing style, emphasizing plot, clarity, and order. Iconoclastic wit and cool, detached intelligence characterize his elegant style.

Because Vidal knows most contemporary public figures—including jet-setters, Wall Street insiders, and Washington wheeler-dealers—many readers comb his writing to glean intriguing bits of gossip. *Two Sisters: A Memoir in the Form of a Novel*, for example, is often read as an account of the lives and loves of Jacqueline Kennedy Onassis and her sister, Lee Bouvier. Some people search Vidal's writing for clues to his own life and sexuality.

Vidal draws from his own rich experience as he creates his fictional world, yet he is a very private person, and he resists people's urge to reduce everyone to a known quantity. He refracts real people and events through his delightfully perverse imagination. The unwary gossipmonger can easily fall into Vidal's many traps.

If readers can learn little of certainty from Vidal's fiction about such famous people as the Kennedys, they can learn much about his major concern, the nature of Western civilization and the individual's role within it. He is interested in politics—how people make society work—and religion, the proper perspective on life as one faces death. In his early novels, one can see Vidal's interest in ideas. Vidal's young male protagonists find themselves entering a relativistic world in which all gods are dead. A "heterosexual dictatorship" and a life-numbing Christian establishment try to impose false moral absolutes. Society tempts the unwary by offering comfort and security and then removes the life-sustaining freedom of those who succumb to the temptation.

The City and the Pillar

In writing his third novel, Vidal probed the boundaries of society's sexual tolerance. The result, *The City and the Pillar*, affected the rest of his career. To Vidal, the book is a study of obsession; to many guardians of moral purity, it seems to glorify homosexuality. In American fiction up to that point, either homosexuality had been barely implied or the homosexual characters had been presented as bizarre or doomed figures. In contrast, Vidal's protagonist is an average young American man, confused by his homosexuality and obsessed with the memory of a weekend encounter with another young man, Bob Ford. While Bob regards the weekend as a diversion to be enjoyed and forgotten, Jim enters the gay world. If he is doomed, it is not because he prefers men to women but because he is obsessed with the past. When he finally meets Bob again and tries to revive the affair, Bob rejects him. Enraged and humiliated, Jim kills Bob. Vidal later issued a revised edition in which Jim forces Bob to submit sexually; in the emotional backwash from the confrontation, Jim realizes the sterility of his obsession.

Vidal later said that he could have been president of the United States had it not been for the homosexual label applied to him. Readers assumed that Vidal must be the character he invented. Vidal is a sexual libertarian who believes that sex in any form between consenting adults is a gift to be enjoyed. He believes, furthermore, that a "heterosexual dictatorship" has distorted human sexuality. "There is no such thing as a homosexual or a heterosexual person," Vidal says. "There are only homo- or heterosexual acts. Most people are a mixture of impulses if not practices, and what anyone does with a willing partner is of no social or cosmic significance." In 1948, people were not ready for that message. Although *The City and the Pillar* was a best seller, such powerful establishment journals as *The New York Times* eliminated Vidal from their lists of "approved" writers. His next few books were failures, critically and financially.

The Judgment of Paris

Two of the books ignored after *The City and the Pillar*, *The Judgment of Paris* and *Messiah*, later found admirers. In these novels Vidal began to develop the style that is so recognizably his own. Moreover, it is in these two books that Vidal fully expresses his philosophy of life: "I have put nearly everything that I feel into *The Judgment of Paris*, a comedic version, and *Messiah*, a tragic version of my sense of man's curious estate."

In *The Judgment of Paris*, Vidal retells the ancient myth of Paris, who was asked by Zeus to choose the most beautiful of three goddesses: Hera (power), Athena (knowledge), and Aphrodite (love). In the novel, Philip Warren, an American innocent, meets Regina Durham (Hera) in Rome, Sophia Oliver (Athena) in Egypt, and Anna Morris (Aphrodite) in Paris. Regina and Sophia offer him, respectively, political power and the life of the intellect. To Philip, political power rests on the manipulation of people, and intellectual life requires the seclusion of the scholar from humanity. He chooses love, but he also leaves Anna Morris. His choice implies that one must accept no absolutes; nothing is permanent, not even love. One must open oneself to love and friendship and prepare to accept change as one moves through life.

Messiah

Many readers consider *Messiah* an undiscovered masterpiece. Religion, the human response to death and nothingness, has been a major concern in Vidal's fiction, especially in *Messiah*, *Kalki*, and *Creation*. *Messiah* is narrated by Eugene Luther, an old man secluded in Egypt. He is a founding member of a new religion that has displaced Christianity and is spreading over the world. Luther, who has broken with the church he helped build, scribbles his memoirs as he awaits death. The movement was built around John Cave, but Cave was killed by his disciples and Cave's word was spread by an organization using modern advertising techniques. One can readily find in *Messiah* characters representing Jesus Christ, Saint Paul, the Virgin Mary, and Martin Luther. The process by which religious movements are formed interests Vidal. *Messiah* shows, by analogy, how the early church fathers manipulated the Gospels and the Christ figure for their own selfish needs.

Julian

With *Julian*, Vidal again examines the formation of a religious movement, this time looking directly at Christianity. Julian the Apostate, Roman emperor from 361 to 363 C.E., had long been the object of hatred in the West because he had tried to reverse the Christianization of the empire. In the nineteenth and twentieth centuries, Julian began to attract admirers who saw him as a symbol of wisdom and of religious toleration.

Julian, reared as a Christian, lived in an age when the modern Christian church was taking shape. Warring prelates conducted abstract debates that robbed religion of its mystery and engaged in persecutions that ignored Jesus' message of love and peace. Julian was trained as a philosopher. His study of ancient wisdom awakened in him love and respect for the gods of the ancient world and for the Eastern mystery religions then being suppressed by Christianity. When he became emperor, Julian proclaimed religious toleration and tried to revive "paganism."

Like Paris before him and Philip Warren after, Julian was offered the worlds of intellect, love, and power. Julian chose power, but he tempered the absolute authority of emperor with love and wisdom. He was also a military genius who, like Alexander the Great, was tempted by the dream of world conquest. He was killed during an invasion of Persia.

Vidal constructs his novel as a fictive memoir written by Julian and presenting Julian's own view of himself and his world. The novel opens in 380 C.E., seventeen years after Julian's death. Two friends of Julian, the philosophers Libanius of Antioch and Priscus of Athens, correspond as they prepare Julian's memoirs for publication. Their letters and comments on the manuscript provide two other views of the events described by Julian. Because they are writing as the Emperor Theodosius is moving to destroy the ancient religions, Julian's life takes on a special poignancy. Vidal's major point, says biographer Ray Lewis White, is that modern people of the West are the descendants of the barbarians who destroyed the classical world, and that the modern world has yet to be civilized. If Julian had lived, Vidal believes, Christianity might well have remained only one of several Western religions, and Western civilization might now be healthier and more tolerant than it is.

CREATION

In 1981, Vidal took readers even further back into history in *Creation*. In 445 B.C.E., Cyrus Spitama, an elderly Persian diplomat to Athens and grandson of the Persian prophet Zoroaster, begins to dictate his memoirs to his nephew, the philosopher Democritus. Cyrus is angry after hearing the historian Herodotus give his account of the Persian-Greek war, and he decides to set down the truth.

Here Vidal traces the earliest foundations of Western civilization and the formation of major world religions. Cyrus, a diplomatic troubleshooter for the Persian court, takes the reader on a tour of the ancient world. He knows Persian emperors Darius and Xerxes; as a traveler to China and India, he meets the Buddha and Confucius, and he remembers his own grandfather, Zoroaster. In Athens he talks with such famous figures as Anaxagoras and Pericles and hires Socrates to repair his wall. In *Creation*, Vidal shows the global interaction of cultures that goes back to the ancient world. He rejects the provincialism that has allowed historians to wall Western civilization off from its Asian and African sources.

BURR

This master of historical fiction also turned his attention to the United States. Starting with *Washington, D.C.*, Vidal began a sequence of novels covering U.S. history from its beginning to the post-World War II era. In chronological sequence, the novels are *Burr*, *Lincoln*, *1876*, *Empire*, *Hollywood*, *Washington, D.C.*, and *The Golden Age*. Vidal's iconoclastic view of the past may have shocked some readers, but in the turmoil of the Vietnam and Watergate era, many people were ready to reexamine U.S. history. At a time when many Americans held that the old truths had failed, Vidal said that those truths had been hollow from the start.

Burr is one of the most widely admired of Vidal's novels. Aaron Burr, the preeminent American maverick, appealed to Vidal personally. *Burr* is narrated by Charlie Schuyler, who in 1833 is a twenty-five-year-old clerk in Burr's law office. He is an aspiring author who writes for William Leggett and William Cullen Bryant, editors of the *New York Evening Post*. Disliking Martin Van Buren, President Andrew Jackson's heir apparent, Leggett and Bryant set Charlie to work running down the rumor that Van Buren is the illegitimate son of Burr; if the rumor is true, they can use the information to destroy Van Buren. The seventy-seven-year-old Burr responds warmly to Charlie's overtures to write about his life. In the next few years, Burr gives the young writer copies of his journal and dictates to him his memories of the past.

Although Vidal's portrait of the Founding Fathers shocks some readers, his interpretation is in line with that of many of the nation's best historians. Vidal reminds the reader that Burr was one of the most able and intelligent of the Founding Fathers. Vidal allows Burr, from an insider's viewpoint, to demystify the founders of the republic. George Washington, Alexander Hamilton, Thomas Jefferson, and the other Founding Fathers created the republic, Burr says, because it satisfied their personal economic and political interests to do so.

Burr admires some of his contemporaries, especially James Madison and Andrew Jackson, but he detests Thomas Jefferson. Jefferson is a ruthless man who wants to create a nation "dominated by independent farmers each living on his own rich land, supported by slaves." What Burr cannot excuse is Jefferson's cant and hypocrisy:

> Had Jefferson not been a hypocrite I might have admired him. After all, he was the most successful empire-builder of our century, succeeding where Bonaparte failed. But then Bonaparte was always candid when it came to motive and Jefferson was always dishonest.

What are the motives of the Founding Fathers? Burr tells Alexander Hamilton: "I sense nothing more than the ordinary busy-ness of men wanting to make a place for themselves. . . . But it is no different here from what it is in London or what it was in Caesar's Rome." The Founding Fathers write the Constitution because it suits their purposes, and they subvert it when it suits their purposes.

Burr makes no secret of his opportunism, although he does regret his mistakes. He should have realized that the world is big enough for both Hamilton and himself, he says. Instead, Vice President Burr kills Hamilton in a duel and is then accused by Jefferson of heading a plot to break up the United States and establish himself as the king in a new Western empire.

Charlie does find evidence that Van Buren is Burr's son, but Charlie, having come to love the old man, refuses to use it. Van Buren rewards him with a government position overseas.

Lincoln *and* 1876

With *Lincoln*, Vidal surprised those who expected him to subject the Great Emancipator to the same ridicule he had directed at Washington and Jefferson. Vidal's Lincoln is a cold, remote, intelligent man who creates a unified, centralized republic that is far different from the one envisioned by the Founding Fathers. In *1876*, Charlie Schuyler returns to the United States from Europe, where he has lived since 1837. He left in the age of Jackson and returns in the age of Ulysses S. Grant to a booming industrializing, urbanizing nation. He watches, in the American centennial year, as the politicians steal the presidential election from Democrat Samuel J. Tilden. He sees members of the ruling class using the rhetoric of democracy but practicing it as little as they had in the days of Washington and Jefferson.

Empire

In *Empire*, Vidal paints wonderful word portraits of Henry Adams, Henry James, William Randolph Hearst, John Hay, and Theodore Roosevelt, along with the fictional characters of newspaper publishers Caroline and Blaise Sanford and Congressman James Burden Day. The creation of the internal empire, begun by Jefferson's Louisiana Purchase, had already made a shambles of the American democratic promise. Now Roosevelt and other American leaders begin to look overseas for new areas to dominate. Their creation of the overseas empire lays the groundwork for the increasingly militarized republic that emerges in the twentieth century.

Hollywood

Many of these same figures appear in *Hollywood*, set a few years later, in the administrations of Woodrow Wilson and Warren Harding. While the forging of the American empire continues, Vidal turns his gaze on a new force that is corrupting the democratic promise, the mass media. Newspaper publisher Hearst and the Sanfords have long understood the power of the press, but Hearst and Caroline Sanford see that the new medium of film has potential power beyond the printed page. Instead of reporting events, film could create a new reality within which newspapers and politicians would have to work.

Washington, D.C.

In *Washington, D.C.*, Blaise Sanford, his son Peter, Senator James Burden Day, and his assistant, Clay Overbury, are locked in a political and moral drama. Senator Day, a southern conservative, much like Senator Gore, opposes the new republic being created by Franklin D. Roosevelt, Harry S. Truman, and Dwight D. Eisenhower. He has a chance to be president but lacks money. Burden Day gives in to temptation and takes a bribe; his presidential bid fails, and later Clay Overbury, using his knowledge of the bribe, forces Day out of the Senate and takes his seat. Overbury is a young man who cares nothing for friends or ideas or issues. Winning personal power is the only thing that interests this politician, who is modeled on John F. Kennedy.

As Day is dying, he says to the spirit of his unreconstructed southern father: "You were right. . . . It has all gone wrong." Aaron Burr would have understood what he meant.

THE GOLDEN AGE

The Golden Age opens on November 4, 1939, when the U.S. Congress amends the Neutrality Act, allowing the United States to sell weapons to England and France, which are at war with Nazi Germany. Vidal places on center stage those who dominated national life when he was growing up in Washington, D.C., including Presidents Franklin Roosevelt and Harry Truman, Eleanor Roosevelt, Franklin's alter ego, Harry Hopkins, and Vidal's grandfather, Senator Thomas Gore. Peter Sanford, founder of *American Idea*, a political and cultural journal, meets these political leaders, as well as such artists and writers as Leonard Bernstein, Dawn Powell, Tennessee Williams, and a promising novelist named Gore Vidal.

Franklin Roosevelt is a mystery even to those closest to him. Is he a devious political genius scheming relentlessly to create a global empire, even at the cost of war? Or is he improvising, desperately trying to placate an isolationist, antiwar public while scrambling to help Great Britain and France hold off the Nazi onslaught? One thing is clear, Hopkins says: Washington now rules a world empire. The United States, offspring of the Enlightenment, sees itself as a democratic, peace-loving Athens but is actually a warlike, imperial Rome.

Roosevelt believes that the American future lies in Asia. He ruthlessly squeezes and humiliates Japan, deliberately provoking an attack. Senator Gore says that Roosevelt keeps attention riveted on Hitler while he prods Japan into attacking so he can live up to his promise that no American will fight in a foreign war—unless we are attacked first. If attacked, Hopkins says, then we go for the big prize: for global domination. The attack on Pearl Harbor surprised no one, one insider muses, except the American people.

In 1945, Roosevelt dies and Truman takes over. Roosevelt had helped destroy German and Japanese power and had shoved aside the spent empires of Britain and France. Truman now tries to impose his will on the Soviet Union, the one remaining obstacle to American global hegemony. The Soviets resist American pressure, and Truman divides the world into two camps, with Washington at the head of the so-called Free World. The Americans begin their long quest to impose their version of democracy on a restive world. Only the United States, says Secretary of State Dean Acheson, has the power to bend history to its will. In pursuit of that illusion the United States transforms itself into a militarized global empire.

The novel jumps forward to the night of New Year's Eve, 1999. Peter Sanford awaits the new millennium, just hours away. He is amused now at his youthful illusion that in 1945 the United States was entering a cultural Golden Age. The Golden Age lasted five years, just a flare that briefly lit the darkness. Peter and author Gore Vidal meet, both now old men, so old, they say, that they can remember back to when the United States was still a democracy. Peter challenges Vidal: You made me up, he says, and placed me in a book filled with American imperial wars—you should have given me a better world to live in.

MYRA BRECKINRIDGE

If most scholars approved of Vidal's well-researched historical fiction, many readers were shocked at *Myra Breckinridge*. Myra opens her book with the proud proclamation, "I am Myra Breckinridge whom no man will ever possess." She maintains her verve as she takes readers on a romp through popular culture. Because the novel is dead, she says, there is no point in writing made-up stories; the film of the 1940's is the high point of Western artistic creation, although it is being superseded by a higher art form, the television commercial. Myra has arrived in Hollywood to fulfill her destiny of reconstructing the sexes. She has a lesson to teach young would-be stars such as Rusty Godowsky and old cowboy stars such as Buck Loner:

> To be a man in a society of machines is to be an expendable, soft auxiliary to what is useful and hard. To-

> day there is nothing left for the old-fashioned male to do, . . . no physical struggle to survive or mate. . . . only in travesty can he act out the classic hero who was a law unto himself, moving at ease through a landscape filled with admiring women. Mercifully, that age is finished. . . . we now live at the dawn of the age of Women Triumphant, of Myra Breckinridge!

Beneath the gaiety of Myra's campy narrative, a serious purpose emerges. Her dead gay husband, Myron, had been abused and humiliated by many males. Myra carries out her plan to avenge Myron, and to revive the Female Principle, by forcing Buck Loner to submit to her demands to take over his acting studio and by raping with a dildo the macho, all-American stud Rusty.

Myra is brought down by an automobile accident, which upsets her hormonal balance. Her breasts vanish, and she sprouts a beard; she is, in fact, Myron, after gender reassignment surgery. As the book ends, Rusty is gay and Myron/Myra is married and living happily with Rusty's former girlfriend. In a sequel, *Myron*, Myron and Myra struggle for domination of the single body and again have much to say about popular culture, the mass media, and human sexuality.

Perhaps as respites from the scrupulous historicity of the American history novels, Vidal interspersed them with fantasies in which reality is plastic and ever changing. In *Myron*, characters are likely to find themselves in the midst of the old films they are watching. *Duluth* represents a deliberately postmodernist interpenetration of an actual Duluth with a serial television show also called *Duluth*.

Live from Golgotha

Live from Golgotha continues the motif of a reality subject to random change. It is set in 96 c.e., but the first century is being manipulated by forces from the twentieth, operating through psychic channelers and the Hacker, whose computer manipulations apparently can destroy not only records of the past but even memories of those records. Indeed, there is a plan afoot to return to the Crucifixion, televise it live, and perhaps even change the events.

Timothy, the narrator, is the biblical Timothy to whom Saint Paul wrote epistles. He has been chosen to preserve the Gospel story in the face of these computerized depredations, though his knowledge of the event is at best secondhand, coming from Paul, who knows it only through a vision. The story departs radically from the standard biblical story. Timothy and Paul are bisexual, as are most of the first century people depicted. Jesus is thought to have been morbidly obese. Anachronistic terms such as "Mossad" and "intifada" abound. Future figures such as Mary Baker Eddy and Shirley MacLaine make appearances.

Timothy eventually learns that the actual Jesus was a Zealot, a political revolutionary. With electronic assistance, Jesus framed Judas, the fat man Paul saw in the vision, and fled to the twentieth century. There he became the Hacker in order to clear out images of "gentle Jesus meek and mild." He plans to start Armageddon through a nuclear attack on Arab capitals. Timothy uses more advanced technology to prevent Jesus' escape from arrest. The Crucifixion takes place, with the real Jesus, but Japanese technicians add to the image a rising sun and the mother goddess Amaterasu. *Live from Golgotha* has been condemned for its irreverence and blasphemy as well as for the outlandishness of its central conceit, but many readers have nevertheless enjoyed its wit and its lusty portrayal of the first century Roman world.

The Smithsonian Institution

Vidal's next novel, *The Smithsonian Institution*, also deals with retroactive time change, but of a political rather than a theological sort. T., a thirteen-year-old mathematics prodigy in 1939, is summoned to the Smithsonian Institution to take part in a secret scientific experiment. He soon learns that the apparent wax dummies that are part of the project are actually living people. Indeed, T. is seduced by Mrs. Grover Cleveland. T. has an Einstein-like ability to visualize equations dealing with time. Anxious to ward off the coming of World War II because it would lead to the development of terrifying new weapons, the scientists secretly in charge of the Smithsonian (with the assistance of the supposed wax dummies of political leaders) plan to use T.'s ideas to construct a time machine and change the past so that the war will not occur. After one trip that only makes things worse, T. returns to a war in which he saves an alternate version of himself and enables the war to be concluded more quickly, without the weapons development.

Some commentators have said that the audience

Vidal created for himself with his highly regarded historical novels was destroyed by *Myra Breckinridge* and *Myron* and by his later campy fantasies *Kalki* and *Duluth*. Vidal continued to write one best seller after another, however, and his books have steadily gained critical admirers. Vidal's books, essays, and television appearances stimulated, intrigued, and angered a large part of his audience, yet his appeal as a writer and public figure remained compelling. As long ago as 1948, with *The City and the Pillar*, Vidal made a decision to live his life and conduct his artistic career in his own way. To many admirers, he is a symbol of freedom. The turmoil of the modern age makes his civilized voice of reason seem more necessary than ever before. Often accused of cynicism, Vidal has responded that he is a pessimist and a realist who also believes that people can, or must act as if they can, take action to make the world better.

William E. Pemberton
Updated by Arthur D. Hlavaty

Other major works

short fiction: *A Thirsty Evil: Seven Short Stories*, 1956; *Clouds and Eclipses: The Collected Short Stories*, 2006.

plays: *Visit to a Small Planet: A Comedy Akin to a Vaudeville*, pr. 1957; *The Best Man: A Play About Politics*, pr., pb. 1960; *Romulus: A New Comedy*, pr., pb. 1962; *An Evening with Richard Nixon*, pr. 1972.

screenplays: *The Catered Affair*, 1956; *Suddenly Last Summer*, 1959 (with Tennessee Williams); *The Best Man*, 1964 (adaptation of his play); *Last of the Mobile Hot-Shots*, 1969; *Caligula*, 1977.

teleplays: *Visit to a Small Planet, and Other Television Plays*, 1956; *Dress Gray*, 1986.

nonfiction: *Rocking the Boat*, 1962; *Reflections upon a Sinking Ship*, 1969; *Homage to Daniel Shays: Collected Essays, 1952-1972*, 1972; *Matters of Fact and of Fiction: Essays, 1973-1976*, 1977; *The Second American Revolution, and Other Essays, 1976-1982*, 1982; *At Home: Essays, 1982-1988*, 1988; *Screening History*, 1992; *The Decline and Fall of the American Empire*, 1992; *United States: Essays, 1952-1992*, 1993; *Palimpsest: A Memoir*, 1995; *Virgin Islands, A Dependency of United States: Essays, 1992-1997*, 1997; *Gore Vidal, Sexually Speaking: Collected Sex Writings*, 1999; *The Last Empire: Essays, 1992-2000*, 2000; *Dreaming War: Blood for Oil and the Cheney-Bush Junta*, 2002; *Perpetual War for Perpetual Peace: How We Got to Be So Hated*, 2002; *Imperial America*, 2004; *Point to Point Navigation: A Memoir, 1964-2006*, 2006; *The Selected Essays of Gore Vidal*, 2008 (Jay Parini, editor).

miscellaneous: *The Essential Gore Vidal*, 1999 (Fred Kaplan, editor); *Inventing a Nation: Washington, Adams, Jefferson*, 2003; *Conversations with Gore Vidal*, 2005 (Richard Peabody and Lucinda Ebersole, editors).

Bibliography

Altman, Dennis. *Gore Vidal's America*. Malden, Mass.: Polity, 2005. A longtime friend of Vidal and a careful student of his thought and career, Altman explores Vidal's dissection of the gap between the professed American dedication to peace and democracy and its practice of war and imperialism.

Baker, Susan, and Curtis S. Gibson. *Gore Vidal: A Critical Companion*. Westport, Conn.: Greenwood Press, 1997. Presents biographical information as well as criticism and interpretation of Vidal's works, which are divided into his historical novels and his "inventions." Includes bibliographical references and index.

Frank, Marcie. *How to Be an Intellectual in the Age of TV: The Lessons of Gore Vidal*. Durham, N.C.: Duke University Press, 2005. While many critics mourn the death of the public intellectual in America, Frank shows Vidal playing that role with intellectual vigor and astute exploitation of his celebrity to gain access to opinion-shaping media.

Harris, Stephen. *The Fiction of Gore Vidal and E. L. Doctorow: Writing the Historical Self*. New York: Peter Lang, 2002. Discusses Vidal's strong identification with history, as reflected in his writing.

Kaplan, Fred. *Gore Vidal: A Biography*. New York: Doubleday, 1999. Comprehensive work describes the events that shaped the life and career of this important novelist, playwright, scriptwriter, essayist, and political activist.

Kiernan, Robert F. *Gore Vidal*. New York: Frederick Ungar, 1982. Seeks to assess Vidal's place in American literature by exploring his major writings up to the early 1980's. Presents astute descriptions of the Vidalian style and manner.

Parini, Jay, ed. *Gore Vidal: Writer Against the Grain.* New York: Columbia University Press, 1992. Vidal's distaste for much of the academic study of contemporary fiction has been mirrored in a lack of academic study of his work. Parini sought to redress the balance by compiling this work, which deals with both Vidal's fiction and nonfiction.

Peabody, Richard, and Lucinda Ebersole, eds. *Conversations with Gore Vidal.* Jackson: University Press of Mississippi, 2005. Collection of interviews extending over nearly forty-five years reveals in Vidal's own words how he has tied history, politics, and literature together into one tight intellectual bundle.

Stanton, Robert J., and Gore Vidal, eds. *Views from a Window: Conversations with Gore Vidal.* Secaucus, N.J.: Lyle Stuart, 1980. Compilation of interviews is arranged according to themes. Vidal comments on his and other authors' works, on sexuality, and on politics. Vidal edited the manuscript and made corrections, with changes noted in the text.

ELIO VITTORINI

Born: Syracuse, Sicily, Italy; July 23, 1908
Died: Milan, Italy; February 12, 1966

Principal long fiction

Conversazione in Sicilia, 1937 (serial), 1941 (book; *In Sicily*, 1948; also known as *Conversation in Sicily*)
Uomini e no, 1945 (*Men and Not Men*, 1985)
Il Sempione strizza l'occhio al Fréjus, 1947 (novella; *The Twilight of the Elephant*, 1951; also known as *Tune for an Elephant*, 1955)
Il garofano rosso, 1948 (wr. 1933; *The Red Carnation*, 1952)
Le donne di Messina, 1949, 1964 (*Women of Messina*, 1973)
La garibaldina, 1950 (novella; *La Garibaldina*, 1960)
Erica e i suoi fratelli, 1954 (wr. 1936; *Erica*, 1960)
The Dark and the Light, 1960 (includes *La Garibaldina* and *Erica*)
Le città del mondo, 1969 (unfinished)
Le opera narrative, 1974
The Twilight of the Elephant, and Other Novels, 1974

Other literary forms

The works of Elio Vittorini (vee-toh-REE-nee) fit uneasily within traditional genres. Vittorini was, by temperament and by conscious decision, an innovator. His novels, with few exceptions, first appeared in installments in literary journals and only years later were published in book form, extensively reworked and perhaps with changed titles. Given the historical and editorial circumstances surrounding their publication, Vittorini's novels appear as works in progress and are fully integrated with his other activities as a writer, with his journalistic, political, and theoretical concerns.

Vittorini's first major publication was a collection of eight short stories, *Piccola borghesia* (1931; petty bourgeoisie). "La mia guerra" ("My War"), which is first in the collection but last chronologically, foreshadows Vittorini's later atmosphere and pattern of allusions, with the theme of childhood adventure set against the background of the experience of war and travel. "La signora della stazione" ("The Stationmaster's Lady") also is significant, in view of Vittorini's later development of the theme of childhood on a sunny, mythical island.

In 1936, Vittorini published *Nei morlacchi—Viaggio in Sardegna*, a collection of notes he had taken on a trip to Sardinia. The book, which includes a prose poem, acquired its definitive title and format, *Sardegna come un'infanzia* (Sardinia as one's childhood), in its 1952 edition. The book contains a series of brief, partly factual and partly poetic pieces about Vittorini's discovery of the Sardinian universe. An important element emerges here for the first time: Vittorini's sensuous participation in everyday life. A basic Vittorinian theme runs through the text, finding explicit expression in the title and in the closing section, titled "Nevermore": the theme of ancient lands, of a solitary island as "a part of one's childhood, . . . of that magic time . . . gone forever."

Two major volumes gather most of Vittorini's essays. *Diario in pubblico* (1957; public journal) covers the period from 1929 to 1956. Its second edition, published in 1970, contains an appendix that covers the period from 1957 to 1965. The volume collects much that Vittorini wrote on all topics, most of it previously published, some not. Notes on literature and antifascism, culture, and public matters all testify to a long period of participation in Italian and European events and debates. They are brilliant fragments often followed by Vittorini's own later comments and updates, and they offer a striking portrait of a European mind, honest and passionate, curious and open to debate.

Le due tensioni (1967; two tensions) was published posthumously, on the basis of Vittorini's notes taken as he thought and read in preparation for a study on the function of literature, its relation to human culture, and its internal dynamics. The exploratory quality of the text reflects the process of Vittorini's meditation, its openness and richness. Underlying the comments on his readings in anthropology, sociology, linguistics, and other disciplines and other critiques of contemporary writers (including himself), the thread that connects all the fragments is the thesis that two tensions, the rational and the emotional, should appear within literature in a dynamic state of flux, if literature is to remain alive. Vittorini's letters also have been published, in three volumes, and a ten-volume edition of his complete works, *Opere*, was published in 1974.

ACHIEVEMENTS

Elio Vittorini was perhaps the most influential figure on the Italian cultural scene of the middle years of the twentieth century, from 1925 to 1965. While all of his work belongs to that period when Western culture experienced unparalleled social and political upheavals, it is also vitally relevant to the concerns of today.

To grasp the extent and significance of his impact on Italian culture, one must look at several facets of Vittorini's activity. He entered the Italian literary world from an unusual direction, at least for those times; not from the well-to-do class, he attended a vocational school rather than a university. He knew the freedom of the young runaway, and he worked as a manual laborer. His teachers included his fellow workers, such as the printer who helped him learn English, and much of his learning was self-taught. He was an "islander," an outsider, a dreamer of adventures whose first hero was Robinson Crusoe. Although he was a Sicilian, he escaped the deadening weight of the mores of an insular bourgeoisie that had oppressed Giovanni Verga and obsessed Luigi Pirandello. Later in his career, as a prestigious author and influential editor, he counseled and published young writers, among whom he always seemed at ease, with his enthusiasm and his passionate commitment to literature.

That commitment, and his lifelong curiosity about other cultures and literatures, prompted Vittorini to read texts from other traditions, in their original languages, and translate them. With other young intellectuals who clustered around the great publishing houses in Milan and Turin (foremost among them Cesare Pavese), Vittorini worked at opening up the closed world of Italy's elite culture, which the Fascist censors wanted to insulate against outside influences.

Translating and publishing foreign texts was not only an intellectual adventure but also a gamble, a statement with cultural and political overtones. *Americana*, a chronologically ordered anthology of excerpts from all periods of American literature, with introductions and commentaries by Vittorini, is a classic in the history of American studies in Italy—and a classic case of the Italian intellectuals' resistance to fascism. Published by Bompiani in 1943, it was suppressed, reworked by other editors, and published in mutilated form, then reissued posthumously in its original form in 1968.

Vittorini had already introduced William Faulkner, William Saroyan, Erskine Caldwell, and Thornton Wilder to the Italian readers. In his anthology, he proposed an interpretation of American literature that inspired his own work and was vitally significant for Italian culture. For him, American literature was the expression of a fruitful contradiction: It spoke of liberation from the dead weight of ancient worlds, yet it was obsessed with absolutes and abstractions. It was full of "barbaric" vitality, yet also of technical refinements. Its best exponents knew of cruelty and corruption, but all of them spoke to a humanity yearning for a new history on a new soil. The myth of America in Italy in the 1930's and 1940's, with its cultural and political implications signifying a rejection both of fascism and of a fatalistic acceptance of the past, owes much of its power to Vittorini and to his inspired reading of American authors.

The editorial work accomplished by Vittorini had an even greater impact on his contemporaries and on the directions Italian culture took in the 1950's and 1960's. Vittorini saw literature as inseparable from other social phenomena, inevitably connected with all the concerns of human beings, and as the rightful domain of all readers, across class boundaries and beyond national borders. Therefore, the collections he compiled, for Bompiani first, then for Einaudi, included a variety of voices, styles, and genres: He published young Italian authors, translations of new foreign works, travel books, chronicles, war diaries, historical documents, and essays in the most diverse disciplines. He continued to enrich the Italian cultural environment and to open it to the winds of change.

As a journalist, Vittorini established an ongoing dialogue with Italian readers on the topics he thought crucial to his work as a writer and to his function in society as a man of culture. He often wrote texts using various techniques in the gaps between traditional genres: part documentary and part fantasy, part metaphor and part reportage. During the postwar period, he insisted on the rootedness of literature in the lives and traditions of the people; foremost among his concerns was the concept of culture as a tool and a weapon against suffering rather than as a device for consolation.

It would be hard indeed to overestimate Vittorini's importance in the intellectual development of a whole generation of Italians, including writers such as Italo Calvino.

Biography

Elio Vittorini was born in Syracuse, Sicily, on July 23, 1908. His father was a stationmaster who moved with his family from one small Sicilian locality to another, wherever the Italian railroad administration assigned him. Vittorini took a train to go to the nearest school, and also to run away from home, which he did for the first time at the age of thirteen. His formal schooling never went beyond the business courses he took by his father's decision. By the time he was eighteen, he was reading furiously, mostly novelists and philosophers. Wanting desperately to leave the provincial environment, where he felt he was suffocating, he sent his first writings to literary journals published in major Italian cities, had them published, and moved to northern Italy. His jobs on the Continent included bookkeeping, manual labor, and proofreading for a newspaper. By 1930, he was in Florence learning English and was ready to publish his first collection of short stories. Within three years, he was also publishing translations of British and American authors.

By the middle 1930's, even the young Italians who, like Vittorini, had thought that fascism could bring renewal and socialistic reforms to Italian society, were forced to acknowledge their misjudgment. Vittorini had already denounced Fascist nationalism and had associated with intellectuals and publications that favored a culture with a European dimension. As he became more interested in political activism and more vocal about the direction that, in his view, the Fascist Party should have taken, the party became hostile to him and expelled him. Those were the years of the Spanish Civil War, when artists and writers such as Pablo Picasso and Ernest Hemingway created works that marked a turning point in Western culture. *In Sicily*, Vittorini's first major work, was born out of his political and personal crisis.

It is clear even to the casual reader that Vittorini viewed politics as an integral part of his literary activities; in this, he was definitely of his times. From his first pages, when, as an adolescent, he supported a Fascist vision of the Italian reality, through the crisis of the 1930's, and up to the years of his work in the Resistance and his critique of the Communist Party, he remained consistent in his commitment and sense of personal responsibility. At the time he wrote his volume on Sardinia, he was already speaking of his awareness of brute labor, "toil that buys a crust of bread, crust of bread that buys that toil." Through forty years, Vittorini developed the principles that are essential to an understanding of his politics and his career as a writer: Literature, if it is to be vital, must be twice bound to the grass roots of society, by giving a voice to all laboring human beings and by speaking to them in an understandable voice; the writer must be constantly "available," in touch, immersed in the present. For Vittorini himself, that meant moving in the orbit of Socialist thought and working with the Italian Communist Party (PCI). From 1937 to 1945, Vittorini's biography reflects the events of Italian history. He was an editor for the Bompiani publishing house in Milan, became a member of the Resistance, and worked on the underground publication of the Communist newspaper *L'Unità*. He was arrested, then released, and continued his Resistance activities, which included joining the guerrillas in the mountains.

After the war, although he was totally committed to the Left, he began a polemic with the PCI, because—he asserted—an intellectual could not be bound by dogmas or prescriptions dictated by political agendas. He articulated, in a more explicit and sustained manner than most, the arguments brought against party authoritarianism and narrow-mindedness by communist intellectuals all over Europe. Particularly important in this context are two journals: *Il politecnico*, of which he was the editor, from 1945 to 1947, and *Il menabò*, which he coedited with Calvino from 1949 to 1966. They are fundamental to Italy's cultural history. They also show the development of Vittorini's concept of the function of literature, which he entrusted with the task of revealing truly revolutionary needs not voiced or fulfilled by political parties.

The issues raised in articles and documents published in the two journals include the "question of the Italian South," the use of dialect, and, above all, the relationship between literature and industrial society, as Italy emerged from its agrarian past into the 1950's and 1960's, through an almost total transformation of its social and economic structures.

Vittorini lived through the 1960's, intellectually active but tormented, disillusioned by the failures he perceived in Italian political and social life, publishing little, and struggling against severe health problems. He died in Milan on February 12, 1966.

Analysis

Elio Vittorini's novels are, above all, dynamic works whose "unfinished" quality reflects the author's restless search for a type of writing that would tell "the truth" about the world. In an important statement he made about his own activity as a writer, in the preface to the 1948 (Italian) edition of *The Red Carnation*, he spoke of his desire to write not "books" but "a book," that book which one writes and rewrites in order to tell "the truth that must be told." Because that truth changes with a changing world and a changing awareness, the task of pursuing it is never ended.

Looking at Vittorini's novels, one notices that almost all of them moved through successive versions. In addition to interruptions and stylistic corrections, the texts underwent title changes, cuts, additions, and much crucial rethinking of plots and characters. It is true that outside circumstances such as the war and censorship caused certain projects to stall, though not for Vittorini only; such external events impinged on many lives. For Vittorini, the practical obstacles were compounded by self-imposed dilemmas—the result of his integrity as a writer who wanted to "understand," to remain close to the suffering world, to be an interpreter and a witness to the world's becoming.

The same commitment to understanding the world and to changing its social order caused Vittorini to search for a new way of writing. Each novel is an experiment in language and approach, a painstaking effort to subvert the tradition. From *The Red Carnation*, which began as a fairly traditional psychological novel about an adolescent's awakening, only to veer toward the exploration of a social and political *crise de conscience* (crisis of conscience), Vittorini went on to explore the impact of fascism, war, and industrialization on people's lives, feelings, and imagination. His late novel, *Le città del mondo* (cities of the world), which turned back to an earlier interest in a peasant universe mythically interpreted, significantly was left unfinished. In spite of Vittorini's efforts to complete it over a span of fourteen years, its theme and technique revealed an incongruity with Vittorini's new consciousness and with his rejection of a worldview that remained rooted in an agrarian culture.

Above all, there is in Vittorini's work a pervasive conviction that literature, its voice and its experiments, do matter to the world and its history. Vittorini's prose, written in standard, plain Italian, uses repetition, dialogue, and poetic techniques to achieve its effects. Fictional events emerge from the interaction of characters with their societal environment, against the background of the voices and actions of a choral or collective presence. Thus, poetry and history find their confluence in Vittorini's fiction.

The "book" that Vittorini visualized as the ideal goal to which his fictional work tended, relies heavily on recurrent themes and myths. The most important is the theme of childhood, which is closely related to what has been called the Robinsonian myth (*Robinson Crusoe* is mentioned frequently by Vittorini as a work that profoundly influenced him). Immersed in the environment of a mythical island, childhood is the time that transfigures reality. Sicily, Sardinia, and Robinson Crusoe's island become one, as the child repeats gestures, retells stories, reinvents rituals, dreams again ancient dreams. Throughout Vittorini's career, his imagination was drawn back to the island myth, but the contemplation of the privileged moment of childhood (although viewed by him as essential to the development of human consciousness), of an appreciation of the community of people and of the fictional world, became in time a temptation, a means to escape awareness, a regress. One cannot remain in that magic circle of purity and certainty; there are outrages and a grieving world waiting out there.

Thus, traveling is an almost perennial activity for Vittorini's characters. The theme of the journey, though, is not a romantic search for self, to be actuated through the discovery of exotic solitudes. It is, rather, a search into the self through the weaving of a network of human relationships, along the pattern of another network, that of railways and highways in a specific place, the Italian peninsula, at given historical moments. Traveling means leaving one's isolation; it means conversing, meeting people, sharing food, establishing or reestablishing roots. For the adolescent or the inexperienced person, traveling is an education; for the adult, it is an opportunity to engage in narration, to find an audience, to influence and inform other people. As seafarers used to ply the seas in search of comradeship and knowledge, Vittorini's travelers haunt train compartments and truck beds, with a great sense of adventure, in a country where the events have set whole populations in motion. During such travels, one hears about, and at times meets, extraordinary people.

Two of the mythical figures in Vittorini's repertory, the Great Lombard and the Queen Bee, may be met under just such circumstances. The Lombard is the embodiment of the moral tension that lies at the core of Vittorini's world, a man who is "like a king" and is even physically imposing, tall and massive, blue-eyed, flanked and admired by beautiful daughters. He is made restless, however, by a need to tend to "other duties," higher duties that make a man more of a man, duties that go beyond those prescribed by the Judeo-Christian tradition and would satisfy the new yearnings of the human conscience, which is no longer content with the old Commandments. The Queen Bee is woman in her maturity, giving but independent, sensual but clearheaded, protective only when needed, a powerful "blessed old sow," "full of honey." Together, usually presented as Father and Daughter, they embody the images of male and female adulthood in Vittorini's mythology.

In Sicily

In Sicily, the novel that placed Vittorini among the major voices of European literature, brings together all the themes and the concerns of its author. Above all, the style of this novel expresses the intensity and complexity of Vittorini's artistic and political preoccupations at a particularly crucial time in his life.

The protagonist, Silvestro, is a prey to "abstract furies" that have to do with "the lost human race," in a dismal winter in the north, with depression mounting as rainwater seeps into his old shoes. His visit to his childhood island, Sicily, and to his mother's house is a descent into a different world, a journey that heals and exorcizes, as Silvestro looks at landscapes, villages, people, and his own parents with the eyes of an adult. The novel chronicles a journey of mythic dimensions, lingering with sensuous everyday details yet distancing them through the use of poetic language. It is a "conversation," as the Italian title says, a continuous dialogue, repetitious and rhythmic like an incantation; it is also a bitter commentary on the state of the world in the mid-1930's. Finally, it is a work of fantasy, in which a child's imagination and an adult's emotions intertwine. The images, rich and suggestive, stand in striking contrast to the simplicity of the syntax and vocabulary.

The train and boat rides from the urban north to the almost dreamlike south begin the cathartic experience. Silvestro engages in conversation with a number of people, all from Sicily: poor laborers, a Great Lombard, a thin old man with a walking stick that ends in a snake head, two police officers in civilian clothes who are called simply Mustache and No Mustache, and a few others, with varying symbolic functions. As he listens to his traveling companions, and speaks sparingly, something stirs in him. The train travels on and on. The second and third sections of the novel describe Silvestro's visit to his mother in her house in the mountainous part of the island. The mother is a Queen Bee, imposing, womanly, and self-sufficient, with inner resources of sensuality and joy. Her husband has left her, but she feels only a sort of irritated condescension toward him; she goes about her domestic chores singing and whistling, enjoying her solitude. The son, now a man, acts almost as an eavesdropper; he admires the directness of the woman who is his mother and muses on the secret of her serenity. She performs a nurse's duties in the village, so he is invited to follow her around as she visits poor and well-to-do patients, chats with them, and gives them injections. Through her, Silvestro hears the voices of the people of the village.

After several visits, Silvestro needs to be alone, to reflect on the discrepancy between the world as it is viewed by a seven-year-old child and the "injured world" one discovers at maturity. In a series of highly symbolic scenes, Silvestro meets a number of village men, several allegorical figures, and the spirit of his brother, slain in war; he is told about the suffering of all the downtrodden, of the outrages of war, and of the additional outrage perpetrated by all forms of empty rhetoric. After these encounters, Silvestro is ready to leave. He will not speak to an old man who, at the mother's house, back turned and face lowered, weeps silently as the mother helps him wash his feet. He is the father, whom Silvestro remembers as a lean and colorfully costumed young man playing Shakespearean dramas on a makeshift stage. The son leaves without greeting him, for he has already said good-bye to his past, has extracted all the nourishment to be gained from his ghostly journey. He has overcome despair and exorcised childhood; he is ready for his own maturity.

In 1949, Hemingway wrote a preface for the American edition of *In Sicily* (now available in *A Vittorini Omnibus*, 1960). A typically brusque but admiring introduction of the Italian author to the American public, it is particularly significant because Vittorini loved and translated the American authors who were his contemporaries and learned from them some important technical and theoretical lessons.

Women of Messina

In the last version of *Women of Messina*, several components have merged into one fictional entity. Some critics have called *Women of Messina* a collage; Calvino calls the novel a fresco that has been painted and repainted in spots, "each time almost with the same brush strokes, but with a changed consciousness." Without any doubt, the novel is the best example of Vittorini's modus operandi, aimed at translating his concerns into a novelist's practice—concerns both existential and theoretical, as he struggled to testify to the events taking place then and, more important, to take into account his own reassessments of them.

The text includes three major plots. The first is the story of an old man's travels through postwar Italy in search of a daughter who has disappeared. This first story had originally been published as a serial in 1947-1948. Uncle Agrippa enjoys his contacts with other travelers and ends up by continuing to travel mostly out of personal satisfaction. Around him, people move up and down the peninsula, looking for relatives or for work, escaping from the desolation left by the war or from personal problems. A set of characters emerges and becomes the core of the second moment of the novel; these refugees build a village on the ruins of an old one, establishing there a new social order.

The changes made in this portion of the novel from the 1949 text to the 1964 version are substantive and quite interesting. In the first version, the emphasis is on the rebirth of a peasant culture, through almost mythical stages, and the central theme is that of human redemption. A third narrative strand begins here at the heart of the novel, introducing melodramatic elements into the epic flow. Ventura is a former Fascist militiaman who, in that role, had no compassion or respect for people, a "no-man," as Vittorini would have said. He now wishes to change his life, for the love of a woman, and succeeds in bending to the democratic rules established by the group, becoming a leader in the village community. He is a hunted man, however, because of his earlier misdeeds, and when his lover refuses to leave the village to run away with him, the "no-man" still alive in him kills her.

In the 1964 version, the mythical peasant society of the earlier version is shown as an archaic creation in contrast to a rising industrial society, where the city is the place for innovation and rebirth. A biting critique of technological culture does not preclude Vittorini's proposing it as the culture of the future. Ventura's function has changed with this shifting of perspective, for his personal dilemma has now become the problem of the whole community. He chooses apathy and a retreat from the dynamics of history, while other villagers choose to move on and become members of the larger society.

With each new version, major changes were also made at the stylistic level. In the earlier versions, narration, journalistic reportage, and choral commentary were simply juxtaposed, in an effort to convey the discrete channels through which reality can be grasped. The narrative of the final version is less emphatic, more direct and plain. The text has been pruned of lyric passages and has acquired greater unity, although some unevenness remains because of the overly complicated structure. Vittorini wanted only his last version reprinted. In it, he spoke of the creative ferment of the postwar years but also of the disillusionment and the new potentialities brought by the 1950's, which seemed to have betrayed and exhausted the vital charge of the antifascist struggle. *Women of Messina* was meant to be the popular epic of that era in Italian history.

Erica *and* La Garibaldina

With *Erica* and *La Garibaldina*, Vittorini returned to a more exacting but more congenial form. Fablelike elements and political motifs blend in a subtler way within the dimensions of these shorter texts, which necessarily impose a greater discipline. Although these two works differ in style and theme, they share an intense focus on a single central character—in both cases, a woman.

Erica was written by 1936 but was published in 1954. The protagonist is a little girl whose increasing awareness of the world Vittorini follows with sensitivity. Erica's childhood in a big city "after a war" is full of wonder. The family's poverty causes the parents to become gradually estranged from the children, until the latter find themselves abandoned, small and hungry. Nevertheless, Erica finds joy in her own resourcefulness and in her almost magical closeness to the objects of everyday life; particularly effective is Vittorini's evocation of the Robinsonian aura around the self-sufficient city girl. The isolation of purity, the fable of childhood, however, cannot last forever. One must leave one's magic "island." Erica understands the veiled evil, the hypocrisy of "charitable" help; she can make contact with other people only by earning her living through an injustice suffered without illusions or alibis: She becomes a prostitute. As she goes to the food store with "her" money, she knows that money is what it can buy, and she experiences the pride of true adulthood, of lucidity without illusions.

La Garibaldina speaks of another strong woman, an old lady whose almost grotesque silhouette stimulates a humor rarely seen in Vittorini. A train is crossing the desolate Sicilian countryside. On it is a soldier who is going home on furlough but who is being denied permission to stay on that particular train. There is also an old baroness, authoritarian and reactionary, full of vitality, a very mature Queen Bee whose language has aristocratic haughtiness and plebeian force. Her name is Leonilde, and she has a tempestuous past, including a part in Garibaldi's legendary campaign; she calls the young soldier Innocenzo. She insists on helping him by using her considerable authority and sharp tongue; as a consequence, they embark on a journey together, partly by train and partly by foot. They undergo many symbolic encounters. In one climactic, faintly ominous and hallucinatory episode, they pass, at night, through a village full of hidden presences and whispers. At dawn, an absurd chorus of harvesters surrounds the old lady, who is now on horseback in all of her ancient finery; their songs and crude servility give the end of the novel the flavor of the happy finale of an operetta. This is *In Sicily* revisited by an older, if not wiser, Silvestro.

Erica and *La Garibaldina* are among Vittorini's best works. Sadness, fantasy, and playfulness alternate in them, and they are pervaded by a disenchanted humor. Significantly, they exploit the deepest vein of the author's imagination—the familiar themes of a magical childhood, of sensuous maturity, of travel, and of the secret voices of village and fields. These short novels, intense and rich, evenly poised between myth and history, confirm Vittorini's stature and his importance for subsequent generations of Italian writers.

Angela M. Jeannet

Other major works

SHORT FICTION: *Piccola borghesia*, 1931; *Nome e lagrime e altri racconti*, 1972 (collected fragments).

NONFICTION: *Diario in pubblico*, 1957, 1970; *Le due tensioni*, 1967; *Gli anni del politecnico: Lettere, 1945-1951*, 1977 (3 volumes).

MISCELLANEOUS: *Nei morlacchi—Viaggio in Sardegna*, 1936 (prose poem and travelogue; reissued in part as *Sardegna come un'infanzia*, 1952); *A Vittorini Omnibus*, 1960; *Opere*, 1974 (10 volumes).

EDITED TEXTS: *Teatro spagnolo*, 1941; *Americana*, 1943, 1968.

Bibliography

Bonsaver, Guido. *Elio Vittorini: The Writer and the Written*. Leeds, England: Northern Universities Press, 2000. A comprehensive examination of Vittorini's life, work, and times, paying particular attention to the link between his fiction and his political commitments. Includes passages in Italian with English translations.

Gordon, Robert S. C. *An Introduction to Twentieth-Century Italian Literature: A Difficult Modernity*. London: Duckworth, 2005. There are numerous references to Vittorini in this study, which focuses on Italy's "'difficult' entry into modernity," in which the country was in the throes of a "convulsive transformation in both society and culture, accompanied at various stages by war, violence and dictatorship."

Heiney, Donald. *Three Italian Novelists: Moravia, Pavese, Vittorini*. Ann Arbor: University of Michigan Press, 1968. A clear and insightful study of Vittorini as an "operatic" novelist, comparing his work to that of Alberto Moravia and Cesare Pavese. Includes a bibliography.

Jeannet, Angela M., and Louise K. Barnett, eds. and trans. *New World Journeys: Contemporary Italian Writers and the Experience of America*. Westport, Conn.: Greenwood Press, 1977. A study of how Italian writers came to view the United States and American literature. Includes an index and a bibliography.

Pacifici, Sergio. *The Modern Italian Novel: From Pea to Moravia*. 1967. New ed. Carbondale: Southern Illinois University Press, 1979. Includes an essay on Vittorini, placing him within the context of modern, twentieth century Italian literature.

Potter, Joy Hambuechen. *Elio Vittorini*. Boston: Twayne, 1979. A full-length introductory overview, with a biography of Vittorini and a discussion and analysis of his writings. A volume in the Twayne World Authors series.

Re, Lucia. "Neorealist Narrative: Experience and Experiment." In *The Cambridge Companion to the Italian Novel*, edited by Peter Bondanella and Andrea Ciccarelli. New York: Cambridge University Press, 2003. This chapter includes discussion of *Conversations in Sicily*, *Men and Not Men*, and other Vittorini novels, placing them within the context of Italian neorealism.

VOLTAIRE

François-Marie Arouet

Born: Paris, France; November 21, 1694
Died: Paris, France; May 30, 1778
Also known as: François-Marie Arouet

Principal long fiction

Zadig: Ou, La Destinée, histoire orientale, 1748 (originally published as *Memnon: Histoire orientale*, 1747; *Zadig: Or, The Book of Fate*, 1749)
Le Micromégas, 1752 (*Micromegas*, 1753)
Histoire des voyages de Scarmentado, 1756 (*The History of the Voyages of Scarmentado*, 1757; also known as *History of Scarmentado's Travels*, 1961)
Candide: Ou, L'Optimisme, 1759 (*Candide: Or, All for the Best*, 1759; also known as *Candide: Or, The Optimist*, 1762; also known as *Candide: Or, Optimism*, 1947)
L'Ingénu, 1767 (*The Pupil of Nature*, 1771; also known as *Ingenuous*, 1961)
L'Homme aux quarante écus, 1768 (*The Man of Forty Crowns*, 1768)
La Princesse de Babylone, 1768 (*The Princess of Babylon*, 1769)

Other literary forms

Voltaire (vohl-TAYR) is probably the most prolific and versatile writer of any age. He wrote in all the literary forms, and he wrote in them concurrently. His numerous plays fill 6 volumes, and his correspondence 102 volumes. He was especially active toward the end of his life; living at Ferney in his eighties, he wrote pamphlets, many plays, and one of his best philosophical poems, *Épître à Horace* (1772). He went to Paris at the age of eighty-three, shortly before he died, to see a production of his latest classical tragedy, *Irène* (pr. 1778). At the time of his death, he was at work on a new play and rewriting others.

In many ways, Voltaire wished to be considered as a defender of the classical tradition. His plays are mainly classical, embodying the unities and dealing with high-born heroes. *Œdipe* (pr. 1718; *Oedipus*, 1761) was widely acclaimed in Voltaire's day, as were *Zaïre* (pr. 1732; English translation, 1736) and *Mérope* (1743; English translation, 1744, 1749). He also, however, introduced devices and techniques that ultimately led to the demise of classical theater, including local color, such as red togas for members of the Senate in *Brutus* (pr. 1730; English translation, 1761) and real cannon fire in *Adélaïde du Guesclin* (pr. 1734). Voltaire's later plays include a certain amount of tearful sensibility that was a characteristic of Denis Diderot's bourgeois dramas.

Voltaire composed many kinds of poetry. As a young man, he achieved much acclaim with his epic poem *La Ligue* (1723) and *La Henriade* (1728, a rewriting of *La Ligue; Henriade*, 1732). *Henriade*, which narrates Henry IV's successful struggle against the Catholic League, was reprinted through the beginning of the nineteenth century. Today, these poems have no appeal. Voltaire also wrote satiric and philosophical poetry, including *Le Mondain* (1736; *The Man of the World*, 1764). This poem caused a scandal with its suggestion that a pleasurable life on earth is the only positive happiness one can grasp and that one should enjoy it rather than wait for a life after death. This element of audacious irreverence is a quality that spices all of Voltaire's work and was what his admirers appreciated. Voltaire's *Épître à Horace* is one of the best of Voltaire's philosophical epistles.

Voltaire has some renown as a historian. His *Le Siècle de Louis XIV* (1751; *The Age of Louis XIV*, 1752) reveals meticulous research and a journalistic bent. Voltaire praises the reign of Louis XIV in order to criticize the reign of Louis XV. *Essai sur les mœurs* (1756, 1763; *The General History and State of Europe*, 1754, 1759) presents a philosophical review of historic events. Other nonfiction works popularize the accomplishments of Sir Isaac Newton in science and of John Locke in philosophy (*Éléments de la philosophie de Newton*, 1738; *The Elements of Sir Isaac Newton's Philosophy*, 1738). In *Lettres philosophiques* (1734; originally published in English as *Letters Concerning the English Nation*, 1733;

also known as *Philosophical Letters*, 1961), Voltaire, with his powerful satire, praises English customs and institutions as a method of criticizing French society of his day. Censorship, which outlawed much of Voltaire's work, not only added to the satirist's celebrity but also increased the prices charged for his books. The articles that Voltaire wrote for *Dictionnaire philosophique portatif* (1764, enlarged 1769; *A Philosophical Dictionary for the Pocket*, 1765; also known as *Philosophical Dictionary*, 1945, enlarged 1962) were also offensive to the establishment, full of his propaganda on the subject of fanaticism, judicial corruption, and social oppression.

Achievements

Voltaire's career spanned sixty years, and during that time he achieved great fame and even greater notoriety. Voltaire's literary ambitions were revealed when he chose *Œdipe* as the subject of his first tragedy. His ambition was to rival Pierre Corneille, and at the age of twenty-four he was already hailed as a worthy successor to both Jean Racine and Corneille. In the theater, Voltaire considerably delayed the demise of classical tragedy, and he remained an extremely popular dramatist of the age. Between 1745 and 1803, his plays were staged many more times than those of Corneille and Racine. Today, however, Voltaire's plays are no longer of interest to audiences.

Voltaire also enjoyed success in the field of poetry. *La Ligue* was so highly acclaimed that it put epic poetry back in fashion. Voltaire's love of the classical tradition stemmed, no doubt, from his Jesuit education at Louis-le-Grand. His poetry also brought him prestige at court and financial rewards. After the successful production of *La Princesse de Navarre* in 1745, performed at the wedding of Louis XV, Voltaire was given the post of royal historiographer and a pension of two thousand francs a year, and later was made a gentleman of the king's chamber. The following year, 1746, Voltaire achieved another ambition when he was finally elected to the Académie Française. He had been denied this privilege several times before because of the various scandals he had caused. Madame du Châtelet tried to protect him from his own indiscretion; she once locked up his outrageous *La Pucelle d'Orléans* (1755, 1762; *The Maid of Orleans*, 1758; also as *La Pucelle: Or, The Maid of Orleans*, 1785-1786), a scurrilous writing on the subject of Joan of Arc.

Voltaire's philosophical and satiric writings, such as his tales and pamphlets, not only brought him literary fame but also endangered his liberty. For this reason, Voltaire lived much of his life in exile or on the French-Swiss border.

One of the most astonishing aspects of Voltaire is his schizophrenic outlook. He dearly wished to have access to the noble classes (which accounts for his name change), while at the same time he despised the inequality inherent in the privilege of noble birth. A champion of the classical tradition, Voltaire inadvertently eroded its hold on his century by his innovations in drama and the novel. It is surprising that a champion of French classical tragedy and epic poetry should be the prime mover in introducing the latest developments in English literature, philosophy, and science into France. Voltaire's efforts to create a climate for liberty of thought and belief did eventually ameliorate conditions in France. The Ency-

Voltaire. (Library of Congress)

clopedists, with Voltaire at their head, were ultimately responsible for producing a climate of critical thinking and a desire for reform that culminated in the French Revolution. Voltaire's *Philosophical Letters* were burned in public because they did not display the respect due "authority." Voltaire nevertheless would have been horrified to see the revolutionary tide sweep away this authority, even though it was corrupt. He enjoyed the cultivated nobility and the gracious support this class gave to the arts; he would have had no faith in the judgment of unrefined and poorly educated republicans. Still, the new ideas he had promulgated traveled through France and even to North America. Like John Locke, many of whose ideas are to be found in the American Bill of Rights and the Constitution, Voltaire contributed to political philosophy as it was developing in Europe and even in the United States.

It is through his satiric and philosophical writings that Voltaire exercised that influence. Whereas his effect on literature disappeared at the beginning of the nineteenth century, his emphasis on reason and critical thinking still dominates the French mind. The ideals of liberty of thought and justice are his legacy.

Biography

Voltaire was born François-Marie Arouet in Paris in 1694. His father was a highly placed official and belonged to the upper middle class. Voltaire received an excellent classical education at the Jesuit school of Louis-le-Grand in Paris, where he displayed a talent for writing poetry. He also probably acquired his taste for theater there.

The Abbé de Châteauneuf, Voltaire's godfather, introduced the twelve-year-old boy to the Society of the Temple, which was the domain of worldly libertines. Voltaire's taste for witty irreverence and for luxurious living was definitely encouraged by this company. In 1711, Voltaire became a law student. As early as 1716, his satiric writing, aimed at the king's regent and the poet Antoine Houdar de la Motte, caused Voltaire to be exiled twice to the provinces. In 1717, after writing a second time satirizing the regent, Voltaire was imprisoned (fairly comfortably) in the Bastille for eleven months. During this stay, he completed *Oedipus* and began to write *La Ligue*. Upon leaving prison, he changed his name to de Voltaire. He became famous with the success of *Oedipus* in 1718 and *La Ligue* in 1723, and as a result he was invited to the literary and social circles of the wealthy. He even became a habitué of the court and had three of his plays, *Oedipus*, *Mariamne* (pr. 1724; English translation, 1761), and *L'Indiscret* (pr., pb. 1725) performed as part of the celebrations for Louis XV's marriage in 1725.

Late in 1725, Voltaire had a dispute with the chevalier de Rohan, who ridiculed Voltaire's use of a false aristocratic name. Angered by a beating at the hands of Rohan's men, Voltaire challenged the noble to a duel. None of Voltaire's aristocratic friends supported him in the matter, which increased Voltaire's hatred of the unfairness of privilege. A *lettre de cachet* (a letter of arbitrary arrest issued by the king) sent him to the Bastille. Soon—in May, 1726—Voltaire was allowed to go into exile in England, where he spent three years frequenting the literary circles of the day. There he wrote his *Philosophical Letters*, prepared four tragedies, and published *Henriade*. Voltaire returned to France in 1729 and once again gained access to literary circles. In 1730, his play *Brutus* was produced. The influence of William Shakespeare, acquired in England, is obvious in Voltaire's drama. *Zaïre* was presented in 1732 and *Adélaïde du Guesclin* in 1734. In the same year, Voltaire also took a great risk when he published his highly critical *Philosophical Letters* for the first time in France.

From 1734 to 1744, Voltaire lived in the du Châtelet castle at Cirey, where Madame du Châtelet, Voltaire's mistress, restrained Voltaire's volatile literary indiscretions somewhat. This period proved to be a most productive one. Voltaire wrote several plays during this time, including *Alzire* (pr., pb. 1736; English translation, 1763) and *Mérope*. He also wrote his provocative *The Man of the World* while at Cirey. Both Madame du Châtelet and Voltaire took an interest in physics, chemistry, and astronomy; it is at Cirey that Voltaire wrote *The Elements of Sir Isaac Newton's Philosophy*.

For the three years following 1744, Voltaire was involved in life at court. His protectress, Madame de Pompadour, was, like him, of a humble background. The king and queen always distrusted Voltaire. After a thoughtless remark, Voltaire was obliged to flee the court and go to the summer home of the duchesse du Maine, the

Château d'Anet at Sceaux. In *Zadig*, Voltaire satirizes life at court.

In 1747, Madame de Châtelet died in childbirth. Voltaire was extremely pained by this loss. There was no longer a reason to remain in France, and Voltaire spent the years from 1750 to 1753 at the court of Frederick the Great of Prussia. He published *The Age of Louis XIV* in Berlin in 1751. There he also wrote his satiric philosophical tale *Micromegas*. Although he had hoped to discover in Frederick his ideal of the "enlightened" monarch, Voltaire was as independent as Frederick was authoritarian, and the visit soon ended. These two men still respected each other greatly, however, and continued to correspond.

In 1755, Voltaire moved to Les Délices, an estate near the Swiss border. He lived there from 1755 to 1760, and it was there that, still in a depressed frame of mind, he wrote *Candide*.

From 1760 until his death, Voltaire resided in Ferney, on French soil, although situated very close to the Swiss border. Voltaire was extremely active during this period. He wrote some six thousand letters, as well as pamphlets, plays, and tales. In closing his letters, he usually wrote "Écrasez l'infâme" (crush the vile), by which he meant that superstition and intolerance must be eliminated. He wrote philosophical tales here, waging his battle against the usual targets; *Ingenuous* appeared at this time, as did many other philosophical tales. Voltaire championed the causes of the Calas and Sirven families and also of La Barre; all three were cases of the miscarriage of justice and of religious persecution.

Voltaire, taking his own advice at the end of *Candide*, did much to improve the region of Ferney. He built a church, installed a tannery, and established a watchmaking industry. He even had his area exempted from the salt tax. In 1778, at the age of eighty-three, Voltaire went to Paris in triumph to watch a production of *Irène*. His popularity was at its highest, and the accolades and honors he received during his sojourn proved too much for him; he died shortly thereafter.

Analysis

Voltaire was the most influential writer in eighteenth century France. He epitomizes the philosopher of the *siècle des lumières*, the Age of Enlightenment; his curiosity embraces all the developments of his day, whether French or otherwise European, scientific or literary. His faith in human reason does not waver, although his optimism about human progress often does. His writings reflect the changing literary tastes of the century as he defends a waning classical tradition while himself introducing the most outrageous innovations. His theater particularly embodies both of these tendencies, whereas his tales tend to exploit traditional literary forms in order to introduce a unique type of satiric philosophical story.

Voltaire's long fiction includes many rather short stories, which have been called indiscriminately *romans philosophiques* (philosophical novels) or *contes philosophiques* (philosophical tales). According to Henri Coulet, Voltaire himself used the term *histoire* (story). Because satire such as Voltaire's depends on economy of style and the tales have no real development of plot or character, they are limited in length by the genre itself.

Candide is considered to be the most perfect example of the philosophical novel, revealing Voltaire's brilliant irony and vivacious wit. All the tales are humorous tragicomedies and include incidents that are by turns absurd, grotesque, poetic, romantic, and shocking. The unifying element is always the philosophical theme that Voltaire is stressing. Voltaire began writing his tales at the age of forty-five, when his ideas were firmly established; hence, the concerns and reforms he seeks to address remain fairly constant throughout the tales. Despite the fact that these stories are meant to appeal primarily to the intellect, they are eminently entertaining. Voltaire's writings are rooted firmly in the humanistic rationalism of the first half of his century rather than in the literature of pre-Romantic sensibility, which made its appearance in the late 1700's.

Henri Bénac's suggestion that the tales fall into four chronological groups related to the development of Voltaire's thought is widely accepted. Bénac proposes that the first two groups—of 1747 to 1752 and 1756 to 1759—reveal Voltaire's growing realization that war must be waged against evils such as intolerance, injustice, corruption, and ignorance. The first group includes such stories as *Le Monde comme il va* (1748; revised as *Babouc: Ou, Le Monde comme il va*, 1749; *Babouc: Or, The World as It Goes*, 1754; also known as *The World as It Is: Or, Babouc's Vision*, 1929), *Memnon: Or, Human*

Wisdom, and *La Lettre d'un Turc* (1750); *Zadig* and *Micromegas* are the best known of the group. The second group includes *History of Scarmentado's Travels*, which is the outline of *Candide*. In the third group figure *Jeannot et Colin* (1764; *Jeannot and Colin*, 1929), *Le Blanc et le noir* (1764; *The Two Genies*, 1895), and, best known, *Ingenuous*, *The Man of Forty Crowns*, and *The Princess of Babylon*. According to Bénac, the tales in this third group are, like Voltaire's pamphlets, weapons in his war against oppression of all kinds. In the last group, Bénac sees Voltaire searching for a morality on which to base a humane and free society. Tales in this period include *L'Histoire de Jenni* (1775) and *Les Oreilles du Comte de Chesterfield* (1775; *The Ears of Lord Chesterfield and Parson Goodman*, 1826).

ZADIG

The concerns of the early tales recur throughout all the stories, but Voltaire presents the different tales with a rich range of tones. *Zadig*, like other tales of this early group, is imbued with sunny humor and gaiety despite the sardonic irony that underscores the misfortunes of the hero. Voltaire sketches his hero Zadig with an unusually delicate touch, and some passages dazzle momentarily with rare poetry: "He marveled at these vast globes of light which to our eyes appear to be only feeble sparks. . . . His soul flew up into the infinite and, detached from his senses, contemplated the immutable order of the universe."

Memnon: Histoire orientale contained fifteen chapters that reappeared in *Zadig* in 1748. The story of Zadig is in the picaresque tradition, which is to say that the hero, on his travels, meets with many adventures. The plot of such a tale is of necessity episodic and highly imaginative. Zadig, a wealthy, virtuous, and handsome young Babylonian, is about to marry the beautiful young Semire, who loves him "passionately." When a jealous youth, Orcan, attempts to abduct Semire, Zadig bravely rescues his betrothed, receiving a wound that might mean the loss of an eye. Instead of expressing her gratitude, Semire protests that she hates one-eyed men, and she promptly marries Orcan. Zadig recovers quickly and marries another woman, Azora, whose faithfulness he puts to the test by pretending to have died. Unfortunately, Azora fails the test. Zadig encounters difficulties with the law when he makes scientific deductions from observing the tracks of the queen's dog and the king's horse, leading a huntsman to deduce that Zadig stole the animals. Zadig eventually becomes the king's prime minister.

His next misfortune arises through no fault of his own: Queen Astarté falls in love with him. The king, in jealousy, plots to kill them both, and Zadig has to flee. As he arrives in Egypt, he sees an Egyptian beating a woman, who asks Zadig to save her. In the ensuing fight, Zadig kills his adversary. Zadig is arrested and imprisoned for this act, then sold as a slave and taken to Arabia by his master, Sétoc, with whom he becomes close friends. Zadig dissuades a young widow from burning herself on her husband's funeral pyre, as is the religious custom. He also persuades an Egyptian, an Indian, a Chinese, a Greek, and a Celt to worship the same Supreme Being. Zadig is accused of impiety by Arabian priests and condemned to be burned. The young widow whom he saved now helps him escape.

Zadig next goes to the island of Serendib (Ceylon) on behalf of Sétoc. He makes a good impression on the king of the island and helps him to find an honest minister. On his travels, Zadig meets the brigand chief Arbogad and learns that King Moabdar has gone mad and been killed, and Astarté has disappeared. Zadig eventually discovers that Astarté is a captive of Ogul, who is sick with an imaginary illness. Zadig cures Ogul, and the two return to Babylon, where peace is restored. Zadig wins a tournament that is held to decide who shall be the new king of Babylon and marry Astarté. Zadig wins the tournament but is cheated, and his rival claims the victory. In the middle of his despair, Zadig meets a hermit who reveals to him the secret of happiness, and Zadig learns to accept the ways of Providence. Zadig guesses the correct answers to the riddles and finally marries Astarté.

Zadig the hero—whose name in Arabic means "just"—attempts to be happy in a world where goodness is frustrated by absurd and illogical interventions of fate. At one point, Zadig says: "I was sent to execution because I had written verses in praise of the King; I was on the point of being strangled because the Queen had yellow ribbons; and here I am a slave with you because a brute beat his mistress. Come, let's not lose heart; perhaps all this will end."

The absurdity of Zadig's world, which is out of

control and beyond the powers of logical explanation, is not the horror evoked in Franz Kafka's fiction; unlike Kafka, Voltaire does not attempt to create a sense of dreamlike but undeniable reality in either setting or characterization. Voltaire's exotic Eastern novel is in the tradition of the fifteenth century *The Arabian Nights' Entertainments*, also known as *The Thousand and One Nights*, translated from the Arabic by Antoine Gallard and much in vogue after the success of Montesquieu's *Lettres persanes* (1721; *Persian Letters*, 1722). The events are as unreal as those of the fairy tale, and the sensibility of the reader is not touched by Zadig's dilemmas. Instead, Voltaire disturbs the comfort of the reader's reason, logic, and innate sense of order and justice; the irony of Voltaire is at work. The frustration of Zadig becomes that of his audience. The knight Itobad steals Zadig's white suit of armor during the night, leaving his green suit in its place so that Zadig cannot claim the hand of Astarté, and Zadig cannot prove that he is the victor of the tournament, because the combatants must conceal their identities until a victor is proclaimed. Zadig has often been punished unjustly for being good, and here he is once again cheated of a happiness that is almost within his grasp. The audience is robbed of an anticipated happy ending and is frustrated by this anticlimax.

Voltaire was a master of the art of satire, and he often made use of anticlimax as an effective satiric technique. Zadig, after bewailing a list of horrifying punishments he has narrowly escaped, says, "Come, let's not lose heart; perhaps all this will end." This anticlimactic statement satirizes both Zadig's naïve optimism and the ridiculous optimism of the philosophers Gottfried Wilhelm Leibniz and Friedrich August Wolf—that "this is the best of all possible worlds"—which was much in vogue in the eighteenth century.

This leitmotif, the attack on optimism, is one of the many minor satiric barbs that Voltaire uses to spice his tale. Other satiric attacks abound in *Zadig* and reappear throughout the tales. Eighteenth century readers, usually members of the nobility and upper middle class, took delight in synthesizing the apparent subject of Voltaire's narrative with the real and often audacious object of its satire. Voltaire makes a dangerous allusion to the court when the fisherman tells Zadig how archers "armed with a royal warrant were pillaging his house lawfully and in good order." The ironic effect is achieved by the surprising juxtaposition of "pillaging" and "lawfully." Voltaire's irony had its basis in reality: He had been forced to flee the court at Versailles after making disparaging remarks about the courtiers being cheats. In *Zadig*, Voltaire also frequently satirizes the judicial system and judges who are "abysses of knowledge," who "prove" Zadig looked out of a window even though Zadig has answered none of their questions.

Voltaire's anticlericalism and antireligious bent often figure in the satire of *Zadig*. Almona the Arab widow intends to burn herself on her husband's funeral pyre, as the Brahman religion demands. Zadig the philosopher reasons her out of this plan, convincing her that she is about to take a ridiculous course in order to satisfy her vanity and not her religious principles. Zadig also persuades Sétoc that it is ridiculous to worship shining lights (the stars), and he demonstrates his reasons by kneeling and appearing to worship lighted candles. The "bonzes," who represent the monks, "chanted beautiful prayers to music, and left the state a prey to the barbarians." Zadig's rationalism (and Voltaire's) is primarily concerned with people's practical problems in society.

Voltaire's primary philosophical theme, however, is people's concern with destiny. Zadig vacillates between hope and despair as fate deals him many adverse blows. Despite his ingenuity and virtue, which he displays when he acts as the prime minister of King Moabdar, Zadig is presented as the plaything of destiny. The fisherman's story and the hermit incident reinforce the supremacy of this philosophical question as the main theme. How do philosophers explain the sufferings of a good person in the hands of a malevolent destiny? Voltaire resolves this problem happily with a deus ex machina ending. The angel Jesrad, representing divine intervention, tells Zadig to stop his questioning and simply worship Providence. Most men, Jesrad explains, form opinions with limited knowledge. Zadig's virtue triumphs, and he wins his queen and rules with "justice and love. Men blessed Zadig and Zadig blessed heaven." The skies of Zadig remain free of the blackness of *Candide*.

MICROMEGAS

Micromegas, which appeared in 1752, is a philosophical tale in a more literal sense, being primarily a vehicle for ideas on relativity. It is a very short tale, with almost no action (in stark contrast to the episodic *Zadig*) and only two main protagonists. Micromegas (which is Greek for "little big one") is a very tall inhabitant of the planet Sirius who has been banned from court for writing a book about insects that the "Mufti" of his planet has found to be heretical. He goes on an interplanetary voyage, finally arriving on the planet Saturn, where he meets a dwarf. (Voltaire intended his readers to recognize in the dwarf a caricature of his own enemy, Bernard le Bovier de Fontenelle.) The two travelers arrive on Earth and finally discover minute humans in a boat. The travelers attend a banquet at which various forms of philosophical credos are represented, allowing Voltaire to launch a satiric attack on the theories of Aristotle, René Descartes, Nicolas Malebranche, and Leibniz. Voltaire approves of the philosophy of the follower of John Locke. A storm develops, and the philosophers fall into the pocket of Micromegas. Although the giant is angry that such small creatures have so much pride, he gives a book to the philosophers; its pages, however, are blank. Voltaire gives the closing line to the dwarf (his enemy, Fontenelle), who, upon receiving the blank book—supposedly a philosophical treatise revealing the final truth about things—says, "Ah . . . that's just what I suspected." This last line was extremely offensive to Fontenelle, because it implied that he agreed that all of his metaphysical speculations over the past years had been wasted effort—that such truths were impossible to discover and prove. This attack on metaphysics is the main thrust of Voltaire's satire in *Micromegas*. Voltaire ridicules the philosophers in the boat, implying that "our little pile of mud" is relatively unimportant when seen in relation to the rest of the cosmos and that the opinions of its inhabitants are hence practically worthless. The philosophers in the boat all talk at once and all have different opinions. Voltaire shows that this kind of truth is "relative" to the person uttering it, and unreliable.

Voltaire's *Micromegas* is in direct imitation of Jonathan Swift's *Gulliver's Travels* (1726), and Montesquieu had previously used this type of travel story in *Persian Letters*. Voltaire, then, used an established subgenre, the fictional travelogue, as a vehicle for social commentary: The traveler in a strange land, seeing things for the first time, has no prejudice and puts into a new perspective situations that have been seen in only a certain way for centuries. This fresh perspective opens the way for critical appraisal and reform.

In *Micromegas*, Voltaire makes little effort to convince the reader of the reality of his story; the tale must be accepted as fantasy. The satire is less complicated, less adroit, and less sparkling than it is in *Zadig*. The main purpose of the satire is to address subjects of great interest to Voltaire's contemporaries; little of the subject matter of *Micromegas* is of interest to the modern reader. These two early works, *Zadig* and *Micromegas*, do, however, share a lighthearted spirit of enjoyment as Voltaire ridicules general stupidity and personal enemies. In these works, too, Voltaire formulated what would become the constant subjects of his satiric attacks throughout his tales.

Candide

Candide belongs to the second group of tales described by Bénac and is distinguished by its radical pessimism and bitter irony, in contrast to the sunny atmosphere of the previous two tales. *Candide* is considered the epitome of the philosophical tale, and it remains highly relevant today. Unlike Voltaire's other writings, *Candide* is still read everywhere. The tale's atmosphere is dark and often despairing. Voltaire was shocked by the horrors and atrocities of the Seven Years' War, which began in August, 1756, when Frederick the Great invaded Saxony. The Lisbon earthquake in 1755 also horrified Voltaire, causing him to reflect on what kind of Providence could inflict death on the innocent and guilty alike. The optimistic philosophy of Leibniz and Wolf seemed totally absurd in the midst of so much human suffering.

The satire in *Candide* is directed above all against this optimistic philosophy, epitomized in the character Pangloss. The characters in this tale are caricatures, deformed so that each represents only one characteristic or outlook. Candide, the hero, represents naïve, good, and reasonable humanity. The philosopher Martin symbolizes a cynical Manichaeanism that acknowledges the power of evil as well as of good in the world. James, who represents real human goodness and charity, is allowed to drown in stormy seas after rescuing a sailor who had attempted to murder him. Such is the bitter mood of the tale.

The form of this novel is basically picaresque, as in

Zadig, but Voltaire also parodies the novel of adventure and the novel of sentiment. The characters continually die horrible deaths after suffering gruesome tortures in various lands, but they somehow miraculously (and ridiculously) reappear, having been saved or cured. Their tearful reunions are a parody of the sentimental literature that Samuel Richardson's *Pamela: Or, Virtue Rewarded* (1740-1741) introduced to France from England and that infiltrated the bourgeois dramas of Diderot, and indeed of Voltaire's own theater. These reappearances also reinforce the central unity of the novel. A finely orchestrated rhythm unifies the entire tale; it is not simply that the main aim of the satire holds the tale together, as in the other stories. The fates (and philosophies) of secondary characters affect the hero in a rhythmic ebb and flow of alternating hope and despair that echo across the desolate landscape of a sad humanity in the throes of war, persecution, and suffering.

A gloss of the incidents in the tale reveals that there is no development of character or plot as such, and it underlines the rapid and vertiginous pace of the tale's episodes. This brisk pace lightens the seriousness of the atrocities being described, preventing the reader from dwelling on them or taking them to heart. Hence, Voltaire employs a technique of diminution, undercutting the value and dignity of human life.

Candide lives happily in a château in Westphalia with the baron of Thunderten-tronckh. Pangloss, the disciple of the optimistic philosophy of Leibniz, also lives there as tutor, as does Cunegonde, the baron's beautiful daughter, whom Candide loves. Candide agrees with Pangloss that all works out for the best in this wonderful world at the château. The baron, however, discovering the two lovers embracing, chases Candide out of the château. He is carried off forcibly to join an army and fight. After deserting, he goes to Holland, where he meets Pangloss, who has become a beggar and is barely recognizable with the sores of a terrible disease. Candide learns that all the people of the château have been killed.

Candide takes Pangloss to his benefactor, James the Anabaptist, who restores the sick man. The three then set sail for Lisbon, where James has a business engagement. On the way to Lisbon, their ship is wrecked in a storm, and James is drowned, while a sailor who had tried to murder him is saved. In Lisbon, Pangloss and Candide live through an earthquake that kills thirty thousand people. As Candide and Pangloss wander through the destroyed city, Pangloss attempts to comfort the citizens with his philosophy that "all is for the best"—a philosophy that, as Voltaire makes clear in his juxtaposition of Pangloss's theories to the suffering about him, is ludicrous if not cruel. Overhearing Pangloss's remarks, an officer of the Inquisition questions Pangloss about his belief in Original Sin and Free Will. Pangloss, sputtering his rationalizations, is arrested along with Candide—"one for having spoken, the other for having listened with an air of approval." Pangloss is hanged, but Candide is saved by the timely arrival of Cunegonde, who has escaped from the massacre of her family.

As things are beginning to seem more hopeful, Candide is obliged to kill two people, and he has to flee to America. He takes refuge with some Jesuits in Paraguay, where he miraculously meets Cunegonde's brother, who has also escaped the massacre at the château and has become a priest. Although he embraces Candide as a brother, his mood suddenly shifts when Candide announces that he intends to marry Cunegonde, and in the ensuing fight, Candide kills the brother of his beloved. After similar incidents in Eldorado, Surinam, Venice, and Constantinople, Candide finally finds Cunegonde. After all of her suffering, she has become very ugly, but, true to his word, Candide marries her. He then takes the advice of a wise old Turk and installs himself and his companions in an estate. He refuses to ask any more philosophical questions about evil and suffering in favor of hard work and practical reality—thus the novel's famous closing line: ". . . we must cultivate our garden."

In 1759, the year that *Candide* was published, Voltaire bought Ferney, an estate on the French-Swiss border, which has led critics to surmise that Candide's conclusions about work and the happiness to be found in practical progress are those of Voltaire. Once Voltaire was installed at Ferney, he gained confidence and energy and bombarded his public and his enemies with pamphlets, essays, plays, and stories, waging numerous legal battles on behalf of those persecuted for religious reasons. *Ingenuous* was written during this last, very active period of Voltaire's life. Although Voltaire was seventy-three years old when he wrote this work, his incredible intellectual and creative vigor had not diminished.

Ingenuous

Ingenuous is one of the weapons Voltaire used in his unremitting battle against intolerance and injustice and belongs to the third group of novels delineated by Bénac. Voltaire's confidence had returned, and he wrote with a sure hand; none of the tales that follow *Candide* can rival the grandeur of *Ingenuous*.

Ingenuous is the most romantic of Voltaire's stories, and its plot is narrative rather than episodic. The tone of the story is more naturalistic, as are the characters. The device of a voyage is used again; the religious and social systems of France in the time of Louis XIV are seen through the eyes of the Huron stranger, who, without prejudice and with candid reasoning, questions institutions and beliefs that have been taken for granted and must now be considered from a new perspective.

The character of the Huron is in the tradition of the "noble savage" popularized by a missionary, baron de Lahontan, who praised the uncorrupted American Indian. The unity of the tale lies in the unfolding of the story of two lovers: Hercules Kerkabon (as the Huron is later named) and Mademoiselle de St. Yves. The satire used here also unites with the central love theme, targeting the corrupt Catholic Church and its priests, monks, and practices, which are instrumental in separating the lovers and ruining their chance for happiness. Voltaire also satirizes the court officials and Jansenism.

Voltaire's wit has a somewhat subdued tone throughout *Ingenuous*; the satire resides in the calmly reasoned arguments of the Huron, who questions all the basic doctrines of Jesuit and Jansenist alike. Voltaire, using the Huron as his mouthpiece, explains very simply all of his objections to the two religions. At the time of writing this tale, Voltaire was involved in the trials of the Calas family, the Sirven family, and La Barre, and his hatred of religious persecution and his anger at the injustices meted out by a corrupt judicial system were therefore as intense as they had ever been.

The story reflects the century's taste for cosmopolitanism. The Huron has been reared by a Huron tribe in Canada and arrives on the Lower Brittany coast in 1689. It is "discovered" that he is the lost child of the Abbé Yerkabon and his sister. Their brother went to Canada as a soldier and was killed by the Iroquois. The Abbé claims Hercules as his nephew and baptizes him as a Catholic. The beautiful Mademoiselle de St. Yves acts as his godmother. Hercules later falls in love with Mademoiselle de St. Yves but cannot marry his godmother, because the Church forbids it. Mademoiselle de St. Yves is sent to a convent, and Hercules, who is by now a hero for helping to defend the French against an English attack, goes to Versailles to engage the king's help in his marriage scheme. At Versailles, he is arrested and imprisoned in the Bastille, where he meets Gordon, a Jansenist. After much study and discussion, he converts Gordon to Deism. Now Mademoiselle de St. Yves goes to Versailles to save Hercules, but she must submit to a government minister in order to obtain her lover's release. She never recovers from the shame and dies of her chagrin. Hercules is tempted to take his own life but recovers himself and becomes an excellent officer and philosopher. The tale does not end with the expected happy ending for the lovers, but Voltaire suggests that even if ambitions and ideals cannot be attained, there are compromises that can be made and one can be tolerably happy—a message similar to that of *Candide*.

The Man of Forty Crowns

The Man of Forty Crowns, published the year after *Ingenuous*, displays a strong contrast in style. The two tales have in common the underlying interest of Voltaire in practical things. In *Ingenuous*, Voltaire has Hercules recover from his loss and become a good soldier; in *The Man of Forty Crowns*, Voltaire has his protagonist discuss tax reform with a mathematician. There is a great difference, however, between these polemics and those of *Ingenuous*. In the later tale, Voltaire writes for a clever and agile mind able to follow the mathematical bent of his arguments. There is scarcely a plot or an appealing character to enliven the discussion. Voltaire, as usual, satirizes monks (who do not pay taxes), despotic monarchs, unfair judicial systems, and ignorant people who think they know more than they do. This highly polemical tale, amusing for Voltaire's eighteenth century circle, is of little interest today; not even the odd humorous remark, such as the suggestion that smiles and songs be taxed, can redeem the lack of relevance or interest of this story for a modern reader.

Voltaire's tales do suffer a slight impoverishment in translation. The musicality of the French language offsets the dryness of the succinct, economic prose and the laconic, pointed understatement. Polemical tales such as *The Man of Forty Crowns* particularly suffer in English translation.

Of Voltaire's many tales (some two dozen in all), *Candide* remains the most popular. Perhaps it has universal appeal because the evils it portrays persist in today's world. Wars are still waged in the name of religious causes, and political prisoners continue to be tortured and cast into jail without trial. Unfortunately, Voltaire is no longer here to provoke people's consciences and fire their minds with his energetic fury. Without him, the genre of the philosophical tale lies in disuse.

Avril S. Lewis

Other major works

SHORT FICTION: *Le Monde comme il va*, 1748 (revised as *Babouc: Ou, Le Monde comme il va*, 1749; *Babouc: Or, The World as It Goes*, 1754; also known as *The World as It Is: Or, Babouc's Vision*, 1929); *Memnon: Ou, La Sagesse humaine*, 1749 (*Memnon: Or, Human Wisdom*, 1961); *La Lettre d'un Turc*, 1750; *Le Blanc et le noir*, 1764 (*The Two Genies*, 1895); *Jeannot et Colin*, 1764 (*Jeannot and Colin*, 1929); *L'Histoire de Jenni*, 1775; *Les Oreilles du Comte de Chesterfield*, 1775 (*The Ears of Lord Chesterfield and Parson Goodman*, 1826).

PLAYS: *Œdipe*, pr. 1718 (*Oedipus*, 1761); *Artémire*, pr. 1720; *Mariamne*, pr. 1724 (English translation, 1761); *L'Indiscret*, pr., pb. 1725 (verse play); *Brutus*, pr. 1730 (English translation, 1761); *Ériphyle*, pr. 1732; *Zaïre*, pr. 1732 (English translation, 1736); *La Mort de César*, pr. 1733; *Adélaïde du Guesclin*, pr. 1734; *L'Échange*, pr. 1734; *Alzire*, pr., pb. 1736 (English translation, 1763); *L'Enfant prodigue*, pr. 1736 (verse play; prose translation, *The Prodigal*, 1750?); *Zulime*, pr. 1740; *Mahomet*, pr., pb. 1742 (*Mahomet the Prophet*, 1744); *Mérope*, pr. 1743 (English translation, 1744, 1749); *La Princesse de Navarre*, pr., pb. 1745 (verse play; music by Jean-Philippe Rameau); *La Prude: Ou, La Grandeuse de Cassette*, pr., pb. 1747 (wr. 1740; verse play; adaptation of William Wycherley's play *The Plain Dealer*); *Sémiramis*, pr. 1748 (*Semiramis*, 1760); *Nanine*, pr., pb. 1749 (English translation, 1927); *Oreste*, pr., pb. 1750; *Rome sauvée*, pr., pb. 1752; *L'Orphelin de la Chine*, pr., pb. 1755 (*The Orphan of China*, 1756); *Socrate*, pb. 1759 (*Socrates*, 1760); *L'Écossaise*, pr., pb. 1760 (*The Highland Girl*, 1760); *Tancrède*, pr. 1760; *Olympie*, pb. 1763; *Le Triumvirat*, pr. 1764; *Les Scythes*, pr., pb. 1767; *Les Guèbres: Ou, La Tolérance*, pb. 1769; *Sophonisbe*, pb. 1770 (revision of Jean Mairet's play); *Les Pélopides: Ou, Atrée et Thyeste*, pb. 1772; *Les Lois de Minos*, pb. 1773; *Don Pèdre*, pb. 1775 (wr. 1761); *Irène*, pr. 1778; *Agathocle*, pr. 1779.

POETRY: *Poème sur la religion naturelle*, 1722; *La Ligue*, 1723; *La Henriade*, 1728 (a revision of *La Ligue*; *Henriade*, 1732); *Le Mondain*, 1736 (*The Man of the World*, 1764); *Discours en vers sur l'homme*, 1738 (*Discourses in Verse on Man*, 1764); *Poème de Fontenoy*, 1745; *Poème sur la loi naturelle*, 1752 (*On Natural Law*, 1764); *La Pucelle d'Orléans*, 1755, 1762 (*The Maid of Orleans*, 1758; also known as *La Pucelle: Or, The Maid of Orleans*, 1785-1786); *Poème sur la désastre de Lisbonne*, 1756 (*Poem on the Lisbon Earthquake*, 1764); *Le Pauvre Diable*, 1758; *Épître à Horace*, 1772.

NONFICTION: *An Essay upon the Civil Wars of France . . . and Also upon the Epick Poetry of the European Nations from Homer Down to Milton*, 1727; *La Henriade*, 1728 (*Henriade*, 1732); *Histoire de Charles XII*, 1731 (*The History of Charles XII*, 1732); *Le Temple du goût*, 1733 (*The Temple of Taste*, 1734); *Lettres philosophiques*, 1734 (originally published in English as *Letters Concerning the English Nation*, 1733; also known as *Philosophical Letters*, 1961); *Discours de métaphysique*, 1736; *Éléments de la philosophie de Newton*, 1738 (*The Elements of Sir Isaac Newton's Philosophy*, 1738); *Discours en vers sur l'homme*, 1738-1752 (*Discourses in Verse on Man*, 1764); *Vie de Molière*, 1739; *Le Siècle de Louis XIV*, 1751 (*The Age of Louis XIV*, 1752); *Essai sur les mœurs et l'esprit des nations*, 1756, 1763 (*The General History and State of Europe*, 1754, 1759); *Traité sur la tolérance*, 1763 (*A Treatise on Religious Toleration*, 1764); *Commentaires sur le théâtre de Pierre Corneille*, 1764; *Dictionnaire philosophique portatif*, 1764 (enlarged 1769 as *La Raison par alphabet*; also known as *Dictionnaire philosophique*; *A Philosophical Dictionary for the Pocket*, 1765; also known as *Philosophical Dictionary*, 1945, enlarged 1962); *Avis au public sur les parracides imputés aux calas et aux Sirven*, 1775; *Correspondence*, 1953-1965 (102 volumes).

MISCELLANEOUS: *The Works of M. de Voltaire*, 1761-1765 (35 volumes), 1761-1781 (38 volumes); *Candide, and Other Writings*, 1945; *The Portable Voltaire*, 1949; *Candide, Zadig, and Selected Stories*, 1961; *The Complete Works of Voltaire*, 1968-1977 (135 volumes; in French).

Bibliography

Aldridge, A. Owen. *Voltaire and the Century of Light*. Princeton, N.J.: Princeton University Press, 1975. Reexamines the life and career of Voltaire within the context of European intellectual and political history, providing many useful insights. Presents information in a pleasant style equally suited to specialists and general readers. Also offers stimulating readings of *Candide* and other selected works as well as a valuable bibliography.

Bird, Stephen. *Reinventing Voltaire: The Politics of Commemoration in Nineteenth Century France*. Oxford, England: Voltaire Foundation, 2000. Focuses on the critical response to Voltaire in nineteenth century France, where his legacy was both vilified and venerated. Includes bibliography and indexes.

Cronk, Nicholas, ed. *The Cambridge Companion to Voltaire*. New York: Cambridge University Press, 2009. Collection of essays examines Voltaire's life, philosophy, and works. Includes discussions of Voltaire as a storyteller, Voltaire and authorship, and Voltaire and the myth of England as well as an analysis of *Candide* by Philip Stewart.

Davidson, Ian. *Voltaire in Exile: The Last Years*. New York: Grove Press, 2004. Chronicles Voltaire's life during his exile from France, when he actively campaigned against censorship, war, torture, capital punishment, the alliance between church and state, and other perceived injustices. Includes an analysis of much of Voltaire's personal correspondence.

Gray, John. *Voltaire*. New York: Routledge, 1999. Volume in Routledge's Great Philosophers series provides a concise overview of Voltaire's philosophy. Includes bibliography.

Havens, George R. *The Age of Ideas*. New York: Henry Holt, 1955. Often reprinted and providing a model and inspiration for many writers, Havens's witty, informed overview of the Enlightenment and its precursors remains authoritative as a guide to trends and thinkers of the period. Contains groups of chapters devoted to Voltaire, Charles de Montesquieu, Denis Diderot, and Jean-Jacques Rousseau; the four chapters devoted to Voltaire provide an excellent introduction to the man and his work, with brief but perceptive readings of such texts as *Zadig* and *Candide*.

Knapp, Bettina Liebowitz. *Voltaire Revisited*. New York: Twayne, 2000. Good introductory study describes Voltaire's life and devotes separate chapters to all of the genres of his works, including *Candide* and other philosophical tales. Includes bibliography and index.

Mason, Haydn Trevor. *"Candide": Optimism Demolished*. New York: Twayne, 1992. Examination of Voltaire's novel is divided into two parts: The first addresses the work's literary and historical context, including its critical reception, and the second provides a reading of the book's view of history, philosophy, personality, structure, and form. Includes notes and annotated bibliography.

_______. *Voltaire*. New York: St. Martin's Press, 1975. Comprehensive monograph (not to be confused with the biography Mason published six years later, cited below) is intended for the interested undergraduate or general reader. Steers clear of the traditional chronological approach in order to present Voltaire's works by genre, treating first his drama and dramatic criticism and then proceeding to historiography, short fiction, poetry, and polemics. Supplemented by a useful if brief bibliography.

_______. *Voltaire: A Biography*. Baltimore: Johns Hopkins University Press, 1981. Presents a concise but lively survey of the subject's life, clearly relating the major works to their contexts, including their inspiration or—as is especially pertinent in the case of Voltaire—provocation. Closely documented, useful both as biography and as criticism, this volume is recommended to students and general readers alike.

Pearson, Roger. *Voltaire Almighty: A Life in Pursuit of Freedom*. London: Bloomsbury, 2005. Readable, compelling account of Voltaire's life focuses on his love of liberty and how that passion informed his life and work. Includes bibliography, index, and illustrations.

Vartanian, Aram. "*Zadig:* Theme and Countertheme." In *Dilemmas du roman*, edited by Catherine Lafarge. Saratoga, Calif.: Anima Libri, 1990. Analyzes Voltaire's novel and argues that its philosophical theme of impersonal fate is counterpoised against a background theme, creating a contrapuntal movement of the narrative structure. Asserts that the story is told in such a way that its overall meaning emerges from a network of tensions felt among its various elements.

KURT VONNEGUT

Born: Indianapolis, Indiana; November 11, 1922
Died: New York, New York; April 11, 2007
Also known as: Kurt Vonnegut, Jr.

Principal long fiction

Player Piano, 1952
The Sirens of Titan, 1959
Mother Night, 1961
Cat's Cradle, 1963
God Bless You, Mr. Rosewater: Or, Pearls Before Swine, 1965
Slaughterhouse-Five: Or, The Children's Crusade, a Duty-Dance with Death, 1969
Breakfast of Champions: Or, Goodbye Blue Monday, 1973
Slapstick: Or, Lonesome No More!, 1976
Jailbird, 1979
Deadeye Dick, 1982
Galápagos, 1985
Bluebeard, 1987
Hocus Pocus, 1990
Timequake, 1997
God Bless You, Dr. Kevorkian, 1999 (novella)

Other literary forms

Although known primarily for his novels, Kurt Vonnegut (VON-uh-guht) also wrote for Broadway and television and published a children's book and several books of essays.

Achievements

Critical acclaim eluded Kurt Vonnegut until *Slaughterhouse-Five* was published in 1969. An immediate best seller, it earned for the author respect from critics who had previously dismissed him as a mediocre science-fiction writer. Over the course of his career, Vonnegut was honored as the Briggs-Copeland Lecturer at Harvard University, as a member of the National Institute of Arts and Letters, and as the Distinguished Professor of English Prose at the City University of New York. Through his insightful and sympathetic treatment of the psychologically and morally crippled victims of the modern world, Vonnegut earned a reputation as one of the greatest humanist writers of his time.

Biography

Kurt Vonnegut, Jr., was born in Indianapolis, Indiana, in 1922. Both the location and the era of his birth helped shape his distinctive worldview. Growing up in the American heartland in the calm interval between the world wars, Vonnegut had a brief vision of a middle-class world that embraced the values of honesty, decency, and human dignity. For Vonnegut, this was the world as it should be, a world unravaged by violence and war, a world untouched by technology. This period of childhood happiness was, however, merely the calm before the storm in a life that would be rocked by a series of personal and national disasters: the suicide of his mother on Mother's Day; his prisoner-of-war experience in World War II; the deaths of his sister and brother-in-law; the dissolution of his first marriage; the bombings of Dresden and Hiroshima; the assassinations of President John F. Kennedy and the Reverend Martin Luther King, Jr.; the Vietnam War; the death of his first wife, with whom he had maintained a close friendship; and the death of his brother Bernard. All the heartaches of his

Kurt Vonnegut. (Jill Krementz)

family and his nation reverberate through Vonnegut's work, while the artist, through his fiction, stands as advocate for a saner, calmer world.

During the years of the Great Depression, Vonnegut's family suffered emotional and financial setbacks. When Vonnegut entered Cornell University in 1940, his father forbade him to study the arts and chose instead for his son a career in science, which he believed would guarantee job security. In 1943 Vonnegut left Cornell to enlist in the U.S. Army, despite his own public opposition to the war. Less than one year later, he was captured by the Germans and, in 1945, survived one of the greatest massacres of the war, the Allied firebombing of Dresden. This horror pursued Vonnegut for twenty-three years, until he worked through the pain by writing *Slaughterhouse-Five*.

After the war, Vonnegut married and began studies in anthropology at the University of Chicago. After three years, he left college and took a job as a publicist with General Electric (GE), where his brother worked as a physicist. Vonnegut's background in science and the disillusionment he experienced at GE influenced his first two novels, *Player Piano* and *The Sirens of Titan*, both parables of dehumanization in a technological society.

Between 1952 and 1998, Vonnegut wrote more than a dozen novels, numerous essays, a Broadway play, and a musical work, *Requiem*, that was performed by the Buffalo Symphony. He and Joe Petro III had a showing of twenty-six of their silk-screen prints in Denver in 1996. Despite his varied artistic talents, however, Vonnegut has always been known primarily for his fiction. In 1978, Vonnegut remarried, and he and his wife, Jill Krementz, settled in New York City. Vonnegut lived in New York until his death in 2007 at the age of eighty-four.

Analysis

In his novels, Kurt Vonnegut coaxes the reader toward greater sympathy for humanity and deeper understanding of the human condition. His genre is satire—sometimes biting, sometimes tender, always funny. His arena is as expansive as the whole universe and as tiny as a single human soul. Part philosopher, part poet, Vonnegut, in his fictive world, tackles the core problem of modern life: How can the individual maintain dignity and exercise free will in a world overrun by death and destruction, a world in which both science and religion are powerless to provide solutions? The reader will find no ready answers in Vonnegut, only a friendly guide along the questioning path.

Vonnegut himself behaved with a commendable sense of responsibility, dignity, and decency: He labored long to show humankind its ailments and to wake it to the work it has to do. He admitted to having lived comfortably while many of the world's population suffered, but in quoting the words of American socialist Eugene Debs in his dedication to *Hocus Pocus*, he seems to define the position that he himself took as human being and as author and public figure for half of the twentieth century: "While there is a lower class I am in it. While there is a criminal element I am of it. While there is a soul in prison I am not free." He spoke out in many forums for many causes and for all of humankind, and his has been a wide audience.

Player Piano

Ilium, New York, sometime in the near future, provides the setting for Vonnegut's first dystopian novel,

Player Piano. Ilium is a divided city. On one side of the river live the important people, the engineers and managers who program and operate the computers and machines that run people's lives. On the other side of the river, Homestead, live the downtrodden inhabitants of the city, those locked into menial, dehumanizing jobs assigned to them by the central computer.

Paul Proteus, the protagonist, is the brilliant young manager of the Ilium Works, a man being groomed for even greater success. Just as Ilium is a divided city, however, so is Paul divided about his life and his future. Paul suffers a growing discontent with his job at the Ilium Works, where people have been replaced by machines and machines are supervised by computers. Outwardly, Paul has no reason for worry or doubt. He has the best job and the most beautiful wife in Ilium, he is being considered for the highest post in his company, and he is climbing the ladder of success. Nevertheless, Paul's uneasiness increases. At first he seeks escape, settling on a farm in an attempt to get back to nature and free himself from his automatic life. He finds, however, that he has become an automaton, completely out of touch with the natural world, and his attempt at escape fails.

Finally, Paul is drawn to the other side of the river. His sympathy for the dehumanized masses and his acknowledgment of complicity in their plight drive Paul to join the masses in armed revolution. The fighters take to the streets, frantically and indiscriminately destroying all machines. The revolution fails, leaving Paul disillusioned and defeated, realizing that he has been manipulated by leaders on both sides of the conflict. Now he must surrender and face execution.

Paul's manipulation, first by those who would replace people with machines and then by those who would destroy the machines, is symbolized by the "player piano" of the title. The simplest of machines, the player piano creates its music without the aid of human beings, neatly rendering the skilled musician obsolete. Paul is entranced by the music of the player piano, in his fascination manipulated by the machine just as it manipulates its ivory keys.

The most striking symbol of the story, however, is the small black cat that Paul befriends as it wanders aimlessly through the Ilium Works. The cat, symbol of all that is natural and pure, despises the monstrous factory machines. The doomed animal is helplessly sucked into an automated sweeper, which spits it down a chute and ejects it outside the factory. Miraculously, it survives, but as Paul races to its rescue, the cat is roasted on the factory's electric fence, symbolizing humanity's destruction by the forces of technology. With characteristic Vonnegut irony, however, *Player Piano* ends on an affirmative note. Although the price of escape is its life, the cat does escape the Ilium Works. Near the end of the novel, Paul sees beautiful flowers growing outside the factory—flowers rooted in cat excrement, signifying ultimate rebirth and a glimmer of hope for Paul and his world.

MOTHER NIGHT

In his third novel, *Mother Night*, Vonnegut peers even more deeply into the human soul, exploring the roots of human alienation, probing an individual's search for his "real" identity, and uncovering the thin veil that separates reality from illusion. The story is told as the memoir of Howard W. Campbell, Jr., a self-proclaimed "citizen of nowhere." A successful writer and producer of medieval romance plays, Campbell sees himself as a sensitive *artiste*. Nevertheless, he allows himself to be recruited by Major Frank Wirtanen to be an American double agent posing as a Nazi radio propagandist in Germany. Secretly, Campbell sends coded American messages in his propaganda broadcasts, but he does not understand the code and never comprehends the messages he transmits. Still unaware, he even transmits the news of his beloved wife's death.

Publicly, Campbell is reviled as a traitorous Nazi hatemonger, but he does not mind because he enjoys being on the radio. Eventually, however, he begins to lose touch with his "real" self. Is he the sensitive artist, the cruel Nazi, or the American patriot? Like Paul Proteus, Campbell allows himself to be manipulated by those around him. With no will or identity of his own, Campbell is easy prey for those who would use him for their own ends.

Two of Campbell's manipulators are his postwar friend George Kraft and his sister-in-law Resi, who poses as Campbell's long-lost wife, Helga. George and Resi are actually Russian spies plotting to capture Campbell and transport him to Russia. They abandon this plan, however, when they realize their love for

Campbell, and they finally attempt to escape to freedom with him. Before the three can flee together, however, the Russians are arrested by American agents. Campbell is arrested as well but is soon freed by his friend Frank Wirtanen.

Gripped by existential fear at finding himself a free man, Campbell appeals to a Jewish couple in his apartment building, a doctor and his mother, both survivors of the Nazi death camp Auschwitz. Campbell begs to be tried for his crimes against the Jews and soon finds himself awaiting trial in a Jerusalem prison. Before Campbell goes to trial, Frank Wirtanen sends a letter on his behalf, explaining how he had recruited Campbell and honoring him as an American patriot. Campbell, however, can never be a truly free man until he purges his conscience. Upon his release from prison, he is nauseated by the prospect of his freedom, knowing that he is one of the many people "who served evil too openly and good too secretly." In his failure to resist evil and his openness to manipulation by others, Campbell had given up his free will and lost his ability to choose. Coming to this realization, he finally asserts his will to choose and ironically chooses to die, vowing to hang himself "for crimes against himself."

Cat's Cradle

Equally dark is Vonnegut's fourth novel, *Cat's Cradle*. In addition to its broad parody of science and religion, *Cat's Cradle* expands on Vonnegut's earlier themes of the dangerous misuse of science and technology, human beings' moral responsibility in an immoral world, and the importance of distinguishing reality from illusion. The parodic tone is set in the very first line, "Call me Jonah," bringing to mind the Old Testament book of Jonah. Like that Jonah, this protagonist (really named John) faithfully pursues God's directives but never truly comprehends the order behind God's plan. Continuing the parody, John encounters the Bokononist religion, whose bible, The Books of Bokonon, proclaims in its first line, "All of the true things I am about to tell you are shameless lies," an obvious inversion of the Johannine maxim "You will know the truth, and the truth will make you free" (John 8:32). In the world John inhabits, the only real freedom is the ultimate freedom—death.

John is writing a book, "The Day the World Ended," an account of the bombing of Hiroshima. His obsession with the destruction of Hiroshima foreshadows his involvement in the eventual destruction of the world by "ice-nine," a substance that converts liquid into frozen crystals. In *Cat's Cradle*, the atomic bomb and ice-nine are both the doomsday toys of an amoral scientist, Dr. Felix Hoenikker. Hoenikker pursues his work so intensely that he has little time for his three children, who grow up to be emotionally warped and twisted Products of Science. Hoenikker's only legacy to his children is the ice-nine he was brewing in the kitchen before his sudden death on Christmas Eve. After their father's death, the three children—Angela, Frank, and Newt—divide the ice-nine among themselves, knowing that it is their ticket to a better future. Newt, a midget, barters his ice-nine for an affair with a Russian ballerina. The homely Angela uses her portion to buy herself a husband. Frank gives his to Miguel "Papa" Monzano, dictator of the Caribbean Republic of San Lorenzo, in exchange for the title of general and the hand of Monzano's beautiful adopted daughter, Mona.

Pursuing information on the Hoenikker family, John finds himself in San Lorenzo, where he is introduced to Bokononism. The people of San Lorenzo are desperately poor, for the soil of the island is as unproductive as the Sahara. The island's teeming, malnourished masses find their only comfort in Bokononism, which urges them to love and console one another. John finds that, ironically, the religion started as a game by the island's founders. Knowing no way to lift the country from its destitution, they decided to give the people hope by inventing a religion based on *foma*, or comforting lies. The religion encouraged people to find strength in their *karass*, groups of people with whom they are joined to do God's mysterious will. To strengthen the faith of the people, Bokononism was outlawed, its founder banished on pain of death. As the people's faith grew, so did their happiness and their dependence on *foma*, until all the inhabitants of the island were "employed full time as actors in a play." For the inhabitants of San Lorenzo, illusion had become reality.

Soon after his arrival on the island, John finds that Papa Monzano is critically ill; it is expected that "General" Frank Hoenikker will succeed Papa and take the beautiful Mona as his bride. Secretly, however, Frank has no desire to rule the island or to marry Mona. He is a simpering mass of insecurities, hiding behind his fake title. Frank's life, like everything around him, has been a lie: He has bought a false sense of dignity, which he wears like a military uniform, but inside he is gripped with fear, the same fear that pulses through the veins of the dying dictator. Papa and Frank become symbols for all people, running scared and grasping at false comforts as they confront brutal reality. Faced with the horror of an agonizing death, Papa clutches his vial of ice-nine, his last illusion of security and power. Uttering the desperate cry, "Now I will destroy the whole world," he swallows the poison and turns himself into an ice-blue frozen statue. Papa's power proves illusory, however, as John and the Hoenikker children clean up the mess and seal off Papa's bedroom.

John, Frank, Angela, and Newt inform the staff that Papa is "feeling much better" and go downstairs to watch a military celebration. Despite their success at covering up Papa's death and hiding their secret, John and the Hoenikker children sense impending doom. As all the islanders watch the military air show, a bomber careens out of control and bursts into flames, setting off a massive explosion and landslide. As his castle disintegrates, Papa Monzano's body is propelled from the bedroom closet and plunges into the waiting sea, infecting all with ice-nine.

As the story ends, only John, Newt, and Bokonon remain, awaiting their imminent death. John recalls Angela's heroic end, remembering how she had clutched her clarinet bravely and played in the face of death, music mocking terror. John dreams of climbing the highest mountain and planting some magnificent symbol. As his heart swells with the vision of being the last man on the highest mountain, Newt mocks him and brings him back to earth. The story concludes with the last verse of The Books of Bokonon, in which Bokonon mourns human stupidity, thumbs his nose at God, and kills himself with ice-nine.

Like many of Vonnegut's satirical writings, *Cat's Cradle* functions as a wake-up call for humanity. For Vonnegut, heroism is not a dream; dignity is not an illusion. Still, he understands all too well the fear that grips an individual on the brink of action, the torpor that invades the soul. In his frustration, all the artist can do is plod on, calling out his warnings as he goes.

SLAUGHTERHOUSE-FIVE

Vonnegut's efforts to touch the soul of humanity are most fully realized in his sixth novel, *Slaughterhouse-Five*, his most moving and brilliant work. Incorporating all of Vonnegut's common themes—the nature of reality and illusion, the question of free will and determinism, the horror of humankind's cruelty to itself, the vision of life as an ironic construct—*Slaughterhouse-Five* produces "an image of life that is beautiful and surprising and deep." This often misunderstood novel leads the reader on a time-warped journey, as popular films say, "to hell and back." Emotionally suffocated by his experience in World War II, Vonnegut waited twenty-three years to tell the story of his capture by the Germans and his survival of the Allied firebombing of Dresden, the calculated annihilation of a quarter of a million refugees and civilians in an unguarded city.

As befits a tale of such distorted experience, *Slaughterhouse-Five* breaks all novelistic conventions. The story is divided into ten sections spanning the years from 1944 to 1968. Opening with a simple, first-person narrative, Vonnegut describes his return to Dresden in 1967. He recounts his life after the war, discusses his wife and children, and relives a conversation with his old war buddy Bernard V. O'Hare, in which he reveals why *Slaughterhouse-Five* is subtitled *The Children's Crusade*. In the original Children's Crusade of 1213, Catholic monks raised a volunteer army of thirty thousand children who were intent on traveling to Palestine but instead were sent to North Africa to be sold as slaves. In the end, half the children drowned en route and the others were sold. For Vonnegut, this incident provides the perfect metaphor for all wars: hopeless ventures fought by deluded children. Thus Vonnegut prepares the reader for this personal statement about the tragedy of war. Nevertheless, the reader remains unprepared for the narrative shape of the tale.

Breaking from his reverie, Vonnegut reads from a Gideon Bible the story of Lot's wife, turned to a pillar of salt for looking back on Sodom and Gomorrah. To Vonnegut, her reaction was tender, instinctively human, looking back on all those lives that had touched hers, and he adopts Lot's wife as a metaphor for his narrative stance. *Slaughterhouse-Five* will be a tale told by a "pillar of salt." Vonnegut assumes the role of a masked narrator, a disinterested party, allowing himself the aesthetic distance he needs to continue his painful journey. When the reader turns to chapter 2, however, another surprise appears, as chapter 2 begins, "Listen: Billy Pilgrim has come unstuck in time."

To increase his emotional distance from the story, Vonnegut, the masked narrator, tells not his own story but the story of pathetic Billy Pilgrim, Vonnegut's mythical fellow soldier. Through time travel over which he has no control, Billy is forced to relive the chapters of his life in seemingly random order. For Billy, as for Vonnegut, his war chronology is too unsettling to confront head-on. Instead of assimilating his life experiences, Billy unconsciously tries to escape the memory of them by bouncing back and forth in time from one experience to another. Not until the end of the tale can he face the crucial moment, the horror of Dresden.

The reader first sees Billy as a forty-six-year-old retired optometrist living in Ilium, New York. Billy's daughter, Barbara, thinks that he has lost his mind. Billy has given up interest in business and devotes all of his energies to telling the world about his travels to the planet Tralfamadore. Two years earlier, Billy had been captured by aliens from Tralfamadore and had spent six months on their planet. Billy's belief in Tralfamadorian philosophy is the great comfort of his life, and he is eager to share this philosophy with the world. The aliens taught Billy, the optometrist, a better way to "see." On Tralfamadore, time is not linear; all moments are structured and permanent, and death is merely one moment out of many moments in a person's life. The Tralfamadorians do not mourn the dead, for even though a person may be dead in one moment, he or she is alive and happy in many others. The Tralfamadorians respond to life's temporary bad moments with a verbal shrug, "So it goes." Their world is a world without free will, without human responsibility, without human sorrow. On an intellectual level, Billy hungrily embraces their philosophy, yet deep inside him (as inside Vonnegut) stirs the need to reconstruct his life, to reconcile his past. So, armed with Tralfamadorian detachment, Billy steps back in time to where it all began.

It is 1944, and Billy, a night student at the Ilium School of Optometry, is drafted into action in World War II. No soldier is more unsuited to war than is Billy. Timid and friendless, he is a chaplain's assistant, a hapless soul with a "meek faith in a loving Jesus which most soldiers found putrid." Billy's marching companion is Roland Weary, a savage young man even by military standards. Weary's father collects ancient instruments of torture, and Weary regales Billy with gruesome tales of cruelty, giving the gentle boy an unwanted view of a monstrous world. Weary, a callous, stupid killing machine, is the natural result of humanity's barbarity. Although physically robust, he is morally depleted, a symbol of the spiritually bankrupt world into which poor Billy has been thrust. Billy—kind, sensitive, tenderhearted—has no natural defenses against the barbarity that surrounds him, so he becomes unstuck in time.

After a brief respite of time travel, Billy returns to the war. He and Weary have been captured behind German lines, taken prisoner by two toothless old men and two young boys. The Germans are accompanied by a guard dog, a female German shepherd named Princess who had been stolen from a farmer. Princess and Billy are confused and shivering from the cold. Of the whole motley group, only the barbarous Weary belongs at war. Billy, Princess, the old men, and the young boys symbolize helpless humanity in the grip of military madness.

Billy and his fellow prisoners, including Vonnegut and Bernard V. O'Hare, are taken to a prisoner-of-war camp before their transport to Dresden. As Billy recalls these moments of his life, he is moved to time-travel many times. He flashes forward to 1948, when, emotionally shattered by his war experience, he checks himself into a veterans' hospital for mental patients. Here the reader is introduced to Valencia Merble, Billy's unlovely fiancé, and Eliot Rosewater, his fellow mental patient. In the hospital, Eliot and Billy devour the science-fiction novels of author Kilgore Trout. They are drawn to Trout's work for the same reason Billy is drawn to the philosophy of Tralfamadore: Human experience on Earth has been too disturbing; life seems meaningless. Escaping to the world of science fiction relieves the pressure, enabling Eliot and Billy to "reinvent" themselves in a kinder universe.

Before Billy returns to his war story, he again relives his adventures on the planet Tralfamadore, where he spends six months in the Tralfamadore Zoo, displayed in a glass cage. Here Billy learns of his own death in 1976. He will be murdered by Paul Lazarro, a former inmate in the prisoner-of-war camp. The maniacal Lazarro, incorrectly blaming Billy for the death of Roland Weary, has plotted revenge since 1944. Naturally, Billy's innocence makes his meaningless death doubly absurd. At this time, Billy also learns of the eventual destruction of Earth by the Tralfamadorians. While testing a new rocket fuel for their spacecraft, they accidentally blow up the universe. "So it goes."

When Billy returns to his war story, he and his fellow American soldiers are in Dresden, working in a factory producing vitamin syrup for pregnant women. Soon, however, there will be no pregnant women in Dresden. The American prisoners of war are quartered underground in a former pig butchery—slaughterhouse number five. On the night of February 13, 1945, Billy (and Vonnegut) nestles safely in the shelter while the city is flattened by British and American firebombs. The next morning, the prisoners go aboveground and find the city as lifeless as the surface of the moon. Only the one hundred American prisoners and their guards had survived.

In chapter 10, Vonnegut himself returns as narrator. It is 1968. In the intervening years, Billy has survived an airplane crash in which all of his fellow passengers died. Valencia, frantically hurrying to see Billy in the hospital, has died of accidental carbon-monoxide poisoning. Robert Kennedy and Martin Luther King, Jr., have been assassinated. The Vietnam War is raging.

Finally, Vonnegut takes the reader back to Dresden. He and Billy are there, where the prisoners of war are digging for bodies, mining for corpses. Billy's digging companion dies of the dry heaves, unable to face the slaughter. Billy's friend Edgar Derby is executed for stealing a teapot. When the corpse mines are closed down, Billy, Vonnegut, and their companions are locked up in the suburbs to await the end of the war. When the war is over, the freed soldiers wander out into the street. The trees are blooming and the birds are singing; springtime has finally arrived for Kurt Vonnegut.

Looking back on the novel, the reader realizes that Billy's time travels have been more than simply a coping device; they provide a learning tool as well. The jumbled events to which Vonnegut subjects Billy are not random and meaningless. Even if Billy remains blankly ignorant of the connections between events in his life, both the reader and the author learn about emotional survival in the modern world. For Vonnegut, who called himself "the canary in the coal mine," Billy's story is a parable and a warning to all humankind: a warning that men and women must resist the temptation to abandon their free will, as Billy had, and an exhortation to keep one's dignity in the face of modern dehumanization.

That *Slaughterhouse-Five* is a story of survival may seem contradictory or ironic, but that is always Vonnegut's approach. It would be hard for the reader to imagine more death than is witnessed here—the slaughter in Dresden and the deaths of Billy, his wife, his father, and assorted soldiers, all culminating in the foretelling of the destruction of the universe by the Tralfamadorians—yet the reader comes to understand that everything about Vonnegut's tale is ironic. Edgar Derby is executed, amid the Dresden corpse mines, for stealing a teapot; Billy, sitting in a slaughterhouse, is saved from destruction. No wonder Billy sees himself as the plaything of uncontrollable forces. Vonnegut knows better, however. Billy, comfortably numbed by Tralfamadorian philosophy, never reinvents himself—but Vonnegut does. Writing this book enabled the author to face his past, his present, and his future. In fact, after writing *Slaughterhouse-Five*, Vonnegut proclaimed that he would never *need* to write another book. *Slaughterhouse-Five* embodied for Vonnegut the spirit of the phoenix: his soul, through his art, rising from the ashes.

After the spiritual and psychological rejuvenation wrought by *Slaughterhouse-Five*, Vonnegut became a totally unfettered artist in his next two books, *Breakfast of Champions* and *Slapstick*. In *Breakfast of Champions*, he sets all of his characters free, disdaining his role as puppeteer. Admitting that, in English poet John Keats's words, he had been "half in love with easeful Death," he asserts that he has rid himself of this dangerous fascination. In *Slapstick*, he becomes frankly autobiographical, abandoning his aesthetic distance, eschewing all masks, facing his uncertain future and painful past with calm equanimity.

GALÁPAGOS

In *Galápagos*, which Vonnegut himself called his best novel, the ghost of Leon Trotsky Trout, son of Kilgore Trout, calmly tells the story of humankind from

1986 to a point one million years in the future. He tells of the end of humankind as known by its "big-brained" twentieth century readers and of the new Adam and Eves and their new Eden. Satirist and atheist that he is, Vonnegut idealizes no part of or party to his story. Knowledge is still the poisoned apple, but naturalist Charles Darwin, not God, is the featured figure of this final record of human life as known to its recorder.

Leon Trout died in the construction of the luxury liner the *Bahia de Darwin*, the launching of which is advertised as "the nature cruise of the century." Worldwide crises, however, cause all but a paltry few to withdraw their names from the list of passengers and crew. The cruise itself is begun by accident, and Mary Hepburn, not the figurehead captain, Adolf von Kleist, guides it to its destination. This unaware Adam and sterile-but-godlike Eve, with six Kanka-bono girls "from the Stone Age," begin the new race according to Darwin's (and God's?) dictum: Having eaten of the rotten apple, humankind, with its big, self-destructive brain, is no longer fit to survive; it is a matter of shrink and swim or die. Humankind thus becomes small-brained fisherkind as witnessed by the curious ghost of Leon Trout—who can now, having so witnessed, travel through the blue tunnel into the Afterlife.

Satirist, moralist, and spokesperson for humankind that he is, Vonnegut, like Jonathan Swift before him, offers in *Galápagos* his modest proposal to a humankind bent on its own destruction. He also offers as epigraph to this tome the words of Anne Frank: "In spite of everything, I still believe people are really good at heart."

HOCUS POCUS

Hocus Pocus is perhaps Vonnegut's grimmest and most powerful indictment of Americans and American life, indicative of why fifteen years later he would title a collection of essays *A Man Without a Country* (2005). The novel is set in 2001, enabling Vonnegut a decade earlier to project his vision of what the United States would soon become. What he sees is revealed by his first-person narrator, his typical war veteran—this time a veteran of the Vietnam War, fittingly for this novel, America's most humiliating military venture. The narrator is presented as the last person to leave by helicopter from the top of the U.S. embassy in Saigon, and the experience enables him to emerge from this personal underground a changed man, convinced that all pro-war propaganda is "hocus pocus," of which he was an admitted master as a military spokesman himself, and now dedicated to trying to tell the truth, without self-serving deception.

What the United States has become in the near future is a schizophrenic, disintegrating world, symbolized both by the college for the wealthy but learning disabled where the narrator finds postwar employment and by the prison for impoverished and uneducated minorities directly across a lake from the college. The U.S. Supreme Court has reinstituted racial segregation, at least in prisons, and while the number of learning-disabled wealthy students has remained a constant at three hundred, the prison population has grown constantly, to ten thousand. Also, the United States is basically under absentee ownership, having been sold bit by bit to foreign nations and individuals by wealthy Americans who "take the money and run," unwilling to be responsible for the country's future. Race- and class-based uprisings are prevalent, including in the South Bronx, and gasoline is so scarce and expensive that it is to be found only in semisecret locations.

In his role as teacher of physics, the narrator attempts to expose the overweening pride and abysmal ignorance that have generated much of the disintegration of America, both represented by the failed perpetual-motion machine created by the college's founder and prominently placed in the foyer of the college library, proof of blind faith in technological solutions by humans who are, in the words of the narrator's dead war buddy, "1,000 times dumber and meaner than they think they are." The narrator's efforts only get him fired as a college teacher, however, with the firing orchestrated by a college trustee who is a conservative television talk-show host and whose daughter used the technology of voice recording to take the narrator's statements out of context and thereby convict him of anti-American teaching. As the narrator notes, a history professor at the college says much worse, but only about the distant past, whereas the narrator, Eugene Debs Hartke (aptly named), talks about America's present inequalities, injustices, and delusional destructiveness.

After he is fired, Hartke is hired by the prison, the director of which is a Hiroshima survivor who was saved from incineration by mere chance when he went into a ditch to retrieve a ball at the time the explosion occurred—a reflection of Vonnegut's belief that time and chance are the prime movers of the universe. Inevitably, given the race- and class-divided world, a prison break occurs, and the nonwhite prisoners (who have had nothing to do in prison except watch television reruns) attack the college and kill the faculty and staff who are present (the students are away on vacation). The prisoners are themselves killed when enough American military forces finally arrive from the Bronx and other intracountry battlefronts to address the prison break. Hartke is then arrested, accused of being the ringleader of the prison break, because he is Caucasian and educated—it is assumed that no members of a minority group could have planned the event. He is imprisoned, from which location and viewpoint he putatively authors the novel.

Unlike in *Galápagos* and *Bluebeard*, there is very little optimism in *Hocus Pocus*, aside from the narrator's humane insight and understanding. The novel conveys Vonnegut's conviction that humans will ultimately destroy themselves, probably sooner than they think, given their arrogance and ignorance and self-deception—their hocus pocus. After *Timequake* was published, Vonnegut admitted that he had struggled mightily in writing one more novel after *Hocus Pocus*, and one reason was probably that he subconsciously realized that he said it all in *Hocus Pocus* and said it incredibly well. *Hocus Pocus* is the powerful culmination of Vonnegut's fiction.

TIMEQUAKE

In *Timequake* Vonnegut has humankind, because of a glitch in time, replay the years 1991 to 2001 "on automatic pilot." He speaks as failed author of a ten-year project, *Timequake One*. Kilgore Trout, whom he personally identifies as his alter ego and as look-alike to his father, plays a crucial role in this novel. Vonnegut reprises his authorial roles as science-fiction writer, fiction writer, autobiographer, and spokesman for humankind.

Vonnegut's fictional story shows characters living and dying, living and dying again, and then waking and reeling from the reintroduction of free will. When humanity is roused from its ten years on automatic pilot, Trout becomes its hero. Because people have had no free will for ten years, they have forgotten how to use it, and Trout shows them the path to readjustment. Trout's words, for which he is celebrated, are, "You were sick, but now you're well again, and there's work to do."

Vonnegut's epilogue honoring his "big brother Bernie," who died toward the end of *Timequake*'s composition, calls to mind his prior references to saints he has known who, in an indecent society, behave decently. His references throughout *Timequake* and this final tribute to Bernard Vonnegut seem a recommendation of that gentle man to the status of saint.

Karen Priest; Judith K. Taylor
Updated by John L. Grigsby

OTHER MAJOR WORKS

SHORT FICTION: *Canary in a Cat House*, 1961; *Welcome to the Monkey House*, 1968; *Bagombo Snuff Box: Uncollected Short Fiction*, 1999.

PLAY: *Penelope*, pr. 1960 (revised pr., pb. 1970 as *Happy Birthday, Wanda June*).

TELEPLAY: *Between Time and Timbuktu: Or, Prometheus-5, a Space Fantasy*, 1972.

NONFICTION: *Wampeters, Foma, and Granfalloons (Opinions)*, 1974; *Palm Sunday: An Autobiographical Collage*, 1981; *Conversations with Kurt Vonnegut*, 1988; *Fates Worse than Death: An Autobiographical Collage of the 1980's*, 1991; *Like Shaking Hands with God: A Conversation About Writing*, 1999 (with Lee Stringer); *A Man Without a Country*, 2005; *Armageddon in Retrospect, and Other New and Unpublished Writings on War and Peace*, 2008.

CHILDREN'S LITERATURE: *Sun Moon Star*, 1980 (with Ivan Chermayeff).

BIBLIOGRAPHY

Allen, William Rodney. *Understanding Kurt Vonnegut*. Columbia: University of South Carolina Press, 1991. Presents critical analysis of Vonnegut's fiction, emphasizing in particular the works produced during his "major phase" in the 1960's, including *Slaughterhouse-Five*. Supplemented with annotated bibliography and index.

Boon, Kevin A., ed. *At Millennium's End: New Essays on the Work of Kurt Vonnegut*. Albany: State University of New York Press, 2001. Collection of eleven essays examines Vonnegut's moral vision.

Klinkowitz, Jerome. *"Slaughterhouse-Five": Reforming the Novel and the World*. Boston: Twayne, 1990. Provides a thorough and modern treatment of *Slaughterhouse-Five* that debunks earlier, fatalistic interpretations of the novel. Includes a comprehensive chronology, a thorough bibliography, and an index.

_______. *The Vonnegut Effect*. Columbia: University of South Carolina Press, 2004. One of the most authoritative scholars of Vonnegut's work presents insightful analysis of all of his major fiction. Provides biographical information and discusses how the events of Vonnegut's life influenced his writing.

_______. *Vonnegut in Fact: The Public Spokesmanship of Personal Fiction*. Columbia: University of South Carolina Press, 1998. Makes a case for Vonnegut as a sort of redeemer of the novelistic form after writers such as Philip Roth declared it dead. Traces Vonnegut's successful integration of autobiography and fiction in his body of work.

Klinkowitz, Jerome, and John Somer, eds. *The Vonnegut Statement*. New York: Delacorte Press, 1973. Collection of essays by various authors constitutes one of the most important accountings of Vonnegut's early career. Establishes the nature and sources of Vonnegut's reputation during this important period, analyzing his career through *Slaughterhouse-Five*.

Leeds, Marc. *The Vonnegut Encyclopedia: An Authorized Compendium*. Westport, Conn.: Greenwood Press, 1995. Provides a comprehensive, descriptive listing that identifies Vonnegut's most frequently recurring images and all his characters. Indispensable for serious students of Vonnegut's work.

Morse, Donald E. *The Novels of Kurt Vonnegut: Imagining Being an American*. Westport, Conn.: Praeger, 2003. Examines Vonnegut's novels against the framework of American history and the literature of the twentieth century.

Reed, Peter J., and Marc Leeds, eds. *The Vonnegut Chronicles: Interviews and Essays*. Westport, Conn.: Greenwood Press, 1996. Collection includes three interviews with Vonnegut and eleven essays on his work by various scholars. Among the topics that Vonnegut addresses in the interviews are postmodernism and experimental fiction. Includes chronology, bibliography, and index.

Tomedi, John. *Kurk Vonnegut*. Philadelphia: Chelsea House, 2004. Presents an informative overall survey of Vonnegut's life and literary work, including his nonfiction.

Vonnegut, Kurt, Jr. Interview by Wendy Smith. *Publishers Weekly*, October 25, 1985. Vonnegut discusses his writing career and his work, with an emphasis on his opposition to book censorship.

JOHN WAIN

Born: Stoke-on-Trent, Staffordshire, England; March 14, 1925
Died: Oxford, England; May 24, 1994
Also known as: John Barrington Wain

Principal long fiction

Hurry on Down, 1953 (also known as *Born in Captivity*)
Living in the Present, 1955
The Contenders, 1958
A Travelling Woman, 1959
Strike the Father Dead, 1962
The Young Visitors, 1965
The Smaller Sky, 1967
A Winter in the Hills, 1970
The Pardoner's Tale, 1978
Young Shoulders, 1982 (also known as *The Free Zone Starts Here*)
Where the Rivers Meet, 1988
Comedies, 1990
Hungry Generations, 1994

Other literary forms

A complete man of letters, John Wain (wayn) published short stories, poetry, drama, many scholarly essays, and a highly respected biography in addition to his novels. Significant among Wain's writings other than novels are several collections of short stories, including *Nuncle, and Other Stories* (1960), *Death of the Hind Legs, and Other Stories* (1966), *The Life Guard* (1971), and *King Caliban, and Other Stories* (1978); and volumes of poetry, such as *Mixed Feelings* (1951), *A Word Carved on a Sill* (1956), *Weep Before God: Poems* (1961), *Wildtrack: A Poem* (1965), *Letters to Five Artists* (1969), *The Shape of Feng* (1972), *Feng: A Poem* (1975), and *Open Country* (1987). Wain also published criticism that communicates a sensitive and scholarly appreciation of good books. Readers should pay particular attention to *Preliminary Essays* (1957), *Essays on Literature and Ideas* (1963), *A House for the Truth: Critical Essays* (1972), *Professing Poetry* (1977), and his autobiography, *Sprightly Running: Part of an Autobiography* (1962). Most readers believe that *Samuel Johnson* (1974) is the best and most lasting of all Wain's nonfiction. In this monumental biography, many of the commitments reflected in Wain's other writings come through clearly and forcefully.

Achievements

John Wain is noted for his observance of and compassion for human sorrow. His writing reflects his determination to speak to a wider range of readers than that addressed by many of his modernist predecessors; it reflects his faith in the common reader to recognize and respond to abiding philosophical concerns. These concerns include his sense of the dignity of human beings in the middle of an oftentimes cruel, indifferent, and cynical world. His concern is with a world caught up in time, desire, and disappointment. His novel *Young Shoulders*, an examination of the ramifications of a fatal accident on the people left behind, won the 1982 Whitbread Best Novel Award.

Biography

Although his world was that of the twentieth century, John Wain was very much an eighteenth century man. He delighted in pointing out that he and eighteenth century writer Samuel Johnson were born in the same district ("The Potteries") and in much the same social milieu; that he attended the same university as Johnson (Oxford, where he served from 1973 to 1978 as a professor of poetry); and that he knew, like Johnson, the Grub Street experiences and "the unremitting struggle to write enduring books against the background of an unstable existence." What chiefly interests the critic in surveying Wain's formative years are the reasons for his increasingly sober outlook. Wain's autobiography, *Sprightly Running*, remains the best account of his formative years as well as offering engaging statements of many of his opinions. In it, the reader finds some of the profound and lasting effects on Wain's writing of his childhood, his adolescence, and his years at Oxford.

John Barrington Wain was born on March 14, 1925, in Stoke-on-Trent, Staffordshire, an industrial city given over to pottery and coal mining. Here, as in other English cities, a move upward in social status is signaled by a move up in geographical terms. Therefore, the Wain family's move three years later to Penkhull—a manufacturing complex of kilns and factories and, incidentally, the setting for Wain's third novel, *The Contenders*—marked a step up into the middle-class district.

From infancy, Wain had a genuine fondness for the countryside. He immersed himself in the sights and sounds and colors of rural nature, all of which made an impression on him that was distinctive as well as deep. This impression developed into an "unargued reverence for all created life, almost a pantheism." On holidays, he and his family traveled to the coast and hills of North Wales—an association that carried over into his adult years, when, at the age of thirty-four, he married a Welsh woman. His feeling for Wales—for the independent life of the people, the landscape and mountains, the sea, the special light of the sun—is recorded in *A Winter in the Hills*. Here and elsewhere is the idea that nature is the embodiment of order, permanence, and life. Indeed, the tension between the nightmare of repression in society and the dream of liberation in the natural world is an important unifying theme throughout Wain's work.

The experience of living in an industrial town also left an indelible imprint on Wain's mind and art. His exposure to the lives of the working class and to the advance of industrialism gave him a profound knowledge of working people and their problems, which he depicts with sympathy and humanity in his fiction. Moreover, Wain's experiences at Froebel's Preparatory School and at Newcastle-under-Lyme High School impressed on him the idea that life was competitive and "a perpetual effort to survive." He found himself surrounded and outnumbered by people who resented him for being different from themselves. His contact with older children, schoolboy bullies, and authoritative schoolmasters taught Wain that the world is a dangerous place. These "lessons of life" were carried into his work. The reader finds in Wain's fiction a sense of the difficulty of survival in an intrusive and demanding world. The worst of characters is always the bully, and the worst of societies is always totalitarian. Beginning with *Born in Captivity*, each of Wain's published novels and stories is concerned in some way with the power and control that some people seek to exercise over others.

To cope with these injustices as well as with his own fears and inadequacies during his early years, Wain turned to humor, debate, and music. For Wain, the humorist is above all a moralist, in whose hands the ultimate weapon of laughter might conceivably become the means of liberating humankind from its enslavement to false ideals. Thus, his mimicry of both authorities and students was used as the quickest way to illustrate that something was horrible or boring or absurd. In both *Born in Captivity* and *The Contenders*, the heroes use mockery and ridicule to cope with their unjust world.

Wain's interest in jazz also influenced his personal and literary development. He spoke and wrote often of his lifelong enthusiasm for the trumpet playing of Bill Coleman, and he admitted that Percy Brett, the black jazz musician in *Strike the Father Dead*, was created with Coleman in mind. Accompanying this interest was a growing interest in serious writing and reading. Unlike many youths, Wain did not have to endure the agonizing doubt and indecision of trying to decide what he wanted to do in life. By the age of nine, he knew: He wanted to be an author. He began as a critically conscious writer who delighted in "pastiche and parody for their own sake," although he had problems maintaining steady plot lines.

Wain matched his writing with voracious reading. His early interest in the novels of Charles Dickens, Tobias Smollett, Daniel Defoe, and others in the tradition of the English novel influenced his later literary style. Like these predecessors, Wain approached his characters through the conventional narration of the realist, and his concerns were social and moral.

The second major period in Wain's life occurred between 1943, when he entered St. John's College, Oxford, and 1955, when he resigned his post as lecturer in English at Reading University to become a full-time writer. Two friends made in his Oxford period especially influenced his writing. One was Philip Larkin, whose "rock-like determination" provided an inspiring example for Wain. The other friend was Kingsley Amis, whose work on a first novel inspired Wain to attempt writing a novel in his spare time. Wain wrote his first novel, not particularly because he wished to be a novelist, but to see if he could write one that would get into print. In 1953, Frederick Warburg accepted *Born in Captivity*, and its unexpected success quickly established Wain as one of Britain's promising new writers.

Wain's exhilarating experience with his first book was, however, poor preparation for the sobering slump that followed. Ill health, divorce proceedings, and the drudgery of a scholar's life pushed him into a crisis of depression and discouragement. He tried to climb out of this crisis by leaving the university for a year and retreating to the Swiss Alps. There, he let his imagination loose on his own problems. The result was *Living in the Present*, a depressing book of manifest despair and disgust. Out of this period in his life, Wain developed a profound awareness of love and loneliness, union and estrangement. The essential loneliness of human beings, and their more or less successful attempts to overcome their loneliness by love, became major themes in his later fiction.

Although Wain was never sanguine about the human condition or the times in which he lived, his life was to be more fulfilling than he anticipated at this time. As a result of his year of self-assessment, in 1955, Wain did not return to the junior position he had held at the University of Reading but instead began working full time at his writing. Little more than a decade later, his reputation had become so well established that he could reenter the academic world as a visiting professor. Eventually, Wain was appointed a professor of poetry at Oxford University, a post he held from 1973 to 1978.

Sprightly Running, published in 1962, was evidence that Wain was much more contented than he had been seven years before. He was now happily married to Eirian James, an intelligent, insightful woman who provided him with companionship and sometimes help with his work (she coedited *The New Wessex Selection of Thomas Hardy's Poetry* in 1978). The couple had three sons, and their life together ended only with Eirian's death in 1987. The following year, Wain married Patricia Dunn.

Despite ill health and diminished vision, Wain labored on courageously at what proved to be his final project, three novels that together constitute the Oxford trilogy. On May 24, 1994, Wain died of a stroke at the John Radcliffe Hospital in Oxford.

ANALYSIS

As a novelist, John Wain has been described as a "painfully honest" writer who always, to an unusual degree, wrote autobiography. His own fortunes and his emotional reactions to these fortunes are, of course, transformed in various ways. His purpose is artistic, not confessional, and he shaped his material accordingly. As Wain himself stated, this intention is both pure and simple: to express his own feelings honestly and to tell the truth about the world he knew. At his best—in *Born in Captivity*, *Strike the Father Dead*, *A Winter in the Hills*, and *The Pardoner's Tale*—Wain finds a great many ways to convey the message that life is ultimately tragic. Human beings suffer, life is difficult, and the comic mask conceals anguish. Only occasionally is this grim picture relieved by some sort of idealism, some unexpected attitude of unselfishness or tenderness. What is more, in all his writings Wain is a thoughtful, literate man coming to terms with these truths in a sincere and forthright manner.

To understand something of Wain's uniqueness as a novelist, the reader must look back at least to the end of World War II. For about ten years after the war, established writers continued to produce successfully. English novelists such as Aldous Huxley, Graham Greene, Evelyn Waugh, C. P. Snow, and Anthony Powell had made their reputations before the war and continued to be the major literary voices of that time. Most of them were from upper-class or upper-middle-class origins and had been educated in Great Britain's elite public schools, then at Oxford or Cambridge. Their novels were likely to center on fashionable London or some country estate. Often they confined their satire to the intellectual life and the cultural as well as social predicaments of the upper middle class.

A combination of events in postwar England led to the appearance of another group of writers, soon referred to by literary journalists as the Angry Young Men. Among these writers was Wain, who, along with Amis, John Braine, John Osborne, Angus Wilson, Alan Sillitoe, and others, turned away from technical innovations, complexity, and the sensitive, introspective protagonist to concentrate on concrete problems of current society. Thus, in the tradition of the eighteenth century novel, Wain fulfills most effectively the novelist's basic task of telling a good story. His novels move along at an even pace; he relies on a simple, tightly constructed, and straightforward plot; clarity; good and bad characters; and a controlled point of view. The reader need only think of James Joyce and Franz Kafka, and the contrast is clear. What most of Wain's novels ask from the reader is not some feat of analysis, but a considered fullness of response, a readiness to acknowledge, even in disagreement, his vision of defeat.

Wain's typical protagonist is essentially an "antihero," a man at the mercy of life. Although sometimes capable of aspiration and thought, he is not strong enough to carve out his destiny in the way he wishes. Frequently, he is something of a dreamer, tossed about by life, and also pushed about, or at least overshadowed, by the threats in his life. Wain's Charles Lumley (*Born in Captivity*) and Edgar Banks (*Living in the Present*) bear the marks of this type. Often there is discernible in his characters a modern malaise, a vague discontent, and a yearning for some person or set of circumstances beyond their reach. Sometimes, this sense of disenchantment with life as it is becomes so great that the individual expresses a desire not to live at all, as Edgar Banks asserts in *Living in the Present* and as Gus Howkins declares in *The Pardoner's Tale*.

Wain is also accomplished in his creation of place and atmosphere. In *Strike the Father Dead*, he fully captures the grayness of a London day, the grayness of lives spent under its pall, the grayness of the people who wander its streets. When Wain describes an afternoon in which Giles Hermitage (*The Pardoner's Tale*) forces himself to work in the subdued light at home, when Arthur Geary (*The Smaller Sky*) walks the platforms at Paddington Station, when Charles Lumley walks in on a literary gathering, or when Roger Furnivall (*A Winter in the Hills*) makes his way home through the Welsh countryside—at such moments the reader encounters Wain's mastery of setting and atmosphere.

The themes communicated through Wain's novels are, like his method, consistent. It is clear that he sees the eighteenth century as a time of dignity, pride, and self-sufficiency—qualities lacking in the twentieth century. Like Johnson, Wain defends the value of reason, moderation, common sense, moral courage, and intellectual self-respect. Moreover, his fictional themes of the dignity of the human being, the difficulty of survival in the modern world, and the perils of success have established him principally as a moralist concerned with ethical issues. In later works, the value of tradition, the notion of human understanding, and the ability to love and suffer become the chief moral values. In all his novels, he is primarily concerned with the problem of defining the moral worth of the individual. For all these reasons, Wain is recognized as a penetrating observer of the human scene.

One final point should be noted about Wain's capacities as a novelist. Clearly, the spiritual dimension is missing in the world he describes, yet there is frequently the hint or at least the possibility of renewal, which is the closest Wain comes to any sort of recognized affirmation. Charles Lumley, Joe Shaw, Jeremy Coleman, and Roger Furnivall are all characters who seem to be, by the end of their respective stories, on the verge of rebirth of a sort, on the threshold of reintegration and consequent regeneration. In each case, this renewal depends on the ability of the individual to come to terms with himself and his situation; to confront and accept at a stroke past, present, and future; and to accept and tolerate the contradictions inherent in all three. Wain's sensitive response to the tragic aspects of life is hardly novel, but his deep compassion for human suffering and his tenderness for the unfortunate are more needed than ever in an age when violence, brutality, and cynicism are all too prevalent.

Born in Captivity

In his first novel, *Born in Captivity*, Wain comically perceives the difficulties of surviving in a demanding, sometimes fearful world. Detached from political causes and the progress of his own life, the hero is a drifter, seeking to compromise with or to escape from such "evils" as class lines, boredom, hypocrisy, and the conventional perils of success. Although the novel carries a serious moral interest, Wain's wit, sharp observations, and inventiveness keep the plot moving. His comedy exaggerates, reforms, and criticizes to advocate the reasonable in social behavior and to promote the value and dignity of the individual.

Born in Captivity has the characteristic features of the picaresque novel: a series of short and often comic adventures loosely strung together; an opportunistic and pragmatic hero who seeks to make a living through his wits; and satiric characterization of stock figures rather than individualized portraits. Unlike the eighteenth century picaro, however, who is often hardhearted, cruel, and selfish, Wain's central character is a well-intentioned drifter who compromises enough to live comfortably. His standby and salvation is a strong sense of humor that enables him to make light of much distress and disaster. Lumley's character is revealed against the shifting setting of the picaresque world and in his characteristic response to repeated assaults on his fundamental decency and sympathy for others. He remains substantially the same throughout the novel; his many roles—as window cleaner, delivery driver, chauffeur, and the like—place him firmly in the picaresque tradition. Lumley's versatility and adaptability permit Wain to show his character under a variety of circumstances and in a multiplicity of situations.

Lumley's character is established almost immediately with the description of his conflict with the landlady in the first chapter. The reader sees him as the adaptable antihero who tries to control his own fate, as a jack of all trades, a skilled manipulator, an adept deceiver, an artist of disguises. Wain stresses Lumley's ingenuity rather than his mere struggle for survival; at the same time, he develops Lumley's individual personality, emphasizing the man and his adventures. The role that Lumley plays in the very first scene is one in which he will be cast throughout the story—that of a put-upon young man engaged in an attempt to cope with and outwit the workaday world.

The satire is developed through the characterization. Those who commit themselves to class—who judge others and define themselves by the class structure—are satirized throughout the novel. Surrounding the hero is a host of lightly sketched, "flat," stock figures, all of whom play their predictable roles. These characters include the proletarian girl, the American, the landlady, the entrepreneur, the middle-class couple, and the artist. In this first novel, Wain's resources in characterization are limited primarily to caricature. The comedy functions to instruct and entertain. Beneath the horseplay and high spirits, Wain rhetorically manipulates the reader's moral judgment so that he sympathizes with the hero. In the tradition of Smollett and Dickens, Wain gives life to the grotesque by emphasizing details of his eccentric characters and by indicating his attitude toward them through the selection of specific bodily and facial characteristics.

Wain has also adopted another convention of eighteenth century fiction: the intrusive author. The active role of this authorial impresario accounts for the distance between the reader and the events of the novel; his exaggerations, his jokes, and his philosophizing prevent the reader from taking Lumley's fate too seriously. In later novels, Wain's authorial stance changes as his vision deepens.

Any discussion of comic technique in *Born in Captivity* leads inevitably to the novel's resolution. Ordinarily, readers do not like to encounter "perfect" endings to novels; nevertheless, they are not put off by the unrealistic ending to this novel because they know from the beginning that they are reading a comic novel that depends on unrealistic exaggeration of various kinds. Elgin W. Mellown was correct when he called the novel "a pastiche: Walter Mitty's desire expressed through the actions of the Three Stooges—wish fulfillment carried out through outrageous actions and uncharacteristic behavior." The reader feels secure in the rightness of the ending as a conclusion to all the comic wrongness that has gone on before.

STRIKE THE FATHER DEAD

In *Strike the Father Dead*, Wain further extended himself with a work more penetrating than anything he had written before. Not only is it, as Walter Allen said, a "deeply pondered novel," but it is also a culmination of the promises inherent in Wain's earlier works. Plot, theme, character, and setting are integrated to tell the story of a son who breaks parental ties, thereby freeing himself to make his own way in life as a jazz pianist. Pointing to the foibles of his fellowman and probing the motives of an indignant parent, Wain's wit and sarcastic humor lighten this uncompromising study of the nonconformist's right to assert his nonconformity.

Two later Wain novels—*A Winter in the Hills* and *The Pardoner's Tale*—continue and elaborate on many of the central themes of his fiction, but they surpass the earlier novels in richness and complexity. Both novels exhibit, far more than do his earlier writings, an interest in the tragic implications of romantic love; a greater complexity in character development allows Wain to portray convincingly men whose loneliness borders on self-destruction. Each novel is not simply another story of isolation or spiritual desolation, although it is that. Each hero is cast into a wasteland, and the novel in a sense is the story of his attempts to find the river of life again, or possibly for the first time. One of the themes that develops from this period in Wain's career is that personal relationships are the most important and yet most elusive forces in society.

The plot of *Strike the Father Dead* is arranged in an elaborate seven-part time scheme. Parts 1 and 6 occur sometime late in 1957 or early in 1958, part 2 takes place in the immediate prewar years, and the other divisions follow chronologically up to the last, which is set in 1958. The scene shifts back and forth between a provincial university town and the darker, black-market-and-jazz side of London, with a side trip to Paris.

Wain narrates the story from the points of view of four characters. The central figure, Jeremy Coleman, revolts against his father and the academic establishment in search of self-expression as a jazz pianist. Alfred Coleman, Jeremy's father and a professor of classics, is an atheist devoted to duty and hard work. Eleanor, Alfred's sister and foster mother to Jeremy, is devoted to Jeremy and finds comfort in innocent religiosity. Percy Brett, a black American jazz musician, offers Jeremy his first real parental leadership. Like Ernest Pontifex, in Samuel Butler's *The Way of All Flesh* (1903), Jeremy escapes from an oppressive existence; he has a passion for music, and once he has the opportunity to develop, his shrinking personality changes.

Strike the Father Dead marks a considerable advance over *Born in Captivity* in the thorough rendering of each character and each scene. By employing a succession of first-person narrators, Wain focuses attention more evenly on each of the figures. The result is that the reader comes away knowing Jeremy even better, because what is learned about him comes from not only his own narration but other sources as well. Inasmuch as there are three central characters, *Strike the Father Dead* represents a larger range for Wain. Each interior monologue is a revelation; the language is personal, distinctive, and descriptive of character.

In the manner of a bildungsroman, *Strike the Father Dead* is also a novel that recounts the youth and young manhood of a sensitive protagonist who is attempting to learn the nature of the world, discover its meaning and pattern, and acquire a philosophy of life. Setting plays a vital role in this odyssey. The provincial and London backgrounds and the accurate rendering of the language make the novel come alive. *Strike the Father Dead* moves between two contemporary worlds—a world of rigidity and repression, represented by Alfred, and a world of creativity, international and free, represented by London and Paris. The first world oppresses Jeremy; the second attracts and draws him. He dreams about it and invents fictions about it. Central to this new world is Jeremy's love of jazz. For him, the experience of jazz means beauty, love, life, growth, freedom, ecstasy—the very qualities he finds missing in the routine, disciplined life of Alfred.

Although *Strike the Father Dead* tells the story of a British young man who becomes successful, the success is to a certain extent bittersweet. In his triumphs over his home circumstances, Jeremy loses something as well. There are various names given to it: innocence; boyhood; nature; the secure, predictable life at home. The world beyond the academic life waits for Jeremy, and he, unknowingly, does his best to bring it onstage. With such a life comes a developing sense of injustice, deprivation, and suffering. These concerns become focal points in Wain's subsequent novels, as he turns toward the impulse to define character and dilemma much more objectively and with greater moral responsibility.

A Winter in the Hills

With its setting in Wales, *A Winter in the Hills* marked a departure from Wain's first seven novels, all of which were centered in England. The story expresses, perhaps more comprehensively than any other, Wain's feelings for the provincial world, its cohesion and deep loyalties, and its resistance to innovation from outside.

Here the reader finds Wain's sympathy for the underdog, his respect for decency and the dignity of humanity, and his affirmation of life; here, too, is expressed Wain's deep interest in the causes and effects of loneliness and alienation.

The reader's first inclination is to approach the novel as primarily a novel of character, the major interest and emphasis of which is the constantly developing character of Roger Furnivall himself. Using third-person narration, Wain keeps the focus on his main character as he progresses straight through several months that constitute a time of crisis in his life. Through most of the novel, Roger struggles doggedly against a combination of adverse circumstances, always in search of a purpose. Outwardly, he forces himself on Gareth, for example, as a way of improving his idiomatic Welsh. Inwardly, he "needed involvement, needed a human reason for being in the district." The guilt he carries because of his brother's suffering and death helps to propel him into a more active engagement with contemporary life. His conflict with Dic Sharp draws him out of his own private grief because he is helping not only Gareth but also an entire community of people.

The reader learns about Roger in another way, too: Wain uses setting to reveal and reflect the protagonist's emotions and mental states. Roger's walk in the rain down the country roads, as he attempts to resolve his bitterness and disappointment at Beverley's rejection of him, is vividly depicted. It carries conviction because Roger's anxiety has been built up gradually and artistically. The pastoral world is a perpetually shifting landscape, and Wain depicts its shifts and contrasts with an acute eye for telling detail. Especially striking are the sketches of evening coming on in the Welsh hills, with their rocks and timber and vast expanses of green. Such descriptions help to convey Roger's yearning for happiness in a world that seems bent on denying it to him.

One major theme of the book is the invasion of the peaceful, conservative world of Wales by outsiders who have no roots in the region, and therefore no real concern for its inhabitants. These invaders are characterized by a sophisticated corruption that contrasts sharply with the unspoiled simplicity and honesty of the best of the natives. A related theme is the decline of the town: its economic insecurity, its struggle to resist the progressive and materialistic "cruelty, greed, tyranny, the power of the rich to drive the poor to the wall." Through Roger's point of view, Wain expresses his opposition to the pressures—economic, political, cultural—that seek to destroy the Welsh and, by implication, all minority enclaves. Thus, *A Winter in the Hills* is more than a novel about the growth of one human being from loneliness and alienation to mature and selfless love; it is also a powerful study of the quality of life in the contemporary world, threatened by the encroachments of bureaucracy, greed, and materialism.

The Pardoner's Tale

The somewhat optimistic resolution of *A Winter in the Hills* stands in stark contrast to that of *The Pardoner's Tale*, Wain's most somber novel. In no other work by Wain are the characters so lonely, so frustrated, or so obsessed with thoughts of mutability, lost opportunities, and death. The novel is really two stories: a first-person tale about Gus Howkins, an aging Londoner contemplating divorce, and a third-person narrative (the framing narrative) about Giles Hermitage, an established novelist and bachelor living in an unnamed cathedral town, who gets involved with the Chichester-Redferns, a woman and daughter, while he is working out the story of Howkins. It is the interplay between these two stories that constitutes the plot of *The Pardoner's Tale*.

Giles Hermitage is obviously the figure with whom Wain is the most intimately involved. He is a highly idiosyncratic figure with very recognizable weaknesses; he is easily discouraged (there is an early thought of suicide), and he resorts to excessive drinking. The root cause of his death wish and of his drinking is loneliness. Like Wain's earlier heroes, he is very much a modern man: vague in his religious and humanitarian aspirations, rootless and alienated from the social life of the community in which he lives, and initially weak and confused in his relationships with women. Plagued by anxiety, depression, vague discontent, and a sense of inner emptiness, he seeks peace of mind under conditions that increasingly militate against it. Add to his problems the ever-growing urge toward self-destruction, and the reader begins to recognize in this novel a truly contemporary pulsebeat. Hermitage is a stranger in a world that does not make sense.

Unlike Wain's earlier heroes, however, Hermitage tries to make sense of the world through the medium of his writing by stepping back into what he calls "the protecting circle of art." His approach to writing is autobiographical, personal, even subjective. The hero of his novel is a mask for himself. The author is creating a character who is in his own predicament, and the agonies he endures enable him to express his deepest feelings about life. In Hermitage, Wain presents a character who tries to create, as artists do, a new existence out of the chaos of his life.

The remaining major characters in *The Pardoner's Tale* bear family resemblances to those in other of Wain's novels. If the part of the lonely, alienated hero so effectively carried in *A Winter in the Hills* by Roger Furnivall is here assigned to Giles Hermitage, then the role of the manipulator is assigned in this novel to Mrs. Chichester-Redfern. Although a good deal less ruthless than Dic Sharp, she nevertheless seeks to exploit the hero.

The process by which Mrs. Chichester-Redfern is gradually revealed through the eyes of Hermitage is subtle and delicate. At first merely a stranger, she comes to seem in time a calculating and educated woman, the innocent victim of a man who deserted her, a seventy-year-old woman grasping for answers to some vital questions about her own life. She summons Hermitage under the pretense of wanting to gain insight into her life. From these conversations, the reader learns that she, like Hermitage, is confronted and dislocated by external reality in the form of a personal loss. Also like the hero, she desires to come to some understanding of her unhappy life through the medium of art. Her true motive is revenge, however, and she wants Hermitage to write a novel with her husband in it as a character who suffers pain. Then, she says, "there will be that much justice done in the world."

In addition to the alienated, lonely hero and the manipulator, most of Wain's fiction portrays a comforter. In his latest novel, the comforter is embodied in Diana Chichester-Redfern, but the happiness Diana offers is only temporary. In this novel, love is reduced to a meaningless mechanical act: Diana, also, is living in a wasteland.

The basic tension of this novel is a simple and classic one—the life-force confronting the death-force. As surely as Mrs. Chichester-Redfern is the death-force in the novel, Diana is the active and life-giving presence. She is depicted as an abrasive, liberated, sensual, innately selfish modern young woman who stands in positive contrast to the deathlike grayness of her mother. She is earthy and fulfilled, accepting and content with her music (playing the guitar satisfies her need for proficiency), her faith (which takes care of "all the moral issues") and her sexuality (which she enjoys because she has no choice). Diana goes from one affair to another, not in search of love (she claims she "can't love anybody") but out of a need for repetition. Diana defines love and meaning as the fulfillment of a man or woman's emotional requirements. To her, love does not mean self-sacrifice; rather, love is synonymous with need.

The world of *The Pardoner's Tale* is thus the archetypal world of all Wain's fiction: random, fragmented, lonely, contradictory. It is a world in which wasted lives, debased sexual encounters, and destroyed moral intelligence yield a tragic vision of futility and sterility, isolation from the community, estrangement from those who used to be closest to one, and loneliness in the middle of the universe itself.

Young Shoulders

Amid all this, Wain's unflinching honesty and his capacity for compassion make his definition of the human condition bearable. Both characteristics are evident in *Young Shoulders*. Again, Wain focuses on senseless waste. A plane of English schoolchildren crashes in Lisbon, Portugal, killing everyone aboard. Seventeen-year-old Paul Waterford, whose twelve-year-old sister, Clare, was one of the victims, describes his journey to Lisbon with his parents, their encounters with other grief-stricken relatives, the memorial service they attend, and their return to England. Because he is still untainted by convention, Paul feels free to see the other characters as they are, often even to find them funny; however, he has to admit that he can be wrong about people. The seemingly calm Mrs. Richardson, a teacher's widow, collapses during the memorial service; the restrained Janet Finlayson howls in the hotel lobby that God is punishing them all; Mr. Smithson, whom Paul assessed as a man on his way up, goes crazy on the tarmac; and everyone depends on Paul's parents: the mother Paul saw only as a drunk and the father Paul dismissed as hopelessly withdrawn.

Because Wain has the eighteenth century writer's hunger for universals, we may assume that the real subject of *Young Shoulders* is not how individuals behave in the face of tragedy but what the young protagonist and, by extension, the reader has learned by the end of the novel. Paul comes to see that human beings avoid acknowledging their emotions in so many ways that an outsider's judgment is likely to be inaccurate. He also recognizes the extent to which he deludes himself, whether by imagining a utopian society he will govern or by addressing "reports" to Clare, thus denying that she is dead. By losing his innocence, Paul gains in compassion.

The Oxford trilogy

With its single plot line, its compressed time scheme, and its limited cast, *Young Shoulders* is much like a neoclassical play. By contrast, the three novels composing the Oxford trilogy have an epic quality, as indeed they must if they are to "describe and dramatize the Oxford that has been sinking out of sight, and fading from memory, for over thirty years," as Wain states in his preface to the final volume. The series does indeed cover three decades.

Where the Rivers Meet introduces the protagonist Peter Leonard and takes him through his undergraduate years at Oxford; *Comedies* begins in 1933, with Leonard's appointment as a fellow, and ends after World War II; and *Hungry Generations* covers Leonard's life from 1947 to 1956. There is a multitude of characters, ranging from Oxford intellectuals to the patrons of the pub that Leonard's parents run, each with definite ideas about local politics, world news, and the progress of society. Wain's honesty is reflected in the way he permits all the characters to speak their minds; his compassion is revealed in his attempt to understand even the least appealing of them. These qualities, along with his creative genius and his consummate artistry, should ensure for John Wain a permanent place in twentieth century literary history.

Dale Salwak
Updated by Rosemary M. Canfield Reisman

Other major works

SHORT FICTION: *Nuncle, and Other Stories*, 1960; *Death of the Hind Legs, and Other Stories*, 1966; *The Life Guard*, 1971; *King Caliban, and Other Stories*, 1978.

PLAYS: *Harry in the Night: An Optimistic Comedy*, pr. 1975; *Johnson Is Leaving: A Monodrama*, pb. 1994.

POETRY: *Mixed Feelings*, 1951; *A Word Carved on a Sill*, 1956; *A Song About Major Eatherly*, 1961; *Weep Before God: Poems*, 1961; *Wildtrack: A Poem*, 1965; *Letters to Five Artists*, 1969; *The Shape of Feng*, 1972; *Feng: A Poem*, 1975; *Poems for the Zodiac*, 1980; *Thinking About Mr. Person*, 1980; *Poems, 1949-1979*, 1981; *Twofold*, 1981; *Open Country*, 1987.

TELEPLAY: *Young Shoulders*, 1984 (with Robert Smith).

RADIO PLAYS: *You Wouldn't Remember*, 1978; *A Winter in the Hills*, 1981; *Frank*, 1982.

NONFICTION: *Preliminary Essays*, 1957; *Gerard Manley Hopkins: An Idiom of Desperation*, 1959; *Sprightly Running: Part of an Autobiography*, 1962; *Essays on Literature and Ideas*, 1963; *The Living World of Shakespeare: A Playgoer's Guide*, 1964; *Arnold Bennett*, 1967; *A House for the Truth: Critical Essays*, 1972; *Samuel Johnson*, 1974; *Professing Poetry*, 1977; *Samuel Johnson, 1709-1784*, 1984 (with Kai Kin Yung); *Dear Shadows: Portraits from Memory*, 1986.

CHILDREN'S/YOUNG ADULT LITERATURE: *Lizzie's Floating Shop*, 1981.

EDITED TEXTS: *Contemporary Reviews of Romantic Poetry*, 1953; *Interpretations: Essays on Twelve English Poems*, 1955; *International Literary Annual*, 1959, 1960; *Fanny Burney's Diary*, 1960; *Anthology of Modern Poetry*, 1963; *Selected Shorter Poems of Thomas Hardy*, 1966; *Selected Stories of Thomas Hardy*, 1966; *Thomas Hardy's "The Dynasts,"* 1966; *Shakespeare: Macbeth, a Casebook*, 1968 (revised 1994); *Shakespeare: Othello, a Casebook*, 1971; *Johnson as Critic*, 1973; *The New Wessex Selection of Thomas Hardy's Poetry*, 1978 (with Eirian James).

Bibliography

Bayley, John. "Obituary: John Wain." *The Independent*, May 25, 1994. In this biographical sketch of Wain's life and literary career, Bayley compares him with Kingsley Amis and praises his biography of Samuel Johnson.

Burgess, Anthony. *The Novel Now: A Guide to Contemporary Fiction*. 1967. Reprint. New York: Faber & Faber, 1972. Expanded from an earlier study, Burgess's work groups Wain with other class-conscious British fiction writers.

Gerard, David E. *John Wain: A Bibliography*. Westport, Conn.: Meckler, 1987. Contains a comprehensive, if dated, annotated bibliography of Wain's work. Lists materials of critical and biographical interest, including radio, television, and sound recordings. Also includes other critical and biographical references and reviews of works by Wain.

Gindin, James J. "The Moral Center of John Wain's Fiction." In *Postwar British Fiction: New Accents and Attitudes*. Berkeley: University of California Press, 1962. Gindin's chapter on Wain discusses the writer's use of morality as a thematic and structural device and claims that each novel contains a central statement of the moral worth of the individual.

Hatziolou, Elizabeth. *John Wain: A Man of Letters*. London: Pisces Press, 1997. The first extensive biography to be published after Wain's death. Includes an index.

Heptonstall, Geoffrey. "Remembering John Wain." *Contemporary Review* 266 (March, 1995): 144-146. A brief discussion of Wain's central themes of faithlessness and the assumption that there are no assumptions. Examines Wain's rejection of realism and his intention to speak imaginatively.

Rabinovitz, Rubin. "The Novelists of the 1950's: A General Survey." In *The Reaction Against Experiment in the English Novel, 1950-1960*. New York: Columbia University Press, 1967. Rabinovitz places Wain in the context of novelists who embraced traditional values rather than those who experimented with unconventional ideas or forms, aligning Wain's novels with those of Arnold Bennett and eighteenth century picaresque novelists.

Salwak, Dale. *Interviews with Britain's Angry Young Men*. San Bernardino, Calif.: Borgo Press, 1984. This useful resource characterizes Wain as an "eighteenth century man." Engages Wain in a discussion of the role of criticism in the author's life, his goals as a writer, his response to the phenomenon of the Angry Young Men, and the sources and themes in several of his novels.

_______. *John Wain*. Boston: Twayne, 1981. Part of Twayne's English Authors series, this work is the first book-length study of Wain and is a useful introduction to Wain's life, career, and works.

Taylor, D. J. *After the War: The Novel and English Society Since 1945*. London: Chatto & Windus, 1993. An attempt to define the nature of postwar writing. Wain is grouped with William Cooper and Kingsley Amis as antiromantic and as antimodernist, that is, opposed to the psychological emphasis and stylistic complexity of James Joyce and Virginia Woolf.

ALICE WALKER

Born: Eatonton, Georgia; February 9, 1944
Also known as: Alice Malsenior Walker

Principal long fiction

The Third Life of Grange Copeland, 1970
Meridian, 1976
The Color Purple, 1982
The Temple of My Familiar, 1989
Possessing the Secret of Joy, 1992
By the Light of My Father's Smile, 1998
Now Is the Time to Open Your Heart, 2004

Other literary forms

Alice Walker has published many volumes of short fiction, poetry, and essays in addition to her novels, as well as several children's books. Walker was an early editor at *Ms.* magazine, in which many of her essays first appeared. Her interest in the then little-known writer Zora Neale Hurston led her to take a pilgrimage to Florida to place a tombstone on Hurston's unmarked grave and to her editing of *I Love Myself When I Am Laughing . . . and Then Again When I Am Looking Mean and Impressive: A Zora Neale Hurston Reader* (1979);

she also provided an introduction to Robert Hemenway's *Zora Neale Hurston: A Literary Biography* (1977). In her collection of essays titled *We Are the Ones We Have Been Waiting For: Light in a Time of Darkness* (2006), Walker advocates an appreciation for the times in which we live, when social, political, and environmental progress is needed and can be made.

Achievements

Alice Walker's literary reputation is based primarily on her fiction, although her second book of poetry, *Revolutionary Petunias, and Other Poems* (1973), received the Lillian Smith Award and a nomination for a National Book Award. Her first short-story collection, *In Love and Trouble: Stories of Black Women* (1973), won the Rosenthal Award of the National Institute of Arts and Letters. In addition, Walker has been the recipient of a Charles Merrill writing fellowship, an award for fiction from the National Endowment for the Arts, and a Guggenheim Fellowship. She has also been a Bread Loaf Scholar and a fellow at the Radcliffe Institute. Walker's books have been translated into more than twenty-four languages.

Her first novel, *The Third Life of Grange Copeland*, was widely and enthusiastically reviewed in publications as varied as *The New Yorker*, *The New Republic*, and *The New York Times Book Review*, although journals aimed primarily at a black readership were often silent on the work or critical of its violence and graphic depiction of rural black life. With the publication of *Meridian*, Walker's second novel, her work as a poet, novelist, essayist, editor, teacher, scholar, and political activist came together. *Meridian* was universally praised in scholarly journals, literary magazines, popular magazines, and black-oriented journals. Some critics, mainly black male reviewers, objected again to the honest, straightforward portrayals of black life in the South and to Walker's growing feminism, which they saw as being in conflict with her commitment to her race. Walker's third novel, *The Color Purple*, was widely acclaimed. Feminist and *Ms.* editor Gloria Steinem wrote that this novel "could be the kind of popular and literary event that transforms an intense reputation into a national one," and Peter Prescott's review in *Newsweek* began by saying, "I want to say at once that *The Color Purple* is an American novel of permanent importance." These accolades were substantiated when Walker received both the American Book Award and the 1983 Pulitzer Prize for fiction.

The Temple of My Familiar has been compared to Thomas Pynchon's *Gravity's Rainbow* (1973) in its revision of Western history as it has traditionally been understood and in Walker's use of various techniques such as oral storytelling, letters, and journals. This novel has also been criticized for what some have seen as its sentimental and clichéd language, however. Critics have appreciated *Possessing the Secret of Joy* for Walker's willingness to expose and critique the African practice of female circumcision, which Westerners find abhorrent. Some critics argue, however, that the novel is written from an ethnocentric viewpoint and does not consider the practice within the context of African culture. Reactions to *By the Light of My Father's Smile* have been widely varied, with some critics praising Walker's treatment of issues of sexuality, particularly the need for fathers to understand their daughters as sexual beings, and others asserting that Walker let her own political agenda steer the novel's plot and style. Similarly, while Walker's prose style in *Now Is the Time to Open Your Heart* has been described as fluent and evocative, the novel has also been criticized for a heavy-handed New Age spirituality.

Biography

Alice Malsenior Walker was born in Eatonton, Georgia, on February 9, 1944, the last of eight children of Willie Lee and Minnie Lou Grant Walker, sharecroppers in rural Georgia. Her relationship with her father, at first strong and valuable, became strained as she became involved in the civil rights and feminist movements. A moving depiction of her estrangement from her father occurs in her essay "My Father's Country Is the Poor," which appeared in *The New York Times* in 1977. For Walker, a loving and healthy mother-daughter relationship has endured over the years. An account of that relationship is central to her essays "In Search of Our Mothers' Gardens" and "Lulls—A Native Daughter Returns to the Black South" and in Mary Helen Washington's article "Her Mother's Gifts," in which Walker acknowledges that she often writes with her mother's

Alice Walker. (Jeff Reinking/Picture Group)

voice—"Just as you have certain physical characteristics of your mother . . . when you're compelled to write her stories, it's because you recognize and prize those qualities of her in yourself."

One of the central events in Walker's childhood was a BB gun accident that left her, at age eight, blind in one eye. Scar tissue from that wound, both physical and psychological, seems to have left her with a compensating acuteness of vision, despite the conviction that she was permanently disfigured. Walker was affected enough by the accident to say in a 1974 interview with John O'Brien, "I have always been a solitary person, and since I was eight years old (and the recipient of a disfiguring scar, since corrected, somewhat), I have daydreamed—not of fairy-tales—but of falling on swords, of putting guns to my heart or head, and of slashing my wrists with a razor." Walker's partial blindness allowed her to attend Spelman College in Atlanta on a scholarship for the handicapped, following her graduation from Butler-Baker High School in 1961. She left Spelman after two years—which included summer trips to the Soviet Union and to Africa as part of a group called Experiment in International Living—for Sarah Lawrence College, from which she graduated in 1965.

Walker's political activity governed her movements during the years immediately following her college graduation: She spent the summer of 1965 in the Soviet Union and also worked for civil rights in Liberty County, Georgia. The next year she was a caseworker for New York City's Department of Social Services, and then a voter-registration worker in Mississippi. In 1967, she married Melvyn Leventhal, a civil rights lawyer, and moved to Jackson, Mississippi, where she continued her civil rights work, lived in the heart of the South as part of an interracial couple, and taught at Jackson State University, while continuing to write stories, poems, and essays. Walker's daughter, Rebecca Grant, was born in 1969. Walker taught at Tougaloo College in Mississippi for a year before returning to the East, where she was a lecturer in writing and literature at Wellesley College, an editor at *Ms.* magazine, and an instructor at the University of Massachusetts at Boston. By 1977, she had divorced her husband, accepted a position as associate professor of English at Yale University, and written six books, before moving to San Francisco in 1978 and writing a books of poems, *Good Night, Willie Lee, I'll See You in the Morning* (1979) and editing *I Love Myself When I Am Laughing . . . and Then Again When I Am Looking Mean and Impressive*, a collection of writings on Zora Neale Hurston, in the same year. These were followed by *You Can't Keep a Good Woman Down* (1981), a book of short stories.

After her 1982 novel *The Color Purple* won critical acclaim, Walker and her family shared the success with Eatonton. Walker's sister established The Color Purple Educational Scholarship Fund, and Walker adopted three elementary schools to help provide needed supplies for students who maintained above-average grades. Walker continued her activities in political forums as well, working for civil rights and protesting against nuclear weapons. She became a devoted and vocal objector to the practice of female genital mutilation ("female circumcision") in Africa, through public speaking and through her novel *Possessing the Secret of Joy* and her nonfiction book *Warrior Marks: Female Genital Mutilation and the Sexual Blinding of Women* (1993), which focus on the horrors and scars of this practice.

Walker also used her success to help other female writers. She advocated for classes in women's literature and helped promote the works of neglected female and black writers. In 1984, she began her own publishing company, Wild Trees Press. In 1994, Walker changed her name to Alice Tallulah-Kate Walker, and in 1997, the Alice Walker Literary Society was chartered at Spelman College. In 2007, Walker agreed to place her personal and literary archive at Emory University.

Analysis

The story of Alice Walker's childhood scar provides the most basic metaphor of her novels: the idea that radical change is possible even under the worst conditions. Although she was never able to regain the sight in one eye, Walker's disfigurement was considerably lessened:

> I used to pray every night that I would wake up and somehow it would be gone. I couldn't look at people directly because I thought I was ugly. . . . Then when I was fourteen, I visited my brother Bill [who] took me to a hospital where they removed most of the scar tissue—and I was a *changed person*. I promptly went home, scooped up the best-looking guy, and by the time I graduated from high school, I was valedictorian, voted "Most Popular," and crowned queen!

The idea that change and personal triumph are possible despite the odds is central to all of Walker's writing. Her work focuses directly or indirectly on the ways of survival adopted by black women, usually in the South, and is presented in a prose style characterized by a distinctive combination of lyricism and unflinching realism. Walker's women attempt not merely to survive, but to survive completely with some sense of stability, despite the constant thread of family violence, physical and mental abuse, and a lack of responsibility on the part of the men in their lives. Walker is simultaneously a feminist and a supporter of civil rights, not only for African Americans but also for oppressed minorities everywhere.

Walker's vision was shaped in part by a work from the first flowering of black writing in America: Jean Toomer's *Cane* (1923). She said in 1974 about Toomer's book that "it has been reverberating in me to an astonishing degree. *I love it passionately*; could not possibly exist without it." Like *Cane*, the first part of which centers mainly on women in the South, Walker's novels are made up of nearly equal parts of poetry, portraiture, and drama, broken up into a series of sections and subsections. Other important literary influences on Walker include Zora Neale Hurston, from whom she inherited a love of black folklore; Flannery O'Connor, who wrote of southern violence and grotesqueries from her home in Milledgeville, Georgia, less than ten miles from Walker's childhood home; and Albert Camus, whose existentialism speaks to the struggle for survival and dignity in which Walker's characters are engaged.

Walker herself has defined her "preoccupations" as a novelist: "The survival, the survival *whole* of my people. But beyond that I am committed to exploring the oppressions, the insanities, the loyalties, and the triumphs of black women." *The Third Life of Grange Copeland*, on the surface a novel about the cycle of rage and violence torturing the lives of a father and his son, is as much about the recipients of that rage—the women and children whose lives are directly affected. Although the novel is unremitting in its picture of desperate poverty's legacy of hatred, hopelessness, and cruelty, it concludes optimistically with Ruth Copeland's hope for a release from sorrow through the redemption promised by the early days of the Civil Rights movement and by the knowledge and love inherited at the sacrificial death of her grandfather. These threads of political awareness and spirituality run throughout Walker's work.

The Third Life of Grange Copeland

Writing in 1973, Walker observed that her first novel, *The Third Life of Grange Copeland*, "though sometimes humorous and celebrative of life, is a grave book in which the characters see the world as almost entirely menacing." This dark view of life is common to Grange Copeland, the patriarch of a family farming on shares in rural Georgia, his son Brownfield, and the wives and daughters of both men. For all these characters, the world is menacing because of the socioeconomic position they occupy at the bottom of the scale of the sharecropping system. Father and son menace each other in this novel because they are in turn menaced by rage born out of the frustration of the system. Although the white people of the book are nearly always vague, nameless, and impersonal, they and the system they represent have the ability to render both Grange and Brownfield powerless.

It is not accidental that these characters' names have agricultural connotations. "Grange" suggests a late nineteenth century association of farmers, a feudal farm and grain storage building, and a combination of graze and range, while "Brownfield" and "Copeland" are self-explanatory—for the inability to cope with the land is what leads both male characters along virtually parallel paths. For the father, the mere appearance of the white farm boss's truck is enough to turn his face "into a unnaturally bland mask, curious and unsettling to see." The appearance of the truck causes the son to be "filled with terror of this man who could, by his presence alone, turn his father into something that might as well have been a pebble or a post or a piece of dirt." Although Grange is, in this same image, literally a piece of land, he eventually returns to the South and learns to live self-sufficiently, farming a section of soil he tricked his second wife into giving to him. Brownfield, in contrast, is never able to escape from the sharecropping system, although he sees that, like his father, he is "destined to be no more than overseer, on the white man's plantation, of his own children." Brownfield is able to live obliviously on a farm in Georgia, content to blame all his problems on others. The poor rural black workers of this novel are themselves little more than a crop, rotated from farm to farm, producing a harvest of shame and hunger, cruelty and violence.

Unlike the men of the novel, the women are menaced by both blacks and whites, by both the agricultural system and the "strange fruit" it produces. Margaret, Grange's first wife, is both physically and mentally degraded by her husband and then sexually exploited by a white truck driver, resulting in her second pregnancy. Unable to cope with this situation, Grange deserts his family, after which his wife poisons both her child and herself. Following his father's pattern, Brownfield marries and begins to work the land, but after "a year when endless sunup to sundown work on fifty rich bottom acres of cotton land and a good crop brought them two diseased shoats for winter meat." he too begins to abuse his wife.

Although Brownfield's wife, Mem, is a schoolteacher intelligent enough to try to break the cycle of raising others people's crops, her brief rebellion against her husband's malevolent beatings and mental tortures is a failure: He is able to subjugate her through repeated pregnancies that sap her rebellion as they turn her once rich and strong body into a virtual wasteland of emaciation. Because her body, which represents the land of the South, is still able to produce children despite its depleted condition, Brownfield is enraged enough to murder her in retaliation for her physical shape: "He had murdered his wife because she had become skinny and had not, with much irritation to him, reverted, even when well-fed, to her former plumpness. . . . Plumpness and freedom from the land, from cows and skinniness, went all together in his mind." Despite his irrational abuse of her, Mem is not ashamed "of being black though, no matter what he said. . . . Color was something the ground did to the flowers, and that was an end to it."

What the ground did to these generations of southern black people is the subject of Walker's novel—the whole lurid history of violence, hatred, and guilt that she chronicles in this story of one family's griefs. By the book's end, Brownfield Copeland has murdered his wife and an unnamed albino baby, while Grange Copeland has murdered his son Brownfield—first spiritually, then physically—and indirectly has killed his first wife and her infant.

Walker's characters are allegorical representations of the classic modes of survival historically adopted by black Americans in dealing with their oppression. Brownfield identifies with whites by daydreaming of himself on a southern plantation, sipping mint juleps, and then by bargaining for his freedom with the sexual favors of black women. Both of Grange's wives attempt to be true to the white stereotype of black women as promiscuous sexual beings, free of any moral restraints. Brownfield's wife, Mem, attempts the passive resistance advocated by Martin Luther King, Jr., but she is destroyed by what her husband calls "her weakness . . . forgiveness, a stupid belief that kindness can convert the enemy." Brownfield's daughter, Daphne, who calls herself the Copeland Family Secret Keeper, tries the strategy of inventing a falsely romantic history of the past, of the good old days when her father was kind, echoing those historical revisionists who try to argue that slavery was not that bad. Brownfield's other daughters try to stay away from their father altogether, regarding him "as a human devil" of whom they were afraid "in a more distant, impersonal way. He was like bad weather, a toothache, daily bad news."

Each of the title character's three lives (at home in the South as a sharecropper married to Margaret; in the North as a hustler of alcohol, drugs, and women; and finally back in the South as a farmer married to Josie and rearing his granddaughter Ruth) parallels a traditional survival strategy, which Grange summarizes as follows: "The white folks hated me and I hated myself until I started hating them in return and loving myself. Then I tried just loving me, and then you, and *ignoring* them much as I could." To put it another way, Grange tries at first to adapt to the system by believing what whites say about blacks; then he turns to the classic escape of the runaway slave—heading North to freedom; finally, he tries the technique of praising black life while ignoring whites altogether. A large part of the novel's devastation is caused by the repeated use of these techniques, not against whites, but against other members of the Copeland family. Only Ruth, the granddaughter through whom Grange seeks redemption, is able to deal with whites in an intelligent, balanced, nondestructive yet independent way. She has learned from her grandfather, and from her family history, that pure hatred becomes self-hatred, and violence begets self-violence; she therefore becomes the novel's symbol of the new black woman, ready to assume her place in black history as a courageous worker in the Civil Rights movement, which the rest of her family has been groping to discover.

MERIDIAN

Walker's second novel, *Meridian*, picks up chronologically and thematically at the point where her first novel ends. *Meridian* describes the struggles of a young black woman, Meridian Hill, about the same age as Ruth Copeland, who comes to an awareness of power and feminism during the Civil Rights movement, and whose whole life's meaning is centered in the cycles of guilt, violence, hope, and change characteristic of that dramatic time. Thematically, *Meridian* picks up the first novel's theme of self-sacrificial murder as a way out of desperate political oppression in the form of the constant question that drives Meridian Hill: "Will you kill for the Revolution?" Meridian's lifelong attempt to answer that question affirmatively (as her college friends so easily do) while remaining true to her sense of responsibility to the past, her sense of ethics, and her sense of guilt of having given to her mother the child of her teenage pregnancy constitutes the section of the novel titled "Meridian."

The second third of the novel, "Truman Held," is named for the major male character in the narrative. The third major section of the novel, "Ending," looks back at the turmoil of the Civil Rights movement from the perspective of the 1970's. Long after others have given up intellectual arguments about the morality of killing for revolution, Meridian is still debating the question, still actively involved in voter registration, political activism, and civil rights organization, as though the movement had never lost momentum. Worrying that her actions, now seen as eccentric rather than revolutionary, will cause her "to be left, listening to the old music, beside the highway," Meridian achieves release and atonement through the realization that her role will be to "come forward and sing from memory songs they will need once more to hear. For it is the song of the people, transformed by the experiences of each generation, that holds them together."

In 1978, Walker described *Meridian* as "a book 'about' the Civil Rights movement, feminism, socialism, the shakiness of revolutionaries and the radicalization of saints." Her word "about" is exact, for all of these topics revolve not chronologically but thematically around a central point—the protagonist, Meridian Hill. In some ways, Meridian *is* a saint; by the book's end she has sustained her belief in the Civil Rights movement without losing faith in feminism and socialism, despite family pressures, guilt, literally paralyzing self-doubts, the history of the movement, and the sexism of many of its leaders. In contrast, Truman Held represents those males who were reported to have said that "the only position for a woman in the movement is prone."

Although Truman Held is Meridian's initial teacher in the movement, she eventually leaves him behind because of his inability to sustain his initial revolutionary fervor and because of his misogyny. Unlike Brownfield Copeland, Truman argues that women are of less value than they should be, not because of skinniness, but because "black women let themselves go . . . they are so fat." Later in the novel, Truman marries a white civil rights worker whose rape by another black man produces disgust in him, as much at his wife as at his friend. When Truman seeks Meridian out in a series of small southern hamlets where she continues to persuade black people to register to vote and to struggle for civil rights, he tells her that the movement is ended and that he grieves in a different way than she. Meridian answers, "I know how you grieve by running away. By pretending you were never there." Like Grange Copeland, Truman Held refuses to take responsibility for his own problems, preferring to run away to the North.

Meridian's sacrificial dedication to the movement becomes a model for atonement and release, words that once formed the working title of the book. *Meridian* could also have been called "The Third Life of Meridian Hill" because of similarities between Meridian's life and Grange Copeland's. Meridian leads three lives: as an uneducated child in rural Georgia who follows the traditional pattern of early pregnancy and aimless marriage, as a college student actively participating in political demonstrations, and as an eccentric agitator—a performer, she calls herself—unaware that the movement has ended. Like Grange Copeland in another sense, Meridian Hill is solid proof of the ability of any human to change dramatically by sheer will and desire.

Meridian is always different from her friends, who, filled with angry rhetoric, ask her repeatedly if she is willing to kill for the revolution, the same question that Grange asked himself when he lived in the North. This question haunts Meridian, because she does not know if she can or if she should kill, and because it reminds her of a similar request, posed in a similar way by her mother: "Say it now, Meridian, and be saved. All He asks is that we acknowledge Him as our Master. Say you believe in Him . . . don't go against your heart." In neither case is Meridian able to answer yes without going against her heart. Unlike her college friends and Truman Held, who see the movement only in terms of future gains for themselves, Meridian is involved with militancy because of her past: "But what none of them seemed to understand was that she felt herself to be, not holding on to something from the past, but *held* by something in the past."

Part of the past's hold on her is the sense of guilt she feels about her relationships with her parents. Although her father taught her the nature of the oppression of minorities through his knowledge of American Indians, her strongest source of guilt comes from her mother, who argues, like Brownfield Copeland, that the responsibility for all problems stems from outside oneself: "The answer to everything," said Meridian's mother, "is we live in America and we're not rich." Meridian's strongest sense of past guilt comes from the knowledge she gains when she becomes pregnant: "It was for stealing her mother's serenity, for shattering her mother's emerging self, that Meridian felt guilty from the very first, though she was unable to understand how this could possibly be her fault."

Meridian takes the form of a series of nonchronological sections, some consisting of only a paragraph, some four or five pages long, that circle around the events of Meridian's life. The writing is clear, powerful, violent, lyrical, and often symbolic. Spelman College, for example, is here called Saxon College. The large magnolia tree in the center of the campus, described with specific folkloric detail, is destroyed by angry students during a demonstration: "Though Meridian begged them to dismantle the president's house instead, in a fury of confusion and frustration they worked all night, and chopped and sawed down, level to the ground, that mighty, ancient, sheltering music tree." This tree (named The Sojourner, perhaps for Sojourner Truth) expands symbolically to suggest both the senseless destruction of black ghettos by blacks during the turmoil of the 1960's and Meridian Hill herself, who receives a photograph years later of The Sojourner, now "a gigantic tree stump" with "a tiny branch, no larger than a finger, growing out of one side." That picture, suggesting as it does the rebirth of hope despite despair, also evokes the last vision of Meridian expressed by the now-shamed Truman Held: "He would never see 'his' Meridian again. The new part had grown out of the old, though, and that was reassuring. This part of her, new, sure and ready, even eager, for the world, he knew he must meet again and recognize for its true value at some future time."

The Color Purple

Like Walker's first two novels, *The Color Purple* is unusual in style: It presents the author's familiar and yet fresh themes—survival and redemption—in epistolary form. Most of the novel's letters are written by Celie, an uneducated, unloved black woman living in rural Georgia in the 1920's; Celie's letters are written in what Walker calls "black folk English," a language of wit, strength, and natural humor. Ashamed of having been raped by her stepfather, a man whom Celie thinks at the time is her father, she begins to send letters to God, in the way that children send letters to Santa Claus, because her rapist told her to tell nobody but God. Although her early letters tell of rape, degradation, and pain, of her stepfather's getting rid of the two children born of his cruelty, the tone is nevertheless captivating, ironic, and even humorous. Soon the despair turns into acceptance, then into understanding, anger, rebellion, and finally triumph and loving forgiveness as the fourteen-year-old Celie continues to write until she reaches an audience, some thirty years later. Like the author, who began writing at the age of eight and has turned her childhood experiences in rural Georgia into novels of violence, hatred, understanding, love, and profound hope for the future, Celie is a writer, a listener, a thinker, and a promoter of Walker's constant theme: "Love redeems, meanness kills."

Like Meridian Hill, Celie compares herself to a tree. After her stepfather's repeated rapes, Celie is sold into a virtual state of slavery to a man who beats her, a man she does not know, love, or talk to, a man she can never call anything but Mr. ——, an ironic throwback to a convention of the eighteenth century English epistolary novel. Celie tries to endure by withholding all emotion: "I make myself wood. I say to myself, Celie, you a tree. That's how come I know trees fear man." Like The Sojourner, or like the kudzu vine of the deep South that thrives despite repeated attempts to beat it back, Celie continues to express her fears and hopes in a series of letters written in a form of black English that is anything but wooden. The contrast between the richly eccentric prose of Celie's letters and the educated yet often lifeless sentences of her sister Nettie's return letters supports Walker's statement that "writing *The Color Purple* was writing in my first language." The language of the letters is at first awkward, but it is never difficult to follow. As Celie grows in experience, in contact with the outside world, and in confidence, her writing gradually becomes more sophisticated and more like standard written English, but it never loses its originality of rhythm and phrase.

Based on Walker's great-grandmother, a slave who was raped at age twelve by her owner, Celie works her way from ignorance about her body and her living situation all the way through to an awakening of her self-worth as well as to an understanding of the existence of God, the relations between men and women, and the power of forgiveness in uniting family and friends. Much of this transformation is brought about through the magic of a blues singer named Shug Avery, who guides Celie in understanding sexuality, men, and religion without causing her to lose her own fresh insights, naïve though they are.

The letters that make up the novel are something like the missives that the protagonist of Saul Bellow's novel *Herzog* (1964) writes but never sends, in that they are often addressed to God and written in an ironic but not self-conscious manner. Because of the combination of dark humor and despair, the letters also evoke memories of the desperate letters from the physically and spiritually maimed addressed to the hero of Nathanael West's *Miss Lonelyhearts* (1933). Although Celie is unlettered in a traditional sense, her ability to carry the complicated plot forward and to continue to write—first without an earthly audience, and then to her sister, whom she has not seen for more than twenty years—testifies to the human potential for self-transformation.

Discussing Celie's attempts to confirm her existence by writing to someone she is not certain exists, Gloria Steinem says, "Clearly, the author is telling us something about the origin of Gods: about when we need to invent them and when we don't." In a sense, Shug Avery becomes a god for Celie because of her ability to control the evil in the world and her power to change the sordid conditions of Celie's life. Early in the book, when Celie is worrying about survival, about rape, incest, beatings, and the murder of her children, her only source of hope is the name "Shug Avery," a name with a magical power to control her husband. Not even aware that Shug is a person, Celie writes, "I ast our new mammy bout Shug Avery. What it is?" Finding a picture of Shug, Celie transfers her prayers to what is at that point only an image: "I see her there in furs. Her face rouge. Her hair like somethin tail. She grinning with her foot up on somebody motocar. Her eyes serious tho. Sad some. . . . An all night long I stare at it. An now when I dream, I dream of

Shug Avery. She be dress to kill, whirling an laughing." Shug Avery becomes a god to Celie not only because she is pictured in the first photograph Celie has ever seen but also because she is dressed in a style that shows a sense of pride and freedom.

Once Celie's sister's letters begin to appear, mailed from Africa, where Nettie is a missionary, the ironic connection between the primitive animism of the Africans and Celie's equally primitive reaction to Shug's picture becomes clear. Although Nettie has crossed the ocean to minister to a tribe of primitive people, her own sister is living in inhuman conditions in Georgia: ignorance, disease, sexism, lack of control of the environment, and the ever-increasing march of white people. When Shug explains her own animistic religious beliefs—which include the notion that God is not a he or a she but an it (just as Celie once thought Shug Avery was an it)—Celie is converted to a pantheistic worship that makes her early identification with trees seem less naïve.

When the narrator of Herman Melville's "Bartleby the Scrivener" (1853) tries to explain Bartleby's withdrawal from life, he thinks of the dead-letter office in which the scrivener was rumored to have worked and says, "On errands of life, these letters speed to death." In contrast, Celie's and Nettie's letters, ostensibly written to people long thought to be dead, speed across the ocean on errands of life, where they grow to sustain not only the sisters in the book but also all those lucky enough to read them. As the author says of *The Color Purple*, "It's my happiest book . . . I had to do all the other writing to get to this point." For the reader who has gotten to this point in Walker's career by reading all of her other books, there is no question that Walker's name could be substituted for Celie's in the author's statement about her most recent novel: "Let's hope people can hear Celie's voice. There are so many people like Celie who make it, who come out of nothing. People who triumph."

Possessing the Secret of Joy

The novels *By the Light of My Father's Smile* and *Possessing the Secret of Joy* share strong characters whose sexual identities suffer because of the need of the individuals to conform to the societies in which they live. Only through death can Tashi and Mad Dog become complete and escape the male-dominated world and its restrictions.

Walker combines fact and fiction in *Possessing the Secret of Joy* to illustrate the effects that female genital mutilation has on the women who are subjected to the procedure. The main character, Tashi, an African tribal woman, willingly undergoes the traditional ritual of genital mutilation because of her desire to conform to her culture and feel complete. The procedure, however, leaves her physically and mentally scarred. Tashi realizes that she has been destroyed emotionally and made to feel as if she were something other than her true self. After her mutilation, she marries Adam Johnson and moves to the United States. She is renamed Evelyn Johnson, and the shift of her chapter headings from "Tashi" to "Evelyn" demonstrates the conflict within her as she struggles to find her true identity. That conflict leads her to madness.

Tashi strives to understand her insanity and to interpret her recurring nightmares of a tower. With the help of her therapists, Mzee and Raye, and the members of her family, Tashi realizes the reasons for her insanity and gradually becomes stronger and able to face her nightmares and what they represent. The story is related through the eyes of all the main characters, a technique that provides insight into the effects that Tashi has on those around her. Through its main characters—Tashi, Olivia, and Adam—*Possessing the Secret of Joy* is connected to, but is not a sequel to, Walker's previous novels *The Color Purple* and *The Temple of My Familiar*.

By the Light of My Father's Smile

Walker's sixth novel, *By the Light of My Father's Smile*, follows the Johnson family on a journey through life and to rebirth through death. Magdalena, referred to as Mad Dog, discovers her sensuality and its connection with her spirituality while living with her parents in Mexico, where the parents are pretending to be missionaries in order to do an anthropological study of the Mundo people. Magdalena is acutely aware of her emotions and sensuality, and she is severely beaten by her father when he discovers her sexual activity.

Magdalena's sister Susannah, shadowed by Magdalena's anger and frustration, is awakened to her true desires by her friend Irene, who is able to survive and accept life on her own terms despite the restrictions placed on her by her society. Susannah realizes that her unhappiness is the result of having been "sucked into the black cloth" and hypocrisy of the world. All of the members of the Johnson family suffer through life searching for true love and happiness, which they find only in death. The story moves between the spiritual world and the physical world as the father watches his two daughters come to terms with their anger and their true spirits. As characters pass into the spiritual world, they are enlightened to their failings in the physical world and make amends with those they have injured. Only when acceptance of each soul is obtained can the four family members cross the river and live in eternity.

Now Is the Time to Open Your Heart

In *Now Is the Time to Open Your Heart*, Walker continues her theme of sexual and spiritual exploration. The novel opens with Kate Talkingtree, a fifty-seven-year-old African American woman, meditating in a group, in a large hall surrounded by redwood trees. When the group's teacher begins to speak, Kate notices his southern European appearance and notes the description on the program that shows he has had a privileged upbringing among "educated and cultured people"; he has studied and lived in Europe and has been a "prominent professor at one of the country's most famous universities." As Kate looks around the circle, she notices that others in it have what she considers the same air of entitlement and that she is the only person of color there; for Kate, this makes what the teacher has said about "hot" revolutions in such countries as Africa and Cuba being less successful than the "cool" one introduced by Buddha twenty-five hundred years ago seem disingenuous. Unable to meditate from this point on and then awakening from a dream in which she has found an anaconda in her freezer and feels the need to kill it before it thaws, Kate decides that she must have a different kind of spiritual adventure.

As her lover, Yolo, watches her leave, Kate departs for a rafting expedition on the Colorado River with other women who are also seeking spiritual enlightenment. Although the pitching and plunging of the boat makes Kate ill, the nurturing and care that she receives from the other women contribute to a cleansing process as Kate remembers failed relationships, including the husband who became physically abusive when she suggested that they spend time apart and the opportunistic woman she married, who, it turned out, only wanted Kate for what she could get from her financially. At the same time Kate is having her spiritual retreat, Yolo is on his own quest, vacationing in Hawaii, where he encounters on the beach the body of a young man who has died from an overdose of crystal methamphetamine. Yolo meets the man's mother, Alma, who explains that the drug has taken over the island.

Meanwhile, Kate listens to the stories of other women on the rafting expedition, including Lalika, who explains that she has been "incested" from the time she was able to crawl and was raped and beaten by patrolmen in the prison where she was incarcerated after murdering a man who raped her. Through the guidance of leaders Armando and Anunu, Kate begins to discover her own spiritual strength. When Kate and Yolo return from their adventures—Kate having healed her own wounds by communing with others among the walking wounded, and Yolo having helped a grieving mother heal as well as learning about the destructiveness of colonialism to indigenous Hawaiian culture—they realize that they are each other's spiritual partners and invite those they met on their journeys to their nontraditional wedding.

Timothy Dow Adams; Mary A. Blackmon
Updated by Holly L. Norton

Other major works

Short fiction: *In Love and Trouble: Stories of Black Women*, 1973; *You Can't Keep a Good Woman Down*, 1981; *The Complete Stories*, 1994; *Alice Walker Banned*, 1996 (stories and commentary).

Poetry: *Once: Poems*, 1968; *Five Poems*, 1972; *Revolutionary Petunias, and Other Poems*, 1973; *Good Night, Willie Lee, I'll See You in the Morning: Poems*, 1979; *Horses Make a Landscape Look More Beautiful*, 1984; *Her Blue Body Everything We Know: Earthling Poems, 1965-1990 Complete*, 1991; *Absolute Trust in the Goodness of the Earth: New Poems*, 2003; *A Poem Traveled Down My Arm: Poems and Drawings*, 2003.

Nonfiction: *In Search of Our Mothers' Gardens: Womanist Prose*, 1983; *Living by the Word: Selected Writings, 1973-1987*, 1988; *Warrior Marks: Female Genital Mutilation and the Sexual Blinding of Women*, 1993 (with Pratibha Parmar); *The Same River Twice: Honoring the Difficult*, 1996; *Anything We Love Can Be*

Saved: A Writer's Activism, 1997; *The Way Forward Is with a Broken Heart*, 2000; *Sent by Earth: A Message from the Grandmother Spirit After the Attacks on the World Trade Center and Pentagon*, 2001; *We Are the Ones We Have Been Waiting For: Light in a Time of Darkness*, 2006.

CHILDREN'S LITERATURE: *Langston Hughes: American Poet*, 1974; *To Hell with Dying*, 1988; *Finding the Green Stone*, 1991; *There Is a Flower at the Tip of My Nose Smelling Me*, 2006; *Why War Is Never a Good Idea*, 2007.

EDITED TEXT: *I Love Myself When I Am Laughing . . . and Then Again When I Am Looking Mean and Impressive: A Zora Neale Hurston Reader*, 1979.

Bibliography

Bates, Gerri. *Alice Walker: A Critical Companion*. Westport, Conn.: Greenwood Press, 2005. Well-crafted work presents biographical material and also discusses Walker's major works, tracing the themes of her novels to events in her life.

Bloom, Harold, ed. *Alice Walker*. New York: Chelsea House, 1989. Collection of important critical essays, arranged chronologically, examines Walker's fiction, poetry, and essays from a variety of perspectives. Provides useful discussions of her first three novels and assessments of her social and political views in connection with her works and those of other African American female authors. Includes an informative editor's introduction and a chronology of Walker's life.

_______. *Alice Walker's "The Color Purple."* Philadelphia: Chelsea House, 2000. Collection of essays by such eminent critics as Henry Louis Gates, Jr., and bell hooks examines the themes and techniques in Walker's most popular and critically acclaimed novel.

Bloxham, Laura J. "Alice [Malsenior] Walker." In *Contemporary Fiction Writers of the South*, edited by Joseph M. Flora and Robert Bain. Westport, Conn.: Greenwood Press, 1993. Provides a general introduction to Walker's "womanist" themes of the oppression of black women and change through affirmation of self. Also presents a brief summary and critique of previous criticism of Walker's work.

Dieke, Ikenna, ed. *Critical Essays on Alice Walker*. New York: Greenwood Press, 1999. Collection of essays pays particular attention to Walker's poetry and to her developing ecofeminism.

Dixon, Henry O. *Male Protagonists in Four Novels of Alice Walker: Destruction and Development in Interpersonal Relationships*. Lewiston, N.Y.: Edwin Mellen Press, 2007. Examines the roles that male characters play in four of Walker's early novels: *The Third Life of Grange Copeland*, *Meridian*, *The Color Purple*, and *The Temple of My Familiar*.

Gates, Henry Louis, Jr., and K. A. Appiah, eds. *Alice Walker: Critical Perspectives Past and Present*. New York: Amistad, 1993. Collection presents reviews of Walker's first five novels and critical analyses of several of her works of short and long fiction. Also includes two interviews with Walker, a chronology of her works, and an extensive bibliography of essays and texts.

Lauret, Maria. *Alice Walker*. New York: St. Martin's Press, 2000. Offers provocative discussion of Walker's ideas on politics, race, feminism, and literary theory. Of special interest is the exploration of Walker's literary debt to Zora Neale Hurston, Virginia Woolf, and even blues singer Bessie Smith.

Montelaro, Janet J. *Producing a Womanist Text: The Maternal as Signifier in Alice Walker's "The Color Purple."* Victoria, B.C.: English Literary Studies, University of Victoria, 1996. Examines the themes of feminism and motherhood in Walker's novel.

Wade-Gayles, Gloria. "Black, Southern, Womanist: The Genius of Alice Walker." In *Southern Women Writers: The New Generation*, edited by Tonette Bond Inge. Tuscaloosa: University of Alabama Press, 1990. Provides an excellent, thorough introduction to Walker's life and literary career. Emphasizes Walker's voice as a black, southern woman throughout her works and argues that Walker's commitment is to the spiritual wholeness of her people.

White, Evelyn C. *Alice Walker: A Life*. New York: W. W. Norton, 2004. Comprehensive biography chronicles the events of Walker's life. Draws on interviews with Walker, her family members, and her friends.

DAVID FOSTER WALLACE

Born: Ithaca, New York; February 21, 1962
Died: Claremont, California; September 12, 2008

PRINCIPAL LONG FICTION

The Broom of the System, 1987
Westward the Course of Empire Takes Its Way, 1989 (novella)
Infinite Jest, 1996

OTHER LITERARY FORMS

David Foster Wallace's writing showcases a remarkable talent, as adept at the novel as at the short story and as skillful in nonfiction as in fiction. Although the literary heft and cultural impact of *Infinite Jest* may have led critics during Wallace's lifetime to consider him primarily a novelist, he was a writer capable of excellent work in any genre, and in years to come his versatile contributions to the short-story and nonfiction forms will doubtless add to his reputation as much as did his second novel. In *Girl with Curious Hair* (1989), his first collection of short stories, Wallace demonstrated his keen eye for representing the complexities of life in the late twentieth century. He would follow with later short-story collections *Brief Interviews with Hideous Men* (1999) and *Oblivion* (2004).

As an essayist, he published detailed philosophical explorations of the death of the author and on the love-hate relationship between fiction and television in the United States as well as humorous travel reports such as "A Supposedly Fun Thing I'll Never Do Again" (originally published as "Shipping Out"), a chronicle of his misadventures aboard a mass-market luxury Caribbean cruise liner. During his visit to the Illinois State Fair in "Getting Away from Already Being Pretty Much Away from It All," Wallace weaves his way among pungent livestock and nauseating rides and indulges in too many prizewinning desserts when he is mistaken for a contest judge. Other essays, including personal profiles of film director David Lynch and tennis player Michael Joyce, provide insights into Wallace's artistry and excellence. The compilation of these essays into *A Supposedly Fun Thing I'll Never Do Again: Essays and Arguments* (1997) established Wallace as a significant commentator on the modern American lifestyle; he cemented his reputation as a skilled nonfiction chronicler with the essays (published in venues as diverse as *Gourmet*, *Rolling Stone*, and *Harper's* magazines) collected in *Consider the Lobster, and Other Essays* (2005). In 1990, Wallace published *Signifying Rappers: Rap and Race in the Urban Present*, which he coauthored with novelist (and college roommate) Mark Costello. Wallace also published *Everything and More: A Compact History of Infinity* (2003), a treatise on the mathematical premise of infinity and the nineteenth century mathematician Greg Cantor.

ACHIEVEMENTS

David Foster Wallace achieved a remarkable degree of recognition early in his career. In addition to numerous prizes awarded for individual short stories, he was honored with several prestigious awards, including the Whiting Foundation's Writers' Award in 1987 and a National Endowment for the Arts Writer's Fellowship in 1989. His cultural analysis of rap music, *Signifying Rappers*, written with Mark Costello, was nominated for the 1991 Pulitzer Prize in nonfiction. *Girl with Curious Hair* earned the Quality Paperback Club New Voices Award for fiction in 1991, and Wallace was a National Magazine Award finalist in both 1995 (for "Ticket to the Fair") and 1997 (for "David Lynch Keeps His Head"). He won the Lannan Foundation Award for Literature in 1996 and in 2000, and received a MacArthur Foundation Fellowship in 1997.

BIOGRAPHY

Born in Ithaca, New York, in 1962, David Foster Wallace was raised in central Illinois, where his father was a philosophy professor at the University of Illinois in Urbana and his mother was a professor of English. Growing up among the geometric grids of rural Illinois farmland, Wallace developed an acute sense of angles, which, he argues in the essay "Derivative Sport in Tornado Alley," enabled him to become a successful player on the competitive junior tennis tournament circuit between the ages of twelve and fifteen. Wallace attended his father's alma mater, Amherst College, where he majored in both philosophy, specializing in math and logic, and English. At Amherst he became acquainted with his long-term friend Mark Costello, who would go on to become an attorney and also a novelist.

The anxiety attacks and problems with depression that first manifested in Wallace's teens recurred while he was in college, and he was briefly hospitalized; after returning to school he wrote part of *The Broom of the System* for his senior thesis project before graduating summa cum laude in 1985. After graduation, he completed the novel and received an M.F.A. degree in 1987 from the University of Arizona. Wallace's early success contributed toward some self-destructive experimentation in his personal life, which a few reviewers speculate might have provided some of the material on addiction that appears in *Infinite Jest*. He was briefly institutionalized at McLean Psychiatric Hospital, an institution affiliated with Harvard University. He began using the antidepressant Nardil and managed to emerge from his downward spiral around 1990. During this time he met novelist Jonathan Franzen, who became one of his best friends.

Wallace served as an editor for the *Review of Contemporary Fiction* and as a contributing editor for *Harper's*; from 1993 to 2002 he was an English professor at Illinois State University in Normal, Illinois. In 2002 he became the Roy E. Disney Distinguished Professor in Creative Writing at Pomona College in Claremont, California. Shortly after moving to Claremont, he met painter Karen Green, and they married on December 27, 2004. After serious onslaughts of depression in the first part of 2008, Wallace committed suicide on September 12, 2008, hanging himself at his home in Claremont.

David Foster Wallace. (Redferns/Getty Images)

Analysis

David Foster Wallace's name is often linked with those of other innovative postmodernist authors, such as John Barth, Robert Coover, and Thomas Pynchon; however, his writing incorporates the intricate intellectual hilarity of these authors at the same time it includes a postironic sincerity and a puzzlement with the predicament of living in postmodern America. Throughout his writing, Wallace examines themes of loneliness and desire, detachment and self-awareness, and mass culture and spectacle. Claiming that books are saturated with the uniform sameness of the messages in commercial media, Wallace maintained that fiction's role for the contemporary reader is "[to make] the familiar *strange* again."

Knowledge is learned through language. To this end, Wallace's work foregrounds narrative as an act that mediates the reader's experience of the world through language. His short stories are often fragmented and defy simple summary, while his long fiction involves twisting, multidirectional sentences and interconnecting plots that rely heavily on contingency and uncertainty. His work is uncompromising in its use of multiple points of view and disparate plot lines that are often left unresolved, but rather than merely frustrating readers' expectations, this openness demands that readers collaborate with the author in the experience of taking meaning from the text. One of Wallace's primary achievements as a writer is his ability to develop creative and experimental structures that serve to reflect the themes interwoven throughout the text. In his story "The Soul Is Not a Smithy" (published in the collection *Oblivion*), for example, the attention deficit disorder of the narrator is reflected in the story's dislocated style. Wallace also makes great use of footnotes continuously in works of both fiction and nonfiction; he manages to delve into multiple, parallel narratives and themes simultaneously through footnotes.

The Broom of the System

Wallace's first novel, published in 1987, employs diverse viewpoints and narrative styles that foreshadow the same techniques used in his later work, from the short story "Order and Flux in Northampton" to the masterfully encyclopedic *Infinite Jest*. Set in the near future (around 1990), *The Broom of the System* is a bizarre quest narrative populated by characters with strange names—Biff Diggerence, Candy Mandible, Clint Roxbee-Cox, Rex Metalman, Judith Prietht—and even stranger events, which have encouraged critical comparisons with Thomas Pynchon's *The Crying of Lot 49* (1966).

The central character, Lenore Stonecipher Beadsman, is emotionally adrift on the edge of the Great Ohio Desert (abbreviated G.O.D.). As Lenore struggles to understand the mysterious disappearance of her grandmother, also named Lenore Beadsman, who has vanished from a Cleveland nursing home with twenty-five other elderly residents, she must also deal with her enigmatic and manipulative family. The elder Lenore and the other patients feel lost in a meaningless, static existence, until Lenore, Sr., manages to persuade the Stonecipheco baby-food company, run by Lenore, Jr.'s father, to develop Infant Accelerant, a drug that is reputed to increase the rate of language acquisition in children. The elder Lenore has learned about the drug from a nurse whose husband researched the product, and she steals the test data from the Stonecipheco corporation, feeding the samples to her granddaughter's pet cockatiel, Vlad the Impaler. The bird develops enhanced speaking abilities and at the end of the novel seems destined for stardom on the Reverend Hart Lee Sykes's *Partners with God* television program.

Lenore's grandmother was once a student of the philosopher Ludwig Wittgenstein, whose *Tractatus Logico-Philosophicus* (1921) concerns the possibilities and limits of language as a medium for representing things in the world. Significantly, the novel's linguistic system revolves around the relevance of words themselves: Definitions, misunderstandings—including one character who calls his telephone a "lymph node" so that he can tell his family he does not own a "phone"—and stories proliferate throughout Wallace's text. The younger Lenore is a switchboard operator for a publishing company, engaged in a halfhearted affair with her boss, Rick Vigorous.

While Lenore feels comforted when Rick reads her the stories he has received for the literary magazine he publishes, she also feels disoriented, imagining that she has no identity except as a character in the stories other people tell about her. A minor character sums up this difficulty of finding a stable identity amid the confusion of an ever-changing world: "How to begin to come to some understanding of one's place in a system, when one is a part of an area that exists in such a troubling relation to the rest of the world, a world that is itself stripped of any static, understandable character by the fact that it changes, radically, all the time?"

In contrast with critics of *Infinite Jest* who have complained that that novel lacks narrative resolution, readers of *The Broom of the System* often feel the novel's rapid conclusion is too contrived. Whereas Wallace chooses to end *Infinite Jest* without neatly summing up the story, in his first novel he does not allow readers to forget that their experience of the text is mediated, as the plot that Lenore (and readers) have been attempting to understand through the fragmented pieces of Wallace's narrative is miraculously explained.

Westward the Course of Empire Takes Its Way

Published as part of *Girl with Curious Hair*, Wallace's novella *Westward the Course of Empire Takes Its Way* parodies John Barth's "Lost in the Funhouse" (1967), a classic metafictional story that debunks the illusion that realistic fiction presents an unmediated view of life. A fictional patricide of its metafictional forefather, *Westward the Course of Empire Takes Its Way* presents a cogent account of the absorption of Barth's once-transgressive metafictional aesthetic by contemporary commercial culture. The story recounts the journey of D. L. Eberhardt and Mark Nechtr to Collision, Illinois, for the televised reunion of every person who has ever appeared in a McDonald's restaurant commercial. D. L., a self-proclaimed postmodernist who constructs poems made entirely of punctuation, and Mark, a talented but blocked writer, are students of Professor Ambrose (a stand-in for Barth) in the East Chesapeake Tradeschool Creative Writing Program. Accompanying D. L. and Mark is Tom Sternberg, a claustrophobic actor who has one eye turned around in his head, although, the narrator informs us, "he doesn't talk about what the backward eye sees."

The other plot line of *Westward the Course of Empire Takes Its Way* describes a successful advertising executive's courting of Professor Ambrose and his scheme to license a nationwide chain of funhouse franchises. While Wallace praises the groundbreaking work of Barth and Coover, he sharply criticizes the imitators of these metafictional masters, who borrow experimental techniques for no substantive thematic purpose. According to Wallace's diagnosis, television usurped metafiction's business of irony and self-reference and thus robbed the metafictional novel of its power to critique televisual culture. What worries Wallace in *Westward the Course of Empire Takes Its Way* is not Professor Ambrose's "selling out," but that "they want to build a Funhouse for lovers out of a story that does not love."

Infinite Jest

The media frenzy surrounding the publication of *Infinite Jest* hailed Wallace's massive novel as the literary spectacle of the 1990's. Set in a dystopian postmillennial near future—when the calendar is subsidized (years are sponsored: "Year of the Tucks Medicated Pad," "Year of the Whisper-Quiet Maytag Dishmaster," "Year of the Depend Adult Undergarment") and huge catapults launch garbage projectiles into a wasteland referred to in the United States as the Great Concavity and in Canada as the Great Convexity—*Infinite Jest* presents a huge cast of characters and their stories. As an encyclopedic novel, it is a compendium of filmmaking, pharmacology, postmillennial politics, and literary history, supplemented with hundreds of footnotes that Wallace uses to fracture the surface of the primary text.

One of the novel's main narrative threads concerns Don Gately, an ex-burglar and oral narcotics addict, who is trying to break his addiction at the Ennet House Drug and Alcohol Recovery House (the redundancy is telling). The other major story chronicles the elite Incandenza family: Hal, a tennis prodigy who memorizes dictionaries; his two brothers, Orin, a professional football punter, and Mario, a dwarf; and their father, James, an "après-garde" filmmaker who apparently committed suicide by sticking his head in a microwave oven.

To deal with his loneliness after his father's suicide, Hal loses himself in tennis and drugs, a pattern that is replicated throughout the novel, as every character struggles with some form of addiction. The novel's title, which alludes to Hamlet's graveyard tribute to Yorick from William Shakespeare's 1600-1601 play, refers to the title of one of James's films, which showcases an entertainment so spectacular that anyone who watches it becomes instantly addicted. Enraged by U.S. president Johnny Gentle's plan to catapult American garbage into their country, a group of wheelchair-bound Canadian assassins plan to disseminate the tape in the United States.

The mysterious film features Joelle van Dyne, who was Orin's girlfriend before he lost her to his father; in the novel's present, she is a radio host who appears at Ennet House after a suicide attempt, where Don falls in love with her. Despite numerous connections between different narrative threads, the novel eludes a clear-cut ending, circling instead back to its beginning. Near the end of the novel, Wallace posits an inclusive vision of a "radical realism" that contains "every single performer's voice" in the foreground. To Wallace's credit, the novel, which contains at least fifteen different points of view, does not degenerate into meaningless chaos. Like James Incandenza's "anticonfluential" film, Wallace's *Infinite Jest* has been called "a stubborn and possibly intentionally irritating refusal of different narrative lines to merge into any kind of meaningful confluence," reflecting

Wallace's refusal to reduce the complexities of his characters' lives artificially into a neat resolution.

Trey Strecker
Updated by Scott D. Yarbrough

OTHER MAJOR WORKS

SHORT FICTION: *Girl with Curious Hair*, 1989; *Brief Interviews with Hideous Men: Stories*, 1999; *Oblivion*, 2004.

NONFICTION: *Signifying Rappers: Rap and Race in the Urban Present*, 1990 (with Mark Costello); *A Supposedly Fun Thing I'll Never Do Again: Essays and Arguments*, 1997; *Up, Simba! Seven Days on the Trail of an Anticandidate*, 2000; *Everything and More: A Compact History of Infinity*, 2003; *Consider the Lobster, and Other Essays*, 2005; *This Is Water: Some Thoughts, Delivered on a Significant Occasion, About Living a Compassionate Life*, 2009.

EDITED TEXT: *The Best American Essays 2007*, 2007.

BIBLIOGRAPHY

Blythe, Will, ed. *Why I Write: Thoughts on the Practice of Fiction*. Boston: Little, Brown, 1998. Collection of twenty-five essays on fiction writing includes Wallace's "The Nature of the Fun."

Boswell, Marshall. *Understanding David Foster Wallace*. Columbia: University of South Carolina Press, 2003. Full-length study considers Wallace's work through the theoretical prisms framed by Ludwig Wittgenstein and Jacques Lacan as well as in the tradition of postmodern literature.

Bruni, Frank. "The Grunge American Novel." *The New York Times Magazine*, March 24, 1996. Offers an author profile of Wallace in the midst of the excitement generated by the publication of *Infinite Jest*. Nominates him as the literary spokesman for the 1990's generation.

Burn, Stephen. *David Foster Wallace's "Infinite Jest": A Reader's Guide*. New York: Continuum, 2003. Insightful guide to the novel explains its relation to "encyclopedic novels" and expertly details the work's complex structure.

Giles, Paul. "Sentimental Posthumanism: David Foster Wallace." *Twentieth Century Literature* 53, no. 3 (Fall, 2007): 327-344. Comprehensive essay considers Wallace's overall body of works in the context of his views on contemporary American life.

LeClair, Tom. "The Prodigious Fiction of Richard Powers, William T. Vollmann, and David Foster Wallace." *Critique* 38, no. 1 (Fall, 1996): 12-37. Compares Wallace's *Infinite Jest* with the ambitious novels of his contemporaries, Richard Powers's *The Gold Bug Variations* (1991) and William T. Vollmann's *You Bright and Risen Angels* (1987). Explores the root of the word "prodigious," demonstrating how these authors display a vast range of encyclopedic information in their fiction in order to reorient readers with the natural world.

Olsen, Lance. "Termite Art, or Wallace's Wittgenstein." *Review of Contemporary Fiction* 13, no. 2 (Summer, 1993): 199-215. Demonstrates the ways in which philosopher Ludwig Wittgenstein greatly influenced Wallace's writing, noting that both use cynicism as a means to an end rather than as an end in itself.

Scott, A. O. "The Best Mind of His Generation." *The New York Times*, September 21, 2008. A posthumous appreciation of Wallace's place in the contemporary literary canon.

Wallace, David Foster. "*E Unibus Pluram*: Television and U.S. Fiction." In *A Supposedly Fun Thing I'll Never Do Again: Essays and Arguments*. Boston: Little, Brown, 1997. Argues that the self-conscious irony of metafictionist writing has been absorbed by the mass media. Asserts that innovative art must posit new values rather than merely expose false ones. An indispensable text for students of twentieth century American literature.

_______. "An Interview with David Foster Wallace." Interview by Larry McCaffrey. *Review of Contemporary Fiction* 13, no. 2 (Summer, 1993): 127-150. In an extensive and cerebral interview, Wallace demonstrates the outspokenness and intelligence for which his work is often lauded.

EDWARD LEWIS WALLANT

Born: New Haven, Connecticut; October 19, 1926
Died: Norwalk, Connecticut; December 5, 1962

Principal long fiction

The Human Season, 1960
The Pawnbroker, 1961
The Tenants of Moonbloom, 1963
The Children at the Gate, 1964

Other literary forms

The brevity of Edward Lewis Wallant's literary career did not allow for a long list of publications. He did contribute three short stories to the *New Voices* series: "I Held Back My Hand" appeared in *New Voices 2* (1955), "The Man Who Made a Nice Appearance" in *New Voices 3* (1958), and the posthumously published "When Ben Awakened" in *American Scene: New Voices* (1963). Wallant also wrote an essay on the art of fiction that was published in the *Teacher's Notebook in English* (1963). In addition, a sizable collection housed at the Beinecke Library at Yale University includes unpublished manuscripts, the final drafts of Wallant's first two unpublished novels, about one-half dozen short stories, various drafts of his published novels, the first act of a play, his journal and his notebooks, and miscellaneous loose notes and fragments.

Achievements

Edward Lewis Wallant's literary output was so small and his career so short that it is difficult to assess his place in postwar American fiction. Wallant's work is best seen in its relationship to kindred works in the late 1950's and early 1960's. Although he is still little known to the public, Wallant's four novels rank with J. D. Salinger's *Franny and Zooey* (1961), Saul Bellow's *Henderson the Rain King* (1959), Bernard Malamud's *A New Life* (1961), and Ken Kesey's *One Flew over the Cuckoo's Nest* (1962) as examples of what has been described as the "new Romanticism." Wallant's novels reflect an outlook on life that led him to write about the unfortunate, the outcast, and the common person, whom he portrayed with compassion and dignity. His unwaveringly realistic perception of life and its often painful demands leaven his general optimism. In each of his fictions, Wallant's central character is shocked out of a moral lethargy and into action on behalf of his fellow human beings. This shock is preceded by a submersion into the contemporary human condition, which provides Wallant the opportunity to explore the interconnections and disconnections of modern urban life.

Wallant was a committed writer whose commitment acknowledged the darker side of the lives of his characters. It is not surprising, then, that while some critics should emphasize the positive nature of Wallant's work, his "happy endings" and his optimism, there should also be those who find in his work a note of despair and a presentiment of his own early death. It was Wallant's achievement to fuse the qualities of an old-fashioned novelist with the perceptions of a modern urban realist. The combination resulted in novels that offer a particularly clear view of the 1960's.

Biography

Edward Lewis Wallant was born in New Haven, Connecticut, on October 19, 1926. His father, who was disabled by a mustard-gas attack during World War I, was almost continuously hospitalized during Wallant's early years, and he died when his son was six years old. Wallant, an only child, was reared in a shabby although respectable middle-class neighborhood by his mother, Anna, and two aunts. Except for his Russian-born grandfather, who told him stories of the old country, it was a household without adult males. During his years at New Haven High School, Wallant held a number of jobs, including plumber's assistant, delivery boy for a drugstore across the street from a Catholic hospital, and hot-dog hawker at Yale football games. Although his academic career in high school was not remarkable, he did attend briefly the University of Connecticut. He soon left, however, to join the U.S. Navy.

The final months of World War II found Wallant serving as a gunner's mate in the European theater of operations; after his discharge from the Navy in 1946, he enrolled in Pratt Institute to prepare for a career as an artist. In 1947, he married Joyce Fromkin, a woman he had known since childhood; in 1948, they moved to Brooklyn. After his graduation from Pratt in 1950, he was hired by the L. W. Frohlich advertising agency, where he became art director for a Westinghouse account. In the same year, he also enrolled in creative writing courses at the New School for Social Research in New York City, where he studied with Charles Glicksberg and Don Wolfe. Under their guidance, Wallant wrote a group of short stories and an unpublished novel, "Tarzan's Cottage."

In 1953, Wallant moved to the advertising agency of Doyle, Kitchen, and McCormick. He also moved his family from New Rochelle, New York, where a son, Scott, had been born in 1952, to Norwalk, Connecticut. In 1954, his daughter, Leslie, was born. In 1955, his short story "I Held Back My Hand" appeared in *New Voices 2: American Writing Today*, edited by his writing instructor, Wolfe. It was Wallant's first publication. During the late 1950's, Wallant submitted to various publishers his early novels *Tarzan's Cottage* and *The Odyssey of a Middleman*, but neither met with any success. Wallant changed jobs a third time in 1957, moving to McCann Erikson as an art director, a position he was to hold until shortly before his death. His second daughter, Kim, was also born the same year. Another story, "The Man Who Made a Nice Appearance," was published in 1958 in *New Voices 3*, edited by Glicksberg.

Wallant's third novel was accepted within twenty-four hours of its submission to Harcourt, Brace. Originally titled "A Scattering in the Dark," it appeared in 1960 as *The Human Season*. Although it received few reviews, some were enthusiastic and helped to create a small, underground reputation for his work. In spite of its limited commercial success, the novel received the Harry and Ethel Daroff Memorial Fiction Award from the Jewish Book Council for the best novel on a Jewish theme. The publication of *The Pawnbroker* in 1961, also by Harcourt, Brace, established Wallant's reputation as a novelist. The book was nominated for a National Book Award, and the screen rights were sold to Sidney Lumet, who in 1965 made a critically acclaimed film starring Rod Steiger.

The modest success of *The Pawnbroker* came at a crucial period in Wallant's life. For years, he had balanced his work as an advertising art director with his after-hours vocation of writing, and he was having increasing difficulty in reconciling his two lives. A resolution of sorts seemed imminent when he received a Guggenheim Fellowship in 1962, which allowed him to travel in Europe and to write full time. For three months, he traveled abroad. Joyce joined him briefly in Italy, and then Wallant went on to Spain. He returned home with the idea for a comic novel, to be called *Tannenbaum's Journey*, based on his travels. He also resolved to devote his life to full-time writing and resigned his position with McCann Erikson. He took a small room in New York to use as a retreat for his work. In spite of feeling tired, Wallant was excited by his prospects; the European trip had given him inspiration. Then, quite suddenly, he was stricken by a viral infection and lapsed into a coma. He died of an aneurysm of the brain a week later on December 5, 1962.

At the time of his death, Wallant had two novels, *The Tenants of Moonbloom* and *The Children at the Gate*, under consideration by Harcourt, Brace, and it fell to his editor, Dan Wickenden, to finish these projects. *The Tenants of Moonbloom* was published in 1963, as were two other pieces: a story, "When Ben Awakened," in *American Scene: New Voices*, again edited by Wolfe, and an essay, "The Artist's Eye," for the *Teacher's Notebook in English. The Children at the Gate*, although written before *The Tenants of Moonbloom*, was not published until 1964.

ANALYSIS

Just before his death, Edward Lewis Wallant wrote, "I suggest that most people are nearsighted, myopic in their inability to perceive the details of human experience." It was a condition he found perfectly normal; there is simply too much energy used up in everyday life, having families, supporting oneself, and living in a community, for much insight into the lives of fellow human beings, except as they relate to one's own immediate needs. Yet there are times, Wallant noted, when people experience an unrecognized yearning to "know what lies in the hearts of others." "It is then," he wrote, "that we turn to the artist, because only he [sic] can reveal even the little corners of the things beyond bread alone." It is revealing that Wallant, first trained as a graphic artist, should title the one essay in which he set forth his artistic credo "The Artist's Eye." In this essay, Wallant explores the relationship between the observable, everyday world and the interpretation of that world through the writer's heightened sense of awareness.

In all four of Wallant's published novels, this theme of heightened perception is central. The protagonist, who has become emotionally insulated from life, experiences a reawakening of feelings and rejoins the world around him. This spiritual and emotional rebirth comes as the result of the death of someone who has become close to the protagonist. The impact of this death, which often happens in a shocking way and with suddenness, penetrates the emotional barriers Wallant's characters erect against the onslaught of modern, urban life: Joe Berman escapes the past, Sol Nazerman is rescued from both the past and the dim recesses of his pawnshop, Angelo DeMarco gets beyond his streetwise sassiness, and Norman Moonbloom overcomes his inertia and learns to act. In each case and with each novel, Wallant takes his readers into the lives of his characters and reveals the little corners of the human heart.

The Human Season

Wallant's first novel, *The Human Season*, is the story of a middle-aged, middle-class man who must come to grips with himself following the death of his wife, Mary. Joe Berman is recognizably a twentieth century Everyman who lives a life barely distinguishable from that of his neighbors. He is a Russian Jew who immigrated to the United States when he was a little boy, and he seemingly has attained the American Dream, founding his own plumbing business, owning his own modest home, marrying, and fathering three children.

Mary, of "obligatory blonde, American prettiness," as one critic has described her, dies prior to the beginning of the novel, leaving Berman alone to face life and his largely unrecognized emotions. The structure of the novel intensifies the tension between past and present by alternating scenes from the present, in which Wallant skillfully renders Berman's daily life through a series of highly detailed episodes, with incidents from the past, each of them exposing some traumatic memory. In their reverse progression into the earlier years of Berman's life, these dreams deepen one's understanding not only of Berman's character but also of the formation of his emotional paralysis. Beginning on April 30, 1956, the day of Mary's fatal stroke, the dreams go back to September, 1907, when Berman was a little boy of nine years living in Russia. The dreams contrast sharply in their emotional vividness with the increasingly comatose quality of Berman's present life. He has become an automaton, living without connection in an environment increasingly alien to him. He lashes out at the objects that remind him of his wife's delicacy and sensitivity as he succumbs to his "numbing, disorienting grief." Finally, Berman tries to kill himself.

As he becomes more and more blind to the real world, the world of his dreams, his past, becomes more vivid until it begins to intrude into his present, waking life. Increasingly, Wallant returns to images of the natural sources of Berman's earlier feelings in his memories of his father and of his life in Russia. Although there is a pastoral quality to these memories. Wallant does not suggest a return to some agrarian ideal. Berman's dreams remind him of his human capacities and inaugurate his search for something that will approximate the bond with the nature of his youth. Among the dreams are recollections of his father and Judaism. Berman realizes how neglectful he was of his own son, who was killed in the war, and how estranged from the healing qualities of his Jewishness he had become. The death of his wife, after all, merely provides a catalyst for his sickness, causing his self-doubt and sense of alienation to surface. The initial moment of his illumination quite literally comes as a shock: In an attempt to fix a faulty television set, Berman is thrown across the room, and in his fear and astonishment, he begins to pray in a jumble of English, Yiddish, and Russian. In that moment, he discovers the meaning of all the months of his suffering: He is alone.

It is from this revelation that he begins to reconstruct his life, one that will be authentic and will result in a new self. He discovers a craving for people; his dreams no longer haunt him but rather provide him with soothing images that strengthen his zest for self-renewal. In a scene that elevates the fiction to a mythical dimension, Berman is born again as he walks home in the rain after having "witnessed" the life around him. As the novel ends, Berman is waiting in his empty house for his son-in-law to take him home for a family dinner. In this final chapter, Wallant convincingly depicts a poignant example of people's infinite capacity for self-renewal.

THE PAWNBROKER

Wallant abandoned work on a comic fiction, *Gimple the Beast*, to write his second novel, *The Pawnbroker*. As in his first novel, the central character is a middle-aged Jewish immigrant. Sol Nazerman, however, did not arrive in the United States as a youth; instead, the forty-five-year-old former professor from the University of Kraków fled Europe and the death camps in which he had been a prisoner during World War II. Now he is the operator of a pawnshop in a black ghetto in New York City. The shop is owned by a minor underworld figure who uses it as a drop point for the transferral of illegal money. Nazerman is aware of the criminality of the operation but does not protest. He uses his income to support his sister and her family, who live in the suburbs. He also contributes to the support of his mistress, Tessie Rubin, who lives with her dying father. The novel brings together the nightmare world of the concentration camp as Nazerman remembers it with the corrupt urban world of the pawnshop.

As in *The Human Season*, the central character has walled himself off from the pain and suffering of the world around him. Amid the grotesques who visit his shop, Nazerman remains private and isolated. The novel is the story of his spiritual reawakening, which is largely brought about through the intervention of Jesus Ortiz, the black, Catholic assistant who works in the business, and whose energy and ambition awaken sympathy from Nazerman. The death of Ortiz during an attempted robbery of the shop, which occurs on the fifteenth anniversary of the destruction of Nazerman's family in the death camps, provides the shock that penetrates the insulation with which Nazerman has wrapped his feelings in order to maintain his delicate sense of survival. He recognizes the part he willingly plays in the chain of human exploitation of which his pawnshop is a microcosm, and he is forced to acknowledge the community of grief to which he belongs and from which he has so long isolated himself.

The novel concludes with three acts of atonement for Nazerman as he rejoins the world. He telephones his nephew, Morton, and asks him to become his new assistant, thereby opening a father-son relationship with the young man who has been wanting it for so long. After the phone call, Nazerman sleeps and dreams, not a nightmare as he usually does, but a dream in which he is able to lay the dead past to rest. Finally, he, like Berman, learns to mourn and goes to Tessie to help her grieve over the death of her father. As in the previous novel, this act is an important sign of his rebirth.

The connections between Wallant's first two novels are more than superficial. The two protagonists, who have much in common, experience similar awakenings. Both novels interweave dreams with the narrative thread. Both men must expiate their guilt over the death of their sons. Berman never did respond to his son, who died in the war unaware of his father's love; Nazerman must seek forgiveness for the guilt he feels for the death of his son, who slipped out of his grasp and suffocated on the floor of a cattle car on their way to the death camp. Both men are finally free from their past when they can fully and properly mourn the dead; then they can rebuild their lives again in the present. *The Pawnbroker* is the darkest of Wallant's books and seems to have provided a release for the marvelously comic voice of the last two novels.

THE CHILDREN AT THE GATE

During the summer of 1961, while he was awaiting the outcome of his Guggenheim application, Wallant underwent a radical shift in attitude concerning his vocation as a writer. In the little more than six months he took to complete the manuscript of *The Pawnbroker*, he drafted the first version of *The Children at the Gate*, a completed version of which was left with his editor before he began his European travels with the fellowship money.

The novel concerns the relationship between the literal-minded, nineteen-year-old Angelo DeMarco, who makes the rounds of a Catholic hospital to take orders among the patients for the pharmacy where he works, and Sammy Cahan, a clownish Jew who is an orderly in the hospital. DeMarco, who clings to a rationalism as a defense against the horrors of his life—his disabled sister, his fatherless home, his obsessively religious mother, and the dying patients among whom he must spend his days—is redeemed by the antics of Cahan, whose essentially emotional view of life provides DeMarco with his spiritual change. Unlike Berman and Nazerman, Cahan seems to have inherited his life-giving vision, which he is able to spread throughout the hospital. As with the pawnshop and later the apartment houses of *The Tenants of Moonbloom*, the hospital setting provides a microcosm for the world's suffering humanity against which the drama of the central character's spiritual growth can take place.

Once again, it is a death, Cahan's, that shocks DeMarco awake to the final recognition of his stifling life and the possibility of rebirth, a recognition that is made concrete in DeMarco's ministrations to his developmentally disabled, childlike sister, who has been raped by their father. Like Berman and Nazerman before him, DeMarco reveals his growing humanity through his acts of kindness and tenderness.

The centrality of the dreamworld that played so important a part in the previous novels is replaced here by a living world of dreams that DeMarco must shatter before abandoning his barricade of toughness. It is no coincidence that he first discovers Cahan in the children's ward at the hospital, for it is the childlike simplicity of the orderly, his trust and innocence, that DeMarco must rediscover in order to be reborn. *The Children at the Gate* reveals the intermingling of Christian and Jewish myths that Wallant used to such great effect in all of his novels. It is not only the accumulation of religious artifacts or references in the novel but also Cahan's portrayal as the religious fool and his martyrdom in the Christlike crucifixion on the hospital gates that sets the tone. Just as the death of the assistant, Ortiz, in *The Pawnbroker* precipitated Nazerman's rebirth, so here Cahan's death reveals to DeMarco the path he must follow. The roles of teacher and priest, the relationship between suffering and redemption, and the confluence of death and rebirth form a religious nexus that gives this book its especially powerful message of commitment, community, and love.

Although there were comic elements in *The Children at the Gate*, it was only in *The Tenants of Moonbloom* that Wallant's comic genius flowered. His last novel exhibits a certainty of handling and a smoothness of execution that were the results of his growing confidence as a writer. Wallant had thrown over his job in advertising and had made a commitment to literature.

The Tenants of Moonbloom

The Tenants of Moonbloom traces the emergence of Norman Moonbloom, an introverted rent collector who manages four decrepit apartment buildings for his brother, and who emerges from his passivity as the result of his contact with the urban flotsam and jetsam who inhabit his apartments. Moonbloom, who is thirty-three at the time of the story, has finally settled down after years of college and a number of majors. He is a rather average young man who has spent his life retreating from people, and although he would prefer to hide in the womblike security of his apartment, his tenants persistently intrude on his consciousness. Finally unable any longer to retreat from the world, Moonbloom plunges into his past, like Berman and Nazerman, to search for a base on which he can build a relationship with life. Through a series of seemingly disconnected visions, Moonbloom awakens to an understanding of the humanity that he shares with even the most bizarre of his tenants. He launches a "holy war" of rehabilitation in order to try to respond to the needs of those human beings placed into his trust.

Through a series of jolts, not unlike the ones received by Wallant's other antiheroes, delivered by the various inhabitants of Moonbloom's apartments, he is transformed. This is accomplished during three visits he makes to his tenants. Each successive visit further shocks him into responding. His reaction culminates in the frenzy of activity in which he engages to bring the buildings and by extension the lives of his tenants up to some sort of standard. Although Moonbloom, a former rabbinical student, is Wallant's final Christ figure, this novel relies far less than its predecessors, most notably *The Children at the Gate*, on biblical imagery and allusions, despite Moonbloom's messianic zeal to convert his tenants into full-blown human beings. In his last novel, Wallant was to integrate the comic and the tragic. As one critic has written, Wallant moved from being a cautious optimist to become "the comic celebrant of man's capacity to live an energetic, courageous, and spiritually dedicated existence."

Wallant's reputation rests firmly on a small body of fiction that he wrote with much passion and energy. Necessarily, this reputation has been enhanced by the tragedy of his untimely death and the unfulfilled promise of his career. His prose reflects a joyful celebration of life, life in all of its manifest complexities. Although he has often been compared to two other Jewish writers, Bruce

Jay Friedman and Nathanael West, Wallant did not succumb to the absurd fantasies of the first or to the despair of the second. Perhaps his importance as a modern novelist is best summarized by a critic who wrote that it was Wallant's cautious refusal to accept "the existential despair and the universal isolation of modern man" that distinguished him from his contemporaries and led him to affirm quietly the worth and joy of life. Wallant's novels are a testament to the continuing resilience of the human spirit.

Charles L. P. Silet

Bibliography

Ayo, Nicholas. "The Secular Heart: The Achievement of Edward Lewis Wallant." *Critique: Studies in Modern Fiction* 12 (1970): 86-94. Focuses on the religious element in Wallant's characters. Compares Wallant to Fyodor Dostoevski, maintaining that Wallant has Dostoevski's ability to convey grim realism and to emphasize changes of heart.

Codde, Philippe. *The Jewish American Novel.* West Lafayette, Ind.: Purdue University Press, 2007. Codde analyzes the unprecedented success of novels written by Jewish Americans in the years following World War II. He focuses on the work of several novelists of the era, including Wallant.

_______. "'No Enemy, No Betrayer, No Bearded Torturer': The Death of God, the Holocaust, and Existentialism in Wallant's *The Human Season.*" *English Language Notes* 43, no. 1 (September, 2005): 63-77. Codde examines Wallant's novel, providing an overview of the book and analyzing its use of Holocaust imagery and its representation of the death of God and of existentialism.

Galloway, David. *Edward Lewis Wallant.* Boston: Twayne, 1979. A full-length treatment of Wallant's life and writings. Includes a chronology, notes, and an annotated bibliography. A good introduction to his work.

Gurko, Leo. "Edward Lewis Wallant as Urban Novelist." *Twentieth Century Literature* 20 (October, 1974): 252-261. Examines Wallant's metaphoric use of the city: ugly, perverted, dangerous, and cruel. Gurko claims, however, that in its sprawling vitality, the city also contains "seeds of its own reconstruction."

Kerner, Howard A. "*The Pawnbroker.*" In *Holocaust Literature*, edited by John K. Roth. Pasadena, Calif.: Salem Press, 2008. An overview and analysis of the novel, describing its characters, stylistic influences, and place within Jewish American literature. Includes a bibliography.

Lewis, Robert W. "The Hung-Up Heroes of Edward Lewis Wallant." *Renascence* 24 (1972): 70-84. This substantial discussion examines all of Wallant's novels, especially *The Pawnbroker*, paying particular attention to his sensitive, intellectual characters and his themes of suffering and rebirth. Also looks at Wallant's use of myth.

McDermott, John V. *Flannery O'Connor and Edward Lewis Wallant: Two of a Kind.* Lanham, Md.: University Press of America, 2005. A comparison of the works of the two American writers, focusing on their philosophical views. McDermott demonstrates how both writers are concerned with spirituality, the meaning of existence, and humankind's relationship to God.

Schulz, M. F. "Wallant and Friedman: The Glory and Agony of Love." *Critique: Studies in Modern Fiction* 10 (1968): 31-47. Compares Wallant and Bruce Jay Friedman, particularly in their use of humor and the theme of love. Finds Wallant's characters examples of growth in sensibility and his novels affirmations of order and rebirth.

Stanford, Raney. "The Novels of Edward Wallant." *Colorado Quarterly* 17 (1969): 393-405. Examines some of Wallant's characters and themes, concentrating especially on *The Tenants of Moonbloom* and *The Pawnbroker.* Maintains that Wallant's characters tend to undergo rebellion that leads to their rebirth.

JOSEPH WAMBAUGH

Born: East Pittsburgh, Pennsylvania; January 22, 1937

Also known as: Joseph Aloysius Wambaugh, Jr.

Principal long fiction

The New Centurions, 1970
The Blue Knight, 1972
The Choirboys, 1975
The Black Marble, 1978
The Glitter Dome, 1981
The Delta Star, 1983
The Secrets of Harry Bright, 1985
The Golden Orange, 1990
Fugitive Nights, 1992
Finnegan's Week, 1993
Floaters, 1996
Hollywood Station, 2006
Hollywood Crows, 2008

Other literary forms

In addition to several nonfiction works, including *The Onion Field* (1973), *Echoes in the Darkness* (1987), and *Fire Lover: A True Story* (2002), Joseph Wambaugh (WAHM-baw) has written screenplays for the film adaptations of his works *The Onion Field* (1979) and *The Black Marble* (1980) and teleplays for *Echoes in the Darkness* (1987) and *Fugitive Nights* (1993). He has also served as creative consultant for the television production of his novel *The Blue Knight* and for the television series *Police Story*.

Achievements

Joseph Wambaugh is widely regarded as an outstanding storyteller and the most respected and prolific American novelist in the field of police procedure novels. All of his fiction and nonfiction works have been best sellers, and, given his cinematic feel for character and scene, many of his works have been developed into television and film projects. With works defined by gritty realism and realistic and vivid characters, Wambaugh has received a range of prestigious genre awards, most notably the Mystery Writers of America's Special Edgar Allan Poe Award for Nonfiction in 1974 (for *The Onion Field*) and the 2004 Grand Master Award, a lifetime achievement recognition presented by the same organization.

Critics have long praised Wambaugh's ability to combine objectivity and empathy in realistic depictions of contemporary life on an urban police force. Few genre novelists have so effectively conveyed the feelings of horror, isolation, despair, frustration, and helplessness experienced daily by police officers, as well as their reactions to these intense psychological pressures. Wambaugh vividly brings to life the heroism and cowardice, anger and compassion, dedication and laziness, insight and ignorance of the average police officer on the beat. His believable portraits of police officers, both men and women, are matched by cogent explorations of the sociopathic personalities of the criminals they battle, all of which draw the reader into a complete and compelling world of drugs, crime, alcoholism, and social and moral decay.

Biography

Joseph Aloysius Wambaugh, Jr., was born in 1937 in East Pittsburgh, Pennsylvania, the son of a small-town police chief. Following in his father's footsteps was not young Wambaugh's original intention. He entered the U.S. Marine Corps in 1954 and soon thereafter married his high school sweetheart, Dee Allsup. Discharged from the military in 1957, Wambaugh settled in Ontario, California, where he became a steelworker and went to college part time at night. He planned to be a teacher and eventually completed both a B.A. and an M.A. in English. In 1960, however, while in his senior year at California State College in Los Angeles, Wambaugh decided instead to become a policeman. Over the next fourteen years, he worked his way up to detective in the Los Angeles Police Department (LAPD) and was eventually promoted to sergeant, despite several well-publicized run-ins with his superiors. Many of these conflicts were occasioned by the publication of Wambaugh's first novel (and best seller), *The New Centurions*, in which the hierarchy of the LAPD is irreverently satirized.

Wambaugh continued to be both detective and novelist until 1974. By that time, he had become so famous that his celebrity status had begun to limit his job effectiveness. He regretfully gave up police work for full-time writing. In 1983 Wambaugh moved from Los Angeles, dividing his time between the suburban areas of Orange County and Palm Springs. In 1993 he moved farther south to the Point Loma district of San Diego. Then, for more than a decade, Wambaugh turned to true-crime writing, most notably his account of a California serial arsonist who was also an arson investigator, *Fire Lover*, which brought Wambaugh his second Edgar Allan Poe Award for best fact crime in 2003. His return to fiction—and to stories of the LAPD—in 2006 was hailed by critics and by fans.

Wambaugh continues to pursue numerous projects, such as the adaptation of his 2006 novel *Hollywood Station* as a television series. In addition, recognizing the impacts that film and television have had on the development of police fiction and the public perception of the process of criminal investigation, he regularly guest lectures on screenwriting and screen adaptation at the University of California at San Diego.

Analysis

All of Joseph Wambaugh's novels deal with police officers, primarily in Southern California. Their environment is completely outside the experience of most middle-class Americans, for it is populated with drug dealers, drifters, pimps, prostitutes, addicts, panhandlers, murderers, and thieves. Supplementing the bad guys are the outcasts, outsiders, and victims: welfare mothers and their families, abused children, old and disabled pensioners, illegal immigrants, the mentally incompetent, and the chronically disaffected. Middle-class values have disappeared, and what are usually considered normal attitudes and behaviors seem nonexistent. In the cultures of the barrio and the ghetto, and even among the wacky rich, police officers are charged with representing and upholding a legal system overwhelmed by the morass of modern society. Because Wambaugh himself is a veteran of the streets, the reader experiences his world through the mind of a policeman: It is full of darkness, desolation, and, above all, a sense of helplessness, for the fate of an individual, as well as the solution to a case, often turns upon trivial, capricious accidents.

This depressing background of urban decay sets the stage on which Wambaugh presents several themes. The most persistent is that real police work is very different from typical public perceptions influenced by television, motion pictures, and traditional police stories, which depict cops as superheroes who always get the bad guys and put them away. Again and again, Wambaugh's police officers express their frustration with juries who demand to know why it takes three officers with nightsticks to subdue a single, unarmed suspect, or why a police officer did not "wing" a fleeing felon rather than shoot him to death. Everyday people who have never been involved in real fistfights or attempted to aim a weapon at a moving target simply do not understand the realities of these situations. Police officers are not superhuman; they are normal people thrown into extremely abnormal situations.

Often, it seems as if the police are at war with a judicial system that elevates form over substance and technicalities over the determination of guilt or innocence. To

Joseph Wambaugh. (Library of Congress)

the average patrol officer, vice-squad officer, or homicide detective, the courts are arenas where shifty, politically motivated defense lawyers and prosecutors conspire to overturn common sense, where judges and juries view police procedures and conduct with twenty-twenty hindsight, and where the rights of defendants have triumphed over the suffering of victims. It is the average officer who most often encounters the anguish and suffering of those victims. These experiences alienate and isolate police officers from the rest of normal society.

Within the police force itself, the officers on the street are responsible to a hierarchy of brass who, for the most part, have never themselves worked a beat. In Wambaugh's view, the brass are primarily concerned with ensuring their own advancement and have little concern for the welfare of their officers. He paints high-level officers, often with brutal humor, as buffoons who spend much of their time trying to seduce female officers, avoiding real responsibility, and protecting their reputations. That acerbic critique of authority continues in Wambaugh's later fiction when he specifically looks at the consequences of bureaucratic directives to compel political correctness and sensitivity in the wake of a bruising series of scandals involving the LAPD in the late 1990's.

Given that he is a street veteran himself, Wambaugh's sympathies clearly lie with his former comrades, yet what makes his novels extraordinary is his realistic appraisal of these officers, warts and all. Many of them are crude racists, many abuse alcohol, and most resent the forced acceptance of women within their ranks, which began in the 1960's. Attempting to shield themselves from the sheer terror and pain intrinsic to their jobs, they exude cynicism and disgust with nearly everything and everybody, even themselves. They respond to the daily brutality they encounter, and that they must occasionally employ, with gallows humor, sexual promiscuity, alcoholism, and, far too often, "eating their pieces"—suicide. Only in his later novels, after his hiatus from fiction in the late 1990's, does Wambaugh's evident compassion for streetwise cops permit a celebration of the profession. Indeed, his later fiction evidences his own reinvestigation of the police procedural itself—he shifts his attention from the intricacy of investigation and the dogged pursuit of solution and the focus on a single complex criminal act to a more character-driven narrative with embedded anecdotes that reflect less Wambaugh as a seasoned cop and more Wambaugh as a gifted storyteller.

The New Centurions

Wambaugh's first novel, *The New Centurions*, follows the progress of three rookies from their training at the Los Angeles Police Academy in the summer of 1960 to their accidental reunion during the Watts riots of August, 1965. Serge Duran is a former athlete and former marine who has attempted to escape his Chicano heritage, Gus Plebesly is an undersized overachiever who is exceedingly afraid of failure, and Roy Fehler thinks of himself as a liberal intellectual making merely a temporary detour from an academic career in criminology. In their development as police officers, all three face situations that force them to examine their beliefs about themselves. Initially assigned as a patrolman in a barrio precinct, Duran meets a Hispanic woman who teaches him not to be ashamed of his ethnic identity. Under the tutelage of a veteran patrolman, Kilvinsky, Plebesly gains the professional and personal assurance to become a competent officer. Fehler, however, fails to reconcile his intellectual views with the emotional realities of race relations on the street: He blinds himself to his own prejudices, tying himself into a psychological knot. His failure is dramatically symbolized at the end of the novel, when he is shot and dies.

The plot of *The New Centurions* develops chronologically and in episodes focusing on each of the rookies in turn. As Duran, Plebesly, and Fehler receive new assignments, Wambaugh takes the opportunity to display the operational peculiarities of the various divisions within the police force—street patrols, vice, homicide, juvenile, and narcotics—as well as to introduce a host of minor characters, both police and civilians, who reveal all the quirks and propensities of their world. Whenever a new character appears, Wambaugh adds believability and depth by interrupting the narrative to discuss some incident that has shaped this person's life and attitudes. These brief digressions are often darkly humorous and also allow Wambaugh to illustrate further the vicissitudes of life in the LAPD.

It is apparent that Wambaugh regards the Watts riots as a kind of watershed for civilized society and the rule of law. Until the summer of 1965, the Los Angeles police force generally dealt with specific crimes committed by and against individuals. The Watts riots, however, represented a fundamental rejection of the structures of lawful authority by almost the entire black community, and the department was astonished and overwhelmed by the senseless violence of mobs of ordinarily law-abiding citizens. At the end of the book it is clear that, though a few officers seem to have guessed that some sort of qualitative change in social attitudes has occurred, most assume that the situation will soon return to normal.

The Blue Knight

One of the main themes of *The Blue Knight*, Wambaugh's second novel, is that the situation did not, in fact, return to normal. Hostile media coverage of the riots focused on the LAPD's lack of community-relations efforts, incompetence, and alleged brutality, while government investigations reported widespread racism and corruption throughout the department. Stung by criticism, department executives became increasingly image-conscious and ordered significant changes in training and operational procedures. One result was that the time-honored tradition of the individual policeman walking his beat was replaced by the two-person patrol-car unit. In the past, officers generally had been granted a large amount of latitude in dealing with situations on their beats and were usually trusted to keep order as they saw fit. The wise policeman developed a commonsense attitude, allowing certain kinds of violations to slide while dealing with others immediately and often severely. The new breed of patrol officer, however, was supposed to stay close to his unit, maintain constant radio communication with his precinct, and limit his activities to those precisely within the law. The new policy was intended to ensure both the safety and the good behavior of officers, whose individual initiative was drastically curtailed.

The Blue Knight takes place in the midst of the transition from the old to the new; its main character is a traditional beat officer, William H. "Bumper" Morgan, a twenty-year veteran on the brink of retirement. Wambaugh examines Bumper's last three days on the police force, using the first-person viewpoint to help the reader perceive events directly through Bumper's eyes and ears. Though Bumper has been forced to trade walking his beat for driving a police unit, he insists on working alone and spends most of his shift out of his car and out of radio contact with his precinct.

Bumper's long experience has made him something of a sociologist and philosopher, and his observations represent Wambaugh's slightly irreverent tribute to the old police view of the world. As he makes his rounds, Bumper recalls for the reader many of the events of his twenty years on the force, as well as what he learned from them. Through these recollections, he reveals the essence of his approach to successful police work: Never give or accept love, and always remain impersonal and uninvolved on the job. Unfortunately, Bumper's philosophy is a self-delusion. The excitement and danger of police work isolate him from everything and everyone outside his beat, the only environment in which he is truly in control. In fact he is so completely involved that his life is nothing but his job. Thus, at the end of the story, despite postretirement plans for marriage and a cushy position as a corporate head of security, Bumper decides that he cannot give up his badge.

Though Bumper is clearly meant to be a sympathetic character, Wambaugh also endows him with flaws. He is overweight and indulges himself in vast feasts provided free by the restaurateurs on his beat. He is crude and flatulent, angry and vengeful, egotistical and very expansive in interpreting his powers as a representative of the law. He imbibes copious amounts of liquor and is certainly no paragon of sexual morality. Sometimes, despite his experience, he even makes stupid mistakes, such as allowing himself to be drawn alone into a dangerous confrontation with student demonstrators. Bumper is softhearted but also tough, violent, and often frustrated. Ultimately, he appears as a tragic figure, unable to break with a career that casts him as a permanent outsider.

The Choirboys

After leaving the LAPD in 1974, Wambaugh apparently felt the need to give free rein to some of the anguish and bitterness he felt about his career as a police officer. These emotions are expressed in his third novel, *The Choirboys*, which differs significantly from his previous works in both style and substance. In its structure, grim humor, and overall feeling of hopelessness, *The Choirboys* resembles Joseph Heller's *Catch-22* (1961), with the LAPD substituted for Heller's Army Air Corps. Like the military officers in *Catch-22*, the ten officers who make up the choirboys are losers and misfits: several alcoholics, a sadist, a masochist, a violent racist, and the like. Each chapter introduces a new character and relates a series of especially harrowing incidents that lead to the calling of a "choir practice," in which the group meets in a park to get drunk and vie for the sexual favors of two overweight waitresses. Choir practice allows the officers to let off steam and serves as a coping device against the horrifying realities they have faced. The sessions frequently get out of hand, however, and eventually lead to the unintended death of a civilian and the suspension of several of the group.

With its uninhibited street language, unrestrained cynicism, emotional violence, and unrelieved sense of futility, *The Choirboys* is saved only by the brutal hilarity of its bumbling protagonists and the ironies they suffer. The situations into which Wambaugh's policemen stumble are so outrageous that the reader cannot take them very seriously. Thus, even though Wambaugh's characters are incisive and believable, the world in which they operate is so impossibly awful that the reader maintains the objectivity necessary for laughter

The Black Marble

After *The Choirboys*, Wambaugh's novels became both more conventional in structure and more sentimental in tone. His main characters are still losers, and the sense of blind fate and the prominence of coincidence continue to dominate his plots, but, in the end, his protagonists seem to be at least somewhat redeemed; the climaxes always result in some kind of catharsis. Each of his succeeding books revolves around a single case, a kind of puzzle that is resolved not through brilliant police work but through dogged determination and serendipitous accidents. An excellent example is his next novel, *The Black Marble*, whose hero is Sergeant Andrei Mikhailovich Valnikov, an absentminded, broken-down alcoholic who is also a consummate and very touching gentleman. Valnikov was once a top homicide detective, but after he investigated a string of cases of sexually abused and brutally murdered children, he developed constant nightmares and started drinking to forget. Eventually, he suffered a breakdown and was reassigned to the robbery division.

Valnikov is paired with Natalie Zimmerman, an ambitious female detective who is bitter generally about the discriminatory attitude of the LAPD toward women and specifically about being stuck with Valnikov. She believes that her Russian-born partner is not only a drunk but crazy as well, especially when he begins to devote all of his still-considerable abilities to the solution of a case she regards as ridiculous: the theft of a prize schnauzer. Wambaugh follows their misadventures in discovering that the dog has been stolen by a trainer seeking to extort money from the owner, a formerly wealthy divorcée now unable to pay the ransom. As always in a Wambaugh novel, along the path to the solution of the case the reader becomes acquainted with a cast of wacky police officers and civilians, until Valnikov finally catches the criminal and wins the love and respect of his partner.

All of Wambaugh's subsequent novels have followed the pattern established by *The Black Marble*: the often-coincidental solution of a crime by not-very-heroic police officers or former officers. Though he himself regards *The Choirboys* as his best work, it is not representative of his style. In later novels Wambaugh solidified his reputation as a master of the crime novel with stories featuring the flawed characters, dark humor, intricate plots, and dangerous constructions exhibited in his earlier works.

The Glitter Dome

Few Wambaugh novels reflect the dark urgency of his outraged moral sensibility (rooted in his Catholic upbringing) better than *The Glitter Dome*—this is a novel, as Wambaugh suggests in his own foreword, full of venom. As such, it holds a particular place in Wambaugh's development: It is something of a nadir; from this point, his novels will follow a steady trajectory toward affirmation more appropriate to the procedural genre in which, traditionally, complex mysteries yield to resolution and a moral order is confirmed in the end.

The Glitter Dome, like other Wambaugh works, is a character-driven procedural, an ensemble narrative that traces four sets of partners who work the seedy districts of Hollywood. There, amid the world of the sordid and the kinky, officers struggle to assert a code of morality. It is Wambaugh's conviction, however, that the police are at best a fragile stay against the moral confusions and brutality of the criminal element. Here police careers follow a grim trajectory from cockiness to compromise and ultimately to despair; successes are rare and often the result not of brilliant police work but rather of guesswork and luck. Indeed, the novel starts with a cold case, a killing that has eluded solution—a film studio executive has been shot in a bowling alley parking lot.

The narrative focus rests on partners Aloysius Mackey and Martin Welborn. Wambaugh again examines the psychological effects of police work: the two partners represent the extremes, the hard-souled survivor (Mackey) and the idealistic innocent (Welborn). The borderline alcoholic Mackey, at forty-three years old paying alimony to multiple ex-wives and living with a cat, toys with the idea of suicide but survives by virtue of his cynicism and his grim sense of humor (the Glitter Dome is a raucous bar where cops go to vent). Welborn, however, struggles in a moral miasma—a lapsed seminarian who finds the order and ritual of the Catholic Church comforting, he seeks that same order in the night-world of Hollywood. He is haunted by memories: of an informant whose name he accidentally revealed who is subsequently murdered; of a child abuse victim, a bed wetter, whose penis was cut off by his father. Like the elaborate contraption he uses to try to repair his back injury, Welborn sees police work as a way to correct failures that Wambaugh sees, with unsettling honesty, are uncorrectable parts of the twisted human psyche.

As Welborn and Mackey investigate, they stumble into a plan to make a so-called snuff film (a film of a real killing) in Mexico, and they become entangled in the seamiest reaches of Hollywood, coming into contact with child pornographers, drug dealers, and sadomasochists. Here, Mackey points out, there is no evil—evil has a dignity and grandeur. Rather, this is simple opportunism and garden-variety greed. By the same token, there are no noble forces of good—detective work here is the product of coincidence and chance executed by imperfect officers who struggle with demons of their own. Appropriately, the final break in the case is entirely capricious—as it turns out, the studio executive was the victim of a spontaneous burglary that had simply gone wrong, and that information only comes from the dying confession of one of the robbers after he is shot. The reader is then denied the satisfying feeling of a case solved—it is merely closed—and that is further complicated by Welborn's suicide as he is overwhelmed by his own surrender to the amorality of the streets (the reader is given disturbing evidence that he may have participated in the robber's shooting as a way to assert some viable moral force). Although the case is technically cleared, like the smog that hangs about the Hollywood streets, a pall of uneasiness hangs about the narrative.

THE GOLDEN ORANGE *and* FUGITIVE NIGHTS

With *The Golden Orange* and *Fugitive Nights*, Wambaugh enters into the "ex-cop" phase of his work in the persons of Winnie Farlowe and Lynn Cutter, both former officers and heavy drinkers who become drawn into complicated crimes requiring considerable application of their skills. All the while they must strive to surmount the accumulation of personal demons engendered and nurtured by years of police work. In both novels the upscale settings—Newport Harbor in *The Golden Orange* and Palm Springs in *Fugitive Nights*—serve as effective foils for the trademark cop chatter and streetwise daring of the heroes.

In the ex-cop's world, saloons serve as substitute offices where former officers and off-duty policemen congregate to conduct business and male bonding on the side. Wambaugh's ex-cops are tough yet vulnerable, especially when they place their trust in others who, on the surface, seem worthy of it. In *The Golden Orange*, the moment arrives for one of the author's gritty veterans to address what he terms the Cop's Syllogism, a condition that could be applied to nearly all of Wambaugh's fictional constructions. It simply states, "People are garbage. I am a person. Therefore——." Once the syllogism is avowed, only something bad can happen. It "has led thousands of burned-out, overwhelmingly cynical members of the law enforcement business into alcoholism or drug addiction, police corruption, or suicide." It affirms why, in an interview, the author took issue with the notion that his works are police procedurals. "I was the first person, I think, to write a book about cops that was not a police procedural," he said. "A police procedural is a novel that attempts to show how a cop acts on the job. I wasn't interested so much in that. So, I turned it around. I thought I'd like to show how the job acts on the cop."

FINNEGAN'S WEEK

In *Finnegan's Week* another of Wambaugh's hero-detectives, Finbar Finnegan, teams up with Nell Salter, a district attorney's office investigator, and Bobbie Ann

Doggett, a navy law enforcement official, to solve a crime involving a stolen truck loaded with lethal pesticide. As usual, the drinks, jokes, sexual repartee, salty dialogue, and verbal and physical clashes flow freely. At times they almost careen out of control, whipsawing the reader to a conclusion that is judicious and sensible.

Floaters

Floaters features an aquatic theme, as Wambaugh pairs a couple of harbor cops and vice officers in an investigation of a scheme by a business tycoon to sabotage a competitor's entry in the America's Cup yachting race. As in previous works, the author demonstrates a knack for juxtaposing characters who are very different. In addition to the unlikely cops, the characters include a yachting enthusiast, an expensive call girl and masseuse, a vicious pimp, and a band of rowdy Australian crewmen. Though the plot is slow paced at the beginning, the events leading up to the climax are vintage Wambaugh. In all his fiction, Wambaugh has explored essentially the same themes: the basic humanity of police officers and the pressures they face, the decline of traditional values in modern society, and the haphazard and accidental nature of fate.

Hollywood Station

After more than a decade working exclusively on documentary treatments of true crimes, a series of successful (and controversial) best sellers in the manner of Truman Capote's *In Cold Blood* (1966), Wambaugh returned to fiction in 2006. It was less a return to form than a reinvention of it. Intrigued by requests from longtime fans and respected colleagues to revisit the LAPD in the wake of nearly a decade of scandals (very public investigations of botched procedures, coerced confessions, evidence tampering, excessive violence, racial profiling, and illegal searches), Wambaugh hesitated only because he was not sure he was still in touch with the psyche of the contemporary street cop. To reignite his fictional sensibility, Wambaugh hosted a series of dinners with a range of LAPD officers and listened to their conversations about life on the streets—he found the process cathartic as he gathered a wealth of vivid anecdotal material, and in the resulting novel, *Hollywood Station*, Wambaugh acknowledges the nearly fifty cops who participated.

Although on the surface *Hollywood Station* is a familiar Wambaugh novel—an ensemble novel set in the gritty underworld of Hollywood—it is a striking departure. It lacks a riveting central investigation: Here, a small-time criminal, a methamphetamine freak who is marginally competent as a thief, ends up tangling with a Russian crime lord (who is himself something of a clownish presence) and a succession of more daring and more dangerous thefts. It is a slender plot—Wambaugh is far more interested in creating the psychological lives of the investigating officers, a collection of vivid characters led by the Oracle, a fifty-ish captain who centers the novel with a steadying moral vision in a universe of chaos and absurdities. The anecdotes that the characters tell, full of streetwise humor, underscore Wambaugh's Irish love of storytelling. Given the range of characters (each with defining interests and signature dialogue—one a new mother, another an aspiring actor, two others veteran surfers), the compelling humor, and the episodic vignettes of these officers struggling to assert some measure of dignity and order, the novel recalls less the traditional police procedural and more Joseph Heller's *Catch-22*, by Wambaugh's admission a seminal text in his evolution as a writer.

Wambaugh (like Heller) is motivated not only by an instinct for compelling stories but also by a caustic critique of what he sees as bureaucratic absurdities—specifically, a complex of federal regulations that tried to create a politically correct environment but that undercut the effectiveness of the street cops and made the old-school camaraderie of the force strained and artificial. Unlike his earlier fictions, however, in which cops are imperfect and at times overwhelmed by the insidious pull of the criminal world they patrol, *Hollywood Station* presents a clear endorsement not only of the LAPD but also of police work generally. Public scandals trained attention, Wambaugh argues, on a slender element of the LAPD—and, as the Oracle says, there is no work more fun than police work. It is that spirited endorsement of the profession that distinguishes Wambaugh's return to fiction. Writing in his seventies, Wambaugh enthusiastically praises the work, determination, compassion, and moral authority of the cops he has chronicled for more than forty years.

Thomas C. Schunk; William Hoffman
Updated by Joseph Dewey

Other major works

screenplays: *The Onion Field*, 1979 (adaptation of his book); *The Black Marble*, 1980 (adaptation of his novel).

teleplays: *Echoes in the Darkness*, 1987 (adaptation of his book); *Fugitive Nights*, 1993 (adaptation of his novel).

nonfiction: *The Onion Field*, 1973; *Lines and Shadows*, 1984; *Echoes in the Darkness*, 1987; *The Blooding*, 1989; *Fire Lover: A True Story*, 2002.

edited text: *The Best American Crime Writing, 2004*, 2004.

Bibliography

Dunn, Adam. "Burning Down the House." *Book* 22 (May/June, 2002): 19. Provides background information on Wambaugh's first book after a six-year hiatus.

Jeffrey, David K. "Joseph Wambaugh: Overview." In *St. James Guide to Crime and Mystery Writers*, edited by Jay P. Pederson. 4th ed. Detroit, Mich.: St. James Press, 1996. Focuses on critical analysis of Wambaugh's work, but also provides some biographical information.

Marling, William. "Joseph Wambaugh." In *Hard-Boiled Fiction*. June, 2007. Case Western Reserve University. http://www.detnovel.com/Wambaugh.html. Accessed January 29, 2009. Presents helpful analysis of the principal themes in Wambaugh's work that place his novels within the tradition of police procedurals.

Van Dover, J. Kenneth. *Centurions, Knights, and Other Cops: The Police Novels of Joseph Wambaugh*. San Bernardino, Calif.: Brownstone Books, 1995. Presents a critical study of Wambaugh's first fourteen books. Includes an excellent chronology of his life.

Wambaugh, Joseph. Interviews, May 17, 2002, and March 28, 2008. Bookreporter.com. Http://www.bookreporter.com/authors/au-wambaugh-joseph.asp. Accessed January 29, 2009. Wambaugh provides extensive discussion of his methods for creating believable police officers in his fiction and for maintaining readers' sympathy for these characters in an era of scandals involving police misconduct. Also examines the relationship between his fiction and his extensive catalog of nonfiction works.

_______. "Ship to Shore with Joseph Wambaugh: Still a Bit Paranoid Among the Palms." Interview by Andy Meisler. *The New York Times*, June 13, 1996. Wambaugh offers his observations on what he considers the erosion of the American judicial system in the late twentieth century and also provides an overview of his own career as a Los Angeles detective and novelist.

ROBERT PENN WARREN

Born: Guthrie, Kentucky; April 24, 1905
Died: West Wardsboro, near Stratton, Vermont; September 15, 1989

Principal long fiction

Night Rider, 1939
At Heaven's Gate, 1943
All the King's Men, 1946
World Enough and Time: A Romantic Novel, 1950
Band of Angels, 1955
The Cave, 1959
Wilderness: A Tale of the Civil War, 1961
Flood: A Romance of Our Time, 1964
Meet Me in the Green Glen, 1971
A Place to Come To, 1977

Other literary forms

Robert Penn Warren wrote successfully in so many genres that Charles Bohner called him "the pentathlon champion of American literature." In addition to his novels, he published short stories, numerous volumes of poetry, and a considerable amount of nonfiction. Warren's fiction and his poetry often consider the same philosophical themes: the meaning of history, the loss of innocence and the recognition of evil in the fallen world, and the difficulty of finding a moral balance in a world in which traditional Christian values seem to be faltering. For example, in his book-length poem *Brother to Dragons: A Tale in Verse and Voices* (1953), Warren begins with a historical event—a brutal murder of a slave by Thomas Jefferson's nephew, Lilburne Lewis—and creates a philosophical examination of people's fallen nature. Warren does something very similar in his novel *World Enough and Time*. The story is based on a murder that occurred in 1825, but the novel, like the poem, becomes an examination of people's fall from innocence and the difficulty of establishing moral ideals in a fallen world.

Warren's concerns over history and morality are also evident in his earliest, nonfiction works. In his first book, a biography, *John Brown: The Making of a Martyr* (1929), Warren contends that Brown did not tread the path of morality quite so righteously as Ralph Waldo Emerson had thought he had; in his fallen condition, Brown mistook his own egotism for pure idealism. Warren's neo-orthodox insistence on people's fallen nature and his skepticism about the possibilities of pure idealism, both of which are reflected in his novels, led him to accept the traditionalist attitudes of the southern intellectuals who made up the Fugitive Group, and he contributed to the agrarian manifesto *I'll Take My Stand* (1930). Warren did, however, espouse a more liberal attitude toward racial matters in his later nonfiction works *Segregation: The Inner Conflict in the South* (1956) and *Who Speaks for the Negro?* (1965).

Warren's social criticism ultimately proved less influential than his literary criticism. His *Selected Essays* (1958) contains perceptive studies of Samuel Taylor Coleridge's *The Rime of the Ancient Mariner* (1798), Joseph Conrad's *Nostromo* (1904), William Faulkner, Ernest Hemingway, and Katherine Anne Porter. These essays are important not only for what they say about these authors but also for what they reveal about Warren's own work. Even more important than these essays, however, was Warren's collaboration with Cleanth Brooks. Their textbooks, *Understanding Fiction* (1943) and *Understanding Poetry* (1938), helped to change substantially the way literature was taught in the United States.

Warren continued to publish literary criticism at intervals throughout his life; indeed, *New and Selected Essays* appeared in the year of his death, 1989. With a poetry-writing career that spanned fifty years, however, he was at least equally well known as a craftsman in that genre. His poems have been widely anthologized, and he is recognized as one of the foremost American poets of the twentieth century.

Achievements

For most readers, Robert Penn Warren's name is probably most associated with his novel *All the King's Men*, for which he won both the Pulitzer Prize for fiction and the National Book Award. He also won the Robert Meltzer Award from the Screen Writers Guild for the play based on that novel. Warren's short story "Blackberry Winter" also has been highly acclaimed and widely anthologized. Other readers think of Warren primarily as a poet, and with good reason; he won the Pulitzer Prize for poetry twice, first for *Promises: Poems, 1954-1956* (1957), which also won the Edna St. Vincent Millay Prize and the National Book Award for poetry, and a second time for *Now and Then: Poems, 1976-1978* (1978). *Selected Poems: New and Old, 1923-1966* (1966) won the Bollingen Prize from Yale University, and *Audubon: A Vision* (1969) won the Van Wyck Brooks Award and the National Medal for Literature. Warren was elected to the American Philosophical Society in 1952 and to the American Academy of Arts and Sciences in 1959. He was named first poet laureate of the United States in 1986.

Biography

Robert Penn Warren's background and experience had a tremendous impact on the thematic concerns of his fiction. He demonstrated the need, common to so many southern writers, to cope with the burden of the past. He also wrote out of a scholar's familiarity with and devotion to certain prominent literary artists, past and present, particularly the Elizabethan and Jacobean dramatists Conrad, Faulkner, and T. S. Eliot. Warren's academic studies, pursued in a long career as an English professor, may have had a great deal to do with the structure of his works and their typically tragic mode. His recurring subject, however, was the peculiar experience of the South; a love-hate relationship with a dying heritage runs throughout his work.

Born to Robert Franklin and Anna Ruth Penn Warren on April 24, 1905, in the tiny Kentucky town of Guthrie, Warren grew up in an almost classic southern situation. His father, a banker and businessman struggling to support a large family, did not initially fire the young Warren's imagination as his grandfather did. The emotional bond between Warren and his maternal grandfather, Gabriel Thomas Penn, ripened during long summers spent on his grandfather's tobacco farm. Here, Warren experienced the pastoral charms of agrarian life, soaked up the nostalgic glow of the American Civil War from his grandfather, and absorbed the rhetoric and humor that permeates the southern storytelling.

Gabriel had been a cavalryman during the Civil War, and he spent many an afternoon with his grandson reliving the legendary time. It is not surprising that the boy looked upon the Civil War as America's great epic, as imbued with nobility and tragedy as Homer's *Iliad* (c. 750 B.C.E.; English translation, 1611) He was not blind, however, to the irony and ambiguity of his grandfather as representative of the values of the aristocratic horse soldier. Warren commemorated his realization that the romantic image of the Confederate cavalryman had its darker side in the poem "Court Martial" in *Promises: Poems, 1954-1956*, which is about his grandfather's hanging of bushwhackers without benefit of legal trial. Because this poem was written much later, however, it is possible that the ambiguous view of the grandfather was partially constructed from a more mature understanding. The event, however, was a true one that evidently made a deep impression on the young Warren. In any case, Warren was absorbing background for a number of later novels, such as *Wilderness: A Tale of the Civil War* and *Band of Angels*. In neither of these does he write as an apologist for the Old South, but he does expose the moral shortcomings of Northerners, much as he does in his early biography of John Brown.

Warren also was absorbing the local tales of tobacco war, when the growers of dark-fired tobacco banded together to boycott the tobacco company that regulated prices. Warren's first novel, *Night Rider*, was written from childhood memories of such local stories. Warren's brother, Thomas, who became a grain dealer, knew all the farmers of the region and was adept at repeating such tales.

Robert Penn Warren. (Washington Post/D.C. Public Library)

The young Warren loved nature; collected butterflies, snakes, rocks, and leaves; and aspired to paint animals (an interest reflected in his poem about John Audubon). Later, he hunted with his brother and learned taxidermy. These experiences were more important, perhaps, to the content of his poetry than to his fiction. In spite of his persistent affinity for nature, he usually recognized in his fiction its essential amorality: "The blank cup of nature," he calls it in *World Enough and Time*.

In spite of the contribution to his early imaginative development by his grandfather and his agrarian milieu, the influence of Warren's father was subtle and pervasive, perhaps more significant in the long run to the human relationships explored in his novels. Ambiguous father-son relationships appear over and over in such novels as *All the King's Men*, *The Cave*, *At Heaven's Gate*, and *A Place to Come To*. None is modeled on Warren's actual relationship to his own father, but they reflect a combination of admiration, guilt, and mystery that suggests some deep personal involvement in the issues they raise.

Warren often admitted to an odd sense of guilt about "stealing his father's life." Robert Franklin Warren had wanted to be a lawyer and a poet but had become a businessman instead, because of financial responsibilities not only to his own family but also to a family of half brothers and sisters left without a provider when his father died. One of Warren's favorite reminiscences was about finding a book with some poems written by his father in it and carrying it with delight to him. His father summarily confiscated the book, and his son never saw it again. Warren thought perhaps his father had been embarrassed or pained at this reminder of a goal long since set aside. According to Warren, his father never regretted the obligations that dictated the terms of his life. Indeed, he took joy in them. Warren speaks with an admiration bordering on awe of the seemingly effortless rectitude of his father and of the ideal relationship between his father and mother.

As the result of an accident when he was fifteen years old, Warren lost his sight in one eye and was thus prevented from pursuing a career as a naval officer, as he had planned. Warren went, instead, to Vanderbilt University and came under the influence of John Crowe Ransom and the Fugitives, a group of academics and townspeople who met regularly to discuss philosophy and poetry. Ransom soon recognized Warren's unusual ability and encouraged him to write poetry.

Warren graduated summa cum laude from Vanderbilt in 1926 and pursued a master of arts degree at the University of California, Berkeley. While there, he became an ardent student of Elizabethan and Jacobean drama, which perhaps struck a responsive chord in an imagination already steeped in the violence and melodrama of southern history. He started to work on a doctorate at Yale University but left as a Rhodes scholar for Oxford, England, where he received a bachelor of letters degree in 1930.

During this period, Warren wrote his first book, *John Brown*. To some extent, this book grew out of an impulse shared with a number of his Vanderbilt friends and other writers of the Southern Renaissance. They were concerned about the exclusively Northern bias of most historians dealing with events leading up to and during the Civil War and its aftermath. Certainly, Warren presents a jaundiced view of the radical abolitionist. Brown seems to have provided a nucleus for Warren's meditations about the effects of power and the misuses of altruism that were to be explored in a number of later novels, especially *Night Rider* and *All the King's Men*. He also wrote his first fiction while at Oxford, a short story called "Prime Leaf," about the impact of the Kentucky tobacco war on an old man, his son, and his grandson. The old man has a role similar to that of the elder Todd in *Night Rider*, the wise man who bows out of the organization when it resorts to vigilante tactics.

Warren taught at a number of universities, including Louisiana State, where he lived in the legendary ambience of the southern demagogue Huey Long, whose presence lies behind the fictional Willie Stark of *All the King's Men*. Warren later said that he knew nothing about the real Long, but the mythical Long was on everyone's lips. Even casual conversations often dwelled on questions of power and ethics, of means and ends, and of "historical costs." In an essay titled "*All the King's Men*: The Matrix of Experience," in John Lewis Longley's *Robert Penn Warren: A Collection of Critical Essays* (1965), Warren writes,

> Melodrama was the breath of life. There had been melodrama in the life I had known in Tennessee, but with a difference; in Tennessee the melodrama seemed to be different from the stuff of life, something superimposed upon life, but in Louisiana people lived melodrama, seemed to live, in fact, for it, for this strange combination of philosophy, humor and violence. Life

> was a tale that you happened to be living—and that "Huey" happened to be living before your eyes.

These remarks demonstrate that Warren was not primarily a historical novelist; rather, he was a classicist, fascinated with the universal patterns in particular experience. He thus discouraged close comparisons between Willie Stark and Long, pointing out that he wrote the first version of the story as a verse drama in Italy, as he watched Benito Mussolini consolidate his power.

In Warren's writing career, the years from 1943 to 1950—though a dry period for poetry—were productive ones for fiction and literary criticism. In addition to *All the King's Men*, he produced *At Heaven's Gate*, about the unscrupulous liaison between government and industry, and *World Enough and Time*, about a nineteenth century murder case. When Warren was poetry consultant for the Library of Congress in 1944-1945, Katherine Anne Porter, who was fiction consultant that year, threw on his desk the confession of Jeroboam Beauchamp, hanged for murder in Kentucky in 1826. Porter announced cryptically that she was giving him a novel. This was, indeed, the germ for his most complex novel, *World Enough and Time*.

Warren's dry period in poetry eventually ended after he divorced his first wife, Emma Brescia, married the writer Eleanor Clark, and fathered two children. He began writing excellent poetry and produced several more novels. A long association with Yale University began in 1950.

In 1986 Warren was named the first poet laureate of the United States, a post he held for two years. He died of cancer in 1989 at his summer home near Stratton, Vermont.

Analysis

Often, what Robert Penn Warren said about other writers provides important insight into his own works. This is especially true of Warren's perceptive essay "The Great Mirage: Conrad and *Nostromo*" (in *Selected Essays*), in which he discusses the enigmatic speech of Stein in Conrad's *Lord Jim* (1900):

> A man that is born falls into a dream like a man who falls into the sea. If he tries to climb out into the air as inexperienced people endeavor to do, he drowns—*nicht wahr*? . . . No! I tell you! The way is to the destructive element submit yourself, and with the exertions of your hands and feet in the water make the deep, deep sea keep you up.

Warren interprets the dream here as "man's necessity to justify himself and his actions into moral significance of some order, to find sanctions." The destructiveness of the dream arises from humans' nature as egotistical animals with savage impulses, not completely adapted to the dream sea of ideas. The one who learns to swim instead of drowning in the unnatural sea of ideas is he who realizes that the values he creates are illusion, but that "the illusion is necessary, is infinitely precious, is the mark of his human achievement, and is, in the end, his only truth." Warren calls *Nostromo* "a study in the definition and necessity of illusion." This phrase could also describe most of Warren's works of fiction.

Warren's classification of thematic elements in Conrad's stories could also be applied to his own. Warren writes that Conrad is concerned with the person who lacks imagination but clings to fidelity and duty (like the old captain in *Youth*, 1902), the sinner against human solidarity and the human mission (like Kurtz in *Heart of Darkness*, 1902, and Decoud in *Nostromo*), and the redeemed individual (Jim in *Lord Jim* and Dr. Monygham in *Nostromo*). Warren says that Conrad is most interested in the latter—"the crisis of this story comes when the hero recognizes the terms on which he may be saved, the moment, to take Morton Zabel's phrase, of the 'terror of the awakening.'"

One might note that in Warren's novel *At Heaven's Gate*, Jerry's dirt-farmer father fits the pattern of natural rectitude, while Slim Sarrett, the nihilistic, cynical artist, is certainly the sinner against human solidarity. No one seems to be redeemed in *At Heaven's Gate*, though Jerry might have a chance in a hypothetical future, since he has acquired considerable self-knowledge. Mr. Munn in *Night Rider* has also stripped away his own illusions, but he dies, like William Shakespeare's Macbeth, without redemption. In other novels of this period, however, Jack Burden in *All the King's Men*, and perhaps even the murderer in *World Enough and Time*, achieve some kind of absolution. Warren and Conrad share this deep obsession with the need for redemption, and though the sentiment is religious and may be expressed in Christian imagery, it is consistently humanistic in emphasis. The world they both recognize is a naturalistic one, but people must live in two worlds, the world of facts and the world of ideas, which they create themselves. Warren's notion of submission to the realm of ideas is analogous, perhaps, to Hemingway's code of the hunter, the fisherman, the bullfighter, or the soldier, which provides existential meaning in a meaningless world.

Warren's early novels, particularly *Night Rider*, *All the King's Men*, and *World Enough and Time*, which critics generally agree are his best, trace a pattern of increasing complexity in the theme of people's vacillation between the fantasy of dreams and the reality of facts. After *World Enough and Time*, which is almost too densely packed and convoluted in theme, Warren relaxed his insistence that everything must be said on the subject of illusion and reality in one novel. Later works, such as *Meet Me in the Green Glen* and *Wilderness*, though not conspicuously different in theme, concentrate on a particular manifestation of the problem—on the nature of love in *Meet Me in the Green Glen*, and on the nature of altruism in *Wilderness*.

Actually, Warren's examination of the apposition between the world of ideas and the world of facts begins in his first book, *John Brown*. Warren portrays the militant abolitionist as not so much obsessed with freeing slaves as with starring in his own myth. Brown is encouraged in this role by the unqualified praise of Ralph Waldo Emerson, whom Warren believed to be a writer of empty words, with little perception of the real world; Warren quotes Emerson as saying of Brown, "He is a man to make friends wherever on earth courage and integrity are esteemed—the rarest of heroes, a pure idealist, with no by-ends of his own." Warren did not for a moment believe that Brown was a "pure idealist"; moreover, Warren had a continuing distrust of "pure idealists," whoever they might be. In his fiction, Warren was inclined to show abstract idealists as lacking in self-knowledge, capable of self-righteous violence because they refuse to acknowledge their own irrational impulses. The best example of this personality-type in Warren's fiction is Adam Stanton, in *All the King's Men*, who assassinates Willie because Willie, the man of fact, seduced Adam's sister.

John Brown, however, as one who uses exalted ideas to inflate his own self-image, is more akin to Warren's Professor Ball, Dr. MacDonald, and Mr. Munn of *Night Rider*; Bogan Murdock, the industrialist, and Slim Sarett, of *At Heaven's Gate*; and Wilkie Barron, the manipulative false friend of Jeremiah Beaumont, in *World Enough and Time*. Willie, though categorized by Jack as the "man of fact," in contrast to Adam, the "man of idea," has his own idealistic dream of the people's hospital, free to anyone who needs it. Whether that dream was truly altruistic, however, or tinged by the secret need for a personal monument to his existence, is ambiguous.

Night Rider

Warren thus suggests that the self is itself part of the dream sea of ideas. Warren's protagonists are often initially passive persons whose emptiness is filled by other more dynamic personalities. Having acquired a somewhat fictitious self under such influence, they proceed to act in the real world as though that dream were true—often with tragic results. Thus, Mr. Munn seems an innocuous, ordinary young lawyer when he first appears in *Night Rider*, but he is drawn irresistibly to his more dynamic friend, Mr. Christian, who has a legitimate concern for the plight of the tobacco growers at the mercy of the price-controlling tobacco company. Munn learns to savor his new role as labor leader. He is ripe, then, for indoctrination by more conniving, professional agitators, Professor Ball and Dr. MacDonald, who preach a secret society that will scrape the fields of uncooperative growers and punish backsliders who dare to violate the embargo.

What begins as a lawful strike by the downtrodden majority becomes lawless action by a vigilante group that destroys crops, burns warehouses, and commits murder. In the case of Munn, the crisis of this psychic change in direction comes when he realizes that his assigned task to assassinate the tobacco farmer Bunk Trevelyon, whom he once defended in court on a murder charge, is not only his "duty" to the group; it also satisfies something very personal in himself that he has not yet recognized. Trevelyon had committed the murder of which he was once accused, and the African American who was hanged for that murder was innocent. Trevelyon thus becomes the symbol for Munn's half-conscious cooperation in framing the African American, or, to use another favorite term of Warren, Munn's original sin. In this ritual of retribution, the shared myth of community justice fuses with Munn's private myth of killing the shadow self, an act of both self-condemnation and deliberate concealment of a secret crime.

After this private confrontation and ritual killing of his shadow self, Munn makes no more moral objections to anything Ball and MacDonald want to do. The three lead a concerted assault on the company warehouses, which results in a number of casualties. One person who dies is young Benton Todd, who had been an ardent admirer of Munn. Moreover, Todd hoped to marry Mr. Christian's daughter, Lucille, who has been having a secret affair with Munn. If Trevelyon symbolizes the murderous shadow self that Munn has hated to acknowledge, Benton Todd suggests the lost idealism, the better dream that Munn has betrayed.

Munn's subsequent flight to the West to escape prosecution for a murder he did not commit might have resulted in redemption, but it does not. The pattern of redemption is presented to him obliquely by the story of Proudfit, the impoverished farmer who is sheltering Munn. Proudfit tells of his own checkered career in the West, as a buffalo hunter and hide-tanner, with companions as rough and wild as himself. Eventually, however, he lives in peace among American Indians. When he becomes ill, the Native Americans care for him, using all their resources of natural healing and religious ritual. In his fever, he eventually has a vision of Kentucky, where he was reared, and a young woman waiting beside a stream. His strength then begins to return, so he leaves the Native American friends and goes back to find the very woman he saw in his vision, now his wife, and the very hill he saw, which is now his farm.

Proudfit's story is both an engrossing dialect narrative and a unique version of the underlying myth of death and resurrection. Proudfit's humble redemption contrasts with the myth of sin and damnation implied in Munn's career. Both Proudfit and Munn have a period of withdrawal (Proudfit, among the American Indians; Munn, on Proudfit's remote farm), time to rethink their past lives and future goals. This experience is analogous, perhaps, to the withdrawal and contemplation that the mythic hero undergoes before he returns to his homeland as a new man. Munn, however, is not transformed. He does become mildly obsessed with the innocent African American who died in Trevelyon's stead, but he cannot even remember the man's name. Perhaps his inability to name the scapegoat is intended to suggest Munn's distance from the redemption offered by Christ's sacrifice. This does not mean that Warren was advocating Christianity; he was admitting, at least, a moral vacuum where traditional values have been eliminated in a society concerned primarily with power and wealth.

All the King's Men

The polarity of idea and fact receives more explicit development in *All the King's Men.* Again, an essentially passive person, Jack Burden, feeds emotionally on a more dynamic personality, Willie Stark. Jack calls himself—somewhat cynically—an idealist, but his idealism consists mostly of a fastidious preference for not getting his hands dirty with some of Willie's more questionable political maneuvers. Willie is good-naturedly tolerant of Jack's moral preferences, since he has Tiny Duffy to do his dirty work.

Jack considers himself a good judge of character and motives, but when a cherished image about the purity and goodness of his old girlfriend, Anne Stanton, is proven to be false, he is devastated and lost in self-doubt. Anne, who is quite a passive, unfulfilled person herself, has become Willie's mistress. Jack's first impulse is to flee, to escape, to drown, to fall into what he calls the Great Sleep. From this symbolic death, Burden is born again into a bleak but emotionally insulating belief in the Great Twitch—an understanding of the world as completely amoral and mechanistic, wherein no one has any responsibility for what happens. Here, indeed, Jack has stepped out of the fantasy of dreams into the reality of facts.

Jack can now consent to let Willie use the information he has uncovered concerning Judge Irwin's long-forgotten political crime. Jack soon discovers how brutal the world of fact can be, when Judge Irwin's suicide reveals that the judge was actually Jack's own father. Hardly recovered from this blow, Jack recognizes a measure of responsibility for the deaths of Willie and his best friend, Adam, who is shot by Willie's bodyguard after the assassination. Through his passivity and noninvolvement, Jack had virtually handed over Anne to his more dynamic boss, and thus set the stage for assassination.

The novel is a fascinating study of symbiotic relationships, of which the most striking is that between Willie, the practical politician, and Adam, the puritanical idealist and perfectionist. Warren also suggests a politically symbiotic relationship between the demagogue and the people he represents. In social terms, the world of *All the King's Men* is more complex than that of *Night Rider*. Munn's career is essentially that of the tragic hero, the good but not exclusively good man who is corrupted by power. Willie, however, is sustained not only by his own drive for power but also by the concerted will of his constituency, who feel themselves to be socially and politically helpless. He is probably more significant as an antidote to their depression than as an answer to their physical needs. Even though Willie wants to change the world of facts for their benefit—build roads, bridges, a free hospital—it is for his psychological impact, exemplifying the triumph of the common person over the privileged elite, that he is beloved. Thus, even the man of facts floats in the symbolic sea of ideas.

World Enough and Time

If the relationship between dream and reality is complicated in *All the King's Men*, in *World Enough and Time* it becomes intricately complex. Seldom have human aspirations been so relentlessly exposed, one after another, as frail illusions. Though it might be termed a historical novel because it is based loosely on an actual event, or a philosophical novel because it comments repeatedly on the abstract meaning of human behavior and aspiration, *World Enough and Time* is better termed a psychological novel, or more precisely, perhaps, an examination of the psychological motivations for philosophizing. It is certainly not, like Andrew Marvell's poem "To His Coy Mistress," to which the title ironically alludes, a neat argument for seizing pleasures while one may. It is not a neat argument for any philosophical position, but it illuminates the sequential confusion of a reasonably thoughtful, well-meaning person trying to identify himself and justify his actions.

Jeremiah Beaumont, the orphaned son of an unsuccessful Kentucky farmer in the early nineteenth century, becomes the loved protégé of Colonel Cassius Fort, a well-known lawyer and statesman of the region. Jerry's exalted view of Colonel Fort receives a cruel blow from his dashing friend Wilkie Barron, a popular man-about-town and dabbler in politics. Wilkie tells Jerry of a beautiful woman he once loved in vain, who was seduced by an older man who had come to console her when her father died. When the young woman, Rachel Jordan, had a stillborn child, the older man abandoned her. The knave who wronged her was the unimpeachable Colonel Fort.

The persuasive Wilkie succeeds in promoting in a somewhat passive Jerry a romantic vision of wronged womanhood. From this point on, Jerry creates his own drama of love and revenge, though Wilkie continues to manipulate him in ways he never understands until near the end of his life. Jerry repudiates Colonel Fort, his surrogate father, and woos and eventually wins the lovely Rachel, who is in a neurotic state of depression, not because of the supposed perfidy of Colonel Fort but because of her baby's death. Jerry, blind to the real source of her despondency, hounds her into commanding him to defend her honor. Fort refuses a duel with Jerry, however, and the honorable vengeance seems destined to fizzle. Rachel is again pregnant, and Jerry is fitting into the comfortable role of country squire. An unknown messenger brings to Rachel a slanderous handbill in which Colonel Fort, presumably denying to his political opponents his affair with Rachel, claims that Rachel had slept with a slave. Fort had gallantly claimed paternity of the child as a chivalric gesture. This shocking document, which is actually a forgery written by Wilkie, precipitates Rachel's labor, and Jerry's child is also born dead. Jerry, in remorse, kills Fort—not openly in a duel, as he had planned, but secretly, letting it appear to be a political assassination.

Jerry's trial is a bewildering process where deceit and truth become inextricably mixed. Wilkie appears, however, and reveals Jerry's vow to kill Fort, the reaction Wilkie had himself orchestrated even before Jerry had met the wronged lady. All is lost, and Jerry is sentenced to hang. Rachel comes and stays with him in his basement jail cell, where they indulge in a passionate interlude—a veritable frenzy of love in the face of imminent death.

The unpredictable Wilkie appears at the last minute, after the lovers have unsuccessfully tried to commit suicide by drinking laudanum. Wilkie rescues them and sends them west to live in the desolate island refuge of a notorious bandit. This is a return to nature, but a nature devoid of its original innocence, incapable of healing the scars of "civilization." Jerry sinks into a bestial pattern and Rachel into insanity, eventually killing herself. Jerry, who finds out that the slanderous handbill came from Wilkie, is himself murdered as he seeks to find his way back to the hangman, resigned now to the most austere prize of all—neither love nor honor, but simply knowledge.

The flight to the West seems an almost gratuitous extension of suffering, especially since the real Jereboam Beauchamp, who murdered Colonel Solomon Sharp in 1825, did hang for his crime. The real trial and death of Beauchamp and his wife, Ann Cook, were only slightly less miserable, however, than Warren's fictional account.

Warren's extension to allow further demoralization of the lovers does help to explore all possible approaches to the problem of reconciling the ideal and the real. At first, Jerry believes that the idea must redeem the world: The mental context defines the object. Unfortunately, this route leads to an idealism divorced from action and allows a further evil to develop in the world—the death of his child. Then he believes that the world will redeem the idea—that is, the act of killing Fort will vindicate the idea of honor. In his flight to the West, he commits a third error, the opposite to his first: to deny the idea completely and embrace the physical world—"to seek communion only in the blank cup of nature."

Perhaps this tortured journey through innocence and experience should arrive at some reconciliation of opposites, but, if so, that too seems more dream than reality. "There must be a way whereby the word becomes flesh," muses Jerry in his last days. Even so, "I no longer seek to justify. I seek only to suffer." If this is not a particularly lucid analysis of philosophical possibilities, it may nevertheless be true psychologically to the mental and moral confusion in which people live. Perhaps it is intended to represent the "terror of the awakening" that Warren finds in Conrad's *Lord Jim* when the "hero recognizes the terms on which he may be saved."

In his later novels, Warren continued to deal with the tension between the ideal and the real. The central mystery is usually the self, which the protagonist does not know except through a painful dialectic between exalted idea and gross fact. The protagonist also suffers from an inability to identify his real father or the real home where he belongs. Jack Burden and Jeremiah Beaumont both have several surrogate fathers, but they are responsible for the deaths of those to whom they owe the greatest filial loyalty. In *At Heaven's Gate*, Jerry Calhoun rejects his real father, the man of natural rectitude and love, and gives his devotion to Bogan Murdock, who, in Conrad's phrase, is hollow at the core.

A Place to Come To

Even in Warren's last novel, *A Place to Come To*, the protagonist's first act is to despise his father and flee from his homeland; his last is to return to his hometown and make peace with the gentle stepfather he had never wanted to meet and the deaf father who had humiliated him as a child. As Warren wrote in "The Ballad of Billie Potts," the son must always return to the father, who often represents the flawed and fallen world that is our heritage.

Wilderness

The struggle between the ideal and the real in Warren's later novels is most explicit in *Wilderness*, about an idealistic young Jew from Bavaria who comes to the United States to fight for the freedom of the slaves. When his father, a political prisoner in Berlin, dies, Adam Rosenzweig realizes that he has "lived only in the dream of his father's life, the father's manhood, the father's heroism." The trip to America is a way to star in his own heroic story. Adam's career in America is a progress in disillusionment; the telltale symbol of the compromising world of physical fact is his clubfoot, which he has desperately sought to hide in a specially constructed boot. If *World Enough and Time* is Warren's most complex treatment of idealism, *Wilderness* is his most direct treatment of this recurring subject, uncluttered by secondary themes or plots. Some critics prefer it for that reason, though it lacks the depth and humanity of Warren's earlier epic treatment of romantic idealism.

Meet Me in the Green Glen

Meet Me in the Green Glen is a pastoral novel about the nature of love. The love of a homeless young Italian immigrant for a dowdy country wife begins with carnal passion devoid of any attempt to idealize sexual attraction. The ironically named Angelo has distinct similarities to Conrad's "natural man," Nostromo, who lives in the physical world with little thought of any other. In fact, Angelo protects himself from any really serious bond with Cassie, the frustrated wife of a paralyzed man, casting her in the more tawdry dream of "scarlet woman" with gifts of a tight red dress and cosmetics. Only at the last, when she pleads for his life in court by confessing to the murder of her husband, of which Angelo is accused, does he recognize a love that transcends the merely physical. Just as Adam in *Wilderness* becomes more human when he admits the strength of flawed reality, so Angelo becomes more human when he recognizes the strength of dreams. In spite of Cassie's confession, Angelo is condemned to die, because, in his ignorance of the racial situation, he violates the mores of the community. Cassie, unable to save her lover, drifts off in the dream sea of ideas, forgetting the sordid elements of their affair and only retaining the dream that transcends the body's need.

In these and other episodes in his fiction, Warren showed his fascination with what he called, in his Conrad essay, "the Great Mirage." It is a dark vision that sees all human values as illusions, yet insists—with the passion that fueled six decades of creative work—that such illusions are necessary, and that humanity must continue to invent itself.

Katherine Snipes

Other major works

SHORT FICTION: *Blackberry Winter*, 1946; *The Circus in the Attic, and Other Stories*, 1947.

PLAYS: *Proud Flesh*, pr. 1947; *All the King's Men*, pr. 1958 (adaptation of his novel).

POETRY: *Thirty-six Poems*, 1935; *Eleven Poems on the Same Theme*, 1942; *Selected Poems, 1923-1943*, 1944; *Brother to Dragons: A Tale in Verse and Voices*, 1953; *Promises: Poems, 1954-1956*, 1957; *You, Emperors, and Others: Poems, 1957-1960*, 1960; *Selected Poems: New and Old, 1923-1966*, 1966; *Incarnations: Poems, 1966-1968*, 1968; *Audubon: A Vision*, 1969; *Or Else—Poem/Poems, 1968-1974*, 1974; *Selected Poems 1923-1975*, 1976; *Now and Then: Poems, 1976-1978*, 1978; *Brother to Dragons: A New Version*, 1979; *Ballad of a Sweet Dream of Peace*, 1980 (with Bill Komodore); *Being Here: Poetry, 1977-1980*, 1980; *Rumor Verified: Poems, 1979-1980*, 1981; *Chief Joseph of the Nez Percé*, 1983; *New and Selected Poems, 1923-1985*, 1985; *The Collected Poems of Robert Penn Warren*, 1998 (John Burt, editor).

NONFICTION: *John Brown: The Making of a Martyr*, 1929; *Modern Rhetoric*, 1949 (with Cleanth Brooks); *Segregation: The Inner Conflict in the South*, 1956; *Selected Essays*, 1958; *The Legacy of the Civil War: Meditations on the Centennial*, 1961; *Who Speaks for the Negro?*, 1965; *Democracy and Poetry*, 1975; *Portrait of a Father*, 1988; *New and Selected Essays*, 1989; *Cleanth Brooks and Robert Penn Warren: A Literary Correspondence*, 1998 (James A. Grimshaw, Jr., editor); *Selected Letters of Robert Penn Warren*, 2000-2001 (2 volumes; William Bedford Clark, editor).

EDITED TEXTS: *An Approach to Literature*, 1936 (with Brooks and John Thibault Purser); *Understanding Poetry: An Anthology for College Students*, 1938 (with Brooks); *Understanding Fiction*, 1943 (with Brooks); *Faulkner: A Collection of Critical Essays*, 1966; *Randall Jarrell, 1914-1965*, 1967 (with Robert Lowell and Peter Taylor); *American Literature: The Makers and the Making*, 1973 (with R. W. B. Lewis).

Bibliography

Blotner, Joseph. *Robert Penn Warren: A Biography*. New York: Random House, 1997. Blotner began this work while Warren was still alive and had the good fortune to have the cooperation not only of his subject but also of the larger Warren family. This book is straightforward and chronological, and it makes a good beginning for a study of Warren.

Bohner, Charles. *Robert Penn Warren*. 1962. Rev. ed. Boston: Twayne, 1981. This lucid survey encompasses details of Warren's literary career and an analysis of his major themes. It also provides a study of the development of Warren's art as evidenced in his novels and short fiction, his poetry (through *Being Here: Poetry 1977-1980*), and his major essays. Includes a detailed chronology and a valuable select bibliography.

Burt, John. *Robert Penn Warren and American Idealism*. New Haven, Conn.: Yale University Press, 1988. Burt describes his book as traversing "regions" of Warren's work: the elegies, the narrative poems, and three major novels—*Night Rider*, *All the King's*

Men, and *World Enough and Time*. What unifies these works, Burt maintains, is Warren's ambivalence about experience, an ambivalence endemic to American idealism.

Clark, William Bedford, ed. *Critical Essays on Robert Penn Warren*. Boston: G. K. Hall, 1981. A comprehensive collection of criticism by leading literary scholars of Warren's major work as novelist, poet, biographer, and essayist. Among the contributors are Harold Bloom, Malcolm Cowley, Carlos Baker, John Crowe Ransom, and Randall Jarrell. The collection includes a valuable 1969 interview with Warren by Richard Sale.

Ferriss, Lucy. *Sleeping with the Boss: Female Subjectivity and Narrative Pattern in Robert Penn Warren*. Baton Rouge: Louisiana State University Press, 1997. A feminist analysis, focusing on Warren's novels. Ferriss argues that although Warren wrote in a traditional masculine style, his narratives contained a "female voice" with the potential to change a plot's direction.

Gray, Richard, ed. *Robert Penn Warren: A Collection of Critical Essays*. Englewood Cliffs, N.J.: Prentice-Hall, 1980. Many of the essays in this collection date from the 1960's, and about two-thirds of them deal with Warren's novels. Represented in the volume are a number of recognized Warren specialists, among them James Justus, Leonard Casper, and Victor Strandberg. A competent and comprehensive essay prefaces the volume, which contains a short bibliography helpful to general students.

Grimshaw, James A. *Understanding Robert Penn Warren*. Columbia: University of South Carolina Press, 2001. An introduction to and commentary on Warren's novels and other works. Chapter 2 focuses on the early fiction, from 1939 to 1955, while chapter 3 examines the later fiction, from 1955 to 1977. Includes notes, a bibliography, and an index.

Guttenberg, Barnett. *Web of Being: The Novels of Robert Penn Warren*. Nashville: Vanderbilt University Press, 1975. Examines Warren's nine novels from *Night Rider* through *Meet Me in the Green Glen*, with emphasis on their existential element. Advances the premise that through all the novels the individual struggles to attain the true being of selfhood through self-awareness.

Hendricks, Randy. *Lonelier than God: Robert Penn Warren and the Southern Exile*. Athens: University of Georgia Press, 2000. Hendricks examines the theme of exile in Warren's work, maintaining this subject is crucial to understanding Warren's theories of language, ideas about race, and his regionalism.

Justus, James H. *The Achievement of Robert Penn Warren*. Baton Rouge: Louisiana State University Press, 1981. A cogent study. Justus argues that Warren's work largely derives from the cultural circumstances of time and place in his career. The book is divided into four sections examining Warren's themes, poetry, nonfiction prose, and novels.

Madden, David, ed. *The Legacy of Robert Penn Warren*. Baton Rouge: Louisiana State University Press, 2000. A collection of critical and biographical essays on Warren's life and work, including discussions of *All the King's Men*, his poetry, and Warren as a mentor and a moral philosopher. Includes bibliographical references and an index.

Watkins, Floyd C., John T. Hiers, and Mary Louise Weaks, eds. *Talking with Robert Penn Warren*. Athens: University of Georgia Press, 1990. A collection of twenty-four interviews, extending from 1953 to 1985, in which Warren talks about his work with characteristic honesty, openness, folksiness, and wit from the joint perspective of writer, interpreter, and critic. The group of interviewers includes Ralph Ellison, Marshall Walker, Bill Moyers, Edwin Harold Newman, Floyd C. Watkins, and Eleanor Clark.

FRANK WATERS

Born: Colorado Springs, Colorado; July 25, 1902
Died: Arroyo Seco, near Taos, New Mexico; June 3, 1995
Also known as: Frank Joseph Waters

Principal long fiction

Fever Pitch, 1930 (also known as *The Lizard Woman*)
The Wild Earth's Nobility, 1935
Below Grass Roots, 1937
The Dust Within the Rock, 1940
People of the Valley, 1941
The Man Who Killed the Deer, 1942
River Lady, 1942 (with Houston Branch)
The Yogi of Cockroach Court, 1947
Diamond Head, 1948 (with Branch)
The Woman at Otowi Crossing, 1966
Pike's Peak: A Family Saga, 1971 (rewritten, one-volume novel based on *The Wild Earth's Nobility*, *Below Grass Roots*, and *The Dust Within the Rock*)
Flight from Fiesta, 1986

Other literary forms

In addition to his long fiction, Frank Waters wrote a number of books that combine history, ethnography, mythology, and speculative essay. All of these are centered in the American Southwest, and all deal, in whole or in part, with American Indian subjects. Of these, *Book of the Hopi* (1963) comes closest to ethnography in the strict sense, being the actual Hopi versions of their mythology, ritual, and belief, which Waters recorded from the words of tribal spokesmen. *Masked Gods: Navaho and Pueblo Ceremonialism* (1950) covers analogous material in relation to the Navajo and Pueblo tribes, and contains substantial sections in which these traditional beliefs are compared to the teachings of the Far East (particularly Tibetan Buddhism) and with the findings of nuclear scientists.

Pumpkin Seed Point: Being Within the Hopi (1969) is a personal account of Waters's three-year residence among the Hopi, while he was compiling material for *Book of the Hopi*. *Mexico Mystique: The Coming Sixth World of Consciousness* (1975) treats the history, myth, and science (particularly calendrical) of Mexico. *Mountain Dialogues* (1981) is more eclectic in style, a series of essays ranging in subject matter from the relation of mind and matter to the bipolar symbolism reflected in the land around Waters's New Mexico home.

Waters's three biographies all deal with Western subjects: *Midas of the Rockies: The Story of Stratton and Cripple Creek* (1937) is the biography of Winfield Scott Stratton, and *To Possess the Land* (1973) is the biography of Arthur Rockford Manby. *The Earp Brothers of Tombstone* (1960) is based on the recollections of Virgil Earp's third and last wife, Allie Earp, and material from Waters's own research.

In 1946, Waters published *The Colorado* as part of the Rivers of America series (Farrar and Rinehart), and in 1964, an art monograph, *Leon Gaspard*. From 1950 to 1956, he was a regular contributor to the *Saturday Review* with reviews of books about the West. Numerous periodicals contain his essays on ethnography, history, and literary criticism, as well as a few short stories.

Achievements

Frank Waters gave the American Southwest its finest and most complete literary rendering. In both his fiction and his nonfiction, he sought to give literary vitality to the spirit of place imbuing that section of the American continent and to show how this spirit variously affects the different peoples who live there, finding its expression in mythology, lifestyle, architecture, and ritual, all reflecting, in their different ways, the "vibratory quality of the land itself." Whether he portrays life by presenting the facts of history (as in his nonfiction) or in the symbols of his novels, or whether he writes about the mythological realm that occupies the zone between the two, his work captures the deep resonance of his locale and thus the significance of place to people's development.

Waters is probably best known for his work on and about American Indians, and he was one of the few writers whose work earned the respect of both the literary establishment and the American Indian communities. He was also one of the few writers who could work successfully both in ethnography and in prose fiction. His first-hand knowledge of the Indian tribes of the Southwest and his deep respect for their traditions and their connections to their locale made it possible for Waters to write about these matters without romanticism, and thus to reveal not only the rugged dignity of their lives but also the value of their wisdom.

Thus, *The Man Who Killed the Deer*, Waters's most popular novel, has long been recognized as a classic in the literature on the Native American, just as *Book of the Hopi* is a landmark in ethnography. In the late twentieth century, the relevance and quality of his other work resulted in a greater degree of recognition, made tangible by the republication of much of his fiction.

Biography

Frank Joseph Waters was born on July 25, 1902, and spent most of his childhood and youth in Colorado Springs. These years provided much of the material for his early novels *The Wild Earth's Nobility*, *Below Grass Roots*, and *The Dust Within the Rock* and consequently for their revised version, *Pike's Peak: A Family Saga*. Waters's grandfather became the model for Joseph Rogier, the main character of these books, and Waters's boyhood experience in the Cripple Creek mining camps provided much of the background. His experiences as an engineering student at Colorado College (from 1922 to 1925) and as a day laborer in the Salt Creek oil fields are also incorporated into these early novels.

After his work at Salt Creek, Waters traveled to California, where he was employed by the telephone company in the border town of Calexico. It was there, among Chinese laborers, opium dens, and general degradation, that he came across Tai Ling, who became the protagonist of *The Yogi of Cockroach Court*. This novel was actually drafted before his Colorado novels, but technical problems prevented its completion until some years later.

The move to California marks a dividing line in Waters's treatment of his material. The personal experiences from before the move went into novels of a semi-autobiographical nature. Those that drew their material from after the move were not autobiographical, though they continued to draw their characters from people Waters knew, their settings from places where he had lived, and even their incidents from actual events. (The ending of *The Yogi of Cockroach Court*, for example, was taken directly from newspaper accounts.)

Waters moved to the town of Mora in the Sangre de Cristo Mountains of New Mexico. There he wrote *The Dust Within the Rock* and planned *People of the Valley*, drawing again on his youth in Colorado. The latter novel takes its material from the Mora locale, an isolated valley that is inaccessible for most of the year and that was settled by Spanish-speaking peoples from Mexico. It was in Mora, too, that Waters witnessed the rituals of the Penitente cult, which he incorporated into the novel.

After leaving Mora, Waters moved to Taos. From there, in the late 1930's, he drew the material (again, based on actual events) for *The Man Who Killed the Deer* and later for two nonfiction works, *Masked Gods* and *Mountain Dialogues*. He continued to make Taos his home, returning there after the war and working as editor for *El crepusculo*, a local Spanish-English newspaper; he also worked from 1953 to 1956 as an information consultant at Los Alamos Scientific Laboratory. These latter two positions are reflected in *The Woman at Otowi Crossing*, though it is evident from *Masked Gods*, published sixteen years earlier, that Waters had long been concerned with the curious juxtaposition of atomic research facilities and Indian kivas in the Four Corners area.

In 1977, Waters was married to Barbara Hayes; thereafter, the couple divided their time between homes in Taos and in Tucson, Arizona. In his later years, Waters devoted his attention principally to the writing of nonfiction. He died on June 3, 1995.

Analysis

The writing of Frank Waters is always concerned with the tensions that underlie human existence: male and female, reason and instinct, conscious and unconscious, progress and tradition, linear and nonlinear, matter and energy (or spirit). His fictional characters are involved in efforts to reconcile these tensions, either within themselves or in the world of events. The search for reconciliation is inseparable from what Waters called the spirit of place: Once one is able to embody the unconscious rhythms of one's locale, one may move more completely toward the reconciliation of these tensions.

In another sense, Waters attempted to give literary expression to this spirit of place. Viewed sociologically, his novels show how this spirit imbues the various racial types of the Southwest. The spirit of place is found in the blood, experienced as a "blood-power" from which one can never quite break free. Because of these instinctual or biological ramifications, the novels about "racial types" are not mere sociological studies but expressions of a spiritual search.

Waters said that the three novels *People of the Valley*, *The Man Who Killed the Deer*, and *The Yogi of Cockroach Court* express his interest in the racial types of the West: the Spanish or Mexican, the Native American, and the mestizos, or those of mixed race. *The Woman at Otowi Crossing*, which deals primarily with Caucasians, completes this study of racial types. *Pike's Peak* portrays the mingling of various racial types, but here Pikes Peak itself is portrayed as an active agent.

This late novel thus makes graphic what in the previous novels was a subtle but powerful undercurrent: In all of Waters's work, the earth itself plays a dominant role. It is the matrix that reconciles polarity. Fruitful and destructive by turns, benevolent or menacing, it resists people's efforts at domination or comprehension yet demands of them that continuing process of individuation that is inseparable from the reconciliation of polarity. The earth, the source of life, embodies a mystery that cannot be overcome but must be understood through faith. As the beginning and end of people's essential polarities (such as life and death, summer and winter), it is both a material fact and a rhythmic energy with which one must be in harmony.

Harmony, however, does not indicate a static equilibrium. Waters's novels end with reconciliation, yet the reconciliation leads to ongoing movement. As Waters points out in an explication of the Nahuatl hieroglyph "Ollin" (movement), the tension between dualities results in movement. This movement is found not only in the processes of the natural world but also inside the heart of people. This ancient Nahuatl concept is reflected in all of Waters's novels. The central reconciliation is in the human heart, as the characters attempt to find that harmony in movement that enables them to be part of the great pattern of Creation.

People of the Valley

People of the Valley was Waters's first nonautobiographical novel to be published. The most obvious social polarity—progress and tradition—is the main impetus of the plot. The government is going to build a dam that will uproot all the people of the Beautiful Blue Valley. The name is significant: The color blue symbolizes the abiding faith of the people in their traditional ways and in the faithful fruitfulness of the valley itself. (This symbolic use of the color blue returns in other novels, most notably *The Man Who Killed the Deer*, where Dawn Lake, the center of the Pueblo religious life, is referred to as the Blue Eye of Faith.) In this period, when their faith is threatened, the people of the valley look to Maria, a local *bruja*, for her reaction and her strength, her wisdom and her faith.

Maria has been in the Beautiful Blue Valley for as long as anyone can remember and has become, in the minds of its inhabitants, synonymous with the valley itself. She knows its secrets and its cures and has lived through its periods of fruitfulness and flood. She is, then, an embodiment of the spirit of place; by turns, she is a goad and a comfort, a shrewd businesswoman and a prophet. As the story progresses (a chapter is devoted to each period of her life), it becomes clear why she is the repository of the implicit faith of the people: She is trusted because of her own implicit trust in the earth, in the essential trustworthiness of its rhythms, even of its floods. Because she accepts the earth in all of its many moods, she is the spokesperson for its wisdom. Like the earth, she can be sharp and repelling, or healing and comforting. Like the earth, she accepts all who come to her, whether as lovers, questioners, or even husbands. Within change, however, she abides in a faith that grows, year by year.

In addition, Maria makes the welfare of the earth—of the valley—synonymous with her own welfare. She has reconciled the duality of self and other by making her own wealth inseparable from that of the valley, and hence of its people. The clearest example of this comes from her early life, when, destitute, she survived by gathering discarded wheat-seed from the local fields. This seed she divided into superior and inferior. The latter she used for food; the former she kept until spring, when she would trade it for a double measure to be collected at the next harvest. This process she repeated yearly. Because she kept the best seed for replanting, the wealth of the valley's wheat increased; because she received a double measure at harvest, her own wealth increased as well. Her wealth, however, was never monetary; rather, it was in the natural yield of the earth, and in the faith that such a yield is sufficient for all purposes.

In the end, it is this faith that makes Maria significant. Faith, too, is the essence of the people of the valley, and of their traditions. Without such faith, life there is not possible. This faith, as she points out, is not a concept, but a baptism into life itself, into the rhythmic experience of harmony, which comes from giving oneself wholly to the spirit and energy of one's locale, the spirit of place. The significance of the dam is that it stops the flow of faith, which is likened to water. Faith refreshes life and gives it meaning; the dam causes stagnation, a break in natural rhythms. The example of Maria shows, however, that if one's faith is deep enough, it will not be disrupted by surface events. In the end, this faith is in the heart, and what one sees in the external world corresponds to one's inner nature.

The Man Who Killed the Deer

The idea of faith carries over into Waters's next novel, *The Man Who Killed the Deer*. Whereas Maria had grown slowly into her faith and had never been torn from it, Martiniano must find a faith within the exacerbated polarities of his nature. The disruptions of progress had not come to Maria until she was an old woman; they come to Martiniano during his formative years. Because of this, his search is one of finding what he has lost, not simply deepening what he already knows.

Half Apache and half Pueblo, Martiniano's mixed blood indicates the duality of his nature, the spirit of independence and rebellion opposed to the spirit of acceptance and harmony. Sent away to a government school at an early age and thus deprived of his initiation into the kiva at the proper age, Martiniano must be taught to find harmony, not only with his world but also within himself, where the pole of masculine independence has not recognized the pole of the "female imperative."

The story of the novel is, on the surface, a simple one. Martiniano has killed a deer out of season, against regulations of the U.S. government as well as against those of the pueblo. The matter seems simple, but as the story unfolds, it becomes clear that the apparently simple event has many layers. It is not so much that Martiniano has broken the white person's law, but that his insistence on his own independence of action indicates an inner disharmony and a lack of wisdom. It indicates, finally, a lack of connection with the mystery of life itself. In place of this connection is a belief that a person can be free when alone, when cut off from society or the earth, from the source of faith, symbolized by the lake in the mountains above the pueblo, "The Blue Eye of Faith," the center of the pueblo's religious-ceremonial life.

The deer that Martiniano has killed becomes for him a totem, appearing to him in various places and guises to demonstrate that there is something in his situation that he cannot defeat by confrontation, something that he first must understand, to which he must submit. Eventually, the deer appears in his wife, Flowers Playing; as she grows with child, with the mystery of life, Martiniano begins to lose connection with her.

Martiniano learns, slowly, that even his own sense of manhood is held in bondage to the feminine part of his being and that until he reconciles this polarity, he will never feel fully alive. This is best symbolized by the description of the Deer Dance (in a passage found in both *The Man Who Killed the Deer* and *Masked Gods*). Flowers Playing is one of the Deer Mothers in the ceremony, the embodiment of the mystery of organic life. The Deer Dance symbolizes how the male force of independence and escape is held bondage, unwillingly but necessarily, by the female imperative, the rhythms of Earth that are deeper than the ego. The dance offers another vantage on the spirit of place, here appearing as the "blood power" from which people can never break free and on which they are dependent for the development of wisdom.

There is another sense in which Martiniano's action was not done in isolation: His killing of the deer has repercussions that are felt in the wider sphere of politics. It has made more difficult the pueblo's case for restoration of Dawn Lake. As the pueblo elders point out again and again, one person's action is like a pebble dropped into a pool; the ripples extend far beyond the action itself. The effort of the elders enables Martiniano to see that much wider whole, of which he is an integral part and without which he is an incomplete human being.

The pueblo elders embody a different way of knowing from that of the white race, which has control of the lake. The polarity is rational-linear opposing nonrational-nonlinear. The method of the elders is intuitive, and, while it does not deny the validity of rational methods (any more than the female imperative denies the validity of the male drive for independence), it does indicate a deeper level of wisdom. The elders know the eventual result of their legal disputes over Dawn Lake far before these results come over the telegraph, even when all indications (relayed, of course, over the telegraph) point to the futility of their case.

To the elders—as, it seems, to Waters himself—linear or rational knowledge is not as encompassing or effective as the more intuitive method of the Indians. The difference between these two methods of knowing is a duality to which Waters returns in later books, particularly *The Woman at Otowi Crossing*. It is interesting to note, in this context, that just as the pueblo elders correctly predicted that they would regain their Dawn Lake, so Waters himself, in his novel, predicted the actual political event; for just as in the novel the Native Americans regain rights to their lake, so, thirty years later, did they do so in fact, through a congressional decision in December of 1970.

THE YOGI OF COCKROACH COURT

Waters's next novel, *The Yogi of Cockroach Court*, takes the working of polarities one step further to juxtapose Eastern mysticism (particularly Buddhist) to life in a Mexican border town. Sociologically, Waters is here concerned with the mestizo culture. Barby is an example of this type. Orphaned as a child, he is brought up by Tai Ling, who runs a small shop, The Lamp Awake, beside the prostitute district, Cockroach Court. The name of the shop itself introduces the duality of light and dark, associated respectively with the clarity of the mind and the darkness of the senses. Tai Ling is repeatedly pictured meditating by his lamp, amid the swirl of a violent, dark world.

Barby and Guadalupe (Barby's lover, and another person of mixed race) cannot detach themselves from that dark world, which to Tai Ling is the result of blindness, the working out of karma. Their relationship is a tempestuous one, fueled by Barby's impotent desire for control. This impotence results from Barby's rootless feeling of inferiority, from his inner division. Where Barby is at the mercy of his internal division, Guadalupe is at the mercy of external ones. In the daytime, she is alive in the absorption in her own physical vitality; at night, she comes under the domination of Barby.

These complexities are interwoven with the life of Tai Ling, whose lamp illumines the darkness of the physical world in which he sits, even as his search for a way to transcend the play of polarities illumines the darkness of his mind. Inherent in Tai Ling's search for transcendence, however, is yet another polarity: The life of transcendence is itself polarized with life in a physical body. In this way, Tai Ling is still involved in duality, or karma, and in the end, just as Barby cannot dominate Guadalupe except in darkness, so Tai Ling cannot subdue the ongoing karma of the physical world until the darkness of death surrounds him.

Both Barby and Tai Ling bring about their own deaths by attempts to conquer the physical world. The difference between them is nevertheless a significant one: Barby dies while blinded by passion, aggression, and ignorance; Tai Ling, whose mind is clearer, finally sees and accepts his inner polarity, accepts his karma and his situation, and sees the folly of trying to transcend the world by separating oneself from it. Tai Ling, therefore, achieves a reconciliation, and though it comes at the moment of death, there is great hope in it, as Tai Ling finally comes to a unity with his world, comes to true knowledge.

Tai Ling's realization is not a rational one. He uses rationality to dissect his ego, but his realization is intuitive. He speaks of the difference between those who see that life's journey is a spiral and those whose vision is so limited that the curve of the spiral seems a straight line. To people of unconsidered action, whose vision is limited to the rational, horizontal plane, all seems linear, not cyclic. The person of contemplation, however, sees the nonlinear nature of things that underlies the linear but does not negate it. Thus, the treatment of two ways of knowing is here given an additional perspective.

THE WOMAN AT OTOWI CROSSING

The Woman at Otowi Crossing deals primarily with Anglos and thus completes the cycle of novels dealing with racial types. It also brings many of Waters's concerns into a contemporary focus. As in previous books, the action develops out of the tension between polarities. The developing, intuitive awareness of Helen Chalmers is juxtaposed to the development of the atomic bomb on the mesa above her. Both developments signal people's evolutionary potential, and both involve the unification of matter and energy.

Helen has come from a broken marriage to operate a small teahouse at the edge of Pueblo Indian land. Coincident with the beginning of the Los Alamos Research Laboratory—called The Project—she discovers a growth on her breast. Her assumption that it is cancerous, and the resultant immediacy of death, triggers in her a chain reaction of explosively expanding awareness, an explosion that radically alters her view of the world around her and her relationship with it.

The scene of Helen's discovery ends with Facundo, a member of the pueblo kiva, tossing pebbles against her window. The moment is significant, for in the kiva, the American Indians continue their attempt to understand and ensure the unity of matter with energy, or spirit. Facundo's response to Helen's condition is one of immediate comprehension, but his response is undramatic. He simply points to the sun, the source of life, empowered by the same unity of energy and matter that the people of the project seek to harness. Facundo's emphasis, however, is on the presence of that process, that reality, in each moment.

Thus, Helen's task becomes what will eventually become the task of everyone: to integrate her newfound knowledge with the tangible events of her life. The discovery of the bomb requires the same integration; the two discoveries together create a new world order in which one must learn to live. Again, the methods of the Native Americans point the way to reconciliation, for they have shown how the development of insight and the knowledge of the unity of matter and spirit can be integrated into, and are in fact a necessary part of, a stable, viable society.

Waters draws a number of additional parallels between the activities of the Pueblo kiva and those of the project. Both are shrouded in secrecy, and both have their selected initiates who take on new identities vis-à-vis the rest of their society. (Members of the kiva take on the identity of cosmic forces; project members take on new, common names: Niels Bohr becomes Nicholas Baker.) Both kiva and project exclude women, and in both there is an attempt to empower the mystery of life, to make use of the unity within the duality represented by matter and energy, matter and spirit. (These parallels echo Waters's speculations in *Masked Gods*, where he writes of the common search of all people, whether in a Tibetan monastery, an Indian kiva, or an atomic research laboratory.)

Along with these parallels, however, the book demonstrates obvious differences as well. Primary among these is that the rituals of the Pueblo are to ensure the ongoing life of all creatures, whereas the activity of the project is directed toward death. The method of the kiva, being intuitive and nonrational, includes and embraces polarity, whereas the method of the project, being rational, divides one entity from another. Even this polarity, however, can result in a reconciliation, not in the external world, necessarily, but within the individual heart. The scientists involved in creating the bomb are presented in warm, human terms. Gaylord, a young scientist and the lover of Helen's daughter, comes to a more intuitive, even mystical awareness as a result of his exposure to radiation.

PIKE'S PEAK

Pike's Peak is a kind of summing up of Waters's work. This may be understood literally, because the novel is a rewritten and shortened version of three early novels, the titles of which are retained as major divisions of the new novel. It may also be understood symbolically, because in its panoramic scope, *Pike's Peak* encompasses many of Waters's lifelong concerns.

Joseph Rogier, the protagonist, is largely a fictionalized version of Waters's grandfather; Waters himself, like the character March (grandson of Rogier and part Native American), spent much of his youth in the mining camps of Cripple Creek, went to college as an engineering student, and worked in the Salt Creek oil fields. The novel transcends the category of autobiographical fiction, however, because of Waters's use of symbolism, in particular that of Pikes Peak itself, which stands as both tangible fact and intangible symbol. A mystery to be understood, an ungraspable meaning that one feels impelled to grasp, it stands at the borderline between the conscious and the unconscious, at once numinous and tangible.

The peak both draws and repels Rogier, who seeks within it for its golden heart. The pull is irresistible, and in his effort to plumb the peak, Rogier slowly lets go of all his social responsibilities. His building firm deteriorates, his family becomes near destitute, and he loses the respect of the community and becomes an object of mockery. His search is an obsession, not for mere gold, and not for riches (though he is not above their temptation), but for the symbolic golden heart, within himself as it is within Pikes Peak, shining in the center of the dense granite, or in the center of the flesh.

The method of his search combines the rational and the irrational. The obsession is irrational, and at its service he places his considerable rational gifts and material wealth. Yet, despite his knowledge of engineering and geology, he cannot strike a significant vein, while those of lesser knowledge, and without his material resources, make seemingly lucky strikes, literally at the drop of a hat. Rogier's situation has parallels to that of Martiniano, for he, like Rogier, finds something in his search that he cannot conquer by rational means or external manipulation. Rogier's attempts to find gold—symbolic or literal—lead him increasingly deeper into darkness and isolation. Like the deer for Martiniano, the peak for Rogier becomes a sort of totem, appearing as a lure, as a guide, or as an obstacle—a truth he cannot grasp, but that is constantly within his sight.

The tragedy of Rogier is that his view of the world is linear. As a miner, he has literal and symbolic tunnel vision. By going straight ahead, mining a vertical shaft, he hopes to find the essence of the mystery symbolized by the mountain itself. Its apparent tangibility as real gold draws him irresistibly, but Rogier's linear viewpoint blinds him to the world around him, isolating him from the sympathies and understanding of his family. His search for truth takes place at the expense of human warmth and community, and he finds, as does Martiniano, that such obsessive pride—even if it seems to be a search for truth—is doomed to futility. Where Martiniano is finally able to understand his folly and arrange for his son to enter the kiva and so live in the harmony it had taken him so long to achieve, Rogier dies in psychological isolation, unable to release his passion into genuine human community.

For all that, however, the tragedy contains a triumph. March, Rogier's grandson, carries on a search encompassing many of Rogier's ideals. Of mixed race, March shows promise of reconciling the intuitive ways of his American Indian blood with the rational methods of his grandfather. Despite himself, Rogier has passed on to March a profound respect for depth and knowledge; one feels for him a deep sympathy, because for all his gruffness, even his selfishness, he has somehow managed to give March a profound respect for enduring value and the determination to search for it, for the enduring gold within the dense rock of material being.

The search for eternal value in the middle of flux is a final polarity. Tai Ling sought it in his meditation and Maria found it in her inseparability from natural cycles; even Martiniano found it by acquiescing to the Pueblo's ways. For Helen Chalmers, the search was for a way to integrate eternal value into the apparently mundane particulars of everyday living. Thus, even the discovery of eternal verities is not a final resting point. The eternal is continually juxtaposed to and interwoven with the mundane, and just as the action of the novels is given impetus by this polarity, so the movement of the world both rises from it and expresses it. As each new layer is peeled off, new polarities emerge.

Waters's writing reveals an attempt to penetrate and illuminate these symbolic and literal layers, and to find within movement the enduring values of human life. His characters seek these values within the temporal, within enduring change, the first cause and final truth. Thus, in Waters's novels, the Nahuatl hieroglyph "Ollin" comes to literary expression: that eternal movement comes from the tension between polarities. The reconciliation between polarities is found in the movement of tangible existence—in concrete substance, not abstract form; in the harmony within activity that expresses harmony with greater cycles, such as those of society, of one's locale, or of the earth. In this sense, the expression of the spirit of place is an expression of the unity of humankind, for all are subject to the same enduring, cyclic existence. In a wider sense, Waters's writing is rightly considered mystical, concerned with the oneness of people with others, with the earth, with all that exists.

Tim Lyons

OTHER MAJOR WORKS

NONFICTION: *Midas of the Rockies: The Story of Stratton and Cripple Creek*, 1937; *The Colorado*, 1946; *Masked Gods: Navaho and Pueblo Ceremonialism*, 1950; *The Earp Brothers of Tombstone: The Story of Mrs. Virgil Earp*, 1960; *Book of the Hopi*, 1963; *Leon Gaspard*, 1964 (revised 1981); *Pumpkin Seed Point: Being Within the Hopi*, 1969; *To Possess the Land: A Biography of Arthur Rockford Manby*, 1973; *Mexico Mystique: The Coming Sixth World of Consciousness*, 1975; *Mountain Dialogues*, 1981; *Brave Are My People: Indian Heroes Not Forgotten*, 1993; *Of Time and Change: A Memoir*, 1998; *Pure Waters: Frank Waters and the Quest for the Cosmic*, 2002 (Barbara Waters, editor).

MISCELLANEOUS: *A Frank Waters Reader: A Southwestern Life in Writing*, 2000 (Thomas J. Lyon, editor).

BIBLIOGRAPHY

Adams, Charles L., ed. *Studies in Frank Waters*. Las Vegas, Nev.: Frank Waters Society, 1978-1990. Contains a number of excellent critical essays on Waters.

Blackburn, Alexander. *A Sunrise Brighter Still: The Visionary Novels of Frank Waters*. Athens: Ohio University Press, 1991. Chapters on each of Waters's novels, with an introduction that surveys the writer's purposes and his career, and a conclusion arguing that Waters is a major American writer. Includes detailed notes and an extensive bibliography.

Deloria, Vine, Jr., ed. *Frank Waters: Man and Mystic*. Athens: Ohio University Press, 1993. Memoirs of Waters and commentaries on his novels, emphasizing his prophetic style and sense of the sacred. Also provides criticism and interpretation of Waters's work, looking specifically at his place in the history of Western literature and of mysticism in literature.

Dunaway, David King, and Sara L. Spurgeon, eds. *Writing the Southwest*. Rev. ed. Albuquerque: University of New Mexico Press, 2003. Collection of interviews, bibliographies, criticism, and excerpts from writers of the Southwest. This updated edition of the book is accompanied by a compact disc, featuring excerpts from the authors' interviews.

Lynch, Tom. "Toward a Symbiosis of Ecology and Justice: Water and Land Conflicts in Frank Waters, John Nichols, and Jimmy Santiago Baca." In *The Environmental Justice Reader: Politics, Poetics, and Pedagogy*, edited by Joni Adamson, Mei Mei Evans, and Rachel Stein. Tucson: University of Arizona Press, 2002. In this examination of the worldwide environmental justice movement Lynch compares the representation of water and land conflicts in the works of Waters and the two other authors.

Lyon, Thomas J. *Frank Waters*. New York: Twayne, 1973. Analyzes Waters's themes and artistic style. After sketching Waters's life, Lyon examines his major fiction and nonfiction, showing him to be a writer of ideas with a sacred theory of the earth and Hopi mythic values. Lyon also discusses his minor works, his book reviews, and his essays on writing. Includes a chronology, notes and references, an annotated bibliography, and an index.

Nizalowski, John. "Frank Waters: Prophet of the Sixth World Consciousness." In *Reading Under the Sign of Nature: New Essays in Ecocriticism*, edited by John Tallmadge and Henry Harrington. Salt Lake City: University of Utah Press, 2000. This analysis of Waters's work is included in a collection examining environmental themes in selected works of prose and poetry.

Waters, Barbara. *Celebrating the Coyote: A Memoir*. Denver, Colo.: Divina, 1999. A memoir by Waters's last wife. Barbara Waters discusses her grief at losing her husband but recalls that their life together was not without its difficulties.

EVELYN WAUGH

Born: London, England; October 28, 1903
Died: Combe Florey, Somerset, England; April 10, 1966
Also known as: Evelyn Arthur St. John Waugh

Principal long fiction

Decline and Fall, 1928
Vile Bodies, 1930
Black Mischief, 1932
A Handful of Dust, 1934
Scoop, 1938
Put Out More Flags, 1942
Brideshead Revisited: The Sacred and Profane Memories of Captain Charles Ryder, 1945 (revised 1959)
Scott-King's Modern Europe, 1947
The Loved One, 1948
Helena, 1950
Men at Arms, 1952
Love Among the Ruins: A Romance of the Near Future, 1953
Officers and Gentlemen, 1955
The Ordeal of Gilbert Pinfold: A Conversation Piece, 1957
The End of the Battle, 1961 (also known as *Unconditional Surrender*)
Basil Seal Rides Again: Or, The Rake's Regress, 1963
Sword of Honour, 1965 (includes *Men at Arms*, *Officers and Gentlemen*, and *The End of the Battle*)

Other literary forms

Evelyn Waugh (waw) wrote seven travel books, three biographies, an autobiography, and numerous articles and reviews. The only completed section of Waugh's planned three-volume autobiography, *A Little Learning* (1964), discusses his life at Oxford and his employment as a schoolmaster in Wales—subjects fictionalized in *Brideshead Revisited* and *Decline and Fall*. The autobiographical background for virtually all of Waugh's novels is evident in his travel books, his diaries, and his letters. His articles and reviews for English and American periodicals include a wide range of topics—politics, religion, and art—and contribute to his reputation as a literary snob, an attitude Waugh himself affected, especially in the 1940's and 1950's.

Achievements

Evelyn Waugh is esteemed primarily as a satirist, especially for his satires on the absurdly chaotic world of the 1920's and 1930's. His ability to make darkly humorous the activities of the British upper class, his comic distance, and his vivid, at times brutal, satire made his early novels very popular among British and American literary circles. His shift to a more sentimental theme in *Brideshead Revisited* gave Waugh his first real taste of broad popular approval—especially in America—to which he reacted with sometimes real, sometimes exaggerated, snobbishness. Waugh's conservative bias after the war, his preoccupation with religious themes, and his expressed distaste for the "age of the common man" suggested to a number of critics that he had lost his satiric touch. Although his postwar novels lack the anarchic spirit of his earliest works, he is still regarded, even by those who reject his political attitudes, as a first-rate craftsman of the comic novel.

Biography

Evelyn Arthur St. John Waugh was born in Hampstead, a suburb of London, in 1903 to Arthur and Catherine Waugh. He attended Lancing College from 1917 to 1924 and Hertford College, Oxford, from 1921 to 1924, from which he left without taking a degree. Although Waugh turned to writing novels only after aborted careers as a draftsman, a schoolmaster, and a journalist, his family background was literary; his father directed Chapman and Hall publishers until 1929, and his older brother Alec published his first novel, *The Loom of Youth*, in 1917.

Waugh's years at Oxford and his restless search for employment during the 1920's brought him experiences that were later fictionalized in several of his novels. After leaving Oxford in 1924, he enrolled in the Heatherley

School of Fine Art, where he aspired to be a draftsman; later in that year, he was apprenticed to a printer for a brief period. His employment as a schoolmaster in Wales in 1925 and in Buckinghamshire in 1926 formed the background for his first novel, *Decline and Fall*. His struggle to establish himself as a writer and his participation in the endless parties of London's aristocratic youth during the last years of the 1920's are fictionalized in his second novel, *Vile Bodies*.

In 1927, Waugh was engaged to Evelyn Gardner and, despite the objections of her family, married her in 1928 when his financial prospects seemed more secure after the publication of his life of Dante Gabriel Rossetti and his first novel. In 1929, while Waugh was working in seclusion on *Vile Bodies*, his wife announced that she was having an affair; the couple, temperamentally unsuited to each other, were divorced that year.

The next seven years of Waugh's life were a period of activity and travel. Two trips to Africa in 1930 and 1931 resulted in a travel book and provided Waugh with the background of *Black Mischief*. A journey through Brazil and British Guiana in 1932 resulted in another travel book and his fourth novel, *A Handful of Dust*. In addition, Waugh traveled to the Arctic and once more to Africa; he was a correspondent for the London *Times*, reviewed books for *The Spectator*, and wrote a biography of Edmund Campion, a British Catholic martyr. During this unsettled period, Waugh converted to Roman Catholicism in 1930, an event that provided much of the stability of his later life. In 1933, he met Laura Herbert, a Catholic, whom he married in 1937, after securing an annulment of his previous marriage from the Catholic Church.

Waugh's experiences during World War II are fictionalized in *Put Out More Flags* and the *Sword of Honour* trilogy. After several months unsuccessfully seeking military employment, Waugh joined the Royal Marines in 1939 and was part of an ineffectual assault on Dakar in 1940. Later in 1940, Waugh joined a commando unit with which he served in the Middle East, taking part in the battle of Crete in 1942. In 1943, after an injury in parachute training, Waugh was forced to resign from the commandos, and, in 1944, he was granted military leave to write *Brideshead Revisited*. In the last year of the war, he served as a liaison officer with the British Military Mission in Yugoslavia, where he struggled against the persecution of Roman Catholics by the partisan government.

Waugh's life from 1945 to 1954 was relatively stable. The success of *Brideshead Revisited*, a Book-of-the-Month Club selection in the United States, brought him moderate financial security and several offers from filmmakers. Although none of these film offers materialized, they resulted in the trip to Hollywood in 1947 that inspired *The Loved One*, and in several commissioned articles for *Life* magazine. During this nine-year period, Waugh published four short novels and the first volume of the World War II trilogy. In the first three months of

Evelyn Waugh. (Library of Congress)

1954, on a voyage to Ceylon, Waugh suffered the mental breakdown that he later fictionalized in *The Ordeal of Gilbert Pinfold*.

Waugh led a relatively reclusive life during the last ten years, avoiding the public contact that had made him notorious earlier. In this period, he finished the war trilogy and published a biography of Ronald Knox, another travel book on Africa, the first volume of his autobiography, a revision of *Brideshead Revisited*, and the recension of the war trilogy into a single volume; he also began several other projects that were never completed. Waugh died on Easter Day in 1966.

Analysis

Evelyn Waugh's novels are distinguished by the narrative detachment with which they survey the madness and chaos of the modern age. His characters participate in a hopeless, often brutal, struggle for stability that hardens them to the absurdities of civilization and leads them, ultimately, to an unheroic retreat from the battle of life. Ironic detachment, thus, is Waugh's principal comic technique and his principal theme as well.

Because each of Waugh's novels reflects actual experiences, the nature of this detachment changes through the course of his career. In his early works, which satirize the havoc and instability of the 1920's and 1930's, he achieves comic detachment by splicing together the savage and the settled, the careless and the care-ridden, the comic and the tragic. Victims and victimizers alike are caught in the whirlwind of madness. Waugh's satiric method changes in his postwar novels: Comically ineffectual characters still wage battle against the absurdities of life, but one is more aware of their struggle to maintain or recapture spiritual and moral values amid the absurdity. Waugh maintains comic distance in these novels by recommending a quiet sort of spiritual heroism as the only source of people's happiness in the uncertain postwar world.

Decline and Fall

Waugh's first novel, *Decline and Fall*, traces the misadventures of Paul Pennyfeather, a temperate, unassuming student of theology at Scone College, Oxford. He is "sent down" for indecent behavior when drunken members of the university's most riotous (and, ironically, most aristocratic) club assault him, forcing him to run the length of the quadrangle without his trousers. Like Voltaire's Candide, Pennyfeather is an innocent victim temperamentally ill suited for the world into which he is thrust. Indeed, *Decline and Fall* owes much to *Candide: Ou, L'Optimisme* (1759; *Candide: Or, All for the Best*, 1759): its Menippean satire, its cyclical "resurrection" of secondary characters, and the hero's ultimate resignation from life.

The action itself provides a thin framework for Waugh's satire on modern life. Pennyfeather finds employment, as Waugh himself did, as a schoolmaster in Wales—the only occupation, Pennyfeather is told, for a young man dismissed from the university for indecent behavior. At Llanabba Castle, he meets three characters with whose stories his own is interlaced: Grimes, a pederast and bigamist who pulls himself out of the continual "soup" he gets into by feigning suicide; Prendergast, a doubting cleric who becomes a "modern churchman" and is eventually murdered by a religious fanatic; and Philbrick, the school butler, a professed impostor, jewel thief, and arsonist who manages to secure a continual life of luxury by his preposterous stories about his criminal life. At Llanabba, Pennyfeather also meets Margot Beste-Chetwynde, a rich socialite to whom he becomes engaged; he is arrested the afternoon of their wedding for unknowingly transporting girls to France for her international prostitution ring. His innocent association with Margot thus leads to his conviction for another act of "indecent behavior," this time leading to a prison sentence in Blackstone Gaol—a "modern" penal institution.

What strikes one about the novel is not the injustices served Pennyfeather, but the very madness of the world with which his innocence contrasts. Characters with criminal designs—Margot, Philbrick, and Grimes—are unaffected by changes in fortune; those in charge of social institutions—Dr. Fagan of Llanabba Castle and Sir Lucas-Dockery of the experimental prison—are eccentrically out of touch with reality. Their absurdity, when contrasted with Pennyfeather's naïve struggle, defines Waugh's theme: The only sanity is to become cautiously indifferent to the chaos of modernism. At the end of the novel, when Pennyfeather returns to Oxford under a new identity and continues his study of the Early Church, he assumes the role of a spectator, not a participant, in the madness of life.

Although *Decline and Fall*'s narrative structure is more derivative and its characters less fully rounded than those of Waugh's later novels, it displays techniques typical of his fiction at its best. The callous descriptions of the tragic—little Lord Tangent's death from Grimes's racing pistol or Prendergast's decapitation at Blackstone Gaol—and their fragmented interlacement into the plot are hallmarks of Waugh's comic detachment. Tangent's slow death from gangrene is presented through a series of casual offstage reports; the report of Prendergast's murder is incongruously worked into verses of a hymn sung in the prison chapel, "O God, our Help in Ages Past." The tragic and the savage are always sifted through an ironic filter in Waugh's novels, creating a brutal sort of pathos.

A Handful of Dust

Waugh's fourth novel, *A Handful of Dust*, was his first to present a dynamically sympathetic protagonist. Pennyfeather, from *Decline and Fall*, and Adam Symes, from *Vile Bodies*, attract one's interest largely because they provide a detached perspective from which one can observe the chaos of modern civilization. Basil Seal in *Black Mischief*, although a participating rogue, is amiable largely because of his comic disregard for the mischief he makes. Tony Last of *A Handful of Dust*, however, is a fully sympathetic character as well as a pathetic victim of the modern wasteland to which the title alludes. Unlike Paul Pennyfeather, Tony is not simply an observer of social chaos: His internal turmoil is set against the absurdity of external events, and in that respect, his quest for lost values anticipates that of Charles Ryder in *Brideshead Revisited* and of Guy Crouchback in *Sword of Honour*.

Waugh's theme is the decadence of tradition, emblematized, as it is in many of Waugh's novels, by the crumbling estates of the aristocracy. Tony's futile effort to maintain his Victorian Gothic estate, Hetton Abbey, thus symbolizes his struggle throughout the plot. He is wedded to the outmoded tradition of Victorian country gentlemen, while his wife, Brenda, embraces the social life of London. She eventually cuckolds Tony by having an affair with the parasitic John Beaver, whose mother, an interior decorator, sees in her son's affair an opportunity to "modernize" Hetton with chromium plating and sheepskin carpeting.

The pathos one feels for Tony is ultimately controlled by the absurd contexts into which Waugh sets the pathetic scenes. When his son, John Andrew, dies in a riding accident, Tony is left emotionally desolate, yet the cause of the accident is ironic; John Andrew's horse is startled by a backfiring motorcycle, a modern "horse." Later, one is made brutally aware of the irony of Tony's grief when one learns of Brenda's initial reaction to the news of her son's death: She assumes it was John Beaver, her lover, not John Andrew, her son, who died. In the same way, Tony's later divorce from Brenda empties him of values he traditionally respected. He consents to the legal convention that he should give evidence of his infidelity, even if his wife has been the unfaithful partner. His evidence incongruously turns into an uncomfortable weekend with a prostitute and her daughter at Brighton, and the absurdity of this forced and inconsummate infidelity further defines Tony's loneliness. Ironically, it provides him with a means to deny an exorbitant divorce settlement that would force him to sell Hetton Abbey.

In the end, Tony searches for his Victorian Gothic city in the jungles of South America and suffers a delirium in which his civilized life at Hetton Abbey is distorted; these scenes are made comically pathetic by interlaced scenes of Brenda in London trying to regain the civilized life she lost in her estrangement from Tony. Ultimately, she does not find in London the city she sought, nor does Tony in South America. Tony does find, instead, an aberration of his vision; he is held captive by an illiterate who forces him to read aloud from Charles Dickens's novels in perpetuity.

Perhaps Waugh's emotional reaction to his own divorce from Evelyn Gardner prior to the publication of the novel accounts for the increase of pathos in *A Handful of Dust*. Perhaps Waugh realized that thinness of characterization in his earlier novels could lead only to stylistic repetition without stylistic development. Whatever the reason, this novel depicts characters struggling for moral equilibrium in a way that no previous Waugh novel had done.

Brideshead Revisited

Brideshead Revisited is different from Waugh's earlier novels in two important ways. First, it is the only novel Waugh finished that employs the first-person point of view. (He had attempted the first person in "Work Suspended" in 1942, but either the story itself faltered or Waugh could not achieve a sufficient narrative detachment to complete it.) Second, *Brideshead Revisited* was the first novel in which Waugh explicitly addressed a Roman Catholic theme: the mysterious workings of divine grace in a small aristocratic Catholic family. As a result, it is Waugh's most sentimental and least funny novel. Although it departed radically from his earlier satires, it was Waugh's most popular and financially successful work.

The narrative frame creates much of what is sentimental in the novel but also provides a built-in detachment. Charles Ryder's love for Sebastian Flyte during his years at Oxford in the 1920's and for Julia Mottram, Sebastian's sister, a decade later, live vividly in Ryder's memories when he revisits the Brideshead estate during a wartime bivouac. His memories tell the story of Sebastian's and Julia's search for happiness, but because they are remembered by an emotionally desolate Ryder, the novel is a study of his spiritual change as well.

Before he meets Sebastian, Ryder is a serious-minded Oxford undergraduate, not unlike Paul Pennyfeather at the end of *Decline and Fall.* Like Pennyfeather, he is drawn into a world for which he is unprepared, yet unlike Waugh's earlier protagonist, Ryder is enthralled by a make-believe world of beauty and art. The Arcadian summer Ryder spends with Sebastian at Brideshead and in Venice are the most sumptuously written passages in any of Waugh's novels, reflecting—as Waugh admitted in his 1959 revision of the novel—the dearth of sensual pleasures available at the time of its composition. The change in style also reflects a change in theme. Sebastian's eccentricities about his stuffed bear, his coterie of homosexual "aesthetes," and his refusal to take anything seriously would have been the object of satire in Waugh's earlier novels. In *Brideshead Revisited*, however, the absurdities are sifted through the perspective of a narrator aware of his own desperate search for love. When Sebastian's make-believe turns to alcoholism, the narrator himself becomes cynically indifferent.

Ryder's love for Julia ten years after he has left Brideshead is an attempt to rediscover the happiness he lost with Sebastian. One is more aware, in this second half of the narration, of Ryder's cynicism and of the discontentment that cynicism hides. When he and Julia fall in love on a transatlantic voyage back to England, they are both escaping marriages to spouses whose worldly ambitions offer no nourishment for the spiritual emptiness each feels. Julia's return to the Church after the deathbed repentance of her father causes Ryder to realize that he has fathomed as little about Julia's faith as he had about Sebastian's. The narration itself thus ends on a note of unhappiness that recalls the separation of Ryder and Sebastian. In the epilogue following Ryder's memories, however, Waugh makes it clear that the narrator himself has converted to Catholicism in the intervening years. Ryder sees in the sanctuary light of the chapel at Brideshead the permanence he sought with Sebastian and Julia and finds contentment, if not hope for the future.

It is easy to overstress the religious implications of the novel. Indeed, many critics find Julia's hysteria about sin, Lord Marchmain's return to the Church, and Ryder's conversion strained. Some, such as Edmund Wilson, see the novel as an adulation of the British upper classes. *Brideshead Revisited*, however, is less a Roman Catholic novel than it is a lament for the past and a study in spiritual and artistic awakening. It was a turning point in Waugh's fiction: His novels after *Brideshead Revisited* dealt less with the absurdity of life and more with the spiritual values that have disappeared as a result of the war.

The Loved One

Perhaps the grimmest of Waugh's satires, *The Loved One* presents a sardonic vision of American culture. Its principal satiric target is Forest Lawn Memorial Park—a place that in many ways served for Waugh as the epitome of American pretensions to civilization. In "Half in Love with Easeful Death," an essay he wrote for *Life* in 1947 after his visit to Hollywood, Waugh describes Forest Lawn as it would appear to archaeologists in the next millennium: a burlesque necropolis, like the tombs of the pharaohs in its aspirations, but, in fact, the product of a borrowed, devalued culture. His version of Forest Lawn, Whispering Glades, is a distorted wonderland in which the cosmetic and the artificial substitute for beauty and in which banality is glorified and substitutes for the poetic vision.

It is fitting that the protagonist, Dennis Barlow, be a

poet—even though an unproductive one who has been seduced to Hollywood by a consultantship with Megalo Studios. Like many of Waugh's other protagonists, he is the filter through which one sees absurdities satirized. Like Basil Seal in *Black Mischief* and *Put Out More Flags*, he is an opportunist, flexible enough to engineer a profit for himself out of the chaotic world into which he is thrust. His vision is grimly sardonic, however, in a way that even Seal's is not.

When he first enters Whispering Glades, he is intrigued, as Seal would be, by its absurd glamour and by the potential of using that glamour to improve his own position at The Happier Hunting Grounds, a pet mortuary where he is employed. Whispering Glades, however, has a far deeper attraction; it would be the kind of place, if it were real, that would appeal to any poet, but Barlow is enchanted by its very fraudulence. At the human-made Lake Isle of Innisfree (complete with mechanized humming bees), Barlow falls in love with a mortuary cosmetician and enchants her by the very fact that he is a poet. The enchantment is false, just as everything is at Whispering Glades; he sends her plagiarized verses from *The Oxford Book of English Verse* and pledges his troth to her by reciting a stanza from Robert Burns's "A Red, Red Rose" at The Lover's Nook near the Wee Kirk o' Auld Lang Syne.

If plagiarism lies at the heart of Barlow's involvement at Whispering Glades, it also lies at the heart of Whispering Glades itself and the characters who work there—even though the place and the people are possessed by the utmost seriousness. The girl with whom Barlow falls in love is named Aimee Thanatogenos. Although she professes to be named after Aimee McPherson—the American huckster of religion whom Waugh satirized in *Vile Bodies*—her given name and her surname both translate into the euphemism that embodies all of Whispering Glades's false coating: "The loved one." Her enchantment with Barlow eventually takes the form of a burlesque tragedy. She is torn between Barlow and the head mortician, Mr. Joyboy—a poet of a different sort, whose special art is preparing infant corpses.

Aimee's tragedy results from a bizarre sequence of events, comic in its effects. When she discovers Joyboy's mother fixation and Barlow's fraudulence, she seeks advice from her oracle, the Guru Brahman, an advice columnist. When the Guru, Mr. Slump—fired from his job and in an alcoholic funk—advises Aimee to jump off a roof, she kills herself in the more poetic environment of Whispering Glades. Her suicide by drinking embalming fluid gives a doubly ironic force to her name and to the title of the novel. The tragedy ends with a darkly humorous catharsis. Joyboy, fearful that Aimee's death on his table might mar his lofty position at Whispering Glades, consents to Barlow's extortion and to Barlow's plan to cremate their beloved Aimee at The Happier Hunting Grounds. The novel's conclusion, thus, strikes the grimmest note of all: Barlow sits idly by, reading a cheap novel, while the heroine—a burlesque Dido—burns in the furnace.

In some ways, *The Loved One* is atypical of Waugh's postwar novels. In *Scott-King's Modern Europe* and the *Sword of Honour* trilogy, Waugh turns his satiric eye to political issues. *The Loved One*, however much it satirizes American values, transcends topical satire. Barlow lacks the spiritual potential of Charles Ryder in *Brideshead Revisited*, even though he displays Ryder's callousness. Barlow is an artist in search of beauty, but he leaves California, ironically, with an artist's load far different from what he expected. It is the view of an ironist, like Waugh himself, who could hardly make a better travesty of Whispering Glades than it makes of itself.

Sword of Honour

The *Sword of Honour* trilogy, like *Brideshead Revisited*, is infused with a predominantly religious theme; it traces Guy Crouchback's awakening to spiritual honor—a more active form of spiritual growth than Charles Ryder experienced. Like *Brideshead Revisited, Sword of Honour* is more somber and more deliberately paced than Waugh's satires in the 1920's and 1930's, but it shares with his early works a detached satiric framework. Each volume is composed at a distance of ten or more years from its historical occurrence and, as a result, reflects a greater consciousness of the long-range implications of the absurdities presented.

Men at Arms

Men at Arms concerns the chaos of Britain's first entry into the war, much like Waugh's wartime satire *Put Out More Flags*. One is immediately aware, however, of the difference in Waugh's detachment. *Put Out More Flags* was the product of a writer in his mid-thirties looking wryly at the days of peace from the middle of the war. Its protagonist, Basil Seal, is a mischief-making opportunist for whom greater chaos means greater fun and profit; the novel satirizes the madness of a world that leaves the characters trapped in the ever-changing insanity of war. *Men at Arms*, however, and, indeed, the entire trilogy, looks back from the perspective of the author's later middle age, with a sense of disappointment at the final results of the war. Appropriately enough, Guy is an innocent at the outset of the war, not a mischief maker like Basil Seal. He is a middle-aged victim who is literally and figuratively cast into a battle for which he is ill prepared.

Guy's heroic illusions are shattered in three successive stages through the separate volumes of the trilogy. *Men at Arms* concerns Guy's search for the self-esteem he lost eight years earlier after his divorce from his wife. As an officer-trainee in the Royal Corps of Halberdiers, Guy temporarily finds self-respect, but the elaborate traditions of the Halberdiers and his traineeship at commandeered preparatory schools cause Guy to revert to adolescence. His physical awkwardness, his jealousy of fellow trainees, his vanity about growing a mustache, his ineffectual attempt to seduce his former wife on Saint Valentine's Day, and the blot he receives on his military record at the end of the novel all seem more appropriate for a schoolboy than for an officer preparing to lead men into battle.

As in Waugh's earlier novels, the comedy of *Men at Arms* depends not on the protagonist, but on the events and characters that he encounters. Apthorpe, a middle-aged *miles gloriosus*, and Ben Ritchie-Hook, Guy's brigadier, represent two forms of the military insanity for which Guy trains. Apthorpe's preoccupation with boots, salutes, and his portable field latrine, the "Box," makes him an unlikely candidate for leading men into battle; Ritchie-Hook, whose only notion of military strategy is to attack, makes an elaborate game out of officer training by booby-trapping Apthorpe's "Box"—a prank that causes Apthorpe to sink deeper into his madness. The confrontation between Apthorpe and Ritchie-Hook defines an absurd pattern that recurs later in the trilogy. Seeming madmen control the positions of power, and the protagonist is unwittingly drawn into their absurd worlds.

Officers and Gentlemen

Officers and Gentlemen further trains Guy in the illogic of military life, this time focusing on the efforts of gentlemen soldiers to re-create the comforts of their London clubs during the war. The novel ends on a more somber note, however, than did *Men at Arms*. Guy finds temporary solace in the commando unit to which he is transferred after his disgrace as a Halberdier and believes again that he will find some honorable role to play in the war, but the British defeat at Crete at the end of this volume negates whatever notions of honor he entertained.

Even more than *Men at Arms*, *Officers and Gentlemen* relentlessly parodies esprit de corps and pretentions to heroism. Ian Kilbannock's gentlemanly service as a military journalist, for example, is to transform the ineffectual Trimmer into a propaganda hero for the common person. Julia Stitch's yacht, the *Cleopatra*, brings the comforts of the English social world to the Mediterranean war. The burrowing Grace-Groundling-Marchpole absurdly continues the secret file he began in *Men at Arms* about Guy's supposed counterintelligence activities. All of these events occur while England is suffering the first effects of German bombing and while the British disgrace at Crete looms ahead.

For a time, Guy imagines that the commandos are the "flower of England"; he even sees Ivor Claire as the ideal soldier, the kind of Englishman whom Hitler had not taken into account. The flower withers, however, in the chaotic retreat of British forces from Crete. Although Guy himself manages to maintain an even keel through most of the ordeal, the officers with whom he serves prove unheroic. His commander, "Fido" Hound, suffers a complete mental collapse in the face of the retreating troops; Ivor Claire, unable to face the prospect of surrendering, deserts his men and flees to India, where he is protected by his genteel birth. Eventually, Guy unheroically joins a boat escaping from the island and, exhausted, suffers a mental collapse. Guy initially resists Julia Stitch's efforts to cover up Claire's disgrace, but eventually he destroys his own diary recording the orders to surrender when he learns that nothing will be done about Claire's desertion and when he learns of England's alliance with Russia. Unlike the first volume, the second volume ends with Guy's realization that he is an ineffectual player in a war that has lost a sense of honor.

It is curious to note that Waugh announced in the dust-jacket blurb for *Officers and Gentlemen* that, although he had planned the series for three volumes, he wanted his readers to regard it as finished with this second volume. The grimness of Guy's disillusionment thus sheds a somber light on Waugh's personal dilemma during the mid-1950's. After completing about a third of the draft of this second volume, Waugh suffered the mental collapse he later fictionalized in *The Ordeal of Gilbert Pinfold*. Guy's hallucination at the end of *Officers and Gentlemen* probably owes some of its vividness to the madness Waugh himself endured in 1954, and perhaps the numbness that affects Guy at the end of the novel reflects Waugh's own consciousness of his failing physical and mental powers.

THE END OF THE BATTLE

Men at Arms and *Officers and Gentlemen* each deflate Guy's illusions about honor. *The End of the Battle* follows the same pattern in terms of wartime politics and in terms of Guy's military life, but in personal terms, Guy achieves a kind of unheroic, unselfish honor by the end of the novel. As a soldier, Guy accomplishes nothing heroic; even his efforts to liberate the Jewish refugees from partisan Yugoslavia is unsatisfying. Although most of the refugees are liberated, the leaders of the group—the Kanyis—are imprisoned and presumably executed. Guy's struggle with the Yugoslavian partisans and his disgust at Britain's alliance with the Communist-bloc countries further define the dishonorable end that Guy and Waugh see in the war.

Unlike the two previous volumes, however, *The End of the Battle* ends on a note of tentative personal hopefulness, effected by Guy's renewed Roman Catholic faith. In the first two novels of the trilogy, Guy's religion lay dormant—a part of his life made purposeless since his divorce from Virginia. In *The End of the Battle*, the death of Guy's piously religious father causes Guy to realize that honor lies not in the "quantitative judgments" of military strategy, but in the spiritual salvation of individual souls. Guy's efforts to rescue the Yugoslavian Jews is selflessly honorable, even if ultimately futile. His remarriage to Virginia, who is pregnant with Trimmer's baby, is directed by the same sense of honor. Guy has little to gain emotionally from his remarriage; he does it for the preservation of the child's life and, implicitly, for the salvation of its soul. It is a different sort of heroism than he sought at the beginning of the war, possible only because Virginia has died.

Sword of Honour is, in many ways, a fitting climax to Waugh's literary career. It poignantly expresses his reverence for religious values yet recognizes the anomalous existence of those values in the modern world. It burlesques the eccentric and the absurd, yet moves beyond superficial satire to a more deeply rooted criticism of postwar politics. It displays Waugh's masterful ability to capture minor characters in brisk, economical strokes while working them thematically into the emotional composition of the protagonist. Waugh's importance as a novelist lay in his ability to achieve this kind of economy in a traditional form. He kept alive, in short, a tradition of the comic novel that reaches back to the eighteenth century.

James J. Lynch

OTHER MAJOR WORKS

SHORT FICTION: *Mr. Loveday's Little Outing*, 1936; *Work Suspended, and Other Stories Written Before the Second World War*, 1948; *Tactical Exercise*, 1954; *Charles Ryder's Schooldays, and Other Stories*, 1982; *The Complete Stories of Evelyn Waugh*, 1999.

NONFICTION: *Rossetti: His Life and Works*, 1928; *Labels: A Mediterranean Journal*, 1930; *Remote People*, 1931; *Ninety-two Days*, 1934; *Edmund Campion: Jesuit and Martyr*, 1935; *Waugh in Abyssinia*, 1936; *Robbery Under the Law*, 1939; *The Holy Places*, 1952; *The Life of the Right Reverend Ronald Knox*, 1959; *Tourist in Africa*, 1960; *A Little Learning*, 1964; *The Diaries of Evelyn Waugh*, 1976 (Michael Davie, editor); *A Little Order: A Selection from His Journalism*, 1977; *The Letters of Evelyn Waugh*, 1980 (Mark Amory, editor); *The Essays, Articles, and Reviews of Evelyn Waugh*, 1984.

BIBLIOGRAPHY

Carens, James F., ed. *Critical Essays on Evelyn Waugh*. Boston: G. K. Hall, 1987. Contains twenty-six essays divided into three sections: general essays, essays on specific novels, and essays on Waugh's life and works. A lengthy editor's introduction provides a chronological overview of Waugh's literary work and a discussion of Waugh criticism. Includes index and bibliography.

Cook, William J., Jr. *Masks, Modes, and Morals: The Art of Evelyn Waugh*. Rutherford, N.J.: Fairleigh Dickinson University Press, 1971. Considers Waugh's novels squarely in the ironic mode, tracing the author's development from satiric denunciation to comic realism to romantic optimism to ironic realism. Presents lengthy analyses of the novels and argues that they move from fantasy to reality and from satire to resignation. Includes bibliography and index.

Crabbe, Katharyn. *Evelyn Waugh*. New York: Continuum, 1988. Informative volume provides a chronology of Waugh's life, a short biography, five chapters of detailed criticism on Waugh's major novels, and a concluding chapter on Waugh's style. Includes bibliography and index.

Davis, Robert Murray. *Evelyn Waugh: Writer*. Norman, Okla.: Pilgrim Books, 1981. Drawing from previously unavailable manuscript materials, Davis examines Waugh's artistic technique, his extensive revisions, and his reworkings of his novels. Begins with a chapter on Waugh's biography of Dante Gabriel Rossetti and then focuses exclusively on the novels, *Brideshead Revisited* and *Sword of Honour* in particular. Includes index.

Hastings, Selina. *Evelyn Waugh: A Biography*. Boston: Houghton Mifflin, 1994. Excellent, lively biography is not an academic work such as that written by Stannard (cited below) but instead represents an attempt to capture Waugh's personality as it appeared to him and to his friends.

Lane, Calvin W. *Evelyn Waugh*. Boston: Twayne, 1981. Relatively brief work contains a detailed chronology, a biography stressing the factors that influenced Waugh's literary career, and lengthy treatments of his novels. Includes four interviews with Waugh and a bibliography. Indispensable for Waugh scholars.

Patey, Douglas Lane. *The Life of Evelyn Waugh: A Critical Biography*. Cambridge, Mass.: Blackwell, 1998. Discusses Waugh's life within the context of his work, providing critical assessments of his novels and other writings. Devotes one chapter to an in-depth examination of *Brideshead Revisited*.

Stannard, Martin. *Evelyn Waugh: The Early Years, 1903-1939*. New York: W. W. Norton, 1987.

_______. *Evelyn Waugh: The Later Years, 1939-1966*. New York: W. W. Norton, 1992. Scholarly, well-documented two-volume account of Waugh's life and literary career provides valuable publication details about the novels and uses Waugh's diaries and letters as resource materials. Includes many photographs and illustrations, a genealogical chart of Waugh's ancestry, a selected bibliography, a general index, and an index of Waugh's works.

Villa Flor, Carlos, and Robert Murray Davis, eds. *Waugh Without End: New Trends in Evelyn Waugh Studies*. New York: Peter Lang, 2005. Collection of essays originally presented at a 2003 symposium examines such topics as Waugh and Catholicism, Waugh's representation of the English gentleman, homosexual themes in his work, and *Brideshead Revisited*.

Waugh, Alexander. *Fathers and Sons: The Autobiography of a Family*. London: Headline, 2004. Evelyn Waugh's grandson chronicles four generations of his family, focusing on their father-son conflicts and their literary achievements. Includes illustrations, bibliography, and index.

FAY WELDON

Born: Alvechurch, Worcestershire, England; September 22, 1931
Also known as: Franklin Birkinshaw

PRINCIPAL LONG FICTION

The Fat Woman's Joke, 1967 (also known as *. . . And the Wife Ran Away*, 1968)
Down Among the Women, 1971
Female Friends, 1974
Remember Me, 1976
Words of Advice, 1977 (also known as *Little Sisters*, 1978)
Praxis, 1978
Puffball, 1980
The President's Child, 1982
The Life and Loves of a She-Devil, 1983
The Shrapnel Academy, 1986
The Heart of the Country, 1987
The Hearts and Lives of Men, 1987
The Rules of Life, 1987
Leader of the Band, 1988
The Cloning of Joanna May, 1989
Darcy's Utopia, 1990
Growing Rich, 1992
Life Force, 1992
Affliction, 1993 (also known as *Trouble*)
Splitting, 1995
Worst Fears, 1996
Big Women, 1997 (also known as *Big Girls Don't Cry*)
Rhode Island Blues, 2000
The Bulgari Connection, 2001
Mantrapped, 2004
She May Not Leave, 2005
The Spa Decameron, 2007 (also known as *The Spa*)

OTHER LITERARY FORMS

Fay Weldon began her writing career with plays for radio, television, and theater, but she soon transferred her efforts to novels, and it is her novels for which she has become best known. She has also published short stories and a good deal of nonfiction. The latter includes a biography of Rebecca West; an introduction to the work of Jane Austen in fictional form, *Letters to Alice on First Reading Jane Austen* (1984); an "advice book" for modern women, *What Makes Women Happy* (2006); an autobiography, *Auto da Fay* (2002); and a collection of her journalism, *Godless in Eden* (1999). Her collections of short fiction include *Moon over Minneapolis: Or, Why She Couldn't Stay* (1991) and *Wicked Women* (1995). She has also put her comic gifts to work in three books for children, *Wolf the Mechanical Dog* (1988), *Party Puddle* (1989), and *Nobody Likes Me* (1997).

ACHIEVEMENTS

In addition to a successful career as an advertising copywriter, Fay Weldon has enjoyed a long career as a television scriptwriter, a playwright (for television, radio, and theater), and a novelist. Her radio play *Spider* (1972) won the Writers' Guild Award for Best Radio Play in 1973, and *Polaris* (1978) won the Giles Cooper Award for Best Radio Play in 1978. Weldon has earned growing acclaim for her humorous fictional explorations of women's lives and her biting satires that expose social injustice, and her novel *Praxis* was nominated for the prestigious Booker Prize. In 1983, Weldon became the first woman chair of judges for the Booker Prize. She was recognized for her many achievements in 1997, when she received the Women in Publishing Pandora Award. In 2000, she was made a Commander of the Order of the British Empire.

BIOGRAPHY

Fay Weldon was born Franklin Birkinshaw in the village of Alvechurch, England, in 1931. Her mother, who wrote under the name Pearl Bellairs, her maternal grandfather, Edwin Jepson, and one of her uncles were all novelists. While still a child, Weldon emigrated with her family to New Zealand, where her father worked as a doctor. When she was six years old, her parents divorced, and Weldon eventually returned to England with her mother and sister to live with her grandmother. This experience of being reared by a single mother in an era that did not easily accommodate single-parent families gave Weldon early insight into the lot of women living beyond the pale of the nuclear family; she was able to observe, at first hand, both the trials women faced and the importance of family and of humor in overcoming these difficulties.

In 1949, Weldon earned a scholarship to St. Andrews University in Scotland, and in 1952 she graduated with an M.A. in economics and psychology. Her first marriage, to Ronald Bateman, a man twenty years her senior, lasted less than two years, leaving her to support her son, Nicholas, as a single mother. She drifted through a series of jobs involving writing of various sorts: writing propaganda for the Foreign Office, answering problem letters for a newspaper, and, finally, composing advertising copy. In this last career she was quite successful, producing many jingles and slogans—a few of which stuck in the memory beyond their use in specific campaigns—and honing her talent for concision, wit, and catchy, memorable phrasing.

In 1960, she married Ronald Weldon, a London antiques dealer; they settled in a North London suburb, where they had three children: Daniel (born 1963), Thomas (born 1970), and Samuel (born 1977). Beginning in the mid-1960's, Weldon combined professional and family responsibilities with a burgeoning career as a writer. Her first efforts were directed toward writing plays. Her one-act play *Permanence* was produced in London in 1969 and was followed by many successes. For British television, Weldon wrote more than fifty screenplays, including an award-winning episode of the series *Upstairs, Downstairs*. Writing for television led to fiction: Weldon's first novel, *The Fat Woman's Joke*, in 1967, began life as a television play. Her third novel, *Female Friends*, solidified her reputation, and Weldon quit her job in advertising. She earned further acclaim for *Praxis* and *The President's Child*, but *The Life and Loves of a She-Devil* proved a breakthrough work, introducing her work to a mass audience when it was made into a motion picture, *She-Devil* (1989), starring Meryl Streep and Roseanne Barr.

Her eventual divorce from Ronald Weldon in 1994 caused a certain amount of bitterness, which she expressed in some of her subsequent fiction. She later married poet Nicholas Fox; they lived briefly in Hampstead before moving to Shaftesbury in Dorset. Weldon seemed to mellow after her marriage to Fox, and she experienced something of an existential break when she had a vision of "the gates of paradise" (or possibly Hell) during a near-death experience suffered in 2005 when an allergic reaction caused her heart to stop. Even though the gates in question seemed hideously tacky and vulgar, she subsequently had herself baptized after being a committed atheist for most of her life. She had already begun to suggest in both her fiction and her nonfiction that she had recanted some of her earlier views, although she sacrificed none of her acerbic sarcasm in making the point. Her widely quoted opinion that men had gotten a rough deal as a result of the advancement of feminism seemed to some of her former admirers a particularly painful item of moral treason. Her combative "advice book," *What Makes Women Happy*—a title that suggests, perhaps presumptuously, that she now knows the answer—argues that the apparent reply is sex, chocolate, and shopping but that slightly deeper analysis would suggest a more refined alliterative triad of family, friends, and food.

Analysis

Fay Weldon's fiction explores women's lives with wit and humor in the cause of a determined opposition to the clichés of romantic fiction. Weldon is caustic in her implicit condemnation of injustice but avoids preaching by satirizing both sides of every issue and by revealing the gulf between what characters say and what they do. Despite their realistic settings, her novels blend fable, myth, and the fantastic with satire, farce, and outlandish coincidence; the combination produces highly distinctive tragicomedies of manners.

Weldon's admiration for writers such as Jane Austen (whose work she has adapted for television) is expressed openly in *Letters to Alice on First Reading Jane Austen*, but it is also evident from the parallels in Weldon's own work. In a typical early Weldon novel, a limited cast of characters interacts in a defined setting. A series of misunderstandings or trivial coincidences initiates the action, which then takes on a momentum of its own, carrying all along with it until an equally trivial series of explanations or coincidences brings closure and a resolution that restores all to their proper place. The theme is often a minor domestic drama, such as a marital crisis, rather than an epic upheaval, but such personal interactions are seen to represent in microcosm society as a whole and therefore have a universal appeal.

Over time, her novels have become more wide-ranging in their settings, narrative devices, and claims, sometimes recruiting fantastic devices in order to attempt deeper analyses of the issues at stake, but generally her works still convey the impression that Weldon is not much given to elaborate planning, preferring to allow her characters and story lines to develop their own momentum. This has sometimes taken her into unexpected narrative terrain, but she always retains a keen intelligence and a trenchant wit. Although her works focus primarily on the lives of women, Weldon comments on a wide-ranging number of issues with relevance to all. Her work reveals a deep yet unsentimental compassion for all human beings, an understanding of their weaknesses and foibles, and a celebration of their continued survival and ability to love one another in the face of adversity.

. . . And the Wife Ran Away

This structure is present even in Weldon's early work, no doubt because it is a formula that works well for television. In her first novel, originally titled *The Fat Woman's Joke* but renamed . . . *And the Wife Ran Away* for its American publication in 1968, Weldon takes as her subject the crisis in the marriage of a middle-aged, middle-class couple, Esther and Alan Wells, when Alan decides to have an affair with his young and attractive secretary, Susan. The beginning of Alan's affair coincides with Esther and Alan's joint decision to go on a diet, a symbolic attempt, Weldon suggests, to recapture not only their lost youthful figures but also their youthful love, ambition, and optimism. Infidelity, the novel therefore subtly suggests, is related to aging and to a more deep-seated identity crisis. Weldon frequently uses hunger or the satisfaction of food as a metaphor for other, more metaphysical and intangible, needs, and this theme recurs in a number of her works (for example, in the short story "Polaris," 1985).

The influence of Weldon's background as a scriptwriter (and the novel's origin as a play) is also evident in this book's form. Esther, who has left her husband at the opening of the novel, recounts her version of events to her friend Phyllis as she gorges herself on food to compensate for the self-denial she has suffered during the diet. Esther's narrative is intercut with scenes of Susan telling her version of events to her friend Brenda. The novel is thus almost entirely conveyed through dialogue describing flashbacks seen from the perspectives of the female characters. This technique is evident elsewhere in Weldon's early work—for example, in *Female Friends*, where parts of the novel are presented in the form of a script.

Fay Weldon. (© Miriam Berkley)

The Life and Loves of a She-Devil

The Life and Loves of a She-Devil stands as one of Weldon's most accomplished works. It represents the themes that are the hallmark of Weldon's fiction (a concern with women's lives and the significance of human relationships such as marriage) while encompassing her use of fantasy in one of her most carefully constructed and formally satisfying novels. The plot tells the story of a middle-class, suburban housewife, Ruth, whose accountant husband leaves her for a rich and attractive writer of romance novels. Unlike the typical wife, however, Ruth does not simply bow to the inevitable. When her husband calls her a "she-devil" in a moment of anger, this becomes her new identity, and she musters a formidable array of resources to live up to it. Through a series of picaresque adventures, she makes the life of her husband, Bobbo, and his new love, Mary Fisher, impossible. She has Bobbo framed and then imprisoned for embezzlement, destroys Mary's ability and will to write, and finally undergoes massive plastic surgery so that she looks just like her now-dead rival and can assume her place in Bobbo's broken life. The configuration at the end of the novel thus mirrors the beginning, but with the variation that the power dynamics of the relationship have been inverted: Ruth is now in command, while Bobbo has been humiliated and accepts his fate like a downtrodden wife.

The tale not only presents a certain kind of symmetry reminiscent of fairy stories but also evokes a poetic magic in the telling of it. Many of the chapters begin with a variation on the opening line of the novel: "Mary Fisher lives in a High Tower, on the edge of the sea." These incantations, repeated with variations, have the hypnotic quality of a witch's spell, reinforcing both Ruth's supernatural power and her obsession with Mary Fisher (whose residence in a tower evokes a fairy-tale princess). This poetic refrain also unifies the narrative and gives a cyclical structure to the plot.

THE SHRAPNEL ACADEMY

On the surface, *The Shrapnel Academy* is a variation on the stale British motif of the "country house weekend." A group of characters, most of them unknown to one another, are seen arriving at the Shrapnel Academy, a military institute, for a weekend. Bad weather will ensure that they remain confined to the academy, cut off from the outside world and forced to confront one another and the problems that arise.

While many novelists fail to acknowledge the presence of the host of servants who make such country weekends possible, Weldon's novel takes the reader below stairs and into the lives of the hundreds of illegal immigrant servants and their extended families and camp followers—as in *Upstairs, Downstairs*, the early 1970's television series about an upper-class Edwardian family and its servants to which Weldon contributed an award-winning episode. *The Shrapnel Academy* ventures beyond realist conventions by presenting a clash between shortsighted, class-based militarism and the struggle for survival and dignity in the microcosm of the academy, eventually extending into quasi-apocalyptic allegory.

As in most of Weldon's novels, no single villain is responsible for the misfortunes that befall the characters in *The Shrapnel Academy*; all the characters bear some degree of responsibility for the accumulation of trivial choices and decisions that combine to make up the climactic "frightful tidal wave of destiny." Many continual thematic elements of Weldon's work recur in *The Shrapnel Academy*, including revenge fantasy, food symbolism, and transfigurations of myth and fable. Formally, too, the novel displays typical characteristics of Weldon's work (short narrative passages with aphoristic asides, the use of dialogue) as well as innovative and experimental qualities. The author interrupts the narrative at frequent intervals, sometimes to offer satirical summaries of military history, highlighting advances in warfare or giving accounts of famous battles. Weldon brings out the absurdity of celebrating such "progress" and uses her fine wit to draw the reader's attention to the Orwellian doublespeak and underlying assumptions of military thinking. At other times, Weldon interpellates the reader directly, apologizing for the delay in getting on with the story or inviting the reader to put him- or herself in the place of one of the characters—invitations that pointedly drive home the lesson that the reader is no better than the characters he or she is inclined to judge.

LIFE FORCE

Weldon also breaks strategically with her readers' expectations in *Life Force*, which, instead of being an indictment of male callousness and infidelity, is a lusty tribute to male sexuality. The central figure in the book is Leslie Beck, a man with no virtues except his power to please women through the skillful use of his huge genitalia and his equally outsized imagination. Structurally, *Life Force* follows the pattern established in Weldon's earlier novels: It begins with a seemingly unimportant incident that stimulates the narrator to relive and reassess complex relationships; that incident eventually becomes a crucial element in a dramatic resolution, in which a woman avenges herself upon a man who has wronged her.

When Leslie Beck turns up at the Marion Loos Gallery, carrying a large painting by his late wife Anita, it does not seem possible that this unappealing, sixty-year-old man could for so long have been the Lothario of upper-middle-class London. However, the owner of the gallery, who at this point is the first-person narrator, explains to the reader why she is so shocked when she sees the unimpressive painting that her former lover expects her to sell on his behalf. Its subject is the bedroom and the bed in which Leslie once gave Marion so much pleasure. Naturally, the painting prompts Marion to recall her involvement with Leslie and to wonder how much Anita knew about the affair.

Nothing in this novel is as straightforward as it seems, however. In the second chapter, Weldon not only changes narrators—now telling the story through the eyes of Nora, another of Beck's former lovers—but also has Nora admit that it was she, not Marion, who actually wrote the first chapter, simply imagining herself as Marion. Although the two narrators continue to alternate as the book progresses, from time to time the author reminds us that Marion's narrative is Nora's fiction, based as much on gossip and guesses as on fact. Weldon thus suggests that since the only approach to truth is through what human beings see and say, what we call reality will always include as much fiction as fact.

Growing Rich

Growing Rich describes the harassment of three adolescent girls by a Mephistophelian figure who has promised one of them as a prize to the wealthy businessman with whom he has made a Faustian pact. Cast in the same mock-folkloristic mode as *The Life and Loves of a She-Devil*, this novel seems to be casting around for a different moral but cannot in the end discover one. The demon is incarnate as the businessman's chauffeur and is thus referred to as "the Driver," which implies that the novel's presiding proverb is "Needs must when the devil drives"—and, indeed, even the novel's primary heroine, Carmen, cannot in the end avoid his driving. Carmen withstands his subtler temptations easily enough, although her friends Annie and Laura are not nearly so fortunate, but she cannot ultimately prevail against his nastier threats. In the end, the fact that she is not required to yield everything demanded by his blackmail cannot conceal the fact that she does yield.

The Driver is an intriguing literary creation: an apt devil for the modern age, whose acid observations reveal as strong a kinship with Alain-René Lesage's Asmodeus as with Christopher Marlowe's Mephistopheles. *Growing Rich*, like most of Weldon's works, is so exuberantly good-humored that even its blackest comedy is little more than black-edged, and the same is true of the marginal gothic elements of many of its predecessors and successors among her long fiction, including the mock-Dickensian melodrama *The Hearts and Lives of Men*, the mock-science-fictional *The Cloning of Joanna May*, and the similarly fantasized *Splitting* and *Mantrapped*. Like many modern authors, Weldon simply cannot take the fantastic seriously enough to make the most of its inherent narrative energy, but the frothy frivolity with which she invests it carries its own rewards.

Trouble

In *Trouble*, Weldon again turns her attention to a society that permits men to victimize women. The protagonist of this novel, which was first published in England under the title *Affliction*, is Annette Horrocks, a woman who, after ten years of trying, has finally become pregnant, only to find that her once-devoted husband, Spicer, has become monstrous. Not only does he now seem to loathe Annette, but also none of his tastes, opinions, and prejudices are what they were just a few months before.

Eventually, Annette discovers the source of the problem: Spicer has been seduced by a pair of unscrupulous, sadistic New Age psychiatrists. Before she is finally cured of what she comes to recognize as her addiction to Spicer, Annette loses her home, her baby, and very nearly her mind. If in *Life Force* Weldon shows the battle of the sexes as essentially comic, in *Trouble* she tells a story with tragic overtones. Again she points out how vulnerable women are in a society that believes men have a monopoly on the truth, but in this case she shows what can happen when the male version of reality is reinforced by the self-seeking therapy industry, the primary target of satire in this novel.

Worst Fears

Worst Fears is one of Weldon's novels most clearly marked by the scars of her 1994 divorce. Its protagonist, Alexandra, an actor, is suddenly precipitated into crisis by the unexpected death of her husband, Ned, and is required, as conventional parlance has it, to "put his affairs in order." This involves her in a disquieting sequence of discoveries about the "true identity" Ned had succeeded in hiding from her for many years, which eventually extend to nightmarish extremes. Members of all of the professions that Weldon learned to hate in the course of her own divorce—especially therapists and lawyers—become targets for her bile here, although the burden of the role of primary traitor within the plot falls on a child-care provider: a dangerous cuckoo in the domestic nest.

Rhode Island Blues

In *Rhode Island Blues*, Weldon presents an elaborate examination of female family ties, dominated by the character of eighty-five-year-old Felicity, whose granddaughter Sophie, a film editor—the novel's primary protagonist—undertakes a quixotic quest to find the old woman's "lost" granddaughter. In the process, Sophie uncovers a great deal of family history extended over the generations and begins to reassess her relationship with her own mother. The novel's transatlantic movements, occasioned by the fact that Felicity was a war bride, add an extra dimension of cultural comparison, while a fantastic edge is added by Felicity's consolatory delusions.

The Bulgari Connection

The Bulgari Connection is an interesting experiment in novelistic product placement, as the writing of the work was financed by the Italian jewelry company. This connection is, however, incidental to the network of the plot, which develops a version of the eternal triangle. Businessman Barney Salt deserts his wife, Grace, for television personality Doris Dubois, thus inviting a she-devil-like revenge. The revenge in question is duly visited after Grace takes up with artist Walter Wells and receives a new lease on life that is quite literal—an aspect of the plot explicitly modeled on Oscar Wilde's *The Picture of Dorian Gray* (1890).

As on several previous occasions, Weldon picked up themes from this novel for further extrapolation in her next work, the identity-exchange comedy *Mantrapped*, whose heroine awakes one morning to find herself in a man's body. There, as in *The Bulgari Connection*, elements of Weldon's own autobiography are clearly recycled, but the fantastic embellishments in both books serve as useful distancing devices for putting "reality" into a broader and more comfortable perspective.

She May Not Leave

She May Not Leave is an elaborate expansion of the child-care-worker subplot from *Worst Fears*, complicated by intergenerational issues echoing those in *Rhode Island Blues*, both elements being carefully ameliorated by a conscientious attempt to strike an evenhanded balance. The protagonist, Hattie, is busily employed in a literary agency and has trouble juggling her relationships with her partner, Martin, a political journalist; her grandmother, Frances, who is busy tracing the family history; and her daughter, Kitty. Polish au pair Agnieszka is an extremely dubious godsend, but she might well be indispensable no matter how problematic she eventually proves to be. As in many Weldon novels, the eventual "resolution" of *She May Not Leave* is unashamedly artificial and rather tokenistic, but the breezy tone illustrates the author's recovered sense of well-being and the essential irrepressibility of her character.

The Spa Decameron

In a plot that echoes *The Shrapnel Academy* but lacks that novel's male/militaristic component, *The Spa Decameron* features wealthy female guests who are snowed in for ten days at a Cumbrian health spa over the Christmas/New Year holidays. As the facilities gradually begin to fail and the staff who maintain the guests' comforts and privileges begin to desert or rebel, the women pass the time by telling one another their instructive life stories, somewhat after the fashion of the plague-beleaguered characters in Giovanni Boccaccio's classic *Decameron: O, Prencipe Galeotto* (1349-1351; *The Decameron*, 1620). *The Spa Decameron* is, however, much more tightly organized around a thematic core than is its model; it really is a novel in spite of its discursive structure.

The characters' experiences gradually add up to a grotesque survey of the possibilities open to modern women and the threats facing them, including adultery, gender reassignment surgery, incest, abortion, husband murder, lesbian sexuality, and child abuse—to name but a few. The principal viewpoint character, Phoebe, is able to supplement the tales she hears further by virtue of her (possibly imaginary) ability to hear other people's thoughts; she does not tell her own story, partly—the reader suspects—because it cannot withstand melodramatic comparison with the stories the other characters tell, but also, and more appropriately, because it still remains to be equipped with a satisfactory sense of closure.

Melanie Hawthorne;
Rosemary M. Canfield Reisman
Updated by Brian Stableford

Other major works

SHORT FICTION: *Watching Me, Watching You*, 1981; *Polaris, and Other Stories*, 1985; *Moon over Minneapolis: Or, Why She Couldn't Stay*, 1991; *Angel, All Innocence, and Other Stories*, 1995; *Wicked Women: A Collection of Short Stories*, 1995; *A Hard Time to Be a Father*, 1998.

PLAYS: *Permanence*, pr. 1969; *Time Hurries On*, pb. 1972; *Words of Advice*, pr., pb. 1974; *Friends*, pr. 1975; *Moving House*, pr. 1976; *Mr. Director*, pr. 1978; *Action Replay*, pr. 1979 (also known as *Love Among the Women*); *After the Prize*, pr. 1981 (also known as *Woodworm*); *I Love My Love*, pr. 1981; *Tess of the D'Urbervilles*, pr. 1992 (adaptation of Thomas Hardy's novel); *The Four Alice Bakers*, pr. 1999; *The Reading Group*, pb. 1999.

TELEPLAYS: *The Fat Woman's Tale*, 1966; *Wife in a Blonde Wig*, 1966; *Dr. De Waldon's Therapy*, 1967; *Fall of the Goat*, 1967; *The Forty-fifth Unmarried Mother*, 1967; *Goodnight Mrs. Dill*, 1967; *What About Me*, 1967; *Hippy Hippy Who Cares*, 1968; *Ruined Houses*, 1968; *£13083*, 1968; *The Three Wives of Felix Hull*, 1968; *Venus Rising*, 1968; *Smokescreen*, 1969; *The Loophole*, 1969; *Office Party*, 1970; *Poor Mother*, 1970; "On Trial," 1971 (episode of television series *Upstairs, Downstairs*); *Hands*, 1972; *The Lament of an Unmarried Father*, 1972; *A Nice Rest*, 1972; *Old Man's Hat*, 1972; *A Splinter of Ice*, 1972; *Comfortable Words*, 1973; *Desirous of Change*, 1973; *In Memoriam*, 1974; *Aunt Tatty*, 1975 (adaptation of Elizabeth Bowen's story); *Poor Baby*, 1975; *The Terrible Tale of Timothy Bagshott*, 1975; *Act of Rape*, 1977; "Married Love," 1977 (episode of television series *Six Women*); *Honey Ann*, 1980; *Life for Christine*, 1980; *Pride and Prejudice*, 1980 (adaptation of Jane Austen's novel); "Watching Me, Watching You," 1980 (episode of television series *Leap in the Dark*); *Little Miss Perkins*, 1982; *Loving Women*, 1983; *Redundant! Or, The Wife's Revenge*, 1983.

RADIO PLAYS: *Spider*, 1972; *Housebreaker*, 1973; *Mr. Fox and Mr. First*, 1974; *The Doctor's Wife*, 1975; *Polaris*, 1978; *All the Bells of Paradise*, 1979; "Weekend," 1979 (episode in radio series *Just Before Midnight*); *I Love My Love*, 1981.

NONFICTION: *Letters to Alice on First Reading Jane Austen*, 1984; *Rebecca West*, 1985; *Sacred Cows: A Portrait of Britain, Post-Rushdie, Pre-Utopia*, 1989; *Godless in Eden: A Book of Essays*, 1999; *Auto da Fay*, 2002; *What Makes Women Happy*, 2006.

CHILDREN'S LITERATURE: *Wolf the Mechanical Dog*, 1988; *Party Puddle*, 1989; *Nobody Likes Me*, 1997.

EDITED TEXT: *New Stories Four: An Arts Council Anthology*, 1979 (with Elaine Feinstein).

Bibliography

Barreca, Regina, ed. *Fay Weldon's Wicked Fictions*. Hanover, N.H.: University Press of New England, 1994. Collection of eighteen essays, five by Weldon herself, deals with leading themes and techniques in Weldon's fiction and various issues raised by her work, such as her relation to feminism and her politics and moral stance.

Cane, Aleta F. "Demythifying Motherhood in Three Novels by Fay Weldon." In *Family Matters in the British and American Novel*, edited by Andrea O'Reilly Herrera, Elizabeth Mahn Nollen, and Sheila Reitzel Foor. Bowling Green, Ohio: Bowling Green State University Popular Press, 1997. Points out that in *Puffball*, *The Life and Loves of a She-Devil*, and *Life Force*, dysfunctional mothers produce daughters who are also dysfunctional mothers. Argues that Weldon agrees with the feminist position that mothering cannot be improved until women cease to be marginalized.

Dowling, Finuala. *Fay Weldon's Fiction*. Rutherford, N.J.: Fairleigh Dickinson University Press, 1998. Examines the themes and techniques in Weldon's fiction, with the principal emphasis on the novels.

Faulks, Lana. *Fay Weldon*. New York: Twayne, 1998. Provides a good introduction to Weldon's life and work, with a focus on the novels. Describes Weldon's fiction as "feminist comedy," contrasting with feminist writing that depicts women as oppressed. Also examines Weldon's experiments with narrative techniques.

Ferreira, Maria Aline Salgueiro Seabra. "Cloning and Biopower: Joanna Russ and Fay Weldon." In *I Am the Other: Literary Negotiations of Human Cloning*. Westport: Conn.: Greenwood Press, 2005. Presents a critical discussion of the role of cloning in Weldon's novel *The Cloning of Joanna May*.

Mitchell, Margaret E. "Fay Weldon." In *British Writers*, Supplement 4 in *Contemporary British Writers*, edited by George Stade and Carol Howard. New York: Charles Scribner's Sons, 1997. Presents detailed information on Weldon's life and work, divided into sections titled "Weldon's Feminism," "The Personal as Political," "Nature, Fate, and Magic," "Self and Solidarity," and "Fictions."

Paloge, Helen. *The Silent Echo: The Middle-Aged Female Body in Contemporary Women's Fiction*. Lanham, Md.: Lexington Books, 2007. Discusses the depiction of middle-aged women in the novels of Weldon, Margaret Atwood, Joan Barfoot, Joyce Carol Oates, and others.

Weldon, Fay. "Nature, Science, and Witchcraft: An Interview with Fay Weldon." Interview by Joanna Zylinska. *Critical Survey* 12, no. 3 (2000): 108-122. Weldon discusses her writing, particularly her novels and their inspirations.

Wilde, Alan. "'Bold, But Not Too Bold': Fay Weldon and the Limits of Poststructuralist Criticism." *Contemporary Literature* 29, no. 3 (1988): 403-419. Focuses primarily on literary theory, using *The Life and Loves of a She-Devil* as an arena to pit poststructuralism against New Criticism, offering some useful comments regarding moderation versus extremism in this novel.

H. G. WELLS

Born: Bromley, Kent, England; September 21, 1866
Died: London, England; August 13, 1946
Also known as: Herbert George Wells

Principal long fiction

The Time Machine: An Invention, 1895
The Wonderful Visit, 1895
The Island of Dr. Moreau, 1896
The Wheels of Chance: A Holiday Adventure, 1896
The Invisible Man: A Grotesque Romance, 1897
The War of the Worlds, 1898
When the Sleeper Wakes: A Story of the Years to Come, 1899
Love and Mr. Lewisham, 1900
The First Men in the Moon, 1901
The Sea Lady, 1902
The Food of the Gods, and How It Came to Earth, 1904
Kipps: The Story of a Simple Soul, 1905
In the Days of the Comet, 1906
Tono-Bungay, 1908
The War in the Air, and Particularly How Mr. Bert Smallways Fared While It Lasted, 1908
Ann Veronica: A Modern Love Story, 1909
The History of Mr. Polly, 1910
The New Machiavelli, 1910
Marriage, 1912
The Passionate Friends, 1913
The Wife of Sir Isaac Harman, 1914
The World Set Free: A Story of Mankind, 1914
Bealby: A Holiday, 1915
The Research Magnificent, 1915
Mr. Britling Sees It Through, 1916
The Soul of a Bishop: A Novel—with Just a Little Love in It—About Conscience and Religion and the Real Troubles of Life, 1917
Joan and Peter: The Story of an Education, 1918
The Undying Fire: A Contemporary Novel, 1919
The Secret Places of the Heart, 1922
Men Like Gods, 1923
The Dream, 1924
Christina Alberta's Father, 1925
The World of William Clissold: A Novel at a New Age, 1926 (3 volumes)
Meanwhile: The Picture of a Lady, 1927
Mr. Blettsworthy on Rampole Island, 1928

The King Who Was a King: The Book of a Film, 1929
The Autocracy of Mr. Parham: His Remarkable Adventure in This Changing World, 1930
The Buplington of Blup, 1933
The Shape of Things to Come: The Ultimate Resolution, 1933
The Croquet Player, 1936
Byrnhild, 1937
The Camford Visitation, 1937
Star Begotten: A Biological Fantasia, 1937
Apropos of Dolores, 1938
The Brothers, 1938
The Holy Terror, 1939
All Aboard for Ararat, 1940
Babes in the Darkling Wood, 1940
You Can't Be Too Careful: A Sample of Life, 1901-1951, 1941

Other literary forms

H. G. Wells's short stories appear in several collections, including *The Stolen Bacillus, and Other Incidents* (1895), *Tales of Space and Time* (1899), *The Country of the Blind, and Other Stories* (1911), and *A Door in the Wall, and Other Stories* (1911). In *The Outline of History: Being a Plain History of Life and Mankind* (1920) and *Experiment in Autobiography: Discoveries and Conclusions of a Very Ordinary Brain Since 1866* (1934), Wells extended his literary range. His sociological essays include *A Modern Utopia* (1905) and *Mind at the End of Its Tether* (1945).

Achievements

H. G. Wells is best known for his science-fiction novels, several of which have been adapted as popular films. A socialist and Fabian, he was a spokesman for women's rights and international peace movements, for which he wrote books of advocacy in essay and fictional form. Wells was also an effective novelist of social satire and comedy.

Biography

Herbert George Wells was born in 1866 at Bromley in Kent, England, to Joseph and Sarah Neal Wells. He attended a commercial academy from 1874 to 1880. Having run away from his apprenticeship in a drapery shop, he taught in a preparatory school. Then he attended the London Normal School of Science from 1884 to 1887, studying biology under T. H. Huxley. In 1891 he was married to Isabel Mary Wells, and he published "The Rediscovery of the Unique." *The Time Machine* brought him fame in 1895, the same year that he divorced Isabel to marry Amy Catherine Robbins.

In 1901, Wells's son George Philip was born; Frank Richard followed in 1903. In 1914, having visited Russia, Wells published a prophecy, *The War That Will End War*; that year his son Anthony West was born to Rebecca West. After visiting soldiers on the front lines of World War I, Wells supported a "League of Free Nations" and entered the propaganda effort against Germany. In 1920 he made another trip to Russia, to meet Vladimir Ilich Lenin, and published *Russia in the Shadows*.

Wells was defeated as a Labour candidate for Parliament in 1922, and Amy Catherine died in 1927. He coauthored a book on biology before visiting Russia and the United States in 1934 to meet Joseph Stalin and President Franklin D. Roosevelt. In 1935 he wrote film scenarios for *Things to Come* and *The Man Who Could Work Miracles*. In 1938, Orson Welles's radio broadcast of an adaptation of Wells's novel *The War of the Worlds* frightened many people in the United States, paving the way for Wells's successful lecture tour there in 1940. Wells died in London on August 13, 1946.

Analysis

H. G. Wells's early scientific romances begin with *The Time Machine* and conclude with *The First Men in the Moon*. His social satires and comic romances commence with *Kipps* and end with *The History of Mr. Polly*. Didactic fiction dominated his last decades, from *Ann Veronica* to *You Can't Be Too Careful*. Throughout is a struggle between science and socialism. Visions of doom alternate with calls for reform and renewal; individuals acquire knowledge of science but lose control of their destinies.

The Time Machine

Wells's early novels are journeys of ironic discovery. The enduring point of *The Time Machine* is in the Time-Traveller's frightening discovery in the year 802701. He

H. G. Wells. (Library of Congress)

encounters the Eloi, who have been terrorized by the Morlocks, molelike creatures who prey on the flesh of the Upper-worlders. They are the fruits of an evolutionary process of separating capitalists from workers. Before he returns to his own time, the Time-Traveller accidentally moves even further into the future, to an Earth about to fall into a dying Sun.

The Island of Dr. Moreau

Edward Prendick, narrator of *The Island of Dr. Moreau*, is a castaway, grateful to reach Moreau's island—until he realizes its horrors. He thinks that Moreau is turning people into animals, but when he finds the Beast-people, he realizes his mistake. Moreau explains that pain is animality, and he excises pain to humanize animals, but they kill him as they revert to their animal natures. Prendick barely escapes becoming an animal before he returns to civilization, where he has anxiety attacks about people's animality.

Pessimism is never far from the surface of Wells's writing. Losing faith in reason, he turned to prophetic satire, as in *The Invisible Man*. In this story, Griffin, having failed to anticipate the awful effects of losing visibility, has lapsed in ethical responsibility because he had no training or economic opportunity to make better use of his knowledge. Lacking love, he lacks constructive purpose for his power. His invisibility represents knowledge itself, as either destructive or constructive. Knowledge and power combine without sympathy in *The War of the Worlds* to result in catastrophe. The narrator is a frightened man struggling to compete for survival of the fittest. He believes that the Martians are little more than brains, dispassionate reason threatening annihilation. All brain with no sympathy threatens civilization, but so does instinct with no brain. The Martians are near success when suddenly they begin to die, ironically having succumbed to some of Earth's tiniest life-forms, bacteria.

The First Men in the Moon

Wells reverses the cosmic journey in *The First Men in the Moon*, as Bedford accompanies eccentric scientist Cavor to mine the Moon, adding private enterprise to science. The heroes find an intoxicating mushroom, which prompts Bedford to speculate that his private motive for profit will produce public benefits—even for the Moon itself. This madly grandiose notion is subverted when Bedford and Cavor are captured by the antlike Selenites, who live under the surface of the Moon. When Bedford escapes alone to Earth, Cavor sends messages that he is to be executed to prevent Earth inhabitants from returning with their violent ways, to do to the Moon what Wells had envisioned in *The War of the Worlds*, where Earth was invaded by Martians.

The Food of the Gods, and How It Came to Earth

The Food of the Gods, and How It Came to Earth edges beyond science and humor into socialism and satire. Experiments with Boomfood on a chicken farm cause mass destruction through the creation of giant chickens, rats, and wasps; human babies become giants, and ordinary mortals grow terrified. Wells is on the giants' side, because they can make a new world by destroying the faults of the old. People accommodate to preserve old ways, but they shut their eyes to truth, eventually causing a crisis of choice between old and new. The story ends as the giants prepare for a war with the little people.

IN THE DAYS OF THE COMET

With *In the Days of the Comet* Wells presents a more optimistic view of changes that can be made in the world. Willie Leadford describes life before the great "change," when a comet turned Earth into paradise. The power of the novel, however, is in the rhythm of rage and hate that accelerates as Willie pursues the woman he loved, to kill her and her new lover. This momentum is accented by other accelerating events, including economic crisis and war with Germany. The comet changes all, including Willie and his beloved, Nettie, who offers to live with both lovers. In a new world, people learn to accept polygamy as natural and right.

KIPPS

Kipps: The Story of a Simple Soul is a story like Charles Dickens's *Great Expectations* (1860-1861, serial; 1861, book). The aunt and uncle who reared Kipps expected him to become a store clerk; Kipps has not been very skilled at anything he has undertaken, and he proves no better at handling an unexpected inheritance. Kipps has a dreary existence: He gains no real pleasure from life, not even from reading. Life in lower-middle-class commercial and shopkeeping society is without substance, imagination, or purpose. Kipps's first thought is to buy a banjo, though he cannot play it. Thinking more seriously of his prospects, he asks his art teacher to marry him, and she proceeds to teach him to speak and dress properly. Kipps tries and hopes, until he encounters an old love, Ann Pornick, working as a maid. He snubs her and in his guilt asks her forgiveness; she not only forgives him but also marries him. Thus, Kipps has stumbled through mistake after mistake, from education to apprenticeship to courtship and marriage. Finally, when he loses most of his fortune, he and his wife resign themselves to a restricted life and open a bookshop.

Wells's satire is directed at Kipps for trying to be more than he can be, for misplacing values in a system of manners; indeed, Wells intensely scorns the social superficialities. The protagonist of *Tono-Bungay*, George Ponderevo, has much in common with Kipps, but George is less simple and more reflective. His early life is like Kipps's (and Wells's) in that he resists training for trade, shows a talent for science, marries above his class, divorces, and rediscovers a childhood romance, through scenes of satiric analysis of the social snobs, religious bigots, and capitalist cutthroats of England. More sympathetic is ambitious Uncle Teddy, who makes a fortune with Tono-Bungay, a bogus medicine, and launches a disastrous career in the "romance of modern commerce." George Ponderevo is more a master of his destiny than is Kipps. After the collapse of his uncle's financial empire, George turns to engineering as a means of commitment to scientific objectivity. He is beyond society and governments, as he is alone in the world of love.

Science triumphs over socialism and capitalism in *Tono-Bungay*, while individual vitality triumphs over all ideas in *The History of Mr. Polly*, another of Wells's best comic novels from his middle period. This story begins with a discontented middle-aged shopkeeper, Mr. Polly, contemplating his boredom, indigestion, and proud misuse of English. He decides to burn his shop and cut his throat. Having succeeded in his arson but having forgotten to cut his throat, he deserts his wife for happy obscurity as a fat woman's handyman, forgetting the life he detested. Although Mr. Polly is an absurd creature, surrounded by stupid, unambitious people, he is sympathetic because he rebels against that absurdity and stupidity. Wells rewards Mr. Polly well for his rebellion.

ANN VERONICA

Wells also rewards the heroine of his infamous novel *Ann Veronica*, which takes up more fully the themes of free love and women's rights. Ann Veronica Stanley rebels against her father's authority and flees to London, where she attends university lectures in biology. Having thrown herself into the cause of women's suffrage, she is arrested and imprisoned. Then she elopes with her biology instructor, a married man, to Switzerland. This unconventional woman, however, receives a very conventional reward: She marries her lover, has children, and becomes reconciled with her father.

Having put new ideas into old literary forms with *Ann Veronica*, Wells set the direction of his writing for the rest of his life. In his later novels, ideas, argument, debate, and intellectual analysis become prominent, often at the expense of literary form. Feminist causes give way to issues of world peace in books dealing with the world wars, the one that was and the one to come. *Mr. Britling Sees It Through* is one of the best, though it is a troubling confusion of political despair and comic resignation. Touches of good humor keep the book going with scenes of absurdity, as when Mr. Britling tries to drive his car or Mr. Direck tries to understand British manners. This good humor erodes, however, under the pressure of the events of World War I. Mr. Britling's son is killed, his children's German tutor also is killed, and his private secretary is terribly wounded. The war nearly destroys Mr. Britling, but he sees it through, clinging to a religious hope of divine struggle through human suffering. He commits himself to the cause of world peace, but in the course of writing a letter to the German parents of his children's tutor, he gradually gives way to outrage against Germany and finally collapses in grief. The novel ends when Mr. Britling gets up from his writing to look out his window at the sunrise.

Such an ending hints of an uncertainty in Wells's own commitment to hope. His novels analyze the dead end of civilization and call for redirection through peaceful applications of scientific discoveries. Wells's bitterness at the barbarism of World War I emerges again in *Mr. Blettsworthy on Rampole Island*, whose hero, driven by an unhappy love affair and a failing business, travels to forget. This is one of Wells's most interesting later works, combining anthropology and psychology with experimentation in form. Mr. Blettsworthy's experience with cannibals on Rampole Island may be a fantasy of his madness or an insight into reality, but his experience on the battlefield of World War I is a plunge into an all-too-real madness. Blettsworthy's romantic life of optimism finally yields to a cynical discontent with reality. His perspective is not, however, Wells's final word, since Blettsworthy's business partner, Lyulph Graves, speaks at the end for a philosophy of "creative stoicism," like the attitude that is assumed by Mr. Britling and, perhaps, by Wells himself. Certainly there were differing points of view in Wells's imagination. These differences may express intellectual confusion, but they gave substance to his fiction and saved it from succumbing utterly to his tendency to preach.

The Autocracy of Mr. Parham

The opposition of Blettsworthy and Graves is repeated in the relationship of Mr. Parham with Sir Bussy Woodcock in *The Autocracy of Mr. Parham*, which envisions a time when humankind might destroy itself through another barbarous world war. Mr. Parham voices the Fascist call (by Benito Mussolini) to traditional discipline and order as a way to prevent self-destruction; Sir Bussy expresses suspicion of dictatorship, social discipline, and intellectual utopias. Wells employs an entertaining device for exposing the differences between his protagonists: He brings them into a fantasy of the future as the result of a séance.

Possessed by a Nietzschean force calling itself the "Master Spirit," Mr. Parham's ego is loosed upon the world as the British dictator Lord Paramount. He goes to war with the United States and Germany, aiming for Russia, but he cannot command the obedience of Sir Bussy, who refuses to use a powerful new gas to destroy the opposition. After the séance, Mr. Parham discovers that Sir Bussy has had a dream very much like his own fantasy. Wells's use of comic irony is very strong in the conclusion, as Mr. Parham is deflated by Sir Bussy's plans to preach peace through the very means by which Mr. Parham had hoped to reach the world himself: journalism. Mr. Parham is a smug intellectual who knows where the world ought to go, if it would only follow his instructions; Sir Bussy is a muddled businessman, limited by the contingencies of immediate events and satisfied with the disorganized vitality that distresses Mr. Parham. This difference between creative capitalism and intellectual autocracy is imaged as a difference in personalities caught in a play of life's ironies.

Wells's scientific romances display an optimistic hope for a future made better by scientific discoveries, countered by the pessimistic doubt that humankind could make the necessary choices for social and political progress. Wells shows sympathy and scorn for the stunted characters of his middle novels, for Kipps, George Ponderevo, and Mr. Polly; he exposes their inadequacies, largely as products of a narrow, stultifying environment, but he also rescues them in life-affirming conclusions. Finally, between the great wars, H. G. Wells, like his Mr. Britling, "saw it through," exercised the "creative stoicism" of Lyulph Graves, and occasionally managed to rise above his pamphleteering style to produce entertaining novels of lives muddled by uncertainty, conflict, and contradiction.

Richard D. McGhee

Other major works

short fiction: *The Stolen Bacillus, and Other Incidents*, 1895; *The Plattner Story, and Others*, 1897; *Thirty*

Strange Stories, 1897; *Tales of Space and Time*, 1899; *The Vacant Country*, 1899; *Twelve Stories and a Dream*, 1903; *The Country of the Blind, and Other Stories*, 1911; *A Door in the Wall, and Other Stories*, 1911; *The Short Stories of H. G. Wells*, 1927 (also known as *The Complete Stories of H. G. Wells*, 1966); *The Favorite Short Stories of H. G. Wells*, 1937 (also known as *The Famous Short Stories of H. G. Wells*, 1937).

NONFICTION: *Honours Physiography*, 1893 (with Sir Richard A. Gregory); *Text-Book of Biology*, 1893 (2 volumes); *Certain Personal Matters*, 1897; *A Text-Book of Zoology*, 1898 (with A. M. Davis); *Anticipations of the Reaction of Mechanical and Scientific Progress upon Human Life and Thought*, 1902 (also known as *Anticipations*); *The Discovery of the Future*, 1902; *Mankind in the Making*, 1903; *A Modern Utopia*, 1905; *The Future in America: A Search After Realities*, 1906; *Socialism and the Family*, 1906; *This Misery of Boots*, 1907; *First and Last Things: A Confession of Faith and Rule of Life*, 1908; *New Worlds for Old*, 1908; *The Great State: Essays in Construction*, 1912 (also known as *Socialism and the Great State*); *An Englishman Looks at the World: Being a Series of Unrestrained Remarks upon Contemporary Matters*, 1914 (also known as *Social Forces in England and America*); *The War That Will End War*, 1914; *God, the Invisible King*, 1917; *The Outline of History: Being a Plain History of Life and Mankind*, 1920; *Russia in the Shadows*, 1920; *The Salvaging of Civilization*, 1921; *A Short History of the World*, 1922; *Socialism and the Scientific Motive*, 1923; *The Open Conspiracy: Blue Prints for a World Revolution*, 1928; *Imperialism and the Open Conspiracy*, 1929; *The Science of Life: A Summary of Contemporary Knowledge About Life and Its Possibilities*, 1929-1930 (with Julian S. Huxley and G. P. Wells); *The Way to World Peace*, 1930; *What Are We to Do with Our Lives?*, 1931 (revised edition of *The Open Conspiracy*); *The Work, Wealth, and Happiness of Mankind*, 1931 (2 volumes); *After Democracy: Addresses and Papers on the Present World Situation*, 1932; *Evolution: Fact and Theory*, 1932 (with Huxley and G. P. Wells); *Experiment in Autobiography: Discoveries and Conclusions of a Very Ordinary Brain Since 1866*, 1934 (2 volumes); *The New America: The New World*, 1935; *The Anatomy of Frustration: A Modern Synthesis*, 1936; *World Brain*, 1938; *The Fate of Homo Sapiens: An Unemotional Statement of the Things That Are Happening to Him Now and of the Immediate Possibilities Confronting Him*, 1939; *The Common Sense of War and Peace: World Revolution or War Unending?*, 1940; *The New World Order: Whether It Is Obtainable, How It Can Be Attained, and What Sort of World a World at Peace Will Have to Be*, 1940; *The Conquest of Time*, 1942; *Phoenix: A Summary of the Inescapable Conditions of World Reorganization*, 1942; *Science and the World Mind*, 1942; *Crux Ansata: An Indictment of the Roman Catholic Church*, 1943; *'42 to '44: A Contemporary Memoir upon Human Behaviour During the Crisis of the World Revolution*, 1944; *Mind at the End of Its Tether*, 1945.

CHILDREN'S LITERATURE: *The Adventures of Tommy*, 1929.

BIBLIOGRAPHY

Batchelor, John. *H. G. Wells*. New York: Cambridge University Press, 1985. Important work, intended as an introduction to Wells as both writer and thinker, examines the entire body of his writings. Includes bibliography and index.

Bergonzi, Bernard. *The Early H. G. Wells: A Study of the Scientific Romances*. Toronto, Ont.: University of Toronto Press, 1961. Classic study is still among the most knowledgeable accounts available of Wells's early fantasies. Focuses on the remarkable affinity of the content of these novels and short stories with the search for new worlds and behavior that characterized the period around the beginning of the twentieth century.

Coren, Michael. *The Invisible Man: The Life and Liberties of H. G. Wells*. London: Bloomsbury, 1992. Biography contradicts other authors' flattering portraits of Wells. Argues that Wells was often on the "wrong side" of literary and political debates, as evidenced by his anti-Semitic comments, belief in racial eugenics, and advocacy of concentration camps.

Costa, Richard Hauer. *H. G. Wells*. Rev. ed. Boston: Twayne, 1985. Provides a sympathetic survey of Wells's career and influence, with an emphasis on the major novels in the context of literary traditions before and after Wells. Includes a chronology, a review of trends in Wells criticism, notes, an annotated bibliography, and an index.

Hammond, J. R. *An H. G. Wells Chronology*. New York: St. Martin's Press, 1999. Presents detailed information on the events of Wells's life and his literary works. Includes bibliographical references and index.

_______. *An H. G. Wells Companion*. New York: Barnes & Noble Books, 1979. An indispensable tool for the Wells scholar. Part 1 describes Wells's background and his literary reputation, part 2 is an alphabetical listing and annotation of every title Wells published, part 3 provides succinct discussions of his short stories, part 4 contains a brief discussion of his book-length romances, part 5 addresses individual novels, and part 6 is a key to characters and locations. Includes an appendix on film versions of Wells's fiction and a bibliography.

_______. *A Preface to H. G. Wells*. New York: Longman, 2001. Concise volume presents an overview of Wells's work as well as biographical information; critical commentary on Wells's fiction, particularly *The Time Machine* and *Tono-Bungay*; and a discussion of his literary reputation.

Haynes, Roslynn D. *H. G. Wells, Discoverer of the Future: The Influence of Science on His Thought*. London: Macmillan, 1980. Presents a thorough discussion of the influence of science on Wells's fiction and sociological tracts. Shows how science helped Wells to achieve an analytical perspective on the problems of his time, from art to philosophy. Includes bibliography and index.

Huntington, John, ed. *Critical Essays on H. G. Wells*. Boston: G. K. Hall, 1991. Collection of essays includes contributions that address Wells's major writings, including *Tono-Bungay* and *The History of Mr. Polly*, as well as discussions of his science fiction and his treatments of social change, utopia, and women.

MacKenzie, Norman, and Jeanne MacKenzie. *The Life of H. G. Wells: The Time Traveller*. Rev. ed. London: Hogarth, 1987. Excellent, comprehensive work is one of the most detailed scholarly biographies of Wells available.

Rinkel, Gene K., and Margaret E. Rinkel. *The Picshuas of H. G. Wells: A Burlesque Diary*. Urbana: University of Illinois Press, 2006. "Picshuas" is the term Wells used for the sketches and cartoons he drew for his second wife, Jane. The sketches reproduced in this book convey the dynamics of their relationship and provide readers with fascinating insights into Wells's psyche and personal life. This work serves as an excellent addition to Wells biographies and as a complement to his own writing.

Wagar, W. Warren. *H. G. Wells: Traversing Time*. Middletown, Conn.: Wesleyan University Press, 2004. Analyzes all of Wells's work, focusing on the author's preoccupation with the unfolding of public time and the history and future of humankind. Demonstrates how Wells's writings remain relevant in the twenty-first century.

EUDORA WELTY

Born: Jackson, Mississippi; April 13, 1909
Died: Jackson, Mississippi; July 23, 2001
Also known as: Eudora Alice Welty

Principal long fiction

The Robber Bridegroom, 1942
Delta Wedding, 1946
The Ponder Heart, 1954
Losing Battles, 1970
The Optimist's Daughter, 1972

Other literary forms

In spite of her success and acclaim as a novelist, Eudora Welty always regarded herself as essentially a writer of short stories. In an interview that appeared in the fall, 1972, issue of *The Paris Review*, she said, "I'm a short-story writer who writes novels the hard way, and by accident." In 1980, all of her previously collected short fiction and two uncollected stories were published in one volume, *The Collected Stories of Eudora Welty*. Another new collection, *Moon Lake, and Other Stories*, was published in the same year, and *Retreat* was released in 1981. Prior to that, some had appeared in *Short Stories* (1950) and in *Selected Stories of Eudora Welty* (1954). Other early short-story collections are *A Curtain of Green, and Other Stories* (1941); *The Wide Net, and Other Stories* (1943); *The Golden Apples* (1949), regarded by some as a loosely structured novel but considered by Welty to be a group of interconnected stories; and *The Bride of the Innisfallen, and Other Stories* (1955). Welty also published numerous essays and reviews, some of which were collected in *The Eye of the Story: Selected Essays and Reviews* (1978). In addition, she published a book for children, *The Shoe Bird* (1964), and books of her own photographs, *One Time, One Place: Mississippi in the Depression, a Snapshot Album* (1971) and *Eudora Welty: Photographs* (1989). A memoir, *One Writer's Beginnings*, appeared in 1984.

Achievements

Although it was not until she wrote *Losing Battles* and *The Optimist's Daughter* that Eudora Welty's name began to appear on the best-seller lists, her work had long been recognized and appreciated by discerning readers. In five decades of writing and publishing, she received nearly every major award for fiction offered in the United States. Among them are the prestigious William Dean Howells Medal of the American Academy of Arts and Letters for the most distinguished work of American fiction for the years 1950 through 1955, the National Institute of Arts and Letters Gold Medal for the Novel in 1972, the Pulitzer Prize for fiction in 1973, and the National Medal for Literature at the American Book Awards ceremony in 1980. In addition, she was awarded several honorary doctorates, Guggenheim fellowships, special professorships, and membership in the National Institute of Arts and Letters.

Uninterested in either fame or fortune, Welty simply wanted the opportunity to write and the assurance that there are readers who enjoy her work. She repeatedly expressed gratitude to such writers and editors as Robert Penn Warren, Cleanth Brooks, Albert Erskine, Ford Madox Ford, and Katherine Anne Porter, who were among the first persons of influence to recognize her ability and to promote interest in her early stories. Warren, Brooks, and Erskine accepted some of her first stories for the *Southern Review* and thus opened the door for subsequent publication in such magazines as *The Atlantic Monthly*, *Harper's Bazaar*, and *The New Yorker*. This exposure to a national audience also facilitated the publication of her first volume of stories.

Biography

Eudora Alice Welty was born in Jackson, Mississippi, on April 13, 1909. She would spend most of her life in Jackson. She was the only daughter of Christian Webb Welty and Mary Chestina Andrews Welty; she had two younger brothers. Soon after their marriage in 1904, Welty's parents moved to Jackson. Her father, who came from Ohio, where his father owned a farm, was president of the well-established Lamar Life Insurance Company. Her mother, a West Virginian, was descended from pre-Revolutionary War Virginia stock, engendered by country preachers, teachers, and lawyers. Welty, who claimed that she would feel "shy, and discouraged at the very thought" of a biography about her, felt that a "private life should be kept private." Still, though she insisted that it is the writer's work, not his or her life, that is important, she did finally write a memoir of her family history and her early years, *One Writer's Beginnings*, which was published in 1984 and received positive critical comment.

Perhaps one reason she suggested that her own biography would not "particularly interest anybody" is that she lived for the most part in the mainstream of American society. As Porter aptly observes in her introduction to *A Curtain of Green*, Welty was not the "spiritual and intellectual exile" that typifies the modern artist. She attended Central High School in Jackson, then was at Mississippi State College for Women, in Columbus, for two years before transferring to the University of Wisconsin in 1927. After graduating with a bachelor of arts degree in English in 1929, she enrolled in the School of Business at Columbia University, where she studied advertising for one year. By then, the United States was in the throes of the Depression, and she returned to Jackson to seek work.

During the next several years, Welty held a variety of jobs in advertising, radio scriptwriting, and part-time newspaper work. She also began writing stories. Possibly the most important of those early jobs was the position of junior publicity agent with the U.S. Works Progress Administration (WPA) from 1933 to 1936. In this position, Welty was required to travel extensively through Mississippi doing newspaper stories on various WPA projects. Her work involved taking photographs, talking with a great variety of people, and, perhaps most important, listening to them. As Welty herself confessed, she had a "good ear" and a visual imagination, qualities that enabled her to hear and observe things and people during those three years that she would use in her fiction throughout her life.

A number of the photographs she took while on her WPA assignment were displayed for one month in the gallery of a small camera shop in New York. Later, some of the photos appeared in her published collection of photographs *One Time, One Place*. Only after several years of discouraging rejection slips did Welty finally publish a story, "Death of a Traveling Salesman," in a small magazine called *Manuscript* in 1936. Soon after that, her talent was discovered by Robert Penn Warren, Albert Erskine, and Cleanth Brooks. Then, John Woodburn of Doubleday, Doran became interested in her work, and with his support, her first collection of short stories, *A Curtain of Green, and Other Stories*, was published in 1941. The next year, her first novel, *The Robber Bridegroom*, appeared. Two of her books have been successfully adapted for the stage, *The Ponder Heart* as a New York stage play in 1956 and *The Robber Bridegroom* as a Broadway musical in 1974.

Humane, thoughtful, and generous, Welty modestly accepted the many honors that came to her. Scarcely a year would pass after 1940 in which she would not receive a major award of some kind. She also gave abundantly of her time to schoolchildren, scholars, interviewers, and aspiring writers. She was active in community causes in Jackson, gave scores of lectures and readings, assisted numerous charities, and even provided recipes for cookbooks.

Welty asserted in a famous article, "Place in Fiction," in *South Atlantic Quarterly* (1956), that a deep sense of place is vital to a writer's development. She herself spent her entire adult life in the neo-Tudor house her father built in 1926 across the street from the campus of Belhaven College in Jackson. In fact, as a young woman she would listen, through the open window of her bedroom, to the melodious sounds emanating from the music building on the Belhaven campus. Music, as well as the visual arts, became an important motif in her fiction. Welty said that aspects of two women characters in her fiction most greatly illustrate qualities of her own life—the high regard for art held by Miss Eckhart, the piano teacher in "June Recital" (in *Golden Apples*), and the great concern of Laurel McKelva Hand (*The Optimist's Daughter*) with her family's past. However, Laurel, unlike Miss Eckhart, is able to deal with her conflicts and achieves "a separate peace."

Eudora Welty. (Richard O. Moore)

During the years of severe unrest over civil rights issues, Welty's critics attacked her for not actively taking up that cause in her fiction. She answered those critics eloquently in a 1965 *Atlantic Monthly* essay titled "Must the Novelist Crusade?" However, in *The New Yorker* the next year, Welty published a short story, "Where Is the Voice Coming From?," attacking the ugly racism of the South that resulted in the murder of a black civil rights leader.

In her introduction to *The Collected Stories of Eudora Welty*, Welty expresses characteristic gratitude for the help and encouragement she received during her career. In her memoir she speaks of her good fortune in being reared in a family that encouraged the reading of books. She had a particular love for myths, fairy tales, and legends, and she believed it her good fortune to have grown up in a region where, as she said, people love talking and delight in a good yarn. Even though she was teased as a child for having a "Yankee" father, her work is deeply rooted, like its creator, in the South as a place. Still, neither she nor her fiction could be called "regional" in any narrow sense of the term. In fact, she balked at the regionalist title. Her work, for all its down-home southern flavor, attests the universality of her vision and the capacity of her art to elude easy labels. Her subject is not the South, but humanity.

ANALYSIS

Paramount in Eudora Welty's work is the sense of what "community," or group membership, means in the South and how it is expressed through manners, attitudes, and dialogue. Clearly, it provides a special way of seeing and responding. In Welty's published essays and interviews, certain concerns keep surfacing—the relationship between time and place and the artistic endeavor, the importance of human relationships in a work of fiction, the necessity for the artist to be grounded in real life and yet be aware of life's "mystery," the value of the imagination, and the function of memory. These concerns find expression in her work principally in the tension between what is actual, what is seen and heard in a specific time and place, and what is felt or known intuitively. Welty uses the sometimes conflicting demands of the community and the self, the surface life and the interior life, to describe this tension in her novels. On one hand is the need for community and order; on the other is the need for the separate individual life, which often works against community and order.

Typically, a Welty novel swings between overt action, including dialogue, and individual contemplation. This is especially evident in *Delta Wedding*, where Welty almost rhythmically alternates dialogue and action with the inner musings of her principal female characters. In *The Optimist's Daughter*, only Laurel Hand's thoughts are set against the exterior action, but it becomes apparent that her father, as he lies unmoving in his hospital bed, is silently contemplating the mystery of life and human relationships for perhaps the first time in his life. Her mother, too, near the end of her life, had begun speaking out the painful things she must have harbored for many years in her dark soul. Even Edna Earle Ponder in *The Ponder Heart* seems to talk incessantly to keep the inner life from raising itself into consciousness. In *Losing Battles*, where Welty says she consciously tried to tell everything through speech and action—she had been accused of obscurantism in previous works—the pattern still emerges. Instead of swinging between action and cerebration, however, this novel swings between action and description. Still, the effect is surprisingly similar, though the pages of action and dialogue far outnumber the pages of description and the transitions between the two modes of narration are very abrupt. Even so, the young schoolteacher who chooses love and marriage against her mentor's advice slips occasionally into Welty's meditative mode. The alternation of thought and action is also the basic structural pattern of the stories in *The Golden Apples*.

Thus, in Welty's novels, external order is established through speech and action that sustain community, either the social or family group. In fact, the novels are often structured around community rituals that reinforce the group entity against outside intrusions and shore up its defenses against its most insidious foe, the impulse to separateness in its individual members. *Delta Wedding* is set entirely in the framework of one of these community-perpetuating rituals. For the moment, the wedding is everything, and members of the group pay it homage by gathering, giving gifts, feasting, and burying their individual lives in its demands. *Losing Battles* is also framed by a community ritual, the family reunion. The threat from individual outsiders is felt constantly, and the family takes sometimes extreme measures to ward off influences that might undermine its solidarity.

There are at least two rituals that provide structure for *The Ponder Heart*, the funeral and the courtroom trial. The first of these is conducted in enemy territory, outside the acceptable group domain; the second is conducted in home territory, and acquittal for the accused member of the group is a foregone conclusion. A funeral is also the major external event of *The Optimist's Daughter* and becomes the battleground in a contest for supremacy between two opposing groups or communities. Several of the stories or chapters in *The Golden Apples* are also structured around community rituals, including the June piano recital, the girls' summer camp, and the funeral.

In addition to these large, highly structured observances, there are the multitude of unwritten laws that govern the group. Welty's community members attach great importance to certain objects and practices: a treasured lamp given to the bride, a handcrafted breadboard made for a mother-in-law, the establishment of family pedigrees, the selection of one male member of the community for special reverence and heroic expectation, the protection of the past from intrusion or reassessment, and, perhaps most important of all, the telling of stories as an attestation of the vitality and endurance of the group.

Underlying all of this attention to ritual and group expectation, however, is the unspoken acknowledgment that much of it is a game the participants have agreed to play, for their own sake and for the sake of the community. Some of the participants may be fooled, but many are not. Aware but fearful, they go through the motions of fulfilling community requirements in an effort to hold back the dark, to avoid facing the mystery, to keep their individual selves from emerging and crying for existence. They sense themselves to be at what Welty called "the jumping off place" and are afraid to make the leap in the dark. They agree to pretend to be fooled. They tell stories instead of rehearsing their fears and uncertainties. The bolder ones defy the group and either leave it or live on its periphery. In every book, there are moments when a character confronts or consciously evades the dark underside of human personality and experience, and memory becomes a device for dealing with the effects of that confrontation or for evading it.

Paradoxically, storytelling, an important ritual for securing the past and bolstering community against passion, disorder, the intimations of mystery, and the erosive effects of individual impulses and yearnings, assists in the breakdown of the very group it was intended to support. The risk of indulging in rituals is that they sometimes set people to thinking and reevaluating their own individual lives and the lives of others close to them. The ritual is performed by the group, but it may stir the solitary inner being to life and to the kind of probing contemplation that jeopardizes the group's authority. Such a countereffect may be triggered by the storytelling ritual even though that ritual is meant to seal up the past for ready reference whenever the group needs reinforcement. Because storytelling relies on memory, it can become an exercise of the individual imagination. It tends to lapse, as one commentator observes, "into the memory of a memory" and thus shifts sides from the group's activities into the realm of mystery. The community's habit of setting up straw men for heroes can similarly erode community solidarity because it too relies on imagination and memory. It glorifies the individual rather than the group spirit.

As Welty presents this conflict, then, between the self and the group, and between the intuitive and the actual, she writes into her work a sense of foreboding. The community, especially the traditional southern community, is doomed. It cannot forever maintain itself on the old terms, for it is dependent on the acquiescence of separate individuals who seem increasingly impervious to the efforts of the group to contain them. Welty's work also suggests that some of the things the community prizes and perpetuates are merely gestures and artifacts with little intrinsic value or meaning. When the meanings behind what a community treasures have been lost or forgotten, that community cannot long endure. In actively laboring to exclude others, the group works against its own best nature, its capacity for loving and caring. Threats to order and community may indeed come from the outside, but Welty insists that the more serious threats come from the inside, from that part of the human heart and mind that seeks to go its own way.

THE ROBBER BRIDEGROOM

Welty's first novel, *The Robber Bridegroom*, is quite unlike her others. Its most noticeable differences are its setting in a much older South, on the old Natchez Trace in the days of bandits and Native Americans, and its fairy-tale style and manner. Even with these differences, Welty establishes what becomes her basic fictional stance. She achieves tension between the actual and the imaginary by freighting this very real setting with fabulous characters and events. The legendary characters are transformed by Welty's imagination and deftly made to share the territory with figures from the Brothers Grimm. Welty indicated the double nature of her novel, or novella, when in an address to the Mississippi Historical Society she called it a "Fairy Tale of the Natchez Trace."

A favorite of William Faulkner, the book is a masterpiece, a delightful blend of legend, myth, folklore, and fairy tale that swings from rollicking surface comedy and lyrical style to painful, soul-searching explorations of the ambiguities of human experience. Although it deals with love and separateness—Warren's terms for the conflicting needs of communities and individuals in Welty's work—it does not deal with them in the same way that the later novels do. Clement Musgrove, a planter whose innocence leads him into marriage with the greedy Salome and an excursion into humanity's heart of darkness, learns what it is like to face the cold, dark nights of despair comfortless and alone. His daughter, Rosamond, is beautiful and loving, but she is also an inveterate liar who betrays her husband's trust in order to learn his "real" identity. Jamie Lockhart, who leads a double life as both bandit and gentleman, keeps his true identity hidden even from her whom he loves. Thus, like so many Welty characters, the principal actors in *The Robber Bridegroom* have interior lives that threaten the equilibrium of their exterior worlds.

In another sense, too, *The Robber Bridegroom* is closely linked with Welty's other novels. In writing the book, Welty testifies to the value of stories and the storytelling ritual that buttresses community, a theme that reappears in all of her novels. She finds common ground with her readers in this novel by spinning a yarn full of their favorite childhood fairy tales. Then, too, fairy-tale worlds, imaginative though they are, sustain surface order, for they are worlds of sure answers, of clear good and evil, of one-dimensional characters, and of predictable rewards and punishments. As such, they confirm what the community collectively believes and perpetuates. Just as imagination, intuition, and the pondering of the individual human soul jeopardize the codes a community lives by in other Welty novels, so do they undercut the basic assumptions of the fairy tale in this novel. Here, answers are sometimes permanently withheld, people are complex and unpredictable, the richest prize is found in human relationships rather than in kingdoms and gold, appearances are deceiving, and evil may lie in unexpected places. It is worthy of note that Welty began her novel-writing career with a book that delights in the fairy tale at the same time that it questions community assumptions about fairy-tale morality.

Delta Wedding

The tension between community expectations and individual yearnings and apprehensions is central to *Delta Wedding*. The narrative takes place in the Mississippi delta country, during the week of Dabney Fairchild's wedding. The Fairchild family, after whom the nearby town is named, is of the social elite and has moderate wealth, mostly in property. The wedding provides an occasion for the family to gather and exercise the rituals and traditions that bind them together and strengthen their sense of community. The wedding itself is the principal ritual, of course, with its attendant food preparation, dress making, rehearsal, and home and yard decorating. Welty's eye for manners and ear for speech are flawless as the Fairchilds deliberate over the consequences of George Fairchild's having married beneath him and Dabney's seemingly unfortunate repetition of her father's mistake. The Fairchilds still claim George, however, even though they have little use for his wife, Robbie Reid, and they will continue to embrace Dabney in spite of her choosing to marry an outsider, Troy Flavin. It is the habit of community to maintain order by defining and placing people and things in relation to itself. A person either does or does not have legitimate ties to the group.

The Fairchilds also repeat family stories in order to keep the past secure and give stability to the present. Their current favorite story is also one that makes a hero out of the male heir apparent. George's dead brother was apparently more remarkable than he, but George is the one survivor, and the family's hopes rest with him. At least a dozen times in the book, some version is told of

George's staying on the railroad track with his mentally retarded niece whose foot was caught in the rails. Instead of leaping to safety with the others, he stayed to face the oncoming train. Luckily, the engineer of the Yellow Dog was able to stop the train in time. By choosing to stay with Maureen instead of answering his wife's plea to save himself, George made a reflexive choice for honor and blood over marital obligation. Later, he again chooses family over wife when he comes for the prewedding activities instead of looking for his absent, heartbroken wife.

Running counter to the speech and actions that affirm order and community, however, is an undercurrent of threat to that order. Welty intersperses the overt actions and attitudes of the family, especially of the aunts, whose sole desire is to perpetuate the clan structure, with individual ruminations of other female characters who are part of that structure and yet somewhat peripheral to it. Ellen, who married into the Fairchilds and has never dared resist them, has moments of personal doubt that would be regarded as treasonous were they known by her aunts. Dabney also wonders, in a brief honest moment, about the homage paid to the wedding ritual for its own sake. Further, she accidentally breaks a treasured lamp, a family heirloom given her by the aunts as a wedding present. Little Laura, having lost her mother, has also lost her basic tie to the family. From her position on the edge of the Fairchild clan, she questions the community tenets that exclude her. Even George seems ready to violate community expectations by his apparent willingness to deprive two of the aunts of their home.

The novel's essential statement, then, is that the community is losing its hold. In an interview published in 1972 by the *Southern Review*, Welty is asked the question, "Is Shellmound [the home of the Fairchilds] with its way of life and its values doomed?" She replies, "Oh, yes. I think that was implicit in the novel: that this was all such a fragile, temporary thing. At least I hope it was." She adds, "Well, you're living in a very precarious world without knowing it, always." The community's position is inexorably altered in the face of individual yearning and independent action.

The Ponder Heart

There are two large community rituals in *The Ponder Heart*: the funeral of Bonnie Dee Peacock and the trial of Uncle Daniel Ponder for her murder. Such narrative matter sounds ominous enough to one unfamiliar with Welty's capacity for comedy, but to the initiated, it promises a hilarious display of southern talk and manners. Still, *The Ponder Heart* is troubled, as Welty's other novels are, by an ominous current running beneath its surface action. Like the Fairchilds of *Delta Wedding*, the Ponders have social position and wealth—perhaps greater than that of the Fairchilds. They are on the decline, however, in spite of the efforts of Edna Earle Ponder, Welty's first-person narrator, to maintain the family and its image. Symbolic of the failing family or community image that Edna Earle seeks to perpetuate and protect are two buildings that the family owns, the Beulah Hotel, run by Edna Earle, and the Ponder home a few miles out of town. In the end, both buildings are virtually empty. The family has shrunk to two members, and the future holds no promise.

The story line tells of middle-aged Uncle Daniel's marrying the young Bonnie Dee Peacock, losing her, regaining her, losing her again, reclaiming her, and then finally losing her by tickling her to death in the aftermath of an electric storm. Uncle Daniel's mental age is considerably lower than his chronological age, but he is blessed with a generous nature. He gives away everything he can get his hands on, and has to be watched continually. Not that Edna Earle cares to restrain him very much, for he is the revered scion, like George in *Delta Wedding*, without whose approbation and presence the community would totter. Her duty is to protect and sustain Daniel, and she will not even permit herself private doubts over what that duty requires. The entire novel is the report of her conversation about Uncle Daniel with a visitor who is stranded at the Beulah. Clearly, Edna Earle's talk and actions are designed to maintain order and community as she has known them all her life. She believes that if she relaxes her vigil, the structure will collapse.

The ritual of the Peacock funeral is important because it is grossly inferior to the Ponder notion of what constitutes a funeral. The Peacocks are what the Ponders (except Daniel, who in his innocence would not know the difference) would call "country"; in other words, they are regarded as comically inferior beings who have no business marrying into the Ponder family. The trial is more to Edna Earle's liking, though it is threatened by the presence of the low-bred Peacocks and a prosecuting shyster lawyer who is an outsider. Edna Earle gets caught in a lie designed to protect Daniel, but the day is saved when Daniel begins passing out greenbacks in the courtroom. The jury votes for acquittal in record time, and Daniel cheerily dispenses the whole family fortune. He discovers to his sorrow afterward, however, that people who have taken his money can no longer face him. Thus, in the end, Daniel, who wanted nothing more than company and an audience for his stories, is left lonely and friendless. Though Edna Earle tries to inject new hope through the promise of a new audience—her captive guest at the Beulah—doom is on the horizon for the Ponders even more surely than it was for the Fairchilds.

The collapse of community structure in this novel, as in *Delta Wedding*, can be laid partly to the failure of the community's rather artificial system of supports—rituals, traditions, family stories, pedigrees, and a family "hero." It must also be laid, however, to the fact that Uncle Daniel, in his innocence, breaks away and acts as an individual. He is not capable of the contemplation that undermines community in *Delta Wedding*, but neither can he be restrained to act as a member of the group instead of as himself.

Losing Battles

In *Losing Battles*, Welty partially turns the tables on what she had done with the conflict between community and self in her previous two novels and in *The Golden Apples*. Here, she shows that community, though mildly ruffled by individual needs and doubts, can prevail when it is sustained by strong individuals who are also loyal group members. Welty indicates in a *Southern Review* interview that she deliberately chose as her setting the poorest section of Mississippi during the time of the Depression, so that her characters would be shown on a bare stage with themselves as their only resource, without "props to their lives." Thus, the artificial structures built of money and status that support community in *Delta Wedding* and *The Ponder Heart* are not available to the Vaughn-Beecham-Renfro clan in *Losing Battles*. Perhaps that is one reason for their greater durability.

The story is told almost entirely through dialogue and action, interlaced with occasional lyrical descriptions of setting and even less frequent ruminations of the story's principal outsider, Gloria Renfro, the hero's wife. The action takes place entirely in one day and the following morning, with details of the past filled in through family storytelling. Jack Renfro, the young grandson who has been exalted by family hope and expectations, bears some resemblance to George Fairchild and Daniel Ponder. On him lies the chief burden of sustaining the family, of guaranteeing its survival as a unit. He returns home from the state penitentiary to the waiting family reunion that is celebrating old Granny Vaughn's birthday. He finds there not only his bride but also a baby daughter he has never seen. The family has believed, has had to believe, that things will be better once Jack has returned home. Jack himself believes it, and, as Welty indicates, the others take their faith from his. Through a series of wild, funny episodes—and more than a few tender moments—the family prevails. Welty said that in this comic novel she intended to portray the indomitability, the unquenchable spirit of human beings. Folks such as these may be losing the battles, but they are still fighting them, and that is what counts.

Welty described "the solidity of the family" as "the strongest thing in the book." She also recognized that, in a clan such as this, a character sometimes has to be him- or herself before he or she can reinforce the unity of the group. Welty said that such a "sticking together," as is seen in *Losing Battles*, "involves both a submerging and a triumph of the individual, because you can't really conceive of the whole unless you *are* an identity." The extended family of *Losing Battles* engages in rituals to maintain itself just as the Fairchild family does in *Delta Wedding*. It acknowledges milestones reached by its members, milestones such as weddings and ninetieth birthdays; it tells stories, creates a hero, and works painstakingly to establish and affirm blood relationships with any who might seek entrance into the group. All is done with the honor of the clan—or the individual as member of the clan—in mind, whether it is going to jail or rescuing a car from a cliff on Banner Top.

In spite of the prevailing unity and the optimistic conclusion to the novel's events, there are small rumblings of individual assertion against community. Gloria loves Jack, but she does not want to be a member of his family. She envisions a smaller community, made up of just her, Jack, and their baby, Lady May. The group, however, will not allow her to build a community of her own. Against her will, it tries to reconstruct a parentage for her that would make her a blood relation. The relatives perform a rather cruel ritual of pouncing on her and forcing her to eat watermelon, but she remains adamant. She also remains steadfast in her admiration for Miss Julia Mortimer, the schoolteacher who picked Gloria as her successor and who fought a losing battle all her life against the joyful ignorance of the likes of Jack's family.

Thus, there are several influences in the book that threaten, though not seriously, the sense of community. Gloria and her child, and Miss Julia, are the most obvious ones. It becomes apparent, though, in the very style of the narration, which repeatedly turns from family action and talk to brief imaginative description, that the ordering of the actual and the real according to community necessity does not entirely carry the day. There is another side to experience, the imaginative, the intuitive—a part of the individual soul that resists allegiance.

The Optimist's Daughter

In *The Optimist's Daughter*, Welty returns to a more balanced combination of action and contemplation. The book's perceiving eye is Laurel Hand, daughter of Becky and Judge McKelva. The abiding question for Laurel is why, after the death of the intelligent, sensitive Becky, the Judge married a crass, tasteless woman half his age. Laurel helplessly watches her father's still form as he silently reviews his life in a hospital room, ironically set against the backdrop of the Mardi Gras festival. She repeats her helpless watch as he lies in his coffin at Mount Salus while his wife, Wanda Fay Chisom, performs her gnashing, wailing ritual of bereavement and his old friends perform their ritual of eulogy. The Chisom family, who nod appreciatively as Fay grossly mourns, are the same breed as the Peacocks in *The Ponder Heart*, entirely out of context in the McKelva home. Laurel, however, is equally uncomfortable with her own group's rites of community preservation—telling stories about the Judge that make a hero of him, despising the intrusive outsider, urging Laurel to stay and bolster the old relationship. Laurel's husband Phil was killed in military service many years ago, and Laurel herself is working in Chicago, but the women who were bridesmaids at her wedding have kept that group intact and still refer to themselves as "the bridesmaids."

Laurel's last night at home is spent in anguish. Trapped by an invading chimney swift in rooms full of memories, she is caught hopelessly in the past. In the course of the night, she is forced to examine the protective structure she had built around her parents' marriage and her own. In doing so, she must allow memory and imagination to reinterpret the past that she had wanted to keep sealed away in the perfection of her own making, and she must relinquish her old idea of what constitutes group unity and loyalty. The Wanda Fays of the world will always claim their space, will always intrude. The secret for surviving their intrusion, Laurel discovers, is to withdraw one's protective walls so that the Fays have nothing to knock down. Laurel at last allows truth to dismantle the edifice of community as she had conceived it, and she finds, through the imagination and the heart, a new source of strength in watching the artificial construct tumble. Thus, the foreboding and pessimism arising from the impending doom of community in *Delta Wedding* and *The Ponder Heart*, diverted for a time in the paradoxical optimism of *Losing Battles*, are to some extent reversed in Laurel's final acceptance in *The Optimist's Daughter*. *The Golden Apples* had foretold such an outcome, for a number of its characters must also deal with the relationship between their individual lives and the group life.

The miracle of Welty's work is the skill with which her imagination bears on the actual and makes a reconciliation out of the conflicting demands of the community and the private life, out of that which can be perceived by the senses and that which can be known only intuitively. For Welty, the actual was mainly the realities of Mississippi life. In her work, however, the reality of Mississippi became a springboard rich with possibilities for an imagination that knew how to use time and place as doorways to the human heart.

Marilyn Arnold
Updated by Philip A. Tapley

Other major works

short fiction: *A Curtain of Green, and Other Stories*, 1941; *The Wide Net, and Other Stories*, 1943; *The Golden Apples*, 1949; *Short Stories*, 1950; *Selected Stories of Eudora Welty*, 1954; *The Bride of the Innisfallen, and Other Stories*, 1955; *The Collected Stories of*

Eudora Welty, 1980; *Moon Lake, and Other Stories*, 1980; *Retreat*, 1981.

NONFICTION: *Music from Spain*, 1948; *The Reading and Writing of Short Stories*, 1949; *Place in Fiction*, 1957; *Three Papers on Fiction*, 1962; *One Time, One Place: Mississippi in the Depression, a Snapshot Album*, 1971; *A Pageant of Birds*, 1974; *The Eye of the Story: Selected Essays and Reviews*, 1978; *Ida M'Toy*, 1979; *Miracles of Perception: The Art of Willa Cather*, 1980 (with Alfred Knopf and Yehudi Menuhin); *Conversations with Eudora Welty*, 1984 (Peggy Whitman Prenshaw, editor); *One Writer's Beginnings*, 1984; *Eudora Welty: Photographs*, 1989; *A Writer's Eye: Collected Book Reviews*, 1994 (Pearl Amelia McHaney, editor); *More Conversations with Eudora Welty*, 1996 (Prenshaw, editor); *Country Churchyards*, 2000; *On William Hollingsworth, Jr.*, 2002; *On Writing*, 2002 (includes essays originally published in *The Eye of the Story*); *On William Faulkner*, 2003; *Some Notes on River Country*, 2003.

CHILDREN'S LITERATURE: *The Shoe Bird*, 1964.

MISCELLANEOUS: *Stories, Essays, and Memoir*, 1998; *Early Escapades*, 2005 (Patti Carr Black, editor).

Bibliography

Bloom, Harold, ed. *Eudora Welty*. Updated ed. New York: Chelsea House, 2007. Collection of essays analyzing Welty's work, including discussions of her novels *Delta Wedding*, *Losing Battles*, and *The Optimist's Daughter*. Includes essays by American writer and literary critic Robert Penn Warren and British writer Elizabeth Bowen.

Champion, Laurie, ed. *The Critical Response to Eudora Welty's Fiction*. Westport, Conn.: Greenwood Press, 1994. Champion has compiled a selection of criticism dating from the first appearance of Welty's individual works of fiction through the 1990's. This book also includes an introduction, in which Champion provides an overview of Welty's writings and the criticism they received, and a bibliography.

Devlin, Albert J. *Eudora Welty's Chronicle: A Story of Mississippi Life*. Jackson: University Press of Mississippi, 1983. Devlin analyzes certain works, such as *Delta Wedding*, in great detail. He offers insightful criticism and suggests that Welty's writing contains a historical structure, spanning from the territorial era to modern times.

Evans, Elizabeth. *Eudora Welty*. New York: Frederick Ungar, 1981. This accessible survey discusses both Welty's fiction and her essays and reviews. The brief literary biography of Welty in the opening chapter is useful, examining her relationship with her publishers and editors in the early part of her long literary career.

Manning, Carol S. *With Ears Opening Like Morning Glories: Eudora Welty and the Love of Storytelling*. Westport, Conn.: Greenwood Press, 1985. An advanced book offering a critical interpretation of Welty's writing. Manning believes that the root of Welty's creativity is the southern love of storytelling. Offers a select bibliography.

Marrs, Suzanne. *Eudora Welty: A Biography*. Orlando, Fla.: Harcourt, 2005. Literary biography provides insight into Welty's life and writing and serves to refute some popular conceptions of the writer. Marrs, a friend of Welty, maintains the writer was not the perfect southern lady described by other biographers.

_______. *One Writer's Imagination: The Fiction of Eudora Welty*. Baton Rouge: Louisiana State University Press, 2002. A combination of critical analysis and memoir written by a longtime friend of Welty who is also a scholar and the archivist of Welty's papers. Discusses the effects of both close personal relationships and social and political events on Welty's imagination and writing.

Mississippi Quarterly 50 (Fall, 1997). A special issue on Welty, with essays comparing Welty to William Faulkner, Edgar Allan Poe, and Nathaniel Hawthorne; discussions of the women in Welty's stories; and a look at Welty's political thought and her treatment of race and history.

Prenshaw, Peggy Whitman, ed. *Conversations with Eudora Welty*. Jackson: University Press of Mississippi, 1984. A collection of interviews with Welty spanning the years 1942 to 1982. Welty talks frankly and revealingly with interviewers such as William F. Buckley, Jr., and Alice Walker about her fiction and her life, her methods of writing, her southern background, her love of reading, and her admiration for the works of writers such as Faulkner, Bowen, and Porter.

Thornton, Naoko Fuwa. *Strange Felicity: Eudora Welty's Subtexts on Fiction and Society*. Westport, Conn.: Praeger, 2003. An analysis of Welty's major works that uncovers her views about the social and literary roles of her fiction. Includes a bibliography and an index.

Waldron, Ann. *Eudora Welty: A Writer's Life*. New York: Doubleday, 1998. The first full-length, unauthorized biography of Welty provides a great deal of detail about Welty's life and literary career but derives commentary about Welty's work from reviews and other previous criticism.

Westling, Louise. *Sacred Groves and Ravaged Gardens: The Fiction of Eudora Welty, Carson McCullers, and Flannery O'Connor*. Athens: University of Georgia Press, 1985. Westling examines Welty's fiction, along with the work of other eminent female southern writers, as part of a tradition of southern women's writing. Provides a feminist reading of southern women's writing as myth, the issue of sexuality, and the symbolic power of place. Welty's fiction is analyzed as a feminine celebration of a matriarchal society in which women can find freedom and fulfillment outside the traditional southern social strictures.

FRANZ WERFEL

Born: Prague, Bohemia, Austro-Hungarian Empire (now in Czech Republic); September 10, 1890

Died: Beverly Hills, California; August 26, 1945

Principal long fiction

Nicht der Mörder, der Ermordete ist schuldig: Eine Novelle, 1920 (*Not the Murderer*, 1937)

Verdi: Roman der Oper, 1924 (*Verdi: A Novel of the Opera*, 1925)

Der Tod des Kleinbürgers, 1927 (novella; *The Man Who Conquered Death*, 1927; also known as *The Death of a Poor Man*, 1927)

Der Abituriententag: Die Geschichte einer Jugendschuld, 1928 (*Class Reunion*, 1929)

Barbara: Oder, Die Frömmigkeit, 1929 (*The Pure in Heart*, 1931; also known as *The Hidden Child*, 1931)

Die Geschwister von Neapel, 1931 (*The Pascarella Family*, 1932)

Kleine Verhältnisse, 1931 (novella; *Poor People*, 1937)

Die vierzig Tage des Musa Dagh, 1933 (*The Forty Days of Musa Dagh*, 1934)

Höret die Stimme, 1937 (*Hearken unto the Voice*, 1938)

Twilight of a World, 1937 (novellas)

Der veruntreute Himmel: Die Geschichte einer Magd, 1939 (*Embezzled Heaven*, 1940)

Das Lied von Bernadette, 1941 (*The Song of Bernadette*, 1942)

Stern der Ungeborenen: Ein Reiseroman, 1946 (*Star of the Unborn*, 1946)

Cella: Oder, Die Überwinder, 1954 (wr. 1937-1938; *Cella: Or, The Survivors*, 1989)

Other literary forms

In addition to the novels listed above, Franz Werfel (VEHR-fehl) authored the novellas included in the collection *Geheimnis eines Menschen* (1927; *Saverio's Secret*, 1937). Werfel's voluminous lyric work was published in a number of collections, among them the influential expressionist ones: *Der Weltfreund* (1911; friend to the world), *Wir sind* (1913; we are), *Einander* (1915; to one another), and *Der Gerichtstag* (1919; Judgment Day). In addition, Werfel wrote a number of internationally successful dramas: an adaptation of Euripides' *The Trojan Women* (415 B.C.E.) titled *Die Troerinnen des Euripides* (pb. 1915); *Spiegelmensch* (pb. 1920; mirror man), dealing with the theme of the alter ego; *Bocksgesang* (pb. 1921; *Goat Song*, 1926), a mythic drama; *Juárez und Maximilian* (pb. 1924; *Juárez and Maximilian*, 1926), a drama about the Habsburg emperor of Mexico, which became Werfel's first international success; and *Paulus unter den Juden* (pr., pb. 1926; *Paul Among the Jews*, 1928), which treats the historical moment when Christianity broke away from Judaism.

Werfel's greatest American success was *Jacobowsky und der Oberst* (1944; *Jacobowsky and the Colonel*, 1944), the story of a Polish officer and a Jew who manage to escape from advancing German soldiers in France. Most works have appeared in *Gesammelte Werke* (1948-1975, 16 volumes; collected works), edited by Adolf D. Klarmann.

Achievements

During his early career, Franz Werfel was one of the most outstanding representatives of German expressionism, giving voice to the world-embracing attitude of this literary movement. This feeling of oneness with all humankind is best exemplified by his famous verse line "My only wish is to be related to you, O Man!" His drama *Spiegelmensch* incorporated one of the most popular expressionist themes, that of the alter ego, which was to find its way into many contemporary films, such as *The Cabinet of Dr. Caligari* (1919). Today, however, Werfel is remembered primarily for his novels, which made him one of the most widely read German-speaking writers of his time.

Werfel's main achievement in his novels lies not in his language or his style, which is traditional and similar to that of other writers of the 1930's and 1940's, but rather in his insistence on the importance of people (no doubt a heritage of expressionism) and his belief in the importance of people's spiritual well-being. He is concerned about people finding their places in relation to others and to God rather than about their material welfare. Werfel fought against all materialistic, "areligious," agnostic, and nihilistic elements of his time, including science and technology, against an "age that with mockery, anger and indifference is turning away from these ultimate values of our life," as Werfel himself put it. This insistence on the validity of metaphysics was at the same time the reason for his declining popularity during the late 1950's and the 1960's, when a settling of accounts with the German Nazi past and a present of newly gained affluence became the hallmark of social-critical German literature.

Biography

Franz Werfel was born in 1890 in the city of Prague, the son of a wealthy Jewish glove manufacturer and merchant. During his high school years in Prague, he became a personal friend of Willy Haas and Max Brod, who were also to become writers. After his graduation, Werfel attended lectures on law and philosophy at the German University of Prague. His mandatory one-year military service was spent in an artillery regiment in Prague. His father's attempt to make him a merchant by sending him as an apprentice to a freight company in Hamburg failed: Werfel showed no inclination or talent for becoming a merchant. In 1911, his first book of poetry, *Der Weltfreund*, appeared, evidently influenced by Walt Whitman's *Leaves of Grass* (1855, 1856, 1860, 1867, 1871, 1876, 1881-1882, 1889, 1891-1892).

Because of the success of this collection, Werfel was able to obtain a position as an editor with the Kurt Wolff publishing company in Leipzig in the fall of 1912, where he stayed until 1914—an extremely productive time. In July of 1914, he had to follow the call to arms; during the first months of World War I, he wrote a number of antiwar poems. In 1917, he was ordered to the war press headquarters in Vienna, where a number of other authors, among them Rainer Maria Rilke, Hugo von Hofmannsthal, Robert Musil, Peter Altenberg, and Franz Blei, were able to survive. During this time, he met Alma Mahler—the widow of composer Gustav Mahler, then the wife of the architect Walter Gropius. During the revolutionary turmoil at the end of the war, Werfel participated in meetings and rallies of the leftist Red Guards, which had been founded by young authors, an activity that he later regretted.

The years from 1918 to 1938 Werfel spent in and around Vienna, interrupted only by a number of extended trips. In 1925, for example, he and Alma took a long trip to the Middle East that inspired Werfel to write the drama *Paul Among the Jews*. Conversations with the dramatist Hermann Sudermann at the Italian Riviera, who told him about the hardships of his youth, induced him to write the novel *Class Reunion*. During a visit to Paris in the spring of 1928, Werfel conceived the idea of writing the novel *The Pure in Heart*. In July, 1929, Werfel and Alma were married. On a second trip to the Middle East in 1929, he was so overcome by the plight of the half-starved Armenian refugee children in Damascus that he decided to write a novel on the persecution of the Armenian people by the Turks, *The Forty Days of Musa Dagh*. The story of *The Pascarella Family* had its origin in a long conversation Alma had with an Italian woman in a hotel in Santa Margherita, Italy. The idea for *Hearken unto the Voice* evolved when, in 1936, Werfel was restlessly pacing the streets of Locarno; looking for new material, he bought himself a Bible and by chance began reading the book of Jeremiah.

During March, 1938, when Adolf Hitler annexed Austria in the Anschluss, Werfel was in Italy. He did not return to Austria but instead met Alma in Milan, from where they traveled to Zurich. Shortly thereafter, their exile led them to Paris. Apart from essays for newspapers and magazines, Werfel was then working on the novel *Embezzled Heaven*, which appeared in 1939, issued by the émigré publishing company Bermann-Fischer in Stockholm. After suffering a heart attack, Werfel moved to Sanary-sur-Mer, a French fishing village where a number of other prominent German exile writers were living, including Lion Feuchtwanger, Robert Neumann, Friedrich Wolff, and Arnold Zweig.

Franz Werfel. (Library of Congress)

After Belgium capitulated on May 28, 1940, Alma and Werfel went to Marseilles and from there to Lourdes, where Werfel vowed to write a book on Saint Bernadette if he should succeed in reaching the United States. Finally, the Werfels managed to get to Portugal and from there to the United States, where they arrived on October 13, 1940; a home that friends had rented was waiting for them in Los Angeles. Werfel immediately started working on *The Song of Bernadette*—which, against his expectations, became his greatest success as a novelist. His drama *Jacobowsky and the Colonel*, which first appeared in English translation, was equally successful in the United States. Werfel was able to complete the utopian novel *Star of the Unborn* ten days before his death on August 26, 1945, at his home in Beverly Hills, California.

Analysis

Although it is impossible to label the entire work of Franz Werfel with the name of one conventional literary movement, his early work (before 1924) clearly shows all the characteristics of expressionism. The style of the work of his middle period (1925-1938) is similar to that of other neorealistic writers of the time. His novels written during his exile show an increased interest in strictly Christian-Catholic themes, similar to the work of Catholic authors such as Stefan Andres, Gertrud von Le Fort, and Elisabeth Langgässer. In his late work *Star of the Unborn*, the mythic element becomes stronger, paralleling other works of the time, such as Thomas Mann's trilogy *Joseph and His Brothers* (1933-1943) or Hermann Hesse's utopian *Magister Ludi* (1943; also known as *The Glass Bead Game*).

A number of themes characterize Werfel's work in particular and, in combination, set it apart from the works of his contemporaries. The father-son conflict, typical of the expressionist period, not only is the hallmark of the work of the early Werfel but also permeates even some of the works of his middle period, such as *The Pure in Heart* and *The Forty Days of Musa Dagh*. The same applies to the theme of Judgment Day, which is not only the main theme of the expressionist Werfel but also part of many of his works in the form of forensic self-justifications and the scrutinizing of one's conscience. Not only *Not the Murderer* but also *Class Reunion* and *Spiegelmensch* are prime examples. Finally, in *Star of the Unborn*, Judgment Day takes place without the use of fictional mediating characters. Many of Werfel's works contain a strong musical element that encompasses their language and structure. The novel *Verdi*, with its musical theme and structure, is the best example. Another structuring device found in many of Werfel's works is a clearly defined polarity between protagonist and antagonist.

Although Werfel, like Franz Kafka, was not convinced of the value of psychoanalysis, his works lend themselves very well to psychoanalytical interpretation, because people's motivations and their consciences are at the center of Werfel's concerns. Indeed, Werfel was a profoundly religious writer. Under the childhood influence of his Czech nursemaid, he was exposed to Catholicism early in his life. He did accept Christianity, but he was never baptized. Christian religion pervades his writings, from an early essay, *Die christliche Sendung: Ein offener Brief an Kurt Hiller* (1917; the Christian mission: an open letter to Kurt Hiller), to *Star of the Unborn*. Using Christianity and a concern about people as a point of departure, Werfel is against all modern ideologies, against all "-isms" (communism, Marxism, national socialism, militarism, materialism), against technology and all attempts to make people subservient to institutions. In all of his works, humankind is at the center—human conscience, human relationships to other people and to God.

NOT THE MURDERER

The most typically expressionist of Werfel's early prose works is *Not the Murderer*, which, in the German subtitle, Werfel calls a novella. The work nevertheless has all the earmarks of a short novel. Consequently, critics have either simply called it Werfel's first novel (Annemarie von Puttkamer) or his first major book of prose (Lore B. Foltin, Werner Braselmann). The book is a first-person narrative.

The fictional, supposedly autobiographical narrator is Karl Duschek, the son of an Austrian officer, who first tells about his difficult childhood. His father has sent him to a military academy with only one goal in mind: to make him an officer. Whereas the father manages to advance to the rank of general, the son becomes a lieutenant who excels in his unmilitary attitude and behavior. He finally joins a group of anarchists who plan to assassinate the Russian czar. After having been arrested during a raid, Karl is brought before his father, who humiliates him in front of other officers by hitting him in the face with his riding whip. In the evening, Karl returns and threatens his father with a dumbbell, chasing the old man around the table. When the father surrenders, Karl does not kill him. After his imprisonment for resisting arrest, Karl immigrates to America. Before he leaves, he returns to an amusement park that he had once visited with his father and learns that the son of an amusement-stand owner had been arrested for killing his father. He remembers that it was here that he himself had thrown a ball into his own father's face, and he realizes that he had meant to hurt him. He sends a letter to the public prosecutor pointing out the general, classical nature of the case before him.

The title of the book goes back to an old Albanian proverb. Werfel got the idea for the plot from an actual killing that took place in the Viennese Prater amusement park, which had prompted him to write a letter to the public prosecutor. The letter contained in the book is a slightly adapted version of the original. The main theme is one of the most popular themes of German expressionism, the father-son conflict, which was treated in plays such as Walter Hasenclever's *Der Sohn* (1914; the son).

In Foltin's interpretation, Werfel sees the father problem as the basic problem of state, society, and military—the basic problem of any kind of authority. He has the speaker of the anarchists explain it to Karl as underlying religion (God as the father of people), the state (the king or president as the father of the citizens), the court (judges and police supervisors as the fathers of those whom human society calls criminals), the army (the officer is the father of the soldiers), and industry (the entrepreneur is the workers' father). *Patria potestas*, authority, is unnatural, is the negative principle as such. Werfel takes these thoughts up again in a letter to the public prosecutor in which he states that every father is Laius, the sire of Oedipus, thus suggesting an interpretation in Freudian terms. Independent of the social level, the guilt of the sons necessarily presupposes the guilt of the fathers. In his letter, Duschek/Werfel not only examines his own conscience but also indicts the generation of the fathers for defending its authority and its inability to abdicate control. He sees the guilt of the generation of the sons who fight their fathers because they are the fathers. Werfel does not support the anarchists' fight—he was against the kind of political activism that many expressionists advocated—but he analyzes what he conceives as being a patriarchal world order.

The father-son conflict is a theme that occupied other writers from Prague, too. There are, for example, numerous parallels between *Not the Murderer* and Kafka's works, particularly *The Sentence* (1913, 1916; also known as *The Judgment*) and *Letter to His Father* (1952, wr. 1919). Later, in *The Pure in Heart*, Werfel took up the father-son problem again; it is also one of the main themes of the novel *The Forty Days of Musa Dagh*, which deals with the gruesome persecution of the Armenian people by the Turkish government in 1915-1916.

The Forty Days of Musa Dagh

Based on a detailed study of historical source material, *The Forty Days of Musa Dagh* remains one of Werfel's best-known works. When the order for relocation reaches five Armenian villages on the Syrian coast, the majority of the inhabitants decide to resist. Five thousand of them collect food and barricade themselves on the Musa Dagh (the Mountain of Moses), which lends itself well to defense purposes. Under their leader, Gabriel Bagradian, they succeed in fighting back several assaults by Turkish troops, and in the end, the survivors are saved by warships of the Allied powers and brought to Egypt.

Only Bagradian himself stays behind (and is killed by the Turks), because for him the events have completed his life—or, rather, the process of self-finding that is central to the story. Thus, the novel is not only the heroic epic of the Armenian people but also the story of an individual, Bagradian, who has lived as a scholar in Paris for many years and has become an "abstract" man, who is theoretical and culturally refined, and who has lost his emotional contact with his people, the Armenians.

In the course of the novel, Bagradian returns to his origins, finds his identity as an Armenian, and learns to fulfill his duty as the leader of his people. He forgets about his cultured exterior refinement and becomes a practical politician, administrator, and officer who, with the help of his fellow citizens, simple farmers and artisans, manages temporarily to hold at bay the military forces of a large country. His counterpart is his French wife, Juliette, who can live only in luxury and ultimately falls prey to the advances of a Greek adventurer. In spite of his love for his son, Stephan, Bagradian fails to understand him; Stephan tries to prove himself in various deeds of daring until he is captured and murdered by the Turks.

Werfel intended to write not a historical epic, restricting himself to historical, social, or political forces and their interaction, but primarily a novel about people and their search for self-understanding. Therefore, to criticize Werfel for making the process of Bagradian's "way to himself" too important in relation to the historical events, the heroic fight of a small group of Armenians, is asking something of him that is counter to his nature and intention. *The Forty Days of Musa Dagh* is both a historical epic about the last stand of a group of Armenians against the Turks and the story of a fictional Armenian leader who returns to his true self.

Because the book contains numerous instances in which Werfel parallels the persecution of the Armenians with the persecution of the Jews, the work was received throughout the world and even in Germany as a prophetic book dealing with the fate of the Jews. Its greatest appeal, of course, was to the Armenian people, and even today the novel is a best seller in Armenian translation.

The lifelong religious struggle of Werfel, a Jew who believed in Christ, had earlier found expression in the play *Paul Among the Jews*. It had manifested itself in the naïvely pious maid, Barbara, and her intellectual counterpart, the Jew Alfred Engländer, who believed in Christ, in *The Pure in Heart*, and also in *Hearken unto the Voice*. In this novel, Jeremiah resists his calling and becomes a prophet and admonisher in his time. In this manner, Werfel met the challenge of national socialism by drawing from Jewish antiquity, just as Lion Feuchtwanger did with *Josephus* (1932) and as Thomas Mann did in the trilogy *Joseph and His Brothers*.

Embezzled Heaven

During his exile, Werfel continued writing novels with religious themes, but with a decidedly Catholic content. The first of these novels is *Embezzled Heaven*, which consists of two parts. First are the memories of the exiled writer, who now lives in Paris and remembers the family of the Argans and their generous hospitality in Grafenegg, Austria.

He remembers the seemingly happy summer of 1936, which comes to an abrupt end with the accidental death of the Argans's son. The author interprets the ensuing collapse of the family as the "revenge of the spirit of the times," which encompasses the inevitable catastrophe, the dissolution of Europe's intellectual world. The old bohemian maid of the Argans is Teta Linek, who slowly moves to the center of attention.

Teta is certain to gain eternal life because she believes she is to have the priestly mediation of her nephew, Mojmir, who has been studying theology at her expense. At the age of seventy, however, she finds out that Mojmir has swindled her out of her money so that her life plan is ruined. She embarks on a pilgrimage to Rome during which she meets the young chaplain Johannes Seydel. In confession to him, she realizes that she lacked love, that she merely wanted to buy God's grace. Although she suffers a stroke in an audience with the pope, her life is not lived in vain, because she has discovered meaning in love in her relationship with Seydel.

Interesting, too, is the intertwining of her fate with the political happenings of the time, the annexation of Austria and the narrator's exile, to which he alludes time and again. Viewed from that perspective, Teta's case becomes a model for our time, which has "embezzled heaven"; which has revolted against metaphysics by making time, work, and money more important than religion; and which has replaced metaphysics by such substitute religions as communism and national socialism. Werfel himself advances this interpretation in a conversation between the exiled author and the chaplain on one of the last pages of the book.

The Song of Bernadette

The focus of Werfel's next novel, *The Song of Bernadette*, seems, at first glance, to be totally different. Faithful to his vow, Werfel tells the story of the fourteen-year-old girl Bernadette Soubirous, who, on February 11, 1858, saw a "lady" in the cave of Massabielle near Lourdes, France, and did not change her story when questioned by secular and Church authorities. The lady calls herself "the immaculate conception." The miracle of a spring that originated in the cave after it had been announced by the lady leads to healings. Bernadette is ultimately (posthumously) canonized in 1933.

In this novel, there is no inner struggle in Bernadette, who always remains the same: a girl who believes and does not question. Thus, Werfel places emphasis on the mystery of the appearance and on the innocence of his heroine. He defends simple, unquestioning belief in a world of intellectual doubt.

The Song of Bernadette is structured according to the rosary, in five divisions of ten chapters each. Accordingly, the fiftieth chapter bears the heading "The Fiftieth Ave." Against Werfel's expectations, the novel became his greatest international success.

Star of the Unborn

Star of the Unborn, Werfel's last work, is a utopian novel. The original subtitle, *Ein Reiseroman*, means "a travelogue"; thereby, Werfel placed his novel in the tradition of Daniel Defoe, Jonathan Swift, and Dante. The novel's narrator, F. W., is summoned by means of spiritualism from the realm of the dead into the "astromental" world of California in the year 101945. He is the guest of honor at a wedding between members of two respected astromental families. He is greeted and guided by his former friend, B. H. (Willy Haas), who has learned the art of reincarnation in the monasteries of Tibet.

The astromentals have overcome all natural threats to human existence, such as sickness, poverty, and even death. They live in underground quarters and take in liquid food only. There is only one language left in the world. All work is performed in the Workers' Park, which has hills, valleys, springs, and herds of diminutive sheep and goats, whereas the landscape of the astromentals is flat. The astromental university, the Djebel, is an artificial mountain that the boys enter and do not leave before the end of their lives at the age of two hundred. Death itself has been eliminated in favor of "retrogenesis" in the winter-garden inside the earth, where two-hundred-year-old people are developed back into children, into embryos, and finally into marguerites if everything goes well. When the astromentals are defeated in a war with "the jungle" at the outskirts of the astromental world, where primitive, barbaric people live, they go to the winter-garden to avoid natural death. Only one boy refuses and accepts death, thus redeeming the astromental world by believing in something that cannot be proven. F. W. and B. H. manage to leave the winter-garden, and F. W. finally finds himself in his home in Beverly Hills.

Star of the Unborn is a highly religious novel that contains the total of Werfel's thinking and beliefs, as Hesse's *The Glass Bead Game* embodies that writer's thought. Like many other utopian novels, it includes the author's criticism of his own time by painting a picture of another world. In contrast to other utopias, however, the astromental world is by no means perfect. Rather, it constitutes the final result of the development of the human world, should the contemporary tendencies be allowed free rein and development. As the Grand Bishop points out to F. W., the nineteenth and twentieth centuries were much better than the astromental era because the latter is much more removed from God. The old civilizations accepted suffering and death, whereas the astromental one tries to avoid work, suffering, and death, thus defying the curse of the archangel. The astromentals cannot experience deep emotions, neither suffering nor true happiness. What presented itself as progress turns out to be the opposite in religious terms, an argument that is much more powerful than the regret about lack of diversity and fullness of life. F. W. realizes quickly that philosophy and metaphysics have not made any progress whatsoever. The final representatives of the astromental era characteristically are the Grand Bishop and the Jew of the Era, who are witnesses to an eternal community between Jews and Christians that, according to Werfel, was to outlast all changes of history.

Although one might criticize some parts of the book for being silly, tedious, or pointless, in many other parts Werfel shows more imagination and fantasy than in any other work. The ironic tone and the humor pervading it take away from the seriousness of the reflections and discussions, adding a touch of lightness to the whole. *Star of the Unborn* is, without a doubt, Werfel's most mature book and his legacy as a thinker.

Hans Wagener

Other major works

SHORT FICTION: *Geheimnis eines Menschen*, 1927 (*Saverio's Secret*, 1937); *Erzählungen aus zwei Welten*, 1948-1952 (part of *Gesammelte Werke*).

PLAYS: *Der Besuch aus dem Elysium*, pb. 1912; *Die Versuchung*, pb. 1913; *Die Troerinnen des Euripides*, pb. 1915 (a free adaptation of Euripides' *The Trojan Women*); *Die Mittagsgöttin*, pb. 1919; *Spiegelmensch*, pb. 1920; *Bocksgesang*, pb. 1921 (*Goat Song*, 1926); *Schweiger*, pb. 1922 (English translation, 1926); *Juárez und Maximilian*, pb. 1924 (*Juárez and Maximilian*, 1926); *Paulus unter den Juden*, pr., pb. 1926 (*Paul Among the Jews*, 1928); *Das Reich Gottes in Böhmen*, pr., pb. 1930 (*The Kingdom of God in Bohemia*, 1931); *Der Weg der Verheissung*, pb. 1935 (*The Eternal Road*, 1936); *In einer Nacht*, pr., pb. 1937; *Jacobowsky und der Oberst*, pr. 1944 (*Jacobowsky and the Colonel*, 1944).

POETRY: *Der Weltfreund*, 1911; *Wir sind*, 1913; *Einander*, 1915; *Der Gerichtstag*, 1919; *Poems*, 1945 (Edith Abercrombie Snow, translator).

NONFICTION: *Die christliche Sendung: Ein offener Brief an Kurt Hiller*, 1917.

MISCELLANEOUS: *Gesammelte Werke*, 1948-1975 (16 volumes; Adolf D. Klarmann, editor).

Bibliography

Brender, Edwige. "'Neither as a Cowboy nor as a Goldhunter, but Simply as a Refugee': Franz Werfel's Debate with His American Publishers, Translators, and Adapters." In *Exile and Otherness: New Approaches to the Experience of the Nazi Refugees*, edited by Alexander Stephan. New York: Peter Lang, 2006. A study of the lives and work of Austrian and German writers, artists, and intellectuals who fled the Nazis and settled in other countries. The chapter about Werfel discusses his life in the United States.

Everett, Susanne. *The Bride of the Wind: The Life and Times of Alma Mahler-Werfel*. New York: Viking Press, 1992. This biography of Alma Mahler-Werfel, who was married to Werfel, describes the couple's life together. Includes a bibliography and an index.

Heizer, Donna K. *Jewish-German Identity in the Orientalist Literature of Else Lasker-Schüler, Friedrich Wolf, and Franz Werfel*. Columbia, S.C.: Camden House, 1996. Heizer studies the representation of Asia in the works of Werfel and two other authors. Examines Werfel's novel *The Forty Days of Musa Dagh*, in which he uses the conflict between the Turks and Armenians as a means of exploring his German-Jewish identity. Includes a bibliography and an index.

Huber, Lothar, ed. *Franz Werfel: An Austrian Writer Reassessed*. New York: St. Martin's Press, 1989. A collection of papers presented at an international symposium on Werfel, discussing his life and works. Includes analysis of his novels *Verdi* and *The Pure in Heart*. Includes a bibliography.

Jungk, Peter Stephan. *Franz Werfel: A Life in Prague, Vienna, and Hollywood*. New York: Grove Weidenfeld, 1990. A biography of Werfel that focuses on the incidents of his life, including his marriage, his alienation from his Jewishness, and his years in exile. Includes a bibliography and indexes.

Kirby, Rachel. *The Culturally Complex Individual: Franz Werfel's Reflections on Minority Identity and Historical Depiction in "The Forty Days of Musa Dagh."* Lewisburg, Pa.: Bucknell University Press, 1999. Kirby examines the themes of identity in Werfel's works, describing his changing views on the subject. She focuses her study on Werfel's novel *The Forty Days of Musa Dagh*, discussing his treatment of identity and historical community and the reception and literary response to the book. Includes notes, a bibliography, and an index.

Michaels, Jennifer E. *Franz Werfel and the Critics*. Columbia, S.C.: Camden House, 1994. Michaels discusses the critical reaction to Werfel's works, devoting a chapter to his novels and other prose. Chronicles trends in Werfel criticism and describes the critical response to his religious and political beliefs. Includes a bibliography and an index.

Minasian, Edward. *Musa Dagh: A Chronicle of the Armenian Genocide Factor in the Subsequent Suppression, by the Intervention of the United States Government, of the Movie Based on Franz Werfel's "The Forty Days of Musa Dagh."* Nashville, Tenn. Cold Tree Press, 2007. Minasian recounts the history of Werfel's novel, describing the book's creation, the successful reception of its English translation, and Metro-Goldwyn-Mayer's (MGM) plans to produce a film adaptation. However, the Turkish government protested the planned film, and Minasian explains how the Turkish authorities, the U.S. State Department, and the Hays Office (the Hollywood censorship bureau) pressured MGM to cancel the project.

Wagener, Hans. *Understanding Franz Werfel*. Columbia: University of South Carolina Press, 1993. Chapter 4 contains a detailed study of Werfel's novels and other prose works, with each major title receiving a separate discussion. Includes notes and an annotated bibliography.

GLENWAY WESCOTT

Born: Kewaskum, Wisconsin; April 11, 1901
Died: Rosemont, New Jersey; February 22, 1987

Principal long fiction

The Apple of the Eye, 1924
The Grandmothers: A Family Portrait, 1927
The Pilgrim Hawk: A Love Story, 1940
Apartment in Athens, 1945

Other literary forms

Glenway Wescott's first published work was *The Bitterns: A Book of Twelve Poems* (1920); another volume of poetry, *Natives of Rock: XX Poems, 1921-1922* appeared in 1925. Two of his short stories were privately published in France by friends as separate books: *. . . Like a Lover* (1926) and *The Babe's Bed* (1930). A collection of stories with a long title essay, *Good-bye, Wisconsin*, was published in 1928. Other books include a variety of forms: *Fear and Trembling*, a collection of essays (1932); *Twelve Fables of Aesop* (1954); and *Images of Truth: Remembrances and Criticism* (1962). Several uncollected poems and stories appeared in literary journals, along with a number of personal and critical essays. Perhaps Wescott's most imaginative work is "The Dream of Audubon: Libretto of a Ballet in Three Scenes," in *The Best One-Act Plays of 1940* (1941), which holds the key to Wescott's extensive use of bird imagery and symbolism.

Achievements

After his beginnings as a published poet, Glenway Wescott often reviewed books of poetry and fiction. His critical pieces reveal that from the time of his earliest experiments in prose fiction, he was forming his idea of the novel and the aims of the art that it best embodied: to present images of reality and the truth of experience.

Even after his first two novels were published, critics disagreed as to whether Wescott was a novelist. The skepticism had several causes, mostly related to form. The first section of his first novel, *The Apple of the Eye*, was published separately as the story "Bad Han" in two parts in *The Dial*. Wescott then expanded it with two more parts to make a novel. *The Grandmothers*, accepted as a novel by the Harper's Prize judges, was a series of portraits of individual characters. Today, these books are recognized as formally innovative: They focus on the process of self-discovery, and they are unified by the relation of the parts to the experience of the protagonist.

The short stories in *Good-bye, Wisconsin* seemed to support the critics' judgment that Wescott was essentially a short-story writer and their further pigeonholing of him as a regional realist attacking the narrowness of culture in the Midwest and as a typical expatriate writer. Doubts about Wescott's capacities as a novelist were permanently laid to rest, however, with the triumph of *The Pilgrim Hawk*, which was hailed as a masterpiece of its genre and later reprinted in two anthologies of great short novels.

The Pilgrim Hawk, set in France, and the next novel, *Apartment in Athens*, showed that Wescott could go beyond regional materials. The latter, however, although chosen by the Book-of-the-Month Club, was not a critical success, probably because its propagandistic aims were too obvious.

Wescott spent many years in service to literature. He was president of the National Institute of Arts and Letters from 1958 to 1961. He wrote and delivered a number of introductory and presentation speeches, later published in the *Proceedings of the American Academy of Arts and Letters*. He also became a member of the National Commission for the United Nations Educational, Scientific, and Cultural Organization (UNESCO). He gave many talks and readings, appeared on radio and television, participated in symposia and writers' conferences, and served on various committees for the institute and for the Authors' Guild. He edited *The Maugham Reader* (1950) and *Short Novels of Colette* (1951), writing the introduction for the latter.

At times considered an unfashionable writer, Wescott should be read in any survey of the great decades of the American novel from 1920 to 1940. A revival of critical interest in his work is long overdue.

Biography

Glenway Wescott was born in Kewaskum, Wisconsin, on April 11, 1901, the first of six children. According to the autobiographical portrait of Alwyn Tower in *The Grandmothers*, he was a sensitive, imaginative, and solitary child. His nature was antipathetic to the physical and cultural poverty of the farm life in which he spent his boyhood. At age thirteen, because of difficulties with his father, he left home, and he lived with an uncle and others while going to high school.

In 1917, Wescott entered the University of Chicago, began writing poetry, and soon joined the poetry club. The following year, he became engaged, but he did not marry then or later; the engagement was broken in 1921. During this period, Wescott tried fiction, beginning the story "Bad Han," which became part of his first novel. Because of ill health, he withdrew from Chicago after a year and a half, thus ending his formal education. Shortly thereafter, he went to New Mexico for an extended visit with Yvor Winters, a period that he referred to as one of the happiest of his life.

In 1920, after a visit to his family, Wescott went to Chicago to stay with Monroe Wheeler, with whom he was to share his travels abroad and much of his life in the United States and to whom he dedicated his 1962 volume of essays. He traveled with Wheeler to New York City, then to England and Germany, before returning to the United States and embarking on a career of serious writing.

In 1925, Wescott moved to France, beginning eight years as an expatriate but returning yearly for a visit to his family. He used the experience of an expatriate looking back at his pioneer family in Wisconsin as the framework for *The Grandmothers*, which was written during the first year of his stay abroad. Winning the prestigious Harper's Prize, the book was a critical and popular success. With the publication of a volume of short stories the following year, Wescott's position in the forefront of talented young writers seemed assured.

During his stay abroad, Wescott spent extended periods in Germany, leading him to write the essays in *Fear and Trembling* and later, during wartime, to try to explain the German character in the novel *Apartment in Athens*. In 1933, Wescott moved back to the United States, dividing his time between New York City and the farm in New Jersey where his family had moved. He went to Europe with his brother and the latter's bride, Barbara Harrison, in 1935 and again traveled abroad in 1938, before finally settling in the United States.

The year 1940 marked a period of renewed creativity for Wescott with the appearance of his acclaimed short novel *The Pilgrim Hawk*, a ballet libretto, several lyrical essays, and, in 1945, *Apartment in Athens*, a war novel set in Greece (which Wescott had never visited). Thereafter, he produced less, leading the life of a public man of letters. Besides the distractions of that role, he suggested another reason for his diminished literary output in later life, saying, "I am an incorrigibly copious letter-writer, and doubtless have wasted time in that way."

Wescott's father, with whom he eventually became reconciled, died in 1953, and his mother, to whom he was extremely devoted, died in 1960. Wescott lived on the family farm in rural New Jersey until he died on February 22, 1987.

Analysis

When Glenway Wescott left his native Wisconsin, returned, and left again, each time it was to move farther east, first to Chicago, then New York, then Europe. It was also to plunge into the major literary currents of the day: imagism in poetry, regionalism in fiction, criticism of American culture and society by the expatriates, focus on the self as a major theme, and revolt against traditional forms and experiments with new ones. If he was typical of the young writers of the 1920's, then he was also—like F. Scott Fitzgerald, Ernest Hemingway, and William Faulkner—a distinctive voice whose contributions to this innovative period of American fiction should be studied along with those of his greater contemporaries.

The Apple of the Eye

Published when Wescott was twenty-three years old, *The Apple of the Eye* was considered an impressive, although not faultless, first novel by such reviewers as Kenneth Burke and Ruth Suckow. In content, it is a typical initiation story, following the self-discovery of the hero, Dan Strane, as he rebels against midwestern puritanism, finds an affirmative meaning in life, and departs to live it his own way. In form, the novel is more original, with its tripartite structure. Its style reveals, even this early, the author's mastery of what Ira Johnson calls the "lyric, disciplined, imagistic prose of sensibility."

Book 1 elaborates on a sort of legend that Wescott's mother once told him about an old servant. Hannah

Glenway Wescott. (Library of Congress)

Madoc, called "Bad Han," is a "secular saint" who accepts love and lives life as it comes, without the common tortures of guilt. Han's lover, Jules Bier, influenced by his father, leaves her to marry Selma Duncan, who represents puritanism, the "evasion of experience." Book 2 introduces Rosalia and tells of her love affair with Dan's new friend, Mike Byron. Mike begins Dan's initiation by explaining that while puritanism appeals to the imagination, it is unhealthy in its division of the flesh from the spirit. Dan turns away from his beloved mother and her religion, while Mike initiates in him an awareness of the pleasures of sensuality. Meanwhile, Mike's and Rosalia's affair gains momentum, then dies, and Rosalia is deserted by Mike. Maddened by sorrow and guilt, she dies in the marsh.

In book 3, Dan's uncle, Jules Bier, retells the story of Bad Han as an object lesson in what is wrong with the local religious views, which have brought Rosalia and others tragedy. Bad Han becomes a powerful symbol, leading Dan to feel he is her spiritual son. Completing his separation from the sterile, frustrating environment, he departs for college, at the same time realizing that he has been blessed by experiencing several kinds of love and has felt a "sense of awakening."

Dan Strane is the first of Wescott's several autobiographical portraits. The natural setting, the rural poverty, the roughness of farm life, the puritanism—all were elements of the author's boyhood against which he rebelled. Even some of the most intimate aspects of Dan are tied to Wescott's life: the devotion to the mother, the conflict with the father, the despair and thoughts of suicide (Wescott had attempted suicide when he was eighteen years old), the implied homosexual attachment.

Most striking for a first novel is Wescott's lyrical style, with its piling of images into central symbols with many facets. The meaning of a symbol such as the marsh changes with the season of the year and the perception of it by a character or the omniscient narrator. It appears variously fecund, barren, ominous, even sexual. Bad Han, herself a creature of the marsh, also assumes symbolic import. A natural symbolist from the beginning, Wescott grew ever more powerful in his control of this tool of meaning, reaching finally its near-perfect use in *The Pilgrim Hawk.*

Even in this first novel, bird imagery and symbolism are pervasive, with passages about bitterns, turkeys, pigeons, wild geese, and crows. Later, in his ballet libretto, "The Dream of Audubon," Wescott sums up the key to his bird symbolism: "We are all hunters; and our heart's desire, whatever it may be, is always somehow a thing of air and wilderness, flying away from us, subject to extinction in one way or another."

The Grandmothers

In addition to the search for self-knowledge, Wescott was preoccupied with the search for an organic form to fit his materials; in his second novel, *The Grandmothers*, he found one of great originality. An expatriate poet, Alwyn Tower, puts together a series of individual histories to create a family portrait. As a third-person participant narrator, looking back from the "tower" of Europe at his origins, Alwyn treats time as fluid, moving from the self-present to the self-past when as a child he heard fragments of stories from his paternal grandmother. His curiosity roused, he watched his grandparents' life, caught glimpses of their past life, and now as an adult is able imaginatively to re-create it, as he does the lives of his parents and of other relatives. The task the adult Alwyn sets himself, at his desk in a Riviera hotel, is a purposeful search for usable knowledge needed by the self, the "all" that he will "win":

> For the personages in rocking-chairs, the questionable spirits leaning over his cradle, had embodied not only the past, but the future—his own wishes and fears; and he was not to be content until an everyday light had unveiled all their faces.

Devoting himself to the acceptance of life and the creation of art, once he has exorcised their spirits, Alwyn can find meaning where they failed. His close examination of the family, and all the misguided ambition, anxiety, pride, and stubbornness of its members, remembered and imagined with compassion, will result finally in the detachment needed for the full creation of the self.

The first chapter shows Alwyn as a small boy in Wisconsin, remembered by the adult Alwyn in Europe, sensing the rich, mysterious layers of family history in his grandmother's rooms, hearing hints and half-explanations, and being tantalized by curiosity about the whole of the stories. In the second chapter he sees the Towers as making up a

> composite character, the soul of a race; something so valuable that one recognized it only as an atmosphere, a special brightness, or a peculiar quality of the temperaments and customs and fortunes of Americans; as if it were the god of place.

Despite his affinity for Europe, Alwyn loves his country and his family; in fact, he feels they are one and the same.

In the next twelve chapters, the narrator reconstructs and reflects on the lives of family members in the two preceding generations. The reader learns snatches of their stories as the boy learns them. Such suspense as there is in the essentially plotless book comes from waiting with him to get the answers: Why did his Grandmother Rose marry Henry Tower instead of his brother, Leander, who was her sweetheart before he went off to war? What happened to their brother, Hilary, who went with Leander and never came home? Why did his Aunt Flora look like "a girl of thirty" and die early? These questions and more are answered in relation to love, family, religion, and historical context, although whether the answers are actually remembered or are imagined is always a guess.

Through this one family, Wescott explores the many ways of love and how it makes the Towers its victims. Henry and Rose, the grandparents, each lose their first romantic love: Henry, when his first wife, Serena, dies; Rose, when Leander will not marry her and she has to settle for his brother. Rose marries her second choice, Henry, because she wants to escape from her own family of rough boys, and she wants "nothing in the world . . . but to be acceptable" to the Towers. Throughout the novel, events and their interpretation hinge on the family—its honor (the boys go to fight in the Civil War), its pride (the one who deserts cannot come home), its narrowness (James cannot choose a career in music), its prejudices (the spinster cannot marry a Catholic). For its members, love of family and of place are all-important and almost identical. Even though it means facing Rose, whom he jilted, Leander decides to return to Hope's Corner from California. The deserter, Evan, returns for visits, even though he knows his father will spurn him. Hope's Corner, poor as it is, symbolizes what has been the dream of the American pioneers, now changed: "The West, that point of the compass which had glittered with hope like a star, came to resemble the East—the light went out of it. . . . Every hope had a rendezvous with disappointment."

"Mother" and "home" are important themes in the novel. In its beginning, the author protagonist hears a drunken sailor on the quay below crying, "I want my mother!" While exploring memory, Alwyn discovers that, beginning with Rose and certainly including his own mother, the strong women who have married the Tower men have been their salvation, and he proclaims America a matriarchy. He finds in himself some of the characteristics of the Tower men and realizes that he will have to accommodate them somehow in his artist self.

Many kinds of love abound in these portraits, but in the conclusion, Wescott develops the theme of incest, making of it a complex metaphor for what Alwyn is doing. He looks back from the "tower" of Europe at his nineteenth year, when he spent many nights watching by the bed of his dying grandmother, Rose Tower. His other grandmother, Ursula Duff, in the confusion of age has called him by the name of her eldest son and also called him her sweetheart. He thinks of this as oracular, "a menace or a promise" that must be interpreted. In the effort, he mediates on the incest taboo, and he also recalls the tradition that the breaking of that law may sometimes create a legendary hero—or god. This idea, in turn, symbolizes his way of becoming self-created: "Memory was incest. . . . The desire to understand was, after all, desire." If the word "mother" means "that which had produced one," then it includes the wilderness, Wisconsin, the family, its "squalor, ideals, manias, regrets, sensuality, what consolations there had been." He had broken the law by going back to what had produced him, going back in imagination and going forward again: "Alwyn thought with rather unreasonable pride that he had become a man in as nearly as possible the way that men had become heroes or gods."

THE PILGRIM HAWK

In his third autobiographical novel, *The Pilgrim Hawk*, Wescott again treats the themes of the self and love, again evokes their essences through symbolism, and for the second time places the development of the story inside the consciousness of a narrator, this one with a first-person viewpoint. Here the self is not, as in *The Grandmothers*, primarily a member of a family or an evolving artist, but a practicing artist exploring the difficulties of his vocation and probing the extent of his talent as well as his own problems of love.

Geographically, there is a reversal: The narrator, Alwyn Tower, the protagonist of *The Grandmothers*, has been an expatriate in France but is now in America about ten years later, looking back at that other place and time. The historical context is the world on the verge of war; he visualizes gun emplacement in the idyllic countryside he once visited. Again, the structural framework makes possible a double layering of time. Tower remembers what happened on one May afternoon and how he speculated on the meaning of the events; in present time, he meditates and elaborates still further on those meanings.

On that day, Alwyn Tower is at the home of his friend, Alexandra Henry (who later meets and marries his brother), when the Irish Cullens arrive. From the beginning, all attention is centered on Lucy, the pilgrim hawk Madeleine Cullen carries on her leather-encased wrist. The bird, along with the lore of falconry, is fascinating to Tower. Even more so is the conundrum of the triangular relationship of the two Cullens and the hawk. Tower sees the hawk, its needs and activities, as vastly symbolic, even of certain aspects of himself.

The events of that day, presented chronologically, can be summarized briefly as following the patterns established by the hawk. The account is interspersed with the reflective analogies drawn by the narrator. He first notes Lucy's "hunger," which can be a "painful greed, sick singlemindedness"; it reminds Tower of "human hungers, mental and sentimental," for example, his own hunger to be a literary artist, which, because no one warned him that he did not have enough talent, "turned bitter, hot and nerve-racking." Then, because his work has not been going well, he thinks of her as "an image of amorous desire," which would be a "natural consolation" to the weary artist.

The hawk bates—that is, throws herself headlong off her perch on the wrist and hangs helpless, upside down. While Mrs. Cullen brings her under control and soothes her, the narrator meditates on the woman's apparent need to dominate, and the group debates the value of independence. Larry Cullen, who is tethered to his wife as firmly as Lucy is, says that such yearning for freedom is the only human characteristic of hawks.

Later in the novel, Tower hears Cullen express embarrassingly frank sexual feelings toward his wife, as well as resentment at the way Lucy, constantly on his wife's arm, interferes with his embraces while traveling. These comments about sexual desire continue the hunger imagery. Tower, also, has been thinking of his own need for love: "Old bachelor hungry bird, aging-hungry-man-bird, and how I hate desire, how I need pleasure, how I adore love, how difficult middle age must be!"

With his jealousy fully roused, Cullen goes to free Lucy, who has been left weathering in the garden. Thus he, in his own way, bates. Having observed the act, Tower quietly informs Mrs. Cullen, and she is able to recapture the bird.

Jealousy also erupts in a subtriangle: Jean, the cook, is enraged by the flirtation of his wife, Eva, with Ricketts, the Cullens's chauffeur. Disturbed by both episodes, the Cullens leave early, only to return immediately. Mrs. Cullen enters the house with the news that her husband has tried to shoot someone; whether the chauffeur—of whom he is also jealous—or himself is not clear. In other words, he has bated again. She goes to toss the gun into the pond in the garden and returns to make a final farewell. Tower and Alexandra linger on the scene, discussing what it all has meant, at the same time concluding from sounds in the garden that Jean and Eva have been reconciled.

The ridiculousness of Mrs. Cullen's appearance while she enacts this drama with Lucy still clutching her wrist makes the bird, too, seem funny to Tower; he begins to unload all the symbols he has piled on her and to see more realistically. The narrator is amused at "how often the great issues which I had taken this bird to augur come down in fact to undignified appearance, petty neurasthenic anecdote." The bird's—and Cullen's—"poor domestication" reminds him of "the absurd position of the artist in the midst of the disorders of those who honor and support him, but who can scarcely be expected to keep quiet around him for art's sake." So it goes, while brick after brick of the carefully built, towering symbol is pulled down.

In his final meditations, the narrator becomes ashamed of the intricate theories he has spun during the afternoon and dubious about their validity. They may be only projections of the artist's self. He calls them "guessing," "cartooning," "inexact and vengeful lyricisms" and says,

"Sometimes I entirely doubt my judgment in moral matters; and so long as I propose to be a story-teller, that is the whisper of the devil for me." While Alex absents herself to attend to household duties, he tries to "compress the excessive details of the afternoon into an abstraction or two," even though he knows that "abstraction is a bad thing, innumerable and infinitesimal and tiresome."

Abstraction—that is, the expression of truth in statement rather than in images—is what Wescott could not or would not give up. In William H. Rueckert's opinion, "Without absurdity, it can be said that Wescott slays himself as an artist in this work." The work itself remains a jewel of art.

Apartment in Athens

Wescott, through the persona of Alwyn Tower in *The Pilgrim Hawk*, appeared to reject further attempts at the art of fiction. Meanwhile, however, he had thought about what the ideal novel should be like: objective, written "with precise equivalents instead of idioms, a style of rapid grace for the eye rather than sonority for the ear," one out of which the self, its prejudices, and its parochial origins "will seem to have disappeared." His next book, *Apartment in Athens*, is a traditional novel, and it suffers by comparison with his more original works.

The chief problem with the novel is its didacticism, arising from its design as propaganda. Since he was ineligible for the draft, Wescott said, he wanted to contribute to the war effort by embodying in a novel his understanding of the German mentality gained on several visits to Germany. He got the idea of setting the story in Athens in meetings with a hero of the Greek underground who was visiting in the United States.

When a Nazi officer, Captain Kalter, is billeted in the apartment of the Helianoses, a Greek family of four, they become his "slaves," constantly harassed and abused. Somehow, though, the parents, an aging couple, find their love renewed by the experience. After leave in Germany, Kalter comes back a changed man, and the Helianoses are baffled by his kindness. When he reveals that he has lost his whole family in the war, Mr. Helianos offers sympathy and blames Adolf Hitler, whereupon the Nazi flies into a rage, beats him, and has him arrested. With her husband in jail, Mrs. Helianos and her children, Alex and Leda, expect more abuse, but Kalter, although obviously declining in health, continues to be kind. When he commits suicide, he leaves a note to a friend in the military suggesting that his death may be charged against this Greek family and used to get information from them about the underground. His friend declines to pursue the suggestion. Helianos is executed anyway. His wife, who has refused to become involved in the Resistance, now joins it and resolves to dedicate her children also to the eventual freedom of Greece.

Told in plain style, from the omniscient point of view, thus without the voice and play of intellect of a participating narrator, *Apartment in Athens* is not an artistic success. Although Edmund Wilson praised this novel and it was a Book-of-the-Month Club selection, it lacks the rich imagery and symbolism of Wescott's previous novels, and it is also marred by long stretches of exposition and argument. One chapter amounts to a lecture by Kalter on the Nazi view of German superiority in all things; another is mostly given over to a letter from prison expressing the views of Helianos on the threat of Germany and the prospects of Greece.

Wescott found his materials in his own life, primarily among the people of the farms and small towns of Wisconsin, with their hard work, cultural poverty, and puritanical outlook, but he wrote of them with nostalgia and compassion rather than with the satiric venom of many midwestern writers of the period. He dwelt on the themes of self, love, family, and home, showing how they interacted with one another and the environment to determine the fate of his characters. His major theme was the self-discovery of the artist, a participant narrator, in his two best novels, who is also an expatriate. Because of the established distance in time and place, the narrator is able to reflect not only on the events he is recounting but also on himself as an artist. The memories are laden with rich imagery, often linked in a matrix of symbols in the narrator's mind. When Wescott abandoned his distinctively subjective, symbolic style, he seemed to have lost his impulse as a storyteller, although he continued to be active as a man of letters.

Eileen Tarcay

Other major works

SHORT FICTION: . . . *Like a Lover*, 1926; *Good-bye, Wisconsin*, 1928; *The Babe's Bed*, 1930; *Twelve Fables of Aesop*, 1954.

PLAY: "The Dream of Audubon: Libretto of a Ballet in Three Scenes," pb. 1941.

POETRY: *The Bitterns: A Book of Twelve Poems*, 1920; *Natives of Rock: XX Poems, 1921-1922*, 1925.

NONFICTION: *Elizabeth Madox Roberts: A Personal Note*, 1930; *A Calendar of Saints for Unbelievers*, 1932; *Fear and Trembling*, 1932; *Images of Truth: Remembrances and Criticism*, 1962; *The Best of All Possible Worlds: Journals, Letters, and Remembrances, 1914-1937*, 1975; *Continual Lessons: The Journals of Glenway Wescott, 1937-1955*, 1990 (Robert Phelps and Jerry Rosco, editors).

EDITED TEXTS: *The Maugham Reader*, 1950; *Short Novels of Colette*, 1951.

Bibliography

Benfey, Christopher. "Bright Young Things." *The New York Times*, March 21, 1999. A review that comments on Wescott's fussy style but claims that his novella *The Pilgrim Hawk* is a brilliant work that can stand comparison with works by William Faulkner or D. H. Lawrence. Asserts the central image of the novella comes from Wescott's relationship with George Platt Lynes.

Cowley, Malcolm. *Exile's Return*. New York: Viking Press, 1951. A notable book on the expatriate movement of the 1930's that explores writers who were once called the lost generation. Helpful in placing Wescott in this movement and defining his relation to the times.

Cunningham, Michael. "*The Pilgrim Hawk* by Glenway Wescott." In *Unknown Masterpieces: Writers Rediscover Literature's Hidden Classics*, edited by Edwin Frank. New York: New York Review of Books, 2003. Part of a collection of essays by prominent writers who discuss the little-known but much-admired works of other authors. Novelist Michael Cunningham explains why Wescott's *The Pilgrim Hawk* may be the finest short novel in twentieth century American literature.

Johnson, Ira. *Glenway Wescott: The Paradox of Voice*. Port Washington, N.Y.: Kennikat Press, 1971. An incisive look into Wescott's career. The book explicates and criticizes each of Wescott's works in detail, and it also demonstrates how each work reflects Wescott's development as a writer.

Pohorilenko, Anatole, and James Crump. *When We Were Three: The Travel Albums of George Platt Lynes, Monroe Wheeler, and Glenway Wescott, 1925-1935*. Santa Fe, N.M.: Arena, 1998. Recounts the triangular relationship among Wescott, Lynes, and Wheeler, who were close friends and lovers. This book contains photographs of their travels, with text that describes their relationship and how they sparked one another's talents and creativity. Includes biographical information about Wescott.

Rosco, Jerry. "An American Treasure: Glenway Wescott's *The Pilgrim Hawk*." *Literary Review* 15 (Winter, 1988): 133-142. Rosco's analysis of Wescott's novella is taken from information provided by Wescott himself during his last interview. Wescott's personal reflections regarding how he wrote the novella and how he was influenced by W. Sommerset Maugham are particularly revealing.

_______. *Glenway Wescott Personally: A Biography*. Madison: University of Wisconsin Press, 2002. A biography, focusing on how Wescott came to terms with his homosexuality. Rosco, who coedited Wescott's journals, recounts the writer's early fame and later struggles to write, his relationship with museum curator Monroe Wheeler, his work with sex researcher Alfred Kinsey on homosexuality, and his friendships with other artists and writers.

Rueckert, William H. *Glenway Wescott*. New York: Twayne: 1965. An introductory biographical overview and the first book-length appraisal of Wescott. Attempts to revise Wescott's reputation as a writer who produced only one minor masterpiece.

Vargo, Marc. *Noble Lives: Biographical Portraits of Three Remarkable Gay Men—Glenway Wescott, Aaron Copland, and Dag Hammarskjöld*. New York: Huntington Park Press, 2005. Devotes a chapter to Wescott, providing a concise biography and focusing on the connections between his sexuality and his literary career. Includes a bibliography and an index.

NATHANAEL WEST
Nathan Weinstein

Born: New York, New York; October 17, 1903
Died: El Centro, California; December 22, 1940
Also known as: Nathan Weinstein

Principal long fiction

The Dream Life of Balso Snell, 1931
Miss Lonelyhearts, 1933
A Cool Million: The Dismantling of Lemuel Pitkin, 1934
The Day of the Locust, 1939

Other literary forms

Nathanael West often used the short-story form for preliminary sketches of characters and themes that later appeared in his novels. Between 1930 and 1933 especially, he wrote stories with a broader focus and in a more sophisticated style than his first work, *The Dream Life of Balso Snell*. The stories include "The Adventurer," "Mr. Potts of Pottstown," "Tibetan Night," and "The Sun, the Lady, and the Gas Station," all unpublished. After the publication of *Miss Lonelyhearts* in 1933, West also worked as a scriptwriter in Hollywood for several years, producing such works as *Born to Be Wild* (1938) and *Men Against the Sky* (1940).

Achievements

Since Nathanael West's death in an automobile accident in 1940, his work has steadily gained critical attention. His characters' hysterical pitch of loneliness, their frustration, and their inability to find a source of relief have gradually interested a wide audience, especially since World War II. Stripped of their professional masks, the people in West's novels reveal a talent for cruelty. They tease, exploit, or murder to ensure their own survival in a world reminiscent of T. S. Eliot's *The Waste Land* (1922), but their world is without Eliot's hint of redemption or spirituality. In *Miss Lonelyhearts*, the world is dead; in *The Day of the Locust*, it is corrupt and jaded, a modern Sodom that West symbolically destroys. This last novel was made into a film in the 1970's; although it never became a box-office hit, West would have approved of its powerful treatment of dreamers and misfits.

Biography

Nathanael West was born Nathan Weinstein in New York City on October 17, 1903. His father's and mother's families had known one another before they emigrated to the United States from Russia. His father's side used construction skills learned in the Old World to become successful contractors in the new country, taking advantage of the building boom of the turn of the century. His mother's side was well educated, and Anna Wallenstein Weinstein wanted her son Nathan and her two daughters to have all the perquisites of an upwardly mobile, middle-class life.

Soon after settling in New York City, the Weinsteins learned to enjoy their comforts and to value them highly. They also assumed that their son would receive the finest possible education, pursue a professional career, or at least join the family business. West was an avid reader but a much less ambitious student. He attended a variety of grammar schools before his parents placed him in DeWitt Clinton High School. West, however, preferred exploring Central Park during the day and the theater district in the evenings. He was particularly attracted to the vaudeville shows, his first exposure to techniques such as slapstick and stereotypes, which he later used in his fiction.

West was not very disciplined, but his clever and adventurous nature helped to get him into Tufts University without a high school diploma. After one unsuccessful year there, he attended Brown University. West's biographer attributes Brown's acceptance of West to a complicated mismatching of transcripts with another student whose name also was Weinstein, though whether this was planned or accidental is not absolutely certain. Whatever the case, West graduated from Brown in 1924 with a degree in philosophy, which he earned in only two and a half years.

Neither West nor his parents had much nostalgia for their Jewish Lithuanian roots; instead, they concentrated on rapid assimilation. In 1926, he legally changed his name to Nathanael West. Even so, the subject of roots still appears in most of his work. The degree of corruption in Lemuel Pitkin's hometown in *A Cool Million* is nothing compared to what he finds elsewhere in the country. The protagonist in *Miss Lonelyhearts* suffers from acute isolation despite his efforts to communicate, and this seems to stem from his earliest memories of childhood; he is estranged from his Baptist upbringing and has only a single comforting memory of his youth. Tod Hackett in *The Day of the Locust* leaves the East Coast, where he was an undergraduate at the Yale School of Fine Arts, for Hollywood. He observes other new arrivals and decides that they have come to California to die in one way or another. Although he does not include himself in this category, it is clear that he too succumbs to the superficial glitter and wastefulness.

Nathanael West. (Courtesy, New Directions Publishing)

West's parents encouraged him to pursue a dependable career, but their son was not interested, and he convinced them to send him to Paris in 1926. He enjoyed the artistic and literary circles there, but signs of the coming Depression were being felt in the construction industry and West had to return to New York after three months. Relatives managed to find him a job as a night manager of a midtown hotel, providing West with an income, a place to write, and a steady flow of guests to watch. West found these people fascinating, and so it is not surprising that seedy hotels and their transient occupants find their way into *The Day of the Locust*. Working as a night manager also gave West time to revise *The Dream Life of Balso Snell*, which he had begun while in college. William Carlos Williams liked the manuscript and recommended that the company Moss and Kamin publish the work; five hundred copies were printed in 1931.

S. J. Perelman, also a student at Brown, married West's sister Laura. Through Perelman, who worked at *The New Yorker*, West met other writers and artists. It was also through his brother-in-law that West conceived of the controlling idea for *Miss Lonelyhearts*. Perelman knew a writer named Susan Chester who gave advice to readers of *The Brooklyn Eagle*. The three of them met one evening in 1939, and she read samples of the letters. West was moved by them and eventually used an advice-to-the-lovelorn column and a tormented newspaper columnist for what is probably his most famous novel. *Miss Lonelyhearts* was published by Liveright in 1933.

West soon went to Southern California to work on film scripts. His experience with the less glamorous aspects of Hollywood and the film industry, with the masses of aspiring actors, with people who had little talent to begin with but compensated for that with their dreams, helped provide the themes, landscapes, and characters of West's final novel, *The Day of the Locust*. In 1940, West married Eileen McKenney, the sister of Ruth McKenney, who worked with Perelman at *The New Yorker*. West's careless driving was known to all his friends, and a few months after his marriage, he and his wife were killed in an automobile crash.

Analysis

Although all of Nathanael West's fiction is concerned with certain recurring themes, it gradually matures in tone, style, and subject. *The Dream Life of Balso Snell*, his first novel, has a clever but sarcastic and ugly adolescent tone. *The Day of the Locust*, his last novel, is also satiric and sarcastic, but its greater maturity and empathetic tone make it both disturbing and profoundly moving.

West's Miss Lonelyhearts dreams that he is a magician who does tricks with doorknobs: He is able to make them speak, bleed, and flower. In a sense, this conceit explains all of West's work. His protagonists travel across dead landscapes that they try to revivify. In *The Dream Life of Balso Snell*, the landscape is mechanical, wooden, purely farcical; in *A Cool Million*, West shows one American town after another, all equally corrupt. *Miss Lonelyhearts* is set in the dirt and concrete of New York City, and *The Day of the Locust* is set in the sordid but irresistible Southern California landscape.

West's typical protagonist is a quester, intent on bringing life wherever he travels; Miss Lonelyhearts especially is obsessed with the challenges of a savior. The task of making a dead world bloom, however, seems hopeless. Life may surface in a moment of communication or lovemaking, but something is likely to go awry, as the moment reverses itself into an unnatural distortion. For example, as Miss Lonelyhearts tries to comfort an old man he meets in Central Park, he suddenly has the urge to crush and destroy him. Shrike, his employer at the newspaper office, compares making love to his wife with sleeping with a knife in his groin. This dichotomy is at the heart of West's vision. Characters driven by benevolent ambitions are thwarted—by themselves, by those in need of their help, by cosmic and divine indifference—until they become grotesque parodies of their original selves. Innocence and success can be recalled only through dreams. At best, the world is passively dead; at worst, it is aggressively violent.

The Dream Life of Balso Snell

The quester of *The Dream Life of Balso Snell* does not take himself seriously, and the novel itself seems to be an extended literary joke. Balso Snell describes a dream in which he encounters the famous wooden horse of the Greeks in ancient Troy. A brash and distinctly modern tour guide leads him through the interiors of the horse, which quickly become the subject of numerous adolescent witticisms. The inside of the horse expands to a landscape that Balso explores for the rest of his dream. West's purpose is humor and parody, which he accomplishes mercilessly although unpleasantly, beginning even with the title of this first book. Following his "path," Balso meets a Catholic mystic, and West has the opportunity to mock the literary lives of saints. Then Balso meets a schoolboy who has just hidden his journal in the trunk of a nearby tree. Balso reads its entries, which serve as a parody of the nineteenth century Russian novel. Balso then meets the boy's teacher, Miss McGeeny, who has been busily writing a biography of a biographer's biographer; West parodies another literary genre.

The Dream Life of Balso Snell is not a significant work of fiction, but it is useful for readers to appreciate how quickly West's style and perspective deepened. His later novels have the same piercing quality, and West never lost his tendency to satirize, but the later novels are finely and precisely directed. West's later fiction also has the same motifs—quester, mechanical or obsessive journeys, dreams, and suffering humanity—but West examines them much more seriously in the later novels.

Miss Lonelyhearts

West is in superb control of his material in *Miss Lonelyhearts*, published only two years after *The Dream Life of Balso Snell*. The vituperative tone of the earlier work is balanced by greater development of plot and diversity of character. Following his preference for fast action and exaggeration, West uses comic-strip stereotypes: the meek husband and the bullying wife, Mr. and Mrs. Doyle; the bullish employer, Shrike, and his castrating wife, Mary; and Miss Lonelyhearts's innocent but dumb girlfriend, Betty. Miss Lonelyhearts himself is only somewhat more developed, primarily because he is in almost every episode and because the third-person voice sardonically presents his private thoughts.

As in *The Dream Life of Balso Snell*, a central quester travels a barren landscape. Between the newspaper office and the local speakeasy is Central Park. As Miss Lonelyhearts walks across it, he realizes that there should be signs of spring but, in fact, there are none to be seen. Then he recalls that last year, new life seemed wrenched from the soil only in July. Miss Lonelyhearts's job as a newspaper columnist thrusts him into the position of a quester, and he makes a highly unlikely candidate. Simultaneously attracted to and repelled by his mission to assuage the grief of his readers, he makes attempts to get close to some of them, such as Mr. and Mrs. Doyle, but he then suddenly feels a compulsion to keep separate from them. This dichotomy keeps him in motion, reeling him like a puppet from one person's apartment to another, building a pressure that is released only when Miss Lonelyhearts has a final breakdown.

In each new location, the newspaperman tries to make a meaningful connection with another human being. Strict chronology becomes vague as the protagonist's state of mind becomes increasingly disturbed. He reaches toward Betty when they are sitting on the couch in her apartment but suddenly has no interest in her. He does remain sexually interested in Mary Shrike, but she refuses his advances as long as they stay in her apartment, and in the restaurant she teases him sadistically. He telephones Mrs. Doyle, a letter writer, saying he will advise her in person. He exploits her unhappiness to satisfy his own need but, not surprisingly, is disappointed in the results. Rather than help others, the quester of this novel uses them as targets for venting his own anger. As he is increasingly frustrated in his task of bringing beauty and gentleness into the world, Miss Lonelyhearts takes to the isolation of his own room.

Another kind of quest occurs here, one that parodies the earlier quest. Rather than embark on further quests from one location to another in New York City, Miss Lonelyhearts hallucinates a journey; his bed serves as his mode of transportation. It appears to him a perfect world and a perfect journey, sanctioned by God, who finally communicates to him that he has chosen the right conclusion to his quest. Miss Lonelyhearts feels that he has become a rock, perfect in its design not because God has helped to create it, but because it is impenetrable to all but its own existence. It is ironic that the driven quester actually drives himself into a blissful delusion of isolation.

Reality intrudes. Mr. Doyle, incensed at being cuckolded, rushes up the stairs to the apartment. Miss Lonelyhearts rushes down the stairs, hoping to meet him and welcome what he assumes is Doyle's conversion. Instead, there is a scuffle and Doyle's gun fires. Only in dreams do doorknobs blossom and human beings turn into gentle and compassionate creatures—at least in West's novels. Miss Lonelyhearts dies, a victim of his own miscalculation.

A Cool Million

The protagonist of *A Cool Million* is another miscalculating quester. Pitkin is an idealistic young man who leaves his hometown to seek his fortune. The fact that the immediate cause of his departure from Ottsville, Vermont, is the dishonest foreclosing of his mother's mortgage does not dampen his enthusiastic belief that his nation is the land of limitless possibilities. He has faith in himself and in those who insist they are using him for his own good.

Mr. Shagpole Whipple, former president of the United States and now director of the Rat River National Bank in Ottsville, becomes Lemuel's earliest supporter. He advises his young friend that America "is the land of opportunity," a land that "takes care of the honest and the industrious." Lemuel is inspired and sets out in what becomes a parody of the Horatio Alger myth. On the train to New York City, he enjoys a conversation with a Mr. Mape, who was left "a cool million" by his father. Lemuel is impressed, especially since, he explains, he must make his fortune starting with only the thirty dollars in his pocket. By the end of the trip, he has been divested of that thirty dollars. Lemuel is the fall guy for another scheme, so that he, and not the thief, is apprehended by the police, brought to trial, and declared guilty. Being sent to prison is only the first of a long series of misfortunes. Lemuel is always someone's dupe or prey, but he bounces back to try again, although he repeatedly gets nothing out of his adventures. In fact, the more he travels, the less he has. Lemuel loses his teeth, his scalp, his eye, part of a hand, one leg; each time there is someone close by who can benefit from his new loss. Lemuel is used by entrepreneurs and thieves of all varieties.

A Cool Million is fast-paced and episodic. Its characters are pure stereotypes—the ingenuous dupe, the patriot, the innocent young girl, the deceitful villain. Everyone and everything is satirized: midwesterners, Jews, southerners, capitalists, and socialists. *A Cool Million* shows how West was beginning to use his material for clearly defined purposes and to control his sharp-edged humor and black comedy in order to make a point. This novel, however, remains a minor work in comparison to *Miss Lonelyhearts* and *The Day of the Locust*. In these works, pathos emerges from West's stereotypes and seems all the more powerful because of its sources. *A Cool Million* is clever and biting but not poignant or profound.

The Day of the Locust

West is at his best in *The Day of the Locust*. Tod Hackett, the central quester, comes to Hollywood from the East to learn set and costume designing. The people he gets to know are desperately in need of beauty, romance, and renewal, but, as in *Miss Lonelyhearts*, the harder they struggle to achieve these goals, the farther away they are.

The story is about dreamers who have traveled to what they believe is the dream capital of America, which West portrays as the wasteland of America. In addition to Tod, there is Faye Greener, beautiful but exploitative, making up in vanity what she lacks in intelligence. Homer Simpson is a thickheaded but sincere middle-aged bachelor from the Midwest. He has run from his one attempt to break through his dull-witted loneliness because the memory of failure is too painful. Characters such as Faye and Homer are particularly successful; although they are stereotypes, they still have something unpredictable about them. This quality usually manifests itself involuntarily by a spasm or quirk. For example, Faye is obviously a second-rate actor, but Tod sees through her tawdry facade to a deep archetypal beauty. Faye is unaware of any such quality; even if she knew, she would not appreciate it, because it has almost nothing in common with the self she has created. Homer has difficulty controlling parts of his body. He does not fall asleep easily because waking up is so arduous. His hands seem disassociated from his psyche; he has to put them under cold running water to rouse them, after which his fingers seem to follow their own rhythms. Like Faye, he has a structural purity without means to express it. Like Miss Lonelyhearts, his emotions swell in intensity, causing pressure that eventually must find release.

Faye becomes Tod's obsession. If he is a quester, she is his grail, and a most difficult challenge. Tod can neither support her nor further her acting career. Instead, he becomes a voyeur, watching her tease Earle Shoop, the cowboy from Arizona, and Miguel, the Mexican. He settles for simply painting Faye in a mural he calls "The Burning of Los Angeles." Tod observes that people come to California to die, despite their ambitions, and the mural reflects their disappointments. In the mural, a mob chases Faye, who seems oblivious to imminent danger and maintains a calm, detached expression. Those who realize they have failed need to express their anger, and those who think they have succeeded exist in a state of happy but dangerous ignorance. As in all of West's fiction, the challenge is as impossible as turning doorknobs into flowers. As the dreamers recognize the gap between their desires and accomplishments, thwarted ambition leads to frustration, and frustration to violence. The power of *The Day of the Locust* derives from the last few chapters, which describe the mindless and destructive product of such frustrated dreams.

It is the evening of a motion-picture premiere; violet lights run across the sky, and crowds of fans are kept under control by police barricades. The premiere provides the opportunity for fans to see face-to-face the "stars," the ones who have made it. The tension is too great, however, and the control too tenuous. The crowd begins to charge toward the theater, and Tod is caught in the pressure. *The Day of the Locust* is a tight, "pressured" novel, but all gives way at the end. As the crowd surges, it builds up strength from the people whose lives are filled with boredom and mistakes. There is mass pandemonium. Homer, moving like a robot, mechanically and swiftly murders a child who has been teasing him. Tod, submerged in the crowd, is hurt, but steadies himself at the base of a rail. In agony, he begins to think about his mural, "The Burning of Los Angeles," until reality and his thoughts merge. He thinks of the burning city, of mobs of people running into the foreground with baseball bats, and he and his friends fleeing from the mob. He actually believes he is painting the flames when police officers grab him from the rail and lift him into a police car. When the siren begins, Tod is not sure whether he or the siren has been making the noise. In effect, he succumbs to the chaos around him.

The Day of the Locust is a bleak novel, reflecting West's belief that recognizing limitations is difficult for humanity, which prefers to think that all things are possible. West shows limitations to be everywhere: within the masses, within the questers trying to save them, within the arid landscape itself. As the limitations prove insurmountable, natural ambitions and desires for harmony are inverted. Love becomes pantomime and compassion a veil for selfish and sadistic purposes. West's characters and settings desperately need to be renewed, but the job of salvation is difficult, one that West's protagonists fail to achieve.

Miriam Fuchs

Other major works

SCREENPLAYS: *Follow Your Heart*, 1936 (with Lester Cole and Samuel Ornitz); *The President's Mystery*, 1936 (with Cole); *Ticket to Paradise*, 1936 (with Jack Natteford); *It Could Happen to You*, 1937 (with Ornitz); *Born to Be Wild*, 1938; *Five Came Back*, 1939 (with Jerry Cady and Dalton Trumbo); *I Stole a Million*, 1939; *Men Against the Sky*, 1940.

MISCELLANEOUS: *West: Novels and Other Writings*, 1997 (includes long fiction, letters, and unpublished writings).

Bibliography

Bloom, Harold, ed. *Nathanael West*. New York: Chelsea House, 1986. This useful collection includes essays on all of West's work in a representative selection. S. E. Hyman's essay is a valuable introduction to West. Includes a bibliography.

_______. *Nathanael West's "Miss Lonelyhearts."* Philadelphia: Chelsea House, 2005. Collection of essays analyzing West's novel, examining such subjects as the novel's modernist antihero and West's use of debased iconography. Includes an introduction by Bloom, a bibliography, and an index.

Bombaci, Nancy. "Nathanael West's Aspiring Freakish Flâneurs." In *Freaks in Late Modernist American Culture: Nathanael West, Djuna Barnes, Tod Browning, and Carson McCullers*. New York: Peter Lang, 2006. Bombaci focuses on West's fascination with genetically maimed and distorted people, examining how his representation of these marginalized characters challenges modernist aesthetics and social values.

Dunne, Michael. "Nathanael West: 'Gloriously Funny.'" In *Calvinist Humor in American Literature*. Baton Rouge: Louisiana State University Press, 2007. Calvinist humor, in Dunne's definition, is the perception of humankind's imperfection. He demonstrates how this humor is used in works by West and other American writers whose fiction is populated with flawed characters.

Martin, Jay. "Nathanael West: *Miss Lonelyhearts*." In *A Companion to Modernist Literature and Culture*, edited by David Bradshaw and Kevin J. H. Dettmar. Malden, Mass.: Blackwell, 2006. Martin's analysis of West's novel is included in this student guide to modernist literature. In addition to essays examining selected works of literature, the book contains general information about modernist art, film, music, dance, architecture, photography, and aesthetics.

Rhodes, Chip. "Nathanael West: Desire, Art, and Cynicism." In *Politics, Desire, and the Hollywood Novel*. Iowa City: University of Iowa Press, 2008. Rhodes examines *The Day of the Locust* and other novels that depict the influence of the film industry upon American politics and ideas of romance.

Siegel, Ben, ed. *Critical Essays on Nathanael West*. New York: G. K. Hall, 1994. Divided into two sections—reviews and essays. In addition to the comprehensive introduction surveying West's life and career, the essay section provides studies of individual novels and of West's work as a whole. Includes notes and an index.

Veitch, Jonathan. *American Superrealism: Nathanael West and the Politics of Representation in the 1930's*. Madison: University of Wisconsin Press, 1997. Contains separate chapters on each novel, as well as an introduction discussing the "crisis of representation in the 1930's." Includes detailed notes.

Widmer, Kingsley. *Nathanael West*. Boston: Twayne, 1982. Widmer's introductory overview concentrates on "West as the prophet of modern masquerading, role-playing, and its significance," while offering useful analyses of West's work. Includes lengthy notes and an annotated bibliography.

Wisker, Alistair. *The Writing of Nathanael West*. New York: St. Martin's Press, 1990. Contains chapters on each novel and a series of appendixes on various aspects of West's work, including his handling of violence, his unpublished fiction, and revisions of his work. Includes notes and a bibliography.

PAUL WEST

Born: Eckington, Derbyshire, England; February 23, 1930
Also known as: Paul Noden West

Principal long fiction

A Quality of Mercy, 1961
Tenement of Clay, 1965
Alley Jaggers, 1966
I'm Expecting to Live Quite Soon, 1970
Caliban's Filibuster, 1971
Bela Lugosi's White Christmas, 1972
Colonel Mint, 1972
Gala, 1976
The Very Rich Hours of Count von Stauffenberg, 1980
Rat Man of Paris, 1986
The Place in Flowers Where Pollen Rests, 1988
Lord Byron's Doctor, 1989
The Women of Whitechapel and Jack the Ripper, 1991
Love's Mansion, 1992
The Tent of Orange Mist, 1995
Sporting with Amaryllis, 1996
Terrestrials, 1997
Life with Swan, 1999
O.K.: The Corral, the Earps, and Doc Holliday, 2000
The Dry Danube: A Hitler Forgery, 2000
A Fifth of November, 2001
Cheops: A Cupboard for the Sun, 2002
The Immensity of the Here and Now: A Novel of 9.11, 2003

Other literary forms

Paul West is a remarkably prolific novelist whose literary interests also include poetry, criticism, and other nonfiction. In addition to his books of verse, *Poems* (1952), *The Spellbound Horses* (1960), *The Snow Leopard* (1964), and *Tea with Osiris* (2006), West has published memoirs. These include *I, Said the Sparrow* (1963), which recounts his childhood in Derbyshire; *Words for a Deaf Daughter* (1969)—one of West's most popular works—which poignantly relates the experiences of his daughter, Mandy, who is deaf; and *Out of My Depths: A Swimmer in the Universe* (1983), which describes the author's determination to learn to swim at middle age. His short stories were collected in *The Universe, and Other Fictions* in 1988.

Besides his numerous essays and book reviews in dozens of periodicals, journals, and newspapers, West has published *The Growth of the Novel* (1959), *Byron and the Spoiler's Art* (1960, 1992), *The Modern Novel* (1963), *Robert Penn Warren* (1964), *The Wine of Absurdity: Essays in Literature and Consolation* (1966), and a four-volume series titled *Sheer Fiction* (1987-2007). *A Stroke of Genius: Illness and Self-Discovery* was published in 1995, and he published several other volumes of nonfiction, including *The Secret Lives of Words* (2000), *My Father's War* (2005), and *The Shadow Factory* (2008).

Achievements

When Paul West arrived on the literary scene as a novelist, he was regarded as an author who possessed a compelling voice but also as one who wrote grotesque and verbally complex fictions. The unevenness of critical reaction cannot overshadow, however, the regard with which serious readers have approached his work, and a list of his fellowships and awards clearly indicates a writer of significant stature: He is the recipient of a Guggenheim Fellowship (1962), a Paris Review Aga Kahn Prize for Fiction (1974), the National Endowment for the Humanities summer stipend for science studies (1975), the National Endowment for the Arts Fellowship in Creative Writing (1980), the Hazlett Memorial Award for Excellence in the Arts (1981), the American Academy and Institute of Arts and Letters Award in Literature (1985), and a National Endowment for the Arts Fellowship in Fiction (1985). In 1998, the French government decorated him Chevalier of the Order of Arts and Letters. Besides teaching at Pennsylvania State University from 1962 to 1995, West was a visiting professor and writer-in-residence at numerous American universities. As his fiction developed, West has shown himself to be a highly imaginative, experimental, and linguistically sophisticated writer. Critics usually commend him for his original style and note the striking diversity of his oeuvre.

Biography

Paul Noden West was born in Eckington, Derbyshire, England, on February 23, 1930, one of two children, into a working-class family. After attending local elementary and grammar schools, West went to Birmingham University, then to Lincoln College, Oxford, and in 1952 to Columbia University on a fellowship. Although profoundly attracted to New York life, West was forced to return to England to fulfill his military service in the Royal Air Force and there began his writing career.

Once he concluded his service, West taught English literature at the Memorial University of Newfoundland, wrote a volume of poems, and did considerable work for the Canadian Broadcasting Corporation. In 1962, he was awarded a Guggenheim Fellowship and returned to the United States, where he took up permanent residence. He was a member of the English and comparative literature faculties at Pennsylvania State University from 1962 to 1995, dividing his time each year between teaching and writing in New York. Upon his retirement, he devoted himself to writing and guest lectureships at Goucher College, University of Miami, Cornell University, and the U.S. Air Force Academy. He became a U.S. citizen.

Analysis

Paul West has long insisted that what is most important to him as a writer is the free play of the imagination. What the imagination invents, he contends, becomes something independent and actual. West himself states the case most clearly when noting that "elasticity, diversity, openness, these are the things that matter to me most." Thus, his fictions often revolve, both thematically and structurally, around the interplay between the individual and his or her imagination and an absurd, threatening universe. Often these fictions rely heavily on dreams of one sort or another, with characters living in their dreams or living out their dreams or becoming confused about where dreams leave off and the world begins.

Consequently, West's fictions often abound with a sense of precariousness as characters who are constrained in one form or another struggle to free themselves and find their places in the world. Sanity frequently becomes the central issue in these lives, with protagonists taking on the forces of conventionality in their private wars with the drab and mundane. Typical West heroes are outsiders, often marginal or largely inconsequential figures, who will not or cannot conform to the forces about them and who, in striking out on their own, pay steep prices for their individuality.

A Quality of Mercy

A Quality of Mercy, West's first novel and a work that he largely disowned, deals with a collection of embittered and failed lives overseen by Camden Smeaton, the novel's central consciousness. The novel is otherwise unmemorable except that it anticipates concerns that West more successfully developed in later novels: alienation, immersion in dream and illusion, the idea of an irrational universe, and the use of stylistic fragmentation.

Tenement of Clay

On the other hand, *Tenement of Clay*, West's second novel, stands as a far more accomplished work, controlled, stylistically inventive, morally probing. Here West introduces the reader to the voices of two narrators, each of whom is compelling and unique. The work is divided into three chapters, the two shortest forming a frame offered by Pee Wee Lazarus, a dwarf wrestler whose direct idiom immediately assaults the reader and demands his or her attention.

West's desire is to "involve" the reader in his tale, a story that revolves around Papa Nick, narrator of the middle section, who along with Lazarus meets a taciturn giant he names Lacland. Lacland appears to have no home or clear destination, so Nick takes him back to his rooms, where Nick presides over a private flophouse for local bums. Kept in the darkened basement, Lacland soon develops, under Lazarus's perverse tutelage, a sexual appetite and his own abusive language. After a series of horrible misadventures, Lacland reverts to his despondency and silence and eventually becomes Nick's legal ward.

All these events, extreme and dramatic as they may appear, actually operate as a backdrop to Nick's personal turmoil. For years he has carried on a fitful relationship with Venetia, a former film actor, who exhorts him to abandon his altruism toward the derelicts and to run off with her to a life of leisure. When Nick physically collapses from the burden of Lacland and Lazarus's escapades, Venetia nurses him back to health, leaves him when he returns to his bums, and dies in a car crash in Florida.

The novel's soul comes in the form of Nick's constant ruminations, which offer a way of coping with and sometimes solving the dilemmas of his existence. Gradually the line between straight narration and Nick's hallucinations begins to dissolve; the two become one, and the reader learns something fundamental about this world: Dream and reality invade each other; there is no escaping one for the other.

The novel is furthermore important for the moral questions it raises. Perhaps the most telling of these involves one's responsibilities to other human beings; in particular terms, is Nick responsible for the lives he admits into his home? As Lacland and Lazarus demonstrate, Nick has assumed the role of a Dr. Frankenstein and created his own monsters, whom he has unwittingly unleashed on the world. Is the answer to this dilemma incarceration? Lacland's temporary internment in the basement suggests that it is not.

For Nick, these are the questions that finally come with life itself, and his failure to arrive at any fixed solution suggests a form of authorial honesty about the complexity of modern existence. In this context, the epigraph from Samuel Beckett makes sense: "If there were only darkness, all would be clear. It is because there is not only darkness but also light that our situation becomes inexplicable."

The novel's title comes from a passage in John Dryden's *Absalom and Achitophel* (1681-1682), and certainly the images of tenements abound in the work: all the buildings in this metropolis Lazarus calls New Babylon, especially Nick's flophouse, the grave into which Venetia is lowered, and the human body itself, which contains and in many cases entraps the spirit. In their concerns with their corporeal selves, most of these characters miss the important questions Nick poses throughout. Life, then, amounts to inhabiting one vast tenement, and the point is never escape, but how one chooses to live that life.

Alley Jaggers

With his next novel, *Alley Jaggers*, West moved even further into depicting a consciousness at odds with the rest of the world. Alley is as compelling a narrator as Lazarus or Nick, and like them he speaks in a language that is distinct and unique, an idiom that oddly combines Irish brogue, Midlands accent, and personal argot.

Alley is a profoundly frustrated little man who realizes that he is unfulfilled by his job and marriage but who has no idea how to remedy his situation. He spends his most satisfying moments dreaming of horses and the elaborate names owners concoct for them and creating airplanes in his attic retreat. Alley wants desperately to make an impression of some kind, and one of his creations, an androgynous, semihuman form emitting a silent scream, both intrigues his fellow workers and stands as an effigy of his own condition.

Eventually his boredom and frustration explode into violence when he accidentally kills a young woman during an unsuccessful sexual tryst. In fear and confusion, he wraps her body in plaster and makes a companion for his own statue. When the police inevitably discover the body, Alley has finally and inadvertently stumbled into prominence: In the police he finds his first willing audience in years.

West's purpose here is far more sophisticated than the old cliché of the criminal as artist or as misunderstood noble creature. Instead, Alley represents the alienated individual, the small person cut off from any meaningful existence who struggles in hopeless confusion to make his life somehow mean something. Alley is locked in the prison of himself, both convict and jailer at once, and remains in fundamental confusion about what to do. Nevertheless, his most vital moments are spent in his imagination, which is infinitely more extravagant and vital than his quotidian existence.

I'm Expecting to Live Quite Soon

The second novel in the Jaggers trilogy, *I'm Expecting to Live Quite Soon*, represents an entirely different turn in West's career. Here he not only shifts his attention from Alley to his much maligned wife, Dot, but also creates a more controlled, straightforward type of narrative. The real daring in this work comes in West's attempt to enter the consciousness of a woman, to take the same world of the first novel and shift the perspective to see through the eyes of another member of the family.

Where Alley was frustrated and irresponsible to anyone outside himself, Dot lives a life of devotion and caring: attending to Alley's irascible mother, ministering to her dying father in a nursing home, and visiting Alley in the mental hospital. Like Alley, she needs a release from boredom and conventionality, which eventually she achieves through immersion in her sensual self. The measure of her change can be seen in her eventual decision to throw over her old life and run away to Birmingham with Jimsmith Williams, a black bus driver.

Bela Lugosi's White Christmas

Bela Lugosi's White Christmas, the final volume in the trilogy, finds Alley (now referred to as AJ) in analysis with Dr. Withington (With) in a state institution. Who is counseling whom becomes vague as With is drawn increasingly into AJ's fractured mind, and the two eventually reverse roles, thus effecting AJ's temporary freedom and With's incarceration.

More than any of the previous novels, this one dramatically stakes its claim to stylistic and linguistic experimentation. Attempting to enter AJ's mind as fully as possible, West fashions one of his densest, most verbally complex fictions. While the reader is often at a loss to understand the exact meaning of many passages, what one does comprehend is AJ's indefatigable desire to experience as much as he can as quickly as he can. The result is criminal melee with AJ commandeering a bulldozer and digging up graves in search of his dead father, threatening customers in a bar, sodomizing and murdering a cow, covering himself with the animal's blood and sawdust, and starting a fire in a factory near his mother's home.

AJ's immersion in his own mind becomes so complete that, like a Beckett character, he reaches a state of almost total silence by the end of the novel. Once again, West examines the line between madness and sanity, originality and convention, but like all of his fictions, the work is no polemic; AJ is neither saint nor hopelessly depraved misanthrope but a tortured human being who desperately wants "a bit of individuality." The work is also significant for the fact that West actually intrudes on the fiction in spots, first in a long footnote in which he explains the eccentricities of his characters' names and ends by noting that "in this text, optical illusion is empirically sound," and later in another footnote announcing his own presence throughout the narrative. The point in both cases is to assert artifice as a fictional construct: Fictions are both stories about people and about fiction itself.

Caliban's Filibuster

West deals with some of these same concerns in *Caliban's Filibuster*, the novel that was published immediately before *Bela Lugosi's White Christmas*. This work represents West at his most experimentally extreme as he takes his deepest plunge into an individual's consciousness. Cal, the narrator, is yet another of West's profoundly frustrated protagonists, in this case a failed novelist-cum-screenwriter who chafes at bastardizing his talent for decidedly mercenary ends. As he travels over the Pacific Ocean with his companions Murray McAndrew, a ham actor, and Sammy Zeuss, a crass film producer and Cal's employer, voices representing various of Cal's divided selves carry on endless debates about his artistic aspirations. Thus, the reader is not only taken fully into the character's mind but also given access to the dimensions of his troubled psyche.

To appease these voices and satisfy himself, Cal concocts three separate yet interdependent scenarios in which he and his companions play significant roles. In creating these tales, Cal attempts to convince himself of his abused talent and also to distance himself from his experience, like a viewer before a screen in a theater watching versions of his own life. Like Caliban, his Shakespearean namesake in *The Tempest* (1611), Cal seethes with revenge, cursing those who control him. On his behalf, however, readers must regard his filibuster as an attempt to retain his individuality, which he sees as being eroded by the sterile conventions of his profession.

One way to view the novel is as West's paean to language itself, for it abounds in extravagant verbal complexities: anagrams, puns, malapropisms, acronyms, rhymes, and alphabet games. Language operates as not only Cal's professional tool but also his saving grace; it literally keeps him sane, affording him the diversity of experience that the world denies. Like so many of West's heroes, Cal feels himself trapped, contained by forces that inexorably press against and threaten to destroy him. Language becomes his one potent defense.

Colonel Mint

In *Colonel Mint*, West operates from a seemingly straightforward, but by no means uncomplicated, premise: An astronaut in space claims that he has seen an angel. Whether he has or not is beside the point; instead, the fact that he *thinks* he has and that others want to disabuse him of this belief becomes the subject of this alternately humorous and morally serious work. For his comment, Mint is shunted off to the hinterlands of Washington State and is forced to undergo endless hours of interrogation. If he recants he can go free; otherwise, he must indefinitely remain a prisoner of the space program.

The more Mint refuses to cooperate, the more clever and depraved the methods used against him become. After threats, physical beatings, and sexual sadism fail to make Mint waver, his tormentor, General Lew R., begins—like Dr. With in *Bela Lugosi's White Christmas*—gradually to assume Mint's point of view. He wonders what it would be like to see an angel and what exactly an angel is, and finally he accepts, though he cannot empirically confirm, that Mint has seen an angel.

When the two men escape from the interrogation compound for the wilds of the surrounding woods, it appears they have defeated the forces of conformity and conventional thinking. As is the case in so many of West's fictions, however, those forces track the characters down and exact payment: Lew R. is shot and Mint is frozen. Thus, in this novel, to assert one's individuality becomes tantamount to political treason, and the response of the state is swift, final, and utterly unforgiving.

Stylistically the novel is far more straightforward than *Caliban's Filibuster*, but in at least one important respect it recalls a feature of *Bela Lugosi's White Christmas*. The tone of the novel, for all of its physical and psychological horror, is remarkably level, often nonchalant and conversational. Here the narrator, not necessarily the author, addresses the audience directly a number of times. For example, early in the work, when the reader begins to doubt the plausibility of Mint's abduction, the narrator anticipates objections by remarking, "You might ask, now, where is the humanity in all this; where sweet reason went." The effect here and later in the work, when the intrusions continue, is one of complicity; the audience cannot remain at the safe distance of voyeur but must participate, psychologically and emotionally, in the events that transpire. The forces of conformity involve everyone, and the audience becomes uncomfortably aware of this throughout the narrative.

Gala

In *Gala*, West extends the range of his experimentation but also returns to some familiar territory as he develops fictionally the situation described in *Words for a Deaf Daughter*. Here, novelist and amateur astronomer Wight Deulius and his deaf child, Michaela, construct a model of the Milky Way in their basement. The reader takes a stellar journey through the universe, moving increasingly toward what appear to be the limits of the imagination.

What is especially intriguing about this work is the form West's experimentation takes. Recalling the practice of earlier novels, but especially *Caliban's Filibuster*, West fashions a unique structure for the fiction. Where in the latter work he relies on the international date line and the color spectrum (different sections of the novel are devoted primarily to different colors), in *Gala* elements of physics and the genetic code symbols offer the pattern for the story. West explains this practice when remarking, "I am a compulsive exotic and structural opportunist. I have no idea what structures I will choose next—although I do feel that they will probably be from nature rather than from society."

The Very Rich Hours of Count von Stauffenberg

In his ninth novel, *The Very Rich Hours of Count von Stauffenberg*, West once again shifted focus and style to re-create the details of one of Adolf Hitler's would-be assassins. The novel represents the best in historical fiction, a seemingly effortless blending of fact, elaboration, and pure fantasy, with the result that history becomes for the reader felt experience rather than a catalog of dry, distant details. As West points out in a preface, Stauffenberg is important for not only his public persona but also as someone whose military experience recapitulates, to greater or lesser degrees, that of West's father and all those who lived through World War II. Thus the reader comes to understand an important feature of this writer's fiction, which he expresses as follows: "Whatever I'm writing evinces the interplay between it and my life at the moment of writing, and the result is prose which, as well as being narrative and argumentative and somewhat pyrotechnical, is also symptomatic."

While the narrative, on the surface, seems markedly different from the novels that immediately precede it, one can also see characteristic West concerns emerging. For example, most of the novel places the audience squarely in Stauffenberg's mind as he copes with his war wounds, struggles to express the abiding love he feels for his wife and family, ponders the responsibilities that come with his social and military class, and rages increasingly at the psychopathic perversity of Hitler, the displaced paperhanger. West manages to avoid the obvious trap of the revisionist historian who might be tempted to make Stauffenberg into a martyr or saint. Instead, he emerges as a deeply committed, idealistic man but also one whose psyche is profoundly bruised and disturbed by the events of which he finds himself a part.

The structure of this novel is also just as experimental as that of earlier novels. West had been reading a number of medieval books of hours, lay breviaries that offer devotional prayers alongside richly illuminated paintings. Stauffenberg's rich hours are the last thirty-six of his life; the novel, however, does not stop with his execution. West imaginatively allows the count to speak to the audience from the grave, becoming, then, the most authoritative and omniscient of narrators describing those turbulent last months of the Third Reich.

Rat Man of Paris

Rat Man of Paris, his most popular novel, found West exploring again the effects of the Third Reich on the life of yet another alienated, marginal figure, in this case a boulevardier of modern Paris who spends his time accosting passersby with a rat he conceals in his overcoat. Étienne Poulsifer, the rat man, has survived the Nazi occupation and destruction of his childhood village, and he carries about with him the emotional and psychological baggage of his horrifying past as well as the rats that serve as metaphor for that growing legacy.

When he learns of Klaus Barbie's extradition to France, Poulsifer confuses him with the Nazi commander responsible for his parents' death and goes on a personal campaign to become the conscience of an entire nation. Watching all this is Sharli Bandol, Rat Man's lover, who desperately tries to bring some order and love into the chaos of his condition. The birth of a son appears to temper Poulsifer's extremism, but to the end he retains his eccentricity and thus his individuality.

Like *The Very Rich Hours of Count von Stauffenberg*, *Rat Man of Paris* carefully examines the interplay between personal and public trauma, and as West puts it,

> Everybody who's born gets the ontological shock, and some people get the historical shock as well, and he has both. Because he has the historical shock, he has the ontological shock even worse, and this has blighted his life.

Thus the rat man stands as a contemporary Everyman, radically imperfect, overwhelmed by the world in which he finds himself, but tenaciously determined to make something of his existence.

Also like other of West's protagonists, Poulsifer demonstrates the vitality of the creative imagination. Were it not for his wild musings, the delight he takes in yoking utterly disparate things together in his mind, he would be consumed by history and dreary conventionality. In many ways he is the last free man, an essential primitive who refuses the definitions and restrictions of others for a life created on his own terms.

Terrestrials

West's seventeenth novel, *Terrestrials*, was actually a story over which he had labored for twenty years or more. It involves a pair of American pilots flying a secret reconnaissance jet over Africa. During one routine flight, they are forced to eject over the Danakil Desert. One of the men is put to work by members of a local tribe in the grueling duties of a salt-mining crew, while the other is stranded in his ejection capsule on the ledge of a nearby mountain. Miraculously they are both rescued, ferried off to Turkey, and "debriefed" by junior officers they despise who question their loyalty. They are then returned to the United States and are kept on a base for more questioning. Eventually they escape, open an air touring business, and evade an assassination attempt.

On the surface the plot may seem confusing and unspectacular; however, plotting is neither the novel's primary concern nor the source of its achievement. The novel is a bold attempt to evince some of what two minds undergo as a result of life-altering trauma. Each is oppressed with guilt, feeling that he has betrayed the other, and although the two are not actually friends, they are devoted to and dependent on each other. They grow closer as a result of their shared experience. In many ways the novel can be seen as a paean to friendship and near-filial devotion, and it asserts the intimate interconnectedness of all life.

Life with Swan

Another intimate portrait can be found in *Life with Swan*, a roman à clef about West's early courtship and years with his spouse of more than twenty years, the poet, naturalist, and writer Diane Ackerman (an anagram of her name—Ariada Mencken—is used for that of the female character). Set in the 1970's, the novel follows a middle-aged professor as he falls in love with a younger woman, against the advice of many of his friends and colleagues. The two begin a life that saves him from his excesses. Their mutual fascination with astronomy develops into a full-blown passion and culminates with their being witnesses, at the behest of Raoul Bunsen (a character who is an echo of cosmologist Carl Sagan), to the launches of the Viking spacecraft to Mars and the Voyager to Jupiter. If *Terrestrials* is a paean to friendship, *Life with Swan* is a companion piece that examines and glorifies the saving grace of unselfish love. The prose is lush and extravagant, every page lovingly adorned with West's incomparable lyricism.

Throughout his career, West has drawn criticism for his own stylistic eccentricities and rich verbal texturing. The usual complaint holds that he is self-indulgent and willfully obscure. While indeed his fiction makes considerable demands of his audience, he is anything but deliberately perverse or obscure. In fact, West consistently attempts to reach and communicate with his audience, to involve them, in each of his rich fictional stories. His note at the beginning of *Tenement of Clay*, the interview appended to *Caliban's Filibuster*, the footnotes in *Bela Lugosi's White Christmas*, the moments of direct address in *Colonel Mint*, the announcement in the middle of *Gala* of the novel's particular structure, and the preface to *The Very Rich Hours of Count von Stauffenberg*—all demonstrate that West is fully aware of his audience and always desirous of its sympathetic participation in the fictional experience.

West is committed to the proposition that writing matters and that good writing must present its own unique experience. As he says in his essay "In Defense of Purple Prose,"

> The ideal is to create a complex verbal world that has as much presence, as much apparent physical bulk, as the world around it. . . . This is an illusion, to be sure, but art *is* illusion, and what's needed is an art that temporarily blots out the real.

David W. Madden

Other major works

SHORT FICTION: *The Universe, and Other Fictions*, 1988.

POETRY: *Poems*, 1952; *The Spellbound Horses*, 1960; *The Snow Leopard*, 1964; *Tea with Osiris*, 2006.

NONFICTION: *The Growth of the Novel*, 1959; *Byron and the Spoiler's Art*, 1960, 2d edition 1992; *I, Said the Sparrow*, 1963; *The Modern Novel*, 1963; *Robert Penn Warren*, 1964; *The Wine of Absurdity: Essays in Literature and Consolation*, 1966; *Words for a Deaf Daughter*, 1969; *Out of My Depths: A Swimmer in the Universe*, 1983; *Sheer Fiction*, 1987-2007 (4 volumes); *Portable People*, 1990 (drawings by Joe Servello); *A Stroke of Genius: Illness and Self-Discovery*, 1995; *My Mother's Music*, 1995; *The Secret Lives of Words*, 2000; *Master Class: Scenes from a Fiction Workshop*, 2001; *Oxford Days: An Inclination*, 2002; *My Father's War*, 2005; *The Shadow Factory*, 2008.

EDITED TEXT: *Byron: Twentieth Century Views*, 1963.

Bibliography

Bellamy, Joe David. "Paul West." In *Literary Luxuries: American Writing at the End of the Millennium*. Columbia: University of Missouri Press, 1995. A discussion of West's work is included in this collection of previously published essays written by Bellamy, a literary critic, teacher, and editor.

Lucas, John. "Paul West." In *Contemporary Novelists*, edited by James Vinson. London: St. James Press, 1976. Lucas discusses West's Alley Jaggers sequence of novels, which "deservedly won his reputation as an original novelist," although he faults them for their lack of psychological study. Lists West's works up to 1975 and includes a statement by West.

McGuire, Thomas G. "The Face(s) of War in Paul West's

Fiction." *War, Literature, and the Arts* 10 (Spring/Summer, 1998): 169-186. Traces the persistence of West's rumination on warfare and conflict. Three principal novels—*The Very Rich Hours of Count von Stauffenberg*, *The Place in Flowers Where Pollen Rests*, and *Rat Man of Paris*—form the basis of the argument. The journal also contains an interview with West.

Madden, David W. "Indoctrination to Pariahdom: Liminality in the Fiction of Paul West." *Critique* 40 (Fall, 1998): 49-70. Examines five of West's novels to explain the confusions and violence they frequently contain. Madden argues that each novel presents characters suspended in a liminal state from which they try to extract themselves.

_______. *Understanding Paul West*. Columbia: University of South Carolina Press, 1993. A book-length study of West that provides an overview of his work through 1991. Intended as an introductory study of West's life and fiction, this work traces the development of the themes of identity, artistic creation, and imagination's freedom.

Meredith, James H. "Occupation, Resistance, and Espionage: An Analysis of John Steinbeck's *The Moon Is Down*, Jack Higgins' *The Eagle Has Landed*, and Paul West's *The Very Rich Hours of Count von Stauffenberg* and *Rat Man of Paris*." In *Understanding the Literature of World War II: A Student Casebook to Issues, Sources, and Historical Documents*. Westport, Conn.: Greenwood Press, 1999. This casebook is designed to help students better understand literary works about World War II. Contains an interview with West conducted in 1998.

Seaman, Donna. "Paul West." In *Writers on the Air: Conversations About Books*. Philadelphia: Paul Dry Books, 2005. A collection of interviews that Seaman conducted for her Chicago-based radio program *Open Books*. Her interview with West is included in a section of the book entitled "Genre Crossers."

West, Paul. "Paul West." In *Contemporary Authors: Autobiography Series*, edited by Mark Zadrozny. Vol. 7. Detroit, Mich.: Gale Research, 1988. A beautifully written autobiography, filled with rich images and information about West's early life, his ideas about writing, and other writers who became his friends. Includes a bibliography of his works.

REBECCA WEST

Cicily Isabel Fairfield

Born: London, England; December 21, 1892
Died: London, England; March 15, 1983
Also known as: Cicily Isabel Fairfield

Principal long fiction

The Return of the Soldier, 1918
The Judge, 1922
Harriet Hume: A London Fantasy, 1929
War Nurse: The True Story of a Woman Who Lived, Loved, and Suffered on the Western Front, 1930
The Harsh Voice, 1935
The Thinking Reed, 1936
The Fountain Overflows, 1956
The Birds Fall Down, 1966
This Real Night, 1984
Cousin Rosamund, 1985
Sunflower, 1986
The Sentinel: An Incomplete Early Novel, 2002 (Kathryn Laing, editor)

Other literary forms

Although Rebecca West excelled in a variety of literary genres, she first came to prominence as a book reviewer, a role that she continued throughout her life. From her first critique, which appeared in *The Freewoman* in 1911, to her last, which appeared in the *London Sunday Telegraph* on October 10, 1982, West wrote almost one thousand reviews. Several of these appear in the collection *The Young Rebecca* (1982). Her first book, *Henry James* (1916), which is an evaluation of Henry James's contributions to literature, was considered an audacious project for a young woman. This fearless honesty and willingness to write bluntly about sacrosanct persons and ideas marked West's entire career. After that bold debut, West published several other notable works of literary criticism. *The Strange Necessity: Essays and Reviews* (1928), a collection of essays from the *New York Herald Tribune* and the *New Statesman*, introduced one of West's recurring themes: the necessity of art in human life. *The Court and the Castle* (1957), based on lectures she delivered at Yale University, describes the role of the arts in government and society from the time of William Shakespeare to Franz Kafka.

West was also a prominent journalist and social commentator. Her coverage of the Nuremberg Trials (the trials of Nazi war criminals following World War II) appeared in *A Train of Powder* (1955). One of her most famous books, *Black Lamb and Grey Falcon: A Journey Through Yugoslavia* (1941), a combination travelogue, history, and sociopolitical commentary on the Balkans, is still considered essential reading for those who wish to understand the complexities of that area.

Achievements

Rebecca West was a writer of great perception, encyclopedic knowledge, extensive interests, and great curiosity. It is hard to categorize her work because of its variety and complexity. As a result, West's individual works, both fiction and nonfiction, have not received the critical analysis and acclaim that they deserve. She often received recognition for the body of her work, however. Certain universal themes permeate her writing: the nature of art, the frauds and weaknesses of the social system, the causes and results of treason and betrayal. West received numerous honors because of her ability to portray accurately the social milieu of the twentieth century. In 1937, West was made a member of the Order of St. Sava by Yugoslavia. The French government named her a Chevalier of the Legion of Honor in 1959. She became Dame Commander, Order of the British Empire, in 1959 and was made a Companion of Literature for the Royal Society of Literature in 1968. The American Academy of Arts and Letters inducted West as an honorary member in 1972. She also received the Women's National Press Club Award for journalism.

Biography

Rebecca West was born Cicily "Cissie" Isabel Fairfield, the youngest of three daughters of Charles Fairfield and Isabella Mackenzie. Charles Fairfield pursued several careers, including journalism, yet failed to succeed at any of them. In 1901, he abandoned his family in order to pursue yet another dream in Sierra Leone. Although he returned to England after a few months, he never again lived with his family. Still, West admired her father's Anglo-Irish gentility and charm, finding him a strong and romantic figure. Throughout her life she wrote fondly of him and frequently justified his poor treatment of his family.

After her father's departure, the family was forced to move to Isabella Mackenzie's family home in Edinburgh. West described this as a period of deprivation. Although the family had enough income to survive, they were caught between social classes, not fitting into any established social level. All three of the Fairfield daughters embraced feminism. West's first job, in 1911, was writing for *The Freewoman*, a weekly publication focusing on women's issues. In the spring of 1912, she adopted a pseudonym, Rebecca West, the name of a character she had once played in Henrik Ibsen's play *Rosmersholm* (pb. 1886; English translation, 1889). The character, a strong woman, mistress of a married man, convinces her lover to join her in suicide. Later, West said that this had been a hasty decision and that she liked neither the play nor the character. However, the name took hold, and to all but her family, Cissie had become Rebecca West.

West's reviews gained for her the attention of the London literary establishment. After reading her review of his novel *Marriage* (1912), H. G. Wells wished to meet its author. Although he was married, the two embarked on an intense ten-year affair. On August 4, 1914, West gave birth to a son, Anthony Panther West. Both West and Wells kept his true parentage from their son for many years, primarily since Wells did not wish to make the affair public. West even acquired adoption papers for Anthony in order to formalize her status as his parent.

Rebecca West. (Library of Congress)

Anthony West was particularly bitter about his mother's role in his life, often criticizing her in the press. The relationship between West and Wells was a tempestuous one. They frequently disagreed on social, political, and literary issues, as well as the details of their relationship and on child rearing. In addition, West often felt trapped by motherhood and was resentful of the freedom Wells had. Her literary career, however, met with growing success in both England and the United States. Her first novels received favorable comment. By 1923, her affair with Wells was ending, and she began a brief, unsuccessful liaison with newspaper magnate Max Beaverbrook.

In 1930, West married Henry Andrews, a banker she had met the previous year. Andrews worked for Schroder, a German banking firm. Both he and West became increasingly disturbed by the growing Nazi influence. Andrews, sympathetic to the plight of the Jews, helped many escape from Germany, a role that eventually caused the bank to fire him. During the 1930's, West became fascinated with the politics, history, and social mores of Yugoslavia. This increased her determination to encourage Britain to adopt an active role in combating the Nazi threat. In 1941, *Black Lamb and Grey Falcon*, West's monumental portrait of Yugoslavia, appeared and garnered popular acclaim.

After World War II, West published several works examining treason and justice. Her stance during the late 1940's and 1950's isolated her from many of her literary acquaintances because she felt Communism was a greater threat than Senator Joseph McCarthy and the actions of the U.S. House Committee on Un-American Activities. On November 3, 1968, Henry Andrews died. In spite of illnesses that crippled her during the 1970's, West continued working until her death in 1983.

Analysis

Rebecca West never received the same acclaim for her novels as she did for her critical and journalistic work. While her novels were praised for their complexity, West was often criticized for overintellectualizing her stories. Critics have frequently asserted that her novels lack action. In fact, all her novels are characterized by extended internal monologues. In addition, West uses long, complex sentences; she has frequently been compared to Henry James in both subject matter and style. A West novel demands the reader's close attention. Most of her novels take place during the Edwardian era or explore the values and social behaviors of that period. Within this background, her fiction examines the relationships between men and women, most of which seem doomed to failure. Her stories are presented through a feminine perspective; West's usual narrator is a young woman who is intelligent, sensitive, and clever.

The Return of the Soldier

The title character of her first short novel, *The Return of the Soldier*, is Chris Baldry, a shell-shocked soldier who is suffering from amnesia. This is a story about love rather than war, however. The novel opens as Chris's wife, Kitty, and his cousin Jenny, the narrator, wait to receive a letter from the war front. Instead they are visited by Margaret Grey, a shabbily dressed woman, who tells them that she has received a message from Chris. As a result of his injuries, Chris has forgotten the last fifteen years of his life, including his marriage, the death of his child, and his comfortable life in Baldry Hall. He remembers only Margaret, whom he had loved passionately fifteen years earlier, despite the difference in their social classes.

When Chris returns, he fails to recognize his wife, and he is desperately unhappy; the present has become a prison, keeping him from the person he loves—Margaret. Eventually he arranges to see her, finding that in spite of the ravages that years of poverty have caused, he is truly at ease only with her. Margaret, however, recognizes that because of their obvious class differences the two of them cannot hope for a life together, and she helps him regain his memory. Ironically, this allows him to resume his former life, and he realizes that he was never content. In addition, since he is now cured, he can return to his life as a soldier. The recovery of memory proves to be more tragic than its loss. *The Return of the Soldier* has the strengths common to West's novels: insight into the nature of romantic relationships, vivid descriptions of the influence of social background, and insightful examination of human nature.

The Judge

West's second novel, *The Judge*, a longer, more complex work than *The Return of the Soldier*, is divided into two sections: The first explores a young woman's coming-of-age, and the second centers on the tortured relationships in her fiancé's family. Several critics have complained that these sections differ so much in style and content that they do not form a satisfactory whole. The first part of the novel, set in Edinburgh, contains many autobiographical elements. The main character, Ellen Melville, a secretary for a law firm, is clever, independent, and involved in the woman suffrage movement. She emerges from youth into womanhood, dealing with problem employers and becoming involved with Richard Yaverland, whom she sees as a romantic hero. Ellen is both charming and intriguing as she learns somewhat bitter lessons about a woman's role in society. The engagement between Ellen and Richard leads to the second section of the novel, where the subject and mood shift dramatically.

The focus moves from Ellen to Richard's mother, Marion, as West concentrates on Richard's illegitimate birth and its consequences. During her pregnancy, Marion is attacked by a group of villagers. In desperation, she allows herself to be married to Peacey, the butler of the man she loves. He eventually rapes her, and she bears a second child, Roger, a pale and pathetic figure beside his more vigorous brother. Marion, whose relationship with Richard contains strong sexual overtones, commits suicide in order to allow Richard and Ellen to be free of his ties to her and to his past. Roger blames his brother for the death. The two fight, and Richard kills his brother. In spite of this novel's dramatic content, it has been criticized for its lack of action as well as for its length.

Harriet Hume

West's previous novels utilized the Freudian psychological realism of many twentieth century novels. In her third novel, *Harriet Hume*, she changed her style, creating a fantasy. The two main characters, Harriet, a pianist, and Arnold Condorex, a politician, both have weaknesses that jeopardize their careers: Harriet's hands are too small to span the keys of the piano as she would like; Arnold was not born to a family with power and social class. Both succeed in spite of their difficulties, however. Their relationship is complicated by Arnold's need to be involved with a woman who will aid his political career and by the fact that Harriet possesses psychic powers, which enable her to read the mind of her lover. The novel traces their meetings throughout the years, describing both the fascination they have for each other and the differences in the values that they have embraced. The novel is a fable illustrating some of the main themes of West's work: the necessity of art in love and life as well as the complex reasons men give to justify betrayal.

The Thinking Reed

The Thinking Reed focuses on the lives of the wealthy, in particular, a young widow and the men she pursues and who pursue her. Critics have noted that West deviates from other writers of her time in her depiction of this moneyed social class. *The Thinking Reed* has often been compared with *The Portrait of a Lady* (1881), Henry James's novel that associates wealth with personal liberty, and *The Great Gatsby* (1925), F. Scott Fitzgerald's morality tale that links wealth with decadence. West, in contrast to her American predecessors, compares persons of wealth to wild animals, attributing to them an instinctive desire for power and a dangerous disregard for the well-being of others.

The title of this novel is drawn from Blaise Pascal's seventeenth century defense of Christianity, *Pensées*

(1670; *Monsieur Pascal's Thoughts, Meditations, and Prayers*, 1688), and West begins with an epigram selected from this work. The passage likens man to a vulnerable "thinking reed," noble in pursuing life with passion despite knowledge of certain death. West's heroine is Isabella Terry, a young American who distracts herself from the recent loss of her husband by pursuing a series of men in France, her ancestral country. Isabella is, in succession, the mistress of a French noble, whom she rejects for being controlling; the love interest of a Virginian abroad, who rejects her for her own unseemly behavior; and finally the wife of a French industrialist, whom she marries to spite the rejecting American. Her marriage is unhappy and, following a miscarriage, she considers obtaining a divorce. Her meditations on her situation, however, cause her to reconsider. Eventually, Isabella places the needs of another, her husband, ahead of her own, and she finds in this abnegation of self a measure of happiness.

The Fountain Overflows

The Fountain Overflows is the first of a four-novel series West planned to write centering on the Aubrey family, patterned on her own family. Only the first of these works appeared before her death; two more, *This Real Night* and *Cousin Rosamund*, were published posthumously. She never completed the fourth novel. *The Fountain Overflows* is a childhood memory. It describes the Aubrey children's survival after their father deserts them: Cordelia, the eldest; the twins Mary and Rose; and Richard Quin, the youngest member of the family. Filled with vivid detail, this novel contains not only a rich portrait of family life but also a murder and several supernatural occurrences, all presented from a child's perspective. West's subject matter and style in this novel have been compared to the richly textured writings of Charles Dickens and Arnold Bennett.

The Birds Fall Down

The Birds Fall Down, one of the most popular of West's novels, marks another departure in subject matter. The story, set in 1905, is narrated by Laura Rowen, an eighteen-year-old whose grandfather, a Russian grand duke, has been unfairly exiled by the czar. The main plot deals with treachery and betrayal, set against the backdrop of the political turmoil in Russia during this period. Clearly, however, West is developing themes she explores in her history book *The Meaning of Treason* (1947). As Laura journeys through France with her grandfather, he learns that his trusted aide is a double agent responsible for his disgrace. Her grandfather has a stroke and dies, and Laura has to struggle to escape from the traitor. The secondary plot line describes her father's affair, a betrayal of his wife and family that runs a parallel course to the treachery on the international level.

This Real Night

Published after West's death, *This Real Night* is the second installment in the chronicles of the Aubrey family. The children featured in *The Fountain Overflows* are now young adults beset by problems associated with the modern age. Conflicts in the novel range from the local to the global, from family disputes to world war, with the former acting as a microcosm of the latter. Richard Quin, the only son in the family, remains the favorite sibling of his older sisters. Central to the novel's exploration of modern life is the crisis of World War I. Richard Quin is no warrior, but following his enlistment, he goes to war. His interest in sports—the fencing, boxing, tennis, and cricket of his youth—fails to arm him effectively for battle. After Richard Quin dies at the front, his sisters confront the effects of his permanent absence. For them there is no glory, only loss.

This Real Night continues the psychological exploration of sibling relations begun in *The Fountain Overflows*. West describes Richard Quin in both feminine and masculine terms. Raised in a matriarchy comprising sisters and a mother, Richard Quin develops a feminine sensitivity while embracing the socially prescribed role of man of the house. At home, he is the de facto protector of his sisters. Unfortunately, when Richard Quin is out in the war-torn world, his older sisters can offer no protection to their brother in return. Their isolation as women on the home front, far from the scene of their brother's death, intensifies their grief.

Sunflower

Sunflower, a fictional account of the author's affair with H. G. Wells, was begun in 1925 and later discarded. It is likely that West never intended for the manuscript to be published, but three years after her death it appeared in print, an incomplete sketch. The writing is unique for its dreamlike qualities, and the story shifts between descriptions of events and the character's interpretations of those events relayed through interior monologues. When West began the novel, she was undergoing psychotherapy to reduce her post-Wells trauma. Notes that she composed for those sessions may have made their way into the book in a curious convergence of fiction and life writing. The title character, Sybil Fassendyll, nicknamed Sunflower, is patterned after West. Sunflower is a young actor engaged in an affair with an older, married intellectual, Lord Essington, a depiction of Wells. While the novel chronicles certain events in the author's life, critics have noted that West was far superior to her fictional alter ego. Sunflower appears a bit dimwitted in certain passages, a trait never associated with the intellectual West.

Mary E. Mahony
Updated by Dorothy Dodge Robbins

Other major works

NONFICTION: *Henry James*, 1916; *The Strange Necessity: Essays and Reviews*, 1928; *Ending in Earnest: A Literary Log*, 1931; *St. Augustine*, 1933 (biography); *Black Lamb and Grey Falcon: A Journey Through Yugoslavia*, 1941; *The Meaning of Treason*, 1947 (revised as *The New Meaning of Treason*, 1964); *A Train of Powder*, 1955; *The Court and the Castle*, 1957; *The Young Rebecca: Writings of Rebecca West*, 1982; *Family Memories*, 1987; *Selected Letters of Rebecca West*, 2000; *Survivors in Mexico*, 2003; *Woman as Artist and Thinker*, 2005.

MISCELLANEOUS: *Rebecca West: A Celebration*, 1977.

Bibliography

Glendinning, Victoria. *Rebecca West: A Life*. New York: Alfred A. Knopf, 1986. Presents a detailed account of West's life, focusing particularly on the early years. Provides insight into West's development as a writer.

Lesinska, Zofia. *Perspectives of Four Women Writers on the Second World War: Gertrude Stein, Janet Flanner, Kay Boyle, and Rebecca West*. New York: Peter Lang, 2002. Relies on textual evidence drawn from West's novels, essays, political writings, and correspondence to reveal how her written responses to warfare are distinct from those of her contemporaries.

Norton, Ann V. *Paradoxical Feminism: The Novels of Rebecca West*. Lanham, Md.: International Scholars, 1999. Offers comprehensive analysis of West's novels in terms of their feminist themes, plots, and characters. Includes discussion of the author as a problematic feminist.

Rollyson, Carl E. *Rebecca West: A Life*. New York: Charles Scribner's Sons, 1996. Detailed biography discusses West's importance to twentieth century literature, tracing the development of her long career and illustrating the connections between her fiction and nonfiction.

Schweizer, Bernard. *Rebecca West: Heroism, Rebellion, and the Female Epic*. Westport, Conn.: Greenwood Press, 2002. Argues that West, in her novels and her travel writing, reinvents the epic tradition to serve the cause of feminism. Presents West as a philosopher whose ideas are more spiritual than political in origin.

_______, ed. *Rebecca West Today: Contemporary Critical Approaches*. Newark: University of Delaware Press, 2006. Nearly all of West's works are discussed in this volume, the first published collection of essays devoted to her writing. Included are in-depth analyses of ten novels, two short stories, one essay, and two of her journalistic writings. The chapter that West omitted from her novel *The Real Night* is also discussed at length.

Scott, Bonnie Kime. *Refiguring Modernism*. 2 vols. Bloomington: Indiana University Press, 1995. First volume of this set discusses women of 1928; second volume offers postmodern feminist readings of the works of Virginia Woolf, Djuna Barnes, and West.

Varney, Susan. "Oedipus and the Modern Aesthetic: Reconceiving the Social in Rebecca West's *The Return of the Soldier*." In *Naming the Father: Legacies, Genealogies, and Explorations of Fatherhood in Modern and Contemporary Fiction*, edited by Eva Paulino Bueno, Terry Caesar, and William Hummel. Lanham, Md.: Rowman & Littlefield, 2000. Examines events and characters in West's *Return of the Soldier* in relation to the story of Oedipus. Contends that West updated the tragic Greek character to serve a new age and a new art.

EDITH WHARTON

Born: New York, New York; January 24, 1862
Died: St.-Brice-sous-Forêt, France; August 11, 1937
Also known as: Edith Newbold Jones

Principal long fiction

The Touchstone, 1900
The Valley of Decision, 1902
Sanctuary, 1903
The House of Mirth, 1905
The Fruit of the Tree, 1907
Madame de Treymes, 1907
Ethan Frome, 1911
The Reef, 1912
The Custom of the Country, 1913
Summer, 1917
The Marne, 1918
The Age of Innocence, 1920
The Glimpses of the Moon, 1922
A Son at the Front, 1923
Old New York, 1924 (4 volumes; includes *False Dawn*, *The Old Maid*, *The Spark*, and *New Year's Day*)
The Mother's Recompense, 1925
Twilight Sleep, 1927
The Children, 1928
Hudson River Bracketed, 1929
The Gods Arrive, 1932
The Buccaneers, 1938

Other literary forms

In addition to her novels, of which several had appeared serially in *Scribners*, *The Delineator*, and *The Pictorial Review*, Edith Wharton (HWAWRT-uhn) published eleven collections of short stories and three volumes of poetry as well as a variety of nonfiction works. She wrote an early and influential book on interior decorating and design, *The Decoration of Houses* (1897; in collaboration with architect Ogden Codman, Jr.); a short book on the art of narrative, *The Writing of Fiction* (1925), published originally in *Scribner's* magazine; and a delightful if highly selective autobiography, *A Backward Glance* (1934), which includes, among other things, an amusing account of Henry James's circumlocutory manner of speech.

Wharton, an indefatigable traveler, recorded accounts of her travels in *Italian Villas and Their Gardens* (1904), *Italian Backgrounds* (1905), *A Motor-Flight Through France* (1908), and *In Morocco* (1920). During World War I, she wrote numerous pamphlets and letters to inform Americans about French and Belgian suffering and to enlist sympathy and support. Articles she wrote to explain the French people to American soldiers were later collected in the volume *French Ways and Their Meaning* (1919), and accounts of her five tours of the front lines were published under the title *Fighting France, from Dunkerque to Belfort* (1915). Wharton also published a great many short stories, articles, and reviews that have never been collected. A number of her stories and novels have been adapted for the stage, motion pictures, and television, and have also been translated into French, Italian, Spanish, German, Danish, Finnish, and Japanese.

Achievements

Unlike Henry James, whose readership was small and intensely discriminating, Edith Wharton managed to attract a large audience of general readers and at the same time command the interest of critics and fellow writers as well. Among her admirers were Sinclair Lewis and F. Scott Fitzgerald; Bernard Berenson, the art critic; and Percy Lubbock. Wharton's popularity remained high almost to the end of her career in the 1930's, but critical enthusiasm began to diminish after 1920, when the quality of her fiction declined.

Even in the early years, 1905 to 1920, when Wharton's best fiction was being published, there were reservations expressed or implied by those who thought her a follower of and to some extent a lesser James, a charge easier to disprove than to eradicate. The truth is, though Wharton learned from James—and a few of her novels, particularly *Madame de Treymes*, reflect Jamesian themes as well as techniques—Wharton had her own manner as well as her own subject, and as she grew older, she continued to discover differences between her fiction and James's. It should also be pointed out (whether in praise or blame will depend on the critic) that James was a more dedicated artist than Wharton; his fiction had a finish and a coherence to be found in only a half dozen of her novels; moreover, Wharton sometimes skated on the thin ice of superficiality, and in one novel, *The Glimpses of the Moon*, plunged through. Toward the end of her career, she also grew increasingly out of touch with life in the postwar world, much of which offended her. Her long residence in France, moreover, not only cut her off from the life of her fellow countryfolk but also—since she spoke French or Italian almost exclusively—loosened her grasp of English, so much so that a critic such as the young Edmund Wilson could complain that there were awkward phrases even in her masterpiece *The Age of Innocence*.

Wharton's major talent was for social observation. Unlike James, whose interest was ultimately metaphysical and whose novels were often invented from the slightest hints and employed few details, Wharton filled her novels with precise accounts of the decoration of houses, of dress and of dinner parties, describing them often down to the cut of a waistcoat and the contents of the soup tureen. This is not to say that such details were signs of superficiality, but rather that Wharton's fictions depended heavily on the notation of manners and were the result of direct observation. Wharton tended to write—again, unlike James—out of her own direct experience. Even novels such as *Ethan Frome* and *Summer*—both set in provincial New England and so different from the world she inhabited in New York and Paris—were created with remarkable attention to surface details, of which the famous cut-glass, red pickle dish in *Ethan Frome* is a familiar example.

Wharton's fiction was (again, unlike James's) significantly autobiographical. Even the novels of provincial life, so different on the surface, treated issues that came out of the tensions of her own restricted upbringing and her unhappy marriage. Marriage was one of Wharton's principal subjects and provided her with a way of exploring and dramatizing her two main themes: the entrapment of an individual, as R. W. B. Lewis puts it in his *Edith Wharton: A Biography* (1975), and the attempt by an outsider, often a vulgar lower-class individual, to break into an old, aristocratic society. There is a sense in which these two themes are contradictory: The first one implies a point of view that identifies with the individual rather than with society; the second one judges from the point of view of society. The apparent contradiction, however, merely points up the range and boundaries of the author's sensibility. In some novels—*Ethan Frome* and *The House of Mirth*, for example—Wharton writes with sympathy of the trapped individual; in others, *The Custom of the Country* and *The Children*, she writes from the standpoint of a traditional society. In her best novels, there is both sympathy for the trapped individual and the invocation of an outside claim—marriage vows, moral code, traditional manners—with the balance of sympathy tipped to the individual.

Wharton's major work was written between 1905, the year *The House of Mirth* was published, and 1920, when *The Age of Innocence* appeared. Interesting novels were still to come: *The Mother's Recompense*, *The Children*, and *The Buccaneers*, which has the best qualities of her earlier fiction; but the major works of the late 1920's and early 1930's, *Hudson River Bracketed* and *The Gods Arrive*, betray a serious falling off of energy and of talent. In these novels, Wharton was attempting to judge the contemporary world by the values of the past, but was so out of sympathy with the life around her and so out of touch with its manners that her representation of it in these later books can hardly be taken seriously.

Despite this later decline, however, and despite the undeniable influence of James on some of her early work, Wharton produced a considerable body of original fiction, high in quality and superior to most of what was being published at the time. Her fiction also influenced other, younger American writers, notably Sinclair Lewis and F. Scott Fitzgerald. After a long decline in readership and a period of critical indifference, there now appears to be a renewal of interest in her writing, both by critics and scholars of the American novel and by feminist scholars interested in extraliterary issues.

BIOGRAPHY

Edith Wharton was born Edith Newbold Jones on January 24, 1862, in New York City. Her parents, George Frederic and Lucretia Rhinelander Jones, were descendants of early English and Dutch settlers and belonged to the pre-Civil War New York aristocracy, families whose wealth consisted largely of Manhattan real estate and who constituted in their common ancestry, landed wealth, and traditional manners a tightly knit, closed society. With the industrial expansion that occurred during and immediately after the Civil War, the old society was "invaded" by a new class of self-made rich men such as John Jacob Astor and Cornelius Vanderbilt. Whereas the old society had lived unostentatiously, observing, outwardly at least, a strict code of manners—the women presiding over a well-regulated social life and the men making perfunctory gestures at pursuing a profession—the new rich spent lavishly, built expensive and vulgar houses, and behaved in ways the old order found shockingly reprehensible. With its energy, its money, and its easier morality, the new order inevitably triumphed over the old, and this displacement of New York society constituted one of the chief subjects of Wharton's fiction, particularly in *The House of Mirth* and *The Custom of the Country*.

Edith Wharton. (Library of Congress)

Wharton was educated at home by governesses and, later, tutors, and it was expected that she would assume the role young women of her class were educated to play, that of wife, mother, and gracious host. From an early age, however, Wharton showed intellectual and literary talents that, along with an acute shyness, kept her at the edge of conventional social life and later threatened to consign her at the age of twenty-three to a life of spinsterhood—the worst fate, so it was thought, that could befall a young woman of her class. After one engagement had been called off (because the young man's mother opposed it) and a promising relationship with a young lawyer, Walter Berry (who later became a close friend), had failed to develop romantically, Wharton married a man twelve years her senior, Edward "Teddy" Robbins Wharton, a friend of her favorite brother.

Teddy Wharton was a socially prominent Bostonian without a profession or money of his own; James and other friends in England were later incredulous that Wharton could marry someone so obviously her intellectual inferior and so incompatible in his interests. Nevertheless, the marriage in the beginning must have been a liberation, both from the social pressure to marry and from her mother's domination. Wharton was close to her father, but there was a coolness between her and her mother that is frequently reflected in her fiction in the portrayal of mother-daughter relationships. By marrying Teddy, she was at last free to come and go as she pleased; to establish her own residence, which she did on a grand scale at Lenox, Massachusetts; and to travel abroad as often as she liked. In time, however, the marriage to Teddy became irksome, partly from lack of deep affection for him but also because of his increasing bouts of depression and, later, his financial and sexual irresponsibilities. After revelations of his mismanagement of her estate and his adulterous affairs, she divorced him in 1913. In researching for the biography of Wharton, Lewis found that she, too, had had a brief but intense affair in 1908 with an American journalist named Morton Fullerton, and that relationship had a profound influence on her fiction.

Wharton had lived and traveled in Europe as a child with her parents and after her marriage had visited abroad as often as possible, alternating the seasons between her house at Lenox and an apartment in Paris, with shorter visits to England and rural France. In 1903, when she met James in England, there began an important friendship, with frequent visits and exchanges of letters and motor trips in Wharton's powerful automobile. The Whartons always traveled in luxury, and their style and Edith's energy quite overwhelmed James at the same time he delighted in them. Like James, and for somewhat the same reasons, Wharton became in time an expatriate, giving up the newer, rawer life of America for the rich, deeply rooted culture of Europe. She felt at home in the salons and drawing rooms of Paris and London, where art and literature and ideas were discussed freely, where women were treated by men as equals, and where life itself was more pleasing to the senses and to the contemplative mind. Wharton also felt that in Europe, respect for the family, for manners, for learning, and for culture, even among the poorer classes, was very much alive.

Even before the final break with Teddy, Wharton had lengthened her frequent stays abroad and, finally, in 1911, allowed the house at Lenox to be sold. When World War I broke out, she remained in Paris and devoted her time, energy, and money to the relief of French and Belgian refugees; in 1916, she was officially recognized for her services to her adopted country by being made a chevalier of the Legion of Honor. After the war, she bought a house just north of Paris and, later, another in the south of France. She made only one more trip home, in 1923, to receive an honorary degree at Yale. The remainder of her life was spent abroad.

According to those who knew her well, Wharton was a highly intelligent, well-read, brilliant conversationalist, somewhat remote at first, though the grand manner that many complained of was apparently a way of covering up her deep shyness. She read and spoke Italian and French fluently, and her salons in both Paris and Saint Claire were gathering places for literary, artistic, and social luminaries of the time, including such well-known figures as Fitzgerald, Bernard Berenson, Jean Cocteau, Aldous Huxley, and Kenneth Clark. Despite the hectic pace of her social life and her frequent travels, Wharton continued to write regularly, turning out novels and short stories and articles, most of which sold well and brought her a great deal of money. She suffered a slight stroke in 1935, which for a time curtailed her activities; two years later, she was fatally stricken. After a short illness, she died at her home in St.-Brice-sous-Forêt, August 11, 1937. Her body was buried in a cemetery at Versailles, beside the grave where the ashes of her old friend, Walter Berry, had been buried earlier.

Analysis

On a surface level, there is a surprising variety in the kinds of characters and the aspects of life with which Edith Wharton was familiar. In *The House of Mirth*, for example, one of her best novels, she was able to create characters such as the Trenors and the Van Osburghs, who belong to opposite ends of the upper level of old New York society, as well as Nettie Struther, the poor working-class girl who befriends Lily Bart when she has sunk from the glittering world of Fifth Avenue social life to a seedy, boardinghouse existence. In *The Fruit of the Tree*, she created not only the world of the fashionable Westmores but also the factory milieu in which the foreman John Amherst attempts to bring industrial reform. In *The Reef*, she could treat life in a French château, as well as in a sordid hotel in Paris, and in her two brilliant short novels, *Ethan Frome* and *Summer*, she managed to depict a life in rural Massachusetts that she could have known only by observation rather than by direct experience.

It must be admitted, however, that Wharton is at times less than convincing. Some critics consider her attempt to deal with factory life in *The Fruit of the Tree* inept, even ludicrous, though others believe it entirely adequate; and certainly the life of impoverished Nettie Struther is delineated with nothing like the thoroughness of Lily Bart's, whose upper-class milieu Wharton knew at first hand. Still, the extent of Wharton's social range and her ability to create realistic characters from a background quite different from her own is impressive, unrivaled in American fiction of the time.

As for variety of character types, one might cite in particular those to be found in *The House of Mirth*, in the range of male characters—from the fastidious Selden to the rapacious Gus Trenor and the socially ambiguous and vulgar Simon Rosedale, all of them suitors for Lily's attention. Both *Ethan Frome* and *Summer* present a more limited range, but both contain sharply realized and distinctly differentiated characters, including the powerful Ethan, the pretty young Mattie, and Zeena, the neurasthenic wife of Ethan. In *Summer*, Charity Royall, the mountain girl, is vividly created, as is her feckless young lover and her elderly guardian and attempted seducer, Lawyer Royall.

Despite this surface breadth, this impressive range of social observation, Wharton's novels have a rather narrow thematic focus. It has been said that Wharton's chief theme is entrapment. Blake Nevious, in *Edith Wharton: A Study of Her Fiction* (1953), points out how this theme is implicit in the principal relationships among characters in many of the novels, in which a superior nature is caught in a wasteful and baffling submission to an inferior nature. It was a situation that Wharton herself must have experienced, not only with a mother who was obsessed with fashion and propriety but also in a society narrowly given up to the pursuit of pleasure. It was a situation in which she later found herself in her marriage to Teddy, who disliked and resented her interest in social and intellectual life. In novel after novel, one sees this same situation treated—superior individuals trapped in relationships with their inferiors and prevented from extricating themselves by a finer sensibility.

The House of Mirth

In *The House of Mirth*, Lily Bart is impoverished by the bankruptcy and later the death of her father and is obliged to recoup her fortune in the only way open to her, by attempting to marry a rich man. Lily's situation was not Wharton's, but the social pressures on her must have been similar: to make a suitable marriage, with social position certainly, and, if possible, money as well. In the novel, Lily is given a choice that Wharton apparently did not have: an offer of marriage from an emancipated young lawyer of her own class (though Berry, a lawyer, was thought at one time to have been Wharton's suitor). Wharton chose a passionless marriage with Teddy; Lily was not allowed that solution. Selden deserts her at the crucial moment, and she dies of an overdose of sleeping medicine.

In her autobiography *A Backward Glance*, Wharton stated that her subject in *The House of Mirth* was to be the tragic power of New York society in "debasing people and ideas," and Lily Bart was created to give that power dramatic scope. Lily's entrapment by society and her eventual destruction are not the final story. Lily overcomes the limitations of her upbringing and aspirations and acts on principle. She has in her possession a packet of letters that she could use to regain her social position, but the letters would involve the reputation of Selden. She also has an inheritance of ten thousand dollars that she could use to establish herself in a profitable business, but she burns the letters and uses the money to repay a debt of honor. Lily dies, but in choosing death rather than dishonor, she escapes entrapment.

The Age of Innocence

In *The Age of Innocence*, published fifteen years after *The House of Mirth*, the underlying conflict is the same, though the tone of the novel and the nature of the entrapment are somewhat different. Here, the trapped individual is a man, Newland Archer, a young lawyer who is engaged to marry May Welland, a pretty and shallow young woman of respectable old New York society of the 1870's and 1890's. This is the world of Wharton's young womanhood, a society that is narrow and rigid and socially proper.

Into this limited and self-contained world, she brings Ellen Olenska, a cousin of May, who belongs to this world by birth but left it years before and has since married a Polish count. Ellen has now separated from her husband, who has been notoriously unfaithful, and has returned to the bosom of her family for support and comfort. Archer is engaged by the family to help her in her quest for a divorce settlement. The inevitable happens: Archer and Ellen fall in love. Archer is attracted by Ellen's European sophistication, her freedom of thought and manners, and her refusal to take seriously the small taboos of New York society. Archer considers breaking with May and marrying Ellen. The family, sensing his defection, contrive with other members of the society to separate the lovers and reunite Archer with May, his conventional fiancé. Social pressure forces Ellen to return to Europe, and Archer is again thinking of pursuing

Ellen; then May announces that she is expecting a baby. Archer is finally and permanently trapped.

As though to drive home the extent to which Archer has been defeated, Wharton takes him to Paris years later. His son is grown, his wife is dead, and Ellen Olenska is now a widow living alone. Archer makes an appointment to see Ellen but gets only as far as a park bench near her apartment. At the last minute, he decides to send his son to see her, while he remains seated on the bench, telling himself that it would be more real for him to remain there than to go himself to see Ellen. The trap has done its work.

While one can see resemblances between Ellen and Wharton—the expatriation, the charm, the liberated views, perhaps even the slight French accent with which Ellen speaks—Archer is also Wharton, or that side of her that could never entirely escape the past. *The Age of Innocence* was thought by some reviewers to be a glorification of the past, which it clearly is not. Wharton does evoke with some nostalgia the old New York of her youth, but she also sets forth with delicate but cutting irony that society's limitations and its destructive narrowness. Archer has led an exemplary life, one is led to believe, but the happiness he might have had was gently but firmly denied him. Whereas a more popular novelist might have allowed Archer to be reunited with Ellen at the end of the novel, Wharton insists that that would be unreal; for her, personal happiness in the real world is the exception rather than the rule.

ETHAN FROME

Two of Wharton's best novels—also two of her shortest—both deal with protagonists trapped by passionless marriages. The earlier of these, *Ethan Frome*, is about a Massachusetts farmer married to an older, neurasthenic wife, whose pretty young cousin has come to work for her. The inevitable again happens: Ethan falls in love with Mattie and dreams about running away with her. Ethan's jealous wife, however, arranges for Mattie to be sent away, and Ethan is obliged to escort her to the train station. It is winter, and the lovers stop for a brief time together. They embrace, realize the inevitability of separation, and decide to kill themselves by coasting down a steep hill into a great elm tree. During the ride down the steep hill, Ethan accidentally swerves the sled; a crash occurs, in which the lovers are seriously injured but survive. Mattie becomes a disabled whiner, while Zeena, the neurotic wife, takes over the running of the household. Ethan, who is severely disfigured, feels himself like a handcuffed convict, a prisoner for life.

As Lewis has pointed out, the situation in *Ethan Frome* is very much like the situation in Wharton's own life at the time. If one shifts the genders, Frome is Wharton trapped in a loveless marriage with the neurasthenic Teddy and passionately in love with a younger man who shared her interests and feelings, Morton Fullerton. The violent ending, of course, may be seen as Wharton's passionate statement about her own desperate situation. The success of *Ethan Frome*, however, does not depend on making such biographical connections; the book is a brilliantly realized work of realistic fiction that owes its power not to some abstractly conceived pessimistic philosophy of life, but to Wharton's successful transposition of her own emotional life into the language of fiction.

SUMMER

Summer was published six years after *Ethan Frome* and was called by Wharton and her friends the "hot Ethan." As in *Ethan Frome*, there is a triangle: Lawyer Royall, elderly guardian of Charity, a pretty young mountain girl, and a visiting architecture student, Lucius Harney. During the idyllic summer months, an intense and passionate affair takes place between Charity and Harney. Harney returns to Boston, and Charity is left to face her guardian, who is also in love with her, and the prospect of an illegal abortion. The novel concludes with a reconciliation between Charity and her guardian and a secure if passionless marriage with him.

While it would be a mistake to overemphasize biographical parallels, they are unmistakable. The affair of Charity and Harney suggests Wharton's earlier affair with Fullerton, while the intrusive presence of the fatherly Lawyer Royall suggests Teddy's irksome claims on Wharton's loyalties. An interesting alteration of chronology is in making the marriage with the older man follow the affair rather than precede it, as it had in Wharton's own life. *Summer* was written four years after the Whartons were divorced, and by then, she may have had time to view her marriage to Teddy more dispassionately, as the practical solution it must originally have been. Like Lily's death, the surrender to marriage is a defeat as well as a moral triumph. *Summer* is one of Wharton's finest novels, written, according to her own testimony, in a state of "creative joy" and reflecting in its characters, scenes, and symbolic structures the deep well of the unconscious that seems to nourish the most powerful works of American fiction.

The Reef

The Reef, published the year before the Whartons' divorce and commonly acknowledged to be Wharton's most Jamesian novel, again deals with conflicts between the individual and society and the problems of marriage. In this novel, however, the society is remote; the inheritor of the society's standards, Anna Leath, an American widow of a French nobleman, is reunited with an old friend, lawyer George Darrow, also an American, living in Europe. Anna and Darrow become engaged and are about to be married when Anna discovers that Darrow has had an affair with Sophy Viner, her daughter's governess, a girl of a lower class, and that Sophy, who is also her stepson's fiancé, is still in love with Darrow. For Darrow the situation is a matter of diplomatic maneuvering, of steering his way between the two women and the stepson; for Anna it presents a moral dilemma involving, on one hand, an inherited code of conduct that tells her that Darrow must be abandoned and, on the other hand, a personal code that tells her not to give him up.

The moral complexities of the novel are a good deal more intricate than summary can indicate—indeed, they are so ambiguous that one is hard-pressed to decide where the author stands. It is possible, however, to see in this novel situations parallel to Wharton's earlier involvement with Fullerton, and a possible moral dilemma over her own infidelity. In a sense, Wharton is Sophy Viner, but Sophy (and Wharton's affair with Fullerton) seen in the light of a later moral judgment; Wharton is also Anna, attempting to accept the break with conventional morality that led to Darrow's affair with Sophy. The trap in which Anna finds herself is doubly baited, and no matter which way she turns, she must fall, either morally or emotionally. The fact that Anna chooses Darrow after all suggests the same kind of compromise other Wharton protagonists have made, Justine of *The Fruit of the Tree* and Charity Royall of *Summer* especially, both of whom were betrayed by the weakness of the men they loved but settled for what was finally available.

The Custom of the Country

The Custom of the Country is a different sort of work, influenced by the French realist Honoré de Balzac rather than by James. The novel attempts to deal, as did Balzac, with the destruction of an aristocracy by the invasion of uncivilized materialists.

The protagonist of the novel, Undine Spragg, is a handsome young woman from Apex, a city in the American Midwest. Undine's father made a great deal of money in Apex and now has come East to try his hand in New York City. The Spraggs move into an expensive hotel, and the parents would be content to exist on the fringes of New York society. Undine, however, who is as ambitious as she is vulgar, manages to meet and then marry Ralph Marvel, an ineffectual member of old New York society. When life with Marvel grows boring, Undine becomes the mistress of a richer and more aggressive New York aristocrat, Peter Van Degen; when Van Degen drops her, she manages to snare the Marquis de Chelles, the son of an old aristocratic French family. Undine marries de Chelles, but she has learned nothing, being without taste, manners, or ideas; her sole interest is in amusing and gratifying herself. As soon as she gets what she thinks she wants, she becomes dissatisfied with it and wants something she decides is better. She grows tired of having to fit herself into the demands of the feudal aristocracy into which she has married; when she attempts to sell family heirlooms, whose value she does not understand, her husband divorces her. Her third husband is a perfect match, a hard-driving vulgar materialist from Apex, Elmer Moffat, whose chief interest is in buying European art. Moffat also aspires to an ambassadorial post but is barred because he is married to Undine, a divorced woman.

The Custom of the Country is regarded by some critics as among Wharton's best fiction, but, as Blake Nevius has observed, during the course of the novel, Undine ceases to be a credible character and becomes an "inhuman abstraction." Clearly, she came to represent everything that Wharton detested in the America of 1912 and, at a deeper and vaguer level, perhaps also expressed Wharton's fear and resentment at the displacement of her own class by more energetic and less cultivated outsiders. The fact that such fears were real enough and the implicit social criticisms valid does nothing to alter the fact that, measured against books such as *The House of Mirth*, *Ethan Frome*, *Summer*, and *The Reef*, the novel *The Custom of the Country* is crude and unconvincing. James had been right years earlier in advising Wharton to write about that part of the world she knew best, for in attempting to deal with the Midwest in *The Custom of the Country*, and later, in *Hudson River Bracketed* and *The Gods Arrive*, with bohemian circles about which she knew very little, she condemned herself to superficiality and caricature. It is difficult to take seriously Undine of *The Custom of the Country* or Advance Weston, the protagonist of *Hudson River Bracketed* and *The Gods Arrive*, who is said to be from Pruneville, Nebraska, and later Hallelujah, Missouri, and Euphoria, Illinois. Caricature is an expression of outrage, not understanding.

The Buccaneers

Fortunately, the last of Wharton's novels, *The Buccaneers*, published the year after her death, was a return to the territory of her earlier fiction, old New York of the 1870's. The novel was unfinished at her death and lacks the coherence of her best early work, but she could still write with the sharpness and scenic fullness that had characterized *The House of Mirth* and *The Age of Innocence*.

Wharton was a novelist of manners, then, not a chronicler of large social movements. Her real subject was the entrapment of superior individuals who keenly feel the pull of moral responsibility. Her talents for social observation, for noting subtleties of dress and decoration, for nuance of voice and phrase, and for language—precise and yet expressive—were essential instruments in the creation of her novels. Wharton has been unduly charged with pessimism; her characteristic tone is ironic, the product of a sensibility able to see and feel the claims on both sides of a human dilemma. If her voice faltered in her later years and she conceded too much to the popular taste for which she increasingly wrote, she nevertheless produced some of the finest American fiction published in the first two decades of the century, and her name deserves to stand with those of James and Fitzgerald, who outrank her only at their best.

W. J. Stuckey

Other major works

SHORT FICTION: *The Greater Inclination*, 1899; *Crucial Instances*, 1901; *The Descent of Man*, 1904; *The Hermit and the Wild Woman*, 1908; *Tales of Men and Ghosts*, 1910; *Xingu, and Other Stories*, 1916; *Here and Beyond*, 1926; *Certain People*, 1930; *Human Nature*, 1933; *The World Over*, 1936; *Ghosts*, 1937; *The Collected Short Stories of Edith Wharton*, 1968; *Collected Stories, 1891-1910*, 2001 (Maureen Howard, editor); *Collected Stories, 1911-1937*, 2001 (Howard, editor).

POETRY: *Verses*, 1878; *Artemis to Actæon*, 1909; *Twelve Poems*, 1926.

NONFICTION: *The Decoration of Houses*, 1897 (with Ogden Codman, Jr.); *Italian Villas and Their Gardens*, 1904; *Italian Backgrounds*, 1905; *A Motor-Flight Through France*, 1908; *Fighting France, from Dunkerque to Belfort*, 1915; *French Ways and Their Meaning*, 1919; *In Morocco*, 1920; *The Writing of Fiction*, 1925; *A Backward Glance*, 1934; *The Letters of Edith Wharton*, 1988; *The Uncollected Critical Writings*, 1997 (Frederick Wegener, editor); *Yrs. Ever Affly: The Correspondence of Edith Wharton and Louis Bromfield*, 2000 (Daniel Bratton, editor).

Bibliography

Ammons, Elizabeth. *Edith Wharton's Argument with America*. Athens: University of Georgia Press, 1980. Ammons proposes that Wharton's "argument with America" concerns the freedom of women, an argument in which she had a key role during three decades of significant upheaval and change. This engaging book examines the evolution of Wharton's point of view in her novels and discusses the effect of World War I on her work and life. Includes a notes section.

Bell, Millicent, ed. *The Cambridge Companion to Edith Wharton*. New York: Cambridge University Press, 1995. Essays on *The Age of Innocence*, *Summer*, *The House of Mirth*, *The Fruit of the Tree*, and *The Valley of Decision*, as well as on Wharton's handling of manners and race. Bell gives a critical history of Wharton's fiction in her introduction. Includes a chronology of Wharton's life and publications and a bibliography.

Bendixen, Alfred, and Annette Zilversmit, eds. *Edith Wharton: New Critical Essays*. New York: Garland,

1992. Studies of *The House of Mirth*, *The Fruit of the Tree*, *Summer*, *The Age of Innocence*, *Hudson River Bracketed*, and *The Gods Arrive*, as well as on Wharton's treatment of female sexuality, modernism, language, and the gothic.

Benert, Annette. *The Architectural Imagination of Edith Wharton: Gender, Class, and Power in the Progressive Era*. Madison, N.J.: Fairleigh Dickinson University Press, 2007. Benert examines the relationship between Wharton's fiction and her books about architecture and domesticity, including an analysis of the creation of structures and spaces in her prewar novels.

Benstock, Shari. *No Gifts from Chance: A Biography of Edith Wharton*. New York: Charles Scribner's Sons, 1994. A substantial biography of Wharton that is informed by Benstock's investigation of a variety of newly available primary sources.

Farwell, Tricia M. *Love and Death in Edith Wharton's Fiction*. New York: Peter Lang, 2006. An insightful look at Wharton's beliefs about the nature of love and the way they reflect her philosophical views, namely those of Plato and Charles Darwin. Wharton's own shifting feelings on love are revealed in conjunction with the shifting role that love played for her fictional characters throughout her career. An enlightening read for those interested in Wharton's writing, or in the philosophy of love.

Gimbel, Wendy. *Edith Wharton: Orphancy and Survival*. New York: Praeger, 1984. Drawing upon psychoanalytic theories and feminist perspectives, Gimbel analyzes the four works that she sees as key to understanding Wharton: *The House of Mirth*, *Ethan Frome*, *Summer*, and *The Age of Innocence*. The analyses of these works, with their deeply psychological overtones, provide excellent reading.

Haytock, Jennifer. *Edith Wharton and the Conversations of Literary Modernism*. New York: Palgrave Macmillan, 2008. Although Wharton denied she was a modernist writer, Haytock argues that Wharton's fiction contained elements of modernism, as demonstrated by her writing style and the cultural issues she addresses.

Lee, Hermione. *Edith Wharton*. New York: Alfred A. Knopf, 2007. An exhaustive study of Wharton's life from childhood through adulthood. Lee offers valuable insights and points out interesting analogies between Wharton's life and fiction.

Lewis, R. W. B. *Edith Wharton: A Biography*. 2 vols. New York: Harper & Row, 1975. An extensive study on Wharton, described as "the most renowned writer of fiction in America." Notes that Wharton thoughtfully left extensive records, made available through the Beinecke Library at Yale, on which this biography is based. Essential reading for serious scholars of Wharton or for those interested in her life and how it shaped her writing.

Lindberg, Gary H. *Edith Wharton and the Novel of Manners*. Charlottesville: University Press of Virginia, 1975. Presents Wharton's style with a keen understanding of the ritualism of the social scenes in her work. Strong analytical criticism with a good grasp of Wharton's use of irony.

Nettels, Elsa. *Language and Gender in American Fiction: Howells, James, Wharton, and Cather*. Charlottesville: University Press of Virginia, 1997. Nettels examines American writers struggling with the concept and realities of patriarchy.

PATRICK WHITE

Born: London, England; May 28, 1912
Died: Sydney, New South Wales, Australia; September 30, 1990
Also known as: Patrick Victor Martindale White

Principal long fiction

Happy Valley, 1939
The Living and the Dead, 1941
The Aunt's Story, 1948
The Tree of Man, 1955
Voss, 1957
Riders in the Chariot, 1961
The Solid Mandala, 1966
The Vivisector, 1970
The Eye of the Storm, 1973
A Fringe of Leaves, 1976
The Twyborn Affair, 1979
Memoirs of Many in One, 1986

Other literary forms

Patrick White first attempted to achieve literary success as a playwright in London in the 1930's. His work was largely rejected, partly, he implies in his memoir *Flaws in the Glass: A Self-Portrait* (1981), because of his lack of connections in the theatrical world (although he did not deny that his talent was immature at that time). In particular, White believed that his effort to dramatize *The Aspern Papers* (1888), Henry James's famous novella based on an incident in the life of Lord Byron's mistress, might have succeeded, thanks to James's dialogue, had it found a sponsor. Later, however, White successfully published a number of plays, mostly in the 1960's and 1980's; one play, *The Ham Funeral* (pr. 1961), received much attention.

White's collections *The Burnt Ones* (1964), *The Cockatoos: Shorter Novels and Stories* (1974), and *Three Uneasy Pieces* (1987) bring together the best of his shorter fiction published originally in Australian literary journals (for the most part); White also published in *The London Magazine*, where, among others, the fine stories "Clay" and "A Cheery Soul" appeared. White experimented with writing film scripts; one was filmed and received some mildly favorable reviews. His autobiographical memoir, already mentioned, mixes poetic impressionism with trenchant satire.

Achievements

Patrick White's stature as a novelist was already considerable among discerning critics and discriminating readers in the English-speaking world before it was confirmed by his reception of the Nobel Prize in Literature in 1973. The books that established White's reputation after World War II were *The Aunt's Story*, which has been widely recognized as a masterpiece; *The Tree of Man*; and the virtually unforgettable *Voss*. At the same time, White's fiction, though accessible to the general reader, unlike the work of such modernist masters as James Joyce and William Faulkner (or contemporary "experimental" fiction), never achieved a wide readership. It is uncompromisingly addressed to the same discerning public that respects Joyce, D. H. Lawrence, Thomas Mann, and Marcel Proust.

If rather philistine criticism of White's work from intellectual readers as well as from the general public in Australia and elsewhere began in the 1960's, after *Riders in the Chariot*, *The Aunt's Story* is almost universally admired, and *The Tree of Man*, *Voss*, *Riders in the Chariot*, *The Vivisector*, *The Eye of the Storm*, and *A Fringe of Leaves* all have admirers who regard them as virtual classics. White's transformation of Australian history into epic and tragic vision in *The Tree of Man*, *Voss*, and *A Fringe of Leaves* is brilliant, and his vision of the fragmented world of the twentieth century is equally impressive, especially in *The Vivisector* and *The Eye of the Storm*. White's major successes ultimately assure their author a place beside the masters of prose fiction in English, including Joyce, Lawrence, and Graham Greene.

Biography

Patrick Victor Martindale White was born in Wellington Court, London, on May 28, 1912, of parents whose affluence allowed them the opportunity to travel and enjoy the social pretensions available to prosperous Australians able to play the role of landed gentry. White's father, Victor (Dick) White, was one of several brothers who enjoyed prosperity in the family grazier business. Although the Whites could trace their lineage to respectable yeoman stock in Somerset, it was only in Australia that they achieved such success. Ironically, their social aspirations so far as the mother country was concerned were forever tainted by their status as "colonials" and Australians, the former penal colony being one of the least prestigious of the British dominions. White's mother was a Withycombe, and it is to the maternal connection that White attributed most of his imaginative and poetic gifts. At the same time, White disliked his strong-willed and socially ambitious mother, Ruth. Toward his father White was more ambivalent; he pitied Victor White for his weakness but found him impossible because he hid his emotions behind his social role as a landed gentleman. Resenting and distrusting his parents as he did, and contemptuous of their social ambitions and their inclination to conceal their humanity behind public personae, White felt as much an outsider and rebel against the class to which he was born as is his painter hero, Hurtle Duffield, in *The Vivisector*, a working-class child adopted by a prosperous Sydney family.

White tended as a child to identify with his nanny and her working-class husband, a circumstance that helps to account for the persistent scorn and irony in his fiction directed toward the assumptions and manners of the Australian upper class. In addition to being an "outsider" in his relationship to the Australian affluent class, White found that his status in English boarding schools, and later at Cambridge, was that of an outsider by virtue of his Australian citizenship and accent. Hence, throughout his career, White as artist played the role of an outsider in a double sense, a condition intensified by his frequent alternation of residences between Australia and England in childhood and youth.

White's major concentration at Cambridge was modern languages, primarily German, an interest augmented by time spent on the Continent, in the Germany of the Weimar Republic in its waning days and in the early years of Adolf Hitler's rule, during summer vacations from 1932 to 1935. One German city, Hanover, is depicted in White's fiction as the archetypal German cathedral town from which White's characters Voss and Himmelfarb both originate.

After he left Cambridge, White spent a bohemian period in London in the middle and late 1930's, lodging mainly in Ebury Street, where he wrote three unsatisfactory novels and attempted without success to begin a career in the theater as a playwright. During this time, White fell under the influence of various intellectual friends and apprentice artists, the most important being the Australian expatriate Roy de Maistre, who was, like White, gay. (White seems to have accepted his homosexuality in his boarding school adolescence, and to have had little difficulty over it at Cambridge and in the London of the 1930's.)

In 1939, White's unsatisfactory first novel, *Happy Valley*, was published, and soon White voyaged to the United States to try his hand in New York literary circles and to begin a period of dissipation that lasted for several months. During this New York period, he completed his strong second novel, *The Living and the Dead*, a book that shows him mastering and exorcising some of the literary and cultural influences of his youth. The decision of White's working-class hero, Joe, to go to Spain to fight on the Loyalist side is a symbol of commitment; it reflects White's own decision, reached after much guilt and self-analysis, to return to England (unlike some other English expatriates, such as W. H. Auden) and offer himself to the campaign against Hitler.

After receiving a commission in the Royal Air Force's intelligence division, White spent the majority of his war years in North Africa, Alexandria, the Middle East, and Greece. It is clear that his years in the war were a significant rite of passage for him. He gained decisiveness and self-reliance as well as maturity. Equally important, he met Manoly Lascaris, a Greek whose mother had been British; Lascaris was to become White's lover and life partner. Eventually, White and Lascaris decided on permanent residence in Australia, and White arrived there in 1947 with the manuscript of *The Aunt's Story* as a kind of "talisman." Hence, White was an Australian by a conscious choice, however reluctant the choice may have been. At the same time, his country was not always overwhelmed by White's decision, for although White used the Australian heroic past extensively in his fiction, he continued to be an outsider whose work did not always display clear relationships with Australian literary traditions.

Patrick White. (© The Nobel Foundation)

White's long career in Australia flourished primarily at two residences, one of which was the small "farm" called Dogwoods, really only a house, some outbuildings, and a few acres at Castle Hill, just outside Sydney and later incorporated into it. In 1963, White moved to Martin's Road in Sydney. In the Castle Hill period, White and Lascaris kept some cattle and tried to support themselves, partially, by some gardening. In later years, White's writing provided some support.

After he had published numerous novels and a book of short stories, White was awarded the Nobel Prize in Literature in 1973. He used the money to establish a fund for struggling Australian writers of some talent and literary ambition. His later life was marked by increasing fame and some travel and by considerable attention from the mass media and from academic critics and scholars. He died in Sydney on September 30, 1990.

ANALYSIS

Patrick White's fiction is concerned with the psychological depth and the emotional density of experience, and with the perceptions of the solitary self. This obsession with the isolated self in its search for fulfillment, its quest for an experience of unity and the divine, and its attempts to resolve the contradictions of its social heritage and its sexual nature provides the central drama in White's fiction. On one hand, White's fiction is rich in its command of the nuances of dialogue and social intercourse; it is possible to discuss these works in terms primarily of the novel of manners and social comedy. On the other hand, White's fiction is the work of an author obsessed with tragic vision and a religious quest. After *The Aunt's Story*, White's novels contain characters who struggle and overcome obstacles to understanding and vision, and whose lives culminate in visionary or mystical affirmation. Stan Parker in *The Tree of Man* testifies to the unity of holiness of being; Elizabeth Hunter finds the eye of God in the center of her storm; Rod Gravenor in his final letter to Eddie Twyborn asserts the reality of love and faith in God. Such affirmations, though they represent White's own beliefs, if his autobiographical statements are to be accepted, are nevertheless to be seen as dramatic statements, paradoxical assertions aimed at overcoming doubts and confusion, and ultimately as aesthetically correct as the statements of faith in the poetry of the seventeenth century metaphysical poets. Despite all the parallels with Victorian novelists who write family novels with complicated plots, White was essentially a religious visionary akin to poets such as T. S. Eliot and W. H. Auden, and one very much at odds with the dominant spirit of his age.

HAPPY VALLEY

White's first published novel, *Happy Valley*, is regarded by most critics as a failure, and the judgment is accurate. The novel deals with the passions and defeats of a group of characters in an Australian rural setting, but White is not entirely in control of his characters and plot, nor of his own style. The characters are mostly flawed romantics, somewhat obsessed by sex and erotic entanglements, and their emotions are often operatic and even Wagnerian in scope. The novel lacks the saving grace of White's magisterial and sophisticated irony, which tends to control the style in the later books and prevent both author and characters from lapsing into the excesses of emotion. White, however, does use the Australian landscape effectively as a dramatic backdrop for human drama played out under the eye of an inscrutable cosmos.

The Living and the Dead

The Living and the Dead, the second published novel of White's prewar apprenticeship, shows considerable improvement. The novel, set in England, primarily London, casts a critical and retrospective look at the 1930's, but like many novels of the period by English and American writers, it displays a movement from empty intellectualism and social snobbery to political and ideological commitment on the part of some characters. The central figures in the book are Elyot and Eden Standish and their feckless and snobbish mother. Elyot and Eden provide an ironic contrast: Elyot is a skeptical rationalist who wants to withdraw from experience, while Eden is a romantic who accepts life with its attendant suffering. Each finds a suitably ironic reward: Eden gains love with a working-class hero only to lose him when he departs to join the Loyalist cause in the Spanish Civil War; Elyot, fearing involvement with others, is doomed to a life of loneliness until he finds himself exposed to the suffering he has tried to avoid, through the death of his mother and the departure of his sister for Spain. Ironically, the experience of tragedy helps to heal Elyot's loneliness and alienation; at the end of the novel, he finds a satisfying release from the prison of himself.

Literary scholar Brian Kiernan has pointed out that many influences of T. S. Eliot's early poetry are evident in the novel; London is Eliot's "Unreal City" of *The Waste Land* (1922), for example. It might be added that Elyot Standish is White's most Prufrockian character; he represents the same kind of paralyzed and life-evading intellectual that Eliot satirized in his early poetry, and White's portrayal indicates his own aversion to such a figure.

If Elyot is skillfully drawn, his mother, with all her vulgarities and superficialities, is equally effective, and her final spasmodic affair with an English jazz musician is poignant, as is the description of her final illness. Less effectively depicted, but still successful, are Eden, Elyot's romantic sister, and Wally Collins, the itinerant jazz musician just back from America, who is presented as representative of the rootless and uncommitted modern urban person. The weakest figure of all is Joe Barnett, the working-class hero, who is too obviously inspired by the abstraction of the virtuous proletarian that afflicted much of the fiction of the 1930's.

The emphasis on commitment and release from alienation with which the novel concludes is handled with much aesthetic tact and restraint. The adoption of the Loyalist cause in Spain is portrayed as more of a humanist commitment than an acceptance of an ideological or religious imperative, although no doubt White's sympathies were leftist. While White's characters find an exit from the modern wasteland through tragic self-sacrifice, the novel does not provide any assurance that the solution found is an enduring one, either for the characters who accept it or for the author.

The Aunt's Story

With his next novel, *The Aunt's Story*, White established himself as a novelist of stature with a mature tragic vision. One of the most difficult things for a novelist to do, White believed, is to make a "virtuous woman" an interesting character. White accomplished this feat with Theodora Goodman, the aunt, who to all outward appearances lives an uneventful life, save for its tragic denouement. The real "story" of the spinster aunt is rendered through White's depiction of her inner life; despite Theodora's apparently barren existence, her experience is rich indeed.

Theodora's tale is told in three economically narrated sections: an Australian sequence titled "Meroe"; a European interlude, "Jardin Exotique"; and a climactic American adventure, "Holstius." In these sections, Theodora's childhood, youth, and maturity are portrayed. She has a strong, rather masculine sensibility, and an imaginative nature with deep psychological insight, in an unprepossessing feminine body.

In part 1, Theodora's journey from innocence to the experience of young adulthood is chronicled. The contrast between the heroine's strong desire for individuality and the conventional femininity and conformity of her sister is strongly marked. At boarding school in adolescence, Theodora develops one of her strongest relationships, a friendship with the sensitive Violet Adams, who, like Theodora, is fascinated by art and poetry. Theodora here reveals her intense and rather hard inner nature: She would like to be a poet, but her chosen subject would be landscapes and studies of rocks.

In her childhood and youth, too, Theodora shows

more love for her father's country estate than for the city: Meroe is the "Abyssinia," or happy valley of innocence, which provides a romantic metaphor for her years of growth and maturation. Later, following World War I, when Australia, after a brief emergence from its provincial slumber, relapses into a comfortable vacuous middle-class existence, Theodora lives in Sydney and cares for her mean-spirited and snobbish mother in the latter's failing years. In this period, the mysterious murderer Jack Frost provides some excitement and titillation for a bored middle-class population, and serves as a symbol of the mysterious Jungian shadow she longs to encounter. Her major chance for the conventional felicity of marriage and children occurs when she is courted by the apparently strong and manly Huntly Clarkson. In a role reversal typical of many later White novels, however, Huntly soon is revealed as weak and somewhat feminine in his relationship with the resolute Theodora. Her skillfulness and strength strike a deathblow to their courtship.

Released from an unrewarding life by the death of her mother, Theodora finds herself free to seek her destiny abroad, and her journey of initiation to Europe constitutes the central action in part 2, "Jardin Exotique," where she encounters a group of European eccentrics in a "grand hotel" setting on the French Riviera. Here Theodora exercises her talent for living, which had been suppressed and frustrated in Australia. She enters imaginatively into the lives of her companions, identifying with them and living their exotic histories vicariously. Her friends, a seedy group of expatriates, have all built up myths of romantic pasts. Theodora not only is a responsive and sympathetic consciousness for them but also is able to enrich their illusions by her own imagination. Ironically, however, each fantasy life proves to have been an artful lie near the end of part 2, leaving Theodora with the sense of having been cheated when the pathetic reality of a character's past is revealed. The final irony occurs when the Hotel du Midi is destroyed by fire, probably a symbol of the coming war.

This section, rich in fine characterizations and virtuoso stylistic divertissements, is White's portrait of the Europe of the 1930's and his moral evaluation of it. Theodora, at first seduced by Europe and its illusions of a glamorous past and then disillusioned by the emptiness of its reality, emerges from the experience morally tested and unscathed, but still an unfulfilled and psychologically incomplete personality. It is not until part 3, "Holstius," that Theodora confronts her own tragic destiny.

Part 3 takes place in the United States, where Theodora is overwhelmed by a sense of the vastness of the American continent and her own sense of isolation. A chance encounter with a traveling salesman on a train near Chicago results in a conversation that is symbolic: The salesman boasts of America's size and population in the best Babbitt or booster style, while Theodora is impressed with the abstractness of the individual self in a country where enormous numbers—of square miles, people, and sums of money—seem to dominate.

Leaving the train in the mountains of Colorado, Theodora wanders into a lonely canyon, driven by an urge to confront the unknown side of her inner self at last. Alone, at night, she hallucinates an experience of mythic force: a meeting with a stunted little man, almost like a folklore dwarf, who informs her that his name is Holstius (a name that perhaps both combines and caricatures the Jungian "animus," or male self in a woman, and the idea of "wholeness"). In Theodora's encounter with the imaginary Holstius, the masculine side of her nature emerges and speaks to her at last, and her inner conflicts appear to be resolved. The confrontation is traumatic, however, and the cost of it is the loss of Theodora's sanity, for the next day a nearby farmer and his family are forced to take charge of her, regarding her as mad.

The Aunt's Story is an expression of mature tragic vision, a novel that explores the possibilities and anguish of the solitary self in search of wholeness and fulfillment, in a more assured manner than White's first two published novels. Unlike *The Living and the Dead*, it envisions self-discovery and self-fulfillment as a private quest, to which the changing political and social winds are incidental, almost irrelevant. In this respect, and in its hints of a symbolism drawn partly from Jungian psychology, as well as in its masterful weaving of a subtle texture of imagery, *The Aunt's Story* marks the beginning of White's maturity as an artist.

THE TREE OF MAN

White's next three novels were much larger in scope and intention, epic in length at least. They also project a vision of the Australian past and of the middle twentieth century present influenced by that past. The first, *The Tree of Man*, tells the saga of Australia's pioneer past, as seen through three generations, but mainly through the experience of Stan and Amy Parker, homesteaders who wrest a farm from the wilderness. Stan and Amy are attractive characters, although rather conventional, and their lives are given a depth not found in most novels of pioneer life. Moreover, White provides splendid comic relief through their foils, the irresponsible O'Dowds, so that despite its length, the novel has considerable popular appeal, unlike much of White's fiction. While Stan and Amy's life as lonely settlers in the outback often possesses a beauty and quiet dignity, their later lives are frustrating, and their sense of progress and achievement is dissipated in the disappointing lives of their children, and in Amy's later estrangement from her husband.

A brilliant reversal of perspective occurs in the closing pages. Here, the aged Stan Parker, apparently a neglected and forgotten failure living in a suburb of Sydney, rises to heights of tragic dignity. Accosted by an annoying fundamentalist evangelist, Parker rejects the easy formula for salvation the latter offers and asserts his own faith: He identifies God with a gob of spittle. To the evangelist, this is a blasphemous comment, and some have tended to treat it as a defiant and rebellious one, but, as William Walsh and some other critics have claimed, Parker's statement is a confession of faith in the ultimate goodness of life and of the holiness of being. This event marks the beginning of the paradoxical but assured religious affirmation that surfaces at crucial moments in most of White's subsequent novels.

Voss

The sense of an impressive tragic vision is heightened and intensified in White's next novel, *Voss*, which is, like *The Aunt's Story*, one of his better-known works. It describes its hero's Faustian ambition to be the first to conquer the Australian continent by leading an exploratory expedition across it. Voss's noble failure (based on an actual expedition led by the explorer Ludwig Leichhardt) is counterbalanced by his mystical love for Laura Trevelyan, which transforms him from an exponent of the heroic and resolute will (like that celebrated by Friedrich Nietzsche in the late nineteenth century) to a more chastened and forgiving spirit. At the end, Voss is ready to accept his failure and death with a sense of Christian (or at any rate, religious) resignation.

Although a humorless and often exasperating character, Voss is a dynamic force who entices stolid Australian businessmen into financing his enterprise. His nature, however, is more complex than most of the unimaginative bourgeois Australians realize; only Laura, a complicated young woman who privately rebels against conventional Christianity and the age's worship of material progress, perceives the hidden sensitivities and beauty of Voss's character.

In the early stages of the novel, Laura and Voss seem to be in conflict, as their opposed but complementary natures seem to strike sparks from each other. Once Voss and his companions embark on their heroic journey in the Australian desert, however, Laura and Voss appear to communicate through a mystical or telepathic bond. Jungian psychology would consider each a person who has partially suppressed a hidden self: Voss has repressed his feminine qualities by devotion to the ideals of the masculine will; Laura has suppressed her masculine alter ego in the service of femininity. Their mystic communication enlarges and fulfills both their natures.

Defeated by the Australian climate and landscape, the treachery of his companions, and his own miscalculations, Voss meets a tragic end. The heroic grandeur of Voss's failure is impressive, however; White's hero has a strength and ambition beyond that of the protagonists of many modern novels, and in his defeat and death he gains some of the humanity that he had so obviously lacked.

Riders in the Chariot

Voss's acceptance of the Southern Cross as a symbol of his transformation from Nietzschean ideals to a more humane and forgiving outlook prompted some to assume that White himself was espousing doctrinal and institutional Christianity in *Voss*. This is not so, but White does affirm his personal religious vision—a synthesis of Jungian thought, Christian and Jewish mysticism, and poetic vision. His next novel, *Riders in the Chariot*, is perhaps his most ambitious attempt to present the religious vision that undergirds all of his fiction after *The Tree of Man*. *Riders in the Chariot* draws its title from Ezekiel's biblical vision of the chariot, but its prophetic and at times apocalyptic tone comes partially from William Blake, whose visionary conversation with Isaiah and Ezekiel in *The Marriage of Heaven and Hell* (1790) provides an epigraph. The four main protagonists, two men and two women (one black or "abo" painter, one Jewish mystic, one evangelical Christian, and one nature mystic) are all outcast visionaries, who combine to make a gigantic and impressive human mandala.

Himmelfarb is a scholar who turns from enlightened rationalism to the dense but powerful mystical images of the Kabbala, including the "blue fire" of some Kabbalist treatises. White's other seekers in the novel are religious questers who follow different and perhaps equally valid paths to their epiphanies and revelations. Miss Hare's nature mysticism is a naïve affirmation of being that resembles the kind of mysticism preached and celebrated by Ralph Waldo Emerson and Walt Whitman. By contrast, Mrs. Godbold's way is that of orthodox Christian piety, and Alf Dubbo's path is that of the romantic transcendentalist vision, as proclaimed by Blake and others.

Riders in the Chariot asserts the primacy of mystical search over conventional life, and it is also Blakean in its harsh indictment of evil in the modern world and in modern history. Evil is seen in various forms in this novel: in the anti-Semitism and later the Nazism that Himmelfarb encounters; in the smug self-righteousness of decaying puritanism in Miss Hare's tormentor, Mrs. Jolley; in the narcissistic upper-class arrogance and contempt for the less fortunate shown by Mrs. Chalmers-Robinson; and in the feeble and thwarted religiosity of the Reverend Pask and his sister. Above all, it is seen in the working-class bigotry and mule-headed chauvinism, with its suspicion of outsiders, of the Australian workmen, who reenact the Crucifixion as a blasphemous joke on Himmelfarb on Good Friday. Primarily, White is inclined in this novel to see evil as a kind of spiritual blindness or lack of vision "of the infinite," as Blake's epigraph says, although the malice demonstrated by Mrs. Jolley and White's laborers is hard to explain in such simple terms. Nevertheless, White's sense of the overwhelming presence of evil in the modern world, especially "moral evil," or evil for which humans are responsible, is one of the most convincing features of the book. Equally strong is the sense of moral goodness or innocence in his four central characters, however much they may occasionally surrender to their flaws. Whether one is interested in White's attempt to portray the different paths of mysticism, it is hard to forget the strength of his portraits of four characters who remain admirable while enduring great suffering.

The Solid Mandala

White devoted the early and middle years of the 1960's to works that were smaller in scale. In *The Solid Mandala*, which White considered one of his three best novels, his idiosyncrasies emerge more noticeably than in earlier works. This novel affirms White's Jungian religious vision more strongly than ever, and to underscore the theme for the obtuse reader, the noble example of Fyodor Dostoevski is invoked by Arthur Brown, the inarticulate visionary who is in part a spokesman for White. Arthur is set in contrast with his tragic brother, Waldo, a minor fiction writer and critic hampered by excessive rationalism and rendered creatively impotent by fear of his emotions and imagination. Ironically, after failing as a writer and ruining his life by aloofness from humanity, Waldo is ambushed by his repressed sexuality near the end: He becomes a pathetic cross-dresser wearing his late mother's discarded dresses, and thus expressing the thwarted feminine side of his nature.

Arthur Brown's life also ends pathetically in a lonely old age, yet Arthur, one of White's holy simpletons or divine fools, lives a spiritually fulfilled, if obscure and misunderstood, existence. Arthur has a mystical sympathy with animals and nature and with some of the other less articulate characters, especially Dulcie Feinstein, a rich young woman to whom both brothers are attracted. A close communion also exists between Arthur and Mrs. Poulter, a working-class woman who is a kind of surrogate mother and wife to him. Arthur finds meaning in existence through his apprehension of mandalas, the Jungian symbol for the unity and holiness of all being, and of all innocent and life-enhancing forms of existence. Two major mandala symbols dominate Arthur's experience: a large green marble, or "solid mandala," which appears to him to be symbolic of the holiness toward which humanity should strive; and a mystic dance in the shape of a mandala he performs with Mrs. Poulter.

Arthur and Waldo both lead tragic lives, if judged by conventional human standards, and each is an incomplete person: Arthur, the mystic and visionary, lacks a well-developed rational mind; while Waldo, the rationalist, is dead to all spiritual and transcendental existence. The story is thus a fable about the tragic split in humanity between the rational and the mystical faculties of the mind, between—if some psychologists, such as Robert Ornstein, are to be believed—the left and the right sides of the human brain. Despite the tragic nature of the novel, however, White makes Arthur much the more attractive of the two brothers and reaffirms once more one of the themes of *Riders in the Chariot* and other novels: If a choice must be made between reason and mysticism, the path of the mystic, however despised in a rationalistic and technological age, is the more rewarding and redemptive road.

Although beneath the rough and grainy surface of *The Solid Mandala* there are surprising riches and pleasures, its sometimes crabbed and eccentric nature might have suggested to some that White had fallen into a creative decline in the 1960's. The three remarkable novels that followed, however, proved that the converse was true: *The Vivisector*, *The Eye of the Storm*, and *A Fringe of Leaves* not only testify to an impressive sustained surge of creative power but also show White in more masterful control of his material and of his artistic form than ever before.

The Vivisector

The Vivisector describes the life of a rebellious and obsessed painter, Hurtle Duffield, who triumphs over enormous obstacles—an obscure background, a stultifying upper-class education, the cultural sterility of the Australian environment, numerous unhappy love affairs—to achieve triumph as a modern artist, a master of the techniques of Impressionism, Surrealism, and abstract Impressionism, who successfully shapes Australian material into a solid series of enduring works.

In terms of form, *The Vivisector* is one of White's more daring gambles, for it ostensibly follows the shapeless biographical narrative mode of some of the most primitive works of fiction, tracing Duffield's development from his childhood to his death through a series of selected incidents and periods. Close inspection of *The Vivisector* shows, however, that White has made sophisticated use of a naïve narrative form in his treatment of Duffield's struggle. For example, Duffield's experience is rendered in terms of his relationship to a series of Jungian anima figures who serve as lovers, supports, and muses. These range from his crippled foster sister, Rhoda Courtney, a childhood rival but a supporter of his old age; through Ponce Nan, a vital but tragic prostitute; and Hero Pavloussi, the wife of a Greek businessman with whom he enjoys a brief, passionate, but unsatisfying romance.

As a painter, Duffield is a tireless worker and committed visionary whose paintings recapitulate many motifs familiar to White's readers. At one point, Duffield perfects his craft by painting rocks; the action suggests the need to come to terms with the intractable and substantial nature of the visible and phenomenal world. In his early stages, Duffield is a rebellious and defiantly blasphemous painter who charges God with being the great "vivisector," an unfeeling and cruel being who experiments with human suffering as a scientist dismembers animals—or as Duffield and other artists approach human life, seeing it as raw material for art. Guilt over the suicide of Nan, however, for which he feels partially responsible, and compassion for the frustrated gay grocer Cutbush, whom he paints as a Surrealist figure machine-gunning lovers, work in Duffield a more tolerant and forgiving nature, and his work at last becomes more a kind of worship than blasphemy. In his last period, weakened by strokes, he becomes obsessed with painting in indigo and is characterized by a wry humility and kindness. Duffield thinks of his final, fatal stroke as a moment when he is "indiggodd," or departing "into God."

The Eye of the Storm

If *The Vivisector* is rich in vital characterizations and frequently possesses the exuberance of Duffield's raw energy, *The Eye of the Storm* is a splendidly controlled performance that demonstrates once more that when he chose, White could display a sure mastery of the techniques of the English novel of manners as practiced by such writers as E. M. Forster. *The Eye of the Storm* is constructed around the social comedy of the last days of Elizabeth Hunter, a regal but selfish matriarch of Sydney society who at eighty-six is slowly dying in her home on Moreton Drive while her son and daughter scheme to have her removed from the care of her nurses and placed in a nursing home. As is usual with White, however, the social comedy of the novel's surface masks tragedy and religious vision: in this case, the Learesque tragedy of

Mrs. Hunter and her two children, and the crisis of faith suffered by her remarkable nurse, Sister Mary de Santis. Although the present time of the novel amounts to only a few days, White's narration re-creates, through the memories of the characters, the spiritual and psychological histories of their entire lives. Elizabeth Hunter, like White himself the talented offspring of a grazier, has during her life grown from a grazier's wife with social aspirations into a lady of poise and charm. At the same time, this majestic woman is portrayed as a dominating and selfish mother whose poise and beauty have given her untalented and unattractive daughter, Dorothy, an inferiority complex and driven her talented but narcissistic son to become both a successful London actor and a pathetic womanizing failure in private life.

Mrs. Hunter in later life, however, has been transformed during a hurricane on Brumby Island, when, abandoned and alone, she experienced a numinous epiphany in the still of the eye of the storm. As a result, she has become a compassionate, understanding, and deeply religious woman, although her piety is of the unchurched kind. This transformation lends a Lear-like poignancy to her last days, when the poorly concealed malice of Basil and Dorothy is embodied in their effort to move her to a nursing home. The irony in this situation is heightened by the fact that Basil Hunter longs to play Lear himself, as the capstone of his career. Another tragic irony is Dorothy's idolizing of the Duchess Sanseverina in Stendhal's *The Charterhouse of Parma* (1839): Longing to be a masterful woman like the duchess, Dorothy resents her mother, whose social poise and personality recall that Stendhal heroine. The tragic irony in the actions of the children comes to a climax in their sentimental journey to their home ranch, where they finally surrender to their loneliness and huddle together in an act of incest during the night.

In contrast to the bleak and loveless lives of Basil and Dorothy, Mrs. Hunter finds solace in the loving care of Mary de Santis, her nurse and a reluctant believer in Greek Orthodox Christianity. Sister de Santis's care aids Mrs. Hunter in her final days, and in turn, Sister de Santis finds her own provisional faith reaffirmed by an epiphany of numinous divine immanence at the end of the novel in a mystic moment of water, birds' wings, and morning light, recalling biblical images of Revelation.

An interesting and partially comic minor plot in *The Eye of the Storm* involves another of Elizabeth Hunter's nurses, the youthful Flora Manhood, who finds herself caught between resentment of her male lover and a temptation to join her cousin in a lesbian affair. Despite White's obvious sympathy for Flora and her lesbian inclinations, the matter is resolved by her decision to remain heterosexual, while lesbian sexuality is treated with a touch of comic irony. It is curious that White, himself gay, was able to treat homosexuality with enormous sympathy yet finally imply the desirability of a traditional heterosexual identity.

Without a doubt, *The Eye of the Storm* is one of White's most carefully crafted and formally satisfying novels, and the one that most closely approximates the Jamesian ideal of complete mastery of novelistic form. This novel, which might have been considered the crowning work of a lesser career, was followed by other equally challenging works.

A FRINGE OF LEAVES

A Fringe of Leaves has many impressive strengths. Like *Voss*, this epic tale is inspired by the Australian past, specifically the experience of Eliza Fraser, a heroic woman who survived shipwreck, the loss of husband and companions, and captivity by Aborigines to return to civilization and become a legendary heroine. White's heroine, Ellen Gluyas Roxborough, is a woman of enormous appetite for living who undergoes numerous metamorphoses on her road to destiny. At first an imaginative Cornish farm girl who longs to journey to some mystical or fabled sacred place such as Tintagel, Ellen marries a dry country squire, Austin Roxborough, and is made over, on the surface at least, into a polished eighteenth century lady and a dutiful adornment to her husband's estate near Winchester. As Ellen takes a sentimental journey to Australia (or "Van Diemen's Land") to visit her husband's rakish brother, Garnet, her inner self emerges, first in a brief affair with Garnet, then in the ordeal of survival of shipwreck and capture by "savages."

The shipwreck and the captivity sections form the heart of the narrative. In the shipwreck, Ellen gradually has her civilized self stripped from her, along with her clothing, which is removed layer by layer. Later, after losing her husband and becoming a captive of the Australian natives, Ellen is obliged to confront her own authentic humanity. Her will to survive is indomitable; to cling to her sense of being human, she weaves a "fringe of leaves" as a kind of primitive clothing and an assertion of her belonging to a human realm above the world of nature. A central question for her, however, is that of her relationship to her captors. Is she of the same order as the dark-skinned Aborigines? The question is answered when she participates in a ritual feast at the center of the novel; it is a rite of cannibalism that provides not only physical nourishment but also, ironically, a sense of religious fulfillment. At the center of her "heart of darkness," Ellen finds her essential humanity.

The captivity section—which one critic has compared to the captivity narratives of prisoners of the American Indians—is followed by an idyllic interlude that represents a return to innocence for Ellen. In this episode, Ellen meets an escaped convict, murderer Jack Chance, who in London had brutally murdered his wife; Jack atones for that by falling in love with Ellen. With Jack, Ellen enjoys her most satisfying sexual relationship, but this edenic experience, like all others, must end when Ellen crosses the Brisband River (likened to a snake) that separates the Australian wilderness from the settled country.

In the resolution of the novel, Ellen is both a heroine to other pioneers, especially the women, and a penitent. In her own eyes, her guilt over her participation in the cannibal rite and the betrayal of Jack is great, but her will to live triumphs over her sense of unworthiness and self-immolation. At the close of the novel, it is clear she will return to routine and ordered life by marrying a pleasant, but somewhat inarticulate, Australian settler.

In its depiction of the indestructible will to survive, *A Fringe of Leaves* is a masterpiece, perhaps White's finest novel. Its central character, Ellen Roxborough, may well become one of the unforgettable heroines of literature.

The Twyborn Affair

Although *A Fringe of Leaves* has received much favorable comment, White's subsequent novel, *The Twyborn Affair*, was the object of a different reception, especially in the United States. This work is one of White's most controversial, for it attempts to deal with homosexual experience more candidly than ever before in White's fiction. Moreover, the novel is an interesting experiment in technique because it is constructed of three sections that are essentially self-contained units, yet it also attempts to form a greater unity of a lengthy novel covering several decades.

Eddie Twyborn, the hero (and sometimes heroine) of the novel, is presented as a feminine personality in the body of a handsome male: an unusual "prisoner of sex" whose incarceration is indeed tragic. In part 1, Eddie Twyborn appears as the transvestite lover of a likable older man, a somewhat decadent Greek living in France in the pre-World War I period. The couple are spied upon by Joanie Golson, a friend of Eddie's upper-class, overbearing Australian mother, and there is a certain amount of rather strained social comedy here until the affair ends with the death of Twyborn's Greek lover. In part 2, Twyborn returns to Australia after the war as a decorated hero and tries living in the outback as a worker on a sheep ranch. There he becomes emotionally entangled with the brutal foreman, Don Prowse, who finally rapes him, and with the owner's wife, who falls in love with him, misunderstanding his sexual nature while beguiled by his charm and sensitivity.

The failure to live peacefully as a man in part 2 is followed by Twyborn's life in London in part 3, where he surfaces in the late 1930's in female dress. This time, he is the madam of a brothel patronized by the rich and fashionable, and he becomes something of a celebrity. During this period, he suffers from a thwarted love for his patron, Lord Gravenor, who is finally revealed as gay also. A touching reconciliation with his selfish mother, now humbled by age and living in London alone, provides a kind of tragic recognition scene at the novel's end. This is followed by Twyborn's death in the London blitz.

Undoubtedly, Eddie Twyborn—the name is an obvious pun on "twice-born"—is one of the most interesting gay heroes in literature, and perhaps White's theme, the irony of a feminine nature in a male body, has never been treated with such insight. The novel's eccentricities, however, are pronounced, and the social comedy in parts 1 and 3 often becomes tiresome. Like White's other major novels, the work achieves a kind of tragic dignity, despite its flaws, yet it appears vastly inferior to his other novels published in the 1970's.

White's strengths as a writer are many. He is a masterful stylist, and his characterizations are psychologically complex and memorable. His skill at social comedy is complemented by contempt for the arrogance of wealth and power. Beyond these gifts, however, White sought to create tragic fictional works on the Greek or Shakespearean scale in an age of irony and a diminished or disappearing tragic vision. White's fiction also, in the works following *The Aunt's Story*, articulates the author's own prodigious mythology and majestic religious vision. It is a vision drawing on numerous disparate sources—Blake and the Kabbala, Carl Jung, Dostoevski, and the Bible—but it forms a synthesis that affirms the importance of a search for transcendence and the significance of mystical experience. Both his vision and his novels are likely to stand the test of time.

Edgar L. Chapman

Other major works

SHORT FICTION: *The Burnt Ones*, 1964; *The Cockatoos: Shorter Novels and Stories*, 1974; *Three Uneasy Pieces*, 1987.

PLAYS: *Return to Abyssinia*, pr. 1947; *The Ham Funeral*, pr. 1961 (wr. 1947); *The Season at Sarsaparilla*, pr. 1962; *A Cheery Soul*, pr. 1963; *Night on Bald Mountain*, pr. 1963; *Four Plays*, 1965 (revised as *Plays*, 1985-1994; 2 volumes); *Big Toys*, pr. 1977; *Signal Driver*, pr. 1982; *Netherwood*, pr., pb. 1983; *Shepherd on the Rocks*, pr. 1987.

POETRY: *The Ploughman, and Other Poems*, 1935.

SCREENPLAY: *The Night of the Prowler*, 1976.

NONFICTION: *Flaws in the Glass: A Self-Portrait*, 1981; *Patrick White Speaks*, 1989; *Letters*, 1996 (David Marr, editor).

Bibliography

Bliss, Carolyn. *Patrick White's Fiction: The Paradox of Fortunate Failure*. New York: St. Martin's Press, 1986. Offers an excellent introduction to White's overall thematic concerns. Argues that all of White's writing stems from a paradox—that is, the failures so often experienced by the characters can in fact lead to their successful redemption.

Collier, Gordon. *The Rocks and Sticks of Words: Style, Discourse, and Narrative Structure in the Fiction of Patrick White*. Atlanta: Rodopi, 1992. Provides detailed analysis of the themes and techniques in White's fiction, including doublings, narration and character, sentence structure, and indexical detail.

During, Simon. *Patrick White*. New York: Oxford University Press, 1996. Examines White's place in Australian history and culture, arguing that his work reflects the end of the country's colonial relationship with Great Britain. Also analyzes the connection between White's homosexuality and his writing.

Edgecombe, Rodney Stenning. *Vision and Style in Patrick White: A Study of Five Novels*. Tuscaloosa: University of Alabama Press, 1989. Addresses five novels including *The Eye of the Storm*, which Edgecombe considers to be White's greatest. Links the books by exploring the metaphysical thoughts they share and examines White's distinctive style, which affirms his novels' thematic emphasis on alienation, isolation, and the subsequent search for a vision to free the individual from spiritual imprisonment.

Hewill, Helen Verity. *Patrick White: Painter Manqué—Paintings, Painters, and Their Influence on His Writing*. Carlton, Vic.: Miegunyah Press, 2002. Describes how painting was a source of inspiration for White, addressing specifically the influence of twentieth century Australian art and European modernist and Romantic art on his work.

Marr, David. *Patrick White: A Life*. New York: Alfred A. Knopf, 1992. Monumental biography was written with White's cooperation. The dying White found the manuscript painful reading, but he did not ask the author to change a word. Includes detailed notes, bibliography, and helpful appendixes.

Tabron, Judith L. *Postcolonial Literature from Three Continents: Tutuola, H.D., Ellison, and White*. New York: Peter Lang, 2003. Tabron provides her opinions on how to read postcolonial literature, then demonstrates her views by analyzing works by four authors, including a chapter devoted to a postcolonial interpretation of *Voss*.

Weigel, John A. *Patrick White*. Boston: Twayne, 1983. Introduces White and his work by tracing his life and discussing each of his novels and his plays. General work provides a good introduction for the beginning reader of White's fiction. Includes bibliography and chronology.

Williams, Mark. *Patrick White*. New York: St. Martin's

Press, 1993. Presents detailed analyses of all of White's novels as well as discussion centered on the themes and contexts of his works. Includes bibliography and index.

Wolfe, Peter. *Laden Choirs: The Fiction of Patrick White*. Lexington: University Press of Kentucky, 1983. While not taking any particular thematic stand, this book offers a substantial analysis of each of White's novels. Focuses in part on White's style, demonstrating how it affects narrative tension, philosophical structure, and the development of character.

_______, ed. *Critical Essays on Patrick White*. Boston: G. K. Hall, 1990. Wide-ranging collection of essays edited by one of White's most astute critics. Includes a section of autobiographical essays by White and a helpful bibliography.

T. H. WHITE

Born: Bombay (now Mumbai), India; May 29, 1906
Died: Piraeus, Greece; January 17, 1964
Also known as: Terence Hanbury White; James Aston

Principal long fiction

Darkness at Pemberley, 1932
First Lesson, 1932 (as James Aston)
They Winter Abroad, 1932 (as Aston)
Farewell Victoria, 1933
Earth Stopped: Or, Mr. Marx's Sporting Tour, 1934
Gone to Ground, 1935
The Sword in the Stone, 1938
The Witch in the Wood, 1939
The Ill-Made Knight, 1940
Mistress Masham's Repose, 1946
The Elephant and the Kangaroo, 1947
The Master: An Adventure Story, 1957
The Candle in the Wind, 1958
The Once and Future King, 1958 (includes *The Sword in the Stone*, *The Witch in the Wood*, *The Ill-Made Knight*, and *The Candle in the Wind*)
The Book of Merlyn: The Unpublished Conclusion to "The Once and Future King," 1977

Other literary forms

T. H. White's first literary productions were two poetry collections. Several short stories enclosed within the satiric frame narrative of *Gone to Ground* were reprinted along with later items in the posthumously issued *The Maharajah, and Other Stories* (1981). The majority of White's nonfiction books celebrate his strong interest in field sports; *The Goshawk* (1951), which describes his experiments in falconry, is the most notable. The title *The Godstone and the Blackymor* (1959) refers to a legendary monument on the island of Inniskea. White also wrote two books on famous scandals, *The Age of Scandal: An Excursion Through a Minor Period* (1950) and *The Scandalmonger* (1952).

Achievements

T. H. White labored long and hard in relative obscurity before achieving literary success. His most successful work, *The Sword in the Stone*, was considered by many a children's book. White intended from the very beginning, however, that the story should be the introduction to a comprehensive modern rendering of the Arthurian legend. The second and third volumes became increasingly adult in their concerns and much darker in their implications. The fourth part languished unpublished for nearly twenty years, but after it was finally revised to form the conclusion of *The Once and Future King*, the collection was eventually recognized as a masterpiece of modern fantasy. Even that version lacked the original fifth part, however, which remained unpublished for another nineteen years—thirteen years after the author's death. Although the animated film of *The Sword in the Stone* (1963) and the film version of the *Once and Future King*-based stage musical *Camelot*

(1967) have reached a far wider audience than the original novels, the Arthurian sequence can now be seen as a work comparable in ambition and quality to the similar endeavors of fantasy novelist J. R. R. Tolkien.

T. H. White. (William Foster)

Biography

T. H. White, whose full name was Terence Hanbury White, was born in Bombay, India, the son of a district supervisor of police and the grandson of a judge. He spent his first five years on the Indian subcontinent before moving to England with his mother, Constance. His childhood was difficult because Constance—who eventually obtained a judicial separation from her husband but not the divorce that would have allowed her to marry her live-in lover—was mentally disturbed, and White was frightened of her. Removal to Cheltenham College in 1920 provided no relief; mistreatment from classmates maintained his misery, but he still won admission to Queen's College in Cambridge. He might have been happier there were it not for certain anxieties, in which homosexual feelings and alcoholism were joined by the total loss of his early religious faith and irrepressible sadomasochistic fantasies. Also, he contracted tuberculosis while in his second year at Cambridge, and his teachers had to donate money to send him to Italy to convalesce; it was there that he wrote his first novel.

White returned from Italy in much better condition. His determination to stay fit and healthy cemented his interest in field sports, but his triumph over physical frailty was shadowed by an exaggerated awareness of his mortality, which added furious fuel to all his activities. After obtaining a first-class degree with distinction in 1929, he became a schoolmaster—concluding with a four-year stint at one of England's best public schools, Stowe, in 1932-1936—before the autobiographical potboiler *England Have My Bones* (1936) sold well enough to win him a commission to deliver a book every year to his publisher, Collins. He rented a gamekeeper's cottage on the Stowe estate to pursue his new career.

Fearful of conscription into a war he desperately did not want to be involved in, White moved to Ireland (which remained neutral throughout World War II) in 1939, lodging in Doolistown in county Meath and at Sheskin Lodge in county Mayo. In these two locations, living as an exile, he wrote the fourth and fifth parts of the Arthurian series, but Collins ended the book-per-year arrangement after issuing *The Ill-Made Knight*; the subsequent hiatus in his career lasted until 1946. In that year he relocated to the Channel Islands, living briefly in Jersey before settling in Aldernay in 1947; he died in his cabin, apparently of heart failure, while on a Mediterranean cruise in 1964.

Analysis

T. H. White's first five novels, one of which was written in collaboration with R. McNair Scott and two of which were concealed under the pseudonym James Aston, were all naturalistic. White wrote his first novel—

They Winter Abroad—under the pseudonym Aston. This work is of some interest for the insight it offers into his youthful state of mind. Also as Aston he published his second novel, *First Lesson*. His first novel as White was *Darkness at Pemberley*. All three novels were published in 1932. The only one of White's novels from this period that is now remembered is his nostalgic panorama of the Victorian era, *Farewell Victoria*; it is also the only one not solidly rooted in his own experiences.

Earth Stopped *and* Gone to Ground

Earth Stopped is a satiric comedy paying respectful homage to the works of English novelist Robert Smith Surtees, whose addiction to hunting, shooting, and fishing was shared by White. White's similarly addicted friend, Siegfried Sassoon, had introduced him to a reprint of Surtees' 1845 novel *Hillingdon Hall* in 1931. Sassoon's autobiographical novel *Memoirs of a Fox-Hunting Man* (1928) reflects sarcastically on the fact that he had been sent to a sanatorium to save him from a court-martial when he refused to return to the front after being wounded in action in 1917; his influence on White's attitudes was profound.

Earth Stopped introduces the inept revolutionary Mr. Marx into a Surtees-like party gathered for a weekend's sport at an English country house. The party remains blithely good humored until the final chapters, when a world war abruptly precipitated by the forces of communism and fascism breaks out, at which point "the universe split open like a pea-pod, informed by lightning but far transcending thunder."

The story continues in *Gone to Ground*, in which the survivors of the house party swap tall tales while they hide from the catastrophe, taking psychological refuge in fantasy while taking physical refuge underground. Although its prophetic pretensions were supposedly impersonal, this provided an ironic metaphorical account of the subsequent shape of White's life and career. The book ends with the conclusion of the final tale—reprinted in *The Maharajah, and Other Stories* as "The Black Rabbit"—in which Keeper Pan, who was the inventor of panic as well as the god of nature, asserts his ultimate dominion over the objects of human sport.

The Once and Future King

Anticipation of a new world war, which many imaginative people expected to put an end to civilization, overwhelmed English fantastic fiction in the late 1930's. Other English writers were writing apocalyptic fantasies far more terrifying than *Earth Stopped*, but White decided to go in the opposite direction, becoming a connoisseur of playful escapism. The account of the boyhood and education of Arthur set out in *The Sword in the Stone* is as firmly rooted in personal experience as White's earliest novels are, but it is a calculated magical transformation of the oppressions that afflicted the author and his ultimate redemption from them.

The Sword in the Stone begins with an exotic schoolroom syllabus devised for the future Sir Kay by his governess, who cannot punish her noble student but can and does take out her frustrations on his whipping boy, the Wart, who is not recognized as the future embodiment of England and the chivalric ideal until he acquires a far more inspiring tutor in Merlyn. The debt that White owed to his tutor at Cambridge and longtime correspondent L. J. Potts is acknowledged in the fact that Merlyn, whose prophetic gifts result from living his life in reverse, actually served as a Cambridge tutor in the twentieth century, which lay in his distant past.

The account of the childhood of Gareth and his brothers contained in *The Witch in the Wood* is far darker—in spite of comic relief provided by the alcoholic lapsed saint Toirdealbhach and King Pellinore's obsessive pursuit of the Questing Beast—because their lustful, neglectful, and unbalanced mother is a transfiguration of White's own. The characterization of Lancelot in *The Ill-Made Knight* probably owes something to Sassoon as well as to White's perception of himself, and it is significant that the text explicitly compares the greatest of all the Arthurian knights to one of the great sportsmen of the late 1930's, the Australian cricketer Donald Bradman. Lancelot's obsessive anxiety that his forbidden love for Guenevere will sap the strength that makes him England's champion and deny him the chance to find the Holy Grail is a transfiguration of White's anxieties about his homosexuality and terror of military service (both of which were implicated in his decision to live as a recluse as soon as it became economically viable).

Given the deep personal significance of the first three volumes, it is hardly surprising that the dourly harrowing *The Candle in the Wind*, which White wrote in the latter months of 1940, is saturated with his anxiety for the blitzkrieg-devastated England that he had left and the civilization that it represented. He wrote to Potts on December 6, 1940, that he had discovered that "the central theme of the *Morte d'Arthur* is to find an antidote to war." In the fifth volume, Arthur goes underground with his old tutor, and they analyze the dismal failure of the Grail quest and look for a new way forward. While they do so, in *The Book of Merlyn*, they are surrounded by the animals Arthur loved so much as a boy, and Keeper Pan is certainly present in spirit, if not in person. Two key sequences from *The Book of Merlyn* were transposed into the version of *The Sword in the Stone* contained in *The Once and Future King*, and other elements were grafted onto the new version of *The Candle in the Wind* to supply the sense of an ending, but these devices distorted the balance and meaning of the whole, which was not published in its intended form.

J. R. R. Tolkien set out to expand his children's fantasy *The Hobbit: Or, There and Back Again* (1937) into an epic at almost exactly the same time White began to elaborate *The Once and Future King*. Tolkien was a Catholic and an Old English scholar who carefully excluded everything that had arrived in Great Britain with the Norman Conquest (1066) from the mythos of his fantastic secondary world, Middle-earth; however, it was precisely that imported tradition of chivalric romance that White chose for the heart of his own exercise. There is, therefore, a curious sense that the two resultant masterpieces of fantasy are as complementary and opposed as the Universities of Oxford, which was Tolkien's home, and Cambridge, White's spiritual home, to which he remained anchored by his correspondence with Potts.

One might also compare and contrast *The Once and Future King* with the fantasies of an older Cambridge man, John Cowper Powys. Powys, also troubled by inescapable sadomasochistic fantasies, eventually followed up the Grail epic *A Glastonbury Romance* (1932) with a more explicit transfiguration of Arthurian myth, *Porius* (1951), which was never issued in its entirety. Powys tackled the problem of designing a mythology for the much-conquered island of Britain by producing his own syncretism of Anglo-Saxon and Anglo-Norman elements with earlier Celtic and Greek myths.

All three of these writers were trying to construct or reconstruct a neomythological epic for an island that had somehow never contrived to produce a real one, which would also embody and allegorize the crisis at which the contemporary British nation had arrived in the pause between World War I and World War II. Of the three, White's is by far the most lighthearted but also—by virtue of its precipitous plunge into tragedy in *The Candle in the Wind*—the most emotional. It is perhaps ironic that Tolkien, who was not nearly as committed to the politics of escapism as White, should have become the parent of a whole genre of escapist fantasy, while White became best known as the inspirer of a Walt Disney film and a musical comedy. Because of the University of Texas edition of *The Book of Merlyn*, however, modern readers and critics can reconstruct White's masterpiece as he intended it to be read, and to judge its true worth as an epic for the isle of Britain.

Later novels

The three fantasies that White wrote after he recovered from the disappointment of Collins's initial refusal to publish *The Candle in the Wind* are best regarded as footnotes to the main sequence of his novels, displaying a gradual acceptance of the fact that he was seen as a children's writer. *The Elephant and the Kangaroo* is an allegorical comedy in which an English atheist in Ireland witnesses a visitation by the archangel Michael and sets out to build an ark in response to the threat of an impending second deluge. In *Mistress Masham's Repose*, a young girl discovers descendants of the Lilliputians of Jonathan Swift's *Gulliver's Travels* (1726) living on an island and sets out to defend them from commercial exploitation by Hollywood filmmakers. *The Master* is a science-fiction story for children, whose juvenile heroes thwart the eponymous island-based villain's plans for world domination.

Brian Stableford

Other major works

NONFICTION: *England Have My Bones*, 1936 (autobiography); *The Age of Scandal: An Excursion Through a Minor Period*, 1950 (anecdotes); *The Goshawk*, 1951; *The Scandalmonger*, 1952 (anecdotes); *The Godstone and the Blackymor*, 1959 (autobiography); *America at Last*, 1965 (autobiography).

TRANSLATION: *The Book of Beasts*, 1954 (of medieval bestiary).

Bibliography

Brewer, Elisabeth. *T. H. White's "The Once and Future King."* Cambridge, England: D. S. Brewer, 1993. Brewer examines White's tetralogy, with separate chapters on each of the four novels and another on the fifth, unfinished work, *The Book of Merlyn*. She discusses comedy in the tetralogy and places White's work within the context of other Arthurian romances, historical fiction, and fantasy literature. Includes a bibliography and an index.

Crane, John K. *T. H. White*. New York: Twayne, 1974. A competent introductory overview of White, with biographical information, discussion of his works, and a bibliography. Very useful for the beginning student.

Gallix, François. "T. H. White and the Legend of King Arthur: From Animal Fantasy to Political Morality." In *King Arthur: A Casebook*, edited by Edward Donald Kennedy. New York: Garland, 1996. This analysis of *The Once and Future King* is one of sixteen essays that examine how the legend of King Arthur has been recounted in medieval romances, nineteenth century art, and twentieth century literature.

Kellman, Martin. *T. H. White and the Matter of Britain: A Literary Overview*. Lewiston, N.Y.: Edwin Mellen Press, 1988. Kellman discusses all of White's historical fiction, the lesser-known works as well as *The Once and Future King*. Includes a bibliography and an index.

Manlove, C. N. *The Impulse of Fantasy Literature*. Kent, Ohio: Kent State University Press, 1983. Manlove's study of fantasy fiction includes a chapter examining *The Once and Future King*, placing the tetralogy within the context of British fantasy literature.

Matthews, Richard. "Shining Past and Future: The Persistence of Camelot (T. H. White's *The Once and Future King*)." In *Fantasy: The Liberation of Imagination*. New York: Twayne, 1997. A study of fantasy fiction, containing a discussion of the genre's origins and development from antiquity to the present as well as analyses of works by White and other writers. Includes a bibliographic essay, a list of recommended fantasy titles, and an index.

Sprague, Kurth. *T. H. White's Troubled Heart: Women in "The Once and Future King."* Rochester, N.Y.: Boydell & Brewer, 2007. An analysis of the female characters in White's tetralogy. Sprague describes White's misogyny, which was a reaction to his difficult mother, but notes that White also was able to create a charming portrait of Queen Guenevere.

Warner, Sylvia Townsend. *T. H. White: A Biography*. London: Cape/Chatto & Windus, 1967. Warner, a novelist and poet, provides a sensitive portrait of White. Includes a bibliography.

COLSON WHITEHEAD

Born: New York, New York; 1969
Also known as: Arch Colson Chipp Whitehead

Principal long fiction

The Intuitionist, 1999
John Henry Days, 2001
Apex Hides the Hurt, 2006
Sag Harbor, 2009

Other literary forms

Although Colson Whitehead is primarily a novelist, he has also published the collection of essays *The Colossus of New York: A City in Thirteen Parts* (2003), a work that makes clear the importance of place and surroundings for him. Working as a journalist and as a critic of books, music, and television has enabled Whitehead to develop the keen sense of language and its nuances that plays a significant role in his fiction. He has published articles in a wide variety of publications, including *The New York Times*, *Salon*, *Spin*, *New York Magazine*, *Harper's*, and *Granta*.

Achievements

Colson Whitehead was heralded as a talented writer from the publication of his first novel. *The Intuitionist* received the New Voices Award presented by the Quality Paperback Book Club and was a finalist in the competition for the Hemingway Foundation/PEN Award. Whitehead was from this first endeavor opening the way for a new type of novel that defies classification. *The Intuitionist* can be read as an allegory, as a detective novel, or even as a comedic tale. His next novel, *John Henry Days*, further broke the boundaries of the traditional novel with its multilevel structure, its satire, and its probing look at historical and contemporary racism. The work received the Young Lions Award and was a finalist for both the National Book Critics Circle Award and the Pulitzer Prize. Whitehead's ability to create fiction that goes beyond the traditional norms of the genre earned him a MacArthur Fellowship in 2002. His work continues the tradition of the intellectual black novel, which is part of the canon of African American literature.

BIOGRAPHY

Arch Colson Chipp Whitehead was born in Manhattan in New York City in 1969; he grew up in the Fort Greene neighborhood in Brooklyn. He attended Trinity School and Harvard University, and after graduating from Harvard in 1991, he began a career in journalism as a pop-culture critic for *The Village Voice*. At first he wrote about books and music; later, he became the newspaper's television columnist.

Whitehead first decided he wanted to be a writer of fiction when he was a child and began reading Stephen King's books. While in college, he discovered the works of more authors who increased his desire to write, including the fiction of Thomas Pynchon and Ishmael Reed. In 1999, Whitehead published his first novel, *The Intuitionist*. His second novel, *John Henry Days*, followed in 2001. His next publication was the collection of essays *The Colossus of New York*, which appeared in 2003. In this nonfiction work composed of personal memories, vignettes, and meditations, Whitehead captures all of the varied and often contradictory qualities of New York City. In 2006, he returned to fiction with the publication of another novel, *Apex Hides the Hurt*. His fourth novel, *Sag Harbor*, published in 2009, is a semiautobiographical story. Whitehead is a fellow at the Cullman Center for Scholars and Writers.

ANALYSIS

Colson Whitehead writes novels that break the traditional rules of fiction writing. His works defy classification into the standard categories. In *The Intuitionist*, the inclusion of features of the detective story add to the intrigue of the novel, but at the same time the work satirizes the detective story. The novel is really neither satire nor detective fiction per se. The setting of *The Intuitionist* is anachronistic: The city in which the fiction takes place is futuristic in the technology depicted and in the focus of the inhabitants on verticality; in this world, elevators are the cornerstone of society. Ethically and morally, however, the inhabitants of the city resemble people living in a city in the United States in the mid-twentieth century.

In *John Henry Days*, Whitehead experiments even more with the novel form. He exercises his privilege as author to take the narrative where he wishes, ignoring any traditional formula. The work includes many digressions and interpolated stories as Whitehead presents events without regard for chronological order. There is a shooting in the novel that Whitehead recounts very early in the work and then again near the end—and neither time does he reveal who was killed. The novel ends without closure; rather, the reader is left to finish the story.

THE INTUITIONIST

The Intuitionist is a combination of allegory, detective novel, futuristic novel, and social satire that addresses prejudice and racial discrimination. The story is set in a large metropolitan city in the middle of the twentieth century. The society is highly advanced technologically and totally devoted to a cult of elevators. Progress is linked to verticality and its improvement, and modernization and success are equated with upward mobility. Everyone reads *Lift*, a weekly magazine that informs the public about what is happening in the elevator industry. Other aspects of the society contrast sharply with its technologically advanced status, however. Political corruption, exploitation, and racial prejudice govern everyday life. Technologically the society is futuristic, but morally it remains locked in a 1940's or 1950's mentality. Using elements of the detective story of the mid-twentieth century—such as mobsters, abandoned warehouses, and late-night assignations—Whitehead gives the story an ambiance of believability.

The Intuitionist recounts the trials of Lila Mae Watson, an African American elevator inspector. She works for the Department of Elevator Inspectors, which, in this verticality obsessed society, is one of the most powerful departments, possibly the most powerful, in the metropolis. All elevator inspectors adhere to one of two different approaches to elevator inspection: An elevator inspector is either an Empiricist or an Intuitionist. An Empiricist inspects an elevator by getting into the elevator shaft and checking the mechanism to see if it meets the specifications. An Intuitionist, in contrast, evaluates the condition of an elevator by listening and by feeling the mechanism's vibrations, becoming one with the elevator. The department is heavily staffed by Empiricists, and Lila Mae is an Intuitionist. Lila Mae's life is a constant ordeal, as she is marginalized by her race, her sex, and her adherence to Intuitionist theory.

In spite of her exclusion, Lila Mae has an impressive record as an inspector and is assigned to inspect the elevators in the Fanny Briggs Memorial Building. A short time after she has inspected the elevators there, one of the elevators crashes. This is a catastrophe for her, given that it could mean the end of her career, and she becomes determined to find out what happened. The Elevator Guild is in the process of electing a new guild chair; the two candidates are Frank Chancre, an Empiricist, and Orville Lever, an Intuitionist. Lila Mae becomes convinced that Chancre, who is known to have connections to a mob boss, has had the elevator sabotaged.

Whitehead complicates his narrative by adding another intrigue: Suddenly papers from the research of the late James Fulton, father of Intuitionism, start showing up with Lila Mae's name on them. Fulton had been researching a black box, the perfect next-generation elevator. Lila Mae decides that she must find the blueprints for the black box and at the same time exonerate herself in regard to the crash. Whitehead turns his narrative into a detective novel as he relates Lila Mae's search, which involves deceptions, false leads, and mob enforcers, and an ambiance of danger invades the narrative. After he has led the reader as well as Lila Mae down a number of false trails, Whitehead concludes the story in a totally unexpected way. The elevator was not sabotaged, it just did a free fall, as elevators sometimes do. Arbo Elevators believed that Lila Mae had Fulton's papers on the black box, and the company wanted them to avoid bankruptcy. Whitehead then adds a section on Fulton's thoughts during his last working days and concludes the novel with Lila Mae, who has become obsessed with completing Fulton's research, alone in a small room working to create the perfect elevator.

In *The Intuitionist* Whitehead uses the metaphor of verticality to delineate African Americans' difficulty in being upwardly mobile in a racially prejudiced society. He develops this theme through the characters of Lila Mae and James Fulton. Lila Mae's father was an elevator operator in a department store where no African Americans were allowed, with the exception of those who worked there. Lila Mae is determined to achieve upward mobility through her own efforts. She puts up with living in a converted janitor's closet at the elevator inspectors' academy, and nothing—not the ransacking of her apartment, her kidnapping by Chancre's thugs, or her deception by Fulton's false nephew—deters her from her goal. Lila Mae is determined to succeed in spite of a system that puts every obstacle in her way.

James Fulton, a light-skinned African American, had been able to achieve upward mobility because of his ability to pass for white. He had become a respected researcher in verticality, in upward mobility in elevators, but throughout his life he knew that the discovery of his true racial identity would have destroyed his career and denied him acceptance in society. Consequently, infuriated and seeking revenge, he played a joke on everyone by creating the concept of the black box. The perfect elevator that was to transform the city's landscape was not real—it was simply a trick that the clever Fulton played to get back at the prejudiced closed society in which he lived.

John Henry Days

John Henry Days incorporates allegory, comedy, pathos, satire, and social realism while at the same time elucidating the dilemma of keeping history and myth alive in a mechanized, materialistic world of consumerism. The novel is set in 1996 during John Henry Days—a festival honoring the American folk legend—in Talcott, West Virginia. At the same time, the post office in Talcott is issuing a new commemorative stamp featuring John Henry—part of a series honoring other American folk legends as well, such as Paul Bunyan and Pecos Pete. J. Sutter, an African American who is very aware of being a member of a racial minority group, is a junketeer who is trying to set a record for having attended the most consecutive events. Pamela, an African American whose deceased father left a large collection of John Henry memorabilia, is at the Talcott festivities because the town wants to buy her father's collection. Other characters include Albert Miggs, a stamp collector; Lucien Joyce, the owner of a publicity agency that has a list of reporters (including Sutter) ready to cover such events; and Sutter's cronies Dave, Frenchie, Tiny, and One Eye.

The apparent narrative is a sprawling account of the days of the John Henry celebration, which are typical of such small-town festivals. Sutter's motel is just adequate; the food, except for the prime rib, is scarcely exciting; the talent is local. The actor Ben Vereen was scheduled to attend the celebration, but he was taken ill at the last minute. Neither Pamela nor the junketeers are really pleased to be there. Pamela has a purpose beyond the town's interest in her father's collection—she has actually come to bury her father's ashes in the neglected cemetery where John Henry is buried. The junketeers are there for the free food and drink and whatever else they can get for free and because they are on the list—and, of course, Sutter is there because he is going for the record. Miggs is there because he collects railroad stamps, and he wants the new John Henry stamp for his collection.

The real narrative of this novel is found in the digressions, however—in the interpolated stories and the long conversations of the junketeers. In these parts of the book, Whitehead examines a number of concepts and issues. One of the major themes of the novel is consumerism, with a focus on how advertising controls people's lives. Sutter and the other junketeers make their living by going from one publicity event to another and writing about the events for various publications. Lucien Joyce, whose agency employs them, has a reputation for being willing to publicize any event, no matter how trivial, for the right amount of money. The junketeers glory in all the free things they get: food, liquor, motel rooms, and sometimes articles that are being publicized. Receipts are everything; turned in, they produce reimbursement. The John Henry Days celebration is cluttered with John Henry merchandise. Whitehead depicts an America obsessed with material things and the desire to get as much as possible for free.

The legend of John Henry—the railroad steel-driving man who died with a hammer in his hand, competing against a steel-driving machine—as well as a chapter on Pamela's temporary job for an Internet company and the junketeers' lifestyle, especially Sutter's, elucidate the enslavement and dehumanization of people, first by the forces of industrialization and then by those of the digital information age. In chapters about John Henry, Whitehead depicts how John Henry trades his enslavement in the cotton fields for a comparable slavery, driving steel, laying track for the railroad, and buying at the company store.

Sutter and the other junketeer journalists go where the events are. Just as John Henry exists to drive steel, Sutter and the others exist to follow the event circuit. When Sutter enters the Big Bend Tunnel with Pamela, he is enticed but also frightened by the fact that the tunnel cuts him off from the digital information world. Whitehead emphasizes the total lack of interaction among the temporary workers at Pamela's workplace as well as their lack of individuality: All have exactly the same items with which to work, and all make no attempt to personalize their workstations. Whitehead portrays these characters as functions of their work environment. The characters are closed, hiding their inner selves, hiding what Sutter is afraid might be released in the Big Bend Tunnel.

In both the main narrative of *John Henry Days* and in the digressions, Whitehead illustrates the difficulty of being a dark-skinned individual in a racially prejudiced society. John Henry was a black man, yet he is the folk hero of a prejudiced white population. Pamela and Sutter are the only two African Americans at the John Henry Days opening banquet. Sutter is there because he is a journalist who will publicize the event; Pamela is there because she has her father's collection—both characters have something the town wants. The novel ends with Sutter trying to decide if he will leave early with Pamela or stay for the banquet. A shooting takes place, but the outcome is unclear: Has Sutter been killed? Whitehead gives clues, but the reader must decide whether the clues are false.

Shawncey Webb

Other major work

nonfiction: *The Colossus of New York: A City in Thirteen Parts*, 2003.

Bibliography

Bell, Bernard W. *The Contemporary African American Novel: Its Roots and Modern Literary Branches*. Amherst: University of Massachusetts Press, 2004. Discusses Whitehead's work and the work of other African American writers as seeking experimentation in the novel and abandoning the traditions and roots of the African American novel.

Liggins, Saundra. "The Urban Gothic Vision of Colson Whitehead's *The Intuitionist* (1999)." *African American Review* 40, no. 2 (2006): 359-370. Places the novel in the gothic tradition based on its setting and the "horror" created by the allegorical treatment of the black struggle for upward mobility.

Porter, Everette. "Writing Home." *Black Issues Book Review*, May/June, 2002. Offers discussion of Whitehead's obsession with place and its influence on his novels.

Russell, Alison. "Recalibrating the Past: *The Intuitionist*." *Critique* 49, no. 1 (2007): 46-60. Describes *The Intuitionist* as an anti-detective novel and discusses textual authority in regard to race, identity, and history.

Whitehead, Colson, and Walter Mosley. "Eavesdropping." Interview. *Book*, May, 2001. In conversation with author Mosley, Whitehead discusses his goals in writing, the difficulties he encountered in publishing *The Intuitionist*, and his sense of himself as a black writer.

JOHN EDGAR WIDEMAN

Born: Washington, D.C.; June 14, 1941

Principal long fiction

A Glance Away, 1967
Hurry Home, 1970
The Lynchers, 1973
Hiding Place, 1981
Sent for You Yesterday, 1983
The Homewood Trilogy, 1985 (includes *Damballah*, *Hiding Place*, and *Sent for You Yesterday*)
Reuben, 1987
Philadelphia Fire, 1990
The Cattle Killing, 1996
Two Cities, 1998
Fanon, 2008

Other literary forms

An intensely lyrical novelist, John Edgar Wideman has also published numerous short stories based on family members, friends, and neighbors from his childhood community of Homewood, a long-standing all-black subdivision of Pittsburgh, Pennsylvania. Twelve of these pieces are presented as letters in his critically acclaimed collection *Damballah* (1981), which has also been published with two of his novels as *The Homewood Trilogy*. Wideman's autobiographical *Brothers and Keepers* (1984) blends facts with fictionalized characters and incidents as the author scrutinizes his own relationship to his brother, Robert Wideman, imprisoned for life in Pennsylvania's Western State Penitentiary. *Fever* (1989), a collection of twelve stories, combines themes of family and community with those of displacement, estrangement, and cultural loss. Uncollected poetry, reviews, and essays on black American literature by Wideman abound in the foremost scholarly journals and literary digests.

Achievements

When he emerged upon the literary scene in the late 1960's, John Edgar Wideman stood out from his peers as a black American writer who did not address exclusively themes of racial conflict and militant nationalism. He concentrated instead on individual psychological struggles that transcend color lines. His earliest novels having been enthusiastically received; he was lauded as a successor to William Faulkner.

After being asked to teach African American literature and essentially having to "teach himself" the field, Wideman began to centralize racial themes overtly in his writing, most radically with the publication of *The Lynchers*, which begins with a chronology of more than one hundred historically documented lynchings. His primary critical acclaim, however, came with the publications of the Homewood series, engendered by the death of his grandmother, Freeda French, in 1973. *Sent for You Yesterday*, the final work of the Homewood Trilogy, received the 1984 Faulkner Award for Fiction from PEN, the International Association of Poets, Playwrights, Editors, Essayists, and Novelists. Wideman was the first author ever to receive two PEN/Faulkner Awards; he was honored with the second for *Philadelphia Fire*. In addition, he was awarded the Lannan Literary Fellowship for Fiction in 1991 and a MacArthur Foundation Award (a "genius grant") in 1993.

In spite of favorable reviews of his fiction, some critics have accused Wideman of indulging in an unconventional style at the expense of theme. More often than not, however, his experimentation extends meaning by illustrating the impact of the past in addition to the inextricable bonds among generations. His autobiographical *Brothers and Keepers*, which displays some of his innovative techniques, earned a National Book Critics Circle Award nomination. In 1998, Wideman won the prestigious Rea Award, sponsored by the Dungannon Foundation and established to honor a short-story author "for literary power, originality, and influence on the genre." Wideman's critical accolades have been profuse, but it is his range of style, continual formalistic innovation, and his powerful prose that warrant his consideration as one of the best American writers of his generation.

Biography

Born in Washington, D.C., on June 14, 1941, John Edgar Wideman initially aspired to be a professional basketball player. Consequently, he served as both a Benjamin Franklin Scholar at the University of Pennsylvania and captain of the school's championship basketball team. A member of Phi Beta Kappa, he was graduated from the University of Pennsylvania in 1963 with a B.A. in English. Promptly selected as only the second black Rhodes Scholar in history, he received his B.Ph. degree from Oxford University in 1966, specializing as a Thouron Fellow in the eighteenth century novel. He then spent one year as a Kent Fellow at the University of Iowa Writers' Workshop, subsequently returning to lecture at his alma mater, Pennsylvania. While writing and teaching literature at the University of Wyoming, he endured the conviction of his oldest son Jacob, on charges of fatally stabbing another youth during a camping trip in Arizona. This tragedy recalls the imprisonment of his brother Robert for involvement in a robbery and killing. His daughter Jamila, having inherited her father's basketball prowess, garnered a position playing in the Women's National Basketball Association (WNBA) professional league. In 1986 Wideman became professor of English at the University of Massachusetts, Amherst. Since the 1980's he has frequently contributed articles and review essays to *The New York Times Book Review* and to popular magazines such as *TV Guide*, *Life*, and *Esquire*.

Analysis

The recurring thematic emphasis in John Edgar Wideman's novels is on the way history, both collective and personal, and the stories that arise from that history shape notions of reality. From gay college professors to ghetto junkies, Wideman's characters are often uncomfortable with their places in history and unsure that they even understand those few traditions that they do observe. Therefore, they shuttle between the imaginary and the real in order to rediscover the past, revive it, or at least preserve whatever parts they do recall. Despite Wideman's literary beginnings in the racially turbulent 1960's, when blacks in America articulated their estrangement from Africa, his white as well as black characters crave the rootedness that distinguishes those who have come to terms with their backgrounds. Shifting from the anonymous northern cities of his first three novels to the clearly delineated Homewood of *Hiding Place* and *Sent for You Yesterday*, Wideman nevertheless consistently indicates that ignorance of heritage results in isolation and psychological turmoil. The same observation is later applied to Philadelphia, specifically Osage Avenue.

Wideman forgoes strictly chronological plot development, adopting instead an intricate experimental style consisting of stream-of-consciousness narrative, long interior monologues, dream sequences, surrealistic descriptions, and abrupt shifts in time, diction, and points of view. Beginning each novel almost exclusively in medias res, he employs a technique influenced by the works of T. S. Eliot, James Joyce, and Jean Toomer, yet indisputably original. In *The Lynchers*, for example, he illustrates the traditionally victimized status of black Americans with a preface that cites more than one hundred documented lynchings. Reeling between their own ravaged communities and impenetrable white ones, the black protagonists of his first two novels, *A Glance Away* and *Hurry Home*, occupy a jumbled landscape where blues clubs coexist with biblical icons. Similarly, in *Hiding Place* and *Sent for You Yesterday*, Wideman retells the stories of his ancestors until a shack or a cape acquires the same expressive quality as a cross. As the author himself explains, "You can call it experimentation, or you can call it ringing the changes. . . . value spontaneity, flexibility, a unique response to a given situation. . . . Getting too close to the edge but then recovering like the heroes of the Saturday matinee serials. That's excitement."

John Edgar Wideman. (University of Wyoming)

A Glance Away

Dedicated to "Homes," Wideman's first novel, *A Glance Away*, creates thematic excitement with its treatment of two drifting men coming to terms with their pasts. After a year spent at a rehabilitation center for drug addicts, Eddie Lawson, a disillusioned young black man, returns to his listless, decaying urban neighborhood. Rather than celebrating, however, he spends his gloomy homecoming confronting the goblins that drove him to the brink in the first place: his mother Martha Lawson's idealization of his dead older brother, his girlfriend Alice Smalls's rejection of him for sleeping with a white woman, and his own self-disgust over abandoning a secure postal job for menial, marginal employment. Dejected and defeated by nightfall, he drags himself to grimy Harry's Place in order to cloak his memories in a narcotic haze. There, he is reconciled by his albino friend Brother Smalls with another outcast named Robert Thurley, a white college professor struggling with his own record of divorce, alcoholism, and homosexuality. Though discrepancies between wealth and power divide the two homeless men, each manages to urge the other to maintain his faith in people despite his guilt-ridden history.

A Glance Away generated much favorable critical response in particular for Wideman's depiction of the alienated Thurley. In trying to disavow his personal past, this connoisseur of food and art embraces a surfeit of creeds and cultures. "In religion an aesthetic Catholic, in politics a passive Communist, in sex a resigned anarchist," he surrounds himself with treasures from both East and West and indulges in a smorgasbord of the globe's delicacies. Yet as a real measure of the displacement that these extravagances so futilely conceal, he quotes lines from T. S. Eliot's "The Love Song of J. Alfred Prufrock" (1917), in which a similarly solitary speaker searches for intimacy in a world bereft of its cultural moorings.

Emphasizing his protagonists' self-absorption and the estrangement of their family members and friends, Wideman abandons strictly chronological plot development in favor of lengthy interior monologues. Conversations tend to be short; more likely than not they are interrupted by unspoken flashbacks and asides. Using speech to measure isolation, the author portrays both Eddie and Thurley as incapable of communicating adequately. Eddie, for example, becomes tongue-tied around a group of southern travelers, shuddering in his bus seat instead of warning them as he wishes for the reality of the northern mecca that they seek. Similarly, despite the empowering qualities of a gulp of Southern Comfort, Thurley delivers a lecture on Sophocles' *Oedipus Tyrannus* (c. 429 B.C.E.) fraught with "futility and detachment, . . . introspection and blindness." In one brilliant play on this speechlessness, both men suddenly converse as if they were actors on a stage. This abrupt emphasis on what is spoken—to the exclusion of private thoughts—stresses each person's imprisonment within him- or herself. Flowing from a weaker artist's pen, *A Glance Away* would have become a mere exercise in allusive technique and stream-of-consciousness style. On the contrary, it reads with the effortless ease of a masterfully crafted lyrical poem. Key to its success is Wideman's careful alliance of form and content, not to mention his insightful treatment of a rootlessness that transcends the barriers of race.

HURRY HOME

The same compact length as the novel that precedes it, *Hurry Home* similarly focuses on the theme of rootlessness. Its ambitious protagonist, the honors graduate Cecil Otis Braithwaite, is in many ways an upscale Eddie Lawson with a wife and an advanced degree. After slaving through law school, supporting himself with a meager scholarship and his earnings as a janitor, Cecil has lost his aspirations and his love for his girlfriend, Esther Brown. In search of something more, he escapes from his wedding bed to Europe, where he roams indiscriminately for three years among its brothels as well as its art galleries. In the tradition of Robert Thurley of *A Glance Away*, two white men as displaced as Cecil attempt to guide him: Charles Webb, belatedly in search of an illegitimate son, and Albert, a mercenary in Webb's employ who has also abandoned a wife. Too lost to save themselves, however, this pair can offer no enduring words of solace to Cecil.

Hurry Home is more sophisticated than *A Glance Away* in its treatment of the isolation theme. It suggests, for example, that the upwardly mobile Cecil is not merely disturbed by his personal past; he is estranged as well from his African and European cultures of origin. On the other hand, nowhere does *Hurry Home* convey the hope that pervades its predecessor. Cecil travels more extensively than does Eddie to reclaim his past, yet he gains no key to it to speak of. Confronting his European heritage merely confirms his status as "a stranger in all . . . tongues." He flees to the African continent by boat, "satisfied to be forever possessed," only to be forever rebuffed from a past that "melts like a wax casing as I am nearer . . . the flame." When he returns at last to his Washington, D.C., tenement, the fruitlessness of his journey is underscored. There, he finds all the same as when he first entered following his miserable nuptials. Symbolically limning his rootlessness, he switches vocations, abandoning the tradition-steeped protocol of the bar for the faddish repertoire of a hairdresser. Thus, "hurry home," the catchphrase for his odyssey, is an ironic one. Cecil really can claim no place where a heritage nurtures and sustains him, no history that he can truly call his own.

Hurry Home displays a masterful style commensurate with that of the later Homewood novels. In addition to a more controlled stream-of-consciousness technique, recurring Christian symbols, icons of Renaissance art, and fragments from Moorish legend powerfully indicate Cecil's fractured lineage. This second novel being a more refined paradigm than the first, Wideman seemed next inclined to break new ground, to address intently the racial polarization that had unsettled American society by the early 1970's, producing that period's most influential published works.

THE LYNCHERS

Distinguished from the previous two novels by its bawdy humor and portrayal of a professional black woman, *The Lynchers* is set in the generic northeastern slum, pockmarked by the self-inflicted wounds of the 1960's, that has become a Wideman trademark. Central to the action are four frustrated black men: Willie "Littleman" Hall, an unemployed dwarf; Leonard Saunders, a ruthless hustler turned repressed postal clerk; Thomas Wilkerson, a plodding fifth-grade schoolteacher; and Graham Rice, an introspective janitor with a persecution complex. Disenchanted with the superficial changes that the Civil Rights movement has wrought—the "job here or a public office there, . . . one or two black faces floating to the top"—these four conclude that violence is the only means to effect a lasting alteration of the white power structure. With Littleman as the ringleader and mastermind, they plan to flex the latent power of the black community and turn the tables on their oppressors by kidnapping and lynching a white policeman.

The plot falls apart, however, once Littleman is badly beaten by the authorities for delivering a militant speech at Woodrow Wilson Junior High School. Suspicion, distrust, and doubt override the remaining conspirators so that they foil themselves instead of their "white butcher pig" enemy. Thus, in a perverse way the weapons of the executioner do revert to black hands. Lynching becomes a symbol of frustration turned inward, of despairing hearts made so taut in their efforts to beat more freely that they burst.

Unlike *A Glance Away* and *Hurry Home*, *The Lynchers* is a total immersion into blackness. Perhaps the critics wanted another black/white character dichotomy, for their assessments of this novel were at best mixed. Nevertheless, Wideman again displays strong gifts of characterization without diminishing the theme's universal appeal. A continuation of his preoccupation with rootlessness, *The Lynchers* showcases men who feel acutely that they belong nowhere. Wilkerson, for example, is the Cecil type, the black professional who is alienated from his working-class roots, condescended to by whites possessing similar educational backgrounds, and unwelcome in the clubs and restaurants that they patronize. Saunders, like Eddie, is a marginally good citizen, at once attracted to and repelled by "the life" of conning and thieving. In an intricate new twist to this scenario, Wideman depicts the older generation as a group as anchorless as the young. For example, Wilkerson's father, a drunk and a philanderer, stabs a longtime friend to death.

In its familiar inner-city setting and cast of alienated men (a passing reference is even made to Cecil Braithwaite as Littleman's lawyer), *The Lynchers* recalls Wideman's preceding works. In its use of a symbol generated exclusively from the black experience, it acts as a transition between these two novels and Wideman's fourth and fifth endeavors. No longer primarily gleaning symbols from Christianity and the European classics, here Wideman unifies his montage of dialogues with "the hawk," a symbol indigenous to the men's own harsh environment. This frigid, anthropomorphic wind that lashes the streets indicates the blacks' powerlessness and the hollow bravado of their ill-fated intrigue. They cannot even abduct the police officer without using one of their own people, his black girlfriend, Sissie, as a pawn.

Hiding Place

After an eight-year interval during which he researched black American literature and culture, Wideman applied folk sources more fully than ever before in *Hiding Place*, one of the three works of fiction that make up the Homewood Trilogy. Challenged to enlarge his black readership without limiting the universal relevance of his themes, he chose to emphasize one black family based largely on his own Homewood clan. In this novel's swift, uncomplicated plot, Tommy Lawson, a tough, wisecracking youth from the black neighborhood of Homewood, is running from the police for his involvement in a robbery and killing. He seeks refuge among the weedy plots and garbage piles of desolate Bruston Hill, a once-fertile area to which his ancestor Sybela Owens fled from the South and slavery with Charlie Bell, her white owner's recalcitrant son. In the lone residence at the crest of the Hill, a rotting wooden shack sardonically known as "that doghouse," the reclusive "Mother" Bess Owens reluctantly offers her sister's great-grandson a temporary haven. After Tommy regains the courage to elude the authorities eager to convict him for a murder that he did not commit, Bess reaffirms her ties to her kin and ends her self-imposed isolation. Not knowing whether Tommy is dead, has escaped, or has been captured, she burns her shack and prepares to reenter Homewood to retell Tommy's tragic story so that another like it might never happen again.

Though Bess does not leave her longtime home until the novel's final chapter, *Hiding Place* is as much the story of her isolation from family as it is one of

Tommy's. Just as Tommy has shirked his responsibilities as a husband, father, and son, Bess has turned her back on the younger generations of kin whose ways are alien to her. Widowed and childless, she has retreated into an archaic lifestyle, shunning the twentieth century amenities of electricity and phones, in order to avoid intimacy with others. Physically rooting herself among Bruston Hill's ruins, she has been running from the present in her mind by focusing her thoughts on the past, especially the deaths of loved ones that have occurred. Only when she becomes involved in Tommy's affairs does she rekindle her active commitment to the family.

In *Hiding Place*, Wideman's style dramatically differs from those of the canonized white writers who were his early models. With a method many reviewers have compared to jazz, his characters unfold the histories of five generations of Lawsons and Frenches. Bess herself repeats certain key events in the family history several times; one of her favorites is the one in which Mary Hollinger revives her cousin Freeda French's stillborn baby by plunging it into the snow. Yet like a jazz improvisation, where instruments alternately play solo and play together, she retells the tale each time in a different way, varying her approach to it with different bits of superstition, mysticism, and folklore. Even Wideman's Clement, an inarticulate orphan similar to Benjy Compson in William Faulkner's *The Sound and the Fury* (1929), bears the unique stamp of the black American experience. As the author himself avows, Clement's assimilation into Homewood reflects the nature of the black community as a tolerant extended family.

Its legacy of songs, tales, and superstitions notwithstanding, the Homewood that finally draws Bess back is a model of urban blight, a "bombed out" no-man's-land of "pieces of buildings standing here and there and fire scars and places ripped and kicked down and cars stripped and dead at the curb." This dying landscape, and in a similar way Bess's ramshackle Bruston Hill homestead, proclaims the present descendants' dissociation from their ancestors and one another. In *Sent for You Yesterday*, the final installment of the Homewood Trilogy and the 1984 PEN/Faulkner Award winner for outstanding fiction, this undercurrent becomes the novel's predominant theme. Carl French and his lover Lucy Tate relate the stories of a Homewood gone by to the latest generation of listeners, as if the recovery of the past is integral for the entire community's survival and solidarity.

Sent for You Yesterday

Sent for You Yesterday cannot be divided easily into main story and subplots. All the episodes in it are major in scope and significance. The most memorable ones include the saga of the piano player Albert Wilkes, who slept with a white woman and murdered a white policeman; the tragedy of Samantha, whose college education could not shield her from grief and madness; and the bittersweet adventures of the resilient Brother Tate, an albino and best friend of Carl who communicates only with gestures and scat sounds. Retold by Carl's nephew Doot, a former Homewood resident modeled largely after Wideman himself, each tale conveys a lesson to a younger generation. More than mere exempla, however, the stories emphasize the cyclic nature of the human condition: Each generation rises to further, alter, and often reenact the accomplishments of its predecessors. Thus, Uncle Carl's street in Homewood becomes to Doot "a narrow, cobbled alley *teeming* with life. Like a wooden-walled ship in the middle of the city, like the ark on which Noah packed two of everything and prayed for land." This determination to survive that the ark imagery calls to mind impels Carl and Lucy to share Homewood's history. By remembering past lives, by preserving traditions, they ensure their own enduring places in the memories of their heirs.

Reuben

Traditions preserved and memories presented from black America's African past form the backbeat of *Reuben*, Wideman's next novel of community and interracial struggle. From a rusting trailer that his clients describe as part office, part altar to the gods, the dwarf Reuben serves the poor of Homewood in need of a lawyer, a psychologist, a warrior, or a priest. Like West African *griots* or oral scribes, who commit to unerring memory genealogies, triumphs, faults, and names, Reuben relies on a mix of law and bureaucratic legerdemain that he has heard from his own employers and remembered. Like an obliging ancestral spirit shuttling prayers from this world to the next, Reuben negotiates pacts between the ghetto's bombed-out streets and the oak, plush, and marble interiors of City Hall. As he prescribes legal strategies and bestows grandfatherly advice, he also steers his clients to confront and abandon the views that have overturned their lives. When words and contracts alone will not do, Reuben rustles deep within collective memory and knots a charm: "A rag, a bone, a hank of hair. Ancient grains of rice." Reuben transforms garbage into power, excrement into nourishment, gristle into life. He preaches reincarnation and the nature of things dead to rise again, and he catalyzes his clients to seek similar transformations in themselves.

Infused with magic and spiritualism, *Reuben* also is illustrated by the ravaged images of the inner city. Wideman likens ghetto buildings to the rat-infested holds of slave ships and the people in those buildings to roles of both predator and prey. Much of the Homewood population resembles a coffle of freshly branded slaves, slaves who are bound by laws instead of chains, by the welfare system or underworld crime instead of a plantation economy. Others are human versions of rats—snitching, beating, starving, stealing, and otherwise pestering their neighbors with an eat-or-be-eaten mentality. "There were historical precedents, parallels," Reuben understands. "Indian scouts leading long-hairs to the hiding places of their red brethren. FBI informers, double agents, infiltrators of the sixties. An unsubtle variation of divide and conquer." In this bleak landscape, the game of divide and conquer has changed little since enslavement.

Philadelphia Fire

Philadelphia Fire, *The Cattle Killing*, and *Two Cities* are framed within a geographic shift from Pittsburgh to Philadelphia. In keeping with Wideman's fluid notion of history and myth as mutually interlocking categories of representation, *Philadelphia Fire* recasts the 1985 police bombing of the building occupied by the radical MOVE organization. John Africa, MOVE's leader, is represented as Reverend King, who is described as "a nouveau Rousseau." King leads a rebellion against the infringement on African American individual and communal rights couched in the guises of "urbanization" and "integration" by espousing an ideology that embraces a return to nature and a rejection of modern material values. Elsewhere, Wideman asserts that "the craziness of MOVE is their sanity; they were saying no to the system . . . it makes perfect sense. So the myth of integration is analogous to the prophecy of the cattle killing."

The Cattle Killing

This prophecy serves as the guiding metaphor for the novel *The Cattle Killing*, and it refers to the lies told to the African Xhosa people in order to make them believe that to combat European oppression they must kill their cattle. The cattle are their life force, and their destruction leads to the near annihilation of Xhosa culture. The people die as their cattle die, struck down because they believed the lie of the prophecy: "The cattle are the people. The people are the cattle." Wideman subtly extends this metaphor to consider the problem of intraracial crime ravaging American inner cities and connects contemporary circumstances with the diseased and disintegrating conditions surrounding the yellow fever outbreak of eighteenth century Philadelphia.

In all three instances—in Africa, in Philadelphia, in black urbania—there is a potential for annihilation because of an epidemic fueled by hysteria, exacerbated by racist ideology and carried out by those who believe the "lie" and perpetrate their self-destruction. The narrator of *Cattle Killing*, Isaiah, called "Eye," is an obvious recasting of the biblical figure who prophesies the downfall of the nation of Israel. He is a prophet who warns of false prophecies—in this case, the lie of integration, which is intricately entwined with modernization and its attenuating conspicuous consumption, the theme foregrounded in *Philadelphia Fire*. This text's distinction from *Philadelphia Fire*, however, lies in the vision of hope with which readers are left; *The Cattle Killing* is also a love story.

Two Cities

The Cattle Killing and the following novel, *Two Cities*, mark a thematic shift for Wideman. Though harkening back to the theme of love (a kind of communal love) inherent in the Homewood Trilogy, the novels transcend that representation, exploring the healing potential of intimate, spiritual love. *Two Cities*, which links Philadelphia and Pittsburgh, Cassina Way and Osage Avenue, explores the difficulty of loving in troubled times. It overwhelmingly endorses the embracing of love, not merely physical love but also self-love, love of community, and love of life, as the only viable means of refusing and subverting the lies that have threatened to destroy the African American community.

From the beginning of his extensive literary career,

critics have often compared Wideman's prose to the experimental fictions of the eighteenth century English writer Laurence Sterne. The sociable Sterne had befriended Ignatius Sancho, a gregarious former slave, a prodigious correspondent, and host of one of London's most popular salons. Sancho admired Sterne's mock humility and imitated his wit and playful style. In turn, Sterne admired the double entendre, self-scrutiny, and flair for detail in the letters of his African friend.

In Wideman's novels, the voices of the African Sancho and the Englishman Sterne converge. These works present black America from the perspectives of the enslaved and the descendants of the enslaved as well as from the vantage point of those whites who served as either tormentors and oppressors or benefactors and friends. These works warn of the potholes where our elders slipped before, and they expose the reader to the vistas that people often fail to notice and enjoy. They achieve Wideman's goal of "expanding our notions of reality, creating hard, crisp edges you can't swallow without a gulp."

Barbara A. McCaskill
Updated by Heather Russell Andrade

Other major works

SHORT FICTION: *Damballah*, 1981; *Fever: Twelve Stories*, 1989; *All Stories Are True*, 1992; *The Stories of John Edgar Wideman*, 1992; *God's Gym*, 2005.

NONFICTION: *Brothers and Keepers*, 1984; *Fatheralong: A Meditation on Fathers and Sons, Race and Society*, 1994; *Conversations with John Edgar Wideman*, 1998 (Bonnie TuSmith, editor); *Hoop Roots*, 2001; *The Island: Martinique*, 2003.

EDITED TEXTS: *My Soul Has Grown Deep: Classics of Early African-American Literature*, 2001; *Twenty: The Best of the Drue Heinz Literature Prize*, 2001.

Bibliography

Auger, Philip. *Native Sons in No Man's Land: Rewriting Afro-American Manhood in the Novels of Baldwin, Walker, Wideman, and Gaines*. New York: Garland, 2000. Analyzes the representation of masculinity in Wideman's works.

Bell, Bernard W. *The Afro-American Novel and Its Tradition*. Amherst: University of Massachusetts Press, 1987. Provides a short but incisive overview of Wideman's evolving concerns as an African American as well as a postmodernist innovator. Also notes Wideman's evocative uses of history as an imaginative paradigm and identifies as his major theme "the conflict between [his protagonists'] ascribed and achieved identities as black men."

Coleman, James W. *Blackness and Modernism: The Literary Career of John Edgar Wideman*. Jackson: University Press of Mississippi, 1990. Discusses all of Wideman's novels through 1989 and includes an interview with the author. Supplemented with a brief bibliography of critical sources.

Dubey, Madhu. "Literature and Urban Crisis: John Edgar Wideman's *Philadelphia Fire*." *African American Review* 32 (Winter, 1998): 579-595. Examines *Philadelphia Fire* in relation to the novel's implicit critique of urban renewal and its attenuating glorification of consumption and excess, legitimation of law and order, and the resulting dispossession, displacement, and segregation of the city's inhabitants.

Mbalia, Doreatha D. *John Edgar Wideman: Reclaiming the African Personality*. Selinsgrove, Pa.: Susquehanna University Press, 1995. Discusses, among other topics, Wideman's narrative technique. Includes bibliography and index.

Rushdy, Ashraf. "Fraternal Blues: John Edgar Wideman's Homewood Trilogy." *Contemporary Literature* 32, no. 3 (Fall, 1991): 312-345. Begins by suggesting that the narrator of the trilogy utilizes three modes of narrating that are depicted in the three texts, respectively: letters, stories, and the blues. Argues that the narrative voice gains an understanding of self when it finds a "blues voice."

TuSmith, Bonnie, ed. *Conversations with John Edgar Wideman*. Jackson: University Press of Mississippi, 1998. Collection of interviews with Wideman dating from 1963 to 1997 covers a wide range of topics, including the sources of Wideman's fiction, his perspectives on race in the United States, his philosophical thought, and his writing technique.

TuSmith, Bonnie, and Keith E. Byerman, eds. *Critical Essays on John Edgar Wideman*. Knoxville: University of Tennessee Press, 2006. Collection of essays covers all of Wideman's major works and addresses such topics as the cultural context of his fiction, his writing style, and his use of personal narrative. Includes bibliography and index.

Wideman, John Edgar. *Hoop Roots*. Boston: Houghton Mifflin, 2001. Wideman reflects on his enduring relationship to the game of basketball, a sport that has played a pivotal role in his personal life and appears frequently in his fiction.

_______. "John Edgar Wideman." Interview by Kay Bonetti. In *Conversations with American Novelists*, edited by Kay Bonetti, Greg Michaelson, Speer Morgan, Jo Sapp, and Sam Stowers. Columbia: University of Missouri Press, 1997. Wideman discusses the oral tales told to him by his aunt, which he developed into the stories in the Homewood Trilogy. Also addresses the politics of writing in the United States, the risks that writers have to take to write truthfully about themselves and those they love, and his fiction's concern with brotherhood and sisterhood.

ELIE WIESEL

Born: Sighet, Transylvania, Romania; September 30, 1928
Also known as: Eliezer Wiesel

Principal long fiction

L'Aube, 1960 (novella; *Dawn*, 1961)
Le Jour, 1961 (novella; *The Accident*, 1962)
La Ville de la chance, 1962 (*The Town Beyond the Wall*, 1964)
Les Portes de la forêt, 1964 (*The Gates of the Forest*, 1966)
Le Mendiant de Jérusalem, 1968 (*A Beggar in Jerusalem*, 1970)
Le Serment de Kolvillàg, 1973 (*The Oath*, 1973)
Le Testament d'un poète juif assassiné, 1980 (*The Testament*, 1981)
Le Cinquième Fils, 1983 (*The Fifth Son*, 1985)
Le Crépuscule, au loin, 1987 (*Twilight*, 1988)
L'Oublié, 1989 (*The Forgotten*, 1992)
Les Juges, 1999 (*The Judges*, 2002)
Le Temps des déracinés, 2003 (*The Time of the Uprooted*, 2005)

Other literary forms

Since the appearance in 1956 of *Un di Velt hot geshvign* (in French as *La Nuit*, 1958; *Night*, 1960), Elie Wiesel (vee-ZEHL) has published many works of fiction and nonfiction. Among these are *Les Juifs du silence* (1966; *The Jews of Silence*, 1966), a personal testimony of his trip to Russia; *Le Chant des morts* (1966; *Legends of Our Time*, 1968), *Entre deux soleils* (1970; *One Generation After*, 1970), and *Un Juif aujourd'hui* (1977; *A Jew Today*, 1978), collections of essays and short stories; several volumes of biblical portraits and Hasidic tales; the plays *Zalmen: Ou, La Folie de Dieu* (pb. 1968; *Zalmen: Or, The Madness of God*, 1974) and *Le Procès de Shamgorod tel qu'il se déroula le 25 février 1649* (pb. 1979; *The Trial of God: As It Was Held on February 25, 1649, in Shamgorod*, 1979); and a cantata, *Ani Maamin: Un Chant perdu et retrouvé* (1973; *Ani Maamin: A Song Lost and Found Again*, 1973). Some of his later works, the biblical portraits and Hasidic tales, although written in French, were originally published in the English translation by his wife, Marion Wiesel.

Achievements

Elie Wiesel is one of the most important figures in the genre known as "the literature of the Holocaust." He brings to literature a new literary vocabulary, rooted in the Bible, that is at once mystical, legalistic, theological, and historical. As a survivor of the Holocaust, Wiesel considers himself to be a messenger from the dead to the living, and, as a witness, he bears testimony both to the unfathomable events of the death camps and to the current, unfolding history of his people. Wiesel's work, parochial in context, is universal in perception. It speaks to all humankind, for all participated, either actively or silently, in the supreme trial of their humanity. He views the Holocaust as touching upon every facet of one's life and interests, and he perceives humanity's major problem to be survival in the post-Holocaust world.

As a writer, Wiesel is preoccupied with the inadequacy of language, but not in the abstract manner of many contemporary writers. Language affirms a belief in humankind and attests its grandeur. The Holocaust negates humanity. It represents a misuse of language; the failure of imagination; the rule of the depraved; the suspension of the senses, of beliefs, of time; the inversion of order. To capture the Holocaust in language is to impose upon it a decorum that in itself is a betrayal of those victimized by this satanic maelstrom. Wiesel believed, when he began to write, that the tale nevertheless must be told, because the murderer murders not only his victim but also himself. He says, "At Auschwitz, not only man died, but also the idea of man." Awareness of the Holocaust may save the world from self-obliteration.

Wiesel raises questions that are unanswerable, questions intended to arouse the consciousness of a people, the progeny of the indifferent observers of the decade of the 1940's. He also vies with God, not as a defiant disbeliever but as a believer in the biblical tradition of the prophets who have challenged God, remonstrated with him, and protested heavenly decrees. There is no gaiety in Wiesel's works. There is laughter, but it is not a joyous laughter. It is the laughter of a madman defying his creator. Writers, theologians, and humanists of all faiths have attempted to come to terms with the problems that Wiesel presents.

Writing, for Wiesel, is not simply intended as a moral lesson for the post-Holocaust generations. It is also, and perhaps primarily—as he explains in the essay "Mes Maîtres" ("My Teachers"), in *Legends of Our Time*—a monument to the unburied dead, to the millions whose celestial cemeteries are bereft of tombstones.

Wiesel's first publication, *Night*, is in the form of a memoir of his Holocaust experiences. Wiesel did not have an easy time publishing his initial work. It originally appeared in 1955 as an eight-hundred-page manuscript in Yiddish titled *Un di Velt hot geshvign* (and the world was silent) and was published in Argentina by a Yiddish press. It was then condensed to a little more than one hundred pages, translated into French, given the title *La Nuit*, and, with the help of Wiesel's close friend François Mauriac, published in France in 1958. It was an instant success. Stella Rodway translated the French version into English, but major publishing houses in the United States rejected the manuscript because the subject matter was "too sad" to appeal to the general public. Finally, in 1960, the publishing company Hill & Wang accepted the manuscript for publication. Wiesel would continue to write in French; his later books were translated into English by his wife, Marion. The exception is his eyewitness account of his trip to Russia, *The Jews of Silence*, which was originally written in Hebrew as a series of journalistic articles for an Israeli newspaper. It was thereafter put together in its present form. Some of Wiesel's essays first appeared in various magazines prior to their appearance in *Legends of Our Time* and *A Jew Today*.

Wiesel is a celebrated lecturer sought after by various organizations, conferences, and campuses, and he has served on the boards of numerous national and international organizations. He holds honorary doctoral degrees from more than forty colleges and universities and has received awards for literary, academic, and humanitarian contributions from numerous organizations. In 1983 he won the Belgian International Peace Prize, and in 1986 he received the Nobel Peace Prize.

In the period since he received the Nobel Prize, Wiesel has been honored with a great many other awards and recognitions, chief among them the Janusz Korczak Humanitarian Award from Kent State University (1989), named for the Polish teacher and author of children's books who chose to march into the gas chambers at Treblinka with his young students so that they would not have to die alone; the first Raoul Wallenberg Medal from the University of Michigan (1990), named for the Swedish diplomat who attended the university in the 1930's and later saved more than one hundred thousand Hungarian Jews from the Nazis; and the first Primo Levi Award (1992), named for the Italian chemist/author and Auschwitz survivor whose writings have served as testimony to the atrocities of the Holocaust. In 2006, Wiesel was made an Honorary Knight of the British Empire, a title bestowed on him in recognition of his vital contribution to Holocaust education worldwide. Wiesel has also been honored by university chairs and distinguished service awards named for him at such prestigious institutions as the University of Haifa, the University of Florida, and Connecticut College.

Biography

Eliezer Wiesel, the third child and only son of Shlomo and Sarah Wiesel, was born in the village of Sighet, in Transylvania, Romania, on September 30, 1928. He had two older sisters, Bea and Hilda, and one younger one, Tzipporah. His parents were Orthodox Jews. As a child, Eliezer was a profound believer in God and spent his days in religious studies. His father, though religious, was a man of culture and a rational humanist. He taught his son to believe in humanity and saw to it that he learned secular subjects, such as Latin, mathematics, and physics, as well as religious ones. His mother was more spiritual. She taught her son a love of God. The constant argument in the Wiesel home was whether their son should be a professor or a rabbi.

Wiesel's maternal grandfather, Dodye Feig, was a Hasid. The young boy would visit with his grandfather to listen to the tales of the Hasidim and the miracles wrought by the rabbis. Eliezer's talent as a storyteller had its beginnings in the stories told to him by his grandfather. He also evinced an appreciation for music and took violin lessons at an early age. After the war, he earned his keep as a choirmaster. His cantata, *Ani Maamin*, with a musical score by Darius Milhaud, is one of the most moving works to be produced about the Holocaust. At the age of twelve, he studied the Kabbala under the tutelage of his master, Moshe. Wiesel's first literary work, *Night*, commences with the serenity of his youth. The portrait of his grandfather and the conflicting attitudes of his parents are subjects of essays to be found in *Legends of Our Time* and *A Jew Today*.

The tranquillity of Wiesel's life was disturbed in the spring of 1944. Although the war in Europe had been going on since 1939, Hungary was one of the last countries to be invaded by the Germans. The inhabitants of the town of Sighet, protected as they were by the Carpathian Mountains and isolated from the events taking place, did not recognize or believe that disaster was imminent. Immigration, when it was still possible, had never been seriously considered. Suddenly, in a matter of weeks, ten thousand Jews were first placed in ghettos and then deported to Auschwitz. For Wiesel, one of the most bizarre aspects of the deportation was the apathy and indifference of the general public. Friends and neighbors turned their backs on people who had lived with them for generations. Wiesel deals with this in his novel *The Town Beyond the Wall* and also in various essays and lectures.

The four-day ride in a sealed boxcar, the arrival at Auschwitz, the separation of families, his last glimpse of his mother and younger sister, the concentration camp experience (including the loss of faith), the stripping away of his humanity, the march to Buchenwald, the death of his father, and finally liberation by the Americans in April, 1945, are tersely rendered in *Night*. Various aspects of this experience are reflected upon by some of the characters of his other novels and by Wiesel directly in some of his essays. The Holocaust itself, while it remains the impetus and muted background of all his writings, does not appear again as the bulk of any particular work. Instead, Wiesel turns from the memoir to the novel form, from fact to fiction, as his protagonists search, as he has done, for a way to live in the post-Holocaust world with the burden of the unimaginable behind them and with the guilt of living confronting them.

When Wiesel was liberated, at the age of sixteen and a half, he refused to be repatriated to the town that had evicted its Jews one year earlier. Instead, he joined a transport of children that was going to France at the invitation of Charles de Gaulle. Upon his arrival in France, he made the decision that he must testify to what he had experienced, but not until he understood it fully himself. He knew it would take him a long time to prepare himself for that testimony, perhaps ten years. He realized that he needed better communication skills and a keener understanding of what had happened. Meanwhile, he vowed not to speak of his experience of the Holocaust. (This vow of silence later became the subject matter for his novel *The Oath*.) In France, Wiesel learned that his two older sisters were alive. At Versailles, he became acquainted with François Wahl, a young philosopher at the Sorbonne, who taught him French by having Wiesel read French classical literature and classics translated into French.

Wiesel moved to Paris in 1946. There, he earned his livelihood as a choir director and as a teacher of the Bible. In 1948, he enrolled at the Sorbonne to study philosophy, the humanities, and literature, hoping to find the answers to the theological, philosophical, and humanistic questions that were plaguing him. His studies broadened his horizons but did not present him with solutions, and he was becoming restless. Fortunately, he landed a job as Paris correspondent for the Israeli newspaper *Yediot Aharonot*, and he spent the next few years traveling in North America, South America, Europe, North Africa, Asia, and the Middle East. As a journalist, Wiesel covered the Israeli War of Independence, which forms the background of his novella *Dawn*. In 1952, Wiesel traveled to India on an assignment. While in India, he wrote a dissertation comparing the Hindu, Christian, and Jewish religions. He also decided to teach himself English at that time.

One of Wiesel's assignments brought him back to Paris, where he met François Mauriac, who convinced him that he must break his vow and start telling his story. The result of this meeting was *Night*, a memoir in the form of a novella. The years after his liberation and the meeting with Mauriac are reflected in his essay "An Interview Unlike Any Other," in *A Jew Today*.

In 1956, Wiesel was sent to New York to cover the United Nations. He also began writing articles in Yiddish for the *Jewish Daily Forward*. During his first summer in New York, he was almost killed when he was struck by a taxicab while crossing Times Square. He required weeks of hospitalization and months of recuperation during which he could move about only with the help of a wheelchair. This experience became the subject of the novella *The Accident*, which he wrote while he was housebound. During that time, his French visa expired, and he applied for American citizenship.

Wiesel returned to Sighet in 1965. He arrived in the middle of the night. It was an unbearable experience for him, which he poignantly and searingly relates in an essay titled "Le Dernier Retour" ("The Last Return"). The retailing of this incident also appears in the collection *Legends of Our Time* and in "The Watch," in *One Generation After*, and it is recorded with great accuracy in his novel *The Town Beyond the Wall*. Wiesel could not bring himself to spend more than twenty-four hours in the city he had left so abruptly some twenty years before.

Wiesel's first visit to Russia, in 1965, resulted in three works, each in a different form: *The Jews of Silence*, a compilation of newspaper articles concerning the trip; *Zalmen*, a play dealing with the anguish of the rabbi of the Moscow synagogue; and *The Testament*, a novel begun during his trip but set against the background of the Stalinist purge of Jewish writers and poets in 1952. Wiesel returned to Russia again in 1979.

Elie Wiesel. (© The Nobel Foundation)

From 1948 on, Wiesel made several trips to Israel in his capacity as correspondent for *Yediot Aharonot*. His participation in the June, 1967, war provided the impetus for the novel *A Beggar in Jerusalem*. He returned to Israel in 1968, this time to be married in Jerusalem, to Marion Erster Rose, a Viennese, a concentration camp survivor also, and a linguist.

Wiesel joined the faculty at City College of New York in 1972, first as a visiting professor teaching courses on Jewish literature, the Holocaust, and Hasidism, and then, in 1973, as Distinguished Professor. Thereafter, he would teach at Boston University, as Andrew Mellon Professor of the Humanities.

In 1979, Wiesel was selected by President Jimmy Carter to chair the U.S. President's Commission on the Holocaust, which eventually created the United States Holocaust Memorial Museum, dedicated in 1993, in Washington, D.C. In 2004, the country of Romania, where Wiesel's hometown of Sighet is located, published a report on the truth about Holocaust atrocities committed against Jews in that region; Wiesel headed the group that researched and wrote this important report.

In 2006, a new edition of *Night* was published, retranslated by Wiesel's wife, Marion. Concurrent with this new edition, television talk-show host Oprah Winfrey chose *Night* as the featured selection of her book club and traveled with Wiesel to the site of the Auschwitz death camp, an event and interview that was later televised on Winfrey's show. At that time, Wiesel stated that he would probably never return to that horrific place. On another Winfrey show shortly after, Wiesel looked on proudly while student essayists, inspired by *Night*, received recognition for their antihate writings.

In 2007, Wiesel was violently assaulted in a San Francisco hotel elevator by a young American Holocaust denier who demanded that Wiesel recant his shattering Holocaust memoir *Night* and publicly assert that the Holocaust never occurred. The attacker was later captured after posting details of the attack on an anti-Semitic Web site. Ironically, when he was attacked, Wiesel was in San Francisco to speak at a conference on conflict resolution; he returned to the city three months later, heavily guarded, to accept a $250,000 award for his Elie Wiesel Foundation for Humanity.

Wiesel continues to be a passionately caring international educator, scholar, spokesman, and public intellectual. He has engaged and interacted with many other scholars, philosophers, and public figures to study and elucidate the genesis and texture of, and potential cures for, hate and its equally evil twin, apathy.

Analysis

Elie Wiesel has said that all his works are "commentary" on *Night*, his one work that deals directly with the Holocaust. His novels are odysseys of a soul fragmented by the Holocaust, in quest of tranquillity, an attempt to move away from the night, reaching the shores of day. The key to understanding Wiesel, then, is his memoir in the form of a novella, *Night*. It is a slim volume that records his childhood memories of his hometown and his experiences in the concentration camp. It also contains the themes, images, and devices that recur throughout his novels.

Night

The opening chapter of *Night* begins with the social setting of Wiesel's native village of Sighet in Transylvania—its inhabitants, their customs, their beliefs—and his first meeting with Moché, the beadle, a character who forms a link to all his other works. Events occur rapidly. The disruption of normalcy with the invasion of the Germans, the forcing of the Jews into ghettos, their deportation, and the obliteration of the Jewish community are recorded tersely but accurately.

From the moment the Jews of Sighet leave the tranquil setting of their native village until they are liberated, time is suspended. The concentration camp is a universe like no other. There, every day is a waking nightmare. Each day is a repetition of deprivation, starvation, cremation; death, either by torture, gunshot, or fire, is the only certainty. The boys look like old men; the men cry like children. Existence depends on endurance, regardless of age.

Not only is the town obliterated and time obliterated, but also the individual is transformed into an unrecognizable substance. The bestial inhumanity of the victimizers, the divorce from social, moral, and humanistic constraints, marks their apotheosis in the kingdom of Hell. The inmates of the concentration camp's universe are metamorphosed also. The tattooing of numbers on their arms indelibly brands them as objects of inventory, to be used as long as they work well and to be disposed of when they malfunction. *Night* describes this transformation. Early in the work, Wiesel says of himself that he "had become a completely different person."

The work ends after the war. He has survived and has been liberated; he looks into the mirror and sees a corpse staring back at him. The corpse becomes part of his life, and the tension of his works rests on his separating himself from the corpse, which means finding a place for himself among the living and giving the corpse a proper burial in the form of a literary monument. Separating himself from the corpse is not an easy task. It involves personal, social, and theological issues: assuaging his own guilt for having survived and coming to terms with an indifferent society and an indifferent God, who allowed the Holocaust to take place. His future works chart his attempt at reconciliation with life, reintegration into society, rediscovery of his religious heritage, and reaffirmation of his belief in God, in spite of everything. This is accomplished by the use of a dual character or alter ego. In each novel, the personality of the protagonist, a survivor of the Holocaust, is complemented by that of the antagonist, usually someone who was not directly involved in the war. They lead separate lives until their paths cross and their souls fuse. The antagonist then disappears; his existence is no longer necessary.

Within the biographical-historical-psychological framework of Wiesel's works are recurring metaphors, characters, and themes. The Holocaust, the overriding presence in Wiesel's oeuvre, is metaphorically night. The sealed, unlit boxcar bearing Wiesel and his townspeople arrived at Auschwitz at midnight. For the victims, night describes the abyss to which they were consigned; for the oppressors, it indicates the depravity of the soul; for the world, it represents the failure of enlightenment, the blackness in which the world was engulfed during the Holocaust period. For Wiesel, night is a physical and psychological condition. As a victim, he moved like a shadow through the kingdom of Death, communicating with corpses. As a survivor, the corpses still haunt him. In Auschwitz, time lost its significance, and night became the only frame of reference. Night continues to circumscribe the parameters of confinement for the protagonists in *The Town Beyond the Wall*, *The Gates of the Forest*, *A Beggar in Jerusalem*, *The Oath*, and *The Testament*.

The lasting effects of the devastation on the psyche are summed up by Wiesel in an incantatory paragraph that appears early in *Night*:

> Never shall I forget that night, the first night in camp which has turned my life into one long night, seven times cursed and seven times sealed. Never shall I forget that smoke. Never shall I forget the little faces of the children, whose bodies I saw turned into wreaths of smoke beneath a silent blue sky.

Having pledged never to forget, Wiesel makes memory an important aspect of all his writings. His characters, especially his protagonists, are haunted by their memories. Memory controls their lives and motivates their actions. It is also a bridge to their future.

Moché, the beadle of *Night*, survives the massacre of the first roundup of Jews and returns to Sighet to tell the tale and warn the others concerning their impending doom. The townspeople, however, refuse to believe him and think he has gone mad. Moché appears in every book; his role is usually that of messenger in the tale he tells. Madness is an essential element in all Wiesel's works. On the one hand, it is indicative of the malady that struck the world during the Holocaust years. Wiesel, however, treats his madmen sympathetically. Their madness is not clinical but mystical. They are visionaries, saints, or messengers, endowed with the task of saving the world. As such, they become one with humankind, God, and creation. Wiesel's point is that madness can be a force of evil or good. Hitler and his Nazis were mad. Their madness was employed to destroy the world. Most of Wiesel's madmen want to bring about the Messiah; they want to redeem the world.

Another theme that is paramount in Wiesel's works is that of silence. Wiesel's ten years of silence after his liberation afforded him the opportunity for reflection and meditation on past events and future actions. He followed a carefully conceived plan not to speak. It was not that he had nothing to say or that he was indifferent; his decision was prompted by the knowledge that no words could describe what had taken place. His silence was intended as an "eloquent silence, a screaming silence, a shouting silence." Wiesel broke his silence when he decided to write, and in each of his novels, excepting *The Town Beyond the Wall*, the protagonist is confronted with a similar problem and makes a similar decision. Related to the theme of silence is the theme of responsibility, which is expressed in breaking the silence.

To evoke accurately the ravaged soul of the survivor in the post-Holocaust world, Wiesel creates a society of characters different from those one is used to meeting in novels. The characters are beggars, witnesses, messengers, storytellers, and chroniclers.

The Town Beyond the Wall

The Town Beyond the Wall, Wiesel's first novel after his three novellas, depicts his attempt to go home again. After his liberation from Buchenwald, Wiesel refused to return to his native town. He became, like the beggars or messengers in his stories, a *navenadnik*, a wanderer, a lost soul traveling throughout the world to find an inner peace and a place that he could call home. He traveled for ten years and finally, albeit accidentally, settled in the United States. It became home for him, however, only when he could totally and irrevocably sever his ties with his hometown. No matter where he went, he was drawn to the memories of his childhood, the familiarity and tranquillity of those days. He had to return at least once in order to realize that the Sighet of his youth no longer existed. It was a journey, as Wiesel says, to "nothingness."

The Town Beyond the Wall is divided into four parts and is presented in a series of reveries that help the protagonist cope with the torture imposed on him by his captors during his confinement in prison. Michael, a survivor of the Holocaust, has returned to his hometown of Szerencseváros with the aid of his friend, Pedro. The town is now under Communist rule, and he has entered it illegally. He is betrayed, imprisoned, and—because he remains silent and will not inform on his friend—is given the standard treatment, a torture called "The Prayer," which consists of keeping a prisoner on his feet facing a wall until he speaks or loses consciousness. To surmount the pain, Michael devises a method of transcending time by moving back and forth in his consciousness so that the present recedes to his subconscious level and the past moves forward into his consciousness. The reflections relating to his hometown are twice filtered, first as they are told to Pedro and then as he recalls them during his "prayers."

The pendular movement between different levels of consciousness, so that time is obliterated, is suggestive of Wiesel's imprisonment in the concentration camp. It is as if Wiesel is saying that time exists only in society. Once removed from society, people are also removed from time. In fact, they have no need for it. Time stops for them, but because time continues to move on for the world beyond their confinement, they will never be able to retrieve it.

Night hovers over *The Town Beyond the Wall*, as it hovered over Wiesel's first work. The protagonist is enveloped in a physical and psychological darkness. With his eyes closed, shutting out all light and consciousness, he evokes the nightmare world of his past, the fears of his childhood, his reflections on the Holocaust, the death of those who influenced him—Moché, the madman; Varady, his neighbor; Kalman, his teacher; his father; Yankel, his friend from the concentration camp—and the bleakness of life in France. An aspect of this nightmare world is his divided consciousness. This is suggested by the time and place in which he meets Pedro: in Tangiers, an hour before midnight in a dimly lit café, which is under a sign of a black cat. Pedro is his antagonist. He is what Saul Bellow would call "the Spirit of Alternatives." They walk the city together late at night. Pedro listens to Michael, providing him with alternatives to his dilemmas, answers to his questions, and a *modus vivendi*. He is a good friend. Their identities, at the conclusion, fuse, and when Michael is imprisoned, Pedro disappears, living only in Michael's memory in the form of an attitude toward life.

Through his relationship with Pedro, Michael comes to realize that silence in the form of indifference is destructive. People affirm their humanity when they involve themselves with or share in the anguish of humankind. To be a spectator of life is to deny life. That was the reason for Michael's return to Szerencseváros. He wanted to confront the spectator, the man who watched his Jewish neighbors being humiliated, looked on as the children cried of thirst, and then turned his back without any expression of emotion. That is why, at the end of the novel, he decides that he must reach out to his cell mate, who has rejected the world and now exists as a mute on the periphery of life. Michael knows that by restoring an interest in existence to his silent companion, he is also asserting his own essence, giving meaning to his own life. Wiesel later expands on this theme in *The Oath*.

In *The Town Beyond the Wall*, silence is viewed as detrimental. In the opening section, when Michael reflects on his childhood friendship with the renegade Varady, he notes that the community expresses its hatred for him through silence. In the next chapter, Michael's failure to respond to his friend's need results in Yankel's committing suicide. In the third section, Michael tells the tale of a mother and child who attempt to flee the Germans by hiding in the wagon of hay owned by a friendly neighbor who offers to take them to safety. He tells them that their lives depend on their being silent. Silence, however, did not help them; they were killed when the Hungarian officers repeatedly stuck their bayonets through the hay. In the conclusion, Michael's silence, while it may have saved the life of Pedro, may also have cost him his own life.

Wiesel expresses his own equivocation regarding silence in this novel. Words may betray, words may deceive, but speech remains the only expression of civilized people. Language, when properly used and properly understood, is instructive and a means of creating a bond between people. It may not save the world, but it may save one human being. This is the lesson Wiesel learned from Mauriac, which caused him to break his vow.

Madness is presented as the opposite of silence. One takes refuge in being mute, the other in being vocal. The silent one sees without responding; the madman sees and reacts, usually through the use of words that other characters cannot comprehend or that they refuse to comprehend. Wiesel elaborates on this theme in the scene at the insane asylum in *A Beggar in Jerusalem*. In *The Town Beyond the Wall*, Pedro prevents Michael from joining the cadre of madmen. He tells him, "To see liberty only in madness is wrong." Madness is seen as a force of evil in this work. Michael's cell mate is mad; he sees things that are not there and says things that do not make sense, and he finally attempts to kill a third cell mate, Menachem.

It is significant that *The Town Beyond the Wall* ends in the cell. Michael is still a prisoner of his past. He is reaching out toward others, attempting to find his own identity, but he has not yet been able to do so. Wiesel's next novel deals with this problem; each of his novels, excluding *The Testament*, charts his journey away from *Night*.

The Gates of the Forest

While *The Town Beyond the Wall* examines the possibility of going home and acknowledges the impossibility of doing so, *The Gates of the Forest* concentrates on retrieving a lost name and the identity that goes with it. This novel also begins with night and imprisonment. The opening setting is not a cell but a cave in the forest. It is springtime, with its intimations of rebirth and regeneration, but the war once again casts its shadowy reflection over the entire work. Gavriel, a seventeen-year-old Jewish youth, has escaped deportation and is hiding from the German and Hungarian police. He has assumed the name of Gregor to increase his chances of remaining alive. His father was with him in hiding but had gone in search of food three days earlier, and he has not returned. Prior to his leaving, he had admonished his son not to break his silence and betray his whereabouts. A stranger, another Jew, makes his way to Gregor's hideout. The man has no name, and Gregor gives him his. The entire work is devoted to searching out the efficacy of silence and its relationship to an individual's identity.

The Gates of the Forest is also divided into four sections, alternating between the forest and the city. The first two sections establish the protagonist as a man of various masks. In the first section, he gives his name to a stranger who first jeopardizes and then saves his life. In section 2, he assumes two guises: that of a deaf-mute bastard child and that of the betrayer of Christ. After escaping from the forest, Gregor seeks refuge with Martha, the peasant woman who used to work for them. It is her idea that he disguise his identity and become the child of her wayward sister, Ileana. He assumes yet another identity in this village, when the school principal decides to stage a Passion play and bestows on him the part of Judas. Section 2 concludes with Gregor proclaiming his true self—Gavriel.

Now that he has pronounced his name, he has to labor at reclaiming his identity. The second half of the work is devoted to transforming the personality of Gregor into that of Gavriel: the estranged individual into a man of God. He does this by intimately relating to his own people and by refusing to be other than what he is. He joins a Jewish partisan group in the forest. When the war is ended, he meets Clara, who was also a partisan, and marries her. In New York, Gregor joins in a Hasidic celebration and gains an audience with a Hasidic Rebbe. He confronts him with all the problems that have afflicted him since the war, especially his inability to believe in God after what has happened. The Rebbe's answers provide him with a "gate" to the future. It is in the synagogue after his meeting with the Rebbe that Gavriel reclaims his name and his identity as a man of God.

The Rebbe and the stranger are Gregor's antagonists. The stranger at the beginning of the novel has the name Gavriel—"Man of God"; the Rebbe, at the end of the work, *is* the man of God. The stranger disappears early in the work, and Gregor's search for him proves futile. He thinks he sees Gavriel at the Rebbe's house of study, but it is an illusion, a dream. He sees, or dreams that he sees, only another stranger. He insists that the stranger listen to his story. The act of telling the story restores Gavriel's identity. He awakens from his dream knowing what he has to do: help Clara lay her ghosts to rest and restore his relationship with God. The work ends with his recitation of Kaddish, which, while it is a prayer for the dead, affirms the greatness of God. Once again, Wiesel concludes that silence is not a solution. Through the use of words, people not only speak to God but also become "messengers to heaven."

There is in this novel, as in all of Wiesel's novels, much autobiographical detail. Wiesel, as Gavriel-Gregor, the storyteller, presents his attitude toward the Germans, the Christians, and Europe itself, as well as the humanism of his father, the mysticism of his childhood, the isolation and ignorance of the Jews of Transylvania regarding their fate, his inability to cry, his guilt as a survivor, his going to France immediately after the war, his becoming a journalist and traveling to North Africa, the Far East, and the United States, his refusal to say Kaddish upon the death of his father, and his inability to believe in a God who remained silent during the Holocaust. Above all, this work charts the author's slow but certain return to religion and the Hasidism of his childhood. The visits to the Hasidic Rebbe are autobiographical, as is the search for a master or teacher. Wiesel continues to study with a Talmudic master and maintains a close relationship with a Hasidic rebbe in Brooklyn, New York.

Night, in this work, is significant as a general obfuscation of identity. The novel begins at night, in the cave with the protagonist who bears an assumed name, and it concludes in the morning, as Gavriel finds himself. Madness is a force of evil. It connotes the failure of rationality and describes the malady of the times, the frenzy of the mob. It is a condition from which one must be saved. Clara is on the verge of madness, and Gregor attempts to rescue her. The masters (or teachers), the stranger Gavriel, and the Rebbe are storytellers, and storytellers always bear messages. Gregor is both witness and messenger. In his role as Judas, he is witness to the madness of the peasants. Upon entering the partisan camp, he is a messenger bearing news from the outside, telling the group about the massacre of the townspeople. Later, he brings word of the death of Leib, leader of the partisans.

The work concludes in the season of winter with the ushering in of a new day. In its reconciliation with the past, the "gates of the forest" open onto a new life for Wiesel and his protagonists while not fully closing on the darkened phase of his youth.

A Beggar in Jerusalem

A Beggar in Jerusalem is a difficult novel. It is lyric, mystical, sensitive, yet powerful. Written in a mood of ecstasy, the seven-hundred-page first draft was condensed to its present length of slightly more than two hundred pages.

A Beggar in Jerusalem was galvanized by two crucial events in Wiesel's post-Holocaust life: a trip to Israel in 1967 and his marriage in 1968. At the outbreak of the Six-Day War in 1967, between the Arabs and Israelis, with its threat of extermination of the Jews once again, Wiesel went to Israel as a journalist. This work captures and records a victorious moment in Jewish history, the reunification of Jerusalem and, with it, the securing of the Wailing Wall. It also transmits the texture of this experience, the significance that Jerusalem embodies for Wiesel and the Jewish people. It is an emotional presentation, communicating the yearning of a people, the fulfillment of dreams, the "returning" home to Jerusalem. Wiesel was married in 1968 in a synagogue near the Wall. The novel is also a dedication to his wife, Marion. As such, it looks backward into his past and forward into the future. Like *The Town Beyond the Wall* and *The Gates of the Forest*, it, too, is a quest. In this novel, the search is for a new being. Wiesel does not want to rid himself of his past; it becomes an integral part of his life. The new being has to integrate his past experiences with his present identity and his future with his wife.

Silence is not a major issue in this work. It is the telling of tales and memory that are paramount. *A Beggar in Jerusalem* shifts between time periods, suggesting that contemporary events are meaningful only in the perspective of history. The joy of conquest is tempered with the sadness of two millennia of Jewish suffering. As in all Wiesel's works, the Holocaust forms the background and molds and shapes the events of this hauntingly beautiful novel. It is a paean to Jerusalem, but it does not extol the victors. There is no gaiety, no victory celebration. It is a somber novel that concentrates on the anticipation and fear that precede war, acknowledges the human torment that follows war, and focuses on the collective responsibility of humankind.

The aftermath of war is not glorious; instead of heroes, the novel offers a strange array of beggars, vagabonds, madmen, and storytellers. All are Holocaust survivors who left the camps with nothing, had no homes to which to return, were unwanted by everyone, and were treated like beggars everywhere—displaced persons whose lives take on meaning in the sharing of experiences. The beggars—Moché, the madman, among them—meet at night. They exchange tales of anguish as they debate God's justice and their own human condition.

David, the narrator of the work, is also a survivor of the Holocaust. As a representative of the past, he is the witness and the teller of tales. He interrupts the present tale of the Six-Day War with memories, the collective experiences of his people, and stories he has heard from others. He is a beggar and seeks out the company of other beggars, survivors like himself. This narrator-beggar ironically bears the name of the king of Israel, David. David's antagonist, Katriel, is an Israeli officer. He represents the present, a new generation that believes that it can alter its destiny. The work begins as a search for Katriel, who disappears after the war. David's and Katriel's stories move along separate lines, yet they are related. They meet during the war in the army camp and enter into a pact whereby they will remain together, each helping the other to conquer his fear. The survivor will bear witness for the other.

They remain together for the war and the victory. They are together at the Wailing Wall, and both observe the custom of writing a wish on a piece of paper that is slipped into a crack in the wall. The destiny of the antagonists of *The Town Beyond the Wall* and *The Gates of the Forest* befalls Katriel: He vanishes. No one knows what has happened to him. Actually, the personalities of Katriel and David have fused at the Wall in Jerusalem. The present has joined the past to create a new being. That David and Katriel are now one is suggested when David repeats to Malka, Katriel's wife, a story about a beggar told to him by Katriel. He then asks her, "But do you know who the beggar was? Sometimes I tell myself he was Katriel, he was I."

In this novel, Wiesel ends his quest. He no longer searches for a home. He has come to realize the validity of the words of a wandering preacher whom he met as a young boy—that all roads lead to Jerusalem. He also recalls the words of Katriel: "One doesn't go to Jerusalem, one returns to it." He no longer searches for identity or a new being; it has been reshaped by Jerusalem, "the city which miraculously transforms man into pilgrim; no one can enter it and go away unchanged." At the conclusion of *A Beggar in Jerusalem*, both the protagonist and his creator find that Jerusalem, the city of peace, is a concept one carries within oneself.

In *The Town Beyond the Wall* and *The Gates of the Forest*, the protagonists learn of the necessity to involve themselves in the life of other human beings. In *A Beggar in Jerusalem*, Wiesel moves from the single individual to the community: The beggars are comforted by the others in their group, Jewish people everywhere offer their support to the threatened Jewish state, and Israel wins the war, as the narrator states, with the aid of the six million who died.

The Oath

Responsibility, both individual and collective, is the major theme of *The Oath*. In the works that preceded *The Oath*, especially *The Town Beyond the Wall* and *The Gates of the Forest*, the dramatic tension created by the desire for silence gave way to the practical need to speak, yet Wiesel continued to question his decision to speak. In *One Generation After*, he suggests that the horrors of the Holocaust might have been transmitted more eloquently and consequently more effectively by the abjuration of speech. Had the survivors "remained mute, their accumulated silences would have been unbearable: the impact would have deafened the world." *The Oath* addresses itself to this issue. It, too, is a personal statement in which Wiesel works out his own problems regarding his decision to break his vow of silence. *The Oath* seems to resolve the tensions created in the desire for silence, recognizing the futility of explanation and the need for speech. It does not, however, conclude Wiesel's concern with the issue, which he takes up once again in *The Testament*.

The Testament

The Holocaust marked the destruction of East European Jewish life and culture. Not long after World War II, another area of Jewish culture was liquidated. On August 19, 1952, Stalin climaxed his infamous purge of Yiddish artists in the Soviet Union. On that day, thirty Yiddish writers were executed simply because they were Jewish. Hundreds more had been murdered earlier or were killed shortly afterward. These artists were consigned to oblivion, but Wiesel commemorates their achievements and bemoans their loss in *The Testament*. In so doing, he helps "the dead vanquish death."

Like Wiesel's earlier novels, *The Testament* is animated by the dramatic and dialectical tension between silence, or the "futility of all explanation," and the need to recount or bear witness. In this work, father and son are in opposition to each other. The father, Paltiel Kossover, an obscure poet, has substituted the god of Communism for the God of his forefathers, only to realize, too late, that his zeal is misdirected, that the new god has rejected him, and that his destiny is linked to his own people. This is the legacy he transmits to his son, in the form of a testament written in jail prior to his execution. The son, Grisha, a mute—he bit off his tongue so that he would not be able to testify against his father—reads the father's testament in an apartment in Jerusalem, to which he has come in 1972. The document was saved by a witness to the execution, Zupanev, a jailer who is determined not to allow Paltiel Kossover's memory to be obliterated.

The testament binds the present to the past, links the current tragedy to its historical predecessors. Zupanev says that Grisha, as a mute, is an "ideal messenger"—ideal because no one suspects him—who will be able to assimilate the events of the document into his consciousness and then recount them to future generations. Grisha's role as an effective witness is diminished, nevertheless, by his inability to speak.

Among Wiesel's novels, *The Testament* is the harshest in outlook and the darkest in vision. All his other works end on a note of optimism. This one does not. Only the setting of Jerusalem illuminates the night of the novel. The work begins in hope, at the Lod airport, with the ingathering of the Russian exiles. It ends in death and in memory and indicates that Wiesel has little faith in the writer's ability to change humanity and human nature. It is his testament that "mankind didn't change." Nevertheless, Wiesel continues to write. One explanation for his persistence is suggested by the prologue to *The Testament*, which recounts an anecdote concerning a Just Man and his desire to correct injustice. He says: "In the beginning, I thought I could change man. Today, I know I cannot. If I still shout today, if I still scream, it is to prevent man from ultimately changing me."

The Forgotten

The Holocaust and its aftermath would remain powerful themes in Wiesel's writings, as he shows again in *The Forgotten*. The title refers to the things that are forgotten as well as to who is forgotten, for memory, remembrance, and mental and psychological forgetting are all important leitmotifs.

Professor Elhanan Rosenbaum, Malkiel's increasingly sick and senile father, is rapidly losing his memory. To hold on to his dissolving past, he sends Malkiel to his native Carpathian village to retrace the family origins, a mission for which the son is highly qualified. As a *New York Times* reporter, Malkiel specializes in the dead, whether the victims of the Cambodian killing fields or the mighty of the obituary page. In President Nicolae Ceaușescu's Romania the reporter meets a philosophical Jewish gravedigger, who, through his tales told in the style of Hebraic storytellers, is both a witness of Nazi horrors and Jewish heroism and a repository of Jewish folklore and memory. Malkiel learns of his grandfather's self-sacrifice and of his father's courage and also of the fact that, as in so many German-occupied countries, most people actively participated in tracking and killing Jews or did nothing to save them. He also learns that the young Elhanan did not speak out while a comrade took revenge on their worst enemy by raping his widow, a silence that would haunt his father forever.

During lucid moments the father tells the son of his illegal entry into Palestine with Talia, his future wife, and of the intoxicating first days of Israel's independence, which symbolically and dramatically coincide with Malkiel's birth and Talia's death. Woven with the moving and passionate plea not to forget the dead are Malkiel's torturing liaisons with Inge the German and Leila the Arab, each of whom revives a special memory of hatred and pain. On the other hand, Tamar, his Jewish colleague and lover, presents him with a more difficult dilemma when she questions the conduct and ethics of modern-day Israel.

Only through legends, stories, eyewitness accounts—in short, words—can one hope to triumph over forgetfulness and ultimately death itself. From the power of words the spinner of tales survives, and so does his message, however incomplete and lost in the fog of memory. To seize and reassemble those shattered fragments of Elhanan's failing memory, Wiesel uses various narrative devices—letters, flashbacks, journal entries, tape recordings, prayers, unspoken dialogues—complemented by parables taken from Hasidic and Talmudic scholars.

Beginning with the publication of *Night* in 1956, Wiesel established himself as the bard of the Holocaust. *The Forgotten*, though, shines with a luminosity that was often absent from his earlier works, as if Wiesel had come out of his own Night Kingdom, scathed of course, but also full of hope and optimism. All is remembered; nothing is forgotten: "Thanks to him [Elhanan's grandson yet to be born], I shall live on; thanks to you, Abraham lives."

THE TIME OF THE UPROOTED

The Time of the Uprooted begins in 1939 as Gamaliel, a five-year-old Jewish boy, is spirited out of Nazi-overrun Czechoslovakia by his parents and taken to temporary safety in Hungary. When the Nazis overtake Hungary in 1944, Gamaliel's parents leave him with a cabaret singer, Ilonka, who lovingly rears the boy as a Christian, thereby protecting him from certain death in the Holocaust. After the war, Gamaliel is able to return the favor by saving Ilonka from the Russians, who think she was a German collaborator. In 1956, after the failed Hungarian Revolution, Gamaliel leaves Ilonka for a transcontinental odyssey through Vienna and Paris during which he has several unhappy affairs and a failed marriage that results in his wife's suicide and twin daughters who hate him. He drifts to New York City, where he has an unfulfilling career as a ghostwriter and, late in life, associates mostly with fellow refugees. A possible "ghost" from Gamaliel's past unexpectedly returns, however, when a doctor, Lili Rosenkrantz, draws him to the hospital bedside of a disfigured, silent, old Hungarian woman. Could this be Ilonka, his surrogate mother who saved him and whom he saved? The unidentified dying woman brings Gamaliel and Lili closer, and they are soon celebrating the Sabbath together.

In *The Time of the Uprooted*, Wiesel explores the themes of statelessness, perpetual itinerancy, and exile, both physical and psychic, and their damaging effects on the personal identity of the wanderer. Most of Gamaliel's problems, including his seeming incapacity for emotional intimacy, result from his being "uprooted" at an early age and therefore unable to feel that he truly belongs anywhere. Torn from his family's roots in Czechoslovakia, Gamaliel is searching, lost, and disconnected, a drifter from one random location and unfulfilling relationship to another. Even his career as a ghostwriter, in which his name fails to appear on his writing, symbolizes that he is hiding behind someone else, never feeling fully legitimate as his own person.

Wiesel also shows how, mostly without awareness, a person's past shapes who he or she is and who he or she becomes. In this powerful novel, as in all of his works, Wiesel explores the ways in which memory both holds humans captive to our pasts and reminds us of the courage and strength required to live nobly and fully despite our pasts. Through his attempts to explain Ilonka's goodness and heroism to Lili, Gamaliel begins to face where he comes from and who he is. He searches for the courage not to shove the past away but to accept it, to push through it and to find possible redemption for his failed life by beginning to live again. Gamaliel's powerful struggle parallels the challenging conundrum articulated by Wiesel in his Nobel Prize lecture. Wiesel implicitly addressed all Holocaust survivors, all of the cruelly "uprooted," when he said, "Because I remember, I despair. Because I remember, I have the duty to reject despair."

L. H. Goldman; Pierre L. Horn
Updated by Howard A. Kerner

OTHER MAJOR WORKS

SHORT FICTION: *Le Chant des morts*, 1966 (essays and short stories; *Legends of Our Time*, 1968); *Entre deux soleils*, 1970 (essays and short stories; *One Generation After*, 1970); *Un Juif aujourd'hui*, 1977 (essays and short stories; *A Jew Today*, 1978).

PLAYS: *Zalmen: Ou, La Folie de Dieu*, pb. 1968 (*Zalmen: Or, The Madness of God*, 1974); *Le Procès de*

Shamgorod tel qu'il se déroula le 25 février 1649, pb. 1979 (*The Trial of God: As It Was Held on February 25, 1649, in Shamgorod*, 1979).

NONFICTION: *Un di Velt hot geshvign*, 1956 (in Yiddish; in French as *La Nuit*, 1958; *Night*, 1960); *Les Juifs du silence*, 1966 (travel sketch; *The Jews of Silence*, 1966); *Discours d'Oslo*, 1987; *Le Mal et l'exil: Recontre avec Élie Wiesel*, 1988 (*Evil and Exile*, 1990); *From the Kingdom of Memory: Reminiscences*, 1990; *A Journey of Faith*, 1990 (with John Cardinal O'Connor); *Tous les fleuves vont à la mer*, 1994 (memoir; *All Rivers Run to the Sea*, 1995); *Et la mer n'est pas remplie*, 1996 (*And the Sea Is Never Full: Memoirs*, 1999); *Le Mal et l'exil: Dix ans après*, 1999; *Conversations with Elie Wiesel*, 2001 (Thomas J. Vinciguerra, editor); *After the Darkness: Reflections on the Holocaust*, 2002; *Elie Wiesel: Conversations*, 2002 (Robert Franciosi, editor); *Wise Men and Their Tales: Portraits of Biblical, Talmudic, and Hasidic Masters*, 2003; *Confronting Anti-Semitism*, 2006 (with Kofi Annan).

CHILDREN'S LITERATURE: *King Solomon and His Magic Ring*, 1999.

MISCELLANEOUS: *Célébration hassidique*, 1972-1981 (2 volumes; biographical sketches and stories; volume 1, *Souls on Fire*, 1972; volume 2, *Somewhere a Master: Further Hasidic Portraits and Legends*, 1982); *Ani Maamin: Un Chant perdu et retrouvé*, 1973 (cantata; *Ani Maamin: A Song Lost and Found Again*, 1973); *Célébration biblique*, 1975 (biographical sketches and stories; *Messengers of God: Biblical Portraits and Legends*, 1976); *Four Hasidic Masters and Their Struggle Against Melancholy*, 1978 (biographical sketches and stories); *Images from the Bible*, 1980 (biographical sketches and stories); *Five Biblical Portraits*, 1981 (biographical sketches and stories); *Paroles d'étranger*, 1982 (biographical sketches and stories); *Somewhere a Master*, 1982 (biographical sketches and stories); *The Six Days of Destruction: Meditations Towards Hope*, 1988 (with Albert H. Friedlander); *Silences et mémoire d'hommes: Essais, histoires, dialogues*, 1989; *Célébration talmudique: Portraits et légendes*, 1991; *Sages and Dreamers: Biblical, Talmudic, and Hasidic Portraits and Legends*, 1991; *Célébration prophétique: Portraits et légendes*, 1998; *Celebrating Elie Wiesel: Stories, Essays, Reflections*, 1998 (Alan Rosen, editor).

Bibliography

Berenbaum, Michael. *Elie Wiesel: God, the Holocaust, and the Children of Israel*. West Orange, N.J.: Behrman House, 1994. Reprint of *The Vision of the Void*, Berenbaum's thoughtful 1979 study of Wiesel, emphasizes Wiesel's insights about Jewish tradition.

Bloom, Harold, ed. *Elie Wiesel's "Night."* New York: Chelsea House, 2001. Collection of critical essays represents the spectrum of responses to Wiesel's memoir, which holds an important place in his body of work.

Cargas, Harry James. *Conversations with Elie Wiesel*. South Bend, Ind.: Justice Books, 1992. Updated and expanded edition of Cargas's 1976 interviews with Wiesel features Wiesel's own words on topics that include the Holocaust as well as his audience, his craft, and his mission as a witness and writer.

Downing, Frederick L. *Elie Wiesel: A Religious Biography*. Macon, Ga.: Mercer University Press, 2008. Analyzes Wiesel's life and writings, with a focus on the influence of his profound religious faith.

Horowitz, Rosemary, ed. *Elie Wiesel and the Art of Storytelling*. Jefferson, N.C.: McFarland, 2006. Collection of scholarly essays focuses on the ways in which Wiesel's cultural background has influenced his writing and how he maintains the Jewish storytelling tradition. Provides a critical examination of his writing style and the content of his works.

Katz, Steven, and Alan Rosen, eds. *Obliged by Memory: Literature, Religion, Ethics*. Syracuse, N.Y.: Syracuse University Press, 2005. In honor of Wiesel's seventieth birthday, such renowned scholars as Geoffrey Hartman and Cynthia Ozick contribute valuable essays to this collection of insights into the ways in which memory is at the core of Wiesel's writing.

Kolbert, Jack. *The Worlds of Elie Wiesel: An Overview of His Career and His Major Themes*. Snelinsgrove, Pa.: Susquehanna University Press, 2001. Offers a useful starting point for the beginning student of Wiesel's work. Combines biography with literary and philosophical analysis.

Mass, Wendy, ed. *Readings on "Night."* New York: Greenhaven Press, 2000. Includes biographical chapters, a summary of the plot and characters of Wiesel's book, and discussion of the major themes, the author's art, relationships in the novel, literary interpretation, and the legacy of the book.

Rosen, Alan, ed. *Celebrating Elie Wiesel: Stories, Essays, Reflections*. Notre Dame, Ind.: University of Notre Dame Press, 1998. Distinguished scholars reflect on the ethical and religious dimensions of Wiesel's essays and novels.

Sibelman, Simon P. *Silence in the Novels of Elie Wiesel*. New York: St. Martin's Press, 1995. Presents a thorough, intelligent, and stimulating discussion of a dominant theme in Wiesel's fiction.

Sternlicht, Sanford. *A Student Companion to Elie Wiesel*. Westport, Conn.: Greenwood Press, 2003. Presents critical analysis of all of Wiesel's major fiction and nonfiction works and relates the works to Wiesel's own life stories. Intended for general readers.

MARIANNE WIGGINS

Born: Lancaster, Pennsylvania; November 8, 1947

Principal long fiction

Babe, 1975
Went South, 1980
Separate Checks, 1984
John Dollar, 1989
Eveless Eden, 1995
Almost Heaven, 1998
Evidence of Things Unseen, 2003
The Shadow Catcher, 2007

Other literary forms

Marianne Wiggins has written short stories, published in periodicals such as *The Yale Review*, *Granta*, *Los Angeles Times Magazine*, *Ploughshares*, *Harper's*, *Woman's Journal*, and *The Paris Review*. Her published collections of short fiction include *Herself in Love, and Other Stories* (1987), *Learning Urdu* (1990), and *Bet They'll Miss Us When We're Gone* (1991). She has reviewed books for such newspapers and journals as the *Los Angeles Times Book Review*, *The Washington Post*, *The Nation*, and *New Statesman*. She wrote the introduction for *Other Edens* (1994), featuring Nick Waplington's photography, and has written essays for other books on photographic subjects, including *From the Heart: The Power of Photography—A Collector's Choice* (1998) and *Still: Cowboys at the Start of the Twenty-first Century* (2008).

Achievements

In 1989, Marianne Wiggins received the prestigious Whiting Writers' Award and a National Endowment for the Arts grant for fiction. Her novel *John Dollar* received the University of Rochester's Janet Heidinger Kafka Prize, which honors the most outstanding novel each year by an American woman. In 1996, Wiggins's novel *Eveless Eden* was short-listed for the Orange Prize for fiction. *Evidence of Things Unseen* was a National Book Award finalist for fiction in 2003 and a Pulitzer Prize finalist in 2004, and it received the 2004 Commonwealth Club Prize. *The Shadow Catcher* was a 2007 National Book Critics Circle Award fiction finalist and was also named a best book of the year by *Publishers Weekly*, *The Christian Science Monitor*, the *San Francisco Chronicle*, and other major periodicals. Some of Wiggins's books have been best sellers and many have been translated into several languages, including German, Dutch, Hebrew, Czech, and Swedish.

Biography

Marianne Wiggins was born on November 8, 1947, in Lancaster, Pennsylvania, to John Wiggins, a grocer, and Mary (Klonis) Wiggins, the daughter of Greek immigrants. Her father preached at a conservative church established by his father. With her mother, Wiggins also attended Greek Orthodox services, having been baptized in that faith when she was nine years old. Negative religious experiences during her childhood later shaped her literary depictions of religion.

In the spring of 1965, Wiggins graduated as valedictorian of Manheim Township High School class but decided not to attend Vassar College, which had accepted her for enrollment. On June 6, she married Brian Porzak. The couple lived in Europe, residing in several capitals, including Brussels, Paris, and Rome. It was in Rome that Wiggins gave birth to daughter Lara, who later became a professional photographer. Wiggins and Porzak divorced in 1970, the same year her father killed himself.

Wiggins next secured employment in the northeastern United States and started writing what would become her first novel, *Babe*. The story told of a divorced woman, much like herself, who was raising a young daughter. Tillie Olsen's book of essays *Silences* (1978) inspired Wiggins to continue pursuing a writing career. Although most reviewers ignored her early works, she began receiving recognition for her literary talents with her third novel, *Separate Checks*.

In 1985, Wiggins moved to London, England, where she met novelist Salman Rushdie, who shared the same literary agent. They were married on January 23, 1988. Within one year, on February 14, 1989, Rushdie was the target of a fatwa issued by the Ayatollah Khomeini of Iran. The fatwa called for Muslims to kill Rushdie for insulting Islam, the Prophet, and the Qurʾān in his novel *The Satanic Verses* (1989). Rushdie had dedicated that novel to Wiggins. Even while Scotland Yard guarded Wiggins and Rushdie and kept them in hiding, Wiggins tried to keep writing. She has said that she and Rushdie relocated about fifty-six times because of the fatwa. Her short story "Croeso I Gymru" reflects this phase of her life. The dates of stories she wrote, and where she wrote them while in hiding, are noted in her anthology *Bet They'll Miss Us When We're Gone*.

In July, 1989, five months after the fatwa was declared and one month after Khomeini died, Wiggins decided to stop hiding. She resumed living in London (Rushdie, in hiding for another several years, later claimed he requested that Wiggins leave England) and became more politically aware because of the fatwa. She returned to the United States for a publicity tour for her 1989 novel *John Dollar*, which she dedicated to Rushdie. The novel, which had been released when she was in hiding, enhanced Wiggins's literary reputation.

Wiggins and Rushdie divorced in 1993. Three years later, Wiggins lost her London residence because of tax problems. She moved to Southern California and focused on creating long fiction. She arranged for Richard Rhodes, author of *The Making of the Atomic Bomb* (1986), to review for scientific accuracy a galley of what would become her novel *Evidence of Things Unseen*. In the fall of 2005, she began teaching creative writing at the University of Southern California in Los Angeles.

Analysis

Transition is a common theme in Marianne Wiggins's novels, whether this comes through characters deciding to alter their circumstances or by changes that are forced upon them. Wiggins often incorporates autobiographical elements in her fiction, and she has acknowledged that she writes about her own fears. Her adult female protagonists are confronted with such losses as divorce and suicidal relatives. These forms of abandonment transform their lives and both strengthen and weaken those who are left behind to cope with the perceived betrayals. Some critics consider Wiggins's fiction to be feminist. Women secure empowerment and autonomy through employment, responsibility for children, and creativity. Male characters become vulnerable when women they love choose other lovers and futures instead of them.

Family and community shape Wiggins's characters. Her depictions of people helping others heal from emotional crises or even causing additional pain convey themes of love and rejection. Often characters endure abuses and injuries caused by carelessness or cruelties. While some characters respond to conflicts with increased resilience, others suffer mental and emotional breakdowns. Intense losses affect memory. Illusion, too, is a frequent theme in Wiggins's work, as identities occasionally seem unreliable as characters reinvent themselves.

Many critics praise Wiggins's writing style, namely its imaginative use of language. Her detailed landscapes are filled with rivers, animals, stars, and light as dynamic characters. Sounds and silences distinguish urban and rural places. She uses colors to intensify characterizations: reds and earth tones indicate steadfastness and endurance, and pale colors suggest translucency and impermanence. Food and eating represent needed nourishment but also gluttony, which consumes characters. Wiggins's fiction includes many photographs.

John Dollar

Considered Wiggins's most provocative novel, *John Dollar* presents figurative criticisms of male-dominated religious, political, economic, and social practices often associated with Western cultures. Her themes of obedience, conformity, and patriarchy, for example, denounce imperialism, colonialism, materialism, and elitism. She used elements from William Golding's novel *Lord of the Flies* (1954) to create a survival tale of females isolated from rescuers. Her characters show that innocence and savagery can coexist.

The opening scene of an elderly woman's burial and references to her previous death six decades before establishes a sinister tone. Wiggins shifts her omniscient narrative to the past, introducing widowed Charlotte Lewes, who accepts a teaching position in Rangoon, Burma, in 1918. Disliking pretentious English colonists, Charlotte prefers to be alone until she meets sailor John Dollar, savoring how their relationship liberates her emotionally and physically. Imagery of porpoises and mermaids symbolize their joy.

The English sail to an island near Burma to celebrate King George's birthday. Three ships transport John, Charlotte, eight prepubescent girls, who are her students, and others. They picnic on the island's beach, where turtles appear from the sea to bury their eggs in the sand. Lizards rush from the vegetation to devour the eggs. Some of the English join in the feeding frenzy. This scene, along with the discovery of a skull and a reference to cannibals, foreshadows potential violence.

The English men depart to hunt on a different island, leaving two boats and the children with John and Charlotte. The next morning, John sees the boys' ship drifting. When he boards that vessel, he sees that the boys are missing and their berths are bloodied. As John races back to the island, a tsunami hits. After the wave recedes, the girls are alone. Assuming rescuers will arrive and lacking survival skills, they explore the island. The girls locate John, who has been paralyzed, and drag him to higher ground. They also see cannibals killing and cooking their fathers on the beach. Horrified, the girls gather their fathers' bones after the cannibals leave, beginning their transition from being civilized to turning "wild."

John attempts to protect the girls, warning them not to fly a kite, which might alert the cannibals to their presence. He becomes a godlike figure to two girls, who remove flesh from his numb legs to eat, suggesting Eucharistic rituals in the Bible's book of John. The other girls, except for half-Indian outcast Monkey, are killed by quicksand and through other mishaps. Monkey discovers a glade, reminiscent of Eden, and finds a blinded Charlotte, who has despaired of being reunited with John. Together they kill the remaining girls and rescue John's body for burial.

Evidence of Things Unseen

Light fascinates Ray "Fos" Foster, who strives to comprehend science by reading books and conducting experiments in *Evidence of Things Unseen*. Wiggins embraces Herman Melville's *Moby Dick* (1851), using textual allusions and epigraphs from that novel. She incorporates light and nature imagery as a literary element to develop settings, themes, and characterizations. Landscapes, particularly rivers, and weather become characters that affect plot developments, and Moon cycles and seasonal changes measure time as the novel progresses. Scientific terminology reinforces the credibility of depictions, with characters expressing reverence for science, such as when they praise evolution while listening to the Scopes trial on radio. Efforts to control nature and manipulate science often disappoint characters.

Fos, a World War I veteran, owns a photography studio in Knoxville, Tennessee, with a war comrade named Flash. Fos is quiet and steady, while Flash is flamboyant and unreliable. When Fos travels to North Carolina to observe meteor showers, he meets Opal, the daughter of a glassblower, and marries her. In Knoxville, Opal's bookkeeping skills reveal Flash's secret wealth. The trio boat on the Tennessee River, where Flash is stymied in his pursuit of an elusive fish. Also, Fos brings an X-ray machine he built to county fairs and X rays Opal's toes to attract customers.

Deaths alter the realities of characters. Flash's reckless behavior results in him impregnating Lally, the teenage daughter of a prominent politician. She dies from an abortion arranged by Flash. A mob destroys the photography studio and Flash is arrested and imprisoned. Opal and Fos retreat to the Tennessee farm she inherited from her mother. Furious that Flash's selfish desires ruined their business, Opal and Fos despair at their newfound roles as agriculturists. Unable to conceive, Opal still yearns to have children. After Opal's father dies, she and Fos find an abandoned baby on his property. Delighted, they name their foundling son Lightfoot.

The population's hydroelectricity needs force the Fosters from their home, as the Tennessee Valley Authority builds dams, which flood local acreage. Scientists offer Fos a job at Site X, a secret World War II atomic bomb government facility in nearby Oak Ridge. Opal becomes ill with radiation poisoning, but authorities prove she was not exposed to radiation at Site X. Recalling that he frequently X-rayed Opal's feet, Fos thinks science has betrayed him. Lightfoot discovers his parents dead together. Sent to a Knoxville group foster home, he withstands bullies and resolves to determine truths about Fos and Opal, clinging to photographs for clues. He locates Flash in prison and reads letters Opal wrote, which clarify some of his questions. The men travel west after Flash is released from prison. Wooden whales and paint that glows in the dark connect Lightfoot with the past and offer hope.

The Shadow Catcher

In *The Shadow Catcher*, perceptions shape how characters, both past and present, react to crises, create their identities, and accept or reject facts. Modern and historical sections share themes of desire, deception, and grief. Mark Twain's *Adventures of Huckleberry Finn* (1884) inspired Wiggins to develop characters in this novel who either escape from burdens to pursue adventure or endure abandonment and the responsibilities others leave behind. Wiggins uses words and photographs to craft her storytelling, providing both figurative and literal images.

The opening chapters introduce a narrator identifying herself in first person as novelist Marianne Wiggins who has written a biography of American photographer Edward S. Curtis (1868-1952), who photographed the American West and recorded images of American Indians in the late nineteenth and early twentieth centuries. Meeting with a Hollywood film executive interested in making a movie about Curtis, Marianne becomes agitated when she realizes the film version of her nonfiction book will perpetuate myths about Curtis instead of depict him truthfully.

Marianne returns home and is contacted by a Las Vegas hospital representative, who tells her that her father has been admitted to the hospital. Marianne, confused because her father committed suicide decades earlier, tells the caller she is mistaken, but the woman adds that the man has documents containing Marianne's name. Marianne embarks on a trip to Las Vegas to determine if the hospitalized man could be her father.

Historical sections in the novel, told in the third person, explore Curtis's life from his wife's perspective. After their parents die, Clara Phillips and her younger brother Hercules travel from their cultured Minnesota home to Washington Territory to live with the Curtis family. Clara soon is disenchanted by the rustic atmosphere but obediently performs chores. She romanticizes a narcissistic Edward Curtis and ignores his shortcomings. They marry, and Edward purchases a Seattle photography studio. Clara advises him to embrace truth, not the illusions he creates with the clothing and props he uses to impress patrons. Seeking better opportunities, manipulative Edward expects Clara to manage the studio during his extended absences. She pays his debts and endures solitude. When Clara divorces Edward, their children praise him and criticize her.

In Las Vegas, Marianne meets Lester, a Navajo. He says the man claiming to be her father had a heart attack in Lester's daughter's store while trying to sell a bracelet that Lester recognized his father had handcrafted. Lester tells Marianne that his father was Edward Curtis's assistant and that American Indians referred to Edward as Shadow Catcher. Marianne realizes Edward stole the identities of Indians much like the stranger in the hospital stole her father's identity. Photographs and American Indian artifacts aid Marianne and Lester in determining the hospitalized man's identity and his connection to Edward. In the process, Marianne achieves closure regarding her father's death and why Curtis neglected Clara.

Elizabeth D. Schafer

Other major works

short fiction: *Herself in Love, and Other Stories*, 1987; *Learning Urdu*, 1990; *Bet They'll Miss Us When We're Gone*, 1991.

Bibliography

Cokal, Susann. "Marianne Wiggins and the Eight Daughters of Chaos: Narrating the Body (of) the

Text." *Critique: Studies in Contemporary Fiction* 40, no. 2 (Winter, 1999): 99-118. Scholarly examination of *John Dollar* that interprets the novel's symbolism and addresses Wiggins's stylistic use of margin notes to aid comprehension of textual references. These references, in particular, include the physical aspects of human and animal characters.

Dohrmann, Gail V. "*John Dollar*: Marianne Wiggins's Anti-Utopian Novel." *English Journal* 80, no. 4 (April, 1991): 69-72. Provides a plot synopsis and analysis and examines parallels between John Dollar and the fictional sailor Dionysus.

Eder, Richard. "Let There Be Light." *The New York Times Book Review*, July 27, 2003. Evaluates *Evidence of Things Unseen*, noting major plot developments and Wiggins's ability to depict nuances to present realistic characters and settings. Eder considers the novel an epic.

Gorra, Michael. "Washed Ashore Without Parents." *The New York Times*, February 19, 1989. Review of *John Dollar* explores Wiggins's motivation to write the book. Also discusses the selection of Burma as its setting. Examines the historical authenticity of her portrayals.

Greiner, Donald J. *Women Without Men: Female Bonding and the American Novel of the 1980's*. Columbia: University of South Carolina Press, 1993. Considers the dynamics of gender relations in *John Dollar*, arguing that males displayed both domineering and loving behaviors toward females while interactions among females were often violent.

James, Caryn. "The Ayatollah's Other Victim." *The New York Times*, February 28, 1989. Includes biographical information about Wiggins's childhood and her religious experiences and explains how the fatwa affected her writing. Includes comments released by Wiggins when she was in self-exile.

Reder, Michael, ed. *Conversations with Salman Rushdie*. Jackson: University of Mississippi Press, 2000. In this collection of talks with Wiggins's former husband, Salman Rushdie, the famed novelist reveals details about his life with Wiggins after the fatwa forced them into hiding.

Smiley, Jane. "Vanished Past." *Los Angeles Times*, June 3, 2007. Novelist Jane Smiley reviews *The Shadow Catcher*. Admires Wiggins's literary style, inclusion of herself as a character, and skillful presentation of modern and historical perspectives.

OSCAR WILDE

Born: Dublin, Ireland; October 16, 1854
Died: Paris, France; November 30, 1900
Also known as: Oscar Fingal O'Flahertie Wills Wilde

Principal long fiction

The Picture of Dorian Gray, 1890 (serial), 1891 (expanded)

Other literary forms

Oscar Wilde wrote in a number of literary forms. His earliest works were poems published in various journals and collected in a volume titled *Poems* in 1881. His later and longer poems, including *The Sphinx* (1894), were occasionally overwrought or contrived, but his final published poem, *The Ballad of Reading Gaol* (1898), is regarded by many as a masterpiece. Wilde wrote two collections of fairy tales, *The Happy Prince, and Other Tales* (1888) and *A House of Pomegranates* (1891). He wrote several plays, most notably the comedies *Lady Windermere's Fan* (pr. 1892), *A Woman of No Importance* (pr. 1893), the successful farce *The Importance of Being Earnest: A Trivial Comedy for Serious People* (pr. 1895), and the controversial and temporarily banned *Salomé* (pb. 1893 in French; pb. 1894 in English). Finally, Wilde wrote a few short stories, including "The Canterville Ghost" (1887) and "Lord Arthur Savile's Crime" (1887).

Achievements

Oscar Wilde's works remain popular more than a century after his death. This is due in part to the enduring beauty of Wilde's poetry and prose as well as to the timeless insights the works offer about art and morality. Wilde's conclusions are presented with such easy elegance and wit that readers enjoy the seduction of the narrative. No doubt Wilde's provocative statements and iconoclastic poses, as well as the notoriety of his trial, helped to immortalize him and thus to sustain interest in his writings for generations. Wilde received Trinity College's Berkeley Gold Medal for Greek in 1874, and he won the Newdigate Prize for Poetry in 1878.

Biography

Oscar Fingal O'Flahertie Wills Wilde was born to ambitious, successful Irish parents in Dublin in 1854. As a young man he attended Trinity College, and in 1874 (at age twenty) he entered Magdalen College, Oxford, on a scholarship. Wilde was drawn to art criticism and literature in his studies, and he was strongly influenced by several mentors, most notably writers John Ruskin and Walter Pater. At college Wilde discovered, developed, and began to refine his extraordinary gifts of creativity, analysis, and expression. These he pressed into the service of aestheticism, an iconoclastic artistic movement, promoted by Pater, that advocated art for art's sake. Wilde would come to personify aestheticism, with all its intellectual refinement, provocative posing, and hedonistic excess.

Wilde married Constance Lloyd in 1884 and with her had two sons. Although throughout his short life Wilde evinced great love and devotion to his wife and sons, he grew increasingly involved in sexual liaisons with men. Most notably and tragically, Wilde became engrossed in an obsessive and rocky gay friendship with Lord Alfred Douglas, the son of the marquis of Queensberry. Douglas helped to lead Wilde deeper into London's gay underworld. While Douglas at times seemed to love Wilde genuinely, he periodically became impatient, selfish, and abusive toward his older friend. Still, Wilde remained, with increasing recklessness, committed to Douglas.

During the second half of the 1880's Wilde wrote poems, plays, and stories with increasing success. To a large extent, however, it was the provocative and radical remarks he made at public lectures and at the social functions he so frequently attended that gained for him sustained public attention. Wilde was a gifted speaker with a keen sense of timing and an ability to lampoon societal standards with his humorous remarks.

The Victorian public's amusement with Wilde's contrarianism turned to contempt in 1895. In that year the marquis of Queensberry, furious over the writer's continuing relationship with his son, accused Wilde of being a "sodomite." Wilde ill-advisedly sued for libel, maintaining that he was not, in fact, gay. The marquis, to support his claim about Wilde's homosexuality, entered into court various letters and other pieces of evidence. When Queensberry's lawyer was about to produce as witnesses young male prostitutes who had had sexual relations with Wilde, Wilde's lawyer withdrew from the suit. Queensberry was acquitted by the jury, and almost immediately after the trial, Wilde was arrested for violation of England's sodomy laws. By now the public had all but deserted Wilde, and after his conviction even most of his friends disavowed him. Wilde spent two years in prison for his offenses.

Upon his release from prison in 1897, Wilde left England to live in exile, finally locating in Paris. He lived under the alias Sebastian Melmoth, attempting to expunge his notoriety as the humiliated Oscar Wilde. His spirits and his health had been broken by his prison sentence, however, and Wilde died within three years, at age forty-six.

Analysis

Oscar Wilde began his literary efforts with poetry, which was a common approach in his day. He published *Ravenna* in 1878. He would write little poetry after the release of *Poems* in 1881. For the next several years he gave lectures in Europe and the United States, establishing his name on both sides of the Atlantic. He also assumed the editorship of a monthly magazine, *The Lady's World*, which was rechristened *The Woman's World*.

In the late 1880's Wilde wrote two collections of fairy tales as well as a number of short stories, essays, and book reviews. He steadily gained attention as a writer, social critic, and, most of all, aesthete. Literary critics frequently were unenthusiastic, or even hostile,

Oscar Wilde. (Library of Congress)

toward his works, finding them to be overly contrived or recklessly immoral. It is true that Wilde's writing can at times assume a baroque ornamentation and artificiality. There is no doubt that Wilde's characteristic indolence (which he exaggerated for show) constrained his ability to see his works through to the final stages of editing and polishing. It is true also that Wilde's writing frequently ridiculed social conventions, mores, and morals. Wilde was, however, indisputably an ingenious analyst of art and culture, possessing a mastery of prose and verse and equipped with a keen sense of paradox.

THE PICTURE OF DORIAN GRAY

Oscar Wilde's only novel was published in its complete form in 1891. It is not a long book, and some of its features reflect the writer's haste or carelessness. However, the story is a fascinating and engaging one, at once depicting basic elements of human nature and conjuring fantastic, almost gothic images. Its plot is rather simple, but the ideas and issues that the narrative presents are complex and even profound. Perhaps for this reason the book has stood the test of time.

The story centers on three figures: an artist (Basil Hallward), his clever but impudent friend (Lord Henry Wotton), and a young, attractive, and impressionable man (Dorian Gray). Basil paints a full-length portrait of young Dorian and presents it to him as a gift. Lord Henry, who meets Dorian for the first time at Basil's studio, talks at length about the supreme value, but transience, of youth. Immediately drawn to Lord Henry's theories, Dorian observes the just-completed portrait of himself and remarks on "how sad it is" that he "shall grow old, and horrible, and dreadful. But this picture will remain always young. . . . If it were only the other way!" In the first section of the book, therefore, Wilde sets up a framework to examine some fundamental ideas about art and beauty: the transience of beauty, the inevitability of aging and death, the goal of the artist to "capture" beauty in art, and the corruptive influence of ideas, among others.

Wilde uses Lord Henry—whom Wilde later declared to be a depiction of how the public perceived Wilde—to provide the corruptive theories and ideas. Throughout the book Lord Henry utters clever aphorisms and paradoxes in Wilde's celebrated wordplay. Dorian is infatuated by Lord Henry and appears receptive to his theories and values. Readers soon see evidence of the corruptive influence of those theories and values in Dorian's behavior. Dorian becomes smitten by a young actress in a seedy theater. He returns with Basil and Lord Henry to watch her perform, but this time he is disappointed by her acting. After the performance the actress declares to Dorian that he has helped her see how false is her world of acting—the false world of the stage—and she declares her love for him. Dorian, however, spitefully dismisses her, claiming that she had thrown away her artistic genius and poetic intellect. Now, she "simply produce(s) no effect."

Upon returning home, Dorian observes a slight change in the portrait Basil had painted of him. Dorian notes a "touch of cruelty in the mouth." It becomes evident that the painting shows the outward signs of sin and of aging, while Dorian himself does not change appearance. Although first horrified by this, Dorian eventually learns to take advantage of the situation. The narrative traces an ever-worsening degradation of Dorian Gray's soul. He lives for sensations and self-gratification, without regard for the consequences of his actions for others. He is seemingly unbound by any sense of morality—indeed, the very notion of violating moral strictures seems to be an attractive prospect for him. Near the climax of the story Dorian goes so far as to murder Basil.

The story thus raises provocative questions about morality and self-imposed restraint. If a person could be assured that any indulgences, including gluttony, sexual abandon, and avarice, would have no effects on his or her earthly body, would self-control survive? What opportunities and temptations are imposed on a person who possesses unusual and eternal beauty? What is the relationship between virtue and constraint? What are the consequences of unexposed moral degradation? Indeed, what are the causes of immorality?

The Picture of Dorian Gray aroused enormous indignation in Wilde's contemporaries, and it was treated especially harshly by most critics. There seemed to be a consensus that the book itself was immoral, that it could corrupt readers, and that it somehow promoted decadent behavior. One can easily arrive at the opposite conclusion, however. The story clearly emphasizes the costs of self-indulgent, immoral behavior. It literally shows this in the changes that appear in the painting, which is understood to portray the condition of Dorian's soul. The story also makes a point of noting the harm done to others by Dorian's misbehavior: reputations ruined, hearts broken, suicides induced, murders committed. In no way does the book portray the corruption of Dorian Gray in a glamorous or seductive way. Instead, the effect is to repulse the reader.

The book might be somewhat corruptive in its suggestion that immorality may be less a choice than simply a product of circumstances. We have no reason to believe that Dorian Gray is intrinsically evil; rather, if the book's basic premise is that one's soul is normally reflected in one's appearance, then the introduction of Dorian as possessing "youth's passionate purity" conveys the idea that he is especially innocent. Ironically, Wilde himself was accused of corrupting a young man (Lord Alfred Douglas), and his writings (including *The Picture of Dorian Gray*) were held up as evidence of his dangerous ideas. That Wilde responded that he believed there was no such thing as an immoral book, only a badly written one, compounds the irony.

The fatalistic view of sin (which might be consistent with Wilde's religious upbringing, such as it was) is further evidenced when Dorian is unable to change his course toward the end of the book. He feels his past starting to catch up with him as people he has wronged, or their defenders, begin to identify him and his actions. Resolving to abandon his ways, Dorian decides to do a good deed; he cancels an arranged plan to go off with (and undoubtedly take advantage of) a young female acquaintance. When he subsequently examines the portrait for evidence of his good deed, however, he detects only a smirk of hypocrisy.

In a conclusion laden with symbolism, Dorian considers his situation hopeless. He reflects that "there [is] a God who called upon men to tell their sins to earth as well as to heaven." He cannot fathom how he could ever confess his sins, however, and he recognizes that even his attempt to do good sprung from a hypocritical desire to experience new sensations. In desperation, he decides to drive a knife into the loathsome painting, which reflects all his sins. The servants downstairs hear a scream, and when they enter the room they see the portrait, restored to its original beauty, hanging on the wall. Dorian Gray lies on the floor with a knife in his heart, looking just as the figure in the loathsome portrait had moments earlier.

The conclusion creates a striking and stark symmetry, although how it answers the questions raised earlier is unclear. Still, the ending is satisfying in that it allows reality finally to come out of hiding. The parallels to Wilde's life are exceptional. While Wilde noted that the character of the languid iconoclast Lord Henry reflected how people viewed Wilde, he also asserted that it was the artist, Basil, whom Wilde actually resembled, and that it was Dorian himself whom Wilde wanted to be.

Steve D. Boilard

Other major works

SHORT FICTION: "The Canterville Ghost," 1887; *The Happy Prince, and Other Tales*, 1888; *A House of Pome-*

granates, 1891; *Lord Arthur Savile's Crime, and Other Stories*, 1891.

PLAYS: *Vera: Or, The Nihilists*, pb. 1880; *The Duchess of Padua*, pb. 1883; *Lady Windermere's Fan*, pr. 1892; *Salomé*, pb. 1893 (in French; pb. 1894 in English); *A Woman of No Importance*, pr. 1893; *An Ideal Husband*, pr. 1895; *The Importance of Being Earnest: A Trivial Comedy for Serious People*, pr. 1895; *A Florentine Tragedy*, pr. 1906 (one act; completed by T. Sturge More); *La Sainte Courtisane*, pb. 1908.

POETRY: *Ravenna*, 1878; *Poems*, 1881; *Poems in Prose*, 1894; *The Sphinx*, 1894; *The Ballad of Reading Gaol*, 1898.

NONFICTION: *Intentions*, 1891; *De Profundis*, 1905; *The Letters of Oscar Wilde*, 1962 (Rupert Hart-Davis, editor); *The Complete Letters of Oscar Wilde*, 2000 (Merlin Holland and Hart-Davis, editors).

MISCELLANEOUS: *Works*, 1908; *Complete Works of Oscar Wilde*, 1948 (Vyvyan Holland, editor); *Plays, Prose Writings, and Poems*, 1960.

Bibliography

Beckson, Karl E. *The Oscar Wilde Encyclopedia*. New York: AMS Press, 1998. Comprehensive compendium of useful information on Wilde and his times. One of the entries is a lengthy and thorough analysis of *The Picture of Dorian Gray*.

Ellmann, Richard. *Oscar Wilde*. New York: Alfred A. Knopf, 1988. Standard biography draws much insight from Wilde's published works and makes use of many of Wilde's writings and recorded conversations. Extensively documented; includes bibliography and informative appendixes.

Eriksen, Donald H. *Oscar Wilde*. Boston: Twayne, 1977. Brief work provides a corrective to studies of Wilde that see him and his work as anomalies of literature and history. After a brief chapter on Wilde's life and times, Eriksen assesses his poetry, fiction, essays, and drama. Chronology, notes and references, annotated bibliography, and index supplement the text.

Gillespie, Michael Patrick. *"The Picture of Dorian Gray": "What the World Thinks Me."* New York: Twayne, 1995. Maintains that the novel is a fictional model of the moral contradictions in late Victorian society. Includes information about the historical and literary contexts in which the novel was published and the book's critical reception.

Holland, Merlin. *The Wilde Album*. New York: Henry Holt, 1998. Holland, Wilde's grandson, supplements a biographical narrative with various artifacts—including photographs, press clippings, and political cartoons—that document Wilde's emergence as a media celebrity and show how Wilde consciously created his own fame. Includes rare family photographs and all twenty-eight of the publicity portraits made for Wilde's 1882 U.S. tour. This book is a useful complement to the weightier biography by Ellmann (cited above).

Kileen, Jarlath. *The Faiths of Oscar Wilde: Catholicism, Folklore, and Ireland*. New York: Palgrave Macmillan, 2005. Examination of Wilde's work focuses on his lifelong attraction to Catholicism and explores the influence of his Protestant background on his work. Devotes a chapter, "Body and Soul: Nature, the Host, and Folklore in *The Picture of Dorian Gray*," to an analysis of the novel.

Kohl, Norbert. *Oscar Wilde: The Works of a Conformist Rebel*. Translated by David Henry Wilson. New York: Cambridge University Press, 1989. Interprets Wilde's works mainly through textual analysis, although the study includes discussions of the society in which Wilde lived and to which he responded. Argues that Wilde was not the imitator he is often accused of being but a creative adapter of the literary traditions he inherited. Supplemented by detailed notes, a lengthy bibliography, and an index.

McCormack, Jerusha Hull. *The Man Who Was Dorian Gray*. New York: St. Martin's Press, 2000. John Gray, the supposed model for Wilde's most famous character, is profiled in this examination of the life of a decadent poet turned priest. This work reveals much about early twentieth century literary society and the emerging gay culture.

McKenna, Neil. *The Secret Life of Oscar Wilde*. London: Century, 2003. Controversial and groundbreaking biography focuses on how Wilde's sexuality, and homosexuality in the Victorian era, influenced the writer's life and work. Includes illustrations, bibliography, and index.

Pearce, Joseph. *The Unmasking of Oscar Wilde*. London: HarperCollins, 2000. Avoids lingering on the actions that brought Wilde notoriety and instead explores Wilde's emotional and spiritual search. Discusses *The Picture of Dorian Gray* and other works and traces Wilde's fascination with Catholicism.

Varty, Anne. *A Preface to Oscar Wilde*. New York: Longman, 1998. Provides an introduction to Wilde's life and works, particularly the period from 1890 to 1895. Some discussion of the author's earlier work gives some insight into the motivating forces behind Wilde's output. Includes index.

THORNTON WILDER

Born: Madison, Wisconsin; April 17, 1897
Died: Hamden, Connecticut; December 7, 1975
Also known as: Thornton Niven Wilder

Principal long fiction

The Cabala, 1926
The Bridge of San Luis Rey, 1927
The Woman of Andros, 1930
Heaven's My Destination, 1934
The Ides of March, 1948
The Eighth Day, 1967
Theophilus North, 1973

Other literary forms

Thornton Wilder is as well known for his plays as for his fiction. *Our Town* (pr., pb. 1938), *The Merchant of Yonkers* (pr. 1938; revised as *The Matchmaker*, 1954), and *The Skin of Our Teeth* (pr., pb. 1942) are some of his best-known plays. Collections of his short plays were published in *The Angel That Troubled the Waters, and Other Plays* (1928) and *The Long Christmas Dinner, and Other Plays in One Act* (1931). *A Life in the Sun*, commonly known as *The Alcestiad*, was published in 1955, and a collection of his essays, *American Characteristics, and Other Essays*, was published in 1979. A set of cullings from his diaries, *The Journals of Thornton Wilder, 1939-1961*, was released in 1985.

Achievements

Thornton Wilder began his career as a teacher and in a sense never gave up the practice of that profession. He attempted to persuade generations of readers of the power of love, the need for individual integrity, and the importance of maintaining faith in people's essential goodness. His clear style and straightforward narrative earned for him a broad readership, transcending categories of age, class, or education. Though detractors have labeled him middle class and middlebrow, he received enthusiastic praise throughout his career from such critics as Edmund Wilson, Malcolm Cowley, Edmund Fuller, Henry Seidel Canby, and John Updike. Wilder has been less a subject of scholarly research than some of his contemporaries—F. Scott Fitzgerald and Ernest Hemingway, for example—yet he has remained widely read since his first novel was published in 1926, and his versatility as a writer—of two Pulitzer Prize-winning full-length plays and dozens of short plays—has brought him worldwide recognition.

Wilder won a Pulitzer Prize for fiction in 1928, the first National Medal for Literature in 1964, and a National Book Award in 1967. He also received several honorary doctorates.

Biography

Thornton Niven Wilder was born in Madison, Wisconsin, on April 17, 1897, the son of Amos Parker Wilder and Isabella Thornton Niven Wilder. His father, a newspaper editor, moved the family to Hong Kong in 1906 when he was assigned a diplomatic post there. The young Wilder attended the Kaiser Wilhelm School, then the China Inland Mission Boys' School, where he harbored a brief desire to become a missionary himself. When his family returned to the United States, settling in California, he continued his education at the Thacher

School in Ojai, then Berkeley High School, where he first began to write plays and act in class productions.

In 1915, Wilder entered Oberlin College, a school his father chose because it was less socially elite than his own alma mater, Yale. At Oberlin, Wilder continued his involvement in theatrical productions and contributed prolifically to the college's literary magazine. After two years there, Wilder was allowed by his father to enroll at Yale, where, after a period of homesickness for Oberlin, he again proved himself, in the words of professor and literary critic William Lyon Phelps, to be "a star of the first magnitude . . . unusually versatile, original, and clever." Wilder graduated with no specific career goals in mind. His father, believing a European experience would be broadening, sent him to study at the American Academy in Rome for a summer. Meanwhile, he searched for a suitable job for his son and found one at Lawrenceville, a preparatory school in New Jersey.

Wilder soon began a novel with the working title *Memoirs of a Roman Student*, which was published as *The Cabala* in 1926. In the same year, he took advantage of Lawrenceville's proximity to Princeton University to earn his master of arts degree. He took a year's leave of absence from teaching and began work on a new novel, *The Bridge of San Luis Rey*, published to enormous acclaim in 1927 and earning Wilder his first Pulitzer Prize.

In 1929, Wilder was invited to teach at the University of Chicago by an Oberlin classmate, Robert Hutchins, who had just been named president of the prestigious Illinois university. Wilder was writing intensely: *The Woman of Andros* was published in 1930, a collection of short plays in 1931, and *Heaven's My Destination* in 1934. He remained at Chicago until the mid-1930's, teaching one semester and writing during the next. More and more, he was drawn to the theater. He completed *The Merchant of Yonkers*, later revised as *The Matchmaker* (and still later transformed into the Broadway musical *Hello, Dolly!*) in 1937 and then turned to a more serious play, *Our Village*, soon retitled *Our Town*. This play was met with great enthusiasm when it opened in New York in 1938 and earned Wilder his second Pulitzer Prize.

The political upheaval in Europe, soon to involve the United States, found its way into Wilder's next play, *The Skin of Our Teeth*, which evoked a deep response in audiences both in the United States and abroad; the play was awarded a Pulitzer Prize in 1942. Wilder served in the U.S. Army during World War II, and emerged with his optimism intact and his faith in humanity unshaken. In the late 1940's, Wilder again turned to fiction, dealing with the problem of authority and dictatorship in *The Ides of March*. This novel reflects his talks with the poet-writer Gertrude Stein, whom Wilder had met in 1934 when Stein was lecturing at the University of Chicago. They shared ideas on the problem of identity and the creation of a believable reality for readers. Stein attempted to deal with these problems in her own book, *Ida, a Novel* (1941); Wilder took as his subject Julius Caesar.

In 1950, Wilder delivered the Charles Eliot Norton lectures at Harvard, then traveled—always a stimulation and joy for him—and worked on *The Alcestiad*, his retelling of the Greek legend of Alcestis. In the early 1960's, he retreated to Arizona to write *The Eighth Day*. By the end of the decade, his pace had slowed. He worked on short plays and completed his quasi-autobio-

Thornton Wilder. (Library of Congress)

graphical *Theophilus North*. He died in his sleep on December 7, 1975.

ANALYSIS

Thornton Wilder's seven novels, written over nearly fifty years, show a remarkable consistency in theme and tone. His early books, contemporaneous with Theodore Dreiser's *An American Tragedy* (1925) and Sinclair Lewis's *Arrowsmith* (1925), are far from the realism and naturalism that dominated American literature in the 1920's and 1930's. Though he joined groups active in civil rights and social justice, these themes did not find their way into his works in the manner of John Dos Passos or John Steinbeck. His later works, similarly, show none of the interest in psychoanalysis that may be found in the works of Sherwood Anderson, for example, and none of the angry intensity of a Norman Mailer.

Wilder chose not to comment on contemporary politics, social problems, psychological angst, or cultural changes, preferring instead to mine those themes he considered of utmost importance: love, brotherhood, tolerance, and faith. His faith was expressed not in strictly Judeo-Christian terms but in humanistic convictions that incorporated diverse religious beliefs. Without being didactic, Wilder wished to educate, to inspire, to allow his readers to move beyond an obsession with the individual case to a consideration of humankind and its history. His second novel, *The Bridge of San Luis Rey*, is representative of the themes that recur throughout his works, and his final statement in that book well expresses his one abiding conviction: "There is a land of the living and a land of the dead and the bridge is love, the only survival, the only meaning."

THE CABALA

Though Wilder drew on his memories of Rome for his first novel, *The Cabala*, the book is a fantasy, only incidentally autobiographical. The Cabala is an aristocratic social circle in which two Americans find themselves involved. These two, Samuele and James Blair, represent Wilder's interest in duality of personality that recurs in later works and results in part from his having been born a twin (his sibling was stillborn). Samuele is a typical Wilder character: innocent, sensitive, stable, with a deep strain of common sense. Blair is the dry intellectual so obsessed by books that he fears real life.

Samuele is the vehicle by which a number of episodes are linked, since he is asked by various members of the Cabala to intervene in the lives of others. First, he is called in to restrain the impetuous and licentious Marcantonio, but fails: The young man engages in incest and then kills himself. Then, Samuele must console the lovely young Alix, unfortunate enough to fall in love with James Blair. Finally, he must deal with the royalist Astrée-Luce in her plot to "prop up" and empower cynical Cardinal Vaini. Samuele is baffled by these obsessed and decadent characters, and is hardly satisfied by an explanation offered to him that the group is possessed by ancient gods who have passed on their power to unsuspecting mortals. Finally, on advice from Vergil's ghost, Samuele returns to America. For Wilder, Europe, for all its richness of culture, was too deeply mired in the past to allow the spirit to grow. Samuele could thrive only in America, a country of youth and intellectual freedom.

THE BRIDGE OF SAN LUIS REY

In his second novel, *The Bridge of San Luis Rey*, Wilder again uses a structure of separate episodes linked by one thread, this time the collapse of an ancient bridge over a chasm in Peru. Again, he offers a religious figure, but instead of the jaded Cardinal, there is the sympathetic Brother Juniper, who searches for meaning in the deaths of those who perished: the Marquesa de Montemayor; Pepita, her maid; Esteban, a young Indian; Uncle Pio, an aging actor, and his ward Jaime. Brother Juniper finds that the five were victims of love, and those who survive are forced to a change of consciousness by the deaths of those they spurned or misjudged.

As in *The Cabala*, Wilder explores twinness in the tale of Esteban and his twin brother Manuel. The two are extraordinarily close, and when Manuel falls in love with a woman, Esteban becomes despondent. Yet he nurses his brother faithfully after Manuel is injured, suffering his delirious ravings until Manuel dies. Nearly mad with grief, Esteban first assumes his dead brother's identity, then attempts suicide, only to die when the bridge collapses. A sea captain, Alvarado, had offered to sign him on his crew, and tried to console him by reminding him, "We do what we can. We push on, Esteban, as best we can. It isn't for long, you know. Time keeps going by. You'll be surprised at the way time passes." Wilder was always conscious of the brevity of life and the need, therefore, to cling to love where one finds it. In *The Bridge of San Luis Rey*, he urges the celebration and fulfillment of love as the only meaning in the world.

The Woman of Andros

From eighteenth century Peru, Wilder moved to pre-Christian Greece in his third novel, *The Woman of Andros*, again dealing with love; its theme, as in *The Bridge of San Luis Rey*, is "How does one live? . . . What does one do first?" Society on the island of Brynos was not essentially different, according to Wilder, from that of his own America. When Chrysis, the central character, says "Lift every roof, and you will find seven puzzled hearts," she speaks of people's bewilderment in the face of the unknown, their search for communion, their need for love—basic human struggles that are not rooted in any particular time or place.

In 1930, however, a number of critics were disappointed with this message. In a time of economic and social crisis, Wilder seemed to retreat into yet another esoteric setting, far removed from the urgencies of the day. One critic writing in *The New Republic* dubbed Wilder a "Prophet of the Genteel Christ" who wrote for a wealthy elite not interested in social problems. The article touched off a month of debate, with letters supporting or attacking Wilder appearing in each issue of the magazine. At the end of December, Wilder finally received his greatest support when Sinclair Lewis, accepting the Nobel Prize in Literature, praised his fellow writer "who in an age of realism dreams the old and lovely dreams of the eternal romantic."

Heaven's My Destination

Throughout the controversy, Wilder remained silent. He was sensitive to the criticism, however, and in his next novel he attempted to find a setting and characters that would appear relevant to his own time. *Heaven's My Destination* concerns the misadventures of George Marvin Brush, a salesman of religious textbooks who travels across the Depression-ridden United States preaching, moralizing, and interfering in the lives of ordinary citizens. Converted to Bible Belt Christianity by a woman evangelist at Shiloh Baptist College, he has proceeded to spread his own fundamentalist version of the Gospel wherever he goes. Wilder returned to the episodic structure of his first two novels in presenting George's adventures in picaresque form. Unlike Don Quixote, however, with whom George has been compared, Wilder's protagonist is rarely endearing, more often exasperating.

George is different from the "normal" Americans with whom he interacts, yet Wilder is satirizing not only his earnest hero but also those who spurn him. George, after a while, becomes depressed by his society and exclaims, "It's the world that's crazy. Everybody's crazy except me; that's what's the matter. The whole world's nuts." Why, asks this ardent believer, is God "so slow" in changing things?

For all his misconceptions, George does act on truly humanistic beliefs. He takes a vow of poverty and occasionally of silence, refuses his interest from the bank and dislikes raises in pay. "I think everybody ought to be hit by the depression equally," he says, as he gives away his money. Like Samuele, George maintains his integrity in an environment that threatens to corrupt him and is selfless in his efforts to aid those who need him—even if they protest against his interference.

George was Wilder's answer to the critics who dismissed his previous works, and in a sense, he gave them what he thought they deserved—a priggish, monomaniacal American overreacting to mundane occurrences. Even with such a cartoon-strip character, however, Wilder could not help but imbue him with gentleness and humility, and for Edmund Wilson, George emerged as a "type of saint . . . and therefore a universal character."

In part, it was George's earnestness, his reluctance to see evil and his determination to do good, that caused Wilder to exclaim, "I'm George Brush." Certainly his persistent faith in humanity unites him with his character, but there is further correspondence in Brush's essential isolation, the loneliness that causes him to reach out for companionship. For Wilder, such isolation was characteristically American; solitude was to be treasured, but loneliness was threatening. He once noted an adage that he thought well expressed the American spirit: "If you can see the smoke from your neighbor's chimney, you're too near." In his next novel, thirteen years later, he created yet another lonely, questing character, but this time Wilder eschewed satire and humor to deal seriously with people powerful before the world, yet powerless before death.

The Ides of March

The Ides of March, written just after World War II, deals with an archetypal dictator, Julius Caesar. Here, Wilder aimed to revive the spirit of the man from a palimpsest of historical and fictional treatments. The novel, therefore, becomes a study in identity and a technical challenge in creating for readers a believable reality. In structure, *The Ides of March* differs sharply from Wilder's previous work. He assembles fictionalized letters, diary entries, messages, and documents in an effort to offer a vibrant picture of Roman life. Caesar himself is obsessed not only with power but also with death, and he must learn how to celebrate life faced with a dark world and an uncaring universe.

Wilder contrasts Caesar with his friend and counselor Lucius Turrinus, who offers a philosophy that was by then familiar to Wilder's readers: "The universe is not aware that we are here," Lucius tells Caesar. "Hope has never changed tomorrow's weather." Yet love could change the world, and Caesar comes to exclaim, "I wish to cry out to all the living and all the dead that there is no part of the universe that is untouched by bliss."

Caesar's urge to seize life and live it to the fullest causes his companions to label him rash and irreverent; but he feels himself to be above them because he has clearly envisioned his own death, and in so doing believes himself "capable of praising the sunlight." Wilder transfers to the Roman dictator much of the sentiment expressed in his play *Our Town*, where Emily Webb dies and is allowed to return to Earth for one day. Only then does she realize how wonderful life is, how desperately she wants to live, and how foolish most people are in squandering their brief existence. Caesar refuses to be foolish; perhaps he will be ruthless, impetuous, temperamental, passionate—but he will live each moment.

The Ides of March had two major inspirations: the war itself, with its focus on the use and misuse of power, the character of a dictator, and the death of innocents; and Wilder's personal confrontation with death—first that of Wilder's friend and mentor Edward Sheldon, a playwright whose character informs Lucius Turrinus and on whose wisdom Wilder often relied, and then, and most important, the death of his mother, his most ardent supporter and admirer.

The Eighth Day

After *The Ides of March* was published, Wilder devoted nearly two decades to his plays; not until 1967 would he write another novel. In *The Eighth Day*, Wilder returned to an American setting, the turn-of-the-century Midwest, and to traditional narrative. He carefully unfolds the tale of John Barrington Ashley, tried for the murder of his neighbor, Breckenridge Lansing, and found guilty. Five days after being sentenced to death, he escapes with the help of an unknown accomplice. Five years later, Ashley is found innocent on the basis of new evidence. Ashley's flight, which takes him to Chile, is contrasted with the life of his wife and children in a small town that barely tolerates the outlaw's family.

Wilder's concern, however, is not with one family's history, but with the archetypal family, and Ashley represents not one wronged citizen, but the man of the Eighth Day, a new person with faith in humanity and a strong commitment to working toward a better future. Wilder tells his readers that faith and action can bring about a better life. Throughout the novel, he assigns several characters to speak for him, most notably Dr. Gillies, a country physician, who observes,

> Nature never sleeps. The process of life never stands still. The creation has not come to an end. The Bible says that God created people on the sixth day and rested, but each of those days was many millions of years long. That day of rest must have been a short one. Man is not an end but a beginning. We are at the beginning of the second week. We are children of the eighth day.

On the eighth day, people must begin to forge their own futures, and although Dr. Gillies knows there will be "no Golden Ages and no Dark Ages," still he believes in the power of each individual to work toward the collective fate of humankind.

Because the novel is concerned essentially with imparting a message, the characters—as in *The Cabala* and *Heaven's My Destination*—are not fully realized individuals, but instead are one-dimensional representations of predictable types. The Ashley family, ignored and rebuffed by their neighbors, never lose their aristocratic elegance. They persist in their nightly reading of William Shakespeare even when economic problems would seem severe enough to lower their morale. Here, Wilder pleads for art as the true salvation of humankind, its highest achievement, "the only satisfactory products of civilization."

Through Dr. Gillies, who echoes the sentiments of Chrysis in *The Woman of Andros* and Lucius in *The Ides of March*, Wilder reminds his readers that they occupy only a brief span of time when contrasted with eternity and so must exhibit proper humility. They are small specks in a vast universe, and their duty is not to enhance their own egos, but to work together toward a higher good. "We keep saying that 'we live our lives,'" Dr. Gillies exclaims. "Shucks! Life lives us." Wilder had sent this message for forty years; he insisted again, in the turbulent, self-conscious, self-indulgent late 1960's, on attempting to awaken his readers to his own values.

Theophilus North

Wilder was seventy years old when *The Eighth Day* was published, the time of a writer's life when he or she might consider writing his or her autobiography or memoirs. Wilder, however, chose not to reveal his memories or bare his soul; instead, he wrote a last novel, *Theophilus North*, with a protagonist, he once told an interviewer, who was what his twin brother might have been if he had lived.

Theophilus may be Wilder's imaginary brother, but his life bears striking similarities to that of Wilder himself. He has lived in China, attended Yale, and spent a summer in Rome; after teaching at a boys' preparatory school in New Jersey, he leaves his job to explore life and goes to Newport, Rhode Island—a town where Wilder often vacationed—to set his new course. Like Samuele, Theophilus is gentle, well mannered, polite, helpful. These traits endear him to the Newport natives, and he is asked to intervene in several lives. The structure here, as in many previous Wilder novels, is one of loosely linked episodes.

Theophilus succeeds in such tasks as separating mismatched lovers, liberating an aging man from the manipulation of his daughter, allowing a shrewish wife to mend her ways, extricating one man from his unwitting involvement with criminals, bringing home a wayward husband, finding a lover for a maimed young man, and impregnating a woman whose husband is sterile. Throughout, Theophilus is a typical Wilder hero—a man of goodwill, of faith, of sincerity.

Theophilus North is Wilder's only novel in which sexuality is of central importance. The sexual episodes are conducted offstage and seem unbelievable and strained. Theophilus, in his seductions and in his everyday relationships with his neighbors, is curiously unaffected and uninvolved. Although he displays emotion, he seems to lack passion.

Wilder's characters, from Samuele to John Ashley, from the circle of Roman aristocrats to Newport society, remain thin and superficial, emblems rather than specific, rounded human beings. Such characterization was in keeping with Wilder's conviction that each individual was, in the long history of the human race, of but little importance. His trials, anguish, suffering, and joy were not significant when placed in the context of all human suffering and all human joy. Rather than writing about individual human beings, Wilder chose to write about humanity; rather than dealing with the intricacies of individual lives, he chose to compress those lives into brief episodes to demonstrate the multiplicity of life.

Wilder, deeply philosophical and reflective, was always the teacher, the educator, with an abiding concern for the future of humanity. "Hope," he wrote in *Theophilus North*, "is a projection of the imagination; so is despair. Despair all too readily embraces the ills it foresees; hope is an energy and arouses the mind to explore every possibility to combat them." In all his works, he exuded hope and, even in dark times, urged his readers to work together in faith and in love.

Linda Simon

Other major works

PLAYS: *The Trumpet Shall Sound*, pb. 1920; *The Angel That Troubled the Waters, and Other Plays*, 1928 (includes 16 plays); *The Happy Journey to Trenton and Camden*, pr., pb. 1931 (one act); *The Long Christmas Dinner*, pr., pb. 1931 (one act; as libretto in German, 1961; translation and music by Paul Hindemith); *The Long Christmas Dinner, and Other Plays in One Act*, 1931 (includes *Queens of France*, *Pullman Car Hiawatha*, *Love and How to Cure It*, *Such Things Only Happen in Books*, and *The Happy Journey to Trenton and Camden*); *Lucrece*, pr. 1932 (adaptation of André

Obey's *Le Viol de Lucrèce*); *A Doll's House*, pr. 1937 (adaptation of Henrik Ibsen's play); *The Merchant of Yonkers*, pr. 1938 (adaptation of Johann Nestroy's *Einen Jux will er sich machen*); *Our Town*, pr., pb. 1938; *The Skin of Our Teeth*, pr., pb. 1942; *Our Century*, pr., pb. 1947; *The Matchmaker*, pr. 1954 (revision of *The Merchant of Yonkers*); *A Life in the Sun*, pr. 1955 (in German; pb. 1977 in English; commonly known as *The Alcestiad*; act 4 pb. as *The Drunken Sisters*); *Plays for Bleecker Street*, pr. 1962 (3 one-acts: *Someone from Assisi*; *Infancy*, pb. 1961; and *Childhood*, pb. 1960); *The Collected Short Plays of Thornton Wilder*, pb. 1997-1998 (2 volumes).

screenplays: *Our Town*, 1940 (with Frank Craven and Harry Chantlee); *Shadow of a Doubt*, 1943 (with Sally Benson and Alma Revelle).

nonfiction: *The Intent of the Artist*, 1941; *American Characteristics, and Other Essays*, 1979; *The Journals of Thornton Wilder, 1939-1961*, 1985.

translation: *The Victors*, 1948 (of Jean-Paul Sartre's play).

miscellaneous: *Thornton Wilder: Collected Plays and Writings on Theater*, 2007 (J. D. McClatchy, editor).

Bibliography

Blank, Martin, ed. *Critical Essays on Thornton Wilder*. New York: G. K. Hall, 1996. A solid collection of criticism on Wilder. Includes bibliographical references and an index.

Blank, Martin, Dalma Hunyadi Brunauer, and David Garrett Izzo, eds. *Thornton Wilder: New Essays*. West Cornwall, Conn.: Locust Hill Press, 1999. Collection of essays, many by prominent Wilder scholars, which discuss both the novels and plays. Some of the essays examine point of view and narrative technique in the novels, while others analyze *The Ides of March*, *The Eighth Day*, and *Heaven's My Destination*.

Bryer, Jackson R., ed. *Conversations with Thornton Wilder*. Jackson: University Press of Mississippi, 1992. A collection of interviews with Wilder, providing interesting perspectives on his life and his literary works. Includes an index.

Burbank, Rex J. *Thornton Wilder*. 2d ed. Boston: Twayne, 1978. Burbank traces the history of critical controversy surrounding Wilder's work, offers insights into his methods of fictional and dramatic composition, and assesses his work's relative merits. Includes a chronology and bibliography.

Castronovo, David. *Thornton Wilder*. New York: Ungar, 1986. A useful introductory study, providing a biography, discussion of Wilder's major novels and plays, and an analysis of the structure of his works. Includes a chronology, notes, and a bibliography.

Goldstein, Malcolm. *The Art of Thornton Wilder*. Lincoln: University of Nebraska Press, 1965. An early and still useful introduction to Wilder's novels and plays. A short biographical sketch is followed by study of his work through the one-act play *Childhood*. Includes bibliographical notes and an index.

Goldstone, Richard H. *Thornton Wilder: An Intimate Portrait*. New York: Saturday Review Press, 1975. An intimate portrait of Wilder by a close friend who had written previous studies on the subject, had access to personal documents, and interviewed family and friends. Includes notes, a selected bibliography, and an index.

Harrison, Gilbert A. *The Enthusiast: A Life of Thornton Wilder*. New York: Ticknor and Fields, 1983. A chatty biographical study of Wilder by a biographer who was provided access to Wilder's notes, letters, and photographs. Harrison successfully re-creates Wilder's life and the influences, both good and bad, that shaped him.

Konkle, Lincoln. *Thornton Wilder and the Puritan Narrative Tradition*. Columbia: University of Missouri Press, 2006. Wilder was the descendant of Puritans, and Konkle argues that the writer inherited the Puritans' worldview, particularly the Calvinist aesthetic, and drew upon it to create his novels and plays. Includes a chronology, a bibliography, and an index.

Simon, Linda. *Thornton Wilder: His World*. Garden City, N.Y.: Doubleday, 1979. A solid biographical study of Wilder that includes examinations of his published works, as well as photographs, notes, a bibliography, and an index.

Walsh, Claudette. *Thornton Wilder: A Reference Guide, 1926-1990*. New York: G. K. Hall, 1993. A thorough guide to Wilder and his works, through 1990. Includes bibliographical references and an index.

JOHN A. WILLIAMS

Born: Jackson, Mississippi; December 5, 1925
Also known as: John Alfred Williams; J. Dennis Gregory

Principal long fiction

The Angry Ones, 1960 (also known as *One for New York*)
Night Song, 1961
Journey out of Anger, 1963
Sissie, 1963
The Man Who Cried I Am, 1967
Sons of Darkness, Sons of Light: A Novel of Some Probability, 1969
Captain Blackman, 1972
Mothersill and the Foxes, 1975
The Junior Bachelor Society, 1976
!Click Song, 1982
The Berhama Account, 1985
Jacob's Ladder, 1987
Clifford's Blues, 1998

Other literary forms

Known primarily as a novelist but also as a short-story writer, John A. Williams has produced an extraordinary number of nonfiction pieces, many of them journalistic. He was among the first African Americans of his generation to write a fact book about Africa, *Africa: Her History, Lands, and People* (1962). His treatment of 1960's social issues can be found in *The Protectors: The Heroic Story of the Narcotics Agents, Citizens, and Officials in Their Unending, Unsung Battles Against Organized Crime in America and Abroad* (1964) and in *This Is My Country Too* (1965), which documents Williams's travels throughout the United States in 1963-1964, from articles serialized in *Holiday* magazine.

A controversial work, *The King God Didn't Save: Reflections on the Life and Death of Martin Luther King, Jr.* (1970) is a critical look at civil rights leader Martin Luther King, Jr.'s public and private life, and *The Most Native of Sons: A Biography of Richard Wright* (1970) treats the life of the famed black novelist Richard Wright. A comprehensive compilation of articles, some autobiographical, was published in *Flashbacks: A Twenty-Year Diary of Article Writing* (1973). Williams has also produced an award-winning book of poetry, *Safari West* (1998), the play *Last Flight from Ambo Ber* (pr. 1981), dealing with the Falashas in Ethiopia, and the libretto for the opera *Vanqui* (pr. 1999).

Achievements

One of the most prolific and influential writers of his era, John A. Williams infuses his works with self-exploration, reflecting the collective social experience of African Americans. He has lectured widely, contributed extensively to anthologies, and edited numerous collections, such as *The Angry Black* (1962), *Beyond the Angry Black* (1966), *Amistad I* (1970), *Amistad II* (1971), *Yardbird No. 2* (1978), *The McGraw-Hill Introduction to Literature* (1985), *Way B(l)ack Then and Now: A Street Guide to African Americans in Paris* (1992), and *Bridges: Literature Across Cultures* (1994). In the 1970's, he was a contributing editor for such publications as *American Journal* and *Politicks*, and in the 1980's he served in a similar capacity for the distinguished, groundbreaking publication *Journal of African Civilizations*.

Williams has been the recipient of numerous awards, beginning with his recognition in 1962 by the National Institute of Arts and Letters. His other honors and achievements include the Richard Wright-Jacques Roumain Award (1973), the National Endowment for the Arts Award (1977), the Lindback Award for Distinguished Teaching, Rutgers University (1982), the American Book Award for *!Click Song* (1983), the New Jersey Literary Hall of Fame Michael Award (1987), the American Book Award for *Safari West* (1998), and induction into the National Literary Hall of Fame (1998).

Biography

John Alfred Williams was born near Jackson, Mississippi, in Hinds County, to Ola and John Henry Williams. Williams's mother, whose African name means "Keeper of the Beautiful House" or "He Who Wants to Be Chief," had been born in Mississippi; his father's roots were in

Syracuse, New York, where the couple met. When Williams was six months old, he returned with his mother to Syracuse. The family resided in the multiethnic Fifteenth Ward, and Williams attended Washington Irving Elementary, Madison Junior High, and Central High School. He joined the U.S. Navy in 1943 and served in the Pacific. After discharge in 1946 and his return to Syracuse, he completed his secondary education, followed by a brief term at Morris Brown College in Atlanta and then enrollment at Syracuse University, where he studied creative writing.

In 1947, Williams married Carolyn Clopton, with whom he had two sons, Gregory and Dennis. In 1950, Williams earned his bachelor of arts degree and continued at Syracuse to pursue graduate study. During this period, he worked at a variety of jobs—foundry work, social work, public relations, insurance, radio and television—while developing as a journalist. Following the failure of his marriage in 1952 and a brief stay in California in 1954, he was determined to become a professional writer. In 1946, he had contributed pieces to the Syracuse newspaper, the *Progressive Herald*, continuing through 1955 as a reporter for the *Chicago Defender*, the *Pittsburgh Courier*, the *Los Angeles Tribune*, and *The Village Voice*.

John A. Williams. (Library of Congress)

After moving to New York in 1954, Williams worked for a vanity publisher, Comet Press, in 1955-1956 and at Abelard-Schuman in 1957-1958. In 1958, Williams was director of information for the American Committee on Africa, a reporter for *Jet* magazine, and a stringer for the Associated Negro Press. Based in Barcelona for a period, he was employed in 1959 by WOV Radio in New York; his first published novel, *The Angry Ones*, appeared in 1960.

Though Williams was nominated in 1962 for the Prix de Rome by the American Academy of Arts and Letters, his name was withdrawn for reasons that Williams attributed to his upcoming interracial marriage. In 1963, he contributed an article to *Ebony* magazine and began writing for *Holiday*, and in 1964 he was an Africa correspondent for *Newsweek*. In 1965, he married Lorrain Isaac, with whom he had a son, Adam. Williams began his career in higher education in 1968, teaching at the College of the Virgin Islands and the City College of New York. He held positions at the University of California, Santa Barbara; University of Hawaii; Boston University; New York University; University of Houston; and Bard College. From 1979 to 1994, he taught at Rutgers while continuing his literary activities. Following the publication of *Safari West* in 1998, his long-awaited novel *Clifford's Blues* (1998) was published; it was his first novel in twelve years.

Analysis

John A. Williams's novels draw on personal experience, though they are not strictly autobiographical; they reflect the racial issues facing American society, especially during the civil rights period. Williams writes in the clear, readable prose of a journalist; his plot structures mix linear time with flashback passages to achieve a seamless continuity. His characters have been writers, jazz musicians, black mothers, and military veterans, and his themes have addressed the hardships of the black writer, the expatriate in Europe, black family life, interracial relationships, and political conspiracy. The presentation of jazz is a frequent element, and New York City is a repeated setting, though Williams has also depicted the Caribbean and Africa.

The Angry Ones

Williams's initial novel is a first-person narrative drawing on autobiographical elements. Like Williams, Stephen Hill, the African American main character, is a World War II veteran, who works for a vanity press in New York. Early in the novel, Williams refers to African and Native American origins and jazz contexts. The novel is principally about Steve's relationships with his employer, coworkers, and friends. One of Steve's closest associates is Linton Mason, a white former college mate and editor at McGraw-Hill. The novel uses Lint's success in publishing to indicate the racial divide, sexual jealousy, and the benefits of being white in racist America. Another theme is the search for a meaningful relationship, the choice between interracial and intraracial love. The causes of black anger are linked to Steve's frustrating attempts to rise within the company run by Rollie Culver and, generally, the treatment of black men in New York's publishing world, symbolized by the suicide of Steve's black friend, Obie Roberts. The novel presents racism through the day-to-day experiences of the main character.

Night Song

Set in Greenwich Village, New York, in the 1950's, *Night Song* is a jazz novel that mirrors the life of famed alto saxophonist Charlie Parker through the portrayal of Eagle (Richie Stokes), a drug-addicted musician who retains the capabilities of jazz performance despite his debilitation. Eagle befriends the alcoholic David Hillary, an out-of-work white college professor employed in the jazz café run by Keel Robinson, a former black preacher and Harvard graduate involved in an interracial relationship with Della. Each of the characters is fractured, most notably Eagle, whose alcoholism and addiction are implicitly the result of the racist treatment of the black artist. Williams portrays David as a savior and betrayer of Eagle; David's "healing" is the ironic result of his association with Eagle, Keel, and Della.

Sissie

Titled for the mother of two principal characters, Iris and Ralph, *Sissie* is divided into four parts. Through memories, the novel presents the stories of Iris, Ralph, and Sissie Joplin, with Sissie's history revealed in parts 3 and 4, resulting in a Joplin family saga. Iris's story—her failed marriage, her career in Europe, and her relationship with the jazz musician called Time—is the first extended flashback. Ralph's recollections—his experiences in the service, his struggle as a writer in New York—are presented through psychoanalysis, a device that reveals racial issues from the viewpoint of a white psychologist, a symbol of societal norms. Sissie Joplin, a matriarchal figure, has an affair that threatens the stability of her marriage, which undergoes numerous challenges, such as the difficulty of surviving economic hard times and the struggle to find personal fulfillment through love. Sissie is ultimately the catalyst for Ralph and Iris's recognition of their family's conflicted yet sustaining experiences.

The Man Who Cried I Am

Williams's best-received and perhaps most influential work, *The Man Who Cried I Am* revolves around Max Reddick, an African American writer reunited in Amsterdam with his Dutch former wife, Margrit. Williams presents, within a twenty-four-hour time period, the downward spiral of Reddick, a Chester Himes figure, who is suffering from colon cancer. Through flashbacks, Reddick's recollections of a thirty-year past present the social experience of black Americans through the civil rights era. The novel portrays Reddick's association with Harry Ames, a character based on black novelist Richard Wright, who has uncovered the King Alfred Plan, a plot to place America's black population in concentration camps. Other characters in the novel also resemble actual black writers or political figures, such as Marion Dawes, a James Baldwin type; Paul Durrell, a Martin Luther King, Jr., replica; and Minister Q, a Malcolm X parallel. Furthermore, Williams develops African characters, such as Jaja Enzkwu, who reveals the King Alfred Plan to Harry Ames. The involvement of the Central Intelligence Agency (CIA) in Reddick's death points to an international conspiracy against black people, demonstrating Williams's tragic vision of global race relations.

Captain Blackman

An exploration of black contributions in American wars, this novel employs a narrative strategy in which time is fluid. At the outset, Captain Blackman, a soldier in the Vietnam War who teaches his troops the history of black Americans in the military, is wounded and trapped by the Viet Cong. His hallucinations are used to develop scenes in various American wars, from the American Revolution through Vietnam. In these settings, Blackman experiences battle and the racial circumstances affecting black troops. The novel mixes fictional characterizations with historical fact, as in the reference to the Battle of Bunker Hill in the American Revolution. Williams portrays a possible nuclear Armageddon in which black people become the forces of control, though the reversal of power from black to white is itself part of the dream visions of Blackman.

!Click Song

Considered by Williams at the time to be the novel in which he achieved the most effective coalescence of his literary intentions, *!Click Song*, titled after a vocal sound found in the Xhosa language of South Africa, parallels two writers, one black, the other white and Jewish. Using flashbacks, manipulating linear time, the narrative develops the literary careers of Cato Douglass and Paul Cummings. Divided into three sections, "Beginnings," "Middle," and "Endings," *!Click Song* uses the first-person narrator, Cato, as a representation of the journey of the black American writer. Beginning with the funeral of Paul, who committed suicide, the novel returns to the undergraduate experiences of the two veterans pursuing creative writing, circumstances that suggest the author's biography. Parallels to Williams's life are inescapable, especially in the treatment of Cato's career. However, Williams goes beyond mere autobiography by using Cato to symbolize the black artist who resists cultural falsehood, as in the closing section in which Cato in the 1960's offers a countertext to the withholding of information about black culture by major museums.

Jacob's Ladder

Jacob's Ladder explores the predicament of an African American military attaché, Jacob Henry (Jake), caught in the turmoil of American destabilizing efforts in Pandemi, a fictitious West African country, where he had spent part of his youth as the son of a black American missionary. Resembling Liberia, Pandemi is ruled by Chuma Fasseke, Jake's childhood friend. The government of Chuma Fasseke has replaced that of the Franklins, a family descended from nineteenth century repatriated African Americans. The novel also offers a parallel to Nigeria in the portrayal of Taiwo Shaguri, the head of state of Temian. Containing elements of an espionage thriller, *Jacob's Ladder* proposes that an African country can attain nuclear capabilities. Williams humanizes Jake and Fasseke, creating a work deeper than clandestine intrigue. The final sections describe the fall of Fasseke and the takeover of the nuclear power plant by his opposition, assisted by the CIA. The epilogue uses the ironic device of the press release to show the perspective of the international press.

Joseph McLaren

Other major works

plays: *Last Flight from Ambo Ber*, pr. 1981; *Vanqui*, pr. 1999 (libretto).

poetry: *Safari West*, 1998.

nonfiction: *Africa: Her History, Lands, and People*, 1962; *The Protectors: The Heroic Story of the Narcotics Agents, Citizens, and Officials in Their Unending, Unsung Battles Against Organized Crime in America and Abroad*, 1964 (as J. Dennis Gregory with Harry J. Anslinger); *This Is My Country Too*, 1965; *The King God Didn't Save: Reflections on the Life and Death of Martin Luther King, Jr.*, 1970; *The Most Native of Sons: A Biography of Richard Wright*, 1970; *Flashbacks: A Twenty-Year Diary of Article Writing*, 1973; *Minorities in the City*, 1975; *If I Stop I'll Die: The Comedy and Tragedy of Richard Pryor*, 1991 (with Dennis A. Williams); *Way B(l)ack Then and Now: A Street Guide to African Americans in Paris*, 1992 (with Michel Fabre); *Dear Chester, Dear John: Letters Between Chester Himes and John A. Williams*, 2008 (John A. Williams and Lori Williams, editors).

edited texts: *The Angry Black*, 1962; *Beyond the Angry Black*, 1966; *Amistad I*, 1970 (with Charles F. Harris); *Amistad II*, 1971 (with Harris); *The McGraw-Hill Introduction to Literature*, 1985 (with Gilbert H. Muller); *Bridges: Literature Across Cultures*, 1994 (with Muller, author).

Bibliography

Bryant, Jerry H. "John A. Williams and the Realist's Dilemma." In *Victims and Heroes: Racial Violence in the African American Novel*. Amherst: University of

Massachusetts Press, 1997. This analysis of Williams's novels is included in a study of how violence is depicted in African American literature from slave narratives through the late twentieth century.

Campbell, James. "The Man Who Came and Cried: John A. Williams." In *Syncopations: Beats, New Yorkers, and Writers in the Dark*. Berkeley: University of California Press, 2008. Campbell, a columnist for *The Times Literary Supplement*, has compiled a collection of his profiles and essays about writers, including Williams, who wrote after the 1950's.

Cash, Earl A. *John A. Williams: The Evolution of a Black Writer*. New York: Third Press, 1975. This text is the first book-length study of Williams's works, covering the novels through *Captain Blackman* and his nonfiction. Includes a bibliography and an index.

Gayle, Addison, Jr. *The Way of the New World: The Black Novel in America*. Garden City, N.Y.: Doubleday, 1975. Gayle addresses the shift from protest to history in Williams's novels *The Man Who Cried I Am* and *Captain Blackman*.

Muller, Gilbert H. *John A. Williams*. Boston: Twayne, 1984. This introductory overview provides a comprehensive treatment of Williams's life and the themes of his work through *!Click Song*. Includes biographical information, a chronology, a bibliography, and an index.

Nadel, Alan. "My Country Too: Time, Place, and African American Identity in the Work of John Williams." In *Containment Culture: American Narrative, Postmodernism, and the Atomic Age*. Durham, N.C.: Duke University Press, 1995. Nadel's study of "cultural narratives of containment" written during the Cold War includes a chapter on Williams's work, namely *The Man Who Cried I Am*, *Captain Blackman*, and *Sissie*.

Ramsey, Priscilla R. "John A. Williams: The Black American Narrative and the City." In *The City in African-American Literature*, edited by Yoshinobu Hakutani and Robert Butler. Madison, N.J.: Fairleigh Dickinson University Press, 1995. Ramsey provides an overview of selected Williams novels, focusing on their urban realities.

Ro, Sigmund. "Toward the Post-Protest Novel: The Fiction of John A. Williams." In *Rage and Celebration: Essays on Contemporary Afro-American Writing*. Atlantic Highlands, N.J.: Humanities Press, 1984. Ro argues that Williams's novels develop from protest fiction to novelistic treatments of 1960's racial issues.

Tal, Kali. "'That Just Kills Me.'" *Social Text* 20 (Summer, 2002): 65-92. Discusses *Sons of Darkness, Sons of Light* in a study of militant black futurist novels. For advanced students.

A. N. WILSON

Born: Stone, Staffordshire, England; October 27, 1950

Also known as: Andrew Norman Wilson

Principal long fiction

The Sweets of Pimlico, 1977
Unguarded Hours, 1978
Kindly Light, 1979
The Healing Art, 1980
Who Was Oswald Fish?, 1981
Wise Virgin, 1982
Scandal, 1983
Gentlemen in England, 1985
Love Unknown, 1986
Incline Our Hearts, 1988
A Bottle in the Smoke, 1990
Daughters of Albion, 1991
The Vicar of Sorrows, 1993
Hearing Voices, 1995
A Watch in the Night: Being the Conclusion of the Lampitt Chronicles, 1996
Dream Children, 1998
My Name Is Legion, 2004
Winnie and Wolf, 2007

Other literary forms

Despite the regularity with which A. N. Wilson produces novels, he has never been limited to that form alone. He is one of the best-known journalists in Great Britain, having served as literary editor to *The Spectator*, the prestigious weekly journal of conservative social and political opinion, and as the literary editor of the *Evening Standard*. His own writing for these publications has not been confined to reviewing books; he often publishes commentary on social and political subjects. Wilson has a special interest in religion, and aside from his occasional essays on that subject, he has published a study of the layman's dilemma in matters of Christian belief, *How Can We Know?* (1985), and historical biographies of Jesus and of the apostle Paul. He has taught at the University of Oxford and has published biographies of writers Sir Walter Scott, John Milton, Hilaire Belloc, Leo Tolstoy, and C. S. Lewis. After a memoir about Iris Murdoch, he published a life of poet John Betjeman. The latter attracted international attention when it was discovered that Wilson had unknowingly included in his biography a hoax letter. He has also published volumes of essays and reviews, including *Pen Friends from Porlock* (1988) and *Eminent Victorians* (1989), as well as children's books, mostly about cats, such as *Stray* (1987) and *The Tabitha Stories* (1988).

Achievements

The Sweets of Pimlico gained for A. N. Wilson the John Llewelyn Rhys Memorial Prize in 1978, and *The Healing Art* won three prizes, including the Somerset Maugham Award for 1980 and the Arts Council National Book Award for 1981. *Wise Virgin* brought him the W. H. Smith Annual Literary Award in 1983, and his study of Scott, *The Laird of Abbotsford: A View of Sir Walter Scott* (1980), won the Rhys Prize for him once again. Another of his biographies, *Tolstoy* (1988), won the Whitbread Award in 1988. His novel *Winnie and Wolf* was long-listed for the Man Booker Prize.

There are several formidable writers in Wilson's generation, but it is possible to distinguish Wilson as one of the best of the satirists and, as such, one of the most perceptive commentators on Great Britain in the late twentieth and early twenty-first centuries. Given his talent, and his capacity to comment attractively (if sometimes improperly) on the excesses of his society, it is not surprising that he has become something of a public personality, the literary figure most often identified with the "Young Fogeys," that amorphous group of literary, social, and political figures who espouse the principles of landowning Toryism and look with nostalgia back to the old Empire and to the days when High Anglicanism was a spiritual power in the land. Part of their conservatism is sheer mischief-making, part of it a matter of temperament and class, but in Wilson's case, it is a love for the aesthetic detail of what he sees as a richer and more caring society (which does not stop him from making wicked fun of it).

Biography

Andrew Norman Wilson, born in Stone, Staffordshire, England, in 1950, was educated at Rugby, one of the great English public schools, and at New College, Oxford. He won the Chancellor's Essay Prize in 1971 and the Ellerton Theological Prize in 1975. He was a lecturer in English at New College and at St. Hugh's College, Oxford, from 1976 to 1981. He was then appointed literary editor of *The Spectator* for two years and later became the literary editor of the *Evening Standard*. In addition to his fiction, his nonfiction, and his children's books, he has published in *The Times Literary Supplement*, *New Statesman*, *Daily Mail*, *Observer*, and the *Sunday Telegraph*. In 1992, he narrated *Jesus Before Christ*, a presentation by Thames Television Production that presents a demythologized approach to Jesus' life. His declaration of loss of faith and departure from the Church of England in the early 1990's ran parallel with events in the lives of a number of major characters throughout the corpus of Wilson's fiction. His new understanding and interpretation of Jesus and Saint Paul are presented in his biographies, published in 1992 and in 1997, respectively, of those early Christian figures.

During his second year of studies at Oxford, Wilson married Katherine Duncan-Jones, one of his tutors in English at Oxford's Somerville College and a specialist in Renaissance literature. Early in the marriage they became the parents of two daughters. After the marriage ended in divorce, he married Ruth Guilding, an art historian whom he met in 1989 when filming a television episode of *Eminent Victorians*, which he was narrating.

Wilson was made a fellow of the Royal Society of Literature in 1981 and is also a member of the American Academy of Arts and Letters.

Analysis

A. N. Wilson's novels are part of the tradition of sophisticated wittiness—sometimes comic, sometimes satiric—that explores the English caste system (with particular emphasis on the middle and upper middle classes), long a subject for English letters, particularly in the 1930's. The promise that World War II would not only stop international tyranny but also destroy the British social hierarchy was not, in fact, fulfilled. Great Britain may have fallen on hard times economically, and may have become less important politically, but the class structure, though shaken, has prevailed.

The Sweets of Pimlico

Evelyn Waugh was the foremost social satirist prior to World War II and until his death in 1966, commenting on the dottier aspects of life among the well-born, the titled, the talented, and the downright vulgar climbers and thrusters determined to ascend the greasy pole of social, political, and economic success. Wilson's first novel, *The Sweets of Pimlico*, might well have been written by a young Waugh. Thinly plotted but written with astringent grace and wide-ranging peripheral insights into the fastidious improprieties of the privileged, it tells of the bizarre love life of Evelyn Tradescant (whose surname alone is appropriately odd, but whose credentials are established by the fact that her father is a retired diplomat, Sir Derek Tradescant, of some minor political reputation).

By chance, Evelyn tumbles (literally) into an association with a much older man, Theo Gormann—wealthy, pleased by the attentions of a young woman, and mysteriously ambiguous about his past, which seems to have involved close association with the Nazis before the war. While Theo urges his peculiar attentions on Evelyn, so does his closest friend, John "Pimlico" Price, and Evelyn learns that everybody seems to know one another in varyingly confusing ways. Her father and mother remember the Gormann of Fascist persuasion, and her brother, Jeremy, is also known to Theo through his connection with Pimlico, who proves to be an occasional male lover of Jeremy, who in his last year at Oxford is doing little work but considerable loving, including a sudden excursion into incest with Evelyn. Wilson is teasingly and sometimes feelingly successful in exploring the sexual brink upon which Evelyn and Theo hover in their relationship and which convinces Theo to give part of his estate to Evelyn. Pimlico, the present heir, knows that someone is being considered as a joint recipient of the estate, but he never suspects Evelyn, and Theo dies before the will is changed. All is well, however, since Evelyn and Pimlico decide to marry. The novel is farce of high order in which coincidence, arbitrary behavior, and sophisticated silliness are mixed with moments of genuine tenderness (but not so tender as to overcome the sly mockery of money and influence in the smart set of south London).

Unguarded Hours *and* Kindly Light

In his next two novels, *Unguarded Hours* and *Kindly Light*, Wilson eschews the underplayed wit of *The Sweets*

A. N. Wilson. (Getty Images)

of Pimlico for comic excess, reminiscent of P. G. Wodehouse in its extravagant playfulness. These theological comedies are strongly cinematic in their incident and character and they display, if ridiculously, Wilson's strong interest in, and deep knowledge of, English Anglicanism and its constant flirtation with Roman Catholicism as well as his affectionate enthusiasm for the detail, the knickknackery, of religious ceremony and trapping. The two novels ought to be read in the proper chronological order, as the hero escapes in a balloon at the end of *Unguarded Hours* and begins in the next one, having floated some distance away, once again trying to make his way into the clerical life.

The Healing Art

The Healing Art, one of Wilson's most admired works, reveals how wide his range can be, not only tonally but also thematically. The novel is a "black comedy" in the sense that acts that normally offend are portrayed in such a way that readers enjoy the improprieties without worrying about the moral consequences. Two women, one a university don, one a working-class housewife, meet while having surgery for breast cancer and comfort each other, despite the fact that they otherwise have nothing in common. Their doctor, overworked but peremptory, unfeeling, and vain, may have misread the women's X rays and deems one of them cured and the other in need of chemotherapy. The gifted, handsome, successful younger woman, informed of her possibly fatal condition, refuses treatment, energetically determined to live out her life quickly and to explore her personal relations with some fervor. In the process, she learns much about herself and her male friends and becomes involved in a love affair with the cast-off, occasional mistress of the man whom she presumed was, in fact, her lover (even if such love had not, to the moment, been consummated).

Wilson juxtaposes the range of experience open to a woman of the upper middle class, searching for some meaning for the last days of her life, surrounded by the many pleasures and alternatives of her world, to the life of a working-class woman, supposedly healthy but obviously wasting away and ignored by family and by the medical profession as something of a nuisance. Wilson subtly explores the cruelty of it all, and the final ironies for both women are unnervingly sad and comic. Wilson proves with this novel that he is serious and sensitive, particularly in dealing with the emotional lives of the two women.

Who Was Oswald Fish?

In *Who Was Oswald Fish?*, which might be called a contemporary black fairy tale, coincidence simply struts through the novel. The mysterious Oswald Fish, a turn-of-the-century architect and designer whose one church—a Gothic ruin in the working-class district of Birmingham—is to be the center of life and death for the parties drawn together to decide its fate, proves to be related to everyone who matters (and some who do not). In the retrieval of Fish's reputation from the neglect and indifference of twentieth century tastelessness and vulgarity, one suicide, one manslaughter, and two accidental deaths occur, the latter two in the rubble of his lovely old church. No one means any harm (although there are two children in this novel who could put the St. Trinian's gang to flight).

Fanny Williams, former pop star and model and survivor of the English rock revolution of the early 1960's, is, in the late 1970's, famous again as the owner of a chain of trash-and-trend novelty shops dealing in Victorian nostalgia, and she is determined to protect the ruined church from demolition at the hands of soulless civic planners. Sexy, generous, and often charmingly silly, Fanny lives a life that is an extravagant mess, a whirlpool of sensual, slapstick nonsense in which some survive and some, quite as arbitrarily, drown. Behind the farcical escapades lies Wilson's deep affection for the rich clutter of Victoriana juxtaposed to the new efficiency.

Wise Virgin

After the comic excesses of *Who Was Oswald Fish?*, Wilson pulled back into the narrower range of his early work in *Wise Virgin*. There has always been a sense that not only Waugh but also Iris Murdoch influenced Wilson (*The Sweets of Pimlico* is dedicated to her and to her husband, the literary critic John Bayley), particularly in the way in which she uses love as an unguided flying object that can strike any character in the heart at any moment. Love tends to strike arbitrarily in Wilson's fiction, for he, like Murdoch, enjoys tracing the madness of fools in love. Also reminiscent of Murdoch, Wilson works interesting technical detail into his novels, often, as has been stated, of the religious world, but in *Who Was*

Oswald Fish? his interest in Victorian architecture and objets d'art predominates and adds amusingly to the texture of the novel. In *Wise Virgin*, Wilson utilizes his own special knowledge as a literary scholar, since his protagonist, Giles Fox, is a medievalist, working on a definitive edition of an obscure text, *A Treatise of Heavenly Love*, on the relation of virginity and the holy life. Fox, irascible, snobbish, and sometimes vicious, has two virgins on his hands—his daughter, whom he has sought to educate without benefit of twentieth century influence, and his assistant, Miss Agar, who is determined to marry him.

Wilson has been accused of gratuitous cruelty in the way in which he allows his characters to comment on the gracelessness of contemporary British society, and it is true that Fox is a master of the unfair comment and is insensitive to the possibility that some kinds of stupidities, particularly in the less privileged classes, are only innocent gaucheries. Certainly Fox is an unattractive protagonist, but he is also a man who has suffered much, having lost one wife in childbirth and another in an automobile accident, and having himself gone blind in midcareer. He is something of a twentieth century Job (although more deserving of punishment), and the tone and plot of the novel suggest black comedy bordering on tragedy. On the lighter side, Wilson satirizes Fox's sister and brother-in-law, who, suffering from that peculiar kind of arrested development that strikes some people as cute, indulge interminably in the baby talk of the schoolboys whom the husband teaches in a public school that is clearly based on Wilson's own school, Rugby.

Gentlemen in England

Gentlemen in England takes place in the late Victorian period of which Wilson is so fond. With this work, Wilson has written a trick novel, partly in the tradition of Thomas Keneally and E. L. Doctorow, in which actual historical events and characters intrude on, and affect, the action. Wilson, however, refuses to use obvious historical allusions carefully chosen to satisfy the vanities of intelligent, well-informed readers. Much of the historical structure requires a deep knowledge of Victorian England. For example, although the novel definitely takes place in 1880, the exact date is never stated but must be gathered from certain facts mentioned by the characters. Allusions to George Eliot and Henry James might be easy to pick up, but those to public figures of the time, such as Charles Bradlaugh, E. B. Pusey, and Sir Charles Wentworth Dilke, require a formidable cultural memory.

The story centers on a father who has lost his Christian faith in the face of Darwinism; a son who is flirting with the late stages of the Oxford movement in religion, with the more theatrical experiments of High Anglicanism, and with the revival of the Roman Catholic Benedictine movement; and a daughter pursued by a disciple of Alma-Tadema, the popular painter of the time. Wilson recounts their family drama in a Victorian style most reminiscent of the works of Anthony Trollope—slightly arch, witty, but restrainedly so, and inclined to overripe ironies. Like Victorian furniture and design, it is rich and heavy to the point of ponderousness.

Inside this lovingly detailed, historically accurate structure, Wilson plays out pure farce: A mother, still beautiful in early middle age, falls in love with a young painter, who falls in love with the daughter, who is half in love with her mother's old lover, who is half in love with both of them, and who is Wilson's way into the real world of London life. Called, with obvious intent, Chatterway, the former lover is intimately associated with the major figures of London life in that particularly lively year, 1880. *Gentlemen in England* is, in many ways, a work that illustrates Wilson's manipulative curiosity about the ways in which novels can be pushed and pulled about. Kingsley Amis has similar ideas, and he anticipated Wilson in *The Riverside Villas Murder* (1973), with its careful re-creation of a 1930's-style English murder mystery in which content, structure, and language are scrupulous imitations of the real thing.

This awareness of the novel as a form that can be used in many ways allows Wilson many humorous moments. In *Who Was Oswald Fish?*, he introduces, in a minor role, Jeremy Tradescant, the sexually confused brother of Evelyn, the heroine of *The Sweets of Pimlico*. He goes even further in making a comment on the fate of Evelyn's marriage to Pimlico Price, incomprehensible to all but those who have read the earlier novel. Wilson introduces into *Gentlemen in England* a genuinely thoughtful discussion of the problem of Christian faith that is tonally at odds with the clutter of Victorian sexual high jinks. He has, in short, no sense of decorum, not because he does not know but because he knows so well. Sometimes, as in *Scandal* and *Love Unknown*, he seems to have returned to social satire; the latter novel is puzzling until one recognizes that it is based on the most pathetic kind of popular romance. Wilson is off again, manipulating the genre, enriching junk literature by imposing first-class literary technique on banality and turning it into something it hardly deserves.

The Lampitt Chronicles

In a vein similar to his other novels, Wilson's five novels that comprise the Lampitt Chronicles focus on a group of middle- and upper-class English whose lives become intertwined through a variety of typically Wilsonian "coincidences." With its ironic overview of twentieth century English society, this *roman-fleuve* quintet chronicles the life of the first-person narrator, Julian Ramsey, and the lives of several members of the upper-class Lampitt family.

The first two novels recount the early events in Julian's life. In *Incline Our Hearts*, a twelve-year-old orphaned Julian is living with his uncle Roy, the vicar at Timplingham. Roy, obsessed with the Lampitt family, continuously recounts "Lampitt-lore" to Julian, who develops an interest in James Petworth "Jimbo" Lampitt, a minor Edwardian writer whose death begins the novel. This hilarious commentary on English snobbery and English institutions follows Julian at school (the "English Gulag") and through his adolescence. *A Bottle in the Smoke*, a darker satire, records Julian's marriage to Anne, a Lampitt niece. Some of the exasperation, confusion, and emptiness over modern relationships between the sexes expressed in poet T. S. Eliot's *The Waste Land* (1922) is echoed here (and in the next three novels).

The satire continues in *Daughters of Albion*, as Julian becomes "Jason Grainger" on the nationally popular radio series *The Mulberrys*. Raphael Hunter (Jimbo's biographer, who outraged the family by presenting Jimbo as a homosexual) successfully sues a would-be Blakean poet, Albion Pugh, for accusing him of murdering Jimbo. Interspersed with his satire on the world of publishing, radio, and television, Wilson, through both the narrator and Pugh, presents ideas about myth, Christianity, Jesus, and Saint Paul that later find their nonfiction counterparts in Wilson's religious biographies.

Hearing Voices is a mystery as well as a comedy of manners. Ramsey, asked to write an authorized biography of the Lampitts, goes to the United States to do research, and he marries for the second time (unsuccessfully). The murder of the American tycoon who had bought Jimbo's literary papers remains unsolved, as Wilson's emphasis continues to be on human interactions.

In *A Watch in the Night*, Ramsey, in his late sixties and at peace with himself, addresses dramatist William Shakespeare—as Saint Augustine does God in his *Confessiones* (397-400; *Confessions*, 1620)—as he reflects on his life and its intersection with the lives of countless characters. This Proustian summary clarifies major and minor ambiguities in the earlier novels (and resolves the murders).

Dream Children

Texturally rich and convoluted in its plotting, *Dream Children* takes on the indelicate problem of the pedophile. Wilson presents this sexual predator, his novel's central character, as a hugely intelligent, eminently reasonable, and mainly likable man—one who has obsessed over the philosopher Georg Wilhelm Friedrich Hegel and has recently attempted a book on Dante but who finds these intellectual interests paling before the attractions of love.

Oliver Gold was a cult figure on the campus where he taught. He suffered a crisis of confidence, however, followed by deep depression, and he has left academia, on the advice of a friend, an older bachelor. Previously Oliver had become great friends with Cuffe, a young philosophy student, who loves him but accepts his seeming indifference to sex. As do others, she suspects Oliver is gay, or perhaps ascetic. Cuffe, who lives in a household of women, opens to Oliver what seems the perfect opportunity for escape. He joins the household, taking an upper-floor suite where he hopes to pursue his studies in isolation.

Oliver's difficulty is his sexual attraction to children. He has kept his desires well hidden, allowing them full play only when he is alone and behind closed doors. His lovers, the "dream children" of the title, are imaginary ones born, in part, of his meditations on Victorian photographs of naked children.

To his surprise, Oliver now finds himself living in a

house with a small child, a girl named Bobs. As he becomes something of a caregiver and surrogate father for Bobs, he also becomes her lover. Entering into a period of supreme personal contentment, with almost unconscious abandon he writes entire journals chronicling his love affair.

Before unveiling these circumstances, Wilson disarms the reader by starting the novel as if it were a mere romantic comedy. Bobs brings news to the women of the household that Oliver is leaving, having become engaged. His new young woman has given him a considerable token of her love: a sports car. Since Oliver's coming into the household had brought peace among them, the news strikes each of the women deeply, and personally. Aloof though he has appeared, everyone in the household has fallen under the spell of the man who has been so good with Bobs. It is wounding, to them, to think some other woman has captured him after his long exposure to their various charms.

Events proceed with a mix of satiric absurdity and emotional sensitivity, reaching an ending that is, in its ethical implications, horrifying. It dawns gradually on the reader that injury is being done to every soul in the novel but the one who bears the deepest and most serious problem. While some of the novel's characters fail to ring true, especially its American ones, *Dream Children* excels in its impressive depiction, executed with subtle judgment, of an appalling sickness within society.

MY NAME IS LEGION

With *My Name Is Legion*, Wilson reintroduces the troubled priest as a major character and continues his exploration of the relationship between adults and those children who are made adult too soon. The child in this case is Peter, a schizophrenic, also a sexual victim of his social worker. His clearly divided personalities—one is based on P.G. Wodehouse's Bertie Wooster—interact internally and then act externally in ways that puzzle and alarm those around him. As intelligent and charming as Peter can be, he also displays pronounced cruelty and violence—to such a degree that his actions have triggered the mental breakdown of his father-in-law.

That Peter's problems lead to his death is made clear to the reader from the prologue, when the priest is shown on his deathbed, with a gunshot wound. In this flash-forward scene, Peter's mother sobs at the bedside—for Father Vivyan is not only wounded, but he has also shot the boy.

My Name Is Legion is also a tale of tabloid journalism, of the least news-oriented and most opportunistic variety. Lennox Mark is the proprietor of the *Legion*, among the worst of these papers. He has ties to Vivyan, whom he sees as embodying his weakened conscience. The two had encountered one another in the copper-rich African country of Zinariya, where the young Mark had given every sign of having opened his eyes to the crimes of his mine-owning family. Both, too, had befriended the young Bindiga, who would become the military dictator of Zinariya. Bindiga is supported, now, by the *Legion*'s proprietor and opposed by the priest. Mark and Vivyan are bound together in another way not known to them, for both engaged in indiscretions that make them equally likely fathers of Peter.

In this entertaining and troubling novel, Wilson's satiric focus is fully engaged, not only on the world of the tabloids but also on a weak-willed British government swayed by such lordship-seekers as Lennox Mark and an overreaching United States. The world of the novel is such that wolfish and capricious columnists, some of them fallen from a kind of intellectual grace, become the tools of deceit and disruption, to be engaged against the most well-meaning.

WINNIE AND WOLF

Where *My Name Is Legion* invents an African country, *Winnie and Wolf* invents the love child of a remarkable but not too far-fetched union—between the English-born promoter of the Wagner Festival at Bayreuth and the soon-to-be führer of the Third Reich. The promoter is Winifred Williams, the wife of convenience to Siegfried, gay son of opera composer Richard Wagner. The "Wolf" of the title is Adolf Hitler, that being his nickname in the Wagner household.

The novel is narrated by Siegfried's secretary, who, along with Winifred Williams, is of the intellectual class that was duped, or that duped itself, into believing the atrocities of Nazism to be passing unpleasantness. Questions of intellectual honesty, blindness, and hypocrisy are central to the novel. That Williams is English-born is of significance, since the novelist points to British Empire precedents, in terms of racist and camp-segregation policies, for Third Reich practices.

Wilson's abiding interest in historical and biographical questions may have encouraged him to indulge more deeply in extended exposition in this ambitious work. His tendency in his novels to state character backgrounds and traits rather than to dramatize them may have made it all too easy for him, here, to become a lecturer on points of opera, philosophy, and history.

Although Wilson's satiric tone varies in his novels from caustic to gentle, his works are generally amusing, perceptive about the human condition, and memorable for their characters (despite their chaotic lives). His insight into English society and its institutions, past and present, reflects the deep confusions not only of contemporary England but also of contemporary Western civilization. Whether he should be grouped primarily with Angus Wilson and Evelyn Waugh for serious farce, with Iris Murdoch and Joyce Cary for analytical comedy, or with Kingsley Amis for caustic irony, it is clear that Wilson is one of the twentieth century's major English authors.

Charles H. Pullen; Marsha Daigle-Williamson
Updated by Mark Rich

Other major works

NONFICTION: *The Laird of Abbotsford: A View of Sir Walter Scott*, 1980; *The Life of John Milton*, 1983; *Hilaire Belloc*, 1984; *How Can We Know?*, 1985; *Pen Friends from Porlock*, 1988; *Tolstoy*, 1988; *Eminent Victorians*, 1989; *C. S. Lewis*, 1990; *Jesus*, 1992; *The Rise and Fall of the House of Windsor*, 1993; *Paul: The Mind of the Apostle*, 1997; *God's Funeral: The Decline of Faith in Western Civilization*, 1999; *Iris Murdoch as I Knew Her*, 2003; *The Victorians*, 2003; *London: A Short History*, 2004 (also known as *London: A History*); *Betjeman: A Life*, 2006.

CHILDREN'S LITERATURE: *Stray*, 1987; *The Tabitha Stories*, 1988; *Hazel the Guinea Pig*, 1989.

EDITED TEXTS: *The Faber Book of Church and Clergy*, 1992; *The Faber Book of London*, 1993.

Bibliography

Atlas, James. "'A Busy, Busy Wasp.'" *The New York Times Magazine*, October 18, 1992. Profile of Wilson, published at the time his work *Jesus* first appeared, provides background on the author.

Hoyle, Ben. "One-Upmanship Follows Hoax in Battle of the Biographers." *The Times* (London), November 21, 2006. Reports on the hoax perpetrated against Wilson during his writing of a biography of poet John Betjeman.

Landrum, David W. "Is There Life After *Jesus*? Spiritual Perception in A. N. Wilson's *The Vicar of Sorrows*." *Christianity and Literature* 44 (Spring/Summer, 1995): 359-368. Presents a discussion of Wilson's first novel after he declared his unbelief in Christianity, in which the author deals much more seriously with the problem of evil and other difficult religious questions than in his other fiction.

Lyall, Sarah. "In Literary London, the Strange Case of the Steamy Letter." *The New York Times*, August 31, 2006. Gives a useful overview from an American perspective of the disagreements between Betjeman biographers Wilson and Bevis Hiller, which made Wilson the object of international interest.

Weinberg, Jacob. "A. N. Wilson: Prolific to a Fault." *Newsweek*, September 13, 1988. Brief, well-written essay is interspersed with comments by Wilson on his novels and biographies. Also concerns Wilson as a "Young Fogey," a term used to describe young members of the Conservative Party in England.

Wolfe, Gregory. "Off Center, on Target." *Chronicles* 10, no. 10 (1986): 35-36. Discusses Wilson's affinities with Evelyn Waugh, particularly in terms of their styles and in their perspectives on Western Christianity. Also asserts that Wilson writes in the tradition of P. G. Wodehouse, who epitomized the light comic novel, but in Wilson's hands that novel becomes a vehicle for satire and social criticism.

ANGUS WILSON

Born: Bexhill, East Sussex, England; August 11, 1913
Died: Bury St. Edmunds, Suffolk, England; May 31, 1991
Also known as: Angus Frank Johnstone Wilson

Principal long fiction

Hemlock and After, 1952
Anglo-Saxon Attitudes, 1956
The Middle Age of Mrs. Eliot, 1958
The Old Men at the Zoo, 1961
Late Call, 1964
No Laughing Matter, 1967
As If by Magic, 1973
Setting the World on Fire, 1980

Other literary forms

Angus Wilson started his literary career in 1946, at the age of thirty-three, by writing short stories. The earliest stories were published in *Horizon*. *The Wrong Set, and Other Stories* (1949), *Such Darling Dodos, and Other Stories* (1950), and *A Bit off the Map, and Other Stories* (1957) deal with the same problems and use the same imagery as his novels. Wilson also wrote drama, and in the 1970's, he became a leading reviewer of fiction. His literary journalism and criticism for *The Spectator*, *The Observer*, and *The London Magazine* center mainly on the problem of the English novel. The range of writers he discussed in articles, introductions, or lectures is wide and includes, among others, the Victorians, the Bloomsbury Group, Aldous Huxley, D. H. Lawrence, John Cowper Powys, Leo Tolstoy, Fyodor Dostoevski, Irving Shaw, Robert Penn Warren, and William Golding.

Wilson also published three full-length literary monographs: *Émile Zola: An Introductory Study of His Novels* (1952), *The World of Charles Dickens* (1970), and *The Strange Ride of Rudyard Kipling: His Life and Works* (1977). Wilson's many lectures and articles display his concern with a wide range of problems relevant to the second half of the twentieth century. Most important for the study and understanding of his art is the volume *The Wild Garden: Or, Speaking of Writing* (1963), which contains lectures given in California in 1960. Some of his criticism was collected in *Diversity and Depth in Fiction: Selected Critical Writings of Angus Wilson* (1983). Written over several decades are the essays collected in *Reflections in a Writer's Eye: Travel Pieces* (1986).

Achievements

Most critics agree that by the 1980's, Angus Wilson had secured a place among the most distinguished contemporary British novelists. He even became recognized outside the English-speaking world, particularly in France. In the 1960's and 1970's, the number of interviews with the artist increased, signifying his growing recognition among critics. Whether the critics use Stephen Spender's terminology of "modern" and "contemporary" or speak of experimental, psychological, aesthetic, or modern versus the traditional, sociological English novel, they all try to assess Wilson in relation to these categories. Some contend that Wilson's main concern rests with the sociological aspects of human life, but almost all critics concede that his interest goes beyond social issues. Without abandoning his commitment to depicting reality, Wilson was always committed to probing deeper into the dark depths of the human self. This concern with the inner self separates him sharply from the "angry" writers who also wrote in the 1950's: Kingsley Amis, John Wain, and Alan Sillitoe. Wilson, however, was dedicated to experimenting both in content and method. In his novels and critical writings, he emerged as a champion for a new type of novel, standing between the traditional and the experimental.

Biography

Angus Frank Johnstone Wilson was born in Bexhill, Sussex, England, on August 11, 1913, the sixth son of a middle-class family. His father was of Scottish extraction; his mother came from South Africa, and he spent some time there as a child. In constant financial troubles, his parents tried to maintain pretense and appearance, which left a deep impression on Wilson: At a very early age, he became aware of the chasm separating the real world and the world of fantasy into which many people escape to avoid the unpleasant facts of their lives. Frequently lonely (he was thirteen years younger than his next older brother), he realized that his clowning ability made him popular with the schoolchildren. He attended prep school in Seaford; from there he went to Westminster School and then to Merton College, Oxford. At the University of Oxford, his history training was on the Marxist line; that fact and his left-wing political activities in the 1930's account for his Labour sympathies.

In 1937, Wilson started work at the British Museum and, with an interruption during World War II, he stayed there until 1955. During the war, he was associated with an interservice organization attached to the foreign office, and for a while he lived in the country in a home with a Methodist widow and her daughter. During this time, he had a serious nervous breakdown; his psychotherapist suggested creative writing as therapy. In 1946, Wilson rejoined the staff at the British Museum and, at the same time, started writing seriously. His first published writing, the short story "Raspberry Jam" (1946), reflects his personal crisis and foreshadows the dark atmosphere of most of his work to come. The whole experience at the British Museum, situated in London's sophisticated Bloomsbury district and especially his job as deputy superintendent at the Reading Room, provided him with an understanding and knowledge of the cultural establishment and of the management of cultural institutions, which he used later in *The Old Men at the Zoo*. Also, observing scholars, book addicts, and eccentric visitors to the Reading Room gave him material for creating some of his fictional characters, such as Gerald Middleton in *Anglo-Saxon Attitudes*.

In 1952, Wilson published his first novel, *Hemlock and After*, and a critical monograph, *Émile Zola*. He gave talks on the novel for the British Broadcasting Corporation that were later published in *The Listener*. In 1955, a contract with Secker and Warburg as well as his ongoing reviewing activity for *The Spectator* and *Encounter* made it possible for him to resign his post at the British Museum. He then retired to the Sussex countryside, thus reviving his childhood garden-dream. As a result of his freedom from job-related responsibilities, he published four novels in a rapid sequence: *Anglo-Saxon Attitudes*, *The Middle Age of Mrs. Eliot*, *The Old Men at the Zoo*, and *Late Call*. Furthermore, his participation in the cultural and literary life of England as a journalist, critic, and lecturer became more extensive. In 1963, he started his association with the University of East Anglia as a part-time lecturer, becoming professor in 1966. Also in 1966, he became chair of the literary panel of the Arts Council of Great Britain. In 1967, he lectured at Berkeley, California, and in the same year published *No Laughing Matter*.

In 1968, Wilson was made Commander of the British Empire and honorary fellow of Cowell College of the University of California, Santa Cruz. He honored the Dickens Centennial in 1970 with *The World of Charles Dickens*. Between 1971 and 1974, he served as chair of the National Book League while receiving two more distinctions in 1972, becoming a companion of literature and a chevalier de l'Ordre des Arts et des Lettres, the latter a sign of his growing reputation in France. A sixth novel, *As If by Magic*, appeared in 1973; in it he made use of his teaching experience and involvement with young intellectuals. He continued to live in the country, his many activities including travel. His Asian journey resulted in his book *The Strange Ride of Rudyard Kipling*. He was a visiting professor at Johns Hopkins University in 1974, and, in 1977, a distinguished visiting professor at the University of Delaware; he also lectured at many other American universities. In 1980, he published another novel, *Setting the World on Fire*. His manuscripts, deposited at the library of the University of Iowa, provide ample material for researchers. After suffering a stroke, Wilson died on June 1, 1991, in a nursing home in the southeast of England.

Analysis

"Self-realization was to become the theme of all my novels," declared Angus Wilson in *The Wild Garden*. Self-realization does not take place in a vacuum; the process is closely linked with a person's efforts to face and to cope with the world. Wilson's childhood experience, among déclassé middle-class people living in a fantasy world, initiated the novelist's interest in the conflict between two worlds and in the possibility or impossibility of resolving the conflict. The rapidly changing scene in England as the Edwardian Age gave way to the postwar 1920's, with the cultural dominance of Bloomsbury, and then to the radical leftist 1930's, impressed on him the urgency of such a search. His encounter with Marxism at Oxford intensified his tendency to see the world as one of opposing forces. The dichotomy of town and country, of the classes, and of old and new forms the background of Wilson's fiction as the remnants of Edwardian England disappeared and the dissolution of the British Empire left the island nation searching for its place in the modern world.

Angus Wilson. (Getty Images)

In *The Wild Garden*, Wilson describes his creative-writing process in terms of a dialectic; he reveals that he "never felt called upon to declare allegiance to either fantasy or realism," but then he adds that "without their fusion I could not produce a novel." Wilson is desperately looking for syntheses to all kinds of conflicts and insists that self-realization is an absolute necessity to achieve them. His own breakdown as well as Sigmund Freud's impact on his generation pushed Wilson in the direction of psychoanalysis and the search for identity. In an age of tension, violence, and suffering, he insists on the necessity of self-realization in order to overcome despair.

Wilson's heroes all have crippled, wasted lives and broken families, and the novelist explores their "cherished evasions." Bernard Sand in *Hemlock and After* has to be shocked into self-knowledge by facing sadism in his own nature; Gerald Middleton, in *Anglo-Saxon Attitudes*, gets a new chance for a satisfactory, if not happy, life in old age when he is ready to resume responsibility as a scholar and to reveal a shameful hoax. Both of these heroes are presented in their private and public lives because, in Wilson's view, both of these aspects of life are equally important to modern people. This view of human life in the dialectic of the private and the public is even more important for Meg Eliot, the heroine of *The Middle Age of Mrs. Eliot*; after many frustrations she emerges at the end of the novel as a career woman. Similarly, Sylvia Calvert in *Late Call* discovers a meaningful (retirement) life of her own, independent of her family.

Wilson was a very "British" writer with a subtle sense for the typical English understatement, while his Hegelian drive for reconciliation of conflicts agrees with the spirit of the traditional English compromise. He was constantly searching for ways to save the remnants of the liberal, humanistic values that have remained dear to him in a world that did not seem to have any use for them. His heroes and heroines, saved from final disintegration, are restored to some kind of meaningful life through self-knowledge and are brought closer to other people in defiance of loneliness and despair.

Hemlock and After

In his first novel, *Hemlock and After*, Wilson extends the exploration of the theme of self-knowledge to both the private and public life of his hero. The novel is about Bernard Sand's troubled conscience, a most private matter; but Bernard is an important public figure, described as "the country's own ambassador to the world outside," and a successful, self-confident novelist who organizes a subsidized writers' colony, Valden Hall, in order to support young talent. Overtly successful, his family life is in shambles. His wife, Ella, lives in "neurotic misery"; his son is a staunch conservative in strong disagreement with Bernard's liberal views; his unmarried daughter, a journalist, feels lonely and unhappy. As an indication of the overhanging disaster, Bernard's first novel is titled *Nightmare's Image*.

In the title of Wilson's novel, "Hemlock" suggests poisonous wrong, evil, and even violence. Poisoning and violence occur in a "massacre of innocence," as related to Eric, Bernard's young gay partner, and to the little girl Elzie, whom the disreputable Mrs. Curry wants to make available to Hugh Rose. Wilson deliberately links the fate of the two young people by calling them both "rabbits." Rose and Mrs. Curry strike their deal at the "Lamb" Inn.

The word "After" in the title refers to the aftermath of knowledge: self-knowledge. A crucial scene occurs at the end of book 1 when a still complacent and self-confident Bernard watches the arrest of young gays at Leicester Square and is shocked suddenly by the discovery that he experienced sadistic enjoyment in watching the terror in the eyes of those youths. This discovery has a devastating effect on Bernard's life and destroys not only him but also Valden Hall. The long-awaited opening of the young artists' colony becomes a total disaster, as its erupting violence grows into a symbol of the modern predicament. Wilson describes the scene as one of chaos, disorder, disappointment, strain, and hostility.

After this startling event, Bernard's life goes downhill very rapidly; self-knowledge paralyzes his will, and he is entirely unable to act. The discovery of sadistic tendencies makes him suspect his own motives. He realizes with frightening clarity the abyss of the human soul and is driven to utter despair about the motivation behind any action. He has a horrifying vision of the subtle difference between intention and action, and as a consequence, Bernard loses his determination to deal with Mrs. Curry. At the same time, Ella almost miraculously recovers from her nervous breakdown and, after Bernard dies, acts on his behalf in arranging efficient management at Valden Hall and a prison sentence for Rose and Mrs. Curry. Rose commits suicide in prison, while Mrs. Curry earns an early release with her good behavior. It is briefly indicated that she might continue her former activity; thus the epilogue ends the novel on an ambiguous note of qualified optimism.

ANGLO-SAXON ATTITUDES

The title *Anglo-Saxon Attitudes*, derived from Lewis Carroll's *Alice's Adventures in Wonderland* (1865), suggests a typically English atmosphere; it is Wilson's most Victorian novel, a broad social comedy. At the same time, it displays experimental technique in the use of the flashback, which provides all the background to Gerald Middleton's crisis in his private and public life. The hero, a sixty-year-old failure, is a historian. In the beginning of the novel, sitting by himself at a Christmas party given by his estranged wife, Inge, Gerald overhears broken sentences of conversation that remind him of the most significant episodes of his life. Wilson makes it very clear that self-knowledge is important for Gerald; it is both a psychological need to him and a matter of "intellectual honesty," a duty to the professional community of historians.

Gerald's crisis of conscience concerns a cruel hoax that occurred back in 1912 when he participated with a team in an excavation. Young Gilbert Stokeway, a disciple of T. E. Hulme and Wyndham Lewis and the son of the leader of the team, put a fake idol in the tomb under research at Melpham. His hoax was successful, and the fake came to be hailed as a pagan idol. At that time, Gerald was a Prufrock-like antihero: disabled physically by a sprained ankle and disabled emotionally by his love for Gilbert's wife, Dollie. His affair with her played an important role in his silence about the fake idol. Gerald's feelings of guilt center on "the two forbidden subjects of his thoughts," his marriage and the hoax. His life, "rooted in evasion," appears to him empty, meaningless, and futile. His professional career fell victim to his decision not to reveal the hoax. Because of his affair with Dollie, he evaded dealing with Inge's inadequacies as a mother.

In fact, none of the minor characters has a happy, self-fulfilling life. While Gerald still believes in the liberal tradition, neither of his sons adheres to his beliefs. His elder son, Robert, a businessman, stands rather to the right and the younger son, John, is a radical, and they have violent clashes whenever they meet. Both sons are unhappy in their personal relationships as well. Robert is married to the conventional Marie-Hélène but loves the more modern Elvira Portway. John has a short-lived sexual relationship with an unruly young Irishman, Larry, who is killed in a wild drive in which John loses a leg. Gerald's daughter, Kay, has a serious crisis in her marriage to the smart right-wing young sociologist, Donald. Wilson employs specific imagery to drive home to the reader the overwhelming atmosphere of frustration of all these people. Expressions such as "flat and dead" and "deadly heaviness" abound, referring to the behavior of people at parties when communication is impossible. Gerald's house is "noiseless as a tomb," and during the Christmas party at the home of the "Norse Goddess" Inge, all those present "shivered" in spite of the central heating.

Realizing the failure of his family, Gerald has to admit that he is to take the blame; when he selected Inge to be his wife, he decided for second-best. Yet, at the end, Gerald manages to pull himself out of his dead life. By revealing the hoax, he succeeds in restoring his professional status, and after a long silence, he becomes active again in research. The novel, however, like *Hemlock and After*, ends on a note of qualified optimism as Gerald remains estranged from his family. The picture of Gerald's life, combined with the divergent subplots, reveals a world in which relationships do not last, where options are limited.

The Middle Age of Mrs. Eliot

Critics believe that they can recognize Wilson in most of his central characters; the novelist, however, admits the connection only in the case of Meg Eliot, the heroine of his third novel, *The Middle Age of Mrs. Eliot*. "Meg," he says, "is in large part modelled on myself," while David Parker's nursery recalled to Wilson childhood memories of a garden of a friendly family.

Meg Eliot, a well-to-do barrister's childless, worldly, spoiled wife, experiences sudden tragedy when her husband dies from a gunshot wound as he tries to protect a local minister. The novel depicts Meg's nervous breakdown and painful recovery: her journey to self-knowledge. She is first revealed to be holding desperately to her old friends; yet, their lives are no more secure than hers. Lady Pirie in her "decaying genteel jail" is preoccupied with her son only; bohemian Polly Robinson lives a kind of "animated death"; and Jill Stokes is obsessed with the memory of her dead husband. These "lame ducks" cannot help Meg, nor can drugs. Meg's brother, David Parker, who runs the nursery with his gay partner, is sheltered in the pleasant quiet atmosphere, which suggests a return to lost innocence. Yet, Wilson is ambiguous about the validity of the garden image, since David's nursery is commercial, an irony in itself. Meg cannot share her brother's lifestyle, his abnegation of action and the human world. Wilson does not censure David for his contemplative lifestyle, but it is evident that he prefers Meg's choice "to be with people!"

Meg is determined to find meaning in life, in a life with people. She is strikingly reminiscent of George Eliot's heroines; similar to them, she used to live in self-delusion and is shocked into consciousness by the "remorse of not having made life count enough" for her husband. Moreover, again like the Victorian woman, she returns to a fuller life. Two factors are important in her recovery. First, she refuses any kind of opium, an Eliot ideal; second, she is determined to build herself a meaningful, useful life. While she admits that she "used to be Maggie Tulliver," she also resembles Gwendolen Harleth from Eliot's *Daniel Deronda* (1876). She shares with her an unhappy childhood and the horrors of remorse, but she shares also in Gwendolen's way of redemption. Like the Victorian heroine, Meg too had to learn in a painful way that the outside world could intrude into her life at any time and destroy it if she is taken unaware. As she takes a paying secretarial job, Meg is full of confidence in her farewell letter to David: "At any rate in a few years at least, the modern world won't be able to take me by surprise so easily again."

The Old Men at the Zoo

From the omniscient narrator of his early works, Wilson shifts to a more modern device in *The Old Men at the Zoo* by creating a first-person narrator in Simon Carter. In the beginning of the novel, Simon is a gifted, dedicated yet disabled naturalist, very much like Gerald Middleton at the time of the excavation. He is prevented from continuing research in Africa because of amoebal dysentery. He joins the London Zoo as an administrator at a crucial time when the zoo itself becomes a battleground of conflicting ideas, reflecting a conflict of values in British politics. Wilson creates an armed conflict between England and Allied Europe, followed by a fascist invasion of England when all standards of civilized behavior collapse and give way to brutality. When the war breaks out, the fascists want to put on a spectacle with prisoners of war fighting the zoo animals. Simon is horrified, but as he later tries to drive the animals to safety, he finds himself killing his favorite badgers to feed a boy and his mother.

Almost an antihero, trying to avoid any kind of involvement with people, an administrator following orders, Simon emerges at the end of the novel ready to face the world, to be involved with people, even running for director. Because of his loyalty to the zoo under three different administrations, representing three different political ideologies, some are inclined to view him as a Vicar of Bray. In the twentieth century, however, many people had to face Simon's fundamental dilemma: whether to follow orders or to take up independent responsibility. Simon's American-born wife, Martha, disapproves of his behavior; she would like him to give up his job. Simon refuses, saying, "What do you think I am, a weathercock?" There is cruel irony in this remark; however, Wilson's irony is not pointed at Simon but rather at the general human predicament of a rapidly changing world in which choices are limited and people are continuously bombarded with dilemmas.

Simon's only independent action is his attempt to save the animals, which ends in disaster. In him, Wilson presents modern society struggling with despair in a desperate race to catch up with challenges. Simon's painful adjustment commands respect; he almost achieves heroic status when, after all the horrors and violence, he describes this modern world as "a demie-paradise." In this sense, *The Old Men at the Zoo* is Wilson's least pessimistic novel.

No Laughing Matter

No Laughing Matter is one of Wilson's most complex novels and requires close reading. The narrative is interwoven with dramas, enacted by the characters and reflecting various dramatic styles, including the absurd. Pastiches and parody of writers are important features of the novel, and literary references abound. A chronicle of the Matthews family like that of the family of John Galsworthy's 1922 *A Forsyte Saga*, *No Laughing Matter* is also a historical document covering the twentieth century to 1967. The father, Billy Pop, a Micawber of the twentieth century, is a failure in his writing profession and ineffectual in his family life, letting his selfish wife dominate the children. All six of them have a crippled childhood and are deprived of privacy. By the end of the novel, they all achieve some kind of success in their professional lives; some even attain fame, such as Rupert, the actor, and Quentin, the political journalist, later a celebrated television commentator. Success does not make him lovable, and his cynicism, enjoyed by a million common viewers, questions the role of the media.

The final scene, in 1967, brings the whole clan together. While Margaret and her gay brother, Marcus, an art dealer, are discussing and quarreling about Margaret's art, Hassan, who will inherit Marcus's cooperatively run scent factory, makes a final statement: the last words of the novel. He considers Marcus's ideas of a cooperative absurd. Hassan admires "ambition, high profit and determined management." His coldly calculating thoughts cast a dark shadow on the future; they underline once again Wilson's skepticism about the survival of liberal humanistic ideals in the modern world.

A strong moral sense links Wilson to Eliot, and his sense of the caricature and the grotesque shows affinities with his favorite author, Charles Dickens. At the same time, his fiction is full of experiments into new literary methods. With almost each novel, Wilson made an important step forward in his search for new techniques. Tragedy and laughter coexist in his novels; there is tragedy in the private lives of the characters, but Wilson has a grotesque view of people's behavior, and his ability to create atmosphere through concentrating on speech habits promotes laughter.

In his commitment to duty, in his moral seriousness, Wilson is definitely akin to Eliot, but he differs from the Victorian in that he cannot believe in "meliorism." Eliot firmly maintained that self-awareness would lead to self-improvement and, in consequence, to the individual's improved performance in the human community. Wilson is much more skeptical. Like E. M. Forster, he, too, is painfully aware of the decline of liberal hopes. In *The Middle Age of Mrs. Eliot*, he came to the sad conclusion that "self-knowledge had no magic power to alter," and in his sixth novel, he killed magic with finality.

As If by Magic

In *As If by Magic*, magic, the ultimate evasion, is destroyed forever for the two central characters. Moreover, this time they are not middle-aged or elderly intellectuals paralyzed by frustration; they are young people. Wilson's teaching experience in Britain and America caused him to concentrate on the young, the future generation.

Hamo Langmuir is a dedicated young scientist on a worldwide fact-finding tour to study the benevolent effects of his "magic" rice, destined to solve the problem of starvation in underdeveloped countries. His goddaughter, Alexandra Grant, in the company of her fellow hippies, is also on a world tour in search of an occult answer to all human problems. A bewildered Hamo must find out that his magic rice solution has introduced a farming method for which natives are not yet prepared and, consequently, it is causing more damage than good. Hamo falls victim to the anger of a crowd at a moment when he is ready to get involved in the human aspects of research. He, like Alexandra, who gets to Goa at the same time, had to learn through experience that the intrusion of Western ways into radically different cultures can cause disruption and many unnecessary tragedies. At the end of the novel, a sober Alexandra, cured of her hippie ways, resumes the responsibility of building a normal life for her son, a legacy of the hippie venture. A millionaire through an inheritance, she is ready to support and subsidize food research, but she knows by now that the possibilities are limited and that no easy answers are available; magic of any kind is only for the neurotics who are unable to face reality or for the power-hungry who use it to dominate others.

Setting the World on Fire

Wilson's concern with human nature and with what it means for the future of the world dominates *Setting the World on Fire*. This novel is a family chronicle like *No Laughing Matter* but more condensed, more limited in time (1948-1969) and in the number of characters. Indeed, the writer concentrates on two brothers, Piers and Tom, the last generation of an old aristocratic family. Literary references are replaced by other arts: theater, music, architecture, and painting. Piers hopes to dedicate his life to the theater, and as a promising student, he earns the admiration of family, friends, and teachers with his stage-managing and directing abilities. The final part of the novel is about the preparations for the first performance of a new play, with the younger brother, Tom, supporting Piers as best he can in the hectic work. Everything is set for success when, unexpectedly, Scotland Yard intervenes and orders the premises emptied because of a bomb threat. The author of the play, an old employee of the family, masterminded the plot, simultaneously aimed at the family and at the government.

Tom saves Piers's life by knocking him down, but he himself gets killed. On his way home from the hospital where Tom died, Piers is on the verge of a breakdown and about to give up hope as well as artistic ambitions, because what good are the wonders of art in "a chaotic universe"? He calms down, however, and decides to stage the play anyway; he must not "lose the power to ascend the towers of imagination," he says. The tragedy brought Piers to a fuller realization of his duty as an artist, which means doing the only thing left to him: to create in, and for, a world threatened by chaos, violence, and destruction.

Wilson, a mixture of a twentieth century Dickens, Eliot, and Forster, with an increasingly dark vision of the modern predicament, rededicated himself, the artist, to his moral obligation. He continued writing in a desperate attempt to impose some kind of order on chaos and, by making people aware, to try to save humankind from itself.

Anna B. Katona

Other major works

short fiction: *The Wrong Set, and Other Stories*, 1949; *Such Darling Dodos, and Other Stories*, 1950; *A Bit off the Map, and Other Stories*, 1957; *Death Dance: Twenty-five Stories*, 1969.

play: *The Mulberry Bush*, pr., pb. 1956.

nonfiction: *Émile Zola: An Introductory Study of His Novels*, 1952; *For Whom the Cloche Tolls: A Scrapbook of the Twenties*, 1953 (with Philippe Jullian); *The Wild Garden: Or, Speaking of Writing*, 1963; *Tempo: The Impact of Television on the Arts*, 1964; *The World of Charles Dickens*, 1970; *The Strange Ride of Rudyard Kipling: His Life and Works*, 1977; *Diversity and Depth in Fiction: Selected Critical Writings of Angus Wilson*, 1983 (Kerry McSweeney, editor); *Reflections in a Writer's Eye: Travel Pieces*, 1986.

Bibliography

Brooke, Allen. "The Mimetic Brilliance of Angus Wilson." *New Criterion* 15 (October, 1996): 28-37. In this biographical essay, Brooke describes Wilson's childhood and youth, his early literary career, his gay relationship with Tony Garrett, his disillusionment with communism, and his declining final years.

Cavaliero, Glen. "Matter for Laughter: Angus Wilson." In *The Alchemy of Laughter: Comedy in English Fic-*

tion. New York: St. Martin's Press, 2000. The comic style of Wilson's novels is examined in this analysis of English fiction, in which Cavaliero discusses how parody, irony, satire, and other types of humor are evident in these works.

Conradi, Peter. *Angus Wilson*. Plymouth, England: Northcote House, 1997. A solid introduction to Wilson's work, including a biographical outline, chapters on his major novels, a section on his stories, notes, and a useful annotated bibliography.

Drabble, Margaret. *Angus Wilson: A Biography*. New York: St. Martin's Press, 1995. A detailed biography of Wilson in which his friend Margaret Drabble reveals the autobiographical sources of much of his fiction in his early years. Drabble describes Wilson's long-term gay relationship with Anthony Garrett and analyzes his obsession with the nature of evil in relationship to his mother's Christian faith.

Furbank, P. N. "No Laughing Matter: A Word on Angus Wilson." In *On Modern British Fiction*, edited by Zachary Leader. New York: Oxford University Press, 2002. Furbank discusses Wilson's fiction, including his novels *Anglo-Saxon Attitudes*, *Hemlock and After*, *No Laughing Matter*, and *The Old Men at the Zoo*.

Gardner, Averil. *Angus Wilson*. Boston: Twayne, 1985. In this general introduction to Wilson's life and art, Gardner provides biographical information and discusses Wilson's novels and short stories. Includes a bibliography and an index.

Halio, Jay L., ed. *Critical Essays on Angus Wilson*. Boston: G. K. Hall, 1985. A collection of reviews, interviews, and criticism covering Wilson's literary career. Includes influential reviews by Edmund Wilson, V. S. Pritchett, Kingsley Amis, and Anthony Burgess, as well as important essays by Malcolm Bradbury, A. S. Byatt, and Margaret Drabble. Halio's overview essay is a concise survey of Wilson's work and a critique of the criticism it has received.

Head, Dominic. *The Cambridge Introduction to Modern British Fiction, 1950-2000*. New York: Cambridge University Press, 2002. This overview of late twentieth century British fiction contains numerous references to Wilson's novels, which are listed in the index. This book helps place Wilson within the broader context of modern British literature.

Mackay, Marina. "Mr. Wilson and Mrs. Woolf: A Camp Reconstruction of Bloomsbury." *Journal of Modern Literature* 23 (Summer, 1999): 95-110. An overview of Wilson's career and works, surveyed with the career and works of Virginia Woolf.

Sinfield, Alan. "Culture, Consensus, and Difference: Angus Wilson to Alan Hollinghurst." In *British Culture of the Postwar: An Introduction to Literature and Society, 1945-1999*, edited by Alistair Davies and Alan Sinfield. New York: Routledge, 2000. Wilson's work is studied in this collection of essays examining how British literature, film, and music reflect the social, economic, and technological changes that occurred in the years after World War II.

ETHEL WILSON

Born: Port Elizabeth, South Africa; January 20, 1888
Died: Vancouver, British Columbia, Canada; December 22, 1980
Also known as: Ethel Davis Bryant

Principal long fiction

Hetty Dorval, 1947
The Innocent Traveller, 1949
The Equations of Love, 1952
Lilly's Story, 1953
Swamp Angel, 1954
Love and Salt Water, 1956

Other literary forms

Eleven short stories and eight essays by Ethel Wilson were published in magazines between 1937 and 1964. Two of the stories, "Hurry, Hurry!" and "Mrs. Golightly and the First Convention," were later anthologized, and two others, "I Just Love Dogs" and "The Window," were selected for *Best British Short Stories of 1938* and *The Best American Short Stories 1959*, respectively. These four stories, and other writings, were collected in *Mrs. Golightly, and Other Stories* (1961). In addition to the stories and essays, seven excerpts from novels also appeared separately as short stories in magazines. One of these, "Miss Tritt," from *The Equations of Love*, was anthologized as a short story.

Achievements

Ethel Wilson was among the Canadian authors of the 1930's who broke away from the frontier tradition of provincial and didactic romances. She adapted to Canadian backgrounds the universal themes and methods of the realistic and psychological novel. She was one of the first Canadians to achieve a critical reputation abroad, not indeed as a major novelist, but certainly as an important minor one. Her novels are in the main current of the British and French realist tradition, especially that of the early twentieth century, showing affinities with the works of E. M. Forster, Virginia Woolf, Arnold Bennett, Ivy Compton-Burnett, and Marcel Proust. Nevertheless, she maintained strong individuality in both theme and form. She wrote that authors can be "endangered by the mould or formula becoming apparent, and then the story has no life." Without being innovative, therefore, her novels have a great deal of variety of theme and approach, so that they are difficult to classify.

Perhaps because Wilson did not attempt to follow literary trends, and perhaps also because she began publishing relatively late in her life, when she was nearly fifty years old, her works did not have a dramatic impact on Canadian letters. She was publishing out of her generation, and her realism and understatement seemed somewhat old-fashioned to those authors of the 1930's who were following naturalistic trends. Still, she was influential in raising the quality of the art in Canada and in quietly introducing the theme of women "finding themselves" in some sense, well before the theme became popular among feminists. Her heroines are not necessarily strong or aggressive but they mature, meet the vicissitudes of their lives with determination and ingenuity, and for the most part succeed in small but important ways. Wilson's treatment of this theme and her impeccable craftsmanship contributed significantly to the maturing of the novel in Canada.

Biography

Ethel Davis Wilson was born in Port Elizabeth, South Africa, on January 20, 1888, to Robert William Bryant and Lila (Malkin) Bryant. Her mother died when she was only two, and her father took her to Staffordshire, England, to be reared by her maternal grandmother and successive aunts and uncles. Her family members were involved in a number of literary activities, including reading, journalism, and translation, and were acquainted with Matthew Arnold and Arnold Bennett. This literary atmosphere no doubt stimulated her interest in letters, and the literary allusions and quotations in her works demonstrate a comprehensive familiarity with the English tradition. Her father died when she was ten years old, and she went to Vancouver, British Columbia, to join her grandmother, who had moved there. Many of these family and early personal experiences are recounted in *The Innocent Traveller*, the semibiographical novel based on the life of her aunt.

In Vancouver, Wilson attended Miss Gordon's School, but she was sent to Trinity Hall School in Southport, England, for her secondary education. In 1907, she graduated from Vancouver Normal School with a Second Class Teacher's Certificate. Between 1907 and 1920, she taught in Vancouver elementary schools.

On January 4, 1921, Wilson married Dr. Wallace Wilson. Their marriage was a happy one, marked by a good deal of traveling in Canada, Europe, and around the Mediterranean, and the successful development of both their careers. Dr. Wilson became a respected physician; he studied internal medicine in Vienna in 1930, represented Canada at the British Medical Association's convention in 1938 and at the World Health Organization in Paris in 1947, and was president of the Canadian Medical Association in 1946 and 1947. The relationship between the Wilsons may have provided details for the happy marriages and the deepening love relationships in *Hetty Dorval*, *Lilly's Story*, and *Love and Salt Water*. The love of travel is also obvious in her work; travel is healing, broadening, and sensitizing to her characters, and Wilson's ability to describe the essential atmosphere of various locales is one of her strongest attributes.

Wilson published her first short story in 1937 and another in 1939 before her career was interrupted by World War II. Although Dr. Wilson was in the Canadian army and Wilson herself served by editing a Red Cross magazine between 1940 and 1945, she made little use of wartime experiences in her novels, except tangentially in *The Innocent Traveller* and *Love and Salt Water*. Only the short story "We Have to Sit Opposite" deals specifically with wartime problems.

It is likely that Wilson's career in writing was encouraged by ill health. She was a victim of arthritis, which by 1956 had become so severe that she could not walk around in London, as she described in her essay "To Keep the Memory of So Worthy a Friend." She wrote, "One of the advantages of being lame is that one can sit and think. . . . And so I often think and think." In her last three novels, several major characters suffer disabilities, either physical or psychological, that affect their relationships with others in various ways and that must be transcended. No doubt her own disability enabled her to interpret this theme sympathetically.

The late 1940's and the 1950's were Wilson's most productive years, all of her novels and most of her short stories and essays being written or published during that period. At the peak of her success, after the publication of *Swamp Angel*, she received three awards: an honorary doctorate from the University of British Columbia in 1955, a special medal from the Canada Council in 1961 for contributions to Canadian literature, and the Lorne Pierce Gold Medal from the Royal Society of Canada in 1964. Wilson lived in retirement in Vancouver until her death in 1980.

Analysis

Although Ethel Wilson's canon is small, it is of high quality. The writing style is direct, simple, and expressive. Only occasionally, in the early books, does the diction or syntax call attention to itself as excellent. In general, only if one should try to paraphrase a passage or change a word would he or she become aware of that rightness of style that is typical of an artist. Passages describing the beauty of nature are most immediately impressive. Wilson's account of the train journey of the Edgeworths across Canada to Vancouver, in *The Innocent Traveller*, offers a vivid impression of the countryside and evokes the haunting vastness of the plains and forests stretching northward from the train track to the Arctic Circle. Magnificent descriptions of the northern lights occur in more than one book, and the mist-shrouded or sun-brightened mountains of the Vancouver area are sketched with a sensitive pen.

Less frequent but equally impressive are descriptions of unsightly scenes, such as the interior of the slovenly Johnson apartment in *Tuesday and Wednesday* (published in *The Equations of Love*). It is not only in description, however, that Wilson excels; her humor is deft, ironic, and humane in passages such as the chapter "Nuts and Figs" in *The Innocent Traveller*, in which Great-Grandfather Edgeworth, in his declining days, proposes to two worthy lady friends in one afternoon and is refused, to the gratification of all three. Thoughtful and philosophical passages are also subtly presented, so that except for a few intrusive statements in the early, less integrated books, the concepts are suggested through economical language and apt symbols.

For Wilson, nature is not only a major inspiration for description but also a method of characterization. Most of her protagonists are close to nature. Their ability to love and the essential civilization of their emotions are measured by their appreciation of the beauties and dangers of the Canadian mountains, forests, and waters. One notable exception is the garrulous Topaz Edgeworth, who exists in her human relationships rather than in nature, and the other is Hetty Dorval, an antagonist, whose appreciation of nature is one of the deceptive charms of her evil. Wilson's characters are firmly rooted in their environments and grow out of them. Her attitude toward them is dispassionately empathetic; they are clearly and humorously drawn, with subtle complexities. All are believable, and the best of them are memorable. She develops understanding of even her most unsympathetic characters, to the extent that plot is often weakened because she is drawn into digressions about the characters, about whom she cares more than she cares about careful plot structure. Topaz Edgeworth, Nell Severance, Lilly Hughes, and Maggie Lloyd are her most convincing creations, and it is the success of their characterization that makes *The Innocent Traveller*, *Lilly's Story*, and *Swamp Angel* her best novels.

If style and characterization are what make Wilson's novels outstanding, the plots are what keep them from being great. Plotting appears always to have been difficult for Wilson. Her admirers defend the inconsequentiality of her plots as true to life, expressing a philosophy about the fortuitous connections, or lack of connections, between the events in a person's history. Wilson minimizes suspense as a plot device; in fact, she often uses a technique of revealing future events, since causality interests her more than suspense. Still, the novels that are most effectively plotted, *Lilly's Story* and *Swamp Angel*, are recognized to be her best.

The Equations of Love

The title of Wilson's third book, *The Equations of Love*, suggests her recurring themes as a novelist. The typical protagonist of a Wilson novel is orphaned or otherwise separated from her family, as Wilson herself was as a child. Deprived of parental love, she becomes independent but lonely. This typical protagonist usually takes a journey, which is both a literal "trip"—aboard ship or into the Canadian wilderness—and an interior voyage of self-discovery. She is both soothed and awed by her insignificance in the natural world, which is beautiful but indifferent. Out of her new self-awareness, she learns to give of herself and to build a relationship, usually but not necessarily marriage, that brings new meaning to her life, either happiness or philosophical maturity. Love is the solution to this symbolic orphanhood, yet love, too, is imperfect. Orphanhood leaves its mark, and people make do with various "equations of love."

This sense of irrevocable loss, of necessary compromise, saves Wilson's love-stories from sentimentality without veering toward cynicism. There is nobility in the aspiration toward love and self-subordination, triumph in even the flawed achievement of those graces. Wilson is impressed by the human ability to transcend egotism through whatever equation of love is possible to each individual.

Hetty Dorval

For a first novel, *Hetty Dorval* is exceptionally good, although a melodramatic climax undercuts the subtleties of its characterization. It introduces Wilson's recurring themes: orphanhood, egotism, and love; the tempering of the ego by nature or travel; the lasting impact of momentary impressions or casual coincidences; the emotional maturation of a young woman. It is the story of Frances Burnaby, and the influence of Hetty Dorval on her maturation.

Hetty crosses Frankie's path only a half dozen times, but the temptation that she represents is very strong. The two are parallel in certain important respects: Both are only children, and both are reared with considerable protection and privilege. Both are attracted by elements of wildness, such as the turbulent Thompson River and the flight of wild geese. Frankie, however, has been reared by her parents with friends and loving discipline. By contrast, illegitimate Hetty's mother, Mrs. Broom, has hidden her maternal role, and with it her model of a loving relationship, to give Hetty a superior social standing: She has pretended to be Hetty's nurse and later her lady's maid, so that Hetty has learned tyranny and self-indulgence. Hetty is seraphically beautiful, with selfish charm, concerned only with her own pleasures. Frankie's mother calls her "The Menace" even before she knows Hetty's full story. Hetty's beauty and charm and her elemental wildness attract Frankie as a child. Even though the younger girl gives up the older woman's friendship, in obedience to her parents' orders, she does not understand the evil in Hetty's character. As she grows up and gains experience, however, in each subsequent contact with Hetty she learns more and comprehends more fully the destructiveness of Hetty's egotism. Frankie's full comprehension of what is morally wrong with Hetty's way of life comes when Richard Tretheway, the man she loves, falls in love with Hetty, and she has to decide what action she should take.

Three of the major characters in the story are orphaned: Frankie loses her father during the course of the story; Richard has lost his mother before Frankie meets him; and Hetty is a psychological orphan, having no publicly acknowledged father or mother. Each has dealt with the problems of isolation in a different way. Frankie grows to love the Tretheway family and builds new familial relationships with them; Richard has tried to substitute as a mother to his younger sister Molly; and Hetty has turned to self-indulgence and the collection and abandonment of men. Each of these compensatory behaviors is one possible equation of love, but Hetty's is not honest or giving. The traits in Frankie's character that are similar to Hetty's are finally subordinated in Frankie as she learns to love. Although Hetty comments near the end of the book about their kinship, Frankie has moved beyond Hetty in self-control and compassion, and has thus ended her egocentric solitude.

The Innocent Traveller

Wilson's second novel, *The Innocent Traveller*, is a radical departure from her archetypal plot line. Topaz Edgeworth is not a solitary orphan, but a beloved child in a large and close family. Family is an all-pervasive concept throughout the book; characters are designated according to their role in the family, which changes as they age. Father becomes Grandfather and finally Great-Grandfather Edgeworth. Topaz herself is defined successively in terms of child, daughter, sister, aunt, and great-aunt. Topaz does lose her mother when she is young, but Father marries Mother's sister, and the family continues with virtually imperceptible interruption. Topaz continues to live with her father until she is middle-aged, and after his death, she lives with her older sister in much the same role of dependent daughter. Even with the death of the sister, she lives with her niece in virtually the same role, as if she were daughter to her niece. Although she moves to Canada, the wilderness does not impress her, nor does the new environment broaden her sympathies.

The Innocent Traveller is a happy book, Topaz a happy woman, with a sense of warmth and security very different from the solitary mood of the other novels. Complementing this happy mood are glowing descriptions of the English and Canadian landscapes and sensitive expressions of a generous, witty, and perceptive philosophy.

What this book contributes to analysis of Wilson's thematic development is the contrast it provides with her recurring story of orphanhood and reconciliation. Topaz is never orphaned; she also never matures. Topaz is characterized as a delightfully irrepressible child, a lovable nonconformist, but gradually (and only between the lines), an irresponsible eccentric, and finally an irritating, futile burden on her family. She is loved, but she does not love deeply in return; she is an affectionate family member, but she does not feel the needs and tragedies of others. She remains childishly egocentric to the last of her life. After her death, "there is no mark of her that I know, no more than the dimpling of the water caused by the wind . . . and when we met together . . . perhaps no one remembers, until afterwards, to mention her name." The contrast between Topaz and Wilson's typical orphaned protagonists is striking. Topaz is never independent and never feels solitary; therefore, she never comes to value loving relationships. She never goes off alone to come to terms with herself and her universe; therefore, she never comes to terms with society. She never feels insignificant in nature; therefore, she never feels the need to establish significance through commitment and love. Having realized these themes from the converse and happy side, Wilson was prepared to use them more powerfully in *The Equations of Love* and *Swamp Angel*.

Tuesday and Wednesday

Tuesday and Wednesday, a novella, the first part of *The Equations of Love*, deals with grotesque and pitiable "equations" in a mood of dark humor or satire. It is the story of the marital relationship of Myrt and Mort Johnson, no longer a marriage of love but an equation of shared resentment and frustration, lightened by moments of sensuality and a habitual tender impulse.

Mort is shiftless, envious, self-deceived, but good-natured and capable of friendship. Myrt is self-pitying, domineering, lazy, sporadically sensual, often spiteful, but kind when it is no trouble to be kind. They live apart from most human contacts; Mort is too feckless and Myrt too lazy to entertain. They have no family except one aunt and one orphaned cousin, Victoria May Tritt, to whom they are indifferently kind because she is even more lonely and repressed than they are. This kindness passes in her mind as beneficence, and her gratitude constitutes a kind of love for them. Mort has a friend, Eddie, whom Myrt dislikes because of his drinking and brawling, but the two men share a bond of camaraderie and wishful thinking. These are the relationships that pass for love in the seedy near slums of the city.

One evening, Mort meets Eddie, drunk; during a search in the dark for Eddie's lost suitcase, the inebriated Eddie falls off a pier and drowns. Mort, in his efforts to save his friend, falls into the water and is dragged under by Eddie to his death. Witnesses testify to Eddie's drunkenness, and the police conclude that both men were drunk, reporting the accident to Myrt in those terms. In her typical spite and self-pity, Myrt is not grieved, but affronted by Mort's drinking, abandoning her, and damaging her reputation by his association with the brawling Eddie. To salvage her self-esteem, she bitterly adopts the role of martyr. Victoria May has seen the meeting of Eddie and Mort, however, and knows that Mort was not drunk. In her love for both Myrt and Mort, she tells not only that part of the story but also the fiction that Mort dived after Eddie in a heroic attempt to save his friend. Thus, in her love for this unlikely pair, she both redeems Mort and comforts his wife by recalling Myrt's love for Mort, restoring her self-esteem, and establishing her right to grieve.

Even though *Tuesday and Wednesday* is darkly satiric, the story is in some ways the clearest of Wilson's statements about the success, however flawed, of the human drive for love as a solution to loneliness. Antagonistic though they may be, Myrt and Mort nevertheless love each other in their own way and cling together against their isolation. Mort's love for Myrt, with so little to thrive on, is sad and admirable. Myrt's need for Mort to pierce the shell of her egotism is believable and moving. Victoria May is almost heroic in her lie for Mort. Such unsatisfactory substitutes for love are pitiable, but they transcend the dingy and uninspiring atmosphere in which these characters live.

Lilly's Story

Lilly's Story, the second half of *The Equations of Love*, approaches the equations in a more positive way, although the heroine begins even more unpromisingly than Myrt and Mort. Lilly is an abandoned child, growing up like an alley cat. Never having experienced love, she expects none, and her first equation of love is the lust she excites to acquire food and stockings from men. Running away from the police, she gets a job as a waitress in a small town some distance from Vancouver and finds another equation of love, a man who provides her some temporary security, like "a kennel into which a bitch crawls." When this man leaves, and she finds she is pregnant, she goes to another small town farther into the wilderness and gets a job as a maid.

In this new environment, Lilly knows love for the first time, her love for her baby; and for her baby's sake, she invents a dead husband and behaves with such circumspection that she earns the respect of the couple whom she serves. Respect is a new equation of love. In this wilderness location, she also learns a new identification with nature that she could not have known in the slums of Vancouver. She lets Eleanor grow up in touch with this natural environment. Lilly also admires the pretty home and gentle manners of her employers, and she allows Eleanor, her child, to receive training from Mrs. Butler, determined that Eleanor will have a better life than her own. Eventually, Lilly leaves the Butlers and finds employment as housekeeper in a hospital. She and the Matron become close friends, and Lilly begins to build relationships that are overcoming her circle of self-protection. Eleanor grows into a lady and goes to nursing school, where she meets and marries a young lawyer. It is from this marriage that Lilly learns what love can be and what she has missed, when she sees Eleanor

> come up to her husband with her face raised, and on her face a revealed look that Lilly had never seen on Eleanor's face nor on any face. . . . She had lived for nearly fifty years, and she had never seen this thing before. So this was love, each for each, and she had never known it.

Soon after this, a threat from Lilly's past drives her to Toronto, where she meets a widower and marries him, not with the passion that she has observed in Eleanor, but at least with "the perfect satisfaction which is one equation of love."

Lilly could be another Mrs. Broom (*Hetty Dorval*), but instead of hiding her motherhood and spoiling her child, Lilly drags herself out of that egocentric circle in order to prevent egocentrism in Eleanor, and in so doing, she finds loving relationships that almost transform her. Lilly starts off too badly and is too warped by her orphanhood ever to be totally transformed by love, but at least her story is a triumph of the power of love over egocentrism.

Swamp Angel

Maggie Lloyd, the protagonist of *Swamp Angel*, is triply solitary: Her mother died when she was a baby, her young husband in the war, and her baby and her father shortly thereafter. Maggie, unlike Wilson's other orphaned heroines, is never trapped in egocentrism by her loneliness. She has too much giving in her nature, and makes a second marriage out of compassion. Her story opens when she leaves that mistaken equation of marriage and goes into the wilderness, not to find but to reestablish herself. She finds a job as cook and assistant manager to a fishing lodge owner who has been lamed and can no longer manage alone. His wife, Vera, is the orphan in this story who has been warped and damaged by her loneliness. Vera finds no comfort in the beauty of the wilderness that restores Maggie after her separation. Vera, to the contrary, longs to return to the city from which she came, and instead of building new relationships that might redeem her, she nags at her husband and grows jealous of his admiration for Maggie. She eventually tries to commit suicide but cannot, and the story ends with Maggie trying to think how to break through Vera's egocentrism to help her.

Another pair of "orphans" in this story are Maggie's friends Nell Severance and her daughter Hilda. Although their story constitutes a subplot, in some ways they are more important to the theme than is Vera. Nell is a widow who has had more than her share of excitement and romance. She used to be a juggler on the stage, and she met and married a man she loved deeply. Because of her career and eventful marriage, however, she neglected Hilda to the extent that Hilda has always felt a degree of isolation and alienation from her mother. Nell's loved memento from her past life is a small revolver, the Swamp Angel, which was part of her juggling act. Hilda has always resented the revolver, as it reminds her of her neglect as a child, but she has never told her mother of her feelings: This is her gift of love to her mother. Nell is aware of Hilda's aversion to the gun, although she does not know the reason; one day she boxes it and sends it to Maggie: This is her gift of love to her daughter. Hilda goes away on a vacation, and comes back with new self-knowledge and recognition of her love for Albert Cousins, whom she marries not long before Nell dies. Thus, she builds new relationships to end her sense of solitude. These are very loving relationships, successful resolutions to the problems of isolation.

Swamp Angel makes use of two important symbols that specify more clearly than any of Wilson's earlier books the meanings of wilderness/egotism and orphanhood/love. While in the wilderness, Maggie goes swimming. She feels happy, strong, elemental, and in control of her movements. She can swim wherever she wishes; she is alone and completely independent. She also realizes, however, that this feeling is an illusion: She is not a god. The water is sensual and comforting, but it could drown her as impartially as it now buoys her. She swims back to her boat and returns to the lodge, to the things of civilization and the friends she serves in her job. The other key symbol is the Swamp Angel itself. It is a symbol of Nell's past, and she clings to it until she realizes that it makes Hilda uncomfortable. She gives it to Maggie to discard, reflecting that the symbol is less important than the reality, which cannot be taken away but which grows less important as she grows nearer to death. Like the water in which Maggie swims, the gun symbolizes independence and control, but it also symbolizes egotism. In giving it away, Nell severs herself from the past in order to build a better relationship with her daughter. Unlike Maggie and Nell, Vera clings to her past, cannot find herself in nature, and so cannot build loving relationships with her husband and son. She tries to drown herself in the same lake where Maggie swims and where she throws Nell's gun.

Wilson's books can be summed up as minor masterpieces of style, insightful, witty, believable, and intelligent. They are prevented from being major works by faults in plotting, and they have not had a great influence on literary trends. Nevertheless, they are all readable and entertaining, and the best are compelling. They deserve renewed attention in this age of increased receptivity to literature by and about women.

Carol I. Croxton

Other major works

short fiction: *Mrs. Golightly, and Other Stories*, 1961.

miscellaneous: *Ethel Wilson: Stories, Essays, and Letters*, 1987 (David Stouck, editor).

Bibliography

Klein, Verena. *Mothering Her Self: Mothers and Daughters in Ethel Wilson's Work.* Trier, Germany: WVT, 2006. Klein focuses on the absence of mothers and the impact of this absence on the female protagonists in Wilson's fiction. She argues that Wilson may have used her work to resolve her own experience of being orphaned at a young age.

McAlpine, Mary. *The Other Side of Silence: A Life of Ethel Wilson.* Madeira Park, B.C.: Harbour, 1989.

The first biography, written by a close friend of Wilson. McAlpine recounts the major events of Wilson's life and recreates the milieu of early twentieth century Vancouver, British Columbia, society in which Wilson lived.

McMullan, Lorraine, ed. *The Ethel Wilson Symposium.* Ottawa, Ont.: University of Ottawa Press, 1982. A collection of papers presented at a conference held in 1981 at the University of Ottawa in Canada. McMullan's introduction is especially useful.

McPherson, Hugo. "Fiction: 1940-1960." In *Literary History of Canada: Canadian Literature in English*, edited by Carl Frederick Klinck. 2d ed. Vol. 2. Toronto, Ont.: University of Toronto Press, 1976. Wilson's fiction is discussed in the context of a "search for identity" that infused Canadian literature's development in the mid-twentieth century. McPherson notes a contrary individuality in Wilson's writing that transcends her failure at times to reconcile her creative impulses as both "artist and sibyl."

Mitchell, Beverley. "Ethel Wilson." In *Canadian Writers and Their Works: Fiction Series*, edited by Robert Lecker, Jack David, and Ellen Quigley. Vol. 6. Toronto, Ont.: ECW Press, 1985. Wilson's life and complete works are thoroughly examined. An exhaustive bibliography follows Mitchell's straightforward, readable analysis, making this study a must for Wilson readers.

Pacey, Desmond. *Ethel Wilson.* New York: Twayne, 1967. This thorough, readable overview of Wilson's long and short fiction is not deeply analytical, but it does consider Wilson's lightly ironic vision and her valuable contribution to Canadian literature despite her relatively short publishing history. Despite its age, the book still contains useful insights. Includes a selected bibliography and an index.

Stouck, David. *Ethel Wilson: A Critical Biography.* Toronto, Ont.: University of Toronto Press, 2003. A critical biography, in which Stouck recounts the events of Wilson's life and analyzes her works. He demonstrates how her writing is characterized by ethical and epistemological uncertainties, anticipates the work of later Canadian writers, and evokes the power of the landscape.

Woodcock, George. "Innocence and Solitude: The Fictions of Ethel Wilson." In *Modern Times.* Vol. 3. in *The Canadian Novel*, edited by John Moss. Toronto, Ont.: NC Press, 1982. Woodcock discusses Wilson's originality and vision as they are expressed in her novels and novellas.

_______. "On Ethel Wilson." In *The World of Canadian Writing: Critiques and Recollections.* Vancouver, B.C.: Douglas and McIntyre, 1980. Slightly revised since its 1974 publication, this reflective personal essay enumerates the strengths of Wilson's personality and her unique works. This volume contains an index of the names of authors mentioned or treated in the book.

JEANETTE WINTERSON

Born: Manchester, England; August 27, 1959

Principal long fiction

Boating for Beginners, 1985
Oranges Are Not the Only Fruit, 1985
The Passion, 1987
Sexing the Cherry, 1989
Written on the Body, 1993
Art and Lies: A Piece for Three Voices and a Bawd, 1994
Gut Symmetries, 1997
The PowerBook, 2000
Lighthousekeeping, 2004
Weight: The Myth of Atlas and Hercules, 2005
The Stone Gods, 2007

Other literary forms

Jeanette Winterson has dramatized several of her own books, most notably *Oranges Are Not the Only Fruit* (1990) for British television. She has written original radio drama and worked on a documentary, *Great Moments in Aviation* (1994), also for British television. She has written short stories, essays, and columns for *The Guardian* and *The Times*. One of her earlier books was a comic book, and she has published several works of children's fiction, including *The King of Capri* (2003) and *Tanglewreck* (2006).

ACHIEVEMENTS

Jeanette Winterson has been in the public eye from the time her first novel won the Whitbread Prize. She was named by *Granta* magazine one of the twenty best young British writers. Other prizes include the Prix d'Argent at the Cannes Film Festival, the Prix Italia, and the BAFTA Best Drama Award for her television adaptation of *Oranges Are Not the Only Fruit*. She won the John Llewellyn Rhys Memorial Prize for *The Passion* and the E. M. Forster Award from the American Academy of Arts and Letters for *Sexing the Cherry*. In 2006, she was awarded the Order of the British Empire (OBE) for services to literature. Her books have been translated into more than one dozen languages.

BIOGRAPHY

Jeanette Winterson was born in 1959 in Manchester, in the northwest of England, and adopted by a childless Pentecostal couple from Accrington, a mill town just outside Manchester. She was raised under strict religious principles and shaped for a career as a missionary. By the age of eight, she was preaching at evangelist tent meetings held by the family's small chapel, and was making converts. Her reading material at home was limited to the Bible and Sir Thomas Malory's *Le Morte d'Arthur* (1485), a strange combination from which she developed a strong feeling for literary style.

At the age of fifteen, Winterson had a lesbian relationship with one of her converts that was strongly denounced by the church. At the age of sixteen, she decided to leave home and took a number of part-time jobs to pay for the academic high school where she was enrolled. When she was eighteen years old, she enrolled at St. Catherine's College, Oxford University, to major in English. She worked for one year at a mental hospital to pay tuition.

After graduation in 1981, Winterson worked in various theaters and began writing what would become her first novel, *Oranges Are Not the Only Fruit*. She finished the novel at the young age of twenty-three years. After it was published in 1985, she began working as an assistant editor for Pandora Press (her early publisher). She began a romantic relationship with Pat Kavanagh, her literary agent. In 1987, Winterson published her second novel, *The Passion*. Its successful reception by readers and critics inspired her to become a full-time writer. The next year she entered a long-term relationship with Peggy Reynolds, an academic and a radio broadcaster. The following year, Winterson published *Sexing the Cherry*.

In 1990, Winterson adapted *Oranges Are Not the Only Fruit* for television in a highly acclaimed dramatization. Her work was embraced in the American market with *Written on the Body* in 1993, ensuring a worldwide readership. Honors and prizes followed, and she became a regular columnist, essayist, writer of children's fiction, and broadcaster. She also bought a delicatessen in central London and a house in Gloucestershire.

ANALYSIS

Jeanette Winterson's novels are at the cusp of modernism, postmodernism, and Magical Realism. Her sheer verbal skills, so evident in her fiction, led to the novels' initial popularity. The novels also were popular because they filled the desire in the mid-1980's for a new lesbian narrative subgenre. In some ways, Winterson steered the postfeminist novel into uncharted territories, especially in terms of narrative. She made gender, along with plot, history, and even narrator, sources of uncertainty. The one certainty in her novels is the story of the truth of love. Other consistent themes include myth and the fairy tale.

Oranges Are Not the Only Fruit, an immediate popular success, is an autobiographical story of lesbian sexuality. The heroine, simply called Jeanette (and later Jess), relates her experiences with a narrow-minded religious sect. With this novel, Winterson joined a long line of writers who were liberated from narrow religious upbringings. (D. H. Lawrence is perhaps the most obvious and most acknowledged of these writers.)

Winterson inherited far more from her religious upbringing than she rejected. She admitted that her readings as a child, narrow and limited as they were, led to her love of words and her sense of style. She became an evangelist, not for religion but for the books themselves, much like the "religion of literature" that the poet Matthew Arnold sought to construct out of the ruins of his childhood faith. Winterson has said that literature, and specifically postmodernist literature, has to redefine the boundaries of truth in terms of love and do so beyond the norms of common sense. As in Lawrence, that love has to be defined in terms of sexuality and passion.

Jeanette Winterson. (Peter Peitsch/Courtesy, Harcourt Books)

Winterson's next two novels, *The Passion* and *Sexing the Cherry*, play with history, with *The Passion* set in the Napoleonic era. Her fourth novel, *Written on the Body*, is a more somber exploration of what became her typical plot structure, the love triangle of a married couple and a single woman, usually lesbian. Love is challenged by disease, as the heroine is diagnosed with cancer. Love and disease break down boundaries, demanding new ones be constructed. The novel has no plot line and the narrator is not clearly gendered. *Art and Lies* and *Gut Symmetries* are similarly constructed.

After publishing the novels *The Power Book* and *Lighthousekeeping*, Winterson turned to children's science fiction. By invitation of a small Scottish press, she turned to pure myth in the novel *Weight*, which is a retelling of the story of Atlas and Hercules. A growing concern with ecological issues led to the novel *The Stone Gods*, set partly in space in the science fiction format and partly on Easter Island, which suffered desertification at the hands of humans.

SEXING THE CHERRY

Sexing the Cherry is an experiment in postmodern fiction, interweaving strands of history, myth, fairy tale, and Magical Realism. The main plot concerns an orphan named Jordan and his adoptive mother, a large Rabelaisian earth-mother type of woman who lives by the river Thames in London. The time is the seventeenth century, and London is in the throes of civil war. Winterson shows herself with this novel to be deeply reactionary in her politics, siding with King Charles against the Puritans. The tale's search, as it develops, is both for new fruit for Jordan and for love and identity, which includes gender identity, for his mother. A banana comes to symbolize the phallus, and Jordan's mother literally bites off a penis as one would bite off part of a banana. The London portrayed is gross, sordid, and decaying, yet the mythic elements, the search for Fortunata the dancer in particular, prioritize the spiritual. The novel is a bold experiment, and it is left to readers to piece together the fragments.

THE POWER BOOK

Winterson considers *The Power Book* the last of a seven-novel cycle of long fiction. The work is another conscious effort to rewrite the English novel on postmodern terms, this time using the metaphor of the computer and, as one of its loci, cyberspace. In *The Power Book*, word processors are shown to erase what one has written and rewrite what one has erased. Networks are shown to help one find parallel information to the story one is working on, but the information comes in fragments. Nothing is whole or finished.

This process of writing becomes a metaphor for individual lives. Winterson's life is consciously "queer," a term she prefers to lesbian. Queer suggests strange, not straightforward, and it also suggests the ambiguity of the phallus. The novel's opening motif is the tulip, which is used as a phallus for the female body to become male. The consciousness of the presence or absence of the phallus in terms of connection and identity runs throughout the book. The novel's subtexts include the story of gender change and ambiguity in Virginia Woolf's *Orlando: A Biography* (1928). The story's themes are the lifelong search for the grand passion, whether for love or tulips, and how humans keep reinventing themselves to find that grand passion; in finding it, one finds one's true identity.

The main plot, such as it is, centers on two lesbian lovers (one of them married) as they meet in Paris and then continue to Capri. In the second half of the book, Winterson introduces autobiographical fragments from *Oranges Are Not the Only Fruit*. A mother tells her adopted orphan daughter that treasure exists out there in the world, if only one searches for it and even if one has to begin that search in muck and filth. This determination to find the treasure through layers of time and meaning, symbolized by the Thames and London archaeology (as in *Sexing the Cherry*), leads to the realization that the treasure lies within.

Lighthousekeeping

By Winterson's own admission, *Lighthousekeeping* uses the remnants of her autobiography that are not resolved in *Oranges Are Not the Only Fruit*. Silver, the narrator of *Lighthousekeeping*, is an illegitimate orphan girl who finds a home in the Cape Wrath lighthouse in the far north of Scotland, where several different seas meet, setting up dangerous currents. The lighthouse keeper, the blind man Pew, teaches her to tell stories, and local history is constructed as narrative. The novel interweaves several stories toward a personal resolution for Silver as she seeks her identity.

The main story weaves around Babel Dark, a Victorian clergyman who was a minister in the local village of Salts and who knew Charles Darwin and the writer Robert Louis Stevenson. Dark lives a double life and is portrayed as the inspiration for Stevenson's classic novel *The Strange Case of Dr. Jekyll and Mr. Hyde* (1886), which forms one of the novel's subtexts. Dark's own life reverses the Jekyll and Hyde scenario, in that the respectable minister suppresses the former fashionable son of a Bristol merchant who had a passionate affair with Molly, a shop assistant. Dark has escaped the affair by retreating to the north of Scotland and living almost a dead man's life, suppressing all emotion. However, he kept two diaries, one respectable and the other wild and passionate, revealing his inner turmoil. Molly reappears twice to offer Dark a second chance, but he refuses, compromising by going to live with her in Bristol for two months under the alias Lux (or light). In the end, he commits suicide. One of Pew's ancestors, also a lighthouse keeper, recounts Dark's confession.

Dark represents some of the emotional suppression of Winterson's own upbringing. In the other main story, Silver has to find her own identity, especially when the lighthouse is automated and Pew and she are out of a job. She goes to Bristol to seek out some of Dark's roots, then undergoes a number of encounters, some of which seem quite autobiographical. She takes a trip to Capri, where she steals a parrot because the parrot can say "Silver," representing the one thing that knows her name and, therefore, her. Eventually, she has a lover and then resolves to return to the lighthouse, say farewell, and realize the strength of love and the choice for passion which must be made to continue living.

David Barratt

Other major works

SHORT FICTION: *The World and Other Places*, 1998.

PLAY: *The Power Book*, pr. 2002 (based on her novel).

TELEPLAYS: *Oranges Are Not the Only Fruit*, 1990 (based on her novel); *Great Moments in Aviation* (1994).

RADIO PLAYS: *Static*, 1988; *Text Message*, 2001.

NONFICTION: *Art Objects: Essays on Ecstasy and Effrontery*, 1995.

CHILDREN'S LITERATURE: *The King of Capri*, 2003; *Tanglewreck*, 2006.

EDITED TEXT: *Passion Fruit: Romantic Fiction with a Twist*, 1986.

Bibliography

Andermahr, Sonya. *Jeanette Winterson*. New York: Palgrave Macmillan, 2008. Late biography of Winterson by a scholar of her work. Places her fiction in historical, critical, and theoretical context and analyzes her experimentation with technique and form.

_______, ed. *Jeanette Winterson: A Contemporary Critical Guide*. Harrisburg, Pa.: Continuum International, 2007. Collection of scholarly essays covering the key themes and styles in Winterson's fiction.

Lopez, Gemma. *Seductions in Narrative: Subjectivity and Desire in the Works of Angela Carter and Jeanette Winterson*. Youngstown, N.Y.: Cambria Press, 2007. Scholarly treatise examining through a poststructuralist lens the themes of desire and self-searching in the novels of Winterson and Angela Carter.

Makinen, Merja. *The Novels of Jeanette Winterson*. New York: Palgrave Macmillan, 2005. Traces the reception to Winterson's novels and places them in the context of modern literary debate. Part of the Readers' Guide to Essential Criticism series.

Onega, Susana. *Jeanette Winterson*. New York: Manchester University Press, 2006. Examines the forms, themes, and ideologies of Winterson's novels within the context of the modern British novel. The first full-length study of Winterson's complete oeuvre.

Pressler, Christopher. *So Far So Linear: Responses to the Work of Jeanette Winterson*. Nottingham, England: Paupers' Press, 1997. Brief but comprehensive survey of modern critical responses and analyses of Winterson's works through 1996.

Reynolds, Margaret, and Jonathan Noakes. *Jeanette Winterson: The Essential Guide*. New York: Vintage Press, 2003. Series of interviews with Winterson in which she discusses four of her most popular novels. Includes a biography, questions for discussion, suggestions for further reading, extracts from reviews, a bibliography, and a glossary of literary terms.

P. G. WODEHOUSE

Born: Guildford, Surrey, England; October 15, 1881
Died: Southampton, Long Island, New York; February 14, 1975
Also known as: Pelham Grenville Wodehouse

Principal long fiction

The Pothunters, 1902
A Prefect's Uncle, 1903
The Gold Bat, 1904
The Head of Kay's, 1905
Love Among the Chickens, 1906
Not George Washington, 1907 (with Herbert Westbrook)
The White Feather, 1907
Mike: A Public School Story, 1909 (also known as *Enter Psmith*, *Mike at Wrykyn*, and *Mike and Psmith*)
The Swoop: How Clarence Saved England, 1909
A Gentleman of Leisure, 1910 (also known as *The Intrusion of Jimmy*)
Psmith in the City: A Sequel to "Mike," 1910
The Prince and Betty, 1912
The Little Nugget, 1913
Psmith Journalist, 1915 (revision of *The Prince and Betty*)
Something Fresh, 1915 (also known as *Something New*)
Uneasy Money, 1916
Piccadilly Jim, 1917
A Damsel in Distress, 1919
Their Mutual Child, 1919 (also known as *The Coming of Bill*)
The Little Warrior, 1920 (also known as *Jill the Reckless*)
Indiscretions of Archie, 1921
The Adventures of Sally, 1922 (also known as *Mostly Sally*)
The Girl on the Boat, 1922 (also known as *Three Men and a Maid*)
Leave It to Psmith, 1923
The Inimitable Jeeves, 1923 (also known as *Jeeves*)
Bill the Conqueror: His Invasion of England in the Springtime, 1924

Sam the Sudden, 1925 (also known as *Sam in the Suburbs*)
The Small Bachelor, 1927
Money for Nothing, 1928
Summer Lightning, 1929 (also known as *Fish Preferred and Fish Deferred*)
Very Good, Jeeves, 1930
Big Money, 1931
If I Were You, 1931
Doctor Sally, 1932
Hot Water, 1932
Heavy Weather, 1933
Right Ho, Jeeves, 1934 (also known as *Brinkley Manor: A Novel About Jeeves*)
Thank You, Jeeves, 1934
The Luck of the Bodkins, 1935
Trouble down at Tudsleigh, 1935
Laughing Gas, 1936
Summer Moonshine, 1937
The Code of the Woosters, 1938
Uncle Fred in the Springtime, 1939
Quick Service, 1940
Money in the Bank, 1942
Joy in the Morning, 1946
Full Moon, 1947
Spring Fever, 1948
Uncle Dynamite, 1948
The Mating Season, 1949
The Old Reliable, 1951
Barmy in Wonderland, 1952 (also known as *Angel Cake*)
Pigs Have Wings, 1952
Ring for Jeeves, 1953 (also known as *The Return of Jeeves*)
Jeeves and the Feudal Spirit, 1954 (also known as *Bertie Wooster Sees It Through*)
French Leave, 1956
Something Fishy, 1957 (also known as *The Butler Did It*)
Cocktail Time, 1958
Jeeves in the Offing, 1960 (also known as *How Right You Are, Jeeves*)
Ice in the Bedroom, 1961
Service with a Smile, 1961
Stiff Upper Lip, Jeeves, 1963
Biffen's Millions, 1964 (also known as *Frozen Assets*)
Galahad at Blandings, 1965 (also known as *The Brinkmanship of Galahad Threepwood: A Blandings Castle Novel*)
Company for Henry, 1967 (also known as *The Purloined Paperweight*)
Do Butlers Burgle Banks?, 1968
A Pelican at Blandings, 1969 (also known as *No Nudes Is Good Nudes*)
The Girl in Blue, 1970
Jeeves and the Tie That Binds, 1971 (also known as *Much Obliged, Jeeves*)
Pearls, Girls, and Monty Bodkin, 1972 (also known as *The Plot That Thickened*)
Bachelors Anonymous, 1973
The Cat-Nappers: A Jeeves and Bertie Story, 1974 (also known as *Aunts Aren't Gentlemen*)
Sunset at Blandings, 1977

Other literary forms

In addition to writing more than ninety novels, P. G. Wodehouse (WOOD-hows) wrote hundreds of short stories, some eighteen plays (of which ten were published), the lyrics for thirty-three theatrical musicals, and a vast, uncollected body of essays, reviews, poems, and sketches. So much of Wodehouse's early work has been lost that it is impossible to measure his total literary output, and collections of his stories published under titles such as "Uncollected Wodehouse" are likely to appear with some frequency for the next twenty years. He also wrote two comic autobiographies, *Performing Flea: A Self-Portrait in Letters* (1953; revised as *Author! Author!*, 1962) and *America, I Like You* (1956; revised as *Over Seventy: An Autobiography with Digressions*, 1957).

Achievements

P. G. Wodehouse has always been regarded as a "popular" writer. The designation is just. "Every schoolboy," wrote Ogden Nash, "knows that no one can hold a candle to P. G. Wodehouse." His novels and short stories were among the best-selling works of their generation, but it should be remembered that Wodehouse's appeal transcended his popular audience. Many of the major writers of the twentieth century have professed a deep admiration for the art of "Plum," as Wodehouse was known to his friends and family. T. S. Eliot, W. H. Auden, Bertrand Russell—all were fanatic enthusiasts of Wodehouse. Hilaire Belloc said that Wodehouse was the greatest writer of the twentieth century, and Evelyn Waugh offered the following tribute to his genius: "Mr. Wodehouse's idyllic world can never stale. He will continue to release future generations from captivity that may be more irksome than our own." It is unfortunately true that critics and readers who expect high seriousness from their literary pleasures will never quite approve of one who makes a lighthearted mockery of most of England's and America's most sacred cows. F. R. Leavis, the celebrated English scholar, pointed to the awarding of an honorary doctorate to Wodehouse as proof of declining literary standards. Other critics have been even more emphatic in their deprecation of Wodehouse's lack of seriousness. For sheer enjoyment, however, or what Dr. Johnson called "innocent recreation," no one can touch P. G. Wodehouse.

Biography

Pelham Grenville Wodehouse was born in Guildford, Surrey, on October 15, 1881, the third of four sons born to Henry Ernest and Eleanor Deane Wodehouse. Wodehouse's father was a member of the English civil service and spent most of his working years in Hong Kong; indeed, it was a mere chance that Wodehouse was not born in Hong Kong. Whether it was miscalculation or the event was premature, his birth occurred during one of his mother's rare and rather brief visits to England.

Wodehouse was reared away from his parents; they were, he often remarked, like distant aunts and uncles rather than parents. Wodehouse entered Dulwich College at the age of twelve and remained there for the next six years. The school was not prominent in the sense that Harrow and Eton were prominent; it was simply a good middle-class school. The headmaster was the most impressive figure, and he may have served as the model for Wooster's nemesis, the Reverend Aubrey Upjohn. The headmaster was not impressed with his student; he once wrote to Wodehouse's parents: "He has the most distorted ideas about wit and humour. . . . One is obliged to like him in spite of his vagaries." The vagaries, apart from the student's drawing stick figures in his classical texts, are unrecorded. In those final years at Dulwich, Wodehouse found his vocation. He was appointed editor of the school paper and sold his first story to a boys' weekly, *The Public School Magazine*. The story won first prize for fiction in that year.

Following graduation in 1900, Wodehouse went to work for the London branch of the Hong Kong and Shanghai Bank. His work there was not a complete disaster for the banking industry, but very nearly so. Wodehouse was no good at checks and balances and served only as an unpleasant distraction for those who were. At night, he continued to write fiction and reviews or plays and was given a position at the newspaper *The Globe* in 1902, the year the first of his many novels was published. The respected humor magazine *Punch* accepted an article from him the next year, and a second novel was also published in 1903. From that time, Wodehouse averaged more than a novel, several short stories, and either a play or musical a year.

In 1914, Wodehouse married Ethel Rowley, a widow with one child. The marriage was a happy one, and the author frequently expressed his gratitude to his wife for the support she gave to his work. For the Wodehouse reader, however, the following year had a much greater significance: *Something New*, the first of the Blandings novels, was published. A few years later, the short-story collection *My Man Jeeves* (1919) appeared, the first of the Jeeves and Wooster saga.

Novels and stories appeared with an unfailing regularity, and in the next two decades, Wodehouse became an acknowledged master. In 1939, Oxford paid tribute to his greatness by conferring on him the honorary doctorate of letters (D.Litt.). The doctorate meant that Jeeves, Wooster, Emsworth, and the rest were accepted as part of the heritage of English literature. *The Times* of London supported the Oxford gesture, noting that the praise given to Wodehouse the stylist was especially apt: "Style goes a long way in Oxford; indeed the purity of Mr. Wodehouse's style was singled out for particular praise in the Public Orator's happy Horatian summing up of Mr. Wodehouse's qualities and achievements."

Wodehouse and his wife had lived in France throughout much of the 1930's, and though war with Germany was believed imminent, Wodehouse returned to France after he received the doctorate at Oxford. In 1940, he was taken prisoner by the Germans. In various prison camps, he made a series of broadcasts over German radio that were interpreted as a form of collaboration with the enemy. Wodehouse was innocent of all the charges, but it was perhaps his innocence, the vital ingredient in most of his heroes, that almost undid him. The closest Wodehouse came to collaboration was his remark to the effect that he was not unhappy in prison, for he was able to continue his work. One scholar has called that broadcast "clearly indiscreet," but those who have read the Wodehouse letters know that he scarcely thought about anything else aside from his work.

After his release, Wodehouse eventually returned to the United States, where he took permanent residence; he became an American citizen in 1955. In 1973 he was knighted, and he died in 1975 at the age of ninety-four.

P. G. Wodehouse. (Courtesy D.C. Public Library)

Analysis

Few of P. G. Wodehouse's novels are ever far from the school environment, for the plots of the later Jeeves and Blandings series of novels frequently derive from the desire of one schoolmate, usually Bertie Wooster, to help another. The early school novels, however, represent a distinct type within the body of Wodehouse's fiction.

The school novels

Perhaps, as one scholar has observed, these eight school novels are no more than "bibliographical curiosities," in that only the most ardent fan of Wodehouse would be led to read them after the later work had been written. Still, the works are different in tone and theme. The novels are set at Wrykyn College, which seems to closely resemble Dulwich, the author's alma mater. The emphasis is on sports, and this emphasis gives a serious tone to the work. Boys are measured largely by their athletic skills. One might suggest that the ever-present sports motif was a symbol of the particular virtues of youth: comradeship, loyalty, and perseverance. Enlarging on these virtues, Wodehouse was following what was almost a cliché in the boy's fiction of the time. The cliché, however, was one particularly congenial to the author, who once noted that he would never be able to write his autobiography, for he had not had one of the essentials in the background of an autobiographer—"a hell of a time at his public school."

Wodehouse loved Dulwich College, and the eight school novels are a record of his affection. The schoolmasters are a decent group, the boys, with few exceptions, are generous and loyal, and the setting of the college is one of great beauty. The distinctive element in the novels is the happiness that pervades them, and the reader need only remember George Orwell's, Graham Greene's, and Evelyn Waugh's accounts of their own school days to notice the sharp difference between Wodehouse and many of his contemporaries. The only curiosity about the novels is not the absence of horror and malice, but that no one in the school novels seems to have learned anything at Wrykyn. It should also be remembered that many of Wodehouse's most celebrated idiots are graduates of Oxford and Cambridge.

Blandings novels

Wodehouse once said of his work: "I believe there are two ways of writing novels. One is mine, making a sort of musical comedy without music and ignoring life altogether." The Blandings series of novels is perhaps the best example of the author's determined resistance to "real life." These twenty-odd novels are centered on the beautiful estate of Lord Emsworth, who serves as unwilling host to almost everyone who goes in and out of his ancestral home. Lord Emsworth is old and absent-minded, and his affections are limited to his younger brother Galahad, his roses, and his pig, the Empress of Blandings. This pig, as Emsworth remarks several times in each of the novels, has won the silver prize for being the fattest in Shropshire County. Only Galahad can really appreciate the high distinction that has been conferred on the Empress, and one feels that even he is not very serious about the pig. The Empress, however, is the catalyst for very nearly all of the actions that take place in the novels. She is stolen, which makes it imperative to effect a rescue; she is painted an outrageous color and introduced into strange bedrooms to make the recipients of such favors "more spiritual" in their outlook; and, on one occasion, her portrait is done at the behest of Lord Emsworth.

This last episode in the life of the Empress occurs in one of the best of the Blandings novels and is a fair measure of the formula used by Wodehouse in the series. *Full Moon*, in which the portrait is commissioned, has all of the characteristics of the Blandings novels. Emsworth has the insane idea that the pig's portrait should be done by an eminent painter, but they have all turned down his request. While this action is debated, Lady Constance, Emsworth's sister, has come to the castle with a young lady in tow. Her intent is to keep the young woman away from the man to whom she has become foolishly engaged, foolishly because the fellow does not have any money, which is the essential requisite for a good marriage in the mind of Lady Constance. Galahad arranges to have the young man invited to the castle on the pretext that he is Edwin Landseer, celebrated painter of animal pictures, including "Pig at Bey." Galahad's ruse works for a while, but the young man's painting is rejected by Emsworth, who complains that the painting makes the Empress look as if she had a hangover. The young man is ejected from Blandings but soon returns, wearing a beard resembling an Assyrian monarch. He makes a tragic mistake when he gives a love note to one of Emsworth's other sisters, thinking that she is a cook. He is again thrown out. By the novel's end, however, he has successfully won the hand of his beloved, and the sisters are all leaving the estate. Galahad has once more succeeded in spreading "sweetness and light" in all directions, except that of his usually irate sisters.

There are few variations in the Blandings series: At least one and sometimes as many as three courtships are repaired; the pig is saved from whatever has threatened it; the sisters have been thwarted, usually in about five ways, by Galahad; and Lord Emsworth has the prospect of peace and quiet in front of him at the novel's end. Still, Emsworth, Galahad, the sisters, and a host of only slightly less important or interesting characters are among the most brilliant comic figures in the whole of English literature. In writing the Blandings novels, Wodehouse followed his own precept: "The absolute cast-iron rule, I'm sure, in writing a story is to introduce *all* your characters as early as possible—especially if they are going to play important parts later." His other favorite maxim—that a novel should contain no more than one "big" character—is seldom observed in the Blandings series. Each of the characters has his or her own element of fascination, and each is slightly crazy in one way or another. As absurd and funny as is Lord Emsworth's vanity about his pig, it is only a little more so than his sisters' vanity about their social position and wealth. If the formula for this series does not vary, neither does the uniform excellence of all the novels in the series.

Jeeves and Wooster novels

More than a dozen novels use Jeeves and Bertie Wooster as the main characters. These novels have commonly been regarded as Wodehouse's "crowning achievement," but the author once noted that the idea of the latent greatness of Jeeves came to him very slowly. In his first appearance in a short story, Jeeves barely says more than "Very good, Sir." Jeeves is the manservant to Bertie Wooster, who is preyed upon by aunts, friends, and women who wish to help him improve his mind as a prerequisite of marriage with him. Wooster has been dismissed as silly and very stupid. Compared to Jeeves, perhaps he is both, but he is also extremely generous with both his money and time, and it is his unfailing willingness to help others that invariably places him in the precarious situation that is the main plot. Wooster is an Oxford graduate, but detective novels are his most demanding reading. He never uses a word of more than two syllables without wondering whether he is using the word properly. Wooster is the "big" character in the Jeeves series, and such a character, according to Wodehouse, is worth "two of any other kind."

The marriage motif is very much a part of the Wooster and Jeeves saga, but frequently the central issue of this series is helping Bertie keep away from the wrong woman. It is not quite accurate to describe him as one of "nature's bachelors," for he has been engaged to nearly a score of females and is threatened with marriage in nearly every one of the novels in the series. Some of these women are insipid and poetic, others are coarse and athletic; the worst are intellectual women who want to improve his mind. He is assigned books to read that he finds boring and incomprehensible, told never to laugh aloud, and threatened, after marriage, with having his membership in the Drones Club revoked. Bertie is quite content with the state of his mind and soul. At the threat of marriage and all the other threats that the novels present, Jeeves comes to the rescue. In spite of Bertie's chronic need of Jeeves's aid, he is ostensibly the main character in the novels and one of Wodehouse's most brilliant creations. It is through the eyes of Bertie that the reader observes and passes judgment on what is taking place in the novel. Such a process was an enormous technical difficulty for his creator: Wooster must be stupid and generous in order for the plot to develop, but not so stupid that the reader casts him off.

The character of Jeeves, perfect as it is, is one of the most traditional aspects of Wodehouse's craft, for the wise servant of a stupid master is a hoary cliché. Jeeves has never been to Oxford, and he has no aristocratic blood flowing in his veins to spur him into action. His central motive for rescuing Bertie and the legions of others who come to him for counsel is a manifestation of what is called in this series of novels "the feudal spirit." Though not a university man, Jeeves knows French, Latin, and the whole of English literature. He quotes freely from the Shakespearean tragedies, and even has at his disposal a host of obscure lines from obscure poets in Latin and English. He is not a gloomy person, but Benedictus de Spinoza is his favorite author. He is well acquainted with psychology, and his rescue of Bertie or others in trouble frequently derives from his knowledge of the "psychology" of the individuals in question. He is moved by the feudal spirit, but he is tipped in a handsome way by his employer for services rendered, and he accepts the just praises of all whom he serves.

The series is also distinguished by a host of lesser figures who threaten to jostle Bertie out of his role as the main character. Gussie Fink-Nottle is an old schoolmate of Bertie, and he is engaged to a particularly insipid woman, Madelaine Basset, a romantic intellectual. She has a poetic phrase for everything, and she drives Bertie and all who know her crazy merely by opening her mouth. Madelaine is one of Bertie's former girlfriends, and she imagines that Bertie is still in love with her. The hero's duty is to see that the pending nuptials between Gussie and Madelaine take place, but Gussie, who is even less intelligent than Bertie, keeps fouling things up. Bertie goes at once to his aid, but nothing works until Jeeves puts his brain to the trial.

Jeeves never fails in his destined role as guardian angel to Wooster, but the plots frequently have an additional twist. Jeeves, though not omniscient as a character, has recourse to a body of information that none of the others shares. As a butler and member of a London club for butlers, he has access to a private collection of anecdotes supplied by other butlers about their masters. It is a point of honor for a manservant to supply all vital information about his employer—tastes, eccentricities, and even weaknesses—so that others will be well advised before taking employment with the same person. The collection has something about almost every rich male in England, and when affairs take on a desperate note, Jeeves is dispatched to London to find out something about the adversary that might serve as blackmail. Thus, one of the silliest of Wodehouse's creations, a proto-Fascist named Spode who is inclined to bully everyone and especially Wooster, is disarmed when it is discovered that he designs ladies' underwear. As Wooster is being threatened with decapitation by Spode, he mentions the name of Spode's company, Eulalie Soeurs, and the man is silent and servile, though it is only at the very end and with the bribe of a trip around the world that Jeeves tells Wooster the meaning of that magic phrase.

The Jeeves novels, then, have at least three plots running through them, and it is in his scrupulous concern for the development of the plot that the author exhibits one of his greatest talents. The key to Wodehouse's concerns for the logic and probability of his plots derives, perhaps, from his lifelong interest in detective novels; Wodehouse frequently avowed that they were his favorite kind of reading. The plots of the great Wodehouse comedies develop like that of a superb mystery: There is not an extraneous word or action in them.

Psmith novels

For most Wodehouse readers, the Blandings and Jeeves series of novels represent the highest level of Wodehouse's art, but there are many other novels that do not fit into either category. In 1906, Wodehouse published *Love Among the Chickens*, which has in it the first of Wodehouse's several "nonheroes," Ukridge. Ukridge has almost no attractive qualities. He does not work; rather, he lives by his wits and is able to sponge off his friends and from many who scarcely know him. Another character who figures prominently in several novels is Psmith. The name is pronounced "Smith," and its owner freely admits that he added the *P* to distinguish himself from the vast number of Smiths. The name is one mark of the young man's condescending arrogance, but he is helpful toward all who seek his assistance. A Psmith novel usually ends with the marriage of a friend or simply a bit of adventure for the central figure. Psmith does not hold a regular job, and like many of the other young male protagonists in Wodehouse novels, he seems to be a textbook study in the antiwork ethic. The heroes in the Psmith series, like the central figure himself, are not ignorant or stupid men, but the novelist's emphasis is on their old school ties and on physical excellence. They are, as one critic noted, "strong, healthy animals." They are good at sports and they triumph over poets and other intellectual types. On occasion, they may drink heavily, but they make up for an infrequent binge by an excess of exercise.

Evelyn Waugh once suggested that the clue to Wodehouse's great success was the fact that he was unaware of the doctrine of original sin. In the Wodehouse novel, virtue is inevitably triumphant, and even vice is seldom punished with anything that might be called severity. In Wodehouse's catalog of bad sorts, one group alone stands out: intellectual snobs. In his frequent descriptions of such types, Wodehouse may have consciously been responding to the disdain with which intellectuals have usually treated his work; in turn, the author had almost no sympathy for the group that he often described as "eggheads." Whatever may have been his motivation, the athletes and the innocents invariably triumph over those who carry on about their own minds or some esoteric art form. It is therefore hard to agree with critics such as George Orwell who find elements of snobbery in the Wodehouse novels. It is true that the creator of Blandings Castle loved big houses and grand vistas, but the aristocrats are too obviously flawed in intellect or temper for any to assume Wodehouse was on their side. It may be, however, that Wodehouse was an inverse snob in his treatment of intellectuals, both male and female. None of them succeeds in his fiction.

There is nothing like a consensus over the source or qualities of Wodehouse's greatness as a writer. Scholars have traced Wooster and Jeeves back through English literature to authors such as Ben Jonson, but source studies do not account for Wodehouse's genius. He has been called the laureate of the Edwardian age, but there is little resemblance between the Edwardian world and that of P. G. Wodehouse. For most readers, the triumph of a Wodehouse novel is in its artistry of presentation. All the aspects of fiction—good story, effective characters, and dialogue that is often brilliant—are present. Wodehouse once summed up his career as well as anyone ever has: "When in due course Charon ferries me across the Styx and everyone is telling everyone else what a rotten writer I was, I hope at least one voice will be heard piping up: 'But he did take trouble.'" Wodehouse did indeed take trouble with his work, but given the rich abundance of that work and the incredible smoothness of each volume, the reader would never know.

John R. Griffin

Other major works

Short fiction: *Tales of St. Austin's*, 1903; *The Man Upstairs, and Other Stories*, 1914; *The Man with Two Left Feet, and Other Stories*, 1917; *My Man Jeeves*, 1919; *The Clicking of Cuthbert*, 1922 (also known as *Golf Without Tears*); *Ukridge*, 1924 (also known as *He Rather Enjoyed It*); *Carry on, Jeeves!*, 1925; *The Heart of a Goof*, 1926 (also known as *Divots*); *Meet Mr. Mulliner*, 1927; *Mr. Mulliner Speaking*, 1929; *Jeeves Omnibus*, 1931 (revised as *The World of Jeeves*, 1967); *Mulliner Nights*, 1933; *Blandings Castle and Elsewhere*,

1935 (also known as *Blandings Castle*); *Mulliner Omnibus*, 1935 (revised as *The World of Mr. Mulliner*, 1972); *Young Men in Spats*, 1936; *Lord Emsworth and Others*, 1937 (also known as *The Crime Wave at Blandings*); *Dudley Is Back to Normal*, 1940; *Eggs, Beans, and Crumpets*, 1940; *Nothing Serious*, 1950; *Selected Stories*, 1958; *A Few Quick Ones*, 1959; *Plum Pie*, 1966; *The Golf Omnibus: Thirty-one Golfing Short Stories*, 1973; *The World of Psmith*, 1974.

PLAYS: *A Gentleman of Leisure*, pr. 1911 (with John Stapleton); *Oh, Lady! Lady!*, pr. 1918; *The Play's the Thing*, pr. 1926 (adaptation of Ferenc Molnár); *Good Morning, Bill*, pr. 1927 (adaptation of László Fodor); *A Damsel in Distress*, pr. 1928 (adaptation of his novel; with Ian Hay); *Baa, Baa Black Sheep*, pr. 1929 (with Hay); *Candlelight*, pr. 1929 (adaptation of Siegfried Geyer); *Leave It to Psmith*, pr. 1930 (adaptation of his novel; with Hay); *Anything Goes*, pr. 1934 (with Guy Bolton and others); *Carry On, Jeeves*, pb. 1956 (adaptation; with Bolton).

SCREENPLAY: *A Damsel in Distress*, 1937 (adaptation of his novel; with others).

NONFICTION: *William Tell Told Again*, 1904 (with additional fictional material); *Louder and Funnier*, 1932; *Bring on the Girls: The Improbable Story of Our Life in Musical Comedy, with Pictures to Prove It*, 1953 (with Guy Bolton); *Performing Flea: A Self-Portrait in Letters*, 1953 (revised as *Author! Author!*, 1962; W. Townend, editor); *America, I Like You*, 1956 (revised as *Over Seventy: An Autobiography with Digressions*, 1957).

EDITED TEXTS: *A Century of Humour*, 1934; *The Best of Modern Humor*, 1952 (with Scott Meredith); *The Week-End Book of Humor*, 1952 (with Meredith); *A Carnival of Modern Humor*, 1967 (with Meredith).

Bibliography

Donaldson, Frances. *P. G. Wodehouse: A Biography*. New York: Alfred A. Knopf, 1982. Informative work provides a more complete account of Wodehouse's life than the biographies that preceded it. Begins with an introduction that offers interesting comments about Wodehouse's humor. Includes illustrations, bibliography, and index.

Green, Benny. *P. G. Wodehouse: A Literary Biography*. New York: Rutledge Press, 1981. Very useful study, arranged chronologically, traces the connections between Wodehouse's personal experiences and his fictional creations. Includes illustrations, chronology, notes, bibliography, and index.

Hall, Robert A., Jr. *The Comic Style of P. G. Wodehouse*. Hamden, Conn.: Archon Books, 1974. Discusses Wodehouse's stories, dividing them into the categories of school tales and juvenilia, romances and farces, and the various sagas. Presents analysis of Wodehouse's narrative techniques and linguistic characteristics that is indispensable for anyone interested in understanding his style. Includes bibliography and index.

McCrum, Robert. *Wodehouse: A Life*. New York: W. W. Norton, 2004. Comprehensive biography identifies Wodehouse's 1941 radio broadcasts from Germany as the defining moment of the writer's life and demonstrates how Wodehouse was tricked into making these controversial broadcasts. Includes illustrations, bibliography, and index.

Murphy, N. T. P. *A Wodehouse Handbook: The World and Words of P. G. Wodehouse*. 2 vols. London: Popgood & Groolley, 2006. Valuable guide for readers covers the world in which Wodehouse lived and describes how he used his personal experiences in his writing in volume 1; volume 2 explains the many references to people, places, and events in his works.

Phelps, Barry. *P. G. Wodehouse: Man and Myth*. London: Constable, 1992. Sympathetic and entertaining biography provides an unusual number of informative appendixes, including a Wodehouse chronology and a Wodehouse family tree, as well as a bibliography.

Sproat, Iain. *Wodehouse at War*. New Haven, Conn.: Ticknor & Fields, 1981. Focuses on Wodehouse's individual psychology and on the sad war events that clouded the writer's life. Sproat, a politician as well as a fan, vindicates Wodehouse in the infamous Nazi broadcasts, which are reprinted here. Includes appendixes of documents in the case.

Usborne, Richard. *After Hours with P. G. Wodehouse*. London: Hutchinson, 1991. A collection of entertaining pieces on Wodehouse's life and death, written somewhat in the spirit of Wodehouse himself.

_______. *Wodehouse at Work to the End*. 1961. Rev. ed. London: Barrie & Jenkins, 1976. Includes individual chapters on Wodehouse's major series characters, helpful appendixes of lists of his books, plays, and films, and an index. For the diehard fan, each chapter is followed by a brief section called "Images," with humorous quotations from the works.

Voorhees, Richard J. *P. G. Wodehouse*. New York: Twayne, 1966. Excellent introductory volume provides information on Wodehouse's life and discusses his public school stories, his early novels, and the development of his romantic and comic novels. Also provides a description of the Wodehouse world and discusses the place of that world in British literature. Includes chronology, notes and references, and bibliography of primary and secondary sources.

LARRY WOIWODE

Born: Carrington, North Dakota; October 30, 1941
Also known as: Larry Alfred Woiwode

Principal long fiction

What I'm Going to Do, I Think, 1969
Beyond the Bedroom Wall: A Family Album, 1975
Poppa John, 1981
Born Brothers, 1988
Indian Affairs, 1992

Other literary forms

Larry Woiwode (WI-wood-ee) was once known primarily for his longer fiction, but as his career has evolved he has shown great diversity and variety. He has published short stories in such prominent literary periodicals as *The Atlantic Monthly* and *The New Yorker*, and several of his stories have been included in anthologies of the best stories published in given years. He has written book reviews and essays for many newspapers, including *The New York Times*. *The Neumiller Stories* (1989), a collection of thirteen previously uncollected stories, including three penned in the 1980's, expands the "family album" of narratives about the Neumiller clan that Woiwode began in his novels *Beyond the Bedroom Wall* and *Born Brothers*.

Woiwode has also published poetry, including the well-received collection *Even Tide* (1977). In 1993, he published another collection of short fiction titled *Silent Passengers: Stories*, and that same year he also published *Acts*, which contains his ruminations on the current state of Christianity and letters. His interest in frontier life and in the North Dakota frontier is explored in *Aristocrat of the West: The Story of Harold Schafer*, which was published by the North Dakota Institute for Regional Studies in 2000. Woiwode returned to narrative prose with *What I Think I Did: A Season of Survival in Two Acts* in 2000; this complex and poetic memoir describes his initiation into the writing life and his apprenticeship to *New Yorker* editor William Maxwell. His second memoir (of a projected trilogy), *A Step from Death*, was published in 2008; like *What I Think I Did*, *A Step from Death* eschews a straightforward, chronological organization, instead following thematic threads in different directions.

Achievements

Larry Woiwode's first novel, *What I'm Going to Do, I Think*, won for him the prestigious William Faulkner Foundation Award for the "most notable first novel" of 1969 and the American Library Association Notable Book Award in 1970 and brought him immediate critical attention. The book was a best seller and was translated into several foreign languages. *What I'm Going to Do, I Think*, and the short fiction Woiwode was publishing, helped him earn a Guggenheim fellowship, awarded for literary excellence. His second novel, *Beyond the Bedroom Wall*, actually begun before *What I'm Going to Do, I Think*, was nominated for both the National Book Award and the National Book Critics Circle Award, and it won the American Library Association Notable Book Award in 1976. It became an even bigger commercial and critical success than his first novel. Woiwode received Bush Foundation fellowships in 1977 and 1978 for his work in fiction.

His third novel, *Poppa John*, was much less successful commercially and critically. The novel's premise and protagonist indeed represented a departure from the regional narrative Woiwode had successfully employed in his previous fiction, but it did earn the Cornerstone Best Book of the Year Award in 1982. In 1991, Woiwode was presented with the John Dos Passos Prize from Longwood University in recognition of the overall excellence of his body of work. His continued work in short fiction (with *The Neumiller Stories* and *Silent Passengers*) earned him the Nelson Algren Short Fiction Award in 1992 and the Association of Writing Programs Award for Short Fiction in 1999. Woiwode received the Lannan Foundation Fellowship for Literary Excellence in 2002 on the strength of his memoir *What I Think I Did*. Furthermore, although he has published only one book of poetry, he was named poet laureate for North Dakota in 1995 for his overall life in letters.

Poppa John notwithstanding, critics are quick to credit Woiwode's idiosyncratic, family-centered narratives with helping indirectly to rehabilitate the family chronicle, a genre long considered out of fashion. After a decade of relative publishing silence, Woiwode returned to this narrative genre in *Born Brothers* and *The Neumiller Stories*. Woiwode's evolving canon of Neumiller narratives depicts prodigal sons and daughters who, no matter where they tread, fulfill their destiny in rediscovering their roots and the family relationships that nurtured them early in their lives. Woiwode unabashedly admires the traditional nuclear family, and his fiction underscores the value of finding one's way by retracing one's steps. His narrative strength is thus seen in the fact that, even among readers accustomed to despondent, "lost" protagonists preoccupied with discovering the mysteries of life in the squalor of the city or some illicit relationship, Woiwode can make such old-fashioned premises seem startlingly fresh and appealing.

In the ebb and flow of many writers' careers, acclaimed first novels often permanently overshadow subsequent efforts, and the disappointment with—and apparent dearth of fresh ideas that followed after—the publication of *Poppa John* provoked many critics and readers to wonder if Woiwode had lost his narrative vision. Such concerns were answered with the publication of *Born Brothers* and *The Neumiller Stories*.

Biography

Larry Alfred Woiwode was born in Carrington, North Dakota, on October 30, 1941. He spent his early years in nearby Sykeston, a predominantly German settlement amid the rugged, often forbidding north-midwestern terrain. No doubt the beauty as well as the stark loneliness of this landscape heightened his appreciation for the effects of nature on individual character. At the age of ten, he moved with his family to Manito, Illinois, another evocatively midwestern environment capable of nurturing the descriptive powers of a budding fiction writer.

Woiwode attended the University of Illinois for five years but failed to complete a bachelor's degree, leaving the university in 1964 with an associate of arts degree in rhetoric. He met his future wife, Carol Ann Patterson, during this period and married her on May 21, 1965. With Carol he would eventually have four children. After leaving Illinois, Woiwode moved to New York City and supported his family with freelance writing, publishing in *The New Yorker* and other prestigious periodicals while working on two novels. He was a writer-in-residence at the University of Wisconsin, Madison, and had extended teaching posts at Wheaton College (Illinois) and at the State University of New York at Binghamton, where he served as a faculty member (intermittently) beginning in 1983. In 1977, he was awarded the doctor of letters degree from North Dakota State University.

Woiwode explains in his memoirs *What I Think I Did* and *A Step from Death* how his nascent Christian faith began to grow and gain strength in his life, and he is now known nationally as a Christian author (although his works are perhaps too complex to relegate him to the shelves dedicated to particularly religious writers).

He and his family returned to North Dakota in 1978 to maintain an organic farm. As detailed in his memoirs, Woiwode would continue to balance the farm life that spoke to him and nourished both his family life and writing with brief academic assignments at the University of North Dakota in Grand Forks and at Jamestown College.

ANALYSIS

To understand Larry Woiwode's craft and achievement, one must finally recognize the essentially religious character of his narratives and their thematic structure. He is an advocate for restoring a moral, even religious, voice to modern letters. While believing that the most important human questions are, in fact, religious ones, Woiwode rejects the notion that there can be legitimate, compelling "novels of ideas"; for him, such fiction connotes mere propagandizing. Woiwode handles such questions not by placing philosophical soliloquies in the mouths of sophisticated, worldly protagonists but by creating authentically ordinary characters and settling them comfortably into the concrete and utterly mundane world of daily life.

In achieving this effective depiction of what might be called heightened normality, Woiwode's prose is consistently active, alive, and unassuming, approaching at times the crisp clarity of Ernest Hemingway but touched with a finely tuned lyricism. While Woiwode has sometimes been criticized for lapsing too easily into didacticism or marring otherwise evocative scenes with excessive detail, his keen eye for the extraordinary ordinariness of life makes his narrative vision compelling and believable.

As a novelist, Woiwode stands apart from most of his contemporaries in refusing to drown his characters in the angst-ridden excesses that have become so conventional in the modern American novel. His characters are not helpless victims of their times but participants in them; they are accountable not so much for what has happened to them but for what they do in response to their circumstances. Their conflicts, from Chris Van Eenanam's enigmatic search for manhood in *What I'm Going to Do, I Think* to Poppa John's drive to recover his self-identity, are not merely contrived psychological dramas played out inside their own consciousnesses; rather, they are compelling confrontations with the very concrete world of everyday life. This is a world that registers as authentic to the reader precisely because of Woiwode's gift for realism.

Woiwode's characters eventually recognize that the answers to their dilemmas are only partly in themselves. In the reestablishment of personal trust in friendships and the nostalgia of forgotten familial relationships, they recover a sense of balance and worth in themselves. However obliquely, each major Woiwode character finds him- or herself in a quest for a transcendent moral order, a renewed trust in God and humanity that will provide a reference point for his or her life. This quest animates the character's rejection of narcissism and a search for a love and security that only marital and familial relationships can foster.

Woiwode's willingness to affirm that these relationships are central to self-fulfillment and to the stability of American culture makes him unique among a generation of writers whose thematic concerns tend to focus on their characters' dehumanization in society and alienation from family life and marital fidelity. Woiwode thus be-

Larry Woiwode. (© Nancy Crampton)

longs in the company of self-consciously moralistic writers such as Walker Percy and Saul Bellow, who are more interested in the ways human beings survive and thrive in a fallen world than in the ways they capitulate to it. Like Percy, however, the importance of Woiwode's struggles with faith in his works (particularly in *Beyond the Bedroom Wall* and *Born Brothers*) takes on more significance as the author's later works follow a more spiritual bent.

When compared with other writers of his caliber, Woiwode cannot be considered a particularly prolific author. Two of his novels, however, have been critically acclaimed, national best sellers, and they are among the best American novels written after 1960. The publication in consecutive years of *Born Brothers* and *The Neumiller Stories* seems to have redeemed Woiwode from the ambivalent response to *Poppa John*, and his reputation as an important American writer in the second half of the twentieth century seems secure.

What I'm Going to Do, I Think

Woiwode's first novel, *What I'm Going to Do, I Think*, is an absorbing character study of two newlyweds, each of whom is originally drawn to the other as opposites proverbially attract. Chris Van Eenanam, the protagonist, is a listless mathematics graduate student, an unhappy agnostic unsure of his calling in life. The novel's title accentuates his self-doubt and indecision, echoing something Chris's father once said in observing his accident-prone son: "What I'm going to do, I think, is get a new kid." Ellen Strohe, his pregnant bride, is a tortured young woman, dominated by the overbearing grandparents who reared her after her parents' accidental death. Neither she nor Chris can abide their interference and meddling.

Despite the fact that little action takes place "live" before the reader, the psychological realism in Woiwode's use of compacted action and flashbacks and the patterned repetition of certain incidents carry the reader along as effortlessly as might a conventionally chronological narrative. The reader learns "what happens" primarily as events filter through the conversations and consciousness of Chris and Ellen Van Eenanam during their extended honeymoon at her grandparents' cabin near the northwestern shore of Lake Michigan. In this retreat from the decisions Chris elects not to face, the couple, now intimate, now isolated, confront a grim modern world that has lost its faith in a supreme being fully in control of his created universe. This loss is exemplified most dramatically in the lives of Chris and Ellen as they try to sort out the meaning of affection and fidelity in their new relationship as husband and wife and as potential parents. Ellen's pregnancy is at first a sign of a beneficent nature's approval of their union, but later, as each has a premonition of the unborn child's death, it becomes a symbol of an ambivalent world's indifference to their marriage and its apparent fruitlessness.

In the absence of a compensatory faith even in humankind itself, a secondary faith arguably derived from faith in God, Chris and Ellen come to realize that they have lost their ability to navigate a hostile world with lasting, meaningful relationships. Neither mathematics nor nature can fill the vacuum left by an impotent faith whose incessant call is to fidelity and perseverance without passion or understanding. In a suspenseful epilogue that closes the novel with an explanation of what has happened to them in the seven years following their marriage, Chris and Ellen return to their honeymoon cabin. Chris retrieves the rifle he has not touched in many years, and, as the action builds toward what will apparently be his suicide, he repeats to himself the beginning of a letter (suicide note?) that he could not complete: *"Dear El, my wife. You're the only person I've ever been able to talk to and this is something I can't say. . . ."*

As he makes his way to the lake, he fires a round of ammunition into a plastic bleach container half buried in the sand. In the novel's enigmatic final lines, Chris fires "the last round from his waist, sending the bullet out over the open lake." This curious ending seems intended by Woiwode to announce Chris's end of indecision—a recognition that his life can have transcendent meaning only through his embracing fully his marriage commitment to Ellen.

Beyond the Bedroom Wall

The expansiveness and comic vitality of Woiwode's second novel, *Beyond the Bedroom Wall*, offer a marked contrast to *What I'm Going to Do, I Think*. In *Beyond the Bedroom Wall*, Woiwode parades sixty-three characters before the reader by the beginning of chapter 3. True to its subtitle, *A Family Album*, *Beyond the Bedroom Wall* is a sprawling, gangly work of loosely connected snapshots of the Neumiller family. An engaging homage to the seemingly evaporating family unit at the end of the twentieth century, the novel's "plot" is nearly impossible to paraphrase, consisting as it does of some narrative, some diary entries, and even its protagonist Martin Neumiller's job application for a teaching position. Given that Woiwode had previously published nearly a third of the forty-four chapters of *Beyond the Bedroom Wall* as self-contained short stories in *The New Yorker*, it is no surprise that the book reads as a discontinuous montage of events, images, and personalities.

The novel opens in part 1 with the funeral of Charles Neumiller, a German immigrant farmer who had brought his family to the United States before World War II, and it continues, to part 5, closing with stories of the third generation of Neumillers in 1970, bringing the Neumiller family full circle from birth to life to death. It is Martin Neumiller, Charles's son, a God-fearing, devoutly Catholic man and proud son of North Dakota, whose adventures and misadventures give the novel any unity it possesses. "My life is like a book," he says at one point. "There is one chapter, there is one story after another." The eccentric folks he encounters in and out of his extended family form a burlesque troupe of characters who boisterously sample both the joys and the sorrows of life on Earth.

In the Neumiller "family album," Woiwode lends concreteness to his notion that reality is a fragile construction, one that sometimes cannot bear scrutiny "beyond the bedroom wall"—that is, beyond the dreamy world of sleep, of its visions of what might be. Woiwode intimates that whatever hope there may be for fulfilling one's dreams, it is anchored in "walking by faith, and not by sight," by trusting in and actively nurturing family intimacy.

The rather sentimental, "old-fashioned" quality Woiwode achieves in this family chronicle, his evocation of once-embraced, now-lamented values, prompted critic and novelist John Gardner to place Woiwode in the company of literature's greatest epic novelists: "When self-doubt, alienation, and fashionable pessimism become a bore and, what's worse, a patent delusion, how does one get back to the big emotions, the large and fairly confident life affirmations of an Arnold Bennett, a Dickens, a Dostoevski? *Beyond the Bedroom Wall* is a brilliant solution."

Woiwode's eye for the rich details of daily life enables him to move through vast stretches of time and space in executing the episodic structure in this novel. His appreciation for the cadences of midwestern speech and his understanding of the distinctiveness of prairie life and landscape and its impact on the worldviews of its inhabitants recall other regional writers such as Rudy Wiebe and Garrison Keillor at their best.

Poppa John

Poppa John is a shockingly short work when compared with the massive *Beyond the Bedroom Wall* and is more a novella than a novel. The book takes its title from the character Ned Daley played for many years on a popular television soap opera. His immense popularity beginning to overshadow the program itself, he is abruptly written out of the show in a dramatic "death." Ned thus finds himself suddenly unable to recover a sense of purpose, as he has lived for so long within the disguise of Poppa John, a fiery father figure who often quoted Scripture to his television family. Now close to seventy, outspoken and Falstaffian in appearance and behavior, he seeks his deeply lost identity. Ned to his wife but Poppa John to everyone else, he is lost in the malevolent nostalgia of growing old without self or self-respect.

The novel opens two days before Christmas, a few months after Poppa John's television death. Facing the Christmas season, broke, broken, and without prospects for the future, Ned and his wife, Celia, wander New York City, squandering their savings on gifts they had always wanted to buy for each other. Forced to "be himself," he finds he has leaned too heavily on the preacherlike Poppa John character, and his life begins to unravel. He is finally forced to face his own inconsistencies, his doubts, and even his sins, as Ned, an "elderly boy," is incapable of trusting in a life beyond the present. Speeding to a climax in its closing pages, the novel depicts Poppa John "coming to himself" on Christmas Day, realizing that he, after all these years, does believe in God, and therefore can come to believe in himself.

Poppa John perhaps deserved a better critical reception than it met on publication; as a more than interesting attempt to portray an elderly actor's disintegrating life, it contains some of Woiwode's most lyrical scenes. In the end, however, it remains an unsatisfying chronicle—in part because the complexity apparent in Poppa John's character is never fully realized, presented as it is in a very compressed time frame. While Poppa John emerges as a potentially authentic character in the early parts of the story, Woiwode gives the reader little insight into the motivations that prompt his sudden conversion experience at the climax.

Born Brothers

In *Born Brothers*, Woiwode returns to the characters, setting, and moral center that brought him his greatest and most uniformly favorable critical attention. Woiwode begins what he calls not a sequel but a "companion volume" to *Beyond the Bedroom Wall* in the middle of the twentieth century, the narration filtered through the consciousness of Charles Neumiller, a lost soul searching his memories for a meaning to life and a purpose for living it. He finds both in exploring his relationship with his brother Jerome. Charles's fragmentary childhood memories in fact become the narrative building blocks for the often elliptical and multiperspective chronicle that unravels before the reader in an even more challenging sequence than that of *Beyond the Bedroom Wall. Born Brothers* contains less a plot than a chain of remembrances; as family members and their ahistorical interactions with Charles are paraded before the reader in a kind of visual patchwork, the reader is compelled to enter Charles's consciousness and see the world through his convoluted epistemology.

Despite his outward sophistication and sense of being, Charles is obsessed with suicide; he seems incapable of conceiving of a meaningful order outside the family structure that had shaped his life and has now dissipated with the death of his mother and the collapse of his marriage. In part, it is Woiwode's intent to explain American society's apparent moral disintegration—rampant promiscuity, unwanted pregnancy, and divorce—by reference to the absence of strong family ties. Charles longs for the bond of brotherhood he once shared, or thinks he shared, with elder brother Jerome. That idyllic childhood in North Dakota, free from the cares and stresses of modern industrial life, impinges without provocation upon Charles's consciousness. Charles's strange career as a "radio personality" who is both interviewer and interviewee is somehow emblematic of his need for conversion, for freedom from self. He needs an "outside," a reference point, which, Woiwode hints, will come only from faith in the transcendent God whose eternal family Charles is invited to join.

Woiwode makes few compromises for the reader unwilling to attend to—or, perhaps, eavesdrop on—Charles Neumiller's open-ended musings. To refer to his ramblings as stream-of-consciousness narration is to give them too precise a label, for not merely a consciousness is under consideration here but the history of a mind and a life as well. The journey to and through that history is not one that the casual reader will be inclined to take, which underscores the main criticism of Woiwode's prose shared even by critics sympathetic to his family chronicle: his apparent inattention to the toll his often exhaustive detail takes on both his characters and his readers. Jonathan Yardley's judgment seems most apt: "It's a pity to see a writer of Woiwode's talent and humanity stuck, at midcareer, in the endless exploration and re-exploration of material that has yielded its last fresh insight if not its last lovely sentence."

Indian Affairs

With its broken sequence of scenes and lack of exposition or resolution of conflicts, *Indian Affairs* has elements of a postmodern novel. Woiwode uses this style to reflect the inner turmoil of Chris Van Eenanam, who appeared earlier as the main character of *What I'm Going to Do, I Think*. Chris and his wife, Ellen, return to an isolated cabin in the Michigan woods so that Chris can write his Ph.D. dissertation on American poet Theodore Roethke's natural philosophy and poetry. Mundane interruptions such as cutting firewood, installing a water pump, shopping, and tavern hopping distract him. A gang of drunken Native American teenagers threatens him when he does not supply them with beer, and a mysterious stalker forces him to keep a loaded gun handy. On a deeper level, Chris undergoes an identity crisis—a need to affirm his masculinity, to cope with religious and moral dilemmas, and to resolve the conflict of whether his roots are Caucasian or American Indian.

Chris and Ellen's childless seven-year marriage has brought them no sense of permanence or hope for the future. Although they are thirty years old, Chris is still a graduate student, and they are dependent on Ellen's wealthy grandparents for use of the cabin. Ellen's previous miscarriage and her ensuing barrenness symbolize the status of their marriage. Ellen resolves her unhappiness by recording her thoughts in a journal. Meanwhile, she joins a feminist discussion group, goes to a bar without an escort, and tries the hallucinogen peyote to ease her feelings of emptiness. Her conflicts disappear when she becomes pregnant again.

Chris spends much time with his bachelor friend Beau Nagoosa, a Chippewa Indian who has dropped out of white culture to build his own cabin. He supports himself as a woodcutter and justifies stealing wood on absentee landowners' property by telling himself it was once Native American land. Beau resents the invasion of white real estate promoters, who claim to represent Volunteers in Service to America (VISTA), yet he accommodates them and compromises his ideals.

Chris and Beau discuss humanity's role within the spiritual harmony of the natural world. For Chris, Roethke's claim that objects in nature are sentient is synonymous with Native American beliefs. Beau introduces Chris to peyote, which stimulates vivid sensory perceptions and fantasies but renders both Chris and Beau unable to cope with their real problems. Frustrated by chaotic events in his life and dissatisfied with the prospect of returning to academe in New York, Chris is overcome with depression. Feeling that nothing can guide him now except his own instincts, he decides to adhere to a line from one of Roethke's poems, "I'll be an Indian." Chris's future role as a teacher or leader is ambiguous.

As Chris begins to identify more strongly with his own Blackfoot Indian heritage and feel reverence for the natural world, conflicts escalate between the segregated white and Native American communities. The natural environment shrinks as urban development expands. Tribal leadership does not extend beyond exhibition dancing at powwows. American Indian families disintegrate, alcoholism and drug use destroy lives, and teenage youths engage in threat making and violence. Woiwode's realistic and tragic portrayal of Native American life offers no solution to the problems.

Readers of *Indian Affairs* will be able to appreciate the work most fully if they have read *What I'm Going to Do, I Think* and if they have more than a passing acquaintance with the philosophies and writings of Theodore Roethke and of the Native American cultural nationalist Vine Deloria. The underlying theme of the novel is that modern Native Americans lack effective leaders to guide them.

Bruce L. Edwards, Jr.; Martha E. Rhynes
Updated by Scott D. Yarbrough

Other major works

SHORT FICTION: *The Neumiller Stories*, 1989; *Silent Passengers: Stories*, 1993.

POETRY: *Poetry North: Five North Dakota Poets*, 1970 (with Richard Lyons, Thomas McGrath, John R. Milton, and Antony Oldknow); *Even Tide*, 1977.

NONFICTION: *Acts*, 1993; *Aristocrat of the West: The Story of Harold Schafer*, 2000; *What I Think I Did: A Season of Survival in Two Acts*, 2000; *My Dinner with Auden*, 2006; *A Step from Death*, 2008.

Bibliography

Cheaney, J. B. "Taming Memory: The Fiction of Larry Woiwode." *World and I* 17, no. 10 (October 1, 2002): 256-260. Presents a biographical sketch of Woiwode that particularly sheds insight on his spirituality and the autobiographical content of his fiction.

Freise, Kathy. "Home Again on the Prairie." *North Dakota Horizons* 23 (Summer, 1993): 19-23. Details Woiwode's connections with the state and its role in his books dealing with the Neumiller family.

Nelson, Shirley. "Stewards of the Imagination: Ron Hanson, Larry Woiwode, and Sue Miller." *Christian Century*, January 25, 1995, 82-86. Profile of the three novelists discusses their works and careers as well as the role of religion in their lives and writing.

Scheick, William J. "Memory in Larry Woiwode's Novels." *North Dakota Quarterly* 53, no. 3 (1985): 29-40. Discusses the importance of memory in *What I'm Going to Do, I Think*, *Beyond the Bedroom Wall*, and *Poppa John*. Identifies two types of memories in the works—those that make a character feel guilt and long for death and those that develop a sense of connection to family—and asserts that the ability to order these allows Woiwode's characters to achieve a balance between them.

Siconolfi, Michael T. Review of *The Neumiller Stories*, by Larry Woiwode. *America* 163 (December 1, 1990): 434-435. Discusses Woiwode's reworking of stories as they become parts of novels and then resurface as the short stories in this collection. Focuses on Woiwode's gift for depicting the "nurturing, eternal feminine" and on the novelist's acknowledgment of his grandmother's influence.

Woiwode, Larry. "Dylan to CNN." *Image: A Journal of the Arts and Religion* 28 (Fall, 2000): 95-101. Woiwode addresses the mass media's interactions with spirituality and religion. Provides some insight into the author's lack of patience with how Christians are sometimes portrayed.

_______. "An Interview with Larry Woiwode." *Christianity and Literature* 29 (Winter, 1979): 11-18. In a revealing early interview, Woiwode discusses the autobiographical nature of his work and the influences that shaped his narrative vision, the Jacob/Esau biblical framework of *Born Brothers*, the mechanics of memory, his religious rebirth, and his future writing plans.

_______. "The Reforming of a Novelist." Interview by Timothy K. Jones. *Christianity Today*, October 26, 1992, 86-89. Woiwode discusses his conversion experience, the role of faith in his writing, and his view of the nonreligious, humanistic approach of the East Coast literary establishment.

_______. "Where the Buffalo Roam: An Interview with Larry Woiwode." Interview by Rick Watson. *North Dakota Quarterly* 63, no. 4 (Fall, 1996): 154-166. Woiwode discusses the influences on his work of the North Dakota landscape and the farming life.

CHRISTA WOLF

Born: Landsberg an der Warthe, Germany (now Gorzów Wielkopolski, Poland); March 18, 1929
Also known as: Christa Margarete Ihlenfeld

Principal long fiction

Der geteilte Himmel: Erzählung, 1963 (*Divided Heaven: A Novel of Germany Today*, 1965)
Nachdenken über Christa T., 1968 (*The Quest for Christa T.*, 1970)
Kindheitsmuster, 1976 (*A Model Childhood*, 1980; also known as *Patterns of Childhood*, 1984)
Kein Ort: Nirgends, 1979 (*No Place on Earth*, 1982)
Kassandra: Erzählung, 1983 (*Cassandra: A Novel and Four Essays*, 1984)
Störfall: Nachrichten eines Tages, 1987 (*Accident: A Day's News*, 1989)
Sommerstück, 1989
Was Bleibt: Erzählung, 1990 (novella; *What Remains*, 1993)
Medea: Stimmen, 1996 (*Medea: A Modern Retelling*, 1998)
Leibhaftig, 2002 (*In the Flesh*, 2005)

Other literary forms

Christa Wolf's reputation rests primarily on her novels. Her short stories were collected into one volume in 1980, *Gesammelte Erzählungen*; this work was updated and translated in 1993 as *What Remains, and Other Stories*. Her most important essays, reviews, speeches, and interviews are found in *Lesen und Schreiben: Aufsätze und Betrachtungen* (1971; *The Reader and the Writer: Essays, Sketches, Memories*, 1977), *Lesen und Schreiben: Neue Sammlung* (1980), *Die Dimension des Autors: Essays und Aufsätze, Reden, und Gespräche, 1959-1985*, 1987 (partial translations *The Fourth Dimension: Interviews with Christa Wolf*, 1988, and *The Author's Dimension: Selected Essays*, 1993), and *Auf dem Weg nach Tabou: Texte, 1990-1994*, 1994 (*Parting from Phantoms: Selected Writings, 1990-1994*, 1997). She has also collaborated on the screenplays of several films and, with her husband, Gerhard Wolf, wrote the script for *Till Eulenspiegel* (1972). Wolf has also published her correspondence with author Brigitte Reimann, *Sei gegrüsst und lebe: Eine Freundschaft in Briefen, 1964-1973* (1993), and her correspondence with author Franz Fühmann, *Monsieur, wir finden uns wieder: Briefe, 1968-1984* (1995). In 2003, she published the unconventional autobiographical work *Ein Tag im Jahr: 1960-2000* (*One Day a Year: 1960-2000*, 2007).

Achievements

Before publishing her first short story, "Moskauer Novelle," Christa Wolf had prepared for her own literary career by working for several years as a reader and reviewer for a variety of East German publications. She rose to the position of editor of *Neue deutsche Literatur*, the periodical of the German Writers' Union (1958-1959). Her fame began with her first novel, *Divided Heaven*, a work that evoked lively discussion in both East and West Germany and that quickly became known beyond the borders of the two German states. She received the National Prize III Class of the Academy of the Arts in 1964 for this novel. In 1972, she shared with Walter Kempowski the Wilhelm Raabe Prize of the city of Brunswick and in 1980 received the prestigious Georg Büchner Prize from the German Academy of Language and Poetry in Darmstadt. In the spring of 1974, she was Max Kade Writer-in-Residence at Oberlin College, Ohio. In 1983, Wolf was a guest professor at Ohio State University, where she received an honorary doctorate. In 1985 she was made an honorary fellow of the Modern Language Association of America (MLA). In 1987, the City of Munich, Germany, awarded her its Geschwister-Scholl Prize, which comes with twenty thousand German marks. Wolf's fortunes then suffered a temporary reversal, and in 1993 the City of Munich attempted to revoke the prize. In 1992-1993, Wolf was a research fellow at the Getty Center for the History of Art and the Humanities in Santa Monica, California. Wolf is an internationally recognized author, the recipient of many invitations, honors, and awards. In 1997, Wolf was the first German to receive the Salon du Livre prize at the Bordeaux Book Fair. She is widely recognized as one of the most significant contemporary German writers by many of her literary peers as well as by critics, Germanists, and the reading public.

The political controversy surrounding several of her works has tended at times to obscure or distort their actual import while at the same time revealing one of their most important thematic concerns: the role and significance of literature in the contemporary technological world. She is a politically engaged writer in the broadest sense of the term. The honesty and the sensitivity with which she has examined the influence of the modern state and of modern society on the individual have struck responsive chords in her readers at home and abroad and have caused those with political axes to grind to regard her as friend or foe, depending on the direction of political currents. Her own self-confidence and clarity of artistic purpose, however, have enabled her to prevail over those who seek to use her works for their own short-range goals.

Biography

Christa Wolf was born Christa Margarete Ihlenfeld, the daughter of a grocer, March 18, 1929, in Landsberg an der Warthe, Germany, now Gorzów, Poland. Her middle-class background and her uneventful youth are remarkable only insofar as they might be seen as typical for many Germans of her generation: those old enough to have been influenced by the twelve years of Nazi rule, but too young at the end of the war to have participated actively in it. Wolf's autobiographical novel *Patterns of Childhood* deals largely with these twelve years and explores the connections that exist between the committed Socialist of the 1970's and the sixteen-year-old girl who confided to her diary that she would die if the Führer should. The flight of Wolf's family westward from her birthplace is documented in *Patterns of Childhood* as well as in several of her other prose pieces. Allusions to her own years of studying German literature in Jena and Leipzig (1949-1953) may be recognized in *The Quest for Christa T.*

She joined the Socialist Unity Party (SED) in 1949, the year that East Germany was founded as a separate state with that party at its head. In 1951, she married Gerhard Wolf, a fellow Germanist and historian, and in the next years had two daughters, Annette (born in 1952) and Katrin (born in 1956). Her work as a reviewer and editor continued throughout these years. In 1959, she followed the suggestion of the SED leadership that writers go to work in the factories in order to gain working-class experience ("the Bitterfeld way to literature"). She worked for a time in a train-car manufacturing plant in Halle. This, along with the overnight construction of the Berlin Wall on August 13, 1961, became the background for *Divided Heaven*.

Christa Wolf. (Getty Images)

Wolf's public activities and her literary concerns became increasingly connected during the 1960's and 1970's. Her conviction that the writer must be personally and actively involved in the workings of his or her society was expressed not only thematically and theoretically in her writings of these years but also in her life. In early 1963, her name was put on the candidate list for the Central Committee of the SED. At the December, 1965, plenary meeting of this body, she defended writers who acknowledged in their works that certain aspects of socialism were as yet unrealized in East German life. This topic had begun to concern her as well, as *The Quest for Christa T.* was soon to show. The defense of such literary works helped to bring her into disfavor with party functionaries, so that in April of 1967 her name was no longer on the SED Central Committee candidate list. Not until 1971 did the political climate in East Germany change enough to allow Wolf's attitudes to be accepted. However, she was removed from the leadership of the Berlin branch of the Writers' Union for having cosigned an open letter protesting the expatriation of the poet Wolf Biermann in 1976. Unlike some other prominent writers and intellectuals who signed the letter, Wolf remained in East Germany and enjoyed the freedom to write, lecture, and travel abroad. She chose to refrain from further criticism of the regime.

East German Communism eventually collapsed, and Germany was peacefully reunified on October 3, 1990. Wolf was then free to publish her account of the costly and absurd surveillance that had intruded into her life for years. The slim volume *What Remains* gave rise to a journalistic attack out of all proportion to the content of the book. The press, not the academics, in West Germany criticized Wolf for not having taken a stronger stand against the Communist regime. Fuel was added to the flames when it became known that Wolf had cooperated with the East German police as a social informant between 1959 and 1962. The facts that she passed on only inconsequential information and came under surveillance herself were ignored. Instead, journalists tried to discredit all of Wolf's work. In an effort to counteract this politically motivated unfairness, her publisher, Luchterhand, put out a thick volume of documentation in 1993, *Akteneinsicht Christa Wolf Zerrspiegel und Dialog* (examining the files on Christa Wolf, distorting mirrors and dialogues). Edited by Hermann Vinke, it contains the state security files on Wolf from 1955 to 1964 and many articles and letters written by others in her defense.

Wolf's collection of essays and speeches, *Parting from Phantoms*, ends with an essay on Germany. Wolf states that the German people did not want the country to be divided into two separate states, East and West, from 1949 to 1990. Now that Germany is reunified, the time has come to work together.

Analysis

In her interview with East German critic Hans Kaufmann (in 1974; reprinted in *Lesen und Schreiben: Neue Sammlung*), Christa Wolf used the term "subjective authenticity" to describe what she believes should be the methodology and the goal of contemporary prose writers: the intense involvement of the author's self in the work, along with an absolutely straightforward presentation of reality, as much as this is possible—given the unavoidable subjectivity of the author. Such an approach to writing prohibits the establishment of distance between the author and the work, the reading public, and society as a whole. It implies that the process of writing is more important than the finished product and therefore prevents the commercialization of literature toward which modern marketing tends. For Wolf, the relationship of the author to the work becomes paradigmatic for the relationship between literary language on one hand and modern secular language on the other, and between the individual's need for self-realization and the pressures for conformity in the technological age. By bridging the gap between author and work through subjective authenticity, Wolf asserts that an intensely reciprocal relationship between author and reader, reader and work is created. At the same time, the dangerous erosion of language in a technological and scientific age is diminished, and the alienation of the individual from society may be abated.

In her acceptance speech for the Georg Büchner Prize in 1980, Wolf warned against alienation of inner, personal life from outer, materialistic life in a contemporary, technological world. She claimed that the dichotomy between the languages of these worlds is not merely a symptom of the separation of the places of work and of living, of the material from the spiritual, but that it has now become a perpetuator of this alienation. Ultimately, it is a threat to the continuation of the human race. The one-sided positive evaluation of modern technology and material advances has been accompanied by a parallel devaluation of the spiritual side of life and its expression in literary language. A deep skepticism toward modern science and technology is an important theme in Wolf's fiction, particularly in the short stories "Neue Lebensansichten eines Katers" ("The New Life and Opinions of a Tomcat") and "Selbstversuch" ("Self-Experiment"). The writer, says Wolf, must combat these modern tendencies by reaffirming the validity of a committed individual viewpoint and its subjective expression in language. The subjectivity of the individual author, because it is founded in the real world and has its purpose outside itself, can thus be a model for individual self-realization. It is not surprising that Wolf's novels all deal with the general problem of individual self-realization within various social contexts. Thematically as well as stylistically, Wolf intends her works to effect "the production of new structures of human relationships in our time," as she told Kaufmann.

In order to examine the problem of modern alienation and as part of the process of developing subjective authenticity, Wolf has drawn heavily on her own life as a literary source. She has looked at East German society in order to understand alienation in herself and others (*Divided Heaven* and *The Quest for Christa T.*). She wrote *Patterns of Childhood* in order to understand herself better as part of a whole generation of Germans who have been alienated from an important era of their lives and history. She has turned to the lives and times of others at the beginning of the technological age, around 1800, when she believes the alienation of the spiritual from the material in art and life and within the modern world in general began. In *No Place on Earth*, she uses the figures of two writers, Heinrich von Kleist and Karoline von Günderode, both early victims of the alienation between art and life, both eventual suicides.

The writer (often represented by the narrator/author) is the quintessential figure in Wolf's works, and the process of narration is often presented as the fundamental act that can reconcile the material with the spiritual, the real with the ideal. The striving toward a whole world that underlies her ideas about writing gives Wolf's work the utopian impulse that she has said is necessary for full human life here and now. The parallels with the philosophical thought of Ernst Bloch (author of *Das Prinzip Hoffnung*, 1954-1959; *The Principle of Hope*, 1986), a professor in Leipzig during Wolf's study there, may be seen in Wolf's concept of utopianism as an attitude of active commitment to contemporary issues. In the foreword to her 1980 edition of Günderode's works, Wolf says, "Writers are, and this is not a lament, predestined to be sacrificial victims and self-sacrificers." They, through language, can bridge the chasm between materialism and spirituality, although they pay a heavy price in the process.

The selection of the long-neglected poet Günderode as the subject not only of the novel but also of this significant essay fits another pattern in Wolf's work: her preoccupation with female figures. Women are the main characters in all her novels and short stories. Where men play prominent roles, it is either as problematic, inwardly torn figures (*Divided Heaven* and *No Place on Earth*) or as destructive forces. Wolf has said that she has focused on female figures because she naturally can identify more readily with women. More than this, however, she has claimed historical reasons for her depiction of women and men in seemingly stereotypical fashion. She asserts that women, because they have been excluded from power in the last two centuries, have also largely escaped the inner alienation from which modern men suffer. They are therefore a potential force for changing and even for saving contemporary human society. The problematic condition of the writer in the modern world is intensified when the writer is a woman.

Wolf, in examining the experiences of earlier women writers (Günderode and Bettina von Arnim) and of incipient, if failed, contemporary women writers (Christa T.), is also examining herself and her own situation. She understands this aspect of her writing as a natural result of an examination of history (women's position in bourgeois society). Her own experiences of the consequences of this historical development then go into her works as part of a general dialogue about women in the Socialist state and as part of her striving for subjective authenticity.

Wolf's life and work are closely intertwined. She maintained her optimism and hope in Socialist society while recognizing its inadequacies. Other East German colleagues were not able to stay on this narrow path without incurring official disfavor. Wolf's own frictions with party functionaries can be seen as proof of the actuality, pertinence, and commitment of her writing. Certainly most of her work would not have taken form without her intense inner and outer involvement with her surroundings. It is not limited to this involvement, however; like all good literature, it goes beyond the configurations of time and place in which it is based to address issues of timeless human interest: the conflict between the individual and society, the problem of self-knowledge, and the endeavor to "heal the world" through writing, as Wolf once put it.

Divided Heaven

The immediate acclaim that was accorded Wolf's first novel, *Divided Heaven*, in both East and West Germany was largely the result of the Cold War climate of the day. The presentation of an unhappy love affair against the background of divided Berlin was interpreted in the West as a veiled protest against this political act. The defection of the negatively portrayed male protagonist and the affirmation of the positive heroine-narrator's life in the East was regarded in East Germany as properly supportive Socialist Realism, in spite of the ideological blurring of the heroine's motivation and the ambivalent Socialist zeal displayed by some of the secondary figures. That the novel is not about divided Germany but about "the reasons people leave one another," as Wolf said, has become clearer in recent years.

The thematic relationship to her later works is also apparent now. Manfred and Rita drift apart because they represent, as Alexander Stephan has noted, the two basic attitudes toward life possible for members of contemporary industrial society. Wolf oversimplifies the dichotomy to some extent by making Manfred the heir of bourgeois materialism and Nazi opportunism through his family, while the two years of Rita's life chronicled in the book almost become a condensation of the Marxist view of historical process: from a close connection to nature through the spiritual and psychological disruptions of bourgeois intellectualism and late capitalism to the healing world of contemporary everyday socialism.

The problems addressed in the book, however, are not so black and white. In *Divided Heaven*, Wolf begins her examination of the elements within Socialist society that prevent individuals from realizing themselves fully. Rita may make the "right" decision in the official view when she parts from Manfred in West Berlin, the day before the Wall is constructed, but her reasons remain unclear to her for some time. Indeed, only several months later, while recuperating from a suicide attempt made soon after the lovers' parting, does she become convinced of the correctness of her decision to participate actively and confidently in the construction of true socialism in her state. Manfred, on the other hand, represents those modern individuals who have become cynical, apathetic, and indifferent to life, alienated by the frustration of their efforts to effect social change, perhaps, or lured by the appeal of fitting into the comfortable routine of a materialistic consumer society. In many ways, Manfred is the central character of the novel. Certainly his self-awareness, his original enthusiasm about contributing to his society, and his ultimate failure to do so make him a more interesting figure than Rita, and also link him closely with the heroine of *The Quest for Christa T.*

In *Divided Heaven*, Wolf had not yet mastered the subjective narrative technique that she used to such advantage in her next novel, although the rather conventional flashback and montage techniques featured in *Divided Heaven* were fairly shocking to East German sensibilities at a time when the insistence on strict Socialist Realist literary principles was only beginning to weaken. More interesting is Wolf's attempt, here supported mainly by repeated imagery and leitmotifs, to show a development toward self-awareness on the part of Rita through her narration of and reflection on the past. This interest in the mutual influence between the narrator and the text prefigures the complex narrative stance of *The Quest for Christa T.* In many ways, *Divided Heaven* is most interesting now for its relationship to later works by Wolf. It established her reputation, for some of the wrong reasons, as an internationally important East German writer, a reputation that needed her next major work, however, to be fully justified.

THE QUEST FOR CHRISTA T.

When Wolf's second novel, *The Quest for Christa T.*, appeared in 1968, it sold out immediately in East Germany. The Luchterhand edition the next year was eagerly awaited and greeted with positive reviews in the West. Within East Germany, however, only two reviews, largely critical, were published, and almost six years passed before a second edition was printed. *The Quest for Christa T.*, like its protagonist, came on the scene before its time. Only several years after its appearance did internal East German cultural politics acknowledge the need for constructive criticism within Socialist society. The potential for social criticism can be seen in one of the main themes of the novel: the question of how an individual can gain self-realization yet also be a productive member of a planned and carefully organized society. The background of East German Socialist society is essential to the novel, unclearly delineated as it seems at times, and unpolitical as the heroine seems to be. Christa T., the incurable individual, believes in the rightness of the new world that socialism is to build yet finds it impossible to develop a role for herself that will make her a useful member of the new society without necessitating her conforming to and stultifying within some given role. Left to assert her individualism outside a social context, she dies.

The extent to which Christa T.'s dilemma reflects Wolf's own experience is unclear; certainly, a close relationship exists among Wolf, Christa T., and the unnamed narrator, the latter's friend and a writer like Wolf. In "Selbst-interview" ("Self-Interview," in *The Reader and the Writer*), Wolf acknowledged the near identity of the three. The biographical background of the novel is sufficiently complex to encourage what becomes an intermingling of personae: Both the narrator and Christa T. share elements of Wolf's biography, and Wolf has claimed that there was a real "Christa T." from whose life and posthumous papers she drew some of the facts and citations included in the work.

Aside from such factual cross-influences, the process of narration encourages identification of the narrator and the author with Christa T. This identification becomes one of the main themes of the novel. The narrator tries to be just to the person Christa T. was—indeed, to "rethink" her and thus let her go on living, for, she says, "we need her now." The English title does not transmit the wordplay that indicates this double function of the reflective, narrative process: both *nachdenken* (to reflect on) and *nach-denken* (to seek and re-create in thought). Christa T., ordinary and insignificant though she may seem, is the proper material for such a reciprocal, productive process. Unwilling and unable to compromise or commit herself and insistent on the necessity of conscience and fantasy for the continuation of the human race, she is an admonition to the narrator/author to maintain her own integrity and not to fall into complacency and self-satisfaction. Christa T.'s life is also a warning to her society. Her failure to find a useful place within it stems from the inconsistencies that result when a society calls for "new human beings" without making their development possible. The narrative process discloses the importance of Christa T. not only to the narrator/author but also to the reader and the society to which she so longed to contribute.

Closely connected to the theme of narration as a creative and healing process is that of writing, for Christa T.

is an aspiring writer, a role she shares with Wolf and the narrator. It is through writing that she seeks to close the "gaps" in life through which the cold, dark, destructive forces pour. For Christa T., as for the narrator and for Wolf herself, writing is a way of constructively processing the past, present, and future. Unlike Wolf herself, Christa T. lacks the strength to prevail against her time, which is still marked by many of the characteristics of the bourgeois and Nazi past. The basic tone of the work is one of optimism, however, just as Christa T. also maintained her optimism and hope for a better future. Critic Andreas Huyssen is correct to point to the utopian philosophy of Ernst Bloch in connection with *The Quest for Christa T.* A better future is posited by the example of Christa T. and by the changes within herself, which the narrator/author acknowledges as consequences of her reflections on her dead friend. The effect on the reader is similar: Christa T. is needed to point the way to a better society in which individual integrity is allowed to take its place as an important contributing factor to the whole.

The tentative quality of Wolf's narrative style in *The Quest for Christa T.* is marked by "the difficulty of saying I," in the heroine's words. The difficulty stems in part from Christa T.'s own reluctance to commit herself to any role. This transmits itself to the narrator, who attempts to be absolutely accurate and at the same time nonautocratic in her statements in order to allow Christa T. to live again on her own terms. This effort causes her to draw closer to and understand her protagonist better and in turn invites a similar effort on the part of the reader to become an active participant in the text. In this novel, Wolf's subjective authenticity is at its best: the provocative evocation of an individual within an identifiable milieu; the weaving of a relationship among author, narrator, protagonist, and reader; and the general utopian impulse pointing the way to a reconciliation of individual fulfillment with common social goals.

Patterns of Childhood

The question of "how we became who we are"—which Christa T. poses—underlies all Wolf's novels. In *Patterns of Childhood*, her autobiographical third novel, Wolf attempts to examine the most problematic period for Germans of her generation: the twelve years of National Socialism. Once again, as in *The Quest for Christa T.*, she is interested in understanding not only the past as such but also its implications for the present and the future. The narrative structure plays an important role here as well. Although the narrator, the protagonist, and the author are the same person, Wolf seems to want to establish some distance between them. She does so by giving her younger self a different name, Nelly Jordan, and, more important, by speaking of this younger self in the second person. In addition, she uses a complex time structure in which there are three levels: the past of Nelly Jordan, from the age of four to sixteen (1933-1945); a trip to her former home of Landsberg, Poland, in July of 1971 along with her husband, brother, and daughter Lenka; and the present, in which she is writing the novel, from November, 1972, until May, 1975.

The evocation of the Nazi years is very convincing, with the scrupulous concern for honesty and completeness that has become characteristic of Wolf's narrative style. The integration of the past with the present is less successful. Wolf attempts to make such connections, for example, through the criticism of contemporary East German institutions and practices voiced by her brother and Lenka, which gives rise to suspicions of continued Fascist tendencies in the Socialist state. She also alludes to historical events in Vietnam and Chile that occur during the writing of the work. The parallelism of such events to others that occurred in the Nazi state is not convincing, mainly because it does not seem to promote the increased self-knowledge that is the goal of the narration. The critical stance toward such events taken by the adult Nelly Jordan as narrator/author does not seem to have its origins in the child she evokes in her reflections. What is missing is the postwar transformation of the Bund Deutscher Mädel girl of the Hitler era to the Freie Deutsche Jugend member of East Germany, as Alexander Stephan has pointed out.

Wolf's attempts to make a personal examination of her own past into a process that would enlighten the present and instruct the future are only partly successful here. This does not mean that her methodology of subjective authenticity, which she pursues here, too, is faulty. Rather, the reason for this partial success probably lies in the enormously problematic nature of the past she is attempting to illuminate. Wolf's novel is a significant attempt to deal with this extremely difficult part of German history as personal history, and it certainly succeeds as personal testimony of that sort. Her efforts to deal with her youth in Nazi Germany as honestly as possible, acknowledging the incomprehensibility of her participation, limited though it was, certainly can provoke an examination of conscience on the part of those Germans who may believe they have "mastered the past." Wolf offers no answer to the question of why so many Germans offered no resistance to the Nazi regime. It is a mark of her uncompromising honesty that one is left with the rather helpless feeling that Wolf herself seems to have experienced after the war when a freed Communist prisoner asked: "Just where were you the whole time?"

No Place on Earth

The utopian import of *No Place on Earth* is indicated by its German title and subtitle, *Kein Ort* (no place) and *Nirgends* (nowhere), being literal translations of the Greek term *utopia*. Here Wolf uses in even more radical form than in her previous works the narrative technique associated with her subjective authenticity. She goes beyond her own past and social environment to examine the lives and times of two writers in the German Romantic era: Heinrich von Kleist and Karoline von Günderode. In her opening lines, she establishes the pertinence of these figures for herself. They are predecessors, for she has their "blood in her shoes." Wolf presents these writers as early victims of the alienation of the artist from society. The deep alienation from the self that ensued led to their youthful suicides. Their fate has broad implications, for it is a prophetic foreshadowing of that awaiting all those who cherish spiritual values in an increasingly materialistic world.

Wolf creates a fictional meeting between Kleist and Günderode in Winkel along the Rhine in 1804. The couple's conversation and inner thoughts are interspersed with commentary by the narrator/author; at times it is difficult to be sure who is speaking. Again Wolf attempts to establish through narrative structure and style a close relationship between subject and object. She succeeds in this by projecting feelings and thoughts into these figures that are consistent with the excerpts from their diaries and letters that she also weaves into the text. Wolf locates here the historical source of problems readers are familiar with from her other works. As in *The Quest for Christa T.*, the artist is the one to sense the alienation between the spiritual and the material and is the most likely to be destroyed by it.

One is reminded of Christa T. when Günderode speaks of the necessity of hope, for, as she says, "when we stop hoping, that which we fear will certainly come." The belief that love can heal the self-alienation that modern materialistic life causes is also posited by Günderode, and this is an important theme in Wolf's fiction, especially in "Unter den Linden" and "Self-Experiment." Again in *No Place on Earth*, a utopian power and vision are ascribed to literature, a power to remind human beings of the need to work continually toward their self-realization and a dynamic vision of humankind that, as Günderode says, is "contradictory to the spirit of every era." Kleist and Günderode may, like Christa T., have "died of their time," but our recognition of this, evoked by Wolf's re-creation of them, can become a first step in ending the historical process that began in their generation.

Sommerstück

Wolf's apolitical novel *Sommerstück* (summer play) portrays private life in the North German province of Mecklenburg. After dissident writer Wolf Biermann was expelled from Communist East Germany in 1976, Wolf refrained from further criticism of the regime. She and her family moved to an island where collective farmers coexisted peacefully with intellectuals in self-imposed exile from the cities. The quiet of the land brought unexpected healing. Wolf's disclaimer at the end of *Sommerstück* is qualified by the coincidence that another writer from the group, Sarah Kirsch, described it more directly in her chronicle *Allerlei-Rauh* (1988).

Wolf uses Kirsch's poem "Raubvogel" (bird of prey) as an epigraph for *Sommerstück* and works the themes into the novel. At the peak of summer, Luisa admires a hawk diving through the sunlight and ascending again with its prey in its talons. "Raubvogel süss ist die Luft/ So stürz ich nicht noch einmal durch die Sonne" (The air is sweet as a bird of prey/ I will not plunge through the sunlight like this again).

The novel is written retrospectively, capturing the poignant essence of a summer so perfect that the characters want to hold and preserve it forever. Wolf's narrative technique of writing from different characters' perspectives creates a broad composite picture, while there are hints of events and interactions not expanded upon. The reader wants to know more and so shares the sense of loss and nostalgia. The people are gone, and their houses burned to the ground.

Medea

Medea was Wolf's first major work after the reunification of Germany in 1990, after which Wolf became the focal point of a general attack on East German literature. Those who are critical of her see the novel as an allegory of her situation and an attempt at self-vindication. Text-immanent analyses show that the novel is concerned with a perennial problem of human nature, the dichotomy between the female emphasis on healing and the male lust for power.

The Medea of Greek mythology killed her brother, her two sons, and her former husband's new wife. Wolf's retelling has the brother dismembered by superstitious hags, the sons stoned by a mob, and the new wife drowning in a well. Central to all these incidents are issues of succession, to the throne of either Medea's native Colchis or her adopted home, Corinth. Only after the fact are the deaths falsely attributed to Medea, as calumny conveniently discredits the woman who knows too much.

Wolf's significant addition to the plot is Medea's unearthing of yet another political murder. Her incautious pursuit of this knowledge brings about her downfall. In retrospect, Medea sees she was wrong to leave Colchis, because Corinth is no better. One king has his son killed, the other king his daughter. Wolf creates multifaceted intrigue by writing from the viewpoints of six different people, none of whom has all the facts. No one, not even a reclusive sculptor, escapes unscathed from the machinations of those determined to remain in power at any cost.

Linda Schelbitzki Pickle
Updated by Jean M. Snook

Other major works

short fiction: *Moskauer Novelle*, 1961; *Unter den Linden: Drei unwahrscheinliche Geschichten*, 1974; *Gesammelte Erzählungen*, 1980 (*What Remains, and Other Stories*, 1993); *Hierzulande, andernorts: Erzählungen und andere Texte, 1994-1998*, 1999; *Mit anderem Blick*, 2005.

screenplays: *Der geteilte Himmel*, 1964 (adaptation of her novel; with Gerhard Wolf); *Fräulein Schmetterling*, 1966 (with Wolf); *Till Eulenspiegel*, 1972 (with Wolf).

nonfiction: *Lesen und Schreiben: Aufsätze und Betrachtungen*, 1971 (*The Reader and the Writer: Essays, Sketches, Memories*, 1977); *Fortgesetzter Versuch: Aufsätze, Gespräche, Essays*, 1979; *Lesen und Schreiben: Neue Sammlung*, 1980; *Die Dimension des Autors: Essays und Aufsätze, Reden, und Gespräche, 1959-1985*, 1987 (partial translations *The Fourth Dimension: Interviews with Christa Wolf*, 1988, and *The Author's Dimension: Selected Essays*, 1993); *Ansprachen*, 1988; *Sei gegrüsst und lebe: Eine Freundschaft in Briefen, 1964-1973*, 1993; *Auf dem Weg nach Tabou: Texte 1990-1994*, 1994 (*Parting from Phantoms: Selected Writings, 1990-1994*, 1997); *Monsieur, wir finden uns wieder: Briefe, 1968-1984*, 1995; *Ein Tag im Jahr: 1960-2000*, 2003 (*One Day a Year: 1960-2000*, 2007).

Bibliography

Bunyan, Anita. "Christa Wolf." In *Landmarks in German Women's Writing*, edited by Hilary Brown. New York: Peter Lang, 2007. Places Wolf's work within the context of her times and describes how being a woman has affected her writing and the reception of her works. Wolf is one of twelve German women writers discussed in this collection of essays.

Drees, Hajo. *A Comprehensive Interpretation of the Life and Work of Christa Wolf, Twentieth Century German Writer*. Lewiston, N.Y.: Edwin Mellen Press, 2002. Ambitious study of Wolf and her work draws connections between her fiction and her life. Focuses on the manifestation of identity, socialization, and artistic expression in Wolf's work.

Finney, Gail. *Christa Wolf*. New York: Twayne, 1999. Provides a thorough introduction to Wolf's life and her works. Argues that Wolf's life and career are both distinctive and representative of those of other writers of her generation.

Fries, Marilyn Sibley, ed. *Responses to Christa Wolf: Critical Essays*. Detroit, Mich.: Wayne State University Press, 1989. Collection of twenty-one essays in English that were originally delivered at a special session on Christa Wolf held during the 1982 convention of the Modern Language Association of

America. Includes a list of secondary articles and books and review articles on each of Wolf's books.

Resch, Margit. *Understanding Christa Wolf: Returning Home to a Foreign Land*. Columbia: University of South Carolina Press, 1997. Provides solid analyses of all of Wolf's major works up to 1990. Supplemented by an informative chronology, a list of selected articles in English, and an annotated bibliography of critical works.

Rossbacher, Brigitte. *Illusions of Progress: Christa Wolf and the Critique of Science in GDR Women's Literature*. New York: Peter Lang, 2000. Discussion of women writers in the former East Germany focuses on Wolf, demonstrating how the writer's criticism of the nation's technological and scientific progress also implied considerations of gender.

Smith, Colin E. *Tradition, Art, and Society: Christa Wolf's Prose*. Essen, Germany: Die blaue Eule Verlag, 1987. Provides lists that cannot be found elsewhere: the seven books edited by Wolf between 1959 and 1985; her many reviews, essays, and articles from 1952 to 1985; and conversations and interviews from 1959 to 1984. Secondary literature is conveniently subdivided into the literature on specific works. Each chapter deals with a single work.

Stamp Miller, G. Ann. *The Cultural Politics of the German Democratic Republic: The Voices of Wolf Biermann, Christa Wolf, and Heiner Müller*. Boca Raton, Fla.: BrownWalker Press, 2004. Examines how Wolf and the other two writers responded to pressures from the East German government, which demanded that they adhere to strict Marxist policies. Eventually, all three dissented and encountered problems with government authorities.

Tate, Dennis. "Christa Wolf: 'Subjective Authenticity' in Practice—An Evolving Autobiographical Project." In *Shifting Perspectives: East German Autobiographical Narratives Before and After the End of the GDR*. Rochester, N.Y.: Camden House, 2007. Chapter on Wolf is part of a larger discussion of five writers from the former East Germany that focuses on works expressing a self-reflexive concern with the writers' own lives, or what Wolf has termed "subjective authenticity." Chronicles the genesis and development of these autobiographical writings, placing them within the context of German history.

Wallace, Ian, ed. *Christa Wolf in Perspective*. Atlanta: Rodopi, 1994. Collection of thirteen essays, eleven in English, deals with Wolf's individual works, her themes and imagery, and her politics, among other topics. Published after Wolf came under attack from Western journalists.

THOMAS WOLFE

Born: Asheville, North Carolina; October 3, 1900
Died: Baltimore, Maryland; September 15, 1938
Also known as: Thomas Clayton Wolfe

Principal long fiction

Look Homeward, Angel, 1929
Of Time and the River: A Legend of a Man's Hunger in His Youth, 1935
The Web and the Rock, 1939
You Can't Go Home Again, 1940
The Short Novels of Thomas Wolfe, 1961 (C. Hugh Holman, editor)

Other literary forms

During his lifetime, Thomas Wolfe published four major works: two novels, *Look Homeward, Angel* and *Of Time and the River*; a collection of short stories, *From Death to Morning* (1935); and his description of his life as a creative artist, *The Story of a Novel* (1936). In addition to his major works, he also sold a few lengthy stories to magazines; *Scribner's* published "A Portrait of Bascom Hawke" (April, 1932) and "The Web of Earth" (July, 1939). Both of these have since been republished as short novels in *The Short Novels of Thomas Wolfe*.

Because Wolfe viewed each piece of his writing as only a part of some larger design, he frequently adapted past material to meet a present need. For example, he modified "A Portrait of Bascom Hawke" for later inclusion in *Of Time and the River*, and "The Child by Tiger" (1937), a short story he published in *The Saturday Evening Post*, appeared two years later with changes in point of view in *The Web and the Rock*. After his death, Wolfe's editor at Harper's, Edward Aswell, put together three posthumous books from two large packing cases of unfinished manuscript that Wolfe left behind. Two of these books—*The Web and the Rock* and *You Can't Go Home Again*—are novels; the third is a volume of stories titled *The Hills Beyond* (1941).

Wolfe began his career (unsuccessfully) as a playwright with *The Mountains*, which he wrote in 1920 but which was not published until 1940 by the University of North Carolina, Chapel Hill, Wolfe's alma mater. Wolfe's letters and notebooks also have been published, allowing for firsthand insight into his personal and creative life.

Achievements

Thomas Wolfe captured the essence of what it meant to be young in his time with the publication of *Look Homeward, Angel*. He further influenced readers of the Depression-plagued 1930's with stories he published in magazines such as *The New Yorker*, *Harper's Bazaar*, *Redbook*, *Scribner's Magazine*, and *The Saturday Evening Post*. Widely read in the United States and abroad, Wolfe was a well-respected author during his lifetime who in a very real sense lived the part of the driven artist. Wolfe is still read, even if not to the extent of his more significant contemporaries, Ernest Hemingway, William Faulkner, and F. Scott Fitzgerald.

In retrospect, Wolfe's achievement is especially remarkable when one considers that his literary life spanned little more than a decade. In 1957, Faulkner ranked Wolfe above all of his contemporaries when he wrote the following:

> My admiration for Wolfe is that he tried the best to get it all said; he was willing to throw away style, coherence, all the rules of preciseness to try to put all the experience of the human heart on the head of a pin.

Wolfe's weaknesses are now recognized, but he is still praised for his strengths. A balanced view of his work has emerged, and his reputation as an important figure in twentieth century American literature is secure.

Biography

Born on October 3, 1900, in Asheville, North Carolina, Thomas Clayton Wolfe was the youngest of the seven surviving children of Julia Elizabeth Westall and William Oliver Wolfe. Of Pennsylvania Dutch-German stock, Wolfe's father had intense vitality. He was a stonecutter who instilled in Wolfe a love of language, whether it be the high rhetoric of Elizabethan poetry or the low vernacular of the mountain people surrounding Asheville. Wolfe's mother was more attuned to the values of commerce than her husband (she was forever speculating in real estate). In fact, one biographer has termed the match an "epic misalliance." Domestic relations in the Wolfe household were often strained; young Wolfe grew up a witness to his father's drunken rampages and his mother's ensuing resentment. From this family cauldron came much of the autobiographical material Wolfe poured forth in *Look Homeward, Angel*.

In September of 1912, Wolfe entered the North State Fitting School, where he came under the influence of his teacher, Margaret Roberts (Margaret Leonard in *Look Homeward, Angel*). Roberts encouraged Wolfe's voracious appetite for reading by introducing him to the best of English literature. In 1916, at the precocious age of fifteen, Wolfe entered the University of North Carolina, Chapel Hill. Six feet tall and still growing (he would eventually reach six feet six inches), Wolfe was a skinny, long-legged youth, sensitive to the criticism of his older classmates. Wolfe's first year at Chapel Hill was unremarkable, but he eventually made a name for himself as an excellent student and a campus literary figure. In March of 1919, *The Return of Buck Garvin*, a play Wolfe had written in a dramatic writing course, was performed by the Carolina Playmakers, with Wolfe performing in the title role.

After graduating in 1920, Wolfe entered Harvard University to pursue his interests as a playwright. He was especially attracted by the famous workshop given by playwright George Pierce Baker (whom he would later depict as Professor Hatcher in *Of Time and the*

River). Wolfe hoped to make a literary name for himself, but after a series of setbacks, he accepted an appointment as an instructor in English at the Washington Square College of New York University and began teaching in February of 1924, continuing to do so intermittently until 1930.

In October of 1924, Wolfe made his first trip to Europe. Many of his experiences there he later incorporated into *Of Time and the River*. Returning to New York in August of 1925, Wolfe met Aline Bernstein, a wealthy married woman who was involved in the theater world of New York. For the next seven years, Wolfe participated in a stormy on-and-off again affair with Bernstein, who was seventeen years his elder. She was the mother-mistress Wolfe seemed to need; certainly, she inspired *Look Homeward, Angel*, which he commenced while abroad with Bernstein in July of 1926.

The popular image of Wolfe as a literary lion is in part caused by the critical success he achieved with *Look Homeward, Angel* but is based mostly on his personal appearance and habits. Often dressed in shabby clothes, he was known to prowl the streets of Brooklyn, where he had settled after another trip abroad in 1931. One night while wandering the streets he was overheard to say, "I wrote ten thousand words today! I wrote ten thousand words today!" Although Wolfe resented efforts to publicize his eccentricities, it was inevitable that his behavior and fame would make him a legendary figure.

In December of 1933, Wolfe began work on what was to become *Of Time and the River*. It was also during this period that Maxwell Perkins, Wolfe's editor at Scribner's, worked closely with the author on the formation of the novel. Wolfe incorporated his experiences at Harvard, in Europe, and with Bernstein into *Of Time and the River*, which picks up the Eugene Gant story where *Look Homeward, Angel* concludes. In 1937, after critics had raised questions concerning Perkins's influence on his work, Wolfe left Scribner's for Harper and Brothers. His editor at Harper's was Edward C. Aswell, and Wolfe left two large crates containing nearly one million words of manuscript with him before leaving on a tour of the West in May of 1938. In July, Wolfe fell ill with pneumonia and was hospitalized near Seattle. In September, having been transferred to Johns Hopkins Hospital in Baltimore, he underwent brain surgery for complications he suffered from tuberculosis. He died on September 15, 1938.

Thomas Wolfe. (Library of Congress)

ANALYSIS

Throughout Thomas Wolfe's fiction there is evidence of a powerful but sometimes uncontrolled mind at work. Few would argue Wolfe's genius, but many have questioned how well he directed it. Part of the difficulty may have come from his self-professed intention to create an American mythology. The result would be the record of an individual, lonely and lost in the flux of time, forever exploring the diversity of American life. Partly because of his early death and partly because of his own difficulties in giving form to ideas, Wolfe never managed to unify the vast body of his work. Add to this the considerable amount of influence his editors exerted on his manuscripts, and some intriguing questions still remain about the interrelationships of segments in the writings and the final form of his novels.

Wolfe wrote with passionate intensity, producing vast quantities of manuscript. His central themes focus on a lonely individual, the isolated artist, in search of self-discovery and the true meaning of the American experience. In *Look Homeward, Angel*, the first of these themes is most pronounced, for this is autobiography thinly veiled. The story of Eugene Gant is in many ways the story of Thomas Wolfe. After the publication of *Look Homeward, Angel*, which was generally well received, some critics began to raise questions concerning the novel's weaknesses, especially the obvious attempt by Wolfe to capture experience at the expense of artistic control. It was not until 1936, however, that the landmark case against Wolfe would be launched with the publication in the *Saturday Review* of "Genius Is Not Enough," Bernard De Voto's indictment of Wolfe and his fiction.

De Voto was responding to *The Story of a Novel*, Wolfe's extremely frank account of his own life as a writer and the work that went into *Of Time and the River*. For Wolfe, writing was a chaotic experience, something done with great pain and toil. De Voto acknowledged that Wolfe was a genius "of the good old-fashioned, romantic kind, possessed by a demon, driven by the gales of his own fury, helpless before the lava-flood of his own passion"; he further argued, however, that such genius was in and of itself not enough. Today the legacy of De Voto's remarks remains manifest in a series of stereotypes: By some readers (especially academics), Wolfe is still thought of as one who never controlled his rhetoric, as one who was unable to organize his work, and as one who sometimes pushed autobiography to the limits of reporting.

To illustrate Wolfe's lack of rhetorical restraint, De Voto pointed to *Of Time and the River*, commenting that Wolfe invested each experience he described with so much raw emotion that a midnight snack took on the same importance as the death of Oliver Gant. As De Voto stated, "If the death of one's father comes out emotionally even with ham-on-rye, then the art of fiction is cockeyed." As for the charge that Wolfe was a writer who never exerted sufficient control over his material, De Voto and others have cited the sprawling sections of his mammoth novels where there is supportive evidence that episodes stand by themselves rather than in relation to others. The extent of Wolfe's involvement with his editors (Perkins at Scribners from 1928 to 1937; Aswell at Harper's from 1937 to 1938) also raises questions about his own ability to revise and organize his novels.

Perhaps the most revealing example of editorial influence on Wolfe's fiction concerns *Of Time and the River*. While Wolfe was working on the novel, Perkins met with him day and night for more than a year in an attempt to help him gain control over the voluminous amount of material he had written. Often Perkins would ask Wolfe to go home and cut a section, only to find that he would return with an episode thousands of words longer. In one of the most dramatic decisions any editor has made with a figure as significant as Wolfe, Perkins, without Wolfe's final approval, sent the manuscript of *Of Time and the River* to the printer in September of 1934. Perkins made the decision because he felt the novel was as complete as Wolfe could make it and that Wolfe needed to get on with other work. Whatever the reasons, the ultimate responsibility for the publication of any book rests squarely on the writer. Because Wolfe was so deferential to his editor and because he was unable or unwilling to see his novel through to the end, he opened himself to questions concerning his craftsmanship, questions that are still being asked today.

Finally, there remains the issue of autobiography in Wolfe's novels. Wolfe himself claimed that autobiography was a part of any serious creative work, but there are in his novels, especially *Look Homeward, Angel*, sections that read like a mere diary. There is also a great deal of artistic invention in his novels, and certainly almost all writers use material based on their own experiences; nevertheless, many of Wolfe's depictions were so thinly fictionalized that individuals were easily recognized, and many were hurt and embarrassed by what they thought were the unflattering portraits Wolfe rendered of them. Wolfe's use of autobiography pushed to journalistic limits raises more questions about his fictional method.

Although Wolfe's rhetoric, his conception of structure, and the autobiographical element within his work have been discussed as weaknesses, these three elements can also be cited as the strengths of his writing. For example, it is true there is ample evidence to support De

Voto's claim that Wolfe's rhetoric is often artificially heightened, but at the same time, one of his most compelling attributes is his ability to depict something as insignificant as a "ham-on-rye" so clearly that readers may suddenly find themselves hungry. More to the point, however, are passages such as the Laura James sections of *Look Homeward, Angel* in which Wolfe manages to capture as well as any writer what it means to be young and in love. There are also numerous passages within his other novels that stand as some of the most poetic set pieces to be found in prose. In large measure, Wolfe is still read because of the magnificence of his style, however extravagant it may be at times.

Wolfe held to an organic theory of art, one in which content dictates form. He was constantly searching for new ways to communicate experience; in this sense, the criticism directed at him for being a "formless" writer may in some ways be unfair. Certainly there is no doubt that in his attempts to depart from traditional formats he sometimes lost control of his material—*Of Time and the River*, for example, is marred by this flaw. On the other hand, he did manage to find an effective structure in "The Web of Earth," his lengthy story written under the influence of James Joyce. The entire work is filtered through the consciousness of an old woman engaged in reminiscence, and it is the finest example of artistic unity in Wolfe's work. In *Look Homeward, Angel*, Wolfe modified a traditional novelistic form, the bildungsroman (the story of a youth initiated by experience into maturity), organizing the novel not around a unified sequence of events but instead around a series of sense impressions. In this way, the loose structure serves to complement the rhapsodic style. The result is a powerful rendering of the book's central theme—that of an artistic youth lost and in search of self-knowledge and self-definition.

As for the contention that Wolfe is too highly autobiographical, that his writing too often approaches mere reportage, there can be no denying that on occasion, he is guilty as charged. In most instances, however, he was by no means a mere reporter of events. His fiction is memorable because he was such an apt interpreter of human beings and everyday experiences. He was able to synthesize experience into art; he himself claimed that everything in a work of art is changed, that nothing is a literal representation of actual experience. Whether he always achieved this transmutation, it can safely be said that Wolfe is still read because his novels stand as a testimony to human experience artistically rendered from a unique and personal vision.

Look Homeward, Angel

Look Homeward, Angel, Wolfe's first and most significant novel, made use of extensive autobiographical material. In many ways, it is the story of his own life, the life of his family, his neighbors, and the region in which he lived. For those who know something of Wolfe's background, there are unmistakable connections between the fictional characters in *Look Homeward, Angel* and the real people among whom Wolfe grew up in Asheville, North Carolina. After the novel's publication, many from his hometown—and indeed many in his own family—were angered by what they took to be unflattering depictions of themselves in the novel. Wolfe's own account of the reaction to his novel can be found in *The Story of a Novel*, wherein he describes the uproar in Asheville and provides his own defense of his fictional method. Essentially, Wolfe believed that the people he described, whatever their faults, were magnificent. As magnificent as he thought his characters were, however, he often described them (no doubt truthfully) with all their faults made highly visible.

The ethics of Wolfe's method can be questioned when one considers how it must have been to have lived in Asheville at the time the novel was published, to have opened its pages and to have found the characters so thinly fictionalized that their real counterparts could be easily identified. The ethical issue is not so much whether Wolfe was accurate in his depictions of the whole range of humanity he described, but rather how one would feel if he or she were identified as the model for the town drunk or as the counterpart of the unscrupulous businessperson. It did not take long for the people of Asheville to start pointing fingers at one another after figuring out who was who in the novel. Perhaps with some justification, all fingers eventually pointed toward Wolfe; the controversy over what he had done to his town and the people in it was so pronounced that he was unable to return to Asheville until seven years after the publication of *Look Homeward, Angel*.

Wolfe departed from the development of a traditional

plot in *Look Homeward, Angel* and instead made use of impressionistic realism to tie events and characters together. The narrator moves in and out of the consciousness of the principal characters, giving readers impressions of their inner feelings and motivations. As much as anything else, *Look Homeward, Angel* is the story of a quest, a search for self-knowledge and for lasting human interaction. The subtitle of the novel is *A Story of the Buried Life*, and much of what Wolfe depicts is concerned with the inner lives of the characters in the novel—what they really think and feel as well as how isolated and alienated they are from one another. In this sense, the novel explores the relationships of time, change, and death as elements that will always frustrate the human desire for happiness and fulfillment.

Look Homeward, Angel was initially titled "O Lost" and then "Alone, Alone." The title on which Wolfe finally settled comes from "Lycidas," John Milton's poem in which the archangel Michael is asked to look back toward England to mourn a young man's death and all the unfulfilled potential it signifies. Eugene Gant is, like most of Wolfe's protagonists, the isolated and sensitive artist in search of meaning and companionship in a hostile world. Given this theme, it is ironic that some of Wolfe's least effective passages are the results of his attempts to describe Eugene's feelings of loneliness and despair. In such segments (which recur in almost all of Wolfe's works), he often lapses into contrived language; rather than arising from natural consequences or from the interplay between one character and another, feelings seem forced by authorial intervention. On the other hand, the novel does contain some of his finest writing, especially when he describes people, places, and things with visionary intensity.

Look Homeward, Angel covers the first twenty years of Eugene Gant's life—his adolescence, his four years at the private school of Margaret Leonard, and his four years at the university. A pattern of potential fulfillment destroyed by frustration is personified in Eugene's parents, Eliza and Oliver, who are modeled on Wolfe's own mother and father. Oliver Gant is a stonecutter who passionately desires to create something beautiful, to carve an angel's head. He is an unfulfilled artist, a man of intense vitality who desires a full and sensuous life. His intensity, his capacity for life, is checked by his wife, Eliza, who is his antithesis: parsimonious, cold, and materialistic.

This pattern of frustrated potential recurs throughout the novel. In one example, after spending his first year at the university and losing his innocence in a brothel, Eugene returns home to spend the summer at Dixieland, his mother's boardinghouse. There he meets and falls in love with Laura James (based on his own first love, Clara Paul). In his descriptions of the young, passionate love that develops between them, Wolfe's prose becomes a lyrical celebration that turns to tragic frustration as Eugene learns that Laura is engaged to marry another young man back home, that she will never be a part of his life again. Thus, potential (in this example, physical and spiritual union between Eugene and Laura) is checked by reality (separation and isolation). This pattern manifests itself in varying ways throughout the novel. The story of a youth coming of age by initiation into experience, *Look Homeward, Angel* is a comprehensive account of the inner life of a sensitive and artistic youth.

With the publication of *Look Homeward, Angel*, Wolfe was thrust (not unwillingly) into the limelight as a legend, a novelist who demonstrated enormous potential. His success was spectacular, but because he was a driven artist (much like his fictional counterpart, Eugene Gant), his initial success created a good many subsequent problems. He immediately felt the burden to surpass his first effort with an even better second novel. At the same time, he ran into difficulty giving form to his expansive ideas (a problem with which he would grapple for the remainder of his life). During this same period, he also began leading a turbulent private life. He was involved with Aline Bernstein (the A. B. to whom *Look Homeward, Angel* is dedicated), and their relationship—as tempestuous as any could conceivably be—would figure heavily in the remainder of his life and work.

Of Time and the River

Composed of eight sections, each of which is named after some epic or mythic figure, *Of Time and the River* exceeds nine hundred pages in length and spans two continents, continuing the story of Thomas Wolfe as personified in the character of Eugene Gant. Wolfe continues the story with Eugene's departure from Altamont for study at Harvard. He stated his ambitious theme for *Of Time and the River* in *The Story of a Novel*; his central idea was to depict the search for a father, not only in a literal but also in a figurative sense. While trying to exemplify his theme, Wolfe also struggled to form *Of Time and the River* out of the vast amount of manuscript he had written (a detailed discussion of that struggle is related in *The Story of a Novel*). The struggle reached its peak when his editor, Perkins, sent the novel to press without Wolfe's knowledge. In one of his letters to Perkins, Wolfe claimed that another six months' work would have allowed him to complete the necessary revisions that would have made the book less episodic.

There can be no doubt that had Wolfe written *Of Time and the River* without Perkins's influence, it would have been a very different novel—perhaps a better one. As it stands, it is, as Wolfe himself noted, episodic; its parts are not always aligned to form a unified plot. Even so, there are fine passages throughout that more than compensate for its ponderous pace and meandering plot. In *The Story of a Novel*, Wolfe describes how he wrote one scene that ran to eighty thousand words (about two hundred pages). He was attempting to capture "the full flood and fabric" of four people simply talking to one another for four continuous hours. This scene, as good as he thought it was, eventually was cut, but it illustrates the massive amount of writing he did for the novel as well as the extensive amount of cutting he did to get it into publishable form.

Perhaps the novel's most magnificent scene is that which describes the death of Eugene's father, who has been slowly dying of cancer. Gant, the paternal figure whose presence was so unforgettable in *Look Homeward, Angel*, is now old and enfeebled. His death, which comes in a final moment of tranquillity, stands in stark contrast to his life, which was lived with violent gestures and howling protests. Often drunk, sometimes violent, he was a hard man to live with, but his death comes as a reminder that life lived intensely—however excessively—is life worth living. The death of his wife, Eliza, would not begin to elicit the intensity of emotion aroused by his final moments, for she stands as a testimony to all that opposes the force and fury of his life.

Other memorable scenes in the novel include those that take place in Boston with Eugene's uncle, Bascom Pentland. Uncle Bascom and his demented wife are two of the more finely drawn eccentrics in the novel. These segments as well as others involving Eugene's dreams to become a playwright, his time spent as an English instructor at a city university in New York, and his eventual travel to Europe, all contribute to Wolfe's attempt to describe the vast array of people, places, and things unique to the American experience.

While working out his central theme of a search for a father, Wolfe developed a three-part vision of time: time present, time past, and time eternal. The first, time present, is the time in which the actual events in the novel take place, the time of reality. The second, time past, represents all of the accumulated experience that affects time present. The third, time eternal, stands for the lasting time of oceans, forests, and rivers, of things that form the permanent backdrop for people's experiences. These three levels of time allow Wolfe to contrast, in a vast and symbolic scale, the relationship of past, present, and eternal experience with the experience of Eugene Gant. The result is an intensely personal search for meaning, an attempt to reconcile opposites, to find something lasting and meaningful.

Throughout the novel, a scene that takes place in the present may be linked with past scenes and eternal scenes. In this way, all three levels of time are united. For example, a train ride taking place in present time provides Eugene with the opportunity to recall the travelers of earlier days, their epic searching, their longing for discovery, for movement. During the same segment, Eugene speculates that other people in the future (eternal time) will also travel the earth in search of one another. The novel frequently develops itself in this way, and it is these segments that give the novel its mysterious, almost haunting, quality. At the same time, however, these same passages become repetitious (if not tedious), and illustrate once again the lack of restraint so evident throughout Wolfe's work. In contrast to these overwritten segments are a good many specific characterizations as well as a variety of satiric passages aimed at mediocre people, middle-class values, and intellectual pretenders. This is a vast and comprehensive book that ends when Eugene sets sail back to the United States. Aboard ship he meets Esther Jack (Aline Bernstein), who, although certainly not the father for whom he is searching, is nevertheless someone who can help him transcend the tormented youth he has endured to this point in his life.

The Web and the Rock

Wolfe claimed that he was turning away from the books he had previously written, that *The Web and the Rock* would be his most "objective" work to date. It should be noted that at that time, Wolfe had become particularly sensitive about the criticism he had received from De Voto and others concerning his alleged inability to exert artistic control over his material. As a result, not only did he claim his new novel to be objective, but also he abandoned his previous protagonist, Eugene Gant, in favor of a new one, George "Monk" Webber. The change was more in name than in substance, however, for Webber, like Eugene Gant, bears a close resemblance to Wolfe himself. Indeed, *The Web and the Rock* is quite similar to Wolfe's earlier works: Its first half parallels *Look Homeward, Angel* while its second half stands as a sequel to *Of Time and the River*.

One of the strongest chapters in the novel is enlightening insofar as it illustrates how Wolfe continually reshaped past material. "The Child by Tiger" was first published in 1937 as a short story, but in the eighth chapter of *The Web and the Rock*, Wolfe reworks the story with changes in character and point of view. It is a moving story about the nature of good and evil, innocence and experience. Dick Prosser, a black man of ability and potential, is the object of the racial prejudice that was so pronounced in the South during the early part of the twentieth century. He befriends several young white boys and teaches them how to throw a football, how to box, and how to make a fire. In short, he becomes a kindly father figure who initiates them into experience.

There is, however, another side to Prosser. Driven to the point of madness by prejudicial treatment, by his own apocalyptic brand of religion, and by his involvement with a woman, he goes on a shooting spree one night, killing blacks and whites alike. Eventually shot by the mob formed to hunt him down, his bullet-riddled body is hung up for display in the window of the undertaker's parlor. In the course of these events, the young men who were Prosser's friends are initiated into a world full of violence and death. For the first time in their lives, they experience profound loss, and they witness evil as it is personified in the bloodthirsty mob. Woven within the story are stanzas from William Blake's poem "The Tyger," from which the chapter title is derived.

In what makes up the second half of the novel, Wolfe deals with his own experiences in New York City. He explores his relationship with Bernstein, depicting her as a sophisticated mistress and himself as a brilliant but egocentric genius. Their relationship is described in detail—from their love-making and eating to their quarrels and reconciliations. These segments are remarkable for their candor and intriguing because of the insight they provide into the tempestuous relationship between the two. Webber's past experiences, the environment in which he was reared, and his ancestry symbolically form the web in which he is snared, and, as Esther Jack becomes a part of that web, he escapes to Germany. His search for the rock, the strength and beauty of vision that is represented by the father figure for whom he longs, is interrupted by his realization at the end of the novel that "you can't go home again." In short, he knows that he must look to the future to escape the past.

You Can't Go Home Again

Continuing the chronicle of George Webber's life and artistic development, *You Can't Go Home Again* metaphorically develops the theme that Webber cannot go "home," cannot return to past places, old ideas, and former experiences because time and change have corrupted them. In this sense, "home" is an idealized vision of the United States as it appeared to George in his youth. These youthful visions come into abrupt contact with reality, and the resulting clash allows Wolfe to explore the very fabric of American society.

The novel begins approximately six months after *The Web and the Rock* ends. Webber has returned home to the United States, and, against his better judgment, he decides to resume his relationship with Esther Jack. He also resumes work on his novel *Home to Our Mountains (Look Homeward, Angel)* and finds a publisher, James Rodney (Scribner's), as well as a sympathetic editor and father figure, Foxhall Edwards (Perkins). Before his book is published, however, he returns home for the first time in years to attend the funeral of his Aunt Maw. Home in this novel is Libya Hill (like the Altamont of *Look Homeward, Angel*, the locale still represents Asheville, North Carolina). On the train trip home, he meets his childhood friend Nebraska Crane, a onetime big-league baseball star. Crane, a Cherokee Indian, is now satisfied to lead the simple life of a family man and part-time tobacco farmer, standing in contrast to Webber, whose intellectual drive and literary ambition make him a driven city man.

Also on the train is Judge Rumford Bland, a blind syphilitic whose corruption serves to symbolize the corruption in Libya Hill toward which Webber is traveling. Upon his arrival, Webber finds that his quiet boyhood town has become crazed from a land-boom mentality that has everyone making huge paper fortunes in real estate (these events parallel those immediately preceding the Depression). Thus, his idealized expectations of home are shattered by the corruption and madness running rampant throughout Libya Hill.

After the publication of his novel, Webber receives abusive letters from the residents of Libya Hill. Typically, Wolfe incorporated his own experiences into his fiction. In this instance, he drew on his unpleasant memories of what happened after he published *Look Homeward, Angel*. An entire book in the novel ("The World That Jack Built") is devoted to the wealthy lives of Esther and Frederick Jack (the Bernsteins). Writing about his own breakup with Aline Bernstein, Wolfe describes Webber's move to Brooklyn and the end of his relationship with Esther Jack. In Brooklyn, Webber learns to love the low-life characters who inhabit the streets—the prostitutes, the derelicts, and the petty criminals—for they are very much a part of the American experience. To ignore them—or worse yet, to explain them away somehow—would be to deny the underbelly of America that Webber (and Wolfe) found so compelling.

After his years in Brooklyn (with scenes devoted to his relationship with Edwards, his editor), Webber tires of New York and sails for Europe. In Germany, he is welcomed with the fame and notoriety he has sought for so long, but he also witnesses the darker side of Nazi Germany. The novel is the story of one man's pilgrimage, a search for a faith that will endure within a society so corrupt that each individual is destroyed by it. *You Can't Go Home Again* is not an entirely cynical book, however, for it concludes with a sense of hope and faith in the future.

Both *The Web and the Rock* and *You Can't Go Home Again* were put together by Aswell, Wolfe's editor at Harper's, and published posthumously as novels. It was not until 1962, when Richard S. Kennedy published *The Window of Memory: The Literary Career of Thomas Wolfe* that the extent of Aswell's influence on the two novels became fully known. Just before his death, Wolfe left a large packing crate of manuscript with Aswell. From that collection of manuscript, it was generally assumed that Aswell found two separate narratives, which he then published as the two posthumous novels. Kennedy discovered, after an extensive study of Wolfe's papers and manuscripts at Harvard University, that Aswell constructed *The Web and the Rock* and *You Can't Go Home Again* from what was a massive—but fragmentary—amount of manuscript that Wolfe apparently intended to condense into a single narrative. Had Wolfe lived, he most certainly would not have published the two novels as Aswell published them. In a very real way, they are as much the product of Aswell's editorializing as they are a product of Wolfe's imagination. Even so, the two novels represent a significant part of Wolfe's creative output, and analysis of them can help put his entire achievement into a clearer perspective.

Throughout his novels, Wolfe explored isolation, death, and the changes wrought by time—themes that exemplify his interest in the darker elements of life. In his attempts to capture the essence of a moment, he often overlooked the artistic demands that the novel imposes on any writer. He was not a craftsman of the novel because he often sacrificed form, unity, and coherence to capture experience. His reputation is linked directly to his ambitious attempts to say it all, and *Look Homeward, Angel*, although only the beginning of the story Wolfe desired to tell, stands as his most satisfying and fully realized work.

Philip A. Luther

Other major works

SHORT FICTION: *From Death to Morning*, 1935; *The Hills Beyond*, 1941; *The Complete Short Stories of Thomas Wolfe*, 1987.

PLAYS: *The Mountains*, pr. 1921; *Welcome to Our City*, pr. 1923 (pb. only in Germany as *Willkommen in Altamont*, 1962); *Mannerhouse*, pb. 1948.

POETRY: *The Face of a Nation: Poetical Passages from the Writings of Thomas Wolfe*, 1939; *A Stone, a Leaf, a Door: Poems by Thomas Wolfe*, 1945.

NONFICTION: *The Story of a Novel*, 1936; *Thomas*

Wolfe's Letters to His Mother, 1943 (John Skally, editor); *The Portable Thomas Wolfe*, 1946 (Maxwell Geisman, editor); *The Letters of Thomas Wolfe*, 1956 (Elizabeth Nowell, editor); *The Notebooks of Thomas Wolfe*, 1970 (Richard S. Kennedy and Paschal Reeves, editors); *The Thomas Wolfe Reader*, 1982 (C. Hugh Holman, editor); *The Autobiography of an American Novelist: Thomas Wolfe*, 1983; *Beyond Love and Loyalty: The Letters of Thomas Wolfe and Elizabeth Nowell*, 1983 (Kennedy, editor); *My Other Loneliness: Letters of Thomas Wolfe and Aline Bernstein*, 1983 (Suzanne Stutman, editor); *To Loot My Life Clean: The Thomas Wolfe/Maxwell Perkins Correspondence*, 2000 (Matthew J. Bruccoli and Park Bucker, editors); *Windows of the Heart: The Correspondence of Thomas Wolfe and Margaret Roberts*, 2007 (Ted Mitchell, editor); *The Magical Campus: University of North Carolina Writings, 1917-1920*, 2008 (Bruccoli and Aldo P. Magi, editors).

Bibliography

Bloom, Harold, ed. *Thomas Wolfe*. New York: Chelsea House, 2000. A compendium of critical essays on Wolfe's oeuvre. Includes an introduction, a chronology, and a bibliography.

Donald, David Herbert. *Look Homeward: A Life of Thomas Wolfe*. 1987. Reprint. Cambridge, Mass.: Harvard University Press, 2003. Donald's fine biography stresses Wolfe's accomplishment as a social historian and his novels as "a barometer of American culture." Like others, Donald admits that Wolfe's work contains much bad writing, but he confesses to responding enthusiastically to the good.

Ensign, Robert Taylor. *Lean Down Your Ear upon the Earth, and Listen: Thomas Wolfe's Greener Modernism*. Columbia: University of South Carolina Press, 2003. An ecocritical interpretation of Wolfe's work, in which Ensign examines the writer's representation of the natural world and his characters' connection with it. Ensign devotes one chapter to a "green" analysis of *Look Homeward, Angel*. Includes a bibliography and an index.

Evans, Elizabeth. *Thomas Wolfe*. New York: Frederick Ungar, 1984. Provides an excellent shorter introduction to Wolfe for both the beginning and the advanced student. Economical and accurate, it is keyed clearly to Wolfe scholarship and is rich in unpretentious literary allusion. Though Evans is cautious in her admiration of Wolfe's fiction, she is appreciative of it as well. Contains a chronology and a good short bibliography.

Holliday, Shawn. *Thomas Wolfe and the Politics of Modernism*. New York: Peter Lang, 2001. A reevaluation of Wolfe, in which Holliday examines how the experimental nature of his fiction and other aspects of his work and life define him as a modernist writer.

Holman, C. Hugh. *The World of Thomas Wolfe*. New York: Charles Scribner's Sons, 1962. An older text, this book is specifically designed for high school and college students. A good cross section of Wolfe criticism is offered, with practical information for further study. Includes suggested topics for library research and term papers.

Idol, John Lane, Jr. *A Thomas Wolfe Companion*. New York: Greenwood Press, 1987. An expression of the resurgence of interest in Wolfe by an unabashed devotee, this handy book is a potpourri of Wolfeana, with glossaries of characters and places, genealogical charts of Wolfe's fictional families, a descriptive and analytic bibliography of primary works, and an annotated bibliography of secondary materials. Also contains information on the various collections of Wolfe material, the Thomas Wolfe Society, and *The Thomas Wolfe Review*.

Johnston, Carol Ingalls. *Of Time and the Artist: Thomas Wolfe, His Novels, and the Critics*. Columbia, S.C.: Camden House, 1996. Johnston examines the bitter relationship between Wolfe and the literary critics, and how he responded to their critiques in his fiction and letters. Re-creates the literary marketplace of the 1920's and 1930's, and examines Wolfe's earliest critical reception.

Kennedy, Richard S. *The Window of Memory*. Chapel Hill: University of North Carolina Press, 1962. Remains indispensable to the study of Wolfe; objective, scholarly, and analytic, this book melds Wolfe's work and life into an artistic synthesis. Particularly valuable as a study of the creative process.

McElderry, Bruce R. *Thomas Wolfe*. New York: Twayne, 1964. An excellent basic introduction to Wolfe's life and work, McElderry's study provides lucid analysis well supported by standard critical opinion. Contains a useful chronology and annotated select bibliographies of primary and secondary sources.

Rubin, Louis D., Jr., ed. *Thomas Wolfe: A Collection of Critical Essays*. Englewood Cliffs, N.J.: Prentice-Hall, 1973. A collection, with an introduction by Rubin, of a dozen stimulating essays by a variety of critics, scholars, and writers ranging from the impressionistic—a mode Wolfe inevitably inspires—to the scholarly. Contains the notorious Bernard De Voto review (1936) of *The Story of a Novel*.

TOM WOLFE

Born: Richmond, Virginia; March 2, 1931
Also known as: Thomas Kennerly Wolfe, Jr.

Principal long fiction

The Bonfire of the Vanities, 1987
A Man in Full, 1998
I Am Charlotte Simmons, 2004

Other literary forms

Tom Wolfe is known as one of the most original and influential of the New Journalists to come to popular attention during the mid-1960's. His collections of essays and original drawings on contemporary American lifestyle include *The Pump House Gang* (1968), *Radical Chic and Mau-Mauing the Flak Catchers* (1970), and *Mauve Gloves and Madmen, Clutter and Vine, and Other Stories, Sketches, and Essays* (1976). In these and other works, Wolfe skewered the foibles of a period he named the me decade. In *The Painted Word* (1975), he addressed what he saw as the false pretensions and theory-driven impulses of modern art, and he took on the similar hoaxing of the general public by architects in *From Bauhaus to Our House* (1981).

Prior to his venture into long fiction, Wolfe's most extensive and successful work was *The Right Stuff* (1979), a lengthy, well-researched, and engrossing study of the manned spaceflight efforts of the United States from their beginnings through the end of the original Mercury program. The book has been widely recognized for its incisive and penetrating exploration of the unique worldview of test pilots and astronauts and for its explanation of the almost inexpressible concept of "the right stuff."

Achievements

During his career, although often attacked by cultural critics, Tom Wolfe has become one of the most recognized and honored of American writers. In 1973, he received the Frank Luther Mott Award for research in journalism, and in 1977 he was named Virginia Laureate for Literature. After the publication of *The Right Stuff*, he was widely recognized, winning the Award in Excellence in Literature from the American Institute of Arts and Letters, the Columbia Journalism Award, and the American Book Award. In 1986 he was given the Washington Irving Medal for Literary Excellence.

An even more important mark of Wolfe's achievement, however, is the fact that he is largely credited with launching an entire literary movement, that of New Journalism, which emerged during the 1960's and 1970's and influenced not only nonfiction writing but also fiction itself.

Biography

Born and raised in Richmond, Virginia, Thomas Kennerly Wolfe, Jr., enjoyed a childhood that exposed him to the world of the arts, especially literature. After graduating from Washington and Lee University, he enrolled at Yale University, where he majored in American studies. Before completing his dissertation but after finishing his course work, he left Yale to work at the *Springfield Union* newspaper, where he began as a city hall reporter. He received his doctorate from Yale in 1957.

In 1959 Wolfe took a position with *The Washington Post*, and then, in 1962, joined one of the most literate and well-written newspapers in the nation, the *New York Herald-Tribune*, as a staff writer for its Sunday magazine supplement. Wolfe quickly established a reputation as one of the paper's finest reporters, with a style that was innovative, energetic, and unique. In 1965 Wolfe angered the literary establishment with a scathing, accurate, and enormously funny dissection of the sacrosanct *New Yorker* magazine.

During these years Wolfe, along with such writers as Norman Mailer, Truman Capote, and Hunter S. Thompson, was establishing what would become known as New Journalism, a genre that blurred or even erased the boundaries between the reporter and the story, and that reveled in subjective and highly idiosyncratic styles. Wolfe's *The Kandy-Kolored Tangerine-Flake Streamline Baby* (1965), a collection of articles chronicling the youth culture of the mid-1960's, was followed by *The Electric Kool-Aid Acid Test* (1968), his in-depth study of author Ken Kesey and his drug-indulging band of Merry Pranksters. In 1979 Wolfe published the quintessential volume of New Journalism, *The Right Stuff*, a history of the formative years of the U.S. space program.

In 1984 Wolfe embarked on a daring and risky adventure, writing a novel to be published in successive issues of *Rolling Stone* magazine. Much as English writers Charles Dickens and William Makepeace Thackeray had done, Wolfe committed himself to producing chapters on a tight deadline. The first installment of *The Bonfire of the Vanities* first appeared in *Rolling Stone* in July, 1984; the twenty-seventh and final installment appeared almost exactly one year later. Wolfe subsequently revised the work substantially, and it was published in hardcover in 1987. The novel became a best seller that also won great critical acclaim. An unsuccessful and much-criticized motion-picture adaptation of the novel was released in 1990.

For almost a decade following *The Bonfire of the Vanities*, Wolfe returned to journalism. It was not until 1998 that he again turned to fiction, publishing *A Man in Full*, about Atlanta real estate entrepreneur Charlie Croker. Like *The Bonfire of the Vanities*, the novel was embraced by critics and the reading public; it too became a best seller and further confirmed Wolfe's ability to write successfully, even brilliantly, in both nonfictional and fictional genres.

Tom Wolfe. (© Nancy Crampton)

Analysis

Tom Wolfe's novels are grounded in the social realism and satire of writers such as Dickens, Thackeray, and Honoré de Balzac, and they are filled with the sharp observations of class and caste characteristic of his nonfiction pieces. Wolfe has stated that he admires Balzac's assessment of himself as "society's secretary" and that he wants his own writing to reflect reality.

The Bonfire of the Vanities

The Bonfire of the Vanities is satire in its clearest and most uncompromising sense, an expression of moral nausea made bearable only by the presence of sharp, mordant humor. The novel's title and much of its theme come from two major sources. The first is the career of the Italian reforming cleric Girolamo Savonarola (1452-1498), who for a brief time convinced the citizens of Florence to destroy their luxury goods in a literal bonfire of the vanities. After their initial exuberance wore off, the Florentines decided to burn Savonarola instead. The second source is Thackeray's novel *Vanity Fair* (1847-1848, serial; 1848, book), which satirizes the excesses of society in early nineteenth century England.

The plot of the novel is relatively simple: Sherman McCoy, a bond trader on Wall Street and self-proclaimed "master of the universe" for his financial dealings, is indulging in an adulterous affair with Maria Ruskin, wife of a wealthy financier. One evening, as Sherman is returning Maria from the airport in his Mercedes, he goes astray and ends up in the unfamiliar and frightening confines of the Bronx. Fleeing what appears to be a bungled highway robbery attempt, Maria, who is driving, accidentally hits a young black man, Henry Lamb, with the car.

When Henry Lamb ends up with a concussion in the hospital, activist Reverend Bacon mobilizes the black community to force Bronx district attorney Abraham Weiss and his assistant Larry Kramer into action. The police find evidence that might link Sherman to the crime, and British tabloid journalist Peter Fallow writes a series of articles about the incident that further inflame tensions in the city. Sherman is indicted, and during the trial he and Maria turn against each other. Her crucial evidence is disallowed on a technicality, and Sherman's indictment is dismissed, resulting in a near riot. In a brief, ironic epilogue cast a year later, many of the major characters have fallen, through divorce, disgrace, or defeat in reelection campaigns. Only Sherman remains, still a defendant, as well as Reverend Bacon, the manipulator of protests and protesters.

The characters in *The Bonfire of the Vanities* are defined by their possessions. The book is a lovingly precise catalog of clothes, shoes, furniture, and accessories, all of fine craftsmanship and artistry, but valued, sometimes worshiped, because of their cost. Additionally, the vanities are appropriately relative: Sherman McCoy's \$1.6 million apartment is juxtaposed with the \$750 rent-controlled love nest that assistant district attorney Kramer takes over from Maria for his own mistress. The antics of Sherman's supposed friends as they try to make their way in the hive of society are no less ridiculous than the efforts of Abraham Weiss to remain district attorney.

The Bonfire of the Vanities falters when it approaches the terrain and the people alien to its hero, Sherman McCoy—the Bronx and its African American population, most of them poor, many of them victimized by crime, some of them criminals themselves. Although Wolfe's ear for speech and nuance is unrivaled, he is less certain about the other aspects of the lives of these characters, more cautious and ambivalent about entering into their minds and psyches. The Reverend Bacon is given minimal treatment, pictured as an accomplished, even sophisticated, shakedown artist skilled at piercing the armor of the white establishment, whether through guilt, fear, or power politics. It is a portrait accurate enough to be satirically truthful but so broad as to be uncomfortably close to stereotype. Roland Auburn, a black youth involved in the aborted robbery attempt, is a man who can arrange for endless deliveries of new white sneakers while imprisoned in the New York City criminal justice system. Beyond Auburn and Bacon, the black characters in *The Bonfire of the Vanities* are "extras" in the crowds during Reverend Bacon's demonstrations.

Still, the novel pulsates with the energy, vigor, and vulgarisms of New York City in the latter half of the twentieth century. Sherman McCoy and his fellow characters may not be up to anything essentially worthwhile in the long-range scheme of things (always a consideration of the satirist), and they are certainly deeply flawed human beings, but they are as destructive as the followers of Savonarola and as active as the puppets Thackeray created.

A Man in Full

An acidly etched survey of the influences of race and wealth, caste, and class on life in the new South, *A Man in Full* is set in the South's unofficial capital, Atlanta, Georgia. This is the city of Charlie Croker, who came roaring out of southwestern Georgia to achieve fame playing both offense and defense as Georgia Tech's "Sixty Minute Man" to become one of Atlanta's most successful and well-known real estate developers. His latest creation, Croker Concourse, gleams proudly northeast of the central city, a symbol of his triumph, but already bank loan officers are demanding that Charlie restructure his company and sell off executive toys such as his jets, and they even cast coldly calculating eyes on his beloved plantation, Turpmtine.

Atlanta lawyer Roger White II (dubbed Roger Too White by his fraternity brother Wes Jordan, now Atlanta's mayor) is asked to secure Charlie Croker's public support of Fareek "The Cannon" Fanon, a star football player at Georgia Tech accused (although neither officially nor publicly) of date rape by the daughter of one of Atlanta's most influential businessmen. In exchange, Roger White can help Charlie by having the banks ease their demands.

In the meantime, Conrad Hensley, a warehouse worker in California for Croker Global Foods, is laid off as part of a drive to cut costs for Charlie's far-flung companies. Before long, in a series of misadventures, Conrad sits in a prison cell, his only diversion a volume of Epictetus, the Stoic philosopher. He begins to read and then to understand. Delivered from prison by an earthquake, Conrad makes his way to Atlanta, where he meets and befriends Charlie Croker and imparts the teachings of Epictetus. At the news conference during which he is expected to support Fanon, Charlie turns away from the banks, the black politicians, and the white power structure to reclaim his own integrity. It is when he renounces those who had a claim on his soul that Charlie Croker truly becomes "a man in full."

As Wolfe glaringly exposes New York City in *The Bonfire of the Vanities*, he goes after Atlanta in *A Man in Full*. The city's acclaimed economic strength, like Charlie Croker's own empire, is an illusion. The towers downtown are deserted when work ends as their inhabitants begin the longest and worst commute in the United States, leaving the inner city 75 percent African American, creating a division that is as fatal as it is fatally ignored. Within the two communities, black and white, there are further divisions, highlighted by degrees of color, levels of wealth, and shades of accents and dialect—all of which, once again, Wolfe captures with a mix of confidence and exuberance.

I Am Charlotte Simmons

In a preface to *I Am Charlotte Simmons*, Wolfe details a scientific study of two groups of cats, those in one group having small portions of their brains removed, those in the other remaining intact. The altered cats begin displaying aberrant behavior, engaging in doglike sexual movements but without stimulus and responding passively to terrifying situations, seemingly unable to sense danger. More intriguing is the reaction of the unaltered cats kept caged in full view of the show: They copy what they see. At first this scenario seems to bear little relationship to what promises to be a typical Wolfe study, this time of campus life at a fictional elite university modeled on several schools he visited in preparing to write the novel. The reader soon sees what he has in mind, however, in his tale of an innocent girl sent into a collegiate den of wolves.

Charlotte Simmons is a star in her backwoods North Carolina town. She has earned a perfect 1600 on her SATs and is enrolled at Dupont University. Her high intelligence and wide reading have not prepared her for the real world, however, where people drink, swear, and have casual sex. She is an outcast, scorned and ridiculed, yet three distinctly stereotypical college types seek her attention. Hoyt Thorpe is the best-looking boy in the best fraternity; he also has a running competition with his fraternity brothers to bed "fresh meat" (freshman girls) within seven hours. Jojo Johansen is the only white starter on the university's basketball team. He appears intellectually challenged, though he eventually manages to earn an inflated C+ on a paper without the writing talent of Charlotte's third pursuer, Adam Gellin, a college tutor. Adam works for the newspaper and sees himself as intellectually superior, belonging to a group of leftist thinkers who have labeled themselves the Millennial Mutants.

These renderings of the worst in any student body are not made easier to bear by the presence of a sympathetic protagonist. Charlotte is at first too rigid, smug, and clueless to be perceived of as intellectually gifted or as one who has any understanding of a world beyond the hills of her home. Then she plunges into the new reality of campus life, however, and begins to assume all the values of the group, viewing intellectual activity as less important than looking good by hanging around with the right people. In other words, in Wolfe's view, Charlotte is the typical college student on a modern-day campus where athletes are adored, fraternities pump out future leaders, and nerds lurk in the shadows thinking deep thoughts. She has observed and then joined in, clearly influenced, as were the intact cats described in the preface.

To a disturbing extent, Wolfe's view may ring true, but he has been faulted for creating caricatures rather than developing characters in *I Am Charlotte Simmons*. His people, as well as their motivations and morals, lack depth. He may want to show the university as a microcosm of the larger society, but he fails to provide the reader with a hint of reality. Somewhere among the status-seeking, morally loose coeds and the slacker, self-important, womanizing frat boys, somewhere among the athletes granted degrees for athletic rather than intellectual prowess and the countercultural types with puffed-up visions of their importance and the lack of worth of others, there are serious students. Do not look for them here.

Michael Witkoski
Updated by Gay Pitman Zieger

Other major works

NONFICTION: *The Kandy-Kolored Tangerine-Flake Streamline Baby*, 1965; *The Electric Kool-Aid Acid Test*, 1968; *The Pump House Gang*, 1968; *Radical Chic and Mau-Mauing the Flak Catchers*, 1970; *The New Journalism*, 1973; *The Painted Word*, 1975; *Mauve Gloves and Madmen, Clutter and Vine, and Other Stories, Sketches, and Essays*, 1976; *The Right Stuff*, 1979; *In Our Time*, 1980; *From Bauhaus to Our House*, 1981; *The Purple Decades: A Reader*, 1982; *Hooking Up*, 2000.

Bibliography

Bloom, Harold, ed. *Tom Wolfe*. New York: Chelsea House, 2001. Collection of important critical responses to Wolfe's work also provides a thorough introduction by Bloom.

Leith, Sam. "Muscular Prose, Soft Centre." Review of *I Am Charlotte Simmons*, by Tom Wolfe. *Spectator*, November 13, 2004. Presents a detailed analysis of the novel, concluding that it is flawed work.

McEneaney, Kevin T. *Tom Wolfe's America: Heroes, Pranksters, and Fools*. Westport, Conn.: Praeger, 2009. Discusses Wolfe's life and writings, both fiction and nonfiction, with a focus on the author's themes, his use of irony, and his interest in pranks.

McKeen, William. *Tom Wolfe*. New York: Twayne, 1995. Provides students and general readers with an introduction to Wolfe's life and career. Especially good in discussing Wolfe's career as a practicing journalist, including his articles, such as his piece on *The New Yorker* that so outraged traditionalists.

Ragan, Brian Abel. *Tom Wolfe: A Critical Companion*. Westport, Conn.: Greenwood Press, 2002. Intended as a guide for students, this book contains a biographical chapter, a contextual chapter introducing the concept of "new journalism" and Wolfe's role in it, and analyses of all of his major works.

Salamon, Julie. *The Devil's Candy: "The Bonfire of the Vanities" Goes to Hollywood*. Boston: Houghton Mifflin, 1991. Focuses on the making of the film version of Wolfe's novel, but useful for helping readers better understand and appreciate the many artistic nuances and insights in Wolfe's carefully layered work that were lost in its translation to the big screen.

Schulman, Sam. "Body and Soul." *Commentary* 119, no. 1 (January, 2005): 67. Presents a thoroughly entertaining critique of *I Am Charlotte Simmons*.

Scura, Dorothy, ed. *Conversations with Tom Wolfe*. Jackson: University Press of Mississippi, 1990. Collection of interviews with Wolfe presents the author's views on numerous topics, including writers he admires, his politics, his use of satire, and his approach to the discipline of writing.

Shomette, Doug, ed. *The Critical Response to Tom Wolfe*. Westport, Conn.: Greenwood Press, 1992. Collection of critical responses to Wolfe's writings over the years addresses primarily his journalistic works, but a section is devoted to the early responses to and criticisms of *The Bonfire of the Vanities*.

VIRGINIA WOOLF

Born: London, England; January 25, 1882
Died: The River Ouse, near Rodmell, Sussex, England; March 28, 1941
Also known as: Adeline Virginia Stephen

Principal long fiction

The Voyage Out, 1915
Night and Day, 1919
Jacob's Room, 1922
Mrs. Dalloway, 1925
To the Lighthouse, 1927
Orlando: A Biography, 1928
The Waves, 1931
Flush: A Biography, 1933
The Years, 1937
Between the Acts, 1941
Melymbrosia, 1982 (wr. 1912; revised 2002)

Other literary forms

To say that Virginia Woolf lived to write is no exaggeration. Her output was both prodigious and varied; counting her posthumously published works, it fills more than forty volumes. Beyond her novels, her fiction encompasses several short-story collections. As a writer of nonfiction, Woolf was similarly prolific, her book-length works including *Roger Fry: A Biography* (1940) and two influential feminist statements, *A Room of One's Own* (1929) and *Three Guineas* (1938). Throughout her life, Woolf also produced criticism and reviews; the best-known collections are *The Common Reader: First Series* (1925) and *The Common Reader: Second Series* (1932). In 1966 and 1967, the four volumes of *Collected Essays* were published. Additional books of essays, reviews, and sketches continue to appear, most notably the illuminating selection of autobiographical materials, *Moments of Being* (1976). Her letters—3,800 of them survive—are available in six volumes; when publication was completed, her diaries stood at five. Another collection, of Woolf's essays, also proved a massive, multivolume undertaking.

Achievements

From the appearance of her first novel in 1915, Virginia Woolf's work was received with respect—an important point, since she was extremely sensitive to criticism. Descendant of a distinguished literary family, member of the avant-garde Bloomsbury Group, herself an experienced critic and reviewer, she was taken seriously as an artist. Nevertheless, her early works were not financially successful; she was forty before she earned a living from her writing. From the start, the rather narrow territory of her novels precluded broad popularity, peopled as they were with sophisticated, sexually reserved, upper-middle-class characters, finely attuned to their sensibilities and relatively insulated from the demands of mundane existence. When in *Jacob's Room* she first abandoned the conventional novel to experiment with the interior monologues and lyrical poetic devices that characterize her mature method, she also began to develop a reputation as a "difficult" or "highbrow" writer, though undeniably an important one. Not until the brilliant fantasy *Orlando* was published did she enjoy a definite commercial success. Thereafter, she received both critical and popular acclaim; *The Years* was even a bona fide best seller.

During the 1930's, Woolf became the subject of critical essays and two book-length studies; some of her works were translated into French. At the same time, however, her novels began to be judged as irrelevant to a world beset by growing economic and political chaos. At her death in 1941, she was widely regarded as a pioneer of modernism but also reviewed by many as the effete, melancholic "invalid priestess of Bloomsbury," a stereotype her friend and fellow novelist E. M. Forster dismissed at the time as wholly inaccurate; she was, he insisted, "tough, sensitive but tough."

Over the next twenty-five years, respectful attention to Woolf's work continued, but in the late 1960's, critical interest accelerated dramatically and has remained strong. Two reasons for this renewed notice seem particularly apparent. First, Woolf's feminist essays *A Room of One's Own* and *Three Guineas* became rallying documents in the growing women's movement; readers who might not otherwise have discovered her novels were drawn to them via her nonfiction and tended to read them primarily as validations of her feminist thinking. Second, with the appearance of her husband Leonard Woolf's five-volume autobiography from 1965-1969, her nephew Quentin Bell's definitive two-volume biography of her in 1972, and the full-scale editions of her own diaries and letters commencing in the mid-1970's, Woolf's life has become one of the most thoroughly documented of any modern author. Marked by intellectual and sexual unconventionality, madness, and suicide, it is for today's readers also one of the most fascinating; the steady demand for memoirs, reminiscences, and photograph collections relating to her has generated what is sometimes disparagingly labeled "the Virginia Woolf industry." At its worst, such insatiable curiosity is morbidly voyeuristic, distracting from and trivializing Woolf's achievement; on a more responsible level, it has led to serious, provocative reevaluations of the political and especially the feminist elements in her work, as well as to redefinitions of her role as an artist.

BIOGRAPHY

Daughter of the eminent editor and critic Sir Leslie Stephen and Julia Jackson Duckworth, both of whom had been previously widowed, Virginia Woolf was born Adeline Virginia Stephen in 1882 into a solidly late Victorian intellectual and social milieu. Her father's first wife had been William Makepeace Thackeray's daughter, James Russell Lowell was her godfather, and visitors to the Stephens' London household included Henry James, George Meredith, and Thomas Hardy. From childhood on, she had access to her father's superb library, and she benefited from her father's guidance and commentary on her rigorous, precocious reading. Nevertheless, unlike her brothers, she did not receive a formal university education, a lack she always regretted and that partly explains the anger in *Three Guineas*, in which she proposes a "university of outsiders." (Throughout her life she declined all academic honors.)

In 1895, when Woolf was thirteen, her mother, just past fifty, suddenly died. Altruistic, self-sacrificing, totally devoted to her demanding husband and large family, the beautiful Julia Stephen fulfilled the Victorian ideal of womanhood and exhausted herself doing so; her daughter would movingly eulogize her as Mrs. Ramsay in *To the Lighthouse*. The loss devastated Woolf, who experienced at that time the first of four major mental breakdowns in her life, the last of which would end in death.

Leslie Stephen, twenty years his wife's senior and thus sanguinely expecting her to pilot him comfortably through old age, was devastated in another way. Retreating histrionically into self-pitying but deeply felt grief, like that of his fictional counterpart, Mr. Ramsay, he transferred his intense demands for sympathetic attention to a succession of what could only seem to him achingly inadequate substitutes for his dead wife: first, his stepdaughter Stella Duckworth, who herself died suddenly in 1897, then, Virginia's older sister Vanessa. The traditional feminine role would eventually have befallen Virginia had Leslie Stephen not died in 1904. Writing in her 1928 diary on what would have been her father's ninety-sixth birthday, Woolf reflects that, had he lived, "his life would have entirely ended mine. . . . No writing, no books;—inconceivable."

On her father's death, Woolf sustained her second incapacitating breakdown, but she also gained, as her diary suggests, something crucial: freedom. That freedom took an immediate and, to her parents' staid friends and relatives, shocking form. Virginia, Vanessa, and their brothers Thoby and Adrian abandoned the Stephen house in respectable Kensington to set up a home in the seedy bohemian district of London known as Bloomsbury. There, on Thursday evenings, a coterie of Thoby Stephen's Cambridge University friends regularly gathered to talk in an atmosphere of free thought, avant-garde art, and sexual tolerance, forming the nucleus of what came to be called the Bloomsbury Group. At various stages in its evolution over the next decade, the group included such luminaries as biographer Lytton Strachey, novelist E. M. Forster, art critic Roger Fry, and economist John Maynard Keynes. In 1911, they were joined by another of Thoby's Cambridge friends, a colonial official just returned from seven years in Ceylon, Leonard Woolf; Virginia Stephen married him the following year. Scarcely twelve months after the wedding, Virginia Woolf's third severe breakdown began, marked by a suicide attempt; her recovery took almost two years.

The causes of Woolf's madness have been much debated and the treatment she was prescribed—bed rest,

Virginia Woolf. (Courtesy D.C. Public Library)

milk, withdrawal of intellectual stimulation—much disputed, especially since Woolf apparently never received psychoanalytic help, even though the Hogarth Press, founded by the Woolfs in 1917, was one of Sigmund Freud's earliest English publishers. A history of insanity ran in the Stephen family; if Virginia was afflicted with a hereditary nervous condition, it was thought, then, that must be accepted as unalterable. On the other hand, the timing of these three breakdowns prompts speculation about more subtle causes. About her parents' deaths she evidently felt strong guilt; of *To the Lighthouse*, the fictionalized account of her parents' relationship, she would later say, "I was obsessed by them both, unhealthily; and writing of them was a necessary act." Marriage was for her a deliberately sought yet disturbing commitment, representing a potential loss of autonomy and a retreat into what her would-be novelist Terence Hewet envisions in *The Voyage Out* as a walled-up, firelit room. She found her own marriage sexually disappointing, perhaps in part because she had been molested both as a child and as a young woman by her two Duckworth stepbrothers.

In the late twentieth century, feminist scholars especially argued as a cause of Woolf's madness the burden of being a greatly talented woman in a world hostile to feminine achievement, a situation Woolf strikingly depicts in *A Room of One's Own* as the plight of William Shakespeare's hypothetical sister. Indeed, the young Virginia Stephen might plunder her father's library all day, but by teatime she was expected to don the role of deferential Victorian female in a rigidly patriarchal household. Once she settled in Bloomsbury, however, she enjoyed unconventional independence and received much sympathetic encouragement of her gifts, most of all from her husband.

Leonard Woolf, himself a professional writer and literary editor, connected his wife's madness directly with her genius, saying that she concentrated more intensely on her work than any writer he had ever known. Her books passed through long, difficult gestations; her sanity was always most vulnerable immediately after a novel was finished. Expanding on his belief that the imagination in his wife's books and the delusions of her breakdowns "all came from the same place in her mind," some critics have gone so far as to claim her madness as the very source of her art, permitting her to make mystical descents into inner space from which she returned with sharpened perception.

It is significant, certainly, that although Woolf's first publication, an unsigned article for the newspaper *The Guardian*, appeared just two months after her 1904 move to Bloomsbury, her first novel, over which she labored for seven years, was only completed shortly after her marriage; her breakdown occurred three months after its acceptance for publication. Very early, therefore, Leonard Woolf learned to keep a daily record of his wife's health; throughout their life together, he would be alert for those signs of fatigue or erratic behavior that signaled approaching danger and the need for her customary rest cure. Rational, efficient, uncomplaining, Leonard Woolf has been condemned by some disaffected scholars as a pseudosaintly nurse who benignly badgered his patient into crippling dependence. The compelling argument against this extreme interpretation is Virginia Woolf's astonishing productivity after she recovered from her third illness. Although there were certainly periods of instability and near disaster, the following twenty-five years were immensely fruitful as she discarded traditional fiction to move toward realizing her unique vision, all the while functioning actively and diversely as a fine critic, too.

After Woolf's ninth novel, *The Years*, was finished in 1936, however, she came closer to mental collapse than she had been at any time since 1913. Meanwhile, a larger pattern of breakdown was developing in the world around her as World War II became inevitable. Working at her Sussex home on her last book, *Between the Acts*, she could hear the Battle of Britain being fought over her head; her London house was severely damaged in the Blitz. Strangely, however, that novel was her easiest to write; Leonard Woolf, ever watchful, was struck by her tranquillity during this period. The gradual symptoms of warning were absent this time; when her depression began, he would recall, it struck her "like a sudden blow." She began to hear voices and knew what was coming. On February 26, 1941, she finished *Between the Acts*. Four weeks later, she went out for one of her usual walks across the Sussex downs, placed a heavy stone in her pocket, and stepped into the River Ouse. Within minutes Leonard Woolf arrived at its banks to find her walking stick and hat lying there. Her body was recovered three weeks later.

Analysis

In one of her most famous pronouncements on the nature of fiction—as a practicing critic, she had much to say on the subject—Virginia Woolf insists that "life is not a series of gig lamps symmetrically arranged; but a luminous halo, a semi-transparent envelope surrounding us from the beginning of consciousness to the end." In an ordinary day, she argues, "thousands of ideas" course through the human brain; "thousands of emotions" meet, collide, and disappear "in astonishing disorder." Amid this hectic interior flux, the trivial and the vital, the past and the present, are constantly interacting; there is endless tension between the multitude of ideas and emotions rushing through one's consciousness and the numerous impressions scoring on it from the external world. Thus, even personal identity becomes evanescent, continually reordering itself as "the atoms of experience . . . fall upon the mind." It follows, then, that human beings must have great difficulty communicating with one another, for of this welter of perceptions that define individual personality, only a tiny fraction can ever be externalized in word or gesture. Yet, despite—in fact, because of—their frightening isolation as unknowable entities, people yearn to unite both with one another and with some larger pattern of order hidden behind the flux, to experience time standing still momentarily, to see matches struck that briefly illuminate the darkness.

Given the complex phenomenon of human subjectivity, Woolf asks, "Is it not the task of the novelist to convey this varying, this unknown and uncircumscribed spirit . . . with as little mixture of the alien and external as possible?" The conventional novel form is plainly inadequate for such a purpose, she maintains. Dealing sequentially with a logical set of completed past actions that occur in a coherent, densely detailed physical and social environment, presided over by an omniscient narrator interpreting the significance of it all, the traditional novel trims and shapes experience into a rational but falsified pattern. "Is life like this?" Woolf demands rhetorically. "Must novels be like this?"

In Woolf's first two books, nevertheless, she attempted to work within conventional modes, discovering empirically that they could not convey her vision. Although in recent years some critics have defended *The Voyage Out* and *Night and Day* as artistically satisfying in their own right, both novels have generally been considered interesting mainly for what they foreshadow of Woolf's later preoccupations and techniques.

The Voyage Out

The Voyage Out is the story of Rachel Vinrace, a naïve and talented twenty-four-year-old amateur pianist who sails from England to a small resort on the South American coast, where she vacations with relatives. There, she meets a fledgling novelist, Terence Hewet; on a pleasure expedition up a jungle river, they declare their love. Shortly thereafter, Rachel falls ill with a fever and dies. The novel's exotic locale, large cast of minor characters, elaborate scenes of social comedy, and excessive length are all atypical of Woolf's mature work. Already, however, many of her later concerns are largely emerging. The resonance of the title itself anticipates Woolf's poetic symbolism; the "voyage out" can be the literal trip across the Atlantic or up the South American river, but it also suggests the progression from innocence to experience, from life to death, which she later depicts using similar water imagery. Her concern with premature death and how survivors come to terms with it prefigures *Jacob's Room*, *Mrs. Dalloway*, *To the Lighthouse*, and *The Waves*. Most significant is her portrayal of a world in which characters are forever striving to overcome their isolation from one another. The ship on which Rachel "voyages out" is labeled by Woolf an "emblem of the loneliness of human life." Terence, Rachel's lover, might be describing his creator's own frustration when he says he is trying "to write a novel about Silence, the things people don't say. But the difficulty is immense."

Moments of unity amid seemingly unconquerable disorder do occur, however. On a communal level, one such transformation happens at a ball being held to celebrate the engagement of two English guests at the resort's small hotel. When the musicians go home, Rachel appropriates the piano and plays Mozart, hunting songs, and hymn tunes as the guests gradually resume dancing, each in a newly expressive, uninhibited way, eventually to join hands in a gigantic round dance. When the circle breaks and each member spins away to become individual once more, Rachel modulates to Bach; her weary yet exhilarated listeners sit quietly and allow themselves to be soothed by the serene complexity of the music. As dawn breaks outside and Rachel plays on, they envision "themselves and their lives, and the whole of human life advancing nobly under the direction of the music." They have transcended their single identities temporarily to gain a privileged glimpse of some larger pattern beyond themselves.

If Rachel through her art briefly transforms the lives of a small community, she herself privately discerns fleeting stability through her growing love for Terence. Even love is insufficient, however; although in the couple's newfound sense of union "divisions disappeared," Terence feels that Rachel seems able "to pass away to unknown places where she had no need of him." In the elegiac closing scenes of illness (which Woolf reworked many times and which are the most original as well as moving part of the novel), Rachel "descends into another world"; she is "curled up at the bottom of the sea." Terence, sitting by her bedside, senses that "they seemed to be thinking together; he seemed to be Rachel as well as himself." When she ceases breathing, he experiences "an immense feeling of peace," a "complete union" with her that shatters when he notices an ordinary table covered with crockery and realizes in horror that in this world he will never see Rachel again. For her, stability has been achieved; for him, the isolating flux has resumed.

Night and Day

Looking back on *The Voyage Out*, Woolf could see, she said, why readers found it "a more gallant and inspiring spectacle" than her next and least known book *Night and Day*. This second novel is usually regarded as her most traditional in form and subject—in its social satire, her obeisance to Jane Austen. Its dancelike plot, however, in which mismatched young couples eventually find their true loves, suggests the magical atmosphere of William Shakespeare's romantic comedies as well. References to Shakespeare abound in the book; for example, the delightfully eccentric Mrs. Hilbery characterizes herself as one of his wise fools, and when at the end she presides over the repatterning of the couples in London, she has just arrived from a pilgrimage to Stratford-upon-Avon. Coincidentally, *Night and Day* is the most conventionally dramatic of Woolf's novels, full of dialogue, exits and entrances; characters are constantly taking omnibuses and taxis across London from one contrived scene to the next.

Like *The Voyage Out, Night and Day* does point to Woolf's enduring preoccupations. It is, too, a novel depicting movement from innocence to maturity and escape from the conventional world through the liberating influence of love. Ralph Denham, a London solicitor from a large, vulgar, middle-class family living in suburban Highgate, would prefer to move to a Norfolk cottage and write. Katharine Hilbery measures out her days serving tea in her wealthy family's beautiful Chelsea home and helping her disorganized mother produce a biography of their forebear, a great nineteenth century poet. Her secret passions, however, are mathematics and astronomy. These seeming opposites, Ralph and Katharine, are alike in that both retreat at night to their rooms to pursue their private visions. The entire novel is concerned with such dualities—public selves and private selves, activity and contemplation, fact and imagination; but Woolf also depicts the unity that Ralph and Katharine can achieve, notwithstanding the social and intellectual barriers separating them. At the end, as the couple leaves Katharine's elegant but constraining home to walk in the open night air, "they lapsed gently into silence, travelling the dark paths side by side towards something discerned in the distance which gradually possessed them both."

The sustained passages of subtle interior analysis by which Woolf charts the couple's growing realization of their need for each other define her real area of fictional interest, but they are hemmed in by a tediously constrictive traditional structure. Except for her late novel, *The Years*, also comparatively orthodox in form, her first two books took the longest to finish and underwent the most extensive revisions, undoubtedly because she was writing against her grain. Nevertheless, they represented a necessary apprenticeship; as she would later remark of *Night and Day*, "You must put it all in before you can leave out."

Jacob's Room

Woolf dared to leave out a great deal in the short experimental novel she wrote next. Described in conventional terms, *Jacob's Room* is a bildungsroman, or "novel of formation," tracing its hero's development from childhood to maturity: Jacob Flanders is first portrayed as a small boy studying a tide pool on a Cornish beach; at twenty-six, he dies fighting in World War I. In structure, style, and tone, however, *Jacob's Room* defies such labeling. It does not move in steady chronological fashion but in irregular leaps. Of the fourteen chapters, two cover Jacob's childhood, two, his college years at Cambridge, the remainder, his life as a young adult working in London and traveling abroad. In length, and hence in the complexity with which various periods of Jacob's existence are treated, the chapters range from one to twenty-eight pages. They vary, that is, as the process of growth itself does.

Individual chapters are likewise discontinuous in structure, broken into irregular segments that convey multiple, often simultaneous perspectives. The ten-page chapter 8, for example, opens with Jacob's slamming the door of his London room as he starts for work in the morning; he is then glimpsed at his office desk. Meanwhile, on a table back in his room lies his mother's unopened letter to him, placed there the previous night by his lover, Florinda; its contents and Mrs. Flanders herself are evoked. The narrator then discourses on the significance of letter writing. Jacob is next seen leaving work for the day; in Greek Street, he spies Florinda on another man's arm. At eight o'clock, Rose Shaw, a guest at a party Jacob attended several nights earlier, walks through Holburn, meditating bitterly on the ironies of love and death. The narrator sketches London by lamplight. Then, Jacob is back in his room reading by the fire a newspaper account of the Prime Minister's speech on Home Rule; the night is very cold. The narrator abruptly shifts perspective from congested London to the open countryside, describing the snow that has been accumulating since midafternoon; an old shepherd crossing a field hears a distant clock strike. Back in London, Jacob also hears the hour chiming, rakes out his fire, and goes to bed. There is no story here in any conventional sense, no action being furthered; in the entire ten pages, only one sentence is direct dialogue. What Woolf delineates is the *texture* of an ordinary day in the life of Jacob and the world in which he exists. Clock time moves the chapter forward, while spatially the chapter radiates outward from the small area Jacob occupies. Simultaneously, in the brief reference to the Prime Minister, Woolf suggests the larger procession of modern history that will inexorably sweep Jacob to premature death.

Such indirection and understatement characterize the whole novel: "It is no use trying to sum people up," the narrator laments. "One must follow hints." Thus, Jacob is described mainly from the outside, defined through the impressions he makes on others, from a hotel chambermaid to a Cambridge don, and by his surroundings and possessions. Even his death is conveyed obliquely: Mrs. Flanders, half asleep in her Yorkshire house, hears "dull sounds"; it cannot be guns, she thinks, it must be the sea. On the next page, she stands in her dead son's London room, holding a pair of Jacob's old shoes and asking his friend pathetically, "What am I to do with these, Mr. Bonamy?" The novel ends.

To construct Jacob's ultimately unknowable biography out of such fragments, Woolf evolves not only a new structure but a new style. Long, fluid sentences contain precise physical details juxtaposed with metaphysical speculations on the evanescence of life and the impossibility of understanding another person. Lyrical descriptions of nature—waves, moths, falling snow, birds rising and settling—are interspersed to suggest life's beauty and fragility. Images and phrases recur as unifying motifs: Jacob is repeatedly associated with Greek literature and myth and spends his last fulfilling days visiting the Parthenon. Most important, Woolf begins to move freely in and out of her characters' minds to capture the flow of sense impressions mingling with memory, emotion, and random association, experimenting with that narrative method conveniently if imprecisely labeled "stream of consciousness."

Jacob's Room is not a mature work, especially with its intrusive narrator, who can be excessively chatty, archly pedantic, and sententious. Woolf protests the difficulties of her task ("In short, the observer is choked with observations") and cannot quite follow the logic of her new method; after an essaylike passage on the necessity of illusion, for example, she awkwardly concludes, "Jacob, no doubt, thought something in this fashion." Even the lovely passages of poetic description at times seem self-indulgent. The book definitely shows its seams. Woolf's rejection of traditional novel structure, however, and her efforts to eliminate "the alien and the external" make *Jacob's Room* a dazzling advance in her ability to embody her philosophical vision: "Life is but a procession of shadows, and God knows why it is that we embrace them so eagerly, and see them depart with such anguish, being shadows."

Mrs. Dalloway

Within three years, Woolf had resolved her technical problems superbly in *Mrs. Dalloway*. The intruding narrator vanishes; though the freedom with which point of view shifts among characters and settings clearly posits an omniscient intelligence, the narrator's observations are now subtly integrated with the thoughts of her characters, and the transitions between scenes flow organically. Woolf's subject is also better suited to her method: Whereas *Jacob's Room* is a story of youthful potential tragically cut off, *Mrs. Dalloway* is a novel of middle age, about what people have become as the result of choices made, opportunities seized or refused. Jacob Flanders had but a brief past; the characters in *Mrs. Dalloway* must come to terms with theirs, sifting and valuing the memories that course through their minds.

The book covers one June day in the life of Clarissa Dalloway, fifty-two years old, an accomplished London political hostess and wife of a Member of Parliament. A recent serious illness from which she is still recovering has made her freshly appreciate the wonder of life as she prepares for the party she will give that evening. Peter Walsh, once desperately in love with her, arrives from India, where he has had an undistinguished career; he calls on her and is invited to the party, at which another friend from the past, Sally Seton, formerly a romantic and now the conventional wife of a Manchester industrialist, will also unexpectedly appear. Running parallel with Clarissa's day is that of the mad Septimus Warren Smith, a surviving Jacob Flanders, shell-shocked in the war; his suicide in the late afternoon delays the arrival of another of Clarissa's guests, the eminent nerve specialist Sir William Bradshaw. Learning of this stranger's death, Clarissa must confront the inevitability of her own.

Mrs. Dalloway is also, then, a novel about time itself (its working title at one point was *The Hours*). Instead of using chapters or other formal sectioning, Woolf structures the book by counterpointing clock time, signaled by the obtrusive hourly tolling of Big Ben, against the subjective flow of time in her characters' minds as they recover the past and envision the future. Not only does she move backward and forward in time, however; she also creates an effect of simultaneity that is especially crucial in linking Septimus's story with Clarissa's. Thus, when Clarissa Dalloway, buying flowers that morning in a Bond Street shop, hears "a pistol shot" outside and emerges to see a large, official automobile that has backfired, Septimus is standing in the crowd blocked by the car and likewise reacting to this "violent explosion" ("The world has raised its whip; where will it descend?"). Later, when Septimus's frightened young Italian wife Rezia guides him to Regents Park to calm him before their appointment with Bradshaw, he has a terrifying hallucination of his dead friend Evans, killed just before the Armistice; Peter Walsh, passing their bench, wonders, "What awful fix had they got themselves in to look so desperate as that on a fine summer morning?" This atmosphere of intensely populated time and space, of many anonymous lives intersecting briefly, of the world resonating with unwritten novels, comic and tragic, accounts in part for the richly poignant texture of nearly all Woolf's mature work.

In her early thinking about *Mrs. Dalloway*, Virginia Woolf wanted to show a "world seen by the sane and the insane, side by side." Although the novel definitely focuses on Clarissa, Septimus functions as a kind of double, representing her own responses to life carried to an untenable extreme. Both find great terror in life and also great joy; both want to withdraw from life into blissful isolation, yet both want to reach out to merge with others. Clarissa's friends, and indeed she herself, sense a "coldness" about her, "an impenetrability"; both Peter and Sally believe she chose safety rather than adventure by marrying the unimaginative, responsible Richard Dalloway. The quiet attic room where she now convalesces is described as a tower into which she retreats nunlike to a virginal narrow bed. Yet Clarissa also loves "life; London; this moment of June"—and her parties. Though some critics condemn her party giving as shallow, trivial, even corrupt (Peter Walsh could make her wince as a girl by predicting that she would become "the perfect hostess"), Clarissa considers her parties a form of creativity, "an offering," "her gift" of bringing people together. For Septimus, the war has destroyed his capacity to feel; in his aloneness and withdrawal, he finds "an isolation full of sublimity; a freedom which the attached can never know"—he can elude "human nature," "the repulsive brute, with the blood-red nostrils." Yet just watching leaves quivering is for him "an exquisite joy"; he feels them "connected by millions of fibres with his own body" and wants to reveal this unity to the world because "communication is health; communication is happiness."

Desperate because of his suicide threats, Septimus's wife takes him to see Sir William Bradshaw. At the center of the novel, in one of the most bitter scenes in all of Woolf's writing (certainly one with strong autobiographical overtones), is Septimus's confrontation with this "priest of science," this man of "lightning skill" and "almost infallible accuracy" who "never spoke of 'madness'; he called it not having a sense of proportion." Within three minutes, he has discreetly recorded his diagnosis on a pink card ("a case of complete breakdown . . . with every symptom in an advanced stage"); Septimus will be sent to a beautiful house in the country where he will be taught to rest, to regain proportion. Rezia, agonized, understands that she has been failed by this obtuse, complacently cruel man whom Woolf symbolically connects with a larger system that prospers on intolerance and sends its best young men to fight futile wars. Septimus's suicide at this point becomes inevitable.

The two stories fuse when Bradshaw appears at the party. Learning of the reason for his lateness, Clarissa, deeply shaken, withdraws to a small side room, not unlike her attic tower, where she accurately imagines Septimus's suicide: "He had thrown himself from a window. Up had flashed the ground; through him, blundering, bruising, went the rusty spikes. . . . So she saw it." She also intuits the immediate cause: Bradshaw is "capable of some indescribable outrage—forcing your soul, that was it"; seeing him, this young man must have said to himself, "they make life intolerable, men like that." Thus, she sees, "death was defiance," a means to preserve one's center from being violated, but "death was an attempt to communicate," and in death, Septimus's message that all life is connected is heard by one unlikely person, Clarissa Dalloway. Reviewing her own past as she has reconstructed it this day, and forced anew to acknowledge her own mortality, she realizes that "he had made her feel the beauty." Spiritually regenerated, she returns to her party "to kindle and illuminate" life.

To the Lighthouse

In her most moving, complexly affirmative novel, *To the Lighthouse*, Woolf portrays another woman whose creativity lies in uniting people, Mrs. Ramsay. For this luminous evocation of her own parents' marriage, Woolf drew on memories of her girlhood summers at St. Ives, Cornwall (here transposed to an island in the Hebrides), to focus on her perennial themes, the difficulties and joys of human communication, especially as frustrated by time and death.

The plot is absurdly simple: An expedition to a lighthouse is postponed, then completed a decade later. Woolf's mastery, however, of the interior monologue in this novel makes such a fragile plot line quite sufficient; the real "story" of *To the Lighthouse* is the reader's gradually increasing intimacy with its characters' richly depicted inner lives; the reader's understanding expands in concert with the characters' own growing insights.

Woolf again devises an experimental structure for her work, this time of three unequal parts. Approximately the first half of the novel, titled "The Window," occurs during a single day at the seaside home occupied by an eminent philosopher, Mr. Ramsay, his wife, and a melange of children, guests, and servants, including Lily Briscoe, an amateur painter in her thirties, unmarried. Mrs. Ramsay's is the dominant consciousness in this section. A short, exquisitely beautiful center section, "Time Passes," pictures the house succumbing to time during the family's ten-year absence and then being rescued from decay by two old women for the Ramsays' repossession. Periodically interrupting this natural flow of time are terse, bracketed, clock-time announcements like news bulletins, telling of the deaths of Mrs. Ramsay, the eldest son Andrew (in World War I), and the eldest daughter Prue (of childbirth complications). The final third, "The Lighthouse," also covers one day; the diminished family and several former guests having returned, the lighthouse expedition can now be completed. This section is centered almost entirely in Lily Briscoe's consciousness.

Because Mr. and Mrs. Ramsay are both strong personalities, they are sometimes interpreted too simply. Particularly in some readings by feminist critics, Mr. Ramsay is seen as an insufferable patriarch, arrogantly rational in his work but almost infantile emotionally, while Mrs. Ramsay is a Victorian earth mother, not only submitting unquestioningly to her husband's and children's excessive demands but actively trying to impose on all the other female characters her unliberated way of life. Such readings are sound to some extent, but they undervalue the vivid way that Woolf captures in the couple's monologues the conflicting mixture of motives and needs that characterize human beings of either sex. For example, Mrs. Ramsay is infuriated that her husband blights their youngest son James's anticipation of the lighthouse visit by announcing that it will storm tomorrow, yet his unflinching pursuit of truth is also something she most admires in him. Mr. Ramsay finds his wife's irrational habit of exaggeration maddening, but as she sits alone in a reverie, he respects her integrity and will not interrupt, "though it hurt him that she should look so distant, and he could not reach her, he could do nothing to help her." Lily, a shrewd observer who simultaneously adores and resists Mrs. Ramsay, perceives that "it would be a mistake . . . to simplify their relationship."

Amid these typical contradictions and mundane demands, however, "little daily miracles" may be achieved. One of Woolf's finest scenes, Mrs. Ramsay's dinner, provides a paradigm (though a summary can scarcely convey the richness of these forty pages). As she mechanically seats her guests at the huge table, Mrs. Ramsay glimpses her husband at the other end, "all in a heap, frowning": "She could not understand how she had ever felt any emotion of affection for him." Gloomily, she perceives that not just the two of them but everyone is separate and out of sorts. For example, Charles Tansley, Mr. Ramsay's disciple, who feels the whole family despises him, fidgets angrily; Lily, annoyed that Tansley is always telling her "women can't paint," purposely tries to irritate him; William Bankes would rather be home dining alone and fears that Mrs. Ramsay will read his mind. They all sense that "something [is] lacking"—they are divided from one another, sunk in their "treacherous" thoughts. Mrs. Ramsay wearily recognizes that "the whole of the effort of merging and flowing and creating rested on her."

She instructs two of her children to light the candles and set them around a beautiful fruit centerpiece that her daughter Rose has arranged for the table. This is Mrs. Ramsay's first stroke of artistry; the candles and fruit compose the table and the faces around it into an island, a sheltering haven: "Here, inside the room, seemed to be order and dry land; there, outside, a reflection in which things wavered and vanished, waterily." All the guests feel this change and have a sudden sense of making "common cause against that fluidity out there." Then the maid brings in a great steaming dish of *boeuf en daube* that even the finicky widower Bankes considers "a triumph." As the guests relish the succulent food and their camaraderie grows, Mrs. Ramsay, serving the last helpings from the depths of the pot, experiences a moment of perfect insight: "There it was, all around them. It partook . . . of eternity." She affirms to herself that "there is a coherence in things, a stability; something, she meant, that is immune from change, and shines out . . . in the face of the flowing, the fleeting." As is true of so much of Woolf's sparse dialogue, the ordinary words Mrs. Ramsay then speaks aloud can be read both literally and symbolically: "Yes, there is plenty for everybody." As the dinner ends and she passes out of the room triumphantly—the inscrutable poet Augustus Carmichael, who usually resists her magic, actually bows in homage—she looks back on the scene and sees that "it had become, she knew . . . already the past."

The burden of the past and the coming to terms with it are the focus of part 3. Just as "a sort of disintegration" sets in as soon as Mrs. Ramsay sweeps out of the dining room, so her death has left a larger kind of wreckage. Without her unifying artistry, all is disorder, as it was at the beginning of the dinner. In a gesture of belated atonement for quarreling with his wife over the original lighthouse trip, the melodramatically despairing Mr. Ramsay insists on making the expedition now with his children James and Cam, although both hate his tyranny and neither wants to go. As they set out, Lily remains behind to paint. Surely mirroring the creative anxiety of Woolf herself, she feels "a painful but exciting ecstasy" before her blank canvas, knowing how ideas that seem simple become "in practice immediately complex." As she starts making rhythmic strokes across the canvas, she loses "consciousness of outer things" and begins to meditate on the past, from which she gradually retrieves a vision of Mrs. Ramsay that will permit her to reconstruct and complete the painting she left unfinished a decade ago, one in which Mrs. Ramsay would have been, and will become again, a triangular shadow on a step (symbolically echoing the invisible "wedge-shaped core of darkness" to which Mrs. Ramsay feels herself shrinking during her moments of reverie). Through the unexpectedly intense pain of recalling her, Lily also comprehends Mrs. Ramsay's significance, her ability "to make the moment something permanent," as art does, to strike "this eternal passing and flowing . . . into stability." Mrs. Ramsay is able to make "life stand still here."

Meanwhile, Mr. Ramsay and his children are also voyaging into the past; Cam, dreamily drifting her hand in the water, begins, as her mother did, to see her father as bravely pursuing truth like a tragic hero. James bitterly relives the childhood scene when his father thoughtlessly dashed his hopes for the lighthouse visit, but as they near the lighthouse in the present and Mr. Ramsay offers his son rare praise, James too is reconciled. When they land, Mr. Ramsay himself, standing in the bow "very straight and tall," springs "lightly like a young man . . . on to the rock," renewed. Simultaneously, though the boat has long since disappeared from her sight and even the lighthouse itself seems blurred, Lily intuits that they have reached their goal and she completes her painting. All of them have reclaimed Mrs. Ramsay from death, and she has unified them; memory can defeat time. "Yes," Lily thinks, "I have had my vision." Clearly, Woolf had achieved hers too and transmuted the materials of a painful past into this radiant novel.

Although Woolf denied intending any specific symbolism for the lighthouse, it resonates with almost infinite possibilities, both within the book and in a larger way as an emblem of her work. Like the candles at the dinner party, it can be a symbol of safety and stability amid darkness and watery flux, its beams those rhythmically occurring moments of illumination that sustain Mrs. Ramsay and by extension everyone. Perhaps, however, it can also serve as a metaphor for human beings themselves as Woolf portrays them. The lighthouse signifies what can be objectively perceived of an individual—in Mrs. Ramsay's words, "our apparitions, the things you know us by"; but it also signals invisible, possibly tragic depths, for, as Mrs. Ramsay knew, "beneath it is all dark, it is all spreading, it is unfathomably deep."

THE WAVES

In *The Waves*, widely considered her masterpiece, Woolf most resolutely overcomes the limits of the traditional novel. Entirely unique in form, *The Waves* cannot perhaps be called a novel at all; Woolf herself first projected a work of "prose yet poetry; a novel and a play." The book is a series of grouped soliloquies in varying combinations spoken by six friends, three men and three women, at successive stages in their lives from childhood to late middle age. Each grouping is preceded by a brief, lyrical "interlude" (Woolf's own term), set off in italic type, that describes an empty house by the sea as the sun moves across the sky in a single day.

The texture of these soliloquies is extremely difficult to convey; the term "soliloquy," in fact, is merely a critical convenience. Although each is introduced in the same straightforward way ("Neville said," "Jinny said"), they obviously are unspoken, representing each character's private vision. Their style is also unvarying—solemn, formal, almost stilted, like that of choral figures. The author has deliberately translated into a rigorously neutral, dignified idiom the conscious and subconscious reality her characters perceive but cannot articulate on their own. This method represents Woolf's most ambitious attempt to capture the unfathomable depths of separate human personalities, which defy communication in ordinary life—and in ordinary novels. The abstraction of the device, however, especially in combination with the flow of cosmic time in the interludes, shows that she is also concerned with depicting a universal pattern that transcends mere individuals. Thus, once more Woolf treats her theme of human beings' attempts to overcome their isolation and to become part of a larger stabilizing pattern; this time, however, the theme is embodied in the very form of her work.

It would be inaccurate, however, to say that the characters exist only as symbols. Each has definable qualities and unique imagery; Susan, as an example, farm-bred and almost belligerently maternal, speaks in elemental images of wood smoke, grassy paths, flowers thick with pollen. Further, the characters often evoke one another's imagery; the other figures, for example, even in maturity picture the fearful, solitary Rhoda as a child rocking white petals in a brown basin of water. They are linked by intricately woven threads of common experience, above all by their shared admiration for a shadowy seventh character, Percival. Their gathering with him at a farewell dinner before he embarks on a career in India is one of the few actual events recorded in the soliloquies and also becomes one of those miraculous moments of unity comparable to that achieved by Mrs. Ramsay for her dinner guests; as they rise to leave the restaurant, all the characters are thinking as Louis does: "We pray, holding in our hands this common feeling, 'Do not move, do not let the swing-door cut to pieces this thing that we have made, that globes itself here.'" Such union, however, is cruelly impermanent; two pages later, a telegram announces Percival's death in a riding accident. Bernard, trying to make sense of this absurdity, echoes the imagery of encircling unity that characterized their thoughts at the dinner: "Ideas break a thousand times for once that they globe themselves entire."

It is Bernard—identified, significantly, throughout the book as a storyteller—who is given the long final section of *The Waves* in which "to sum up," becoming perhaps a surrogate for the author herself. (As a young man at school, worrying out "my novel," he discovers how "stories that follow people into their private rooms are difficult.") It is he who recognizes that "I am not one person; I am many people," part of his friends as they are part of him, all of them incomplete in themselves; he is "a man without a self." Yet it is also he who on the novel's final page, using the wave imagery of the universalizing interludes, passionately asserts his individuality: "Against you I will fling myself, unvanquished and unyielding, O Death!" Life, however obdurate and fragmented, must be affirmed.

The Waves is without doubt Woolf's most demanding and original novel, her most daring experiment in eliminating the alien and the external. When she vowed to cast out "all waste, deadness, and superfluity," however, she also ascetically renounced some of her greatest strengths as a novelist: her wit and humor, her delight in the daily beauty, variety, and muddle of material existence. This "abstract mystical eyeless book," as she at one point envisioned it, is a work to admire greatly, but not to love.

The six years following *The Waves* were a difficult period for Woolf both personally and artistically. Deeply depressed by the deaths of Lytton Strachey and Roger Fry, two of her oldest, most respected friends, she was at work on an "essay-novel," as she first conceived of it, which despite her initial enthusiasm became her most painfully frustrating effort—even though it proved, ironically, to be her greatest commercial success.

The Years

In *The Years*, Woolf returned to the conventional novel that she had rejected after *Night and Day*; she planned "to take in everything" and found herself "infinitely delighting in facts for a change." Whereas *The Waves* had represented the extreme of leaving out, *The Years* suggests the opposite one of almost indiscriminate putting in. Its very subject, a history of the Pargiter clan spanning fifty years and three generations, links it with the diffuse family sagas of John Galsworthy and Arnold Bennett, whose books Woolf was expressly deriding when she demanded, "Must novels be like this?"

Nevertheless, *The Years* is more original than it may appear; Woolf made fresh use of her experimental methods in her effort to reanimate traditional form. The novel contains eleven unequal segments, each standing for a year; the longest ones, the opening "1880" section and the closing "Present Day" (the 1930's), anchor the book;

the nine intermediate sections cover the years between 1891 and 1918. Echoing *The Waves*, Woolf begins each chapter with a short panoramic passage describing both London and the countryside. Within the chapters, instead of continuous narrative, there are collections of vignettes, somewhat reminiscent of *Jacob's Room*, depicting various Pargiters going about their daily lives. Running parallel with the family's history are larger historical events, including Edward VII's death, the suffrage movement, the Irish troubles, and especially World War I. These events are usually treated indirectly, however; for example, the "1917" section takes place mainly in a cellar to which the characters have retreated, dinner plates in hand, during an air raid. It is here that Eleanor Pargiter asks, setting a theme that suffuses the rest of the novel, "When shall we live adventurously, wholly, not like cripples in a cave?"

The most pervasive effect of the war is felt in the lengthy "Present Day" segment, which culminates in a family reunion, where the youngest generation of Pargiters, Peggy and North, are lonely, cynical, and misanthropic, and their faltering elders are compromised either by complacency or failed hopes. Symbolically, Delia Pargiter gives the party in a rented office, not a home, underscoring the uprooting caused by the war. Yet the balancing "1880" section is almost equally dreary: The Pargiters' solid Victorian house shelters a chronically ailing mother whose children wish she would die, a father whose vulgar mistress greets him in hair curlers and frets over her dog's eczema, and a young daughter traumatized by an exhibitionist in the street outside. One oppressive way of life seems only to have been superseded by another, albeit a more universally menacing one.

The overall imagery of the novel is likewise unlovely: Children recall being scrubbed with slimy washcloths; a revolting dinner of underdone mutton served by Sara Pargiter includes a bowl of rotting, fly-blown fruit, grotesquely parodying Mrs. Ramsay's *boeuf en daube* and Rose's centerpiece; London is populated with deformed violet-sellers and old men eating cold sausages on buses. Communication in such a world is even more difficult than in Woolf's earlier books; the dialogue throughout is full of incomplete sentences, and a central vignette in the "Present Day" section turns on one guest's abortive efforts to deliver a speech toasting the human race.

Despite these circumstances, the characters still grope toward some kind of transforming unity; Eleanor, the eldest surviving Pargiter and the most sympathetic character in the novel, comes closest to achieving such vision on the scale that Lily Briscoe and Clarissa Dalloway do. At the reunion, looking back over her life, she wonders if there is "a pattern; a theme recurring like music . . . momentarily perceptible?" Casting about her, trying to connect with her relatives and friends but dozing in the process, she suddenly wakes, proclaiming that "it's been a perpetual discovery, my life. A miracle." Answering by implication her question posed fifteen years earlier during the air raid, she perceives that "we're only just beginning . . . to understand, here and there." That prospect is enough, however; she wants "to enclose the present moment . . . to fill it fuller and fuller, with the past, the present and the future, until it shone, whole, bright, deep with understanding."

Even this glowing dream of eventual unity is muted, however, when one recalls how Eleanor's embittered niece Peggy half pities, half admires her as a person who "still believed with passion . . . in the things man had destroyed," and how her nephew North, a captain in the trenches of World War I, thinks, "We cannot help each other, we are all deformed." It is difficult not to read the final lines of this profoundly somber novel ironically: "The sun had risen, and the sky above the houses wore an air of extraordinary beauty, simplicity and peace."

Between the Acts

Woolf's final work, *Between the Acts*, also deals with individual lives unfolding against the screen of history, but her vision and the methods by which she conveys it are more inventive, complex, and successful than in *The Years*. Covering the space of a single day in June, 1939, as world war threatens on the Continent, *Between the Acts* depicts the events surrounding a village pageant about the history of England, performed on the grounds of Pointz Hall, a country house occupied by the unhappily married Giles and Isa Oliver. The Olivers' story frames the presentation of the pageant, scenes of which are directly reproduced in the novel and alternate with glimpses of the audience's lives during the intervals between the acts. The novel's title is hence richly metaphorical: The acts of the drama itself are bracketed by the scenes of real life, which in turn can be viewed as brief episodes in the long pageant of human history. Equally ambiguous, then, is the meaning of "parts," connoting clearly defined roles within a drama but also the fragmentation and incompleteness of the individuals who play them, that pervasive theme in Woolf's work.

In *The Years*, Woolf had focused on the personal histories of her characters; history in the larger sense made itself felt as it impinged on private lives. This emphasis is reversed in *Between the Acts*. Though the novel has interesting characters, Woolf does not provide much information about their backgrounds, nor does she plumb individual memory in her usual manner. Instead, the characters possess a national, cultural, communal past—finally that of the whole human race from the Stone Age to the present. That Woolf intends her characters to be seen as part of this universal progression is clear from myriad references in the early pages to historical time. For example, from the air, the "scars" made by the Britons and the Romans can be seen around the village as can the Elizabethan manor house; graves in the churchyard attest that Mrs. Haines's family has lived in the area "for many centuries," whereas the Oliver family has inhabited Pointz Hall for "only something over a hundred and twenty years"; Lucy Swithin, Giles's endearing aunt, enjoys reading about history and imagining Piccadilly when it was a rhododendron forest populated by mastodons, "from whom, presumably, she thought . . . we descend."

The pageant itself, therefore, functions in the novel as more than simply a church fund-raising ritual, the product of well-meaning but hapless amateurs (though it exists amusingly on that level too). It is a heroic attempt by its author-director, the formidable Miss La Trobe, to make people see themselves playing parts in the continuum of British history. Thus, the audience has an integral role that blurs the lines "between the acts"; "Our part," says Giles's father, Bartholomew, "is to be the audience. And a very important part too." Their increasing interest in the pageant as they return from the successive intermissions signals their growing sense of a shared past and hence of an identity that both binds and transcends them as individuals.

The scenes of the pageant proceed from bathos to unnerving profundity. The first player, a small girl in pink, announces, "England am I," then promptly forgets her lines, while the wind blows away half the words of the singers behind her. Queen Elizabeth, splendidly decorated with six-penny brooches and a cape made of silvery scouring pads, turns out to be Mrs. Clark, the village tobacconist; the combined applause and laughter of delighted recognition muffle her opening speech. As the pageant progresses from a wicked though overlong parody of Restoration comedy to a satiric scene at a Victorian picnic, however, the audience becomes more reflective; the past is now close enough to be familiar, triggering their own memories and priming them for the last scene, Miss La Trobe's inspired experiment in expressionism, "The Present Time. Ourselves." The uncomprehending audience fidgets as the stage remains empty, refusing to understand that they are supposed to contemplate their own significance. "Reality too strong," Miss La Trobe mutters angrily from behind the bushes, "Curse 'em!" Then, "sudden and universal," a summer shower fortuitously begins. "Down it rained like all the people in the world weeping." Nature has provided the bridge of meaning Miss La Trobe required. As the rain ends, all the players from all the periods reappear, still in costume and declaiming fragments of their parts while flashing mirrors in the faces of the discomfited audience. An offstage voice asks how civilization is "to be built by orts, scraps and fragments like ourselves," then dies away.

The Reverend Streatfield, disconcerted like the rest of the audience, is assigned the embarrassing role of summing up the play's meaning. Tentatively, self-consciously, he ventures, "To me at least it was indicated that we are members of one another. . . . We act different parts; but are the same. . . . Surely, we should unite?" Then he abruptly shifts into a fund-raising appeal that is drowned out by a formation of war planes passing overhead. As the audience departs, a gramophone plays a valedictory: "Dispersed are we; we who have come together. But let us retain whatever made that harmony." The audience responds, thinking "There is joy, sweet joy, in company."

The qualified optimism of the pageant's close, however, is darkened by the bleak, perhaps apocalyptic postscript of the framing story. After the group disperses, the characters resume their usual roles. Lucy Swithin, identified earlier as a "unifier," experiences a typically Woolfian epiphany as she gazes on a fishpond, glimpsing the silver of the great carp below the surface and "seeing in that vision beauty, power and glory in ourselves." Her staunchly rational brother Bartholomew, a "separatist," goes into the house. Miss La Trobe, convinced that she has failed again, heads for the local pub to drink alone and plan her next play; it will be set at midnight with two figures half hidden by a rock as the curtain rises. "What would the first words be?"

It is the disaffected Giles and Isa, loving and hating each other, who begin the new play. In a remarkable ending, Woolf portrays the couple sitting silently in the dark before going to bed: "Before they slept, they must fight; after they had fought they would embrace." From that embrace, they may create another life, but "first they must fight, as the dog fox fights the vixen, in the heart of darkness, in the fields of night." The "great hooded chairs" in which they sit grow enormous, like Miss La Trobe's rock. The house fades, no longer sheltering them; they are like "dwellers in caves," watching "from some high place." The last lines of the novel are, "Then the curtain rose. They spoke."

This indeterminate conclusion implies that love and hate are elemental and reciprocal, and that such oppositions on a personal level are also the polarities that drive human history. Does Woolf read, then, in the gathering European storm, a cataclysm that will bring the pageant of history full circle, back to the primitive stage of prehistory? Or, like W. B. Yeats in "The Second Coming," does she envision a new cycle even more terrifying than the old? Or, as the faithful Lucy Swithin does, perhaps she hopes that "*all* is harmony could we hear it. And we shall."

Eight years earlier, Virginia Woolf wrote in her diary, "I think the effort to live in two spheres: the novel; and life; is a strain." Miss La Trobe, a crude alter ego for the author, is obsessed by failure but always driven to create anew because "a vision imparted was relief from agony . . . for one moment." In her brilliant experimental attempts to impart her own view of fragmented human beings achieving momentary harmony, discovering unity and stability behind the flux of daily life, Woolf repeatedly endured such anguish, but after *Between the Acts* was done, the strain of beginning again was too great. Perhaps the questions Virginia Woolf posed in this final haunting novel, published posthumously and unrevised, were answered for her in death.

Kristine Ottesen Garrigan

Other major works

SHORT FICTION: *Two Stories*, 1917 (one by Leonard Woolf); *Kew Gardens*, 1919; *The Mark on the Wall*, 1919; *Monday or Tuesday*, 1921; *A Haunted House, and Other Short Stories*, 1943; *Mrs. Dalloway's Party*, 1973 (Stella McNichol, editor); *The Complete Shorter Fiction of Virginia Woolf*, 1985.

NONFICTION: *The Common Reader: First Series*, 1925; *A Room of One's Own*, 1929; *The Common Reader: Second Series*, 1932; *Three Guineas*, 1938; *Roger Fry: A Biography*, 1940; *The Death of the Moth, and Other Essays*, 1942; *The Moment, and Other Essays*, 1947; *The Captain's Death Bed, and Other Essays*, 1950; *A Writer's Diary*, 1953; *Letters: Virginia Woolf and Lytton Strachey*, 1956; *Granite and Rainbow*, 1958; *Contemporary Writers*, 1965; *Collected Essays, Volumes 1-2*, 1966; *Collected Essays, Volumes 3-4*, 1967; *The Flight of the Mind: The Letters of Virginia Woolf, Vol. I, 1888-1912*, 1975 (Nigel Nicolson, editor; also known as *The Letters of Virginia Woolf, Vol. I: 1888-1912*); *The London Scene: Five Essays*, 1975; *Moments of Being*, 1976 (Jeanne Schulkind, editor); *The Question of Things Happening: The Letters of Virginia Woolf, Vol. II, 1912-1922*, 1976 (Nicolson, editor; also known as *The Letters of Virginia Woolf, Vol. II: 1912-1922*); *A Change of Perspective: The Letters of Virginia Woolf, Vol. III, 1923-1928*, 1977 (Nicolson, editor; also known as *The Letters of Virginia Woolf, Vol. III: 1923-1928*, 1978); *Books and Portraits*, 1977; *The Diary of Virginia Woolf*, 1977-1984 (5 volumes; Anne Olivier Bell, editor); *A Reflection of the Other Person: The Letters of Virginia Woolf, Vol. IV, 1929-1931*, 1978 (Nicolson, editor; also known as *The Letters of Virginia Woolf, Vol. IV: 1929-1931*, 1979); *The Sickle Side of the Moon: The Letters of Virginia Woolf, Vol. V, 1932-1935*, 1979 (Nicolson, editor; also known as *The Letters of Virginia Woolf, Vol. V: 1932-1935*); *Leave the Letters Til We're Dead: The Letters of Virginia Woolf, Vol. VI, 1936-1941*, 1980 (Nicolson, editor); *The Essays of Virginia Woolf*, 1987-

1994 (4 volumes); *Carlyle's House, and Other Sketches*, 2003 (David Bradshaw, editor).

Bibliography

Barrett, Eileen, and Patricia Cramer, eds. *Virginia Woolf: Lesbian Readings*. New York: New York University Press, 1997. Part 2 of this collection of conference papers focuses on Woolf's novels, with lesbian interpretations of *The Voyage Out*, *Mrs. Dalloway*, *To the Lighthouse*, *Orlando*, *The Waves*, *The Years*, and *Between the Acts*.

Beja, Morris, ed. *Critical Essays on Virginia Woolf*. Boston: G. K. Hall, 1985. Collection is divided into two sections: reviews of Woolf's major works and essays on Woolf's art and artistic vision. The various interpretations reflect the editor's premise that Woolf, although claimed by several ages and schools of criticism, was unique and thus cannot be pigeonholed in any specific way.

Blair, Emily. *Virginia Woolf and the Nineteenth-Century Domestic Novel*. Albany: State University of New York Press, 2007. Describes the influence of nineteenth and early twentieth century literature, particularly its descriptions of femininity, on Woolf's work and compares her novels to those of Elizabeth Gaskell and Margaret Oliphant, two popular Victorian novelists.

Briggs, Julia. *Virginia Woolf: An Inner Life*. Orlando, Fla: Harcourt, 2005. Biography focuses on Woolf's work in relation to her fascination with the workings of the mind. Traces the creation of each of Woolf's books, from *The Voyage Out* through *Between the Acts*, combining literary analysis with details of Woolf's life.

Goldman, Jane. *The Cambridge Introduction to Virginia Woolf*. New York: Cambridge University Press, 2006. Provides a wealth of information designed to help students and other readers better understand Woolf's writings, including biographical details and discussions of the novels. One section places Woolf's life and work within historical, political, and cultural context, including information about the Bloomsbury Group; another section focuses on critical reception of the works from the 1940's through the 1990's and includes contemporary reviews.

_______. *The Feminist Aesthetics of Virginia Woolf: Modernism, Post-impressionism, and the Politics of the Visual*. New York: Cambridge University Press, 2001. Feminist reading of Woolf's works focuses on the influence of literary and artistic modernism and places the works within their historical and cultural context.

Gordon, Lyndall. *Virginia Woolf: A Writer's Life*. New York: W. W. Norton, 1985. Biography looks not only at Woolf's life in Bloomsbury but also at her works, including her unfinished memoirs, the drafts of novels, and some lesser-known and unpublished pieces. Divides Woolf's life into three phases: her childhood, her time of literary apprenticeship and recurring illness, and her mature period of artistic achievement.

King, James. *Virginia Woolf*. New York: W. W. Norton, 1995. Literary biography relates Woolf's life to her works, showing how the chief sources of material for her writing were her life, her family, and her friends.

Lee, Hermione. *Virginia Woolf*. New York: Alfred A. Knopf, 1997. Detailed biography describes Woolf's complex family relationships, her lifelong battle with mental illness, and her relationship to the Bloomsbury Group.

Marder, Herbert. *The Measure of Life: Virginia Woolf's Last Years*. Ithaca, N.Y.: Cornell University Press, 2000. Biography focuses on the events of the final decade of Woolf's life and analyzes the changes in her writings during this period.

Reid, Panthea. *Art and Affection: A Life of Virginia Woolf*. New York: Oxford University Press, 1996. Biography draws on the vast amount of material available about Woolf and her circle to examine Woolf's desires to write and to be loved. Especially strong in providing a psychological explanation for Woolf's artistic choices, such as her decision to abandon conventional representation in her fiction.

Roe, Sue, and Susan Sellers, eds. *The Cambridge Companion to Virginia Woolf*. New York: Cambridge University Press, 2000. Collection of essays by leading scholars addresses Woolf's life and work from a wide range of intellectual perspectives. Includes analyses of her novels and discussions of Woolf in relation to modernism, feminism, and psychoanalysis.

HERMAN WOUK

Born: New York, New York; May 27, 1915

Principal long fiction

Aurora Dawn, 1947
The City Boy, 1948
The Caine Mutiny, 1951
Marjorie Morningstar, 1955
Slattery's Hurricane, 1956
Youngblood Hawke, 1962
Don't Stop the Carnival, 1965
The Lomokome Papers, 1968
The Winds of War, 1971
War and Remembrance, 1978
Inside, Outside, 1985
The Hope, 1993
The Glory, 1994
A Hole in Texas, 2004

Other literary forms

Herman Wouk (wohk) wrote several plays; the first, *The Traitor*, was produced on Broadway in 1949 and was published by Samuel French the same year. His most successful theatrical work, *The Caine Mutiny Court-Martial* (based on his novel published in 1951), appeared on Broadway in 1954 and was published by Doubleday the same year. *Nature's Way* was produced on Broadway in 1957 and was published by Doubleday the following year. Eric Bentley, speaking of *The Caine Mutiny Court-Martial*, said that Wouk showed a gift for crisp dialogue that no other regular writer for the American theater could rival. The musical *Don't Stop the Carnival*, a collaboration with pop musician Jimmy Buffett, was produced in 1998. Wouk collaborated with Richard Murphy in writing the screenplay for *Slattery's Hurricane* (1949). Wouk also wrote teleplays, for *The Winds of War* (1983) and *War and Remembrance* (1988). *This Is My God*, which Wouk first published in 1959 and followed with a revised edition in 1973, is a description and explanation of Orthodox Judaism, especially as it is practiced in America. The volume was a Reader's Digest Condensed Book Club selection and an alternate selection for the Book-of-the-Month Club in 1959.

Achievements

It is a peculiarity of American criticism to denigrate popular success in literature. Almost from the outset of his career, Herman Wouk was a very popular writer; putting aside prejudicial presuppositions, this can be acknowledged as a genuine achievement, for Wouk did not attain his popular status by catering to the baser tastes of his readers. Beginning with *The Caine Mutiny*, his books appeared regularly on best-seller lists. Several of his titles were selections of major book clubs. Wouk was awarded the Pulitzer Prize for fiction in 1952 for *The Caine Mutiny*. That same year, Columbia University presented him its Medal of Excellence, an honor extended to distinguished alumni. Several universities awarded him honorary doctorates.

Wouk might be described as a traditional novelist, in that his writing does not reflect the experimental qualities that are to be found in so much twentieth and twenty-first century American fiction. As with John Updike, he gives primacy of place to the narrative element in fiction; he brings to the novel his own peculiar brand of rough-hewn vigor. At a time when conventional wisdom judged it bad form for a novelist to take a clear stand on moral issues—as if ambiguity itself were a virtue—Wouk consistently declared his moral position in his writings. This was not always to the benefit of his fiction, but by and large, his novels are stronger for his conviction that literary art does not subsist in a vacuum but is part of a larger moral universe.

Biography

Herman Wouk was born in New York City on May 27, 1915, the son of Abraham Isaac and Esther (Levine) Wouk. Wouk's father, an industrialist in the power laundry field, started out as an immigrant laundry worker earning three dollars a week. Wouk was educated at Townsend Harris Hall and at Columbia University, where he graduated with honors in 1934. While at Columbia, he studied philosophy and comparative literature and was editor of the *Columbia Jester*. From 1934 to 1935 he worked as a gag writer for radio comedians, and from 1936 to 1941, he was a scriptwriter for Fred Allen. In

1941, Wouk moved to Washington, D.C., following his appointment to the U.S. Treasury Department as a dollar-a-year man; his job was to write and produce radio shows to sell war bonds.

Wouk left this work to join the Navy. After completing Officer Candidate School, he was commissioned an ensign and assigned to mine sweeper duty in the Pacific fleet. He served in the Navy from 1942 to 1945, first aboard the USS *Zane* and then aboard the destroyer-minesweeper USS *Southard*. Eventually, he was promoted to the position of executive officer of the *Southard*. He was decorated with four campaign stars during the war, and received a unit citation as well. When Wouk was processed out of the Navy in 1945, he held the rank of lieutenant. Wouk married Betty Sarah Brown in December, 1945. They had three sons, Abraham Isaac (who died before reaching his fifth birthday), Nathaniel, and Joseph.

Wouk began his career as a serious writer while he was in the Navy; before his release from the service, he had completed a good portion of his first novel. That novel, *Aurora Dawn*, was published by Simon and Schuster in 1947. The following year he published his second novel, *The City Boy*. Neither of these works gained a great deal of attention for Wouk, but with the publication of *The Caine Mutiny* in 1951 (awarded the Pulitzer Prize the following year), he was quickly established as a writer of consequence. His play *The Caine Mutiny Court-Martial* began its successful run on Broadway in 1954. *Marjorie Morningstar* appeared in 1955 and his nonfiction work on Jewish culture and religion, *This Is My God*, appeared in 1959. The 1960's saw the publication of *Youngblood Hawke* and *Don't Stop the Carnival*. Wouk's sprawling two-volume fictional account of World War II, which he began writing in 1962, was published in the 1970's; the first volume, *The Winds of War*, appeared in 1971, and the second, *War and Remembrance*, was published in 1978. Wouk wrote the teleplay for the eighteen-hour television film based on *The Winds of War*, which was broadcast during the week of February 6-13, 1983. He was coauthor of the teleplay for the television adaptation of *War and Remembrance*, which appeared in 1988.

Unlike many contemporary popular novelists, Wouk shunned the public spotlight throughout his career. Though the Wouks spent more than a decade after they were married in New York, they moved to the Virgin Islands in 1958, partly so that Wouk could find a place to write free of interruptions. In 1964, the family moved to Georgetown, a Washington, D.C., suburb, so that he could be closer to archival materials he needed to consult to write *The Winds of War* and *War and Remembrance*. During the next three decades, Wouk divided his time between his home in the nation's capital and one in Palm Springs, California, occasionally appearing at public events to accept awards or participate in fund-raising or religious events. In 1995, Wouk entered into an agreement with popular singer Jimmy Buffett to write the book for a musical based on *Don't Stop the Carnival*. Featuring a number of Caribbean songs composed by Buffett, the mu-

Herman Wouk. (National Archives)

sical opened in Florida in 1997 and moved to Broadway in 1998.

Wouk's great popular success enabled him to devote his full time to his craft, but on occasion he took academic or semiacademic positions. From 1953 to 1957, he was a visiting professor of English at Yeshiva University, and during 1973-1974, he was scholar-in-residence at the Aspen Institute for Humanistic Studies. He was a member of the Authors Guild and the Dramatists Guild, and he served on the board of directors for institutions and organizations such as the College of the Virgin Islands, the Washington National Symphony, and Kennedy Center Productions.

Analysis

Herman Wouk is a novelist in the tradition of the great English novelists of the nineteenth century; he is also a spiritual descendant of such American writers as James Fenimore Cooper, William Dean Howells, Theodore Dreiser, and James T. Farrell. What he has in common with these writers is narrative prowess, a commitment to realism, and a lively moral consciousness. Furthermore, like these writers, Wouk addresses himself to the population at large. Since World War II, American fiction has seen a distinction between writers who seem inclined to write primarily for other writers or for academic critics and those inclined to write for a general audience. That Wouk is numbered among the latter would appear to be traceable to a definite decision on his part.

Wouk's first novel, *Aurora Dawn*, has the flavor of the experimental fiction that began to proliferate in the postwar period. If one were to have speculated in 1946 on the course that Wouk's literary career was going to take, it would have been a safe guess to say that he would probably continue down the road of experimentation, that he would become more and more concerned with language as an end in itself, and that eventually, he would be writing books destined to be read only in upper-division English courses in universities. This was not what happened, however; in his second novel, *The City Boy*, Wouk followed a conventional narrative pattern and told his story in language that was not constantly calling attention to itself.

In *Aurora Dawn* and *The City Boy*, Wouk was still stretching his muscles and attempting to find his proper level as a writer. He came into his own with *The Caine Mutiny*. In that novel, and in every novel that followed for the next four decades, there is the presence of a central theme, treated in various ways and from varying perspectives. The theme is the conflict between traditional values and a modern consciousness that is either indifferent to those values or flatly antipathetic toward them. The conflict is not treated in abstract terms, but in terms of individuals who are caught up in it, and how the individual fares is in great part determined by the side with which he chooses to ally himself.

Aurora Dawn

Aurora Dawn, which Wouk began writing while serving as an officer in the Navy, is an effort at satire. The butt of the satire is the advertising industry and, more generally, the foolishness of anyone in business whose ethical consciousness is dimmed by avarice. The moral of the story is explicit: Greed is the root of all evil. Andrew Reale, the novel's young protagonist, is bright, energetic, and imaginative, but until he undergoes a conversion at novel's end, his primary concern is getting ahead. He wants to be successful above all else, and to him, success means money. In his scramble to get to the top as quickly as possible, his myopia becomes acute and his values are severely twisted. He is willing to make compromises where compromises should not be made. A connection is intimated between Reale's moral weakness and his failure to continue to adhere to the religious principles according to which he was reared, a recurring theme in Wouk's fiction.

Reale's obsessive pursuit of success leads him to jilt his fiancé, the beautiful and innocent Laura Beaton, so that he can take up with the beautiful but frivolous Carol Marquis, daughter of the despicable but very rich Talmadge Marquis. It leads him to be crassly manipulative in his dealings with the Reverend Calvin Stanfield, who is simple, straightforward, and a good man. Finally, it leads him, in a move of pure expediency, to quit an employer who has been generous with him so that he can join forces with Talmadge Marquis. All Reale's machinations, however, are to no avail. The hastily courted Carol Marquis runs off with an eccentric painter, and Laura Beaton, brokenhearted at Reale's rejection of her, marries an older man. In the end, Reale gets better than he deserves. His thwarted attempt to blackmail Father

Stanfield proves to be the occasion of a conversion experience for him. He suddenly sees the wickedness of his ways and decides to alter his course. Laura Beaton is miraculously released from her unconsummated marriage, so that Reale is able to get the woman of his dreams after all. Fleeing the wicked city, the bride and groom go off to live together in New Mexico.

The novel is not realistic and cannot be judged according to the criterion of verisimilitude. It is a light, playful work in which humor plays an important part. Despite several brilliant passages, however, the novel does not come across as successful satire, and that would seem to be attributable to the fact that Wouk is vacillating and hesitant in what he wants to say. What he takes with one hand, he gives back with the other. The novel is clever, in both good and bad senses. While its language is often lively, it can as well be pretentious and self-conscious at times. The anachronistic devices of addressing the reader directly, inserting explicit authorial commentary on the action, and interspersing the narrative with short philosophical asides do not always work to maximize the effect. The humor of the novel is capable of being right on the mark, but for the most part it is a bit forced; Wouk, the radio gagman, is too much in evidence. The flaws to be found in *Aurora Dawn* are flaws that are not uncommon in a first novel. Despite its weaknesses, however, already in evidence in this work are the two traits that have subsequently become the chief strengths of Wouk's fiction: a vigorous talent for narrative and a lively sensitivity to moral issues.

The City Boy

Perhaps the most striking thing about Wouk's second novel, *The City Boy*, is that, stylistically, it represents a marked departure from the standards he had established in his first novel. The language of the work does not call attention to itself; it is clear, straightforward, and unpretentious. The novel is humorous in tone, and its plot structure is loose.

The book revolves around the adventures—most of which take place in an upstate summer camp—of a New York City boy, Herbie Bookbinder. John P. Marquand's comparison of this novel with Mark Twain's *The Adventures of Tom Sawyer* (1876) is well-founded. In many respects, Herbie is an urban version of the scamp from the midwestern frontier. He is a bright and enterprising lad, and if he is mischievous at times, it is seldom with malice. Much of what he does is calculated to impress Lucille Glass, the object of his single-minded puppy love. Herbie is unlike Tom Sawyer in that he is an outsider as far as other boys are concerned, largely because of his poor athletic skills and his penchant for things intellectual. A goodly number of Herbie's efforts in the novel are given over to his attempts to gain the status of a regular guy. He succeeds, finally, and as a result is welcomed into the full fellowship of his peers. *The City Boy* is a light novel—in some respects a boy's book—but in it, Wouk's moral consciousness is manifested by his underscoring the difference between good and evil in the actions of the characters.

The Caine Mutiny

The Caine Mutiny is Wouk's best novel, the work on which his reputation rests. The novel takes place against the backdrop of war, but it cannot be regarded as a "war story" in any simplistic sense. It is a story about the subtle and complicated relationships that exist among men who are part of the enclosed world that constitutes the military establishment. One of its central themes concerns the matter of authority—how it is exercised within a military context, and how it is abused. The novel explores the manner in which various personality types act and react within a hierarchical, authoritarian structure. In addition, it examines the ways in which the lives of those caught up in the trauma of war are altered, sometimes profoundly. Other themes that the novel treats are loyalty and disloyalty, patriotism, doers versus sayers, personal integrity, and the process by which young men are tested in stressful situations.

The Caine Mutiny can easily be misread. One might conclude that its chief concern is the everlasting battle between despotism and democracy, that Captain Queeg therefore is clearly the villain of the piece, and that its heroes are Lieutenant Maryk, Willie Keith, Tom Keefer, and the others who were involved in the mutiny. It is not that simple. If it were, *The Caine Mutiny* would be little more than a melodrama. Captain Queeg is not a hero, but neither is he a diabolical type. He is a sorry human being; he has serious personal problems (his eccentricity is not amusing—he is, in fact, a sick man); and, perhaps most serious, given his status as a commanding officer, he is incompetent professionally. For all that, he is consistent in trying to do his job to the best of his ability. Queeg's problem is that he is in over his head; he can at times scarcely cope with situations that are his duty to control. The circumstances surrounding the event that lead to the mutiny are sufficiently ambiguous as to render doubtful the claim of the mutineers that, had they not relieved Queeg of command when they did, the ship would have been lost.

Wouk's assessment of the situation seems to be communicated most directly through the character of Lieutenant Greenwald, the young aviator-lawyer who defends Maryk at the court-martial. Greenwald is not sympathetic with the mutineers, but he decides to defend Maryk because he respects the executive officer's personal integrity and because he is convinced that Maryk, in assuming command of the *Caine* during the typhoon, was acting in good faith. Greenwald succeeds in having Maryk acquitted of the charge of mutiny, mainly by drawing out of Queeg in the courtroom telltale signs of his emotional instability, but he takes no joy in his victory.

After the trial, Greenwald puts the damper on the victory celebration being staged by the *Caine*'s officers when he gives them a stinging tonguelashing. His ire is directed particularly at Tom Keefer, whom he perceives correctly as being the chief instigator of the mutiny, but one who refused, when the matter came to a head, to put himself on the line. Greenwald's position seems to be that, while the *Caine*'s officers are legally innocent, they are morally guilty. However sophisticated a rationale they might provide for their actions, what was at the bottom of those actions, in his view, was disloyalty, and disloyalty, for a military officer, is an unforgivable sin. One might say that the trial does not prove either clear-cut guilt or innocence. If anything, it demonstrates the complexity and ambiguity of all human situations. Greenwald's position is that, given the ambiguity, it is always better not to second-guess legitimately constituted authority. It is the chief responsibility of the naval officer to do his duty through thick and thin.

If there is a clear villain in *The Caine Mutiny*, Tom Keefer would appear to be the most likely candidate for the role. Keefer is, in many respects, a preeminently modern man. He is committed to what he presumably regards as the absolute truths of Freudian psychology, which he employs in a reductionist way, as weapons against those who do not share his worldview. He is in the Navy, but not of it, and, in fact, he rather enjoys and exploits his position as an iconoclastic outsider. He maintains an attitude of supercilious superiority toward people such as Queeg, and toward everything that the Navy represents. His view is narrow, restricted by the dictates of his overriding egotism. Keefer is a carping critic of the Navy, but he does not hesitate to take selfish advantage of what the Navy can offer him at every turn. His hypocrisy allows him to talk a big game, but when the pressure is on and when circumstances call for words to be translated into action, he invariably backs off. Perhaps the most damning thing that could be said of Keefer is that he is a coward, as he demonstrates when he is captain of the *Caine* and precipitously abandons ship. By the novel's end, however, Keefer seem to have arrived at a degree of self-awareness that hitherto had eluded him; he confesses to Willie Keith, who succeeds him as commanding officer, that Keith is a better man than he. He is right.

Willie Keith is the central character of the novel; his moral education is the real subject of *The Caine Mutiny*. Willie is an aristocratic rich kid from New York who comes to learn, among other things, the value of democracy. His relationship with Maria Minotti, alias May Wynn, can be interpreted in this way. The bulk of Keith's education, however, takes place in the Navy. When he first comes aboard the *Caine*, he is very much under the influence of Keefer, and he accepts Keefer's cynical interpretation of things as the correct one. Eventually, Keith realizes that the Navy, though imperfect, is not a bad organization. What is more, given the realities of the modern world, it is a necessary organization. Unlike Keefer, Keith is prepared to acknowledge that the Navy in World War II is contributing toward the preservation of the way of life into which both men have been born and to which they are devoted, and that, excepting a total transformation of human nature, navies will probably always be needed to ensure the protection of people's freedom. Keith is not changed into a mindless patriot and militarist, but his criticism of the Navy and its personnel becomes more discriminate, more intelligent, more responsible. He learns to judge matters according to criteria that are not self-centered and develops an appreciation for the larger scheme of things. He takes pride in his work, and, as he rises in rank, his conscientiousness increases; he tries to be the best officer he can.

The world of the Navy in *The Caine Mutiny* is in certain respects a microcosm of the world at large. It is beset by all sorts of problems, but there is no perfect alternative somewhere to which one might flee. A person's maturity is measured by his or her ability to establish standards of excellence and to work assiduously to achieve them in spite of various limitations, sometimes severe—limitations in him- or herself, in others, and in the situation.

Marjorie Morningstar

On the surface, Wouk's fourth novel, *Marjorie Morningstar*, would seem to lead nowhere. It is the story of a young Jewish woman, the daughter of immigrants established comfortably in the middle class of New York, who has been sufficiently Americanized as to have for her chief ambition the desire to become a famous actor, a star. Marjorie Morningstar (née Morgenstern) is a beautiful woman whose theatrical talent, while not scintillating, is probably sufficient to underwrite the realization of her dream, given a lucky break here and there. She is willing to make the sacrifices, within certain bounds, and to invest the hard work that the ascent to stardom inevitably entails. If Marjorie is determined about anything, it is that she is not going to allow herself to lapse into the staid, conventional life that is the destiny of the vast majority of nice, middle-class Jewish girls. She is going to be different; she is going to break out of the mold.

After several fruitless efforts to break into the theater and to make it big, after a sequence of adventures with an assortment of men, chiefly with Noel Airman, Marjorie ends up doing what she vowed she would never do. She marries a Jew, a successful lawyer by the name of Milton Schwartz, and she retires to a plush suburb to live the most conventional of conventional lives. The novel, then, would seem to end on an almost laughably anticlimactic note, but only if one fails to perceive the kind of statement that it is attempting to make.

If *The Caine Mutiny* delineates the education of Willie Keith, the education of Marjorie Morningstar is the primary concern of the novel that bears her name. If Marjorie comes full circle, as it were, and ends by embracing the conventional, it is because she discovers that the conventional is worthy of being embraced, the conventional not only as representing middle-class morality but also, and much more important, as embodying traditional cultural and religious values. The glamorous life to which Marjorie aspired, whether or not she was always fully conscious of the fact, was a life that repudiated traditional values. As a teenager and young woman, she fought her own tradition, particularly as manifested in the Jewish religion; she viewed it as crude and superstitious, a carryover from humankind's primitive past. This tradition, however, was more deeply embedded in her, was more integral a part of her identity, than she was willing to admit, and throughout her various experiences it guided her actions more than she knew.

Marjorie's failure to realize her dream of becoming a star actually represents the triumph of her better, truer self. Her concern shifts from thin, superficial values to those with substance and depth. The drama of her quest for self-realization is played out principally around her long and erratic affair with Noel Airman. When she first meets Noel, who is some ten years her senior, she is scarcely more than a girl, and she is completely enamored of him. He is handsome, intelligent, urbane, and witty, a talented composer of popular songs who shows promise of becoming a success in the theater. Noel represents much of what she wants to become, and all of what she has decided is most valuable in life, which is emphasized by the fact that she throws decorum to the winds and pursues him actively. When she finally catches him, however, she realizes that she does not really want him. The man who was once her ideal, her hero, the man whom she wanted to marry more than anyone else, is at last perceived, albeit faintly, as a god with clay feet.

Who is this Noel Airman? He is Saul Ehrmann, one who has actively repudiated his Jewish identity and its associated traditions but who has failed to come up with a viable substitute for either. He is a rootless vagabond, a shameless Casanova, one who eschews commitment as a matter of principle, and who tries hard to make a profession of cynicism. It would be wrong, however, to think of him entirely in negative terms. He is not a character lacking in complexity, and he is not devoid of critical self-knowledge, which at times can be acute and penetrating. Still, this self-awareness serves only to accentuate his pathetic quality, for in the final analysis, he is impotent to act on his better impulses. He does not have the moral stamina to follow through, and this is so, Wouk implies, precisely because he has cut himself off from his tradition.

The fact that Marjorie arrives at a new state of consciousness that allows her to see Noel for what he is, and accordingly to reject him, is attributable in part to her brief but fateful acquaintance with Michael Eden. Michael, like Noel, is a Jew, but, unlike Noel, he is not in flight from the fact. He is a strong, taciturn man whose personal sufferings have led him to dedicate himself to a melancholy but determined altruism. He is involved in the very risky business of rescuing Jews from Nazi Germany. He is every bit as bright and talented as Noel but has what Noel lacks—integrity and a sense of purpose in life. Although it is not Marjorie's destiny to marry Michael, meeting him has the effect of altering her perception of Noel. Milton Schwartz, the person she marries, has in common with Michael a fundamental decency.

Youngblood Hawke

Wouk's sixth novel, *Youngblood Hawke*, based to some extent on the life of Thomas Wolfe, could be the story of many young American writers of the twentieth century, and for that reason, the novel, besides its intrinsic worth as a work of fiction, has considerable value as a historical document. The story of Arthur Youngblood Hawke is a success story, but it is a story of failure as well. Indeed, Hawke's case is in many respects a tragic one. Hawke is a lanky, down-home Kentuckian who, after being released from the Navy at the end of World War II, moves to New York to conquer the city and the country, by his pen. He comes to his task with a spotty education, with an explosive imagination, and with a seemingly boundless store of energy. Writing is his life, and his engagement in it is passionate.

There is much about Hawke that smacks of the all-American boy. He is crude and unpolished, but straightforward and gentle in his dealings with people—except with those who deserve otherwise. He is honest, in his way, and an assiduous worker. He wants to be a success as a writer. He wants to become a millionaire, not so that he can give up writing but so that, freed from financial worries, he can devote himself to it without distractions. Hawke is in the mold of the rustic innocent who has long played a part in American literature.

Hawke's early success works against him in the long run. His first novel, though receiving rough treatment at the hands of the critics, gains a large popular audience; his second novel wins the Pulitzer Prize and increasing respect from the critics. He is associated with a solid, respectable publishing house whose head values his work, has faith in his future, and is willing to be very generous in making contractual arrangements with him. Hawke's obsessional longing for financial independence, however, prompts him to break ties with his publisher and begin publishing his own books; he also makes some risky investments. His luck turns, and in a matter of months he finds himself on the threshold of bankruptcy. He determines that he is going to write his way out of his debts; leaving behind the plush life that he enjoyed only too briefly in New York, he returns to Kentucky, and there, living in a cabin in the woods, he works furiously to complete what proves to be his final novel. In fact, he overworks, devoting himself not only to the novel but also, earlier, to a theatrical production that he hopes will strike it rich. The strain brought about by his frenetic activities exacerbates an old head injury, and, after a wild chase to South America made in a state of delirium, he ends up back in New York. He is hospitalized there and dies at the age of thirty-three.

As Hawke lies dying, his vaguely addressed prayer is that he might be given more time so that he can work. Everything that he has done he considers as only preparatory exercises to his great multivolume *Comedy*. That his magnum opus was never written is not simply attributable to the fact that Hawke showed poor business sense or that he was careless of his health. There is evidence in the novel to warrant the conclusion that Hawke's failure to fulfill his chief artistic ambition amounts to an exacting payment he has had to make for his sins. There have been two principal women in his life but, by his own admission, there should have been only one.

In the beginning of the novel, before he bursts upon the American literary scene, Hawke meets a young editor, Jeanne Green, who subsequently becomes for him what Maxwell Perkins was for Thomas Wolfe. Jeanne, besides being a very talented editor, is, like Hawke, essentially a small-town person. She is simple, unpretentious, genuine. Hawke falls in love with her almost immediately—his better self tells him that this is the woman in his life, the woman he should marry—but he becomes involved in a torrid affair with a wealthy, sophisticated, fundamentally selfish New Yorker, Frieda Winters. Winters is older than he; she is married, has three children, and is no stranger to adulterous affairs. Hawke is honest enough with himself to admit that he is involved in adultery; the reader is told that he hates both the word and the fact. He does not have the moral courage, however, to extricate himself from the affair—not until, as it turns out, it is too late. His relationship with Winters proves to be an enervating experience; if it does not exactly destroy him, it contributes substantially toward his destruction.

What allowed Hawke to become involved in an affair that he knew to be wrong? One explanation is that he failed to be true to the basic religious principles that he had been taught as a boy but that in his impetuous youth he attempted to reject. Unlike Marjorie Morningstar, whose roots in a religious tradition were sufficiently deep and tenacious to carry her through the hard times, Hawke succumbs to the facile moral standards of a secularized society.

Don't Stop the Carnival

Wouk's next novel, *Don't Stop the Carnival*, is the weakest of his entire corpus. It is a comic novel and it would seem to have some kind of satiric intent, but the humor, instead of carrying the moral import of the tale, more often than not obstructs it. The work's humor is hampered by obtrusive, heavy-handed moralizing, and its seriousness is trivialized by a humor that too often degenerates into tedious slapstick. Most damaging for the novel is that Wouk's narrative talent, which is his forte, serves him poorly here. The plot is too often based on contrivance, and in some instances blatant authorial manipulation is very much in evidence. Add to this fact that characterization is unconvincing, and the sum total is a generally undistinguished piece of fiction that holds the reader's attention only by an adamant act of will. It is not that the novel is completely lacking in substance, but the detectably substantive elements are not allowed to emerge fully. There is, for example, a statement being made about the haplessness of "liberal" types who are awash in a world that in many respects is the result of their own brand of thinking, but the message is befuddled by static of various kinds and one must strain to detect it.

The Winds of War *and* War and Remembrance

Wouk's impressive companion novels, *The Winds of War* and *War and Remembrance*, published in 1971 and 1978, respectively, are in effect a single, sustained work of fiction, and therefore can be discussed together. Wouk spent sixteen years in completing the work, and it seems likely that he regards it as his magnum opus. *The Winds of War* is focused primarily on the European theater during World War II, beginning with the German invasion of Czechoslovakia and Poland, putting special emphasis on the latter. The Battle of Britain is also treated at close range. The book ends with the bombing of Pearl Harbor, the point at which *War and Remembrance* takes up the story. This book, while continuing to trace the course of events in Europe, especially those events having to do with the systematic extermination of the Jews by the Nazis, shifts attention to the Pacific theater and provides poignant descriptions of the major naval battles fought there. The book ends with the dropping of the atomic bombs and the Japanese acceptance of unconditional surrender.

In these two massive volumes, which constitute a single work, an ambitious fictional history of World War II, Wouk once again shows himself to be a master of narrative. This is not a mere chronicle of events; rather, major events of the war are given dramatic immediacy by the tactic of having one of the many key characters in the narrative involved in those events. One is even provided access to the Axis point of view through excerpts from the analytic histories of the German general Armin von Roon, interspersed throughout the work.

The key character in the work is Victor "Pug" Henry, a naval officer who has given thirty years of his life to military service. He is a staid, conservative man, a patriot but not a jingoist, dedicated to professional excellence and quietly guided by deeply embedded religious principles. Following his various adventures in Europe and in the Pacific, one is not only brought into direct contact with important historical personages but treated to his thoughtful reactions to them as well. Wouk is the type of artist who likes to paint on a large canvas, but the canvas he is covering in this work is of mammoth proportions. All the more remarkable, then, is the control he exercises here; nothing gets away from him. There is about this wide-ranging tour de force a satisfying unity and completeness. It is thickly peopled with a vast array of characters, and their attitudes toward the war run the full gamut from self-sacrificing heroism to cold-blooded murderousness.

One of the most interesting characters in the work is Aaron Jastrow, a Jewish American, world-renowned scholar and former Yale professor who at the outbreak of the war is living in active retirement in Italy. In tracing the story of Aaron Jastrow, and that of his Polish cousin Berel, Wouk recounts in moving fashion the sickening circumstances of the infamous "final solution." Aaron himself was born in Poland and reared in a strict Orthodox tradition. As he reached young manhood, he put aside his religion and settled into a benevolent agnosticism. Accompanied by his niece Natalie, he is hounded by the Nazis throughout Europe for years, until he finally ends up in the land of his birth, in a death camp. His life is choked out in the gas chambers. He speaks to the reader directly through *A Jew's Journey*. What one learns from this document is that the most significant journey in the waning months of Jastrow's life is a spiritual one. His personal confrontation with the horrors of Nazism has the effect of returning him to the religion of his birth. When he comes to die, he is possessed of an inner peace his murderers could never know, and he represents a basic human dignity that they have chosen to abandon for themselves and to attempt to destroy in others.

The Winds of War and *War and Remembrance* are about a specific war, but they are about war in general as well. Wouk does not romanticize World War II, but he suggests that it was absolutely essential that the Allied forces emerge as victorious. It was an unspeakably grim yet nevertheless necessary struggle. The bombs that ended the war, however, changed the nature of war forever. If humankind were capable before Hiroshima and Nagasaki of arguing that all-out war, however cruel and crude, was a workable solution to human problems, that argument proved no longer tenable. World War II was perhaps the most gruesome war that human beings have ever inflicted on themselves. Wouk's thesis is that wars in the future will not be avoided simply by proclaiming them to be unthinkable. One must think about them; one must think especially about the most gruesome of wars. Through memory, perhaps a pathway to peace can be found.

Inside, Outside

Wouk's *Inside, Outside* appeared in 1985. *The Caine Mutiny* is by consensus Wouk's single best work of fiction, but *Inside, Outside* could arguably be offered as a legitimate contender for that honor. Here one finds all Wouk's considerable skill in operation: his commanding ability to create characters that live and breathe and convince, telling their interesting and interlocking stories within the context of a fictional world that, while complex, never degenerates into incoherence. Wouk's characters move and make their marks in a world that can be as confused and disorienting as that created by any other modern fictionist. However, the core, the center, of Wouk's world, although subjected to great strain, always manages to hold; that is, although Wouk's characters live in an extremely difficult and demanding world, that world preserves its essential meaningfulness. Wouk does not burden himself with the absurd task of attempting to populate an absurd universe.

It is difficult to specify what makes for the peculiar success of this novel, but certainly at work is Wouk's uncanny ability—which is singularly devoid of self-advertising and therefore easy to overlook—to create what one might call fictional immediacy. Wouk can effect the magic of bringing into being a fictional world that more than half persuades the reader that it is not fictional at all. In other words, he is a maker of art.

Inside, Outside revolves around the life and times of one Israel David Goodkind. It is principally his story, and he tells it with verve. The novel is interestingly structured. The time frame of the narration is 1973. In that year, Goodkind, a successful New York lawyer, finds himself in the rather unusual position—given the fact that he has been a lifelong Democrat—of serving in Washington as a special assistant to President Richard Nixon. The job, though flattering in its way, is anything but exacting, and Goodkind begins to expend his considerable free time in writing; however, this activity is not simply an idle exercise with which to fill the gaps in his undemanding day. He takes his writing quite seriously, and he intends to produce something of real literary worth. He endeavors to fulfill an ambition he has harbored since his youth but that thus far he has not managed to accomplish. He writes about his own life, which takes him back to the turn of the century and the stories of his parents, two Jewish emigrants from Russia. They both arrive in New York; there they meet and marry, and there their children, Israel and Lee, are born.

The reader follows the entire course of Goodkind's life as he recounts its developments, its delays, its assorted dramatic and melodramatic reversals, with meticulous and loving detail. The reader is brought into the very center of Goodkind's world and discovers it to be a world that is at once intensely provincial and intensely cosmopolitan—the kind of combination that is possible perhaps only in New York City. It is a wide world, thickly populated with a rich variety of relatives and friends. The reader is given the opportunity to meet them all and, with differing degrees of completeness, to come to know their stories, too.

Such is the main strand of the novel's narrative. Its secondary strand is no less compelling. Goodkind is interrupted periodically in his recounting of his past by the pressing events that take place around him in 1973 as he continues his writing project. Two significant historical events mark that time period. One is the Israeli-Egyptian War and the other is the resignation of President Nixon in the wake of the Watergate scandal. The first event takes place within the time frame of the novel, and Goodkind reports on it as he writes. The second event draws closer and closer, but the novel ends without the president's resignation having yet taken place. The Israeli-Egyptian War plays an important symbolic role in the narrative because one of the central themes of the novel is the situation of Jews in the modern world.

The "inside" of the novel's title refers to the somewhat self-enclosed, clearly identifiable, but far from homogeneous world of Jewish religion and culture, whereas the "outside" refers to the world at large. Wouk is something of an oddity among contemporary American novelists because of his open and unapologetic commitment to his religious convictions. This fact largely explains the decided and persistent moral tone of his fiction. One can find expressions, more or less strong, more or less developed, of his commitment to Judaism throughout his fiction, but in no other novel, it seems, does his religious faith play so central and integral a part than in *Inside, Outside*.

What Wouk gives the reader in this novel, along with much else, is a dynamic and dramatic picture of the manifold consciousness that constitutes late twentieth century Judaism. The picture he presents is intricate, complicated, and in some respects even contradictory. Wouk deals with the rich reality that is Judaism in a manner that is—variously—intensely objective and intensely subjective. He seems to leave nothing out of the picture; negative elements are treated with as much thoroughness as are positive elements. Nevertheless, Wouk does not treat the heart of his subject matter, the essential identity of Judaism, with anything but respect and reverence.

If by novel's end one cannot identify its protagonist as a typical modern Jew, that is only because one has come to understand that there is no such thing. Goodkind is a representative modern Jew, but so are many who are quite different from him, and Goodkind himself is far from simple. On one hand, Goodkind reflects the "inside" component of his world, but a distinct "outside" dimension to his personality exists as well. Both together, "inside" and "outside," make up who he is. Goodkind is a religious Jew who faithfully practices his religion. He is also a political Jew who sympathizes with the Zionist tradition and takes great patriotic pride in the state of Israel. At the same time, Goodkind is a thorough American. In a larger sense, he is an eminently modern man, one who, even in spite of himself at times, reflects the consciousness of the contemporary Western intellectual, with all the limitations peculiar to it. His judgments on the major issues that impinge on his life have to them a ring of confident cosmopolitanism, which disguises their lack of substantial metaphysical foundations. For example, although he is in many respects exemplary for his perspicacity and sensitivity, he is obtuse in response to some of the clear signs of decadence in modern culture.

Mention might be made of the unorthodox manner in which the novel deals with the character of Nixon. Wouk goes beyond the crude journalistic stereotypes to discover in Nixon not merely a caricature but a real human being. Finally, *Inside, Outside* is simultaneously a serious and a humorous work, and both of these faces complement each other, helping to bring each into greater relief. In some of his other novels, Wouk has demonstrated his facility in handling humor, but that skill is especially in evidence in *Inside, Outside*.

The Hope *and* The Glory

Unfortunately, Wouk was not able to sustain in his next two novels the high level of artistry he achieved in *Inside, Outside*. In *The Hope* and *The Glory* he continues to exploit his interest in Judaic issues, using the techniques that proved successful in *The Winds of War* and *War and Remembrance*. Though published separately, *The Hope* and *The Glory* are much like Wouk's two-volume romance about World War II; collectively they provide a portrait of the early years of the state of Israel, depicting the struggles of the Jewish people to establish a new independent country in their ancestral homeland.

The Hope is set in the years immediately following World War II, when a small but determined group of Zionist freedom fighters ousted the British from Palestine and declared the foundation of the new state of Israel. As he did in *The Winds of War* and *War and Remembrance*, Wouk creates a number of fictional characters whose lives intersect with the real-life heroes and heroines of the new Jewish nation. Wouk offers a vivid account of the 1948 War of Independence, focusing on the struggles of leaders such as David Ben-Gurion and Moshe Dayan to unite the disparate political and paramilitary groups in the region. The climax of the novel is the stunning victory of the Israelis over their Arab enemies in the Six-Day War of 1967. *The Glory* is a sequel, containing many of the same characters. In recounting the tale of the Jewish nation from 1967 to the announcement of the Camp David Peace Accords, Wouk has his fictional characters support the likes of Golda Meir and Menachem Begin.

Though with less success than he realized in his World War II novels, Wouk gives his narrative a sense of immediacy by concentrating his attention on the effects of the Israelis' struggle on the lives of common men and women. To accomplish this, he creates four families whose fortunes are intertwined not only with historical personages of note but also with each other: the Baraks, the Blumenthals, the Pasternaks, and the Luries. Among them are fighters, local politicians, businessmen, and even ambassadors who represent Israel in the United States and at the United Nations. Political issues are paralleled by small acts of love and vengeance, bringing a certain degree of humanity to the large historical canvas on which Wouk depicts the nation he loves.

Like most novels published by Wouk since the appearance of *The Caine Mutiny*, both *The Hope* and *The Glory* attracted a large readership, but neither received praise from critics. The negative critical reaction seems justified. While the historical accounts are accurate and presented with a strong sense of control, at least one reviewer found this extremely complex political subject treated with "only slightly more subtlety than a grade-school Thanksgiving pageant." Knowing that he would be open to criticism because of his strong partisan views, Wouk was careful to offer a note in *The Hope* that he worked hard not to present a caricature of Arabs. Unfortunately, there is a general laxity in dealing with both major and minor Jewish figures. Instead of striving for complexity, Wouk often resorts to stereotypes that create heroes and villains more commonly found in melodrama or popular romances. His men are almost all superhuman, his women submissive handmaids. What could have been a wonderful final performance in a distinguished career as a popular novelist seems to have emerged as little more than a drifting away into contemporary cliché.

Despite his broad popular appeal, Wouk has generally not found favor with the critics, especially academic critics. The common response of the latter has been simply to ignore him. It is difficult to explain precisely why this is so. Perhaps Wouk's very popularity militates against him, as if there existed a necessary relationship between popularity and artistic worth: The more popular a writer, the poorer the quality of what he writes. Perhaps Wouk's traditionalist worldview and forthright advocacy of Judeo-Christian moral principles, to which many critics today are hostile, account in part for the critical neglect of his work.

In any case, Wouk deserves more critical attention than he has received. He is not the greatest among the many fine novelists to appear in the United States since World War II, but neither is he an inconsequential figure. His prose is solid and vigorous, eschewing precosity and self-indulgence. Writing with intelligence and sensitivity, he appeals neither to a small clique of literary aesthetes nor to the lowest common denominator of a general audience. His attitude toward fiction is that shared by all the major novelists of literary history; his fiction is not concerned with itself but with the world at large. His fiction does not attempt the irrelevant task of creating a moral universe from scratch, but accepts and responds to the moral universe that is already in place.

Dennis Q. McInerny

Updated by Laurence W. Mazzeno

Other major works

PLAYS: *The Traitor*, pr., pb. 1949; *The Caine Mutiny Court-Martial*, pr., pb. 1954; *Nature's Way*, pr. 1957; *Don't Stop the Carnival*, pr. 1998 (adaptation of his novel; musical with Jimmy Buffett).

SCREENPLAY: *Slattery's Hurricane*, 1949 (with Richard Murphy).

TELEPLAYS: *The Winds of War*, 1983; *War and Remembrance*, 1988.

NONFICTION: *This Is My God*, 1959; *The Will to Live On: This Is Our Heritage*, 2000.

Bibliography

Beichman, Arnold. *Herman Wouk: The Novelist as Social Historian*. New Brunswick, N.J.: Transaction Books, 1984. A lifelong friend of Wouk, Beichman offers a strident defense of the novelist against those who fault him for his conservative political stance and his decision to stress narrative and action over complex characterization.

Darby, William. *Necessary American Fictions: Popular Literature of the 1950's*. Bowling Green, Ohio: Bowling Green State University Press, 1987. Examines *The Caine Mutiny* as a mirror of 1950's popular values in the United States.

Gerard, Philip. "The Great American War Novels." *World and I* 10 (June, 1995): 54-63. Gerard notes that World War II was "the last public event that defined a generation of novelists." In this essay, he looks at the works of many of these novelists, including Wouk's *The Caine Mutiny*.

Klingenstein, Susanne. "Sweet Natalie: Herman Wouk's Messenger to the Gentiles." In *Talking Back: Images of Jewish Women in American Popular Culture*, edited by Joyce Antler. Hanover, N.H.: University Press of New England, 1998. Klingenstein examines Natalie Jastrow, the American Jewish heroine of *The Winds of War* and *War and Remembrance*. She describes how Wouk uses his character to personalize the Holocaust for non-Jewish readers.

Mazzeno, Laurence W. *Herman Wouk*. New York: Twayne, 1994. Offers a brief biographical sketch and analyses of the major novels through *Inside, Outside*. The book contains excerpts from hundreds of reviews of Wouk's fiction, providing a sense of the contemporary reaction to each of his major works.

Shapiro, Edward S. "The Jew as Patriot: Herman Wouk and American Jewish Identity." In *We Are Many: Reflections on American Jewish History and Identity*. Syracuse, N.Y.: Syracuse University Press, 2005. This collection of Shapiro's previously published essays includes a retrospective review of Wouk's career. Shapiro argues persuasively that Wouk is concerned principally with defining American Jewish identity.

Shatzky, Joel, and Michael Taub, eds. *Contemporary Jewish-American Novelists: A Bio-critical Sourcebook*. Westport, Conn.: Greenwood Press, 1997. Includes an entry on Wouk's life, major works, and themes, with an overview of his critical reception and a bibliography of primary and secondary sources.

RICHARD WRIGHT

Born: Roxie, Mississippi; September 4, 1908
Died: Paris, France; November 28, 1960
Also known as: Richard Nathaniel Wright

Principal long fiction

Native Son, 1940
The Outsider, 1953
Savage Holiday, 1954
The Long Dream, 1958
Lawd Today, 1963
A Father's Law, 2008

Other literary forms

In addition to his novels, Richard Wright published collections of essays and short stories and two autobiographical volumes. Two collections of short fiction, the early *Uncle Tom's Children* (1938) and the posthumously collected *Eight Men* (1961), represent some of Wright's finest writing. Wright himself felt that the characters in *Uncle Tom's Children* were too easily pitied and that they elicited from readers a sympathy that was unlike the tough intellectual judgment he desired. Wright later wrote that his creation of Bigger Thomas in *Native Son* was an attempt to stiffen that portrayal so that readers could not leniently dismiss his characters with simple compassion, but would have to accept them as free, fully human adults whose actions require assessment. Nevertheless, the stories of *Uncle Tom's Children* are carefully written, and the characters, though sometimes defeated, embody the kind of independence and intractability that Wright valued in his fiction.

Two stories from *Eight Men* reveal the themes to which Wright gave sustained development in his novels. In "The Man Who Was Almos' a Man," the main character learns that power means freedom, and although he first bungles his attempt to shoot a gun, his symbol of power, he lies to his family, keeps the gun, and at the conclusion of the story leaves home to grow into manhood elsewhere. In "The Man Who Lived Underground," the main character, nameless at first, is accused of a crime he did not commit. Fleeing underground to the sewers of the city, he becomes a voyeur of life, seen now from a new perspective. The values that served him badly aboveground do not serve him at all below. By the end of the story, he has come to understand that all men are guilty; his name is revealed, and with his new values, he ascends once more to accept responsibility for the crime. Since all men are guilty, it is less important to him that the crime is not his own than that he acknowledge freely that he shares in human guilt.

Even more important than these two collections is the first volume of Wright's autobiography, *Black Boy: A Record of Childhood and Youth* (1945), which opens up a world of experience to the reader. It traces the first seventeen years of Wright's life—from his birth in Mississippi and the desertion of the family by his father through years of displacement as he travels from one relative to another with his ill mother and religious grandmother. The early years find Wright, like his later protagonists, an outsider, cut off from family, from friends, from culture. He is as out of place among blacks as among whites, baffled by those blacks who play the roles whites expect of them, himself unable to dissimulate his feelings and thoughts. Although the work is nonfiction, it is united by powerful metaphors: fire, hunger, and blindness. Wright's inner fire is mirrored throughout the work by actual fires; indeed, his first act is to set afire the curtains in his home. His physical hunger, a constant companion, is an image of his hunger for knowledge and connection, and his two jobs in optical factories suggest the blindness of society, a blindness given further representation in *Native Son*.

What Wright learns in *Black Boy* is the power of words. His early life is marked by physical violence: He witnesses murders and beatings, but it is the violence of words that offers liberation from his suffocating environment. Whether it is the profanity with which he shocks his grandmother, the literalness with which he takes his father's words, or the crude expressions with which he taunts Jewish shopkeepers, he discovers that words have a power that makes him an equal to those around him. When he feels unequal, as in his early school experiences, he is speechless. The culmination of this theme occurs when Wright acquires a library card and discovers through his readings of the works of American social critics of the early part of the twentieth century, such as H. L. Mencken and Sinclair Lewis, that he is not alone in his feelings and that there are others who share his alienation and discontent.

When Wright finally sees his father many years after his desertion, his hatred dissolves: He realizes that his father, trapped by his surroundings, with neither a cultural past nor an individual future, speaks a language different from his own, holds different thoughts, and is truly a victim and therefore not worthy even of his hatred. Wright's characters must never be victims, for as such they hold no interest. At the end of the book, he goes north, first to Memphis and, when that fails, north again to Chicago, pursuing the dream, having now the power of words to articulate it and to define himself.

The record of Wright's years in Chicago is found in the posthumously published second autobiographical volume, *American Hunger* (written in 1944, published in 1977). Largely a record of his involvement and later disillusionment with the Communist Party, this book is interesting for its view of a later, mature Wright who is still struggling with institutions that would limit his freedom.

Achievements

In his best work, Richard Wright gives American literature its strongest statement of the existential theme of alienated people defining themselves. Wright's use of the black American as archetypal outsider gives his work a double edge. On one hand, no American writer so carefully illuminates the black experience in America: The ambivalence of black feeling, the hypocrisies of the dominant culture, and the tension between them find concrete and original manifestation in Wright's work, a manifestation at once revealing and terrifying.

It is not only in his revelation of black life, however, that Wright's power lies, for as much as his writing is social and political, it is also personal and philosophical. The story of alienated people is a universal one; because the concrete experiences of the outsider are so vividly rendered in Wright's fiction, his books have an immediate accessibility. Because they also reveal deeper patterns, they have further claims to attention. Much of Wright's later fiction seems self-conscious and studied, but it cannot diminish the greatness of his finest work.

Biography

Born in Mississippi of sharecropper parents, Richard Nathaniel Wright had a lonely and troubled childhood. His father deserted the family early, and after his mother suffered a stroke, Wright was forced at a young age to work to help support the family, which moved frequently from one relative to another. His portrayal of his mother is of a stern but loving parent, unable to contend with the stronger personality of his extremely religious grandmother. Wright's grandmother believed that all fiction was "the devil's lies"; her chief goal was to force Wright into a religious conversion, a goal in which she was singularly unsuccessful.

Wright's direct connection to family members who had been slaves came through both sets of grandparents. Richard Wilson, his mother's father, had been a slave in the cotton fields and had fled slavery to serve in the Civil War. His anger against whites carried throughout his life and was fueled by the government's refusal to offer disability assistance. This bitter figure was a strong influence on Wright's own angst. Less influential to Wright's ideology was his paternal grandfather, Nathaniel Wright, who had been a slave, a Civil War soldier, and a sharecropper in the post-Civil War south.

Wright moved from school to school, attempting to make friends and make his talents known. Though both tasks were difficult, he became valedictorian of his class. Even this accomplishment was spoiled when the principal insisted that Wright read a speech that the principal himself had written, and Wright refused. An uncle told Richard, "They're going to break you," and society, both black and white, seemed intent on doing so. Wright was determined to resist, not to be claimed by his environment as he felt so many blacks around him were.

Wright left Mississippi for Memphis, Tennessee, had little luck there, and—with money stolen from the film theater where he worked—moved to Chicago. When others stole, Wright disapproved—not for moral reasons, but because he felt stealing did not change the fundamental relationship of a person to his environment. When it offered a chance to change that environment, Wright accepted it.

In Chicago, Wright became involved with others who viewed the country as he did, first in a federal theater project and then with the Communist John Reed

Richard Wright. (Library of Congress)

Club, which supported his writing until Wright's goals differed from their own. In 1937, he moved to New York City to become the editor of the *Daily Worker*. A year later, he published his first important work, *Uncle Tom's Children*, after which he won a Guggenheim Fellowship, which provided him with the time and funds to write *Native Son*. The novel was published to great acclaim and was followed by a second major work, *Black Boy*. Although his writing career was a success, Wright was arguing more frequently with the Communist party, with which he finally broke in 1944, and was becoming less optimistic about the hope of racial progress in the United States.

In 1946, Wright moved to France, where he spent the rest of his life. Although he wrote a great deal there, nothing in his later work, with the possible exception of *The Outsider*, approaches the strength of *Native Son* and *Black Boy*. The existentialism that was always implicit in his work became the dominant theme, but—displaced from his native environment—Wright never again found a convincing dramatic situation in which to work out his preoccupations.

Wright died in France of a heart attack on November 28, 1960. After his death, several more of his works were published, including the novels *Lawd Today* and, much later, *A Father's Law*.

Analysis

Richard Wright's best work is always the story of one man's struggle to define himself and by so doing make himself free and responsible, fully human, a character worthy not of pity but of admiration and horror simultaneously. Typically, the character is an outsider, and Wright uses blackness as a representation of that alienation, though his characters are never as interested in defining their blackness as in defining their humanity. Although many characters in Wright's works are outsiders without being aware of their condition, Wright is never interested in them except as foils. Many of them avoid confronting themselves by fleeing to dreams; religion and liquor are two avoidance mechanisms for Wright's characters, narcotics that blind them to their surrounding world, to what they are and what they might be.

Even Wright's main characters must not think about that world too often: To let it touch them is to risk insanity or violence, and so his characters strive to keep the fire within in check, to keep the physical hunger satisfied. Thus, all of Wright's protagonists are initially trapped by desire and by fear—fear of what might happen to them, what they may do, if they risk venturing outside the confines of black life in America—and the desire to do so. The life outside may be glimpsed in films; Bigger Thomas, for example, goes to a film and watches contrasting and artificial views of black and white society. Yet as untruthful as both views are, they remind Bigger of a reality beyond his present situation. Desire is often symbolized by flight; Bigger, like other Wright characters, dreams of flying above the world, unchained from its limitations.

Most of Wright's stories and novels examine what happens when the protagonist's fear is mastered for a moment when desires are met. The manifestation of desire in Wright is almost always through violence (and it is here, perhaps, that he is most pessimistic, for other, more positive, manifestations of desire, such as love, can come only later, after the protagonists have violently acted out their longings). Violence is central to Wright's fiction, for as important as sex may be to his characters, power is much more so, and power is often achieved through violence; in Wright's world, beatings and murders are frequent acts—central and occasionally creative.

Once the character has acted, he finds himself trapped again in a new set of oppositions, for in acting, he has left the old sureties behind, has made himself free, and has begun to define and create himself. With that new freedom comes a new awareness of responsibility. He is without excuses, and that awareness is as terrifying as—though more liberating than—the fears he has previously known. Although Wright does not always elaborate on what may follow, the characters open up new possibilities for themselves. If one may create oneself by violence, perhaps, Wright sometimes suggests, there are other, less destructive ways as well.

Some of Wright's novels end on this note of optimism, the characters tragically happy: tragic because they have committed violent and repulsive acts, but happy because for the first time they have *chosen* to commit them; they have freed themselves from their constraints, and the future, however short it may be, lies open. Others end simply with tragedy, the destruction achieving no purpose, the characters attaining no illumination.

Lawd Today

Lawd Today, written before *Native Son* but not published until after Wright's death, tells the story of Jake Jackson from his awakening on the morning of February 12, 1936, to that day's violent conclusion. Jackson is Wright's most inarticulate protagonist: He has a banal life, undefined dreams, and a vague sense of discontent that he is unable to explain. Violent and prejudiced, he speaks in clichés, a language as meaningless as his life.

The book incorporates a montage of radio broadcasts, newspaper articles, and religious and political pamphlets into the narration of Jake's day. Divided into three sections, *Lawd Today* opens with Jake's dream of running up an endless staircase after a disappearing voice. That dream gives way to the reality of his life: hunger, anger, and recrimination. Tricked by Jake into an abortion for which Jake still owes five hundred dollars and now claiming to have a tumor that will cost another five hundred dollars to remove, Jake's wife represents his entrapment. In the first section, "Commonplace," Jake reveals his brutish and trivial character: his anger at his wife, a jealousy and resentment that lead him to bait her so he can hit her, a mock battle straightening his hair, and a meeting with friends who work with him at the post office. As they play bridge to pass the time until work, Wright presents without comment their stupid, cliché-ridden conversation.

The second section, "Squirrel Cage," shows the men at work. They are all alienated in meaningless, routine jobs, but Jake's position is the most desperate, for his wife has been to see his boss, and he is now threatened with the loss of his job. Falling deeper into debt by borrowing more money and making mistakes on the job, Jake is trapped by his work—despite his own protestations, as a self-proclaimed Republican and capitalist, that work is liberating. This section, too, ends with a long, rambling, and banal conversation among the men at work.

In the concluding section, "Rat's Alley," the men go to a brothel for a good time on some of Jake's borrowed money. There, Jake is robbed and then beaten for his threats of revenge. Finally, Jake stumbles homeward, his day nearing an end. The February weather, pleasant when the book began, has turned bad. All of Jake's frustration and anger finally erupt; he beats his wife, whom he finds kneeling asleep by the bed in an attitude of prayer. As they struggle, he throws objects through the window. She grabs a shard of broken glass and slashes him three times. The book ends with Jake lying in a drunken stupor, bleeding, while his wife is on her knees, also bleeding, praying for death. Outside, the wind blows mercilessly.

Although some of the experimentalism of *Lawd Today* seems artificial, and although the protagonist is too limited to sustain the reader's interest, this early work is powerful and economical. The situation, if not the character, is typical of Wright's work, and the reader understands Jake's violent frustration. *Lawd Today* has its flaws, but it foreshadows the strengths of Wright's best work and in its own right is a daring and fascinating novel.

Native Son

Along with *Black Boy*, *Native Son* is one of Wright's finest achievements: a brilliant portrayal of, as Wright put it, the way the environment provides the instrumentalities through which one expresses oneself and the way that self becomes whole despite the environment's conspiring to keep it divided. The book parallels Theodore Dreiser's *An American Tragedy* (1925): Both are three-part novels in which there is a murder, in part accidental, in part willed; an attempted flight; and a long concluding trial, in both cases somewhat anticlimactic. Both novels are concerned with the interplay of environment and heredity, of fate and accident, and both have protagonists who rebel against the world that would hold them back.

In the first part of *Native Son*, Bigger Thomas is a black man cut off from family and peers. Superficially like his friends, he is in fact possessed of a different consciousness. To think about that consciousness is for him to risk insanity or violence, so Bigger endeavors to keep his fears and uncertainty at a preconscious level. On the day of the first section, however, he is required by the welfare agency to apply for a job as a menial at the home of the rich Dalton family. Mr. Dalton is a ghetto landlord who soothes his conscience by donating sums of money for recreational purposes. That it is a minuscule part of the money he is deriving from blacks is an irony he overlooks. Mrs. Dalton is blind, a fact that is necessary to the plot as well as being symbolic. Their daughter, Mary, is a member of the Communist Party, and from the moment she sees Bigger, who wants nothing more than to be left alone, she begins to enlist his support.

The first evening, Bigger is to drive Mary to a university class. In reality, she is going with Jan Erlone, her Communist boyfriend, to a party meeting. Afterward, they insist that Bigger take them to a bar in the black part of town. Jan and Mary are at this point satirized, for their attitudes toward blacks are as limited and stereotyped as any in the novel. Bigger does not want to be seen by his friends with whites, but that fact does not occur to Mary. After much drinking, Bigger must carry the drunken Mary to her bedroom. He puts her to bed, stands over her, attracted to the woman he sees. The door opens and Mrs. Dalton enters. When Mary makes drunken noises, Bigger becomes frightened that Mrs. Dalton will come close enough to discover him, so he puts a pillow over Mary's face to quiet her. By the time Mrs. Dalton leaves, Mary is dead.

Wright wanted to make Bigger a character it would be impossible to pity, and what follows is extremely grisly. Bigger tries to put Mary's body in the furnace and saws off her head to make her fit. However accidental Mary's death may appear to the reader, Bigger himself does not regard it as such. He has, he thinks, many times wanted to kill whites without ever having the opportunity to do so. This time there was the act without the desire, but rather than seeing himself as the victim of a chance occurrence, Bigger prefers to unite the earlier desire with the present act, to make himself whole by accepting responsibility for the killing. Indeed, he not only accepts the act but also determines to capitalize on it by sending a ransom note. Later, accused of raping Mary as well, an act he considered but did not commit, he reverses the process, accepting responsibility for this, too, even though here there was desire but no act. His only sign of conscience is that he cannot bring himself to shake the ashes in the furnace; this guilt is not redemptive, but his undoing, for, in an implausible scene in the Dalton basement, the room fills with smoke, the murder is revealed to newspaper reporters gathered there, and Bigger is forced to flee.

He runs with his girlfriend, Bessie Mears. She, like Bigger, has a hunger for sensation, which has initially attracted him to her. Now, however, as they flee together, she becomes a threat and a burden; huddled with her in an abandoned tenement, Bigger wants only to be rid of her. He picks up a brick and smashes her face, then dumps her body down an air shaft. His only regret is not that he has killed her, but that he has forgotten to remove their money from her body.

The rest of the plot moves quickly: Bigger is soon arrested, the trial is turned into a political farce, and Bigger is convicted and sentenced to death. In the last part of the novel, after Bigger's arrest, the implications of the action are developed, largely through Bigger's relations to other characters. Some of the characters are worthy only of contempt, particularly the district attorney, who, in an attempt at reelection, is turning the trial into political capital. Bigger's mother relies on religion. In a scene in the jail cell, she falls on her knees in apology before

Mrs. Dalton and urges Bigger to pray, but toughness is Bigger's code. He is embarrassed by his mother's self-abasement, and although he agrees to pray simply to end his discomfort, his attitude toward religion is shown when he throws away a cross a minister has given him and throws a cup of coffee in a priest's face. In his view, they want only to avoid the world and to force him to accept guilt without responsibility.

Bigger learns from two characters. The first is Boris Max, the lawyer the Communist Party provides. Max listens to Bigger, and for the first time in his life, Bigger exposes his ideas and feelings to another human. Max's plea to the court is that, just as Bigger must accept responsibility for what he has done, so must the society around him understand its responsibility for what Bigger has become and, if the court chooses to execute Bigger, understand the consequences that must flow from that action. He does not argue—nor does Wright believe—that Bigger is a victim of injustice. There is no injustice, because that would presume a world in which Bigger could hope for justice, and such a world does not exist; more important, Bigger is not a victim, for he has chosen his own fate. Max argues rather that all men are entitled to happiness. Like all of Wright's protagonists, Bigger has earlier been torn between the poles of dread and ecstasy. His ecstasy, his happiness, comes from the meaningfulness he creates in his existence, a product of self-realization. Unhappily for Bigger, he realizes himself through murder: It was, he feels, his highest creative act.

If Max articulates the intellectual presentation of Wright's beliefs about Bigger, it is Jan, Mary's lover, who is its dramatic representation. He visits Bigger in his cell and, having at last understood the futility and paucity of his own stereotypes, admits to Bigger that he too shares in the responsibility for what has happened. He, too, addresses Bigger as a human being, but from the unique position of being the one who is alive to remind Bigger of the consequences of his actions, for Bigger learns that Jan has suffered loss through what he has done and that, while Bigger has created himself, he has also destroyed another.

Native Son ends with the failure of Max's appeals on Bigger's behalf. He comes to the cell to confront Bigger before his execution, and the novel closes with Bigger Thomas smiling at Max as the prison door clangs shut. He will die happy because he will die fulfilled, having, however terribly, created a self. *Native Son* is Wright's most powerful work, because his theme, universal in nature, is given its fullest and most evocative embodiment. In the characterization of Bigger, alienated man at his least abstract and most genuine, of Bigger's exactly rendered mind and milieu, and of Bigger's working out of his destiny, *Native Son* is Wright's masterpiece.

Unlike many highly acclaimed books of the 1940's, *Native Son* and *Black Boy* have not become dated. They offer a lacerating challenge to contemporary readers and writers—a challenge to share the relentless integrity of Wright's vision.

The Outsider

Wright's next novel, *The Outsider*, written in France and published thirteen years after *Native Son*, suffers from a surfeit of internal explanation and a failure to provide a setting as rich as that of *Native Son*. Still, its portrayal of Cross Damon and his struggle to define himself, while too self-conscious, adds new dimensions to Wright's myth.

As the novel opens, Damon is trapped by his life. His job with the post office is unfulfilling, his wife is threatening, and his underage mistress is pregnant. He "desires desire," but there is no way for that desire to be completed. "A man creates himself," he has told his wife, but the self Damon has created is a nightmare. He broods, his brooding as close as he comes to religion. Another underground man, Damon gets his chance for new life on the subway. Thought dead after his identification papers are found near the mangled body of another, Damon gets a chance to create himself anew. He must invent, he thinks, not only his future, but also a past to fit with his present; this new opportunity brings with it a different and more potent sense of dread.

From the beginning of this new life, Damon is remarkably successful at the mechanics of creating a past. He easily obtains a birth certificate and a draft card. At a deeper level, however, he traps himself as surely as he has been trapped in his old life, so that his new one becomes a continuous act of bad faith. Even before he leaves Chicago, he hides in a brothel where he encounters a coworker who recognizes him. Damon murders the man and throws his body out a window. The pattern of violence, so typical of Wright's characters, begins in earnest for Damon.

Taking a train to New York, Cross meets two people who will influence his new life, a black waiter who introduces him to the world of Communist politics in New York City, and Ely Houston, the district attorney, who is the most articulate person in the novel and the only one fully to understand Damon. Houston asks Damon why, when all blacks are outsiders, so few seem conscious of this fact. Wright suggests that being human is too much to be borne by people, that the struggle to define oneself is too difficult; the novel is a testament to that suggestion.

The Communist Party members, too, are outsiders, and there is nothing unified about their company. Each one that Damon meets is playing god, hoping to protect and extend his personal power. Their awareness of their motives varies, but they are a threat to Damon, and the action of the book is propelled by a series of murders: Damon himself wants to act like a god. Near the end of the book, Houston comes to understand that Damon is the killer, but—rather than indicting and punishing him legally—Houston allows him to go free, alone with his knowledge of what he is. Damon is horrified by his fate, but he is robbed of even that when he is killed by two Communist Party members who fear him.

The Outsider is both an extension and a modification of Wright's earlier views; it is far more pessimistic than *Native Son*, and the influence of the French existentialists is more pervasive. Like earlier Wright heroes, Damon is engaged in defining the world and himself. "The moment we act 'as if' it's true, then it's true," he thinks, because each person, in the absence of a god, is able to create the world and its truth. From Fyodor Dostoevski, Wright again borrows the notion of underground man and the idea that without a god, all is permitted. Yet as each man plays god, as each becomes criminal, policeman, judge, and executioner, there are no longer limits. People desire everything, and desire is described as a floating demon. People are jealous gods here—the worlds they create are petty, their jealousy destructive. Cross Damon is loved in the novel, but that love, unlike the love in *Native Son*, which is held up as potentially meaningful, is here without promise. Although he creates himself and his world in *The Outsider*, all that is made is violent and brutal, a world without redemption even in the act of self-realization.

At the end of the novel, Cross Damon dies, not with Bigger Thomas's smile, but with the knowledge that alone, people are nothing. Searching in his last moments of freedom for a clean, well-lighted place in which to rest before he confronts the world again, Cross finds only death. Before he dies, he admits his final act of bad faith: He has thought that he could create a world and be different from other men, that he could remain innocent. Like Joseph Conrad's Kurtz in *Heart of Darkness* (1902), Damon dies realizing the futility of that hope; having looked into his own heart of darkness, he dies with the word "horror" on his lips.

It is Wright's bleakest conclusion, the book his most relentless examination of the consequences of his own philosophy. If *The Outsider* lacks the narrative drive of *Native Son*, it remains a strongly conceived and troubling piece of fiction.

THE LONG DREAM

The Long Dream, despite some effective scenes, is one of Wright's weakest novels. The story of Rex "Fishbelly" Tucker's growing up and coming to terms with his environment is a pale repetition of earlier themes. The first section describes Tucker's youth. His father, an undertaker, is the richest black man in town, but his money comes also from a brothel he runs on the side. Tucker admires his father's success while detesting his obsequiousness with whites. When, however, Fishbelly is arrested, he twice faints at the white world's threats. Having presented himself as a victim, he becomes one. Walking home after his father has arranged his freedom, Fishbelly sees an injured dog, which he puts out of its misery. Fishbelly then comes upon a white man who is pinned to the ground with a car door on his body. When the white man calls out to Fishbelly, using the term "nigger," Fishbelly walks on, leaving the man to die.

In the second section, Fishbelly finds a woman, but she and forty-one others are burned to death in a fire at the bar. The rest of the novel is an unconvincing story of the police who want the return of the cancelled checks that Fishbelly's father has used to pay them off, the police's arranged murder of the father, the subsequent framing and imprisoning of Fishbelly for rape, and Fishbelly's keeping the checks for his future use. All of this is seriously contrived. At the end, Fishbelly is on a plane leaving for France, where his childhood friends are stationed in the army, which they describe as exciting. He is talking to an Italian whose father has come to America and found a dream, where Fishbelly himself has known only a nightmare. France, he dreams, will offer him what America has not.

In Fishbelly's attempt to understand himself and his environment, he is a typical Wright protagonist. He is weaker than Wright's usual characters, however, and that shallowness, coupled with an implausible plot, prevents the novel from being entirely successful.

A Father's Law

Julia Wright, Richard Wright's daughter, had *A Father's Law*, his last unfinished novel, published on the one hundredth anniversary of his birth. Along with providing intriguing insight into a partial biographical critique, Julia Wright's introduction to the novel shares her touching memory of finding the manuscript in the months after Wright's death.

The novel is a study in the ironies present in the law that Ruddy Turner must enforce, both as a police officer and as a father. The story begins with Ruddy's promotion from police captain in an African American neighborhood in Chicago to the position of police chief in an affluent white area of the city. The police commissioner hopes to stir up the complacent citizens of Brentwood Park against the crime that runs rampant in the area. As soon as Ruddy assumes his new office, he is confronted with a portion of that crime—five unsolved murders. In the midst of work challenges, Ruddy also faces concerns at home. His relationship with his academically brilliant son, Tommy, is conflicted. He cannot understand either Tommy's ways of thinking or his motivations. Tommy's educational interest in the psychological motivations behind acts of crime further separates the father and son. While Tommy questions why people do not commit crimes, his father questions why they do. Ruddy's lack of comprehension of his son's reasoning and actions leads him to suspect his own son in the murders. The novel's end leaves Ruddy wrestling with his son's very public confession, a confession that undermines the father's law in every way.

The question of guilt is a central focus of the novel. Ruddy, Tommy, and Tommy's former fiancé, Marie, are all engulfed in guilt. Marie, who has been diagnosed with hereditary congenital syphilis, has been jilted by Tommy. She is blameless, yet she is isolated, and it is her guilt that serves as the psychological driving force behind Tommy's guilt—both literally and figuratively. Further, the lack of ability even to acknowledge, let alone feel, guilt is the problem with Brentwood Park, the scene of both men's downfall. Ruddy's own youthful decision to become a law enforcer in an effort to assuage his feelings of guilt ironically turns back on him with his suspicions of his son and Tommy's subsequent confession to the crimes.

Like Wright's other novels, this novel also deals with isolation. Ruddy is isolated from his friends and fellow officers as he worries that his son is a murderer. Marie is isolated from her parents, her lover, and all other human contact when she is diagnosed with an illness that brings moral condescension. Tommy is isolated from his father and his fiancé. While Ruddy's isolation is partially self-inflicted because he does not want others to know of his doubts about his own child, Marie is isolated as a result of other people's choices. She is truly the innocent victim.

A Father's Law is a brilliant reflection on the meaning of law, the motivations of people, the way guilt works in our lives, and the isolation of human beings. Even in its incomplete state, this deeply psychological piece is further evidence of Wright's genius.

Howard Faulkner
Updated by Theresa L. Stowell

Other major works

short fiction: *Uncle Tom's Children: Four Novellas*, 1938 (expanded as *Uncle Tom's Children: Five Long Stories*, 1938); *Eight Men*, 1961.

play: *Native Son: The Biography of a Young American*, pr. 1941 (with Paul Green).

poetry: *Haiku: This Other World*, 1998 (Yoshinobu Hakutani and Robert L. Tener, editors).

nonfiction: *Twelve Million Black Voices: A Folk History of the Negro in the United States*, 1941 (photographs by Edwin Rosskam); *Black Boy: A Record of Childhood and Youth*, 1945; *Black Power: A Record of Reactions in a Land of Pathos*, 1954; *The Color Curtain*, 1956; *Pagan Spain*, 1957; *White Man, Listen!*, 1957;

American Hunger, 1977; *Richard Wright Reader*, 1978 (Ellen Wright and Michel Fabre, editors); *Conversations with Richard Wright*, 1993 (Keneth Kinnamon and Fabre, editors).

MISCELLANEOUS: *Works*, 1991 (2 volumes).

Bibliography

Baldwin, James. *The Price of the Ticket: Collected Nonfiction, 1948-1985*. New York: St. Martin's Press/Marek, 1985. Baldwin's essays "Everybody's Protest Novel" and "Alas, Poor Richard" provide important and provocative insights into Wright and his art.

Butler, Robert. *"Native Son": The Emergence of a New Black Hero*. Boston: Twayne, 1991. Provides an accessible critical look at the seminal novel. Includes bibliographical references and index.

Fabre, Michel. *The Unfinished Quest of Richard Wright*. 2d ed. Urbana: University of Illinois Press, 1993. Update of a work originally published in 1973 remains one of the most authoritative biographies available on Wright.

Felgar, Robert. *Student Companion to Richard Wright*. Westport, Conn.: Greenwood Press, 2000. Basic resource intended for undergraduate readers is composed mainly of biographical information and an introduction to Wright's use of literary elements. Includes a brief bibliography of Wright's works.

Kinnamon, Keneth. *The Emergence of Richard Wright: A Study in Literature and Society*. Urbana: University of Illinois Press, 1972. Valuable study of Wright's background and development as a writer. Covers his writings up to the publication of *Native Son*.

_______. *Richard Wright: An Annotated Bibliography of Criticism and Commentary, 1983-2003*. Jefferson, N.C.: McFarland, 2006. Lists more than eight thousand sources related to Wright's work, including books, articles, and dissertations on African American literature and criticism.

_______, comp. *A Richard Wright Bibliography: Fifty Years of Criticism and Commentary, 1933-1982*. Westport, Conn.: Greenwood Press, 1988. Mammoth work (one of the largest annotated bibliographies ever assembled on an American writer) traces the history of Wright criticism through the early 1980's. An invaluable research tool.

_______, ed. *Critical Essays on Richard Wright's "Native Son."* New York: Twayne, 1997. Collection is divided into sections of reviews, reprinted essays, and new essays. Includes discussions of Wright's handling of race, voice, tone, novelistic structure, the city, and literary influences.

Kinnamon, Keneth, and Michel Fabre, eds. *Conversations with Richard Wright*. Jackson: University Press of Mississippi, 1993. Collection of interviews with Wright, conducted over decades by both American and foreign journalists and scholars, provides insight into the author's views on numerous topics.

Rowley, Hazel. *Richard Wright: The Life and Times*. New York: Henry Holt, 2001. Comprehensive biography places Wright's work within the context of the events of his life. Includes bibliography, photographs, and index.

Walker, Margaret. *Richard Wright: Daemonic Genius*. New York: Warner Publishing, 1988. A critically acclaimed study of Wright's life and work written by a friend and fellow novelist. Not a replacement for Michel Fabre's biography but written with the benefit of several more years of scholarship on issues that include the medical controversy over Wright's death. Walker is especially insightful on Wright's early life, and her comments on Wright's short fiction are short but pithy. Includes a useful bibliographic essay at the end.

WU CHENGEN

Born: Huaian (now in Jiangsu Province), China; c. 1500
Died: Huaian (now in Jiangsu Province), China; c. 1582
Also known as: Ruzhong; Wu Ch'eng-en (Wade-Giles)

Principal long fiction

Xiyou ji, pb. 1592 (also known as *Hsi-yu chi*; partial translation as *Monkey*, 1942; *The Journey to the West*, 1977-1983)

Other literary forms

Wu Chengen (woo chehng-ehn) is remembered chiefly for his great novel, but he was also a skilled poet and a writer of satiric stories, supernatural tales, and essays in the literary language. Only *The Journey to the West* is available in English translation.

Achievements

The Journey to the West is one of the world's great comic adventure novels, a major religious epic, and an amusing and instructive satire on human foibles. In compiling and shaping materials that by the sixteenth century had a rich tradition of their own, Wu Chengen gave them their definitive form, a form that has remained unrivaled by later variations on the story. The imaginative force of this quest by a magic monkey, a pig, a river monster, and a monk to bring Buddhist scriptures back from India can be seen in *The Journey to the West* cartoons, comic books, and cut-paper pictures still popular in China (and Japan) today. The modern Westerner who has the opportunity to attend a performance by a "Chinese opera" troupe is likely to see a scene from one of the plays that were part of the evolution of the novel, and he or she is almost certain to be captivated by the spectacle of the monkey-king's acrobatic antics.

The novel is also one of the works that mark the sixteenth century in China as a heyday for fiction written in the language of the people. For at least five centuries, stories in the vernacular had been told in the marketplaces by professional storytellers, despite the official view of the educated class that fiction, and anything not written in the difficult language of the classics, did not deserve the status of "literature." (Westerners might compare the situation to that of medieval Europe before Dante, when serious writing was done not in French or Italian or Spanish but in Latin.) Love stories, tales of heroism, and narratives about human encounters with the supernatural came to be written down and printed, perhaps as "promptbooks" for the storytellers or perhaps as imitations of such promptbooks for members of the literate middle class—and for some of the literati in their leisure hours.

There existed also an even older tradition of popular Buddhist sermons and homilies that used secular, and sometimes sensational, subject matter to compete with the marketplace storytellers for the attention of busy passersby. *The Journey to the West*, in its use of such traditional techniques as interpolated poems and direct address to the audience/reader ("If you want to know what happened, you must listen to what is told in the next chapter"), applies the achievements of these generations of anonymous makers of fictions to a work of a high order of literary art. The poems are especially deserving of attention, though they were omitted by Arthur Waley from his translation: Wu's gift for casting description, narration, and commentary into well-crafted verse gave great strength to the work.

Another of the author's achievements was the skill with which he arranged existing materials and gave to them the tone, the unifying perspective, the fascinating characterizations, and the structure that they have retained for future generations. The sources of *The Journey to the West* have indeed drawn a great deal of scholarly attention, but it is clear that, whatever the degree of development of his immediate source or sources, Wu did not merely copy; he effectively manipulated the materials for his poetic, comic, and descriptive ends. As Andrew Plaks points out, *The Journey to the West* is not so much the retelling of a popular story as the transformation of that story into the vehicle for the important message of Tripitaka's beloved Heart Sutra, "Form is emptiness and the very emptiness is form."

The Journey to the West has been read and loved by schoolchildren and by scholars from the Ming Dynasty to the post-Mao Zedong era. It stands with Lo Kuan-chung's *San-kuo chih yen-I* (fourteenth century; *The Romance of the Three Kingdoms*, 1925), his *Shui-hu chuan* (fourteenth century; *All Men Are Brothers*, 1933; also known as *Water Margin*, 1937), and the anonymous *Chin P'ing Mei* (sixteenth century; *The Golden Lotus*, 1939; also known as *Chin P'ing Mei: The Adventurous History of Hsi Men and His Six Wives*, 1940) as the Four Great and Wondrous Books of the efflorescence of Chinese fiction during the Ming Dynasty, and it rivals even Cao Xueqin's superlative *Hongloumeng* (1792; *Dream of the Red Chamber*, 1958; also translated as *The Story of the Stone*, 1973-1980, and *A Dream of Red Mansions*, 1978-1980) in the affection it inspires in its readers. Perhaps it is the most accessible work of Chinese literature for the foreign reader; certainly, it invites stimulating comparisons with Western allegories, epics, and satiric narratives.

Although subject to a wide variety of thought-provoking allegorical interpretations—psychological, religious, Marxist-Maoist—the book can be read with simple delight (especially in Waley's abridged version) by a bright eleven-year-old who wants a good story. To what extent the materials of the novel were of the author's own invention and to what extent they were rather a well-used inheritance may never be determined, but his work in creating *The Journey to the West* as we know it was invaluable, and the world's readers are in his debt.

Biography

The attribution of *The Journey to the West* to Wu Chengen has been questioned. In fact, the preface to the oldest extant printed text of the novel claims that the identity of the author was unknown, and the earliest known identification of Wu as the author appeared about forty years after his death (c. 1582). This situation is not, however, uncommon in the history of Chinese fiction, for the publication of work not in the literary language was once considered to be "beneath" an educated person: Many works in the vernacular were published anonymously or under pen names. Nevertheless, most of the novel read today seems to be the work of one person, and what evidence there is points clearly to Wu.

Wu was a minor official of the Ming Dynasty (1368-1644). His biographies tell us that he was a "native" of the Shanyang district in Huai'an Prefecture, which is today part of Jiangsu (sometimes spelled Kiangsu) Province. This does not necessarily mean that he was actually born in Shanyang, but rather that this district, which is located in the lower Yangtze (or Chang) River basin north of modern Shanghai, was his family's ancestral home. He seems to have spent most of his life in this central coastal region, however, and *The Journey to the West* includes many phrases in the dialect of Huai'an. For about eight years, when he was in his forties, Wu lived in Beijing, the capital, but, as Liu Ts'un-yan suggests, he may have preferred life in the central Yangtze city of Nanjing or in the provinces.

Wu was born into a line of educated men, though economic need forced his father to forgo scholarship for business. In 1544, Wu received an academic degree, known as tribute student; he had passed the preliminary examination and had earned the rank of *xiu zai* a decade earlier. The civil service was the career of most literary men in traditional China, and Wu's efforts to secure a post finally succeeded when he was given the position of assistant magistrate of the Changxing district in what is now Zhejiang Province, a few hundred miles south of his home. He retired at the end of the 1560's to a life of "wine and poetry," the conventional pursuits of a slightly nonconformist gentleman of leisure. His biographers note that, though he was married to a woman from an influential family, he had no surviving sons. Liu points out that Wu's childhood observations of his mother's problematic status as a concubine may have led him to eschew the common practice of taking a concubine of his own in order to produce an heir.

In a biography recorded roughly a century after his death, Wu is described as being quite intelligent and a voracious reader. As a child, he read popular fiction and historical romances on the sly, despite the efforts of his father and his tutor to restrict his reading to the orthodox classics that were the basis of a traditional Confucian education. The brief autobiographical passage in one of Wu's essays that mentions this also explains that his taste for the supernatural and his urge to write short fiction comparable to the "strange tales" of the bygone Tang Dynasty grew strong in his early adulthood. Evidently, he published a collection of such stories, but it no longer exists. Wu associated with some of the leading literary men and aesthetes of his day, but in his own lifetime, his reputation seems to have been based chiefly on his talents as calligrapher, satirist, and writer of elegant poetry. It may be that while he was alive *The Journey to the West* circulated only in manuscript. One sign of his fame is his appearance in the local histories of Shanyang and Huai'an in the centuries after his death.

Analysis: *The Journey to the West*

The Journey to the West pleases; it includes slapstick humor, sly satire, eerie monsters such as the Cadaver Demon, marvelous battles, and adventures in countries as odd as Lilliput or Brobdingnag—places such as the Women Nation, Serpent Coil Mountain, and Mysterious Flower Cave. The main characters are an amusing mix: a complaining holy man, an all-too-human pig, a vague but friendly river monster, and the magical king of the monkeys, who calls himself The Great Sage Equal to Heaven and gets into trouble because he refuses to knuckle under to the celestial hierarchy. Their goal is not reached until near the book's end, and the pilgrims' return to China is supernaturally swift.

The novel has a didactic message as well. Before considering what it has to say about human nature, society, and religion, however, it will be useful to consider the centuries-long evolution of its plot and its characters. Much of the novel's richness is the result of the author's wide-ranging perspective, but much, too, is the result of the variety of its long, multilayered development.

Structure

One major strand of materials around which the story grew is the official biographies and the popular hagiographies of a seventh century monk, Xuanzang, who came to be known as T'ang San-tsang, or Tripitaka. Both the first name (which is Chinese) and the second (which is Sanskrit, the language of the Buddhist scriptures) honor him for the sutras he brought back from India to China. Works such as the *Ta T'ang San-tsang ch'ü ching shih-hua* (thirteenth century), the story, with poems, of how the Tang Dynasty monk Tripitaka obtained the scriptures, sketch in a few of the events and themes that appear elsewhere in the tradition, most fully in Wu's *The Journey to the West* itself. Yet numerous brief tales and fragments recorded earlier suggest the gradual accretion of fantastic motifs onto the historical Tripitaka's journey, which—rigorous though it was—was actually only one of many made by devout Chinese west and south to the homeland of Buddhism.

In *The Journey to the West* and its immediate forebears, the Tripitaka tales are mingled with motifs from many legends about magic monkeys. It has been suggested that *The Journey to the West* shows influence from Indian, Tibetan, or Central Asian epics that tell about monkeys of mythic power, and certainly some sharing of themes among the cultures must have taken place, but native Chinese stories also abound with supernatural apes, some of which do acts of religious merit and some of which are evil and must be controlled. (Clearly, both aspects of the indigenous tradition find expression in Wu's Monkey.) Moreover, the evidence suggests that the written transmission to China of figures such as India's Hanuman, the monkey-hero of the Rāmāyana (c. 350 B.C.E.) epic, was limited. What influence there was, then, seems most likely to have been minor. Perhaps the metaphor of ape for human is not so farfetched that it could not be thought of more than once.

In any case, these two main characters—the pilgrim monk and his unruly monkey disciple—appear together long before the composition of Wu's novel. Fragments of dramas dating from the thirteenth century, and a fourteenth century cycle of plays in twenty-four acts called *Hsi-yu chi tza-chü* (the journey to the west variety shows), suggest the range and shape of the novel to come. There still exist two short narratives in the vernacular that, because they were published well before Wu's lifetime yet show marked similarities to passages in *The Journey to the West*, reveal that Wu must have worked from an older text or texts in creating his novel. The two shorter versions of *The Journey to the West* that were published about the same time as Wu's may have been sources for his work or may have been abridgments of it.

There is a further textual problem that affects the modern reader's experience of the novel. The text now ascribed to Wu today includes as its ninth chapter a pious biography of Tripitaka, which may seem somewhat at odds in tone with the rest of the book. This chapter does not appear in the 1592 edition of *The Journey to the West*. Probably it was added later from the wealth of materials about the life of the monk, yet the chapter's appearance in one of the contemporaneous shorter versions mentioned above suggests the possibility of a full version, written by Wu and circulated in his lifetime, that was the basis for an abridgment as well as for the 1592 edition, which for some reason omitted chapter 9. Or perhaps Wu himself—recognizing the need to give the story of Tripitaka's life before the quest, as he does for the other pilgrims—added chapter 9 after releasing the draft that became the basis for the 1592 edition, though stylistic differences make this seem less likely. In any case, other changes since that date are minor, especially when compared to the textual problems associated with other old Chinese novels.

Plot

The structure of *The Journey to the West* suggests something of the complexity of its development in the folk tradition; it also reflects the scope of a novel that places human life in the larger context of the supranatural cosmos. The book may be considered to fall into four parts: the early history of the monkey-king (chapters 1 through 7); the origins of Tripitaka and of the quest for the scriptures, which is prefigured by the Chinese emperor's visit to the underworld (chapters 8 through 12); the pilgrims' adventures (chapters 13 through 97); and the conclusion of the journey (chapters 98 through 100).

The novel begins with the beginning of the universe. Thus, the reader is reminded of the formless, undifferentiated Chaos that—in the traditional Chinese cosmogony—existed prior to existence. Grafted onto this concept in the opening poem is the Buddhist ideal of enlightenment so important to the book's development. This is only the first of many instances of Wu's syncretism, and his blending of elements from the various philosophical and religious schools of his day is a major source of the novel's satisfying complexity and one reason for its popularity. After the narrative describes the primal cosmic day of 129,600 years, the formation of the physical world begins, and the reader's attention is directed to a stone stop an *axis mundi* mountain in the fabulous realms of the paradisiacal Eastern Sea. This immortal stone, which is a kind of microcosm of the universe of space and time, is impregnated by the spiritual energy of the Yin and Yang forces and gives birth to the magic monkey, who recognizes and hence draws on the powers of the "four quarters" (the orderly, created earth) and finally becomes the founder of a nation.

Such is the cosmic frame of reference that gives *The Journey to the West* its epic scope, its mythic force, and the authority for its central theme of illusion versus reality. Like the invocation to the muse at the beginning of the great epics of the West, this opening links the mundane realm to the divine, and the first chapter's conclusion, the monkey-king's acquisition of a name with a strong religious message—he is called Wu-kung, which might be glossed as "one who has become spiritually awakened to the Void that is the true nature of what we take to be reality"—reminds us of the power of language. The name that defines the monkey's ego is also a sign of the truth that everything, even that ego, is illusion—a truth that the pilgrims, and the reader, will have to journey through ninety-nine more chapters to grasp.

Characters and themes

Monkey has much to learn, or unlearn, however, before the name that so delights him becomes altogether accurate. His qualities are the restlessness and daring of the human mind, and his wondrous abilities—to change his bodily form or to travel to a distant continent in the wink of an eye—suggest the slippery tricks of human fancy. When he overreaches and steals peaches of immortality from the heavenly orchard, magic elixir from the palace of the revered Daoist figure Laozi, and jade juice and ambrosia from a celestial banquet, Monkey must be imprisoned for five hundred years beneath a mountain in the desert borderlands of China, until Tripitaka frees him to serve as a disciple on the quest. So, too, must the mind be controlled, and even after he is freed, "the monkey of the mind," as he is sometimes called, remains subject to a thin band of metal that literally surrounds his skull and clamps down when Tripitaka finds it necessary—until the novel's end, when Monkey becomes a Buddha and learns that the band that restricted him has vanished.

Yet there is much of value in Monkey's energy, once it is civilized. His optimism, his ingenuity in matching his magical transformations to the enemy at hand, his straightforwardness and freedom from inhibitions, his generosity toward his dependents—these qualities are as much a part of his appeal as are his bombast and humor.

Central to what makes the reader admire him is his liberation from what muddles more ordinary lives. He views his rights as equal to those of anyone else and simply does not recognize the authority of the heavenly bureaucracy. He has the daring that allows him to step outside society's limitations; even if those ordering limitations seem necessary for daily life, the individual who finds them at times confining is bound to feel a secret glee at Monkey's antics. Most important, Monkey maintains the attitude of nonattachment that is central to Buddhist ideals of right thought and action. His attention is not focused on the goal of the quest, on fretting and imagining; rather, he lives in the moment at hand, solving problems when they present themselves, and is therefore liberated from the ill effects of taking this illusory world too seriously.

Tripitaka, for all the reverent description of his piety in chapter 9, falls short of this ideal of nonattachment. His sentimentality arises, forgivably, from his compassion, but he is also guilty of fear. In part, his fears arise from an awareness of his human physical limitations; this causes him to fret over his bodily needs and leaves him sometimes paralyzed and helpless. Worse is his wrongful willingness to believe in the reality of his senses and the false monsters that they create. Thus, in Tripitaka's first adventure with his new disciple, the monk falls easy prey to the Six Robbers (allegorical representations of those tricksters, the eye, the ear, the nose, the tongue, the mind, and the body), while Monkey wisely laughs them off. Tripitaka, however, does have the great virtue of faith, and he, too, becomes a Buddha at the end—not because he has worked for saintliness, but precisely in spite of his sometimes petty clinging to the letter of monastic law.

Another of Tripitaka's disciples, the river monster Sha Monk (Sha Wuching, or Sandy) is less sharply characterized, but the fourth pilgrim, Pigsy (Chu Pa-chieh, Wu-neng), is unforgettable. The long poem in which he introduces himself aptly begins: "My mind was dim since the time of my youth;/Always I loved my indolence and sloth." As Hsia has pointed out, Pigsy represents the ordinary human being who simply wants a comfortable family life. His greed and his lust make him an object of ridicule, yet in the end he is rewarded—not with Buddhahood, for he has not yet detached himself from his passions, but with a comfortable position clearing up the plentiful offerings of food from Buddhist altars. Thus, he is given a situation suitable to his level of spiritual development, as the book concludes with the "everyone in the right place" ending familiar to readers of Western comedies.

The objects of Wu's satire, then, include the various follies of the pilgrims, and hence of humanity, but that is only the beginning. Early in the novel, when Monkey first leaves his subjects in the monkey kingdom and goes off to learn how to become an immortal, a demon attacks his land; presumably the monkey-folk would not have suffered had their king been fulfilling his social duties rather than seeking personal spiritual growth. Despite Wu's devout espousal of Buddhist beliefs and the high value he places on the spiritual effects of esoteric Daoist practices, such as internal alchemy and breath-control, he does not hesitate to criticize religious practitioners. The bickering and the fruitless dogmas of various schools are revealed as foolishness when Monkey first becomes a pupil of the Patriarch. The satire goes further: This teacher's "secret signs" are somewhat laughable, and the one who deciphers them and wins the coveted right to the secret teachings is, after all, an unruly ape.

In contrast to the quarrelsome and selfish would-be holy ones is the simple woodcutter in chapter 1: He points the way to the Patriarch's cave for Monkey but cannot take time for religious study himself because he has selflessly devoted his life to caring for his aged mother. A similar figure, the tiger hunter who defies all the Buddhist prohibitions against taking life and eating meat, appears at the start of Tripitaka's journey west; although he breaks religious law, he, too, is portrayed as filial, thoughtful, and helpful.

Sometimes, just as human characteristics such as pride and greed are given animal or monster form, female figures are used in the novel as the embodiments of the temptations of lust and the subtler temptation (see chapters 53 and 54) to reproduce, but this misogynous projection of the human sexual drive onto women alone may be viewed rather as a prejudice of Wu's culture than as uniquely his. Also, as in the West, this vision of women is oddly accompanied by a female figure of great virtue, Kuan-yin, the motherly and loving Goddess of Mercy.

Critical reception

Fuller analyses of the Buddhist, Daoist, and neo-Confucian allegorical messages of *The Journey to the West* have been written by Plaks, Yu, Hsia, and a long tradition of Chinese commentators before the present century; there are other possible allegorical readings as well. Certainly, the riotous disruptions of the somewhat pompous courts of the Daoist pantheon or the Dragon King wittily suggest the vulnerability of similar institutions in the human realm. Bureaucratic corruption, too, is given amusingly pointed satiric treatment: It even appears among the divine assistants of the Buddha himself. Several interesting readings of the novel in the light of the Marxist concept of class struggle have been made; these focus on Monkey's defiance of established authority. The author of the brief essay in a volume edited by Margaret Mead and Martha Wolfenstein (cited in the bibliography) offers a fascinating interpretation of the work from the perspective of developmental psychology. Yet to reduce this multivalent work to any one simplistic allegory is to lose sight of many other meanings.

Still, Wu's novel does have a central focus, one that allows for a variety of understandings of the characters, their interrelationships, and the true nature of their journey. The main point of the book is clear: This world is unreal, even absurd, and certainly our perceptions of it are not to be trusted. What we call "reality" shifts and deceives us; the laws of nature may apply to hapless, nervous, human Tripitaka, but not to enlightened beings such as Monkey. To realize this, however, is not to despair; rather, it is to achieve the kind of relaxed acceptance that is modeled by the novel's narrator. If society's hierarchies are to be questioned and if Tripitaka's pietistic concern with maintaining his purity is sometimes looked at askance, their positive values are also recognized. The bitterness of the last part of Jonathan Swift's *Gulliver's Travels* (1726) has no place in this book. Wu Chengen seems to encourage us to see how far short of ideal this world falls—and how that falling-short is inevitable, given its illusory nature. Still, it is the world we have to live in, and he allows his reader to see the joke in that.

Jeanne Larsen

Bibliography

Dudbridge, Glen. *The "Hsi-yu chi": A Study of Antecedents to the Sixteenth-Century Chinese Novel.* 1970. Reprint. New York: Cambridge University Press, 2009. Dudbridge examines Chinese folklore and other sources to find precedents for *The Journey to the West*. Includes a bibliography.

Hsia, C. T. *The Classic Chinese Novel.* 1968. Reprint. Ithaca, N.Y.: Cornell University, East Asia Program, 1996. Hsia studies six novels, including *The Journey to the West*, providing analyses of their structure, style, characters, and moral and philosophical themes.

Li, Qiancheng. *Fictions of Enlightenment: "Journey to the West," "Tower of Myriad Mirrors," and "Dream of the Red Chamber."* Honolulu: University of Hawaii Press, 2004. Li examines how the Buddhist quest for enlightenment has been transformed into narrative in *The Journey to the West* and in two other works of classic Chinese fiction.

Liu Ts'un-yan. *Wu Ch'eng-en: His Life and Career.* Leiden, the Netherlands: E. J. Brill, 1967. A concise biography of the writer to whom *The Journey to the West* is attributed. Includes a bibliography.

Plaks, Andrew H. *The Four Masterworks of the Ming Novel: Ssu ta ch'i-shu.* Princeton, N.J.: Princeton University Press, 1987. A lengthy, critical study of *The Journey to the West* and three other novels written during China's Ming Dynasty. Includes a bibliography and an index.

Subbaraman, Ramnath. *Beyond the Question of the Monkey Imposter: Indian Influence on the Chinese Novel, "The Journey to the West."* Philadelphia: University of Pennsylvania, Department of Asian and Middle Eastern Studies, 2002. Subbaraman examines "remarkable plot similarities" between *The Journey to the West* and two Indian epics, the Rāmāyana and the Mahābhārata. Includes bibliographical references.

Wang, Jing. *The Story of Stone: Intertextuality, Ancient Chinese Stone Lore, and the Stone Symbolism in "Dream of the Red Chamber," "Water Margin," and "The Journey to the West."* Durham, N.C.: Duke University Press, 1992. Wang compares and contrasts the use of stone symbolism in *The Journey to the West* and two other literary works, describing how this symbolism originates in Chinese myth and folklore.

WU JINGZI

Born: Quanjiao (now Chuzhou, Anhui Province), China; 1701
Died: Yangzhou (now in Jiangsu Province), China; December 12, 1754
Also known as: Wu Ching-tse (Wade-Giles); Wu Ching-tzu

Principal long fiction

Rulin waishi, 1768-1779 (*The Scholars*, 1957)

Other literary forms

The most important extant writings of Wu Jingzi (woo jihng-dzee), other than *The Scholars*, is a collection of poems he wrote before he was forty years old. The collection, known as *Wenmu shanfang ji* (1931, 1957; collection of the mountain retreat of literary trees), was secured in 1921 by the scholar Hu Shih, who first established Wu's authorship of *The Scholars*. This work includes strongly autobiographical poems in various traditional forms as well as seven informative prefaces by Wu's acquaintances and poems by his eldest son, Wu Lang. As a result of renewed interest in the People's Republic of China after 1954, twenty-three additional poems were discovered and published in 1956 in the journal *Wen-hsüeh yen-chiu chi-k'an*. Three other poems and two prefaces to works of friends make up Wu's extant oeuvre, which would be undistinguished if not for his novel.

Achievements

Wu Jingzi wrote his novel at a time when fiction occupied the lowest rung on the Chinese literary ladder. The dominant Confucian ideology stressed morality in literature; fiction, especially when written in the vernacular language, was considered frivolous, essentially "the gossip of the alleyways and marketplaces," not worthy of serious attention by men of letters. This was the attitude, even though, at least three centuries before Wu, long fictional narratives of artistic complexity and merit were already being produced and widely read. Moreover, since the early seventeenth century, defenders of such writings were becoming more vocal and more noticed, even though they continued to be regarded as eccentrics. There is good reason to believe that Wu himself was casual about his fiction writing and, following the practice of his time, passed his manuscript around his circle of friends as a source of amusement. Nevertheless, he injected a serious and idealistic morality into his narrative, which he rendered with a quiet and subtle wit. The result was the first piece of extended satire in Chinese vernacular fiction.

In many formal ways, Wu's fiction retains the trappings of its lighthearted and entertainment-oriented tradition: the omniscient narrator, formulaic commentary, a stringing-out of episodes with few causal linkages, and the vernacular language so different from the elliptical and allusive classical one employed in all serious writings of the time. Significantly, however, he introduced a distinctly upper-class sensibility into this fiction, which advances the idealistic ideology of Confucian eremitism with enough understatement and sophistication to demand for its appreciation an alert and educated mind. *The Scholars* is really a hybrid work that marks the end of Chinese fiction's long journey from folksy gossip to refined and committed art, essentially identical to the art of the learned and the leisured.

With the adoption of modernist values in twentieth century China, fiction and the vernacular attained common respectability, and Wu's contribution to Chinese literature came to be generally recognized and applauded. Since the 1920's, when classical Chinese ceased to be the official medium of communication and instruction, Wu's vernacular prose, anthologized in textbooks, has become a model of clarity and grace for generations of students to follow. Since the beginning of the twentieth century, as the Chinese nation has continued its efforts to create a "modern" literature that transmits social morality in a language easily comprehended by a massive reading public, Wu's fiction has been recognized as an important progenitor of the writings dominating the Chinese literary scene.

Biography

Wu Jingzi was born in 1701 into an extended family in the rich and cultured Yangtze Plain of southeastern

China. His family had experienced great success in Chinese officialdom for four previous generations. Beginning with his great-great-grandfather Wu P'ei, members of the family regularly attained honors through the civil service examinations, the standard route to governmental office and the concomitant wealth and status to which all men of ambition aspired. Wu's own branch of the family, however, had begun declining two generations before his birth. His grandfather Wu Tan had to purchase a lower degree and was recorded in the local histories only for his filiality. Wu Linch'i, the father Wu evidently revered, also had a rather mediocre career, holding for some years a minor educational post in northeastern Kiangsu.

Wu's own life spanned the years 1701 to 1754, coinciding remarkably with the lives of many satirists in English literature. At Wu's birth, John Dryden had been dead one year; Alexander Pope was a child of thirteen; Joseph Addison and Richard Steele were both twenty-nine; and Jonathan Swift, at thirty-four, had not yet begun to produce his greatest works. Henry Fielding would be born in another six years, and Samuel Johnson in another eight. The political turmoil that stimulated the satiric style in England, however, did not have its counterpart in China. Wu lived during the reigns of the Ch'ing Dynasty emperors K'ang-hsi (1661-1722), Yung-cheng (1722-1735), and Ch'ienlung (1735-1796), a period that represented the high-water mark of the dynasty's achievement of unity, stability, peace, and prosperity.

The only natural child of his parents (he had an adopted sister of whom he was very fond), Wu was described as serious and introverted as a youth. Like other children from literati households, he was schooled in the Confucian classics, which, to the Chinese of the time, was the repository of all human reason and human morality. After his mother died at the onset of Wu's teenage years, his father devoted much attention to Wu's education, taking him along to his post in neighboring Kiangsu and hiring a special tutor to prepare him for the examinations and for the official life beyond. In the verse of a cousin, Wu is described as a young man of talent and promise, able to "weave smoothly together, with a sweep of the pen, a composition of a thousand words/ Covering the breadth and width of a subject like silkworms munching the leaves of the mulberry." These abilities, however, would never be used as they were originally intended to be used, in the conventional service to the state.

Beginning about 1722, Wu's fortunes began a downward turn. His father resigned his post and was seriously ill on returning home to Ch'üan-chiao. The following year, Wu was sent to compete in the district examinations for the *sheng-yuan* degree, the first of three major steps to high officialdom. The good news of success arrived almost simultaneously with his father's death. "Before a dark scholar's gown could adorn your happy smiles,/" his cousin recalls in verse, "Your hempen garments were like snow, your hair in disarray." The loss was far more than an emotional one for Wu, for it also placed on his reluctant shoulders the tasks of settling his estate and dealing with the various claimants who suddenly descended on him. In later years, he was to describe them as "kite-owls" and "wolves." Troubled by such unfamiliar cares, he sought solace in the pleasure quarters of Nanking, then as now a bustling metropolis accessible by boat from Ch'üan-chiao. Such revels proved expensive. Wu's once-ample inheritance was gradually depleted, and he was forced to sell most of his ancestral property. As he found himself on the threshold of poverty, he became the target of the malicious gossip of his neighbors. "My land and houses all sold," he wrote in early 1731. "In local circles I serve as warning to son and brother." This loss of respect that accompanied his loss of wealth left in him a bitterness that lasted many years.

As if to compound his troubles, Wu's first wife died around 1728, and he recalls her passing in a poem that showed both self-doubt and self-pity. "Would that I could find a good match,/ But who would be willing to wake this Chiang-lang from his slumber?" "Chiang-lang" refers to the sixth century litterateur Chiang Yen, who, according to legend, awoke from dreams to find his talent gone. At the age of only thirty, Wu had given up on himself and on his once-bright future. By 1733, his poetry began to be laced with references to recluses and to a life of retirement. That was the year he moved from his native Ch'üan-chiao permanently to Nanking, marking the event with a long poem written in "extreme grief and resentful anger, with copiously flowing tears." In the tradition of Confucian recluses, he was not withdrawing from human contact but only from involvement with officialdom. In Nanking's urban environment, he would spend his days in intellectual and moral self-cultivation, with ample time to entertain "men of wine and literature from everywhere" who ventured into the city, as an early biographer relates.

With these friends, Wu salvaged a measure of respect. By 1736, his reputation for scholarship and literary talent had grown sufficiently for him to be recommended to take a special examination ordered by the newly installed Ch'ien-lung emperor. No one has been able to ascertain his actual reasons, but Wu eventually declined the opportunity and reaffirmed his eremitic course. Thereafter, he spent the remainder of his funds to finance the construction of a temple to the Confucian sage Ts'ang Chieh and to stage elaborate sacrificial ceremonies there. This act of Confucianist faith, made in honor of the supposed inventor of Chinese writing and historiography, plunged him into deep poverty. For the remaining decade or so of his life, he hovered on the edge of starvation.

In contrast to the bitterness with which he reacted to his earlier troubles, Wu faced the trials of his later life with stoic courage and admirable equanimity. His biographers usually point out his cheerful resignation to a straitened existence so different from the comfort and luxury of his youth. It is told of him that he would go for days without food, that he would go about without so much as an inkstone or a brush, the basic tools of a literatus. In winter, unable to secure the sustenance of food or wine, he would spend the night walking around Nanking's city walls with like-minded friends, and they would sing and shout to one another until dawn; because they had no fuel, that was their way of "warming the feet."

Wu died poor and almost alone, probably from a stroke while on a boat in Yang-chou. Only a few days before, he had "gathered up the remaining cash in his purse" and invited friends to drink with him. Flushed with wine, he had cited the lines of the ninth century eremite-poet Chang Hu that Yang-chou, with its scenic Zen temples, was a fitting place for a man to die. If it were not for his work of fiction written in the final decades of his life, he would have passed into the obscurity that usually followed an eremitic life. In choosing such a life, Wu surely knew the price. Like his fictionalized hero Wang Mien in *The Scholars*, he probably thought he was fated to leave the world without disclosing his name. That his name is now prominently placed in the history of Chinese literature is the result of historical changes he could not have foreseen. Like most authors of traditional fiction, he had not been proud enough of his creation even to mark it as his own.

Analysis: The Scholars

While it has long been out of fashion to link an author's life too closely to his or her created work, the sometimes puzzling fiction produced by Wu Jingzi does become far more understandable when examined in the light of his biography. Written in a tradition that has always played down fictionalization in favor of factual truth, much of Wu's novel can best be seen as a commentary on the actual social conditions of his times and as an apologia for his own decision to live apart from the limitations they imposed. While modern critics generally do consider *The Scholars* in terms of the former, few accord the latter more than perfunctory attention.

Confucian influences

The Confucianist eremitism Wu practiced differs greatly from conventional Confucianism, which is generally contrasted with Daoism by its affirmation of social values and by its justification of active service to the state. Wu's novel clearly criticizes such active service, even as it continues to preach uncompromising adherence to the fundamental Confucian virtues of humanity (*jen*), righteousness (*yi*), propriety (*li*), and, especially, filial piety (*hsiao*), in a way that would be alien to the relativistic and iconoclastic principles of Daoist doctrine. Confucianism has always had an idealistic side, one that cites the sage Mencius to justify the refusal to serve when such service is considered detrimental to the full development of a person's intellect and morality. That *The Scholars* has been regularly misunderstood in modern times can be traced to the ignoring of its basic commitment to this dimension of Confucian doctrine.

This commitment can be seen from many parts of Wu's biography, beginning with his grandfather's and father's relative lack of success in career matters and the justification of their lives in terms of their practice of virtue. For Wu, the age-old conflict between the Confucian directive to render public service and the equally Confucian requirement to be filial occurred almost from the moment he competed in the examinations: He had to leave a dying father in order to do so, and what little success he achieved was tied forever to a great personal tragedy, his father's passing. The image of the dying father figure is prominently featured in his novel, usually voicing warning against the seeking of worldly gains. Moreover, a common criticism the novel advances against examination candidates is their slighting of filial duties once they experience the sweet taste of success.

Critics have also recognized that the biting depictions of small-town gentry in various parts of *The Scholars* can be traced to Wu's residual disgust for the greed, the empty status-seeking, and the general maliciousness of his Ch'üan-chiao neighbors. Clearly, it was such maliciousness that led to his bitter self-exile and premature retirement. By opposing the quest for wealth and status with the full development of morality and intellect, Wu can be seen to be expressing in his novel his condemnation of the Ch'üan-chiao gentry, who ridiculed him for his descent into poverty and obscurity. Away from such provinciality, Wu was free in urban Nanking to devote full attention to the practice of humane virtue and the study of traditional classics, which he equated in his later years with "the sun and the moon in the heavens" for their ability to illuminate the myriad changes in the human world.

In chapter 37 of *The Scholars*, Wu includes an account of the temple sacrifices that marked his final commitment to Confucianist eremitism. In this account, however, he exercised his prerogative as a writer of fiction, changing the sage honored from Ts'ang Chieh to T'ai-po, an ancient prince praised by Confucius for running away to the then-barbaric south in order to yield the throne to a younger brother. The legend recalling the incident also attributes the civilizing of all southern China to this act of idealistic generosity. By referring to T'ai-po, Wu is thus advancing the moral message of his novel and justifying his own renouncement of competition as directly opposed to genuine self-cultivation. This moral message is the key to the understanding of his difficult work.

Structure

For those who do not understand Wu's eremitic orientation, *The Scholars* can appear to be a baffling and loosely structured work full of seeming inconsistencies. This is, in fact, the common impression of Wu's fictional art. The looseness can be explained in two ways. First, in comparison to modern novels, with their dynamic and tightly woven plots, all premodern Chinese novels would appear static, episodic, and carelessly put together; Wu was merely following tradition in making *The Scholars* the same way. Second, *The Scholars* is a satiric work, and satire, even in the West, has an innate tendency to feature "collections of loosely related scenes and business which curls back on itself," as Alvin Kernan demonstrates in *The Plot of Satire* (1965). In addition, there is the nagging question of interpolation in the standard text, traceable to the Wo-hsien ts'ao-t'ang edition of 1803. Sudden shifts of style and tone, especially after chapter 37, make the common practice of wholesale changes and emendations in the text a distinct possibility.

The general concern with looseness comes from those who choose to overlook *The Scholars*' essentially satiric nature and insist on regarding it as a work of realism. It is as satire, however, that the work is most intelligible, since, like all satire, it expresses its morality with witty indirection. Whereas other works in its tradition tend to provide the reader with everything, *The Scholars* achieves its didactic effect by requiring its reader to fill in the blanks and come to the inevitable conclusions as if they were his or her own. When this reader changes from a Ch'ing Dynasty Chinese to a person in the twenty-first century, far removed by time and distance from the original reader's background and concerns, the meaning of the text can become obscured. For this reason, *The Scholars* has undergone an array of divergent interpretations in modern times, and Wu has been seen as anything from a prescient Marxist who exposes the evils of Chinese feudalism to a prescient existentialist who describes the fundamental absurdity of human life.

Actually, the episodes of *The Scholars* are arranged in a definite design that clearly conveys the moral standards by which its many dunces are to be judged. The fifty-five chapters of the standard text (which excludes a disputed final chapter) sandwich their satiric barbs between a prologue and an epilogue that feature paragons of virtue and learning against whom the reader is expected to contrast the lesser characters who inhabit the rest of the work. These paragons—Wang Mien and four eccentric townsfolk—are joined by a moral constant: They are all men of talent who stubbornly adhere to a life of withdrawal, barring their gates to official enticements that they see as impinging on the independence necessary for their own development. As one of them explains it:

> I make six or seven silver cents a day; and when I've eaten my fill, if I want to strum my lyre or do some writing, there's nobody to stop me. I neither covet the wealth or the position of others, nor have to wait on their pleasure. I owe nothing to heaven or earth. Isn't it pleasant?

Most members of society, however, are shown to give up this freedom gladly in their headlong quest for material and social gain. In *The Scholars*, success in the quest is linked to a necessary moral and intellectual decline. In an ironic reversal typical of all satire, what Kernan calls a "wedge" is indeed driven between appearance and reality, so that as scholars seek to magnify themselves with degrees and titles, the magnification itself corresponds to a diminution of their learning and virtue; as they seek to rise in status, the rise becomes a fall in their actual worth; and as they drive forward toward a certain order, the order invariably brings on moral chaos.

Style

In sketching this topsy-turvy world, Wu's technical contribution goes well beyond a skillful use of the vernacular language in description, for which he is usually praised, for he also introduced to the then lightly regarded fictional medium an accomplished narrative style to go with the expression of upperclass values. This style, called *p'i-li yang-ch'iu* (subtly and indirectly indicating critical judgment beneath a noncommittal surface) was derived from a historiographic technique attributed to Confucius himself. In contrast to the mode of garrulous commentary typically found in so much of traditional vernacular fiction, incidents in *The Scholars* are usually related without the narrator's expressed opinions. In traditional fashion, this narrator remains closely identified with the author and retains an omniscience that he exercises while providing points of information; he also maintains the traditional distance from the action. From such an authoritative and detached position, the more complex situations of what R. C. Elliott (in *The Power of Satire*, 1960) calls "the satirist satirized" and the broader range of satiric techniques to which this can lead are not operative. There is neither parody nor burlesque, nor the double irony that can occur when the narrator is himself a dunce. Nevertheless, by strategically presenting each episode in a manner that compels the moral commentary of the reader, Wu's style achieves a rhetorical power beyond what is possible with the traditional preachy narration and its attendant verbal overkill.

Since the beginning of the twentieth century, under the stress of constant political turmoil, Chinese fiction has assumed in full the moral burdens Wu helped introduce to the medium a century and a half before. Few modern authors, however, have been able to match his ability to understate and leave things appropriately unsaid, even as they have followed his lead in developing the vernacular language as a medium for literary art. For this reason, Wu's one novel remains as important a model today as when it was first called to the attention of the would-be creators of a modern Chinese literature.

Timothy C. Wong

Other major works

POETRY: *Wenmu shanfang ji*, 1931, 1957; "Jinling jingwu tu shi," 1956.

Bibliography

Chang, H. C. "Young Master Bountiful." In *Popular Fiction and Drama*. Vol. 1 in *Chinese Literature*. Edinburgh, Scotland: Edinburgh University Press, 1973-1983. Chang's collection of critical studies and translations of Chinese literature includes a chapter on Wu Jingzi's classic novel.

Hsia, C. T. "The Scholars." In *The Classic Chinese Novel: A Critical Introduction*. 1968. Reprint. Ithaca, N.Y.: Cornell University, East Asia Program, 1996. Hsia studies six Chinese novels, including *The Scholars*, providing analyses of their structure, style, characters, and moral and philosophical themes

Lin, Shuen-fu. "Ritual and Narrative Structure in *Ju-lin wai-shih*." In *Chinese Narrative: Critical and Theoretical Essays*, edited by Andrew H. Plaks. Princeton, N.J.: Princeton University Press, 1977. Lin's analysis of the narrative structure of *The Scholars* was first presented at the Princeton Conference on Chinese Narrative Theory held at Princeton University on January 21-22, 1974.

Roddy, Stephen J. *Literati Identity and Its Fictional Representations in Late Imperial China*. Stanford, Calif.: Stanford University Press, 1998. Roddy examines three works of Chinese vernacular literature, including *The Scholars*, written in the eighteenth and nineteenth centuries, demonstrating how these works reflect new perceptions of the Confucian scholar-gentry.

Ropp, Paul S. *Dissent in Early Modern China: "Ju-lin wai-shih" and Ch'ing Social Criticism*. Ann Arbor: University of Michigan Press, 1981. Ropp's examination of *The Scholars* places the novel within the context of social and intellectual developments in eighteenth century China, demonstrating how Wu Jingzi used parable and example to criticize Chinese society.

Shang, Wei. *"Rulin waishi" and Cultural Transformation in Late Imperial China*. Cambridge, Mass.: Harvard University, Asia Center, 2003. In his analysis of *The Scholars*, Shang shows how the novel reflects the intellectual and literary debates in eighteenth century China. Also shows how Wu Jingzi depicts the Confucian elite's attempts to retain moral and cultural authority. Includes a character list, a bibliography, and an index.

Wong, Timothy C. *Wu Ching-tzu*. Boston: Twayne, 1978. Contains a chapter about Wu Jingzi's life, as well as discussion of the satire in his work and the "eremitic ideal" in *The Scholars*. One of the introductory overviews in Twayne's World Authors series. Includes a bibliography and an index.

Y

A. B. YEHOSHUA

Born: Jerusalem, Israel; December 9, 1936
Also known as: Abraham Ben Yehoshua; Avraham B. Yehoshua; Boolie

Principal long fiction

Mot ha-zaken, 1962 (novella)
Sheloshah yamim ve-yeled, 1967 (novella; *Three Days and a Child*, 1970)
Bi-tehilat kayits 1970, 1972 (novella; *Early in the Summer of 1970*, 1977)
Ha-meahev, 1977 (*The Lover*, 1978)
Gerushim me'uharim, 1982 (*A Late Divorce*, 1984)
Molkho, 1987 (*Five Seasons*, 1989)
Mar Mani, 1990 (*Mr. Mani*, 1992)
Shivah me-hodu, 1994 (*Open Heart*, 1996)
Masa' el tom ha-elef, 1997 (*A Journey to the End of the Millennium*, 1999)
Ha-Kalah ha-meshahreret, 2001 (*The Liberated Bride*, 2003)
Shelihuto shel ha-memuneh al mashabe enosh, 2004 (*A Woman in Jerusalem*, 2006)
Esh yedidutit, 2007 (*Friendly Fire*, 2008)

Other literary forms

The writer and philosopher A. B. Yehoshua (yeh-HOH-shew-uh) first came to critical attention with short-story collections he published in the 1960's, such as *Mul ha-ye'arot* (1968; facing the forests). English translations of many of these early stories are collected in *The Continuing Silence of a Poet* (1988). By the 1980's, in addition to novels, Yehoshua began to publish essays and to write plays, among the most notable of which is *Hafatzim* (pr. 1986; *Possessions*, 1993); he has also written children's books. Yehoshua holds strong, and often controversial, political views, which he has defined in his collections of essays as well as through media and academic appearances and interviews.

Achievements

A. B. Yehoshua is one of the most acclaimed and translated of the Hebrew novelists, known for his carefully observed portraits of Jewish life in Israel, with all its moral, political, and psychological conflicts. Among the many literary honors and awards Yehoshua has received in Israel and elsewhere are the Brenner Prize, the Bialik Prize, and the Alterman Prize. *Mr. Mani* was named "Best Novel of the Year" in England in 1992, and Yehoshua has also won the National Jewish Book Award twice (1990 and 1993), the Israeli Prize for Literature (1995), and Italy's Giovanni Boccaccio Prize (2005). In 2003 he received both the Premio Napoli and the Lampedusa Literary Prize for his novel *The Liberated Bride*. In 2005 he was among the nominees for the first Man Booker International Prize, and he was presented with the Viareggio Prize for Lifetime Achievement (Italy). In 2006 his novel *A Woman in Jerusalem* won the Los Angeles Times Book Prize, and in 2008 *Friendly Fire* received the Premio Roma.

Biography

Abraham Ben Yehoshua was born a Sephardic Jew. His father's family was originally from Salonica and his mother's from Morocco, but the families had resided in Jerusalem for five generations, and Yehoshua considers himself simply an Israeli. His family was educated; his grandfather was a rabbi and his father, Yakov Yehoshua, was an Orientalist who wrote twelve books about the history of Sephardim in the Old City of Jerusalem. Historians have a certain prominence in Yehoshua's work, as many characters return to the past in their efforts to understand it.

The young Yehoshua fulfilled his military service as a paratrooper from 1954 to 1957 and then started to publish fiction. He soon became known as one of a "new wave" of Israeli writers whose emphasis on individuals and their relationships contrasted with the social concerns of earlier writers.

In June of 1960 he married Rivka Kirsninski, a psychoanalyst, with whom he eventually had three children. He studied Hebrew literature and philosophy at Hebrew University in Jerusalem, graduating with a B.A. in 1961, and he graduated from Teacher's College a year later. He taught in Paris from 1963 to 1967 and served as dean of students at Haifa University in Haifa, Israel, upon his return. He was promoted to professor of literature at Haifa University in 1997, where he worked until his retirement. Throughout his career he also served as visiting professor at many institutions, including St. Cross College, Oxford, Harvard University, the University of Chicago, and Princeton University.

Analysis

A. B. Yehoshua is sometimes called Israel's best living novelist, and judging from the variety and complexity of his work, this may be true. His art fictionalizes the controversies that are ever present in Israel: the tensions between European-born and native-born Israelis, the tensions between those who live in Israel and those who choose to live in the Diaspora, the conflicts between Sephardic and Ashkenazi Jews, and the conflicts between Arabs and Israelis. Against the opposing forces of such conflicts, Yehoshua delves deeply into his characters' inner lives with astute psychological understanding, using certain archetypal and mythic patterns as well.

The Lover, his first full-length novel, immediately brought him international recognition; this work delineates the disintegration of an Ashkenazi family. Not until he wrote *Mr. Mani*, however—a family epic that spans six generations—did Yehoshua create a protagonist who is Sephardic and whose Sephardic roots play an important role in the story. The technique he employs in *Mr. Mani* is unusual; the novel is composed of five different conversations at five significant moments of history, but only one side of the dialogue is given in each of these conversations, while the other side must be assumed. In this way Yehoshua combines a long historical span with the personal perspectives of the members of the Mani family. The theme of the disintegration of the family is seen here as well as in many of his novels, such as *A Late Divorce* and *The Liberated Bride*. Yehoshua has often been called the Hebrew Faulkner, and in many of his books he deals with the same issues of guilt and penance that are addressed in the works of William Faulkner. The novelist credits Faulkner as one of his sources of inspiration, along with Albert Camus and Franz Kafka.

Always interested in history, Yehoshua switched from contemporary Israeli society with *A Journey to the End of the Millennium*, a historical novel that takes place in the year 999. The novel tells the story of a merchant traveling from Africa to Europe who has taken a second wife, a custom that was accepted in North African Jewish communities but forbidden in Europe. When he sets out on his journey, Ben Attar, the protagonist, intends to

A. B. Yehoshua. (Getty Images)

persuade the Jews of Europe to his way of thinking about polygamy. The novel is rich with the colorful appearance and sophisticated ideas of the African visitors, against which the drab costumes and narrow beliefs of the Rhineland towns Ben Attar visits seem provincial indeed. Ben Attar fails to persuade, however.

The Liberated Bride

The Liberated Bride centers on Yochanan Rivlin, a professor of Near Eastern studies at Haifa University. Rivlin is determined to find out the cause of the divorce of his eldest son, Ofer, and he is also determined to find out the root cause of the ferocity of the Algerian war of the 1990's for a book he is writing. These two quests form the narrative arc of the novel, as they lead Rivlin into adventures that find him far from home and the constraints of his beloved wife, Hagit, a well-respected district judge. Hagit's position involves making judgments on those who break the boundaries of the law and trains her to respect privacy.

When Rivlin is dispatched to Jerusalem to pick up his visiting sister-in-law from the airport, he happens to hear that his former daughter-in-law, Galya, is in mourning for her suddenly deceased father. Seizing on this as an opportunity to see Galya, he stops in to pay his respects while Galya's family is receiving guests. He not only discovers that Galya has remarried but also comes to believe that she is pregnant. These facts do not quench his desire to discover the cause of his son's divorce from Galya five years previously, but he receives no satisfaction. Still obsessed with his hunger to know the causes of Ofer and Galya's divorce, he writes to Ofer and suggests that his son write a letter of condolence to Galya.

Later, when his wife leaves him for a few days to attend a trial in Europe, Rivlin calls Ofer in France to try again to find out the cause of his son's divorce, although Hagit has told Rivlin several times to leave their son in peace. Meanwhile, Ofer sends a letter to his mother telling her of his accidental discovery of his former father-in-law's dalliance with a woman who is not his wife, which led to the breakup of his own marriage when he told Galya.

Hagit returns from Europe and, her suspicions aroused regarding her husband's meddling, cross-examines Rivlin, which leads to a bitter fight about Ofer. Eventually, they declare a truce, and Ofer comes to Israel for a diving expedition with his younger brother, Tsakhi, an officer in the Israeli army. Hagit considers her younger son almost a saint because he has a sense of boundaries and knows right from wrong. Rivlin, who has no sense of boundaries, tries to question Ofer regarding his marriage to Galya, after which his son attacks him as a domineering, pushy traitor and returns to France, where he lives. In the final section of the book, titled "The Liberation," Galya, about to give birth at any moment, shows up at Rivlin and Hagit's home, to which she has summoned Ofer from Paris. She asks his forgiveness for dismissing his report of her father's dalliance, which caused the divorce. She has learned the truth from an employee at her father's hotel. She will not reunite with Ofer, however. While she is in labor at a Haifa hospital, Galya's husband and sister show up there to take her back to Jerusalem.

The Liberated Bride includes a rich subplot concerning Rivlin's graduate student Samaher, which brings Rivlin to cross the line between Israel and the Palestinian Territories in the middle of the night with Rashid, an Arab driver. Rivlin is amazed at how quickly Rashid kicks in the dividing fence, another boundary that Rivlin crosses. The novel is also embellished with acts of plays performed in the novel, with bits of Arabic conversation and Algerian poetry and stories, and with letters written from various characters to other characters. The narrative is further enriched by the differences Rivlin has with his colleagues, their discussions centering on the meaning of "national identity" and minority points of view. The point of view of the novel is always Rivlin's, usually told in the third person by an omniscient narrator and occasionally told in the second person.

Rivlin, driven by a thirst to know facts and causes—owing to his training as a historian—is insatiable, but he is willing to deal with real people in all their confusion and complexity, a character trait that is endearing. Constantly traveling Israeli roads and highways, the professor crosses borders both emotional and physical, annoying his family and friends in his quest for answers. He does not find them, however; he never learns the cause of Ofer and Galya's divorce, and he never learns to respect boundaries. At the end he is seen meddling in his younger son's new occupation as a housepainter, passing himself off as the young man's boss.

A Woman in Jerusalem

As *A Woman in Jerusalem* begins, a past employee of a bakery, a woman in her forties, has died as the result of a bombing. The only identification found with her body is a pay slip from the company, dated after she had quit her job a month previously. Nobody had noticed that she was still on the payroll. Stung by a forthcoming newspaper article about the inhumanity of the company, the prosperous, eighty-seven-year-old owner dispatches his human resources manager (unnamed) to investigate the woman so that he can make a public gesture on her behalf. The human resources manager, himself recently divorced and interested only in rearing his daughter, discovers a romantic entanglement between the worker and the bakery's night supervisor, which accounts for her continuing paychecks. The manager soon becomes obsessed with the deceased, Yulia Ragayev, an engineer from Russia who worked as a cleaner in the bakery. Negative newspaper publicity prods the owner to send the human resources manager to escort Yulia's body back to her home village on the steppes of Russia to be buried, thinking this will exonerate him of his company's former neglect of the woman.

The manager and the body are accompanied on the trip by the newspaper reporter who has been covering the story and his photographer. Their journey becomes saturated with irony and dark humor, and it is in dealing with the absurdities of the journey that the timid and nonassuming human resources manager finds himself, displaying resources of his own that he never knew he possessed. Along the way, as the group travels in a demobilized armored personnel carrier, the manager is forced to pay bribes to the authorities, fends off Yulia's ferocious ex-husband, lives for a time underground in a former bomb shelter because of the onslaught of a fierce winter storm, and survives a devastating illness. The novel turns into a comic tour de force, told mainly from the manager's point of view except for a series of brief, italicized passages that act as a kind of Greek chorus by giving outsiders' views of the action.

The change in the manager's character from a man intimidated by his mother, his ex-wife, and his secretary to a hero of staunch moral integrity is the main trajectory of the novel. The overarching theme of *A Woman in Jerusalem* is the question of responsibility, an issue revisited again and again by the human resources manager, by his mother, by the owner of the bakery, and by Yulia's relatives in Russia. In the final scene, the human resources manager asserts his humanity and, with great honor, resolves the question.

Sheila Golburgh Johnson

Other major works

short fiction: *Mul ha-ye'arot*, 1968; *Three Days and a Child*, 1970 (selection of short stories, including the novella *Three Days and a Child*); *Tishah sipurim*, 1970; *The Continuing Silence of a Poet: The Collected Short Stories of A. B. Yehoshua*, 1988; *Kol ha-sipurim*, 1993.

plays: *Layla be-May*, pr. 1969 (*A Night in May*, 1974); *Tipolim acharonim*, pr. 1973 (*Last Treatments*, 1974); *Two Plays*, 1974 (includes *A Night in May* and *Last Treatments*); *Hafatzim*, pr. 1986 (*Possessions*, 1993); *Tinokot laylah*, pr. 1992.

nonfiction: *Bi-zekhut ha-normaliyut*, 1980 (*Between Right and Right*, 1981); *Israel*, 1988; *Hakir v-h-har*, 1989; *Kohah ha-nora shel ashmah ketanah*, 1998 (*The Terrible Power of a Minor Guilt*, 2000); *Essays*, 2006; *Achizat moledet*, 2008.

children's literature: *Ha-Achbar shel Tamar ve-Gaya*, 2005; *Chaiat ha-machmad shel Ofri*, 2007.

Bibliography

Band, Arnold J. "The Archaeology of Self Deception: A. B. Yehoshua's *Mar Mani*." In *Studies in Modern Jewish Literature*. Philadelphia: Jewish Publication Society, 2003. Provides an in-depth discussion of *Mr. Mani* as part of a larger work concerned with contemporary Jewish literature in general.

Bayley, John. Review of *Mr. Mani*, by A. B. Yehoshua. *The New Republic*, November 5, 1992. Unravels the complexities of this novel, which jumps around in time and point of view.

Ellis, Samantha. "Fiction Turbulent as Life." *Jewish Quarterly*, no. 201 (Spring, 2006): 1-6. Presents an informative survey of Yehoshua's career, with special emphasis on the novels *The Lover* and *Mr. Mani*.

Essex, Ruth. "The Eastern Influence." In *Israeli Writing Against Itself: The Clash of Hellenism and Judaism in Modern Israeli Narrative*. New York: Peter Lang,

2001. Presents analysis of Yehoshua's novel *Open Heart* as part of an examination of the meeting of ancient lore and modern narrative in ten novels by Israeli writers.

Halkin, Hillel. "Politics and the Israeli Novel." *Commentary* 117, no. 4 (April, 2004). A frequent translator of Yehoshua's work offers an insightful discussion of how Israel's political climate determines the fate of many of the characters in the author's novels.

Horn, Bernard. *Facing the Fires: Conversations with A. B. Yehoshua*. Syracuse, N.Y.: Syracuse University Press, 1997. A recognized expert on Yehoshua presents his own interviews with the author that cover many topics, including books, nostalgia, politics, Sephardic Jewry in Israel, and writing.

Morahg, Gilead. "Testing Tolerance: Cultural Diversity and National Unity in A. B. Yehoshua's *A Journey to the End of the Millennium*." *Prooftexts* 19, no. 3 (September, 1999): 235-256. Examination of Yehoshua's novel focuses on the allegorical nature of the work and its depictions of cultural diversity.

Newton, Adam Zachary. "Not Quite Holocaust Fiction: A. B. Yehoshua's *Mr. Mani* and W. G. Sebald's *The Emigrants*." In *Teaching the Representation of the Holocaust*, edited by Marianne Hirsch and Irene Kacandes. New York: Modern Language Association of America, 2004. Compares and contrasts Yehoshua's novel and Sebald's *Die Ausgewanderten* (1992; *The Emigrants*, 1996) from within the context of fiction about the Holocaust.

FRANK YERBY

Born: Augusta, Georgia; September 5, 1916
Died: Madrid, Spain; November 29, 1991
Also known as: Frank Garvin Yerby

Principal long fiction

The Foxes of Harrow, 1946
The Vixens, 1947
The Golden Hawk, 1948
Pride's Castle, 1949
Floodtide, 1950
A Woman Called Fancy, 1951
The Saracen Blade, 1952
The Devil's Laughter, 1953
Benton's Row, 1954
Bride of Liberty, 1954
The Treasure of Pleasant Valley, 1955
Captain Rebel, 1956
Fairoaks, 1957
The Serpent and the Staff, 1958
Jarrett's Jade, 1959
Gillian, 1960
The Garfield Honor, 1961
Griffin's Way, 1962
The Old Gods Laugh: A Modern Romance, 1964
An Odor of Sanctity, 1965
Goat Song, 1968
Judas, My Brother, 1968
Speak Now: A Modern Novel, 1969
The Dahomean: An Historical Novel, 1971
The Girl from Storyville, 1972
The Voyage Unplanned, 1974
Tobias and the Angel, 1975
A Rose for Ana Maria, 1976
Hail the Conquering Hero, 1978
A Darkness at Ingraham's Crest, 1979
Western, 1982
Devilseed, 1984
McKenzie's Hundred, 1985

Other literary forms

In addition to his novels, Frank Yerby wrote poetry and short stories that are often found in anthologies of black literature. One story, "Health Card," first published in *Harper's* magazine, won a special O. Henry Memorial Award in 1944.

Achievements

Frank Yerby wrote many best-selling historical novels over a long career beginning in the 1940's. Most of his best work, however, dates from the 1960's, after he had established himself as a prolific popular novelist. Yerby excelled at creating complicated, fast-moving plots that give vivid impressions of historical eras and periods. Often the novels contradict myths and stereotypes of the periods in question. Almost every novel, too, suggests the futility of finding real truth in the universal confusion of the human condition. While Yerby's protagonists are flawed, often by ruthlessness and infidelity, they are also characterized by a fierce sense of dignity based on the worth of a human life.

Frank Yerby. (Library of Congress)

Biography

Frank Garvin Yerby was born in Augusta, Georgia, on September 5, 1916. He received a bachelor of arts degree from Paine College in 1937 and a master of arts degree from Fisk College in 1938. Subsequently, he did graduate work in education at the University of Chicago.

From 1939 to 1941, Yerby taught English, first at Florida A&M and then at Southern University and A&M College. He married in 1941 and then worked until 1944 at the Ford Motor Company in Dearborn, Michigan, as a technician and then as an inspector at Fairchild Aircraft from 1944 to 1945. In 1944, he won an O. Henry Memorial Award for the short story "Health Card," a story that dealt sensitively with black issues. In 1945, he started work on a novel, *The Foxes of Harrow*, which he aimed to make a commercial success. Thereafter, Yerby wrote many similar melodramatic best sellers. His books have sold millions of copies and have been translated into at least fourteen languages.

Divorced in the 1950's, Yerby moved to France and then to Spain, where he died in 1991. He had four children from his first marriage. His second wife was his researcher and general manager; some of his later novels give evidence of considerable research. He traveled widely, and sometimes his travels involved investigating locales of works in progress.

Analysis

Frank Yerby was a best-selling author, and much of what he wrote has clear commercial appeal, a point on which he made inconsistent remarks. His plots are intricate and involved, but in many of his novels, the characterizations are basically flat. His favorite era is the nineteenth century South, yet he wrote about many other places and times in his more than thirty novels. Occasionally, he set a novel in modern times. The reader of popular best sellers will find in Yerby's novels fast-paced narrative with appropriate amounts of violence and sex.

Yerby was more, however, than a best-selling writer. His short stories written early in his career show promise and develop radically different themes from those of his costume novels. In the 1960's, secure after many commercial successes, Yerby began to do his best work, dealing with larger issues of race and religion, which figure less prominently in his earlier novels. The characters in these later novels are no longer cardboard figures, while the backgrounds are as richly detailed and vividly re-created as ever. Yerby's historical novels must be their children, who are burned in their house except for one daughter, who dies after being repeatedly raped, all of them victims of the Klan. He also helps a black minister escape, but only after the dynamiting of the minister's house, which killed a daughter. At his daughter's funeral, the minister delivers a stern sermon to the Klan members, who then threaten his life so that Paris must again help him. The Klan members finally back off from Paris's house when one accidentally shoots Laurel, still very much a symbol of southern womanhood.

The novel ends with dawn imagery, the night having been endured and the humane whites now waiting for the light of morning. Whether the whites threatened by the Klan can start anew is unclear. Given the implied parallel to modern events, Yerby seems to be saying that it is too soon to tell whether the twentieth century can rise above racial violence; nevertheless, the concluding imagery does suggest hope.

An Odor of Sanctity

In *An Odor of Sanctity*, Yerby is at his best as a historical novelist. It is a long, deftly paced novel that, while using many of the stock elements of Yerby's novels of the 1940's and 1950's, also deals intelligently with a religious theme. Once again, Yerby creates an outsider, Alaric Teudisson, as hero; he is set off by his odor of sanctity, a saintly force in him of which he is not fully aware for most of his life. Teudisson must deal with the complex culture of medieval Spain, a battleground for Christians, Moors, and numerous bands of marauding barbarians.

Like earlier Yerby protagonists, Teudisson is involved in many liaisons and several marriages. Teudisson is a striking blond of Visigoth extraction who, before the male hormones take effect, is so "beautiful" that at one point he is almost made a catamite. Thereafter, Teudisson has numerous sexual encounters, one unconsummated marriage, and finally a marriage to a woman who has been repeatedly raped by bandits, a marriage that shows Teudisson's magnanimity and also brings him genuine happiness and a family.

The religious motif of *An Odor of Sanctity* adds depth to what would otherwise be an entertaining but rather shallow melodrama. Despite himself, Teudisson becomes a saint by the end of the novel. As a man, Teudisson is handsome but scarred by battle, but as a boy, his beauty, so unlike the usual rough Goth face, led his mother and others to think he was marked for the priesthood. He turns from his religious impulses to lead a secular life, however, and while doing so, he finds his saintliness. In dealing with women, he shows a compassion and love that are the basis of his profound sexual appeal; at one point of seeming dissolution, he has numerous prostitutes loving him because he has talked to them and treated them as human beings and not merely as sex objects. Misused by a woman, he always responds with kindness.

By the end of the novel, Teudisson becomes the arbiter between Moor and Christian factions when a certain group of fanatic Christians wants to destroy all tolerance for the predominant Moors. Throughout the novel, Teudisson has been a genuine ecumenist. At the end, Teudisson, doubting his saintly powers because he is unable to save his wife, willingly seeks crucifixion and thus enters sainthood and legend. In losing himself, he gains sainthood.

As in most of his novels, Yerby's greatest strength in *An Odor of Sanctity* is his re-creation of a time, a re-creation imbued with color and action. Again, a humane authorial voice speaks throughout the novel. The book shows that the diversity of medieval Spain is indeed its glory. While the Moorish culture encourages learning and recognizes Christ as a prophet, the contrasting Christian culture (except for Teudisson and a few Church fathers) is dark and intolerant. In showing the clash between these cultures, *An Odor of Sanctity* is first-rate historical fiction.

The Dahomean

If one of Yerby's novels is destined to last, it is *The Dahomean*, a novel unlike any of his others. It is a simple, moving tale of the life of a black man in his African culture before he was sold into slavery. Yerby neither idealizes nor sensationalizes his material but presents a story composed of love, envy, and hatred that reads as a legend, a story of characters and events drawn larger than life. The protagonist, Nyasanu, is like other Yerby protagonists because he is an alien or outsider: He is far less violent and far more handsome than most men of his society. Caught in the ugliness of the American slave system, he has the tragic quality of some of the great existentialist heroes.

Yerby begins the chronological narrative of Nyasanu as he is about to enter manhood, a passage marked by the painful ritual of circumcision. The early parts of the novel present such rituals in convincing detail. Yerby moves the reader from Nyasanu's initiation to an enemy's attempt to destroy his guardian tree to his wedding and the "deflowering" of his bride. In "A Note to the Reader," Yerby explains that the novel is based on research into the customs of the Dahomeans of the nineteenth century, but Yerby adds to his research his own respect for this African culture.

As Nyasanu moves through his period of manhood, Yerby depicts the society of the Dahomeans as a stage for the great primal emotions and forces of life. Nyasanu has encounters with numerous women, but his sexual experiences are never merely sensational, the stuff of popular fiction: Nyasanu has a reality that sets him apart from Yerby's typical protagonists. In addition to his sexual encounters, Nyasanu has the experience of real brotherhood, for his society expects each male to have his three closest friends identified in order. Battles with warring tribes give Nyasanu the chance to show bravery and also to distinguish himself as more sensitive to violence than the average Dahomean. In addition, Yerby shows the diversity of Dahomean society, which includes both male homosexuals and Amazonian warriors.

In a moving discussion with his number one friend, Kpadunu, Nyasanu learns that the generations are all of one fabric. Each generation faces the same problems of love, the family, and death. The old priests, therefore, give answers based on the past to the young and the unsure, and—given the coherence of their society—the answers generally hold. Facing the problem of belief in the gods that these old priests try to inculcate in the young, Nyasanu realizes that their wisdom is not divine but experiential, that the past of his society answers the present needs. Ironically, his friend Kpadunu is trying to help Nyasanu rise above the control of priests by showing where their wisdom resides, yet he actually makes the skeptical Nyasanu believe more than he did, so that he must face the priestly prediction that his life will end in Dahomey but will begin again in another place.

Nyasanu does learn that he can count on the inexorability of fate and not the protection of the gods. In quick succession, he loses his friend Kpadunu, his wife in childbirth, and his father. He comes to see his heroism as mere foolishness in taking risks. Rather than listening to the gods, he simply faces life as chieftain and husband of Kpadunu's widow. Far more than the ritual of circumcision, his acceptance of life and his rejection of the illusion of divine protection mark Nyasanu's adulthood. When Nyasanu next appears in the novel, he is chieftain and has four wives. His life is successful until he is sold into slavery with the aid of his homosexual brother and rival.

The betrayal of Nyasanu has the archetypal pattern of tragedy, the hero fallen from great heights, undone by his own blindness in not facing the evil of his brother and his incestuous brother-in-law and by his pride in not following the past and living with his extended family in the same compound. He faces the guns of his attackers with his sword, only to be told to put his sword down, for in the modern era, swords are powerless against guns. First, he must watch the murder of his mother (the slavers see that she is too old to have children), the subsequent murder of all his children (the slavers know that they would die on the voyage across the Atlantic), and the subjugation of his wives, the rape of some and the suicide of one. His response is disassociation, a silence that lasts the rest of his life.

Like a classical tragedy, *The Dahomean* treats terrible despair in its conclusion but leads to an illumination, Nyasanu's enlightenment. He recognizes the evil of blacks selling blacks into American slavery, although they have no conception of the degradation of this foreign slavery, their domestic slavery being gentle and indulgent. Philosophically, Nyasanu faces the bleakness of life with the realization that there are no answers. Truth is only that there is no truth. Nyasanu acquits himself with honor; like a great tragic hero, he has his dignity, the dignity of silence in the face of the emptiness of the human condition.

Dennis Goldsberry

Other major works

SHORT FICTION: "Health Card," 1944.

Bibliography

Bloom, Harold, ed. "Frank Yerby." In *Modern Black American Fiction Writers*. New York: Chelsea House,

It was not until 1963, with the publication of his first novel, *A Wake in Ybor City*, that he began to utilize fully the rich material that his Tampa-Manhattan connection provided him.

Analysis

There is a special quality to each of José Yglesias's novels, a kind of aura that seems to tell the reader that he or she is entering a fictional world radically different from the Anglo-American tradition. Although each novel is unique unto itself, there is in all of his novels a definite tension underlying the seemingly natural flow of events, a kind of double vision that stems from Yglesias's diverse and at times conflicting heritage. In New York City while still young, he encountered head-on the rather old and impersonal but nonetheless captivating charm of mainstream America. Yglesias never rejected his Latin roots, and he experienced the tenuous acceptance that is given to all those who succeed in Anglo America's melting pot. The result is a unique mestizo portrayal of American reality.

The vision presented in *A Wake in Ybor City*, *An Orderly Life*, *The Truth About Them*, *Double Double*, *The Kill Price*, and *Home Again* is at once reminiscent of the seventeenth century Spanish picaro and the twentieth century New York intellectual. Like the Peruvian novelist José Maria Arguedas, who committed suicide in 1969, Yglesias presents the world through the eyes of one who belongs simultaneously to two distinct realities. Thus, the reader is treated to a rare opportunity: an inside view of the world as seen from the perspective of a semi-outsider.

A Wake in Ybor City

Yglesias returns to the place of his youth, Ybor City, for the setting of his first novel, *A Wake in Ybor City*. An omniscient third-person narrator recounts three days in the life of a Cuban American family in 1958. The novel's simple structure and fluid style pose no problem to the reader, who quickly finds him- or herself more and more involved in a moving depiction of a family's struggle to face several crises that threaten to destroy their uncommonly close ties with one another.

The story is simple. An aging widow, Dolores, anxiously awaits the arrival of her children, who will be visiting her from Havana, Cuba. Elena, the eldest daughter, is married to a wealthy and influential Cuban aristocrat, Jaime. They are scheduled to arrive the next day with Dolores's other daughter, Clara, and her son, Jimmy. During the two days following their arrival, several unforeseen events occur that rock the very foundation of Dolores's family, perhaps foreshadowing the political upheaval that was to undo Fulgencio Batista's Cuba the following year.

Almost immediately, the reader is introduced to Dolores's extended family. First, there are her two widowed sisters, Mina and Clemencia. Then come the children and their families. Mina's son, Feliz, is a weak man, totally dominated by his mother and equally unsuccessful with other women. He has been married four times. Clemencia's son, Roberto, is visiting for the summer from New York City with his Jewish American (non-Cuban) wife, Shirley, and their two children. Roberto is a struggling artist who, in his idealistic youth (he is now thirty-seven years old) was involved with the political left.

Of all the characters, Roberto comes closest to being Yglesias's alter ego. Dolores, besides her two daughters who are visiting from Cuba, has two sons, one in Miami (Mario) and another one, her youngest, Armando. Although Armando is living at home, he previously had served in the Army, during which time he was married to and later divorced from an American (non-Cuban) girl named Katie. Of all the children, Armando seems the most lost. His association with a local gangster, Wally Chase, distresses his mother. One of the two reasons for Elena's visit to Ybor City is to offer Armando a lucrative position in Cuba. Armando initially refuses this offer but later is forced to accept it when his boss is mysteriously killed. Armando is suspected of involvement in the slaying and flees, with the help of his family, to Cuba. The other reason for Elena's return is to obtain permission from her sister's former husband, Esteban, to adopt Jimmy. Jimmy's sudden and unexpected death, a result of complications that arise after an emergency appendectomy, shocks the reader as well as Dolores's entire family.

What might, at first reading, appear to be a typically melodramatic story, whose unexpected and tragic ending leaves the reader stunned and therefore properly entertained, takes on a somewhat deeper significance upon further reflection. What Yglesias has done in fabricating his tale about a wake in Ybor City is to introduce the Anglo-American reader to some of the characteristic elements of Cuban American life that ordinarily are not accessible to mainstream Americans. In particular, *A Wake in Ybor City* focuses on two important aspects of Cuban American life: the family, and the male's ambivalent role in the family structure.

From the outset, it is clear that Dolores, Mina, and Clemencia are the spiritual as well as the political authorities of this Cuban American family. The fact that the reader never learns their surnames suggests that the matriarchal structure portrayed here is representative of the Cuban American family in general. Moreover, their given names reveal some of the qualities of the typical matriarch. Of the three, Mina (a mine of hidden wealth) is the realist. She is a practical woman whose earthy wisdom constantly returns the family to everyday reality where difficult decisions must be made and their consequences accepted. Clemencia ("Mercy") is a compassionate and understanding woman. Dolores ("Sorrows") is the dominant one among the three and embodies the role of the suffering mother. She is a romantic, a writer of heroic dramas and pastoral poems that reflect her subjective and distorted vision of her family. Together, these three women are the heart, head, and loving arms that control and sustain the life of this Cuban American family. Living as an isolated island within the American mainstream, their primary mission is to protect the family at all costs.

As the novel progresses, it becomes clear that the new matriarch who is to succeed the three aging women is Elena. It is her responsibility to take the reins of authority so that the family structure can continue to exist in relative peace and security. Elena has already helped set up her brother Mario in Miami. It is she who arranges Armando's escape to Cuba, and it is she who is organizing the legal adoption of her nephew, Jimmy, before his untimely death. Perhaps Elena's failure to save Jimmy, the family's youngest, from death is a foreshadowing of the eventual breakdown of the matriarchal family structure. To the extent that the younger members, such as Roberto, decide to leave the security of Ybor City and enter into the mainstream of American (non-Cuban) society, the inhibiting influence of the dominant mother figure will diminish.

The undisputed primacy of women in the Cuban American family gives rise to a particular problem concerning the men, commonly referred to as machismo. Since the male's role in the family is ambivalent at best, he feels pressured to prove his manhood outside the family structure. This machismo is expressed by extramarital sexual conquests or by even more violent manifestations of strength and superiority. Except for Roberto, who has abandoned the matriarchal environment of Ybor City, the other male characters fail miserably in their quest for manliness within the family structure. Feliz, who has been married four times, is still an adolescent psychologically. For him, it is baseball that allows a man to prove his worth. Esteban, although a highly committed revolutionary, can only relate to women as sex objects. Armando, whose marriage to Katie failed shortly after he brought her back home to live with his mother, fears any form of adult responsibility. Even Roberto, who is the strongest of the male characters, has difficulty looking directly at women. Jimmy, the youngest grandson, is virtually smothered by the attention given to him by all the women of the family.

Perhaps the best indication of female superiority is Dolores's criticism of God for having allowed her grandson to die. According to Dolores, her status as one of the family's matriarchs has given her the right to scold God. In such a female-dominated environment, there is little place for the man to feel useful, let alone important. With these insightful vignettes of Cuban American life, *A Wake in Ybor City* introduces the American (non-Cuban) reader to a part of America normally outside his or her experience.

An Orderly Life

Unlike Yglesias's first novel, which described an entire family's struggle to maintain its Cuban American identity in the threatening ambience of a changing Tampa, *An Orderly Life* focuses on one individual: Rafael (Rafe) Sabas. In many ways, Rafe resembles Roberto of *A Wake in Ybor City*. If Jimmy's death prefigured the family's eventual loss of Latin American identity by allowing itself to be absorbed into America's amorphous mass of humanity, Rafe represents the extreme to which one may fall prey to the great American Dream while still carrying within him the seeds of his Latin heritage. Narrated in the first person, *An Orderly*

Evergood, it becomes clear that what appears to be a superficial portrayal of the 1960's is actually a highly original re-creation of an era that was both defined and destroyed by the unbalanced interplay between idealism and realism—with Seth Evergood as the embodiment of this conflict.

The Kill Price

In his fifth novel, *The Kill Price*, which focuses on a theme that is too frequently avoided—death and dying—Yglesias displays a growing mastery over the narrative form. The few but well developed characters (a dying man named Wolf, his wife, and three friends) and the concentration of place and time (Wolf's apartment on the night of his death) permit the reader to share in the fear, the frustration, and ultimately the personal revelation that one inevitably experiences on witnessing the death of a loved one.

The feeling of immediacy that is created by such an intense convergence of time and place is counterbalanced by Yglesias's timely retreats into the thoughts and feelings of the protagonist, Jack Moreno, Wolf's closest friend. Besides the intimacy that Jack's interior monologues allow the reader, the necessary distance for reflection is also established. It is Yglesias's skillful juxtaposition of cinematic-like close-ups and fade-outs that make *The Kill Price* a superbly written novel. Whereas the close-ups capture the magnitude of the moment, subsequent fade-outs transport the reader away from the immediate situation and allow for internalization of events.

The first third of the novel recounts Jack's memories as he walks over to Wolf's West Side apartment. Jack is a successful New York journalist whose cosmopolitan, jet-set lifestyle is in conflict with the values of his Chicano upbringing in El Paso, Texas. He reflects about his past, how he abandoned his story on César Chávez and the farmworkers' movement in Los Angeles to be with T. D., Wolf's wife, when Wolf was forced to return a second time to the hospital, and how his efforts to comfort T. D. eventually led to their having an affair. Further reflections inform the reader about Wolf's past, how he was previously married to Mary Anne, had a son by her, and eventually went through a painful divorce that he later used as material for his novel *Breaking Away*.

When Jack arrives at Wolf's apartment, he is greeted by Carol, a New York actor who was Wolf's girlfriend before he and T. D. were married. Although Wolf is suffering from an advanced case of lung cancer and is near death, the three closest people in his life (Jack, T. D., and Carol) act as if there is nothing terribly wrong, for Wolf has been told that he is recuperating from an attack of pleurisy. Although it is obvious that Wolf is aware of the seriousness of his condition, he, too, plays along in the charade. Wolf's former brother-in-law, Perry, arrives shortly after Jack. A longtime acquaintance of both Wolf and Jack, Perry has never managed to penetrate into their inner circle of friendship. He joins in the tacit deception concerning Wolf's illness, directing Wolf's attention from his present condition by requesting the film rights to his novel. He further distracts Wolf by offering to arrange to have his son, whom Wolf has not seen in more than a decade, come and stay with him and T. D. The charade comes to a sudden end, however, when Wolf dies, leaving his friends behind to deal with death's seemingly unchallenged dominion over life.

Although the actions seems to center on Wolf's untimely death, the novel's true focus is on Jack. His friend's death is but the catalyst that awakens him to his own inner emptiness. Wolf's terminal illness is the most dramatic reminder of death to appear in the novel. There is the death of a neighborhood, depicted by the West Side's deterioration; there is the death by drugs of the black celebrity Tiny Dick, whom Jack had once encountered while flying back to New York; there is the death of a lost love, as experienced by Wolf in his painful divorce from Mary Anne; moreover, the nation itself, presently embroiled in the Watergate fiasco, is in a state of moral decay.

Of all the forms of death present in *The Kill Price*, none is more devastating than the death one experiences on rejecting the truth about oneself. In leaving El Paso, first to go to Iowa for his college education and then on to New York for his career as a journalist, Jack was not going *to* some place as much as he was fleeing *from* some reality—his Chicano heritage. It takes the harrowing experience of seeing his best friend unable to express openly the truth of his imminent death, to force Jack to acknowledge that the life he has been living in New York is no life at all, but a lie. As his surname indicates (*moreno* means "dark"), he is Chicano, and it is by embracing his Mexican American heritage that he will truly begin to live, and therefore know how to die—in dignity and peace.

The vision presented in *A Wake in Ybor City*, *An Orderly Life*, *The Truth About Them*, *Double Double*, *The Kill Price*, and *Home Again* allows the reader a rare glimpse into the schizophrenic existence of the Cuban American attempting to enter the mainstream of American society. Yglesias draws deeply from the well of his dual heritage and shares a refreshingly different perspective on American reality. American society may be likened to a finely woven tapestry whose cultural threads weave in and out, creating an endless array of patterns. Yglesias's novels, by focusing on one particular thread, the Cuban American reality, help the reader to appreciate the unfathomable richness of the multicultural heritage of the United States.

Richard Keenan

Other major works

SHORT FICTION: *The Guns in the Closet*, 1996.

PLAYS: *Chattahoochee*, pr. 1989; *The Dictatorship of the Proletariat*, pr. 1989; *You Don't Remember?*, pr. 1989; *New York 1937*, pr. 1990.

NONFICTION: *The Goodbye Land*, 1967; *In the Fist of the Revolution*, 1968; *Down There*, 1970; *The Franco Years*, 1977.

TRANSLATIONS: *Island of Women*, 1962 (also known as *Sands of Torremolinos*; of Juan Goytisolo's novel); *Villa Milo*, 1962 (of Xavier Domingo's novel); *The Party's Over*, 1966 (of Goytisolo's collection of short stories).

Bibliography

Baskin, Leonard. "José Yglesias." *Tampa Review* 13 (1996). This article examines Yglesias, the literary influence of his work, and his overall literary life.

Hospital, Carolina, and Jorge Cantera, eds. *A Century of Cuban Writers in Florida: Selected Prose and Poetry*. Sarasota, Fla.: Pineapple Press, 1996. Yglesias is one of the thirty-three writers whose work is included in this anthology of Cuban residents of Florida. The editors' introduction examines the historical importance of the Cuban connection to Florida's heritage.

Ivory, Ann, ed. "José Yglesias." In *Contemporary Authors*. Vols. 41-44. Detroit, Mich.: Gale Research, 1974. One of the few critical resources on Yglesias, and a sympathetic one, too. Contains a chronology of his life and discusses his Cuban American background. Examines his interest in recording the lives of Hispanic people and his travels to Spain, and it includes extracts of reviews of *The Kill Price* and other works.

AL YOUNG

Born: Ocean Springs, Mississippi; May 31, 1939
Also known as: Albert James Young

Principal long fiction

Snakes, 1970
Who Is Angelina?, 1975
Sitting Pretty, 1976
Ask Me Now, 1980
Seduction by Light, 1988

Other literary forms

In addition to his fiction, Al Young has produced nonfiction and numerous volumes of poetry, the first being *Dancing* (1969). His twin themes are the American family and individual maturation. Early in the twentieth century, Ezra Pound warned modern poets that music separated from dance will atrophy, as will poetry separated from music. Accordingly, Young's love of the rhythms of life places music between poetry and dance. His second volume of poems is titled *The Song Turning Back into Itself* (1971). Here, the singer of life confronts images of a Whitmanesque America less musical, choral perhaps, but certainly panoramic: The singer's song becomes the poet's vision. In *Geography of the Near Past* (1976) and *The Blues Don't Change: New and Selected Poems* (1982), the music and the dancing continue along

Young's thematic lines of loving and growing. *The Blues Don't Change* incorporates musical rhythms and quotations from Chinese poets into a collection of poems designed to dance with "laughter in the blood." *Heaven: Collected Poems, 1956-1990* (1992) presents a chronological time line of Young's works. *Straight No Chaser* (1994), not to be confused with the biography of Thelonius Monk with the same title (written by Leslie Gourse), is a tribute to the jazz great as well as homage to Young's love of music and his own musical career. *Conjugal Visits, and Other Poems in Verse and Prose* was published in 1996.

In 1981, Young published his autobiographical *Bodies and Soul: Musical Memoirs*, which makes use of specific pieces of music to provide continuity and to set the tone for related essays, each based on personal recollection. Several more books of a similar nature followed: *Kinds of Blue: Musical Memoirs* (1984), *Things Ain't What They Used to Be: Musical Memoirs* (1987), and *Drowning in the Sea of Love: Musical Memoirs* (1995). In 1989, he published a tribute to jazz musician Charles Mingus, *Mingus/Mingus: Two Memoirs*, written with Janet Coleman.

Young's poetry, fiction, and essays have appeared in such publications as *Antaeus*, *Essence*, *Evergreen Review*, *Harper's*, *Journal of Black Poetry*, *The New York Times*, *Paris Review*, and *Rolling Stone*. His work is also represented in many major anthologies and books. Among them are *How Does a Poem Mean?* (1976, edited by John Ciardi and Miller Williams), *The Wedding Cake in the Middle of the Road: Twenty-three Variations on a Theme* (1992, edited by Susan Stamberg and George P. Garrett), *Moment's Notice: Jazz in Poetry and Prose* (1993, edited by Art Lange and Nathaniel Mackey), *Every Shut Eye Ain't Asleep: An Anthology of Poetry by African Americans Since 1945* (1994, edited by Michael S. Harper and Anthony Walton), *Listening to Ourselves: More Stories from "The Sound of Writing"* (1994, edited by Alan Cheuse and Caroline Marshall), and *Berkeley: A Literary Tribute* (1997). Young has also been translated into over a dozen languages. Young has also written screenplays and scenarios for Laser Film Corporation and Stigwood Corporation in New York and for Verdon Productions, First Artists Ltd., and Universal Pictures in California.

Achievements

During the mid-1960's, Al Young founded and edited *Loveletter*, an avant-garde review that has received awards from the National Arts Council. He was the West Coast editor of *Changes* and in 1975 was guest fiction editor of the *Iowa Review*. With Ishmael Reed, he founded and, for a time, edited the biennial anthology *Yardbird Reader* and *Quilt*, pioneering multicultural arts journals, and he was coeditor of *Yardbird Lives!* (1978; with Reed).

A selection of Young's poems and an introductory essay are included in the 1979 anthology *Calafia: An Anthology of California Poets*. *Calafia* is a widely recognized project that examines the poetry of the West Coast, with recognition of a regional tradition extending back through the nineteenth century.

Young was a Wallace E. Stegner Fellow in 1966 and in 1969 was the recipient of the Joseph Henry Jackson Award for his first collection of poetry, *Dancing*. The California Association of Teachers of English selected Young to receive a special award in 1973. Young was a Guggenheim Fellow in 1974, has been a Fulbright Fellow, and received grants from the National Endowment for the Arts in 1968, 1969, and 1974. In 1980, he received the Pushcart Prize for poetry, and in 1982, the Before Columbus Foundation Award.

Biography

Al Young was born Albert James Young, the son of Mary (Campbell) and Albert James Young. He attended the University of Michigan from 1957 to 1961 before moving to the San Francisco Bay Area in 1961. There he received his bachelor of arts degree in Spanish from the University of California, Berkeley, in 1969. He and his wife, Arline June (Belch), were married in 1963 and have a son, Michael James Young.

Among various other jobs, Young's early career included an acting role in a television documentary about Archie Moore, a year as a disc jockey, and, prior to that, eight years as a professional jazz musician. His love of music deeply influences his writing, and music and musicians are often among its subjects.

Young taught writing at the San Francisco Museum of Art during the late 1960's and was linguistic consultant for the Berkeley Neighborhood Youth Corps. From

1969 to 1973, he held Stanford University's Edward H. Jones Lectureship in Creative Writing. He was the 1979 director of Associated Writing Programs, an organization of graduate university administrators, teachers, and students of creative writing; was writer-in-residence at the University of Washington from 1981 to 1982; and served as consultant to the New York writer's organization Poets and Writers in 1974 and 1975.

Young lectured at numerous universities in the United States and traveled extensively in Canada, Mexico, Portugal, Spain, and France. He has also had presentations of his work produced and broadcast by KQED-TV San Francisco and by the Pacifica Radio Network.

Analysis

Al Young's concern for language, a concern that embraces both mistrust and love, is clearly evinced in his prose. His second novel, *Who Is Angelina?*, and his fourth, *Ask Me Now*, have third-person narrative personae who stand close to their author; they appear hesitant to act freely for want of purpose. Readers of the first and third novels, however, will quickly recognize Young's ability to render in his first-person narrative personae a vibrant male voice of new adulthood (*Snakes*) or sagacious middle age (*Sitting Pretty*).

The author's background as a professional musician enables him to use music descriptively as well as metaphorically. The music of language also affects Young's style. Sparingly, he alters standard syntax and diction, sometimes punctuation, in order to set the speech closer to its natural human tone. His objective is not merely to create contemporary dialect but also to create an enduring contemporaneity, to offer rhythmically, as the poet-musician should, the nonverbal meanings that language can carry in its sounds. Young creates this quality of speech through narrative personae who speak softly or stridently, sometimes too literally, yet with voices constant and sincere.

Love, like a curse or a whimper, extends most intensely from the individual to those nearby. The contemporary American social dilemma is thereby represented in Young's prose just as it appears in his poetry: Each person must somehow maintain the unity, fidelity, and consistency love requires while grappling for the freedom and oneness that American mythology promises. Although *Snakes* and *Sitting Pretty* are more successful, all Young's novels contain graphic portrayals of mainstream urban America—middle-class people who try to be good at being themselves. They emote, they dream, and they reason. At worst, they stand too large on the page; at best, they find purpose to complement the dignity they feel. Whether he narrates with commentary from a third-person point of view, or with the immediacy of first-person sensory experience, Young confronts the problems of individuals growing into their individuality, and the qualities of life central to the congregate American family.

Al Young. (© Miriam Berkley)

Snakes

The narrative persona of Young's first novel, *Snakes*, is M. C. Moore, who recollects his youth and adolescence in the mature, seasoned voice of the novel's master of ceremonies. A novel of formation, *Snakes* is in the bildungsroman tradition and is rendered in a tone of voice at once nostalgic and fatherly. Although he has only snapshots of his true parents by which to remember them, M. C. gradually finds their love implanted in his own initialed name, "so it sound[s] like you had some status," his first lover explains, "whether you did or not." For M. C., the process of learning who he is becomes the composition of his own music.

M. C. discovers music in his soul and he makes music the core of his world. He finds music everywhere, "in the streets, in the country, in people's voices," and "in the way they lead their lives." Providing counterpoint, M. C.'s grandmother, Claude, offers guidance and family history, and M. C. is her captive audience: "I could listen to Claude talk all day long, and did, many a time. Her voice was like music." The association expands as his views of love and music merge, and women ultimately become "lovable fields of musical energy."

While living with relatives in the South, M. C. learns at the age of ten that music will be his life. His uncle Donald, a "night rambler" with a "talent for getting hold of a dollar," turns their impoverished household into a "blind pig," or a Meridian, Mississippi, version of a speakeasy. During his first exposure to the amoral world of adults, M. C. meets Tull, an itinerant jazz pianist who in effect provides the novel's premise:

> You'll get it if you keep at it. Listen, just take your time, one note a time over here with your right hand. Just take your time, that's all it is to playin' the piano or anything else. Take your time and work it on out.

The impression lasts; M. C. goes on to structure his life around his love of music and his faith that music will help him grow.

Literature also has a formative effect on him. It is not literature as found in the classroom or in books—M. C. attends high school in body only, and barely earns his diploma—rather, literature personified in Shakes, his closest friend, whose name is short for William Shakespeare. Shakes has a "greedy memory and a razor tongue." He is bright, musical, and funny: "You hip to Cyrano de Bergerac? Talk about a joker could talk some trash! Cyrano got everybody told! Didn't nobody be messin with Cyrano, ugly as he was."

Yet there is more to know about life than its music and its literature; such knowledge appears in the person of Champ, who exposes M. C. to contemporary jazz and the business hemisphere of that musical world. In his bemusing, self-sacrificial way, Champ also demonstrates his worsening drug addiction and the consequential brutalization of his sensibilities. "Poor Champ," M. C. soon observes while he learns to jam, to feel his music come alive inside himself and issue forth, "who wanted to play an instrument so badly, would stand around working his arms and fingers for hours sometimes, shaping the smoky air in the room into some imaginary saxophone.... We all wanted to get good."

The evil to which Champ submits himself opposes the good that he gives M. C.—music as growth and expression. M. C.'s band, the Masters of Ceremony, discover in their art a meaning that transcends the music they produce, and although the group separates after one demo and some local gigs, M. C.'s early success provides him with a clearer view of the possibilities of his life and a deep sense of wonder. He emerges from his plain, ordinary background complete, communicative, and capable of more, having also achieved his own narrative voice, that husky, now masculine voice the reader has heard maturing since the story's outset. He boards the New York bus a musician, grown: "I don't feel free . . . but I don't feel trapped." Awkwardly, painfully, naturally, M. C. has learned to look for the subtle ironies that enrich both life and art. Ready at last for the rest of what he will be, the young adult takes with him his guitar, his music, and precious recordings of his song "Snakes," which throughout the novel parallels his experience of youth: "The tune sounded simple the first time you heard it, but it wasn't all that simple to play."

Who Is Angelina?

While the narrative voice of *Snakes* provides contrast and consistency—a gradual merging of the maturing young man with his adult consciousness—the narrative voice of *Who Is Angelina?* accomplishes neither. Angelina is already grown, but her adult life has entered a phase of meaningless triviality. This she blames on the shifting cultural milieu of Berkeley. Life in Berkeley seems different now—dangerous—and the people's sense of freedom and fun, that community spirit of festivity, is gone. She uses the burglary of her apartment as the justification, and a friend's convenient cash as the means, to skip town—an act she considers prerequisite to introspection. She flees not only her fictional problems but her reader as well, a character with both brains and beauty who struggles with mere communal ennui is less than sympathetic. Moreover, even the reader who can overlook her escapist behavior needs to know more about her, and most of her background is provided through recollection and reminiscence. The novel's principal events—travel in Mexico, some romantic sex, an emergency trip home to Detroit, an encounter with a street thief—facilitate reflection by the viewpoint character, and the reader must simply accept her gradual appraisals. Dramatically, little takes place. Most of this novel is exposition; what little action there is consists of Angelina's consideration of an adaptation to what goes on around her.

The unifying thematic metaphor of *Who Is Angelina?* is the act of taking away: Angelina is robbed (her reaction is passive), her lover's mysterious occupation suggests more of the same, her father is robbed and nearly killed, and a friend's purse is stolen (her reaction this time is spontaneous and violent). Eventually, Angelina's searching appears to reach some sort of resolution that makes her worthy of new self-esteem. The reader, however, cannot participate in this search but can only observe it, because—unlike the composer-narrator of *Snakes*—Angelina does not experience within the narrative a process of growth.

Plainly, Angelina is a woman experiencing a crisis of self-identity during a series of events that propel her toward introspection. What she ultimately discovers within herself is a typical American complex of contradictions, such as the one she describes to a fellow traveler early in her journey, the contradiction Americans create by equating individuality with isolation:

> Angelina explained that in America it's the individual who matters most and that she and her family, such as it was, lived at separate ends of what's called reality. She too was lonely and fed up with a kind of life she'd been leading.

Whether the narrator addresses the reader directly or through the medium of a letter to a former lover, the exposition continues:

> Everyone nowadays is busy digging for roots. Well, I know them well and it doesn't make a damn bit of difference when it comes to making sense of who I am and why I make the kinds of mistakes I do. In the end, I've discovered, it all comes down to being in competition with yourself.

At moments, Angelina's concern waxes angry and the culturally contemplative author intrudes:

> I'm not so sure that all those chitlins, hamhocks, hog maws, pigsfeet, spareribs and cooking with lard—soulfood so-called—isn't contributing more toward bringing about black genocide, as the phrasemongers would have it, than Sickle Cell Anemia.

An important discovery about herself does take place, however, and this is what her wandering is all about. The exploration has been a contemporary one that many young, single Americans never complete: "The truth was that, most of all, she loved open-hearted vulnerable strangers for whom she wasn't strictly obliged to feel anything."

In the end, Angelina also learns that she has been changing at the same time that her surroundings have been changing. Because she has confused one process with another, separation followed by a reassertion of self followed by a return to her point of departure appears to be cathartic. If so, the reader hopes that she also learns that life is and continues to be a process of change, some small part of which is subject to each individual's conscious control. Angelina's recognition of this consciousness is both the special story and the ordinariness of Young's second novel.

Sitting Pretty

Sidney J. Prettymon, the narrative persona of *Sitting Pretty*, is streetwise, sardonic, and ironically self-conscious. He establishes early a mock superstitious mentality—astronauts may mess up the moon so that it can no longer be full—and verbalizes "the integral aspects of [his] personal philosophy to be cool." Prettymon is dangerously learned: "I cut this article out of the *National Inquirer* that maintain how you can succeed and develop yourself and transformate your whole personality by the buildin' up your vocabulary." His inborn sense of linguistic sound combines comically with his interest in discovering associative meanings ("radical chic" connotes to him the concubine of a politically motivated Arab husband of many wives), but the best humor to be found in *Sitting Pretty* is derived from Prettymon's command of the text. The reader is at all times close to Prettymon, and he exploits the closeness. Having pondered his plot-situation at the story's outset, he describes himself to himself as being "on the threshold of destiny, temptation, and fate." Turning aside, he speaks directly to the reader: "Now, that's bad! [good] Let me run through that one again so y'all can savor it."

The narrative opens below the closing sentence of Mark Twain's *Adventures of Huckleberry Finn* (1884); in many ways, Sidney J. Prettymon is a contemporary, self-possessed Jim. As Twain's narrative control allowed him to elevate linguistic puns through burlesque to high satiric levels, Young's narrative is successful here by virtue of its consistently controlled authorial distance: "All I mean by imagination," Prettymon says, "is the way stuff look when you pull back from it and give it some reflection room." Prettymon as first-person narrative persona allows the author to work most effectively; because his imagination provides Prettymon with overview, it allows him to construct connotative ironies.

The incongruous coexistence of common insight and aesthetic misinterpretation (Huck does not misinterpret aesthetic qualities; he misses them entirely) works through sarcastic understatement: "Carpe Diem, like they say in Latin. Save the day." The author's hand moves subtly, characterizing by misquotation.

Like M. C.'s unknown parents, Prettymon has given his son an inspirational name with which to command respect—Aristotle: "He is a lawyer." Professionally successful, Aristotle is a son ungrateful for his name, and working-class Prettymon must struggle to disguise his pride as resentment:

> He go around callin hisself A. Winfred Prettymon. I'm the one give him his first name and that's his way of gettin back at me. I wanted him to stand out and be distinguished and be the bearer of a name that smack of dignity.

Telephoning his daughter, Prettymon again creates linguistic pandemonium, quoting Ralph Waldo Emerson in order to reinforce some fatherly advice, then addressing the reader as the individualistic, proconsumer Henry David Thoreau:

> I hung up fast, then taken the receiver back off the hook again so the operator couldn't ring me back for that extra ten cent. I ain't got nothing but the vastest contempt for the Phone Company. Leeches and rascals! Need to be investigated.

Sitting Pretty is Young's best novel for three reasons: its consistency of viewpoint, the ingenuity of the narrative persona, and Young's control of the language. The last must be perfect for an author to choose suggestive, convincing variations consistent with popular speech. Young's rendering of black dialect for artistic purpose is found throughout his fiction, and it works effectively here. The novel's language is an unconcealed treasure:

> What with all that racket and commotion and the drink I'd just taken, I was startin to feel randy—a term the Professor use, British word for horney—randy for my own private bottle of sweet wine. Got a job lines up and just *know* Aristotle gon spring my Plymouth loose. Celebratin time! Time to do that quiet furlough down to Adamo's again.

Surprised, uniquely joyful, Sidney J. Prettymon rediscovers his treasure again and again.

Ask Me Now

Whereas Young's first and third novels may be paired according to their points of view and the consistency of their narrative voices, *Ask Me Now*, Young's fourth novel, contains narrative weaknesses similar to those found in *Who Is Angelina?* Like Angelina, Woody Knight also finds himself in a world changing at a pace inconsistent with his own ability to change, a major source of frustration for this retired professional basketball player who has always depended on the musical, built-in rhythms of his game. In life on the outside, it seems to Woody, the court lines keep shifting.

The sequence of events that brings crisis and reunion to Woody's middle-class family is, like the catalytic changes Angelina experiences, rather improbable. As the narrative opens, Woody is not trying to control the ball and the players in motion, but a double armload of groceries, rain, a raucous crowd in a shopping mall, the theft of his car, and his wife's winning of a sweepstakes raffle, all in the time it takes to report his loss to a security man who mistakes him for someone he is not. This complexity of absurd events may be American, middle-class normality, but the midlife, change-related distance Woody discovers growing between himself and his wife (the prize she wins is a trip to Reno, America's emblematic city of the free and the damned), his children, and society becomes less believable as the plot progresses.

The kidnapping of his daughter by the street gang who stole his car and hid cocaine in one of its tires provides crisis and denouement, but at the cost of increasing the distance between Woody and the reader. Secondary characters quickly become contemporary types that provide color, not credibility, and a final chase scene produces climactic anger, not release. On Woody's mind as the final seconds tick away—the police and the mobsters in the mysterious limousine move aside—is the "elbow room" he valued so highly on the court, the kind of elbow room Angelina sought in her flight to Mexico City. Although this moment contains a great burst of energy—Woody charging in to rescue his daughter, his family, and himself—the climax rings false: He finds and then abandons his daughter in order to pursue the criminal, whom the police ultimately must rescue from a murderous Woody. Despite rather than because of his heroics, all ends well. New insights are gained by all, including that minority of readers for whom the fiction maintains its illusion of reality.

The unbelievable crime and the stock family crisis notwithstanding, Young's control of language is complemented by the twin metaphors of basketball as dance and music as movement. Woody works the ball along the novel's narrative line with eloquence and style. If what he does and what others do to him are too pat, too contrived, his responses are genuine. Woody is a man both worthy of respect and capable of love. He proves himself. The crisis past, he finds himself renewed, as did Angelina, yet, for the reader, there remains at best an evanescent certainty that Woody's reaction to events, not himself, and his reaction to selected alternatives, not decisions, have brought resolution. Unlike the courageous M. C. and the umbrageous Prettymon, Woody is yet incompletely his own. His story ends, but his score remains tied with time remaining on the clock.

Young's main characters experience their passages with a fortitude that affects their worldviews. M. C. copes with the pressures of adolescence and street danger while Angelina seeks alternatives to her past; Prettymon nurtures his self-concept, and Woody deals clumsily with his midlife crisis: Their stories inform their thoughts and expression. The music and love in their living are heard and felt; the reader wants to dance with them, to celebrate. "Celebratory" is a good word to describe Young's style. His major characters are able to seek and find better versions of themselves when they become able and willing to celebrate what they already are.

Seduction by Light

For his fifth novel, Young again employs a first-person narrative persona, female and clairvoyant. Mamie Franklin is a woman in her forties, rich in impressions and experience. Having grown up in Mississippi an admirer of her namesake and imaginary tutor-yogi Benjamin Franklin, having made those feelings real through writing, having left home early to perform in the style of Dinah Washington with her husband's group, the Inklings, and having married and begotten her son, Benjie, out of wedlock, she lives now in Santa Monica with Burley, the man she loves and whose love is returned until—cataclysmically—Mamie's past and future upheave into the narrative present.

As in *Snakes* and the adventures of Sidney J. Prettymon, there is a running commentary on situation and circumstance along with a steady stream of verbal ironies and satiric asides. Mamie works part time in Beverly Hills as a domestic for Mr. Chrysler and his French wife, Danielle, who live in "a big stockbroker Tudor" graced with eucalyptus, or "Noxema trees." Mamie has the confidence of her employers, in fact their favor, as she drives her Honda Civic (nicknamed Sweepea) up the front driveway and strolls into the house. There she discovers a strange, unclothed woman with toes and fingernails painted black who looks like "a bleached-out, fuzzy-headed raccoon," and a Monopoly board, which compromises Mr. Chrysler ("that man loves to play Monopoly . . . with real money").

This kind of fun—the world according to Mamie

Franklin—enlivens the novel's complication. Regarding the 1970's, that too-short period when black consciousness merged with African American professional development and economic opportunity, Mamie says, "It mighta looked to the public like anything black was gonna make money . . . but that wasn't nothin but an illusion."

More than witty, these quips come from a woman who made her living as a performer during the 1950's, when the business of entertainment reinstituted racial segregation, and who now sees further deterioration in the filmmaking business: "This old brotherhood junk, funny stuff and jive everybody use to be talkin—all that went out the minute the money started gettin shaky." With a tonal admonition for more education, she observes that the film industry is being run by young white men who "started readin *Variety* and *Billboard* when they were nine." For Mamie, age enables one to "ripen into know-how, or better yet, know-when." After all, she says, "The smarter you are, the harder you smart when you fall."

Throughout the novel, light and light imagery brighten the reader's way like the sunlit flowers of Alice Walker's *The Color Purple* (1982) or the moonlit landscapes of Nathaniel Hawthorne's tales. Mamie's vision captures both the brilliance and the business of the California landscape while nuances of Eastern philosophy energize her sensibility and evoke a mood of resolution. Such evocations occur in dreams or dreamlike experiences, such as the surreal state of shock following the reality of an earthquake or the emotional upheaval of sexual renewal. "It was all done with light," Mamie says of cinematic production and marketing. Like the girl she "use to be" watching a film at the Grand Lux Theatre, Mamie learns that "pretty much every last one of us out here [in California] gettin seduced." As girl and as mother, as woman and as lover, Mamie looks over her shoulder to see "nothin but light, not a thing but light quiverin and makin patterns on a screen."

Throughout her life, Mamie has had enlightening experiences. She recalls a vision of sunlight playing over a leaf, how the light "shimmered all around it; then the leaf sends out this invisible feeler [and] suck up the light around it, drink it up, sip on it like you would a glassa buttermilk." Similarly, when Mamie's housemate Burley returns in spirit, he describes his passage from life: "It was like this hole opened up in the middle of my forehead and the light started pourin into it."

Moreover, Mamie contemplates the textuality of her life by the light of her contemplations, suggesting that this affects the storyteller, too:

> Where do you begin when you start tellin your story and rememberin as you go along? Do you start with the source of light itself, the sun? Or do you start with what the sun touches, the moon? Or do you only deal with what the moonlight touches?

We must consider the light by which we live our lives, Mamie suggests, as we rewrite the texts of our lives:

> It's actually possible in one lifetime to do so much and to get caught up in so many of your own illusions and lies and half lies until it can finally come down to sun versus moon versus moonlight.

Celebratory and down-to-earth, Young's novels glow with human warmth. In the mode of vernacular speech, *Seduction by Light* rings true with contemporary experience while transmuting everyday life into the light of love.

Joseph F. Battaglia
Updated by Daryl F. Mallett

Other major works

POETRY: *Dancing*, 1969; *The Song Turning Back into Itself*, 1971; *Geography of the Near Past*, 1976; *The Blues Don't Change: New and Selected Poems*, 1982; *Heaven: Collected Poems, 1956-1990*, 1992; *Straight No Chaser*, 1994; *Conjugal Visits, and Other Poems in Verse and Prose*, 1996; *The Sound of Dreams Remembered: Poems, 1990-2000*, 2001; *Coastal Nights and Inland Afternoons: Poems, 2001-2006*, 2006; *Something About the Blues: An Unlikely Collection of Poetry*, 2007.

NONFICTION: *Bodies and Soul: Musical Memoirs*, 1981; *Kinds of Blue: Musical Memoirs*, 1984; *Things Ain't What They Used to Be: Musical Memoirs*, 1987; *Mingus/Mingus: Two Memoirs*, 1989 (with Janet Coleman); *Drowning in the Sea of Love: Musical Memoirs*, 1995.

EDITED TEXTS: *Changing All Those Changes*, 1976 (of James P. Girard); *Zeppelin Coming Down*, 1976 (of

William Lawson); *Yardbird Lives!*, 1978 (with Ishmael Reed); *Calafia: An Anthology of California Poets*, 1979 (with Reed and Shawn Hsu Wong); *Quilt*, 1981-1986 (with Reed; 5 volumes); *African American Literature: A Brief Introduction and Anthology*, 1996.

Bibliography

Bell, Bernard W. *The Afro-American Novel and Its Tradition.* Amherst: University of Massachusetts Press, 1987. Bell compares Young's *Snakes* to 1960's novels by Gordon Parks, Kristin Hunter, Rosa Gunn, Barry Beckham, and Louise Meriwether.

Broughton, Irv. *The Writer's Mind: Interviews with American Authors*. Vol. 3. Fayetteville: University of Arkansas Press, 1990. Contains a rare and enlightening interview with Young in which he explains his poetic philosophy. This source is widely available and is useful to undergraduate as well as graduate students.

Carroll, Michael. "Al Young: Jazz Griot." In *African American Jazz and Rap: Social and Philosophical Examinations of Black Expressive Behavior*, edited by James L. Conyers, Jr. Jefferson, N.C.: McFarland, 2001. Carroll examines the centrality of music, particularly jazz and blues, to Young's life and writing, demonstrating this aesthetic with an analysis of *Snakes*.

Kirkpatrick, D. L., ed. *Contemporary Novelists*. 4th ed. New York: St. Martin's Press, 1986. This compilation features a condensed biography of Young plus an extensive listing of the author's works through 1982. A useful guide to Young as an emerging American artist, this reference profiles him among novelists of various ethnic backgrounds.

Raynaud, Claudine. "Coming of Age in the African American Novel." In *The Cambridge Companion to the African American Novel*, edited by Maryemma Graham. New York: Cambridge University Press, 2004. Young's book *Snakes* is included in this discussion of African American novels.

Schultz, Elizabeth. "Search for 'Soul Space': A Study of Al Young's *Who Is Angelina?* and the Dimensions of Freedom." In *The Afro-American Novel Since 1960*, edited by Peter Bruck and Wolfgang Karrer. Amsterdam: Gruner, 1982. Young's novel was written in 1975, a time when few works of fiction by African Americans were being published. Schultz analyzes Young's work in terms of the quest for expression, especially the quest of those who are out of the mainstream.

MARGUERITE YOURCENAR

Marguerite de Crayencour

Born: Brussels, Belgium; June 8, 1903
Died: Northeast Harbor, Maine; December 17, 1987
Also known as: Marguerite de Crayencour

Principal long fiction

Alexis: Ou, Le Traité du vain combat, 1929 (*Alexis*, 1984)
La Nouvelle Eurydice, 1931
Denier du rêve, 1934 (*A Coin in Nine Hands*, 1982)
Le Coup de grâce, 1939 (*Coup de Grâce*, 1957)
Mémoires d'Hadrien, 1951 (*Memoirs of Hadrian*, 1954; also known as *Hadrian's Memoirs*)
L'Œuvre au noir, 1968 (*The Abyss*, 1976; also known as *Zeno of Bruges*, 1994)
Anna, Soror . . ., 1981
Comme l'eau qui coule, 1982 (3 novellas; includes *Anna, Soror . . .*, *Un Homme obscur*, and *Une Belle Matinée*; *Two Lives and a Dream*, 1987)

Other literary forms

Marguerite Yourcenar (yewr-suh-NAHR), although best known as a novelist, wrote in virtually every other literary form as well. Her first published work, *Le Jardin des chimères* (1921), was a poem about Icarus. It was followed by a collection of poems titled *Les Dieux ne sont pas morts* (1922). Of these early works she did not speak highly. *Feux* (1936; *Fires*, 1981) is a collection of prose poems about love centered on such characters as Phaedra, Achilles, Antigone, Sappho, and Mary Magdalene, but shot through with images and allusions that reflect the modern world. *Les Charités d'Alcippe, et autres poèmes* (1956; *The Alms of Alcippe*, 1982) is another verse collection.

Pindare (1932) is a study of the Greek poet, another early work with which Yourcenar later became dissatisfied. *Les Songes et les sorts* (1938; *Dreams and Destinies*, 1999) concerns the mythic aspects of dreams. The collection *Sous bénéfice d'inventaire* (1962; *The Dark Brain of Piranesi, and Other Essays*, 1984) includes essays on such diverse subjects as the engravings of Piranesi, the château of Chenonceaux, Selma Lagerlöf, and Thomas Mann. *Mishima: Ou, La Vision du vide* (1980; *Mishima: A Vision of the Void*, 1986) is a study of the Japanese novelist Yukio Mishima. *La Mort conduit l'attelage* (1934) and *Nouvelles orientales* (1938; *Oriental Tales*, 1985) are volumes of short stories. Yourcenar also wrote many plays and translated a number of works into French: the poetry of Constantine Cavafy and Hortense Flexner; a volume of African American spirituals, *Fleuve profond, sombre rivière: Les Negro Spirituals* (1964); and a selection of Greek poetry, *La Couronne et la lyre* (1979). *Le Labyrinthe du monde* (1990), a three-part chronicle of her forebears, comprises *Souvenirs pieux* (1974; *Dear Departed*, 1991), *Archives du nord* (1977; *How Many Years*, 1995), and *Quoi? L'Éternité* (1988). *Les Yeux ouverts: Entretiens avec Matthieu Galey* (1980; *With Open Eyes: Conversations with Matthieu Galey*, 1984) is a series of interviews in which she talks about her life, her values, and her work.

Achievements

Marguerite Yourcenar's greatest achievement is probably *Memoirs of Hadrian*, a novel in the form of a letter written by the emperor shortly before his death. Like nearly all of her mature works, it had a long gestation period—more than a quarter of a century, in fact. She destroyed some early versions of it, and between 1939 and 1948, she put it wholly aside. *The Abyss* is another novel with a long history. The original impulse goes back to the early 1920's, and the final version is a development of material from the first story in the 1934 collection *La Mort conduit l'attelage*. Such perfectionism is seldom rewarded with popular success, however respectful the critics may be. *Memoirs of Hadrian*, however, was not only very favorably reviewed (like most of her previous works) but also widely read by a large and enthusiastic public. It won the Prix Femina-Vacaresco. Yourcenar was awarded the Légion d'Honneur and the National Order of Merit. Other honors she received included membership in the Royal Academy of Belgium, the Prix Combat (1963), the Prix Femina for *The Abyss*, the Grand Prix National des Lettres (1974), and the Grand Prix de la Littérature de l'Académie Française (1977). In 1980, international attention was focused on Yourcenar and her work when she was elected to the Académie Française, becoming the first woman member in that institution's history.

Biography

Marguerite Yourcenar was born Marguerite de Crayencour in Brussels in 1903. Her mother died a few days after Marguerite was born, and she was reared by her father, who supervised her education at home. They would read aloud to each other in French, English, Latin, and Greek. As a child, she lived sometimes at Mont Noir, the family home near Lille in northern France, and sometimes in Paris or the south of France. Her father took her to England in 1914, in flight from the Germans. A year later, they returned to Paris and then fled to the south of France.

In *With Open Eyes*, Yourcenar says that she felt herself and her father to be contemporaries from the time she was about thirteen. He paid for the publication of her first book, *Le Jardin des chimères*, as a Christmas gift, and he helped her to invent the anagrammatic pseudonym that she later made her legal name. He died when she was in her mid-twenties. His portrait is given at length in the second volume of her family chronicle, *How Many Years*.

Yourcenar traveled extensively. She made her first visit to the United States during the winter and spring of 1937-1938. At the beginning of the war in 1939, she returned to the United States at the invitation of an American friend, Grace Frick, whom she had met in Paris two years earlier. Frick became Yourcenar's lifelong companion and her English translator. What was planned as a visit of six months became a permanent change of residence for Yourcenar. For a while she taught French and comparative literature part time. She and Grace Frick (Yourcenar always referred to her by her full name) first visited Mount Desert Island in Maine in the early 1940's, and they eventually bought a house there. Grace Frick died of breast cancer in 1979.

Yourcenar became an American citizen in 1947. Among her many interests were an active concern for the environment. She contributed to a variety of organizations for reducing overpopulation and pollution and for saving whales, seals, trees—whatever is threatened with extinction by avaricious exploiters.

Marguerite Yourcenar. (Jacques Robert, Editions Gallimard)

Analysis

Some of Marguerite Yourcenar's novels have appeared in English, including *A Coin in Nine Hands*, *Coup de Grâce*, *Memoirs of Hadrian*, and *The Abyss*. *A Coin in Nine Hands*, first published in 1934 and extensively revised in 1959, takes place in Rome in 1933 and is thus unlike the other three novels in having (in its first version at least) a contemporary setting. It is also atypical in the number of its important characters. *Coup de Grâce* has only three major characters. *Memoirs of Hadrian* and *The Abyss* have large casts of secondary figures, but each is firmly centered on a single protagonist. *A Coin in Nine Hands*, in contrast, gives fairly full treatment to about a dozen characters, some of them only tenuously connected to one another. The looseness of structure that might have resulted is guarded by the concentration of the time scheme: Though the novel contains a certain amount of retrospective narrative (the past is always a concern for Yourcenar), the main action is confined to a period of about eighteen hours.

A Coin in Nine Hands

The English title of *A Coin in Nine Hands* refers to a unique structural feature of the novel, its tracing of the passage of a ten-lira piece from one character to another. The nine characters who handle the coin, and several others as well, are linked by a network of relationships, often casual or accidental, although none of them sees the whole pattern. The coin, though it is in itself of no great value to any of them and might seem a facile contrivance to a skeptical reader, in fact takes on considerable symbolic weight. In the afterword to the revised version of the novel, Yourcenar calls the coin "the symbol of contact between human beings each lost in his own passions and in his intrinsic solitude." The casual or mechanical nature of many of these contacts is obvious, and the coin, belonging to anybody and finally to nobody in particular, suggests the inability of the characters to form any real bonds with others. In *With Open Eyes*, she offers another meaning for the coin, saying that it represents the external world, the state, all that is opposed to the intimate, secret lives of people. This meaning is also suggested by the title of the play that Yourcenar adapted from the novel, *Rendre à César* (pb. 1961; *Render unto Caesar*, 1984), an echo of Mark 12:17.

Any coin has two sides, and a symbolic coin may well be allowed several. Another meaning is suggested by the French title for the novel, *Denier du rêve*, literally "denarius of the dream." The coin is associated with the characters' dreams or illusions. The reader first sees the coin in the hand of Lina Chiari, a prostitute who received it from a man who has become a regular client since his wife deserted him. The narrator comments that although love cannot be bought, dreams can be, and adds, "The little money Paolo Farina gave Lina each week was used to create for him a welcome illusion; that is to say, perhaps the only thing in the world that does not deceive." Lina, after learning that she must have a mastectomy, uses the coin to buy a lipstick, makes up her face, and forces a smile that gradually becomes sincere: "Party to an illusion that saved her from horror, Lina Chiari was kept from despair by a thin layer of makeup." The storekeeper who sold her the lipstick buys votive candles to petition the Madonna for relief from his domestic problems, and the candles "maintain the fiction of a hope." The candle vendor, learning of the sale of her childhood home in Sicily, to which she has long dreamed of returning, buys coals to light a fire to asphyxiate herself. Marcella, the seller of the coals, passes the coin to her estranged husband as payment for a gun she stole from him, with which she plans to shoot Mussolini. Her husband is in good standing with the Fascists, and she hates herself for still feeling drawn to him in spite of his politics. The gesture of paying for the gun is intended to free her from any debt to him, to purchase an illusion of independence. He, in turn, uses the coin to buy flowers for a stranger to whom he has made love in a film theater, as if to mitigate the sordidness of the encounter. The flower vendor, uneasy at having been called a miser, proves to herself that the charge is untrue by passing the coin to a man that she takes for a beggar. He is in fact a famous painter, old and frightened by increasingly frequent attacks of angina. He throws the coin into the Trevi Fountain, like those tourists who hope to return, but thinking instead that he may soon see a quite different "Eternal City." Finally, under cover of darkness, a worker scoops up the coin with a handful of others and goes to a tavern to purchase a few hours of exaltation and oblivion in drink. Each character uses the coin to maintain a protective illusion or to soften the pain of a loss.

As the foregoing sketch indicates, death is a prominent theme in the novel. Lina thinks of her impending mastectomy as a death. The attempt on Mussolini's life is the novel's central event, and Marcella expects that even if she succeeds she will be killed. She is right. Her most important confederate, a dissident writer named Carlo Stevo who has been deported to Lipari Island, has exerted a potent influence on her and on several other characters, too. Ironically, the reader learns halfway through the book that Stevo has been dead since before the story began. For Marcella the news is a blow, the more so since Stevo's captors seem to have succeeded in breaking his spirit before he died. His death increases the sense of the futility of Marcella's attempt.

The settings often reinforce the novel's emphasis on death. The darkness in Marcella's little bedroom is mentioned repeatedly. As she moves toward the place where she hopes to kill and knows she will be killed, the street becomes a "river of shades . . . carrying along in its waves inert, drowned corpses who thought they were alive." The film theater that is the setting of the immediately succeeding chapter is a "cave full of specters," a version of the underworld of classical myth. The films offer illusory reflections of real life so distorted that they suggest life's opposite. Moreover, the fact that Marcella has been killed is withheld until the end of this scene. Thus, the whole chapter draws together the themes of illusion and death.

The larger setting, the Eternal City itself, is rendered with remarkable economy. There are no extended descriptions or set pieces, yet the city is vividly evoked. Moreover, Yourcenar succeeds in giving it a kind of double identity. There is the Rome of 1933 and, opening out behind it, the long vista of its past, the Rome of history. The characters, too, transcend their particular historical moments through their connections with mythological figures. The 1959 version reduces the frequency of such mythical parallels, but they are still there, giving added dimension to the characterization. Marcella, moving toward her fatal encounter, is "like a Greek woman in Hades, like a Christian one in Dante's Inferno, carrying a burden as old as History itself." It is not a matter of detailed correspondences in the sequence of events or in the relationships among characters, as in, for example, James Joyce's *Ulysses* (1922). Rather, the mythological references arise out of particular situations and character traits. Moreover, a single character may be associated with several mythological figures and a single mythological figure with several different characters, so that the correspondences have the indefiniteness and flexibility of figures in dreams. Thus, Marcella is called Medusa, Judith, Martha, and Mary, and she resembles Electra as well (Mussolini had betrayed her father). The candle vendor sees her feeding pigeons and is reminded of a statue of Venus with her doves, but the candle vendor's sister, a film star, is also a Venus, and a Narcissus, too. A young friend of Marcella and Stevo is also Narcissus, and he is Thanatos and Hermes as well. There is something of Antigone in the candle vendor. The old flower seller is the earth mother, while the worker who takes the coins from the fountain is a kind of Dionysus.

These parallels would be merely empty gestures, however, if the characterization were not so rich and firm in realistic terms. The dozen or so major figures are all interesting and convincing, and there are a good number of secondary ones who are brought fully to life in the space of a few paragraphs. On the whole, the most effective characterizations are of women, and the women carry the story. The novel therefore takes a special place in the body of Yourcenar's work that is available in English, for (along with most of the prose poems in *Fires*) it constitutes an interesting counterbalance to her male-dominated novels. The men in *A Coin in Nine Hands* are often remarkable, but Marcella, Lina, the candle vendor, and the old flower seller are extraordinary.

Coup de Grâce

Coup de Grâce appeared in 1939, only about twenty years after the time of the events it describes. In spite of its modern setting, it is in a sense a historical novel. In her preface, Yourcenar cites dramatist Jean Racine's view that "remoteness in space . . . is almost the equivalent of distance in time." The story is set in Kurland during the Baltic civil wars in the years immediately following World War I, a place and an episode that drew little attention from the rest of Europe. Because of the remoteness of its setting, the novel required patient research and an effort of imaginative projection of a kind similar to that which later went into *Memoirs of Hadrian* and *The Abyss*, though *Coup de Grâce* was written in a matter of weeks, while the other two took years to reach their final forms.

The civil war makes a fitting background for this story of three people locked in a close and ultimately destructive relationship by feelings that—in two of them at least—oscillate unpredictably between love and repulsion. The story (which the author says she heard from "one of the best friends of the principal person concerned") is told in the first person by Erick von Lhomond, a soldier of fortune with a penchant for lost causes. He is a Prussian with some French and Baltic blood. His best friend, Conrad de Reval, is a Balt with some Russian ancestry. There is between them a physical similarity so close that they are often mistaken for brothers. Erick has chosen to limit his experiences with women to commerce with the least respectable of them; his strongest inclinations are homosexual. The circumstances of the narrative (Erick is telling his story to two auditors met by chance in a train station) preclude his dwelling on the nature of his bond with Conrad; in any case, homosexuality is not the main issue in the novel, and Conrad is the least important of the three main characters. The central conflict is between Erick and Conrad's sister, Sophie.

As a young officer, Erick joins a German volunteer corps supporting the White Russians against the Bolsheviks in Estonia and Kurland. Conrad turns up, and the two are posted to Kratovitsy, Conrad's family estate, which had been briefly occupied by the Reds. There Sophie falls in love with her brother's friend. The mixture of bloodlines in Erick and in Sophie suggests their conflicting emotions, and their relationship develops in a pattern of ironic oscillations that reflect the uncertainties of the political struggle.

Because Erick resembles her brother, Sophie's attraction to him seems to involve a kind of transference of an unconscious incestuous impulse. Sophie and Conrad also resemble each other, a fact that complicates Erick's response to the girl. When she confesses her love to Erick, he is stunned, but they develop an intimacy "like that between victim and executioner"—a simile that foreshadows the novel's conclusion. His attitude toward her fluctuates between insolence and tenderness, and "when she began to mean more to me, I suppressed the tenderness." He comes to see her as an adversary whom, in a "show of bravado," he treats as a friend. In an attempt to arouse his jealousy, she turns to promiscuous relations with other soldiers. He remains indifferent to these activities as long as it is obvious to him that she has no pleasure in them.

The turning point in their relationship comes one night when Erick sees a light in Sophie's window during an air attack. He goes to her room and rebukes her for endangering the lives of everyone in the house, but then he himself leads her out onto the balcony. The language and imagery of this scene in which the two perversely court death is full of references to love and sexual consummation as well as to physical cruelty and death. They embrace, but then, in a characteristically abrupt reversal, Erick's "ecstasy changed into horror," and what Sophie sees in his expression makes her recoil, "covering her face with her upraised arm, like a child who is slapped."

In reaction, Sophie takes a new lover, Volkmar, and this time her choice upsets Erick. As Sophie's resentment of Erick begins to outweigh her love for him, his jealousy, ironically, increases. When she ostentatiously kisses Volkmar at a party, Erick slaps her in public, and the ground of their relationship shifts again, for she comes to his door later that night. For fear of waking Conrad, Erick does not admit her, but he finds himself considering marriage to her.

Volkmar tells Sophie of Erick's homosexuality, and she leaves Kratovitsy after a brief but painful confrontation with Erick. Her sympathies have long been with the Bolsheviks, and she sets out to join them, wearing men's clothing provided by the mother of the young man who had converted her to the Red side.

Erick conceals from Conrad his role in Sophie's departure. Conrad's love for his sister turns to hatred, and he begins to believe that she had long been spying on their band for the Reds. Yourcenar underlines this reversal with one of those paradoxes that are a feature of her gnomic style. Erick says that the brother and sister grew to be complete strangers "such as only two members of the same family can manage to become." In this novel, hatred grown out of love is the strongest kind, just as a civil war is often the bitterest of wars.

It is not long after Sophie's flight that Erick summarizes the political developments that are weakening the anti-Bolshevist cause and comments, "Europe was betraying us." The public events thus seem to reflect the personal situation. They are forced to abandon Kratovitsy. Erick is in command. Conrad is killed in a skirmish with some Cossack cavalry and is thus spared the next engagement, in which Erick's troop captures Sophie with a small band of Bolshevik soldiers. Neither side is taking prisoners. In a final interview, Sophie rejects with indifference Erick's efforts to find a way to save her. Here and in the final scene, the language and certain gestures repeat the love theme in inextricable conjunction with its opposite, as had been the case in the scene on the balcony. The next morning, after the other prisoners have been shot by the butcher from Kratovitsy, who now serves as executioner for the troop, Sophie's turn comes. She indicates to her former family servant that she wants Erick to pull the trigger. He does so. He interprets her request at first as conclusive proof of her love. "But I understood afterwards that she only wished to take revenge, leaving me prey to remorse." He remarks wryly, "One is always trapped, somehow, in dealings with women."

As he prepares to fire at Sophie, Erick says, "I clung to the thought that I had wanted to put an end to Conrad, and that this was the same thing." Conrad had lain dying all night in the cemetery where the Cossacks had attacked them, and Erick says that cowardice prevented his putting an end to his friend's agony. This cowardice, however, is clearly not fear for his own safety, for, at Conrad's request, Erick lights "one of those iron lanterns that they hang on the tombstones in that region," in spite of the risk of its drawing enemy fire.

Through the reference to the possibility that the lantern would draw enemy fire, which recalls the scene between Erick and Sophie on the balcony, and through Erick's thinking of Conrad's death as he fires at Sophie, the link between the brother and the sister is reaffirmed, and it seems that the reader is to regard the terrible end of Sophie as another heroic death. She chooses her own fate and even appoints her executioner, thus gaining the upper hand over Erick, whom she at last forces to do her bidding. Her choice, moreover, raises him to the level of tragic heroism. Erick does not dwell on it (his personality, Yourcenar warns in the preface, often leads him "to offer the least favorable interpretation of his actions"); to administer the coup de grâce in this case surely requires as much courage as to request it. The ending, though grim, fully justifies the connotations of chivalric nobility carried by the novel's title.

Memoirs of Hadrian

Memoirs of Hadrian resembles *Coup de Grâce* in that it is a first-person monologue in which a character confronts his past. This is a device Yourcenar used often and favored, because, as she says in the preface to the earlier novel, it eliminates the author's point of view and puts the reader in immediate contact with a character looking directly at his own life. The monologue is here cast in the form of a letter from the dying emperor to the young Marcus Aurelius. In *With Open Eyes*, Yourcenar says that when she unexpectedly recovered a draft of the opening of the novel in 1948 (in a trunk that had been stored in Switzerland during the war), she found its tone, that of an intimate journal, inappropriate for the character. The Romans kept no journals in the contemporary sense of the term, so something rather more formal and organized was required. Her approach depends heavily on her ability to portray a voice actually speaking; in fact, in "Reflections on the Composition of *Memoirs of Hadrian*" (appended to later editions of the novel), she calls the book a "portrait of a voice."

In *With Open Eyes*, Yourcenar remarks on a similarity between Hadrian and Erick. They are alike in being at once hard and tender, and alike, too, in their lucidity. Another obvious parallel is their bisexuality, though Erick's is actually something of a technicality: He is a misogynist who has had little pleasure in his relations with women. Hadrian's attitude toward women is more positive. As a young man, he had a string of mistresses whom he genuinely enjoyed, and his nonphysical relationship with Plotina, the wife of his predecessor Trajan, shows that his deeper friendships are not limited by considerations of gender. (Here, too, historical authenticity comes into play: Yourcenar notes in *With Open Eyes* that exclusively homosexual individuals were rare in antiquity.) For Hadrian, however, as for Erick, the fully satisfying relationship is with one of his own sex—namely, the Bithynian youth Antinous. Just as Conrad may have died to save Erick's life, Antinous's suicide is a ritual offering that the youth believes will in some mystical way extend Hadrian's life. Hadrian's indirect responsibility for Antinous's death can be compared to Erick's more direct responsibility for Sophie's. Yourcenar has called Hadrian "a man who was *almost* wise." Hadrian fails in wisdom, by a growing insensitivity to the youth's feelings, as he comes to take him increasingly for granted. Antinous's suicide is a complex act. It is both a gift and a reproach, and Hadrian sees that he has been master of Antinous's destiny but that he "must leave to the boy the credit for his own death." Similarly, Erick credits Sophie "with the initiative for her death."

Memoirs of Hadrian, however, is a larger book in every sense than *Coup de Grâce*; the paradoxical link between love and hatred and the mysterious affinity between love and death make up only one of its themes. Antinous, whom Hadrian calls "that fair stranger who each loved one is," is only one of several characters who evoke in the emperor an acute sense of the separateness of others. His friends Plotina and Attianus were present at the death of Trajan and may have been responsible for Hadrian's being named the successor. One of the few other witnesses, an enemy of Hadrian, died suddenly, shortly after Trajan did. Hadrian has never known for certain to what lengths his friends had to go in order to secure for him the imperial succession.

In addition to the impenetrable isolation in which the most fundamental parts of people's experience is wrapped, Hadrian is concerned at the start of the book with the shapelessness of his own life. By the end, however, one's strongest sense is not of shapelessness but of a clearly defined arc, or—to use a figure the author herself invokes in *With Open Eyes*—a pyramid. One follows Hadrian through the years of his education and his preparation for power, to the high point of public glory combined with personal happiness, thence to the loss of Antinous and a correspondingly important defeat in the public sphere—namely, the Jewish revolt under Simon Bar-Kochba. The phase of decline continues through the death of the brilliant and charming Lucius, whom he had adopted as his successor; the struggle for patience under the burden of failing health; and the difficult preparation for the attempt "to enter into death with open eyes." Without ever denying the considerable role of chance, the narrative succeeds in imposing a pattern on experience. Moreover, the emperor overcomes to some extent the isolation of the individual self, for he takes the reader with him virtually as far as he himself can go in the contemplation of his past and in the experience of his approaching death. Indeed, it seems possible to say that the reader comes to know Hadrian better than Hadrian knew Antinous or Plotina.

The convincing characterization proceeds in part from an imaginative identification that Yourcenar has described in terms almost mystical, "a method akin to controlled delirium," as she says in "Reflections on the Composition of *Memoirs of Hadrian*." In *With Open Eyes* (which takes its title from Hadrian's last words), she speaks of the necessity of cultivating an interior silence that enables her to hear what the characters have to say. She also mentions a letter from a university professor who had set his students the exercise of translating a page of the novel into Greek (the language in which the emperor says he thought). Yourcenar decided to try to do the same and found that much of it went easily into Greek, but one or two phrases did not. The reason, she concluded, was that they were hers, not Hadrian's. In "Reflections on the Composition of *Memoirs of Hadrian*," speaking of the choice of a first-person narrative, she remarks, "Surely Hadrian could speak more forcibly and more subtly of his life than could I." She says, too, that at some moments it even occurred to her that the emperor was lying. "In such cases I had to let him lie, like the rest of us." Through her method of intense contemplation, her characters take on an independent reality that she succeeds in conveying to her readers. Speaking in *With Open Eyes* of the death of the central character in *The Abyss*, she says that she loved him too much to be willing to make him suffer greatly.

In spite of the semimystical terms in which Yourcenar discusses this contemplative preparation, it is firmly grounded in preparation of a different kind—long and painstaking historical research. Her bibliographic note attests the thoroughness and range of her reading of both primary and secondary sources, and professional historians have endorsed her scholarship. For her, the public and political aspects of Hadrian's life are at least as important as the private and philosophical. He was a man of action as well as of letters. She says in *With Open Eyes* that she would not have seen the statesman if she had written the novel earlier, and in "Reflections on the Composition of *Memoirs of Hadrian*" she remarks, "The fact of having lived in a world which is toppling around us [during World War II] had taught me the importance of the Prince." With remarkable economy, the novel succeeds in conveying the extent of the emperor's public achievements: his encouragement of trade, his interest in founding and rebuilding cities, his administrative reforms, his fostering of the culture of Greece, his reversal of the expansionist policies of Trajan in order to concentrate on a policy of stability within the existing frontiers of the already vast empire, and his commitment to peace. In Hadrian, supreme political power was united with an incisive and disciplined intellect as well as with a highly developed artistic sense. The convincing presentation of all of his facets evidences Yourcenar's extraordinary gifts, and *Memoirs of Hadrian* is perhaps the most persuasive justification of the often maligned genre of the historical novel that the twentieth century has produced.

The Abyss

The Abyss is a third-person narrative with, for the most part, invented rather than historical characters (though the author's note validates many of the details of the story by citing parallels from the lives of real people). The hero is, like Hadrian, a man who seeks to be useful. Zeno, a physician, identifies himself at one point with the words, "I take care of my fellow men." The novel is set in a time of unrelenting religious and political conflict, the mid-sixteenth century, and it is in every way a darker book. Its theme, as the epigraph to part 1 indicates, is freedom and people's ability to choose. In "Reflections on the Composition of *Memoirs of Hadrian*," Yourcenar says that in the second century "men could think and express themselves with full freedom," and Hadrian's position as emperor made his own freedom all the greater. In Zeno's world, however, freedom is narrowly circumscribed. Zeno must plant obscure passages in his books to avoid being accused of heresy, and even with this precaution his writings are often suppressed. When he returns to Bruges, his birthplace, after half a lifetime of travels, he must conceal his true identity. Figurative and literal references to prisons and traps occur throughout the book. "Who would be so besotted," Zeno asks at the beginning of his travels, "as to die without having made at least the round of this, his prison?" He refers to the body as a prison, and he ends his life in an actual prison. On the eve of his death, he is offered the opportunity to save himself from the fire by recanting: He can win physical freedom at the price of his intellectual freedom. Having concealed a scalpel among the few personal belongings left to him, he has one last liberty of choice, but he realizes that he could be deprived of even this by a chance intrusion of his jailer or a priest. Only at the moment of his death does he finally feel free. He had once heard of a man burned at the stake at the end of a long chain that enabled him to run about in flames until he fell. "I have often reflected that that horror could serve as allegory for the plight of a man who is left *almost* free."

That is one of a large number of references to fire, which serves as the other of the book's two governing images. In an early scene in which Zeno is sitting by a hearth, the narrator calls him "the companion of the fire." Zeno has been a student of alchemy, and the many images of fire are directly or indirectly related to the use of that element in alchemical experiments. Transformations analogous to those at which alchemy aimed are everywhere stressed, though they tend to be baleful ones. The plague transforms its victims overnight. During a rainstorm in Innsbruck, air and water "turn the world into one vast, melancholy chaos." The human bowels perform an alchemy that proceeds constantly, in secret and independent of the conscious will. Life passes into corruption. Neither are these changes restricted to the physical level. Zeno learns that "ideas die, like men." John Calvin's doctrines are "rebellion transformed into law." The hidden meanings Zeno puts into his works "alter the whole." Knowledge and contemplation can be transmuted into power.

In alchemy lie the fumbling beginnings of modern chemistry. This search represents people's attempt to gain control over the processes of nature. In a long chapter at the center of the novel, a chapter whose importance is indicated by its having the same title as the novel itself, Zeno contemplates his past. He had turned away from alchemy, impatient with its encumbrance of arcane metaphors, to study "such sciences as are less imbedded in the stuff of dreams." Now, however, he finds that

> the two branches of the curve, the metaphysical and the pragmatic, were meeting; the *mors philosophica* had been accomplished: The operator, burned by the acids of his own research, had become both subject and object, the experiment that he had thought to confine within the limits of the laboratory had extended itself to every human experience.

Later in the novel, Zeno remarks that alchemy, like magic, postulates the unity of matter, and the chapter titled "The Abyss" describes a kind of visionary insight into that unity. It is full of images of things and people merging and fusing, images of the breaking down of the boundaries of time and space. Zeno himself passes through the changes that turn water to mist and rain to snow, and he unites himself with the element of fire. Zeno's experience in this chapter reflects that phase of alchemical experiment called "the black work" (the novel's French title is *L'Œuvre au noir*). According to the author's note, this is the first and "most difficult phase of the alchemist's process, the separation and dissolution of substance." The term may be applied to both "daring experiments on matter itself . . . [and to] trials of the mind in discarding all forms of routine and prejudice."

The kind of correspondence that the last quotation establishes between two different activities recurs in other forms throughout the book. The Renaissance concept of the relation between macrocosm and microcosm appears in Zeno's statement that mathematics, mechanics, and alchemy "apply to our study of the universe only those same truths which our bodies teach us; for in our bodies is repeated the structure of the Whole." The abyss through which Zeno passes is "both beyond the celestial sphere and within the human skull." Zeno bases his limited faith in astrology on the system of correspondences, and he calls the human heart a "fiery star palpitating in the dark of our bodies." He goes so far as to conceive of the possibility of roads in time like those in space.

Of the various areas of human experience in which transformations comparable to those of alchemy are seen to occur, two gradually assume special prominence in the pattern of the novel: religion and sex. They are linked to each other and to alchemy by a network of analogies and images. Zeno returns to Bruges in the company of the prior of a monastery of the Cordeliers, whom he met by chance in Paris. The two become friends, and the Prior gives the physician the use of a small building attached to the monastery, in which Zeno opens a dispensary for the poor. In one of their conversations, the Prior mentions an alchemical theory that Jesus Christ is the true Philosopher's Stone and that the magnum opus of the alchemists is equivalent to the transubstantiation of the bread and wine into the body and blood of Christ in the Mass. Zeno says that this shows merely "that the human mind has a certain bent," yet it is surely an important indication of the bent of the author's mind. Moreover, the link thus suggested is reinforced by the very fact of the friendship between the scientist and the churchman, a bond so strong that Zeno stays in Bruges longer than is safe because the Prior is dying and the physician will not abandon him. One night, Zeno hears footsteps hurrying toward his door. No one is there, but he goes to the Prior and finds him on the point of death. At the moment of his own death, Zeno again hears footsteps. Yourcenar says in *With Open Eyes* that they are those of the Prior.

A link between sex and religion is established early in the novel, in the powerful chapter describing the way the religious enthusiasm of the Anabaptists in Münster transformed itself into debauchery under the leadership of John of Leyden. More important are the events that lead to Zeno's arrest in Bruges. A young monk named Cyprian, who assists Zeno in the dispensary, tries to lure him to join in the clandestine meetings of several young monks with a girl of good family and her servant. Their orgies involve eating and drinking the consecrated bread and wine and addressing each other in the language of a heretical sect that Zeno thought had been suppressed years earlier. Zeno is arrested on false testimony obtained from Cyprian under torture. Though his judges do not credit Zeno's participation in the debauchery, his revelation of his true identity enables them to charge him with the authorship of heretical books. Zeno reflects more than once on the special severity that the Church reserves for sexual offenses, and, as one of Yourcenar's bisexuals, he is particularly struck by the fact that the punishment for homosexual activity is the same as that for heresy.

The triangle is completed by the figurative linking of sex with alchemy: "The abandoned underground room [in which the monks and the girls were accustomed to meet] was truly a magic chamber; the great flame of carnal desire had power to transmute everything, as did the fire of the alchemist's furnace."

The Abyss is a remarkable example of the kind of historical novel in which the past is clearly related to present realities. It reflects some of the most pressing problems of modern life. In Zeno's world, war rather than peace is the norm, oppressive institutions threaten personal liberties, and change has begun to proceed too rapidly to be readily integrated. The enormously wealthy banking families that have sprung up are "a greater danger to the established order of things than the infidel Turk, or the peasants in revolt"; they are effecting a radical shift in the basis of power. The problems of industrialization and automation are foreshadowed in the passages concerning certain mechanical looms, which in his youth Zeno helped to design and which, instead of easing the lot of the workers, facilitate their exploitation by the owners. Late in life, Zeno realizes that he shares in the guilt for human suffering: As "any other artificer would have done," he sold his formula for liquid fire to the Emir Noureddin. The passage points directly to the ethical problems of individual responsibility that are raised about modern scientific research. Zeno foresees the possibility that "some Phaeton could one day set fire to the earth of his own accord. . . . Who knows but what some baneful comet will emerge one day from our alembics?" His reference to "the stupid and ever-increasing primacy of sheer numbers" is a warning of the dangers of overpopulation. There is even a reference to the theory of relativity when Zeno imagines roads in time like those in space.

Most reviewers judged *The Abyss* a lesser achievement than *Memoirs of Hadrian*. Perhaps it is less accessible in some ways. The lack of a prominent love interest may disappoint some readers, and its vision is, without doubt, a dark and pessimistic one. The narrative line in the earlier novel is a fairly straightforward, chronological one, whereas *The Abyss* tends more toward a fragmented, elliptical, and discontinuous presentation, especially in the descriptions of Zeno's travels. An episode may at first be only sketched or alluded to, with the details filled in later. The sense of disunity that this may create for the hasty reader is exacerbated by the fact that several times in the novel the focus switches to experiences of other characters in which Zeno has little or no part. Such is the episode of the Anabaptists in Münster. The thematic relevance of that chapter, however, is not hard to see, and the same can be said for other scenes that might at first appear to be digressions. Throughout the novel, the author's vivid imagination is controlled by a coherent intelligence. On its own terms, *The Abyss* is a notable achievement, with aims and virtues different from those of *Memoirs of Hadrian*.

John Michael Walsh

Other major works

SHORT FICTION: *La Mort conduit l'attelage*, 1934; *Nouvelles orientales*, 1938 (*Oriental Tales*, 1985); *"Conte bleu," "Le Premier soir," "Maléfice,"* 1993 (*A Blue Tale, and Other Stories*, 1995).

PLAYS: *Électre: Ou, La Chute des masques*, pb. 1954 (*Electra: Or, The Fall of the Masks*, 1984); *Rendre à César*, pb. 1961 (*Render unto Caesar*, 1984); *Le Mystère d'Alceste*, pb. 1963; *Qui n'a pas son Minotaure?*, pb. 1963 (*To Each His Minotaur*, 1984); *Théâtre*, 1971 (partial translation *Plays*, 1984).

POETRY: *Le Jardin des chimères*, 1921; *Les Dieux ne sont pas morts*, 1922; *Feux*, 1936 (*Fires*, 1981); *Les Charités d'Alcippe, et autres poèmes*, 1956 (*The Alms of Alcippe*, 1982).

NONFICTION: *Pindare*, 1932; *Les Songes et les sorts*, 1938 (*Dreams and Destinies*, 1999); *Sous bénéfice d'inventaire*, 1962 (*The Dark Brain of Piranesi, and Other Essays*, 1984); *Souvenirs pieux*, 1974 (*Dear Departed*, 1991); *Archives du nord*, 1977 (*How Many Years*, 1995); *Mishima: Ou, La Vision du vide*, 1980 (*Mishima: A Vision of the Void*, 1986); *Les Yeux ouverts: Entretiens avec Matthieu Galey*, 1980 (*With Open Eyes: Conversations with Matthieu Galey*, 1984); *Le Temps, ce grand sculpteur*, 1983 (*That Mighty Sculptor, Time*, 1988); *La Voix des choses*, 1987; *Quoi? L'Éternité*, 1988; *Le Labyrinthe du monde*, 1990 (autobiography; includes *Souvenirs pieux*, *Archives du nord*, and *Quoi? L'Éternité*).

TRANSLATIONS: *Les Vagues*, 1937 (of Virginia Woolf's novel *The Waves*); *Ce que savait Maisie*, 1947 (of Henry James's novel *What Maisie Knew*); *Présentation critique de Constantin Cavafy*, 1958 (of Cavafy's poetry); *Fleuve profond, sombre rivière: Les Negro Spirituals*, 1964 (of African American spirituals); *Présentation critique d'Hortense Flexner*, 1969 (of Flexner's poetry); *La Couronne et la lyre*, 1979 (of Greek poetry); *Le Coin des "Amen,"* 1983 (of James Baldwin's play *The Amen Corner*); *Blues et gospels*, 1984 (of American songs).

MISCELLANEOUS: *Œuvres romanesques*, 1982.

Bibliography

Armbrecht, Thomas J. D. *At the Periphery of the Center: Sexuality and Literary Genre in the Works of Marguerite Yourcenar and Julien Green.* Atlanta: Rodopi, 2007. Comparative study of the two twentieth century writers focuses on the depiction of homosexuality in their novels and plays. Includes selected bibliography.

Farrell, C. Frederick, and Edith R. Farrell. *Marguerite Yourcenar in Counterpoint.* Lanham, Md.: University Press of America, 1983. Provides an introduction to Yourcenar's novels and essays along with brief biographical material. Includes chronology and bibliography.

Frederick, Patricia E. *Mythic Symbolism and Cultural Anthropology in Three Early Works of Marguerite Yourcenar: "Nouvelles orientales," "Le Coup de grâce," "Comme l'eau qui Coule."* Lewiston, N.Y.: Edwin Mellen Press, 1995. Focuses on Yourcenar's use of symbolism and mythology in her early fictional writings. Introduction and conclusion contain valuable insights into all of her writing. Includes notes and bibliography.

Horn, Pierre. *Marguerite Yourcenar.* Boston: Twayne, 1985. Reliable introductory study presents a biographical chapter, two chapters on *Memoirs of Hadrian*, a chapter on Yourcenar's autobiographical works, and another on her writing in other genres. Includes chronology, notes, and annotated bibliography.

Howard, Joan E. *From Violence to Vision: Sacrifice in the Works of Marguerite Yourcenar.* Carbondale: Southern Illinois University Press, 1992. Offers a textual analysis of Yourcenar's major novels, short stories, and plays, focusing on the episodes of sacrifice in these works and the cultural meanings attached to the sacrifices.

Rousseau, George. *Yourcenar.* London: Haus, 2004. Biography describes Yourcenar's "life of contradictions," one element of which was that she was a lesbian who wrote primarily in the voice of a gay man. Epilogue examines the question "Is Yourcenar a gay writer?" Includes chronology, list of Yourcenar's works, and secondary bibliography.

Saint, Nigel. *Marguerite Yourcenar: Reading the Visual*. Oxford, England: Legenda, 2000. Examines Yourcenar's historical novels, including *Memoirs of Hadrian*, and her lesser-known essays from the perspectives of art history and critical theory. Includes bibliography and index.

Sarnecki, Judith Holland, and Ingeborg Majer O'Sickey, eds. *Subversive Subjects: Reading Marguerite Yourcenar*. Madison, N.J.: Fairleigh Dickinson University Press, 2004. Collection of essays focuses on the issues of self, desire, and "the other" in Yourcenar's work. Includes analyses of *Memories of Hadrian* and *Coup de Grâce*. Contains bibliography and index.

Savignau, Josyane. *Marguerite Yourcenar: Inventing a Life*. Translated by John E. Howard. Chicago: University of Chicago Press, 1993. Provides a reliable and well-annotated account of Yourcenar's life and also examines the significance of the author's literary contributions. Includes family tree, notes, and bibliography.

Shurr, Georgia Hooks. *Marguerite Yourcenar: A Reader's Guide*. Lanham, Md.: University Press of America, 1987. Addresses topics such as Yourcenar's experimental fiction, her fictional studies of politics, and women in her fiction. Devotes a chapter to discussion of *Memoirs of Hadrian*. Includes a chronology, notes, a bibliography of books and articles about Yourcenar, and a bibliography of Yourcenar's works in English translation.

Z

YEVGENY ZAMYATIN

Born: Lebedyan, Russia; January 20, 1884
Died: Paris, France; March 10, 1937
Also known as: Yevgeny Ivanovich Zamyatin; Evgenii Ivanovich Zamiatin

Principal long fiction

Uyezdnoye, 1913 (novella; *A Provincial Tale*, 1966)
Na kulichkakh, 1914 (novella; *A Godforsaken Hole*, 1988)
Ostrovityane, 1918 (novella; *The Islanders*, 1972)
My, 1927 (wr. 1920-1921; corrupt text), 1952 (*We*, 1924)
Bich bozhy, 1939

Other literary forms

The Russian literary lexicon includes a number of terms relating to prose fiction that have no exact equivalents in English. Among these is the term *povest'*, defined by Alex M. Shane in his study of Yevgeny Zamyatin (zuhm-YAWT-yihn) as "a fictional narrative of intermediate length"; as Shane notes, this term "frequently has been translated into English by the somewhat nebulous terms 'long short story,' 'short novel,' or the pejorative 'novelette.'" Shane himself prefers "tale" as a translation of *povest'*, but many readers will find "novella" the most useful equivalent.

Zamyatin published roughly a half dozen *povesti*, or novellas, in addition to several dozen short stories, including fables and other forms of short fiction. The dividing line between his short fiction and his long fiction is not always clear-cut, however, and to trace the development of his distinctive narrative techniques, one must consider his fiction as a whole.

Zamyatin was an influential critic and literary theorist as well as a writer of fiction, publishing articles on such writers as H. G. Wells, O. Henry, Anatole France, Andrey Bely, Anton Chekhov, and Maxim Gorky and devoting several broad essays to the evolution of art in general. In these essays, Zamyatin developed an interesting theory of artistic change based on a Hegelian dialectic.

Writing on Russian literature, Zamyatin perceived a "thesis" in the realism of the 1890's and early twentieth century, represented by writers such as Chekhov and Gorky. The "antithesis" came in the form of the Symbolist movement: The Symbolist writers delved into aspects of reality lying beneath the surface of everyday life; their literary techniques became more complex than those of the realists as they tried to capture the inner essence of things. Finally, a synthesis appeared in the form of neorealism, the representatives of which depicted everyday life with the knowledge that there is more to life than appears on the surface. While focusing on everyday reality, they utilized the complex techniques developed by the Symbolists to convey their visions with more power and verisimilitude. Zamyatin considered himself a neorealist along with Bely, Anna Akhmatova, Osip Mandelstam, and others. Zamyatin's observations on Russian art and literature help to illuminate a complicated period in the history of Russian culture.

In addition to his essays and prose fiction, Zamyatin also wrote several original plays, adaptations, and film scenarios. His first two plays, *Ogni svyatogo Dominika* (pb. 1922; *The Fires of Saint Dominic*, 1971) and *Attila* (pb. 1950, wr. 1925-1927; English translation, 1971), depict historical subjects: The former exposes the repressiveness of the Spanish Inquisition, while the latter deals with the epoch of the struggle between ancient Rome and its barbarian invaders. Later works include *Afrikanskiy gost* (pb. 1963; wr. 1929-1930; *The African*

Guest, 1971), an original farce on accommodation to the Soviet system, and several adaptations of other writers' work for the screen. His most successful adaptation was of Gorky's *Na dne* (pr., pb. 1902; *The Lower Depths*, 1912) for Jean Renoir's film *Les Bas-fonds* (1936).

Achievements

Yevgeny Zamyatin's most impressive contribution to world literature is his satiric anti-utopian novel *We*, which he wrote from 1920 to 1921. A biting portrayal of a society in which the human spirit is curbed by a totalitarian state, *We* had an important influence on George Orwell's *1984* (1949). In his own country, however, Zamyatin's shorter prose works made a greater impact than his novel, which was not published in the Soviet Union until 1988. His innovative approach to narrative technique helped to shape the writing style of a number of contemporaries, and this impact was doubly enhanced by Zamyatin's role as literary critic and teacher in the post-Revolutionary period. Among those who attended Zamyatin's lectures on art and literature were writers Lev Lunts, Nikolay Nikitin, Veniamin Kaverin, and Mikhail Zoshchenko. Zamyatin's unique prose style and his unrelenting criticism of philistinism and human injustice have lost none of their power over the years, and his work continues to retain its vitality and relevance today.

Biography

The son of a rural schoolteacher, Yevgeny Ivanovich Zamyatin was born in the small town of Lebedyan on January 20, 1884. Located on the Don River, the town lies in the heart of old Russia, and Zamyatin notes that it was famed "for its cardsharpers, gypsies, horse fairs, and the most vivid Russian speech." Provincial Russia would figure prominently in Zamyatin's later fiction, but in his youth, he took little interest in it. Instead, his childhood was marked by a keenly felt isolation. Having few playmates, he regarded books as his real companions. Learning to read at the age of four, he called Fyodor Dostoevski and Ivan Turgenev his "elders" and Nikolai Gogol his "friend."

In 1896, after four years at the local school, Zamyatin enrolled in the *Gymnasium* (college-preparatory secondary school) in Voronezh. Six years later, he finished school with a gold medal, which he immediately pawned when he went to St. Petersburg to study naval engineering. During the next few years, he took classes at the Petersburg Polytechnic Institute, spending his summers working in shipyards and factories throughout Russia. He developed an interest in politics, and he soon joined the Bolshevik Party. During the frenetic political turmoil of St. Petersburg at the end of 1905, Zamyatin was picked up in a mass arrest and was forced to spend several months in solitary confinement; he spent his time in jail writing poetry and studying English. In the spring of 1906, he was released and exiled to Lebedyan, but he could not bear the torpor of the provincial town, and he returned to St. Petersburg illegally. It was not until 1911 that his true status was discovered, and he thus escaped renewed exile for several years.

In the interim, Zamyatin had graduated from the institute and had become a practicing naval engineer; in 1911, he was appointed lecturer at the institute. Moreover, he had just published his first stories: "Odin" (alone), which appeared in 1908, records the saga of an imprisoned student revolutionary who commits suicide because of frustrated love, and "Devushka" (1909; the girl) contains a similarly tragic theme of unfulfilled love. Neither story is the work of a mature artist, but both show that Zamyatin was already experimenting with prose technique. His first successful work was the novella *A Provincial Tale*, which he wrote from 1911 to 1912 during the weeks of seclusion in the country following his exile from the capital. This exposé of stagnation and cruelty in rural Russia sparked a glowing critical response upon its publication in 1913, while his next major novella, *A Godforsaken Hole*, so offended the authorities by its portrayal of inhumanity in a provincial military garrison that they confiscated the magazine in which it appeared.

In 1916, Zamyatin went abroad to work on icebreakers in England, where he wrote and gathered material for two satiric works, *The Islanders* and "Lovets chelovekov" (1922; the fisher of men), which depict the constrained reserve of the British with exceptional skill. After the abdication of Czar Nicholas II in 1917, Zamyatin returned to St. Petersburg and immersed himself in literary activities. During the years from 1917 to 1921, he completed fourteen stories, a dozen fables, a play, and the novel *We*. Zamyatin's works from this period exhibit a wide variety of styles and interests. They include stories that examine the undiluted passions still found in Russia's backwaters, such as "Sever" ("The North," 1966); stories that depict the struggle to preserve humanistic impulses in the difficult conditions of urban life after the Revolution, such as "Peshchera" ("The Cave"), "Mamay," and "Drakon" ("The Dragon"); and ribald parodies of saints' lives, such as "O tom, kak istzelen byl inok Erazm" ("The Healing of the Novice Erasmus").

In addition to writing fiction, Zamyatin gave lectures on writing to young authors in the House of Arts in Petrograd, held significant positions in literary organizations such as the All-Russian Union of Writers, and served as an editor for several journals and publishing ventures, including the World Literature publishing house. The immediate post-Revolutionary period was a time of intellectual ferment. In literature, all topics came under debate—the goals of literature, the proper style and technique for the age, and the relationship of literature to the Revolution itself. On one side of the debate were those groups that called for the creation of proletarian and socially useful literature; on the other were those who believed that literature should be free from any ideological direction. During this period, Zamyatin had considerable influence as a critic and literary mentor. His superbly written articles and speeches attracted a large audience and provoked a wide response.

Throughout his work, Zamyatin adopted the position of a perpetual opponent to the status quo. He attacked every kind of conformity and all attempts to channel a writer's output into an ideologically uniform direction. In his essay "Ya boyus" (1921; "I Am Afraid," 1970), he wrote that "true literature can exist only where it is created, not by diligent and trustworthy officials, but by madmen, hermits, heretics, dreamers, rebels and sceptics." Behind this stand lay a deep, humanistic concern for the individual's spiritual freedom in an era of growing absolutism. The spirit of defiance that had marked his student days in St. Petersburg had not faded, and in fact Zamyatin was in the process of developing a romantic philosophy of revolution that colored many of his articles, speeches, and fictional works.

In essence, Zamyatin believed in perpetual revolution, the ultimate effect of which is to combat what he termed "entropy"—stagnation, philistinism, static and vegetable life. All truths are relative; there is no final truth. It is the obligation of the heretic, the visionary, the imaginative writer to work for the revolution and the distant future. Attainment of one's goal paradoxically becomes defeat, not victory, because the result would be stagnation, not continuation of the struggle. Zamyatin never called for bloody revolution in the streets; on the contrary, he would protest at every manifestation of humankind's inhumanity to humans. His ideal seemed to be a balance of the rational and irrational in people, but his fear of stagnation and regimentation fired his imagination and resulted in his romantic concept of infinite revolution.

Yet, even if one dismisses these ideas as rhetoric, Zamyatin's earnest campaign for the rights of the individual was dangerous enough in a state that condemned individuality and glorified the collective. In 1922, Zamyatin was arrested along with 160 other intellectuals whose activities were considered undesirable. An order for his deportation was signed by the notorious head of the secret police, G. G. Yagoda. Unknown to Zamyatin, however, and very likely against his will, a group of writers and friends succeeded in having the order rescinded. When Zamyatin was released in 1923, he applied for permission to leave the country but was refused.

Zamyatin's production of prose fiction declined sharply after this incident, in part as a result of deepening involvement in his editorial and administrative duties, his growing interest in the theater, and the increasing influence of politics on the realm of literature. The political situation in the Soviet Union became more rigid during the mid-1920's. Joseph Stalin was then in the process of consolidating his dictatorial powers; he introduced the first Five-Year Plan into the economy late in 1928, and with it came a kind of Five-Year Plan in literature, too. A writers' organization named the Russian Association of Proletarian Writers (RAPP), headed by the strident critic Leopold Averbakh, began to dominate the literary arena and with the tacit approval of the party sought to discredit and harass all of those writers who deviated from their ideal of "artisans" producing ideologically sound works about the social benefits of the Five-Year Plan and collectivization.

Zamyatin, who had for some time been known as an "inner émigré," became one of the chief targets of this campaign of vilification. Productions of his plays were canceled, publishing houses were closed to him, and various writers' groups took turns criticizing him. In particular, he was reproached for "extreme individualism" and hostile attitudes toward the principles of Marxism-Leninism and class warfare. Yet Zamyatin, who had written in 1926, "a stubborn, unyielding enemy is far more deserving of respect than a sudden convert to communism," did not break down and confess his "errors" as others did.

Finally, in 1931, Zamyatin wrote a letter to Stalin asking permission to go abroad with the right to return "as soon as it becomes possible in our country to serve great ideas in literature without cringing before little men." Through the intercession of Gorky, Zamyatin's request was granted, and he left in November of that year with his wife. In Paris, he worked on translations, screenplays, and the first part of a novel, *Bich bozhy* (the scourge of God). He hoped to travel to the United States, where he could continue his work in drama and film, but his plans never reached fruition. He died on March 10, 1937.

Analysis

In his essay "Sovremennaya russkaya literatura" (1956; "Contemporary Russian Literature," 1970), Yevgeny Zamyatin contrasts the narrative style of the realists to that of his own generation. He writes,

> By the time the Neorealists appeared, life had become more complex, faster, more feverish. . . . In response to this new way of life, the Neorealists have learned to write more compactly, briefly, tersely than the Realists. They have learned to say in ten lines what used to be said in a whole page.

His own work demonstrates how consistent he was in his search for a concise yet vivid narrative manner. Throughout his career, he experimented with language, imagery, colors, and sounds to craft his own personal narrative voice.

A Provincial Tale

The outlines of Zamyatin's mature narrative manner are evident in his first major prose work, the novella *A Provincial Tale*, written in 1911-1912. Zamyatin traces the life of a loutish brute named Anfim Baryba, from the moment he is thrown out of his house by his father, through an oppressive affair with a fat widow, a career of theft and dishonesty, and the attainment of a job as a police officer as a reward for betraying a close friend through perjury in a criminal court case. Zamyatin's treatment of Baryba's life highlights the callousness and ignorance that prevail in the primitive backwaters of Russia, and reflects his personal antipathy for stagnant, prejudice-ridden life. Heightening the verisimilitude of this dark vision is the colloquial narrative tone Zamyatin adopts in the story. This distinctive tone, in which the neutral language of an objective narrator is replaced by language drawing heavily on the vernacular of spoken Russian, is termed *skaz*, and Zamyatin's use of *skaz* reflects the influence of such writers as Nikolay Leskov and Alexey Remizov.

On the other hand, the devices that Zamyatin utilizes in character description already bear the hallmarks that later distinguish his mature work. A favorite method of characterization is the identification of a character with an object, animal, or distinctive physical attribute. With this device, Zamyatin can stress a character's personality traits and signal the presence of that character merely by mentioning the established association. When Chebotarikha, the widow with whom Baryba has an affair, first enters the story, Zamyatin notes that she was "spread out like dough." Later, when Baryba begins his liaison with her, Zamyatin writes, "Baryba turned around and . . . sunk his hands deep into something soft as dough." The scene concludes, "Baryba drowned in the sweet, hot dough." Finally, when the woman discovers Baryba's infidelity, she "shook like dough that's risen to the edge of the bucket." It is interesting to note that Zamyatin's penchant for concise yet striking forms of expression does not create a feeling of lightness in *A Provincial Tale*. His tone is somber, and images of stasis and grime prevail, as when the narrator sums up the life of his village: "And so they live in peace, sweating like manure in the heat."

By the end of the 1910's, Zamyatin had developed the vibrant, expressionistic style of *A Provincial Tale* to its fullest extent. His depiction in "The Cave" of Petrograd's urban landscape during the arduous winters following the Russian Revolution remains one of the most impressive representations of that city in Russian literature, which has a long tradition of exposing the unreal or fantastic aspects of the city. For this work, Zamyatin isolates the elements of darkness and cold on a winter night in Petrograd and weaves from them a broad "mother metaphor," to apply a term used by the critic D. S. Mirsky in his book *Contemporary Russian Literature, 1881-1925* (1926). Zamyatin once described his predilection for creating extended metaphoric images: "If I firmly believe in the image . . . it will inevitably give rise to an entire system of related images, it will spread its roots through paragraphs and pages."

The central image here casts Petrograd as a prehistoric, Ice Age setting and the city's inhabitants as cave dwellers who have regressed into a primitive lifestyle that includes worshiping the "greedy cave god: the castiron stove." Isolating one couple, Martin Martinych and his wife, Masha, Zamyatin records how the customs of civilization give way to the more primal instincts for survival. Needing fuel for the stove, Martin struggles with his urge to steal his neighbor's wood. As Zamyatin describes it, there were two Martins "locked in mortal combat: the old one, who loved Scriabin and who knew he must not, and the new one, the cave dweller, who knew—he must." In the frozen wasteland of this city, all choices are bad, and Zamyatin's taut narrative manner heightens the aura of entrapment and despair.

We

Zamyatin's other memorable urban setting—the futuristic city of the novel *We*—transcends the boundaries of contemporary Russia and attains dimensions of universality. Influenced by his readings of H. G. Wells's utopian writings and repelled by the inflamed rhetoric of the new Soviet state, Zamyatin constructed an antiutopian novel that both amuses the reader with its ironic humor and unsettles the reader with its startling prediction of totalitarian repression.

Written in the form of a journal by D-503, an engineer building a rocket ship to carry the ideals of the United State to less advanced worlds where people may still languish "in the primitive state of freedom," *We* describes a world in which nearly every action of its citizens is carried out according to strict schedules set by the government and its ruler, the Well-Doer. Even sexual activity is regulated by a rigid system of registration and appointments. Beneath the comic aspects of this society, however, lie such troubling phenomena as rigged elections, denunciations of one's fellow citizens, and the torture and execution of political dissidents.

The plot of the work centers on D-503's discovery of elements within himself that do not harmonize with his belief in order and control—the irrational emotions of love and passion. The object of his arousal is a female number, I-330, a member of a revolutionary group seeking to overthrow the government and to revitalize the world by reintroducing into society the energies of a primitive people who live beyond the Green Wall encircling the United State. I-330's conversations with D-503 contain the ideological message of the novel. An advocate of perpetual revolution, she articulates the fundamental concept that two forces exist in the world—entropy and energy: "One leads into blessed quietude, to happy equilibrium, the other to the destruction of equilibrium, to torturingly perpetual motion." She, of course, prefers the latter, but her revolutionary plans are uncovered by the secret police, the Guardians, and at the end of the novel, the forces of the United State seem to be winning the battle: I-330 has been arrested, and D-503 has undergone an operation to remove the source of his pain—his "fancy."

We unfolds at a rapid pace. D-503's journal entries are laconic, often breaking off in midthought; as in his other works, Zamyatin relies on bold imagery in characterization and description. Thus D-503 notes with shame that he has hairy, apelike hands—an indication of atavistic tendencies within him—while I-330 is distinguished by her black, slanting eyebrows, which form an X on her face—a kind of mathematical variable or unknown that troubles D-503. Zamyatin also makes use of vivid sounds and colors. At times, his manipulation of sounds recalls the prose of Andrey Bely, and his use of color creates an intense network of symbolic associations. Red, for example, is the color of blood and fire, and it is associated with the revolution and surging passion, while pink, a diluted version of red, is the color of the official forms through which the state regulates sexual contact. Zamyatin's handling of color and sound reflects his conviction that "a word has color and sound. From now on, painting and music go side by side."

Mathematics provides another major source of imagery in *We*. D-503 loves the precision of the multiplication tables and abhors imaginary and irrational numbers. Zamyatin's own support for the concept of the irrational in human affairs filters through D-503's opposition to it, and the reader recognizes that the writer owes a substantial debt to the works of Fyodor Dostoevski, particularly his *Zapiski iz podpolya* (1864; *Notes from the Underground*, 1913) and *Bratya Karamazovy* (1879-1880; *The Brothers Karamazov*, 1911). Reminiscent of the former work is the glass-enclosed world of the United State, in which human happiness is calculated according to exact mathematical formulas. This recalls the diatribe of Dostoevski's underground man against a world in which all human facts will be listed in something like logarithmic tables and people will be urged to live in an indestructible crystal palace. Zamyatin even invokes specific imagery used by Dostoevski. The underground man's animosity toward the "stone wall" of mathematics, symbolized in the simple equation $2 \times 2 = 4$, is echoed by D-503's ardent love for this same formula.

From *The Brothers Karamazov*, Zamyatin draws on the parable of the Grand Inquisitor to underscore his distaste for a self-serving ruling order that boasts of having eliminated individual freedom of choice for the sake of human happiness. *We* is a remarkably resonant piece of writing. Fusing dark dimensions of human oppression with light notes of affectionate satire, Zamyatin's novel remains an impressive model of the anti-utopian genre.

After several years of working in the charged narrative mode of the early 1920's, Zamyatin gradually began to simplify his narrative techniques, and the tight austerity of his late fiction endows that body of work with understated power. The writer himself commented on the conscious effort he made to achieve this kind of effective simplicity: "It turned out that all the complexities I had passed through had been only a road to simplicity. . . . Simplicity of form is legitimate for our epoch, but the right to simplicity must be earned."

Zamyatin's evolution as a writer reflects the conscious striving of a dedicated artist, and the work he produced as a result consistently exhibits high quality. His innovative approach to narrative and descriptive techniques lends his fiction a special vibrancy and life, while his sensitivity to the demands of the human spirit and his aversion to all forms of repression add moral depth to his art. Although Zamyatin's work appeared as a draft of fresh air in the 1910's and 1920's, its appeal far transcends that time, and he has earned a place of lasting significance in the history of modern Russian literature.

Julian W. Connolly

Other major works

Short fiction: *Bol'shim detyam skazki*, 1922; *Nechestivye rasskazy*, 1927; *Povesti i rasskazy*, 1963; *The Dragon: Fifteen Stories*, 1966.

Plays: *Ogni Svyatogo Dominika*, pb. 1922 (*The Fires of Saint Dominic*, 1971); *Blokha*, pr. 1925 (*The Flea*, 1971); *Obshchestvo pochetnikh zvonarei*, pr. 1925 (*The Society of Honorary Bell Ringers*, 1971); *Attila*, pb. 1950 (wr. 1925-1927; English translation, 1971); *Afrikanskiy gost*, pb. 1963 (wr. 1929-1930; *The African Guest*, 1971); *Five Plays*, 1971.

Screenplay: *Les Bas-fonds*, 1936 (*The Lower Depths*, 1937; adaptation of Maxim Gorky's novel *Na dne*).

Nonfiction: *Gerbert Uells*, 1922 (*H. G. Wells*, 1970); *Kak my pishem: Teoria literatury*, 1930; *Litsa*, 1955 (*A Soviet Heretic*, 1970).

Miscellaneous: *Sobranie sochinenii*, 1929 (collected works); *Sochineniia*, 1970-1972.

Bibliography

Brown, Edward J. "Zamjatin and English Literature." In *American Contributions to the Fifth International Congress of Slavists*. Vol. 2. The Hague, the Netherlands: Mouton, 1965. Discusses Zamyatin's interest in, and debt to, English literature stemming from his two-year stay in England before and during World War I.

Cavendish, Philip. *Mining the Jewels: Evgenii Zamiatin and the Literary Stylization of Rus'*. London: Maney, 2000. A thorough study of the folk-religious background of Zamyatin's sources of inspiration. It traces his attempts to reconcile the folkloric tradition and the vernacular through his artistic expression. In the process, drawing from the past and from the language of the people, he creates literature that is basically modernistic.

Collins, Christopher. *Evgenij Zamjatin: An Interpretive Study*. The Hague, the Netherlands: Mouton, 1973. In this ambitious study, Collins advances a rather complex interpretation of Zamyatin, mostly of *We*, based on Carl Jung's ideas about the conscious, the unconscious, and individualism.

Cooke, Brett. *Human Nature in Utopia: Zamyatin's "We."* Evanston, Ill.: Northwestern University Press, 2002. Cooke interprets the novel from the perspective of evolutionary psychology, analyzing its creation, style, content, and fascination for readers; he places the novel within the context of other works of utopian and dystopian fiction. Includes an index and a bibliography.

Kern, Gary, ed. *Zamyatin's "We": A Collection of Critical Essays*. Ann Arbor, Mich.: Ardis, 1988. A collection of essays on Zamyatin's magnum opus, covering the Soviet view of the novel, mythic criticism, aesthetics, and influences and comparisons. Edward J. Brown's essay "*Brave New World*, *1984*, and *We:* An Essay on Anti-Utopia" offers a particularly incisive comparison of dystopian novels by Zamyatin, Aldous Huxley, and George Orwell.

Richards, D. J. *Zamyatin, a Soviet Heretic*. New York: Hillary House, 1962. An overview of the major incidents and issues in Zamyatin's life and work; an excellent, brief presentation of all facets of a very complex writer.

Russell, Robert. *Zamiatin's "We."* London: Bristol Classical Press, 2000. In the first part of the book, Russell discusses the novel within the context of the Russian civil war, when readers interpreted it as a satire on Soviet life; he also surveys major trends in modern criticism of the novel. The second part provides his own detailed analysis, based on a close reading of the "entries" in the protagonist's diary.

Shane, Alex M. *The Life and Works of Evgenij Zamjatin*. Berkeley: University of California Press, 1968. An unusually comprehensive overall study of Zamyatin in English. Shane covers Zamyatin's life and the most important features of his works, chronologically, in a scholarly but not dry fashion, and reaches his own conclusions. Includes extensive bibliographies.

Slonim, Mark. "Evgeny Zamyatin: The Ironic Dissident." In *Soviet Russian Literature: Writers and Problems, 1917-1977*. 2d ed. New York: Oxford University Press, 1977. Slonim offers a good portrait of Zamyatin as a leading literary figure of his time.

ÉMILE ZOLA

Born: Paris, France; April 2, 1840
Died: Paris, France; September 28, 1902
Also known as: Émile-Édouard-Charles-Antoine Zola

Principal long fiction

La Confession de Claude, 1865 (*Claude's Confession*, 1882)
Le Vœu d'une morte, 1866 (*A Dead Woman's Wish*, 1902)
Les Mystères de Marseille, 1867 (*The Flower Girls of Marseilles*, 1888; also known as *The Mysteries of Marseilles*, 1895)
Thérèse Raquin, 1867 (English translation, 1881)
Madeleine Férat, 1868 (English translation, 1880)
La Fortune des Rougon, 1871 (*The Rougon-Macquart Family*, 1879; also known as *The Fortune of the Rougons*, 1886)
La Curée, 1872 (*The Rush for the Spoil*, 1886; also known as *The Kill*, 1895)
Le Ventre de Paris, 1873 (*The Markets of Paris*, 1879; also known as *Savage Paris*, 1955)
La Conquête de Plassans, 1874 (*The Conquest of Plassans*, 1887; also known as *A Priest in the House*, 1957)
La Faute de l'abbé Mouret, 1875 (*The Abbe's Temptation*, 1879; also known as *Albine: Or, The Abbé's Temptation*, 1880; better known as *The Sin of Father Mouret*, 1904, 1969)
Son Excellence Eugène Rougon, 1876 (*Clorinda: Or, The Rise and Reign of His Excellency*

Eugène Rougon, 1880; also known as *His Excellency*, 1897)
L'Assommoir, 1877 (English translation, 1879; also known as *The Dram-Shop*, 1897)
Une Page d'amour, 1878 (*Hélène: A Love Episode*, 1878, also known as *A Love Affair*, 1957)
Nana, 1880 (English translation, 1880)
Pot-bouille, 1882 (*Piping Hot*, 1924)
Au bonheur des dames, 1883 (*The Bonheur des Dames*, 1883; also known as *The Ladies' Paradise*, 1883)
La Joie de vivre, 1884 (*Life's Joys*, 1884; also known as *Zest for Life*, 1955)
Germinal, 1885 (English translation, 1885)
L'Œuvre, 1886 (*His Masterpiece*, 1886; also known as *The Masterpiece*, 1946)
La Terre, 1887 (*The Soil*, 1888; better known as *Earth*, 1954)
Le Rêve, 1888 (*The Dream*, 1888)
La Bête humaine, 1890 (*Human Brutes*, 1890; better known as *The Human Beast*, 1891)
L'Argent, 1891 (*Money*, 1891)
La Débâcle, 1892 (*The Downfall*, 1892)
Le Docteur Pascal, 1893 (*Doctor Pascal*, 1893; previous 20 novels [*La Fortune des Rougon* through *Le Docteur Pascal*] collectively known as *Les Rougon-Macquart* [*The Rougon-Macquarts*, 1896-1900])
Lourdes, 1894 (English translation, 1894)
Rome, 1896 (English translation, 1896)
Paris, 1898 (English translation, 1897, 1898; previous 3 novels collectively known as *Les Trois Villes*)
Fécondité, 1899 (*Fruitfulness*, 1900)
Travail, 1901 (*Work*, 1901)
Vérité, 1903 (*Truth*, 1903; previous 3 novels collectively known as *Les Quatre Evangiles*)

Other literary forms

Émile Zola (ZOH-luh) is remembered today chiefly as a prolific novelist and as the outspoken defender of Captain Alfred Dreyfus, who had been falsely sentenced for disclosing French military secrets to German authorities. This defense reached its apex in an open letter to the president of the French Republic. (Georges Clemenceau, editor of *L'Aurore*, the journal in which the letter appeared, titled it "J'accuse.") Although the letter precipitated Zola's trial for libel and his exile to England, it helped bring about Dreyfus's pardon in 1899 and his ultimate exoneration in 1906. While Zola was praised as a man of courage and honesty for his role in the Dreyfus affair, he had already gained national and international renown for his work as a novelist. His literary reputation rests solidly on his fiction, especially on the multivolume work known as *The Rougon-Macquarts*.

Zola had first intended, however, to be a poet. Having come under the influence of Alfred de Musset while a schoolboy, Zola wrote several poems, the most notable of which are the three parts of *L'Amoureuse Comédie* (written 1860; the loving comedy). When he showed his poetry to his employer, the publisher Louis Hachette, in 1862, Hachette advised Zola to turn to prose. As a result, Zola wrote his first book of short stories, *Contes à Ninon* (1864; *Stories for Ninon*, 1895), a mixture of highly Romantic tales in the style of Victor Hugo, a story of disillusionment that shares in the dark side of the Romantic tradition, and the satiric "Aventures du grand Sidoine et du petit Médéric," which takes a Voltairean look at the politics of the Second Empire at home and abroad. Some of the attitudes and themes of *Stories for Ninon* anticipate Zola's concerns in *The Rougon-Macquarts*. This is even more the case with his *Nouveaux Contes à Ninon* (1874; new stories for Ninon), a collection containing several autobiographical pieces, *souvenirs*, and sketches of characters who would appear in one or more of his novels. In addition to these two collections for Ninon, Zola's contribution to the anthology of short fiction *Les Soirées de Médan* (1880), "L'Attaque du moulin" ("The Attack on the Mill"), ranks him as one of the nineteenth century's great storytellers. *Les Soirées de Médan* was inspired by an evening of reminiscing about the Franco-Prussian War and was named for Zola's country house; its publication is an important event in the history of French naturalism, and Zola's particular contribution marks a high point in the development of naturalistic fiction, a point he would surpass with his installment of *The Rougon-Macquarts* for 1880, *Nana*.

Zola's defense of naturalism as a literary and dramatic theory and practice in several of his mature critical works, principally in *Le Roman expérimental* (1880; *The Experimental Novel*, 1893), *Les Romanciers naturalistes* (1881; *The Naturalist Novel*, 1964), and *Le Naturalisme au théâtre* (1881; *Naturalism on the Stage*, 1893), reveal him as a deft controversialist who advanced significantly beyond the prorealist posture of his first collection of essays, *Mes haines* (1866; *My Hates*, 1893). This earlier work, a collection of his journalistic efforts and addresses, provides an interesting view of the young Zola forming opinions and points of view that would surface later in his novels and in his criticism as he progressed from an advocate of realism to the leader of the naturalist movement.

Like his poetry, and unlike his criticism and fiction, Zola's dramatic efforts met with little or no success. *Thérèse Raquin* (pr., pb. 1873; English translation, 1947), a dramatic presentation of his 1867 novel, was a short-lived failure. A much worse critical reception greeted his *Les Héritiers Rabourdin* (pr., pb. 1874; *The Rabourdin Heirs*, 1893), a reception that united him with the fraternity of Gustave Flaubert, Edmond de Goncourt, Alphonse Daudet, and Ivan Turgenev, who met with Zola once a month in 1874 for a "Dinner of the Hissed Authors." After another of his plays, *Le Bouton de rose* (pr., pb. 1878; the rosebud), was judged a complete failure, Zola wisely withdrew from the theater, although the theater greatly attracted him, figured prominently in his critical work, and formed the background against which he set *Nana*.

Achievements

Hailed as "the French Charles Dicken" and, in the funeral eulogy delivered by Anatole France at the Montmartre cemetery, as "a moment of human conscience," Émile Zola claims many achievements, the foremost of which are his place as a great master of French fiction and his campaign to defend Dreyfus. Zola spoke to the people of Paris about their lives, conditions, aspirations, dreams, and failures; he also spoke out, in their hearing, about the injustice perpetrated on Dreyfus and the whitewash of injustice by officialdom—and he suffered self-imposed exile for his outspokenness. He achieved a kind of heroic status, then, by a prodigious literary output and by his courage and will to be heard as a citizen.

His passion for truth in the fictional representation of life is fundamental to his theory of realistic treatment that came to be called naturalism. Likewise, his passion for truth in the Dreyfus affair led him to proclaim in *Le Figaro*, on November 25, 1897, "Truth is on the march, and nothing will stop it." His prediction proved correct; Dreyfus was pardoned in 1899.

Zola's principal achievement is in his advocacy and practice of naturalism. Zola argued for naturalism in the theater as well as in fiction, but while he superbly illustrated that theory in his novels, he did not succeed in doing so in his plays. Zola's dramatic achievement, in fact, lies more in the influence he exerted on dramatists of his time than in his own work as a playwright. His short fiction is, like the novels, remarkable for its realism and naturalism, although some of the early stories clearly hark back to a fresher, possibly more innocent brand of Romanticism than that for which he is famous. Indeed, realism and naturalism may be seen as hybrids, late flowerings of a decayed Romanticism.

Zola's essays, critiques, and reviews from the 1860's onward, in a wide variety of French journals and in the Russian *Vestnik Evropy*, form another dimension of his achievement as an accomplished chronicler of his own times, a keen observer and acute critic of society, a controversial literary theorist, and a political commentator of acuity and courage.

Largely in consequence of the controversial nature of his fiction, the charges of obscenity that attached to it, and the naturalistic portrayal of humanity, Zola never achieved the one honor to which he aspired, election to the Académie Française, for which he presented his name each year from 1890 on. He was elected president of the Société des Gens de Lettres in April, 1891, and was received into the Légion d'Honneur in 1888. The accounts of Zola's state funeral provide some of the most moving tributes to his achievement as a writer and as an individual. His cortege was greeted by the people of Paris with cries of "Germinal!" and "Glory to Zola!" Anatole France's eulogy provoked great applause. Six years later, in June, 1908, Zola's ashes were removed from Montmartre in a formal public ceremony and placed in the Panthéon in Paris, alongside the remains of Voltaire, Jean-Jacques Rousseau, and Hugo; this ceremony raised again the controversies surrounding the Dreyfus case and inflamed public opinion on both sides of the issue. As in life, so well beyond his death, Zola remained and still remains a figure of controversy, not only for his role in the Dreyfus affair but also for the trenchancy of his writing. Zola had also seized the consciousness and imagination of the French in other ways: During his lifetime, such articles as clay pipes, dinner plates, jewelry, pens, and statuettes bore the likenesses of his characters and of Zola himself, all of which added to the folklore of a living legend.

Biography

Born in Paris on April 2, 1840, Émile-Édouard-Charles-Antoine Zola was the only child of a French mother, Émilie-Aurélie Aubert, and an Italian father, Francesco Zola. The Zolas moved to Aix-en-Provence, where Francesco was engaged to work on the municipality's water supply system. Upon his father's premature death in 1847, Émile and his mother began a series of moves to ever less expensive housing, first in Aix and later in Paris. Zola's childhood friends from the Pension Notre-Dame and the Collège Bourbon, Philippe Solari, Marius Roux, Baptistin Baille, and Paul Cézanne, proved to be lifelong friends, and the countryside of Provence, in all its variety, remained in Zola's memory and consciousness long after he moved to Paris in 1858, appearing in many of his novels.

The move to Paris was a major turning point in Zola's life, and the transplantation from rustic Provence to the teeming streets of the city proved difficult. Having failed his *baccalauréat* examination in August and again in November of 1859, Zola appears to have lost interest in further attempts to earn the diploma and in further education, possibly in part because he lacked the money to continue his studies. The period from 1858 to 1862 is not a well-documented one in Zola's life, though some of his early poetry, short stories, and an unfinished play date from this period. The chronic poverty the Zolas faced prompted Émile to try his hand at clerking on the Paris docks in 1860. The same year, Zola had his first love affair, one that cured him, when it ended early in 1861 in disillusionment, of some of his Romanticism and brought him a poverty of a different sort. He finally secured a position with the publishing firm of Hachette in 1862 and was soon promoted to the advertising department by Louis Hachette, who also gave him the sound advice that he should pursue prose rather than poetry as his métier. While Zola was composing the last of his *Stories for Ninon*, his friend Paul Cézanne, the Impressionist painter, made several trips to Paris, taking Zola to see the famous Salon des Refusés of 1863 and introducing him to Gabrielle-Eléonore-Alexandrine Meley, who soon became Zola's mistress and, in 1870, his wife.

In the early 1860's, Zola also became a *chroniqueur* and literary critic for such publications as *Le Petit Journal, Le Courrier du monde*, and *Le Salut public* of Lyons. Later in the decade, beginning in 1866, he wrote for *L'Événement illustré* and, subsequently, for a number of other journals, such as *La Revue contemporaine*, *Le Gaulois*, *La Tribune*, *Le Rappel*, *La Cloche*, and *Le Sémaphore de Marseille*. By the time he published the first volumes of *The Rougon-Macquarts*, in 1871, he had established himself not only as a controversial novelist but also as a critic and social commentator of acknowledged force and insight. In one of his more notable reviews, he defended a work many found indefensible, Edmond and Jules de Goncourt's *Germinie Lacerteux* (1865; English translation, 1887), and praised its extreme realism in depicting the more depraved elements of human life with absolute honesty. This defense of realism and his emphasis on the validity of a writer's individual vision of life take on central roles in Zola's own practice as a novelist.

Zola's first novel, *Claude's Confession*, came under attack for its grim realism in the portrayal of poverty, the sordid side of bohemian life, and the disillusionment of a love affair that cannot succeed. Another early novel, *Thérèse Raquin*, is fully within the naturalistic mode; hailed by some as his early masterpiece, it brought him wide recognition as a serious novelist. *Madeleine Férat* added to his reputation as a forceful writer but fell short of the standard he had set in *Thérèse Raquin*. By the time *Thérèse Raquin* was published, Zola had resigned from Hachette and planned to live as a writer, proposing to write two novels a year to complete a series of ten novels that would incorporate the varied influences of heredity and environment on his characters.

Embarked on this venture to write the natural and social history of a family under the Second Empire—a series that would extend to twenty novels over the next twenty-five years—Zola, however, did not confine himself to writing novels. Shortly after his marriage in 1870 to Alexandrine and the publication of the first serial installment of *The Fortune of the Rougons*, the Franco-Prussian War began (July 19, 1870), and Zola spoke out against the policies of Napoleon III to find himself charged with inciting others to civil disobedience. Although the events of 1870 resulted in the abandonment of the case against him, Zola's frank opposition to official policies and governmental injustice did not abate and would resurface in the 1890's. Zola left Paris for Marseilles in September, 1870; began a short-lived journal there with Marius Roux; served for a time as secretary to Glais-Bizoin, a member of the Government of National Defense at Bordeaux; and returned to Paris in time to witness and chronicle the civil war of the Commune, which officially began on March 18, 1871.

Émile Zola. (Library of Congress)

With the publication of *The Fortune of the Rougons*, Zola's own fortune turned, and he became an even more controversial and respected force in Parisian literary circles. His own circle included Gustave Flaubert, Alphonse Daudet, Ivan Turgenev, Edmond de Goncourt, Paul Alexis, and Joris-Karl Huysmans, among others—writers who shaped the literary consciousness of the late nineteenth century in France and abroad. Zola's novelistic success in the 1870's reached its peak with his *succès de scandale*, *L'Assommoir*, a work that shocked the literary establishment with its intense, unrelieved portrayal of the working class. The volley of criticism aimed at Zola for what many mistakenly took to be his deliberate denunciation of the Parisian workers not only provoked controversy but also helped sales of the book. Zola received recognition as the author of a grim masterpiece and great financial rewards once Charpentier started paying him royalties; in all, about 91,000 copies were printed between 1877 and 1881. Zola's financial success allowed him to purchase a property at Médan, where he spent much of his time writing when he was not in Paris, turning out novel after novel until he surpassed *L'Assommoir* with what many consider to be his greatest work, *Germinal*.

In the late 1880's, Zola entered into the sort of relationship that is at the disillusioning center of much of his fiction and of which he had written with considerable distaste: In 1888, he took as his mistress a woman half his age whom his wife had employed as a seamstress, Jeanne Rozerot, with whom he had two children, Denise and Jacques. Zola's union with Rozerot lasted for the remaining fourteen years of his life, although he remained married to and continued to live with Alexandrine, who, though furious when she discovered the affair, took legal action after Zola's death so that his children could bear his name. His liaison with Rozerot profoundly altered his life in many regards, generally for the better; it brought him, in addition to a happy, satisfying relationship and rejuvenation, renewed inspiration to complete the remaining four volumes of *The Rougon-Macquarts*, to write the trilogy *Les Trois Villes*, and to write three of the projected "Four Gospels" of *Les Quatre Evangiles*.

As Elliott Grant has written, Zola's association with Rozerot became "something fine and beautiful"; in fact, Rozerot became the model for feminine virtue and positive female qualities in Zola's later work.

A major event in Zola's public life was his intervention in the Dreyfus affair, in which Captain Alfred Dreyfus was convicted by a court-martial on trumped-up charges of selling military information to the Germans and was sent to the infamous Devil's Island penal colony in the Caribbean. Zola became Dreyfus's advocate in a series of essays begun in November, 1897, that led to Zola's own trial for libel and his flight to England to avoid imprisonment. After eleven months, new evidence in the Dreyfus case made it appear likely that Zola could return to France; Dreyfus was pardoned in 1899 and, finally, rehabilitated in 1906. By the time of this last event, Zola was dead, asphyxiated by coal dust from a defective fireplace flue on September 28, 1902; some have suggested that the flue was blocked by anti-Dreyfusards bent on assassinating Zola. All of Paris, including Dreyfus, mourned him in a public funeral on October 5; nearly six years later, his ashes were transferred to the Panthéon. Zola was survived by his wife and by Jeanne Rozerot and their children, one of whom, Denise Le Blond-Zola, wrote a biography of her father.

Analysis

Émile Zola's novels, from first to last, may be justly characterized as representing his lifelong quest for truth and its exposition—the truth of human situations and circumstances, of social conditions and of the conventions of his society, of the innermost fears, desires, aspirations, horrors, depravities, and exultations of humanity. As the founder of the naturalist school, Zola attempted to apply the methods of natural science as they emerged in the mid-nineteenth century to the writing of fiction, regarding himself as an "experimental novelist" and "practical sociologist" who took into account both heredity and environment in presenting his characters. Among the notions he espoused and eclectically applied to his own writing were the determinist theories of the critic Hippolyte Taine, Charles Darwin's thoughts on natural selection and evolution, the hypotheses of Dr. Prosper Lucas on heredity, and many other contemporary ideas about physiology, psychology, and positivist philosophy gleaned from varied sources. His literary models, Honoré de Balzac, Flaubert, and Stendhal, predisposed him to write realistic fiction; his scientific studies disposed him to take realism one step further to its logical extension. From all of these studies, he formed a plan to write not the history of an individual but the history of an entire family under the Second Empire of Napoleon III—the scientific study of a family and the effects of his own age on it, "its breakdown through the ravaging passions of the epoch, and the social and physical action of the environment." This plan is the basis for Zola's outstanding series *The Rougon-Macquarts*.

Claude's Confession

Zola had published several novels before he began this multivolume series, and these novels contain elements and concerns that would reappear in his later work; indeed, they form a prelude, however tentative, to *The Rougon-Macquarts*. His first novel, *Claude's Confession*, is an autobiographical inner quest for the true meaning of experience, experience that is presented in the grim and somber tones of Zola's own life and that includes abject material poverty and an emotional poverty resulting from an improbable and impossible love affair that the critic Angus Wilson and others have suggested was an attempt on Zola's part to reclaim a young prostitute. The next of these three novels, *Thérèse Raquin*, explores human motivation from the perspective of lust, murder, remorse, and suicide. Not unlike Flaubert's *Madame Bovary* (1857; English translation, 1886), *Thérèse Raquin* is a scientific study of the temperaments of persons dominated by "nerves and blood" (Zola's phrase), persons who wantonly satisfy their lust for each other, commit murder to that end, are haunted by the horror of their actions, and finally, with all fleshly desire dead between them, commit double suicide. *Madeleine Férat* is as bleak and as obsessed with sex as the first two novels, but it is much more artificially contrived than its predecessors and transgresses the bounds of probability as Zola attempts to illustrate a suspect physiological theory by hinging the novel's action on a series of unlikely coincidences.

The Fortune of the Rougons

Zola's major novelistic enterprise, the fictive history of the Second Empire and of the Rougon-Macquart tribe, begins with Louis-Napoleon's coup d'état late in 1851 and with the ancestry and relations of the clan whose story Zola would unfold over the course of more than two decades. *The Fortune of the Rougons* is set in Plassans (Aix-en-Provence, Zola's boyhood home) and recounts both the defeat of Republican resistance to the coming Empire and the idyllic but tragically doomed love of Silvère and Miette against a background of the grasping, manipulative, and acquisitive actions of the Rougons and of the Bonapartists, who create an empire predicated on the slaughter of the innocents. In Zola's second installment, naturalistic excess triumphs as Zola presents Aristide Rougon (who consented to the killing of Silvère in the first novel) as a money-mad speculator whose rush for the spoils in *The Kill* typifies the graft and corruption possible in the vast urban-renewal projects directed by Baron Haussmann in the late nineteenth century. Social corruption is at the novel's core, a corruption that permeates every level of society but that is fully developed in the lives of the great middle class, the bourgeoisie.

Another sort of corruption is the target of Zola's dual focus, the moral corruption that complements the speculative morass; in this case, it is the deliberate, premeditated, and shocking act of incest between Aristide Rougon's wife, Renée, and his son, Maxime. (In some of his descriptions, Zola appears to have been carried away by the voluptuousness of his own creation and truly exceeds the bounds of any possible convention or propriety as he debases the Phaedra theme and makes it utterly sordid.) Aristide, in need of Renée's signature and agreement, remains complaisant in the face of her incest, thus subordinating any possible moral consideration to a merely financial one.

Savage Paris

Savage Paris is, like its predecessors, a polemical sociopolitical inquiry into the war between the haves and the have-nots. Set in one of the new wonders of reconstructed Paris, Les Nouvelles Halles (today, Les Halles Centrales), the novel places the poor, the lower classes, and the politically alienated on a symbolic food chain that puts them at the mercy of their natural predators, the rapacious middle class. While *Savage Paris* is a novel of considerable originality, it ranks well below *The Kill* and, although ample in its descriptive passages, is decidedly thin in respect to plot.

Three more novels followed the first three before Zola was to achieve recognition and success with *L'Assommoir*: *The Conquest of Plassans*, *The Sins of Father Mouret*, and *His Excellency*. In these novels, Zola applied his formulaic notions of heredity and environment to diverse situations. *The Conquest of Plassans* continues the examination of provincial France that the first novel had begun by presenting the political intrigues that turn Plassans from a Legitimist to a Bonapartist town and ecclesiastical intrigues that complement the political and show the priest, Faujas, undertaking other conquests. *The Sins of Father Mouret* explores the religious questions of the era; here, the conflict between nature and religion assumes mythic rather than naturalistic dimensions. *His Excellency* is Zola's contribution to the political novel in France, a genre Anthony Trollope perfected in England, and contains a biting satire on the empire, the government, and its minions; it is also, on one level, a roman à clef in which the figures of Napoleon III's regime could find themselves unflatteringly portrayed. Taken together, then, the first six volumes of *The Rougon-Macquarts* represent a prodigious effort on Zola's part and form a fascinating group that brings before us many aspects of the empire and many character types common to it.

L'Assommoir

As artistically successful as these works are, the popular success of which he dreamed and for which he labored continued to elude Zola until the publication in 1877 of *L'Assommoir*. In that novel, Zola presented the Parisian proletariat exactly as he saw it; indeed, *L'Assommoir* is virtually the first French novel to do so. The reactions of the mainstream critical community and of the general public were similar: outrage at the naturalistic, despair-ridden depiction of the working class with an honesty and frankness unparalleled by any previous work. Responses to the novel remain divided: Some deem the work a bitter and bleak indictment of the proletariat; others agree that Zola presents a bleak but sympathetic view of the workers. One may approach the novel on many levels: as an exposé of the pervasive, devastating, and debilitating power of drink; as a sociological study of the wearying Parisian working life; as a character study of the psychology of human frailty and weakness and of the small comforts that both relieve an otherwise barren existence and hasten its end. Death in all its brutal, naked force, resulting from exhaustion through work and poverty, is never far from the novel's characters; death is, in fact, a logical and predictable end to, almost a relief from, the already dehumanized existence that Gervaise Macquart and her husband, Coupeau, endure as their lot. The deaths of Gervaise and her husband reinforce in strikingly poignant ways the futility of their lives, their impossible aspirations and broken dreams, and the inexorable fate stemming from the irremediable condition of the poor.

One useful way of considering Zola's artistry in *L'Assommoir* is to reflect on the work's structure; another is to examine its symbolism; a third is to focus on the highly wrought characters it contains. While exploring these three elements represents only a partial foray into this highly complex novel, it does provide some insight into Zola's intentions and achievement. Unlike several of his earlier works, *L'Assommoir* is not full of varied themes, multiple subplots, and a wide range of characters; rather, it has a single emphasis (on Gervaise), relatively few important characters, and a line of dramatic action that is classical in its simplicity. Gervaise's rising fortunes reach an apex when, through an initially fortunate marriage with Coupeau and the kindness of a shy admirer, she finds her hard work rewarded and becomes the proprietress of a small laundry business with employees of her own. Coupeau's literal fall from a high building (and his consequent inability to work) results in Gervaise's metaphoric fall, a downward journey that is entirely unrelieved and ends only as she achieves the oblivion of a death she surely sought. The turning point, Zola clearly and heavy-handedly points out, occurs one afternoon in the laundry, when Coupeau, having been encouraged in his self-indulgence by Gervaise, turns up drunk, falls over the mounds of clothes, and insists on kissing her. That kiss marks the beginning of the couple's decline. Gradually, Gervaise yields to the temptation of drink in Colombe's Bar, where the still appears to be a living, monstrous thing that dispenses poison.

The still is one among many symbols heralding Gervaise's end; like it, other objects seem to assume lives of their own within the novel's pages. Zola uses the physical environment, for example, to signify the impact of the exterior landscape on the interior landscape of his characters. From her first small apartment in Paris, to the laundry room where she works, to the bewildering surroundings of the Louvre, to the succession of buildings in which she lives while she is on her downward spiral, each worse than the last, the physical environment triumphs over Gervaise and modifies her perceptions of life and its meaning. Apart from the most obvious and powerful symbol in the work, the still, another symbol contends for notice: clothes. The heaps and mounds of clothes in the laundry rooms Gervaise inhabits, her unending task of cleaning them, and the disreputable state of her own attire after her fall combine to reinforce the fetid atmosphere of the novel and to form the impression that this atmosphere is inescapable.

Above all, at the core of the novel are Zola's characters. Gervaise's first lover, Lantier, abandons her and their two children as the novel opens, only to reappear and be invited by the sodden Coupeau to lodge with them. Lantier becomes a true *copain* for Coupeau, a drinking buddy whom Gervaise must also support by her hard work and who, predictably, becomes master of the house and, eventually, of Gervaise. Coupeau himself is a case study in frailty who succumbs to his first adversity, the fall, continues through a deterioration of will, and finally abandons himself to drinking away all of Gervaise's earnings and the scant resources their goods bring in from pawnbrokers. He ultimately suggests that Gervaise gain money to satisfy his addiction to alcohol and her own newly acquired drinking habit through prostitution. She has grown so slovenly and has so aged prematurely that no man will have her. Finally, one of the men she attempts to interest, the blacksmith Gouget, who had loaned her the money to set up her own laundry, takes pity on what she has become. She will eat his food but only out of animal instinct; she will neither stay with him nor seek to infect his life with hers.

The central character is Gervaise, whose fortunes form the locus of narration, whose history is the subject of the work, and through whose eyes we see most in the novel. As one example of the intractability of some of Zola's thinking about heredity and environment, she is doomed to the unhappiness he provides for her; as a character whose good intentions are subverted by fate and foiled by chance, she is the object of pity; as a representative of the working class whose best of many dwelling places is in a slum and whose social position can be altered only for the worse, she exists as an indictment of the ruling forces of the Second Empire, the great bourgeoisie, whose members simply ignored the plight of workers and the problems of those below their social level. It is not without significance that a character who receives minor but nevertheless important attention in *L'Assommoir*, Nana, would be the focal point of yet another novel in Zola's series and would provide him with another vehicle for raising similar issues concerning the gulf between the social classes.

NANA

If Zola astounded Paris with *L'Assommoir*, he outdid himself with a second masterpiece, *Nana*. A novel that Zola had planned to write for several years, *Nana* was greeted, like *L'Assommoir*, as a work of great obscenity, in this case for its candid treatment of what Zola termed *la vraie fille* (the true prostitute), who makes her life in the theater. Like the Goddess of Reason in earlier Republican days, Nana assumes a symbolic value in the novel, to become, as we first see her and as she develops, a Venus who not only offers the joy and excitement of sexual abandon but also exercises formidable destructive power, a femme fatale who brings ruin in her wake, ruin that involves the empire's aristocrats and financiers. In some sense, this seductive and destructive offspring of Gervaise Macquart may represent the revenge of workers on their oppressors. Nana's dual nature does, in many senses, mirror Zola's own ambivalent attitudes toward sexuality present in most of his works (certainly in the novels he wrote before his transforming affair with Jeanne Rozerot brought him joy without apparent remorse or destruction). Commenting on the mythic dimension of the novel, Flaubert was quick to point out the work's thorough grounding in the actual world of the Second Empire and characterized the work as Babylonian, something not unlike his own attempt to "fix a mirage" in *Salammbô* (1862; English translation, 1886), in this case a mirage that springs from and undercuts the hothouse world of the grisette.

The novel's mythic aspect is only one facet of this highly controversial study of the Second Empire's decadence. Nana herself assumes mythic proportions in the book's first chapter, as she emulates Venus rising from the sea with her tresses as her only veil. As she becomes Venus onstage, so she becomes Venus offstage, capturing the attention and wealth of Steiner the banker, Count Muffat, a chamberlain of the Second Empire, and several others. There are two sides to this Venus, however: She can please but she can also conquer. The destroying Venus is announced early in the novel, when, having captured the attention of all in Bordenave's theater with her considerable beauty, Nana smiles "the smile of a man-eater." This clearly signals that the major theme of the work, sex as personified in Nana, is not pleasurable but is, instead, compulsive, sordid, furtive, unsatisfying, and arid. To the extent that this is so, sex itself is mythologized and removed from truly human experience to an extrahuman, subhuman plane.

Like *L'Assommoir*, *Nana* has a simple architectural principle: The action consistently rises throughout the novel until immediately before its, and its heroine's, end. Although Gervaise's fall is a long, gradual, and painful one, Nana's is sudden; though fortuitous, it is quite credible. The principle at work, with some minor variation, is to show Nana's rise in relation to the characters present in the first chapter as they seduce or are seduced by her. One chief element the characters share is their dehumanization and reduction to a merely animal state by a Venus-turned-Circe. The most notable example of this transformation is Count Muffat, whose persistence in the face of Nana's rebuffs finally wins him the prize he so intently desires. The progress of Muffat's degradation is a simulacrum of the degradation of the Second Empire's officialdom, of which he is both member and symbol. At one point, Nana forces him into a naked romp in which he must pretend to be a bear, a horse, and a dog; she takes great delight in demeaning him and then of making fun of his unattractive nakedness. A final degradation occurs when Muffat discovers Nana in bed with his father-in-law, a marquis. Throughout the novel, Nana allows herself to be used by a variety of men and also uses them as an antidote to boredom, poverty, and a life in the streets. Zola characterizes her by using a variety of animal images ranging from the tigress man-eater of the first chapter to the horse named for her that wins the Grand Prix de Paris. All of these images reinforce the subhuman depiction of the denizens of Second-Empire Paris.

In the larger context of the empire's history that Zola chronicles in *The Rougon-Macquarts*, Nana becomes a symbol of the empire's decline, her life ending as the government is about to crumble. She breathes her last as an ugly, scabrous smallpox victim in a squalid Parisian hospital while the first salvos of the Franco-Prussian War penetrate Paris. Zola is intent, in his skillful but sometimes too obvious use of myth and symbol, on probing the frailty of his characters and on relating that pervasive frailty to the decay and debilitating weakness of the much-hated Second Empire.

Germinal

L'Assommoir and *Nana* are universally acknowledged masterpieces on which Zola's reputation as a novelist of the first order rests. A third work, *Germinal*, is still, as it was in his own time, acknowledged to be Zola's supreme novelistic achievement (some would add *Earth*, his novel of peasant life, as his fourth major achievement in this series). *Germinal* is a brilliant, if depressing, depiction of a facet of proletarian life quite different from that which he portrayed in *L'Assommoir*. Zola set *Germinal* in the mining town of Montsou, and in it he scrutinizes the issues of the exploitation of workers, attempts at collective action on their part in a bitter strike not uncharacteristic of the era, and the inevitable destruction that awaits them in what becomes an epic class struggle between labor and capital. Zola's is one of the earliest and relatively few nineteenth century novels that examines Marxist thought (embodied in Étienne Lantier, a son of Gervaise Macquart) in more than a superficial and partisan way. While he takes great pains to present the arguments of the mine owners (who are absentee landlords) and of the mine's manager, Zola is emotionally and intellectually on the side of the workers. As in *Savage Paris*, Zola pits the haves against the have-nots and presents their personal dramas with heavy satire of the former and great sympathy and sensitivity toward the latter, a sympathy that informs all of his treatments of working-class life.

Other important works in *The Rougon-Macquarts* are *Earth*, a naturalistic paean to the love of the land and the love of a woman; *The Human Beast*, Zola's most pessimistic work, which treats the railroads and the judicial system while presenting raw human passion; and *The Downfall*, the great war novel he had planned for many years, in which he succeeds in illustrating the utter confusion and horror of war by fictionalizing the fall of Napoleon III at Sedan and the ensuing civil war of the Commune. When he finished *The Rougon-Macquarts* with *Doctor Pascal* in 1893, Zola had chronicled, in an unsystematic way, the history of the Second Empire, from its inglorious inception to its ignominious demise, and had developed an entire world populated by representatives of every class and segment of French society. This panoramic epic of his own times remains as an enduring literary monument to Zola's genius and to his passionate quest for truth. He was never to match, in his later fiction, the intensity and literary worth of *The Rougon-Macquarts*.

Zola's later works, *Les Trois Villes* and *Les Quatre Evangiles*, while containing some brilliant writing and some hard-hitting social criticism, on the whole fail as novels because their propaganda for a socialist utopia overshadows the artistry Zola had brought to bear on the ethical, social, political, and philosophical concerns in *The Rougon-Macquarts*. As Angus Wilson has observed, Zola's happiness with Jeanne Rozerot meant for him a gradual slipping away of his fears and horrors and the consequent decline in the need to sublimate their expression, and his physical paternity "was undoubtedly the precursor of literary sterility."

John J. Conlon

Other major works

SHORT FICTION: *Contes à Ninon*, 1864 (*Stories for Ninon*, 1895); *Esquisses parisiennes*, 1866; *Nouveaux Contes à Ninon*, 1874; *Les Soirées de Médan*, 1880 (contributor); *Le Capitaine Burle*, 1882 (*A Soldier's Honor, and Other Stories*, 1888); *Naïs Micoulin*, 1884; *Contes et nouvelles*, 1928; *Madame Sourdis*, 1929.

PLAYS: *Thérèse Raquin*, pr., pb. 1873 (adaptation of his novel; English translation, 1947); *Les Héritiers Rabourdin*, pr., pb. 1874 (*The Rabourdin Heirs*, 1893); *Le Bouton de rose*, pr., pb. 1878; *Madeleine*, pb. 1878 (wr. 1865); *Théâtre*, pb. 1878; *Renée*, pr., pb. 1887 (adaptation of his novel *La Curée*); *L'Ouragan*, pr., pb. 1901 (libretto; music by Bruneau); *L'Enfant-roi*, pr. 1905 (libretto; music by Bruneau); *Lazare*, pb. 1921 (wr. 1893; libretto; music by Alfred Bruneau); *Poèmes lyriques*, pb. 1921; *Sylvanire: Ou, Paris en amour*, pb. 1921 (wr. 1902; libretto; music by Robert Le Grand); *Violaine la chevelue*, pb. 1921 (wr. 1897).

POETRY: *L'Amoureuse Comédie* (wr. 1860; in *Œuvres complètes*).

NONFICTION: *Mes haines*, 1866 (*My Hates*, 1893); *Le Roman expérimental*, 1880 (*The Experimental Novel*, 1893); *Documents littéraires*, 1881; *Le Naturalisme au théâtre*, 1881 (*Naturalism on the Stage*, 1893); *Nos auteurs dramatiques*, 1881; *Les Romanciers naturalistes*, 1881 (*The Naturalist Novel*, 1964); *Une Campagne*, 1882; *The Experimental Novel, and Other Essays*, 1893 (includes *The Experimental Novel* and *Naturalism on the Stage*, better known as *Naturalism in the Theater*); *Nouvell Campagne*, 1897; *Pages d'exil*, 1898 (*Notes from Exile*, 2003); *La Vérité en marche*, 1901.

MISCELLANEOUS: *Œuvres complètes*, 1966-1968 (15 volumes).

Bibliography

Baguley, David, ed. *Critical Essays on Émile Zola*. Boston: G. K. Hall, 1986. Collection of essays by noted Zola scholars covers a wide variety of topics, including discussion of the experimental novel and Zola's ideology. Contains a select English-language bibliography of works about Zola.

Berg, William J., and Laurey K. Martin. *Émile Zola Revisited*. New York: Twayne, 1992. Focuses on *The Rougon-Macquarts* and employs textual analysis rather than biography to analyze each of the twenty volumes in Zola's widely known series. Berg and Martin use Zola's literary-scientific principles to organize their study.

Brooks, Peter. "Zola's Combustion Chamber." In *Realist Vision*. New Haven, Conn.: Yale University Press, 2005. Chapter on Zola's novels is part of a larger study of realist literature and art in France and England during the nineteenth and twentieth centuries.

Brown, Frederick. *Zola: A Life*. New York: Farrar, Straus and Giroux, 1995. Detailed and extensive biography discusses Zola's fiction and the intellectual life of France, of which he was an important part. Shows how Zola's naturalism was developed out of the intellectual and political ferment of his time.

Gallois, William. *Zola: The History of Capitalism*. New York: Peter Lang, 2000. Interprets *The Rougon-Macquarts* as a history of capitalism, drawing connections between Zola's novels and the work of economists and sociologists Karl Marx, Max Weber, and Émile Durkheim. Includes bibliography and index.

Lethbridge, Robert, F. W. J. Hemmings, and Terry Keefe, eds. *Zola and the Craft of Fiction*. Leicester, England: Leicester University Press, 1990. Collection of ten essays includes six written in English by notable Zola scholars such as David Baguley, Philip D. Walker, and Joy Newton.

Nelson, Brian. *Zola and the Bourgeoisie: A Study of Themes and Techniques in "Les Rougon-Macquart."* New York: Macmillan, 1983. Examines how *The Rougon-Macquarts* depict the middle class and its value structure in nineteenth century France. Explains how the bourgeoisie vilified Zola, whose social vision uncovered the baseness of their class.

_______, ed. *The Cambridge Companion to Émile Zola*. New York: Cambridge University Press, 2007. Collection of essays presents analyses of *Thérèse Raquin*, *Nana*, and *Germinal* as well as discussions of Zola's depiction of society, sex, and gender. Includes a summary of Zola's novels, a family tree of the Rougon-Macquarts, a bibliography, and an index.

Newton, Ruth, and Naomi Lebowitz. *The Impossible Romance: Dickens, Manzoni, Zola, and James*. Columbia: University of Missouri Press, 1990. Discusses the impact of religious sensibility on literary form and ideology in works by Zola as well as works by Charles Dickens, Alessandro Manzoni, and Henry James.

Pollard, Patrick. *Émile Zola Centenary Colloquium*. London: Émile Zola Society, 1995. Collection of essays, originally delivered at a colloquium held in London in September, 1993, examines various aspects of Zola's life and works.

Schom, Alan. *Émile Zola*. London: Queen Anne Press, 1987. Biography considers Zola the journalist, the novelist, and the man and his values. Places Zola within the context of nineteenth century France and shows the artist as crusader against social ills. Includes photographs, illustrations, and select bibliography.

Walker, Philip D. *Zola*. London: Routledge & Kegan Paul, 1985. Biography by a prominent Zola scholar draws on personal research as well as on the work of many other critics, historians, and biographers to depict Zola's life. Includes a select bibliography.

Long Fiction in History

Long Fiction in the Ancient Greco-Roman World

The novel has often been described as a modern genre with little in common with the prose fiction of other periods and cultures. The relationship between the modern novel and the prose fiction of the ancient Greeks and Romans is particularly problematic. In *The Novel Before the Novel* (1977), Arthur Heiserman admits that it is anachronistic to categorize ancient prose works as fiction novels. Ian Watt, an influential scholar, begins his study of the novel in *The Rise of the Novel* (1957) with eighteenth century or, at the earliest, seventeenth century prose fiction. In *The Ancient Novel: An Introduction* (1995), however, Niklas Holzberg argues that the works of ancient authors such as Xenophon of Ephesus and Lucius Apuleius easily fit the broad modern definition of the novel.

Differences in style, form, and content among modern novelists have made any critical definition of the genre difficult. The questions "What makes a good novel?" and "Is this work really a novel?" can be answered only through the application of arbitrary critical rules, for a major feature of the genre appears to be its inability to be restricted or characterized. The novel becomes what it wants to be: descriptive, narrative, or dramatic; ironic, serious, or ambiguous in tone; historical or imaginary; purely entertaining, didactic, or both. As a result, critics such as Robert Scholes and Robert A. Kellogg, in *The Nature of Narrative* (1966), have stressed the diverse and changing nature of the novel form. In *The Ancient Romances: A Literary-Historical Account of Their Origins* (1967), Ben Edwin Perry calls the genre "formless," and in *The Search for the Ancient Novel* (1994), James Tatum describes ancient fiction as oxymoronic because of its many contradictory features. Tim Whitmarsh, in *The Cambridge Companion to the Greek and Roman Novel* (2008), argues that Greek and Roman novels do constitute a "distinctive genre," if the term is used "flexibly." It might be useful to think of such a varied genre as polymorphic, or "many-formed." The protean tendencies of the novel are, perhaps, its defining characteristic.

The ambiguity of the genre applies not only to its form but also to its name. The ancient Greeks, who supplied the terms "epic," "drama," and "lyric," never created a word for their prose fiction, which was obliquely referred to as fictional (*plasmatika*), dramatic (*dramatika*), or, according to Chariton of Aphrodisias, "erotic sufferings" (*erotika pathemata*). Because they were written not in the standard Latin of the time but in the vernacular of the Romance languages, the adventure stories of the medieval period, such as *Chanson de Roland* (c. 1100; *Song of Roland*, 1880), were called romances, which, in the form *roman*, supplied the term for all forms of long prose fiction in French and German. In Spanish and English, however, the words *novela* and "novel" (from *novus*, or "new," in Latin) were created to distinguish from the more idealistic romance a form of prose fiction on contemporary or realistic subjects. As a result, the European languages present a variety of terms for long prose fiction, including "romance," *roman*, "novel," and "novella." The confusion is especially acute in English, which has retained both "romance" and "novel." In theory, "romance" is used for long fiction that is "ideal" and "remote from contemporary life," while "novel" applies to works that are "realistic" and "contemporary," but the distinction is often difficult to apply. Further, the term "romance" itself refers equally to both the chivalric epics of the medieval period and a popular genre of paperback fiction.

The uncertain terminology surrounding long prose fiction is particularly evident with the surviving ancient Greek examples of the genre. Most modern critics call these works "romances" because of their idealistic qualities, and they imply a generic gap between the Greek romances and the modern novel that reinforces the view of the novel as a modern creation; yet many of the features considered characteristic of the modern novel can, in fact, be found in ancient prose fiction. Psychological development of character, time sequencing, narrative form, and realism or verisimilitude (especially an insistence on the illusion of real experiences) are contained in the Greek romances as well as in the modern novel. Ancient prose fiction, like its modern counterpart, tends to incorporate into its fabric many literary forms and modes, so that both, to a certain extent, can be called polymorphic. For these reasons, the term "novel" will be applied in this essay to both ancient and modern examples of long prose fiction.

History and criticism of the Greek novel

The Greek novel received little contemporary critical attention, probably because ancient critics did not consider it a serious literary form, and modern critics have often been more interested in the literary precursors and origins of the Greek novel than in the works themselves. Erwin Rohde's monumental study of the genre, *Der griechische Roman und seine Vorläufer* (1876; the Greek novel and its antecedents), established the theory that the form was a phenomenon of the mid-second through sixth centuries C.E. and was especially the product of rhetorical schools. In particular, Rohde linked the Greek novel with the Second Sophistic, a second century C.E. cultural movement that sought a return to the literary models and language of fifth century B.C.E. Athens.

Papyrus finds of Greek novels, however, have proved Rohde wrong. This genre originated much earlier than Rohde imagined, at least as early as the first century B.C.E., and the extant novels represent only a few examples of a very popular and thriving literary form. A distinction must now be made between the novels of Heliodorus, Achilles Tatius, and Longus, which show many characteristics of the Second Sophistic, and those of Chariton and Xenophon, which predate this period and are therefore called "non-Sophistic" or "pre-Sophistic." Despite major alterations in Rohde's theories, however, his emphasis on the rhetorical features of the Greek novel is still valid. Rhetorical tropes, set speeches, and legal argumentation as taught in ancient schools of rhetoric are indeed an important aspect of the surviving novels, even if the schools themselves can no longer be called the originators of the novel form.

Realization that the Greek novel developed in the late Hellenistic world of the second and first centuries B.C.E. has led to many hypotheses on the sociological background of the genre. Perry has suggested that the diverse nature of the novel reflected the varied literary tastes of the cosmopolitan Hellenistic society that gave it birth, in the same way that the more fixed Greek epic served the needs of an earlier, more uniform age. According to Perry, any talk about the "development" of the Greek novel is useless; the genre did not gradually evolve but was instead a sudden, deliberate creation of an individual unknown author. Tomas Hägg, in *Den antika romanen* (1980; *The Novel in Antiquity*, 1983), associates the earliest novels with a rise in literacy in the late Hellenistic Age and plausibly conjectures that these novels were usually recited in small groups rather than read silently and were probably circulated, if not created, by scribes. The evidence suggests that the Greek novel was a popular rather than a serious literary form, originally meant to entertain rather than to edify. Only in its later, Sophistic manifestations does the novel display clear didactic and sophisticated tendencies.

Another theory on the origin of the Greek novel is that presented by Reinhold Merkelbach in *Roman und Mysterium in der Antike* (1962; novel and mystery in antiquity). Merkelbach associates the novels with various religious sects, especially with the Egyptian cult of Isis, and makes these novels into mystery texts. According to this view, the regular plot of the Greek novel, with its themes of separation, trial, and reunion, parallels the message of the ancient mystery religions, and the text becomes religiously symbolic. While the religious interest in the novels is a valid observation, it is unlikely that Greek novels arose from such a monolithic, theological purpose.

Graham Anderson used Sumerian texts to suggest the Near Eastern origin of the Greek romance. Similarly, Laurence M. Wills compared Greek novels to prose works in the Jewish tradition—such as the biblical books of Tobit, Esther, and Judith—and concluded that both the Greek and the Jewish narrative form, thriving simultaneously in the first century B.C.E., sprang from the same tradition of popular literature in the eastern Mediterranean.

The polymorphic nature of the Greek novel is also suggested by the many literary antecedents proposed for the genre. The influence of the Greek epic, especially of Homer's *Odyssey* (c. 725 B.C.E.; English translation, 1614), is evident in the Greek novel of all periods. Chariton has his characters retell the story at the end of his novel in the same way as Homer has Odysseus retell his odyssey to Penelope in *Odyssey* 23. Achilles Tatius's use of the first-person narrative may be traced back to a similar technique in *Odyssey* 9 to 12. Heliodorus's debt to Homer for beginning in medias res is unquestionable. He also imitates Homer in book 7 when the hero almost fails to recognize the heroine because she, like Odysseus, is dressed in rags.

The frequent description of their works as dramas by Chariton, Achilles Tatius, and Heliodorus points also to the influence of the Greek theater on the novel. Similarities between the two genres are numerous. The Aristotelian dramatic terms "peripeteia" (reversal) and "anagnorisis" (recognition) readily apply to the plots of Greek novels, with their frequent and sudden changes of situation and with their inevitable reunions of the main characters with their separated lovers and their families. In Heliodorus, the dramatic recognition by the Ethiopian king and queen that the heroine is their daughter has many parallels in Greek drama (for example, Euripides' *Ion*). Furthermore, the romantic dramas of Euripides, such as *Ion*, *Helen*, and *Iphigenia in Tauris* (all c. 412 B.C.E.), are, like the novels, filled with intrigues, love, foreign settings, and happy endings. The Greek novels also share themes with the Greek New Comedy as exemplified by Menander, from which the genre may have derived another feature—the stock character of the intelligent slave upon whom the ingenuous protagonist relies for help.

It is, perhaps, to ancient historiography that the Greek novel owes the most. The modern world's distinction between "fiction" and "history" was not generally made in the ancient world, where myths and legends were not distinguished from eyewitness accounts of actual events and where the historian was not expected to recount what was actually said, but what ought to have been said. Herodotus is a good example, for the probable founder of history blends into his historical framework not only the events surrounding the war between the Persians and the Greeks in the early fifth century B.C.E. but also numerous undocumented legends and stories. Such a priority of storytelling over historical method undoubtedly influenced the Greek novel, which does not hesitate to blend historical and fictional elements. Chariton, for example, centers his novel on the apparently fictional daughter of a historical personage, Hemocrates, known from books 6 and 7 of Thucydides' *Historia tou Peloponnesiacou polemou* (431-404 B.C.E.; *History of the Peloponnesian War*, 1550).

The Greek novel's debt to the historian Xenophon of Athens can be seen not only in Chariton's imitation of Xenophon's prose style but also in parallels between several novels and the *Kyrou paideia* (c. 430-355 B.C.E.; *The Cyropaedia: Or, Education of Cyrus*, 1560-1567) of Xenophon. This work, a didactic, fictional biography of a Persian prince, shares themes of travel and love with the Greek novels. The semibiographical *Cyropaedia* also suggests another path leading toward the development of the Greek novel, a path that leads through the ancient tradition of biography and the *Alexander Romance* (c. 300 C.E.).

Finally, Rohde's famous study notes the influence of Greek travel tales and erotic poetry on the novel. Fantastic tales of adventure, such as those by Euhemerus and Iambulus and, especially, Antonius Diogenes' *Ta uper Thoulēn apista* (c. 100 C.E., twenty-four books; *Marvels Beyond Thule*, 1989), were popular in the Hellenistic period and undoubtedly satisfied the same yearning for the exotic that can be found in the Greek novels. The erotic poetry of the Hellenistic age, with its emphasis on local legends about the varying fortunes of young lovers, shares with the Greek novels a similar depiction of the violent eruption of young love. Examples of such tales survive in the *Erotika pathemata* (erotic tales) of Parthenius, written during the first century B.C.E. and accessible in full in Jacob Stern's English translation *The Love Stories of Parthenius* (1992).

Such broad literary debts indicate that the Greek novel did not originate from any single genre; rather, Greek novelists were able to incorporate features from different literary contexts into the fabric of their texts. Modern novelists do much the same.

THE GREEK NOVEL: A SURVEY

In addition to five extant ancient Greek novels, fragments or summaries survive from several other novels. Even these few short pieces provide enough information to create a fuller picture of the genre and its development. Unless otherwise noted, all the material discussed below is available in English translation in the second edition of B. P. Reardon's *Collected Ancient Greek Novels* (2008).

The earliest fragments come from the so-called *Ninus Romance* by an unknown author from about the first century B.C.E. The plot of this novel apparently centers on the adventures of the legendary Assyrian king Ninus and his love for Semiramis, identifiable with the real Assyrian queen Sammu-ramat, who built the famous Hanging Gardens of Babylon. The author's evident alteration of historical fact—Sammu-ramat's real husband was King Shamshi-Adad (r. 823-810 B.C.E.)—parallels the blend of legend and history that can also be found in Chariton's extant novel.

A similar trend can be seen in the fragments of a later novel, the *Parthenope Romance* (also known as *Metiochus and Perthenope*), dated to the second century C.E., by another unknown novelist. In this work, as in Chariton, the principal characters are offspring of prominent figures in Greek history: The heroine, Parthenope, is the daughter of Polycrates, the tyrant of Samos (fl. 540-522 B.C.E.), and the hero, Metiochus, is the son of Miltiades, the Athenian general at the Battle of Marathon (490 B.C.E.). In the extant fragments, the lovers Parthenope and Metiochus are participating in a symposium, or drinking party, at which the topic is the nature of love. One is reminded here of the famous discussion at the end of book 2 of Achilles Tatius on the advantages of homosexual love over heterosexual love.

Fragments from two other works, the *Phoenicia* (also known as *Phoenician Story*) of Lollianus and the *Iolaus* fragment (by an unknown author), both of the second century C.E., are significant for their highly erotic contents. The graphic scene of deflowering in the *Phoenicia* and the vulgar language found in the *Iolaus* contrast sharply with the virtuous poise of the extant novels and suggest that the genre as a whole may have treated the love theme in a more varied fashion than the extant novels suggest.

The *Babyloniaca* (*Rhodanes et Simonis*) survives only in a Byzantine summary. The author, Iamblichus (fl. 161-180 C.E.), was not a Greek but a Hellenized "Oriental," a background that partly accounts for his novel's Eastern setting. Babylon, also the setting for the *Ninus Romance* and books 5 and 6 of Chariton, clearly satisfied the novel reader's taste for the exotic. Iamblichus's plot is similar to those of the extant novels: Two young lovers, Rhodanes and Simonis, suffer the hardships of jealousy and separation but are eventually reunited happily, and Rhodanes becomes king of Babylon.

While papyrus evidence suggests that *Peri Chairean kai Kalliroēn* (c. second century C.E.; *The Loves of Chareas and Callirrhoe*, 1764), in eight books, by Chariton of Aphrodisias, was extremely popular in the ancient world, this novel was the last of the five extant Greek novels to be published in the modern world. Its *editio princeps*, or first printed edition, was in 1750. It is accessible in G. P. Goold's English translation, *Callirhoe* (1995).

Rohde once called Chariton's work the product of the fifth or sixth century C.E., but it is now considered the earliest extant complete novel and can be dated around 125 C.E. or even as early as the first century B.C.E. Some independent archaeological evidence has even been found for the author, Chariton, in his native city of Aphrodisias in ancient Caria (southwest Turkey). In his novel, Chariton identifies himself as the legal secretary to the rhetorician Athenegoras, and Chariton's professional interests are evident especially in the public and legal speeches that highlight his novel. The action of the novel begins with a festival of Aphrodite, the Greek goddess of love, in Syracuse, Sicily, where, historically, the cult of that goddess was not important, and it is possible that Aphrodite's dominance throughout Chariton's novel may in fact be caused by the prominence of Aphrodite in Aphrodisias, her eponymous city and Chariton's home.

Chariton's story centers on two handsome young Syracusans, Chaereas and Callirhoe, the offspring of political rivals, who fall in love at first sight during Aphrodite's festival and are married only after their fathers are persuaded at a public assembly to put aside their feud. The parallels to the plot of William Shakespeare's *Romeo and Juliet* (pr. c. 1595-1596) include not only the Capulet-Montague theme but also a false death and burial of the heroine, who is kicked by her jealous husband and knocked unconscious. Chariton shares this treatment of mistaken death and burial with several other Greek novelists, including Achilles Tatius and Heliodorus. Callirhoe awakes in her tomb only to be carried off by the pirate Theron and sold as a slave in Miletus (eastern Turkey). Chariton's vivid psychological study of Callirhoe's new master, Dionysius, is noteworthy. Recently bereft of a beloved wife, Dionysius is torn between his sudden passion for a new slave and his loyalties to his dead wife, between the absolute power of a master over his slave and the complete subjection of a lover to his beloved. Chariton's portrayal of Dionysius in such emotional turmoil displays a psychological perception usually associated only with modern novels.

Whereas the heroines of all the other Greek novels remain resolutely faithful to their lovers, Callirhoe, upon learning that she is pregnant with Chaereas's child, agrees to marry the childless Dionysius and passes her child off as his. Callirhoe's decision to remarry, albeit based on her difficult circumstances, has been called an act of betrayal of Chaereas. It is also a hint that the standard of absolute chastity that applies to the other extant novels is not a rule of the genre but an accident of preservation. Katharine Haynes explores the meaning of chastity in the Greek novel at some length in *Fashioning the Feminine in the Greek Novel* (2002).

Chaereas eventually learns that his wife is still alive and follows her to Miletus, where he is attacked by pirates and sold into slavery to Mithridates, the Persian governor of Caria (Chariton's homeland), who himself has fallen in love with the heroine. This complicated, spiraling love triangle eventually leads to Babylon and the royal court of Artaxerxes II (r. 404-359 B.C.E.), where a great trial determines the disposition of Callirhoe. The king himself becomes enamored of the girl, but before he can force her to join his harem, he himself is enjoined to leave Babylon to deal with an Egyptian revolt. Chaereas becomes a general for the Egyptians, eventually defeats the king, and wins back his wife. The exciting military scenes are paralleled in the *Ninus Romance* as well as in Heliodorus. The novel ends with the triumphant return of the protagonists to Syracuse, where all the events are recapitulated at another public assembly. Chariton is particularly fond of these scenes of public deliberation, which occur throughout his novel and create within the framework of the plot a collective voice with which Chariton's readers can readily identify.

Chariton's form is unusual in that it is a mixture of prose and verse. This type of composition, called Menippean after its inventor, the cynic philosopher Menippus of Gadara (fl. third century B.C.E.), was particularly popular among Latin authors, including the novelist Petronius, but is not otherwise common in extant Greek novels. Chariton writes in educated Greek in the simple but dramatic style called Asianism that was very popular in his time. His novel, lacking the Attic tendencies of the Second Sophistic, is technically called pre- or non-Sophistic. Chariton also demonstrates a particular fondness for Homer, whose epic dialect is frequently quoted and whose epic techniques, including formulas or repeated phrases, are often imitated.

Approximately contemporary with Chariton is the *Ephesiaca* (second or third century B.C.E.; *Ephesian History: Or, The Love Adventures of Abracoman and Anthia*, 1727; better known as *Ephesian Tale*), in five books, of Xenophon of Ephesus. Nothing is known of the author. His association with Ephesus may result solely from the fact that his story begins and ends in that important ancient city; his name may even be a mere pseudonym, perhaps meant to honor the great Athenian historian by that name. Some scholars suspect the surviving text to be an epitome or summary of a longer work, but this cannot be proven. Like the text of Chariton, Xenophon's novel was published in the modern world only belatedly; its *editio princeps* was in 1726.

Of the five extant Greek novels, Xenophon's is the least popular today and is often criticized as crudely written and poorly developed. In contrast to Chariton's careful psychological studies, Xenophon's characters are often mere puppets in a complicated series of adventurous episodes.

Xenophon's plot has several features in common with Chariton's. The Ephesian hero and heroine, Habrocomes and Anthia, fall in love at a religious festival and are soon married. Sent away from Ephesus because of the prediction of an oracle, the newlyweds are captured by pirates and enslaved in Tyre. A double love triangle develops between the couple and their masters, which leads to a separation that is not resolved until the end of the novel. Prior to their reunion on the island of Rhodes, Habrocomes and Anthia travel separately throughout the eastern half of the Mediterranean, and they are put through a series of trials, tests of fidelity, and escapes from near death.

Several Euripidean parallels can be noted in the novel. Like Hippolytus, Habrocomes is fanatically dedicated to chastity at the beginning of the novel and later gets entangled in a Hippolytus-Phaedra-Theseus triangle in which his mistress first attempts unsuccessfully to seduce him and then falsely accuses him of rape. A nearly certain Euripidean imitation, this time of the *Ēlektra* (413 B.C.E.; *Electra*, 1782), is the marriage of Anthia to a goatherd who honors her chastity.

Religious elements are particularly strong in Xenophon. The fate of the protagonists is sealed by an oracle, and the deities Artemis of Ephesus, Helius (the sun) of Rhodes, and Isis of Egypt play dominant roles.

A distinctive feature of this novel is the appearance of two stories-within-stories that are among the more memorable incidents of the book. The tale of the pirate Hippothoos's tragic homosexual love affair in book 3 contrasts with the happier but bizarre story of the necrophiliac Aigaleus and his wife, Thelxinoe, in book 5. Both tales, recounted in the first person to Habrocomes, highlight the overall love theme of the novel in much the same way that Lucius Apuleius (c. 125-c. 185 C.E.) employs tales in his *Metamorphoses* (second century C.E.; *The Golden Ass*, 1566). (James N. O'Sullivan's *Xenophon of Ephesus: His Compositional Technique and the Birth of the Novel*, 1995, is a good source for further study.)

Ta katà Leukippēn kaì Kleitophōnta (*Leucippe and Cleitophon*), in eight books, of the Alexandrian orator Achilles Tatius, was once considered a fifth century C.E. parody of Heliodorus's novel, but papyrus finds have made necessary a much earlier date, approximately 170 C.E., which makes imitation of Heliodorus virtually impossible. While Achilles Tatius is now dated close in time to the novels of Chariton and Xenophon, his book is stylistically a world apart and reflects, with its simple language and use of literary figures, the learned influence of the Second Sophistic. The *editio princeps* of Achilles Tatius appeared in 1601, but the work was known in Latin translation fifty years earlier.

This novel takes place, in succession, in Tyre, Egypt, and Ephesus. The three settings correspond loosely to the three stages of the story: love, separation, and reunion. As in the other novels, the plot is complicated by several near or apparent deaths and love triangles threatening the union of the lovers. Like Chariton, Achilles Tatius includes a thrilling trial scene, but here the hero is falsely condemned to death for murdering the heroine. Achilles Tatius's effort to create surprise and suspense at every possible turn is also reflected in Leucippe's three near-deaths: the first as a ritual victim at a sacrifice, the second by poisoning, and the third by beheading.

Achilles Tatius is fond of long digressions, mostly in the form of *ecphrasis*, or careful description reflecting the author's learned style. In fact, the novel begins with an *ecphrasis* of a painting of the rape of Europa. This description is not a mere digression for its own sake; it not only broadly parallels the plot but also serves to introduce the hero to the author, who meets Cleitophon while looking at the painting. Like Chariton, the Alexandrian Achilles Tatius can let local pride intrude into his novel. The magnificent description of the city of Alexandria at the beginning of book 5 could only have been written by a patriot. Other digressions can be zoological (such as a description of the hippopotamus in book 4) or erotic (such as a debate on homosexual versus heterosexual love in book 2).

The most striking feature of Achilles Tatius's novel is narrative form: Cleitophon himself is presented as relating the story to the author. This first-person narrative underscores the contemporaneity of Achilles Tatius's story. Leucippe and Cleitophon's experiences have occurred recently enough for the hero himself to relay them to the author, whereas all the other extant novels recall events of the distant past. Although Cleitophon is narrating after the fact and knows how incidents will turn out, he never intrudes into the story as an omniscient narrator. Rather, the reader experiences events as Cleitophon did at the time, without benefit of hindsight. Thus when the hero sees Leucippe sacrificed before his eyes, the reader sees only what Cleitophon sees and learns the happy truth of her escape only when he does.

This narrative perspective also creates between author and hero a distance that permits Cleitophon to relate events without the author intruding his own comments and views. The reader is thus introduced directly to Cleitophon's bumbling affairs; his aborted deflowering of Leucippe and their disastrous elopement in book 2 and his unheroic acquiescence to Melite's advances in book 5 make Cleitophon's escapades quite similar in tone to the adventures of Petronius's antihero Encolpius or to Henry Fielding's protagonist in *The History of Tom Jones, a Foundling* (1749; commonly known as *Tom Jones*). It is, perhaps, this mock-heroic perspective that has made many scholars erroneously believe *Leucippe and Cleitophon* to be a parody of Heliodorus's novel.

The *Ethiopica* (*Ethiopian Story*, 1961; also as *An Aethiopean History*, 1569, reprinted 1895) in ten books of Heliodorus of Emesa, datable as early as 225 C.E. (but a late fourth century date is also possible), brings to a fruitful climax the ancient novel tradition. Heliodorus so masterfully reworked the diverse elements of the form that his novel remained very popular in late antiquity and in medieval Byzantium, was admired in the Renaissance, and became an early model for the prose authors of the seventeenth century. Heliodorus was the first Greek novelist to become available in the Renaissance; his *editio princeps* was in 1534. A 1547 French translation by Jacques Amyot and a 1569 English translation by Thomas Underdowne did much to put Heliodorus into the mainstream of Renaissance literary activity.

The Syrian Heliodorus presents a novel that is the most exotic of its extant Greek counterparts. The heroine, Charicleia, is actually the abandoned daughter of the king and queen of Ethiopia, and the denouement of the novel is the dramatic recognition of the girl by her parents. Anagnorisis is achieved in classical fashion by means of birth tokens left with the girl when she was abandoned as an infant (recalling the recognition scenes in many Greek dramas, including Euripides' *Ion*). "Ethiopia" to Heliodorus and his readers meant not the geographic bounds of the modern nation but the ancient kingdom of Nubia, located in the modern southern Egypt and northern Sudan. The novel, in fact, ends in the capital of ancient Nubia, Meroë, and, except for events in Greece recounted after the fact, all the action of the book takes place along the Nile. Heliodorus manages to restrict the broad wanderings of the genre's typical protagonists but, like so many of his predecessors, features a faraway place in his novel.

The battle scene, found in earlier novels such as those of Chariton and the *Ninus Romance*, is used to great effect by Heliodorus, whose description in book 9 of the siege of Syene is perhaps modeled on the siege of Nisibis in 350 C.E. recounted by Julian the Apostate and is filled with elaborate detail and suspense. This *ecphrasis*, as well as that of a procession at Delphi in book 3, reminds one also of the careful descriptions found in Achilles Tatius.

Heliodorus's novel is also exotic in terms of religious sentiment. The Eastern sun cult, popular in the author's native Emesa and apparently important in Meroë as well, is central to the story. Religious syncretism, common in antiquity, is evident in the association of the sun god with Apollo, whose shrine at Delphi plays a critical role in the history of the hero and heroine. Charicleia's protector, Calasiris, is both a priest of Helius (the sun) and a gymnosophist, an Egyptian wise man. Heliodorus, whose name in Greek means "sun-gift," ends his novel by describing himself as a descendant of the sun.

In no other ancient novels are the protagonists so resolutely chaste. Chastity takes on a deeply religious meaning in *Ethiopian Story*, where Charicleia's virtue is closely associated with her worship of Artemis and Isis.

Characterization in Heliodorus can be particularly complex. Several of the characters present multiple sides to their very human and very realistic personalities. The religious convictions of both Charicleia and Calasiris are intermingled with tendencies toward deception difficult for the modern reader to understand. Theagenes, resolutely chaste and stoic even under torture when his virtue is threatened, lacks a similar fortitude when faced with mere servitude or certain death. He is ingenuous and often unable to understand his beloved's deceptions of others, such as Charicleia's deceit of Thyamis at the end of book 1. Thyamis, the brigand son of the priest Calasiris, temporarily compromises his religious background with the life of a pirate. While some of the minor characters are mere stereotypes, others, such as the Athenian Cnemon, are carefully developed in a sympathetic manner.

Heliodorus's artistry is particularly evident in his narrative technique. The novel begins with a brilliant use of in medias res. An omniscient narrator describes the aftermath of a bitter battle. The only survivors, a wounded young man and the beautiful young woman nursing him, turn out to be the protagonists, Theagenes and Charicleia. Their full identities and the circumstances surrounding the battle come to light only much later in the narrative. Heliodorus's refusal to narrate events in the chronological order standard in the other extant novels creates an intense suspense that is heightened at the end of book 1 when the brigand Thyamis apparently murders Charicleia. Only in the next book does the reader learn that Thyamis has murdered the wrong woman, but not before the hero, Theagenes, also mistakes the corpse for that of Charicleia.

The unusual beginning naturally leads to the use of flashback to bring the reader up-to-date. The flashback is dramatically achieved through a conversation between Calasiris and Cnemon in which the priest recounts past events in the first person. In this instance, Heliodorus is probably imitating the *Odyssey*, with its central flashback narrated by Odysseus himself. The affinity of Heliodorus's technique to that of modern cinema has often been noted.

Calasiris's story itself is not chronologically straightforward. In books 3 to 5, he narrates first how Theagenes and Charicleia met at Delphi and fell in love; then he goes back further in time to relate Charicleia's birth and history; finally, he returns to the first narrative string to describe the escape of the protagonists from Delphi, their capture by pirates, and, at last, the circumstances surrounding the carnage with which book 1 began. Thus only at the end of book 5 does the reader receive all the background information necessary to comprehend the events described in book 1.

Like Xenophon, Heliodorus uses the story-within-a-story technique, but his stories are much more tightly bound into the fabric of the novel. Most notably, the story of Cnemon, recounted in book 1, proves in several ways to be linked with the story of the protagonists.

Heliodorus's intricate narrative form is paralleled by a baroque language. The ancient passion for rhetoric results here in complicated sentence structures with multiple pairs of balanced subordinate clauses. Heliodorus's diction is often poetic and oblique, as even a casual examination of the battle scene in book 1 indicates: Severed limbs quiver, wine goblets become missiles, wine is mixed with blood, the bloody wound of Theagenes makes his white cheek more brilliant, and Theagenes mistakes the living Charicleia for a benevolent ghost. (A good introduction to Heliodorus in English is Gerald N. Sandy's *Heliodorus*, 1982; see also *Studies in Heliodorus*, 1998, edited by Richard Hunter.)

Daphnis and Chloë, in four books, stands out in many ways from the other four extant Greek novels yet has much in common with them. Little is known about the author, Longus of Lesbos, whose association with Lesbos may result merely from the setting of Longus's story, chosen, perhaps, because of the traditional links between the island of Lesbos and the love theme. Dating of the work is mere conjecture: from the late second to the middle of the third century C.E. Of the Greek novels, *Daphnis and Chloë* is probably the best known today. It was translated into French by Amyot in 1559, and the *editio princeps* of the Greek text appeared in 1598. Two very readable English translations are those by Paul Turner (1989) and Ronald McCail (2002).

Longus's tale, like that of the other novels, is of young love, with the standard themes of separation of the lovers, jealousy, love rivals (both heterosexual and homosexual), and eventual union of the lovers at the end. What is distinctive is the novel's simple, bucolic setting. The entire action takes place on the island of Lesbos—quite a contrast with the multiple changes of scene in Xenophon's *Ephesian Tale*. The protagonists, a goatherd and a shepherdess, function in the peaceful, natural surroundings of the Lesbian countryside. The conventional pirate raid is permitted to intrude into this pastoral setting, but only abortively. Pan, the rural deity who oversees the fates of both Daphnis and Chloë, miraculously saves the heroine from the pirates before the ship has left Lesbian waters. The author clearly owes much to the pastoral poetic tradition best known today through Theocritus's *Idylls* (c. 270 B.C.E; English translation, 1684) and Vergil's *Eclogues* (43-37 B.C.E.; also known as *Bucolics*; English translation, 1575), in which "Daphnis" is both a conventional shepherd name and a mythic figure. The artificiality of this poetry, in which the simple setting is described in a highly sophisticated, indirect language, is reflected in the stylized, poetic language of Longus, whose novel, like those of Achilles Tatius and Heliodorus, is labeled "Sophistic." Yet, within this artificial context, Longus's vivid characterization of the stirrings of adolescent love is striking and psychologically perceptive.

The temporal structure of the novel is controlled not so much by a succession of events as by the changes of the seasons, followed through nearly two cycles. The story begins in spring with the first signs of pubescent passion. Winter brings snow and isolation to the lovers. The following spring finds an entirely innocent and sexually naïve pair of lovers trying to consummate their love by imitating their flocks. Summer provides more practical sexual experience to Daphnis, who is successfully seduced by the wife of a neighboring farmer. Here Longus follows all the other extant novelists except Heliodorus in suggesting or admitting sexual experience on the part of the male protagonist, but Chloë, like the heroines of Achilles Tatius and Heliodorus, remains unquestionably innocent until her marriage to Daphnis. The second autumn leads to the recognition of the foundling protagonists by two sets of wealthy, aristocratic, urban parents. Their anagnorises, accomplished through the necessary tokens, are appropriately occasioned by a harvest festival. Daphnis and Chloë, rejecting the city life of their newly found parents, are eventually married among their beloved flocks and lead a bucolic existence for the rest of their lives. Here, again, Longus diverges from his colleagues, who tell their readers nothing about the protagonists' lives following their happy reunions. Daphnis and Chloë are said to have had children, a boy and a girl, and to have "grown old together." (For a more detailed discussion of Longus's novel, see W. E. McCulloh, *Longus*, 1970.)

The foregoing survey of the five extant Greek novels and the fragments of several others has demonstrated that the Greek novel tradition functioned in a context of conventionality. The themes are repetitious: Young lovers, separated on long journeys and tested in terms of their virtue and fidelity by various temptations, are eventually reunited, usually under the guidance of a protective deity. Conventional, too, are the rhetorical style and the borrowings from other genres. Over these conventions, however, is laid a pattern of variety that is a controlling feature of the genre. The protagonists, it turns out, are not always completely virtuous. The time is usually, but not always, the distant past. The tone is not consistently ideal; there are occasional elements of irony and comedy. Characterization differs significantly from novelist to novelist. The mode of presentation, while always narrative, varies from the simple omniscient narrative technique of Chariton, Xenophon, and Longus to the more sophisticated first-person narrative of Achilles Tatius and the extremely complicated combination of third- and first-person narratives in Heliodorus. Each author strives through a different technique to establish the authenticity of his story: by associating the main characters with historical personages (Chariton), by documentary inscription (Xenophon), or even by personal witness (Achilles Tatius). Each author seeks variety as a means of creating suspense and surprise and of establishing his credentials for novelty and originality within the genre. From this point of view, the Greek novel, like its modern counterpart, is indeed polymorphic, open to a diversity of form, theme, and expression.

THE ROMAN NOVEL

Until papyrus fragments radically altered the late dating of the Greek novels, the two extant Latin works of long prose fiction, the *Satyricon* (c. 60; *The Satyricon*, 1694) of Petronius Arbiter and the *Metamorphoses* of Lucius Apuleius, were thought to have been written before the rise of the Greek novel and thus were considered uniquely Roman creations, independent of the Greek romance tradition. With the realization that the Greek novel arose in the late Hellenistic period, at least as early as the first century B.C.E., it is now necessary to view both Petronius's novel of the first century C.E. and Apuleius's work of the late second century in the context of a thriving tradition of novel composition in the Mediterranean world. Both of these works, while unquestionably Roman and original creations, arose out of the peculiar symbiotic relationship of Greek and Latin literature. From the outset of literary Latin writing in the third century B.C.E., the influence of the older and more established Greek literature on Latin authors is constant and strong. Latin writers strove to emulate their Greek counterparts and, at the same time, to create a uniquely Roman literature of high quality.

The literary background to the *Satyricon* and the *Metamorphoses* is a case in point. Petronius and Apuleius both produce original works, but only out of the Greco-Roman literary tradition. Several diverse genres have been proposed as building blocks for the Roman novels. The most prominent source is the Greek novel. While the down-to-earth tone of the Roman novel, usually described as comic or even picaresque, is quite distinct from the generally romantic, idealistic mood of the Greek novel, the Roman novel shares many themes with its Greek counterpart. The Roman novel, however, takes these themes and turns them upside down. This is especially true of the *Satyricon*, which is, among other things, "a parody of the Greek ideal world," according to Hägg.

The same is true, to a lesser degree, of the *Metamorphoses*. Both Latin works contain the themes of travel, divine protection or disfavor, and, especially, love that are central to the Greek novel but treat them in different ways. The virtuous heterosexual relationship normally depicted in the Greek novel becomes, in Petronius, a disastrously comic homosexual ménage à trois, and, in Apuleius, wanton sexuality leads to the transformation of the hero into an ass. Such differences in tone have generally caused the Greek works to be called ideal romances and the Roman ones comic novels, but their structural similarities and historical links cannot be ignored. Greek papyri such as those of Lollianus and the *Iolaus* fragment have even suggested the existence of a Greek comic novel tradition contemporary with the Roman.

In addition to the Greek novel, several other genres are important to the development of the novel in Latin. The epic tradition, represented in Rome by both Homer and Vergil, is an inevitable source of literary material for both Petronius and Apuleius, who create heroes who are the inverse of the epic mold. The bumbling adventures of the naïve Petronian antihero Encolpius and the Apuleian Lucius are striking contrasts to the heroes of epic and have much in common with the blunders of Achilles Tatius's Cleitophon and with the picaresque heroes of seventeenth and eighteenth century novelists.

The influence of the Roman stage, especially of the popular low comedy of the mime, also can be seen in Petronius and Apuleius. The mime, a short, comic skit about everyday life with stock characters using colloquial language, gave the Roman novel its contemporary scenes and characters, its often "low" or realistic tone, and, in Petronius, its sometimes unliterary, colloquial Latin.

The erotic Milesian tales, a collection of racy short stories originating with the Greek Aristides of Miletus in 100 B.C.E. and early translated into Latin, were undoubtedly a model, if not a source, for the often indecorous tales inserted by both Petronius and Apuleius into their works. Several of these tales, including Petronius's "Widow of Ephesus" and Apuleius's "Tale of the Jealous Husband and the Tub" (*Metamorphoses*, 9, 38)—a tale later borrowed by Giovanni Boccaccio in *Decameron: O, Prencipe Galeotto* (1349-1351; *The Decameron*, 1620)—have developed independent literary lives of their own. It is difficult to judge from the fragmentary remains of the *Satyricon* how many short stories Petronius blended into his novel and how closely these tales were related to the plot, but all the tales in Apuleius can be interpreted as part of the larger work. Apuleius, if not Petronius, took the short-story tradition and incorporated it integrally into the novel form. Parallel use of such stories-within-stories can be seen in the Greek novelists Xenophon and Heliodorus and in more recent authors such as Fielding.

Finally, Roman satire exerted a major influence on the Latin novel, especially on Petronius. Inasmuch as the Greeks lacked examples of the genre, the Romans claimed satire as their own creation, which, as developed by Lucilius, Varro, Horace, and Juvenal, was primarily a medley, conversational in tone with an emphasis on variety of form and character. While the best-known Latin satirists, Horace and Juvenal, wrote exclusively in verse, the first century B.C.E. satirist Varro of Reate wrote in a combination of prose and verse called Menippean satire, and Petronius, following Varro's example, wrote the *Satyricon* in the prosimetric form. Of the Greek novelists, only Chariton used both prose and verse. Prosimetry aside, both Petronius and Apuleius owe to Roman satire the variety that is so evident in their novels. Roman satire also offered often biting commentary on contemporary Roman society that Petronius readily followed. Such variety or polymorphy is a feature that the Latin novelists shared with their Greek and modern colleagues.

Any discussion of the antecedents to the Roman novel must also mention the work of Ben Edwin Perry. In *The Ancient Romances*, Perry argues that there was no gradual development of the Latin novel; rather, he claims, both the *Satyricon* and the *Metamorphoses* were individual creations written to serve the unique literary purposes of their authors. Perry's theory remains a caveat for those who overemphasize the literary debts of Petronius and Apuleius instead of their originality.

The *Satyricon* of Petronius survives only in extensive fragments filling about 140 modern pages. The original work may have been at least five times that length. Nearly one-third of the extant *Satyricon* is devoted to the famous "Cena Trimalchionis" ("Trimalchio's Feast"). It is generally agreed by scholars that the author of the

Satyricon was the Petronius Arbiter who is mentioned in Tacitus's *Ab excessu divi Augusti* (c. 116 C.E.; also known as *Annales*; *Annals*, 1598) as Nero's minister of etiquette (*arbiter elegantiae*) and was forced to commit suicide in 66 C.E. The man of polished and elegant voluptuousness, whose very death was so charmingly staged, transferred his personal qualities into his work, which is a perfect product of the licentious elegance of the Neronian age. Petronius's fragments, without the "Cena," were first published in 1482; the "Cena" did not emerge from obscurity until the mid-seventeenth century. Several good modern English translations are available, including those of William Arrowsmith (1959) and of R. Bracht Branham and Daniel Kinney (1996).

The title of the novel is somewhat disputed. Most manuscripts render it *Satyricon*, which seems to refer to the Greek satyr and thus to associate the work with the lascivious nature of that mythological beast. Other manuscripts give the mongrel form *Satiricon*, which could only be the Latin word *satira*, or "satire," transformed into Greek. P. G. Walsh has suggested convincingly that Petronius's title is meant to be ambiguous, that in the novel Petronius is consciously combining the traditions of Greek comic fiction (*Satyricon*) with Roman satire (*Satiricon*). This interpretation goes far in explaining the diverse elements of this novel, with its sympathetic but comic antihero Encolpius, his homosexual passion for Giton, the pathetically comic figure of Trimalchio (whose development owes much to the figure of the bore in Roman satire), and the ironic depictions of the rhetor Agamemnon and the poet Eumolpus. Each of these characters is unquestionably a blend of literary antecedents and contemporary caricatures, so that the novel was topical to its first century C.E. readers and is sometimes arcane to twenty-first century readers, who often miss the allusions. Contemporaneity is also a feature that distinguishes the Roman novel from its more ideal Greek cousin, which usually chooses the distant past as its setting.

The extensive poetry of Eumolpus contained in the text is also a source of controversy. Eumolpus's verses, especially those on the sack of Troy and on the Roman Civil War, are interpreted by Perry to be serious literary creations that are, in fact, the excuse for the novel itself. Perry argues that Petronius, living at the dangerous court of Nero, could produce his serious literature only within the context of a farce and that the *Satyricon* provided the ideal outlet for Petronius's literary genius. Walsh, on the other hand, argues that the poems of Eumolpus are not insertions by Petronius but are meant to be Eumolpus's own verses, ironically in character with the poetic caricature created by Petronius. For Walsh, the *Satyricon* is intentionally a burlesque, not only of contemporary Roman life but also of much Greco-Roman literature, including the Greek novel.

The *Metamorphoses*, in eleven books, is dated to the second century C.E. (first translated as *The Golden Ass*, 1566). The author, Lucius Apuleius, was a native of Madaura in North Africa, studied law at Carthage and Athens, and was fluent in both Latin and Greek. His career as a lawyer brought him fame and respect in his native Africa. His unsuccessful prosecution for witchcraft (c. 158 C.E.), on which his extant *Apologia* (158-159 C.E.; English translation, 1909) is based, as well as the themes of sorcery in the *Metamorphoses* led to the medieval belief that he was a wizard. The *Metamorphoses* was one of the first classical texts published in the Renaissance; its *editio princeps* appeared in 1469. The famous English translation of 1566 by William Adlington, *The Golden Ass* (revised 1915), is still usable today. Julia Haig Gaisser traces the importance of the *Metamorphoses* to later readers in *The Fortunes of Apuleius and "The Golden Ass": A Study in Transmission and Reception* (2008).

Apuleius derived the kernel of his story, the adventures of a man transformed into an ass, directly from a Greek source: a prose story associated with the Greek satirist Lucian (c. 120-c. 180 C.E.). Lucian's *Metamorphoses* survives only in an abridged edition, called the *Onos* or *The Ass* (English translation, 1989). Lucian's tale, filled with sex and magic, undoubtedly springs from the Milesian type of story already discussed. Comparison of the extant *Onos* with Apuleius's novel shows that Apuleius closely followed the plot of his original but added much in terms of characterization. Apuleius's hero, Lucius, is much more developed than in the Greek version, but this impression may be a result of the abridgment of the Greek text. More significantly, Apuleius weaves into the plot a series of short stories, including "Cupid and Psyche," that were not in his original source. Completely Apuleian, too, is the climax of religious conversion in book 11. In the Greek version, the retransformation of Lucius back into his true shape occurs when the ass eats some roses; in Apuleius, the metamorphosis occurs only through the intervention of the Egyptian deity Isis, and the novel ends with the hero dedicating his life to her.

The intent of Apuleius's work has been the subject of much debate. At the beginning of the first book, Apuleius addresses his reader directly and describes his tale as "diverse stories in the Milesian fashion" that will "delight your gracious ears with a pleasant tale." The entertaining goal of the work is reinforced at the end of this introduction, where the reader is asked to "pay attention; you will be amused." Many scholars, including Perry, take Apuleius's words at face value and argue that the work is meant exclusively for entertainment. Other scholars emphasize the intense religiosity of the last book and argue that, while entertaining, the work also has a didactic purpose. Walsh thus sees the *Metamorphoses* simultaneously as entertainment, as fable (especially in "Cupid and Psyche"), and as religious apologia. According to this interpretation, the diverse tales that Apuleius incorporates into his work are not merely amusing anecdotes; rather, each serves to develop the message of the work—the danger of excessive eroticism and curiosity versus religious faith as the sole source of personal salvation.

The *Metamorphoses* is a unique blend of the comic and the ideal, of entertainment and edification. The hero, Lucius, is both an amusing bungler and, ironically, a moral exemplum. Female characters in the tales are both intensely sexual, as in the Milesian tales, and admirably virtuous, as in the Greek novel tradition. Using variations of tone and theme, Apuleius has thus created a unique example of ancient long fiction. The *Metamorphoses*, in itself, exemplifies the polymorphic character of the novel form of which it is a significant ancient example. (The best introduction to both Petronius and Apuleius is Walsh's *The Roman Novel*, 1970.)

Other ancient long fiction

A survey of the novel in the ancient world would be incomplete without a brief discussion of other forms of long fiction that Tomas Hägg has shown to have close ties with the novel form. *Marvels Beyond Thule*, in twenty-four books, by Antonius Diogenes (fl. 100 C.E.) is an example of the travel literature popular in antiquity. While the work survives only in a medieval summary, many parallels between it and the ancient novels can be noted, particularly in the elements of travel, separation, apparent death, and reunion. Significantly, the love motif appears to have been secondary in Diogenes, who emphasizes, as the title suggests, incredible adventures beyond the end of the world. He apparently wove together a complicated narrative consisting of first-person narrative within first-person narrative.

The *Alexander Romance*, attributed falsely to the fourth century B.C.E. historian Callisthenes, is an excellent example of the way fiction and history could be blended in the ancient world. The author, called Pseudo-Callisthenes and writing sometime around the fourth century C.E., seems to have started with a Hellenistic prose biography of Alexander the Great and to have added material gathered from an epistolary romance about the king (dated about 100 B.C.E. and now lost) as well as from several separate longer letters from Alexander to his mother or to his teacher Aristotle. These last letters include descriptions of the king's adventures in India and at the ends of the world, especially his encounter with the gymnosophists of India (recalling the gymnosophists in Heliodorus). The affinities of this peculiar historiography with the Greek novel tradition are based on the travel motif as well as the fictionalization of historical events. The *Alexander Romance* survives in several Greek and Latin versions from late antiquity (fourth to sixth centuries) as well as in many medieval vernacular forms that indicate the popularity of the book in the medieval period. The romance has been translated into English by Ken Dowden in Reardon's *Collected Ancient Greek Novels*.

Also well known in the Middle Ages were the *Troy Romances* of Dictys of Crete and Dares of Phrygia, which were written about the second century C.E. (English translation, 1966). These works—both Dictys's *Ephemeris belli Troiani* (fourth century C.E.; diary of the Trojan War) and Dares's *De excidio Troiae historia* (fifth century C.E., probably written during second or third century C.E.; English translation, 1553)—claimed to be historical accounts of historical events. If the *Alex-*

ander Romance could treat history like fiction, the *Troy Romances* could treat myth like history. So, too, could the ancient novelists.

The anonymous *Historia Apollonii regis Tyri* (c. third century C.E.; *The Old English Apollonius of Tyre*, 1958) is another piece of ancient long fiction extremely popular in the Middle Ages and widely translated into the vernacular. The surviving Latin version, dating from the fifth or sixth century, is probably derived from an original Greek version of the third century to which Christian elements were joined. The plot and style are very similar to Xenophon's *Ephesian Tale* and display the typical novel's blend of love, travel, and adventure, to which folktale motifs such as the suitor contest have been added. The story of Apollonius thus provides an important link between the Greek novel form and the "darkness" of the Middle Ages. An accessible English translation, by Gerald N. Sandy, is in Reardon's *Collected Ancient Greek Novels*.

The popular Menippean satire must also be mentioned as another example of ancient long fiction. The prosimetric form was employed not only in the classical novels of Petronius and Chariton but also in important works of late antiquity: the fifth century allegory *De nuptiis Philologiae et Mercurii* (*The Marriage of Philology and Mercury*, 1977) of Martianus Capella (fl. late fourth to early fifth century) and the sixth century philosophical work *De consolatione philosophiae* (523 C.E.; *The Consolation of Philosophy*, late ninth century) by Boethius (c. 480-524 C.E.). These works, fictional in the way Plato's philosophical presentation of the historical Socrates is fictional, demonstrate the variegated purposes and forms of ancient fiction.

A final form of long prose fiction shows an important link between the "pagan" novel and early Christian literature. Hägg discusses the thematic and structural similarities between the Greek novels and such fictional works as *Paul and Thecla* from the *Apocryphal Acts of the Apostles* (both dating around the second century) and the *Recognitions* (written c. 200 and attributed to Clement of Rome; English translation, 1890). Both works use the novelistic themes of travel, love, separation, and reunion to introduce Christian themes to readers. The same motifs can be seen transmitted into the hagiographic literature of the medieval period. Such lives of the saints as the popular *Barlaam and Joasaph* have proved, upon examination, to be more fiction than fact. The classical disregard for historical fact, the blending of history and fiction—also notable in the ancient novel—continues in this Christian literature well past the medieval period.

THE CONTINUITY AND INFLUENCE OF THE GENRE

While the Sophistic Greek novels of Heliodorus, Achilles Tatius, and Longus, as well as the two Roman novels, were certainly known and read in late antiquity, there is no evidence that any new novels of this type were written after Heliodorus. There are several possible reasons for this. Certainly, the political and social upheavals of late antiquity resulted in a gradual decline in literacy and, logically, in a decrease in the numbers of potential readers of the novel. Also important is the rise of Christianity. While the Greek novels of Heliodorus and Achilles Tatius were admired for their moral edification and praise of virginity, demand for these pagan works was inevitably displaced by more Christian fiction, such as *Paul and Thecla*.

During the medieval period there is little indication that any of the ancient novels were known in the West, but the Greek Sophistic novels continued to be read and enjoyed in the Greek Byzantine Empire. Achilles Tatius and Heliodorus received the praise of Photius, the learned ninth century Byzantine patriarch, and of Michael Psellus, the eleventh century philosopher and diplomat. The twelfth century revival during the Comnenian Dynasty saw the appearance of four Byzantine novels modeled on ancient tales: those of Hysmine and Hysminias, by Eustathius Macrembolites; *Rhodantes et Dosiclis amores*, by Theodorus Prodromus; Aristandros and Callithea, by Constantius Manasses; and Drosilla and Charikles, by Nicetas Eugenianus (the last of these is accessible in an English translation by Joan B. Burton, 2004). Despite the innovation that all but the first were written in verse rather than in prose, each retains a classical, pagan setting as well as many of the standard novelistic themes. Byzantine novels continued to be written nearly until the Fall of Constantinople in 1453, but in these later novels, the genre had already begun to transform under the influences of medieval and folktale traditions and even through Western contacts, especially the

Crusades. The impact of these relatively obscure Byzantine novels on Western literature through cultural links has been little studied but is another potential bond between the ancient and modern genres.

The *Metamorphoses* of Lucius Apuleius was the first ancient novel to reemerge in the West. The novel, dated to the second century C.E. and first translated into English in 1566 as *The Golden Ass*, had a wide circulation from about 1100 onward in Italy and reached France and Great Britain by the thirteenth century. One of the first Latin texts to be published, the *Metamorphoses* gained a large reading public and exerted great influence during the Renaissance. The admiration of Giovanni Boccaccio, who uses three of Apuleius's tales in his *Decameron*, makes Apuleius an important source, especially for stories about cuckolded husbands, in the history of the modern novella or short story. Apuleius's "Cupid and Psyche" has had broad independent influence beginning with Boccaccio's retelling in his *Genealogia deorum gentilium* (1350-1375, 1472; the genealogies of the gods). Since then, "Cupid and Psyche" has been fashioned into epic, drama, ballet, opera, poetic letter, and painting throughout Europe. Apuleius is also influential both in the rise of a popular literature of the ass, especially in Renaissance Italy, and in the development of the picaresque novel, particularly in Spain. Mateo Alemán's *Guzmán de Alfarache* (1599-1604; *The Rogue: Or, The Life of Guzman de Alfarache*, 1622) is modeled, to a certain extent, on the adventures of Apuleius's Lucius. Through such Spanish rogue literature, the Roman novel exerts its influence on the novels of other European languages, including Alain-René Lesage's *Histoire de Gil Blas de Santillane* (1715-1735; *The History of Gil Blas of Santillane*, 1716, 1735) and Henry Fielding's *The History of the Adventures of Joseph Andrews, and of His Friend Mr. Abraham Adams* (1742; commonly known as *Joseph Andrews*).

Petronius's influence in the Renaissance was more subtle than Apuleius's but not insignificant. The fragmentary and often scandalous nature of his novel meant that few had direct contact with the *Satyricon* during this period, but enough was known of Petronius and his novel to encourage imitation of Petronius's mood and structure and to explain the similarities between the *Satyricon* and modern comic novels such as Fielding's. Petronius's novel has even been adapted to the cinema in a famous screenplay by Italian director Federico Fellini (1969).

The three Sophistic Greek novels were all known in the West, either in the original or in translation, by the mid-sixteenth century. Several translations, especially those of Heliodorus by Amyot and by Underdowne, were widely read and particularly influential. Heliodorus, in fact, quickly became a critical model for the Renaissance, which ranked the *Ethiopian Story* together with Aristotle's *De poetica* (c. 334-323 B.C.E.; *Poetics*, 1705) and Horace's *Ars poetica* (c. 17 B.C.E.; *The Art of Poetry*, 1567). The appeal of Apuleius and Heliodorus in the Renaissance results, to a great extent, from the ability of both writers to combine entertainment with edification, the Horatian principles of *utile* (useful) and *dulci* (sweet), which were so precious to the Renaissance. Heliodorus received commendation for his instructional value, both as moral and literary standard, from such Renaissance critics as his French translator Amyot, the great classical scholar J. C. Scaliger, the Italian poet Torquato Tasso, and the Spanish theorist López Pinciano. Critical praise inevitably led to imitation. Some of the more famous and influential works with Heliodoran features include Sir Philip Sidney's pastoral *Arcadia* (1590), Honoré d'Urfé's *L'Astrée* (1607-1628; *Astrea*, 1657-1658), and Miguel de Cervantes' *Los trabajos de Persiles y Sigismunda* (1617; *The Travels of Persiles and Sigismunda: A Northern History*, 1619). The seventeenth century saw Heliodorus's modern heyday, when he gained the admiration of even the French classical dramatist Jean Racine, but, with the gradual rejection of edification as a primary literary goal in the late seventeenth century, Heliodorus's influence quickly waned and has never recovered.

Longus's *Daphnis and Chloë* has maintained its own sphere of modern influence, especially over the sometime popular pastoral. In 1831, the novel even received the glowing commendation of Johann Wolfgang von Goethe for its "perfection" and "great beauty." The work was particularly favored by European book illustrators of the nineteenth and twentieth centuries.

The pre-Sophistic Greek novels of Xenophon and Chariton were not known again in Europe until the eighteenth century and thus have not affected modern literature in the way Heliodorus or Apuleius have. It has been suggested by Paul Turner, however, that the influence of the text of Xenophon rediscovered in 1727 can be seen in the novels of that period, including Fielding's *Joseph Andrews* and *Tom Jones*, and in Charlotte Brontë's *Jane Eyre* (1847). The similarities of plot between the Greek novel and these modern novels is at least a modest caution to those who deny any link between the ancient and modern novel traditions.

Thomas J. Sienkewicz
Updated by Cynthia A. Bily

Bibliography

Anderson, Graham. *Ancient Fiction: The Novel in the Graeco-Roman World.* Totowa, N.J.: Barnes & Noble Books, 1984. Broad examination of the ancient novel begins with the quest for the origin of the Greek novel and uses some Sumerian texts to suggest the Near Eastern roots of the tradition. Also includes chapters on topics such as narrative, love, character, myth, history, sex, and structure in the Greek novels as well as a chapter on Petronius's *Satyricon* and two chapters on Apuleius's *Metamorphoses*.

Hägg, Tomas. *The Novel in Antiquity*. Berkeley: University of California Press, 1983. Offers the general English reader an outstanding introduction to the ancient novel. Includes chapters on the genre in antiquity, plot summaries and analyses, social context and readership, literary antecedents, historical novels, hagiographic novels, Roman comic novels, and the influence of the Greek novel in the Renaissance. Particularly useful to the novice is an introductory note on terms. Also includes a map and seventy-nine black-and-white illustrations depicting ancient artwork and artifacts as well as woodcuts and prints from early modern editions of the novels.

_______. *Parthenope: Selected Studies in Ancient Greek Fiction, 1969-2004*. Edited by Lars Boje Mortensen and Tormod Eide. Copenhagen: Museum Tusculanum Press, 2004. Follow-up to Hägg's *The Novel in Antiquity* is a collection of his work edited by two of his colleagues. The twenty-three essays focus on Chariton, Xenophon, *Parthenope* and its reception, and Apollonius, and include seven reviews.

Haynes, Katharine. *Fashioning the Feminine in the Greek Novel.* New York: Routledge, 2002. Focuses on the strong female characters that lie at the heart of ancient Greek prose, arguing that these characters offered an educated, largely male, readership an instructive way to think about masculinity and empowerment.

Holzberg, Niklas. *The Ancient Novel: An Introduction.* Translated by Christine Jackson-Holzberg. New York: Routledge, 1995. General overview of the genre includes chapters on characteristics and definition of the genre, the historical development of ancient prose fiction, the idealistic Greek novel in the early Roman empire, the Greco-Roman comic-realistic novels, and idealistic Greek novels in the second century C.E.

Panayotakis, Stelios, Maaike Zimmerman, and Wytse Keulen, eds. *The Ancient Novel and Beyond.* Boston: Brill, 2003. Collection of thirty essays, twenty-five in English, originally presented at the International Conference on the Ancient Novel held in the Netherlands in 2000. Sorted into three sections, the essays analyze the ancient novel in context, focus on particular novels, and trace the works' influences on later literature. Written for a scholarly audience, but general readers will find many of the essays accessible and insightful.

Perry, Ben Edwin. *The Ancient Romances: A Literary-Historical Account of Their Origins.* Berkeley: University of California Press, 1967. Influential scholarly study of the origin of the Greco-Roman novel tradition is divided into two parts: The first argues that the first Greek romance was the conscious creation of an individual author in the late Hellenistic period; the second examines features of comic or burlesque romances such as Petronius's *Satyricon*, Lucian's *Metamorphoses*, and Apuleius's *Metamorphoses*.

Schmeling, Gareth L., ed. *The Novel in the Ancient World.* New York: Brill, 1996. Scholarly collection of essays covers a wide range of topics related to the ancient novel, including genre, origin, readership, characterization, religion, portrayals of women and foreigners, and the influence of these works in later periods. Also includes individual essays on each of the major ancient authors and twelve maps illustrating the routes followed by the characters in these novels.

Tatum, James, ed. *The Search for the Ancient Novel.* Baltimore: Johns Hopkins University Press, 1994. Collection of twenty-four scholarly articles includes studies on the origins of the ancient novel, the use of parody and imitation in the genre, the romance or pastoral form, idealized love, representations of reality, religion, and later influence.

Walsh, P. G. *The Roman Novel.* New York: Cambridge University Press, 1970. Scholarly study of the Roman comic novel examines the literary antecedents and sophistication of works such as Petronius's *Satyricon* and Apuleius's *Metamorphoses.* Includes separate studies of the *Satyricon*, the *Dinner of Trimalcio*, the *Metamorphoses*, and the tale of "Cupid and Psyche" as well as a chapter on the influence of these works on later European literature.

Whitmarsh, Tim, ed. *The Cambridge Companion to the Greek and Roman Novel.* New York: Cambridge University Press, 2008. Rather than focusing on individual works, these nineteen original and accessible essays address central themes and issues in the early Greek and Roman novels, including narrative and style, form and genre, religion and politics, sexuality and gender, and culture and class. Includes suggestions for further reading.

Wills, Lawrence M. *The Jewish Novel in the Ancient World.* Ithaca, N.Y.: Cornell University Press, 1995. Examines several examples of prose fiction in the Jewish tradition, including the biblical books of Daniel, Susanna, Tobit, Esther, and Judith as well as the nonbiblical *Joseph and Aseneth* and other Jewish historical novels. Notes similarities between these works and other prose fiction in the eastern Mediterranean, especially that of the Greeks and the Sumerians, and argues that all of these novels spring from a literary tradition popular in the first century B.C.E.

Origins and Development of the Novel Before 1740

The English-speaking world has long considered 1740, the year in which Samuel Richardson's *Pamela: Or, Virtue Rewarded* was published, pivotal in the development of the novel, a broad term that, for several centuries, has been applied to many different forms of long fiction. Richardson's first novel remains a convenient landmark in the history of the form because, at least in England, it went further than any previous work in exploring an individual character's "sensibility," that wonderful mix of perception, culture, logic, sentiment, passion, and myriad other traits that define a person's individuality. *Pamela* has been called the first intellectual novel, that subgenre in which most of the greatest novelists of the nineteenth and twentieth centuries worked.

Nevertheless, while 1740 is an important date in the development of one type of novel, to see all earlier novels as primitive ancestors of *Pamela* would distort the history of this multifarious form. The novel followed substantially different lines of development in Spain, France, and England, three countries notable for their contributions to the early growth of this form in Europe. Moreover, different types of novels exist side by side in every period, each type appealing to a different taste, much as different types of the novel flourish today. Finally, certain earlier works have exerted as profound and lasting an influence on the novel in Europe as that attributed to *Pamela*.

The massive, one-thousand-page *Genji monogatari* (c. 1004; *The Tale of Genji*, 1925-1933) appeared in Japan hundreds of years before the genre developed in the West. *The Tale of Genji* was an immediate success in Japan, and celebrations in the year 2008 marked the one thousandth year since the first recorded mention of the novel appeared in 1008. The author, Murasaki Shikibu, was a lady-in-waiting to the empress, and the story describes courtly, not common, life. Because there was virtually no contact between Japan and Europe at the time, this first great novel in the history of world literature came to have little influence on the Western novel. Unlike in Japan, the woman novelist would not emerge in the West for another seven hundred years; women's contributions to the Western novel emerged alongside those of men, especially during the eighteenth and nineteenth centuries.

The sixteenth century

It could be argued that Sir Thomas Malory's *Le Morte d'Arthur* (1485; the death of Arthur) marks the beginning of the English novel, followed closely by Sir Thomas More's *De Optimo Reipublicae Statu, deque Nova Insula Utopia* (1516; *Utopia*, 1551). Scholars of the genre, however, have usually excluded these works. *Le Morte d'Arthur*, somewhat inaccurately titled, is an English translation of selected and condensed romances from the French. The plot is rambling and unfocused, unlike the novel as a form. *Utopia* is a much more unified work of prose, but it is composed in Latin and therefore technically, and literally, not a work of English literature.

Whereas the French novel underwent constant refinement during the century and a half preceding 1740, with French writers producing masterpieces at intervals throughout the period, the English novel flowered briefly before 1600 and then lay dormant for more than a century until it was revitalized by Daniel Defoe. The seventeenth century in England produced but one work of genius in the form, John Bunyan's *The Pilgrim's Progress* (1678, 1684), a novel ignored by Bunyan's contemporaries in literary society because of its style and theme.

Although overshadowed by the unsurpassed drama of the Elizabethans, the 1580's and 1590's saw an outpouring of original fictional narratives, including one voluminous work and a host of shorter works in the pastoral and satiric modes. Like the French one decade later, English writers were heavily influenced by translations of the late Greek romances as well as by the satires of the humanists, the pastorals of Jacopo Sannazaro and Jorge de Montemayor, and the tragic love *novelle* of Matteo Bandello. Other influential sources were the manuals of courtly behavior and noble ethics written by the Italians Baldassare Castiglione (*Il libro del cortegiano*, 1528; *The Book of the Courtier*, 1561) and Stefano Guazzo (*La civil conversazione* (1574; *Civil Conversation*, 1581-

1586). These inspired similar guides in England and provided a format of learned discourse imitated by writers of fiction.

The most distinctive feature of the English novels of that time is their commitment to moral improvement of the individual and of the state as a whole. Since, with the exception of Sir Philip Sidney, the principal novelists of that time were sons of the middle class, much of their writing was suffused with middle-class values: hard work, thrift, cautious ambition. As the period advanced, fictional works became more overtly addressed to the middle class, with more middle-class characters taking principal roles. In the 1580's, this bourgeois appeal typically took the form of the romance intended to instruct the upwardly mobile reader in courtly ways; later, satire held sway, a satire moved by the spirit of reform rather than by the resigned contempt of the Spanish picaresques.

The most influential fiction early in this period was John Lyly's *Euphues, the Anatomy of Wit* (1578), actually less a novel than a moral handbook for wealthy, budding scholars. In it, bright young Euphues exchanges academic arguments with wise old Eubolus on the issue of worldly experience versus the codified wisdom of the ages. Euphues fails to heed Eubolus's sage advice and decides to taste the world, only to become the emotional captive of Lucilla, a courtesan who strips him of his money and his dignity. A chastened Euphues vows to spend the rest of his life contemplating philosophy and warning the young. *Euphues, the Anatomy of Wit* was a continuing hit with a wide audience, and Lyly's peculiar style established a fashion that persisted for a decade. Called euphuism, this style features the culling of exotic lore from the pseudohistories of the ancients, primarily the Roman scholar Pliny. In euphuistic argumentation, these strange bits are used as evidence for or against certain courses of action. That euphuism succeeded where other linguistic experiments such as *marivaudage* failed shows the hunger of Lyly's audience for a mode of discourse that would make them appear learned.

Lyly's most enthusiastic follower, Robert Greene, was a highly original novelist in his own right who composed an amazing variety of euphuistic romances between 1580 and 1587. In Greene works such as *Mamillia: A Mirror or Looking Glass for the Ladies of England* (1583, 1593), *The Mirror of Modesty* (1584), *Morando: The Tritameron of Love* (1584, 1587), and *Euphues, His Censure to Philautus* (1587), one can see clearly the amalgamation of sources—Italian *novelle*, the Bible, Castiglione, Greek epic—in Elizabethan fiction. Unlike Lyly, however, Greene brings to these romances a spirit of comic realism that invests his characters with greater fullness and sympathy than Lyly's characters demonstrate. Greene's later romances (such as *Menaphon*, 1589, and *Greene's Never Too Late*, 1590) reject euphuism in favor of a more colloquial conversational style better suited to his more realistic characters.

When Greene turned away from Lyly in 1588, he was responding to the new fashion for pastoral love stories established by Sidney's huge romance, *Arcadia*, which had been circulating in manuscript since 1580 but was not published until 1590 (revised in 1593 and 1598). *Arcadia*, an aristocratic work similar to Honoré d'Urfé's *L'Astrée* (1607-1628, 1925; *Astrea*, 1657-1658), shows the blending of the Greek romances, with their pastoral and heroic elements, and the intensely emotional love pastorals of Sannazaro and the Elizabethan sonneteers, including Sidney himself. There is a good deal of the chivalric spirit present here, too, as knightly combats, with armor and emblems vividly described, are the primary means of settling disputes. Amid the shipwrecks, kidnappings, heroic rescues, and seemingly endless love laments of the sexually frustrated heroes, Musidorus and Pyrocles, two genuinely sympathetic characters emerge: Amphialus and his wife, Parthenia. Theirs is a tragic tale of the Homeric conflict between a soldier's sense of duty and his regard for his wife, whose desire for his safety leads her to endanger herself and ultimately lose her life. The power of this story within *Arcadia* derives from Sidney's almost Shakespearean refusal to take sides—his willingness to let the story unfold and allow the reader to judge. Had the novel's main plot—his heroes' often silly attempts to win the favor of a pair of princesses—been exchanged for a serious investigation of ethical issues, Sidney might have produced a work of the stature of Miguel de Cervantes' *Don Quixote de la Mancha* (1605, 1615). Cervantes' novel—one of the greatest in literary history—has had an influence on popular fiction, drama, and film in the West that can scarcely be overstated.

Thomas Shelton translated part 1 of *Don Quixote de la Mancha* into English shortly after its original publication. Poet and playwright William Shakespeare may well have read Shelton's translation. In fact, some scholars have speculated that one of Shakespeare's lost plays was a dramatization of *Don Quixote de la Mancha*. Henry Fielding imitated the manner of Cervantes in *The History of the Adventures of Joseph Andrews, and of His Friend Mr. Abraham Adams* (1742; commonly known as *Joseph Andrews*). Fielding also composed a ballad-opera titled *Don Quixote in England* (pr., pb. 1734). Tobias Smollett, Daniel Defoe, and many later English writers paid the tribute of imitation to the knight of La Mancha.

Among the traits that limited Sidney as a novelist was his contempt for the common people, as shown in several episodes in *Arcadia* that caricature plebeians as stupid, greedy, and bestial. Since the future of publishing in England meant appealing to the powerful London middle class, it was inevitable that novels would emerge with middle-class heroes and heroines. Greene's later romances are of this category, as are the works of Thomas Deloney, a silk weaver, whose *The Pleasant History of John Winchcomb in His Younger Days Called Jack of Newbery* (1597; better known as *Jack of Newbery*) and *Thomas of Reading: Or, The Six Worthy Yeomen of the West* (c. 1600) feature romanticized artisan heroes within vividly authentic backgrounds of English town and rural life.

Deloney's contribution to English literary history was much disputed by scholars of the twentieth century. Although some considered him "an astonishing genius" and others disregarded him entirely, most current critics and historians take a middle view of Deloney's significance as a prose writer. While not a genius, Deloney was one of the first English authors to write for and about the rising middle class. His perceptiveness of the prevailing literary climate, whether educated or merely fortuitous, was accurate, for his popularity among the middle class was unsurpassed. His works, within only a few years of their publication, were literally read out of existence. The realistic novel of the twentieth and twenty-first centuries owes a substantial debt to Deloney, for his early portrayal of middle-class values, concerns, and language.

That Deloney became a spokesperson for the middle class was only a portion of his accomplishment. Another reason for the popularity of his works was that they were written in prose. Prior to Deloney's time, written works were composed in verse or dramatic form, making the exploration of rising social issues a challenge. Less artificial, prose fiction was better suited to addressing such subject matter, and Deloney proved himself a more talented master of the form than most prose fiction writers of his time.

Two elements that make Deloney's fiction outstanding are his skillful use of dialogue and his excellent characterizations. Presenting three-dimensional middle-class characters drawn from his hardworking colleagues, Deloney engages them in dialogue fit for the stage, yet instead of the lofty language familiar only to kings and nobles he captures the idiomatic speech and straightforwardness of the common people of his day.

Deloney's plot development is less remarkable, although it should not be lightly dismissed. *Jack of Newbery*, considered his most unified prose work, is a tale about a young man who works for a wealthy clothier and eventually becomes the master of the business when the owner dies, leaving the conscientious young Jack (known as John) to marry the widow. The majority of the work centers on John's adventures after his wife has died and he has become a wealthy man. *Thomas of Reading* is a less unified work, yet it reaches a level of plot sophistication higher than that of *Jack of Newbery*. In it, King Henry I is made aware of the value of the clothing industry in England, and, by deliberately supporting the clothiers, he enables them to raise their social positions. Such a change in social status was finally an attainable goal for the working class, and thus a tale of this type appealed to a wide audience.

While many of Deloney's characters grasp the beneficent hand of capitalism, Deloney ensures that they do not succumb to the snobbishness common to those who already enjoy aristocratic freedoms. After diligently earning their wealth, these protagonists liberally distribute it, thus allowing the entire community to prosper from their good fortune. Despite the indirectness of his moralizing, Deloney was accepted as the militant spokesman for the middle class, and the political disjunction between his views and those of Sidney gives evidence of the social rift that would lead to civil war in the next century.

Class and religious tensions—the fires fanned by economic decline—were already sparking sharp satires, some obviously political, others less partisan in their scourge of social abuse. In the latter group are Greene's tales of "connycatching" (1591-1592), which purport to expose the methods of actual thieves and con artists so that decent citizens may beware. These contributed to the development of fiction in England because Greene's reproving tone is a thin veil for his real interest in exploring the romantic, sympathetic side of the criminal stereotype. Such characters as Ned Browne, Nan the whore, Laurence the cutpurse, and Cuthbert Connycatcher blend the picaros with the courageous imps of the medieval jestbooks. The candor and colloquial discourse of these stories created a fashion for rogue books that persisted through the seventeenth century and influenced Defoe.

Brilliantly capitalizing on the connycatching fad was Greene's boon companion Thomas Nashe, one of literature's sharpest tongues and quickest wits. After achieving notoriety through vicious anti-Puritan pamphlets and personal attacks on literary foes, Nashe penned the age's premier satiric novel, *The Unfortunate Traveller: Or, The Life of Jack Wilton* (1594). Lacking the fellow feeling of a Lazaro, a Gil Blas, or even one of Greene's connycatchers, Nashe's Jack Wilton astounds the reader with the range of his amoral exploits and the depth of his depravity. He satirizes through deeds as well as words: He outcheats the greatest cheats, plots the deaths of murderers, tortures the heartlessly cruel. Though he makes a perfunctory repentance at the end of the novel, Jack is a thorough villain who satirizes not from a sense of moral outrage but because his clever foes are so gullible or have the audacity to be as villainous as he. His attacks on Italy, for example, are inspired by the Italians' allegedly unquenchable thirst for vengeance, a trait that Jack has much reason to fear.

Just as outrageous as the character of Jack are those in Nashe's cast of minor figures: King Henry VIII, Thomas More, Desiderius Erasmus, and other notables of the early sixteenth century. Jack spends a good deal of the novel as the servant of Henry Howard, earl of Surrey, and together they romp through dangerous escapades. History as rewritten by Nashe is a pageant composed for Jack Wilton, poor in birth but inexhaustibly rich in wit. The plot and the person are incredible, but Nashe so deftly appeals to the cynical reader that it is easy to see this book as a realistic fiction rather than what might more accurately be described as a fantasy of revenge. The dark tragedies of Cyril Tourneur, John Webster, George Chapman, and Thomas Middleton in the Jacobean years partake of this same spirit and were surely influenced by *The Unfortunate Traveller*.

The seventeenth century

Because satiric fiction of the next decades returned to the pattern and subject matter of the connycatching works, prose writers who followed Nashe perhaps found his brilliance inimitable. The best of these writers, Thomas Dekker, presented collections of jests and stories carefully describing the shifts of London thieves and beggars in his *The Bellman of London* (1608) and *Lanthorn and Candlelight* (1608, 1609; revised as *O per se O*, 1612; *Villanies Discovered*, 1616, 1620; *English Villanies*, 1632, 1638, 1648), both heavy-handed condemnations of the outlaws from the perspective of the outraged citizen demanding protection. Dekker achieves neither Greene's sympathy nor Nashe's worldly-wise cynicism. Because his works create no real characters, they cannot really be called novels.

Just as the French religious wars of the sixteenth century precluded the growth of the novel in France, so the strides in English fiction taken during the Elizabethan years were halted during the seventeenth century as the economy worsened and religious tensions increased. Though novel readers continued to demand reprints of Elizabethan fictions, no significant works in this genre were produced in England until well after the Restoration of the monarchy in 1660. The appetite for novels during the first two-thirds of the century was satisfied by translations of contemporary French works, with Honoré d'Urfé's *Astrea* and the heroic novels of Madeleine de Scudéry enjoying great popularity. Ironically, when the century did produce a great English novelist, John Bunyan, he was ignored by the readers of French novels because of his allegorical method and his Puritan views.

Bunyan's masterpiece, *The Pilgrim's Progress*, was partly written during his second imprisonment for unauthorized preaching. This occurred some six years after his first imprisonment (1660-1672), during which he had written his spiritual autobiography, *Grace Abounding to the Chief of Sinners* (1666), an intensely moving study reminiscent of Saint Augustine's *Confessiones* (397-400; *Confessions*, 1620). It would be misleading to say that *The Pilgrim's Progress* was influenced by any literary source except the Bible, since the uneducated Bunyan is not known to have been familiar with any other of the earlier seminal works. This partly explains why Bunyan's style avoids affectations that make most fiction of this period indigestible for modern readers. Also, Bunyan wrote for an audience as simple as himself, one that did not demand the veneer of learning applied by aristocratic writers.

If the Bible did influence Bunyan's masterpiece, one can find in Revelation the source for his use of the dream-vision framework, as well as such features as the castlelike Heaven, the goal of Christian's journey. The allegorical hindrances that the pilgrim encounters on his trek, such as the Castle of Despair and the Hill of Difficulty, seem original with Bunyan, though certainly the mode of the allegorical journey is familiar from Edmund Spenser's *The Faerie Queene* (1590, 1596), a work probably known to Bunyan. Undeniably original are Bunyan's characters, such as Timorous, Mistrust, and Talkative, who not only embody the vices for which they are named but also talk as authentically as actual people in whom one recognizes these dominant traits. The arguments of these characters are so plausible that the reader sympathizes with the character Christian's frequent doubts about how to proceed and whom to believe. Moreover, Bunyan's characterizations are so concise, his observations so exact, that a character's presence for one or two pages is sufficient to sharply define him or her. For example, though Christian is accompanied by Faithful through only a small portion of part 1 of *The Pilgrim's Progress*, the reader builds up enough sympathy for this character to feel shocked when he is murdered by the citizens of Vanity Fair.

Bunyan as a novelist works so economically, so unselfconsciously, that the reader quickly loses the sense of artifice, even though the work is in an unorthodox form. In other words, *The Pilgrim's Progress* is one of those rare works of fiction that readers usually do not regard as fiction because they apprehend it as truth. Passing directly into the cultural mainstream of the people without having been authorized, as it were, by literary society, Bunyan's allegory can be said to have influenced most English writers since the mid-eighteenth century, although its traces are often hard to mark because it has been so well assimilated.

Beginning just after the appearance of *The Pilgrim's Progress*, though in no way inspired by Bunyan's work, the novelistic career of Aphra Behn appealed to the aristocratic and city audience to which Bunyan gave no thought. Predictably, Behn's novels and stories follow the French heroic pattern, with its idealized, beautiful characters and exotic settings. In her best work, *Three Histories* (1688), a collection that includes the notable *Oroonoko: Or, The History of the Royal Slave*, Behn adds a wrinkle that makes her heroic works irresistible: The stories purport to be true, and she includes sufficient London names and places to make the assertion believable. At a time when London society craved gossip about the fashionable and saw the roman à clef as a way to satisfy that craving, readers preferred to accept the illusion of allegedly real people performing impossibly heroic acts rather than explicit fiction attempting the accurate portrayal of reality. In *Oroonoko*, for example, a pair of African lovers (with ideal European aristocratic manners) are swept across continents and oceans from one harrowing scrape to another until both are murdered. Despite the implausibility of the events, readers accepted Behn's claim that the incidents actually occurred.

THE EARLY EIGHTEENTH CENTURY

Behn's popularity occasioned many imitators. In competition with them were the writers of sensational accounts of authentic voyages to exotic places. Both forms appealed to the taste, present in every age, for examples of individual survival or death in the midst of calamitous events. It was to suit this taste that the most famous adventure novel of modern times, Daniel Defoe's *Robinson Crusoe* (1719), was written. Drawing on numerous accounts of travelers' shipwrecks, isolation, and survival, Defoe created a study of the individual in collision with environment that surpassed in realism any previous English fiction, except perhaps *The Pilgrim's*

Progress. Defoe's *Robinson Crusoe* and *The Fortunes and Misfortunes of the Famous Moll Flanders, Written from Her Own Memorandums* (1722; commonly known as *Moll Flanders*) created a fashion for realistic characterization that made possible the character studies of Richardson, Fielding, and their successors.

Firmly established as a journalist, political propagandist, and editor of popular periodicals, Defoe brought to the writing of *Robinson Crusoe* an unerring sense of public taste and a sure knack for the detail or turn of phrase that would convince the reader of the authenticity of a story. Though the central fact of the book, an Englishman's survival on an uninhabited island for twenty-eight years, is as fanciful as many of Behn's turns of plot, Defoe makes the entire story plausible through his scrupulous attention to even the tiniest fact of Crusoe's existence. Where Behn or one of her imitators might have focused on the emotional trauma of shipwreck and isolation, Defoe, eminently practical in all his endeavors, focuses on the mundane how of existence: how to ensure a supply of meat when all the gunpowder and bullets are gone, how to make a shovel without iron, how to bake bread without an oven. Nevertheless, Defoe does not slight Crusoe the moral and emotional creature; perhaps the masterstroke of the novel is that Defoe first makes the reader confront and gradually accept the narrator's aloneness before presenting the fearsome truth that Crusoe is not alone. Though Defoe's sincerity as an ethical writer has often been questioned, there is nothing feigned about Crusoe's confused response to his savage visitors. Behn's *Oroonoko* has been called the first novel to make racial equality an issue, but Crusoe's profound dilemma over his proper reaction to the Indians' cannibalism is an authentic grappling with the issue.

Following the immediate success of *Robinson Crusoe*, Defoe wrote two sequels in the same year, one a series of further adventures and the other Crusoe's reflections on his miraculous life. Meanwhile, Defoe's prolific imagination was at work on a new project, the "private history" of a London woman who, originally a poor orphan, grows up to lead an exciting, inevitably scandalous life before finally achieving security and station. *Moll Flanders* differs in plot and setting from *Robinson Crusoe*, but the psychological authenticity of this purportedly true memoir is brought about by standard Defoe methods. Where Crusoe lovingly recounts his ingenious solutions to minute logistical problems, Moll recalls verbatim the coolly calculated speeches, the nuances of dress and gesture, that have been her making or her undoing in romantic affairs. These are Moll's tools of survival just as surely as Crusoe's odds and ends are his, and Defoe, through his everlastingly coy narrator, convinces the reader that her predicament within society is perhaps more precarious than Crusoe's without. Moreover, one accepts the extremity of her situation because she, like Crusoe, wastes few words bewailing it, instead moving immediately from the recognition of disaster to the search for means to survive. One does not pity Moll; rather, one sees oneself in her plight and soon comes unconsciously to share her values.

The reader accepts Moll's authenticity as an autobiographer because she is neither more nor less conscious of her motives than one would expect her to be. She is intuitively ethical, knowing that her need for money does not justify her thievery, especially from people no better off than she is; nevertheless, she is not so aware of herself as to realize that her panic-stricken repentance in Newgate is not real. Neither she nor Defoe is hiding tongue in cheek when she vows to live honestly, then immediately lies. When, at the end, Moll, rich and secure, says that she and her husband (the fourth of five, but the only one surviving) will spend the rest of their days in penitence, the reader can stand back and chuckle. With the realization that it would be useless to demand that the protagonist be more introspective, the reader understands that Defoe has established Moll as the child of a society where money is everything and only the rich can afford to be morally precise. The greatness of the novel is that Defoe never mentions this point; the closest Moll comes is to say that a woman without a dowry is lost and that a woman without looks or a dowry is truly lost.

The irony of the novel is that Defoe, in his preface, would have the reader believe that *Moll Flanders* is a story of despicable deeds fervently repented rather than one of inevitable deeds and a sprinkling of penitent words. With his eye on the prejudices of his audience, he could not bring himself to say that Moll could not repent because society could not forgive and because it was really society that needed repentance. He, like his flesh-

and-blood heroine, dared give the lie to his public time and again, in one "true" history after another, but he, like she, dared not take off the mask.

Not much later, on the Continent, Voltaire produced *Histoire de Charles XII* (1731; *The History of Charles XII*, 1732). His interest in the extraordinary character of Sweden's great soldier-king moved Voltaire to write the king's biography, but he did so emphasizing details of the monarch's personal, not public, life. The history thus reads like a novel, and Voltaire would eventually use the techniques developed in writing this book in his creation of two philosophical novels at midcentury. By the third decade of the eighteenth century, then, Defoe had successfully exploited fiction disguised as history, and Voltaire had written history that read like good fiction.

Christopher J. Thaiss
Updated by Patrick Adcock

Bibliography

Donovan, Josephine. *Women and the Rise of the Novel, 1405-1726.* New York: St. Martin's Press, 2000. Examines early modern novellas and romances in English, French, Italian, and Spanish, tracing the contributions of women writers to the development of the Western novel. Argues that in this period women's fiction emerged as a distinct form, one concerned with women's lives, dangers, and agency.

Gilman, Stephen. *The Novel According to Cervantes.* Berkeley: University of California Press, 1989. Discusses how *Don Quixote de la Mancha* not only influenced great picaresque novels that would later be written in English—including Henry Fielding's *The History of Tom Jones, a Foundling* (1749) and Mark Twain's *Adventures of Huckleberry Finn* (1884)—but also firmly established several stock characters for generations of popular novels, plays, and films: the comic sidekick, the idealized and unresponsive maiden loved by the hero, and the elusive villain orchestrating the hero's woes from the shadows.

Novak, Maximillian E. *Daniel Defoe: Master of Fictions—His Life and Ideas.* New York: Oxford University Press, 2001. Biography of Defoe pays special attention to his work as a journalist and propagandist, his experiments with fictional forms, and his composition of *Robinson Crusoe.*

Owens, W. R., and Stuart Sim, eds. *Reception, Appropriation, Recollection: Bunyan's "Pilgrim's Progress."* New York: Peter Lang, 2007. Collection of ten essays examines how *Pilgrim's Progress* has been read in the many years since its publication as well as how the work has influenced other writers.

Salzman, Paul, ed. *An Anthology of Elizabethan Prose Fiction.* 1998. Reprint. New York: Oxford University Press, 2008. Contains modernized editions of John Lyly's *Euphues, the Anatomy of Wit*, Thomas Nashe's *The Unfortunate Traveller*, Thomas Deloney's *Jack of Newbury*, and two other works. Includes bibliographies, a glossary, and explanatory notes.

Sambrook, James. *The Eighteenth Century: The Intellectual and Cultural Context of English Literature, 1700-1789.* 2d ed. White Plains, N.Y.: Longman, 1994. Provides a good introduction to the intellectual currents of eighteenth century England. Traces the impact of social, political, and aesthetic thought on the literature of the period, including the novel.

Smith, Grahame. *The Novel and Society: Defoe to George Eliot.* Totowa, N.J.: Barnes & Noble Books, 1984. Devotes two chapters to a broad discussion of the relationship of literature—in its several forms in different countries during different periods—to society, then presents an examination of Daniel Defoe, Tobias Smollett, and the rise of the novel in England. Includes discussion of Samuel Richardson and other novelists who wrote between 1740 and the late nineteenth century.

Spacks, Patricia Meyer. *Novel Beginnings: Experiments in Eighteenth-Century English Fiction.* New Haven, Conn.: Yale University Press, 2006. Study intended for the general reader examines the variety of fiction produced in eighteenth century England, including such early works as *Robinson Crusoe* and *Pamela* as well as Eliza Haywood's *Love in Excess* (1719-1720). Looks backward to the fiction of the seventeenth century and identifies a concern with ordinary life as a characteristic of the emerging novel form.

Tatum, James, ed. *The Search for the Ancient Novel.* Baltimore: Johns Hopkins University Press, 1994. Twenty-four essays trace the influence of ancient

Greek, Roman, Byzantine, and Arab romances, pastorals, and tales on such novelists as François Rabelais, Miguel de Cervantes, Samuel Richardson, and Frances Burney.

Todd, Janet M., ed. *Aphra Behn.* New York: St. Martin's Press, 1999. Collection of eleven feminist and new historical essays reflect the reappraisal of Behn's work that occurred at the end of the twentieth century. Five essays explore Behn's fiction, with special attention to the author's exploration of race and gender in *Oroonoko* and other works.

Williamson, Marilyn L. *Raising Their Voices, 1650-1750.* Detroit, Mich.: Wayne State University Press, 1990. Discusses the contributions of women to the Enlightenment in England. Notes that Aphra Behn firmly established the place of women in novel writing with the popular *Oroonoko*, proving that a woman who could describe sensational adventures in exotic settings would find a reading audience. Although in the next century the gothic romance was introduced into England by a man, Horace Walpole, it soon became the domain of women novelists.

ORIGINS AND DEVELOPMENT OF THE NOVEL, 1740-1890

No primary genre of literature has been so often defined and redefined as the novel, and still, no consensus has been reached. Several scholars have suggested that the only valid definition of the novel is the history of the genre itself. The origins of the modern novel, however—the novel as it appears in the early years of the twenty-first century, encompassing both serious fiction and best sellers—are more easily traced. The modern novel in the eighteenth century and its rise in the nineteenth coincided with the rise of the middle class. In consequence, as Ian Watt observes in *The Rise of the Novel* (1957), one of the paramount features of the novel has been its focus on a detailed re-creation of the bourgeois interior: the clothes, the furnishings, the belongings of the middle class. The novel is also distinguished, Watt points out, by its emphasis on individual characterization, an emphasis that can be related to the social and political movements of the eighteenth and nineteenth centuries. These movements recognized the dignity of the individual and the equality of all people. Despite all its transmutations and variations, the novel today performs the same function it has served since the eighteenth century: It offers reports on (to borrow a title from Anthony Trollope) "the way we live now."

Since American literature was, in its early stages, merely an outgrowth of English literature, this survey will treat the development of the English novel before turning to the history of the form in America. It is well to note at the outset, however, that there are several notable differences between the English novel and the American novel. While generalizations about "the novel" in a given nation must always be hedged, it is true that, as Richard Chase observes in *The American Novel and Its Tradition* (1957), "the American novel tends to rest in contradictions and among extreme ranges of experience," while "the English novel has followed the middle way." Frederick R. Karl, in *A Reader's Guide to the Nineteenth Century British Novel* (1972), argues that "unlike the American novel, the English novel principally takes place in time, not space." He then maintains that the temporal emphasis of the English novel, as opposed to the spatial aspect of the American novel, is related to the greater "blandness" of English fiction, since people who live in a restricted space must pay closer attention to time and also must modify their behavior more rigorously than those who occupy large areas, feel no sense of crowding, and need give much less heed to the passage of time and the markings of its flow.

More important than such dissimilarities, however, are the general likenesses, one of the most significant of which is the tendency traced in Erich Kahler's study *The Inward Turn of Narrative* (1973). Kahler's thesis is that throughout the eighteenth and nineteenth centuries the consciousness of Westerners turned more toward an inner vision of reality, and the novel reflects this slow but momentous shift in human attention. As Watt indicates, the "realism of the novel allows a more immediate imitation of individual experience" than do other literary forms, and "this surely explains why the majority of readers in the last two hundred years have found in the novel the literary form which most closely satisfies their wishes for a close correspondence between life and art."

The narrative element of the novel can be traced back to preliterate eras when storytellers recounted long narratives, such as the Sumerian Gilgamesh epic, which dates to about 2000 B.C.E. In some ways, Gilgamesh is not so different from the protagonist of a contemporary novel. During the course of the epic, he changes: He grows, then declines. Initially, he is a bad, oppressive king. Then, under the beneficent influence of his dear friend, Enkidu, he grows into a good king whose reign is marked by great deeds. At Enkidu's death, Gilgamesh is overcome by grief and despair. He undertakes an arduous journey in search of the secret of everlasting life. When he finds and then loses the secret, he returns to Uruk, sickens, and dies.

Such narratives, however, were in the form of verse, which facilitated memorization; narrative prose fiction was a much later development. Precursors of the modern novel can be found in every literate culture, ranging from Greek romances such as Chariton's *Peri Chairean kai Kalliroēn* (c. second century C.E.; *The Loves of Chareas and Callirrhoe*, 1764) to *Genji monogatari* (c. 1004; *The Tale of Genji*, 1925-1933), written by Murasaki Shikibu in eleventh century Japan. Like a novelist of the nineteenth or twentieth century, Murasaki portrays her society in exquisite detail. It is not, however, a bourgeois society; it is the society of the imperial court. The novel as it is now known began in the eighteenth century, following related but distinct lines of development in England, in Spain, and on the Continent.

Eighteenth century background

Many factors contributed to the birth of the English novel in the eighteenth century. An important social phenomenon was the growing trend of country people gravitating to the cities, especially London. Although no reliable figures are available, the population of London appears to have at least doubled, from around 350,000 to 700,000, between 1650 and 1750. With the growth of the city came attendant blessings and curses: more rapid and wider spread of ideas, easier dissemination of reading material, and the development of a more commercial society (although England's economy remained primarily agrarian until the Industrial Revolution) as well as the miseries of urban crime (which had been flourishing since the Elizabethan era, but never so widely), unhealthy living conditions, insufficient housing, disease, and what has been called the greatest social curse of the period, the high incidence of drunkenness. As late as 1780, infant and child mortality was still at a shockingly high level; it was rare for a family to have more than half of its children reach adulthood.

Such a lively and perilous time was, in a sense, made for Daniel Defoe (1660-1731), regarded by many critics as the first significant English novelist. As a small businessman (often a failed one), occasional spy, prolific writer under various names in a number of genres, Dissenter (one who refused to accept the established Church of England, though still a Protestant), and generally energetic citizen (who was accused of being a Trimmer, a person who switched from Whig to Tory, or vice versa), Defoe seems to represent nearly all the conditions that prepared the way for the appearance and popular acceptance of the English novel. These conditions include an emphasis on the individual, both as a social entity and as a being with a soul, and an interest in the individual's daily affairs (Defoe displays this emphasis clearly in *The Fortunes and Misfortunes of the Famous Moll Flanders, Written from Her Own Memorandums*, 1722; commonly known as *Moll Flanders*) as well as the treatment of narrative in measured time rather than in eternal time (thus the novel deals with events in a more specific temporal frame than that of the heroic romance; Henry Fielding's *The History of Tom Jones, a Foundling*, 1749—commonly known as *Tom Jones*—is perhaps the quintessential example of such a careful temporal treatment). Other conditions in Defoe's works that prepared readers for the novel are as follows: depictions of people acting in real settings, including earning a living, eating, drinking, and making love; an interest in improving one's social and economic status, usually by legal means, but not exclusively so (Moll Flanders tries to live honestly, but circumstances force her into thievery); a growing independence, of children from parents, citizens from their government, parishioners from the Church, and everyone from traditional ideas and beliefs, especially those received from the past and from authoritative sources; an emphasis on interior scenes and urban experiences (though the countryside was to figure prominently in the English novel for two centuries, much of the most important action takes place indoors, with the most detailed description being saved for interiors—the classic later example of this accent is the work of Charles Dickens, 1812-1870); and, finally, an unprecedented attention to the interests and aspirations of women.

Defoe represents as well as anyone that most significant fact about the English novel: It is the ultimate expression of the middle class. No literary form was written and read by the ever-growing middle class as much as the novel. By the time Samuel Richardson (1689-1761) published *Pamela: Or, Virtue Rewarded* (1740-1741), the reading public was rapidly expanding, though it was still very small by modern standards. Again, no reliable numbers are available, but scholarly estimates indicate a figure of about seventy or eighty thousand, which was only 1 or 2 percent of the total population. The figure increased as the century waned, but even by 1800, only a small fraction of the population, perhaps some 100,000 people, was capable of reading a novel.

The same process was under way in the East, though probably at a somewhat lesser rate. Between 1740 and 1750, Cao Xueqin (or Ts'ao Hsüeh-ch'in; 1715[?]-1763), born in China into a once-prominent family then in decline, wrote the first eighty chapters of *Hongloumeng* (1792; also known as *Hung-lou meng*; *Dream of the Red Chamber*, 1958; also translated as *The Story of the Stone*, 1973-1982, and as *A Dream of Red Mansions*, 1978-1980). The manuscript circulated for several years after the author's death, and later writers added chapters until the first published version appeared in 1792. This classic novel embodies the cultural identity of China at the middle of the eighteenth century.

1740 to 1764

In 1740, potential novel readers were chiefly interested in family life, the details of everyday living, and the problems of morality on an individual basis. Wide generalizations concerning what constituted ethical conduct, as were found in Alexander Pope's poetry, may have been widely quoted, but they were not taken much to heart; also, the novel could do what no verse essay—even one by so skilled a versifier as Pope—could do: It could show morality being lived. Richardson's *Pamela* satisfied these interests, and the book was extremely popular. The fact that Richardson tells most of the story by way of letters is an indication of the particularity of detail and expression and the interest in the individual that engaged the attention of readers near the middle of the century.

As to the economy and the stability of the government, the nation was in reasonably good condition. At this point, England was enjoying a rewarding trade relationship with its colonies in the New World and was in the initial stages of taking over India. The wars in which it engaged took place on foreign soil. George II (r. 1727-1760) was not a skilled ruler, but the country was controlled chiefly by ministers who were intent on keeping or increasing their power, always with an eye, however, to avoiding open conflict with the people. The most notable civil disorders of the era (not counting the abortive attempts to restore the Stuarts to the throne, which had little effect on the lives of ordinary citizens) were the Gordon Riots, an anti-Catholic outburst, which did not take place until 1780 and were confined to small sections of London, lasting but a few days.

Although the period was called the Age of Reason, and although the official philosophy was one of rationalism, the actual lives of most people were not lived according to such theories; this fact is more clearly reflected in the novel than in any other form of literature. The best-known heroes of the early novel are either criminals, such as Moll Flanders, or rebels against a hostile society, such as Clarissa Harlowe from Richardson's *Clarissa: Or, The History of a Young Lady* (1747-1748) and Sophia Western from *Tom Jones* (the former running away from home and being drugged and seduced, the latter escaping from her father and nearly being raped). Tom Jones is turned out of his benefactor's house on very slender evidence of wrongdoing; he is then beaten, robbed, and almost hanged, and it takes almost eight hundred pages for him to establish his innocence. (Typical of the increasingly middle-class morality of the time, one of the chief themes of *Tom Jones* is that virtue is what a person owes to others, while prudence is what one owes to oneself.) These works deal primarily with the lives of one or two central characters, further evidence of the eighteenth century emphasis on the individual.

Individuality, as a concern and thematic focus, is most strikingly advanced in the entertaining but often nearly surrealistic *Tristram Shandy* (1759-1767), by Laurence Sterne (1713-1768). Some critics believe that Sterne's book did more than any other to open the way for the later psychological novel. A concern for individuality was also indicated by the spread of Methodism, whose first meetings were held in 1729. In its early stages, before it hardened into an established denomination, it was an emotional movement that went back to the individualistic roots of Protestantism. The focus on the life of the individual is also reflected in the earlier, and continuing, enthusiasm for biography. Defoe augmented this tradition by basing *Robinson Crusoe* (1719) largely on the experience of the Scottish sailor Alexander Selkirk, who was marooned on an island for some four and a half years. Typically, Defoe transforms Crusoe into a resourceful, God-fearing middle-class man who hardly changes at all during more than twenty-five years on the fictional island—unlike Selkirk, who emerged from his experience in a half-bestial state.

Along with an increasing emphasis on the particulars of people's lives, the early novel depended heavily on a flexible, readable prose style that was far from the inflated expression of the romances of earlier times. Much of the brevity and liveliness of this new style was the product of journalists and "hack" writers who were compelled to produce considerable quantities of material for a general audience in short periods. Defoe is again a classic example. He did not start writing long fiction until he was sixty years old, by which time he had produced hundreds of expository works of a very readable nature, most of them published in periodicals. On a more lofty plane, but still of a vigorous composition, were the widely admired informal essays of Joseph Addison (1672-1719) and Richard Steele (1672-1729), published chiefly in the popular periodicals *The Tatler* (1709-1711) and *The Spectator* (1711-1712). The styles of Richardson and Fielding (1707-1754) are also somewhat more elevated, as befits the stories of more socially eminent characters (Fielding was the more literary, having had a superior education and an admirable career in the law, along with previous experience as a successful dramatist), but Tobias Smollett (1721-1771) wrote in a very plain style, displaying the "common touch" to a high degree and attaining a much-enjoyed earthy humor.

One reason that prose fiction sold so well during this era was the Licensing Act of 1737, directed at the theater, which amounted to a form of censorship enforced by a sensitive government under the leadership of Prime Minister Sir Robert Walpole, who had been the butt of several satirical passages in popular plays. In effect, this law forced Fielding to turn from drama to the novel; it also encouraged bland theater, thus winning a greater readership for contentious periodicals such as the famous *Spectator Papers* by Addison and Steele, which led a growing list of well-written and topical journals. The emphasis on individualism during this period was further reflected in the new esteem for portraiture, leading to illustrious careers for such great portrait painters as Sir Joshua Reynolds (1723-1792), a popular member of Samuel Johnson's celebrated Club, and Thomas Gainsborough (1727-1788). Johnson's group, which met more or less regularly in the 1760's and 1770's, was a culmination of another eighteenth century tendency that exhibits the desire of people to come to know others on a quasi-individual basis: the popularity of the coffeehouses, establishments where upper-middle-class men gathered to discuss events of the day, the latest articles in the current periodicals, and one another. One of Johnson's salient criticisms of men he did not like was that they were "unclubbable."

Since the novel was written chiefly for the middle class and selected most of its characters from the ranks of this group, it reflects the lamentable fact that nearly all the truly charitable work that was done during this midcentury period (and there was an unfortunate paucity of it, by modern standards) was accomplished by the middle class. It was this stratum of society that instituted the parish groups that gave to the poor and looked after unwed mothers and orphaned offspring (although, as *Moll Flanders* clearly demonstrates, the care was woefully inadequate for many). The two institutions that would be expected to take the lead in such endeavors—the government and the church—simply failed to do so in any meaningful fashion until the next century; both were more determined to promulgate their primacy and power than to form any effective organized assistance for the unfortunate. Foreign wars and economic shifts created a large body of needy people; indeed, former military people who become idlers appear as minor characters in decades of British fiction.

Perhaps the chief cultural irony of this period is that the novel protested against the conditions of society and yet depended on them for its existence. The cosmic concerns expressed by earlier writers (John Milton, 1608-1674, is perhaps the most obvious example) no longer attracted the interest of readers. People were more interested in how to get along, live successfully and morally, and come to terms with the rapidly changing times. For such guidance, it was not the philosophers or great poets to whom most readers turned but the novelists, for these middle-class authors spoke to the real needs and concerns of their readers. Addressing this issue, Johnson's moral strictures against licentious material in the newly popular novels were severe but were based on a genuine concern for the virtue of the readership, many of whom were "the young, the ignorant, and the idle." Apart from the ethical aspect of this influential declaration of concern, Johnson's remarks, in an essay published in *The Rambler* in 1750, also reveal the great effect that fiction was having on a number of its readers, who, Johnson notes, "regulate their own practice" on the models of the leading characters in novels.

Two of the major historical events that captured the imagination of the everyday reader were the voyage around the world from 1740 to 1744 of Lord Anson (1697-1762) and, later, the Pacific explorations from 1768 to 1779 of James Cook (1728-1779). The passages in Smollett's *The Adventures of Roderick Random* (1748; commonly known as *Roderick Random*) dealing with the hero's experience on a naval vessel were thus of considerable relevance to the novel reader. As the feats of explorers and colonizers became known, a greater sense of empire, as well as the recognition of ever-increasing opportunities for trade, began to be felt in the populace. England's navy, strong for centuries, was now the guardian of a lively British maritime commerce around the world, with the colonies providing invaluable raw materials and opening areas for further colonization and economic development for enterprising adventurers.

1764 to 1800

The date 1764 is of special significance in the history of long fiction because it clearly marks the beginning of a distinct change in the direction of English culture, especially as reflected in the novel. The first genuine gothic novel (the novel of suspense, terror, exotic setting, and effects) was published in that year. *The Castle of Otranto* (1765), by Horace Walpole (1717-1797), enjoyed enormous success and signaled a shift in public taste toward the exotic, the extraordinary, and violent passions—toward the Romantic movement, adumbrations of which can be found this early.

Another early sign of Romanticism is a different sort of novel, also the first of its kind: *The Vicar of Wakefield* (1766), by Oliver Goldsmith (1728 or 1730-1774), regarded as the harbinger of the novel of sensibility, another signal of the Romantic "temperament." These two impulses, the gothic and the sentimental, were to gain an even greater hold on the interests and reading habits of the late eighteenth century English. Further evidence of this shift in enthusiasm can be found in the seemingly unrelated art of architecture. The early eighteenth century had seen the construction of practically designed and constructed buildings, with symmetrical proportions and even measurements (the double cube was a popular design)—a kind of "proper" organization also found in the well-trimmed and geometrically planned formal gardens of the time (the topiary art reached its highest point in this era). The later age preferred wild countrysides spotted with ruined or half-ruined castles or rude country dwellings, charming in their quaint rusticity. These "wild" settings became increasingly common in novels and were a staple feature of the Romantic novel to come.

Another important strand of Romanticism was anticipated by the publication of Bishop Thomas Percy's *Reliques of Ancient English Poetry* (1765), which brought to its clearest exposure an interest in the medieval past that had been growing since early in the century. The enormous popularity of the volume by Percy (1729-1811) testified also to the wider interest in ancient and exotic poetry that came to characterize Romanticism. Further, nature, which was to play so large a part in later novels—notably those of the Romantic Sir Walter Scott—is secondary to the concern for human welfare, especially in terms of emotional states.

Such pre-Romantic tendencies were not confined to England. One of the most popular novels of sensibility was *Die Leiden des jungen Werthers* (1774; *The Sorrows of Young Werther*, 1779) by Johann Wolfgang von Goethe (1749-1832), a pathetic tale of unrequited love and sad but eloquent protestations of passion and self-pity. It has been claimed that the suicide rate among young readers rose sharply soon after this novel was published. Goethe's novel reveals a typical connection between the novels of sensibility and gothicism, in that much of the scenery in his tale is wild and natural. The pre-Romantic tendencies revealed in these novels can also be discovered in the often socially critical, homespun Scottish poetry of Robert Burns (1759-1796) and the mystic verses of William Blake (1757-1827).

Probably the most extreme manifestation of sensibility is to be found in Henry Mackenzie's *The Man of Feeling* (1771); in this short novel, the hero falls to weeping more than fifty times. This sentimentality (which was, in later novels, to be the basis of some extremely humorous satire, as in Jane Austen's *Northanger Abbey*, 1818) was in part an expression of the flowering social consciousness of the age. This imperative to develop sensitivities to the needs and concerns of others allied itself with the perennial didactic element in the novel and in the national consciousness. Just as the early novelists often claimed a morally elevating purpose in order to have their works accepted by the public and not roundly condemned from the pulpit, so the writers of this era genuinely believed that their novels were stimulating readers to loftier sentiments and more generous acts. In Parliament, the moving and eloquent speeches by the liberal Edmund Burke (1729-1797), many of which were devoted to opposing the government's narrow-minded policy of taxation in the American colonies, officially ratified the growing belief that people had a right to be helped by others and that the willingness to help was a sacred duty for any who were able. A popular idea in the novel of sensibility asserted that the true gentleman was never an indifferent spectator of misery in others. This attitude assumed, of course, that human nature is essentially benevolent, a notion that did not take hold in popular fiction until this period.

The notion that human nature is, when uncorrupted by evil forces, naturally good was urged upon the English nation by the influential French philosopher Jean-Jacques Rousseau (1712-1778), whose asseveration that humans in their natural state are moral gave rise to a widespread discussion of the doctrine of the "noble savage." This theory relates to the whole atmosphere of primitivism that is found in the ballad revival (intensified by Percy's volume) and associated phenomena, such as the novel of ideas, a genre that usually endorsed liberal educational and social concepts. Typical of the genre was Thomas Day's *The History of Sandford and Merton* (1783-1789), a humorless tract in the form of a novel that tries to prove that a "natural" education is better than an excessively structured one and that morality is always rewarded. Many novels of ideas dealt with education in Rousseauistic terms, but the most striking novel of liberal tendencies was William Godwin's *Things as They Are: Or, The Adventures of Caleb Williams* (1794; also known as *The Adventures of Caleb Williams: Or, Things as They Are*; best known as *Caleb Williams*), which has the distinction of being one of the earliest novels of propaganda and also perhaps the first novel of crime and detection.

These novels of social concern illustrate an important phenomenon: The novel was beginning to occupy a position formerly held by the drama. While a few excellent satires can be found near the close of the century—such as Goldsmith's *She Stoops to Conquer: Or, The Mistakes of a Night* (pr., pb. 1773) and Richard Brinsley Sheridan's *The Rivals* (pr., pb. 1775) and *The School for Scandal* (pr. 1777)—generally, the burgeoning concern for human rights and social reform is to be found most fully developed in the novel, though a number of poems also reveal such concerns. In *English Literature from Dryden to Burns* (1948), Alan D. McKillop argues that the novel "entails a critical or analytical attitude toward characters represented under actual or conceivable social conditions" and that the "critical attitude is directed toward both individual character and the social situation." He suggests that the novel was coming ever closer to the real lives of its readers as the eighteenth century came to a close. Despite the excesses of the sentimental novel and the novel of terror, the central trend of prose fiction was an attempt to grasp and come to terms with the world as it had to be dealt with every day.

Perhaps the best example of this tendency is the work of Fanny Burney (1752-1840), whose moralistic but readable novels of domestic life contain a great deal of sensible advice—either by demonstration or by declaration—for their readers, especially young women. The extensive readership attained by her novels illustrates another aspect of the times: More women were beginning to read and write novels. Burney had a great many followers in the field of domestic fiction. This trend helped to prepare the way for the woman who is, in the view of numerous critics, the best female novelist in the language, Jane Austen (1775-1817).

In 1759 the fierce French satirist Voltaire (1694-1778), Rousseau's philosophical and literary archenemy, had published his masterpiece of dark comedy, *Candide: Ou, L'Optimisme* (*Candide: Or, All for the Best*, 1759; also known as *Candide: Or, The Optimist*, 1762). This fast-moving combination of farce and biting satire sweeps its naïve hero along from one disaster to another and evokes from the reader laughter rather than horror. One character is hanged, a second has a sword thrust into his belly up to the hilt, and a third is repeatedly raped and stabbed. All reappear later in the novel, still alive. The plot races from Europe to South America, back to Europe, and finally to the Middle East. Voltaire's influence on the English novel extended well into the twentieth century. *Candide*-like comic novels about rootless and irreverent young people—*Decline and Fall* (1928) and *Vile Bodies* (1930) by Evelyn Waugh (1903-1966), *Afternoon Men* (1931) by Anthony Powell (1905-2000), and *Highland Fling* (1931) by Nancy Mitford (1904-1973)—flourished for a time and constituted almost a "school" of the period.

It could be argued that, for common people, the Industrial Revolution was more important than any political unrest. For intellectuals, however, among them many novelists, the disappointment over the Reign of Terror, which was seen as a betrayal of the worthy liberal sentiments that had inspired the revolution, was deep and long. The youthful William Wordsworth (1770-1850) was among the most grimly unsettled of the poets, shocked by the bloody course that the insurrection took; the young Sir Walter Scott (1771-1832), though not as morbidly struck as the poet, was deeply disappointed. The reason for the perhaps greater significance of the industrial advance among the lower and middle classes was that individual lives were more directly affected. This fact is of signal importance in the development of the English novel, because this genre, like no other, concentrates on the inner lives of people. Whether the author achieves a detailed delineation of the thoughts and emotions of a character (as does Richardson) or a clear demonstration of a character's motives by action (as does Fielding), the novel depends on single people, both in their relationships with others and in their interpretations of the meaning of their own lives, for most of its interest and value. This dependency was to increase in the ages following the eighteenth century. That the trend was to be informed by what could be considered a semi-revolutionary bent (the single person pitted against society or a tradition) was only the predictable result of the tenor of the times.

1800 to 1832

The first decades of the nineteenth century were the peak of Romanticism in English literature, its chief exemplars being the five great Romantic poets John Keats (1795-1821), Percy Bysshe Shelley (1792-1822), William Wordsworth (1770-1850), Lord Byron (1788-1824), and Samuel Taylor Coleridge (1772-1834). These artists wrote verse that emphasized the imaginative intuition of the individual as the way to achieve truth.

Scott was a powerful force in the popularization of both Romantic poetry and the Romantic novel. His *Minstrelsy of the Scottish Border* (1802-1803) capitalized on the widening interest in old ballads and folktales, especially of the rural type. Scott turned to the novel as an act of self-defense when Byron became so popular that the verse of other poets could no longer command an adequate market. At the time, Scott had no idea of what a favor was being accorded him. The publication of *Waverley: Or, 'Tis Sixty Years Since* (1814), the first of the so-called Waverley novels—all set in the past and many providing insightful, if not fully accurate, visions of historical events and people—marked the commencement of a groundswell of enthusiasm among readers for depictions of wild Scottish scenery and vigorous actions performed by impossibly virtuous and somewhat leaden heroes in the defense of improbably sweet and chaste heroines. Scott's talent for characterization was never highly praised, except in his portraits of lower-class characters such as thieves, pirates, and gypsies, but his powers of description were unequaled in his day. In his better works, such as *The Heart of Midlothian* (1818) and *The Bride of Lammermoor* (1819), he attained gothic effects that rival those in any of the novels in the genre, even the works of Ann Radcliffe (1764-1823) and Charles Robert Maturin (1780-1824).

While verse was the prevailing form during the Romantic period, the novel was still popular; the growth of the population, especially in cities, and the proliferation of lending libraries permitted a wider dissemination of fiction and thus greater economic rewards for writing and publishing novels. There was, however, still a stigma attached to both the writing and the reading of fiction. Scott published his first several novels anonymously, and Jane Austen took considerable pains to conceal from all but members of her family that she was writing novels. A period that can boast the wide sweep and narrative drive of Scott's historical fiction and the elegant but barbed domestic vignettes of Austen is rich indeed.

An additional aspect of the novel in this era was the fairly new emphasis on regional fiction. Maria Edgeworth (1767-1849) dealt with the problems, charms, and complexities of life in Ireland with sensitivity and perception. Relations between Ireland and England had been strained since the time of Elizabeth I. In response,

Edgeworth offered some penetrating arguments in favor of the Irish side of the question, most notably on the injustice of the English practice of absentee landlordism. Although satire was not the predominant tone of the fiction of the period, the novels of Thomas Love Peacock (1785-1866) provide an entertaining vision of the romance as seen through more modern eyes, with lively touches of humor. The very titles of some of his most popular works indicate the nature of his approach: *Headlong Hall* (1816), *Nightmare Abbey* (1818), and *Crotchet Castle* (1831).

1832 to 1870: The early Victorian age

Although Victoria did not gain the throne until 1837, several events suggest the year 1832 as a suitable date to designate the opening of the era that bears her name. The designation indicates the complexity of the cultural and historical period. It followed epochs that have been labeled according to their obvious characteristics: the Age of Reason, the Enlightenment, the age of Pope, the age of Johnson, the Romantic age. A seventy-year period named after the reigning monarch is something of an evasion, but the era was so complicated and contradictory that the choice is understandable. As Walter Houghton notes in *The Victorian Frame of Mind* (1957), "Studies in this area have emphasized only a few characteristics, notably moral earnestness and optimism, to the obscuring of others, equally important, like enthusiasm and anxiety." He goes on to explain how difficult it is to capture the spirit of the period because it is composed of so many divergent and, at times, contradictory elements.

Indeed, anxiety underlay a great deal of the surface optimism for which Victorian England is famous. Thus the celebrated response by Matthew Arnold (1822-1888) to an English industrialist's ignorant remark about the era's wonderful condition makes a great deal of sense. Another indication of the anxiety and conflict that pervaded the period can be found in the Oxford, or Tractarian, movement, which started in 1833 and persevered until 1841. This movement was an attempt to elevate the position of the Church of England in the lives of the people. There were complicated theological and even political reasons for the zeal of the reformers, but one can perceive in this intense conviction that there was a need for such a radical change, an aura of uncertainty and even anxiety about the cultural substance of the life of the time.

The novelist who epitomizes the Victorian era, Charles Dickens (1812-1870), published his first major work beginning in 1836. *Pickwick Papers* (1836-1837, serial; 1837, book) demonstrates an additional aspect of the Victorian personality: a delightful sense of humor, chiefly based on charming eccentricity of character. It is typical of the age, however, that the tone of Dickens's novels almost steadily darkened throughout his lifetime. Indeed, one can trace an increasing tendency toward grimness as the century passed in novelists from Dickens through Thomas Hardy (1840-1928).

In part, the increasing pessimism of the Victorian age reflected a growing awareness of urban blight, of the complex consequences of the Industrial Revolution. There were few novels specifically about industry, but Dickens's impassioned plea for more humanity and less materialism, as found in *Hard Times* (1854; originally published as *Hard Times for These Times*), was echoed in the works of lesser writers who were popular in their day. Dickens protested against a variety of social abuses, from inhuman schools for poor children, as in *Oliver Twist* (1837-1839, serial; 1838, book), to the corruption and inefficiency of the courts of chancery, as in *Bleak House* (1852-1853, serial; 1853, book); particularly intense was his resistance to the cruel working conditions created by the factory system, presented most sharply in *The Old Curiosity Shop* (1840-1841, serial; 1841, book), a work whose excessive emotional stress causes it to cross the border into bathos, a common failing of the era's novels. Despite these social concerns, the central thrust of the novel in the Victorian period remained toward a revelation of the ways by which more or less common people attempt to meet the challenges of life.

The spiritual crises that afflicted many of the artists and thinkers of the Victorian era—particularly the conflicts with Charles Darwin's evolutionary hypothesis, but also with other challenges to orthodox Christianity, such as higher criticism of biblical texts—lent the later novels of this period a philosophical depth and seriousness unprecedented in English fiction. The most impressive novelist who wrote in this vein was George Eliot (1819-1880), in whose works one of the most iterated principles of Thomas Carlyle (1795-1881) is demonstrated repeatedly: the assertion that life can take on its true meaning only when the individual is willing to renounce earthly glory and material possessions. The theme of renunciation that resounds through Eliot's *Adam Bede* (1859), *The Mill on the Floss* (1860), *Silas Marner* (1861), and *Middlemarch* (1871-1872) is an echo of the same stress placed by Carlyle on this human recognition of limited claims and the virtue of humility. These two philosophers of the period, Carlyle being the earlier, reveal two diverging tendencies in the Victorian attitude toward prominent people. While Carlyle, in his famous essay *On Heroes, Hero-Worship, and the Heroic in History* (1841), praises the hero in history as the kind of person who makes historical events happen, Eliot presents her leading characters as simple people who demonstrate the Victorian trend away from the usual vision of the lofty, noble, aristocratic hero of the past, as in Scott's historical novels. As Mario Praz establishes in *The Hero in Eclipse in Victorian Fiction* (1956), the romantic hero gave way to the middle-class man or woman who exhibited worthy moral traits, some bravery, and a lack of egotism. Such central characters allowed Eliot and a host of other writers to explore the intellectual and emotional depths of people who appear common (they certainly occupy common places in society) but display profound levels of sensitivity and spiritual resources. Eliot's often-noted remark that she found God inconceivable but duty indispensable illustrates an attitude typical of many of the respected authors of the middle and later Victorian period.

1870 to 1890: The late Victorian age

The era referred to as the late Victorian age is often said to include the last decade of the nineteenth century; it is also known as the realistic period. The generation opened with the death of Dickens in 1870 and the publication of Darwin's *The Descent of Man and Selection in Relation to Sex* in 1871. In the same year appeared one of Hardy's early novels, *Desperate Remedies*. This gloomy title not only indicates the grim philosophy that Hardy revealed in nearly all of his novels but also suggests the plight of many of the inhabitants of Great Britain, who had encountered several political and cultural realities: the repressive policies of Lord Palmerston, prime minister in 1855-1858 and 1859-1865; the positivistic interpretation of history in the works of Hippolyte Taine (1828-1893), whose four-volume *Histoire de la littérature anglaise* (1863-1864) was translated as *History of English Literature* in 1871; and the naturalism of Émile Zola (1840-1902). The potato famine that had struck Ireland in 1846 was a harbinger of the hard times to strike the rest of the British Isles. As the previously burgeoning economy began to slow down and settle into less expansive patterns, the competition from other industrial nations, especially the United States and Germany, began to take a severe toll. The near monopoly in international trade that England had enjoyed for decades was irrevocably broken. For the laboring classes, the results were catastrophic. There were extended periods of unemployment, and the rate of emigration, before but a trickle, rapidly rose. It is estimated that some twenty thousand English citizens emigrated to the United States in 1886 and that an even greater number left in the following two-year period.

An inevitable result of the ruptures in the previously booming economy was an increased interest in socialistic projects and leaders. In 1880 three Labor Party candidates won seats in Parliament; soon afterward, several socialistic organizations were founded, the most remarkable being the Fabian Society, started in 1884, which was later to count H. G. Wells (1866-1946) and George Bernard Shaw (1856-1950) among its members. The disorder in society that this sort of expedient implies was indeed present. Faith in a number of institutions, such as the church, the monarchy, Parliament, the economic system, religion, and even science, began to wane.

By an odd quirk of psychology, the novels of Anthony Trollope (1815-1882) found their popularity largely on the basis of their calm tone, the certitude of a pleasant outcome (now and then, Trollope stops the story to inform the reader that there is no cause for anxiety, as he has arranged it so that all will be well), and the relatively trivial concerns of the characters, many of whom are country parsons with very little of serious import in their actions and conversation. This phenomenon was repeated during the anxious days of World War II, when Trollope was again popular. This impulse to escape was to be expressed in a much different manner in the 1890's by the Decadents, who championed the notion of art for art's sake on the theory that art is far above life and therefore should not soil its hands trying to deal with it. The most famous of the Decadents was Oscar Wilde (1856-1900), whose semigothic supernatural novel *The Picture of Dorian Gray* (1891) was a sort of fictional announcement of the bizarre extremes of this movement.

Thus, while the empire was expanding abroad, life at home for the lower classes—the upper middle class was not harmed much by the unemployment and the emigration—was a struggle. Writers strenuously resisted the principles of expansion of the empire and the heartless exploitation of foreign and domestic laborers. In the novel, one finds such impassioned propagandistic works as Hardy's *The Mayor of Casterbridge* (1886) and George Gissing's *Workers in the Dawn* (1880).

From a more purely literary standpoint, however, the age was a rich one, as the novel achieved a wider scope and a greater depth than it had yet known. Though George Eliot is best known for her novels of domestic life, such as *Middlemarch*, she also took up social causes with an intensity and thoughtfulness not found before in the English novel—the prime example is *Daniel Deronda* (1876), which deals with "the Jewish question." Although England had a skilled Jewish prime minister, Benjamin Disraeli (1804-1881), in office for several long periods in the nineteenth century, anti-Semitism was still widespread and often institutionally sanctioned. Eliot, along with Hardy and George Meredith (1828-1909) in particular, also helped create what was to become known as the psychological novel. Certainly, writers of the realistic school—most notably the French realists Honoré de Balzac (1799-1850), Stendhal (Marie-Henri Beyle, 1783-1842), and Gustave Flaubert (1821-1880)—had assisted in opening the paths to psychological realism, but the English novelists of the late nineteenth century carried this tendency to a lofty height. British literary historians occasionally claim that the American-born Henry James (1843-1916), who could be classified as the most insightful of all psychological realists, was more of an English novelist than an American one, since he lived the last thirty-five years of his life in England and wrote a great deal more about English society than he did about that of his native land. The claim is hotly contested, however, by students of the novel in the United States, and there is much in James's work that proclaims its author as essentially American, wherever he chose to reside.

The period ended with the death of Robert Browning (1812-1889). This most Victorian of writers, whose optimistic poems are so well known as to mislead casual readers, is a fitting representative of the era. The way was already prepared for the more modern writings of later poets such as Rudyard Kipling (1865-1936), a severe critic of the empire-building practices of the government, and William Butler Yeats (1865-1939). The novelists to follow included Robert Louis Stevenson (1850-1894), Joseph Conrad (1857-1924), Arnold Bennett (1867-1931), and D. H. Lawrence (1885-1930). The works of these authors, and of the other imposing figures who were to carry this magnificent genre down to the present, would not, however, have been possible without the efforts of the countless writers of long fiction who opened the avenues of what F. R. Leavis has aptly called the great tradition.

BACKGROUND OF THE AMERICAN NOVEL

By general consent, the first American novel was *The Power of Sympathy: Or, the Triumph of Nature* (1789; also known as *The Triumph of Nature Founded in Truth*), attributed to William Hill Brown. Numerous literary achievements had been seen in America since the founding of the settlements at Jamestown, Virginia, in 1607, and at Plymouth, Massachusetts, in 1620, but no memorable fiction was produced until late in the next century. Most of the earliest works were practical, semihistorical pieces, such as Captain John Smith's *A True Relation of Such Occurrences and Accidents of Noate as Hath Hapned in Virginia Since the First Planting of That Collony* (1608) and *A Description of New England: Or, Observations and Discoveries of Captain John Smith* (1616). A substantial body of religious literature began to appear, including the famous *Bay Psalm Book* (1640), which had the distinction of being the first book to be printed in America, Roger Williams's *Bloudy Tenent of Persecution, for Cause of Conscience, Discussed* (1644), the poetry of Edward Taylor (c. 1645-1729), and the fiery sermons and tracts of Increase Mather (1639-1723) and Cotton Mather (1663-1728). These and similar works, well into the eighteenth century, provided information, attitudes, some impressive poetic imagery, and much moralizing; what they lacked was any recognizable belletristic quality. This was especially true of the prose. Fiction did not begin to find a general readership until the second half of the eighteenth century, and most of the fiction published at that time in the colonies was either British (no international copyright law existed, and much importing and pirating of novels from the mother country occurred) or closely based on British models, chiefly novels by Daniel Defoe, Samuel Richardson, and Henry Fielding.

The delay in the appearance of native fiction of high quality is attributed to a variety of causes, both cultural (a heavy dependence by the colonies on Britain for literary forms and techniques, which endured until long after the American Revolution, 1776-1781) and natural (the enormous land mass of the "new" continent and the regionalism it stimulated). Many scholars believe that the primary reason for the delayed and tentative beginning of American long fiction, apart from the influence of British examples, was simply the absence of an indigenous culture rich in tradition; in Henry James's formulation (*Hawthorne*, 1879), it requires "an accumulation of history and custom . . . to form a suggestion for the novelist."

It has been noted that this paucity of social and historical substance compelled American novelists to discover or create other bases for their themes, founded on more abstract material. The result, claim scholars who are favorably impressed by this phenomenon, was a fiction rich in symbolism and allegory, a literature abundant in metaphysical significance and elevated by a textual density. Of special interest in this connection is the massive achievement of *Moby Dick* (1851), in which Herman Melville (1819-1891) created a symbol of evil (or of something far more complex) that may represent the highest attainment in the English language of a thematic expression. Nathaniel Hawthorne's (1804-1864) "romances," as he wished his fictions to be designated, are almost by definition apart from the British genre of the realistic novel of social life. It is inviting to speculate about what Mark Twain (1835-1910) would think, given his preliminary instructions to readers to eschew a search for any motive, moral, or plot, of the scholarly attention given to *Adventures of Huckleberry Finn* (1884), which discovers in the novel archetypal characters such as Jim (interpreted as a surrogate, spiritual father to Huck) and events such as the journey down the Mississippi River (elucidated as a recapitulation of the quest motif found in primitive myth). In *Form and Fable in American Fiction* (1961), Daniel Hoffman makes a persuasive case for the enormous reliance of American novelists on folklore and their extensive utilization of allegorical and symbolic modes of signification.

Because the United States comprises such a vast expanse of territory, and this area includes regions settled by peoples with diverse backgrounds and ambitions, it has been customary to divide the country into several regions. A measure of the linguistic importance of this regional aspect of America may be seen in the fact that, at the First Continental Congress in 1774, many of the delegates were frustrated because they found themselves nearly unable to comprehend the speech of other members. The differences among these regions demonstrate the rich variety of American literature. For a considerable time, the cultural life of America was synonymous with the cultural life of New England, and Boston was judged the cultural capital of the country as well as its publishing center—the first printing press in America was established in Cambridge in 1639—until well into the nineteenth century, when it relinquished that distinction to New York City. More isolated by topographical features than any other major division of the nation, New England was marked by an often-overstated Puritan fervor and a moralistic emphasis. The middle states—usually regarded as including New York, New Jersey, Pennsylvania, and perhaps Maryland and Delaware—were distinguished by the great diversity of their settlers and the resulting manifold qualities of thought and concerns. By contrast, the South developed a more homogeneous culture, a sort of feudal society based on the establishment of slavery. From a literary standpoint, the chief cultural benefit of the plantation system was that it allowed the growth of a leisured class of aristocrats who had the time and the education to read widely and write articulately.

The last general division in the national consciousness, which was soon to be broken into constituent regions, was the West, an area that was unknown and untraveled, and thus possessed, for the first settlers and many later immigrants, an awesome charm. As the frontier moved west, more and more was learned that removed the mystery from the land, but until late in the nineteenth century, the image of the West held by many Americans and foreign visitors was still marked by a sense of romance, unreality, freedom, and unlimited opportunity.

In establishing the periods of American literature, great variance is found, and quarrels continue regarding delineation of the periods. The wisest deduction would appear to be that American literature is so complex, despite the evident relative simplicity of the nation's history and culture, that clear separations are just not possible or legitimate. The person who most historians agree was the first American professional author, Charles Brockden Brown (1771-1810), did not publish until near the end of the eighteenth century, and then he was only moderately successful.

As in England, the novel in America was chiefly the product of middle-class authors and the reading material of middle-class citizens. These middle-class writers, however, were not as close to social and political subjects as were their British counterparts. There existed a severe tension between opposing impulses and enthusiasms: between the intense desire for freedom and the fact of slavery, between the opposing attractions of Romanticism and rationalism, and between the desire for economic power and what Leslie Fiedler calls "the need for cultural autonomy." One result of these tensions and the difficulty of obtaining a unified vision of American society was that the most important authors tended to resort to forms of escape, distancing them from the people. James Fenimore Cooper escaped to the frontier, Hawthorne fled to the past with his insightful studies of the Puritan ethos, Melville found liberation in distant settings and on the sea, Twain escaped to the near past and the West, and James went to Europe to find suitable subject matter for his art.

1789 to 1820

Several conditions prevailed prior to that period in England that hindered the development of the novel there. These conditions also existed, but with greater impact, in the colonies until the time of the American Revolution and afterward, lessening as the decades passed; they are important in understanding why the American novel did not develop as quickly as its European model. Apart from the problem of colonial, then state, loyalties (Alexander Cowie, in *The Rise of the American Novel*, 1948, points out that most citizens, even after a national identity had been established, would identify their "country" as the state from which they came), the conditions included a scattered population, making the dissemination of books difficult and expensive; an uneven and low level of public education, an area in which America lagged sadly behind Europe; and, finally, a lack of publishers. Although more than fifty new magazines were published in the last decade of the eighteenth century, few had any chance of persisting, and almost all were content either to print fiction from abroad or to focus on practical, expository material. This emphasis on the pragmatic had a further dampening effect on the production of worthy native fiction.

The early American novels that were set in America and dealt with distinctively American concerns were almost entirely of a moralistic nature, since the moral strictures that had militated against lively, imaginative novels in England were felt in America as well; in some regions, mainly New England, they were felt with even more force than in Britain. As a consequence, the fiction that was turned out well into the nineteenth century tended to be both didactic and imitative of English forms, such as the novel of domestic life, the sentimental novel (these categories often overlapped), the gothic romance, and the historical novel.

William Hill Brown's *The Power of Sympathy* fits into the category of the novel of domestic life with more than a suggestion of the qualities of the sentimental novel, and it has a heavily moralistic dedication; yet it is replete with sensational elements such as near incest, seduction, abduction, and violence. The influence both of the story of Moll Flanders—the lowborn protagonist of Defoe's tale of suffering, thievery, and intrigue—and of Richardson's account of the grim adventures of the upper-middle-class Clarissa Harlowe is seen here. Equally lively but better written—Brown's style is ponderous, in the vein of lesser-known English authors of the eighteenth century—is Susanna Rowson's popular *Charlotte: A Tale of Truth* (1791; also known as *Charlotte Temple*, 1797), which also displays the effects of the pressure of a Puritan morality and probably a sympathetic reading by the author of the works of Fanny Burney. Other novels of this type, written chiefly by women, established this subgenre in American literature for decades to come.

The gothic romance, while presented in some impressive early examples, mostly those of Charles Brockden Brown, did not flourish as had the domestic and sentimental novels. The most apparent reason for this weakness was the lack of didactic themes. The gothic setting and plot did not encourage moralizing on the author's part. There was often a touch of the picaresque in these productions, which tended to discourage moral lessons. Like the British models, such as William Beckford's *Vathek: An Arabian Tale* (1786; original French edition, 1787) and Matthew Gregory Lewis's *The Monk: A Romance* (1796; also published as *Ambrosio: Or, The Monk*), the American gothic novel developed a body of gothic machinery designed to terrify. As in England, the form stimulated a number of parodies of its most extreme features: unlikely plots, bizarre settings, and unwholesome characters whose actions often descend into the lunatic.

As a reaction against these types developed in the form of the early historical novel—marked by the introduction of American Indians as important characters—the quality of fiction in the New World began to rise, but at a slow pace. It is noteworthy that it was not until nearly fifty years after the American Revolution that American novelists dealt significantly and seriously with that event. The delay was once again largely the result of a powerful British cultural influence on the new nation. When that influence was overcome, and as the country became more unified (improved roads and modes of travel had a great deal to do with this advance), the ground was laid for important literary achievements.

1820 to 1865

The unrest at the heart of the American novel, especially in the nineteenth century, is particularly evident in the work of James Fenimore Cooper (1789-1851). It is not so evident in a lesser book, such as *Satanstoe: Or, The Littlepage Manuscripts, a Tale of the Colony* (1845), as in the more famous novels: *The Last of the Mohicans: A Narrative of 1757* (1826), *The Prairie: A Tale* (1827), *The Pathfinder: Or, The Inland Sea* (1840), and *The Deerslayer: Or, The First War-Path* (1841)—the central titles in his famous Leatherstocking Tales, which recount the adventures of one of the most influential characters in early American fiction, the redoubtable Natty Bumppo. Cooper's presentation of this interesting personage's experiences on the frontier could be said to have brought about the development of the Western genre, or at least to have brought it to the highest point to which it aspired (the culmination of the trend may perhaps be found in Owen Wister's *The Virginian*, 1902, which, while a more sophisticated work, still emphasizes the virtues of Western heroes in contrast with the evils and corruption of the East). As Richard Chase declares in *The American Novel and Its Tradition*, Cooper is at his best when he can "accept without anxiety or thought the vivid contradictions of Natty Bumppo and his way of life." Chase and many other literary historians point out that the unrest was the result of unresolved disunities in a nation that had been formed largely from disparate elements: progressive thinkers and conservative traditions, European influence and American innovation, and what would later be termed the "highbrow" versus the "lowbrow."

Such oppositions might well be expected in a new country whose physical borders were still expanding, with new states being added every several years, and whose population was still being enlarged by immigration at a rapid pace (more than fifty million people traveled to the United States from Europe and Asia during the nineteenth century). The lack of serenity in American political and economic life was mirrored by the artistic sphere. A sort of inferiority complex in the arts persisted in the United States long after the insulting remark by the British writer Sidney Smith in 1820: "In the four quarters of the globe, who reads an American book? Or goes to an American play? Or looks at an American picture or statue?" Many Americans were forced to agree that the artistic accomplishments of the new nation were slight. As late as the 1840's, Margaret Fuller (1810-1850), the scholarly author and friend of most of the Transcendentalists (whose most illustrious member was Ralph Waldo Emerson, 1803-1882), asserted that for America to produce a literature of its own, "an original idea must animate this nation." Few of these fresh concepts were to be found in a culture that was influenced by Europe and the chief concerns of which were advancing its political growth and consolidating its economy.

Into this wasteland of artistic sterility came the imposing figure of Nathaniel Hawthorne, who turned to his Puritan forebears for material for some of the finest short stories and at least two of the most impressive novels (*The Scarlet Letter*, 1850, and *The House of the Seven Gables*, 1851) of the nineteenth century. One of Hawthorne's ancestors had been a judge at the Salem witch trials and had participated in the condemnation to ghastly torture of innocent women. The sensitive descendant of this old, honored, and guilty family could not rid himself of the sense of wrongdoing and, fortunately for his art, developed a haunting penetration into the nature of good and evil. Also of benefit to his writing was a distinctive and lofty prose style. Many scholars would concur with Irving Howe's judgment in *The Literature of America: Nineteenth Century* (1970) that Hawthorne is "the first great American novelist."

Writers as diverse as Herman Melville and Mark Twain not only produced American novels of high quality but also helped to legitimate American fiction in the United States. Their success was partially a result of nonartistic phenomena, such as the nation's rapid increases in population and territory. Prosperity led people to take pride in their accomplishments and provided more leisure in which to read fiction. While the stress on personal advancement sometimes took the form of self-aggrandizement, Americans had a countervailing impulse toward endorsement of the leveling effects of democracy. This conflict, like so many others appearing in the United States toward the middle of the nineteenth century, can be discovered as an underlying theme in the better novels of Melville: *Redburn: His First Voyage* (1849), *White-Jacket: Or, The World in a Man-of-War* (1850), *Moby Dick*, and *Billy Budd, Foretopman* (a novella not published until 1924 but now considered one of his finest works).

The midcentury also saw the growth of "local color" fiction, which ranged in the following decades from the Western sketches of Bret Harte (1836-1902) to the poetic realism of Sarah Orne Jewett (1849-1909). To some extent, the local colorists were preserving or re-creating a simpler, preindustrial America in the nostalgic mood of Twain's *The Adventures of Tom Sawyer* (1876). Though Twain produced only one generally accepted masterpiece, *Adventures of Huckleberry Finn*, the influence of his stories, especially the early ones, was enormous. It is perhaps not too much to say that this emotionally troubled author (particularly in his later years) assisted America in realizing how much it had lost with the westward spread of civilization.

Harriet Beecher Stowe (1811-1896), a then little-known writer from the civilized East, fond of reading the romances of Sir Walter Scott, has been credited with awakening the conscience of the North to the horrors of slavery. *Uncle Tom's Cabin* (1852) is hardly a great book, and its romantic elements are at times humorous, or would be were the subject of the novel not so serious. Abraham Lincoln was no doubt exaggerating when he remarked upon meeting Stowe that he was pleased to greet the "little lady" who had started the big war, but there is no question that this novel contributed greatly to the abolitionist movement. In so doing, it proved that a work of fiction could have profound social and political effects on the nation.

This period also saw the publication of the first novel by an African American, William Wells Brown's *Clotel: Or, The President's Daughter* (1853; as *Miralda: Or, The Beautiful Quadroon*, 1860-1861; *Clotelle: A Tale of the Southern States*, 1864; and *Clotelle: Or, The Colored Heroine*, 1867). Brown, himself an escaped slave, wrote the novel to flesh out the now-confirmed rumors that Thomas Jefferson had fathered children with Sally Hemings, a woman who was his slave. Perhaps unpublishable in the United States, *Clotel* was published in London. In 1859, the first novel by an African American woman, Harriet E. Wilson's *Our Nig: Or, Sketches from the Life of a Free Black, in a Two-Story White House, North. Showing That Slavery's Shadow Falls Even There*, became also the first novel by an African American to be published in the United States.

The post-Civil War period, satirically named the Gilded Age by Twain and his collaborator, Charles Dudley Warner (1829-1900), in their 1873 novel of that title, was also perceived, especially by later historians, as the age of realism. Novels with realistic elements had appeared before the war, but the forthright recognition by novelists of the harsh realities of the Reconstruction period justifies that designation. James emphasized psychological realism. While he did live mostly in Europe and often wrote about Europeans, he never lost his interest in the American personality; his novels are filled with fascinating American characters, often seen in conflict with, or corrupted by, the older society of Europe, such as the charming Isabel Archer of *The Portrait of a Lady* (1881) and the very American Christopher Newman of *The American* (1877). Even when James was writing chiefly about European characters who visit the United States, as in *The Europeans* (1878), the attentive reader gleans more information about the nature of American morals and attitudes, as with the Wentworth family in that story, than about those of the foreign characters. James's psychological realism influenced his good friend and constant admirer William Dean Howells (1837-1920), most notably in *The Rise of Silas Lapham* (1885). However, Howells was more concerned with external reality and much cruder in his treatment of emotional nuances than was James.

Indeed, under the influence of naturalism, Howells went so far as to claim that art should be eliminated altogether and fiction turned into a sort of factual, semiscientific report of life as it is. He never attained this goal, but some of the naturalistic writers came close to doing so: Howells's influence on Frank Norris (1870-1902), Stephen Crane (1871-1900), and Theodore Dreiser (1871-1945) was considerable. In a larger way, James and Twain affected the course of American long fiction for a longer time. As depth psychology came into vogue, the examinations of characters' motives and states of mind so highly evolved in James's novels—the later ones, such as *The Wings of the Dove* (1902) and *The Ambassadors* (1903) are especially impressive for this achievement—became very influential. Although his popularity with readers has never equaled Twain's, James had a powerful effect on later writers.

The spread of literacy, which accelerated sharply after the Civil War, helped create a market for fiction, and a great number of minor authors emerged. Some of them had superior credentials, such as the historical novelist Francis Marion Crawford (1854-1909), who, during his travels and studies, attained a reasonable fluency in more than fifteen languages. Most of these authors are, unfortunately, little read today. Stylistically, the most prominent influence on the period was Twain, to whom, much later, both William Faulkner and Ernest Hemingway would admit a debt. In another way, Twain's increasing pessimism encouraged the advance of the naturalist movement, which has been defined as realism with predilection for the nasty. This gloomy outlook, largely the result of business reverses (Twain was a poor businessman, and the expanding economy encouraged unwise investments), can readily be seen in the naturalistic writers.

The dejection in Twain's later work, most sharply revealed in the posthumously published *Mark Twain's Mysterious Stranger Manuscripts* (1969), was not without valid cause. The Gilded Age had followed the Civil War, which some experts consider the first truly modern war, characterized by the participation of large numbers of civilians, the massing and action of large bodies of troops, and the phenomenon of individual battles becoming massacres; also, it has been judged the first war in which victory was primarily the result of an industrial superiority. The epoch was modern in other ways as well, which, though not so bloody, were distressing: The growth of the economy created new industries and sudden fortunes at the same time it brought into being a new class of urban poor and the beginnings of extensive slum areas. These grim conditions inevitably led to clashes between corporations and nonorganized workers, impelling the rapid expansion of the labor movement.

By 1890 the United States was well on its way to becoming a modern country, with all the blessings and curses that such a development implies. Novelists tended to fix their attention on the curses, yet this penchant could be regarded as something of a duty for novelists, especially in the modern era. When the liberal educator and writer Thomas Wentworth Higginson (1823-1911) was asked how one could best learn about "American society in its formative process," he recommended reading the novels of Howells. It might not be too much to say that Americans who desire to understand the most significant trends in the early development of their nation and their people would be well advised to peruse the novels produced by their own varied and energetic culture.

Fred B. McEwen; Patrick Adcock
Updated by Cynthia A. Bily

Bibliography

Clayton, Jay. *Romantic Vision and the Novel.* New York: Cambridge University Press, 1987. Addresses the theme of transcendence in the English novel, with discussion of *Mansfield Park* by Jane Austen, *Wuthering Heights* by Emily Brontë, *Little Dorritt* by Charles Dickens, *Adam Bede* by George Eliot, and *Women in Love* by D. H. Lawrence.

David, Dierdre, ed. *Cambridge Companion to the Victorian Novel.* New York: Cambridge University Press, 2001. Collection of eleven essays analyzes such issues as readership, publishing, aesthetics, gender, sexuality, economy, and science in the Victorian novel. Includes an extensive bibliography.

Davidson, Cathy N. *Revolution and the Word: The Rise of the Novel in America.* 2d ed. New York: Oxford University Press, 2004. Expanded and revised edition of a classic study of the parallel rise of a new nation and the rise of the novel in America. Argues that the idea that early American fiction imitated European works is exaggerated.

Ellis, Markman. *The Politics of Sensibility: Race, Gender, and Commerce in the Sentimental Novel.* New York: Cambridge University Press, 1996. Offers a thoughtful examination of the sentimental novel, with consideration of politics, race, slavery, and the treatment of women in fiction.

Harris, Sharon M., ed. *Redefining the Political Novel: American Women Writers, 1797-1901.* Knoxville: University of Tennessee Press, 1995. Collection of nine essays discusses the contribution of women writers to the political novel. Two essays deal with the famous authors Louisa May Alcott and Mary E. Wilkins Freeman, whereas the others examine the work of lesser-known female novelists.

Perosa, Sergio. *American Theories of the Novel: 1793-1903.* New York: New York University Press, 1983. Presents discussion of the colonial background of the American novel, followed by chapters titled "The Debate over Realism in the 1870's and 1880's," "Henry James and the Art of Fiction," "Genteel Realism and Regionalism," "Naturalism, Veritism, and Impressionism," and "The New Romance."

Samuels, Shirley. *A Companion to American Fiction, 1780-1865.* Malden, Mass.: Blackwell, 2004. Examines important American authors, including Cooper, Hannah Foster, Hawthorne, Melville, and Stowe, and explores such issues as race, gender, religion, and political identity in their works. Also devotes discussion to dime novels, Western novels, and novels for children.

Spacks, Patricia Meyer. *Novel Beginnings: Experiments in Eighteenth-Century English Fiction.* New Haven, Conn.: Yale University Press, 2006. Study intended for the general reader examines the variety of fiction produced in eighteenth century England, including the novel *Tristram Shandy* and gothic fiction, the political novel, and the novel of manners. Discusses *Tristram Shandy* as an important step toward the development of the true novel.

Origins and Development of the Novel, 1890-1980

The environment in England during the 1880's and 1890's was especially fertile for the development of new trends in literature. As the century came to a close, all the giants of the novel, except George Meredith, had either died or stopped writing. Even Thomas Hardy, who can be justly classified as either "Victorian" or "modern," quit writing prose in 1895 and turned to poetry. The great Victorian poets, too, were disappearing: Matthew Arnold died in 1888, Robert Browning in 1889, and Alfred, Lord Tennyson in 1892. The Victorian stage, for decades the province of producers and directors who spared no expense to provide "spectacle" to audiences whose penchant for grand performances demanded ever-greater mechanical wonders on the boards, was becoming the province of men such as George Bernard Shaw. His plays, while amusing at times, generally abandoned the grandiose for the middle class and did so with a striking (and sometimes disturbing) sense of realism. Upstarts such as Oscar Wilde and Walter Pater were turning their backs on "traditional" subjects in art and presenting material that the general populace could only describe as decadent.

The younger generation of writers had turned away from their English ancestors, seeking inspiration from French novelists whose naturalistic treatment of subjects glorified the commonplace and vulgar while minimizing the good in traditional morality; Honoré de Balzac and Émile Zola became the luminaries whom budding authors copied with dedication and fidelity. Among this generation of writers and readers, the Victorian notion of "high seriousness" was giving way to a concern for subjects only whispered about during the heyday of that glorious queen who gave her name to the period. That aging lady still occupied the throne, but everyone knew that she was to die soon, and with her would pass an "age" in English life.

The American novel, 1880-1900

On the other side of the Atlantic, the novel was also undergoing a transformation. By the close of the nineteenth century, most American novelists had declared their independence from their English forebears. Whether one agrees with Ernest Hemingway that "all American literature springs from one book," Mark Twain's *Adventures of Huckleberry Finn* (1884), it is nevertheless true that by the 1880's, American writers had turned to their own country for literary inspiration. The heritage of the American past, the attitudes and concerns of the founding fathers and the Puritan heritage they had bequeathed to their heirs, the legends of the original American Indian inhabitants of the land, and the particular curiosities associated with the various regions of the country had supplanted earlier tendencies to anglicize American situations and frontier characters. Whereas the Indians in James Fenimore Cooper's Leatherstocking Tales speak (and often act) like eighteenth century gentlemen, those of late century novelists exhibit no such artificiality. American writers had become interested in American society, a society that had, in a period of barely more than one century, grown from adolescent imitation of the English culture that had given it birth to an adult life that was in many ways different from that of its parent.

The absence of a society that dated back a thousand years made it difficult for Americans to write social novels in the manner of Jane Austen, George Meredith, or George Eliot, for, as Alfred Kazin has observed, the social novel most often flourishes in a society "deeply settled," one that "knows itself thoroughly" and "takes itself for granted." While British writers such as Matthew Arnold could dismiss America as "uninteresting," and the expatriate Henry James lamented the absence of the castles, kings, and monuments that in Europe heralded links to the past of a thousand or more years, most American writers of the last decades of the nineteenth century took a look around them, found what they saw of interest to themselves and to their countrymen, and wrote about it with fidelity not to British literary tradition but to their own growing awareness of the unique qualities of their own country.

What American writers lacked may have been a handicap in the 1830's, but by the 1880's they had abandoned their attempts to imitate their British counterparts; instead, they turned to the problems and the people around them for inspiration and found ample material for their work. The American experience had been, for almost three hundred years, one of change and development, characterized by the ever-present challenge of conquering the frontier. America was not, and had in fact never been, one society; rather, it was a collage of many societies. Its various regions—South, Northeast, Midwest, Pacific Coast—developed separate cultures in which political homogeneity was often the only common link to other areas in the vast expanse of the country. American novelists, turning from romance to realism, found their subjects in the various regions about which they chose to write. As a consequence, novelists as diverse as William Dean Howells and Mark Twain were both realists in depicting the American scene, though they differ significantly in subject matter and technique. Both treat American life, but life in the Northeast was quite different from that in the Far West or along the Mississippi River. Hence the modern American novel, born of a drive to portray a country and its people realistically, became for almost half a century a novel of regions and subcultures.

By the end of the nineteenth century, the novel had gained acceptance in the United States as a serious literary form, but even then there was strong sentiment among readers that novels were purely entertainment unless some explicit moral was woven into the narrative. Beginning in the 1880's, however, a young American, a New Yorker by birth, a Bostonian by upbringing, and an expatriate by choice, began to change that perception, both in his homeland and in England.

Henry James

Henry James may well be considered the first modern critic of the novel, and since the modern novel is the product of self-conscious artists who are concerned with their craft as well as their message, it is well to begin a discussion of the development of the modern novel with James. Considering his own works to be art as well as social commentary, James spent four decades explaining, in essays and prefaces he affixed to the collected edition of his works, how good prose fiction may be identified and judged. James's essay "The Art of Fiction" (1884), written as an answer to Walter Besant's 1884 essay of the same title, comes closer than any other document published during the final decades of the nineteenth century to being a manifesto for the modern novelist. Besant's essay had summarized the Victorian position on the role and limits of the novel: It was to provide wholesome entertainment, treat certain subjects only, avoid others at all costs, attempt verisimilitude but not at the expense of moral education, provide swift and unrelenting justice for moral offenders (especially where sexual transgressions were involved), and support the aims of society at large. In his response, James struck out against almost all of these notions. The only requirement a novelist has, James says, is to be "interesting." "We must grant the artist his subject matter," he insists, and judge the value of the work by the artist's success in executing his (or her) own design. No subject should be taboo, James argues; no artificial strictures should be placed on the novelist's creativity as long as that talent is put in the service of depicting life as it really is. Where Besant had tried to develop appropriate classifications for novels (similar to those used to describe various forms of poetry), James swept away such prescriptive categories, asserting that novelists must be free to explore incidents and characters and develop their stories in such a way as to be pleasing to the reader.

James fancied himself the consummate realist, interested in portraying life as it is lived by sensitive individuals full of thought and reflection. Much like Jane Austen, he limited his artistic gaze to a narrow segment of society, forgoing the panoramic techniques of the romancer and the historical novelist and avoiding the sweeping pronouncements of the social novelist to explore the nuances of social life among the upper classes. James has been called the first international novelist, and he was undoubtedly the first major figure to explore the clash of American and European cultures; in *The American* (1877), *The Portrait of a Lady* (1881), *The Ambassadors* (1903), *The Golden Bowl* (1904), and numerous other works, he presents American men and women, usually naïve and optimistic, confronting the wiser but more jaded men and women of England and the Continent.

A late masterpiece, *The Golden Bowl*, may serve as an example of James's method. In that novel, a young American girl, Maggie Verver, falls in love with an Italian nobleman, Prince Amerigo. Amerigo is charmed by Maggie's naïveté but apparently prefers the company of her more worldly-wise and well-traveled American friend, Charlotte Stant, with whom Amerigo has apparently had an affair some time before. Because Maggie is rich, he agrees to marry her, and only after the two are already married does Maggie discover the true nature of the relationship between her friend and her husband. At the end of this sordid tale of social intrigue and betrayal, Maggie emerges victorious—after a fashion. Charlotte marries Maggie's father and returns with him to America, leaving to the heroine a prince who is apparently reformed enough to recognize where his loyalty should lie. In winning, however, Maggie loses, too; her father, whom she adores, returns to America, never to see her again, and she is at best a sadder and wiser woman for the "victory."

As an allegory of the conflict of cultures, James's novel is largely pessimistic about the modern condition. Such an attitude is clearly characteristic of the realists in general, who, looking scientifically at the contemporary scene, found little to cheer about in the condition of society. These men and women were willing to express their displeasure openly, despite the threat of censure from a reading public accustomed to having their literary lessons presented either in romantic garb or in stark allegorical narrative. James and his contemporaries who examined the American or British scene under their figurative microscopes would not allow their readers to maintain a comfortable distance from their subject.

James's novels and his critical pronouncements signaled a change in the attitude toward the novel shared by several of his contemporaries who were just beginning to regard themselves as artists as well as (or rather than) social reformers or educators, or mere entertainers. From James, it is only a short step to Joseph Conrad, who declared in his preface to *The Children of the Sea: A Tale of the Forecastle* (1897; republished as *The Nigger of the Narcissus: A Tale of the Sea*, 1898) that "any work which aspires to the condition of art must carry its justification in every line." Conrad's own works testify to his constant concern for selecting the right word or phrase to characterize the situation he chooses to create. Always the careful observer of people in conditions that test their fortitude and challenge their values, Conrad wrote of the sea as a constant metaphor for the human condition in general. In his works, events take on a significance beyond the literal, but Conrad is no simple allegorist whose story serves as an excuse for presenting a philosophical proposition. For the most part, his men and women are interesting as people, not merely as representations of abstract principles. In *Heart of Darkness* (1902), for example, the "horror" that Kurtz sees as he lies on his deathbed in the heart of Africa strikes the reader as especially poignant because no one in the story is really larger than life; the simple possibility that men could be so corrupted makes the tale a chilling commentary on the tenuousness of civilization as a means of staving off the bestial side of human nature.

Writers such as James and Conrad concerned themselves with the structure of their works, with choosing incident and detail to give the works a sense of balance and completeness that satisfies the reader's aesthetic sensibilities. Quietly, these novelists were redefining their readership: No longer would they write for the general audience (though they may have claimed to do so); rather, they would write for those discerning few who could detect what James would call in another essay "the figure in the carpet." No longer would plot, action, and moral pronouncement be the glue to bind the parts of the novel to the whole or to solidify the bond between the reader and writer. Artists were becoming aware that they could communicate with the reader—albeit a certain kind of reader—by other means: through patterns of images that would themselves suggest larger themes than the story conveys (symbolism, leitmotif), through conscious attempts to balance or juxtapose incidents and characters whose stories are often unrelated on the literal level, and through clear links with the great literature or folk culture of the past. The fragmentation of the audience for fiction that had begun at least a decade before James began writing became complete by the decade after he died.

While James was abroad writing pronouncements on the status of American and British fiction, his friend and contemporary William Dean Howells remained at home and did the same. Using his position as editor of several popular magazines, Howells influenced the taste of countless readers by promoting the kind of fiction he believed best suited the public's needs. Like James, he was a realist: His own novels display a careful concern for realistic presentation of information, often a meticulous attention to detail and an extraordinary accumulation of facts, and a concern for the contemporary social and political milieu in his own country. Howells, less daring than James, remained faithful to nineteenth century moral ideals and practices; hence, his realistic vision is limited by his moral sensibilities. In *The Rise of Silas Lapham* (1885), for example, Howells combines his penchant for providing realistic detail with his strong sense of moral purpose to create a portrait of American society and American business that shows how the drive for material betterment can often lead to spiritual poverty and, eventually, to ruin—in this world and possibly in the next. As a portrait of American commerce it is most unflattering, but it is typical of both Howells's own outlook and that of many other realistic novelists who were looking around them and finding little to like in the contemporary scene.

Thomas Hardy and Theodore Dreiser

Two novelists, one English, one American, may serve to characterize the naturalistic movement in the English-language novel during this period of transition from Victorian to modern sensibilities. Like other naturalists, both Thomas Hardy and Theodore Dreiser were followers of the school of realism: Their works are filled with minute descriptions of ordinary places and events, with scenes and characters from the middle and lower classes, and neither makes any attempt to glorify his heroes and heroines by raising them to epic proportion.

Hardy's novels, usually set in the Wessex district of England, depict the life of common folks who struggle to eke out an existence against an unforgiving nature. Influenced by the theories of Charles Darwin and Herbert Spencer, Hardy displays in his novels a world where natural selection and determinism are the primary moving forces and where chance is ever present to ruin the best designs of even the best persons. *The Mayor of Casterbridge* (1886) offers a good example of Hardy's philosophy of determinism and the role that chance plays in human lives. In this novel, Michael Henchard, a man of strong will but somewhat irrational temperament (in the opening scene, a drunken Henchard sells his wife and daughter), rises by his own industry to become a wealthy farmer and prominent citizen in his local community. As chance would have it, however, he soon falls victim to a series of setbacks: He finds his wife again and, believing he should win her back to make restitution for his earlier behavior, abandons a woman who loves him; he loses all his money to another farmer, largely because the weather favors the other's crops; and he loses his wife again to this rival, who also supplants him as mayor of the town. He is reduced at the end of the novel to a penniless beggar who wanders off to die alone in the barren countryside.

This note of extreme pessimism characterizes Hardy's other works and is, in fact, typical of many naturalistic novelists. The work of Frank Norris in the United States, especially in a novel such as *McTeague* (1899), bears a striking resemblance to Hardy's fiction. Like most naturalists, Hardy ignored the Victorian conventions prescribing subject matter for fiction and turned to issues that would eventually cause him to be rejected by the British public of his day. In *Tess of the D'Urbervilles* (1891), his heroine, forced to yield to a young nobleman who abandons her after he has used her, suffers the fate one would expect for prostitutes in Victorian England; Hardy's Tess, however, evokes not horror but pity in the reader, a feeling that apparently made many Victorian readers uncomfortable. In *Jude the Obscure* (1895), Hardy abandons any pretense of dealing out Victorian justice or shying away from taboo subjects. In this novel, he frankly and sympathetically treats the extramarital, adulterous relationship of Jude Fawley and Sue Bridehead. They struggle to maintain a life built on genuine love in a society whose conventions work against their ever being happy. As in other Hardy novels, chance intervenes to bring misery to both hero and heroine, destroying them for no apparent reason. *Jude the Obscure* was Hardy's last novel, for he was sternly criticized for his open treatment of adultery, a subject he felt he had only touched on and not fully explored in this work. Disappointed that the public was unwilling to face contemporary issues head-on, Hardy abandoned the novel and turned to poetry.

The kind of restraints that caused Hardy to abandon the novel worked against American novelists as well; Dreiser's experience is a good example. Dreiser was initially stymied in his attempts to publish *Sister Carrie*, which was finally published in 1900, because that work dealt openly with the problems of an impoverished girl who becomes a man's mistress as a means of preserving her life. The book was derided in literary and religious circles, for it suggests that submission to evil, even in extremity, does not necessarily lead to a life of ignominy. Unlike Hardy's Tess, Carrie succeeds by using her wits and feminine charm. Without the least hint that he believes his heroine has been wrong in her actions, Dreiser traces Carrie's rise to prominence in society while simultaneously portraying the decline and eventual suicide of her original benefactor, Hurstwood. There is in this novel, and in most of Dreiser's others, a strong implication that the common person in the United States can succeed only by abandoning the platitudes preached both in the pulpit and in the public forum, and that those who succeed do so at the expense of others.

Regardless of the methods one uses, however, there is no guarantee of success. In the greatest of his novels, *An American Tragedy* (1925), Dreiser portrays the sad results of the American Dream gone awry. His protagonist, Clyde Griffiths, a shallow young man, self-centered and greedy for the "good things in life," enters the world of business and society to find that success depends much more on birth and chance than on honest striving for advancement. Clyde is made to look like a fool in the high society where he seeks membership. Through foolish behavior, he impregnates an innocent farm girl who really loves him. When he discovers that she is a hindrance to his chances to climb the social ladder, he plots to kill her, only to discover that he is too much the coward to commit the deed. Cruel chance does for him what he cannot do for himself, however, as the girl accidentally falls from a boat and drowns (the kind of death Clyde had planned for her). Ironically, Clyde is accused of committing the crime he had plotted but failed to carry out and is eventually convicted.

It is impossible not to see an intellectual kinship between Dreiser and Hardy, both of whose characters succeed or fail according to circumstances over which they have no control. The works of these novelists provide some of the finest statements of naturalism, the stepchild of scientific determinism and literary realism.

THE EDWARDIAN NOVEL

The death of Queen Victoria in 1901 and the ascension of Edward VII marked the beginning of a new political age in England, but the fiction of the next two decades continued to show strong ties to that which had preceded it. On more than one occasion, the literature of the period has been disparagingly dismissed as mere journalism. That journalistic style, however, was often a facade that covered serious treatments of problems plaguing England as it entered the new century. Novelists in early twentieth century England, much more than artists in the United States, felt the impact of the intellectual advances that had been made during the preceding century. Living in what John Batchelor, in *The Edwardian Novelists* (1982), has called "a contracting moral universe, in which the received moral imperatives had lost their urgency," they attempted to find substitutes for religious imperatives in secular ones. Duty in society replaced obedience to God as the principle of right living for many Edwardians, and novelists reflected that attitude in their works.

Heroes were needed, of course, but heroism seemed impossible in the modern environment. Further, the English countryside that had provided a wholesome counterpart to the squalor of the city for earlier novelists was fast disappearing as suburbs spread out around the metropolitan areas. The growth of the suburbs was paralleled by the retreat of the empire, as Great Britain's worldwide system of colonial enterprise was clearly in danger of falling apart. The "glory that was England" under Victoria was fading, and the impending conflict with Germany, foreseen as early as 1900, caused concern among the populace and influenced the works of Edwardian novelists. The period was characterized by a general anxiety about the state of the individual and society. The major figures of the period—John Galsworthy, Arnold Bennett, H. G. Wells, Ford Madox Ford, E. M. Forster—adopted the form of the novel that their Victorian predecessors had bequeathed them, but they were living in a society quite changed both intellectually and politically. It is small wonder that one of the most popular images in Edwardian novels is the abyss.

On the popular front, two voices emerged as the spokesmen for the novel in England: Bennett and Galsworthy. Bennett's popularity was important to him, and some critics have complained that he prostituted a fine talent to satisfy his desire to be regarded as a social lion. A disciple of realism, in his best works, such as *The Old Wives' Tale* (1908), he demonstrates a keen eye for detail and an ability to make the lives of commonplace people interesting and significant. He and Galsworthy did much to popularize the chronicle novel, multiple volumes dealing with the same character or characters. Others among Bennett's works, such as *The Grand Babylon Hotel* (1902; also known as *T. Racksole and Daughter*), are predecessors of the modern documentary novels that explore life in particular institutions or forms of business. Galsworthy achieved success as both a playwright and a novelist, giving Edwardian England a portrait of its Victorian heritage and its contemporary problems in his famous series *The Forsyte Saga* (1922).

Both Galsworthy and Bennett paid close attention to external detail, but their unwillingness or inability to explore the motivations and inner feelings of characters with the same sensitivity made them targets for writers who believed that the job of the artist is not to substitute for the photographer but to explore the reality of experience that cannot be seen on the surface. Virginia Woolf's famous essay "Mr. Bennett and Mrs. Brown" (1924) provided the rationale for certain post-World War I novelists to reject traditional realism.

Ford and Forster bridged the gap between the Edwardian period and the 1920's. Ford had achieved recognition during the early years of the war with the publication of *The Good Soldier* (1915), but in his Tietjens sequence of four novels (1924-1928) he examines the changes that had occurred in society and their effect on the hero, who is carefully drawn to represent the traditionally good English gentleman. Forster published four novels before 1910, all of them typical English social novels that are, at times, melodramatic. His most significant work, *A Passage to India*, did not appear until 1924, and while the style and method of narration recall his own earlier works and those of the novelists of the turn of the century, the book's theme reflects both the effects that the war had on sensibilities in England and a timeless concern for the paradox of human experience that Forster shared with other members of the literary circle to which he belonged, the Bloomsbury Group (which included Woolf). More than in any of his other novels, Forster depicts in *A Passage to India* a certain tragic quality about human life. One of his characters, Mrs. Moore, reflects at one point, "Pathos, piety, courage—they exist, but are identical, and so is filth. Everything exists, nothing has value." For anything in life to have value, humans must make that thing worthwhile; no values are preordained. That philosophy, the product of modern science strengthened by the experiences of World War I, links Forster to as unlikely a colleague as Ernest Hemingway, whose characters often express the same idea and act to establish meaning for their own lives in the face of certain defeat.

THE AMERICAN NOVEL, 1900-1920

During this same period in the United States, the novelists who rose to prominence were often much like their British counterparts. In *The Modern Novel in Britain and the United States* (1964), Walter Allen calls the first two decades of the twentieth century a period of comparative sterility in American fiction. If one excludes Henry James and Theodore Dreiser, that description may be just, for no giant of American literature emerged until after World War I. The American populace was being swept away by sensationalism, as the new journalists captured the country's interest with their exposés of business, politics, and life in the cities and the country. Novelists such as Upton Sinclair achieved popular acclaim for fiction that called attention to the rot at the core of American institutions; Sinclair's *The Jungle* (1906), which graphically displays the horrors of the meatpacking industry, was read for its sociological impact as much as for its literary merit. It became fashionable for the novelist to look deeply into the American scene and expose the corruption or absence of value in institutions that had long been considered honorable.

Among American novelists who focused their gaze in this fashion, none was more popular than Sinclair Lewis, whose works consistently drew attention to the inadequacies of the American Dream. Like Dreiser and Sherwood Anderson, Lewis was a midwesterner by birth. A student of the American realists, he concentrated on mid-America, depicting the pettiness and emptiness of life in what was generally regarded as the bastion of modern American morality in *Main Street: The Story of Carol Kennicott* (1920), *Babbitt* (1922), and other earlier works. Lewis pointed out to Americans and readers abroad (where he achieved a certain degree of popularity) that the heartland of America was filled with George Babbitts, whose lives consisted of belonging to clubs that gave members status by telling them what to think, men whose advancement in society was always at the expense of someone less fortunate. Lewis was awarded the Nobel Prize in Literature in 1930, the first American so honored.

Also writing in the United States during this period were other authors whose works were less sensational but of considerable literary merit. Edith Wharton, a writer of the Jamesian school of social realism, turned to East Coast society for her subject and created novels that rival James's for their penetrating insights into social situations and the impact on character that society can have. The American penchant for local color and regionalism continued unabated, and among novelists who provided this kind of literature were Willa Cather and Ellen Glasgow. In her stories of the Nebraska plains where she was reared, the Virginia area where she was born, and other regions, Cather constantly reminded her readers of the plight of the individual in modern society. Her insight into contemporary America rivals, and often surpasses, that of Lewis. Glasgow's region was the old South, where she was born and reared. Her stories showed the fixation of the South on its past, and her vision was pessimistic. A fine novelist in her own right, she is also important as a forerunner of the southern writers who were to form a literary subculture in the United States during the later decades of the twentieth century.

World War I provided a distinct dividing line between the nineteenth century sensibility and the new age in both England and the United States. Although Americans had had, in their Civil War, a preview of the kind of destruction modern warfare could produce, few people in either country were psychologically prepared for the carnage of World War I. In both countries, the postwar period was characterized by rapid social change and a heightened sense of the tenuousness of modern life in the face of total war. Though it is hard to offer a generalization that can encompass all English and American novelists, it is safe to say that in both countries the 1920's were characterized by a certain gaiety of spirit that masked a genuine disillusionment with institutions and in Britain with the class system. This feverish gaiety gave way to the Great Depression, reflected in British and American novels by a growing sense of concern for the future of a society based on capitalism, a growing trend toward social violence, and an increasing tendency to look for solutions to social problems outside the existing political frameworks that had been functioning in these countries for so long.

As one might expect, a large number of novels were written about the war itself, many of them by men who had taken part in the fighting. Several of these novels have taken their place among the modern classics: John Dos Passos's *Three Soldiers* (1921) and Hemingway's *A Farewell to Arms* (1929) fall into this category. The impact of the war on the literature of the next decades extended far beyond the novelists whose works deal directly with battlefield events. Institutions that had stood for a century or more had been shaken by the conflict. The worth of the individual, already called into question by the discoveries and theories of nineteenth century science, had been almost shattered by the wholesale destruction that the machinery of modern warfare had wreaked. Such events left many sensitive young men and women in shock, and those who turned to the novel as a means of expressing their dismay reflected the general disillusionment of the populaces of both countries.

MODERNISM

The breakdown of public agreement about what is significant in human life, the new view of the nature of consciousness introduced by the study of psychology, and a desire to discover new ways to reach their audience caused writers of the post-World War I period to experiment with the form of the novel. In fact, the period immediately following the end of hostilities on the Continent can best be described as the age of experimentation. The tendency to try new ways of representing reality is most noticeable in novelists who abandoned traditional narrative conventions, adopting instead the method suggested by William James in his discussions on psychology. Determining that reality cannot best be portrayed by a simple recitation of physical detail, these writers attempted to put down on paper the thought processes of characters, to re-create the stream of consciousness. The term "stream of consciousness" was first used by William James as a metaphor to describe the way thoughts pass through the mind just below the surface level, prior to their being formulated into intelligible patterns that are normally expressed as sentences. The technique of limiting the perspective of the novel to a single character was nothing new: Daniel Defoe's *Robinson Crusoe* (1719) makes use of the first-person narrator, as do myriad other eighteenth and nineteenth century works. That one could further limit the perspective, and hence more closely approximate the way in which reality was really apprehended, was first argued explicitly by Henry James, who, in the preface to *The Ambassadors*, discussed his method of limiting his descriptions to whatever might impinge on the "center of consciousness" of his hero. James's hero, however, is presented as having already formulated his thoughts, so that what one reads in a James novel are the intellectual reflections of a character who has observed something outside himself, rather than the record of those impressions as they first impinge upon his consciousness. The great experimenters in the modern novel—Dorothy Richardson, Virginia Woolf, and James Joyce in Britain and Nobel laureate William Faulkner in the United States—attempted to record the stream of consciousness itself.

In her essay "Mr. Bennett and Mrs. Brown," Woolf observed that "human character changed" decisively "on or about December 1910." Despite the whimsical precision of her statement, the sentiment was real; during the decade from 1910 to 1920 a number of literary figures, captivated by the new way of apprehending reality, began experimenting with the form of the novel. Woolf herself provided a key to understanding both the purpose and the method of the new movement. In an essay appropriately titled "Modern Fiction" (1925), she dismissed the efforts of Galsworthy, Bennett, and Wells as materialistic, condemning them for "spend[ing] immense skill and immense industry making the trivial and the transitory appear the true and the enduring" without capturing life as it really exists. Those novelists were hidebound by the tradition of the novel, which had always found in external events and relationships the proper material for fiction; if one should look within, Woolf says, "life, it seems, is very far from being 'like this.'" Instead, Woolf says, life is the action of the mind in contact with the outside world.

> The mind receives . . . impressions—trivial, fantastic, evanescent, or engraved with the sharpness of steel. From all sides they come, an incessant shower of innumerable atoms. . . . Life is not a series of gig lamps symmetrically arranged; but a luminous halo, a semi-transparent envelope surrounding us from the beginning of consciousness to the end.

The job of the writer is to abandon conventions and seek to display this inner life. Woolf continues with the following:

> Is it not the task of the novelist to convey this varying, this unknown and uncircumscribed spirit, whatever aberration or complexity it may display, with as little mixture of the alien and external as possible? We are not pleading merely for courage and sincerity; we are suggesting that the proper stuff of fiction is a little other than custom would have us believe it.

In her own novels, Woolf repeatedly tried to capture life as a series of impressions upon the minds of sensitive characters such as Mrs. Ramsay in *To the Lighthouse* (1927) and Bernard in *The Waves* (1931). Abandoning conventional concerns for plot, Woolf tried to reproduce—through asyntactical language, parenthetical digressions, juxtaposed sentences whose meanings appear to have no causal relationship, and other similar techniques—the immediacy of the human mind encountering the world around it.

When Woolf wrote "Modern Fiction," she was not introducing a theory so much as commenting on the works of novelists who had recently entered the literary scene. Early experimenters included Dorothy Richardson, who attempted to capture in toto the workings of a single, ordinary mind. Miriam, the heroine of Richardson's thirteen-volume *Pilgrimage* (1938, 1967), is revealed to the reader solely through the associative patterns of thoughts that race through her consciousness as she goes about her ordinary tasks. Though Richardson's notions of psychology may be pre-Freudian and though she may avoid with a curious Victorian reticence certain subjects and actions that no doubt would have been on her heroine's mind at some time, she is nevertheless a critical figure in the development of stream-of-consciousness fiction. Another early experimenter whose novels reflect an awareness of Freudian psychology was May Sinclair. Better than Richardson, Sinclair seems to have understood the real frustrations of women in late Victorian England, and she captures the psychological turmoil of her characters in narratives that are a curious blend of the Jamesian center of consciousness and Richardson's more free-form technique.

Unquestionably the greatest experimenter in this age of the experimental novel was James Joyce. His *A Portrait of the Artist as a Young Man* (1916), a semiautobiographical work about the upbringing of a young Irish Catholic Dubliner, is told with a degree of objectivity previously unknown in novels. Not once does the author intrude to tell the reader how he or she should respond to the hero's actions; even descriptive adjectives are carefully omitted so that the reader is forced to interpret feeling and motive directly from the character's action and speech. The same penchant for authorial self-effacement characterizes Joyce's later masterpieces, *Ulysses* (1922) and *Finnegans Wake* (1939). In these, Joyce abandons the conventions of plot and narrative to present events in a method best described as collage: Incidents are set in parallel, compared and contrasted so that meaning must be inferred, gleaned by the reader in the act of judging the text itself, not from authorial intrusions telling the reader what to believe or what to make of this strange mixture of dialogue, stream-of-consciousness narrative, soliloquies, dramatic vignettes, and other curious interjections of prose that often mystify all but the most careful, attentive reader.

In *Ulysses*, Joyce resorts to a device typical of many modern authors who aim not at the general reader but at one who brings to the work a strong background in classical and modern literature. By suggesting correspondences between his work and Homer's *Odyssey* (c. 725 B.C.E.; English translation, 1614), Joyce forces the reader to look for parallels between the world of modern Dublin and the mythic world of Homer's poem. The drive to raise the significance of modern events to the level of myth has become commonplace among many novelists who consider themselves serious artists, and the works of writers as diverse as Albert Camus and William Faulkner share this tendency to some degree.

In *Finnegans Wake* the tendency toward myth is still present, but punning and other forms of wordplay dominate that work and have baffled most readers, leading to the production of numerous handbooks explaining what Joyce "means" in his novel. Some critics have thrown up their hands at *Finnegans Wake*, dismissing it in exasperation as not a novel at all. Its "narrative" is circular (the book begins in midsentence and ends with the first half of that sentence), and even the stream-of-consciousness method seems secondary to Joyce's continual play with the multiple meanings of words. In fact, *Finnegans Wake* is often cited as the primary example of what is wrong with the experimental novel by critics and novelists who adhere to the more traditional methods of narrative and who feel that the novel should not abandon its historical function as a bearer of news about the way people live.

Experimentation with form was not confined to writers in England or on the Continent. A number of American novelists quickly adopted wholly or in part the technique of stream of consciousness and other methods of nontraditional narration. Dos Passos used a kind of collage of narrative forms to achieve the panoramic effect he sought as a means of capturing the expanse and variety of his native land in his *U.S.A.* trilogy (1937). Faulkner carried on experiments with the form of the novel that included juxtaposing stream of consciousness with traditional narrative techniques (*The Sound and the Fury*, 1929), collecting disparate stories with related themes to form a single work (*Go Down, Moses*, 1942), and presenting two seemingly unrelated stories in parallel (*The Wild Palms*, 1939). Adding an elaborate style to these other rhetorical devices, Faulkner moved the novel in the direction of modern poetry, where the reader is often called upon to work to discover meaning amid a collection of images. The use of stream of consciousness and other nontraditional techniques has now become commonplace in modern fiction.

D. H. Lawrence

The reaction to experimentation with form has been strident, perhaps more vehement in England than in the United States. Since 1923, when D. H. Lawrence dismissed the efforts of Joyce, Richardson, and Woolf as "childish" and "absorbedly self-conscious" in his essay "Surgery for the Novel—or a Bomb," many critics and novelists have lashed out against the trend to abandon the intellectual bond between the writer and the general reader. Novelists who believe in the efficacy of fiction as social documentary have been loudest in their protests, and their work has remained close in both form and content to the traditional novel as written by their eighteenth and nineteenth century forebears. In *The Realists* (1978) C. P. Snow, always a staunch believer in the value of the story in the novel, described the trend to "regard novels, and compose novels, as verbal puzzles to be worked out by persons cleverer than the original writer" as a sign of a "period of decline not only in the art itself, but also in the society from which it derives." It is no wonder that Snow's own novels, especially those in the *Strangers and Brothers* series (1940-1970), are traditionally realistic chronicles of English society that focus on intellectual dilemmas and social quandaries faced by men and women who are immediately recognizable to the reader. The swing back toward more traditional forms of narrative after World War II was hailed by British critic Paul West, who saw the return to convention as a kind of recovery after sickness: "The English novel has recovered from the flux, and only Lawrence Durrell makes much use of it."

Though he distrusted the experimental fiction of his time, Lawrence now is ranked as a great innovator himself. Along with Woolf and Joyce, he stands as a preeminent figure of the period between the wars. Like Joyce, he had already published a work of some distinction before the war, distinctly exhibiting modern sensibilities in his first autobiographical novel, *Sons and Lovers* (1913). Though similar in some respects to the traditional bildungsroman, *Sons and Lovers* clearly shows the influence of Freudian theories of psychology; in it, Lawrence depicts the classical Oedipal conflict. In the 1920's, an age that glorified anti-intellectualism, Lawrence was right at home. He rebelled against the modern industrial society because it had, in his view, cheapened the quality of human experience. Intellectualism was at best a form of escape from the fullness of life's experiences, and at worst it ruined all that was worthwhile in life; not surprisingly, almost all of Lawrence's villains are intellectuals. Only those who feel deeply and act vigorously (even violently) are worthy of praise in his works.

The theories of Sigmund Freud and other psychologists had made the world aware of the submerged part of the human mind that often drives people to actions they cannot explain, and Lawrence found in these theories fertile ground for his fiction. In a style often reminiscent of Romantic poetry, Lawrence tried to convey the power that these subliminal urges have to drive men and women to act. Unlike Joyce or Woolf, he did not abandon conventional narrative techniques or traditional forms of organization for his works; in fact, *The Rainbow* (1915), one of his best novels, is in many respects a fine chronicle novel in the fashion of Galsworthy or Bennett. Lawrence was always interested, however, in trying to convey what literary critic Eliseo Vivas called the "felt quality of experience," the "ebb and flow of the affective life, particularly the felt quality of erotic passion and of religious emotion." As much as any novelist of the period, Lawrence created in his works powerful symbols that could evoke multiple levels of meaning for discerning readers. A man of strong passions himself, he was ultimately disappointed with the public response to his works, complaining on one occasion that his "psychological" stuff simply did not sell well. What did sell well was *Lady Chatterley's Lover* (1928), but for the wrong reasons—the book developed a reputation as a pornographic masterpiece.

The brilliance of Joyce, Woolf, and Lawrence has often overshadowed the accomplishments of other British novelists whose careers were contemporary with theirs. Aldous Huxley, the preeminent exponent of the novel of ideas, published his first novels in the years immediately following the armistice. Though remembered by succeeding generations principally for *Brave New World* (1932), his dystopian analysis of a future society controlled by scientists, Huxley explored the problems of post-World War I Britain in a number of provocative novels, including *Antic Hay* (1923) and *Crome Yellow* (1921). Through careful selection of character types and careful construction of plots that juxtapose characters in situations where they must talk with one another at length, Huxley managed to satirize the more extreme forms of English character and society while retaining a focus on what he saw as an irreconcilable problem: Human actions, however noble, inevitably lead to frustration and evil, and humankind's highest intellectual and artistic aspirations exist in beings who have inescapable biological urges and needs.

Joining Huxley among the ranks of the social comedians were Evelyn Waugh and Anthony Powell. Both were skilled crafters of the novel, and Waugh especially donned the satirist's mantle to shock people into recognizing the moral vacuity of modern life. Graham Greene first surfaced as a novelist concerned with the social condition of his country; he quickly turned to popular forms of the day—the thriller, for example—taking them over for his own use and making them the vehicles for serious discussion of moral and theological questions. While none of these novelists practiced experimentation in forms that matched the works of Joyce or Woolf, they often displayed the marks of influence in their close treatment of the inner psychology of character.

A host of lesser-known novelists round out the complement of figures whose works provide an insight into the post-World War I period: David Garnett, T. F. Powys, John Cowper Powys, William Gehardi, and others all wrote novels that reflect the impacts of contemporary events and ideas. L. H. Myers, whose best work was done in the 1930's, was a product of this period. Richard Hughes's *A High Wind in Jamaica* (1929; also known as *The Innocent Voyage*) provided one of the most original treatments of childhood in any British novel. A bleaker vision of maturation appears in William Golding's *Lord of the Flies* (1954), in which the author examines the responses of a group of isolated young boys to their first encounter with the darkness dormant in the human heart.

The rebellion in the novel that became evident in the new experiments with form extended far beyond technical boundaries. As Irving Howe has observed, "modern novelists," those who began writing after the earlier works of Henry James had been published, "had been committed to a peculiarly anxious and persistent search for values." The novelists of the 1920's and 1930's tested values by juxtaposing their characters against sets of fixed social norms—the business community, the political hierarchy, the wealthy class. The values of these social groups were clearly identifiable and often open to question. Certainly, in the period between the two world wars there was ample reason to challenge the worn-out institutions that had led Europe and the United States into a frenzy of destruction and had wreaked havoc over a continent. Many of the young novelists of the period, especially those in the United States, did exactly that.

F. Scott Fitzgerald and Ernest Hemingway

The most prominent American novelists of the 1920's were F. Scott Fitzgerald and Ernest Hemingway. Fitzgerald's novels generally reflect the moral degeneracy of the Jazz Age; his characters, often nouveau riche, often pretenders to social status, are usually defeated because they aspire to false values. Fitzgerald's *The Great Gatsby* (1925) remains the best illustration of the sad decay of the American Dream. The hero, Jay Gatsby, is a self-made man from the West who has come east to reap all the benefits that money can buy. He appears to possess unlimited riches, and he attempts to buy his way into Long Island society through lavish parties and extravagant affairs at his home. The secret to his success, however, is "dirty money": He made his fortune as a bootlegger, changed his name to avoid his Jewish heritage, and never achieved the one thing he really wanted, the love of his sweetheart from more innocent days, Daisy, who is now the wife of the boorish Tom Buchanan. Gatsby's world comes tumbling down around him when, through a series of misadventures, he is murdered by the husband of Tom Buchanan's mistress. For all his pretensions and foibles, however, Gatsby himself is drawn quite sympathetically by Fitzgerald. It is hard to dislike him, and his brand of heroism has a certain charm about it that suggests that the old virtues of the American character, so often derided as both unobtainable and psychologically damaging, are a tragic alternative to the sterility of life in American high society of the Jazz Age. For Fitzgerald, there appeared to be no way of winning.

The importance of Hemingway to American literature cannot be overestimated. During the 1920's, Hemingway developed three things that were to ensure his success: a writing style characterized by a simplicity unmatched by any writer of equal stature before or after him; a "code," or philosophy, by which men must live and die if they wish to be great; and a lifestyle, based in part on the code, that was to gain him notoriety for several decades and make him as controversial for his personal life as for his fiction. Like many writers of his generation, he had gone to the war, and its experiences had made an indelible impression on him. Unlike many of them, however, Hemingway found a certain dignity in violent action; it was one way for humans to express themselves in defiance against a universe that seems not to care for the individual. His novels, beginning with *The Sun Also Rises* in 1926, develop in fiction the code that Hemingway himself lived by publicly: gusto for life, distrust for institutions, commitment to duty. His *A Farewell to Arms* (1929) may be the best novel about World War I and ranks with Stephen Crane's *The Red Badge of Courage: An Episode of the American Civil War* (1895) as one of the finest American war novels ever written. When he turned his attention to the Spanish Civil War in the mid-1930's, Hemingway again produced, in *For Whom the Bell Tolls* (1940), a literary work that captures at once the futility of war and the opportunities for true heroism that war offers the brave.

Hemingway wrote for four decades, always clinging to his original artistic premise that good art must be simple and suggestive. A late work, *The Old Man and the Sea* (1952), shows Hemingway's method of simplicity at its best: The hero, an old fisherman who has failed to catch anything for eighty-four days, goes out alone into the Gulf Stream off Florida, where he hooks a magnificent fish and finally lands it after a three-day battle, only to have the carcass eaten by sharks on the trip back to his dock. The reader suffers with the hero, feels his triumph at the catch, and experiences his despair when the fish is taken away by the agents of nature. One is left with a curious feeling, however, that the hero has triumphed despite the apparent failure; this feeling is precisely the one that Hemingway sought to convey in all of his works.

It soon became fashionable for young novelists to imitate the Hemingway style, spare prose devoid of complex sentences and elaborate rhetoric. Hundreds of popular adventure stories, filled with toughs and soldiers of fortune, rogues from every walk of life, filled book stands across the United States; some writers and readers even went so far as to try to adopt the Hemingway code as a model for living. Since the virtues he promoted—courage in the face of overwhelming odds, bravery, self-sufficiency—were the ones that had traditionally been associated with the American hero, Hemingway soon developed a large following both among the general public and in academic circles. Always subject to criticism for his aggressively masculine persona, Hemingway has been judged with increasing severity as the values that he embodied have become increasingly unfashionable. His legacy to American literature, however—and, indeed, to world literature—cannot be ignored.

The Great Depression

With the Depression, many young novelists turned with renewed interest to social and political issues. Any hope that may have begun to grow during the 1920's was shattered during this decade of mass unemployment and the growing spread of fascism. In the United States, novelists concerned with the plight of victims of the Depression used realistic methods to depict graphically the effects of economic privation. James T. Farrell's *Studs Lonigan: A Trilogy* (1935) is one of the best of American works during the period that present, according to Walter Allen, "a corrupt and vicious social order that [the novelist believed] must be destroyed." Farrell was one of a number of writers on both sides of the Atlantic who adopted communism as an alternative to the capitalism that was apparently responsible for the condition of life in the Western world in the 1930's.

During the same period, another significant American novelist first began to publish. John Steinbeck's *In Dubious Battle* (1936) deals directly with the problems of workers and the possibilities and restrictions communism offered. From Steinbeck, the United States received its greatest literary treatment of the effects of the Depression. *The Grapes of Wrath* (1939) is the story of the Joad family, poor farmers who leave the Dust Bowl of Oklahoma for a better life in California, only to find that conditions there are no better, sometimes worse. Because the plight of the Joads and the other families in the novel appeared so typical and because their stories were presented so poignantly (often melodramatically), *The Grapes of Wrath* became a parable of the American migrant. Much like early works of Charles Dickens or Harriet Beecher Stowe's *Uncle Tom's Cabin* (1852), the novel provided a rallying point for reformers, a propaganda piece in the hands of those attempting to aid the victims of a decade of hard living and inhuman suffering.

While daring young men and women in England were experimenting with the form of the novel and their counterparts in the United States were fulfilling their role as members of the lost generation, a large number of writers, less concerned with artistry than with entertainment, continued to provide the public with what is now referred to as popular literature. Much of the best-seller material of the 1920's and 1930's lasted no more than a season. One form of popular fiction, however, rose to a new level of prominence and achieved notice for its artistry from contemporary critics and in succeeding decades. Detective fiction, developed by Edgar Allan Poe almost one century earlier and brought to fame by Sir Arthur Conan Doyle at the beginning of the twentieth century, reached a new level of artistic merit during the period between the wars, often called the golden age of detective fiction. In England Dorothy L. Sayers and Agatha Christie entered the literary scene, creating detective heroes who would rival the legendary Sherlock Holmes in the public eye. In the United States Dashiell Hammett led the way for a number of gifted storytellers whose brand of detective thriller differed noticeably from the British version. The genteel, intellectual pursuit of the criminal characteristic of Sayers's Lord Peter Wimsey and Christie's Hercule Poirot was replaced by the tough-guy tactics of hard-boiled characters such as Hammett's Sam Spade. In England, Graham Greene explored in his thrillers, especially *Brighton Rock* (1938), the violent world that had recently received much attention in the newspapers. During the next fifty years, bookstores and public libraries were filled with the novels of these early mystery writers and their many successors; the works of the best of them—writers such as Hammett, Raymond Chandler, and Ross Macdonald—gradually achieved the recognition generally reserved for mainstream fiction. The novels of English writer P. D. James, who began publishing mysteries in the 1970's, have been considered equal in literary merit to those of her contemporaries writing more mainstream fiction.

THE SOUTHERN NOVEL

During this period of exceptional literary activity, the novels of a single Mississippi author highlighted the emergence of southern fiction. William Faulkner had been writing for a decade and had already published three novels and several short stories when *The Sound and the Fury* appeared in 1929. It was followed in rapid succession by *As I Lay Dying* (1930), *Sanctuary* (1931), *Light in August* (1932), and *Absalom, Absalom!* (1936), all of which depict the fate of the South through the lives of generations of men and women in Faulkner's mythical Yoknapatawpha County. Earlier novels and stories had provided some details about these characters, and later ones, notably *Go Down, Moses* (1942), *Requiem for a Nun* (1951), and the trilogy consisting of *The Hamlet* (1940), *The Town* (1957), and *The Mansion* (1959), round out the portrait of a community that is representative of its region in a way that is unlike any other work by an American author.

Faulkner also dealt with philosophical issues that may have been apparent only to readers steeped in the American South; what he had learned and what he attempted to portray both in his stories and through the texture of his prose was the inextricable link between past and present. The evils upon which southern society had been built, especially the evil of slavery, remain to entrap those who try to put the past behind them. Comprehensive in his view of society, Faulkner presents a cast of characters from all walks of life who share the plight of the southerner and who are ultimately destroyed by it: the Compsons, the Sutpens, and African Americans such as Charles Bon (*Absalom, Absalom!*) and Joe Christmas (*Light in August*). He also presents characters who endure: Dilsey the black housekeeper, the poor farm girl Lena (*Light in August*), and the chameleon-like Snopes family, who attain the reader's grudging admiration for their stubbornness and adaptability, despite their overriding amorality.

Faulkner stands at the forefront of southern writers, many of whom emerged during the period between the wars and were influenced in one way or another by the Fugitives, a coterie of artists and academics early in the twentieth century at Vanderbilt University in Nashville, Tennessee. Allen Tate and Robert Penn Warren, both members of this group, wrote works that attempted to define and explain the special conditions that set the South apart from the rest of the United States. Warren's *All the King's Men* (1946), a fiction based on the political career of Louisiana demagogue Huey Long, achieved popular success and has been critically acclaimed for its sensitive portrait of the characters whose lives fall under the spell of the political tyrant. Carson McCullers, like Faulkner, focuses on the rural and small-town South, presenting a kaleidoscope of characters, many of them physically impaired, to suggest the moral condition of the region. Flannery O'Connor fuses the grotesque and the transcendent in a distinctively southern vision that has exercised a great influence on other fiction writers, not only in the South but also in the other regions.

THE WAR NOVEL

The end of the 1930's found the world once again aroused to arms in a conflict that, like its predecessor, would change the shape of both serious and popular fiction. Novelists' reactions to World War II, however, were quite different from the reactions to World War I. Before England's and, later, the United States' first encounters with the realities of modern warfare, people had shared a tenuous kind of idealism; the novels of the post-World War I period reflected the disillusionment, horror, and cynicism of those who had seen for the first time what such a war was really like. Works about World War I were often crude, but the sentiments they expressed were shocking to their audience. The novels of World War II, by contrast, were more sophisticated, but serious novelists found themselves reacting to a different kind of problem from that which had faced their predecessors after World War I.

During the first two decades after World War II, a great many war novels were published, far more than had been generated in the 1920's and 1930's. Many of these works, however, were merely popular potboilers, not serious attempts to investigate the causes or conditions of the conflict. Among novels that did make an attempt to come to grips with the impact of World War II on those who participated in it, Norman Mailer's *The Naked and the Dead* (1948) offered a portrait of life in battle as it affects men of different geographical and ideological backgrounds. In Mailer's work, one can see the irony that characterizes many of the new war novels. Through a careful juxtaposition of scenes, Mailer depicts the common soldier plodding through the seemingly meaningless tasks that war brings and the grand strategy of those in charge. The goal of the army in this novel is the capture of an island in the Pacific. That goal is achieved not through brilliant planning or heroic action but through accident and blundering. To make matters worse, the success of the army accomplishes nothing to help the war effort. Mailer's novel is a study in the effects of power in men's lives and the changes that war may bring into their lives, but it does not appear to be saying something new about the nature of modern warfare.

Mailer's inability to offer something new is characteristic of many writers of this period. The novelists writing about World War II lacked the advantage of "shock value" as a means of gaining their readers' attention and sympathy. Although the machinery of mass destruction was more devastating than in World War I, World War II produced almost no real surprises except for the destructive power of the atomic bomb, which has been one of the most pervasive, if subtle, influences on literature since the 1940's.

THE POSTWAR NOVEL

The explosion of the atomic bomb provides a new dividing line for fiction, but one must be careful not to insist too strongly that all literature changed immediately and irrevocably after August, 1945. As had happened after World War I, in both England and the United States, many novelists who had established their reputations before the conflict continued to publish during the first postwar decade, and much of their work followed themes worked out either completely or partially in earlier novels. Greene continued to explore religious and moral questions under the guise of thrillers. Evelyn Waugh continued to write satire. Anthony Powell, who had published five novels in the 1930's, began his masterpiece, *A Dance to the Music of Time*, a series of twelve novels published between 1951 and 1975. Hemingway's novels of the late 1940's and 1950's show little advance in theme over those of the 1930's. Faulkner continued his saga of the Yoknapatawpha County, crystallizing a world within the borders of this Mississippi region.

The new voices in literature were different, however; the young novelist now faced the horror that at any time, humans could conceivably destroy themselves—the ultimate achievement of Western civilization was, sadly, the perfection of destruction. Novels that deal directly with the possibility and the effects of a nuclear holocaust have been surprisingly few. The subject has not lacked treatment in nonfiction, but in fiction it has been largely the purview of popular novelists whose sensationalistic treatments have titillated the reading public and aroused momentary curiosity or fear without providing serious study of either the problem or its potential solution. With few exceptions, the modern writer, choosing to avoid direct confrontation with the issue, has opted instead to examine the experience of people who live daily in the shadow of the threat that total destruction poses.

The Cold War and the threat of nuclear holocaust did give rise to a host of thrillers—spy stories, tales of adventures and intrigue, conventional mysteries—that adapted the traditional formulas that had made these kinds of novels popular since the beginning of the century. The international spy novel achieved a new level of prominence, and Ian Fleming's slim volumes about a British intelligence agent gave his own country and the United States a new hero, James Bond. A combination of bravado, exceptional knowledge and intelligence, charm, and sex appeal made Bond and the dozens of other characters who populate the world of the spy novel immediate successes with the mass reading public as many people sought escapism rather than serious investigation of modern problems. Not all spy novels, however, are to be dismissed as escapist fare written in the slapdash manner of the Bond saga. The novels of John le Carré, for example, distinguished works by any standards, capture the ambience of the Cold War years, the "climate of betrayal," with great authority and insight.

Perhaps the primary issue for the artist of this period became the assertion of the self in a society that promoted anonymity. The new writers who emerged after World War II in Britain have often been classed with their fellow dramatists as the Angry Young Men. Writing about a society in which mobility among classes was becoming much easier, novelists such as John Wain, Kingsley Amis, John Braine, and Doris Lessing struck out against institutions that remained to signal the vestiges of class distinction. Some, like Amis, turned to comedy as the medium for social commentary. Others, including Lessing, who was awarded the Nobel Prize in Literature in 2007, composed sociological dramas in which the line between fiction and reportage is often blurred.

Curiously, many of these writers turned away from the experimental methods of the giants of literature in the preceding generation, finding that older forms of narrative better suited their purposes. The British novels of the 1950's and after often appeared to be throwbacks to their predecessors of a century or more: Picaresque, farce, even the massive sweep of society that characterized the Victorian novel appeared once again in the hands of men and women whose avowed purpose was to hold the mirror up to contemporary society.

What makes these novelists quite different from their predecessors is the relativism—moral as well as social—that characterizes their fiction. Even the novelists of the 1920's and 1930's wrote with a sense that absolutes may exist or do exist. That certainty is almost completely absent in the works of the new generation. The heroes of post-World War II novels are most likely to be existential people given to establishing their own norms and defining their existence by setting themselves up against the flux of experience that they encounter. Beneath the comedy of Amis's *Lucky Jim* (1954) or the political arguments of Lessing's early novels is a strain of metaphysical existentialism that links these works to those of Camus and Jean-Paul Sartre as closely as their form or ostensible subject may link them to their British ancestors.

The reason for this is simple. As James Gindin has observed, "Almost all the contemporary novels are searches for identity, efforts on the part of the hero to understand and to define who or what he is." The search to find or define the self, to establish an identity that sets one apart from mass society, is often the goal of the modern hero. Unlike earlier heroes, however, the modern hero is often self-questioning, a kind of antihero given to failure and sometimes the victim of acute neurosis or even paranoia.

The protagonist as antihero is a staple of the works of John Updike, perhaps the most prolific and controversial American novelist of the postwar period. A chameleon writer who excelled in short and long fiction, poetry, and essays, Updike produced a major work nearly every year from 1957 to 2008. Principally concerned with domestic issues and questions of morality and convention, Updike combined exceptional insight into American society and the human condition with a unique command of style to produce novels that highlight the individual's difficulty in establishing a sense of selfhood and self-worth in a postindustrial society.

In virtually every one of his novels, Updike wrote about questions of religion and sex, two issues that for him defined the human condition in its spiritual and physical dimensions. Updike's most extensive analysis of the problems common people face in modern society is the work detailing the life of Harry Angstrom, a character affectionately known to family and friends as Rabbit. *Rabbit, Run* (1960), the first novel in the series, depicts Angstrom's life in a small Pennsylvania town where the boom caused by industrialism is fading. Noted only for his basketball prowess in high school, Rabbit is unable to cope with the pressures of adulthood. Married to a woman almost as immature as himself, he constantly runs away from his responsibilities to his wife, his newborn baby, and his job. Rabbit longs for the nostalgia of his youth, when he was important and when others handled his problems for him. In subsequent parts of the series, the novels *Rabbit Redux* (1971), *Rabbit Is Rich* (1981), and *Rabbit at Rest* (1990) and the novella *Rabbit Remembered* (2000), Rabbit begins to understand his weaknesses and comes to accept the sad comedy of his existence. Updike also used this series of novels to critique changes in American society from the end of World War I through the end of the twentieth century. Throughout the series, Updike presents his unsophisticated, materialistic, and often self-centered protagonist with great sympathy, making him a reflection of many in modern society who also long for a less complex time when answers to ethical, epistemological, and theological questions were more readily forthcoming.

One of the more common methods adopted by postwar novelists to portray the conflict between the individual and society is the use of an outsider as hero or protagonist. A great number of American novels have such characters as heroes: Truman Capote's gays, Saul Bellow's and Bernard Malamud's Jews, and the black heroes of James Baldwin and Ralph Ellison.

Two novelists who emerged in the 1950's, Bellow and Malamud, may serve to represent the course that writers in the mainstream of modern fiction took for the next three decades. As observers and recorders of modern American society, both Bellow and Malamud captured the essential frustration that the individual feels when facing the leviathan that modern society has become. In the case of Bellow, much of his fiction was influenced by his Jewish background, but that often provided merely a point of departure for works that explore the modern condition in much broader terms. His *The Adventures of Augie March* (1953), for example, a picaresque novel set in the era of the Great Depression, displays the universal struggle of the individual to gain freedom from the shackles of society. In *Henderson the Rain King* (1959), Bellow's hero abandons modern society in favor of a more primitive mode of living in Africa, in order to be reborn, as it were, into a new life of self-awareness and to develop a deeper appreciation for himself and others.

Malamud—like Bellow, of Jewish background—introduced his heritage into works such as *The Assistant* (1957). In this novel, the universal problem of the human desire to achieve moral excellence is treated with irony, as the hero, an assistant in a small store run by a Jewish family, first tries to take advantage of the family members (stealing from the store, seducing the daughter) but then undergoes a change of heart and carries on the business when the father dies. The hero's acceptance of others' burdens gives the story a poignant quality that borders on the melodramatic yet never becomes so.

In the case of both writers, the hero is often on the fringe of society (Bellow's Augie March) or a subgroup of society (the Gentile assistant in Malamud's novel), or he consciously abandons modern, urban society to find personal meaning outside it (Henderson), suggesting that to meld with society is to become faceless, a kind of nonperson who counts for nothing. Because life has meaning only in the here and now (the existentialist view certainly dominates these works), the nonperson who fades into the anonymity of the mass society is lost forever. A rage to assert the self against the forces that foster anonymity burns within the hearts of many modern heroes.

As a result, it is not surprising to find social causes that promote individual identity and individual worth being celebrated in novels that treat the question of identity. During the 1950's and 1960's in the United States, several important works about African Americans and identity made a mark on the literary scene. Although works depicting the African American experience had been circulating for some time, particularly since the start of the Harlem Renaissance around 1925, only a few, such as Richard Wright's *Native Son* (1940) and Ralph Ellison's *Invisible Man* (1952), had received widespread critical attention. Fine works such as Arna Bontemps's *Black Thunder* (1936), a historical novel about Gabriel Prosser's aborted slave rebellion in the early nineteenth century, and Zora Neale Hurston's *Their*

Eyes Were Watching God (1937) had gone largely unnoticed.

The interest in African American culture generated during the late 1960's and the 1970's, among Americans both black and white, led to the "discovery" of numerous writers whose works have expanded the boundaries of American fiction. These authors produced powerful testimonies to the struggle that oppressed people face in preserving identity and dignity in a world hostile toward them. Critic Tony Tanner called Ellison's *Invisible Man* "quite simply the most profound novel about American identity since the war." Among African American writers who began to receive acclaim in the 1950's, Baldwin emerged as a major literary figure whose writing presented the experiences of African Americans and of gay men candidly and forcefully in novels that are artistically excellent. Baldwin's ability to portray the anger and the pathos of his characters without preaching or moralizing makes works such as *Go Tell It on the Mountain* (1953) and *Another Country* (1962) stand out among the thousands of post-World War II books that dramatize contemporary American social problems.

While a number of major novelists were exploring contemporary issues in traditional forms, others, employing a method designated as "fabulation" by the critic Robert Scholes, abandoned attempts at verisimilitude and opted instead to create conscious artifices that moved "away from direct representation of the surface of reality" but approached "actual human life by way of ethically controlled fantasy." Many important novelists, among them William H. Gass, Robert Coover, Kurt Vonnegut, Donald Barthelme, and John Barth, produced works that clearly share the qualities of fabulation: concern with design and structure, use of the absurd or surreal, a tendency toward allegory, and formal and narrative characteristics of the romance tradition as opposed to those normally associated with the novel. At the center of the aesthetic of the fabulators is a belief expressed succinctly by one of their exemplars, John Hawkes, that "the true enemies of the novel [are] plot, character, setting, and theme." For Hawkes, "structure—verbal and psychological coherence" is the primary concern. For such writers, realism is no more than one of many formal constructs available to the novelist.

Laurence W. Mazzeno

BIBLIOGRAPHY

Batchelor, John. *The Edwardian Novelists*. New York: St. Martin's Press, 1982. Discusses the major British novelists of the first decades of the twentieth century, explaining how these figures form a bridge between their Victorian forebears and the modern novelists who followed them.

Breen, Jennifer. *In Her Own Write: Twentieth-Century Women's Fiction*. New York: St. Martin's Press, 1990. Offers a method of reading novels that privileges the values and aspirations of women. Focuses on British novelists, but the method described is useful for examining American women novelists as well.

Gindin, James. *Postwar British Fiction: New Accents and Attitudes*. Berkeley: University of California Press, 1962. Explores the persistence of British novelists' concern with conduct and class, noting how World War II changed both the political climate and the social climate in England. Discussion focuses on the heroes created by novelists such as Alan Sillitoe, Kingsley Amis, Doris Lessing, John Wain, Iris Murdoch, and William Golding.

Graham, Maryemma, ed. *Cambridge Companion to the African American Novel*. New York: Cambridge University Press, 2004. Collection of fifteen essays traces the history and development of the African American novel beginning with slavery and the slave narrative. Writers discussed include Richard Wright, Ralph Ellison, James Baldwin, and Toni Morrison.

Klein, Marcus, ed. *The American Novel Since World War II*. New York: Fawcett, 1969. Collection of essays by a number of distinguished critics provides analysis of the social and political background to novels written during the period 1940-1960. Includes a section on the underground novel, writings protesting mainstream American values.

Knight, Stephen Thomas. *Crime Fiction, 1800-2000: Detection, Death, Diversity*. New York: Palgrave Macmillan, 2004. Presents a full history of the development of the crime novel and its many variants. Includes a chronology of primary works and a bibliography of the most useful criticism published on the genre.

Lamb, Robert Paul, and Gary Richard Thompson, eds. *A Companion to American Fiction, 1865-1914*. Malden, Mass.: Blackwell, 2005. Collection of essays provides analyses of traditions, genres, contexts, and themes as well as discussion of major authors, including William Dean Howells, Henry James, Edith Wharton, Stephen Crane, and Theodore Dreiser. Illustrated.

McCormick, John. *Fiction as Knowledge: The Modern Post-romantic Novel*. New Brunswick, N.J.: Transaction, 1999. Examines the stream-of-consciousness novel, the rise of the antihero, and metaphysical and epistemological themes.

Meredith, James H. *Understanding the Literature of World War I: A Student Casebook to Issues, Sources, and Historical Documents*. Westport, Conn.: Greenwood Press, 2004. Presents analyses of six novels, including Hemingway's *A Farewell to Arms*. Supplemented with historical documents and records that illuminate the historical events depicted in the works.

_______. *Understanding the Literature of World War II: A Student Casebook to Issues, Sources, and Historical Documents*. Westport, Conn.: Greenwood Press, 1999. Discusses several long prose works about World War II alongside journalism articles and other primary documents written during the war and interviews conducted afterward. Includes a chronology of the war.

Parrinder, Patrick. *Nation and Novel: The English Novel from Its Origins to the Present Day*. New York: Oxford University Press, 2006. History of the development of the novel in England from 1485 demonstrates how the nation's political and economic influenced style and theme.

Spiller, Robert E. *The Cycle of American Literature: An Essay in Historical Criticism*. New York: Macmillan, 1955. Still-useful review provides insight into the development of the modern American novel by analyzing it in the context of its nineteenth century forebears. Discussions of Theodore Dreiser, Ernest Hemingway, William Faulkner, and Thomas Wolfe explain the social context in which these authors wrote and the political and literary milieus that helped shape their fiction.

Postcolonial Long Fiction

A discussion of postcolonial literature must first acknowledge the scope and complexity of the term "postcolonial." Temporally, the term designates any national literature written after the nation gained independence from a colonizing power. According to this definition, all literature written in the United States after 1776 could qualify as postcolonial. Because the United States has occupied the position of an economic and political world power since the nineteenth century, however, it is today regarded more as a historically colonizing force than as a former colony of Great Britain. Within this field of literary studies, "postcolonial" refers to those nations that gained independence between the last quarter of the nineteenth century and the 1960's.

Geographically, "postcolonial" is a global term: It designates nations of the Caribbean, Central and South America, Africa, the South Pacific islands, and Malaysia. It applies equally to India, Ireland, Australia, New Zealand, Canada, and the Philippines. The colonizing powers to which these countries were subjected and with which they have continued to contend after gaining independence are Great Britain, France, Spain, Portugal, Belgium, Germany, and the United States.

Postcolonial studies are not limited by geography or time, however. They treat a broad span of concerns: the functioning of different empires during the colonial period and varying administrative systems left as legacies to the former colonies; the specific conditions under which independence was gained in each case; cultural, economic, and linguistic imperialism that persists after independence; and the local concerns of education, government, citizenship, and identity. Postcolonial literature tends to address opposition to imperial forces as it seeks to define autonomous national identity. In that quest, postcolonial literature explores issues of cultural alienation, and it struggles to express the specificity and particularities of indigenous cultures in languages that are not generally the original languages of the indigenous peoples but rather the languages of the former colonizers. The Kenyan writer Ngugi wa Thiong'o decided in 1981, after his imprisonment and exile for coauthoring and producing two Kikuyu-language plays that criticized the postcolonial Kenyan government, to switch from English to Kikuyu as the language for his writing. Similarly, the Irishman Samuel Beckett chose to live in France and write in French because this location and language did not carry the baggage of Ireland's struggles for independence from Britain. For many postcolonial writers, then, to write in the language of the colonizing power is an act of acceptance and acquiescence to that power, even if that power is no longer physically present.

The issue of language is complex, however. Although writing in the language of the colonizers implies some complicity with their power and cultural dominance, there are questions of circulation and counterdiscourse to consider. Can the circulation and readership of Ngugi's writings be as wide in Kikuyu as in English? Can the postcolonial voice of resistance against dominance and hegemony of the empire be heard in a Caribbean patois? To express postcolonial struggles and establish national identity in the languages of the colonizing powers—English, French, or Spanish—is to form a counterdiscourse that can be heard at the center of the empire.

To express oneself in a language that is not one's own, a language that does not belong to one's land but has been violently imposed on it, is a source of tension that gives rise not only to feelings of alienation and uncertainty regarding the legitimacy of the mother tongue but also to confusion regarding identity. To what degree is a citizen from India truly Indian, having been educated in English, writing in English, and even communicating with fellow Indians in the language of the British Empire? Although India possesses national identity, history, literature, and cultural practices, how can these remain purely Indian after two hundred years of British rule? Just as postcolonial Indian literature finds expression in English, not in one of the hundreds of Indian languages, so does it strive to define and establish an identity that can no longer be pure. This postindependence, postcolonial identity must admit that it is a hybrid, a mix of colonial and national identities transmitted through education, government, religion, and social practices.

The dynamics of foregrounding and theorizing a plurality of identities, mixing of cultures, and interdependence between colonizer and colonized, as well as localized political concerns, create a reciprocity between postcolonial fiction and postcolonial theory. The interdependent development of postcolonial fiction and theory constitutes postcolonialism.

The association with poststructuralism and postmodernism is not accidental: These schools of literary and cultural criticism serve to validate the margins of artistic production by deconstructing centers of truth. These forms of criticism posit that truth, meaning, and identity are never axiomatic; they are in a constant state of production, wholly dependent on the contexts in which they appear. Postcolonial theorists stress that colonial identity is created by the ruling, colonizing powers. For example, Edward W. Said's seminal work *Orientalism* (1978) argues that the "Orient" is a set of images and assumptions constructed by the Western literary canon and projected onto colonized nations. Along with Said, Gayatri Chakravorty Spivak and Homi K. Bhabha argue that these fabricated, projected images of the Oriental "other" provide a framework and support for the enlightened European subject. India's Subaltern Studies group, led by Ranajit Guha and Spivak, rereads the history of British occupation for the purposes of asserting versions of cultural identity free from imperial constructions. Just as the Oriental other was given form through writing, so the postcolonial subject seeks expression through literature. With each postcolonial novel that is written, a new version of postcolonial subjectivity is told, and a new theory of cultural difference as well as political and intellectual autonomy is formulated. In postcolonialism, fiction and theory work together to define, shape, and stretch each other's boundaries.

Among the principal themes developed in postcolonial fiction are those of exile and alienation; rebellion, struggle, and opposition against colonial powers; and mixing or confusion of identities, multiculturalism, and the establishment of cultural autonomy free from imperial forces.

Exile and alienation

Exile and alienation are represented both physically and figuratively in postcolonial fiction. Exile occurs when the protagonist or another character, usually a member of an indigenous people subjected to the colonial power, travels to the land of the colonizers for the purpose of education or finding work. Becoming a marginal member of society in the colonizing nation, the subject takes on certain characteristics and values of the oppressing culture. Thereafter, returning to the land of birth is nearly impossible because of psychological changes the postcolonial subject has experienced while away. Physical exile also occurs for political reasons: The subject either acts out against the government and is sent away or chooses to leave the homeland because colonial and postcolonial rules have wreaked such change on the native environment that it becomes unlivable.

Figuratively, the theme of exile is expressed as alienation and represents a search for the self. Colonial conditions in the native land render native culture, language, and education inferior to the culture and governing systems of the colonizers. Such cultural repression and validation of the imperial other provoke in the postcolonial protagonist an identity crisis and prompt him or her to search for a legitimate and positive image of the self. In order to embark on this quest for the self, the protagonist must first be split, shattered, or called into question, leading to alienation from society. Alienation is similar to exile in that the subject is no longer "at home" either physically or psychologically in the native land. Physical alienation occurs when an otherwise respectable inhabitant of the native land is considered criminal or subversive by colonial law, leading to imprisonment or the revocation of societal privileges for the subject. More often, alienation is represented as psychological in postcolonial fiction: It is the state of not belonging, of not having a true home. Postcolonial subjects are alienated by Eurocentric, imperial systems that will never fully accept them, either culturally or racially; at the same time, they are alienated by native cultures that have either acquiesced to the colonial system or rejected them because they speak the language of the colonizers or have received the education of the empire.

One of the most in-depth explorations of cultural exile and quest for the self is presented in James Joyce's *Ulysses* (1922). Although its main characters, Stephen Dedalus, Leopold Bloom, and Molly Bloom, never leave

Dublin, the novel draws a modern parallel to Homer's *Odyssey* (c. 725 B.C.E.; English translation, 1614), the epic story of a man's alienation from his home, exile to strange lands, and search for a way back home (metaphorically, a search for the self). On the surface, Joyce's novel does not appear to be concerned with Ireland's struggle for freedom from centuries of British rule. The action of the novel takes place in one day; the plot consists in Bloom and Stephen going about their day and in Bloom making his way home. Yet the novel operates on many levels—literally, metaphorically, and mythically—one of which emerges from its many references to the British occupation of Ireland and the Irish struggle for political autonomy. Following Bloom in his journey through Dublin, the novel depicts his departure from home and his return to home at the end as an exploration of Irish subjectivity. What the reader discovers, as the many layers of meaning unravel, is that Bloom is neither a pure Irishman nor a pure product of British colonial rule. The novel makes references to Bloom's Jewish descent; his wife, Molly, grew up in Gibraltar, the geographical gateway for British imperial expansion; and Bloom's English is a multicultural mix of Irishisms and Italian and Greek words. This modern odyssey with colonial concerns shows that a search for the self leads to the revelation of an identity that is not culturally pure. The novel also shows that as soon as one leaves home, all notions of a pure, unified self are lost.

A prototypical novel of exile and alienation is George Lamming's *In the Castle of My Skin* (1953). This autobiographical bildungsroman presents the author's childhood in Barbados from his point of view at the age of twenty-three while living in London. He is led into retrospection by the alienation he experiences in the capital of the colonizers. The childhood that he revisits and that forms the narrative chronologically parallels the last stages of colonialism in the Caribbean and unfolds against the backdrop of rising nationalism. The author's childhood development meaningfully parallels the loss of cultural innocence as destructive floods, a general strike across the island, and riots mark his ninth year, and the land of the village is sold to business just before he takes his first job in neighboring Trinidad. As the protagonist leaves Barbados, his village falls apart, thus producing an analogy between loss of childhood innocence and the disruption of cultural identity, between exile and alienation and the destruction of native lands by colonization. Only from the point of view of physical and spiritual alienation can the narrator look back and understand the destruction of his homeland. Only from this state of exile can he narrate his story; the only home to which he can return is the one that is rendered fictional, the one that constitutes his story. As the title suggests, in the state of exile that colonialism has forced upon him, the narrator is left with only his body, which has become his home.

The theme of alienation and exclusion of people not only from a dominant culture but also from their own land, language, and cultural practices has extended the boundaries of postcolonial literature to include feminist concerns regarding the oppression of women by men. Anita Desai's novel *Fire on the Mountain* (1977) addresses the cultural and social alienation of women in India with an unusual twist on the theme of exile. The novel's protagonist, Nanda Kaul, has retired to a mountaintop in the Punjab after fulfilling the duties of wife and mother. This exile into retirement in her old age foreshadows the transformative exile that awaits Nanda. The novel first depicts her as the image of Indian womanly perfection: stately, gentle, upstanding, and refined in her manners. Nanda paints her life as a young woman in the colors of happiness: her childhood, what her parents offered her as a child in a society that typically holds girls in contempt, and her marriage. By the end of the narrative, she reveals the unhappy reality of her past: Her father was usually absent when she was a child, and he never brought home nice gifts; her husband never loved or respected her, and he kept a mistress throughout his marriage to Nanda; and she never enjoyed a closeness with her children, who were in fact responsible for placing her atop a mountain in order to be rid of her. So that Nanda's story does not appear to be tragic or out of the ordinary for women in India, the novel presents a minor character, Ila Das, whose life story is indeed tragic and unlucky. Ila is a childhood friend of Nanda who has not grown up; she is vulgar, ill mannered, and rather stupid. Ila has also been unlucky: Her father died when she was young, her mother was an invalid, and her brothers squandered the family fortune. Nanda and her husband rescue Ila many times from poverty by procuring jobs for her that she fails to keep. She is well-intentioned but has no social graces to compensate for her lack of survival skills. One day, just after having tea with Nanda, Ila is raped and killed in the streets. This event marks a turning point for Nanda, who admits to the social alienation she has experienced her whole life. She then performs the exit ritual and becomes one with the fire god, Agni, the bearer of the flame of eternal life, by walking into hot coals. Her act of exile from the physical realm represents her alienation and at the same time raises her life to a higher, symbolic, transformative level.

Struggle and opposition

Aside from the themes of alienation, exile, confusion of identity, and search for the self, postcolonial fiction is also characterized by tensions between colonizer and colonized or between the old colonial society and the emerging postcolonial one. These multiple themes that seek to define the postcolonial condition are often present in and overlap within the same novel, but it is just as often the case that one theme stands out above the others.

When the theme of social and political tension upstages the others, it can take the form of direct confrontation between colonizer and colonized. For example, in E. M. Forster's novel *A Passage to India* (1924), colonial tensions make their way to the courtroom when the respectable Indian citizen Dr. Aziz is accused of attacking a visiting Englishwoman, Adela Quested, during a friendly outing to some regionally famous caves. Everyone in town takes a side as the polemics surrounding the trial against Aziz reach an explosive level. The Indians believe strongly in Aziz's innocence, while the occupying British remain convinced that Aziz is a local savage incapable of restraining himself around a white woman. The trial marks the climax of the novel, and the turning point occurs when Adela takes the witness stand only to waver in her testimony and withdraw her charges against Aziz. Here, colonial tensions are played out on a symbolically legal level; the confrontation between colonized and colonizer is expressed as a life-or-death issue of guilt or innocence to be decided by emotional fervor and resentment of the colonial situation only thinly veiled by justice. In the end, justice prevails in that Adela recants her accusation, but the readiness of the British to bring Aziz to trial and the Indians' protest against such an act of oppressive power reveal the prejudices, and exemplify the hatred and mistrust, that colonialism promotes on each of the opposing sides. The novel encapsulates colonial hatred and mistrust in a legal issue, the trial, yet it is a legal issue—one country's government forcibly taking over another country's rights to govern itself—that provokes this hatred and mistrust.

In the novel *Things Fall Apart* (1958), by the Nigerian author Chinua Achebe, struggle, confrontation, and rebellion are evident from start to finish. The protagonist, Okonkwo, is leader of an Igbo village and has built a reputation from his youth as a great wrestler. He develops fierce, warrior-like ways in opposition to his father, who died a man of weak, "woman-like" character. Okonkwo is a strict ruler, adhering closely to the traditions of his religion and culture. He does not defy tradition when community elders command the execution of his adopted son; he obediently accepts the traditional punishment of seven years of exile when he inadvertently kills a clansman. Okonkwo is a warrior whose principal cause is to preserve his culture even if it means rebelling against his father and, at times, cruelly beating his wives. Ironically, in obeying the dictates of tradition by serving the sentence of exile, Okonkwo allows his culture to be destroyed. During the seven years of his absence, British missionaries move in and proselytize. In exile, Okonkwo learns from a friend that when people in a neighboring village killed a missionary, more white men came and annihilated the village's entire population. Okonkwo returns to his community to find that a district commissioner, a representative of the British government, has established a council. The climax of the novel stems from a conflict of religious interests: When the villagers burn down the missionaries' church because of sacrilege committed against their religion by a convert, the commissioner performs an act of retribution by imprisoning a group of Igbo men, including Okonkwo, until a fine is collectively paid. In the final confrontation between colonized and colonizer, Okonkwo kills a British messenger, knowing immediately after the fact that this reckless act of violence has ruined his possibility of successfully combating the British with warrior-like integrity. When the district commissioner arrives at Okonkwo's home to arrest him for the murder, he finds the warrior hanging from a tree, having committed suicide. The novel ends with the commissioner's musings about how to integrate Okonkwo's story as either a chapter or a paragraph in his book, *The Pacification of the Primitive Tribes of the Lower Niger.*

Achebe's novel depicts struggle and conflict within the Igbo community before and during colonization. It is precisely this contrast, as well as the focus on customs and interpersonal relations in the village, that sends a message: Conflicts did indeed exist among the Igbo people of this community prior to colonization, but they could be reckoned with and resolved; with colonization came the destruction of Igbo religion, and conflicts soon led not to resolution but to violence and death. The last words of the novel, the title of the district commissioner's book, reflect the British appropriation of African history: The chronicle of an Igbo village and the life of its leader becomes, by the end of the novel, a mere episode in the history of British colonization.

Multiculturalism and identity

Colonial rule—the control and assimilation of other nations, their cultures and histories—was not executed without conflict, struggle, and opposition; furthermore, it has left its subjects, colonized peoples, in a state of alienation and either physical or psychological exile from places that were once unquestionably their homes. While colonialism has created two distinct categories of people, colonized and colonizer, each on the opposite side of the power divide, historically it has also caused a blending of races, languages, cultures, and systems of beliefs and values. This mixing of cultures is another principal theme in postcolonial fiction, and it is often developed in the broader context of establishing identity. With what identity are the people of a colonized nation left after centuries of foreign occupation and rule during which their neighbors were exported for labor or they themselves left home in search of legitimating education and experience in Europe? On what cultural identity can an Indian family, for example, depend when the parents speak Hindi yet their children speak only English? What historical legitimacy can a community enjoy when its history has been rewritten by colonizers and when its laws have been overruled by the laws of a foreign land?

The need for an identity not imposed by occupying forces comes from a lack created by the violent intrusion and disruption of "home" by foreign powers. In V. S. Naipaul's *A House for Mr. Biswas* (1961), the house that a Hindu resident of Trinidad, Mr. Biswas, insists on buying but cannot afford becomes a symbol of independence and identity. His is an unlucky life fraught with poverty, lack of love, and failure. Analogous to oppressive, colonizing powers is the Tulsi clan to whom Biswas's wife remains faithful and who hold him in contempt. Having had enough of homelessness and rambling, Biswas buys the house, no better than a shack, and it stands for his pride, a fortress of autonomy towering above the prejudice and cultural oppression from which he suffers. His house also symbolizes the poverty and weakness that members of minority groups experience in establishing cultural autonomy. The house of Mr. Biswas is a metaphor for his identity: It is at once poor and ramshackle, yet it belongs solely to him. In 2001, Naipaul was awarded the Nobel Prize in Literature for his "works that compel us to see the presence of suppressed histories."

Salman Rushdie's *The Satanic Verses* (1988) deals in more complex terms with the issue of establishing cultural identity in postcolonial Britain and India. Regarding the formation of the postcolonial subject, this novel underscores ambivalence and posits that identity is composed through hybridity. Neither the British subject nor the Indian subject is constituted in a culturally pure fashion; the identities of both consist in effects and qualities of the other. Postcolonial identity is split between the cultural identity produced in the land of the colonizers and that of the colonized land, between British history and Indian history, between formation under British rule, with its concomitant values and customs, and the values and customs of the indigenous culture. From the moment the two cultures meet and clash as part of the colonizing project, neither culture can remain pure or unaffected.

The Satanic Verses expresses this process in terms of good and evil. Rushdie blurs the distinction between the colonizers as evil and the colonized as good by transforming the characteristics of the two protagonists, Gibreel Farishta and Saladin Chamcha. Gibreel was a poor orphan who became a movie star in Bombay (now known as Mumbai). He achieved stardom by acting the parts of Hindu gods in theological films, and all the women of Bombay desire him. Aside from the divine roles he plays and the archangel his name denotes, he develops the physical attributes of an angel. After the start of the novel, he quickly acquires a halo and the power to entrance whomever he meets. In terms of postcolonial subjectivity, Gibreel initially represents the purity of Indian culture and identity, but by the end of the novel he has become disturbed and delusional, transforming into Azraeel, the angel of death. Gibreel parades around London blowing Azraeel's trumpet, provoking fires, and pronouncing destruction. Thematically, Gibreel is in London to colonize the land of the colonizer. As archangel, he fancies himself the harbinger of change for humanity, and he declares to the city of London that he intends to "tropicalize" it. In transforming from benevolent angel into the angel of death and destruction, Gibreel represents the absolutist system of values imposed on India by the British. Gibreel, the postcolonial subject, is both good and evil; he is both the culturally pure colonial native and a violent, invading force. His insanity and subsequent death suggest that such absolute, inflexible identities lead to totalitarianism and destruction. In order to thrive, the postcolonial subject must be constituted by a working blend of cultural attributes.

By contrast, Saladin Chamcha is a "brown Englishman," an Indian made in Britain. Bombay-born, he was sent to English schools as a boy, and there he remained. He has made a career of providing the voices for inanimate objects in British television commercials as well as for the animated cartoon character Maxim Alien. Saladin proves to have the most malleable of British accents, with which he can can pass for a catsup bottle, a proud Englishman, or an alien at will. He has expelled the Indian from himself—lifestyle, face, and voice—and represents the postcolonial Indian subject who has completely subscribed to British ways. It is not surprising that shortly after the start of the novel Saladin begins to grow horns. As the Indian who has betrayed his culture and national identity, Saladin is a product of postcolonial evil. He metamorphoses into a full-blown, eight-foot, goatlike devil. Just as Gibreel undergoes a qualitative transformation from good to bad angel, so Saladin rehumanizes himself upon admitting his hatred for "Mister Perfecto," Gibreel, who betrayed Saladin at the time of the latter's unjustified arrest. In the end it is Saladin who makes of himself a successful postcolonial subject: Having received a British education and understanding the position of fellow immigrants in London, he returns to his native Bombay, to his dying father's side, and there he decides to stay.

The start of the novel presents the situation that brings Saladin and Gibreel together. They take the same plane to London from India, and the plane is hijacked by Sikh militant separatists. They spend more than one hundred days hovering over the British Isles until the plane explodes; Saladin and Gibreel are the sole survivors. As they descend toward English soil, the two protagonists are transmuted into devil and angel, first passing through a state of being one. The process of uniting Saladin and Gibreel in order to separate them as devil and angel represents the cultural and symbolic splitting of the postcolonial subject. The novel then renders ambiguous their respective identities as Gibreel becomes a demonic angel and Saladin develops his sense of humanity through his experience as a devil. Above all, the novel posits that postcolonial identity is not stable, absolute, or fixed; it is always in a process of renegotiating itself. The postcolonial subject is neither a culturally pure colonized native nor a completely converted object of colonizing discipline and control. Postcolonial identity is necessarily a dynamic blend of the qualities, mentalities, and cultural formations of both colonized and colonizer.

Postcolonial fiction is not limited to the themes of exile and alienation, struggle and opposition, and cultural hybridity. Many postcolonial novelists have developed other themes, such as American and European enslavement of Africans, the historical oppression of black people in the United States, and the forced assimilation in North America of minority cultures such as Native Americans, Latinos, and Asian immigrants. Some have addressed the lives of North Africans and their descendants in France and of Turkish immigrants in Germany. Regardless of the topic or setting, however, the postcolonial novel concerns itself with the cultural and political situation created by the colonial project, the necessarily violent and oppressive encounter between colonizer and colonized.

Nirmala Singh

Bibliography

Ashcroft, Bill, Gareth Griffiths, and Helen Tiffin. *The Empire Writes Back: Theory and Practice in Post-colonial Literatures*. 2d ed. New York: Routledge, 2002. Important categorical study of postcolonial fiction in English defines the genre in its relation to English literary studies, divides postcolonial fiction among critical models, and defines and examines the textual strategies used in producing this fiction. Also offers critical analyses of exemplary works and discusses various postcolonial literary theories according to geographic divisions.

Bhabha, Homi K. *The Location of Culture*. New York: Routledge, 1994. Twelve essays, including the widely read "DissemiNation: Time, Narrative, and the Margins of the Modern Nation," examine the formation of the colonial subject, whether colonizer or colonized. One of the principal aims of Bhabha's work is to reveal the possibilities for developing a minority discourse and expressing cultural difference.

Boehmer, Elleke. *Colonial and Postcolonial Literature: Migrant Metaphors*. 2d ed. New York: Oxford University Press, 2005. Highly regarded historical and critical overview of colonial and postcolonial literature in English presents close readings of important texts and a clear explanation of postcolonial theory. Includes an extensive annotated bibliography.

Harrison, Nicholas. *Postcolonial Criticism: History, Theory, and the Work of Fiction*. Malden, Mass.: Blackwell, 2003. Important theoretical work relies less on abstractions and jargon than do many books in the field. Explains theoretical concepts through close reading of several major works.

Lazarus, Neil, ed. *The Cambridge Companion to Post-colonial Literary Studies*. New York: Cambridge University Press, 2004. Collection of thirteen essays provides an introduction to the field, an overview of its social and historical contexts, and close examinations of such major issues as globalization, feminism, and nationalism. Includes a chronology of historical and literary events.

McLeod, John. *Beginning Postcolonialism*. Manchester, England: Manchester University Press, 2000. Textbook intended for undergraduates just beginning their study of postcolonial fiction. Guides students through the major theoretical texts, including Said's *Orientalism*, and the major novels, including those by Ngugi and Achebe.

Mohanram, Radhika, and Gita Rajan, eds. *English Post-coloniality: Literatures from Around the World*. Westport, Conn.: Greenwood Press, 1996. Collection of essays discusses postcolonial literature in English according to regional cultures. The final section addresses indigenous literatures.

Said, Edward W. *Orientalism*. New York: Pantheon, 1978. Classic and boldly critical study of European cultural imperialism argues that the intellectual and artistic formation of the "Oriental other" by the West was the necessary precursor for physical colonization. Exposes and denounces European discursive constructions of the Orient in literature and history that persist and continue to colonize the literary imagination.

Salhi, Kamal, ed. *Francophone Post-colonial Cultures: Critical Essays*. Lanham, Md.: Lexington Books, 2003. Twenty-nine critical essays, arranged geographically, discuss major authors, themes, and terms in postcolonial literature. Includes summaries of major primary texts and an extensive bibliography.

Spivak, Gayatri Chakravorty. *In Other Worlds: Essays in Cultural Politics*. New York: Routledge, 1988. Collection of Spivak's essays is divided into three sections: The first explores feminist strategies for rereading canonical literature, the second critically examines French feminism and the production of ideology in Western universities, and the third develops methods for reading developing world literature by analyzing the work of Indian author Mahasweta Devi and the subaltern studies group.

Wisker, Gina. *Post-colonial and African American Women's Writing: A Critical Introduction*. New York: St. Martin's Press, 2000. Introduces and analyzes African American women's fiction and then moves on to examine the writings of women from the Caribbean, Africa, the Indian subcontinent, Australia, New Zealand, Canada, Singapore and Malaysia, Oceana and Cyprus, as well as the work of black women authors in Great Britain.

Contemporary Long Fiction

It is generally agreed that the postmodern period of world literature begins immediately following the end of World War II and extends at least through the fall of the Berlin Wall (1989) and the dissolution of the Soviet Union (1991). Perhaps this period of the novel's development is identified most of all with experimentation. Worldwide, postmodern novels have flown in the face of much that preceded them, yet the novel remains an evolving, thriving genre. Testimony to its vitality is the fact that this formerly Eurocentric, male-dominated genre of literature now counts among its preeminent practitioners women from countries not traditionally identified with the novel at its best.

To appreciate such a turn of events in the novel's development, one must know something about the history of the novel and its traditions. The novel is the only genre today that cannot also be found among the classical literatures of Rome and Greece, although these societies had their own forms of long fiction. The novel emerged as a budding literary form while philosophical thought and everyday life were undergoing changes of staggering breadth during the Age of Enlightenment in the seventeenth century. The Enlightenment championed human reason at a time when God and the Church had begun to recede from the forefront of European consciousness as the defining elements of human existence, as evidenced by philosopher René Descartes's dictum, "I think, therefore I am." A new formulation of value and worth was in the offing as well, one imposed by humanity rather than by the heavens. Rising in tandem with the gold standard, international trade, and modern economics, the novel found its initial audience and practitioners amid a flowering, newly educated, secular middle class of people who had begun to appear on the horizons of mercantile Europe.

Like the flourishing mercantile environment from which it sprang, the novel traditionally championed individual initiative, choosing for its protagonists not high-ranking nobility, as was true of the literatures of ancient Rome and Greece, but rather unremarkable, often common men and women with recognizable emotional and physical desires. These characters resembled the reader. With their capacity to reason, such protagonists were given the opportunity to understand the world around them and, through such understanding, the chance to satisfy their physical needs and emotional desires by choosing one alternative over another. What brings readers to a novel may well be the chance it gives them to participate in the wishes, dreams, desires, and emotions of its characters, but what propels a novel forward are the characters' decision-making processes and their capacity to make well-informed choices. By bringing what they have learned in the past to bear on their current situations, the protagonists of traditional novels have opportunities to control their destinies in ways that would have boggled the minds of the ancients, held in the grip of the fates as they were. The linear concept of time—that is, that a past bears directly on a present that allows one to determine a future—came hand in hand with a new sense of space that emerged with the Enlightenment thought of Descartes, Baruch Spinoza, Thomas Hobbes, and John Locke. As world trade flourished and as the globe became navigable through spatial coordinates such as longitude and latitude, this new and relatively sophisticated sense of space was reflected in the novel as a literary form.

The conventional novels that grew out of the Enlightenment reflected the age's confidence in the human being's ability to navigate a world based on scientific laws. Conventionally, the first 10 to 20 percent of a novel introduces the major characters, especially the protagonist, and locates those characters in a particular time and a particular spatial realm. Then follows an event, choice, or dilemma—something that sets the plot into motion. Plot development begins as a character responds to this initial event, choosing *A* over *B* in an attempt to resolve a dilemma. That choice is usually successful only in part, resulting in a new event, choice, or dilemma to which the protagonist must respond. How well characters fare in manipulating their circumstances to achieve their goals is eventually determined by some central and final occurrence, the climax of the plot. The reader's identification with the characters compels the reader's interest. Moreover, novels suppose not only an ever-changing world but ever-changing characters as well. The reader expects the characters—at least the central characters—to change and evolve emotionally and intellectually as they live through the experiences the novel puts before them.

THE NEW NOVEL

The single most important change in the novel after World War II was the degree to which it challenged and reacted against what the novel had been traditionally. Within a decade of the war's end, signs were afoot that the modernist period of literature—a literary movement that had begun after World War I—had probably run its course. The watchword of the modernists had been "alienation." As the Industrial Revolution of the mid-nineteenth century had flowered at the beginning of the twentieth century, momentous changes had taken place that called for new ways of understanding the world and the people in it. A machine age was beginning. For the first time in the history of Western civilization, large numbers of people were abandoning the rural environment and agrarian life in favor of cities and a life of mercantilism premised upon the mass manufacture of material goods. If the literature of the period is to be trusted, this shift wrenched humankind from the most trusted human verities and demanded new ways of conceiving what it means to be human.

Within a decade of the end of World War II, modernism's "alienation" seemed to be transmogrifying into something other. New watchwords such as "isolation" and "anxiety" were in the offing, and new, postmodern considerations came to the fore. With the development of the atomic bomb, humankind had in its hands enough power to destroy civilization. Fundamental concepts from the Enlightenment—attempts to understand the world through temporal and spatial coordinates as well as through cause-and-effect relationships, assumptions of the primacy of reason in the human experience, and assumptions of the primacy of the individual—were challenged, questioned, and defied by a new generation of novelists who appeared after 1945.

This change has been reflected in a wide variety of names, most of them suggesting reaction against the status quo or rebellion against constraint. American critics called it "antiliterature" or the "antinovel," while in France experimental forms of fiction were variously labeled *écriture blanche*, *chosisme*, *école du regard*, or *école de minuit*. In both Europe and the United States, the form eventually came to be called the *nouveau roman* or, loosely translated, the New Novel.

Spearheaded by a number of authors—among them the French writers Alain Robbe-Grillet, Nathalie Sarraute, Michel Butor, Claude Simon, Robert Pinget, Marguerite Duras, and Jean Cayrol, and the Irishman Samuel Beckett—the *nouveau roman* was to have far-reaching, liberating effects on the novel in the decades ahead. The *nouveau roman* looked for its subject matter not in the world at large but rather in the consciousnesses of its protagonists, for it grew out of an assumption that in an unstable world only human consciousness can be known for certain. Conventions of plotting, characterization, and narrative based on linear time and stable space were put to the side as writers explored the workings of minds struggling to structure, often through language, a world that in the wake of two world wars defied comprehension.

With *Murphy* (1938), *Watt* (1953), and his mid-1950's trilogy of novels—*Molloy* (1951; English translation, 1955), *Malone meurt* (1951; *Malone Dies*, 1956), and *L'Innommable* (1953; *The Unnamable*, 1958)—Beckett set out what would be his primary novelistic interests over the next twenty-five years. Beckett's focus is human solitude, and, understandably, the protagonists of his novels are often monologists. They are generally incapacitated, crippled, and immobile, doing their best to understand where they are and how they got there. Readers generally meet them just as their bodies are dying or, more precisely, at the point when they become aware of the dying process, yet their minds race on, refusing to quit even though their flesh is prepared to surrender. Unable to distinguish between illusion and reality or between memories of actual events and figments of their imaginations, they speak in a void, gradually becoming more aware of their own narrative voices and the futility of their need to tell their stories when no one is there to listen. That does not stop them from speaking. It should. Certainly they would like it to stop. Their consciousnesses will not allow it, however. Despite all odds, human consciousness needs to make sense of experience; hence their monologues continue to their final, dying breaths. As Beckett writes in the concluding lines of *The Unnamable*, "You must go on, I can't go on, I'll go on, you must say words as long as there are any, until they find me, until they say me."

Robbe-Grillet, perhaps the most articulate spokesperson for the New Novel—as attested by his 1963 *Pour un nouveau roman* (*For a New Novel: Essays on Fiction*, 1965)—dealt with similar issues. Robbe-Grillet's first novel, *Les Gommes* (1953; *The Erasers*, 1964), was published while he was freshly associated with the influential French publishing house Éditions de Minuit, but it was *Le Voyeur* (1955; *The Voyeur*, 1958), which won the Prix des Critiques, that brought Robbe-Grillet to world prominence. He announced shortly after its publication, "What is important for me in the novel is structure." His plots appear, in their first few pages, to be conventional, but as one reads, one enters plots of labyrinthine complexities—one of Robbe-Grillet's later novels, in fact, is titled *Dans le labyrinthe* (1959; *In the Labyrinth*, 1960). There is no dramatic conclusion, no logical climax to a Robbe-Grillet novel; rather, one enters a narrative in which attempts to comprehend events through chronology and space, and through cause-and-effect relationships, lead only to dead ends.

Sarraute's first significant postwar work is *Martereau*, published in 1953 (English translation, 1959). However, it was the short-story collection *Tropismes* (1939, 1957; *Tropisms*, 1963) with which she is most often identified. The "tropisms" of the title are fleeting responses to the world, the experiences people sense in themselves that are not translatable into language. Her concern is how Western thought teaches people to privilege language, reason, and what cannot be known through the five senses, and how it subjugates tropisms to the level of whim or emotion. People's real lives are being lived on levels of consciousness that they have been trained to ignore. Sarraute's novels contain story lines and characters of sorts; however, like Robbe-Grillet, her foremost concern is demonstrating that readers are too willing to trust the artifice of fiction.

Women novelists

The novel flowered internationally following World War II. Despite all that has been written about the decline of print literature and the rise of electronic media after 1945, the depth and breadth of talented novelists have arguably never been greater than in this single period. Witness Sarraute and Robbe-Grillet in France, the Soviet Union's Aleksandr Solzhenitsyn, India's Salman Rushdie, Germany's Nobel laureate Günter Grass and Heinrich Böll, and Mexico's Carlos Fuentes; the trend continued as a younger generation of enormously talented novelists, England's Graham Swift and Julian Barnes to name but two, began to take their rightful place in world letters. Many women may be counted among the preeminent novelists of the postwar period, particularly South Africa's Doris Lessing and Nadine Gordimer, both of whom won the Nobel Prize in Literature, Canada's Margaret Atwood, and Chile's Isabel Allende. That these women hail from countries not normally identified with the forefront of the Western world's letters attests to the growing internationalization of the novel.

Lessing's two most widely read novels are *The Golden Notebook* (1962) and *The Four-Gated City* (1969). First published before the second-wave feminist movement had received high recognition, *The Golden Notebook* became a feminist landmark with its ambitious, unyielding account of the political, personal, and professional lives of writer Anna Wulf. Attempting to reconcile her inner self with the self that she shows to the world at large, Wulf turns to her notebooks. The struggle to define herself as a woman and as a person is played out in four different notebooks: one for her political self, another for her personal self, a third for her self as an author confounded by writer's block, and a fourth, the "golden notebook" of the title, in which she brings the other three together.

This idea of creating a whole that is more than the sum of its parts is central to Lessing's writing, as is maintaining one's mental stability in an unstable world. Both themes are dealt with in *The Four-Gated City*, the fifth and last installment of her Children of Violence pentology, five works published individually as *Martha Quest* (1952), *A Proper Marriage* (1954), *A Ripple from the Storm* (1958), *Landlocked* (1965, 1991), and *The Four-Gated City*. Lessing's protagonist, Martha Quest, is her most compelling and certainly most complex heroine. The pentology follows Martha from her youth as a rebellious teenager through her middle age, during which she copes with teenagers of her own. A woman not unlike what is known about Lessing from her autobiography *Walking in the Shade* (1997), Martha takes up residence in London and becomes politicized as she finds herself involved in the communist scares of the period and deeply involved in the lives of people she encounters. Many of Martha's actions are daring, risky, and sometimes foolish, for experience is Martha's goal—to experience life in a manner different from how, as a woman, she has been taught to live. Commitment, however, is the lesson to be taken to heart. The act of commitment stands apart from politics, from the cause itself; Lessing suggests that in a world of contradiction and confusion, commitment is the only way to affirm life in a particularly human fashion. Lessing won the Nobel Prize in Literature in 2007, recognized as an "epicist of the female experience."

Gordimer, who won the Nobel Prize in Literature in 1991, published the novel *Burger's Daughter* in 1979. Its protagonist, Rosa Burger, has survived her two politically active parents, both of whom suffered for their antiapartheid convictions. With her parents dead, Rosa struggles to find her place in South African culture and to reconcile her parents' legacy with the current political climate of her homeland, discovering as she does that every private act carries with it a public dimension. Many of these same concerns are dealt with in Gordimer's *The House Gun* (1998). Its protagonists are the Lindgards, Harald and Claudia, a middle-aged, upper-class couple living in postapartheid South Africa who are forced to confront their country's legacy of violence and racism when their son Duncan is arrested, imprisoned, and tried for the murder of his lover. Facing a postapartheid legal system, the Lindgards hire a black attorney to be their son's representative, thinking that will be all they need, only to discover themselves becoming enmeshed in a legal and personal process in which they are powerless to act effectively or even understand what is going on. Imprisonment is the central theme of the book. The story explores the generational differences that separate parents from child, but it also explores the walls that the Lindgards have erected around themselves in order to avoid dealing with the darkest realities of South African culture.

Atwood's *Surfacing* (1972) is set in northern Quebec on a remote island. The nameless female protagonist, the protagonist's lover Joe, and their friends Anna and David set out to find the protagonist's father, who has been reported missing. Their search returns the protagonist to the area where she was raised; in the course of searching for her father, she finds, most of all, herself. She finds in her own psyche memories and levels of understanding that have little to do with the definition of herself she has established through her artwork and her social relationships. Atwood also deals with the ways in which women define themselves in such later novels as *The Handmaid's Tale* (1985), *Cat's Eye* (1988), *Alias Grace* (1996), and *The Penelopiad: The Myth of Penelope and Odysseus* (2005).

The Handmaid's Tale, a thought-provoking, scathing satire rather than a journey of self-discovery, is set at the millennium in the mythical Republic of Gilead. In this parody of the biblical story of Rachel, a social movement akin to America's Moral Majority has blurred the separation of church and state and institutionalized a mind-numbing version of domestic tranquility. Young women, including the protagonist, Offred, are required to breed in order to repopulate a world devastated by birth control gone awry, ecological mismanagement, and nuclear fallout. Offred and the other handmaids of Gilead remain uneducated and in positions of servitude, their primary—in fact their sole—social identity being their fertile ovaries.

Allende, a seasoned journalist, debuted as a novelist with *La casa de los espíritus* (1982; *The House of the Spirits*, 1985), a chronicle of three generations of the Trueba family in an unnamed South American country from the beginning of the twentieth century through the 1980's. The novel's central character is Clara del Valle-Trueba, a hypersensitive youngster who is just discovering her own telepathic powers. The death of her sister Rosa silences Clara for nearly a decade. When Rosa's fiancé, Esteban Trueba, returns to his homeland, Clara recognizes him as the figure who has been coming to her in her dreams and speaks for the first time since her sister's death. Esteban and Clara marry and take up residence in the house of the novel's title. In addition to bearing and raising a family, Clara fills the house with artists, spiritualists, and an assortment of other visionaries until the mansion becomes a world unto itself. However,

Esteban's attachment to his estate points his attention outward to the world beyond his property. There, an amalgam of uneasy political forces is gradually drawing the country toward a volatile period of socialist reforms that threaten Esteban's hold on his land. Esteban fails to recognize what, for Clara, is the most fundamental tenet of life—namely, that what people seek to possess will, in the end, take possession of them, rather than the other way around. Consequently, over the years, Esteban's opposition to a socialist state draws him and his loved ones into political upheavals that jeopardize their lives, their property, and their love for one another.

Magical Realism

Allende attempted to reconcile the political novel with the epic in *The House of the Spirits*, just as she attempted to reconcile the effect of people on history and the effect of history on people, the private world of a family and the public world in which people's lives are finally lived, and the hold nature has on people's minds and the hold the supernatural maintains on their souls. Allende's subsequent novels, such as *El plan infinito* (1991; *The Infinite Plan*, 1993) and *Hija de la fortuna* (1999; *Daughter of Fortune*, 1999), have been somewhat less ambitious but no less skillfully written. Her prose is filled with vivid, often surprising imagery. To read her work is akin to waking from a dream only to find that one has not been dreaming, for her spiritual world is as faithfully and realistically rendered as are her accounts of revolutions.

Allende's work has been associated with Magical Realism, a genre of writing that appeared after World War II. Magical Realists make little or no distinction between the real and the surreal; characters seem to inhabit a world where the magical is no less substantial than the commonplace event. The term "Magical Realism" has been used in discussions of the works of a wide variety of fiction writers, including Graham Swift, Sandra Cisneros, Peter Carey, Alusaine Dunbar, B. Kojo Laing, Milan Kundera, V. S. Naipaul, Tomaso Landolfi, Jorge Luis Borges, Italo Calvino, and Marina Ama Omowale Maxwell. Ordinarily, however, Magical Realism as a description is reserved for the work of those writers who draw from particular South American and Spanish traditions of the absurd or the grotesque, predominantly Laura Esquivel, Horacio Quiroga, Carlos Fuentes, Alejo Carpentier, Roberto Gonzalez Eschevarria, Julio Cortázar, and José Saramago, who won the 1999 Nobel Prize in Literature.

Of the Magical Realists, Colombia's Gabriel García Márquez, who won the Nobel Prize in Literature in 1982, is perhaps the most well known. His novel *Cien años de soledad* (1967; *One Hundred Years of Solitude*, 1970), one of several works set in the village of Macondo in the South American lowlands of Colombia, relates the history of the Buendía family from about 1830 to 1930. The novel is less a family chronicle than a physical and metaphysical exploration of human life. García Márquez is capable of stunning physical description. In that sense, he demonstrates all the capacities of the finest of realist writers, but his aim is to demonstrate that a "realistic" depiction of the world is misleading. His sentences can run on for pages, making readers lose the point in the process. The family tree at the book's beginning proves of less help than expected: Several different characters share the same name at the same time, and the referents for pronouns such as "he" or "they" are often difficult, if not impossible, to locate. The past flows into the present without warning, and plot and subplot become so intertwined that it is nearly impossible to distinguish one from the other. One senses, however, that ordering principles exist beneath the apparent confusion.

García Márquez's depiction of life in the community of Macondo reveals that the village's political history is one of violence, mayhem, and chaos. Yet an order belies this chaos, if one is perceptive enough to detect it. In one of the novel's most famous sequences, for instance, a character is pushed up against a wall, then shot within view of his loved one, Rebecca, who exacts revenge by shooting someone else. In a long section rendered in minute and breathtaking detail, her victim's blood trickles through the town, finally passing by this victim's loved one, Ursula, just as she is separating thirty-six eggs in the course of baking bread. Ursula follows the trail in reverse, discovering, at last, her dead loved one and Rebecca.

The patterns that inform the world of García Márquez's *One Hundred Years of Solitude* have little to do with what can be learned from history books or courses in empirical science, much less what one expects to learn from a book-length family chronicle. This same worldview is to be found as well in his later novels, such as *El amor en los tiempos del cólera* (1985; *Love in the Time of Cholera*, 1988). This novel is set in a mythical country on the Caribbean coast of South America and accounts for about fifty years in the lives of its three main characters. As young men, Florentino Ariza and Juvenal Urbino fall in love with Fermina Daza. Although she marries Urbino, Ariza remains in love with her, and she becomes his primary reason for living. Upon the death of Urbino many years later, Ariza declares his feelings for Daza at last, woos her as if she were still a young girl, and loves her in his bed despite the fact that her beauty has long passed.

One of the major themes of the novel is time. As measured by a calendar, many years pass in the course of the plot. For Ariza, however, no time has passed at all. Time is meaningful only if one can know how it is experienced, and, similarly, one can understand the life Ariza has lived only once given a privileged view of his heart. Ariza might appear to the world to be a lecher, for instance, or at the very least a libertine—a reputation that might be shared by the protagonist of García Márquez's novella *Memoria de mis putas tristes* (2004; *Memories of My Melancholy Whores*, 2005). Ariza reports that he has brought to his bed more than six hundred women, and one of these was his ward, a fourteen-year-old girl. Fermina Daza, however, is the woman to whom he has been trying to make love. Paradoxically, by becoming Urbino's wife rather than Ariza's, she has become the center of Ariza's life in ways she could not have had she married him.

THE POSTMODERN AMERICAN NOVEL

Not surprisingly, much that changed in the novel worldwide after World War II also changed in the American novel—sometimes more so. Perhaps the most important development in American novels after the war, however, was the manner in which America itself and the place of its citizens within it were portrayed. What kind of country was the United States to become, now that Europe was disabled and the United States was so unthinkably strong? Was it possible that modernism's sense of alienation was now going to be institutionalized, employed, made part of the social infrastructure? Modernism had chronicled the assimilation of immigrants into the American grain. Much of that assimilation was complete by the end of World War II. Postmodern literature seemed to question the price at which this assimilation had come about. To participate in America as a "melting pot" had meant that those who traveled to the United States from distant lands gave up old ways of life in favor of new ones. New authors began to consider whether the melting pot was a myth and whether it was possible to give up one's roots completely and become, first and foremost, an American.

World War II cost some 350,000 Americans their lives in battle, and more than double that number were wounded; yet in a war that counted more than 50 million dead in all, America was spared much of the suffering endured by the nations of Europe. The United States emerged more prosperous and powerful than any other nation on Earth. Change was in the air. This was true as well in literature. Thomas Wolfe had died in 1938; F. Scott Fitzgerald and Nathanael West in 1940; Sherwood Anderson in 1941. Other modernist novelists who had been at the forefront of American letters since World War I, such as William Faulkner and Ernest Hemingway, had already done their best work, and though they would be lauded in the years ahead, they were stepping to the side as younger novelists sought a voice in literature, many of them military veterans, most of them university educated, and all of them coming into their own as adults. The first signal of this change was the publication of a spate of popular, middlebrow novels that appeared within a few years of the war's end that chronicled wartime experience: John Hersey's *A Bell for Adano* (1944), Gore Vidal's *Williwaw* (1946), John Horne Burns's *The Gallery* (1947), Irwin Shaw's *The Young Lions* (1948), James Gould Cozzens's *Guard of Honor* (1948), Herman Wouk's *The Caine Mutiny* (1951), and James Jones's *From Here to Eternity* (1951). It soon became clear that the new novelists were doing more than adding their voices to those of their elders, however. This generation brought to their work thematic concerns that were different in kind and degree from those seen in the works of the novelists who had preceded them.

No three or four novels can demonstrate the depth and breadth of such matters, but perhaps Norman Mailer's

The Naked and the Dead (1948), Ralph Ellison's *Invisible Man* (1952), and Saul Bellow's *The Adventures of Augie March* (1953) can serve as a place from which to begin. Though its form was seriously indebted to the work of modernist novelist John Dos Passos, Mailer's *The Naked and the Dead* was a war novel that touched on what would become postmodern fare in the years ahead; it is arguably the first postmodern war novel in the American canon. Freudian thought had recently become a standard component of many liberal arts curricula in American universities, and the Harvard-educated Mailer made use of what he had learned. Mailer's platoon of soldiers tasked with taking an island in the Pacific during the final months of the war are drawn as characters with both conscious and unconscious levels to their psyches, characters only partially aware of their own motives and the motives of others. They are complicated and confused characters, unable to make their own experience of the United States coincide with the country's myths. They are drawn in ways that suggest that anxiety is a central feature of the human experience. Literature had always included fearful, anxious characters, but these were conditions that could be mitigated or overcome. Not so in Mailer's work. Postmodern people were anxiety-ridden figures, unable to understand or appreciate the complexities of their situations, ever aware that they had less control of their fate than they told.

More important, Mailer had his finger on what would become a new and disturbing concept of the United States itself, one that would become familiar in American novels in the coming years. As the United States became the world's most powerful nation, American authors began focusing on Americans who had less power than ever before in history. Postmodern Americans were forced to find their place in a culture that touted individualism and self-sufficiency yet denied both in practice as it attempted to enter an era of high technology, mass culture, and anonymous suburban life.

One of Mailer's characters, the brilliant General Cummings, continually debates the shape of the postwar world with his subordinate Lieutenant Robert Hearn. Hearn argues that much of American military life is dangerously close to fascism. Cummings counters that fascism is singularly suited to meet the challenges of a country as rich and diverse as the United States will be in the years ahead. If anything, Cummings instructs Hearn, the military environment is a preview of what the United States will be like after the war is over. It will continue to appear to be a free and democratic nation, paying lip service to the importance of the individual and other outmoded patriotic verities, but the truth of the matter will be otherwise. In order to harness the kinetic energy of the country so it can take its place as a world power in an age of high technology, American society will have to be rigidly structured from top to bottom. There will be little or no place for the free-thinking individual. People will be forced to accept their places in a "fear ladder," afraid and envious of their superiors and threatened by their subordinates' ambitions and eager to keep them in their place. According to Cummings, "The only morality of the future is a power morality, and a man who cannot find his adjustment to it is doomed. There's one thing about power. It can only flow from the top down."

The nameless protagonist of Ellison's *Invisible Man* is a black college student at an all-black southern institution funded by white benefactors and run by a distinguished black educator, Dr. Bledsoe. Early in the novel, the protagonist protests when Bledsoe moves to have him expelled unfairly. The protagonist threatens to make his case public. Bledsoe's speech is reminiscent of that of Mailer's General Cummings. Here, Cummings's "power morality" becomes Bledsoe's "power set-up."

> "Tell anyone you like," [Bledsoe] said. "I don't care. . . . Power doesn't have to show off. Power is confident, self-assuring, self-starting, self-stopping, self-warming and self-justifying. . . . This is a power set-up, son, and I'm at the controls. You think about that. When you buck me, you're bucking against power, rich white folks' power, the nation's power—which means government power. . . . You're nobody son, you don't exist—can't you see that?

These last few words direct a reader to the central conceit of the novel. Ellison's protagonist is as "invisible" to powerful black people as he is to powerful white people. He has no significant individual identity. As a person, he exists only insofar as he accepts a role in the agenda of the people in power.

A related concept is to be found in Bellow's *The Adventures of Augie March*. Bellow first appeared on the literary scene with *Dangling Man* in 1944. For much of that novel, Bellow's protagonist, Joseph, "dangles" between two alternatives, both of which he finds unsatisfactory. As Joseph awaits induction into the U.S. Army, he tries to decide whether he should accept his induction notice and become part of an institution that he finds morally repugnant or be true to his own conscience, suffer the immediate consequences, and accept that he will spend the rest of his life defined by this choice, always on the fringes of mainstream American community. Joseph's is a sticky decision to make, but it pales in comparison to the world faced by Augie March in *The Adventures of Augie March*. Augie's world is one of dizzying complexities. As the Jewish Augie tries to take his place in mainstream American culture, he finds that good and evil, right and wrong, are simpleminded tenets. So is individual identity. In his way, Augie is as "invisible" as Ellison's protagonist. The only thing Augie can know for sure is that everyone seeks power. Each person comes to a given situation with his or her own agenda in hand, eager to make others a part of it, eager to offer them identities that serve the person's immediate ends.

> You invent a man who can stand before the terrible appearances. This way he can't get justice and he can't give justice, but he can live. And this is what mere humanity always does. It's made up of these inventors or artists, millions and millions of them, each in his own way trying to recruit other people to play a supporting role and sustain him in his make-believe. The great chiefs and leaders recruit the greatest number, and that's what their power is. There's one image that gets out in front to lead the rest and can impose its claim to being genuine with more force than the others. . . . Then a huge invention, which is the invention maybe of the world itself, and of nature, becomes . . . the actuality. That's the struggle of humanity, to recruit others to your version of what's real.

This identifiably postmodern consideration of the United States and American life in literature, in which individuals are defined by their incapacities as much as by their strengths, by their confusions as much as by their insights, became a predominant theme of novels written through the time of the Vietnam War. No longer was the United States a country premised on the rights and prerogatives of the individual. One had to take one's proper place in the culture, like it or not; predictably, the protagonists of American novels did not like it.

The postmodern era has been called the era of the antihero. This would suggest that the protagonists of many novels of this time are bounders, wasters, simpletons, and fools when, in fact, they demonstrate many of the same strengths as conventional heroes. What changes is that they are so rarely successful in achieving what they set out to do. This is another way of saying that what changes is not the American hero but America itself. The protagonists of novels published ten to fifteen years after World War II test four central courses of action—assimilation, accommodation, flight, and rebellion—and find each to be as ineffective as the next.

Perhaps the two authors most associated with the perils and peculiar difficulties of assimilation into American culture after the war are John Updike and James Purdy. The issue surfaced with Updike's *Rabbit, Run* (1960) and became a concern with which he would deal throughout his career, particularly the subsequent installments of the Rabbit Angstrom series, *Rabbit Redux* (1971), *Rabbit Is Rich* (1981), *Rabbit at Rest* (1990), and the novella *Rabbit Remembered* (2000). Purdy staked a collateral claim to these concerns in his first published work, a collection of short stories titled *Color of Darkness* (1957), then explored it in more depth in such early novels as *Malcolm* (1959) and *Cabot Wright Begins* (1964). This theme has been explored by a wide variety of postmodern American fiction writers: Protagonists attempt to embrace the values of the culture, take their place, and make do with what they were given. This course of action is rarely, if ever, successful. The values of American culture are no longer clear, and they seem to center on money, mercantile success, upward social mobility, power, and secular values; even if one were to succeed, the victory would be a hollow one.

Another approach was to accommodate the culture, but only in part. This was the tactic explored by Ellison in *Invisible Man* and Bellow in *The Adventures of Augie March*. For a time it seemed to be the domain of Jewish American novelists, particularly Bellow, Philip Roth, and Bernard Malamud, suggesting that accommodation was the domain of novelists focusing their attention on the search for the American Dream among minority groups. Accommodation, however, was explored by a wide range of authors, and the results were largely the same in each case: One plays a daily role, taking what one can from the marketplace but always keeping some of oneself in reserve, only to discover in the end that such a preservation of "self" is virtually impossible. Insofar as "we" accommodate culture, "we" become "them," whether or not "we" realize this is happening.

Flight was yet another response to the new American life. Protagonists in American novels had been fleeing civilized American life in favor of the frontier since the nineteenth century; in fact, such protagonists as James Fenimore Cooper's Natty Bumppo and Mark Twain's Huckleberry Finn were legendary for it. Flight, however, was no longer a possibility. The United States had become urbanized and suburbanized, and it no longer contained a frontier. Although this lack stopped many novelists dead in their tracks, others, such as William S. Burroughs and Richard Brautigan, looked for less terrestrial alternatives and a redefinition of new and fertile landscapes. Burroughs's *The Naked Lunch* (1959; republished as *Naked Lunch*, 1962) explored drug addiction and retreat into the recesses of the human psyche, while Brautigan's *Trout Fishing in America* (1967) and *In Watermelon Sugar* (1968) offered the human imagination as the last frontier in which the America of mythology could be found.

Rebellion is as American as the United States itself, as is clear from the history of the American Revolution. Yet rebellion no longer seemed viable either. Novels no longer made it clear who the enemy was, and it was difficult to determine whom one should rebel against in order to prosper. Ken Kesey's *One Flew over the Cuckoo's Nest* (1962) articulated such dilemmas for the youthful countercultures of the turbulent 1960's, particularly the dilemma of the rebel. Kesey's protagonist, Randle Patrick McMurphy, checks himself into a mental institution in an attempt to get off a work detail during a sentence he is serving in prison. He does battle with Nurse Ratched, the supervisor of the mental ward to which he is committed. Prior to McMurphy's arrival, the narrator of the novel, Chief Bromden, has found a way to accommodate her and the ward she runs by passing himself off as deaf and mute. McMurphy's presence brings Bromden to his full senses, and McMurphy's willingness to confront and rebel against Nurse Ratched inspires Bromden to daring, selfless acts of his own. Any pleasure of victory he might feel is tempered, however; after all, one nurse in one mental ward is not really the problem. In the novel, Mailer's "power morality" and Ellison's "power set-up" become what Bromden calls the "Combine." He says about McMurphy,

> He says he don't think getting her out of the way would really make much difference; he says that there's something bigger making all this mess and goes on to try to say what he thinks it is. He finally gives up when he can't explain it. McMurphy doesn't know it, but he's onto what I realized a long time back, that it's not just the Big Nurse by herself, but it's the whole Combine, the nation-wide Combine that's the really big force, and the nurse is just a high-ranking official for them.

Black humor

The problem that Bromden ponders is a familiar one in postmodern novels. If the Combine, rather than Nurse Ratched, is the enemy, how is one to rebel against it? The Combine is tantamount to postmodern American life itself. Therefore, the enemy is everywhere yet, paradoxically, nowhere to be found. Can acts of rebellion be heroic in a world so absurd, one in which the enemy is everywhere and nowhere, or are they simply self-destructive? These and similar questions became the focus of what has come to be called the black humor novel. It is marked by a darkness of authorial vision and an absurd, sometimes surreal, depiction of contemporary life. Mostly, however, it is definable through its sense of gallows humor. This school of darkly comic novels is generally considered to be a Cold War phenomenon, but the black humor novel first entered the American canon of letters at the end of the modernist period with the works of Nathanael West: *The Dream Life of Balso Snell* (1931), *Miss Lonelyhearts* (1933), *A Cool Million: The Dismantling of Lemuel Pitkin* (1934), and *The Day of the Locust* (1939).

Among the most noteworthy postmodern practitioners of this form are James Purdy, John Hawkes, Jerome Charyn, Max Apple, Barry Hannah, Bruce Jay Friedman, J. P. Donleavy, Thomas Pynchon, Terry Southern, Vladimir Nabokov, William Gaddis, T. Coraghessan

Boyle, Don DeLillo, and John Barth. Were one to choose a single novelist to be the dean of this school, however, it would probably have to be Joseph Heller. The title of Heller's first novel, *Catch-22* (1961), has become part of American lexicography—one can find it in dictionaries. The title refers to a phenomenon one encounters when dealing with powerful bureaucratic institutions. Situations appear to offer the individual a choice between mutually exclusive alternatives, but there is always a "Catch-22." Either alternative brings the same result: The institution wins, the individual loses.

The novel recounts the wartime experiences of Yossarian, a U.S. Army Air Corps bombardier stationed in Italy during the last two years of World War II. Yossarian begins to realize that the occupying German forces are no more his enemy than the regime of which he is a part: Neither cares for his well-being, and both would just as soon see him dead. The most important distinction in the world is not between the Allies and the Axis or the Americans and the Germans, nor is it between right and wrong, the just and the unjust; rather, the world is only really divisible between those with power and those without it, and those without it will always lose. Yossarian spends much of the novel trying to survive by accommodating the whims of his commanding officers and the shifting winds of fate, reasoning that when one's enemies are everywhere, there is nowhere to flee and no one to rebel against. In the novel's final pages, however, he chooses a higher course. For much of the novel he has done everything in his power to get out of combat and be sent home. When that opportunity finally presents itself, he opts instead to perform one unselfish act, risking life and limb in the process, to save one child and take her to Sweden. He is told that what he intends to do will accomplish little of substance, but that, Yossarian realizes, is not the point. As a human, he knows that he is not relieved of the responsibility to behave humanely simply because the world no longer cares for humanity, nor is he relieved of responsibility for the evil of the world simply because it is not in his power to stop it. Yossarian thinks, "Someone had to do something sometime. Every victim was a culprit, every culprit a victim, and somebody had to stand up sometime to try to break the lousy chain of inherited habit that was imperiling them all."

Metafiction

The form of *Catch-22* might be said to reflect its theme. The novel begins in the middle of Yossarian's tour of duty, then moves back and forth through time and space without warning or guidance on the part of the author. Such a curious sequencing of events is dizzying, even to those willing to read the novel repeatedly, but then, that is the point. That is precisely the kind of lesson Yossarian would have readers take to heart from what he has learned. Temporal and spatial coordinates no longer tell people where they are; when the world has gone mad, one bombing run is the same as any other, and one enemy the same as all the enemies one may encounter.

Such an authorial strategy has been termed metafiction; many postmodern novels share this impulse to play form and content against each other. However, this is not what is meant by the term "metafiction" per se. The metafictional novel is one that draws the reader's attention not only to the story being told but also to the means through which the novel tells a story. Perhaps the best example of the form is the Italian author Italo Calvino's *Se una notte d'inverno un viaggiatore* (1979; *If on a Winter's Night a Traveler*, 1981), which is about a reader attempting to read a novel called *If on a Winter's Night a Traveler.*

The metafictional novel reminds readers that the conventions of the traditional novel are just that—conventions, or formal properties, that emerged several hundred years ago. Conventions of plot, character, setting, and theme are acts of artifice, a way of giving artistic structure to a depiction of human life; the metafictional novel suggests that such a conventional form of novelizing may have outlived its time.

Many of the foremost black humorists have found their place in the metafictional school, particularly John Barth, Robert Coover, Gilbert Sorrentino, Ronald Sukenick, Donald Barthelme, Thomas Pynchon, and Vladimir Nabokov. Both schools intend for readers to realize that life is less stable than they would like to let on and that precision is only approximate. Reason is a more limited means of comprehending life than people are apt to admit.

As surely as filmmaker Alfred Hitchcock made it a practice to appear momentarily in his own films, reminding viewers that, after all, they are watching a movie, so metafictional novelists make sure that readers know they are in their own novels. Late in Pynchon's *Gravity's Rainbow* (1973), after readers have grappled with hundreds of characters and dozens of interwoven plots, the author declares that the reader "will want cause and effect," assuming, and rightly, that readers are at a point in the book where they are sure to be confused. Likewise, the narrative voice of Nabokov's *Ada or Ardor: A Family Chronicle* (1969), aware that the novel cannot be understood on one reading alone, steps forward and addresses the reader as "re-reader."

Published in 1958, Barth's novel *The End of the Road* was the first to articulate the unique relationship between reader and writer that the metafictional novel posits.

> Everyone is necessarily the hero of his own life story. *Hamlet* could be told from Polonius's point of view and called *The Tragedy of Polonius, Lord Chamberlain of Denmark*. He didn't suppose he was a minor character in anything, I dare say. . . . So in this sense fiction isn't a lie at all, but a true representation of the distortion that everyone makes of life. Now, not only are we the heroes of our own life stories—we're the ones who conceive the story, and give other people the essences of minor characters. But since no man's life story as a rule is ever one story with a coherent plot, we're always reconceiving just the sort of hero we are, and consequently just the sort of minor roles that other people are supposed to play.

The metafictional novel is self-conscious, then, but with a larger purpose in mind than drawing attention to itself alone. This is also to remind readers that everyone is a storyteller. People cast themselves as the protagonists in their tales, "star" in their own stories, as it were, attributing a particular cause to a particular effect; people assume that experiences they have had in the past can inform what they are experiencing at any given moment. They attribute motives to those around them, casting some in minor roles and others in larger roles such as villain or antagonist. They create narrative structures they know to be false, or at least not indisputable, in an attempt to understand the world around them and their place within it.

The Native American novel

Among the developments in the American novel during this period was the degree to which it began to privilege gender and ethnicity as defining factors in the American experience. New categories began to appear in literary criticism and on the shelves of bookstores: the Native American novel, the Asian American novel, the Latina/Latino novel, the African American novel, and the feminist novel. Novels written by Native Americans, such as Louise Erdrich's *Love Medicine* (1984; revised and expanded 1993) and *The Plague of Doves* (2008), have brought new and important perspectives to bear on the established canon of American literature. While only a few of these have earned a full position in that canon, any number of Native American novels would have to be counted among the more significant written after World War II, among them James Welch's *Winter in the Blood* (1974) and *Fools Crow* (1986), Greg Sarris's *Watermelon Nights* (1998), Paula Gunn Allen's *The Woman Who Owned the Shadows* (1983), Michael Dorris's *A Yellow Raft in Blue Water* (1987), D'Arcy McNickle's *The Surrounded* (1936) and *Wind from an Enemy Sky* (1978), Linda Hogan's *Power* (1998) and *People of the Whale* (2008), Gerald Vizenor's *Darkness in Saint Louis Bearheart* (1978; revised as *Bearheart: The Heirship Chronicles*, 1990), Louis Owens's *The Sharpest Sight* (1992), Thomas King's *Green Grass, Running Water* (1993), Leslie Marmon Silko's *Ceremony* (1977), N. Scott Momaday's *House Made of Dawn* (1968), Guy M. Madison's *The Res: An American Novel* (1998), and Sherman Alexie's *Reservation Blues* (1995) and *Flight* (2007).

Erdrich's *Love Medicine* was the first of these to receive widespread acclaim, garnering, among other honors, the National Book Critics Circle Award; it was also perhaps the first novel by a Native American to receive deep and widespread critical attention. The characters introduced in *Love Medicine* reappeared in such subsequent works as *The Beet Queen* (1986), *Tracks* (1988), and *The Bingo Palace* (1994). The lives of the families chronicled in Erdrich's work span several generations. Later generations are inevitably caught between the world of white, industrialized America and that of Native American culture. Consequently, her youngest characters have a clearer idea of who they are not than they do of who they are. For instance, Lipsha Morrissey, the protagonist of *The Bingo Palace*, returns to his Chippewa reservation on the North Dakota plains after moving away to work in Fargo's sugar beet factories. His return to a winter powwow is chronicled in these words:

> We saw [Lipsha] edge against the wall to watch the whirling bright dancers, and immediately we had to notice that there was no place the boy could fit. He was not a tribal council honcho, not a powwow organizer, not a medic in the cop's car in the parking lot, no one we could trust with our life. . . . He was not even one of those gathered at the soda machines outside the doors, the ones who wouldn't go into the warm and grassy air because of being drunk or too much in love or just bashful. He was not the Chippewa with rings pierced in her nose or the old aunt with water dripping through her fingers or the announcer with a ragged face and a drift of plumes on his indoor hat.
>
> He was none of these, only Lipsha, come home.

In the hope of bringing in revenue from beyond the reservation, the tribe is building the bingo palace of the title on a sacred lake, and in the course of the novel both Lipsha and the reader come to understand that what a white man might perceive to be chance occurrence or luck is actually the doing of Lipsha's dead ancestors, now part of the spirit realm. Such a turn of events can come as no surprise to Erdrich's regular readers. Much in her work attempts to bridge the workings of contemporary America with those of Native American religion and tradition.

Something of the same might be said about the formal properties of her novels. For structure, her novels draw on both the oral traditions of her Chippewa roots and the printed narrative patterns of American novels. *Love Medicine*, for instance, spans some fifty years. The lives of several Chippewa families during this period are presented in overlapping fragments, most from the mouths of the central characters. This is appropriate to a culture less affected by print than by an oral tradition, a culture where news comes in bits and pieces as what a white world might dismiss as "gossip," for each speaker modifies the account as he or she brings prejudices and unique perspectives to bear. The end result is the formation of a community based on shared experiences, one that transcends familial and tribal differences, and this perception is central to what Erdrich is about. While neither traditional tribal structures and ways of life nor the structures of white modern America seem to serve her characters, Erdrich holds out the possibility of yet a third sense of community, one that might serve as salvation for all of those involved.

The Asian American novel

Among Asian American novels of significance are Gus Lee's *China Boy* (1991) and *Honor and Duty* (1994), Lisa See's *Flower Net* (1997), Mako Yoshikawa's *One Hundred and One Ways* (1999), Maxine Hong Kingston's *Tripmaster Monkey: His Fake Book* (1989), Gish Jen's *Typical American* (1991) and its sequel *Mona in the Promised Land* (1996), Yiyun Li's *The Vagrants* (2009), and Amy Tan's *The Joy Luck Club* (1989), *The Kitchen God's Wife* (1991), and *Saving Fish from Drowning* (2005). All of these deal with the clash of Western and Eastern cultures and explore this clash by placing their central characters in family units that extend for several generations.

Jen's *Typical American*, for instance, explores how time, traditions, social boundaries, and social customs are central to the Chinese understanding of human experience: "Everywhere there are limits," one of her characters says. For Jen, those limits are central to understanding the Chinese world as it runs headlong into the United States. It is no wonder, then, that when her Chinese characters emigrate to the United States, they are baffled by what they find. At one point, a character's car is stolen, and what impresses him most is the way the thief drives. Unlike the speaker, the thief is completely comfortable behind the wheel, heedless of danger and anyone who might be in his way: "He was a natural driver for whom the wheel seemed a natural extension of his hands. Anyone would have thought he'd invented the automobile."

Tan deals with similar matters in *The Joy Luck Club*. Set in San Francisco's Chinatown, the novel focuses on two generations of Asian women—Chinese mothers and their Chinese American daughters—and the bonds that hold them together as well as the tensions that force them apart. Foremost among these tensions is how the two generations view the world. For the mothers, the world is a cosmos of carefully balanced structures (ancestral hierarchies, for instance) and natural forces (earth, wind, fire, and water) in which people must find their proper place. With that place properly found, one achieves *nengkan*, a strength or capacity to survive and prosper. Says one of the narrators,

> It was this belief in their *nengkan* that had brought my parents to America. It had enabled them to have seven children and buy a house in the Sunset district with very little money. It had given them the confidence to believe their luck would never run out, that God was on their side, that the house gods had only benevolent things to report and our ancestors were pleased, that lifetime warranties meant our lucky streak would never break, that all the elements were in balance, the right amount of wind and water.

Born and reared in China, the mothers in the novel take their immediate identity as women from their place in a family unit. For instance, many of their memories of China deal with being "orphaned" in one form or another, their greatest fear. In fact, they cannot perceive an identity apart from that unit. To their educated, liberated, Americanized daughters, such outmoded beliefs are just one step away from believing in magic dragons. For them, a woman's identity comes from her taking charge of her own fate, not from her finding her place in some larger, preestablished order, and certainly not from finding her place as a homemaker in her own family or as a dutiful daughter in her mother's.

Readers see what these two generations can appreciate only in part. Neither way of understanding the world and one's place in it is proportionately better than the other. Certainly the daughters are not happier for being liberated and Americanized. Their relationships with men are troubled and troubling; the rewards of the careers they choose leave them sleepless and unsatisfied. Readers come away from the narratives wishing that the daughters could speak as easily to their mothers as they seem to be able to speak to the readers.

The Latino/Latina novel

Rudolfo Anaya's *Bless Me, Ultima* (1972) and Tomás Rivera's *. . . y no se tragó la tierra/. . . and the earth did not part* (1971; also known as *This Migrant Earth*, 1985; *. . . and the earth did not devour him*, 1987) both represent the essence of the Latino/Latina novel. Published within months of one another, these pioneering efforts in the establishment of a postwar Mexican American literature reaffirmed traditional verities at a time when so much of postmodern literature seemed to be putting them aside.

Rivera's characters try to reconcile their Catholicism and their belief in a higher pagan power with the cruelties and hardships that make up so much of their daily experience. Backbreaking manual labor is their life. They struggle to make sense of their experience by looking first to laboring for their own survival, then to the heavens, and finally to a netherworld of good and evil spirits where pagan gods control the sun, droughts, rain, and floods. Valued most of all in Rivera's work are human life and the dignities that human beings can muster against all the things that go wrong. In one passage, the young protagonist is in danger of losing his father to illness. He has recently learned that he is in danger of losing his younger brother as well, and despite his mother's warnings, he curses God out of grief.

> He cursed God. Upon doing it he felt the fear instilled in him by time and by his parents. For a split second he saw the earth open up to devour him. But, although he didn't look down, he then felt himself walking on very solid ground; it was harder than he had ever felt it. Anger swelled up in him again and he released it by cursing God. Then he noticed that his little brother no longer appeared quite so ill. . . . He was no longer worried about his father nor about his brother. All he looked forward to was the new day, the coolness of the morning. . . . He left for work and he was faced with a very cool morning. There were clouds and for the first time he felt himself capable of doing and undoing whatever he chose. He looked toward the ground and he kicked it and said to it, Not yet, you can't eat me yet. Someday. But I won't know.

Much of this same sense of the world is found in *Bless Me, Ultima*. Anaya's novel is set in the Santa Rosa area of central New Mexico, midway between Albuquerque and Tucumcari, not far from New Mexico's nuclear testing grounds during a period in which nuclear testing was under way. It is a grown man's memoir of a time during his childhood when his grandmother, Ultima, came to live with his family. Ultima is a *curandera*, a sorcerer who is in touch with a supernatural world of witches, both good and bad, and has magic at her fingertips. The story is set at a time in the boy's life when innocence has made him open-minded, when the wonders of nuclear power are no more or less amazing than his grandmother's magic; the boy tests these wonders, and others, against the Catholicism in which he is being raised and his father's secular way of life as a rancher. The novel ends with the protagonist struggling to make sense of what he has experienced, aware, as an adult, that the answer must be found in a synthesis between a belief in God and a belief in the supernatural, between sacred beliefs and secular beliefs, between high technology and what the earth has to teach.

The Latino/Latina novel is much more diverse than many readers appreciate. While Anaya and Rivera are perhaps the most well known of Latino novelists, their work is not necessarily representative of a body of literature that includes José Antonio Villarreal's *Pocho* (1959), John Rechy's *City of Night* (1963), Alfredo Véa, Jr.'s *La Maravilla* (1994), Arturo Islas's *The Rain God* (1984), María Amparo Escandón's *Esperanza's Box of Saints* (1999), Oscar Hijuelos's *The Mambo Kings Play Songs of Love* (1989) and *Empress of the Splendid Season* (1999), Julia Alvarez's *In the Time of the Butterflies* (1994), Sandra Cisneros's *The House on Mango Street* (1984), and Junot Díaz's *The Brief Wondrous Life of Oscar Wao* (2007). For example, Cisneros's roots are Mexican American, and her setting is the American Southwest. *The House on Mango Street* is a fragmented narrative, a journal of civic events distilled by the author into stunning lyric moments. Díaz's Pulitzer Prize-winning *The Brief Wondrous Life of Oscar Wao* is even less conventional, told through several points of view and featuring extended footnotes, with a strong narrative voice describing the brutality of Rafael Trujillo, the dictator of the Dominican Republic, where the author was born. The novel combines elements of Magical Realism, metafiction, science fiction, and fantasy in telling the story of a Dominican American's search for identity in urban New Jersey. By contrast, the Pulitzer Prize-winning Hijuelos writes rather conventionally structured novels. Of Cuban descent, Hijuelos focuses on the collision of an immigrant's dreams with the realities of life in large, East Coast cities. How does one maintain a distinctly Cuban identity in a country where the key to survival seems to be to reinvent oneself repeatedly? How does one convey Cuban identity to one's children? His *Empress of the Splendid Season* explores the lives of one Cuban American family over fifty years, taking readers from pre-Fidel Castro Cuba to the 1990's by passing the narrative from one character's point of view to another's.

The African American novel

A relatively clear pattern can be found in the development of novels written by African American men. This literary tradition began with slave narratives in the nineteenth century, such as those of Frederick Douglass. It developed through the Harlem Renaissance of the 1920's—where jazz music influenced the poetry of Countée Cullen, Claude McKay, and others—and reached new heights just before and just after World War II with the novellas and novels of Richard Wright (*Uncle Tom's Children*, 1938; *Native Son*, 1940) and James Baldwin (*Go Tell It on the Mountain*, 1953; *Giovanni's Room*, 1956). After World War II, Ellison and younger writers such as Ernest J. Gaines (*A Gathering of Old Men*, 1983), David Bradley (*The Chaneysville Incident*, 1981), Charles Johnson (*Dreamer*, 1998), and Randall Kenan (*A Visitation of Spirits*, 1989) chronicled, in relatively conventional forms, the difficulties of African Americans in finding personhood in a predominantly white culture while still keeping intact what is strongest about their own heritage. Meanwhile, Amiri Baraka (*The System of Dante's Hell*, 1965), Ishmael Reed (*Yellow Back Radio Broke-Down*, 1969; *Mumbo Jumbo*, 1972), and others began to experiment with language, blur the distinctions between conventional narrative forms, and explore alternative systems of beliefs.

No such clear developmental pattern can be found in the work of African American women, yet the body of literature they have produced is impressive, including Toni Cade Bambara's *The Salt Eaters* (1980), Alice Walker's *The Color Purple* (1982) and *Possessing the Secret of Joy* (1992), Gloria Naylor's *The Women of Brewster Place: A Novel in Seven Stories* (1982), and Jamaica Kincaid's *Lucy* (1990) and *The Autobiography of My Mother* (1996). Of the African American women writers who emerged after World War II, the greatest longevity was demonstrated by Paule Marshall, whose *Brown Girl, Brownstones* (1959) chronicles a young Barbadian girl's experiences as an immigrant in an

American city. Although initially ignored, the novel was reissued in 1981 to great acclaim, and Marshall's popularity increased with her later work, including *Praisesong for the Widow* (1983), *The Chosen Place, the Timeless People* (1969), *Daughters* (1991), and *The Fisher King* (2000).

Toni Morrison, who won the Nobel Prize in Literature in 1993, has produced an impressive body of work: In addition to plays and works of nonfiction, she has published many well-respected novels, including *The Bluest Eye* (1970), *Song of Solomon* (1977), *Tar Baby* (1981), the Pulitzer Prize-winning *Beloved* (1987), *Paradise* (1998), *Love* (2003), and *A Mercy* (2008). Morrison's central concerns are the relationships between black men and women; the necessity for black women to find, within a community of women, new ways of understanding themselves beyond the identity taken from the men in their lives; and the manner in which these women pass on to their children what is best in themselves and their pasts. The Bible, myth, legend, and the supernatural play significant roles in her writing. She has explained that one of her intentions is

> to blend the acceptance of the supernatural and a profound rootedness in the real world at the same time with neither taking precedence over the other. It is indicative of the cosmology, the way in which Black people looked at the world. We are a very practical people, very down-to-earth, even shrewd people. But within that practicality we also accepted what I suppose could be called superstition and magic, which is another way of knowing things.

Morrison is certainly to be counted among the best novelists in the United States. *Beloved*, perhaps her finest novel, is a slave narrative and nineteenth century family saga that blends the natural and the supernatural. The title character is a ghost, the lost daughter of the novel's protagonist, Sethe, who escapes from brutal slave masters. Sethe kills the child when her masters catch her rather than allow Beloved to live a life of enslavement. Sethe subsequently spends her days trying "to beat back the past," without much success. The house in which she lives is filled by the child's restless spirit. Sethe's experiences as a slave remain so fresh in her memory that she calls them "rememories," for they are as present and immediate as any experience she might be having at the moment. The task Morrison sets her protagonist is to get that past behind her somehow and get on with her life. This process begins when Beloved's spirit materializes. She appears on Sethe's property in the flesh, demanding a place in Sethe's life and her world. Beloved's presence threatens the weak hold that Sethe has on her living daughter, Denver, as well as Sethe's relationship with a man, Paul D. It is only after Sethe can come to terms with Beloved that she can reaffirm her relationships with Denver and Paul D and step outside her house toward the future.

The feminist novel

Several African American women, such as Audre Lorde, Patricia J. Williams, Barbara Smith, and Alice Walker, are often classified as feminist writers, although Walker prefers the term "womanist" to describe the perspective of women of color. During the 1970's, feminist literature was associated with a particular left-of-center political agenda that connoted a call for political activism. Marge Piercy, Rita Mae Brown, Allison Lurie, Susan Fromberg Schaeffer, and Erica Jong were included in this category. Readers of these authors' novels often expected certain themes to be addressed, certain plot situations to be explored, and characters to develop in particular ways. However, the body of work produced by women novelists after World War II has been so much richer than these expectations that to speak of a feminist novel today is probably to refer to a novel in which the main characters are female and the novel itself has been written by a woman who explores issues thought to bear more immediately on the lives of women than on those of men.

Since World War II, numerous women have been recognized for their writing achievements. The highly esteemed National Book Critics Circle Award provides examples: Women who have received this honor include Louise Erdrich for *Love Medicine*, Morrison for *Song of Solomon*, Anne Tyler for *The Accidental Tourist* (1985), Carol Shields for *The Stone Diaries* (1993), Penelope Fitzgerald for *The Blue Flower* (1996), Marilynne Robinson for *Gilead* (2004), and Kiran Desai for *The Inheritance of Loss* (2006). Among Jewish American writers, Cynthia Ozick's work is as important as the later work of

Roth or Bellow as a chronicle of the Jewish experience. While skillful artisans with wide and faithful followings such as Robert Stone, Thomas Berger, and John Irving produced novels such as *Damascus Gate* (1998), *The Return of Little Big Man* (1999), and *A Widow for One Year* (1998), respectively, Rosellen Brown, E. Annie Proulx, and Barbara Kingsolver moved to the fore as serious and popular novelists of their generation. Similarly, with novels such as *Barn Blind* (1980), *Ten Days in the Hills* (2007), and her Pulitzer Prize-winning *A Thousand Acres* (1991), a novel based on William Shakespeare's *King Lear* (pr. c. 1605-1606), Jane Smiley demonstrates great literary breadth.

In the twenty-first century, novels by and about women continue to demonstrate the diversity of female experience. Jhumpa Lahiri, who won the Pulitzer Prize for her first collection of short stories, tells the tale of a contemporary couple who emigrate from India to the United States in *The Namesake* (2003). Geraldine Brooks won the 2006 Pulitzer Prize for fiction for *March* (2005), a historical novel based on Louisa May Alcott's *Little Women* (1868). While major writers, including Morrison and Joyce Carol Oates, continue to publish highly regarded work, new writers, including lesbian authors Sarah Waters and Carissa Halston, Arab American Diana Abu-Jaber, and Dominican American Angie Cruz, experiment with new themes and ideas while working within largely traditional forms.

Literature is not a contest; it is not gender war. To frame matters in these terms is simply to acknowledge that American women novelists began to come into their own after World War II and to suggest that the novels they have produced may be changing the American novel itself. One of the changes is the importance assigned to family. From its outset, the American novel has been most at home with lone male figures setting out on their own or with other male companions to perform heroic acts in the open spaces of America. Examples include Natty Bumppo and Chingachgook in the forests of the upper East Coast, Huckleberry Finn and Slave Jim floating south on the Mississippi, Ishmael and Queequeg shipping out aboard the *Pequod* to hunt whale, and, later, Hemingway's characters at war on foreign shores or hunting in Africa. In any case, American novels have favored self-sufficient men establishing their presence far afield from where family really matters. If anything, wives, children, and family have been equated with the civilizing forces of middle-class life, which has been depicted as the proper domain of women rather than men. This tradition can still be seen in such contemporary novels as *One Flew over the Cuckoo's Nest*. When McMurphy seeks to restore the inmates of the asylum to a proper state of manhood, he removes them from the purview of the nurse, taking them out to sea, "where men are men, and boats are boats."

Many women have responded to the same postwar disorientation explored by lonely, isolated, anxious protagonists. Theirs is certainly not an affirmation of the middle-class nuclear family; if their books are to be trusted, the nuclear American family is in desperate trouble, maybe in irreparable shape. What they have proffered instead is an alternative to being lost and alone. A new kind of "tribal" family may be on the horizon, one in part composed of blood relationships but in larger part depending on a loose community of people with shared experiences coming together in support of one another.

Another change in American novels concerns space, specifically interior, domesticated space. Literally and metaphorically, much in the American grain has pointed protagonists toward the open frontier. This was where real life was to be lived. What readers have longed for in protagonists is the great deed, and only in such an untrammeled space could an American protagonist impose himself fully on the landscape. Women provide a counterpoint. The title of Smiley's *A Thousand Acres*, for instance, refers to one thousand acres of rich farmland with which the patriarch of the family, Larry Cook, identifies a lifetime's work. It exists for him in time and space; he can touch it with his hands. Readers gradually realize that the defining moments in the family saga take place indoors, however, not in the fields; to ignore this fact is to miss more than half of the story. In Marilynne Robinson's *Home* (2008), the protagonists Glory and her brother, Jack, end their years of wandering—physically and emotionally—when they return to the small town and the home where they were raised.

Another change is seen in the rituals through which people create communities. Gossip, birthing, household chores, and preparing, serving, and eating food—matters that have been ignored or mocked in the American traditional novel—are now being given credence as paramount moments of human experience. In Smiley's *A Thousand Acres*, for instance, eating together signals more than filling one's stomach, just as preparing and serving food become defining moments in a family's well-being. To eat without being a community is to be a family in desperate trouble.

Finally, there seem to be two evolving views of the world that are apt to come into conflict with each other. It is often said that men are vilified in many novels by women, but, in fact, vilification is less the issue than how the men in these novels make sense of their lives. The men are much more trusting in the powers of logic and reason than are the women. Whether using myth, legend, the spirit world, the supernatural, or simply intuition—a "sixth sense"—the women are more likely than the men to be open to alternative modes of understanding.

The novel after the Cold War

The post-Cold War novel, which includes much of what is called postcolonial literature, comprises the work of novelists such as Paul Scott (*The Raj Quartet*, 1979) and Salman Rushdie (*The Satanic Verses*, 1988), who explore the cultures of developing nations as they emerge from domination by declining world empires. The term has also been used more loosely, however, to categorize Charles Frazier's *Cold Mountain* (1997), an American Civil War epic that chronicles with methodical detail the realities of nineteenth century battle, and David Guterson's popular *Snow Falling on Cedars* (1994), which blends a World War II-era history of the American Northwest with an oddly lyrical murder mystery.

The novel after the Cold War changed from its earlier modernist and postmodernist manifestations. Postmodernism has been identified with a period of history during which the fate of the world was defined by the tensions between two new superpowers, the Soviet Union and the United States. This brings up questions of whether the collapse of the Soviet Union has caused the world, and its literature, to change diametrically and whether a new era, a "post-postmodern" era, has begun. What is certain is that novels are changing, and they will continue to be much richer than the categories that have been employed in attempts to appreciate them.

By privileging gender and ethnicity, critics may well have created categories that obscure as well as inform an understanding of literature. The concerns of women and people of color, as well as others claiming their place in the literary arena—gays and lesbians, people of different faiths, members of different socioeconomic classes—may well be part of something still more profound, an attempt to find alternative means of understanding human experience. The novel no longer has full faith in what the Enlightenment had to teach. Reason is more limited than one might suspect for negotiating a confused and confusing world. Logic can take one only so far.

When it was first published, Jay McInerney's *Bright Lights, Big City* (1984) was hailed as his generation's anthem to life on the fast track. In retrospect, it may be something more. It may well be in line with precisely this sentiment. With the failure of his brief marriage and the departure of his bride, the protagonist loses his job and surrenders to a devastating cocaine addiction that he has been battling. Only after he has lost everything of value near the novel's climax does he begin to understand his dilemma. It is not the loss of his bride that has brought him to this point, but rather the death of his mother and his estrangement from his own family. He has brought disastrous values to the fast track of upwardly mobile, big-city life, and this has left him unprepared to cope with daily living. In the book's final moments, he is in front of a bakery at dawn. Strung out on drugs, he is reminded by the smell of baking bread of his last visit home while his mother was alive. A deliveryman throws him a bag of bread as one might toss such a bag to an indigent. The novel ends with these words:

> You get down on your knees and tear open the bag. The smell of warm dough envelops you. The first bite sticks in your throat and you almost gag. You will have to go slowly. You will have to learn everything all over again.

Jay Boyer
Updated by Cynthia A. Bily

Bibliography

Aldridge, John W. *Talents and Technicians*. New York: New York University Press, 1992. Addresses developments in the American novel at the end of the twentieth century through discussion of the works of Jay McInerney, Ann Beattie, Donald Barthelme, Brett Easton Ellis, and others of their generation. Aldridge is a noted scholar whose *After the Lost Generation* (1951, 1985) is a landmark study of American modernism; his *The American Novel and the Way We Live Now* (1983) addresses the novel's transition from modernism to postmodernism.

Bell, Bernard W. *The Contemporary African American Novel: Its Folk Roots and Modern Literary Branches*. Amherst: University of Massachusetts Press, 2004. Presents a history of the development of the African American novel beginning in 1853, with analyses of modernism, postmodernism, metafiction, and genre literature.

Bilton, Alan. *An Introduction to Contemporary American Fiction*. New York: New York University Press, 2003. Offers a critical and theoretical introduction to postmodern writers Don DeLillo, Paul Auster, Cormac McCarthy, Rolando Hinojosa, E. Annie Proulx, Bret Easton Ellis, Douglas Coupland, and Thomas Pynchon. Includes biographical information, a glossary, and bibliographies.

Geyh, Paula, Fred G. Leebron, and Andrew Levy, eds. *Postmodern American Fiction: A Norton Anthology*. New York: W. W. Norton, 1997. First volume of the Norton Anthology series devoted solely to postmodernism, and one of the best samplers available on postmodern American fiction. Offers a wide range of readings and informative guides.

Harvey, David. *The Condition of Postmodernity: An Enquiry into the Origins of Cultural Change*. Reprint. Cambridge, Mass.: Blackwell, 2008. Classic study of postmodernity in art, architecture, economics, and post-World War II culture in general. Establishes a context for the reading of contemporary literature.

Levitt, Morton. *The Rhetoric of Modernist Fiction from a New Point of View*. Lebanon, N.H.: University Press of New England, 2006. Offers examinations of various aspects of contemporary fiction, including point of view, narration and narrators, internal monologue, and metafiction.

Millard, Kenneth. *Contemporary American Fiction*. New York: Oxford University Press, 2000. Presents discussion of dozens of the central works in American contemporary long fiction, including novels by Toni Morrison, Barbara Kingsolver, Alice Walker, Cormac McCarthy, and John Updike.

Muller, Gilbert H. *New Strangers in Paradise: The Immigrant Experience and Contemporary American Fiction*. Lexington: University Press of Kentucky, 1999. Focuses on writings by immigrants displaced by the Holocaust as well as by immigrants from Latin America, the Caribbean, and Asia.

Sakrajda, Mira. *Postmodern Discourses of Love*. New York: Peter Lang, 1999. Explores the topic of love in fiction and its absence from the works of Thomas Pynchon, John Barth, Robert Coover, and other contemporary novelists.

Tabbi, Joseph. *Postmodern Sublime*. Ithaca, N.Y.: Cornell University Press, 1995. Ambitious study addresses postmodern literature from Norman Mailer to the cyberpunk genre. Posits that an ambivalence toward technology unites otherwise disparate literary texts.

Wirth-Nesher, Hana, and Michael P. Kramer, eds. *The Cambridge Companion to Jewish American Literature*. New York: Cambridge University Press, 2003. Fifteen essays address various issues in Jewish American literature, including gender, race, politics, and identity. Also discusses the influence of Hebrew and Yiddish literature on the works of American Jewish authors.

World
Long Fiction

African Long Fiction

The term "African," when applied in this essay to the novel and other literary genres, does not include the Arab states of the north or the peoples of European descent who may have settled in Africa. It refers to the black, indigenous peoples in the southern two-thirds of the continent who, to a limited extent, share a common culture. The geographical area extends from Senegal in the west to Kenya and Somalia in the east and southward to the Cape of Good Hope. It encompasses more than thirty-five countries, which are themselves often arbitrary divisions that cut across tribal groups with different languages and customs. It might seem strange amid all of this diversity to speak of an African novel, rather than, for example, a Kenyan or a Yoruba novel. A few countries, in fact—notably Nigeria—have established their own written literary traditions. What makes the situation even more complicated is that African novels, with a few exceptions, have not been written in African but in European languages, such as French, English, or Portuguese. Thus, most scholars, both African and foreign, attempting to understand the totality of the fiction, while not having to deal with multiple African languages, nevertheless do face a language barrier. In spite of these obstacles and differences, the African novel is a meaningful and manageable category.

Though the history of written African prose goes back at least as far as Olaudah Equiano's *The Interesting Narrative of the Life of Olaudah Equiano: Or, Gustavus Vassa, the African, Written by Himself* (1789), that is, to the era of the slave trade, and even further back if one includes the Islamic presence in the Sahel and cultural centers such as Timbuktu during the medieval period, the African novel itself is a relatively recent phenomenon. The first African novel is thought to have been *Ethiopia Unbound: Studies in Race Emancipation* (1911), written in English by Joseph Ephraim Casely Hayford (also known as Ekra-Agiman), who lived in what is now Ghana. Published a decade later, René Maran's *Batouala* (1921; English translation, 1922), pretended to be an attack on colonialism but actually reflected European perceptions. Its author, son of Guyanese parents but born in Martinique, did not spend an extended period of time in Africa until he was twenty-three. Other examples of prose fiction before the 1950's include the famous African tales of Birago Diop, various oral chronicles in written form, and novels derivative of the French. D. O. Fagunwa's *Ogboju Ode Ninu Igbo Irunmale* (1939; translated by Wole Soyinka as *Forest of a Thousand Daemons*, 1984), written in his native Yoruba, and Amos Tutuola's *The Palm-Wine Drinkard* (1952), written in a dialect of English that captures the primitive tone of oral folk tales, both transform traditional myths and legends into a longer structure that approaches novel form but captures a truly African spirit.

Though Peter Abrahams of South Africa anticipated the movement by about ten years with *Mine Boy* (1946), the true flowering of the novel came in the 1950's with Camara Laye's *L'Enfant noir* (1953; *The Dark Child*, 1954; also known as *The African Child*), Cyprian Ekwensi's *People of the City* (1954; revised 1963), and Chinua Achebe's *Things Fall Apart* (1958). Since that time, the novel has been a consistently popular form, especially in francophone and anglophone regions. From a multitude of rising novelists, several have emerged as accomplished artists and have attained an international reputation and classic status. Among these writers from francophone countries are Cheikh Hamidou Kane and Ousmane Sembène of Senegal, Ferdinand Oyono and Mongo Beti of Cameroon, Camara Laye of Guinea, and Yambo Ouologuem of Mali. Anglophone novelists include Ayi Kwei Armah and Ama Ata Aidoo of Ghana; Buchi Emecheta, Chinua Achebe, Wole Soyinka, and Ben Okri of Nigeria; Ngugi wa Thiong'o and Grace Ogot of Kenya; Nuruddin Farah of Somalia; and Peter Abrahams, Ezekiel Mphahlele, Bessie Head, and Alex La Guma of South Africa. This impressive array of novelists is part of a genuine literary revival in Africa, coinciding with political resistance to colonialism after 1945 and the declarations of independence in the late 1950's and early 1960's. There is a nearly unanimous feeling of responsibility among these writers toward their own peoples, but also toward the continent as a whole. At the same time, they form an elite literary community that is acutely aware of itself, within which literary influences are common; they have begun to create a written African literary tradition. This fact, together with the brevity of its history, makes it still possible to view the African novel holistically.

Furthermore, in the contemporary world, being African as well as Senegalese or Ghanaian is a political reality. The African novel has developed within an international context; the novelists have undergone extensive exposure to the West, and the subject of the novels was, until the 1980's and 1990's, almost exclusively the impact of colonialism. There is a feeling of commonality among black Africans because they have shared the same history over the past several centuries: the slave trade, economic exploitation, colonialism, liberation, and political and economic instability during the postindependence years. They have undergone a common psychological experience. Whatever the particular tribal myths and customs might have been, the immediate problems of survival in the face of foreign intimidation have prompted a self-consciousness and a common purpose. In a sense, the West has made Black Africa aware of itself. The novel has played a significant role in this coming to awareness.

Finally, there is a powerful ideological factor responsible for African unity. Behind the violent initiation into the industrial age, there was not only an expansionist policy of exploitation and conquest but also an assumption among the colonizers that the old Africa was primitive and superstitious, that its cultures were markedly inferior to those cultures that colonized it. In order to counter and modify that image, certain African thinkers as early as the eighteenth century, but especially in the nineteenth and twentieth centuries, who had lived in the West and had received a Western education, challenged the primitive image and insisted on the value of their own culture.

Léopold Senghor of Senegal coined the term "negritude" to identify the black peoples of the world, including those peoples no longer living on the African continent. For him, it indicated the collective consciousness of the race. He distinguished African individuals by their different mode of consciousness: Theirs was essentially an emotional response to things, not an intellectual one. Their reason was intuitive, not analytical. Rather than the Cartesian "I think, therefore I am," Senghor posited the African "I feel, I dance the other." This definition of the African was long perceived as a francophone response to the French assimilation policy that tried to create a French mentality among the colonized. Abiola Irele, however, convincingly showed in *The African Experience in Literature and Ideology* (1981) that the concept of an African personality—developed among anglophone Africans in the nineteenth century—was essentially the same, emphasizing the communal, religious sense of the world as characteristic of all Africans, regardless of tribe or region. Both concepts, the one epistemological, the other ontological, are Pan-African and have as their purpose the establishing of a positive, dynamic image for the oppressed peoples of the subcontinent. As a concept within the literary world, negritude, or the African personality, has had such influence and aroused such controversy as to warrant special attention.

Negritude and the novel

The concept of negritude, perhaps because of its emotive and mystical dimension, originally found literary expression in poetry rather than fiction. Léopold Senghor himself was a poet as well as a philosophical apologist and political leader. Nevertheless, it appears as a basic assumption in the novel as well, especially those by such francophone writers as Cheikh Hamidou Kane, Camara Laye, and Mongo Beti. Kane's classic work, *L'Aventure ambiguë* (1961; *Ambiguous Adventure*, 1963), presents the tragic psychological and spiritual confrontation of two mentalities. Nurtured as a child within the rituals and mystical atmosphere of an African animism modified by Islam, in which he experienced a spiritual oneness with the universe, the hero, Samba Diallo, becomes a student in a French educational system that is characterized by Cartesian dualism. His fate is to end his life with no identity at all, torn between the two worlds. The only way he has to rejoin the universe that was once his is to die, a service symbolically performed by a madman on his home soil. Though Kane was himself from the French colony of Senegal, as is his hero, the novel seems designed to represent the archetypal situation of a Western-educated African during the 1950's. It laments the loss of spiritual fulfillment and, at the end, reasserts its primacy. Laye, in his autobiographical novel *The Dark Child*, gives an even more complete picture of traditional life, this time in a Malinké village of French Guinea: the ancient customs, the daily presence of the supernatural, the animism, the honored craft of the goldsmith, and the terrifying ritual of circumcision.

Laye's second novel, one of the most impressive creations by an African writer, *Le Regard du roi* (1954; *The Radiance of the King*, 1956), is perhaps the most striking example of the concept of negritude incorporated into fiction. Laye dramatizes Senghor's idea that the West needs the imaginative and spiritual qualities of the black race as much as the African has needed the technical and intellectual lessons of the colonizers. The hero is a white man, Clarence, a rarity in African fiction. At the beginning of the novel, he is the typical arrogant expatriate, with the usual sense of superiority to the blacks around him—even though, with his careless sense that as a white man he is invulnerable, he is practically destitute. Laye puts him through a series of adventures, in particular a long symbolic journey through Africa and the life of a stud in a harem. His journey is in search of the African King, who holds court in the south. Though he originally believes that his race qualifies him to speak to the king, by the end he has cast off his Western assumptions about time, money, work, and inalienable rights and has humbled himself before the mysteries of things, of the senses, and of spiritual transcendence. Laye has thus done more than assert the difference between the West and Africa; he has dramatized the primacy of the senses and the spirit, which the West has lost but which the African still possesses.

Certainly not all francophone writers place such faith in the endurance of an African consciousness. Though Mongo Beti often draws striking contrasts between the two cultures, his satiric purpose either throws emphasis on the insidious danger of Western education and religion or exposes the naïveté and vulnerability of traditional village life. In Beti's *Le Pauvre Christ de Bomba* (1956; *The Poor Christ of Bomba*, 1971), it is primarily the central character, the Reverend Father Drumont, who represents the intolerance and insensitivity of the Catholic Church as it attempts to stamp out pagan practices. By the end of the novel, as his failure to convert the natives drives him back to France, he comes to a notional awareness of the inadequacy of himself and his religion, but, as Eustace Palmer has demonstrated in *The Growth of the African Novel* (1979), he remains blind to his real responsibility for the changes in Bomba and continues to sadistically project his frustrations through his punishments of the young girls at the mission who have violated his rule of chastity. Lying behind the Catholic vision of reality is the indigenous sense of the sacred and the natural purity of sex, but they seem already removed from their original state. The narrator, Dennis, an acolyte in the Mission of Drumont, has long since lost the mentality of the native village. He exits the novel to work for a Greek merchant.

In another of Beti's novels, *Mission terminée* (1957; *Mission Accomplished*, 1958; better known as *Mission to Kala*), the sixteen-year-old narrator, Jean-Marie, returns to his native village after attending school in the French educational system. He has recently failed his examination, and his education has obviously been incomplete, but the village perceives him as a hero. It is not Jean-Marie, however, who truly knows the world, but the peers he left behind. Gradually, he is initiated into the traditional life of the village and experiences sexual fulfillment. In making a comment on the degrees of usefulness in the education provided by the two societies, Beti assumes a negritudist view of traditional African life. Still, the description is double-edged. Beti satirizes the Kalans for their romanticizing of foreign learning and attacks the father in particular, as Palmer notes, for his authoritarian insistence on his son's getting a Western education. The father's tyranny, which may reflect a flaw in the traditional society, drives Jean-Marie away. He, like so many other African heroes, is left wandering between the two worlds. Beti seems pessimistic about the African clinging to a traditional consciousness.

One francophone writer in particular, Yambo Ouologuem, completely rejects the notion of negritude; the naturalistic panorama of African history in his chronicle-novel, *Le Devoir de violence* (1968; *Bound to Violence*, 1971), unmasks the naked truth. What characterizes Africa (and humankind in general), according to myth, legend, and history, is a penchant for violence, sexual perversion, and political subjugation. Skepticism toward negritude, though it does not elsewhere reach this extreme, is most prevalent among anglophone writers, who have tended to see it as idealistic, needlessly theoretical, and impractical. This idea seems to reflect an "English" insistence on fact and may be the result, to some extent, of English education and English colonial policy. Chinua Achebe, for example, has written two novels that are anthropological rather than theoretical in emphasis: *Things Fall Apart* and *Arrow of God* (1964).

Nigerian playwright and novelist Wole Soyinka attacked the concept of negritude directly with his now famous and influential statement that the tiger does not declare his "tigritude." Yet Soyinka is among the most consistent defenders of African tradition. He objects to what he regards as the backward-looking, nostalgic flavor of the negritudist theory, as well as its vague simplicity and especially its implied acceptance and even glorification of the exploiter's myth about the African personality. Soyinka contends, in *Myth, Literature, and the African World* (1976), for example, that the blacks on the subcontinent are not simply intuitive, sensuous beings, but are as practical, analytical, and sophisticated as their Western counterparts. When he returns to the past and the essential African spirit, it is to recall and reinterpret the myths of his own Yoruban culture, to bring them alive within the contemporary setting. In his novels (as well as his plays), his modern characters are often embodiments of mythical figures; the creator or poet is the servant of the traditional Promethean-Dionysian god, Ogun, and the situations are repetitions of archetypal patterns.

Soyinka's first novel, *The Interpreters* (1965), captures this sense of the past impinging on the present. His "interpreters" are Western-educated Nigerians futilely trying to balance the two worlds in their psyches, to change a society that has imitated and perpetuated the worst features of the new and the old. Although Soyinka uses particular details from his own Yoruban myth and theology, his aim, as his political pronouncements indicate, is Pan-African. Soyinka's second novel, *Season of Anomy* (1973), although somewhat more sensational and melodramatic, follows archetypal patterns, including a paradisal view of precolonial Africa, that assume generalizations about the African continent and, at the same time, provide a point of contact with a foreign consciousness.

Another anglophone novelist, Ayi Kwei Armah, based two of his novels on the myth of an African way of life, kept alive by religious leaders, warrior priests, and their followers, who pass the secret down from generation to generation in anticipation of an age when the entire society will be ready to accept it. One is tempted to assume that Armah regards himself and other African intellectuals as members of this secret community. While Armah has a mythical imagination and pan-African aspirations, he does not fit easily into the negritudist concept of Africa. Ousmane Sembène, much more clearly, though a French-speaking African from Senegal, exhibits certain practical, political instincts that place him in the Anglophone camp. In Sembène's novel *Le Dernier de l'empire* (1981; *The Last of the Empire*, 1983), the major character rejects Senghor's romantic vision of Africa in favor of native social values that are not simple responses to a myth of Africa perpetuated by white people. Though originally Marxist-inspired, as is evident in the earlier novels, Sembène seems to be envisioning a truly African socialism drawn from traditional sources. Again, however, even when the negritudist position is called into question, the alternative is not usually an insistence on local or provincial values but on values that include the entire subcontinent.

The language problem

From the point of view of negritude, of the African personality, or of an alternative, there emerges a concept of Africa as one entity that has to some extent contributed to the shaping of an African novel. That is, African writers seem to have a consciousness of themselves that extends beyond their tribal origins or "national" identity. Theirs is a rather special situation in the modern world. What makes it even more special is the language they choose for their works. In the brief history of the African novel, practitioners have in most cases been at least bilingual. They have their own tribal language, which often offers no written tradition, and they have the language of the European country that colonized their regions—in whose educational system they received their introduction to Western culture and literature. Almost without exception, African novelists have expressed themselves in the official European language. Obviously, the choice of a foreign linguistic medium works against the expression of an indigenous African personality, for it is extremely difficult to communicate the mentality of a tribe (or a race) without using the language in which the instinctive responses to life are learned. To put them into another language is tantamount to translating the rhythms of native speech into a foreign idiom. This concept has raised the basic aesthetic problem that writing a novel in French, English, or Portuguese would seem to deny the importance of its Africanness.

Without dismissing the significance of this fact, one must also admit that choosing a European language has enabled writers to cross tribal and national boundaries. Not that the use of a foreign tongue was entirely a matter of choice; certain conditions dictated it. It was through the study of the novel in the foreign idiom that the first generations of African novelists learned their craft. Their audience was not, in the beginning, within Africa but in Europe, and indeed the early novels, satiric attacks on Western culture and defenses of a traditional African culture, were largely addressed to a foreign readership. In addition, financial realities dictated foreign publication. Now that there is an established Western-educated elite in Africa, readership has expanded and evolved. Still, in order to speak to the entire continent, and not only to one tribe within one or two countries whose members speak the novelist's mother tongue, European languages have remained the primary means of communication.

Sembène found film, not the novel, to be an effective means of using the local language. After writing three successful novels in English, Ngugi wa Thiong'o renounced the language of the British colonizers and began writing only in his native Kikuyu and in Swahili, the lingua franca of much of East Africa. In his novels *Caitaani Mũtharaba-Inĩ* (1980; *Devil on the Cross*, 1982), *Matigari ma Njiruungi* (1986; *Matigari*, 1989), and *Mũrogi wa Kagogo* (2004; *Wizard of the Crow,* 2006), Ngugi speaks directly to the Kikuyu people in Kenya by writing in their common language. *Devil on the Cross* was popular enough to go through three editions in Kikuyu; he then translated the novel into English, trying to preserve the native idiom.

Ngugi aside, because the African novel has usually been written in the language of the colonizer, it has had to contend with a corollary issue: whether it is, in fact, an appendage of the mother country—that is, an extension of French or English literature. One of the literary issues facing the African novel, then, is its uniqueness. Has the novelist been able to manipulate the language so that it has become an African medium, or is language itself so essentially a part of culture that Africans must use their own to express their Africanness? Dealt with in this way, the issue is not political but aesthetic, and it has plagued chauvinist sentiment since the inception of the novel in the 1950's. Ngugi explores the full implications of language for African writers in *Decolonising the Mind: The Politics of Language in African Literature* (1986).

Chinua Achebe was perhaps the most successful in dealing with the problem, both in his criticism (*Morning Yet on Creation Day*, 1975) and in his novels. The two set in a traditional village during the colonial era (*Things Fall Apart* and *Arrow of God*) overcome the barrier by imitating the pattern of Igbo thought in the structure of the English sentence, relying on images and figures of speech from the local setting, and sprinkling traditional proverbs throughout the narrative and dialogue. The novels set in more modern times (*No Longer at Ease*, 1960, *A Man of the People*, 1966, and *Anthills of the Savannah,* 1987) continue this practice to some extent, but they rely also on the pidgin English of contemporary Nigeria. Achebe's predecessor in Nigeria, Amos Tutuola, who achieved a kind of notoriety through his use of nonidiomatic English in *The Palm-Wine Drinkard*, raises his own aesthetic and generic problems. Some novelists, such as Achebe, Soyinka, Ngugi, and Ahmadou Kourouma, seem to have found a satisfactory linguistic compromise. Others have not seen the issue as crucial or have found different ways to reflect an African quality in the total structure and technique. While novelists in Africa have had to experiment with the form, a slowly developing tradition led away from formal realism toward Magical Realism in the 1980's and 1990's, influenced no doubt by Latin American authors.

The major theme: A quest for identity

Whatever else may be said to distinguish the African novel from its Western counterparts—whether a unique consciousness significantly modifies the conventional form—there can be no doubt about its content. The African novel has had as its subject the African experience, and formal realism has been one of the essential modes in presenting it. Colonialism is at the center of this experience. Western industrial society has forced Africa to repeat its 250-year transition within a matter of decades. The Western novel has developed over that same period; in Africa, as it evolved during the second half of the twentieth century, it became an instrument in Africa's response to the West's cultural and economic imperialism.

Formal realism has allowed African writers to describe their situation in a convincing manner and attack both foreign presumptions and local acquiescence. The novel, born of an economic era that stressed the reality of things, money, upward social mobility, materialism, and individualism, proved to be appropriate for the kind of existence the West was forcing Africa to live. The African novel is both description and critique, but it has an ultimate goal. Its subject, viewed holistically, is a search for identity. Africa presents a special instance of this significant theme in modern literature, which Robert Langbaum, in his study *The Mysteries of Identity* (1977), explores in such "romantic" figures as William Wordsworth, William Butler Yeats, and D. H. Lawrence. For Langbaum, identity and humanity are interchangeable. The denial of humanity by industrial and technological progress, however, is compounded in Africa by the attempt of the West over the past several centuries to assert its superiority in all aspects of culture. The West has put Africans in the position of denying the value of their past. In order to recover that past, defend it, put it into perspective, and deal with the modern threat and its consequences, novelists have examined the various stages of Africa's contact with the West. Four periods in African history have come under scrutiny: the precolonial era, when the African village was supposedly intact; the colonial era, during which the central motif was a conflict of cultures; the resistance movement and the establishment of independent states; and finally the ensuing period of self-rule, dominated by economic distress, political corruption, and what Ngugi calls "neocolonialism." In this final phase, experimental novelists suggested new directions in thought and aesthetics. A few novels from the last half of the twentieth century and the beginning of the twenty-first attempt to give a panoramic view, but most concentrate on one or two of these phases.

The precolonial era

The attempt to re-create African society before the arrival of Europeans is generally a defense of African culture and hence of its humanity. Such depictions are often idealistic and even improbable—thus the advantage of the novel form that uses formal realism to establish the illusion of reality. Laye, in *The Dark Child*, nostalgically describes experiences that were no doubt his own in a village untouched by the outside world. Everything takes place in an atmosphere of mystery, spiritual presences, magical interactions between humans and animals, and rituals that have real and sacred meanings. The absolute faith of the young narrator as he tells the actual events of his early life in unpretentious, simple language lends credibility to the implied argument that such occurrences actually happened. This is not legend, but "fact." The sacred nature of things is named as part of the identity of the old life.

The experience of Samba Diallo in Kane's *Ambiguous Adventure* is similar, though here Islam has become an integral part of African animism and encourages an even more mystical and metaphysical identification with cosmic forces and death. When Ngugi alludes to precolonial days, as in *The River Between* (1965), he also suggests an idyllic existence; rather than re-create it, however, he usually relies upon the myths and legends about the origins of Kenya. Armah, on the other hand, in both *Two Thousand Seasons* (1973) and *The Healers* (1978), makes a daring attempt to create a timeless society that maintains the values of community and self-sacrifice. Consisting as it does of exiles who become guerrillas fighting for the restoration of old Africa, it hardly becomes credible on a realistic level. In Armah's case, the moral purpose of the search makes the demand of formal realism almost irrelevant.

On the opposite end of the spectrum is Ouologuem's *Bound to Violence*, which argues that precolonial Africa was not essentially different from its subsequent history of sadism, violence, and treachery. It is difficult to see this novel as anything but an attempt to debunk the nostalgic view of the past. Achebe, who strives to create an impression of complete objectivity, presents an interpretation of traditional African culture between the two extremes. Rather than glorify the past, he takes pains to describe its daily life, the heroism and failings of ordinary inhabitants of the village. The legends become tales that mothers tell their children. The rituals have a perceivable function within the seasonal cycle. The proverbs are practical ways of dealing with other people, with natural forces, and with the gods. Though there are protagonists in both *Things Fall Apart* and *Arrow of God* who reflect the traditional life, and though one of them is, in fact, the chief priest of the tribe, Achebe does not insist upon a mystical reality among the Igbo to which European civilization is insensitive. Both protagonists are practical, pragmatic members of society whose downfall, nevertheless, results from the human failings of pride, stubbornness, and self-interest.

The emphasis in Achebe is not so much on the cultural values as it is on the humanity of the African, which differs in no essential respect from that of the invading European, though the rhetorical argument of the novels emphasizes the African's humanity at the expense of the particular breed of Englishman representing the British Empire in Nigeria. Achebe's precolonial Africa is a rational, ordered, self-sufficient society, with a legal system capable of coping with violations to the social order, a belief in a supreme being, and a concept of the gods as human creations designed to serve human needs. He also acknowledges that certain customs in traditional life were needlessly cruel and superstitious. The balancing of the virtues and failings makes the total picture believable and lends credibility to the underlying argument that the Western view of African primitivism is prejudicial and self-serving.

The colonial era: A conflict of cultures

Though numerous African novels attempt to identify traditional life, either through an extensive treatment, as in Achebe's works, or through brief glimpses of the recent or distant past, few confine themselves exclusively to that era, recognizing perhaps the impossibility of return and the necessity of redefining the African identity within an international context. In fact, until the mid-1960's, at which time most African states had achieved their independence, the dominant subject of the novel was the initial contact between Africa and the West and the disruption of tribal life. Underlying the conflict of cultures in these novels is racism on the part of the West, which the African was not prepared to cope with, making it difficult to reestablish a clear sense of self. European culture pervaded every part of African life. European mentality and the various institutions that reflected it—the church, education, the law, and the economic system—gradually insinuated themselves into the social fabric.

Achebe's *Things Fall Apart* is a classic example of the process, modified by the author's own premise that resilience and adaptation are essential for human survival. Okonkwo is an aggressive, ambitious individual who has difficulty accommodating himself even within his own traditional world, which is in most cases flexible enough to tolerate his defiance and admire his material success. His concern over his masculine image and his unpredictable resistance to authority—natural, supernatural, or human—prove to be his downfall, however, when it is not his own tribal custom that rises to chastise him but the foreign English authority. Okonkwo's life covers the crucial period of transition between the old and the new. Though he has passed his youth and achieved his social status within a traditional framework, he has to maintain his success and his image in a changing society.

During his enforced exile of seven years for accidentally killing a member of the clan, English institutions infiltrate his native village. He returns to see his own status diminished and his fellow villagers adopting English ways. When Achebe comments on this process, he presents the typical sequence experienced in practically every African country. The missionary moves in with a new religion and a new god. The clan innocently tolerates his presence and even ridicules him, because he attracts only the social outcasts and builds his church on accursed land. In spite of expectations, the church thrives and continues to make converts, one of whom is Okonkwo's own son, rebellious against his father's authoritarian treatment. Achebe calls the church the knife that cuts the ties binding the society together: Without spiritual cohesiveness, the tribe falls apart. Into this disintegrated society enter the government and its legal system. Now Okonkwo is in danger of violating not only his own social codes but also those of white people. It is when the English administration tries to establish control over the village that Okonkwo asserts his manhood—his sense of self defined by his life within traditional society. Okonkwo symbolically lashes out by attacking a representative of the new order and, rather than be humiliated by becoming a victim of English justice, hangs himself.

Meanwhile, the third significant institution has already begun its encroachment on the minds of the villagers: Okonkwo's Christian son has been receiving an English education. He has learned how to speak and write English—the crucial first step in the new system. When the novel ends, he is already studying in a teachers' college so that he can enter the ranks of a Westernized bureaucracy. Okonkwo is symbolic of the dying order. The issue in the novel is the inevitability of change, the necessity of adaptation, and the intense desire, nevertheless, to somehow retain a sense of one's integrity, which is certainly not to be found in the unattractive picture of English character that closes the novel, the district commissioner reducing the tragedies of the village and Okonkwo to one paragraph in his projected study, *The Pacification of the Primitive Tribes of the Lower Niger*.

In much more strident and emotional fashion, Ngugi traces the same process of English exploitation. His language becomes more and more that of a revolutionary, intensified by his disenchantment with Christianity, his Marxist ideology, and the particular nature of colonialism in Kenya, which attracted not only European and American industrialists but also settlers who bought and occupied fertile Kenyan lands and subjugated the inhabitants to the role of tenants. Ngugi's strategy is often to decry this exploitation of the land. To the Kikuyu tribe, land is sacred, its possession sanctioned by the gods. Ngugi draws a parallel between the biblical story of Eden and the Kikuyu myth that defines Kenya as the garden granted to descendants of the original parents. This appeal to myth and the sacred arouses passions that Achebe chooses not to inject into his works. Still, like Achebe, Ngugi points to the Christian Church as the initial culprit in the disasters that befall his country: Missionaries are the prophets of capitalism, and hence their message is tainted. They lull the inhabitants into an acceptance of the foreigner. The education they provide seems to be the wisdom of the future, to contain the "light" of salvation. *Weep Not, Child* (1964) has as its main motif the exposure of this panacea: Acceptance of Western education and religion means submission to Western imperialism.

It is primarily in *The River Between*, however, that Ngugi presents the head-to-head conflict between traditional culture and the new Christian faith. He symbolically uses a river to separate the adherents to traditional custom and the new Christian converts. The protagonist, Waiyaki, educated within the British system but sympathetic to the spiritual life of the past, tries to unite the two. His role is complicated by his being in love with the daughter of the pastor who puritanically leads the Christian element of the population. Like Achebe, Ngugi does not see the situation as a simple black-white melodrama. Waiyaki's defeat is at the hands of devious elements within traditional society, and the Christian intruder is not a white missionary but an African who has become obsessed by the Christian message. Thus, Ngugi's attack is directed as much against the dupes of Western imperialism—who become traitors to Kenya—as against the foreign force itself. Waiyaki himself carries within him the taint of his mission-school education: He is a messianic hero, his language is sprinkled with biblical images, and his fate is that of a "Christian" martyr who, however, achieves nothing.

It is difficult to determine whether, in this early novel, Ngugi admires the young romantic individualist or looks at him ironically for his narcissism and his want of political savvy. He nevertheless offers evidence that the alien society has infiltrated the consciousness of the people and has set the old and the new forces on a collision course that a simple romantic idealism cannot prevent. The great enemies of traditional culture, for Ngugi, are Christianity and capitalism. It is the former that occupies Ngugi in this early novel and attracts more and more of his venom as his pessimism and his social and political involvement deepen.

Perhaps the most devastating critique of Christianity's impact on African culture is Beti's *The Poor Christ of Bomba*. It presents a striking contrast between the natural, uninhibited sexual attitudes and social forms of the native people of Cameroon and the Church's absolute notions of sexual purity, abstinence, and monogamy. The Reverend Father Drumont's mission to convert the natives leads not to the virgin ideal but to either total rejection of his dogma or a deceitful subversion of it that spreads syphilis throughout the region. This has both a real and a symbolic significance. The Church has not really succeeded in establishing itself, but it may, nevertheless, have contaminated the rhythms of life it has tried to replace. The novel is also a philosophical analysis of the Catholic menace. In this *roman à thèse*, Father Drumont engages in periodic discussions with the local administrator, Vidal, who views Christianity in the skeptical European manner but who regards it as an essential weapon in the struggle against Marxism in Africa. Specifically, Vidal confirms Ngugi's and Achebe's contention that the role of the missionary is to soften the natives' resistance to political and economic exploitation. At the same time, he is convinced that the introduction of French civilization is for the Africans' benefit.

Father Drumont had never shared these assumptions but had come to Cameroon as an idealist to save the natives for Christ, naïvely believing that his religion so clearly represented the truth that the lost, unfortunate natives would hunger after it. Whatever Father Drumont's failings may be at the end of his experience, he does eventually admit his ignorance and youthful innocence. In his last conversation with Vidal, he rejects his role as a prophet for capitalism. Besides, he has seen clearly that the natives' acceptance of Christianity is superficial, a purely formal one arising first out of curiosity, then out of fear and self-defense. He has never reached their souls. In addition, he recognizes that they have, almost from the start, seen through the subtle process of exploitation. Though he still makes statements that indicate an insensitivity toward their culture, he has begun to admit their intelligence and their humanity, thus emphasizing, as do other aspects of the novel, the dominant motif of colonial fiction—the insistence on an independent African identity.

These, then, are three among many African novels that treat the challenge to African identity during the initial conflict with the West. Where white characters appear, they are either stereotypes—thus reversing expectations and pointing up the depth of the African character by contrast—or, in the exceptional case of *The Poor Christ of Bomba*, complex individuals exposing the immorality and deficiency of the European in Africa. Here, it is the African who perceives and interprets human nature. These novels are set within the village, where white people are anomalies, albinos, ghosts riding their iron horses—comic precursors of doom. In these novels, one also finds the transition already beginning between the old and new orders. A few Africans have adopted Western ways, become Christian, joined the administration, learned to read and write. They have assumed an importance in society because they have the foreign government behind them. The black missionary is a potent force. It would appear that the only way to survive is to change allegiances.

Sembène, because of his atypical education and experiences among the poor, presents a special variation of the transition. His novel, *Ô pays, mon beau peuple!* (1957; oh my country, my beautiful people), is also, for the most part, set in a rural community, the Casamance region of Senegal, but establishes its ties with the urban seat of government and with the mother country, France. More important, it has as its protagonist Oumar Faye, a son of the region who has fought in the European wars, has had extensive experience in France, and has discovered and defended his identity among white people. He returns home to a people who have not yet learned that they can face up to the white political and economic leaders who are controlling their lives. His mission is to unite the farmers into a cooperative strong enough to resist pressures from the white businesspeople—a community effort that draws upon African and Marxist ideals—but also open enough to introduce technological knowledge from the West.

Again, white people tend to be stereotyped, but Sembène at least makes an attempt at compromise here, too, through a mixed marriage. Oumar brings back with him a Frenchwoman who sincerely joins in with the traditional life, eventually wins over Oumar's family, and ends the novel pregnant with a symbolic union of the two races and cultures. Sembène has obviously moved beyond a definition of the conflict toward a political and ideological solution. To some extent, he re-creates the traditional life in the family and in the fishing and farming communities, but his attitude, shaped as it is by contact with the West, tends to be critical of those customs that militate against reason, individualism, and practical adaptation to the contemporary world. Yet, through all of this, one continues to sense a loyalty to Africa, a love of the land, and a preservation of tradition.

Other novels, which transport the African to the city, deal with a later stage of the colonial period and are mainly concerned with the phenomenon of alienation and disorientation. No longer surrounded by traditional custom, the protagonists must adapt to the white people's world. Perhaps the writer who deals with this situation most extensively is Cyprian Ekwensi. This prolific storyteller has attempted to describe practically every phase of African life, including the old precolonial era, but such accounts as found in his *Burning Grass* (1962), about the Fulani herdsmen of northern Nigeria, seem more like tales than novels.

One can almost say the same about Ekwensi's stories of city life: *People of the City, Lokotown, and Other Stories* (1966), *Jagua Nana* (1961), and *Jagua Nana's Daughter* (1986). *People of the City,* the first Nigerian novel to reach an international audience, introduces a common motif: the youth who has left the village and is trying to make his way in the city. Ekwensi's rather improbable (and Western) choice to make his hero, Amusa Sango, a crime reporter and a part-time trumpeter in a dance band nevertheless gives him the opportunity to introduce practically every facet of the city's teeming life. However, improbabilities, so uncharacteristic of what one expects in a novel, plague the development of Amusa's adventures.

Ekwensi defines Amusa as the most eligible bachelor in the entire metropolis of Lagos, anxious to achieve success but addicted to pleasure and especially to women. His irresistible charm (never made convincing) almost appears to be authorial wish-fulfillment, as not only the loose women of the city but also the respectable seek him out and involve him in seemingly inextricable situations. Aina, a Moll Flanders type, enters the novel as his mistress, soon goes to jail as a thief, and eventually uses her pregnancy (by another man) to appeal to his conscience, while her vindictive mother, thinking he is responsible for her imprisonment, unsuccessfully tries to implicate him in an illegal racket. Beatrice, a social climber who attaches herself to numerous successful men, but especially white men, also becomes Amusa's mistress. Then there is Elina, Amusa's childhood fiancé, whom he tries his best to abandon because she is plain and holds none of the excitement of city life. The fourth attraction is a well-educated, respectable girl, also named Beatrice for some curious symbolic reason, who apparently combines the best of two worlds but whom Amusa cannot marry until Aina has a miscarriage. Aina's mother suffers a miraculous change of heart, Beatrice the First is mauled to death by women whom she had slighted in her ambitious seductions, Amusa's own mother dies (leaving him to choose his own wife), and Beatrice the Second's fiancé commits suicide after failing his medical examinations. The novel ends as Amusa and Beatrice incredibly set off into the sunset in a lorry bound for Ghana (the Gold Coast).

Amusa's adventures have involved him in all the "romance" of the city: theft, murder, prostitution, political and economic corruption, and swindling and racketeering, as well as an election and a labor march mourning the death of a spiritual leader who is described as an African Gandhi. The message is clear that money has replaced the old values, in particular loyalty to relatives and to the people of one's own country. Amusa has to experience it all before he can accept the responsibility of doing something and becoming something—that is what his self-imposed exile is all about. It is difficult to take this romantic, melodramatic, chaotic novel seriously. Yet Ekwensi wrote better works, and this is his first. For a long time it was pointed to as the first anglophone novel to be widely read outside Africa. It is thus historically important. It is also an unfortunate example of some of the worst elements in Western fiction and illustrates what appears to a Western reader to be a complete loss of an African perception. It is difficult to distinguish Amusa's goal of success from a Western one, or from Ekwensi's. His father's challenge to seek opportunities in the new world, to do something, to become something makes success a definition of one's humanity. Thus, *People of the City* is, above all, in both its story and its point of view, a record of the moral confusion that Western civilization has incited in such urban centers as Lagos in West Africa.

In *Jagua Nana*, Ekwensi is again in Lagos, and the protagonist is a female version of Amusa Sango, a forty-five-year-old prostitute with dreams of marrying into the elite. She plans to achieve her goal by sending her young lover, Freddie Namme, to England to get a degree in law. When he abandons her for a younger woman and then dies in a political vendetta, she returns to her native village and dreams of setting herself up as an independent merchant. Ekwensi fleshes out this skeletal plot with almost as many varied adventures as make up *People of the City* and with the same titillating language. The male protagonist, Freddie, is even closer than Amusa to the fictional type that dominates the late colonial period: the young, Western-educated African—usually a "been-to"—whose main goal is to imitate white people, enter the elite of the city, drive a car, have money, and attract women. That is, he not only has rejected but also is ashamed of his past and wants to be completely independent of the old ties of loyalty. Unlike Amusa, Freddie must pay for his selfishness and betrayal with his own death, but Jagua Nana herself survives and returns to moral sanity. Jagua Nana became such a popular character in Nigeria that Ekwenski returned to her twenty-five years later with *Jagua Nana's Daughter*. In the sequel, Liza, the daughter, has reaped the benefits of the struggles of her mother's generation. She is educated, sophisticated, and ultimately happy.

Achebe, in *No Longer at Ease*, also examines the experience of the "been-to." However, rather than allow the melodramatic elements to get out of hand, Achebe uses various devices, such as flashbacks, juxtaposition, point of view, irony, and humor, to force a judgment of the protagonist, Obi Okonkwo (grandson of the hero in *Things Fall Apart*). The novel begins with his trial and indictment, for example, and the plot moves inexorably toward a financial and moral indebtedness that tempts him into the widespread practice of accepting bribes. Though he begins his life in Lagos with a sense of mission, to remain above the prevailing moral corruption, he eventually succumbs but is not clever enough to succeed. Through Obi and his experience, Achebe indicts the entire Nigerian society for its unfair demands on the young, for the corruption of the older members in both the city and the native village, for the false values that have replaced the traditional ones, and for the vanity and naïve expectations of the young. Nor do the racist British bosses escape blame. *No Longer at Ease* may not have the firm sense of place and authority found in *Things Fall Apart* and *Arrow of God*, but it convincingly reveals the loss of identity and integrity in the transition from village to city.

Both Achebe and Ekwensi are Nigerians, with Lagos providing their common example of the new culture in Africa, but their perception is not essentially different from that of observers in other regions with somewhat different colonial histories. Lenrie Peters, from Gambia and Sierra Leone, describes a similar situation in his novel *The Second Round* (1965). In this case, however, the protagonist, Dr. Kawa, retains his integrity. He returns from England with his medical degree and with high ideals of serving his country but finds Freetown a divided city, European civilization having modified the traditional society. Uncomfortable in the superficial, materialistic environment and unable to satisfy the expectations of his mother and friends, Kawa decides to transfer to a country hospital in hopes of washing off the stain of moral contamination. In spite of his moral integrity and his attack on superficial Western values, Kawa remains a contemporary man. This novel is at a far remove from the negritudist perception of an African personality that one finds in the novels of Laye.

The same can be said of the novels of city life that come out of South Africa, an area that poses a special problem to readers of African literature. Until the 1990's, it represented an entrenched colonialism, a white minority that controlled the political, social, and economic situation under the system of apartheid. On the other hand, South Africa has long been so highly industrialized that relations between the races resemble the American experience in that black writers are often far removed from their tribal roots. The return to an African identity that shapes literature through much of the continent has not been a major motif in South African work.

This can, at least, be said for one of the country's most prolific novelists of the colonial period, Peter Abrahams, born in a Johannesburg slum, son of a black father and a colored mother. Early in his life, he made the breaking down of the color barrier a major conviction and goal, and rejected negritude, which seemed to glorify blackness and emphasize racial distinctions. For him, spiritual freedom and individualism, Western values with an early touch of Marxism, ignored distinctions of race. Eventually, as his later novels reveal, he argued that political freedom must precede individual freedom. His novel of city life, *Mine Boy*, written in his mid-twenties, already indicates these directions of his thought. Its purpose is to expose the evils of apartheid, which denies the humanity of blacks and either maims or kills them. Xuma, a strong young man from the country, comes to the city with illusions of money and success. He receives evidence of the city's destructiveness in the form of disheartened men and women, hears advice from Leah, a magnificent mother-protectress, but remains in his ignorance until he goes to work in the mines.

Once on the white people's ground, he begins to feel his inferiority. It requires the support and wisdom of his Irish boss, Paddy O'Shea—a Marxist and hence a rare example of tolerance among white people—before he recovers his sense of integrity. He then becomes aware of the political situation that will not allow him his humanity, and this, in turn, prompts him to lead a strike against his white bosses at the mine. Though still subject to apartheid law at the end of the novel, he declares himself a spokesman for his people—the role that Abrahams himself has assumed. Through all of this, it is evident that Abrahams makes no appeal to tribal values. It is the Westerner, Paddy O'Shea, who guides him, and, though Marxism may be at the root of the economic struggle, it is Western individualism that wins him over. Abrahams himself insists that racism, prejudice, and provincialism are prevalent in every culture and that international understanding and pluralism are the answer.

Abrahams's critique of society, in particular the city, is tame and romanticized in comparison with that of another South African, Alex La Guma, who relies extensively on realistic and naturalistic detail. His attack is almost exclusively against the evils of apartheid, which necessitates underground resistance (*In the Fog of the Seasons' End*, 1972) and results in large portions of the nonwhite population spending their lives in prison for politically or economically motivated crimes (*The Stone Country*, 1967). In the former novel, La Guma inserts a typical interrogation of a nonwhite by a white authority who details the endless regulations that control the nonwhite's movements within the country. Both of these novels deal with urban blacks, but La Guma's earlier work, the short novel *A Walk in the Night* (1962), gives the clearest picture of what it is like for a nonwhite to live in a South African city. It recounts the events of one evening in the life of a Coloured, Michael Adonis—a bitterly ironic choice of names—who has recently been fired from his factory job for speaking disrespectfully to his white superior.

Frustrated and angry, Michael wanders the streets, frequents old restaurants and bars, is interrogated by a policeman, comes into contact with the lower elements of society, and ends up at the house of his neighbor, Mr. Doughty, an old Irishman and formerly successful actor whom life has beaten into alcoholism. In a drunken fit of passion and resentment over Doughty's philosophizing, but especially over his whiteness, Michael hits him with a wine bottle and kills him. He has a series of psychological reactions to this, his first murder—rationalization, indifference, a sense of superiority, entrapment, and fear. Ironically, it is not Michael whom an informer names as the guilty party, but Willieboy, one of his acquaintances in the streets. In a brutal sequence of scenes, the police constable, Raalt, chases Willieboy like an animal, shoots him, and allows him to die in the back of his van while he stops to buy cigarettes on the way to the station. Michael has no idea that Willieboy has died in his place, that he is a "sacrificial victim." The old Irishman who futilely quotes William Shakespeare to Michael, describing life as the ghost of Hamlet's father walking the night, cannot become his spiritual father. The only culture in these streets is in the gangsters and cowboys at the cinema. Joe, the young vagabond who wanders through the novel, warns Michael to preserve his integrity, but this advice, too, fails.

Michael decides to join a band of thieves. Hope seems impossible. La Guma ends the novel with a cockroach gorging itself on a mixture of liquor and vomit in old Mr. Doughty's room; John Abrahams, the informer, living in shame and helplessness; Joe escaping the city for the sea; and the anonymous Frank Lorenzo, with his five children and his pregnant wife, Grace, looking to the dawn. The irony of Michael Adonis's name continues to the bitter end. The experience of the black South African is almost a thing apart. It seems closer to Ralph Ellison's *Invisible Man* (1952) than to colonial literature in the rest of black Africa. Nevertheless, the need for community, which Michael is able to find only in a robber gang and which Joe seeks in Michael, is as real in its absence as in Armah's *The Beautyful Ones Are Not Yet Born* (1968). Identity within the community is an essential motif within these African novels.

From resistance to independence

The theme of resistance to apartheid, strongly suggested in such novels as *Mine Boy*, *A Walk in the Night*, and *The Stone Country* and treated directly by *In the Fog of the Seasons' End*, finds its parallels in the countries to the north. Throughout the colonial period, before the final achievement of independence in the early 1960's, there were pockets of resistance to foreign intervention. Armah presents this phenomenon mythically in *The Healers* and *Two Thousand Seasons*, the former concentrating on the defeat of the Ashanti during the British conquest of Ghana in the late nineteenth century, the latter tracing the resistance to exploitation over the past one thousand years. Armah raises the issue of the slave trade, a rarity in African fiction, and accuses his own people of complicity and betrayal in this and in the turning over of power to British authority. In both novels, however, he contends that a group of spiritual leaders has continued to preserve the old African traditions and has periodically engaged in guerrilla warfare in order to survive.

Mongo Beti of Cameroon attempts a more realistic account of the struggle in *Remember Ruben* (1973; English translation, 1980). It deals with the exploits of a trade union leader, who first opposes the French through political means but eventually must become a guerrilla leader. The novel has a romantic strain as well: Mor-Zamba, the true protagonist, attains heroic status in the eyes of his fellows. It is his realization that constitutes the message of the novel, that the struggle has nothing to do with individual personalities or personal gain, that the goal is not simply political power or economic control but African identity and spiritual independence of foreign cultural domination.

Meja Mwangi of Kenya, in his *Carcase for Hounds* (1974), relies even more than Beti on pure realistic detail. He examines the role of one particular group of Mau Mau fighters, the carryover of tribal ferocity into the struggle for liberation, and, in particular, the quest of the legendary General Haraka for the heads of tribal chiefs who side with the British. More gruesome, however, is the loyalty code that demands success or death. The novel ends with Kimamo, who functions as the main focus of narration, nursing his wounded and feverish general, watching him execute a fellow terrorist who has failed in a mission, and then watching his own execution for the same reason. The final paragraphs reintroduce the almost inevitable but ambiguous romantic note of the soul's survival in a paradisal afterlife in which Kimamo and General Haraka reunite. The hyena's sardonic chuckle, which had floated as a motif in earlier scenes, dimly qualifies the spiritual affirmation.

Some mythologizing of the resistance movement is almost inevitable. The resistance fighters must become heroes of legend, especially within the African context, in which such transformation is basic to the oral literature. Ngugi, in his resistance novel, however, has his legendary figure recede into the background and concentrates on the psychological realities of betrayal, deception, and cowardice. *A Grain of Wheat* (1967) is many things at once: a mythical but humanized treatment of the guerrilla fighter Kihika; a clever merger of Christian myth within the thematic structure of divine mission and Judas-like betrayal; and a satiric portrait of the anemic white administration in the last days of the colony. Its purpose, however, is to raise essential questions about motives and aspirations of the combatants and to suggest, finally, the ambiguity surrounding heroism, cowardice, and the personal struggle that is even more intense than the public one. Mugo, the betrayer of the legendary hero Kihika, endures the most intense moral struggle among the participants; ironically, his public avowal on the day of independence, which leads to his execution by people of less moral stature, is too late to have any effect on the political situation. Gikonyo returns from a detention camp to find his wife pregnant by Karanja, a subordinate for the white administration. Despite the ambiguity surrounding her submission to Karanja, Ngugi seems to insist on her essential integrity and puts the burden on Gikonyo to accept her in an act of faith. Again, this struggle is as real in the novel as any directly connected with the resistance movement. Contained in *A Grain of Wheat* are the seeds of success and of failure in the postindependence society.

Like Ngugi, Sembène carries the resistance movement up to the moment of independence. His novel *Les Bouts de bois de Dieu* (1960; *God's Bits of Wood*, 1962) is a fictional account of an actual event in the Western Sudan, the railway strike of 1947-1948. He treats its success as a temporary triumph against oppressive French authority and treats its leaders as romanticized heroes. It is an epic portrayal relying upon realistic detail, romantic gesture, communal loyalty, and a touch of Marxist ideology. Sembène's next novel, *L'Harmattan, livre I: Référendum* (1964), treats events in an anonymous African country in the late 1950's. He shifts focus from the band of Marxist revolutionaries endorsing a vote for independence on the referendum to the personal and public life of Dr. Tangara, who sympathizes with their goal but not their ideology and methods and who must make a decision for or against them. Though the referendum results in independence in only one of the French colonies, the revolutionary forces have not lost heart, and the hesitant politicism of such rare humanistic figures as Dr. Tangara withdraws from the scene. Sembène in these novels is much less pessimistic about the future of Senegal than Ngugi is about the capacity of Kenyans to maintain a high level of resistance to the temptations of Western civilization. Like Sembène, Ngugi eventually turns to Marxism as an ideology that better suits the African sense of community, but more than Sembène, he desperately needs to recover and reinstate traditional African values—hence, perhaps, his deeper pessimism about the future.

This pessimism is also evident in two other novelists, Armah and Abrahams. Armah's *Why Are We So Blest?* (1971) is a unique version of the revolutionary theme. The action takes place entirely outside black Africa. This universalizes the revolutionary struggle and, in fact, turns it into a conflict of races. The colonial situation in the sub-Sahara is essentially no different from that in America and North Africa, and Armah holds out no hope of success. Of the three protagonists, the white American girl, Aimée, has motives that are suspect; the young African student at Harvard, Modu, dies while naïvely trying to join the revolution; and the mature Solo, also an African, is too skeptical about revolution and the callous organization that runs it to commit himself. His contribution will apparently remain that of a philosophical literary exile.

Abrahams, in *A Wreath for Udomo* (1956), likewise carries the struggle outside Africa, to a core of political leaders residing in London. Their job is to conduct a propaganda campaign that forces the British government to turn power over to the indigenous population. Michael Udomo, in rather unconvincing fashion, soon becomes the center of the group, wresting power and influence from the country's idol, who has lost touch with the real political situation. Although he returns to "Pan-Africa" to prepare the way for Lanwood, by the time the latter arrives, Udomo is firmly established in the seat of power and has changed markedly from the rash, irresponsible youth he was in London to an astute politician, sure of himself and his goals. He no doubt represents the voice of Abrahams in the novel, but as a result, it brings both him and the author into conflict with the voice of tribalism. Udomo uses his power to modernize and industrialize his country; he works to defeat the tribe, which stands for everything evil, superstitious, and savage. This goal drives him to a temporary compromise with Pluralia (South Africa) and a betrayal of his best friend, who heads a resistance group within that country.

Whether such actions go beyond Abrahams's own convictions is difficult to say, but Udomo seems to retain his romantic image to the very end. Abrahams's pessimism does not, it would seem, arise from the necessity of compromise but from his awareness that the enemy, tribalism, is a powerful force. Udomo dies a sacrificial death at its hands in a savage and terrifying ritual ceremony. The intellectual of the novel, Paul Mahbi, in a letter to Lois, Udomo's white mistress whom he had abandoned for the African cause, composes an eloquent defense of his greatness in spite of his violation of private moralities. Whatever Abrahams's intentions, the conflict in the novel suggests the necessity of compromise between the new civilization and the old and makes one wonder if the tribe does not, after all, have values that Abrahams and Udomo do not allow to surface. In any case, *A Wreath for Udomo* is a remarkable novel, written as it was in 1956, some years before the majority of the African countries had achieved independence. It is prophetic in its anticipation of the internal struggles that were to ensue.

Postindependence and neocolonialism

Many of the new African states that achieved independence after 1960 have borne out Abrahams's fears, and fictional representations of these states have been harsh. Return of political power to African hands has not been complete—for economic control has remained, for the most part, with international conglomerates and with "black Europeans" who reflect foreign interests. The new political leaders themselves have been corrupt or incapable of controlling the competing factions and often corrupt forces within the country. Another problem is the basic ideological conflict that Abrahams identifies.

In practically every novel dealing with contemporary Africa, the temptations of Western materialism—the dream of social advancement, status symbols, the luxuries of modern civilization and technology, and the power that makes their attainment possible—and the capitalistic ideology that lies behind them receive the brunt of the attack, but now it is not usually the foreigner who is the villain. The novelist points to the African who betrays his heritage. The rare individuals who maintain their integrity either have no visible or respected sanctions for their morality or more or less vaguely inherit it from the traditional past. In the most pessimistic of the novels, the individual becomes a helpless and alienated victim of corruption and various economic and sociopolitical forces. Among the many who have set their novels in the postcolonial period are the canonical figures in African literature: Aidoo, Achebe, Emecheta, Soyinka, Sembène, and Ngugi.

The most erudite novelist and critic of the contemporary scene is Wole Soyinka, the recipient of the Nobel Prize in Literature in 1986. His first novel, *The Interpreters*, is a masterpiece of virtuosity, ironic commentary, philosophical probing, and mythic intimations. Though it touches every level of society, it concentrates on the social elite: those people who belong to the hypocritical majority and the few intellectuals, educated abroad but spiritually bound to Africa, who try to act, to find a place for themselves, and to interpret their situation. They include Egbo, the son of a tribal chief whose dilemma is to reconcile his obligations to the past and the present and whose conflicting sexual attractions to the sensuous Simi and a young university student provide a specific locus for his choice. Egbo's return with the other interpreters to visit his tribal home vividly depicts the power of tradition over the minds of the descendants. His private encounter with Ogun—the Dionysian god of creation and destruction—puts him into spiritual contact with the natural world and is only one of many ways that the mythic impinges on the daily lives of the interpreters.

Kola, the painter, makes contact through his art—Ogun himself being the patron of artists—as he struggles to finish his masterpiece, a merging of contemporary personalities into the forms of the Yoruba gods. Egbo is Ogun, the god of contradictions, repeating the god's symbolic journey from the traditional world of spirits to the contemporary world of the living. Kola's sculpture, *The Wrestler*, is a heroic elevation of a comic incident involving another of the interpreters, Sekoni. This idealist and spiritual inspiration within the group is already dead but has become a legendary hero. After his attempt as an engineer to construct an electric power station in a rural community is rejected by provincial and corrupt politicians, he goes insane, for the power station represents for him not simply a technological achievement but a harnessing of natural power through human creativity and was to give meaning to his new life in Africa. This failure haunts the other interpreters. They see his death in terms of a ritual sacrifice.

Sagoe seems in some respects to be a practical member of the group. As a reporter for a Lagos newspaper—a position he obtains in a strange and comic way—he investigates curious happenings in the city. He is also bound to one of the female protagonists in a relatively conventional fashion. Yet his strange and symbolic philosophy of "Voidancy"—spiritual elevation being achieved through complete relieving of the bowels—gives him an opposite dimension. The philosophy is not only comic playfulness, but it is also part of the motif of excrement and filth, of fertility and sterility, in contemporary Nigerian society. Finally, there is Bandele, apparently the cohesive force of the group. Generally a detached observer, quiet and pragmatic in his actions, he is a professor of English at the university and may be Soyinka's authorial voice, the *raisonneur*.

While these characters exist on many different levels, from the profoundly sacred to the farcical, the characters representing a hypocritical society reside in a world of satiric comedy, and Soyinka is brilliant as a Molière in exposing them to ridicule. Faseyi, Sir Derinola, Chief Winsala, Professor Oguazor, and Dr. Lumoye are "petrified" brains, concerned only with facades and trivia. Through them, Soyinka attacks the materialism and utilitarianism that inhibit the interpreters from realizing their creative energies within the social fabric. A third group of characters introduces the strange world of evangelical religions so prevalent in modern Nigeria and a common theme in Soyinka's other work. The interpreters visit the church of the prophet Lazarus, who claims to have risen from the dead. Soyinka seems to use the religious service—which is fraught with theatrics—as well as the other pseudo-Christian rites and avowals, to emphasize the quest for spiritual values in the void of contemporary life. The activities of the interpreters themselves are part of the same quest.

Rather than provide answers, however, the novel seems to end in paradox and mystery. There is a strange equation of disciples and thieves, of sinners and martyrs. The mystery of death and resurrection is present throughout the novel but reappears at the end with the symbolic, nightmarish drowning of Joe Golder, a black American, in a vat of black dye. Golder, who has no identity, who is black and yet an American rather than an African, obsessively defends the principle of negritude. Yet Soyinka also identifies him as homosexual and, in the eyes of Sagoe, a pervert. While Soyinka defends the integrity of the African tradition, he does not make it a matter of color and rejects here as elsewhere the negritudist definition of the African. His vision of the African is complex. It is not even clear that he has intellectually sorted it out or wishes to do so in any dogmatic or analytical way. He states as much in his second novel, *Season of Anomy*.

The Interpreters ends as a night of severance: The disciples are separated, and the Savior has not come. The interpreters are "apostates," but to what, they are not sure: to the new world that demands their acquiescence, to the real or imagined past that still has a spiritual hold on them, or to the inner self as the final sanction for responsible and heroic action? Bandele usually remains quiet in the face of the irreligious society that sacrifices its young to the preservation of itself, but he is the one who gives the parting ironic shot: May they all live to bury their own daughters.

While Soyinka's first novel focuses on the lives of intellectuals during the early sixties, and his second, *Season of Anomy*, on the Nigerian Civil War (1967-1970), others writers such as Armah, Achebe, Ngugi, and Sembène turned their attention to the political leadership and its effect on the citizenry. Armah's *The Beautyful Ones Are Not Yet Born* looks at national corruption, as condoned and even encouraged by politicians, through the eyes of an unnamed protagonist, "the man," a controller in a railway office. He is the only moral force in the society, surrounded by images of filth and excrement, by fellow workers who take bribes, by a family whose material desires pressure him to do likewise, by a cynical "Teacher" friend who has retreated from society, and by a former schoolmate, Koomson—the main human symbol of social degradation, who has used corrupt means to rise to political prominence and who is using the man and his family in yet another of his illegal activities. Armah transforms the protagonist into a hero—a model of moral behavior—in the second half of the novel when, after a military coup, with absolutely no ulterior motive, he risks his own life to save Koomson's. Armah's indictment of the new African leadership is achieved largely through scatological imagery and character foils: the indulgent materialism of Koomson and the reflective sensitivity and compassion of the man.

Achebe presents similar portraits of political leaders in *No Longer at Ease* and *A Man of the People*, but most impressively in his fifth novel, *Anthills of the Savannah*. Using shifting points of view, overlapping time sequences, and periodic flashbacks, he focuses on incidents surrounding a military coup in present time in an imaginary African country (actually a thinly disguised Nigeria in the early 1980's). Kangan's president, familiarly known as Sam, has gone the way of other political figures in postcolonial Africa, abandoning his revolutionary ideals and abusing his newly gained power. The main characters are Sam's former schoolmates, who react in various ways to his betrayal: Chris, minister of information, who tries to guide Sam back to public responsibility; his friend Ikem, editor of the city newspaper, who attacks Sam in his columns; and Beatrice, a secretary and priestess in love with Chris and confidant of Ikem. When Sam refuses to acknowledge the needs of the people, specifically ignoring a delegation of elders from the drought-plagued north, a military junta assassinates him and assumes authority. At the end, with both Chris and Ikem dead, Beatrice hosts a symbolic communal meeting of friends that suggests the ideal future direction of the country. The novel reflects, through its various techniques, a contemporary experimentation with fictional form; through Beatrice the growing feminist voice in Africa; and through the use of myth, folktale, and legend the continuing attempt of novelists to explore the relevance of tradition in modern Africa.

In Kenya, Ngugi continued to develop as a novelist as well, and to respond in fresh ways to the postcolonial situation in his country. In *Devil on the Cross* and *Matigari* he asserted his indigenous culture by writing in his native Kikuyu before producing English versions and by adapting oral techniques to the novel form. Both works attack corruption of the neocolonialists. The former specifically targets Western capitalism and patriarchy, using griot narration, folktale monsters, ritual repetition, and a female folk hero to rouse the public against blatant abuses of power. The latter targets government and economic abuse through parabolic characters and stories that mix social satire and fantasy in a form of Magical Realism. A folk hero-father returns to his native country after fighting wars of revolution only to find that imperialist forces are still in power behind the scenes. In his search for truth and justice, he rescues a prostitute and a child-thief to form a new African family but is chased out of the country, wounded and perhaps killed, with only his "son" to carry on the cultural war. The satirical novel, *Wizard of the Crow*, is set in the fictional Free Republic of Abruria, governed by a tyrannical figure known only as the Ruler. Ngugi again attacks corruption—all of the authority figures in this novel are greedy and destructive—but uses humor as a device to offer a degree of hope.

Likewise, Sembène, first in *Xala* (1973; English translation, 1976), then in *The Last of the Empire*, attacks neocolonialism from an African socialist perspective. *Xala* focuses on the chamber of commerce in Dakar, in particular on one representative member, El Hadji, who follows the typical literary pattern of neocolonial capitalists. He forgets his revolutionary ideals before independence and becomes a corrupt opportunist, taking advantage of the economic system to acquire wives, material possessions, and social standing. Sembène traces his gradual fall at the hands of the people he has disenfranchised and impoverished, led by a beggar-griot who, through the curse of impotence, reminds him of his crime, its human consequences, and the necessary cure: an identification with the community of Senegal. In *The Last of the Empire*, in a political plot similar to Achebe's *Anthills of the Savannah*, the "chamber" is that of the government, the ministers who serve under Léon, the president of Senegal. The main character is the minister of justice, the conscientious elder Cheikh Tidiane, who at the beginning of the narrative resigns his post just as Léon mysteriously disappears. The novel is itself a mystery, which gradually reveals the reason for the disappearance, exposes the egotistic struggles for power of Léon's subordinates, provides the stimulus for Tidiane's realization of his social role as writer-griot, and sets the stage for Sembène's own political agenda in support of feminism, social responsibility, and sanity in dealing with issues of religion, polygamy, property, and education. All of these writers—Achebe, Armah, Ngugi, and Sembène—assume the role of traditional griot, assessing the needs of contemporary African society in the light of indigenous traditions and colonial influences.

Other voices on the literary scene include a second generation of male writers and a growing number of female writers to complement such established names as Aidoo, Emecheta, and Head. While they continue some of the same social and political themes, following the African aesthetic of writing for the people's sake, they also often exhibit a highly experimental style, sometimes resembling the Magical Realism of Latin American novelists. Among the most distinguished of the male artists are Ben Okri of Nigeria and Nuruddin Farah of Somalia. Farah published ten novels between 1970 and 2007, including *From a Crooked Rib* (1970), a sympathetic, even feminist, portrait of a Somali woman, and two sets of trilogies with political themes (a third trilogy saw its first two novels published in 2004 and 2007). The first novel in the trilogy Variations on the Theme of an African Dictatorship, *Sweet and Sour Milk* (1979), led to his exile of almost twenty years from his native country. His works, fictional manifestations of Edward Said's Orientalism argument, are exquisitely written assertions of Somalian identity in the face of Western "othering" of Third World, or developing world, peoples. Okri, who has expressed the wish to be known as a writer, not simply as an African writer, is a superb stylist who mixes realism with mythical and magical qualities that draw on African folk literature and themes. *The Famished Road* (1991) and *Songs of Enchantment* (1993), for example, present as the protagonist an *ogbangi* child, the literary prototype for which is Ezinma in Achebe's *Things Fall Apart*. His characters move through fabulous worlds reminiscent of Tutuola's narratives and African folktales. Okri won several literary prizes in recognition of his technical skills, and his moral commitment to the

African people is a visible part of his fictional achievement. Several other writers emerged at the end of the twentieth century and the beginning of the twenty-first, including Henri Lopès and Labou Tansi of the Congo, Tierno Monénembo of Guinea, South Africa's Zakes Mda and Zoë Wicomb, and Nigeria's Chimamanda Ngozi Adichie.

One of the most encouraging signs in the literature of this period was the emergence of new women authors, including novelists. Few women of the first generation continued to write. Ama Ata Aidoo of Ghana was mainly known for her poems, short stories, and plays until 1977, when her 1966 African feminist novel, *Our Sister Killjoy: Or, Reflections from a Black-Eyed Squint*, was finally published; in 1993 she published a second novel, *Changes: A Love Story*. Another West African writer, Emecheta of Nigeria, wrote some fifteen novels between 1976 (*The Bride Price*), and 1994 (*Kehinde*). Her most famous and important novel, *The Joys of Motherhood* (1979), offers a wrenching account of a wife and mother in the modern city of Lagos, bound by the tradition of polygamy and spousal inheritance that forces a second wife into her already established monogamous marriage. Grace Ogot of Kenya was the first and is perhaps the best known East African female novelist. Her early novel *The Promised Land* (1966) and her collection of literary folktales, *Land Without Thunder* (1968), established the themes and folkloric style for her later works that deal with the impact of tradition on modern life and the plight of women. Her novel *The Graduate* (1980), about women in postcolonial Kenya, like her first, was written in English, but her later work, including *Miaha* (1983; *The Strange Bride*, 1989) and *Simbi Nyaima* (1983), was written in her native language, Luo. Among francophone women, Mariama Bâ followed up her widely read *Une si longue lettre* (1980; *So Long a Letter*, 1981), which raises serious questions about polygamy, with *Un Chant écarlate* (1981; *Scarlet Song*, 1986), which deals with mixed marriages within the particular cultural expectations of postcolonial Senegal.

Among women novelists of the second generation, one of the most productive is Aminata Sow Fall, a francophone writer from Senegal. Fall's novels, including *Le Revenant* (1976; the ghost), *La Grève des bàttu* (1979; *The Beggars' Strike*, 1981), *L'Appel des arènes* (1982; the call of the arena), *Ex-père de la nation* (1987; ex-father of the nation) and *Festins de détresse* (2005; feasts of distress), focus on unstable socioeconomic and political situations that make victims of everyone in society. *Ex-père de la nation* traces the life of an imprisoned former president of an African country to show that neither the "fathers" nor the "mothers" in Africa are fulfilling their nurturing roles. They promise no future for Africa until individuals assume communal responsibility. Although Fall studied in France at the Sorbonne, she made a conscious determination that her writing would not reflect Western influences or experiences. Other novelists who have received critical attention are Calixthe Beyala and Werewere Liking of Cameroon, Angèle Rawiri of Gabon, and Véronique Tadjo of Ivory Coast. They offer a variety of perspectives on the personal, familial, and social positions of women in Africa. Yvonne Vera, an anglophone writer from Zimbabwe, was poised to become another canonical figure, but she died at the age of forty, having produced five novels: *Nehanda* (1993), *Without a Name* (1994), *Under the Tongue* (1996), *Butterfly Burning* (1998), and *The Stone Virgins* (2002). Her books, four of which won major literary prizes, are psychological studies of women in exile caught between a disturbing past and an uncertain future.

An emerging writer from Nigeria is Chimamanda Ngozi Adichie, who tells the story of the failed struggle for Biafran independence from Nigeria in *Half of a Yellow Sun* (2006). Called "the twenty-first century daughter of Chinua Achebe," Adichie presents a picture of a Nigeria that has accepted the colonists' notions of class and bureaucracy while retaining ancient tribal practices and prejudices. By focusing on a few main characters—the sisters Olanna and Kainene, their lovers Odenigbo and Richard, and a houseboy—she provides both brutal detail of violence, hatred, and greed and a compassionate and ennobling view of struggle. *Half of a Yellow Sun,* like much of the literature from this period, is a realistic novel based on recent history, not on oral culture, but it depicts urban, Westernized characters with lingering ties to rural, traditional ways. The voice of this novel is clearly a woman's voice—unusual for a novel about war—a trend that flourished throughout African literature in the postindependence period.

Generations of African writers have lived part of

their lives outside their native countries, and this trend has continued into the twenty-first century, with writers living in Europe and North America while continuing to write about Africa. Adichie, who was named a 2008 MacArthur Fellow, settled in the northeastern United States in 1996. South African novelist Zoë Wicomb, author of *David's Story* (2001) and *Playing in the Light* (2006), moved to Glasgow, Scotland, where she has taught postcolonial literature. Her novels deal with racial identity issues in South Africa, particularly among the mixed-race people known as "coloureds"; her short-story collection, *The One That Got Away* (2008), contains stories set in Capetown and in Glasgow. Even in the age of globalization, leaving Africa for a better education, or more political freedom, or wider access to publishing and the arts is a good career choice—especially for those who seek a worldwide readership.

Conclusion: A critical evaluation

Throughout its brief history, the African novel can be characterized as theme and variation on the issue of identity. An internalized sense of inferiority and the threat of cultural extinction contributed to its rise, usually as a mode of defense and a means of preservation. What the novels often lament is the loss of community, and of customs, rituals, values, and sanctions that give meaning to an individual life. When the incursion of an alien culture began to destroy cultural cohesiveness, alienation was an inevitable result. While some novelists, such as La Guma and Mwangi, stress the anonymity that comes with the loss of tradition, others make an effort to integrate the past with the contemporary world. In any case, the novel is not only a literary phenomenon in Africa but also a social document that traces the history of Africa during the past one thousand years. Furthermore, as Kenneth Harrow has argued in *Thresholds of Change in African Literature: The Emergence of a Tradition* (1994), the written tradition is now at least fifty years old and has begun to build on itself. In these documents containing the gradual and then the sudden introduction of Africa to the West, that is, in these various commentaries on the threat to traditional African identity, one motif stands out, that of initiation.

To personalize the conflict, the novelist almost inevitably has created a narrator or a central character who undergoes an initiation experience. This technique is a common theme in Western novels as well, but it seems particularly appropriate to Africa in its period of sudden transition to a society that still practiced age-old initiation rites as an integral part of its communal life. Eileen Julien, in *African Novels and the Question of Orality* (1992), sees initiation as one of three genres from the oral tradition still practiced by African male novelists. In *God's Bits of Wood*, Sembène explicitly states that participation in the protest march to Dakar is a realistic and practical substitute for the ritual of initiation. The usual pattern in the initiation process is a character's introduction to Western culture, ordinarily through education; a resulting split in personality and loyalties; alienation from the old community and a failure to integrate into the new one; at the extreme, a total exile from the country or a mental breakdown; and finally, in rare cases, a recovery and the beginning of efforts to reestablish ties or create a new community. Novels that end in alienation are likely to be realistic in mode; those novels that project a cure are likely to emphasize the archetypal aspects of the motif and rely on the romantic and mythic mode. No African novel, however, is written exclusively in one mode or the other. The novel that is perhaps the best example of the entire process is, ironically, Laye's *The Radiance of the King*, which forces a white man to discover the cultural realities of black Africa.

This is only a hint at the variety one finds in the African novel. Certainly there are other archetypal motifs. Initiation itself can merge gradually into the quest, as is the case with Soyinka's *Season of Anomy*. The sacrificial scapegoat is a common motif that arises out of the historical situation, though often the victim's death does not seem to have any immediate benefits, except perhaps in its effect within the fictional rhetoric. It is partly through the use of archetypes that the novelist, consciously or unconsciously, appeals to an international audience while reflecting local realities. The myth of paradise is a common device to contrast the old life with the new. In numerous novels, symbolism breaks through the realistic description. In some novels, local color—sociological and anthropological documentation—is a significant part of the structure. In others, the novelist explores the psychological impact on a highly sensitive individual reared in one culture but educated into another. Often the primary purpose is social or political satire. Some novels are structured as histories in imitation of traditional chronicles told by the griots. Others are highly experimental, attempting to incorporate Western devices into the African context or carry over folk and mythic qualities from the past into the contemporary novel form.

In the light of this variety, it may seem somewhat surprising that the African novel has come under fire from Western critics, especially the formalists. African intellectuals have often been sensitive to outside criticism; Achebe is a case in point. They question whether the foreigner really has enough knowledge of African history, the African oral tradition, the African mentality, the contemporary situation, or, more particularly, the biographies and intentions of individual authors. Formalist critics would tend to downplay such factors anyway, and they complain that African novelists are so concerned with social purpose that they neglect aesthetic matters. Achebe's response is that the purpose of literature is first of all humanistic and that this obligation pertains especially in Africa.

Perhaps the best way to evaluate the African novel is through such a sociological critic as Kenneth Burke, who defines all literature as essentially a strategy to deal with reality. His emphasis is on the reality imitated, as is the case in the African novel, but he also stresses the importance of a complex strategy—how well and how convincingly it responds to the situation. This allows some latitude for the pedagogical function that Achebe sees as essential, for the satiric attacks on Western exploitation and African assimilation, and for the general quest for a new African image. This is somewhat the approach Eustace Palmer takes in his 1979 study *The Growth of the African Novel*. The novel began as a response to a new situation; it has provided not only complex presentations of it but also a variety of strategies to deal with it. Significantly, Burke uses the proverb to illustrate the way literature deals with reality. It is a way of coping. Achebe himself defines the proverb as "the palm oil with which words are eaten." He and other African novelists respect the aesthetic medium, and some, including Achebe, Soyinka, Ngugi, Laye, Kane, Okri, and Farah, achieve a high level of artistry that deserves recognition, especially considering the short history of the form in Africa. The fact that the novelist uses that artistry primarily in the service of a humanistic and social purpose should not be an object of criticism but a source of admiration.

Thomas Banks
Updated by Cynthia A. Bily

Bibliography

Booker, M. Keith. *The African Novel in English: An Introduction*. Portsmouth, N.H.: Heinemann, 1998. Provides an introduction addressed specifically to a Western audience, a brief history of the African novel, and essays on eight anglophone African novels—four by men and four by women. Selections represent the variety in the African novel as well as the social and historical contexts of three different regions.

Harrow, Kenneth W. *Thresholds of Change in African Literature: The Emergence of a Tradition*. Portsmouth, N.H.: Heinemann, 1994. Applies formal and deconstructive theory in tracing the development of modern African fiction from the 1950's to the 1990's, from novels that witness to those that revolt, and finally to complex discourses that are not realistic or easily accessible.

Hay, Margaret Jean, ed. *African Novels in the Classroom*. Boulder, Colo.: Lynne Rienner, 2000. College instructors provide introductions to twenty important African novels, including works by Abrahams, Achebe, Emecheta, Farah, and Soyinka. Each essay describes why and how the novel is taught and lists supplementary readings and materials.

Irele, Abiola, and Simon Gikandi, eds. *The Cambridge History of African and Caribbean Literature*. New York: Cambridge University Press, 2004. Offers a sweeping introduction to the major themes and issues in African literature, including orality, empire and colonialism, and the various African regions and languages.

Ker, David I. *The African Novel and the Modernist Tradition*. New York: Peter Lang, 1997. Comparative study of anglophone African novels attempts to show that the authors—Wole Soyinka, Kofi Awoonor, Ngugi wa Thiong'o, Ayi Kwei Armah, and Gabriel Okara—consciously adapted British and American models by experimental novelists to African cultural and historical contexts. Places African fiction within an international modernist setting but asserts that modernism's response to cultural chaos is particularly appropriate to postcolonial Africa.

Lindfors, Bernth, ed. *Africa Talks Back: Interviews with Anglophone African Authors*. Trenton, N.J.: Africa World Press, 2002. Presents interviews with twenty-eight writers, including Chinua Achebe, Kofi Awoonor, Cyprian Ekwensi, Aubrey Kalitera, Ken Lipenga, Es'kia Mphalele, Meja Mwangi, Peter Nazareth, Njabulo Ndebele, and Grace Ogot.

Loflin, Christine. *African Horizons: The Landscapes of African Fiction*. Westport, Conn.: Greenwood Press, 1998. Analyzes landscapes, or horizons, of various types—natural, communal, domestic, social, political, economic, and religious—as defined from within by the African novelists themselves, not dictated by Western perspectives.

Nfah-Abbenyi, Juliana Makuchi. *Gender in African Women's Writing: Identity, Sexuality, and Difference*. Bloomington: Indiana University Press, 1997. Uses the novels of nine anglophone and francophone women to help redefine African feminist and postcolonial theory and to place the power of self-definition in the hands of the women themselves regarding such issues as education, home, politics, and sexuality.

Okafor, Dubem, ed. *Meditations on African Literature*. Westport, Conn.: Greenwood, 2001. Collection of essays discusses major works—mostly novels—and their origins and influences. Two essays examine the roles of women in African literature, and several focus on literature from Nigeria.

Owomoyela, Oyekan, ed. *A History of Twentieth-Century African Literatures*. Lincoln: University of Nebraska Press, 1993. Collection of essays on language and literature in Africa includes three on fiction from West, East, and South Africa and one on francophone fiction. Others deal with culture and identity, the use of European rather than African languages, the development of women's writing, and the status of publishing in various regions of the continent.

Palmer, Eustace. *The Growth of the African Novel*. London: Heinemann, 1979. Important early study of the African novel argues that novels from Tutuola's *The Palm-Wine Drinkard* in 1952 to Ngugi's *Petals of Blood* in 1977 should be evaluated within an African context concerning their social and human relevance as well as aesthetic matters such as structural coherence, character portrayal, and technique.

Salhi, Kamil, ed. *Francophone Post-colonial Cultures: Critical Essays*. Lanham, Md.: Lexington Books, 2003. Approximately one-third of the essays in this volume pertain to African literature. Includes essays on negotiating identity, colonialism, and major authors.

Woods, Tim. *African Pasts: Memory and History in African Literatures*. New York: Palgrave, 2007. Examines genres in African fiction, including the imprisonment narrative and resistance poetry, before turning to modern and postmodern works.

The Australian Novel

Australian novels enjoy a wide reception around the world, yet recognition of Australian novelists came slowly, taking place for the most part after World War II. History helped the Australian novel to be accepted around the world. Following the war, Australia shed its British cocoon and entered the larger world. In particular, it strengthened its relationship with the United States, a situation that not only influenced the country's social structure and literary art but also opened the door to an immense audience. Some observers suggest that the distribution of Australian films in the early 1980's and their popularity abroad helped to introduce Australian fiction to a larger readership. During this period, as well, government support of the arts increased, and novelists benefited from financial grants and subsidized publishing. The appearance of a major figure in Australian literature, Patrick White (1912-1990), also helped bring the Australian novel to world attention. Initially published and recognized in the United States and Great Britain, White received the Nobel Prize in Literature in 1973, the first Australian writer to do so.

The Australian novel emerged long before, however; while many of the nineteenth century novels hold more historical than literary interest, a few have become classics. During the first half of the twentieth century, several notable novelists published books that found an Australian readership and in some instances received attention overseas. Today, long after the appearance of White's last book in 1986, the literary scene remains a lively one.

Convicts and settlers: 1788-1900

Australia's European settlement began in 1788, when the First Fleet of convicts and their keepers arrived in Sydney Harbor. This brutal and uneducated society hardly encouraged literary production. Instead, those in charge kept diaries and wrote reports on the settlement's development, the exotic flora and fauna, the land's geographical oddities, and the Aboriginal inhabitants. Australia's first novel appeared in 1830: *Quintus Servinton*, an undistinguished book by a convict named Henry Savery (1791-1842), an educated man who had been transported to Australia for forgery. Although the author died in Australia after further criminal activities, the book's hero, Quintus, makes a fortune in the new land and returns happily to England. This plot line characterized many of the novels that followed. Written by homesick settlers, not convicts, the books treated the colony's rugged life harshly and allowed their heroes to go home to England with money they had accumulated by exploiting the country's resources.

The Transportation System (the euphemism for sending English convicts to the colony) lasted into the 1830's. One other convict, James Tucker (c. 1808-1888), wrote a novel about his experiences. The manuscript, dated around 1845, was not discovered until the 1920's and first appeared in an authentic edition in 1952. Tucker's *Ralph Rashleigh*, unlike Savery's book, depicts the convicts as overcoming the injustice dealt them and showing pride in their new country, where they hoped to lead a better life. In spite of the significance of the convict settlement and its inherent drama, only one other novel from the nineteenth century treated the Transportation System fully, and it was written by a free British settler, Marcus Clarke (1846-1881). His novel, *For the Term of His Natural Life* (1882), records the misadventures of Rufus Dawes, transported to Australia on false charges to suffer every degradation the Transportation System had to offer. Clarke's fictional version of the convict experience is generally considered to be the most important Australian novel from the 1800's.

As the nineteenth century progressed, the makeup of the country altered. The Transportation System was disbanded, the old convicts vanished, and free settlers arrived with plans to stay and advance the colony, attracted by the discovery of gold and the fortunes to be made in sheep. They shunted aside the colony's ignominious beginnings as an embarrassing happenstance. In 1838, Anna Maria Bunn, the daughter of a retired military man and the wife of a merchant mariner, published *The Guardian; A Tale*, using the pen name An Australian. Published by a newspaper printer in Sydney, where the author lived, this Gothic romance set in Ireland and England was the first novel published in Australia. It was not until the mid-twentieth century that novelists again addressed the convict experience, in books such as Eleanor Dark's *The Timeless Land* (1941), Hal Porter's *The Tilted Cross* (1961), Thomas Keneally's *Bring Larks and Heroes* (1967) and *The Playmaker* (1987), Jessica Anderson's *The Commandant* (1975), and Patrick White's *A Fringe of Leaves* (1976).

A new theme had now emerged: life in the bush. This theme embraced the severity of a land tormented by fire, dust, drought, flies, and untold hardships. It also created the bushman: individualistic, brave, unpretentious, self-deprecating, and, above all, loyal to his fellows—a much-prized quality known as mateship. In this predominantly male world, the long-suffering female settler usually remained invisible. A Sydney newspaper, the *Bulletin*, established in 1880, encouraged a brand of literary nationalism that promoted literature by Australians and about Australians out in the bush. Ironically, most Australians lived in the growing cities, including many of those who wrote bush stories. Although little of the short fiction published by the *Bulletin* lasted long, the newspaper's literary theory had a profound impact on Australian literature well into the twentieth century.

Two noteworthy novels from this era, both of which could be called bush romances, are *The Recollections of Geoffry Hamlyn* (1859), by Henry Kingsley (1830-1876), and *Robbery Under Arms* (1888), by Rolf Boldrewood (pseudonym for Thomas Alexander Browne, 1826-1915). Kingsley chronicles the fates of three families who confront unbounded misfortunes and personal calamities but at last prevail. Although it has often been dismissed as too British in its sensibility and too romantic in its approach, the novel successfully captures a period in Australian history. More engaging and more faithful to Australia, *Robbery Under Arms* offers a lively narrative that follows the adventures and destruction of a gang of bush rangers: lawless men, sometimes former convicts, who pillaged and terrorized the countryside.

The bush tradition: 1788-1900

On January 1, 1901, the six separate colonies on the vast continent united to become the Commonwealth of Australia. The move toward federation had started in the 1840's but did not gain momentum until the late 1800's. Through the nineteenth century literary advancement of the bush myth and the chauvinistic attitudes it incorporated, writers had taken an active part in the political maneuvering that led to federation. In the nationalistic fervor that dominated at the turn of the century, it was generally assumed that Australian literature would focus on what was considered authentic Australia and genuine Australians—that is, the bush and its inhabitants. While this prescribed framework produced a body of forgettable fiction in the first half of the century, it also brought forth a number of memorable novels that adhered to the tradition but overcame its limitations.

One writer who mastered the bush tradition was Katharine Susannah Prichard (1883-1969). *The Black Opal* (1921), for example, deals with the rigors of opal mining, while *Working Bullocks* (1926) depicts the lumber industry. Both are set in Western Australia, and both are politically charged. A dedicated Communist, Prichard saw literature as a way to improve Australia's social structure. The most admired of her novels, *Coonardoo: The Well in the Shadow* (1929), examines the tragic encounter between the Aboriginal and the white settler and was one of the first books to treat the Aboriginal in a sympathetic and honest manner. Another writer who took up the conflict between Australia's white and Aboriginal inhabitants was Xavier Herbert (1901-1984). His first major work, *Capricornia* (1938), is set in the vast, unsettled Northern Territory and traces the day-to-day lives of its assorted and colorful inhabitants. A tireless proponent of the superiority of the bush over the city, Herbert may well have been the last member of the nationalistic movement and his monumental book *Poor Fellow My Country* (1976) the last of its novels. This sprawling, fourteen-hundred-page narrative expands on the setting and people in the earlier novel and indicts modern Australia for turning its back on the virtues that the bush myth embodies.

Barbara Baynton (1857-1929) offers a striking alternative to the bush romance by showing that country life could be grim and oppressive, especially for women. These themes dominate her novel, *Human Toll* (1907), and her collection of short stories, *Bush Studies* (1902). Miles Franklin (1879-1954), although she wrote several books recording bush life, remains best known for *My Brilliant Career* (1901), which was made into an internationally acclaimed film of the same title (released in 1979). This narrative undermines the romance of the bush by exposing how miserably women fared on the land. To encourage Australians to create literature, Franklin left the bulk of her estate to establish what became the Miles Franklin Award, given to honor the best Australian novel or play each year.

Some of the most lasting novels from this era, at least in popular terms, are the mystery tales of Arthur Upfield (1888-1964), who continued to publish into the 1960's. Relating the adventures of a half-white, half-Aboriginal detective named Napoleon Bonaparte, the books brim with bush lore and provide an honest account of Aboriginal life. Among the best known are *The Sands of Windee* (1931) and *Death of a Swagman* (1947). Although not great literature, the novels are entertaining and continue to draw readers from around the world.

From a purely literary standpoint, though, the finest work to come from this period is *The Fortunes of Richard Mahony* (a trilogy first published as one volume in 1930), by Henry Handel Richardson (pseudonym for Ethel Florence Lindesay Robertson, 1870-1946). Interestingly, Richardson left Australia for Germany at the age of eighteen, then settled in England, where she spent the rest of her life, except for one brief visit to Australia. Although her other novels take Europe as a setting, *The Getting of Wisdom* (1910), a narrative based on Richardson's time in a Melbourne girls' school that was made into a successful film, and the trilogy return to the Australia of her childhood. For the most part, Richardson based *The Fortunes of Richard Mahony* on her own family's intermingling of tragic and fortunate circumstances in Australia from the gold rush days of the 1850's to her father's death and their impoverishment in the 1880's. In painstaking detail, Richardson re-creates colonial society, both its strengths and its defects, and in particular scrutinizes the role of women. This absolutely Australian exposition of the dark and the bright sides of colonial life fulfills the bush tradition but at the same time subverts it.

Divergence of theme and form: The novel after 1946

The bush myth in Australian fiction did not simply vanish in the postwar period. Its champions fought hard to maintain its literary conventions. That is one reason Patrick White's work gained only limited recognition at home until he received the Nobel Prize in 1973. In a 1958 essay, "The Prodigal Son," published in *Australian Letters*—a rebellious journal determined to promote cultural modernism—White called Australian critics "dingoes . . . howling unmercifully" and expressed his desire to prove the Australian novel as "not necessarily the dreary dun-coloured offspring of journalistic realism."

Although most of White's twelve novels are set in Australia, he handled the inherited materials in new ways by turning away from the realistic form of Australian fiction and moving into metaphysical realms. His first postwar novel, *The Tree of Man* (1955), unfolds the lives of an ordinary Australian farm couple, but at the same time it probes the possibilities of their inner being. On one level, the book consolidates the elements of the bush heritage—the tyrannies of nature, such as drought, bushfires, dust, and floods, along with the patience and understated valor of the pioneer. At the same time, the narrative undermines these conventions, reversing them to explore the visionary's longing. The same could be said of *Voss* (1957), which inverts the myth of heroism as it traces the Australian desert explorations of Voss, whose tortured journey evolves into a metaphysical one. White continued to give new meaning to sanctioned Australian materials in novel after novel, a practice that culminates in *A Fringe of Leaves* (1976), which retells an Australian legend of a woman captured by Aborigines. In this version an escaped convict rescues her. On the surface, the narrative resembles a classic bush romance, but in truth it deals with the deeper understanding its heroine gains through her trials. White's style, especially his tortured syntax, is inseparable from what is being said. In all respects, White opened up fresh possibilities for a fiction once characterized by stark realism.

While only a handful of Australian critics recognized the impact these novels would have on their literature, many emerging writers realized that they were no longer required to "write Australian," as Michael Wilding (born 1942) described the demands of the bush tradition. Wilding, Frank Moorhouse (born 1938), and Murray Bail (born 1941) write in an experimental fashion far exceeding White and base their work on the urban experience. Another writer, Thea Astley (1925-2004), said in an interview that no Australian novelist who picked up a pen after White began writing could escape his influence. Publishing her first novel in 1958, Astley remained faithful to the Australian stock-in-trade and to the landscape. Yet she employed these familiar rudiments to place her characters in a position to seek and possibly to find what she called the spiritual "center," a theme that dominates her work. Like White, she forsakes the cheerful bushmen and long-suffering pioneer women for what she called "misfits," those who confront an often bitter vision as they exorcise what Astley describes as the "sore fruit of their souls."

Even after White's death in 1990, some writers and critics complained that he continued to dominate Australian fiction like a colossus under whose shadow novelists must work. That is an exaggeration. Although his massive achievement will endure and remain a landmark in the Australian novel—and in the world novel in English—he freed novelists from the demand that they "write Australian." As a result, Australian fiction flourishes. Australian novelists are published abroad; their books are well reviewed and are honored with international awards. Two writers in particular, Peter Carey and David Malouf, deserve special notice.

Carey writes mainly about Australia, and his work is distinguished by wit, flights of imagination, cosmopolitan traits, and a metaphysical dimension. Critics have compared him with Jorge Luis Borges and Gabriel García Márquez. In *Illywhacker* (1985), whose title comes from an Australian slang term for confidence artist, Carey undermines the national myth in a tour de force that demonstrates how lies dominate the nation's history. He received the Booker Prize for *Oscar and Lucinda* (1988), a novel about colonial Australia that moves from reality into the fanciful. In *The Unusual Life of Tristan Smith* (1994), Carey invents a postcolonial nation that resembles Australia, which is in conflict with another imaginary nation, a powerful country that brings to mind the United States. In *Jack Maggs* (1998), he revisits Charles Dickens's *Great Expectations* (1860-1861, serial; 1861, book) to unfold the history of the Australian convict Magwitch, who figures peripherally in the original novel. *True History of the Kelly Gang* (2000) is a historical novel about Ned Kelly, who settled with his family in Australia when his Irish father was transported there as a criminal. The settings of Carey's later works have reached beyond Australia; in *His Illegal Self* (2008), for example, a small boy is taken from New York City, where Carey has lived since about 1990, to a hippie colony in the Australian Outback. By 2009, Carey had won the prestigious Booker Prize twice—one of only two authors to do so—and the Miles Franklin Award three times.

Equally original in his writing, Malouf sometimes sets his work in Europe but has placed his best novels foursquare in the Australian milieu. He examines the plight of the artist in a postcolonial society through the depiction of a painter in *Harland's Half Acre* (1984), and in *Remembering Babylon* (1993) and *The Conversations at Curlow Creek* (1996) he returns to the colonial era. Malouf does not handle that material in the prescribed manner of the bush tradition but uses the settlers, convicts, and bushrangers to make a contemporary statement. Publishing first as a poet, Malouf writes in a luminous poetic style. In 1993 he received the prestigious IMPAC Dublin Literary Award for *Remembering Babylon*. Following the publication of *The Conversations at Curlow Creek*, Malouf devoted much of his writing time to forms other than long fiction, publishing several volumes of short stories and novellas, poems, and essays as well as a play.

No discussion of the Australian novel would be complete without attention to the enigmatic figure Christina Stead (1902-1983). Born in Australia, she left for England in her mid-twenties and for the next forty years lived in Europe and the United States. At the end of her life she returned to Sydney, where she died. Except for *Seven Poor Men of Sydney* (1934), an impressionistic account of city life, and the first half of *For Love Alone* (1944), none of her fiction takes place in Australia. Her reputation depends in great part on *The Man Who Loved Children*, set in the Washington, D.C., area. First published in 1940 but largely ignored until it was reissued in 1965, the novel has since then become an international classic. Her highly original, penetrating, at once bold and subtle narrative style is unparalleled in the Australian novel. Long ignored in Australia, Stead has found a secure place in the national literary canon.

Although Australia's original inhabitants have figured in Australian fiction throughout its history—too often not very favorably or authentically—there were few or no known novels by Aboriginals to give a firsthand account of their lives in a colonized condition. The man considered by many the founder of Aboriginal writing is Mudrooroo (born 1938), who was born and who published as Colin Johnson until he took his tribal name in 1988. His first two novels, *Wild Cat Falling* (1965) and *Long Live Sandawara* (1979), are conventional in structure and depict alienated Aboriginal men living on the fringes of society. In one of his most noted works, *Doctor Wooreddy's Prescription for Enduring the Ending of the World* (1983), Mudrooroo relates the history of the Tasmanian Aboriginals who were slaughtered during the nineteenth century. He tells this horrific story in an impressive and inventive way, as the title suggests. Since this novel appeared, he has continued to work in the postmodern mode while employing Aboriginal materials to make statements about the precarious condition of Aboriginality. Many other Aboriginal writers have emerged, excelling more fully in drama, poetry, and the short story than in the novel.

Mudrooroo is undeniably an important writer and a leading voice in the effort to promote literature by Australia's indigenous people, whom the English named Aborigines. In 1990 he began a new movement with his influential *Writing from the Fringe: A Study of Modern Aboriginal Literature in Australia* (also known as *The Indigenous Literature of Australia: Milli Milli Wangka*). His own status among indigenous authors, however, has been controversial since his family revealed in 1996 that Mudrooroo's mother was Irish and English and his father was Irish and African American. Mudrooroo explained that he had felt, since he was a young child, that he was in fact Aborigine, and that his true identity was with that group. After the controversy erupted, the author stopped talking about his ancestry, saying instead that his literature is a postmodern exploration of racial identity. In a 1999 interview he stated, "Whatever my identity is, it rests on my history of over fifty years and that is that."

In the twenty-first century, new voices in Aboriginal novel writing include Alexis Wright (born 1950), whose second novel, *Carpentaria* (2006), won the Miles Franklin Award; and Tara June Winch (born 1983), whose first novel, *Swallow the Air* (2006), was highly acclaimed. Other important Australian novelists of the late twentieth and early twenty-first centuries have reached beyond Australia for their settings and themes. Janette Turner Hospital (born 1942), has written nine novels, including *Borderline* (1985), a thriller about smuggling Salvadoran refugees into Canada; *Oyster* (1996), about a charismatic cult leader in the Outback; and *Orpheus Lost* (2007), a terrorist thriller set in Cambridge, Massachusetts. Thomas Keneally (born 1935), one of Australia's most prolific and most widely known writers, has published more than thirty novels, including *Schindler's Ark* (1982; also published as *Schindler's List*, 1983). Keneally's first international success was *The Chant of Jimmie Blacksmith* (1972), which is based on the true story of an Aborigine who committed several murders in a rage over his exploitation. Years later, Keneally reflected that if he were to write the novel again he would not presume to use the voice and point of view of an Aborigine—a viewpoint he did not feel qualified or entitled to use. Keneally has won the Booker Prize twice, for *The Chant of Jimmie Blacksmith* and for *Schindler's Ark*, and he has won the Miles Franklin Award four times.

The bush tradition in Australian long fiction has faded. Realism in the Australian novel has been replaced by a fiction employing a mixture of experimental techniques. Standardized prose has been transformed into a melange of styles. The Australian novel still flourishes, an inheritor of the very traditions it has relegated to literary history.

Robert L. Ross
Updated by Cynthia A. Bily

Bibliography

Birns, Nicholas, and Rebecca McNeer, eds. *A Companion to Australian Literature Since 1900*. Rochester, N.Y.: Camden House, 2007. Thirty critical essays are divided into five sections: "Identities," "Writing Across Time," "International Reputations," "Writers and Regions," and "Beyond the Canon." Includes discussion of Australian popular writing, science fiction, children's literature, and gay and lesbian fiction.

Gelder, Kenneth, and Paul Salzman. *After the Celebration: Australian Fiction, 1989-2007*. Carlton, Vic.: Melbourne University, 2009. Examines key themes and issues in Australian fiction since 1989, the year of the country's bicentennial. Topics covered include postcolonial novels, crime fiction, feminist writing, and cultural identity.

Jones, Joseph, and Johanna Jones. *Australian Fiction*. Boston: Twayne, 1983. Surveys the development of Australian fiction and provides an extensive partially annotated bibliography of novels and critical works.

Kossew, Sue. *Writing Woman, Writing Place: Contemporary Australian and South African Fiction*. New York: Routledge, 2004. Explores the works of women writers in the two former British colonies and how they approach "place, space, and gender." Among the Australian writers discussed are Kate Jennings, Kate Grenville, and Gillian Mears.

Mudrooroo. *The Indigenous Literature of Australia: Milli Milli Wangka*. Melbourne: Hyland House, 1997. The controversial figure Mudrooroo presents a major critical survey of the oral and written literature of the indigenous peoples, or Aborigines, of Australia.

Scheckter, John. *The Australian Novel, 1830-1980: A Thematic Introduction*. New York: Peter Lang, 1998. Traces the development of the Australian novel from its beginning to 1980, with full discussions of many major works. Examines how specific themes have been repeated and refined over the years.

Walker, Shirley, ed. *Who Is She?* New York: St. Martin's Press, 1983. Considers the treatment of women in works by fifteen Australian novelists, both male and female, from the nineteenth century to the early 1980's.

Webby, Elizabeth, ed. *The Cambridge Companion to Australian Literature*. New York: Cambridge University Press, 2000. Collection of essays explores the major writers, literary movements, styles, and genres of Australian literature from the beginning. Discusses writings by the indigenous people as well as by the colonialists and includes criticism by Australians. Also includes suggestions for further reading and a chronology.

Willbanks, Ray. *Australian Voices: Writers and Their Work*. Austin: University of Texas Press, 1991. Provides in-depth interviews with sixteen contemporary Australian novelists who talk about their work and the state of the art in Australia.

Wolfe, Peter, ed. *Critical Essays on Patrick White*. Boston: G. K. Hall, 1990. Collection of critical essays provides a comprehensive introduction to White's work, examining various aspects of his themes and style. A long introduction by the editor surveys White's development as a writer.

Central and Southeastern European Long Fiction

The Central and Southeastern European literatures—Polish, Czech, Slovak, Hungarian, Serbian, Croatian, Slovenian, and Macedonian—have a long history, yet their long fiction did not develop until the second half of the nineteenth century, long after the genre had established itself in Western literatures. There had been earlier manifestations—in 1810 in Serbian literature, in 1836 in Hungarian, in the 1840's in Polish—but they were only beginnings, while the full bloom would come decades later. There is a valid reason for this delay. All these countries lived under a similar historical handicap: They were all dominated, until some time in the nineteenth century, by foreign powers that prevented them from fulfilling their national potential. While the novel flourished in other, more fortunate nations, the Polish, Czech, Slovak, Hungarian, and South Slavic lands were either in the process of liberating themselves from a centuries-old yoke or were still under domination. For the same reason, the literary movements that prevailed in Western and Russian literatures in the eighteenth century and the first half of the nineteenth century came to Central and Southeastern European literatures decades later. Furthermore, all of these peoples found themselves, around the middle of the nineteenth century, in the middle of a powerful national revival, during which literature began to flourish suddenly and, understandably, in a somewhat emotional and romantic manner. It is normal that, at such times, genres other than the novel—poetry, drama, even the short story—occupy prominent positions. (Three poets from this region have won the Nobel Prize in Literature since 1980.) All of these factors contributed to the slow rise of the novel in these literatures.

As these national reawakenings began to draw to a close, the novel began to grow. Because romanticism lingered and the euphoria of the national renaissance was still in the air, there were still romantic, patriotic, and historical novels. Thus, the national renaissance contributed after all to the growth of the novel in the second half of the nineteenth century, which would eventually—and organically—lead to a flood in the next decades. The flood swelled as realism reached these literatures, again belatedly, and social conditions and problems swayed writers to pay more attention to them. The readership, hitherto rather small, grew to the extent that it demanded more substantial works, such as the novel. It is no surprise, therefore, that the rise and full blossoming of the novel (quantitatively, if not qualitatively) coincided with the growth of social consciousness.

The enthusiasm centered on national revival and increased social awareness were the two main forces that enabled the novel to come into its own in this region. There were, however, other common features. Because these societies were in the nineteenth century overwhelmingly rural, the novelists concentrated on the life of the peasants and identified with them. As these societies became more urbanized, the focus of the writers shifted accordingly; around the middle of the twentieth century, novels about city life—whether they focused on urbanites or on newcomers from the villages—greatly outnumbered those with rural themes. By the same token, as social problems sharpened, often to the point of confrontation, novelists' interest in these problems grew. Consequently, the number of socially engaged, even revolutionary, writers in this area is disproportionately large.

One additional common feature in all of these literatures is the interest in, and the influence of, larger and more advanced literatures, especially those of Western Europe, Russia, and the United States. There is no denial that these writers were, to a greater or lesser extent, shaped by the models abroad, despite their deep roots in the native soil. The earlier the period, the greater was that influence. Today, this process is still taking place, although on a much more sophisticated level and with an increasing mutuality.

Finally, similar historical circumstances have brought on similar literary developments, especially in the sequence of literary movements, almost always in the same order. The simple fact that these countries, except Yugoslavia to some degree, suffered the same political fate after World War II also accounts for similar literary experiences. All of these factors have led to striking similarities in the literatures, especially in the novel, of the entire region. Yugoslav novelist Ivo Andrić, however, attracted international acclaim when he was awarded the Nobel Prize in 1961. Among his works, the historical novel *Travnička hronika* (1945; *Bosnian Story*, 1958; better known as *Bosnian Chronicle*), part of the author's Bosnian trilogy, received special notice. Andrić's experiences are illustrative of the special circumstances surrounding literature from this region: He was born in what is now Bosnia and Herzogovina but was then under the Ottoman Empire; before World War II he was a diplomat in what was then the Kingdom of Yugoslavia; he died in Belgrade, in what is now Serbia. He was ethnically Croatian and politically allied with the Serbs. His Nobel Prize citation made note of "the epic force with which he has traced themes and depicted human destinies drawn from the history of his country."

One should not always speak about the literatures of Central and Southeastern Europe in the same breath. On the contrary, they arise from separate countries that differ from one another in many ways—ethnically, culturally, linguistically, and even historically. For example, the fact that Polish, Czech, Serbian, Croatian, Slovenian, and Macedonian literatures are Slavic does not make them interchangeable; one cannot be read intelligently by the readers of another (Serbian and Croatian are the only exceptions). Moreover, the fact that Slavic countries have often been closely connected through common or related historical experience does not eliminate the inevitable and often basic differences between them. Therefore, to speak of their literatures together or separately is simply a matter of personal preference or convenience.

Long fiction in the Central and Southeastern European countries reflects both the similarities and the differences of the countries' respective literatures and is, perhaps more than any other genre, a true mirror of their successes and travails, their riches and limitations.

Vasa D. Mihailovich

THE POLISH NOVEL

While the history of the Polish novel in the strict sense goes back only a little further than two hundred years, the beginnings of Polish long fiction can be traced back as far as the Middle Ages and the Renaissance. The fifteenth and sixteenth centuries gave birth to numerous chronicles, hagiographies, legends, and apocrypha, in which the proportion of fictional and nonfictional elements varied. Even a genre as apparently factographic as the chronicle usually included fictional or fantastic passages, and apocrypha were purely fictional variations on biblical motifs. The subsequent development of long fiction in the late Renaissance and the long period of the baroque (which lasted approximately until the middle of the eighteenth century) moved along two distinctly different routes. In terms of the sociology of literature, the difference can be seen as a gradually widening rift between the cultural elite and the popular readership, as well as between "high" and "low" literary genres. The genre of verse epic evolved from among the "high" genres to acquire the greatest significance in the seventeenth century. Of the "lower" genres, medieval legends and apocrypha developed into the special genre of "histories," popular tales loosely based on historical, mythological, or biblical plots. Meanwhile, nonfictional genres such as memoirs, itineraries, and diaries, which flourished particularly in the seventeenth century, also laid foundations for the emergence of the Polish novel, insofar as they provided it with specific models of construction and style.

The creation of the genre of the novel in Poland, however, would have been delayed still further if a sudden outburst of interest in Western literatures had not occurred around the middle of the eighteenth century. The period of the Enlightenment, which in Poland coincided with the reign of the last Polish king, Stanisław August Poniatowski (r. 1764-1795), was marked by the rapidly increasing popularity of English, French, and German novels, which were read both in the original and in translations or loose adaptations; in particular, translations of Daniel Defoe, Jonathan Swift, Henry Fielding, Tobias Smollett, Samuel Richardson, Voltaire, Jean-Jacques Rousseau, and Johann Wolfgang von Goethe were available from about the 1760's.

Both foreign and native influences can be detected in the first Polish novel, *Mikołaja Doświadczyńskiego przypadki* (the adventures of Nicholas Doświadczyński), which was published in 1776 by the most prominent poet of the Polish Enlightenment, Ignacy Krasicki (1735-1801). In full accord with the didactic role assigned to literature in that epoch, with *Mikołaja Doświ-*

adczyńskiego przypadki, Krasicki initiated the genre of the "educational novel," in which the central character goes through various stages to demonstrate how Prejudice and Error can be finally overcome by Reason. Krasicki's novel, a liberal mixture of satiric, realistic, utopian, and didactic elements, gave the initial stimulus to the more far-reaching experiments in the field of the newly created genre. Authors such as Dymitr Krajewski (1746-1817), Józef Kossakowski (1738-1794), and Stanisław Kostka Potocki (1752-1821) produced other educational novels and "novel-treatises"; Krasicki (in another novel), Franciszek Salezy Jezierski (1740-1791), and Anna Mostowska (c. 1762-1833) created the Polish version of the historical novel; the sentimental novel, sometimes including both elements of psychological insight and realistic portrayals of society, was represented by Ludwik Kropiński (1767-1844), Maria Wirtemberska (1768-1854), and Klementyna Tańska-Hoffmanowa (1798-1845); the novels closest to the realistic mode were written by Julian Ursyn Niemcewicz (1757-1841) and Fryderyk Skarbek (1792-1866), who was also influenced in other of his novels by the style of Laurence Sterne.

In spite of the generally rationalistic character of the Enlightenment, the first Polish gothic novels (chiefly by Mostowska) also emerged; the most masterful example of this genre was that of Jan Potocki (1761-1815), *Manuscrit de Saragosse* (*The Saragossa Manuscript*, 1960), written in French between 1803 and 1815 and published in Polish as *Rękopis znaleziony w Saragossie* only in 1847. As far as its poetics was concerned, the Polish novel of the Enlightenment was characterized by its didactic purpose, personal narrator, and frequent use of "authenticating" devices (for example, epistolary or diaristic forms, or the convention of the "found manuscript").

In Poland, the subsequent epoch of Romanticism was the period of the greatest triumphs of the nonprosaic genres, such as poetry and poetic drama—though certain epic poems, such as the famous *Pan Tadeusz: Czyli, Ostatni Zajazd na litwie historia Szlachecka zr. 1811 i 1812 we dwunastu ksiegach wierszem* (1834; *Pan Tadeusz: Or, The Last Foray in Lithuania, a Tale of Gentlefolk in 1811 and 1812, in Twelve Books in Verse*, 1917), by Adam Mickiewicz (1798-1855), can be said to represent long fiction in verse. The novel, however, was far from insignificant in this period. On the contrary, the first half of the nineteenth century was marked by the rapid evolution of realistic techniques in the novel, developed principally under the powerful influence of Honoré de Balzac (Stendhal, Charles Dickens, and—in the field of the historical novel—Sir Walter Scott were also important influences). Another source of inspiration was the subjective and fantastic prose of Sterne, Nikolai Gogol, Jean Paul, and E. T. A. Hoffmann.

The towering figure in the Polish novel of the first half of the nineteenth century was Józef Ignacy Kraszewski (1812-1887), an amazingly prolific author of hundreds of novels ranging in subject matter from historical topics to contemporary life; his chief undertaking was an enormous sequence of novels that presented the history of Poland at various stages from its legendary beginnings until the end of the eighteenth century. Zygmunt Kaczkowski (1825-1896) was another important historical novelist of the period, while Józef Korzeniowski (1797-1863), Józef Dzierzkowski (1807-1865), and Walery Łoziński (1837-1861) were the most prominent novelists to deal with contemporary themes in a realistic manner. A special place is occupied by Ludwik Sztyrmer (1809-1886), who represented an extreme in his narrative subjectivism and fascination with psychopathology, and by Henryk Rzewuski (1791-1866), who drew from the seventeenth century tradition to create a specifically Polish genre of *gawęda* (a first-person tale told in "oral" style).

After the defeat of an uprising against Russia in 1863 and 1864, Polish literature entered the epoch of positivism, which was characterized by, among other things, an abrupt turn from poetry to prose. Realistic description of society's woes became the principal task of literature, and the novel seemed the most fit genre to perform it. Bolesław Prus (the pen name of Aleksander Głowacki, 1845-1912) was the most accomplished novelist of Polish positivism. A journalist turned fiction writer, he wrote a number of excellent novels, ranging in theme from that of *Faraon* (1897; *The Pharaoh and the Priest*, 1902), a novel on the mechanisms of political power as exemplified by ancient Egypt, to that of *Lalka* (1890; *The Doll*, 1972), a panorama of Polish society after the failure of the 1863 uprising. Eliza Orzeszkowa (1841-

1910) was the most outspoken champion of positivist ideas among female writers; in several novels she dealt with specific social issues, such as the emancipation of women and the fate of the Jewish minority, while her chief work, *Nad Niemnem* (1888; on the bank of the Niemen), is another vast panorama of society's life. Henryk Sienkiewicz (1846-1916) was particularly well known in the West, thanks to his novel on ancient Rome, *Quo vadis* (1896; *Quo Vadis: A Narrative of the Time of Nero*, 1896), which helped to win him the Nobel Prize in Literature; in his own country, however, he enjoyed tremendous popularity for his novels on Poland's historical past, *Krzyżacy* (1900; *The Knights of the Cross*, 1900; also known as *The Teutonic Knights*, 1943) and the trilogy consisting of *Ogniem i mieczem* (1884; *With Fire and Sword: An Historical Novel of Poland and Russia*, 1890), *Potop* (1886; *The Deluge: An Historical Novel of Poland, Sweden, and Russia*, 1891), and *Pan Wołodyjowski* (1888; *Pan Michael: An Historical Novel of Poland, the Ukraine, and Turkey*, 1893; also known as *Fire in the Steppe*, 1992).

The traditional kind of realism that had reigned in the positivist novel at the end of the nineteenth century developed, under the visible influence of Émile Zola, into the naturalistic trend in Polish fiction. This naturalism, however, was often heavily indebted to the poetics of Symbolism, which at the same time began to flourish in poetry. The most prominent fiction writer of the postpositivist generation, Stefan Zeromski (1864-1925), can be considered an inventor of a specific form of novel in which a realistic, sometimes naturalistic, vision is contrasted with a highly emotional, lyric style. Władysław Reymont (1867-1925), another Polish Nobel Prize winner, was close to naturalism in his unflinching portrayal of the industrial city of Łódź in *Ziemia obiecana* (1899; *The Promised Land*, 1927) and in his epic picture of peasant life in the four-volume *Chłopi* (1904-1909; *The Peasants*, 1924-1925). Wacław Berent (1873-1940) also began his career as a naturalist, but he later devoted himself to seeking new technical solutions in both contemporary and historical fiction. His highly original novel *Ozimina* (1911; winter wheat), for instance, employs an innovative device of shifting points of view in order to present a cross section of Polish society's attitudes. Other experimental options in novelistic narration and construction were sought by Stanisław Brzozowski (1878-1911) and Karol Irzykowski (1873-1944), both of whom were better known for their literary criticism; it was only later that their novels began to be appreciated as they deserved to be.

In the interwar period of 1918 to 1939, Polish novelists continued their search for new technical devices and thematic areas, although there was no lack of conservative solutions. Such an extreme of traditional storytelling was represented, for example, by Maria Dąbrowska (1889-1965) and her family saga *Noce i dnie* (1932-1934; nights and days). Two other female novelists, Zofia Nałkowska (1884-1954) and Maria Kuncewiczowa (1899-1989), explored the theme of the subconscious with great subtlety. The works of Juliusz Kaden-Bandrowski (1885-1944) introduced a new kind of political novel, a combination of roman à clef with expressionistic deformation. The echoes of naturalism and expressionism could still be heard in the novels of Józef Wittlin (1896-1976) or Zbigniew Uniłowski (1909-1937). At the same time, the three most important fiction writers of the interwar period were, in their own individual ways, experimenters in both artistic philosophy and technique. Stanisław Ignacy Witkiewicz (1885-1939), in his loosely constructed novels such as *Nienasycenie* (1930; *Insatiability: A Novel in Two Parts*, 1977), offered a half-catastrophic and half-grotesque prophecy of the approaching totalitarianism. Bruno Schulz (1892-1942) published two collections of short stories that can be considered segments of a complex whole; the mythologized world of his private obsessions is reflected in a highly subjective narrative technique. Finally, Witold Gombrowicz (1904-1969), in his prewar novel *Ferdydurke* (1937; English translation, 1961)—complemented, after the war, by three other of his novels—concealed under a seemingly absurd plot a profound analysis of the mechanisms of interhuman relations.

In post-1944 Poland, long fiction retained its prominent place among other literary genres despite the censorship troubles that seemed to affect the novel more than any other genre. Although the reign of Socialist Realism (from 1949 to 1955) brought a visible decline in artistic quality of the novel, Polish fiction gained momentum after the 1956 "thaw" in cultural policies of the state, and it continues vigorously to seek new creative solutions. The most prominent postwar novelists are Jerzy Andrzejewski (1909-1983), who, after the realistic *Popiół i diament* (1948; *Ashes and Diamonds*, 1962), shifted toward parabolic fiction in *Ciemonosci kryją ziemię* (1957; *The Inquisitors*, 1960) and *Bramy raju* (1960; *The Gates of Paradise*, 1962) before returning to direct social criticism in *Miazga* (1972; English translation, 1980); Kazimierz Brandys (1916-2000), whose fiction often employs nonfictional genres, such as the diary, letter, and essay; Jacek Bocheński (born 1926), author of parabolic novels on ancient Rome; Tadeusz Konwicki (born 1926), who offered catastrophic and bitter visions of contemporary Poland in *Sennik współczesny* (1963; *A Dreambook for Our Time*, 1969), *Kompleks polski* (1977; *The Polish Complex*, 1981), *Mała apokalipsa* (1979; *A Minor Apocalypse*, 1983), and *Nowy Swiat i okolice* (1986; *New World Avenue and Vicinity*, 1991); Julian Stryjkowski (1905-1996), author of *Austeria* (1966; *The Inn*, 1971) and other novels that revive the history of Jews in Poland; Tadeusz Parnicki (born 1908), a unique innovator in the field of the historical novel; and Stanisław Lem (1921-2006), an equally original writer of science fiction and philosophical parables. Lem became one of the most widely read science-fiction novelists in the world, known best perhaps for *Solaris* (1961; English translation, 1970), which has twice been made into feature films, including a 2002 version starring George Clooney. Among a younger generation, Janusz Głowacki (born 1938) and Janusz Anderman (born 1949) scored artistic successes with their novels on contemporary Poland.

In the twenty-first century, Dorota Masłowska (born 1983) wrote an acclaimed postmodernist novel, *Wojna polsko-ruska: Pod flagą biało-czerwoną* (2002; *Snow White and Russian Red*, 2005), which drew controversy because of its use of language that some critics labeled as vulgar. Daniel Koziarski (born 1979) was heralded for his debut novel, *Kłopoty to moja specjalność, czyli kroniki socjopaty* (2007; troubles are my specialization, or the chronicles of a sociopath), and its sequel, *Socjopata w Londynie* (2007; sociopath in London). One of the most popular Polish writers at the beginning of the twenty-first century is the novelist and poet Olga Tokarczuk (born 1962). Her novels include *Podróż ludzi księgi* (1993; the journey of the book people), *E. E.* (1997), *Prawiek i inne czasy* (1996; *Primeval and Other Times*, 2009), and the loosely structured *Dom dzienny, dom nocny* (1998; *House of Day, House of Night*, 2002).

Stanisław Barańczak

The Czech novel

Although Czech literature is the oldest of the Slavic literatures, its long fiction appeared relatively late, in the nineteenth century. This may be the result of the twofold handicap of the Czech culture mentioned by the great Czech critic Arne Novák (1889-1939): religion and nationalism.

Religion, particularly dissenting religion, or Protestantism, mixed with the national cause, first isolated Bohemia from the European cultural context, and when, during the Counter-Reformation, it was forcibly reattached to it, the national cause suffered. The latter meant that Czech publications were discouraged, and only at the end of the eighteenth century and then gloriously in the nineteenth did a national revival take place. This revival invested literature with tremendous responsibilities: Literature represented the nation. It set out with a grand aim to prevent the nation from perishing, and it accomplished that goal. It also laid the foundations for the future independent state. This nation-building role was fulfilled primarily by poetry; fiction had a relatively less prominent part in it. Nevertheless, considering the shortness of time, Czech fiction developed remarkably quickly and in astonishing variety, perhaps as a result of the central position occupied by the Czechs in the reigning cultural and particularly literary world at the time. Czechs were aware of the German culture as well as the triumphs of the Russian novels. They read the English as well as the French masters. Most important, the Czech novel embarked on a mission that continues to this day and that could be considered the most notable of all literary endeavors: the mission of self-discovery. It is in this vein that the first Czech masterpiece of note must be approached.

Humbly titled *Babička* (1855; *The Grandmother*, 1891), this novel by Božena Němcová (1820-1862) is a portrait of her grandmother, whose gift was the power to transform the life of her grandchildren, who were doomed by modest circumstances. Hailed as the major fictional artistic legacy of the post-Romantic era, the novel succeeds in bringing to life an admirable character whose grace, charm, and wit have endeared Němcová to generations of readers.

A direct antithesis to Němcová is Karolina Světlá (1830-1899). While Němcová still represents a woman who honors tradition, occasionally transcending it in the name of love, Světlá is a feminist often compared to George Sand and George Eliot. Contemporary problems, set against a background of country settings and picturesque local customs, are typical of her fiction. Representative of this type of novel is her *Vesnický román* (1867; a village romance), which proved to be a generic predecessor of a group of novels by writers predominantly concerned with the village novel but who belong to a later generation, such as Karel V. Rais (1859-1926), Vilém Mrštík (1863-1912), and Josef Holeček (1853-1929). In fact, the novels of Světlá foreshadow, in a curiously incomplete and often frustrating manner, the main directions of Czech fiction in the nineteenth century: the social, the village, and the historical. An attempt has been made to place *The Grandmother* into the category of the social novel, but the works of Gustav Pfleger Moravskyá (1833-1875), Matej Anastasia Šimáček (1860-1913), and Josef Karel Šlejhar (1864-1914) better exemplify this type.

By far the most influential type of novel written in the nineteenth century was the historical novel. Here, the Czech Protestant cause—its defeat and what followed it—proved irresistible to nationalist-minded Czech novelists: V. Beneš Třebízsk (1849-1884), Zikmund Winter (1846-1912), and, most important, Alois Jirásek (1851-1930). Jirásek covered the whole range of Czech history, and his importance is analogous to that of Henryk Sienkiewicz in Poland. It is no exaggeration to say that Jirásek consciously blended historical material into myths designed to augment the nation building that was going on in his lifetime. That this effort was often accompanied by distortions, simplifications, and whitewashing, to say nothing of the fact that it ignored the obviously negative consequences of at least some historical Czech actions, is beyond doubt. Also beyond doubt is Jirásek's powerful historical vision, his ability to project himself to distant times and to grasp or re-create the motivation of historical characters in a spellbinding and often emotionally moving manner. This is true of his *Proti všem* (1893; against everyone) and his trilogy *Bratrstvo* (1899-1908; the brethren), as well as of his numerous historical novels, with the exception of those treating a more recent, revivalist past, such as his tetralogy *U nás* (1896-1903; in our land).

The period of realism announced in the work of K. Čapek-Chod (1860-1927) can be understood either as a transitional period leading up to the three most important interwar novelists, Jaroslav Hašek (1883-1923), Karel Čapek (1890-1938), and Vladislav Vančura (1891-1942), or as the beginning of an as yet unconcluded period of realism of many different varieties. Hašek's *Osudy dobrého vojáka Švejka za světove války* (1921-1923; *The Good Soldier: Švejk*, 1930; also known as *The Good Soldier Švejk and His Fortunes in the World War*, 1973; better known as *The Good Soldier Švejk*) is a masterpiece of the satiric novel, while Čapek's trilogy comprising *Hordubal* (1933; English translation, 1934), *Povětroó* (1934; *Meteor*, 1935), and *Obyčejný život* (1934; *An Ordinary Life*, 1936) offers a fine example of the philosophical novel. Vančura's experimentation was stylistic and, of the three, is least accessible to a foreign reader; these three authors taken together represent a firm foundation for the flourishing of the novel after World War II. Somewhat isolated seems Jaroslav Durych (1886-1962), a brilliant novelist who is an antipode to Jirásek in his own historical novels concerned with the same Hussite period, to which Durych takes a contrasting, Catholic approach.

The novel, as well as all Czech literature, suffered after the Communist takeover in 1948, when a large-scale Sovietization of cultural life was enforced, together with the absurd requirements of Socialist Realism: to write in a way that would not anger the authorities. The tragic 1950's ended in gradual liberalization and the appearance of three great novelists: Bohumil Hrabal (1914-1997), Josef Škvorecký (born 1924), and Milan Kundera (born 1929). Hrabal was a narrative genius with an unerring eye for the surreal and the grotesque in everyday life. In his fiction, accidents, violence, sex, and drinking are mixed with sentimentalism and the moving pathos of unexpected lyric passages. Even though after initial prohibition Hrabal was allowed to publish, he was forced to make many compromises with state censors, as is evident in those works that have been published abroad.

Škvorecký and Kundera, in that order, were forced to emigrate after the liberalization of the 1960's abruptly ended in the Soviet invasion of Czechoslovakia in 1968. This exile was a mixed blessing; whatever the discomforts of the authors, the world gained two great novelists. Kundera's *Le Livre du rire et de l'oubli* (1979; *The Book of Laughter and Forgetting*, 1980; in Czech as *Kniha smíchu a zapomnění*, 1981) and, even more, his *L'Insoutenable Légèreté de l'être* (1984; *The Unbearable Lightness of Being*, 1984; in Czech as *Nesnesitelná lehkost bytí*, 1985), as well as his many essays published in leading literary magazines in the West, made him the leading spokesman for the endangered entity of Central Europe, whose roots and sympathies lie in the West. Kundera's prose carries the influence of Hašek, Čapek, and Vančura into a synthesis always grounded in a philosophical theme approached with irony and sometimes even misanthropy. (In 2008, a controversy erupted when Kundera, who took up residency in France in 1975, was accused in a Czech newspaper of having been a secret police informer in 1950. Eleven well-known writers, including Nadine Gordimer, Gabriel García Márquez, and Salman Rushdie, issued a public announcement of support for Kundera.)

Škvorecký's *Zbabělci* (1958; *The Cowards*, 1970) is a masterpiece of dramatic action seen through the eyes of an adolescent interested in girls and jazz. Much more ambitious, but less successful, is his *Příběh inženýra lidských duší*, 1977 (*The Engineer of Human Souls: An Entertainment on the Old Themes of Life, Women, Fate, Dreams, the Working Class, Secret Agents, Love, and Death*, 1984), in which the narrator, like Škovrecký himself, an émigré Czech professor at a university in Toronto, Canada, deals with personal and political problems with the help of his experiences under the Nazi and then the Communist regimes in Bohemia. His well-received *Obyčejné životy* (2004; *Ordinary Lives*, 2008) recounts the life of his recurring narrator, Danny Smiricky, and the ideological waves he faces over fifty years of Czech history. Škvorecký's work, although informed by a powerful intellect, is less elaborate than the work of Hrabal or Kundera. A quiet sense of rationality and moderation radiates from Škvorecký's writing, which is infused with a gentle humor.

One of the most popular Czech writers of the late twentieth and early twenty-first centuries is Michal Viewegh (born 1962), author of humorous novels about contemporary relationships. His *Báječná léta pod psa* (1992; the blissful years of lousy living), *Výchova dívek v Čechách* (1994; *Bringing Up Girls in Bohemia*, 1997), and *Román pro ženy* (2001; woman's novel) were all made into feature films. He published *Román pro muže* (man's novel) in 2008. Czech author Michal Ajvaz (born 1949) has published several works of Magical Realism, and Pavel Řezníček (born 1942) works in the surrealist style. The works of Ajvaz and Řezníček have not yet been translated into English.

Peter Petro

The Slovak novel

Slovak literature, and consequently Slovak fiction, is less well known than the neighboring Czech fiction. This could be a negative consequence of having a binational state. The country was, until it split into the Czech Republic and Slovakia in 1993, known as Czechoslovakia, and if one thought about translating anything of "Czechoslovakian" literature, one thought first of Czech literature, not Slovak literature. (Some encyclopedias published post-1993 contain articles about "Czechoslovakian" literature.)

In addition to good poetry, interesting and occasionally brilliant works are to be found in Slovak literature. This fiction is very much unlike the fiction of any of Slovakia's neighbors, perhaps because it reflects radically different living conditions: Slovakia, like Switzerland, is a country of mountains, of shepherds and lumberjacks, but also of rapidly growing cities; its capital, Bratislava, always had a cosmopolitan atmosphere because of its German and Hungarian populations. The center of gravity of Slovak fiction, then, not surprisingly, lies in the exploitation of the country's mountainous geography. The Slovak village novel is characteristically concerned with unspoiled, natural people; the traditional lifestyle of the people of the mountains is juxtaposed to the artificial existence offered by the cities. This contrast is particularly well developed and fortified by an indigenous Slovak tradition of lyric prose. Indeed, while there are urban Slovak novels and experimental novels that betray common Central European—that is, Western—heritage, the main accomplishment of Slovak long fiction is the development and establishment of the rich genre of lyric prose.

Jozef Ignác Bajza (1755-1836) stands at the beginning of Slovak prose with his novel *René mládenca príhodi a skúsenosti* (1783; the adventures and experiences of the young man René), published even before the codification of the Slovak language (1843). The novel bears traces of the influence of Voltaire and Christoph Martin Wieland.

The first half of the nineteenth century was taken up with the gradual establishment of the revivalist movement, expressed in literature mainly through poetry. Prose reaffirmed itself in the second half of the century with *Reštaurácia* (1860; the elections), by Ján Kalinčiak (1822-1871), wherein the world of the Slovak gentry's life is pictured in Hungary before 1848, the revolutionary year. The problem of Slovak politics in the absence of a Slovak state (for Slovakia was then a part of Hungary) is indirectly posed through the gentle satire of manners and politics.

Far more valuable are the works of a leading man of letters, Svetozár Hurban Vajanský (1847-1916), who dealt sensitively with a wide range of problems—social, domestic, national, and philosophical—in his *Letiace tiene* (1883; fleeting shadows) and *Suchá ratolesť* (1884; the withered branch).

Martin Kukučín (1860-1928), often considered the best Slovak novelist, spent much of his life abroad, forced by unbearable conditions to leave his motherland. Indeed, millions of his fellow Slovaks began leaving their country toward the end of the nineteenth century, settling in the United States, Canada, and elsewhere in such numbers that, one hundred years later, there were more Slovaks abroad than in Slovakia. Kukučín's work, in five volumes, *Mať volá* (1926-1927; mother is calling), deals with the fate of Croatian emigrants in Latin America, but his short stories, plays, and other novels are firmly rooted in Slovak soil.

A follower of Kukučín and in many respects his superior in the scope, quality, and the ambitiousness of his novelistic enterprise is Jozef Cíger-Hronský (1896-1961), best known for his novel *Jozef Mak* (1933; English translation, 1984), which deals with the life of a silent villager in a sensitive, lyric manner imbued with a pathos based on a Christian worldview. Among Hronský's other novels, particularly brilliant are two in which it is possible to trace connections with *Jozef Mak*, thus establishing a "trilogy": *Pisár Gráč* (1940; Gráč the clerk) and *Andreas Búr Majster* (1948; Andreas Búr, master). This trilogy of masterpieces is unequaled in Slovak literature. No one has matched Hronský's ability to capture the spirit or essence of Slovak existence and to express what it meant to be a Slovak in some key and dramatic periods of the modern history of Slovakia.

Milo Urban (1904-1982) received considerable attention for his *Živý bič* (1927; the living whip), which, together with Hronský's *Jozef Mak*, belongs among the outstanding novels of the interwar period. This period was particularly rich and represents an explosion of talents and styles: the decadent experimentation of Gejza Vámoši (1901-1956), the proletarian novels of Peter Jilemnický (1901-1949), and the gradual establishment of lyric prose through the work of L. Ondrejov (1901-1962), Margita Figuli (1909-1995), František Švantner (1912-1950), and Dobroslav Chrobák (1907-1951).

After 1948, the Communist takeover slowed down the promising coming-of-age of Slovak long fiction but could not stop its development in the hands of F. Hečko (1905-1960), Franko Král' (1903-1955), and their younger followers, such as Vladimir Mináč (1922-1996) and Dominik Tatarka (1913-1989), who later developed into a fiercely independent spirit best known for his *Prútené kreslá* (1962; straw chairs) and *Démon súhlasu* (1963; the demon of acquiescence).

Strangely enough, the most successful and original of a newer generation of Slovak novelists, Vincent Šikula (1936-2001), tried to link up with the prewar novel; his model is Hronský. This is clear from his trilogy *Majstri, Muškát, Vilma* (1976-1979; masters, geranium, Vilma). In addition to books of poetry and children's fiction, Šikula wrote more than twenty books of fiction for adults, including *Ornament* (1991; ornament) and *Požehnaná taktovka* (2003; blessed wand).

The various ups and downs of Communist literary politics during the late twentieth century notwithstanding, Slovak literature continued to flourish, even though the price may have been a compromise—flight into history or even the inability to publish. This paradoxical situation can be explained by a strong showing of new talent and a great variety of approaches observable in the incoming novelistic production. Contemporary Slovak fiction bears all the attributes of modern urban literature. Juraj Červenák (born 1974) is a best-selling writer of historical fictions and novels drawing on mythology. Dušan D. Fabian (born 1975) writes in the horror and fantasy genres; his first two novels are *Invocatio Elementalium* (2006) and *Pestis Draconum* (2008). More conventional and highly regarded literary fiction is also a part of the twenty-first century Slovak literary scene, created by writers such as Michal Hvorecký (born 1976), who has won literary prizes at home as well as in Germany and the United States.

Peter Petro

The Hungarian novel

In contrast with Western Europe, where the history of the modern novel had its beginnings with the rise of the Third Estate, in Hungary this genre appeared around the end of the eighteenth century, at the time when a sizable and nationally conscious native bourgeoisie did not yet exist. The most bourgeois of literary forms was thus championed by the more enlightened representatives of the privileged classes. Another peculiarity of late eighteenth century Hungarian literary life was that while nearly every intellectual realized the necessity to develop a sovereign national cultural atmosphere, imitations of Western European forms continued to prevail. In the case of the novel, the example of the English model, with its moderate, moralizing sentimentality, and of the French writers, with their cooler, rational detachment, were particularly strong influences. The German trends were also prominent on the scene, but, in part because of the uncomfortable presence of Habsburg domination, a number of Hungarian writers were reluctant to follow them.

In accordance with what many Hungarian intellectuals adopted as their motto, "The chief hope of a country's happiness lies through knowledge," the earliest novels were earmarked by enlightened curiosity and newly gained erudition. The various aspects of Neoclassicism were mixed with the baroque and rococo elements of the Habsburg culture, while faint signs of sentimental and Romantic attitudes foreshadowed the developments that were to take place during the nineteenth century.

Popular interest in the novel was increasing, but works of long fiction were available to Hungarian readers mostly in the form of poor translations (or, more often, adaptations) based on foreign works of questionable value. The term *roman* even acquired a pejorative connotation among some intellectuals, who criticized the genre as much for its "immorality" as for its lack of aesthetic standards. Among the earliest examples of original Hungarian novels, the most successful were those that catered to the sentimental outlook of the women readers and the nationalistic pride of the men. Thus, in a country where lyric and narrative poetry were traditionally considered the chief forms of literary expression, the novel was well on its way to becoming the new, modern national epic.

After the beginning of the nineteenth century, a small but determined group of intellectuals initiated a thorough reform of the Hungarian language. They emphasized originality, individuality, and new aesthetic principles, and they revealed their concern for the development of a less feudalistic and tradition-bound society by coining phrases and words to fit timely concepts, thus opposing the linguistic (and social) isolationism of their opponents. They may have broken some of the rules of grammar and "offended the spirit of the language," as their critics claimed, but the majority of their linguistic innovations passed into literary and everyday use. Their campaign also brought literature to the center of Hungarian public life. Shrewd publishers offered more and more novels to satisfy popular demand. The quality of these writings improved rather slowly, and imitations and adaptations continued to prevail for decades; nevertheless, by the 1840's a number of significant novels dealing with the social problems of the past and the present appeared. Exhibiting the positive influence of the French and English Romantics, Hungarian writers introduced well-drawn characters in fast-paced action, and their manner of depiction also became more convincing.

In addition to offering plenty of adventure and excitement to the readers, Romanticism was also in perfect accord with the birth or revival of national consciousness sweeping Europe during the nineteenth century. One important aspect of this process was that men of letters made the study of folk life and folk literature one of their aims, in order to depict better the lives of, and eventually to give voice to the long-neglected aspirations of, the commoners. In Hungary, this trend held out the promise of a more democratic approach to national characterization as well as to literary activity in general. Romantic philosophy was domesticated by equating the concept of True Man with that of the True Hungarian. During what came to be called an "era of the people," populist aesthetic principles and practices came to prevail, and increasingly realistic elements were introduced into the essentially Romantic prose of the mid-nineteenth century. To a certain extent, this was true even in the case of Mór Jókai (1825-1904), the greatest and most prolific Romantic storyteller of Hungary, whose imaginative power, spontaneously allied with the prevailing sentiments of his countrymen, was supremely responsible for the creation of many national illusions.

Romanticism continued to dominate the Hungarian novel, even though there were writers, most notably József Eötvös (1813-1871), whose works approached in quality the best that European realism had to offer. The problems and contradictions of society, however, became the central theme of long fiction only after the 1867 Compromise between the Habsburg ruler and his formerly rebellious Hungarian subjects. Influenced by imported positivist, utilitarian, and even socialist ideas, a number of middle-class writers came to view themselves as members of an "unnecessary" generation and vented their feelings of disappointment in a flood of bitterly critical bildungsromans.

After the policies of Dualist Hungary achieved a certain degree of "consolidation," the tendencies toward objective realism and social criticism again were neglected. Johann Strauss the Younger's operetta *Der Zigeunerbaron* (1885; *The Gypsy Baron*, 1954), based on an 1885 Jókai novel of the same title, could with some justification be considered the representative artistic creation of the period. The anecdotal approach of Jókai and his followers was so prevalent that, even as the fin de siècle brought more of the problems of society to the surface, Hungarian writers clung to the genre of the melancholy, resignation-filled short story in their presentation of the new realities. Kálmán Mikszáth (1847-1910) may be considered the most successful exception: In his novels, the influence of the best and worst traits (imaginative, dramatic narration and anecdotal provincialism) of Jókai were gradually replaced by a bitingly critical, though never combative, strain of social satire. As the first major Hungarian writer whose Romanticism was subordinated to realism, the influence of Mikszáth on subsequent generations of prose writers was decisive.

Many Hungarian writers were associated with the literary journalism of the growing cities, and this experience was instrumental in their adopting subjective and relative aesthetic values and, consequently, shocking their audiences with adventurous free-association techniques. They struggled hard to present their society successfully, as that society was troubled by sharp contradictions between the glitter of Budapest and the squalor of the villages, between the impressive economic growth and the self-destructive process of mass emigration, and between the prevalence of national complacency and the intellectual ferment brought about by an illustrious generation of thinkers and artists. The periodical *Nyugat* (meaning "west"), published from 1908 to 1941, financed by "new money," and cultivated mostly by urban intellectuals, attracted a loose coalition of artistic and literary talent, difficult to classify into any single category but strongly influenced by the fashionable "isms" of contemporary Western Europe. Paying more attention to style than to content, and remaining a largely apolitical platform throughout its existence, *Nyugat* (and the publishing house associated with it) rejected many conventions and provided an independent forum for every new, exciting trend and idea. The *Nyugat* novelists were served by the principle that in literature anything was justified if the writer had the talent to achieve his intended effect.

The literature of Hungary during the interwar period is frequently labeled as nationalistic and conservative, but a conscientious examination reveals that many kinds of writings, including even those of the noncommunist Left, were allowed to reach the readers, and critical realism continued to be in ascendance. Having shed some of their nationalistic presumptions and addressing instead the issues of modern human existence, the best of Hungary's writers strove to make their public aware of the burning need to alter their society. Since realism was relatively late arriving in Hungary, its energies were still fresh, and the extreme social polarization lent it a special virulence. The works of Zsigmond Móricz (1879-1942) stand out with their carefully balanced duality: They bore the stamp of naturalism in presenting the joys and sorrows of poor people's lives, while they continually affirmed the idealistic, nearly prophetic commitment of the writer to improving the lot of the underprivileged. An entire generation of writers following Móricz's lead, and their ethnocentric orientation continues to make its effect felt even in today's Hungarian prose.

The neopopulists of the 1930's advocated a "third road" course for Hungary and proclaimed the potentials of peasantry for leading a national revival. Their "revolution of quality" was to prepare the country for the changes that were foreseeable after the end of the war. On the other hand, the writings of the important novelists among the "urbanists" were marked by a desire to reveal the unsettling dichotomy between surface appearance and reality and by an ability to capture the substance of individual lives in seemingly insignificant gestures. Populist and urbanist groups had little sympathy or understanding for each other, and the resulting split in intellectual leadership was one of the genuine tragedies of twentieth century Hungary.

The defeat and occupation of Hungary by the Soviet armies brought about major changes in the literary life of the country as well. After the initial postwar years of democratic coalition, during which various voices were allowed to be heard, there followed the subjugation of literature to the often ludicrous political course of the times. Many promising talents fell victim to the war and persecution, and many more to a different brand of barbarism during the subsequent years. The ill-defined principles of Socialist Realism proved to be a straitjacket into which only the writings of a few hacks fit comfortably. The best-known Hungarian socialist writer, Tibor Déry (1894-1977), repeatedly came up against the stone wall of unappreciative official criticism, while many of his best contemporaries were prevented from publishing their works. Although its aftereffects are felt to this day, this period of heavy-handed repression proved to be neither long-lasting nor entirely successful. Hungarian literature did not lose its inherited resilience, and the 1954 "explosion of talent" contributed to raising public consciousness to the level that made the 1956 revolution inevitable. The role of the printed word in the revolution was convincingly affirmed when the Soviet-installed Kádár government imprisoned or silenced a number of writers and disbanded the Writers' Union.

After the end of World War I, millions of Hungarians came under the jurisdiction of the neighboring successor states, and since then they have faced formidable odds in striving to preserve their cultural traditions. Their writers produce some of the most relevant works in contemporary Hungarian prose, most significantly in Transylvania, a land that long nurtured its own intellectual heritage. The oppressive policies of the Romanian authorities during later years made this literary activity even more noteworthy. In comparison, the output of Hungarian novelists living in the West, presumably under more favorable conditions, remained by and large unimpressive.

In Hungary, the post-1956 "consolidation" amounted to little more than an admission by the rulers of the country to the effect that writers have the right to be apolitical and mildly experimental. The reorganized Writers' Union was given the task of preserving the position of hegemony that was occupied by Marxist-Leninist aesthetics, while, somewhat ironically, the freedom of non-Marxist but "well-meaning" writers was loudly proclaimed. Within a smoothly running system of self-censorship, a relatively liberal publishing practice was realized, with the result that barely tolerated (or suppressed) pieces of Hungarian prose attracted considerable attention at home and abroad. However, Hungarian Jewish author Imre Kertész (born 1929), a Holocaust survivor, won the Nobel Prize in 2002 for his historical novels that uphold "the fragile experience of the individual against the barbaric arbitrariness of history." His best-known novel is *Sorstalanság* (1975; *Fateless*, 1992; also known as *Fatelessness*, 2004), about a teenage boy's experiences in three Nazi concentration camps.

The writer Péter Esterházy (born 1950) is widely known in Hungary and throughout the Western world. Many of his novels have been translated into English, including *A szív segédigéi* (1985; *Helping Verbs of the Heart,* 1991), *Egy nő* (1993; *She Loves Me,* 1994), and *Harmonia Cœlestis* (2000; *Celestial Harmonies,* 2004). Esterházy's works have been translated into more than twenty languages, and he has won nearly every literary award given in Hungary as well as several international prizes. The most significant woman writer in Hungary during the late twentieth and early twenty-first centuries was Magda Szabó (1917-2007), who wrote poetry and criticism as well as highly regarded novels.

András Boros-Kazai

The Serbian novel

Slavic tribes in Southeastern Europe developed their cultures separately beginning in the tenth century. Only in the second decade of the twentieth century were they united in one state called Yugoslavia. Even then, Yugoslav literatures went their own ways despite the ethnic, linguistic, and cultural kinship. For that reason, it is best to discuss fiction of Serbian, Croatian, Slovenian, and Macedonian literatures separately.

Serbian fiction did not fully develop, or show worthwhile results, until the nineteenth century. The main reason is that the Serbs were militarily occupied by the Turks from the end of the fourteenth century almost to the middle of the nineteenth century. Little literature, except for oral epics, was possible. The earlier forms resembling fiction, biographies of saints and kings, the folk epics, and the translations of medieval novels were either not novels or not original creations and therefore belong to the prehistory of the Serbian novel. The Serbs, who had migrated to Austrian lands in the north, slowly began to revive cultural activity in the late eighteenth century. The first novelist of significance was Milovan Vidaković (1780-1841), a writer of limited skill but unlimited ambition. Imitating both the European baroque adventure novel and the Greek love novels of late antiquity, he wrote several of his own that, though of meager artistic value, were very popular with the readers. The ensuing Romanticism, lasting approximately four decades (1830-1870), emphasized poetry and drama and showed little interest in the novel. The Serbian novel came into its own in the second half of the nineteenth century. The writer most responsible for this development was Jakov Ignjatović (1822-1889). He began by writing historical novels but soon turned to the realistic depiction of the life of his people in Austro-Hungary. Even though he wrote most of his novels when Romanticism was still dominating Serbian letters, it was his interest in everyday life and his attention to minute detail (which he acquired during his stay in Paris and through contacts with French realists) that made him the founder of the realist novel in Serbian literature. He possessed sharp observation, keen understanding of the life around him, and boundless energy. His glaring artistic weaknesses prevented him from becoming an outstanding novelist in the mold of Honoré de Balzac. Nevertheless, Ignjatović's works formed the firm basis for further development of the Serbian novel.

It was not until the last decade of the nineteenth century that other realist novelists appeared. For the most part, they depicted the Serbian village, following the lead of the short story. Furthermore, they tended to emphasize their own region, drawing from its rich folklore and thus bringing that region into the limelight. These writers—Janko Veselinović (1862-1905), Simo Matavulj (1852-1908), Stevan Sremac (1855-1906), and Svetolik Ranković (1863-1899)—brought the Serbian novel closer to the European realistic novel, though not to the same artistic level. They were also very much concerned with social problems, which began to preoccupy the Serbian society, and through their psychological probings they revealed the influence of the nineteenth century Russian realists.

In the twentieth century, the fragile realistic tradition continued while new modernistic tendencies began to make inroads, not dramatic at first but increasingly evident. While Borisav Stanković (1876-1927) and Ivo Ćipiko (1869-1923) also wrote about provincial regions, Milutin Uskoković (1884-1915) attempted to write a city novel about Belgrade, in contrast to the existing literature, which was almost entirely about either village or small-town life. The true modernists, however, appeared after World War I, spurred by their traumatic war experiences and keeping in step with the dramatic changes in their country. A noticeably enhanced artistic value of their novels, imbued with a pronounced poetic atmosphere, as manifested in the novels of Rastko Petrović (1898-1949) and Miloš Crnjanski (1893-1977), finally brought the Serbian novel to the level of world fiction after a century of lagging behind.

The culmination of this advance is embodied in the three novels by Ivo Andrić (1892-1975) published in 1945. His magnum opus, *Na Drini ćuprija* (1945; *The Bridge on the Drina*, 1959), combines the epic tradition with modern approaches to the novel, notably those of psychological penetration and mythmaking. Andrić stands at the watershed of the preceding century and the contemporary period. After World War II, the Serbian novel was characterized by increased output, improved artistic quality, and the tradition adapting to developments in other literatures.

The leading contemporary novelists are Dobrica Ćosić, Meša Selimović, Danilo Kiš, and Milorad Pavić. Ćosić (born 1921) deals in the four-volume *Vreme smrti* (1972-1979; *A Time of Death*, 1978; *Reach to Eternity*, 1980; *South to Destiny*, 1981; also known as *This Land, This Time*, 1983 [includes *Into the Battle*, *A Time of Death*, *Reach to Eternity*, and *South to Destiny*]) with the momentous event in Serbian history, World War I, and with the struggle of the Serbian army against overwhelming enemies. In the three volumes of *Vreme zla* (1985-1990; a time of evil), he dissects the experience of Serbs with Communism, tracing the painful road from the early idealism of true believers to the internecine fight symptomatic of totalitarian movements. In the two-volume *Vreme vlasti* (1996, 2007; a time of power), he follows that experience to the next logical step, the inevitable corruption of power and painful betrayal of initial goals. Even though Ćosić bases his novels on historical and political themes, he creates strong, credible characters and builds skillful plots. He represents best the neorealistic trend in contemporary Serbian novels, using the political scene as a background to underscore the need for morality in everyday life.

In one of the best contemporary Serbian novels, *Derviš i smrt* (1966; *Death and the Dervish*, 1996), Selimović (1910-1982) grapples with some of the basic ethical problems. Drawing from his personal experience—the loss of his brother at the hands of his Communist brethren—he weaves a powerful story of love and loyalty. His philosophical musings and psychological probing lead to a charming fusion of the East and the West and to a thoughtful quest for the meaning of life within a Muslim frame of mind.

Among the younger writers, Kiš (1935-1989) impressed critics and readers, both at home and abroad, with his novels *Bašta, pepeo* (1965; *Garden, Ashes*, 1975) and *Grobnica za Borisa Davidoviča* (1976; *A Tomb for Boris Davidovich*, 1978). In his early works he dealt with the tragic loss of his Jewish father at the hands of the Nazis, creating in him an almost mythical character. In his later novels he used a modernistic approach to deal with burning political and ideological questions of the time. *A Tomb for Boris Davidovich*, consisting of seven loosely related stories yet with an organic unity, follows the crisscrossing paths of several victims of the totalitarian Communist ideology. It was illogical to Kiš to oppose one form of dictatorship, Nazism, while disregarding or even supporting its sibling, Communism. In *Enciklopedija mrtvih* (1983; *The Encyclopedia of the Dead*, 1989), which is similarly a collection of nine loosely related stories but is treated also as a novel, he deals mostly with the syndrome of death, intertwining documentary and fictitious material. Kiš's insistence on authenticity of his subject matter, which he achieved by meticulously studying historical documents, led to a peculiar mixture of fact and fiction, transformed by the author's unmistakable artistry into internationally acclaimed works of fiction.

Pavić (born 1929), a leading representative of postmodernism in Serbian fiction, achieved significant international success with his *Hazarski rečnik: Roman leksikon u 100,000 reči* (1984; *Dictionary of the Khazars: A Lexicon Novel in 100,000 Words*, 1988) as well as with other novels. In *Dictionary of the Khazars*, Pavić employs dazzling flights of imagination, spanning centuries and bringing together a colorful array of characters, in order to show that reality and fantasy are constantly interchanged and that their borderlines are therefore deliberately blurred. This pervasive relativity is underscored by the fact that the story is presented in three versions—the Christian, the Islamic, and the Hebrew. Laden with many possible interpretations, the novel is a perfect example of postmodernism, which has taken a strong hold among Serbian novelists. Pavić continues in a similar vein in *Predeo slikan čajem* (1988; *Landscape Painted with Tea*, 1990), and *Unutrašnja strana vetra: Ili, Roman o Heri i Leandru* (1991; *The Inner Side of the Wind: Or, The Novel of Hero and Leander*, 1993), using striking metaphors, similes, paradoxes, hyperboles, maxims, and other tropes, making the novel just as complex yet delightful to read. Pavić has become most representative of the present trends in Serbian long fiction.

Other significant novelists are Mihailo Lalić (1914-1992), Branko Ćopić (1915-1984), Aleksandar Tišma

(1924-2003), Miodrag Bulatović (1930-1991), Dragoslav Mihailović (born 1930), Borislav Pekić (1930-1992), Živojin Pavlović (1933-1998), and Slobodan Selenić (1933-1995). Each has contributed at least one memorable novel, such as Lalić's *Lelejska gora* (1952, revised 1962, 1990; *The Wailing Mountain*, 1965), Bulatović's *Crveni petao leti prema nebu* (1959; *The Red Cock Flies to Heaven*, 1962), Tišma's *Upotreba čoveka* (1976; *The Use of Man*, 1988), Mihailović's *Kad su cvetale tikve* (1968; *When Pumpkins Blossomed*, 1971), Pekić's *Vreme čuda* (1965; *The Time of Miracles*, 1976), and Selenić's *Ubistvo s predumišljajem* (*Premeditated Murder*, 1996). While following their own paths, they have contributed to a sophisticated, innovative, and lasting brand of fiction. They are not reluctant to explore the formalistic possibilities of the modern novel while having their characters persistently cope with the dilemmas and difficulties of everyday life.

Serbian novelists of a younger generation are preoccupied with the difficult situation in which Serbs find themselves, especially after the war in Bosnia. Even though writers such as Pavić and Pekić tend to use the extraneous events only as a distant background for their novels, others use the everyday events as direct stimuli. Among the more successful ones are Vladimir Arsenijević (born 1965) and Radoslav Petković (born 1953). Arsenijević enjoyed great success with the first of his five novels, *U potpalublju* (1995; *In the Hold*, 1996), in which he uses the war between the Serbs and the Croats in 1991 as a background governing the fate of all the characters involved and their efforts to avoid being drawn into and destroyed in the war's vortex. Arsenijević does not limit himself to the depiction of the war; he delves into Belgrade's drug culture, black marketeering, and crime, along with desperate flights into emigration of the young people and suicides. The author's control over the subject matter, his subliminal moral messages, and the novel's high literary quality make it not only excellent literature but also a harbinger of a new spirit in Serbian fiction. The novel was translated into twenty languages, making Arsenijević one of the most widely read Serbian writers outside his native country.

Petković, in his most successful novel, *Sudbina i komentari* (1994; destiny and comments), traces in a wide sweep covering more than three hundred years the destinies of several characters to establish the connections between events in the past and the present. Using a postmodernist technique, he probes the relationship between history and literature, thus lending the modern Serbian novel a much wider and more universal scope.

Vasa D. Mihailovich

THE CROATIAN NOVEL

Croatian fiction had an early beginning in Petar Zoranić's *Planine* (1569; mountains), but that was an isolated case. Like the Serbs, the Croats were dominated by a foreign power for centuries, this time the Austro-Hungarian Empire. The true development began with August Šenoa (1838-1881), who wrote several historical novels during the Romantic period in Croatian literature. Šenoa approached his novels more like a realist, especially when describing social conditions. Historical events and figures from the fourteenth to the eighteenth centuries were used by Šenoa to inspire his people in their struggle for independence and social order. Toward the end of his life, he turned entirely to topics from everyday life, foreshadowing several realist novelists concerned almost exclusively with social problems. Ante Kovačić (1854-1889), Eugen Kumičić (1850-1904), Josip Kozarac (1858-1906), Vjenceslav Novak (1859-1905), Ksaver Šandor Djalski (1854-1935), and Janko Leskovar (1861-1949) attempted, in their individual ways, to cope with the pressing problems besetting their people while striving to advance the novel. Some novelists reflected a local milieu, while others showed the influence of Honoré de Balzac, Gustave Flaubert, Ivan Turgenev, and the naturalists. Although they were usually successful with one or two novels, they all helped in establishing a tradition in Croatian fiction that was lacking before and that would later bring forth outstanding works.

Around the beginning of the twentieth century, realism lost its vitality, and new currents, spurred by developments in West European literatures, especially the French, began to take hold. A movement called *Moderna* (modern) established itself as the leading literary trend, as it did in Serbian literature on a smaller scale. Leading novelists of this period—Milutin Cihlar Nehajev (1880-1931), Dinko Šimunović (1873-1933), and Janko Polić

Kamov (1886-1910)—advocated close ties with European literatures, considered form as important as content, and demanded full independence for the artist. Their efforts were soon overshadowed by the most dominant writer in Croatian literature between the two world wars—indeed, in all of Yugoslav literature in the twentieth century—Miroslav Krleža (1893-1981). His political activism, based on humanitarian communism, colored his approach to literature as well, primarily in the topic selection and in his treatment of social problems. His favorite theme, the rise and fall of the bourgeois society in Austro-Hungary, is designed to show the obsequious role of the Croatian upper classes in that society as well as the suffering of the lower classes. Thanks to his artistic prowess, Krleža succeeded in keeping his social criticism from slipping into preaching, and a certain long-windedness is compensated by a wealth of pertinent detail, exquisite character sketches, fine nuances, and a sharp eye for shape and color. Krleža is a master of hint and allusion, and he knows how to keep his distance. His pessimism—even nihilism, at times—and his irony, often turning to sarcasm, are tempered with humor and compassion. All of these characteristics, coupled with his enormous erudition and savoir faire steeped in Central European culture and tradition, made Krleža a very important writer, not only in Croatian literature but in world literature as well.

Other novelists at this time, though writing in Krleža's shadow, helped create a lively atmosphere and great literary ferment in this period. They were preoccupied with social and political problems much more than writers in other Yugoslav literatures, and the main reasons were Krleža's influence and the specific conditions present in the Croatian part of Yugoslavia after 1918.

The postwar era is characterized by a large number of gifted novelists who continued the traditions of the prewar period while striking new paths. Versatility is perhaps the most telling feature of the contemporary Croatian novel. Also, for the first time, the novel reached the same level of importance as the short story, which had dominated Croatian fiction from the beginning. Although most of the new novelists were under the heavy influence of Krleža, many of them were able to free themselves of this influence in their later development. Petar Šegedin (1909-1998), Vladan Desnica (1905-1967), Ranko Marinković (1913-2001), Vjekoslav Kaleb (1905-1996), Mirko Božić (1919-1995), Vojin Jelić (1921-2004), and Slobodan Novak (born 1924) have addressed new themes and problems, both artistic and social, with sophistication and verve seldom seen before in Croatian literature. The general growth of the novel, paralleling that of other Yugoslav literatures, reflects maturity and familiarity with world standards of the genre.

A newer generation of novelists, led by Ivan Aralica (born 1930), Pavao Pavličić (born 1946), Goran Tribuson (born 1948), and Dubravka Ugrešić (born 1949), among others, is showing even greater versatility, maturity, and affinity with modern tendencies in world fiction. Aralica frequently uses historical themes of his native Dalmatia in order to comment on later events, combining the elements of medieval chronicles, oral folklore, and contemporary jargon, as in *Psi u trgovištu* (1979; dogs at the market), *Put bez sna* (*Journey Without Sleep*, 1982), *Duše robova* (*Souls of the Slaves*, 1984), and *Okvir za mržnju* (*Frame for Hatred*, 1987). Pavličić writes in a light, entertaining style, dwelling on urban, unusual, and sometimes esoteric themes, as in his novel *Večernji akt* (1981; evening act). Tribuson, one of the most popular of the Croatian writers, creates detective novels in a postmodernist vein, including *Zavirivanje* (1985; peaking), *Noćna smjena* (1996; night shift), *Gorka čokolada* (2004; bitter chocolate), and the other novels in the detective Nikola Banić series. Ugrešić's novel *Forsiranje romana-reke* (1988; *Fording the Stream of Consciousness*, 1994), is a quasi-detective novel about a literary meeting in Zagreb, written in a humorous and ironic vein castigating the self-aggrandizement of the literary world. The so-called fatherland war of the 1990's has become an increasingly popular subject in Croatian contemporary literature, including long fiction. As might be expected, Croatian novelists have begun attempting to join the world scene even more than before the war. For example, Ugrešić's criticism of nationalism in the early 1990's created a backlash that led her into exile in 1993; her novel *Ministarstvo boli* (2004; *The Ministry of Pain*, 2005) deals with the struggles of Yugoslavian exiles.

Vasa D. Mihailovich

THE SLOVENIAN NOVEL

Like their South Slavic brethren, the Slovenes were suppressed by a foreign power, Austria, for almost ten centuries and were not allowed to develop their self-government, let alone their culture. For that reason, Slovenian fiction made a late appearance; the first novel, *Deseti brat* (the tenth brother), by Josip Jurčič (1844-1881), was published in 1866. Although it lagged somewhat behind other Yugoslav literatures, Slovenian fiction has proved to be a valuable contribution to the genre. The early novels were based mostly on the native folk narratives, but they were much more than imitations; rather, they transformed the folkloric material into genuine works of literature. While the short story was dominant in the nineteenth century, the novel made quick and significant strides. In addition to Jurčič, Josip Stritar (1836-1923), Janko Kersnik (1852-1897), and Ivan Tavčar (1851-1923) wrote in a style showing either a mixture of Romanticism and realism or straight realism. The main feature unifying them was a strong preoccupation with social conditions of their people who, unlike other Slavic tribes, did not gain full independence until 1918. Because most of the writers were of peasant origin, they depicted most often the plight of the peasantry oppressed by foreign rule and exploited by domestic upper class.

With Ivan Cankar (1876-1918), one of the greatest of Slovene writers, Slovenian fiction reached its high point in the first two decades of the twentieth century. A leader of the Slovenian *Moderna*, with his several novels he laid the solid foundation of contemporary Slovene fiction. At first affected by the spirit of Decadence and Symbolism at the beginning of the twentieth century, he later developed his own style without severing ties with the *Moderna* yet going beyond its purely artistic objectives. On the par with Ivo Andrić and Miroslav Krleža, he ushered in a new spirit and a new era in Slovene literature.

The post-*Moderna* novelists were neither numerous nor artistically accomplished, but they aided the development of the genre through a great variety of approaches, partaking of almost all literary movements prevalent in world fiction between the two world wars and afterward. While some, such as F. S. Finžgar (1871-1962), were still closely tied to their native soil or, like Prežihov Voranc (1823-1925), were preoccupied with social conditions, others, such as Ivan Pregelj (1883-1960) and Miško Kranjec (1908-1983), were psychologically oriented or imbued with lyricism. The younger, postwar generation—Andrej Hieng (1925-2000), Lojze Kovačič (1928-2004), Pavle Zidar (1932-1983), Rudi Šeligo (1935-2004), and Vitomil Zupan (1914-1987), among others—made great strides in expanding novelistic horizons and overcoming the staple themes that dominated the Slovenian fiction for almost a century.

One of the most popular contemporary Slovenian writers is Drago Jančar (born 1948), who has published essays and plays as well as novels; his works of long fiction include *Petintrideset stopinj* (1974; thirty-five degrees), *Severni sij* (1984; *Northern Lights*, 2001), *Posmehljivo poželenje* (1993; *Mocking Desire,* 1993), and *Graditelj* (2006; the builder). Other important Slovenian writers in the early twenty-first century include Igor Škamperle (born 1962) and Damijan Śinigoj (born 1964).

Vasa D. Mihailovich

THE MACEDONIAN NOVEL

Macedonian literature was officially recognized only after World War II, although it has existed in a subterranean fashion for centuries. Given that Macedonian literature bypassed entire literary movements and had no tradition of its own on which to draw, it is not surprising that the novel would take some time to appear. After the first novel—*Selo zad sedumte jaseni* (1953; the village behind the ash trees), by Slavko Janevski (1920-2000)—the Macedonian novelists not only asserted themselves fully but also caught up, to a large degree, with other Yugoslav writers. Understandably, the novelists dealt at first with basic changes in Macedonian society, especially the village, after the war. Soon, however, they began to probe more deeply the inner world of their characters and experiment with more advanced approaches to the novel. While there is no single dominant figure, several novelists, especially among the younger writers, have written promising works that can take their place alongside other achievements in South Slav long fiction.

In retrospect, several common features are discernible among South Slav novelists. They all started rather late because of the specific developments of their societies. For that reason, they lagged behind the developments in other world literatures. They were spurred on, at the beginning, by other literatures, mostly those of Western Europe, but they also tried to express the indigenous narrative tradition rooted in folklore and national epics. In addition, most of them have been preoccupied with the conditions in their respective societies, and this concern has somewhat hampered their development in the pure artistic sense. As a compensation, however, they wrote novels that transcended their artistic value or intent. As they matured and built up their own tradition, they kept looking abroad for improvement, especially toward the German, Russian, and French literatures. Today, the South Slav novelists have, for the most part, made up for lost time and have reached the world standard in several excellent accomplishments, some of which have been translated into many languages.

Two important Macedonian writers of long fiction at the end of the twentieth century were Slavka Maneva (born 1934) and Vidoe Podgorec (1934-1997). Bozin Pavlovski (born 1942), who lives in Australia, has written more than a dozen novels in Macedonian, several of which have been translated into English and other European languages. Žarko Kujundžiski (born 1980) has reached a large international audience with his metaphysical novels, including *Spectator* (2003) and *Amerika* (2006), but his works have not yet been translated into English.

Vasa D. Mihailovich

Bibliography

Barac, Antun. *A History of Yugoslav Literature*. Ann Arbor: Michigan Slavic Publications, 1973. Solid overview, written by a leading literary historian, traces the development of the Yugoslav novel. Dated but still valuable.

Bogert, Ralph. *The Writer as Naysayer: Miroslav Krlema and the Aesthetic of Interwar Central Europe*. Columbus, Ohio: Slavica, 1991. Presents wide-reaching references to the literature, including long fiction, of Yugoslavia as seen through analysis of the works of the greatest contemporary Croatian writer.

Eekman, Thomas. *Yugoslav Literature, 1945-1975*. Ann Arbor: Michigan Slavic Publications, 1978. Complementary volume to Antun Barac's work discusses the main Yugoslav novelists and novels of the three decades after World War II.

Hawkesworth, Celia, ed. *A History of Central European Women's Writing*. New York: Palgrave, 2001. Collection of essays from this emerging field of study begins with the writings of women in medieval Bohemia and continues through 1990. Explores major authors and themes as well as the growing feminist movement.

Holý, Jirí. *Writers Under Siege: Czech Literature Since 1945*. Brighton, England: Sussex Academic Press, 2007. Chronologically arranged overview includes biographical sketches of the most important writers, a list of Czech literature anthologies in English, and a bibliography of secondary works in English and in Czech.

Mihailovich, Vasa D., ed. *South Slavic Writers Before World War II*. Vol. 147 in *Dictionary of Literary Biography*. Detroit, Mich.: Gale Research, 1995.

_______. *South Slavic Writers Since World War II*. Vol. 181 in *Dictionary of Literary Biography*. Detroit, Mich.: Gale Research, 1997. This and the preceding volume offer extensive biographies and expert critical analyses of all important Southeast European novelists, written by the best scholars in the field.

Petro, Peter. *A History of Slovak Literature*. Buffalo, N.Y.: McGill-Queen's University Press, 1995. Provides an overview of the literature from the Great Moravian period, around 800, to modern writers in 1990. Includes a bibliography of criticism in English.

Pogačnik, Jože. *Twentieth Century Slovene Literature*. Ljubljana, Slovenia: Milan Simčič, 1989. A leading Slovene literary historian presents a thorough survey of Slovene literature of the twentieth century.

Vucinich, Wayne, ed. *Ivo Andrić Revisited: The Bridge Still Stands*. Berkeley, Calif.: International and Area Studies Publications, 1995. Collection of scholarly essays addresses various aspects of Andrić's works, with emphasis on the novels.

Zagajewski, Adam, ed. *Polish Writers on Writing*. San Antonio, Tex.: Trinity University Press, 2007. Collection of pieces by twenty-five twentieth century Polish authors focuses on the art of writing.

Chinese Long Fiction

In surveying some six centuries of the Chinese novel, from the first major accomplishment, *Sanguo yanyi* (fourteenth century; *The Romance of the Three Kingdoms*, 1925), to the novels of the twenty-first century, some important distinctions must be observed. First, a Chinese novel's style depends on whether it belongs to the tradition of the "old novel" (*jiu xiaoshuo*)—written before the launching of the Literary Revolution in 1917—or to that of the "new novel" (*xin xiaoshuo*), written after 1917. Both kinds of novels are said to be written in the vernacular and cover a broad spectrum in respect to writing. For a written work to be regarded as literature in ancient China, it first had to be written in the literary idiom of *wenyan*, a highly formalized style that is commonly known today as classical Chinese. Because the novel ordinarily contained colloquialisms adopted from common speech, it was considered by nearly all scholars and critics, if not by many of its readers, "impure" in style as well as frivolous in content and hence outside the pale of genuine literature. The vernacular style of the traditional novel, however, despite its use of colloquialisms—actually confined mostly to dialogue—bore little resemblance to informal speech, for classical Chinese remained an essential ingredient of this style.

Indeed, a comparative inspection of the language of the traditional Chinese novel reveals a kind of evolutionary process in respect to the proportion and purpose of colloquialisms embedded in the literary idiom. For example, *The Romance of the Three Kingdoms* follows the standard history of the turbulent Three Kingdoms so closely as to quote the state documents verbatim and in full. On the other hand, the sixteenth century *Jin Ping Mei* (*The Golden Lotus*, 1939; also known as *Chin P'ing Mei: The Adventurous History of Hsi Men and His Six Wives*, 1940) employs a larger count of colloquial particles than do some of the much earlier short tales called *huaben*, which were based on oral telling and whose heyday was the twelfth and thirteenth centuries. The early eighteenth century *Rulin waishi* (*The Scholars*, 1957) is relatively free of *wenyan*, *guanhua* (official speech), and *liyan* (slang). The late eighteenth century *Honglou meng* (1792; *Dream of the Red Chamber*, 1929; also known as *The Story of the Stone*, 1973-1986; and as *A Dream of Red Mansions*, 1978) shows a considerable advance over the previous novels in individual characterization, which is accomplished mostly by idiomatic speech uttered by its principal characters. The new novel of modern times came into being following the launching of the Literary Revolution in 1917 and the introduction of Western novelistic standards. Its leaders, Hu Shi and Chen Duxiu, despised classical Chinese and advocated that the written vernacular, *baihua*, replace it in all writing. Their view eventually obtained general acceptance: The modern Chinese novel is written exclusively in the colloquial language and in terms of Western, not traditional Chinese, literary standards.

Second, the traditional Chinese novel must be viewed in the light of its own history, literary tradition, and narrative standards. The novel in the West emerged during the eighteenth century predominantly out of the epic, collections of novellas, and various modes of the romance—chivalric, classical, pastoral, picaresque, allegorical, gothic, and historical. In China, on the other hand, the traditional novel appeared during the fourteenth century under the dominant influence of historiography and oral techniques of the professional storytellers. The first major Chinese novel, *The Romance of the Three Kingdoms*, adheres closely to standard history and is concerned predominantly with historical characters; few ahistorical figures or fictional episodes appear. Hence the novel is not a historical novel in the Western sense but rather dramatized history produced by skillful narrative architectonics, especially a closely knit internal structuring of incidents, rendered in an elegant style. Thus, the line between historiography and fiction in old China is not easy to draw. If novels after *The Romance of the Three Kingdoms* move further in the direction of fiction, history often serves as a starting point and a baseline.

The strong influence of the technique of oral storytelling is another marked feature of the traditional Chinese novel. This feature is evident in the largely colloquial speech of the characters, which sometimes descends into slang and even into billingsgate. Apart from the colloquial idiom of the dialogue, however, the traditional novel contains other oral conventions: the quoting of popular songs, the adapting of popular tales, and the creating of pseudohistory. An important oral convention is the simulation of the oral storytelling situation by using a single narrative point of view that represents a generalized storyteller speaking to a generalized reader. This method contrasts prominently with that employed in the Western novel, in which a variety of simulacra, limited or unlimited, are used and often individualized. In the dialogue of the novel, the Chinese author provides no hint of the emotion implicit in a speech; he or she simply uses such terms as *Ta shuo dao* (He said as follows), *Song Jiang jiao dao* (Sung Chiang shouted), or *Ta yue* (He said), and so on, without the "stage directions" often found in the Western novel, particularly in popular fiction: "'I agree,' he said haltingly" or "'I won't,' she angrily replied."

Furthermore, prefixed to each *zhang* (chapter) of the old novel conventionally appears an antithetical couplet of verses whose meaning is related to the contents of the chapter. Also, chapters commonly end on a note of crisis or suspense that is emphasized by a conventional formula amounting to: "If you don't know what happened afterward, then *listen* to the *telling* of the next chapter" (italics added). Finally, the episodic development of the narrative is a feature of the inherited orality of the old novel. Here, the term "episodic" means the intricate interweaving of incident and coincidence throughout the whole narrative without any evident concern that the whole will finally assume some discernible shape identifiable with that unity of structure that Western critics tend to demand of the novel.

In short, whatever social or psychological realism the traditional Chinese novel manages to convey to the Western reader—a mimetic aim never envisioned by the Chinese author—that effect is both restricted and aided by its oral conventions. On the other hand, the new novel in China is a product of the rejection of the previous Chinese literary tradition in favor of Western literary standards and conventions, whether bourgeois or proletarian.

Third, the episodic orientation of the old novel was ultimately a product of the traditional Chinese cosmology shared by most educated people. Rejecting the notion that the cosmos and the humans in it had come about as the result of some ultimate cause, they conceived of the universe as a self-generating, finite, dynamic process—a single, organic whole whose parts interacted in harmony. Humanity was viewed as an intimate part of this holistic, creative process. Employing the "Rule of Three," these educated people abstracted the principal parts of the cosmic organism as Heaven, Earth, and Man, seeing their relationship as triadic and symbolizing it emblematically as an equilateral triangle. If the Chinese rejected the idea of an ultimate cause or external force in terms of the transcendent, the anthropomorphically conceived Jewish Jehovah or Christian God, Heaven (*tian*) was nevertheless regarded as Providence, an immanent force that silently directed both the workings of the physical world and the affairs of humans. Hence, Confucians spoke of the "Mandate of Heaven" (*tianming*); Daoists spoke of "The Way and the Power" (*daode*), referring to the power of nonbeing that "does things without doing them"; and Buddhists spoke of "The Great Void" (*wu*), by which they also meant nonbeing, and "moral retribution" (*baoying*), meaning "present retribution in this life" according to a person's just deserts as dictated by the law of karma.

This sort of worldview accounted for the lack of emphasis on causality in the traditional Chinese novel. Events are presented in a different arrangement and with a different focus from those commonly found in the Western novel. According to Western thinking, an event is the consequence of a previous happening: It is an "outcome" and a result. As such, events in a Western novel are presented in a linear and temporal fashion as a sequence of cause-and-effect occurrences. That is, each event (E) has its proximate cause in some preceding event (C_1), the occurrence of which, in the circumstances prevailing at the time, necessitated the occurrence of E—that is, made it happen. If traced backward through some intermediary steps, E may also have some remote cause (C_2). Cause and effect are thus considered an event, but the things, substances, or people that affect or are affected by this happening, and thereby undergo some change, are considered agents or receivers. In a narrative, "agents" imply actors, which in turn imply action. "Receivers" imply those people, things, and substances that experience the action and may be affected by it. "Things" and "substances" imply setting and atmosphere. A sequence of causally connected events arranged in some meaningful pattern constitutes the plot, or the line of action, of a narrative from the Western standpoint. Additionally, it is the principal factor that structures the story and gives it a shape that is supposed to possess unity. The acceptance of this view of causality has led Western authors to choose between two possible foci: The focus will be directed either at character or at action. The former gives rise to the novel of character and the latter to the novel of adventure. Either character or action becomes the principal force imparting motion and momentum to the sequence of cause-and-effect events. Indeed, the Western conception that human experience is a process opposed to stasis eventually placed the emphasis on internal rather than external events; the former were put into the realm of consciousness or subconsciousness.

The traditional Chinese worldview, however, was not wedded to a causal interpretation of events. The universe is a dynamic process, to be sure, whose parts interact with one another, but not in a linear, progressive fashion. Rather, it is a complementary, reciprocal process, a dual interrelation in which the duality remains constant, hence neither progressive nor dialectical but simply cyclic. Unlike Georg Wilhelm Friedrich Hegel's philosophy, which proposed that when a thing is negated, a new thing arises at a higher level, traditional Chinese philosophy held that when a thing is negated, it simply repeats the old. The Great Harmony initiates the forces of *yin* and *yang*, whose interaction brings all things into form but eventually destroys their forms. Still, because things cannot be dispersed without forming again, their perpetuation is spontaneous, inevitable, and cyclic. Thus, motion (*yang*) becomes rest (*yin*), and rest becomes motion once more. This process continues ad infinitum in a spatiotemporal universe that is a finite whole. Hence, the Chinese did not think of events as causally linked. Furthermore, because motion is opposed to rest, events have their opposite in nonevents, and events are interwoven in the tapestry of the universe with nonevents as woof and warp. Events are connected merely by succession or coincidence—not causally linked—and are juxtaposed to nonevents. In this way, both events and nonevents are spatialized into a pattern of dynamic and static episodes.

This traditional Chinese worldview was responsible for the focus and the structure of the old novel. The traditional novel does not focus on a single character or a single event to the extent that one or the other serves to unify the whole. The interest tends to embrace many people in their interrelationships in a variety of social contexts. The principal characters may not change—may neither develop nor decline, as they frequently do in Western novels—but simply remain the same.

In dealing with the fortunes of a series of protagonists, the novelist presents a series of cycles in each of which a different protagonist is featured. First one and then another character or incident takes the lead in forwarding the linear progress of the narrative on the printed page. The novel is developed by a system of linked plots, usually governed by some central issue, and these plots together structure the novel as a whole.

In dealing with an individual protagonist, a conflict-resolution pattern (proceeding through the stages of point of contention, confrontation, conflict, and resolution) is linked to that of the next individual protagonist, but emphasis is placed on nonevents nearly as much as on events. In other words, this "overlapping" of events takes into consideration what has been called "the interstitial spaces between events." In this procedure, the novelist sets his or her "clearly defined events" into "a thick matrix of nonevents" such as static descriptions, set speeches, formal banquets, and discursive digressions. The effect is to give the reader a sense of the continuity of discrete events that are not causally linked.

This spatial, noncausal, and nonlinear structuring typical of the traditional Chinese novel is in part obscured by the necessarily temporal, line-by-line arrangement of the narrative language. If the novel were a Chinese landscape painting—whose principles of organization stem from the same cosmological theory, in which the iconology is presented to the eye simultaneously within the confines of the picture plane—this kind of structuring would be immediately apperceptible. In painting, Chinese artists do not aim at the realistic representation of surface appearances. They are not interested in presenting an illusion of depth, for instance, by imitating visual phenomena according to certain optical principles. Rather, they follow the Law of Three Sections: They place the foreground low; depict trees, a pond, and a fisherman in a boat in a middle area; and then sketch the mountains above. Making use of intervals of space and rhythmic lines, Chinese artists seek to induce in the viewer a sense of the "life breath" and the "life motion" of the cosmic organism. Indeed, they regard the lines of their configurations as a vascular network made up of "dragon veins," and they seek to depict the pulse of the universe.

In sum, these discriminations are the first and foremost that the Western-oriented reader must draw in attempting an appraisal of the Chinese novel, whether old or new, from an aesthetic standpoint. It is therefore a mistake to arbitrarily take Western fiction as a standard against which to appraise Chinese traditional fiction. Aesthetic standards and techniques differ in terms of time, place, cultural orientation, and aim. In respect to the Chinese new novel, the critic must distinguish between those novels that have bourgeois aesthetic aims and those composed according to the aesthetic principles of the proletariat revolutionary movement, especially those laid down by Communist Party chairman Mao Zedong in *Zai Yan'an wenyi zuotanhui shang de jianghua* (1942; *Talks at the Yenan Literary Conference*, 1965), which later became the literary program of the New China.

Origins and development

In the European tradition, epic verse was an important forerunner of long fiction, but such was not the case in China, where special historical and intellectual conditions precluded the production of folk epics. Chinese fiction originated from its oral traditions of myth, folklore, legend, and history, in ballads to be sung and tales to be told. Hence, Chinese fiction emerged from certain other oral practices and forms as well as from certain rhetorical techniques common to fiction that appeared in written histories, philosophies, and religious texts such as narratives, descriptions, biographies, and dialogues.

The premodern view of fiction in China differed significantly from that held in the Western world. To the ancient Chinese, fiction was termed *hsiao-shuo* (small talk). They regarded it as something trivial and frivolous that had little or no literary merit. To them, orthodox literature consisted of but four genres: classics (the "Four Books" and the "Five Official Classics"), histories, philosophies, and belles lettres (poetry, literary criticism, and miscellaneous essays on sundry subjects). Thus, fiction in China received little respect and less attention from scholars and critics until the twentieth century.

The late Tang Dynasty (618-907 C.E.) scholars who wrote the earliest Chinese fiction, short stories called *chuangi* (tales of the marvelous), did so as practice exercises for the public civil-service examinations. Hence, these stories were also known as *wenquan* (warming-up scrolls). Furthermore, these stories were written in classical Chinese and not in the vernacular favored by later writers of short stories and novels. Those scholars who wrote vernacular stories and novels were not anxious to reveal their true identities and thus tarnish their reputations, so they concealed them by leaving their works anonymous, using a pseudonym or "studio name," or citing an earlier (deceased) writer as the original source. Consequently, many Chinese authors of traditional fiction remain unknown or were identified only in later scholarship.

By the fall of the Han Dynasty in 220 C.E., the scholar class had practically become the exclusive custodian of the Chinese written language. In their hands, the written script broke away from the common speech of the people and went its separate way. The characters were normally given sounds (either imaginatively, in silent reading, or aloud, in recitation) in some dialect because the script had no pronunciation of its own. This style, called *wenyan* (classical or literary Chinese), came to be used exclusively for all serious writing. At the same time, the written script was also used to simulate the vernacular favored by later writers, and the colloquial forms were mixed with the classical. The colloquial style was called *baihua* (plain speech). Thus, Chinese literature as a whole came to have two contrasting prose styles—literary Chinese, or *wenyan*, and colloquial Chinese, or *baihua*. *Wenyan* was also developed in two contrasting styles—*pianwen* (parallel prose) and *guwen* (ancient prose)—but the latter replaced the former for most serious writing by the ninth century C.E. Not until the Yuan (Mongol) Dynasty (1279-1367 C.E.) were dictionaries produced giving the Chinese characters in Mandarin pronunciation. At any rate, the history and development of Chinese fiction closely parallel the history and development of both literary and colloquial prose.

Although written records prove that public storytelling in China was a common social institution as early as the Tang Dynasty, such an activity goes much further back into history. The major writings of the Zhou Dynasty (1122-221 B.C.E.), such as the *Shujing* (*The Book of Documents*, 1950), the *Guoyu* (conversations from the states), the *Zhanguo Ce* (fifth to second century B.C.E.; intrigues of the warring states; English translation, 1970), and the *Lun yu* (late sixth or early fifth century B.C.E.; *Analects of Confucius*) are all within the oral tradition. While primitive conventions of narrative form and technique stem from this oral tradition, both traditions—oral and written—continued to influence narrative until the twentieth century. Even when written in classical Chinese, this narrative, especially the novel, continued to reflect the colloquial idiom.

Although the downfall of the Zhou led to the creation of the first Chinese empire under Emperor Shi Huang Di, only two developments took place during the short-lived Qin Dynasty (221-207 B.C.E.). The autocratic Shi Huang Di harshly censored and burned all books of which he disapproved. A more significant development for the future of literature was the standardization of the Chinese script.

The Han Dynasty (207 B.C.E.-220 C.E.), however, was a more fruitful literary period. The Han emperors actively promoted literary scholarship and rewarded worthy scholars with official appointments and promotions. Scholars tried to reconstruct the texts of the burned books, and the Confucian classics were edited, redacted, and "fixed." The first etymological dictionary was prepared. The civil-service examination system was firmly established. A reliable and effective historiography was founded through the efforts of Sima Qian (c. 145-c. 85 B.C.E.) and Ban Gu (32-92 C.E.). Two new poetic forms, the *fu* (rhyme-prose) and the *yuefu* (lyrics and ballads), were devised, and Indian Buddhism was introduced in the Former Han (207 B.C.E.-24 C.E.) to compete with the indigenous Confucian and Daoist creeds.

All the developments already described contributed to the later development of Chinese fiction. The examination candidates of the Tang Dynasty were to create the first literary short stories, the *chuangi*, as practice exercises. The essence of history is narrative, and later Chinese fiction would draw heavily upon Chinese historical narrative, particularly the novel. The new poetic *fu* and *yuefu* were narrative forms. Finally, Indian Buddhism was to have a profound impact on the Chinese imagination.

The fall of the Han Dynasty resulted in relative political chaos in China for four centuries, a period known as the Six Dynasties (220-589 C.E.). During this time, the two chief indigenous systems of thought, Confucianism and Daoism, reacted to the introduction of Buddhism, the foreign creed from India, prompting an increased interest in mysticism and metaphysical speculation. This led to a distortion of the heretofore practical system of ethics that Confucianism had espoused. Mystical meanings were interpolated into the Confucian classics, while the more speculative and metaphysical Daoism rose in popularity. Eventually these trends led to a new school of philosophy called *xuanxue* (dark, or subtle, learning). This philosophy sought to encourage metaphysical speculation by means of dialogues studded with wit and humor called *qingtan* (pure conversations), which were recorded in writing. One such compendium, entitled *Shishuo Xinyu* (fifth century B.C.E.; *A New Account of Tales of the World*, 1976), was made in the fifth century by Liu Yiqing (404-444 B.C.E.). The contribution of the institution of *qingtan* to later fiction was no doubt greater than that made to philosophical speculation. Rooted in speech rather than in *wenyan*, it minimized the importance of the content of the essay and focused on the wit, encouraging a search for choice words and phrases.

Another side effect of the introduction of Buddhism was the revival of the ancient Chinese spiritualist cult of the *wu*. A *wu* was a shaman or priest who acted as a mediator between spirits and humans. The cult's preoccupation with gods and ghosts was enhanced by the teachings of Buddhism. Members of the cult adopted the practice of writing stories about gods and ghosts. These stories became so popular with the people that noncult writers began to compose such stories for entertainment. Even scholars took an interest in them and began to collect and publish them. One such collection was published about the beginning of the third century under the title *Liyizhuan* (c. 220; strange tales); the identity of its author or editor is unknown, though it has been ascribed to Caa Bei. Other collections were brought out by Zhanghua

(232-280), Gan Bao (fl. c. 300), and Wu Qun (469-519). The adherents of Buddhism and Daoism also wrote similar tales.

Such "ghost stories" were called *qigui* (tales of the supernatural). Although the scholars of the Six Dynasties period took an interest in them, they did not take them seriously as literature, referring to them as *qigui xiashuo*. Actually, the *qigui* were simply journalistic recordings of folklore or religious propaganda. Nevertheless, they are significant in the history of fiction because they were among the first attempts at imaginative writing and point to the Buddhist and secular *pianwen*, which began to appear near the end of the Six Dynasties period.

The introduction of Buddhism into China resulted in an imaginative expansion of Chinese mythology and legend that later provided stock for fiction. Legendary tales were scattered in various ancient books such as the *Shijing* (c. 500 B.C.E.; *The Book of Odes*, 1950); the *Zuozhuan* (c. 450 B.C.E.; *The Tso Chuan*, 1989), which covered political, social, and military events from 722 to 463 B.C.E.; and the *Shanhai jing* (c. 200 B.C.E.; *The Classic of Mountains and Seas*, 2000). The Chinese began learning of Buddhas and Bodhisattvas; numberless universes; many heavens and hells; endless cycles of rebirths; Gautama Buddha; Amitabha Buddha, the ruler of the Western Paradise; Vairochana, the primordial eternal Buddha; and Maitreya, the Laughing Buddha, who will come again. There were legends, too, of Siddhartha Gautama sitting under the bo tree, the dream of Emperor Ming Di, and Bodhidharma meditating before a wall at the Shaolin Monastery and then teaching his novices the art of *quanfa* (the law of the fist).

Buddhism also had an impact on the Chinese language and on prose style. With its introduction, there was an urgent demand for translations of the Buddhist sutras (sacred texts). New words and concepts had to be interpreted and translated from Sanskrit into Chinese. The translators saw that Daoist words and concepts could be used to explain Buddhist ideas; this method was called *geyi* (interpretation by analogy). In other cases, if no Chinese words could be substituted for the Sanskrit, transliteration was employed. Thus, the Sanskrit *nirvāna* became the Chinese *nipan*. Truth and comprehension were paramount in the eyes of the translators, and they made every effort to keep their prose style plain and unadorned, perfectly clear, and as faithful to the original as possible.

The Buddhist narrative compositions, the *pianwen* (changed composition), were the products of peripatetic Buddhist monks who recited them before temple audiences. Composed in alternate prose and verse, the *pianwen* were creative popularizations of passages selected from the Buddhist scriptures that were illustrated by stories taken from the life of Gautama Buddha, the founder of Indian Buddhism. Because these "sermons with exempla" were popular adaptations of sacred scriptures, they were regarded as "changed compositions." These changes included an irregular alternation between the use of verse and prose, as well as the bridging of the compositional process by means of the episodes taken from the Buddha's life.

The Buddhist *pianwen* became so popular with Chinese audiences that similar types of secular narratives were modeled after their religious prototypes. Specimens of *pianwen*, both religious and secular, were among the numerous manuscripts dating from 406 to 995 recovered at Dunhuang. Among them is a religious *pianwen* of the Five Dynasties period (907-960) referred to as *Mulian pianwen* (the story of Mulian). It is the story of a young man who becomes a Buddhist monk and his effort to rescue his mother from hell. There is also a secular *pianwen* called *Shunzi qi xiao pianwen*, which may be the earliest fictional account of the legendary Emperor Shun, the Chinese model of filial piety. At any rate, the *pianwen* substantially influenced later Chinese fiction.

These first attempts at formal imaginative writing seen in the *qigui* and the *pianwen*, as unsophisticated, crude, and awkward as they were, prepared the ground for the emergence of the first mature Chinese fiction, the literary short prose romances called *chuangi* that reached their greatest vogue in the late Tang Dynasty. Written in *wenyan*, or literary Chinese, in the new prose style called *guwen*, these short stories were written by the literati (*rusheng*) for other literati. As romances, they were longer, more sustained, better organized, and superior in style to previous fictions. Although written in *guwen* classical prose instead of the vernacular, the dialogue portions of the stories showed an attempt to approximate living speech. In terms of the literary tradition, the *chuangi* was the main fictional form of the Tang period. At the same time, the manuscripts of the Denhuang caves show that popular fiction in the form of the *pianwen* was produced throughout the Tang period and well into the Song Dynasty (960-1279).

During the Northern Song period (960-1126), however, the art of the oral storyteller had reached such a state of perfection that the literati turned from the writing of *chuanqi* to the writing of short tales in colloquial Chinese based on the art of the popular oral narrators of fiction. These vernacular stories were called *huaben* (story roots) because the literati derived them from the promptbooks that the *shuohua ren*, or speech makers, prepared to jog their memories when they found that necessary. By the Southern Sung period (1127-1279), the vogue of the *chuanqi huaben* had diminished to such an extent that the *huaben* had become the dominant fictional form. Indeed, the greatest *huaben* stories written by literati were produced during the Southern Song period.

During the Ming Dynasty (1368-1644), however, interest in *chuanqi* was revived for a time by the stories of Ch'ü Yu (1347-1433), who had used the Tang *chuanqi* as his models. Most of the extant Tang tales had been preserved in a collection made at the insistence of the Song emperor Taizong. During the Ming Dynasty, at the time of this brief revival of interest, some further collections were made.

A more potent revival of the *chuanqi* form, however, occurred during the Qing (Manchu) Dynasty (1644-1911), which inspired the most famous of all such tales by the masterly hand of Pu Songling (1640-1715) published in 1679 under the title *Liaozhai zhiyi* (*Strange Stories from a Chinese Studio*, 1880). Although his range of subject matter is in line with earlier *chuanqi*, his tales display an unusual command of literary Chinese and the ability to make the improbable, sometimes even the impossible, convincing. His work inspired many imitators. As for the *huaben* stories, there are no extant Song or Yuan collections. Several collections of such stories, however, were made during the Ming Dynasty. The earliest of these stories were printed by Hong Pian, around 1550, in six volumes. Although sixty tales were originally preserved, only twenty-nine of them have survived. In the 1620's, a major anthologist and writer, Feng Menglong (1574-1646), published a three-volume collection known as the *Sanyan* (three words), each volume containing 40 stories, or 120 tales altogether. Most of them are of the *huaben* type written during the Yuan Dynasty or even earlier, but some are Ming pieces. These collections were followed by the inspired writing of Ling Meng-qu (1580-1644) and Li Yu, or Li Liweng (1611-c. 1680), who wrote their own *huaben* fiction. Such tales continued to be written until the twentieth century.

In comparison to the short tale, the novel was long in coming in China, not emerging until near the close of the fourteenth century. If the term "novel" is used in its general sense to mean "a long prose fiction with a relatively complex plot or pattern of events," then the first major Chinese novel is *The Romance of the Three Kingdoms*, attributed to Luo Guanzhong (c. 1320-c. 1380). This novel was partly inspired by a previous fictional form that originated with the oral storytellers of the Southern Song period and flourished in conjunction with the *huaben*. Some oral storytellers specialized in telling long narratives of fictionalized history that required serial development. Even more than the *huaben* tellers, they needed promptbooks in writing. These serialized stories were called *pinghua* (common talk) because, like the shorter *huaben*, they were written in the vernacular (actually Mandarin mixed with classical Chinese). Their development seems to parallel that of the Southern drama.

Pinghua promptbooks in their original condition, although lost in China, were preserved in Japan, all printed between 1321 and 1323, during the reign of Yuan Yingzong of the Yuan Dynasty. These texts retain the formal properties of their Song predecessors. Beginning with a prologue setting forth a small story analogous to the main tale to be told and suggesting its moral, the *pinghua* is a much longer narrative than the *huaben* type of short story and belongs to a different genre. It is the transitional fictional form between the vernacular short story and the vernacular novel, and it points directly toward the colloquial novel that was to come. The *pinghua* that partly inspired Luo was the *Sanguozhi pinghua* (1321-1323; a *pinghua* of the history of the Three Kingdoms), but he also made use of a reliable official history and a commentary on it.

Following Luo's *The Romance of the Three Kingdoms*, the vernacular novel completely dominated the Chinese tradition. Although the *guwen* style of *wenyan* had proved effective for short narratives, it was not a satisfactory instrument for extended fiction in which dialogue played a prominent part. Sung writers of short fiction had abandoned the literary Chinese of the *chuanqi* in favor of the vernacular of the *huaben*. It was natural, therefore, that Luo should have adopted the *pinghua* as his model.

Although some novels were written in classical Chinese, especially during the Qing Dynasty, none is comparable to the best vernacular novels. A Qing *guwen* novel entitled *Yin shi* (c. 1800; the tale of a silver fish), by Tu Shen (1744-1801), has enough magic to be relatively successful. A more lengthy effort, however, a 300,000-word novel in *pianwen* (parallel prose) written by the eccentric Chen Qiu, entitled *Yan Shan waishi* (c. 1810; the informal history of Yan Shan), and whose style is involved and complex, is virtually unreadable.

The vernacular novel tradition brought forth the greatest masterpieces. The next major effort after Luo was *Shuihu zhuan* (fourteenth century; translated by Pearl S. Buck as *All Men Are Brothers*, 1933; also known as *Water Margin*, 1937), attributed to Shi Nai'an (c. 1290-1365), about whom nothing is known. Although written in the fourteenth century, the earliest known edition dates from the middle of the sixteenth century. Following this work, novel writing seems to have been eclipsed by the Yuan drama. Two centuries elapsed before another masterpiece appeared, *Xiyuo ji* (1592; also known as *Hsi-yu chi*; *The Journey to the West*, 1977-1983; abridged by Arthur Waley as *Monkey*, 1942), by Wu Chengen (c. 1500-c. 1582).

In the late Ming Dynasty, a great novel appeared that was quite different in character from those preceding it. This was the novel of manners called *Jin Ping Mei* (*The Golden Lotus*, 1939; abridged as *Jin Ping Mei: Adventurous History of Hsi Men and His Six Wives*, 1940), traditionally attributed to Wang Shichen (1526-1590), although this attribution has been questioned. A one-hundred-chapter novel, it was circulated in manuscript in the 1590's, and the first printed edition appeared around 1610. The previous masterpieces are of a semi-historical character and have a close alliance with Chinese historiography. Although the *Jin Ping Mei* purports to show the dissolute manner of the time of Emperor Hui Zong of the Song Dynasty, it actually depicts, realistically and with considerable precision, the manners of the author's own time. This Ming novel was followed by perhaps the greatest masterpiece in the history of the Chinese novel, *Dream of the Red Chamber*, by Cao Xueqin (c. 1715-1763). The story of the decline of a wealthy aristocratic family of the author's own time, centering on the romantic love affair of the two teenagers, Jia Baoyu and his cousin and playmate Lin Daiyu, the narrative is infused with Buddhist and Daoist myth.

After the appearance of these five—*The Romance of the Three Kingdoms*, *Water Margin*, *The Journey to the West*, *Chin Ping Mei*, and *Dream of the Red Chamber*—nothing comparable followed in the Chinese novel tradition. There are, however, other novels of considerable value and significance. Two are of special importance: *Rulin waishi* (1768-1779; *The Scholars*, 1957), an early Qing work by Wu Jingzi (1701-1754) that satirizes pseudoscholarship and the civil-service examination system; and a late Qing work, *Lao Can youji* (1904-1907, serial; *The Travels of Lao Ts'an*, 1952; revised 1990), by Liu E (1857-1909; also known as Liu Tieyun), a delightful story of an itinerant Chinese physician concerned about his country's condition and opposed to injustice and harsh government.

Originating in Chinese myth, legend, and folklore, the oral tradition of Chinese literature strongly influenced written literature. Although the Chinese literary language became divorced from common speech, an alliance between writing and speech was maintained from early to modern times. Traditional Chinese fiction, like Western fiction, is divisible into the short story and the novel, but unlike Western fiction it is also divisible into fiction written in the literary as opposed to the vernacular language. This latter distinction is as important as the former.

With the Literary Revolution in 1917, the character of Chinese fiction drastically changed. The acceptance of *baihua* (common speech) for all forms of literature, as well as the acceptance of Western forms and standards, meant the complete rejection of the ancient Chinese literary tradition and the culture that accompanied it. Therefore, modern Chinese literature is a special study in itself. The fiction of the Chinese renaissance of 1930 to 1937, based on Western literary criteria, showed promise, if not fulfillment. The Sino-Japanese War (1937-1945) and the subsequent civil war, however, stopped this progress.

With the establishment of the People's Republic of China in 1949, Chinese fiction quickly became a propaganda instrument of the state, and the sanctioned literary production was strictly controlled. Although the communist hierarchy prescribed the rejection of Western influences and a return to the Chinese tradition, this meant the tradition of the folk but not of the literary elite. Furthermore, communist fiction turned to formula and dogma, and writers were required to express themselves solely according to the Marxist-Leninist view of the world. No vital and authentic fiction has as yet emerged under these circumstances.

The traditional vernacular novel

The first great vernacular novel produced in China was *The Romance of the Three Kingdoms*, attributed to Luo Guanzhong, a playwright and writer of the late Yuan and early Ming periods. If he modeled his novel on the oral form of the *pinghua*, which he saw recorded in the promptbook *Sanguo zhi pinghua*, which was fictionalized history, Luo also turned to reliable official history to keep his facts straight. Indeed, in his novel he adhered closely to the official history of Chen Shou (233-297 C.E.), the *Sanguo zhi, juan* 36, but also consulted the commentary on it made by Pei Songzhi (fl. 400-430 C.E.). He may also have been indebted to Yuan drama for some structural principles.

The story told in *The Romance of the Three Kingdoms* occurs during the Three Kingdoms period (220-265 C.E.), actually extending from 168 to 265 C.E. Following the eclipse of the Han Dynasty, the three states of Wei, Shu, and Wu contended for dominance and the reunification of China. Contrary to Chen, who regarded Wei as the legitimate successor to Han, Luo considered Shu the rightful heir. Presenting his hero, Liu Bei, who becomes the King of Shu, as the legal successor to the Han family, Luo sees the struggle for power as a great historical drama involving opposite moral principles. Consequently, he pits Liu Bei, whom he depicts as the personification of legitimacy, righteousness, and honor, in alliance with Sun Quan, who has inherited the Wu kingdom, against Cao Cao, the founder of the Wei and the embodiment of falsehood, treachery, and cruelty. At Liu Bei's side is his friend Guan Yu, the ideal feudal Chinese knight, who, though good and pure, is also foolhardy and arrogant. Liu Bei's prime minister and generalissimo, Zhuge Liang, combines loyalty, sagacity, and resourcefulness with amazing examples of military strategy. Another prominent hero-knight is Zhang Fei, who represents physical prowess, reckless bravery, and impetuous temper. Although Luo obviously intends to glorify Liu Bei and his friends and vilify Cao Cao and his supporters, he does not fail to humanize his characters and displays their weaknesses as well as their strengths. They are not stereotypes; rather, they are well-rounded, complex human beings. Although the novel is concerned mainly to show forth the vain ambitions of humans and their inability to control their own destinies, it is also a novel of character.

The term *yanyi* in the Chinese title of the novel has commonly been translated by Westerners as "romance," but it literally means "an expansion of the text in a popular version." In short, it means "popular history." To regard *The Romance of the Three Kingdoms*, however, as nothing more than popularized history, as some critics have, detracts much from the full measure of the author's achievement. Reacting against the superstitions and vulgarities of a cyclic tale told many times over by oral storytellers, Luo sought to create in writing a long narrative of the *zhang-hui* (chapter division) type which would be more artistically designed and more elegant in style than the folk version. Purging the story of most of its vulgar elements, he blended popular legend with authentic history, eliminating or selecting incidents to suit his purposes. He invented incidents to fit the personalities of his characters and changed the nature of historical personages to suit himself. Although the oral version supported the Buddhist theme of *baoying*, or "moral retribution" according to the law of karma, he substituted the Confucian theme of *tian ming*, or the "Mandate of Heaven," by which all events are determined. Working in this manner, Luo stitched together a strong internal pattern of military campaigns, political intrigues, small exciting incidents of various kinds, and vivid human relationships. Out of the multiplicity of characters and heroes,

Zhuge Liang emerges as the principal hero and the model of intelligence, wisdom, competence, resourcefulness, and selfless service to his prince. *The Romance of the Three Kingdoms* was a great pioneering effort and remains an important landmark in the history of Chinese fiction.

Possibly written as early as 1358 and circulated in handwritten manuscript, nothing of which is extant, the first printed edition of *The Romance of the Three Kingdoms* dates from about 1545. During the Qing Dynasty, around 1679, Mao Lun and his son Mao Zonggang edited a revised version of the novel together with a commentary. This Mao edition has been regarded as the standard since 1925, when C. H. Brewitt-Taylor brought out an English translation of the novel in two volumes, which is relatively complete and reads smoothly. A reprint of this translation with an introduction by Roy Andrew Miller appeared in 1959.

If *The Romance of the Three Kingdoms* is a great re-creation of an exciting historical period, which is also relatively authentic history, the next major effort in the history of the Chinese novel, *Water Margin*, is a creation of a historical epoch which is almost wholly fictitious. In seventy chapters in the standard edition, *Water Margin* is the story of 108 heroes who have rebelled, not against the government itself but against the activities of corrupt officials in the government, and who are living the life of outlaws. The term *shui hu* means "water margin"; in this context, it refers to a region in present-day Shandong Province, Liangshanbo. It is in this area, composed of Mount Liang (Liangshan) and the marshes that surround it, that the brigand-heroes, under the leadership of Song Jiang, have established their headquarters. Although the novel is almost entirely imaginative, this situation had a historical basis. A similar band of outlaws, including the historical Song Jiang, were active at this location in a similar manner from about 1117 to 1121, or immediately prior to the collapse of the Northern Song Dynasty in 1126. The historical Song Jiang and his outlaw band surrendered to the government in 1121. According to some historical sources, the government then enlisted the band in a campaign to quell a much more threatening revolt led by the rebel Fang La.

The story of Song Jiang and his outlaw band was a favorite topic with the oral storytellers of the Southern Song Dynasty; it also became a popular subject with the Yuan Dynasty playwrights. The Mongol historian T'o T'o mentions the activities of Song Jiang and his outlaws in his dynastic history, the *Songshi* (1345). Finally, an early Yuan fiction, apparently based on a Song *pinghua* promptbook, also tells this tale. *Water Margin* must have been inspired by these sources as well as by popular legend.

Unlike *The Romance of the Three Kingdoms*, whose tight internal structure results from the interweaving of narrative strands and interrelated conflict situations, *Water Margin* is composed of a sequence of cycles, each of which features a different hero. Hence, although its internal structure is weaker than that of *The Romance of the Three Kingdoms*, its overall structure is stronger. Jin Shengtan's 1641 redaction in seventy chapters, which has become the standard edition, ends with the brigand-heroes assembled in the Hall of Loyalty and Righteousness. They are assembled to receive the Heavenly Tablet, on which their names are inscribed together with the mottoes "Carry Out the Will of Heaven" and "Fidelity and Loyalty Complete." Although Jin's ending was actually designed to avoid heaping praise on the outlaws, it nevertheless underscores their lofty principles and the grandeur of their mission. It was no wonder that the Jin version of the novel scored such a hit with the Chinese people.

It must be pointed out, however, that the Jin edition is an arbitrary redaction of a 120-chapter version possibly edited by Yang Tingqian in 1614. The ending of the story in this edition differs significantly from the one provided by Jin in 1641. In the Yang edition, the story ends tragically, the heroes dying one by one with their missions unfulfilled. Jin actually retained seventy-one chapters of the Yang version but converted chapter 1 into a prologue. Jin's ending, therefore, was both new and arbitrary. It was motivated not by any aesthetic consideration but by political morality, slanted by Jin's personal dislike for the rebel leader Song Jiang. The Jin edition became the standard simply because of its great popularity. An edition prior to Yang's also once existed. This was the Guo Xun edition of about 1550, which consisted of one hundred chapters. It is this edition that states that Shi Nai'an was the author and Luo Guanzhong the editor. Although only five chapters of this edition have survived, the whole appeared in a Kangxi reprint of 1589. The problem of the definitive text of the novel, therefore, is complex.

At any rate, *Water Margin* in the Jin edition is perhaps the finest example of *wuxia xiaoshuo* (military knight fiction) in Chinese literature. Pearl S. Buck produced an English translation of the novel in 1933 under the title *All Men Are Brothers*, issued in two volumes, and J. A. Jackson issued an English translation as *Water Margin* in 1937, also in two volumes. Jackson's translation is more condensed and less literal than that of Buck. Although Buck's contains some expurgations, it is faithful to the original text, yet it lacks the spirit of action and movement that Jackson's conveys. There are many inaccuracies in both translations.

With these two masterpieces of the late Yuan period, *The Romance of the Three Kingdoms* and *Water Margin*, the Chinese novel came of age. No doubt because of the popularity of Yuan and Ming drama and other types of theatrical entertainment, however, a hiatus in novel writing set in for nearly two centuries, and it was not until the 1560's that another novelistic masterpiece finally appeared. This work was *The Journey to the West*, by Wu Chengen, a writer, poet, scholar, and official of the middle Ming period. The discovery of the novel's true author did not occur, however, until the twentieth century. Previously, its composition had been ascribed to Qiu Zhuqi (1148-1227), a great traveler who was an adviser to Genghis Khan.

On the literal level, *The Journey to the West* is the story of the journey from China to India of a Chinese Buddhist monk named Xuanzang, or Tripitaka, who is accompanied by four animal spirits who serve as his disciples. In fact, it is not the monk who is the hero of the story but one of his disciples, a monkey spirit named Sun Wukong. The other disciples are a pig spirit named Zhu Bajie, a fish spirit named Sha Heshang, and the monk's white horse, who is a dragon prince in disguise and understands human speech. Consisting of one hundred chapters, the novel is divided into four parts. The first deals with the birth and early life of the monkey spirit. Born of an egg-shaped rock, he becomes king of the monkey tribe. Highly intelligent, he studies Buddhism and Daoism, acquires magical powers and superhuman abilities, and becomes an immortal. A resident in Heaven, his ego is so inflated that he seeks to replace the Jade Emperor on the throne. After causing havoc in Heaven, he is subdued by Buddha himself and imprisoned beneath the Mountain of Five Elements. Five hundred years later, he is released to serve Tripitaka. The second division is the story of the early life of Tripitaka and the origin of his quest. The third division relates the adventures of Tripitaka and his disciples on their way to India. After fourteen years, the pilgrims reach their destination, where they collect numerous scriptures. Not until their return to China, however, do they attain enlightenment and Buddhahood. The journey is described in a lively and rapid narrative embracing many episodes and numerous trials, tribulations, and confrontations with demons and monsters. The fourth part presents the conclusion of the journey.

Despite its supernatural cast, the tale had a small basis in fact. There was a historical Chinese Buddhist monk named Xuanzang who was known by the religious name of Tang Sanzang (or Tripitaka—the collection of Buddhist scriptures). He traveled to India and was absent from China for seventeen years (629-645). When he returned to China, he became a national hero and a favorite of the emperor. He spent the rest of his life translating the Indian texts and teaching his disciples. He dictated his account of his journey to a disciple, Pianqi, entitling it *Da Tang xiyu ji* (seventh century; *On Yuan Chwang's Travels in India, 629-645 A.D.*, 1904-1905). Xuanzang and his journey became a popular subject of the oral storytellers. The Tripitaka legend became as popular with the Chinese as the Liangshan legend of Song Jiang and his outlaw band.

Wu Chengen's fantastic novel, however, appears designed to suggest much more than its literal level of presentation, as interesting, exciting, and amusing as that is. Although the author good-naturedly pokes fun at the three Chinese religions and the governmental hierarchy and its bureaucracy, underneath or beyond that is a serious thrust, a satire upon the nature of humanity itself and an effort to explain the fundamental process through which any human, regardless of his or her particular religious orientation, comes to enlightenment and consequent peace of mind. It is clear that Tripitaka represents Everyman. An ordinary physical mortal, he is fearful, humorless, not too bright, gullible, preoccupied with his own well-being and safety, yet also filled with love and compassion. All too human, he is a model of unenlightened human behavior, a *ying'er* (a babe in the woods). At the same time, he and his animal spirit friends also clearly represent the various aspects of the human self. He is referred to in the text as "the body of the Law" (*fashen*), "the original nature" (*benxing*), and the "primal spirit" (*yuanshen*).

On the other hand, the monkey spirit obviously represents the human mind at its most efficient and is referred to as the "mind-monkey" (*xinhou*). He is smart, nimble, clever, rampant, courageous, arrogant, and vainglorious. He personifies the genius of humans, and he calls himself "The Great Sage, Equal to Heaven." Yet as Lucifer could not outwit or best God, so Monkey cannot outwit or best Buddha, who is simply the Enlightened One and no divinity. The pig spirit represents humanity's gross nature and sensual appetites; he is lazy, lecherous, gluttonous, jealous, envious, and stupid. The fish spirit, a water monster who lived in the River of Flowing Sands prior to joining Tripitaka, is a coward and a bluffer who seeks to deceive through a ferocious appearance and a bold front; he represents people's self-deceptions, illusions, and fears. The white dragon/horse symbolizes humanity's will and determination, an indomitable spirit and sense of responsibility and a willingness to take on a burden and see it through to the end.

These are but some general observations on the complex range of meaning with which the novel is infused in terms of symbolization and allegory. This range of meaning supports the novel's main concern, which is Wu Chengen's explanation of the process of human salvation. This state comes about by self-cultivation of the whole person, mind and body. With discipline and humility, humans can arrive at a mental and physical equilibrium, their minds in tune with the corporeal world, the total human in harmony with self and the universe. It is only through corporeality that humans can arrive at the necessary perception of nothingness—a realization that completes the process of enlightenment whereby humans reach complete peace of mind. In short, Wu Chengen's formula is *yisiwukong*—that is, "to perceive the nature of emptiness through the medium of illusion," for the corporeal world, though real, is not Ultimate Reality, which is Void. *The Journey to the West* is not only an outstanding example of a novel on a supernatural theme but also a polysemous, complex, and seminal book.

Arthur Waley's English translation under the title *Monkey*, though including only thirty of the original one hundred chapters, is superb and has long been popular with the general public. Anthony C. Yu, however, produced the first complete translation, published between 1977 and 1983 under the original title in four volumes. Yu's translation is both highly readable and faithful to the original text, and it is supplemented by helpful notes. *The Journey to the West* has been made into a series of feature films and was adapted to the stage as *The Journey to the West: The Musical*, which premiered in New York City in 2006.

Possibly written as early as 1565, the next great masterpiece in the history of the Chinese novel, *The Golden Lotus* (the Chinese title, *Jin Ping Mei*, consists of parts of the names of three women characters), is of uncertain authorship. Its composition generally has been attributed to Wang Shichen, a scholar and writer who is alleged to have written it as an instrument of revenge against an official who had ruined the author's father, another official. This attribution, however, has been questioned, and several other candidates have been proposed, including Xu Wei (1521-1593), a writer and painter, and Li Kaixian (1501-1568), a poet and playwright. At least one handwritten manuscript of the one-hundred-chapter novel was in circulation during the 1590's.

The first printed edition appeared around 1610, but it met with destruction. The earliest extant edition, known as the Wanli edition, was published around 1617 under the title *Jin Ping Mei Cihua* (Jin Ping Mei, a vernacular novel with songs). Sometime between 1666 and 1684, the critic and writer Zhang Zhupo (c. 1654-c. 1694) prepared an edition with a commentary entitled *Zhang Zhupo ping Jin Ping Mei* (Jin Ping Mei commented on by Zhang Zhupo). This edition has been regarded as standard. The important thing as far as Chinese literary history is concerned is that *The Golden Lotus* was a complete departure in terms of the previous history of the novel. Previous novels had dealt either with people who were of epic proportions or with characters who were different in kind from humans, such as immortals, spirits, demons, and monsters. As specific fictional forms, they are "romances." *The Golden Lotus*, however, deals with ordinary people in the context of social relations and manners. Indeed, it is a "novel of manners," a "novel" in the specific formal sense, the first such long narrative in China.

Although *The Golden Lotus* purports to show the dissolute manners of the time of the Song emperor Huizong, it actually depicts those of the author's own time, the first half of the sixteenth century. Set in the town of Qinghe in present-day Shandong Province, the story is primarily concerned with the town's leading citizen and businessman, Ximen Qing, and his six wives. The wealthy owner of an apothecary shop and an underworld figure as well, his principal activities are making money, gaining social prestige, and searching for fresh sexual experience, particularly by seducing married women. The novel delineates representative figures at most levels of Ming society; it was the first Chinese novel to adequately characterize women. Although the original title of *The Golden Lotus* (*Jin Ping Mei*) may be read literally to mean something like "plum blossoms in a golden vase," it actually refers to three women in Ximen Qing's life: "Jin" to Pan Jinlian (Golden Lotus), the fifth wife; "Ping" to Li Ping'er (Little Vase), the sixth wife; and "Mei" to Chunmei (Spring Plumblossom), Lotus's maid, whom Ximen debauches. The other women of Ximen's household are Yueniang (Moon Lady), who holds the honored position of first wife; Li Qiao'er, the second wife; Meng Yulou, the third wife; and Hsüeh-o, the fourth wife; of these, only Moon Lady is a decent person. It is Golden Lotus, a veritable femme fatale, who is the dominant character of the book. She promotes her husband's financial ruin and contributes to his early death.

Although the novel progresses by episodes, the tension developed between the parts and the whole is, for the first time in Chinese long fiction, satisfactorily resolved. Its explicit descriptions of sexual activity have frequently been termed pornographic, but they are in fact supportive of the novel's individualized characterizations and naturalistic view of life. Its naturalism, however, is not based on the Western notion of the influence of heredity and environment in human makeup but on the Buddhist notion of moral retribution, in which humans are a product of the quality of their deeds throughout their previous states of existence. The personal view of the author, however, appears more Confucian than Buddhist because he has taken pains to show the folly of those men and women who become trapped in the net of a hedonistic and materialistic world. He appears to regret the necessity of the novel's religious solution when Moon Lady permits her only son, the fifteen-year-old Hsiaoko, to enter a Buddhist monastery to become a monk to save his father's soul. Although the author derived the opening of his novel from chapter 22 of *Water Margin*, introducing the reader to the famous military knight Wu Song, he quickly shifts the focus from him to Golden Lotus, who murders her husband, Wu Song's brother, in order to marry Ximen, with whom she is having an adulterous affair. On this and other sources, the author shows but little dependence. *The Golden Lotus* is primarily a work of a single imagination and a unified and effective narrative. Although heavily erotic, the novel is a strong work of social criticism.

In 1939, Clement Egerton issued an English translation of *Jin Ping Mei*; the erotic passages, however, are rendered in Latin. A revised version, for the most part complete and unexpurgated, was published in 1972 and is readable and fairly accurate. An excellent and readable translation by David Tod Roy has been published, although only three of the five volumes have been completed: *The Plum in the Golden Vase, or Chin P'ing Mei: Volume One: The Gathering* (1993), *The Plum in the Golden Vase, or Chin P'ing Mei: Volume Two: The Rivals* (2001), and *The Plum in the Golden Vase, or Chin P'ing Mei: Volume Three: The Aphrodisiac* (2006).

Although *The Golden Lotus* has been highly regarded by some critics, the consensus is that the greatest masterpiece in the history of the Chinese vernacular novel is *Dream of the Red Chamber*, by Cao Xueqin, the scion of a wealthy family that inherited the office of supervisor of the imperial textile factory at Nanjing but suffered a fall from prosperity to poverty. In 120 chapters altogether, the first 80 chapters were thoroughly completed by Cao about 1763 and circulated in handwritten manuscript. The novel in this form included a commentary prepared by an older cousin of the author, Cao Yufeng, known by his pen name, Zhiyan Zhai. Cao Xueqin died at about this time, leaving behind a forty-chapter conclusion to the novel in a rough draft. Nearly thirty years later, Go E and a contemporary, Cheng Weiyuan, edited the last forty chapters and issued the whole in a printed edition in 1792 under the new title *Dream of the Red Chamber*. The novel is presumed to be at least partly autobiographical because it relates the story of the wealthy Jia family and its decline and fall and thus duplicates to some degree the experience of the author himself.

Actually, *Dream of the Red Chamber* tells what might be called three stories in one, arranged in three insetting frames, the smallest set within the border of a larger and that larger set within the largest. The smallest story is concerned with the tragic love affair between two teenagers, Jia Baoyu (Precious Jade), the hero of the novel, and Lin Daiyu (Black Jade), his cousin and playmate, the heroine. The larger narrative is concerned with the decline and fall of the Jia family, within the context of which the romance takes place, but it features Baoyu's widowed grandmother, Jia Mu (Matriarch), who presides over the Rungquofu household, and Wang Xifeng (Phoenix), the wife of the Matriarch's grandson, Jia Lian, and the crafty manager of the household who, however, contributes to the family's ruin.

The largest narrative, the one that frames the others, utilizes a Chinese creation myth about the goddess Nügua and her efforts to repair the Dome of Heaven with pieces of rock. One such rock being left unused laments its fate to two passersby, a Buddhist monk and a Daoist priest. It expresses the wish to be transported to the earth so that it might experience life in the "red dust" (*hongchen*). While waiting at the court of the Goddess of Disillusionment to be thus transported, the celestial rock cares for a celestial plant by watering it daily with dew. This loving care makes the plant blossom into a fairy who vows that if she may accompany the rock to earth, she will repay his love with tears of gratitude. When Baoyu is born into the Chia family, he is "born with a piece of jade in his mouth" and obviously is the rock incarnate in the earthly setting. He falls in love with his cousin Lin Daiyu, who, sickly and temperamental, is like a sensitive plant and is clearly the plant fairy incarnate on earth. In her romance with Baoyu, she cries many tears, but they are tears of self-pity and jealousy rather than tears of gratitude. After the Jia family requires Baoyu to marry another cousin, Xue Baochai (Precious Clasp), instead of the unsuitable Daiyu, who soon dies, Baoyu begins to undergo a severe disillusionment. He begins to see desire, whether for love, status, wealth, or knowledge, as the root of all suffering. Longing to free himself from suffering, he decides to renounce the world, or life in the "red dust," to become an unattached monk. He is last seen disappearing into the horizon accompanied by a Buddhist monk and a Daoist priest. Thus, through Buddhist wisdom and Daoist grace he has achieved enlightenment after having experienced the sufferings of a man in this life. The myth rounds out the novel.

The autobiographical background of *Dream of the Red Chamber* and its treatment of its subject have prompted various interpretations as to its real meaning. Some of the interpretations are simply silly. It is not easy to decide whether Cao Xueqin intended his novel to be an attack on Confucian ideals and morality and on the feudal system generally, or a vindication of Confucianism and the feudal system (by demonstrating that sensual indulgence, the neglect of the cultivation of Confucian morality, and the irrationality of romantic love can wreck not only the individual but also an entire family), or a compromise with Confucianism and the feudal system (by advocating a Buddhism-Daoist form of escapism). It appears that the novel is actually a complex response to the whole Chinese cultural tradition and that the device of ambiguity is its watchword. This ambiguity is given expression by the author's attitudes of detachment, toleration, and compassion, which foster a subjective interpretation of the novel's meaning at the hands of every reader. To a Confucian, romantic love is disastrous, and the ending is a regrettable form of escapism. To a Buddhist or Daoist, romantic love can mean only suffering, and the ending points out the proper solution. To a Chinese taken by Western democratic ideals, Confucianism and the feudal system were cruel anachronisms whose destruction was overdue in the eighteenth century. To a Chinese communist, the novel is a direct attack on Confucianism and the feudal system, and its ending is a regrettable capitulation to superstition. It would seem that Cao Xueqin himself was more concerned with rendering a tragic sense of life than championing any one of these interpretations.

Dream of the Red Chamber is notable for a variety of qualities, some of which mark an important advance over previous Chinese novels. The plot, though complex, is carefully framed and tightly knit in its development to the end. The characterization is outstanding, particularly in respect to older women. The portrait of the widowed grandmother, Jia Mu, is certainly one of the finest characterizations of an elderly woman to be found in any novel, and that of Wang Xifeng is also vivid and forceful. The characters of the young girls, Lin Daiyu and Xue Baochai, are well defined and individualized. Baoyu's character is developed step-by-step through dialogue, through his reactions to various situations and through his dreams until he is well understood by the reader. The novel is outstanding for its psychological analysis and penetration. The author rarely indulges in didacticism or authorial comment but allows the opposition between the attitudes of detachment and compassion to develop the ambiguity necessary for subjective judgment. He also makes subtle use of poetry to guide the reader's feelings. The style he employs is a polished, refined, and highly expressive form of the colloquial that is unusually advanced. Altogether, *Dream of the Red Chamber* is a work that is both realistic and imaginative. It is a close study of the everyday life of a wealthy and aristocratic Chinese family of the eighteenth century, a precise analysis of the ravages of a romantic love affair, and a profound religious and philosophical commentary on the nature of human life.

The standard Chinese text of *Dream of the Red Chamber* is the Chengqao edition, published in 1792. It was reprinted in Taibei (Taipei) in a two-volume edition under the title *Tsu-pen Hung-lou mêng* (1957). A variorum edition in four volumes, however, was published in Beijing in 1958. This work was prepared by Xu Pingbo and Wang Xishi and issued under the title *Honglou meng bashi wei chao ben*.

There are several English translations of *Dream of the Red Chamber*. One translated from a German version by Franz Kuhn was done by Florence McHugh and Isabel McHugh and published in 1958. Another was done by Wang Qichen and published in the same year. Neither is completely satisfactory, for different reasons. David Hawkes and John Minford published a fine five-volume English translation under the title *The Story of the Stone* from 1973 to 1980; an abridged version of this translation was released by Penguin books in 1996 with the title *The Dream of the Red Chamber: A Chinese Novel of the Early Ching Period*.

In addition to the five outstanding masterpieces of the Chinese novel already discussed, there are two other traditional vernacular novels of significance: the eighteenth century *The Scholars*, by Wu Jingzi, and the early twentieth century *The Travels of Lao Ts'an*, by Liu E. *The Scholars* (the Chinese title literally means "unofficial history of the forest of scholars") is an attack on pseudoscholarship and hypocrisy and an exposure of the ill effects produced by the civil service examination system, especially after the emphasis put on the writing of the *bagu wen* (eight-legged essay). Wu Jingzi came from a well-to-do family that had produced many scholars and officials. He himself, however, was of a nonconforming temperament. He shunned an official career and took no interest in preparing for the civil service examinations. Indeed, he preferred the company of poets, painters, writers, monks, prostitutes, and actors rather than that of officials and bureaucrats. Although his novel is satiric, it is also good-humored. It displays his sincere Confucian convictions, the first and last chapters describing paragons of Confucian virtue who are ignored by high officialdom. In the rest of the book, he satirizes both the worst elements produced by the civil service system and the rest of the social order as well. In addition to being the first effective novel of exposure, it is also a roman à clef, because many of the book's characters are based on either famous historical people or personal acquaintances of the author. Although the novel is composed of episodes that are lacking in unity, the characterization is individualized and well-rounded and is perhaps the most distinguished feature of the novel.

In his epilogue, Wu Jingzi presents his own moral vision. Although still in resistance against corrupt and hypocritical authority, he introduces four humble scholar-artist recluses who represent the Four Noble Pastimes of the Chinese scholar: the playing of the *guqin* (a particular kind of lute); the playing of *weigi* (Chinese checkers; called *go* in Japan); the practice of *shufa* (writing with the brush or calligraphy); and the practice of *wen ru hua* (literary painting, the art that combined painting, calligraphy, and poetry). Through these four figures, Wu suggests that if the world is easily misled by degrees, official rank, and material success, there are in the background genuine scholars and true artists. If they are unknown and in humble circumstances, they practice their scholarship and their noble pastimes with sincerity and moral sensibility. Such men can carry forward the cause of culture and morality in China even if others have failed.

There is an adequate English translation of *The Scholars* by Hsien-i Yang and Gladys Yang, published in Beijing in 1957. The full-scale Chinese text was published in Taibei in a fourth printing under the title *Ju-lin wai-shih* (1957).

Liu E's *The Travels of Lao Ts'an* is the most important Qing novel produced after the end of the nineteenth century. Written between 1904 and 1907, it was given partial publication in a magazine and a newspaper. The first complete version appeared in book form in 1909. Its literary value, however, was not fully appreciated until the publication of the Ya Dong edition of 1925, which included an introduction by the renowned scholar and critic Hu Shi (Shih), who had in 1917 successfully advocated the use of vernacular Chinese (*baihua*) in "respectable" literature. Like *The Scholars*, *The Travels of Lao Ts'an* is a novel of exposure (and also a roman à clef). The novel of exposure became particularly fashionable during the declining years of the Qing period. Some critics think that these "muckraking" novels reflect the transition between the traditional and the modern vernacular novel. *The Travels of Lao Ts'an* launches an attack on official corruption and harsh government and shows Liu E's concern over the declining state of China in his time. At the same time, he celebrates in lyric style the pleasures of living and remains optimistic about China's future.

It is generally taken that Lao Ts'an is a self-portrait of the author. Although Liu E was born into a scholar-official family, he declined to prepare for the civil service examinations and instead devoted himself to a variety of studies: medicine, law, astronomy, engineering, music, poetry, and oracle bone inscriptions. He began his career by practicing medicine. Later, at various times, he operated a tobacco shop, a printing shop, and a mining company, and he tried to organize a railroad company. He also supervised flood-control operations and took an interest in criminal justice. The Lao Ts'an of the novel is an itinerant physician who practices traditional Chinese medicine. He is fond of music and poetry and enjoys the drum-tale recitations of the Fair and the Dark Maids. He is interested in good and just government, flood-control measures, and the criminal justice system. He acts the part of the famous eleventh century judge-detective, Bao Zheng, by intervening in a sensational murder case, thwarting the harsh official, Gang Bi, and saving the lives of thirteen members of the Jia family. Like his creator, he is a man of varied interests, wide learning, practical competence, independent courage, and humanitarian compassion. He is a lover of people, nature, art, and life. Although a spokesman for the author, Lao Ts'an is at the same time a credible character and a real human being in his own right.

The Travels of Lao Ts'an, which in a genuine edition consists of twenty chapters, is mainly concerned with the fate of China and the sufferings of its people in Liu E's time. Quite loosely organized, the book divides itself into three main parts. At the beginning, in the preface and the first chapter, Liu compares the Chinese state to the endgame in chess, the onset of old age, and a leaky ship, which, though floundering in tempestuous seas and on the verge of sinking, refuses any outside assistance. The first part, however, is mainly concerned with the wanderings through Shandong Province of the itinerant physician Lao Ts'an and with the reports he hears of a harsh official, Yu Xian. The second part is mainly a philosophical interlude in which a woman philosopher, Yu Gu, and a hermit-sage, Yellow Dragon, offer their views on various philosophical problems. The third part is mainly about Lao Ts'an's investigation of the murder case being prosecuted by another harsh official, Gang Bi, and his exposure.

Despite the novel's loose construction, the entire work has a pattern. The first and last parts constitute a third-person journal of the travels of a highly interesting person and his observations, conversations, and reflections. The middle section gives his responses to what he has seen, heard, and meditated upon—in short, it gives his responses to his own times. The book ends with Lao Ts'an saving thirteen innocent lives and then taking one of the unfortunate singsong girls for a concubine. Thus, the two contrasting sides of his nature are shown—his humanitarian idealism and his capacity to enjoy the pleasures of life. Technically, the novel exhibits several unusual qualities: the effective use of the third-person narrator, the skillful use of the character of Lao Ts'an as a persona for the author, the artistry displayed in the vivid descriptions of scenery, and, finally, the adroit harmonizing of a lyric style with the dissonance of sociopolitical concerns. On the whole, the novel is a delight to read. An excellent, complete English translation of *The Travels of Lao Ts'an* by Harold Shadick was published in 1952. Another version, *The Travels of Lao Can* (1983) translated by Yang Xianyi and Gladys Yang, omits sections of the text that the translators have deemed apocryphal.

The modern movement

The twentieth century saw the Manchu rulers of the Qing Dynasty enter into their last days. It was evident on every side that drastic reforms were needed if China were to overcome its backwardness and catch up with the progress made in the West. Although the monarchy initiated various reforms, it failed to satisfy the new Chinese revolutionaries led by Sun Yat-sen (Zhongshan). While Sun was abroad, his followers in China rebelled in 1911. With Russian communist support, they overthrew the Manchu monarchy, and China became, at least technically, a republic. Although Sun was chosen the first president, he soon resigned in favor of army commander Yuan Shikai, who possessed sufficient military strength to defeat the republic if he wished.

The new "republic" faced enormous problems on every side: economic distress among the masses, steadily increasing indebtedness to foreign nations, contentions among foreign nations on Chinese soil for railroad concessions, and disunion. Army commanders, or "warlords," in various areas of the country were powers unto themselves and not subject to the control of the central government. China entered World War I on the side of the Allies, hoping to improve its international position. These hopes were frustrated by the growing power of Japan. China stood in desperate need of all sorts of reforms.

In 1917, the Western-educated scholar and critic Hu Shi (Shih) launched the Literary Reform Movement, which was to have widespread effects on Chinese education and the future of Chinese literature. In an article published on January 1 of that year, in a magazine called *Xin Qingnian* (new youth), Hu Shi argued that *wenyan*, or literary Chinese, had outlived its usefulness as the language of communication and should be replaced by *baihua*, or vernacular Chinese. His argument proved convincing. Yet, because there were many local dialects of colloquial Chinese, this complication posed a problem. If there were to be a national language, one of these dialects would have to be chosen as the standard. Considering that the Mandarin dialects of the north were understood by ninety percent of the Chinese population, the dialect of Beijing was selected as the standard. It, therefore, received the designation of *guoyu*, or "national language."

In 1920, the Chinese government decreed that standardized *guoyu* be taught in the first two grades of elementary school. By 1928, this decree was extended to the junior middle schools, and textbooks in classical Chinese were banned from these grades. This new attitude toward *baihua* prompted a reevaluation of those old novels, short stories, plays, and folk poems that were written in a style close to the colloquial but had no respectable standing as literature. By this time, also, many translations of Western books had made their appearance, and Chinese intellectuals had begun to read Western literary masterpieces. They were amazed to learn that in the West short stories, novels, plays, and poems written in the vernacular were regarded as great works of art. Therefore, when Chinese authors began to write fiction and other literary forms in *guoyu*, they imitated the Western literary forms that enjoyed such high prestige. They ignored the fact that China had, for centuries, possessed a vernacular literature of its own. Although a few intellectuals insisted that traditional Chinese vernacular literature had artistic merits of its own, they were unable to convince others that this opinion had any validity; it took almost a generation before the idea gained wide currency.

Few Westerners realize the full significance of the Literary Revolution, which may be said to have actually begun with the abolition of the civil service examination system in 1905 and was completed by the rejection of literary Chinese for modern writing in 1920. It was not merely that the classical language had been replaced by the vernacular of *guoyu*. More important for the future of Chinese literature was the fact that the reading audience that had enjoyed the perusal of literary Chinese and traditional vernacular literature was also dispensed with, together with its entire culture, and replaced with an entirely new audience, a popular audience. At the same time, however, this popular audience was rejected by the new intellectual class. In rejecting the elite audience and its culture, the new intellectuals also rejected the traditional popular culture that was the inheritance of the mass person. The new intellectuals were therefore cultureless in the Chinese sense. Having stripped themselves of their Mandarin robes and insignia and donned plain Western garb, they attempted to graft Western culture to the new mass person whom they had created in the laboratory of their imaginations but who did not yet exist. They set themselves the difficult task of creating not only a new literature but also a new audience.

When Sun Yat-sen died in 1925, the former director of the Wangpu Military Academy, Chiang Kai-shek (Jiang Jieshi), emerged as the new leader. His immediate object was the reunification of China through conquest of the northern warlords, and he launched his "northern expedition" against them in 1926. Meanwhile, the communists within the Guomingdang (Kuomintang) attempted to organize the workers and peasants to support their cause. Rightly suspecting that the communists were bent on taking over the Guomindang, Jiang expelled them from that body in 1927. In 1928, he succeeded in overcoming the Beijing government and thus reuniting China more than it had been since 1911, but genuine reunification was never achieved. Some warlords still held out against Jiang's leadership, and the communists, largely driven from the cities, established themselves in the hinterlands under the leadership of Mao Zedong and Zhu De. China was therefore continually engaged in domestic warfare until the Japanese invasion of China in 1937. The modern Literary Reform Movement therefore labored under unusually adverse conditions from 1920 to 1937, when it practically ground to a halt. From 1937 until the Japanese defeat, most Chinese writers believed that it was their patriotic duty to support the war effort to defeat and expel the foreign invader. If they wrote fiction at all, it became an instrument of patriotic propaganda. With the Japanese surrender in 1945, civil war broke out between the communists and the Guomindang; it ended when, in 1949, mainland China fell to the communists and the Nationalist Government fled to Taiwan.

The first writer of the Literary Reform Movement to gain enduring fame was Lu Xun (1881-1936), whose real name was Zhou Shuren. In 1918, he published his first short story in the May, 1918, issue of *Xin Qingnian*, "Kuangren Riji" ("The Diary of a Madman"), an attack on Confucian morality. It is considered the first work of modern Chinese fiction. He is most widely known, however, for his novella *Ah Q zhengzhuan* (anthologized 1923, published separately, 1946; *The True Story of Ah Q*, 1927), which he wrote in 1921 as an illustration of the failure of the revolution of 1911. He did not write many stories, and *The True Story of Ah Q* is the nearest he came to novel length. He devoted himself mainly to writing polemical essays.

The period 1930 to 1937 proved the most productive for the new literature; some critics have dubbed this period the Chinese Renaissance. Many poems, short stories, and novels were produced during this time, but perhaps the finest work was done in the short story. Several novels, however, have gained considerable fame. They are the work of Mao Dun (pseudonym of Shen Yanbing, 1896-1981), Lao She (pseudonym of Shu Qingchun, 1899-1966), Shen Congwen (1902-1988), and Ba Jin (pseudonym of Li Feigan, 1904-2005). All of these writers also wrote short stories.

Mao Dun's second novel, *Zi ye* (*Midnight*, 1957), published in 1933, is regarded as his finest effort and is considered a masterpiece in the People's Republic of China. Set in Shanghai during the years 1925 through 1927, it concerns the owner of a silk mill, Wu Sun-fu, and the struggle between capitalists and workers. The point of view is anti-Trotsky. The novel presents a panorama of the industrial and business activity of the great city of Shanghai and its environs.

Lao She grew up in poverty, a condition that developed in him a philosophy of fatalism. His most famous novel is *Luotuo Xiangzi*, which English-speaking readers know in Evan King's 1945 translation by the title *Rickshaw Boy*, or by the title of the 1981 Shi Xiangzi translation, *Camel Xiangzi*. Published in 1938, it is the story of an honest, sensitive, and industrious rickshaw boy who fails to survive in the face of destructive socioeconomic forces.

Shen Congwen, hailing from Hunan Province, had a military rather than a conventional academic background. Of the modern writers, he has paid the least attention to Western influences. As a youth, he served in the army and saw many places and many people. His fiction is peopled with garrison soldiers, bandits, peasants, landlords, civil servants, scholars, artisans, sailors, and prostitutes. He wrote many novels and an abundance of stories. His finest novel is generally considered to be *Chang he* (1949; the long river), which he wrote about 1937. It is a sensitive pastoral story that is realistically and objectively presented. Interwoven with social criticism and Daoist wisdom, it shows a profound understanding of human nature.

Ba Jin grew up in a landowning family in Sichuang Province. As a youth, he absorbed the anarchistic ideas of the Russians Mikhail Bakunin and Pyotr Kropotkin. Having revolted against the Chinese family system and Confucian morality, he dramatized his feelings in his autobiographical novel *Jia* (1933; *The Family*, 1964). It immediately became popular with radical Chinese youths. While it made its author famous, to modern audiences it can seem overwrought, sentimental and immature.

After the founding of the People's Republic of China, a series of measures was taken by the ruling Communist Party to make writers faithful tools of the dictatorship of the proletariat. All the writers became members of writers' federations under the control of the party. As *ganbu* (cadres), writers were paid fixed salaries and were required to follow the policy laid down by Mao: Art and literature must serve workers, peasants, soldiers, and the party's political agenda.

Most of the novels published during the period of 1949 to 1966 exemplify what Mao called "revolutionary realism" combined with revolutionary romanticism and glorify Mao or ordinary revolutionaries under his leadership. Among these novels are Wu Qiang's *Hongri* (1957; *Red Sun*, 1961) and Hao Ran's *Jinguang dadao* (1972; *The Golden Road*, 1981). Few works depicting intellectuals and business people were allowed to be printed, and all of them had to reflect the ideological remolding of the intellectuals and the transformation of business people by the party. Yang Mu's *Qingchun zhi ge* (1958; the song of the youth) serves as an example. Almost no novels were written by such writers as Lao She and Bao Jin, who had established themselves before 1949.

Members of writers' federations had to undergo rigid ideological reform by studying Marxism-Leninism and Maoism, undergoing relentless political examinations under the supervision of party organizations, and living and working among factory workers and poor and lower-middle class peasants to become aware of the difference between "the pettiness of their bourgeois thinking" and the admirable qualities of the rank and file revolutionaries. Moreover, they were subjected to repeated and merciless political purges ordered by Mao. Survivors of one major purge might not escape the next one. Among the major purges was the Suppression of the Counter-Revolutionaries in the early 1950's, with Hu Feng and his close colleagues being the most famous victims in the literary circle. During the Anti-Rightists Movement in 1957, such famous writers as Ting Lin, Ai Qing, Wang Meng, and Liu Binyan were condemned as antiparty rightists and sent to forced labor camps without a trial. However, all these persecutions of writers and other intellectuals, though already cruel and illegal, were simply dwarfed by the Cultural Revolution started by Mao in 1966.

Mao's zealous followers publicly humiliated, physically brutalized, psychologically tortured, and in many cases even murdered those they considered to be anti-Mao elements. Such elements included Liu Shaoqi (1898-1969), vice chairman of the party and president of the republic, who died in solitary confinement, and Zhao Shuli (1906-1970), author of *Xiao Erhei jiehun* (1943; Xiao Erhei getting married), who was beaten to death by Red Guards. To protest the ceaseless, unlawful persecutions of innocent people and preserve their dignity, a large number of artists committed suicide. One of them was a literary giant in modern Chinese history, Lao She, who threw himself into the Weiming Lake at the most prestigious institution of higher learning in China, Beijing University. Those who happened to survive the first waves of vicious assault by Mao's followers were then dispatched to the countryside to do forced labor, all in the name of what Mao called "reeducation" by the workers and peasants.

The rampage of Mao's revolution eventually came to an end with his death and the fall of the Gang of Four headed by his wife in 1976. Then, one by one, almost all the writers victimized by Mao's constant purges were rehabilitated. Literary creation resumed. What first appeared on the scene was *shonghen wenxue* (literature of the wounded), with personal or family tragedies under Mao's tyranny as the only logical and inevitable subject matter. One of its earliest representatives was Lu Yanshou's *Tianyunshan chuanqi* (1980; legend of the Tainyun mountain), also made into a feature film. In 1979, New Realism emerged with the publication of several important novellas, such as Shen Rong's *Ren dao zhongnian* (1980; *At Middle Age*, 1987) and pieces of reportage literature (*baogao wenxue*), such as Liu Binyan's *Ren yao zhijian* (1982; *People or Monsters?, and Other Stories and Reportage from China after Mao*, 1983).

New Realism differed from the literature of the wounded in that the former endeavored to reveal the disparity between the ideals of socialism and the reality of corruption and bureaucracy, while the latter attempted to recall the historical tragedy. Whatever their difference was, both were daring and successful attempts to break away from the fetters imposed by Mao, thus paving the way for a new generation of writers who could afford to ignore what Mao had said about literature. Among the new writers were musician and fiction writer Liu Suola (born 1955), interested in experimental fiction, whose novels in English translation include *Hun dun jia li ge leng* (1991; *Chaos and All That*, 1994); Mo Yan (born 1955), author of *Hong gaoliang jiazu* (1987; *Red Sorghum: A Novel of China*, 1993), devoted to depicting life as lived by ordinary people with real strengths and weaknesses, moral aspirations, and sexual desires, and other novels, many available in English translations; and Eryuehe (born 1945), author of *Kangxi dadi* (1985; Emperor Kangxi), fascinated by the important lessons people can learn from Emperors Kangxi, Qilong, and Yongzheng instead of from Mao's workers, peasants, and soldiers.

After Mao's death, many taboos were broken, and a degree of freedom emerged. Writers were no longer forced to serve as tools of the party or undergo ideological remolding. Many felt freer to experiment with literary forms and ideas, led by the novelists Zhang Xinxin (born 1953) and Zong Pu (born 1928) in the early1980s, and later by Su Tong (a pseudonym of Tong Zhonggui, born 1963) and Ge Fei (a pseudonym for Liu Yong, born 1964). Others, in the Xungen ("Search for Roots") Movement, worked to reconnect Chinese literature to its ancient roots. Han Shaogong (born 1953), for example, draws on Chinese folklore and myth for material but looks to Western genre models. His novels include *Maqiao ci dian* (1996; *A Dictionary of Maqiao*, 2003) and *An shi* (2002; intimations). Nevertheless, an awareness of the existence of a line that no one was allowed to cross remained; in other words, no one was allowed to challenge the legitimacy or authority of the ruling party. The consequence of breaking this ultimate taboo was unmistakably demonstrated by the massacre of students at Tiananmen Square on June 4, 1989.

After the events at Tiananmen Square, and with the increasing importance of China in the global marketplace, Chinese fiction opened up in many ways, becoming more welcoming to commercial genre fiction and to fiction by and about contemporary women. With advancements in electronic communication, Chinese writing also became harder to censor and control—although the government's General Administration of Press and Publication tries to regulate all commercial publications. Wang Anyi (born 1954), who writes realistic portrayals of women's lives in Shanghai, is among contemporary Chinese writers who have drawn an international audience. Her novels include *Chang hen ge* (1996; *The Song of Everlasting Sorrow*, 2008). Eileen Chang (Zhāng Ailíng; 1920-1995) also wrote about women in Shanghai, and a number of her works of fiction have been published in English translation, including *Qing cheng zhi lian* (1996; *Love in a Fallen City*, 2007) and *Se, jie* (1994; *Lust, Caution*, 2007).

In the early years of the twenty-first century, a new generation of sexually liberated writers emerged who defied governmental attempts to keep them from writing. The work of Zhou Weihui (born 1973) was banned and condemned as "decadent" in China, but her autobiographical novel *Shanghai baobei* (1999; *Shanghai Baby*, 2001) has become the best-selling Chinese novel of all time, selling more than six million copies in more than thirty languages. Mian Mian (born 1970) wrote the controversial novel *Tang* (2000; *Candy*, 2003), which depicts a gritty life of drugs, prostitution, and gambling in 1990's Shanghai.

Another movement that will shape the future of Chinese literature involves expatriate writers, who may be freer to explore historical and political themes. Yiyun Li (born 1972), for example, who moved to the United States from Beijing in 1996, writes in English about China. Her novel *The Vagrants* (2009), which is set in a small village in China during the Cultural Revolution, criticizes the dehumanizing effects of that period in a way that no writer living in China could hope to do.

Richard P. Benton; Chenliang Sheng
Updated by Cynthia A. Bily

Bibliography

Chi, Pang-yuan, and David Der-wei Wang, eds. *Chinese Literature in the Second Half of a Modern Century: A Critical Survey*. Bloomington: Indiana University Press, 2000. Collection of critical essays on Chinese literature is supplemented with an extensive bibliography.

Hanan, Patrick. *Chinese Fiction of the Nineteenth and Early Twentieth Centuries*. New York: Columbia University Press, 2004. Essays by a distinguished scholar of Chinese fiction include discussions of the missionary novel, the new novel, and the works of Wu Jianren, Chen Diexian, and Lu Xun.

Hsia, Chih-tsing. *The Classic Chinese Novel: A Critical Introduction*. Reprint. Ithaca, N.Y.: East Asia Program, Cornell University, 1996. Provides a good introduction to Chinese long fiction. Includes a bibliography and an index.

Idema, Wilt, and Lloyd Haft. *A Guide to Chinese Literature*. Ann Arbor: Translation Center for Chinese Studies, University of Michigan, 1997. Covers Chinese literature up to the early 1990's. Includes a lengthy bibliography, a glossary, and an index of major works.

Leung, Laifong. *Morning Sun: Interview of Chinese Writers of the Lost Generation*. Armonk, N.Y.: M. E. Sharpe, 1994. Source for studies in literary works by writers of the *zhiqing* generation—that is, those who participated in Mao's Cultural Revolution, then went to the countryside to be rusticated, and finally, after Mao's death, came back to the cities to face a rapidly changing society driven by materialistic desires.

Lévy, André. *Chinese Literature, Ancient and Classical*. Translated by William H. Nienhauser. Bloomington: Indiana University Press, 2000. Presents an insightful and impressionistic introduction to Chinese classics, poetry, prose, and the literature of entertainment.

McDougall, Bonnie S., and Kam Louie. *The Literature of China in the Twentieth Century*. New York: Columbia University Press, 1997. Takes a historical approach to Chinese literature, examining the early century, the return to tradition, the coming of modernism, and literary experimentation at the end of the century.

Mair, Victor H., ed. *The Columbia History of Chinese Literature*. New York: Columbia University Press, 2001. Collection of essays includes analyses of traditional literature and of fiction—including Tang tales, vernacular and classical fiction—and twentieth century fiction. Also discusses the reception of Chinese literature in other parts of Asia.

Nienhauser, William H., ed. *The Indiana Companion to Traditional Chinese Literature*. Bloomington: Indiana University Press, 1986. Encyclopedic guide to Chinese literature completed by nearly two hundred international scholars. Focuses on important authors, representative individual works, and various genres as well as unique types, including Buddhist and Daoist writings.

Rushton, Peter H. *The "Jin Ping Mei" and the Nonlinear Dimensions of the Traditional Chinese Novel*. Lewiston, N.Y.: Mellen University Press, 1994. Examines this important work and its impact on the Chinese literature that followed.

Yang, Xiaobin. *The Chinese Postmodern: Trauma and Irony in Chinese Avant-garde Fiction*. Ann Arbor: University of Michigan Press, 2002. First major work on China's experimental fiction focuses on writers such as Can Xue, Ge Fei, Ma Yuan, Mo Yan, Xu Xiaohe, and Yu Hua.

The English Novel

To a greater extent than any other literary form, the novel is consistently and directly engaged with the society in which the writer lives and feels compelled to explain, extol, or criticize. The English novel, from its disparate origins to its development in the eighteenth century, from its rise in the nineteenth century to its present state, has been strongly influenced by the social, political, economic, scientific, and cultural histories of England. In fact, English writers dominated the novel genre in its earliest stages of development and continued to do so through much of its history. As a realistic form, the novel not only reflects but also helps define and focus society's sense of itself, and as the novel reflects the growth of England first into a United Kingdom, then into an empire, and its decline to its present role in the Commonwealth of Nations, it does so predominantly through the eyes of the middle class.

Indeed, the origins and development of the English novel are most profitably examined in relation to the increasing growth and eventual dominance of the middle class in the course of several hundred years. Typically concerned with middle-class characters in a world largely of their making, the novel sometimes features excursions into the upper reaches of English society; with more frequency, it presents incursions by members of the upper class into the familiar world of the solid middle class. As a form of realistic literature intended primarily for the middle class, often for their instruction and edification (or excoriation), the novel frequently depicts the worlds of the lower orders of society—not only the exotic cultures subjugated by Imperial Britain but also the familiarly strange domestic worlds of the "criminal classes," a subculture with its own hierarchies, vocabulary, customs, and occupations.

As distinguished from allegory and romance, the English novel has for its primary focus the individual situated in society and his or her emotions, thoughts, actions, choices, and relationships to others in complex and often bewildering environments. Set against backgrounds that realistically reflect all facets of the English experience, the "histories" or "lives" of the novels' protagonists must hold a necessary interest for readers who, in turn, seek to make sense of, master, cope with, escape from, or become fully assimilated into the society in which they, like their heroes and heroines, find themselves. While any attempt to trace with great particularity the multiple relationships between the history of the English novel and the larger patterns of English society remains necessarily imperfect, the general outlines of those relationships can be sketched.

Origins of the English novel

Although long-standing debates about the origin of the English novel and the first English novel continue, it is both convenient and just to state that it is with the fiction of Daniel Defoe (1660-1731) that the first novel appeared, especially in the sense that term came to have in the late eighteenth century and continues to have today. Without considerable injustice it may be said that the novel first developed out of a series of false starts in the seventeenth century and a series of accidents in the eighteenth. The reading public, having been exposed to large amounts of novelistic material, fictions of various lengths, epics, and prose romances, appears to have been ready to receive a form that went beyond Aphra Behn's *Oroonoko: Or, The History of the Royal Slave* (1688), John Bunyan's *The Pilgrim's Progress* (1678, 1684), and the prose works of earlier masters such as Sir Thomas Malory, John Mandeville, Robert Greene, Thomas Dekker, and Thomas Nashe. Such a form would emphasize unified action of some plausibility, individualized and articulate characters, and stories presented with such verisimilitude that the readers could find in them highly wrought illusions of the realities they knew best.

The literary children of the eighteenth century, the novel and its sibling the short story, created a taste for fiction of all varieties in a middle-class readership whose ranks were swollen by a newly literate mercantile class. This readership appears to have wanted and certainly received a literary medium of their own, filled with practically minded characters who spoke the same middle-class English language and prized the same middle-class English goals (financial and familial success) as they themselves did. In general, the novel helped make the position of the individual in new, expanding, and increasingly urban social contexts more intelligible; frequently addressed directly to the "dear reader," the novel presented unified visions of individuals in society, reflected the cultural and social conditions of that society, and supported the presumed rationalist psychology endemic to the age, which was fostered by Francis Bacon, Thomas Hobbes, and John Locke.

The novel was influenced by historic events and societal developments, especially tidal changes that involved the class structure of English society. The merchant class had existed for centuries and had steadily grown in the Age of Discovery and during colonization in the seventeenth century. In that century, a number of events conspired to begin the disestablishment of the feudal, medieval world, a disestablishment that would become final in the early nineteenth century. The beginning of the English Civil War (1642) marked the most noteworthy outbreak of religious and class strife England had yet seen. The subsequent regicide of Charles I in 1649 and the abolition of monarchy and the House of Lords by the House of Commons in that year signaled the formation of the Puritan Commonwealth (1649-1660) and the first rise to political dominance of the middle class, a much-contested context. In the Glorious Revolution of 1688, Parliament invited William of Orange and his wife, Mary, the Protestant daughter of the Catholic James II, to rule England. James II (the "Old Pretender") fled to France with his son Charles (the "Young Pretender" or Bonnie Prince Charlie), established himself in exile, and began plotting a return to power that would eventuate in the Scottish rebellions of 1715, 1719, and 1745-1746 on behalf of the Stuart monarchy. The Glorious Revolution may, in part, be seen as establishing the principle that the English middle class, through Parliament, could choose their own ruler; it may also be seen as another phase in the growth of power of that middle class.

A war with France (1689-1697) saw the beginning of the national debt, but the late seventeenth and early eighteenth centuries (especially during the reign of Queen Anne, 1702-1714) were marked by material progress, increased mercantilism, drastically increased population, and a rapid and irreversible shift of population from the country to the city. Apart from two major trade monopolies (the Hudson Bay Company in Canada and the East India Company in the Indian subcontinent), trade was open to all after 1689. Free enterprise flourished and with it the middle class, as early eighteenth century England became a mercantile society teetering on the brink of the Industrial Revolution and the concurrent scientific revolution that abetted it. While the governance of England still rested with a relatively small number of families, the hereditary landowners of England had to share power with the new merchant princes of the era.

From this milieu of class conflict emerged the earliest English novels. Rooted both in the picaresque tradition stemming from the anonymous Spanish *Lazarillo de Tormes* (1554; English translation, 1576) and Miguel de Cervantes' *Don Quixote de la Mancha* (1605, 1615) and in the pseudohistorical tradition, Daniel Defoe's novels present their fictions as fact, as the "histories" or "lives" of characters such as Robinson Crusoe, Colonel Newport, and Moll Flanders. Defoe's novels are distinguished by a realism that employs minute and concerted observations, as well as a morality that—despite lapses, an occasional blind eye to folly, and some ambiguous presentations of vice—fits well with the morality of the middle class, especially when erstwhile sinners repent and exemplify the Protestant virtues of seriousness, usefulness, social responsibility, and thrift. Like their many literary descendants, Defoe's characters evince a cheerful triumph of person over place and situation, an eventual mastery of the world and its too-familiar snares in the common and the uncommon adventures that form their educative encounters with the world and with themselves.

Even more obviously in line with middle-class Puritan ethics is the work of Samuel Richardson (1689-1761), whose epistolary novels of personality, sensibility, and moral conflict present the first multidimensional characters in English prose fiction. *Pamela: Or, Virtue Rewarded* (1740-1741) began by accident what Walter Allen calls the "first great flowering of the English novel." Commissioned to compose and print *Familiar Letters* as models of correspondence, moral guides, and repositories of advice to "handsome girls," Richardson expanded the project until it became *Pamela*. The particular virtue rewarded is chastity, in the face of assaults from a member of the Squirearchy, Mr. B., who is, ironically, a justice of the peace. One important artistic concern in the novel is the power of the written word to effect the conversion of wayward characters. One could take the view that Pamela's epistles reinforce traditionally Christian, or social, or merely prudential morality and that they also represent the generally desirable triumph of a member of the lower-middle class over representatives of the upper-middle class and the titled upper class. Virtue is, Richardson suggests, its own reward; it is all the better if it brings other rewards prized by the middle class. The novel's themes of moral courage and virtue reaffirmed bourgeois values and thus helped create an avid reading public.

Following Defoe, whose fiction offered a journalistic facticity, and Richardson, who wrote transparent moral sermons, Henry Fielding (1707-1754) was the first to write avowed novels and depict ordinary English life and the panorama of his age. Like Richardson, Fielding's beginning as a novelist was fortuitous. Sir Robert Walpole served George I and George II as prime minister from 1721 to 1742, and for much of that time he was the object of satire at the hands of several playwrights, Fielding among them. With Walpole's successful introduction of the Licensing Act of 1737, Fielding's career as a dramatist ended, and he turned his ironic and satiric vision to the new prose form, the novel, perfecting that form, many argue, in *The History of Tom Jones, a Foundling* (1749). Before that accomplishment, however, Fielding began his prose efforts by writing a broad satire of Richardson's title character, Pamela Andrews, which he titled *An Apology for the Life of Mrs. Shamela Andrews* (1741). He followed this success with *The History of the Adventures of Joseph Andrews, and of His Friend Mr. Abraham Adams* (1742), concerning Pamela's imagined brother, but took the story in new directions at midnovel. His *Amelia* (1751) is the first novel of social reform and thus was a point of reference for Charles Dickens and the many contributors to the "Newgate novel" in the nineteenth century. In *Amelia*, Fielding clearly exposes social wrongs and provides possible remedies for them. His portrayal of gambling dens, prison life, and the omnipresent Hogarthian gin mills foreshadows the excessive realism (or naturalism) of Honoré de Balzac and Émile Zola in France and George Moore in late Victorian England.

Two other great eighteenth century novelists, Tobias Smollett (1721-1771) and Laurence Sterne (1713-1768), added various dimensions of eighteenth century English life to the novel's inventory. In *The Adventures of Roderick Random* (1748), Smollett brought to the novel the first extended account of one fundament of English trade, prosperity, and adventure: seafaring life. Like Fielding and Defoe, he used English military history as background material for some of the finest English picaresque novels. Sterne, in *Tristram Shandy* (1759-1767), departed from the norm that his contemporaries had established, introducing a stream-of-consciousness technique to refract society through the prism of an individual mind, a technique that would not be further developed until the early twentieth century in the novels of James Joyce and Virginia Woolf.

The gothic novel

By the end of the eighteenth century, both the novel of sentiment and the gothic novel had appeared in *The Vicar of Wakefield* (1766) by Oliver Goldsmith (1728 or 1730-1774) and *The Castle of Otranto* (1765) by Horace Walpole (1717-1797). While Goldsmith's work and others like it continue in prose the situations and characteristics of the highly popular sentimental domestic drama of middle-class life, Walpole's novel exists outside of the conventions of eighteenth century thought and fiction. His is the only novel of those already mentioned that does not take as its premise the world as it exists, society in the country or city, and the generally agreed upon concept of the possible as coextensive with the real. Premised, then, on questions of epistemology and radical uncertainty, one can ascribe to *The Castle of Otranto* the beginnings of gothic traditions in the novel.

An emphasis on shared, common experience and consensus unified society and its conception of itself intellectually, philosophically, and psychologically. This society, in many respects the first truly modern society, emerged near the end of the seventeenth century into the era of Enlightenment and took for its tenets common sense, secular reason, science, and gentility. One fundamental emphasis of this era was upon the necessity to treat life and its problems in the spirit of reason and scientific empiricism rather than in the traditional spirit of appeal to authority and dogma. In this era, the landed gentry and not a few of the merchant princes regarded themselves as "Augustans" and sought to imitate the values and beliefs of the Roman patricians of the age of Augustus. In so doing, they set the intellectual tone of their times by asserting rationalism (and skepticism) as the primary focus of thought and by insisting on symmetry in all phases of life as well as of art, artificial ornament and the preference of artifice to "nature," reserved dignity in preference to any form of enthusiasm, and expansive, urbane sophistication instead of narrow, superstitious thought. It comes, then, as an extraordinary incongruity to find not only Walpole's work but also other novels of horror written, avidly read, and widely praised in this neoclassical Age of Reason.

Nevertheless, Walpole's gothic story was immensely successful, quite probably so in reaction to the restraint of the age, the dominion exercised by the Protestant ethic, and the evangelicalism of the century born in the advent of Wesleyanism and Methodism. In his conscious outlandishness, Walpole set a new course for fiction. His horrific pseudomedieval tale was followed by the gothic novels of Clara Reeve (1729-1807), Ann Radcliffe (1764-1823)—especially *The Mysteries of Udolpho* (1794)—and Matthew Gregory Lewis (1775-1818), and by numerous novels of the Romantic period. The success of this kind of imaginative, experimental writing is most probably what allowed for later development of novels based on fantasy, including science fantasy and science fiction. Mary Wollstonecraft Shelley's *Frankenstein* (1818) continued the gothic strain in the nineteenth century and became the preeminent novel of experimental science.

THE LATE EIGHTEENTH CENTURY

The last quarter of the eighteenth century, a period that saw the beginnings of Romanticism, featured the remarkable first ministry of William Pitt, the Younger (1759-1806), a ministry that laid the foundation for much of the reform movement in the nineteenth century. The intellectual tenets of the Augustan Age, already called into question by the gothic novelists and several poets of the age, were about to suffer a sea change in the triumph of individualism that characterized Romanticism. Economically, however, England maintained rather than altered its newfound tradition of progress, legitimatized by the writings of David Ricardo and Adam Smith. The advances of industry and capitalism begun early in the Augustan Age continued and ensured an economic boom that, with few setbacks, was to characterize the nineteenth century and fuel the expansion of the empire. Culturally, the pre-Romantic period was marked by an extraordinary growth in literacy, helped in great part by the growth of charity schools, the drive to regularize and teach English (if only for commercial purposes), the increasing new opportunities for the education of women, and the establishment and development of circulating libraries.

Two writers of this transitional period—the era, roughly speaking, between the outbreak of unrest in the American colonies in the early 1770's and the accession of Queen Victoria (1837)—stand apart from the mainstream of the rapidly changing world in which they lived. One, Jane Austen (1775-1817), epitomized an age that had already passed; the other, Sir Walter Scott (1771-1832), eschewed his own world except to the extent that he could translate some of its characteristics to other times. Austen's works, unpublished until the second decade of the nineteenth century, are the last novels of the Enlightenment. Unlike those of the other great eighteenth century novels, the characters presented by "the great feminine Augustan" are drawn almost exclusively from the landed gentry. In her novels she presents minute descriptions of the members of that class, their characters, beliefs, aspirations, and hopes in a period marked by a strong desire for stability on the part of the gentry despite the fact that they were surrounded by the armies of change. A supremely accomplished novelist, Jane Austen set the pattern for all subsequent novels of manners and family. Her characters interest themselves in issues of importance only to themselves—social position, socially and financially advantageous marriages, and the orderly passage of property from one generation to the next. The portraits that emerge are absolutely dissimilar to those of Fielding and his fellows and are essentially those of the placid, insulated upper class; as such, they present not only highly wrought pictures of the gentry but also invaluable insights into a social stratum that utterly vanished in the twentieth century.

Scott's Romantic novels, unlike Austen's works, deal with the world as it might have been rather than as it then was. His novels transplant nineteenth century heroes of sense, sensibility, and virtue to remote places or historically distant times. Moreover, his pioneer work in shaping the historical consciousness and national identity of Scotland while recounting its seventeenth century and eighteenth century history, and his novels of medieval and Renaissance Britain won him a place as a universally respected novelist of his century.

Both Austen and Scott are anomalies. Austen clearly summarizes the Augustan Age and its concerns, and Scott is surely the spokesman of a movement that grew in the last decades of the eighteenth century and took hold as the dominant intellectual mode of subsequent centuries, Romanticism. Though his novels rarely treat the world in which he lived, Scott's perceptions were conditioned by the growing intellectual and emotional tenets of Romanticism. Although he sought to explore the political and social conditions of earlier times in English and Scottish history, he consistently chose not to recognize the inescapable facts of the Industrial Revolution, the expensive (both in money and in lives) wars England waged in his own time, and the bloodless social revolution that saw the gentry finally replaced by the middle class as the political and economic rulers of England. The largest element of Scott's Romanticism is a studied medievalism that may be viewed as an escapist alternative (of considerable psychological necessity) to the pervasive and turbulent revolutions in every sector of society and as a reassertion of fundamental and traditional values. One benefit Scott gained by focusing upon Romantic medievalism as his chief fictional concern is that he thereby escaped the social censure and ostracism other Romantics experienced. Not only did he achieve personal respectability as a poet-turned-novelist, but he also created such a large and insatiable reading public for his and others' novels that the novel became the most popular form of literature.

The Victorian novel

The Victorian novelists—Charles Dickens was arguably the greatest of them—mark a new era in the novel, an era in which the primary middle-class emphasis on its own place in society and the reformation of society in its own image came to the fore. Society itself expanded in the Victorian Age to include not only England and the United Kingdom but also an empire upon which, proverbially, the sun never set. In consequence, novelists, in their characters, backgrounds, and plots, often surveyed an empire that extended geographically to all continents, covering fully one-tenth of the earth's surface, and financially to the entire populated world. Trade and tradesmen literally moved the empire, opened Australia and Canada to colonization, brought India into the fold (first via the East India Company and then, in 1857, under the Crown), and brought about the foundation of the corporate world with the Companies' Act of 1862.

The reform movement, in part attributable to the Romantic rebellion and in larger part to the middle-class redefinition of societal ideals, came to partial fruition in the 1820's and flourished in the 1830's and in subsequent decades. The hated and inflationary measure of 1815 prohibiting grain imports, the Corn Law, was modified in 1828; the Combination Acts of the era illustrate the pronounced middle-class opposition to trade unionism; the repeal of the Test Act (1828) and the passage of the Catholic Emancipation Bill (1829) brought about a liberalization of attitudes toward Roman Catholics and extended political franchise to a large number of men; the Third Reform Bill (1832) abolished slavery in the empire; the Factory Act (1833) regulated working hours and required two hours of schooling daily for children under the age of thirteen; and the New Poor Law (1834) represented another phase of regularizing governmental services and social programs. These reforms typify, without nearly exhausting, the great social legislation of this era. Reform was the byword of the early decades of the nineteenth century and the hallmark of the entire Victorian era as English society evolved. Subsequent reforms in suffrage, for example, seem to have moved at a glacial pace and only included women in 1928, but each new enfranchisement under the ministerial guidance of Benjamin Disraeli and William Gladstone added appreciably to the power of the middle class. It was quite natural, then, for the English novel to add social reform to its repertoire of themes.

Conditions for novelists also improved in nineteenth century England. As the eighteenth century marked the end of patronage as the primary support of artists and writers, so the explosion of periodicals, the multiplication of newspapers, the growth of publishing firms, and the extension of consumerism to literary works in the nineteenth century made it possible for more writers to try to live by and from the pen. "Grub Street" had meant, since the mid-eighteenth century, hard times for writers such as Samuel Johnson and Oliver Goldsmith, and in the eighteenth century the supply of writers far exceeded the demand. This, too, was the case in the nineteenth century, but less severely so, and it would remain the case despite the paperback, magazine, and other media revolutions of the twentieth century. It has often been suggested that Dickens,William Makepeace Thackeray, and most popular novelists of the century whose novels were first serialized in journals and magazines wrote at such length because they were paid by the line of print; while padding is one possible consequence of such a method of publication and payment, the leisurely pace of the novel, its descriptiveness and its length, date from the eighteenth century and grew without regard to such payment schedules. Serial publication no doubt influenced how authors arranged their plot developments. Authors provided rising action toward the end of each installment rather than solely toward the end of the entire novel. These suspenseful moments became known as "cliff-hangers" for their ability to tease readers into purchasing the next issue.

The Victorian novel as exemplified in the works of Charles Dickens (1812-1870) not only describes life but competes with it as well. Here one finds a verisimilitude so persuasive that the swarming complexities of Victorian life seem fixed in the novels. While carrying on the traditional celebration of middle-class values, Dickens also tried to make sense of the complex variety of choices open to his readers, of the fabric of society (by explaining, exposing, and mythologizing the middle class), of the ills of his society (by exposing them and calling for their reform), and of the patent injustices of capitalist society (by emphasizing their consequences, the plight of the victims of injustice, and the dehumanization of its perpetrators). To all of these concerns Dickens added a sense of comedy that suffused his early and some of his middle work but that changed to ferocity in his last complete novel, arguably his best after *Bleak House* (1852-1853, serial; 1853, book), *Our Mutual Friend* (1864-1865, serial; 1865, book).

Like Scott and many of his own contemporaries, Dickens is not above providing in his fiction a psychological escape from the mechanized world of his readers, as in *Pickwick Papers* (1836-1837, serial; 1837, book), a genteel picaresque work set in the period before the Age of Steam. Little else but artificially contrived escape exists for the reader and the protagonist of *Oliver Twist* (1837-1839, serial; 1838, book), an intense (and in its initial chapters unrelieved) examination of the workhouse system, one of the more depressing phenomena of the reform movement. Similarly, his descriptions of the criminal classes (so severely criticized, especially in regard to his depiction of prostitutes and child criminals, that he felt compelled to document his observations in the preface to the novel's second edition) illustrate the predatory relationship of this class to all other classes and form an indictment of the society that spawned and neglected them, an indictment that Dickens reiterated in *Bleak House* and elsewhere. Dickens the social reformer achieves some of his most enduring effects by indulging in the sentimentalism inherent in the sort of melodrama popular in the Victorian Age and still popular in some sectors today.

The Chancery Court and the legal system are the objects of Dickens's satiric wrath in *Bleak House*, a novel that amply illustrates that "the Law is a Ass," while in few other novels has the middle-class Gospel of Wealth been so soundly condemned as in *Dombey and Son* (1846-1848, serial; 1848, book). It is significant that in this novel the railway appears for the first time in Dickens's works. Dickens cast a cold eye on another English social institution, debtors' prison, in *Little Dorrit* (1855-1857, serial; 1857, book), in which London's Marshalsea Prison is the primary setting. On a smaller canvas in *Hard Times* (1854), he took on the educational abuses favored by the Gradgrinds of British industrial Coketowns, complete with their belief in the dullest of "facts."

Similar social issues and notions of reform appear in the Newgate novels (picaresque tales of crime and punishment by incarceration in Newgate Prison) and in the important work of the novelist Elizabeth Gaskell (1810-1865). Both Gaskell and Charles Kingsley (*Alton Locke*, 1850) did much to introduce the working-class or proletarian figure as a central focus of fiction, a focus Thomas Hardy would further sharpen late in the century.

William Makepeace Thackeray (1811-1863), a contemporary and sometime friend of Dickens, presented the world of the upper-middle class and limited his novels to that sphere. His *Vanity Fair: A Novel Without a Hero* (1847-1848) eschewed the conventional novel of intrigue and focused on the steady social climb of Becky Sharp from the position of governess to the ranks of the leisured gentry, a new class only possible to the England of empire and Industrial Revolution. Thackeray is at pains to glorify the virtues of the upper-middle class and to bolster them through his fiction: Marriage, home, and children constitute the proper society he portrays. Surely it is still possible to see in these ideals the safe harbors they had become for Victorians: It is also possible to view them as indicative of the societal dichotomy present in nearly every aspect of Victorian thought, a dichotomy that, in this case, emphasized an intense desire for security while positing the need for the adventurous life of acquisition. Like many of his predecessors and contemporaries, Thackeray turned his hand to the historical novel to explore from a nineteenth century perspective the social and literary life of the Queen Anne era, the Jacobite plots to return the Stuarts to monarchy, and the campaigns of the Duke of Marlborough.

Anthony Trollope (1815-1882) brought to the novel two new subject areas drawn from Victorian life: In his Barsetshire novels he introduced the first accurate portraits of English clerics; in his political or parliamentary novels he presented accurate descriptions of English politicians and political life rivaled only by those of Benjamin Disraeli (1804-1881), the first earl of Beaconsfield and twice prime minister of England (1867-1868; 1874-1880). In the novels of Trollope and Disraeli the vast and intricate world of ministries and parliaments, political intrigue, and the multifarious activities of empire in relation to the political process achieve a place in the novelistic tradition of England.

The religious controversies of the era, notably the Oxford Movement and the Anglo-Catholicism it induced, are present as background to Trollope's Barsetshire novels. The controversies are the concerns of several characters in the works of George Eliot (Mary Ann Evans, 1819-1880), and enter into *Sartor Resartus* (1833-1834, serial; 1836, book) by Thomas Carlyle (1795-1881) as well as into numerous other novels of the era, many of which use the historical convention of setting stories in Roman times to explore the religious question. Eliot's explorations of the internal motivations of her characters, in *Middlemarch* (1871-1872), for example, led to a brand of novel sometimes described as "psychological," although the full manifestation of this inside story would be independently delivered by Virginia Woolf (1882-1941) and James Joyce (1882-1941) after the turn of the century. The scientific basis for certain religious controversies, such as the influx of German higher criticism, the use of evidence from the expanding science of geology, and the introduction of the theory of evolution by Charles Darwin (1809-1882), also find their way into the novels of the period. The religious question and its attendant fideist, agnostic, and atheistic responses find novelistic expression in the works of such writers as Trollope; Charles Kingsley (1819-1875), the exponent of "Muscular Christianity"; Edmund Gosse (1849-1928), especially in *Father and Son* (1907); and Samuel Butler (1835-1902), particularly in *Erewhon* (1872), *Erewhon Revisited* (1901), *The Fair Haven* (1873), and *The Way of All Flesh* (1903).

Both abrupt and gradual changes in the religious climate are reflected in many Victorian novels, particularly in the otherwise quite dissimilar works of George Meredith (1829-1909) and Thomas Hardy (1840-1928). Meredith's championing of "advanced ideas" generally and his particular advocacy of woman suffrage, free thought, political radicalism, and evolutionary theory (optimistically considered) combine to form a vision of the Comic Spirit that suffuses his works. Hardy was differently affected by the multiplicity of Victorian controversies and conflicting claims; in his works one finds not comedy but a tragic vision of human life dominated by an inexorable sense that the evolutionary process has produced in man a kind of alien species against which the permanent forces of nature are constantly arrayed. Nowhere is this more evident than in *Jude the Obscure* (1895), a novel so universally condemned by churchmen and the conservative literary establishment that Hardy turned away from the novel to become a poet of considerable importance.

Another element in the continuing debate that the Victorians carried on with themselves springs from the social reform movements of the era and collides with the positivistic thought of Auguste Comte (1798-1857), who coined the term "sociology." This element surfaced in some of Dickens's work (*Bleak House*; *Martin Chuzzlewit*, 1843-1844 [serial], 1844 [book]; *Our Mutual Friend*; and the unfinished *The Mystery of Edwin Drood*, 1870), rose to a different plane in the novels of Wilkie Collins (*The Woman in White*, 1860; *The Moonstone*, 1868), and formed much of the matter of "yellow-back" or pulp novels as "shilling shockers" and "penny dreadfuls." It reached its logical Victorian zenith in the accounts of the world's greatest private consulting detective, Sherlock Holmes, by Arthur Conan Doyle (1859-1930), narratives that range from *A Study in Scarlet* (1887) to *The Case-Book of Sherlock Holmes* (1927).

THE DETECTIVE AND SPY NOVELS

The phenomenon of detective fiction captured the interest and imagination of the Victorian public at all levels of society. Organized police forces were first created in the nineteenth century, the science of criminology was born, and ingenious threats to life and, especially, property from the criminal classes grew apace with the unremitting urbanization of England. The steady progress of the fictional criminal, from the endearing rogues of sentimental fiction to the personification of social evil created by Conan Doyle in his Napoleon of Crime, Professor Moriarty, is directly related to the growth of the propertied middle class, to the swelling population of the "undeserving poor" (in George Bernard Shaw's phrase), to the ample opportunities for anonymity which urban centers and clear class divisions afforded, to the inevitable lure of easy money, and to the multiple examples of corrupt politicians on a national scale. Crime fiction kept pace with developments in crime and in criminal investigation, and in some cases the fiction anticipated developments in criminal science. The crime thriller, mystery story, and detective novel are still staple items of English fiction and have been so for more than a century, thanks to the efforts of Conan Doyle and the prodigious work of such writers as Agatha Christie (1890-1976) and John Creasey (1908-1973).

Still another subgenre linked to the detective novel was born of the armies of empire, international political events, and the information and communication explosions of the nineteenth century—the spy novel. Espionage had run through several Romantic and Victorian novels, but the Secret Service—John le Carré's "Circus" in his novels of the 1960's and 1970's—first came to prominence in *Kim* (1901) by Rudyard Kipling (1865-1936), and revolutionary espionage and anarchy came to the fore in *The Secret Agent* (1907) by Joseph Conrad (1857-1924). The spy novel in the twentieth century had great impetus from the events of World War I and World War II (in *The Third Man: An Entertainment*, 1950, for example, by Graham Greene) but is most closely associated with the post-1945 Cold War.

Both the detective novel of the Victorian Age and the spy novel born in its last days came to emphasize, of necessity, plot and action over character development and so tended to evolve into forms that do not fully coincide with the mainstream novel as the Victorians established it for themselves and their successors. A primary example of this is Ian Fleming's (1908-1964) character James Bond; a notable exception is John le Carré's (born 1931) George Smiley: Both writers and their characters face each other across an abyss. Yet the impulse to both sorts of fiction is historically rooted in the Romantic fiction of Scott and in the Romantic revival of the late nineteenth century, a revival sparked by an ever more urgent necessity to seek in fiction an escape from the complexities and difficulties of the present, and to find in fiction the disordered world set right, a finer or more exotic world, an adventurous world providing a chivalrous alternative to and a definite release from mercantile and corporate life.

In the Romantic revival of the late Victorian era, Robert Louis Stevenson (1850-1894) provided the best and most enduring fictional alternatives to the everyday life of Edinburgh, London, and the great industrial cities of the United Kingdom. Stevenson's novels of Scotland (*Kidnapped*, 1886; *The Master of Ballantrae*, 1889; *David Balfour*, 1893; *Weir of Hermiston*, 1896), *Treasure Island* (1881-1882), and *The Strange Case of Dr. Jekyll and Mr. Hyde* (1886) set a new fashion for tales of adventure and terror with such prime ingredients as soldiers, rebellions, pirates, and a monstrous transmogrification. His example was followed by H. Rider Haggard (1856-1925) in *King Solomon's Mines* (1885), Anthony Hope (1863-1933) in *The Prisoner of Zenda* (1894), Bram Stoker (1847-1912) in *Dracula* (1897), and P. C. Wren (1885-1941) in *Beau Geste* (1924), and by the writers of "best sellers" in succeeding generations. The novels of Alistair MacLean (1922-1987), Frederick Forsyth (born 1938), Jack Higgins (Harry Patterson, born 1929), and the hundreds of novels about World War II continue the Scott-Stevenson tradition, mixing reality with escapism. Further other-world fiction was provided by authors such as H. G. Wells (1866-1946) who, in science fantasies such as *The Time Machine: An Invention* (1895) offered readers hypothetical realities in novels that were sometimes classified as "speculative fiction."

The twentieth century novel and beyond

The end of Queen Victoria's reign and the accession of Edward VII (1901) truly marked the end of an age and of a century in which the novel rose to literary supremacy. On the eve of the twentieth century, England had passed several relatively peaceful decades since the Napoleonic era. The military excursions of the Crimean War (1854-1856), the Sepoy Rebellion in India (1857), a war with China (1857-1858), and the Boer War in South Africa (1899-1902) in no way prepared the empire for the global struggle that began in 1914 in the reign of George V and lasted as the Great War (now, World War I), until 1918. This and other military conflicts of the twentieth century left clearly discernible marks upon the development of the English novel. World War II (1939-1945), the most cataclysmic for England, is also the most notable of the conflicts but not the longest. Wars, "police actions," and skirmishes in the distant corners of the empire, from Suez (1956) or Palestine (1949) to the Falkland Islands (1982), and extending temporally from the Boer War to the Argentinian conflict, may have matched in sporadic intensity but not in overall bitterness the continuing Anglo-Irish struggle, begun many centuries ago and marked in the twentieth century by the Easter Rising (1918), the partition of Ireland (1922), and the move to Commonwealth status (1937) and to Republic (1949) for the South.

World War II, however, justly overshadowed all other military events of the twentieth century and exerted such an influence on the course of the English novel that the number of fictional works about Britain's "finest hour" has grown astronomically since 1945. World War II may have passed into cultural memory, but it remained, for whole generations, a recent event of personal history that also marks the beginning of the "postmodern" world. Shortly after the war, beginning around 1947, the empire was virtually dismantled, and more than one billion people throughout the world gained political independence.

The proletarian novel and the novel of social criticism

The British economy was sapped by expensive modern warfare, the rapid dissolution of the empire, and the immigration of large numbers of the middle class; it was plagued by taxation (marked by the establishment of the first modern social security system, in 1912, and later by the socialistic British welfare state, 1945-1951), devastated by the Great Depression of 1929 and the wholesale destruction of property in the Battle of Britain and the subsequent saturation bombing of London, and eroded by massive unemployment and the steady devaluation of the pound sterling. These events and their economic effects form a background for the rise of the proletarian novel and the novel of social criticism of the 1950's and subsequent decades, including works by Kingsley Amis (1922-1995), John Braine (1922-1986), John Wain (1925-1994), and Alan Sillitoe (born 1928), who are now known as the Angry Young Men.

Social issues that occasioned the protests of the Victorian novelists were largely resolved during the last decades of Victoria's reign, ceased to have the same importance in the years when Edward VII was monarch (1901-1910), and, except for the extension of the voting franchise to women (1928), became legally moot in the early years of George V's reign. A divergent set of social issues replaced them for twentieth century novelists such as John Galsworthy (1867-1933), H. G. Wells (1866-1946), Arnold Bennett (1867-1931), and George Moore (1852-1933). Galsworthy, for example, captured the decline and disintegration of Victorian/Edwardian pillars of the middle class into the "lost generation" of the 1920's, and in so doing raised lapsarian questions that contribute to a "modernist" sensibility. Wells, apart from his socialist propaganda, also examined the possibilities of dehumanization and the inevitable destructiveness of the retrograde evolution of English class, social, and scientific structures. Bennett and Moore, like Galsworthy, pilloried the bourgeoisie and Victorianism generally, and both imported techniques from the French naturalistic novel to do so. Although French and other Continental writers exerted considerable influence on the cultural development of the English novel from roughly the mid-nineteenth century onward (one finds such influences extending from the novels of George Eliot to those of Henry James), it is noteworthy that the anti-Victorian writers should employ the naturalistic technique of Balzac and Zola in their novelistic experiments.

The form of the novel, as established in the eighteenth century, had evolved but had not drastically changed throughout the nineteenth century. With the influx of the French aesthetic, symbolist, and decadent literature in the 1890's, and the experiments of Bennett and Moore, the stage was set for more radical experiments with the English novel, experiments that centered primarily on the traditional focus of the novel, character, and subordinated all else to it. One must look to the Anglicized American, Henry James (1843-1916), as a primary source for the experimental novel, even if James did remain clearly within the confines of the English novelistic tradition. By emphasizing such elements as angle of narration, the capturing of actual experience and the way people are, the primacy of individual psychology, and the disappearance of the traditional hero, James prepared the way for further experiments by Joseph Conrad, James Joyce (1882-1941), Virginia Woolf (1882-1941), D. H. Lawrence (1885-1930), and Lawrence Durrell (1912-1990), among others. In their fiction variations on the modernist questions of ultimate meaning, individual responsibility, and elemental issues of guilt, moral alienation and dehumanization, and atonement find enduring expression as each writer searches for individual answers to similar questions. Whether the scope of the search is global, as in Conrad's settings throughout the empire, or intensely local, as in Joyce's Dublin, Lawrence's Nottinghamshire, or the mind of Woolf's Mrs. Dalloway, it is the same inner search. In the light of the experimental novels of the twentieth century, *Tristram Shandy* no longer seems the oddity it once appeared to be.

Differing from the vast quantity of twentieth century English novels written in the authorized veins of bourgeois or antibourgeois traditions, the abundant novels of adventure, detection, mystery, romance (in all senses), espionage and humor—all forms in which society is reflected and sees itself—the experimental novel provided a different sort of novelistic focus, the novel of social criticism and satire in which the protagonist is no longer concerned with a place in society but is, as his or her American cousins have been since the days of Nathaniel Hawthorne and Herman Melville, most frequently an outsider who seeks to preserve and justify alienation from a disordered and dissolving society and culture. Set adrift from intellectual, social, religious, and cultural stability and identity, the interbellum generation (1918-1939) and the postwar or postmodern generations consistently emphasize the futility of human community under the social contract. Not only the Angry Young Men but also their predecessors, successors, and contemporaries such as Ronald Firbank (1886-1926), Aldous Huxley (1894-1963), Evelyn Waugh (1903-1966), George Orwell (1903-1950), William Golding (1911-1993), Graham Greene, and John le Carré engage in social criticism and satire that ranges from assailing the societal, mechanistic, technocratic trivializing of human dignity to asserting the necessity of a solitary quest for personal ethics in an era that lacks an ethical superstructure and in which organized religion is one among many residual elements of limited use.

Multiculturalism in the Novel

Beginning in the last half of the twentieth century, a reinvigorated strain of fiction came to reflect the growing ethnic diversity of England's people and their multicultural character and global concerns, as many Commonwealth writers and expatriates chose England as their residence and principal forum. In addition, the growing genre of postcolonial fiction gave writers from the former British colonies new themes, genres, and readers. Three writers of the 1980's amply illustrate this diversity. Kazuo Ishiguro was born in Nagasaki in 1954;

his family moved to England in 1960. Ishiguro's first novel, *A Pale View of Hills* (1982), is narrated by a Japanese widow, a survivor of the atomic bombing of Nagasaki, who is living in England. *An Artist of the Floating World* (1986) is the story of an old Japanese painter oppressed by guilt over the prostitution of his art in the service of Japanese imperialism. With his universally acclaimed third novel, *The Remains of the Day* (1989), winner of the Booker Prize, Ishiguro made a bold leap; here his first-person narrator is an English butler in the mid-1950's, a figure at once comic and poignant. The first-person narrator of *When We Were Orphans* (2000) is also an Englishman, but one who grew up in colonial Shanghai in the 1930's. *The Unconsoled* (1995) is Ishiguro's exploration of a dreamscape so ambiguous that it thoroughly upsets traditional narrative concepts. The main character, Mr. Ryder, finds that his conflicted past and his insecurities about his future transform everything he encounters into a surreal dream of reality. This defamiliarization from the real is one of the universal themes that Ishiguro gravitated toward in rejection of the earlier emphasis on the lapse between Japanese and English cultural identities. In either case, his fiction cautions that "we tend to think we're in far more control than we are." This confusion about identity and lack of control is fully realized in Ishiguro's dystopian novel *Never Let Me Go* (2005), which won the Arthur C. Clarke Award for the best British science fiction novel of the year.

Salman Rushdie, born in Bombay (now Mumbai) in 1947, was educated in England. His novel *Midnight's Children* (1981) views the partition of India and the creation of the independent Muslim state of Pakistan through the lens of Magical Realism. The novel was chosen, on the fortieth anniversary of the Booker Prize, as the Best of the Booker, the best of the novels ever to have won the coveted prize. *Shame* (1983) covers much of the same territory. Rushdie achieved international notoriety with his Joycean novel, *The Satanic Verses* (1988), a great wheel of a book that was condemned by Muslim fundamentalists for what they considered blasphemous treatment of the Qurʾān and of the life of Muḥammad. In *Haroun and the Sea of Stories* (1990), a children's book written for adults as well, Rushdie, threatened with death and forced into hiding, answers his critics with a celebration of storytelling and the unconstrained imagination. His return to the context of improbable reality in *The Moor's Last Sigh* (1995) offers readers a heightened emphasis on storytelling as a theme. Rushdie returned to the theme of partition with *Shalimar the Clown* (2005), set in Kashmir, but he set *The Enchantress of Florence* (2008) squarely in the fifteenth century, in Italy, and in the realm of fantasy.

V. S. Naipaul (born 1932), a Trinidadian-born British writer whose heritage is Indian, is a leading figure in postcolonial literature and the winner of the 2001 Nobel Prize in Literature. His novella, *In a Free State* (1971), the first book by a writer of Indian descent to win the Booker Prize, is set in a newly independent East African country, modeled on Kenya, which became independent from Great Britain in 1963. *A Bend in the River* (1979), also set in Africa, is narrated by an Indian shopkeeper who fits in neither with the Africans nor with their former colonizers. In *Half a Life* (2001) and its sequel *Magic Seeds* (2004), Naipaul depicts an Indian writer who moves to London and then to Africa. Naipaul has been criticized by postcolonial theorists for his apparent sympathies with the colonizers rather than with the colonized, but his Nobel citation praised him "for having united perceptive narrative and incorruptible scrutiny in works that compel us to see the presence of suppressed histories."

Women writers have used fiction to tell neglected stories in multicultural Great Britain. Beryl Gilroy (1924-2001) was born in what was then British Guyana, now the independent nation of Guyana. She traveled to Great Britain to study at the University of London, and she became a teacher, a psychotherapist specializing in the needs of black women and children, and a writer. Her first novel for adults, *Frangipani House* (1986), is set among the elderly in Guyana, and *Boy-Sandwich* (1989) depicts the experiences of young black boys in Great Britain's large cities. Bangladeshi British author Monica Ali (born 1967) shows the struggles faced by women in London's Bangladeshi neighborhoods in *Brick Lane* (2003), which was adapted as a feature film in 2007. *White Teeth* (2000), by Zadie Smith (born 1975), is about the moral and psychological struggles of immigrants, and her *On Beauty* (2005) explores the life of a mixed-race family.

Less emphatically concerned with diversity issues, A. S. Byatt (born 1936) and Julian Barnes (born 1946) seem to have inherited the position of authorial status occupied by the writers of the 1950's through the 1970's. Their novels exhibit such sophisticated strategies that in some cases, such as Barnes's *Flaubert's Parrot* (1984) and *Arthur and George* (2005), they are considered "post-postmodern." Byatt's works tend to focus on intellectual problems characteristic of past eras, such as allegorical representation common to the Renaissance, evidenced in *The Virgin in the Garden* (1978), and deistic wrangling over biblical stories, in *Babel Tower* (1996). Byatt translates these pedantic puzzles into contemporary English life, providing relevance for both the society she writes about and the history of ideas that influences them. She often combines modern and historical characters in one novel, as in the Booker Prize-winning *Possession* (1990) and *The Biographer's Tale* (2000), both of which tell the stories of intellectual figures from history and the scholars who study them.

At the beginning of the twenty-first century, Ian McEwan (born 1948) emerged as one of the leading writers of the English novel. The author of several novels as well as short stories, screenplays, poetry, a play, an opera, and books for children, he won the Booker Prize for *Amsterdam* (1998), a novel about a composer and a newspaper editor struggling with moral questions, hatred, and vengeance. A feature film adaptation of *Atonement* (2002), McEwan's most popular work, was released in 2007. This novel also deals with the consequences of making moral missteps.

The English novel, then, to paraphrase William Shakespeare's Hamlet, holds the mirror up to society and shows the very age and body of the time, its form and pressure. Even a brief sketch of the varied patterns of societal influences on the development of the English novel demonstrates that the novel is of all literary forms the most responsive to the changing emphases of an evolving society. Whether in overt reaction to the values of a society, in praise of them or in criticism of them, the novel consistently presents the society as the individual must confront it, explains that society to itself, and helps society to define itself.

John J. Conlon; Scott D. Vander Ploeg
Updated by Cynthia A. Bily

Bibliography

Adams, Percy G. *Travel Literature and the Evolution of the Novel.* Lexington: University Press of Kentucky, 1983. Suggests a correlation between deception in travel stories and the essential (un)trustworthiness of the narrator.

Bradbury, Malcolm. *The Modern British Novel.* London: Penguin Books, 1994. Explores the great variety of twentieth century British literature.

Cavaliero, Glen. *The Supernatural and English Fiction: From "The Castle of Otranto" to "Hawksmoor."* New York: Oxford University Press, 1995. Wide-ranging discussion of the supernatural in English fiction is valuable for its discussion not only of well-known authors such as Ann Radcliffe and Horace Walpole but also of less-familiar writers and novels.

David, Dierdre, ed. *Cambridge Companion to the Victorian Novel.* New York: Cambridge University Press, 2001. Collection of eleven essays covers topics such as gender, sexuality, economy, and science as explored in the Victorian novel. Includes an extensive bibliography.

Horsman, Alan. *The Victorian Novel.* New York: Clarendon Press, 1990. Offers insightful and comprehensive treatment of both the major Victorian authors and many minor authors of the period. Includes a helpful chronology.

Kiely, Robert. *The Romantic Novel in England.* Cambridge, Mass.: Harvard University Press, 1972. Presents an overview of a dozen of the most commonly discussed Romantic and gothic novels published between 1764 and 1847.

McKee, Patricia. *Public and Private: Gender, Class, and the British Novel, 1764-1878.* Minneapolis: University of Minnesota Press, 1997. Surveys the sociological implications of changing roles represented in novels from the early period into the Victorian era.

McKeon, Michael. *The Origins of the English Novel, 1600-1740.* Baltimore: Johns Hopkins University Press, 1987. Provides an aggressive exploration of the philosophical and religious underpinnings of the early English novel.

Parrinder, Patrick. *Nation and Novel: The English Novel from Its Origins to the Present Day.* New York: Oxford University Press, 2006. Examines the development of the British novel from 1485, with an emphasis on political and economic influences.

Richetti, John, et al., eds. *The Columbia History of the British Novel*. New York: Columbia University Press, 1994. A good standard of critical opinion on matters pertaining to the novel.

Roberts, Andrew Michael, ed. *The Novel: A Guide to the Novel from Its Origins to the Present Day*. London: Bloomsbury, 1994. Handy primer on the novel presents informative discussion of contemporary critical trends.

The European Novel

How early was the earliest novel? Critics attempt to establish a beginning for the form in order to make the analytical task manageable. Because the novel, as generally defined, holds many elements in common with drama, epic, folktale, fable, satire, biography, and autobiography, it is impossible to designate one work as the earliest novel. Furthermore, when critics do include certain early works as novels, they are making a distinction that did not exist before the eighteenth century. Thus, literary historians must include as novels many works for which the category did not exist at the time they were written, or that were not considered novels by either their authors or their first readers. For example, Samuel Richardson's *Pamela: Or, Virtue Rewarded* (1740-1741) itself was originally conceived of by its author, a printer by trade, as an illustrative guide to the art of letter writing, not as a work of fiction. Richardson's predecessor, Daniel Defoe, author of *Robinson Crusoe* (1719) and *The Fortunes and Misfortunes of the Famous Moll Flanders, Written from Her Own Memorandums* (1722), called his own works histories and specifically wrote against novels, a class of writing that, he said, "invents characters that never were in Nature."

Beginnings of the novel in Europe

The canon of the novel, then, should probably include all important works, no matter how early, that are read as novels are read today and that have clearly influenced the shape of European fiction. In this light, it makes sense to trace the origins of the novel back to the origins of Western literature, perhaps to Homer's *Iliad* (c. 750 B.C.E.; English translation, 1611) and *Odyssey* (c. 725 B.C.E.; English translation, 1614). Certainly, two of the oldest traditions in fiction, the heroic and the picaresque, maintain these works as prototypes. Among other ancient works, the narratives of the Old Testament have also been of immeasurable influence in shaping the forms and themes of Western fiction. Genesis, for example, can be said to have shown the West how to use character to embody the history and spirit of a people; indeed, the Old Testament is rich in narratives of many kinds. Perhaps even more influential in Western literary history, however, have been the Gospels of the New Testament, which present the archetypal story of the individual versus society, or, more precisely, of the individual's defining his or her personal relationship with the divine, irrespective of society's definition. Because most critics see the growth of the novel in terms of a movement toward realizing unique individuals and away from reiterating stereotypes, one way to view the history of the novel is in terms of its lesser or greater success in achieving the iconoclastic ideal set by the Gospels. Given the Gospels' pervasive influence on Western culture, it is only to be expected that critics will frequently see Christian parallels in the acts of well-known characters. Similarly, the most important novels have been considered radical, even dangerous, books, though perhaps none so radical and dangerous in its time as were the Gospels at the time of their writing.

Because of their importance in the school curricula of the Middle Ages and the Renaissance, and hence in the growth of some forms of the novel, such Roman writers as Vergil, Horace, Plautus, and Terence must also be mentioned. Plautus and Terence, the comic dramatists, gave to European literature a particular character type, the wily slave, versed in the ways of the street, the market, and the noble household and able to outwit anyone he meets—noble, tradesman, or fellow slave. Through the Italian popular drama, this figure made his way throughout the Western Mediterranean countries and into prose fiction of the sixteenth century in the rogue stories of Spain, France, and England. Horace and the other Roman satirists contributed to this same fictional strain by re-creating the milieu of contemporary Rome and peopling it with types of actual citizens. The realistic novel grew out of these satirists' attention to the things and events of everyday life.

The poetry of Vergil was the most eminent model for the Middle Ages and the Renaissance of the idealization of life through literature. His *Aeneid* (c. 29-19 B.C.E.; English translation, 1553) carried forward the epic tradition from Homer and, in Aeneas, gave Europe a model of heroism in peace and in war. The Arthurian romances of the later Middle Ages take much of their inspiration from the Vergilian hero; the tales of Arthur inspired other chivalric romances (such as *Amadis of Gaul*, 1508) that brought the Vergilian ideal into the Renaissance, these romances remaining popular into the seventeenth century and even, albeit in different form, today. Vergil was also the primary model of the pastoral strand in fiction and poetry through the Renaissance. His *Eclogues* (c. 43-37 B.C.E.; also known as *Bucolics*; English translation, 1575) created Arcadia, an idealized landscape somewhat removed from the turmoil of the city and hospitable to the daylong singing of love songs. In Arcadia, shepherds vie without malice for the love of shepherdesses, regret the coldness of their lovers, and lament the foolish ambitions of city folk, who can never know Arcadian serenity. Based on the Greek myth of the Golden Age and the biblical idea of Eden, this pastoral ideal has exerted great continuing force on the literary imagination, producing among its manifestations the pastoral romances of late sixteenth century England and Spain, the aristocratic love intrigues of seventeenth century France, and the romances and high-society novels that fill the paperback racks in stores today.

The influence of the ancients on both the heroic and the pastoral modes was augmented in the sixteenth century by the rediscovery and translation of the Hellenistic romances (c. 200 B.C.E.) of Longus (*Poimenika ta kata Daphin kai Chloen*; *Daphnis and Chloë*, 1587), Heliodorus, and Achilles Tatius. Considered by some critics to be early novels, these long prose tales combined pastoral episodes with violent adventures: wars, shipwrecks, kidnappings by pirates. These books gave European writers an easily imitable format that has proven immensely successful in succeeding centuries.

The Middle Ages to the Renaissance

During the Middle Ages, verse and prose works in the heroic, realistic/satiric, and pastoral modes continued to be written, thus nourishing the soil that produced the long fictions of the Renaissance that modern critics most frequently call the first novels. The dominant heroic form of the early Middle Ages, the lives of Christian saints and martyrs, blended the influences of Vergil with those of the Gospels and the letters of Paul to create a Christian heroic type that would flourish in the later Middle Ages in the epics of Roland, the Cid, and Arthur. The saints' lives also carried forward the Roman satiric mode, primarily in the form of tricks played by the saints on the always greedy, pompous, pagan soldiers and magistrates. In the later medieval period, such satire was most often directed at corrupt clerics and wealthy burghers, with pranks being pulled on them by such masterful imps as the German Tyll Eulenspiegel. The French fabliaux of the thirteenth and fourteenth centuries contain many stories of this type, besides satires in which the trick is a sexual one played by a lusty youth with the wife of a rich, gout-ridden old merchant. Geoffrey Chaucer worked marvelous variations on these themes in *The Canterbury Tales* (1387-1400), and Giovanni Boccaccio worked the same vein in his *Decameron: O, Prencipe Galetto* (1349-1351; *The Decameron*, 1620), both collections providing continuing inspiration for later writers of fiction.

Of incalculable effect on the eventual rise of the intellectual novel, or novel of sensibility, was the introspective devotional literature of the Middle Ages, its greatest example being the *Confessiones* (397-400; *Confessions*, 1620) of Saint Augustine. Using autobiographical narrative in the service of ethical and religious speculation, the *Confessions*, like the greatest novels, grant high dignity and importance to the individual life. The *Confessions* also brought to Western literature that intimacy of tone and truthfulness of thought and feeling that are the essence of the modern intellectual novel.

The invention of movable type and the influence of the Humanists

Perhaps the single most important event in the development of the modern novel was Johann Gutenberg's invention of movable type in 1450. Without the technology to produce thousands of copies, each several hundred pages in length, the novel as it is known today, sprawling in scope of time and place, dependent on a diverse reading public, is inconceivable. In terms of the historical development of the genre, this invention also occasioned the amazing speed with which the influence of major works moved from country to country after about 1500, as works written in one vernacular were translated and made available for other readers only a few years after their first printing. As a result, one sees continual enrichment by foreign sources of the distinctive national traditions.

The clearest example of this multicultural influence is that of the Dutch-born Desiderius Erasmus, whose *Moriae encomium* (1509; *The Praise of Folly*, 1941) and *Colloquia familiaria* (1518) affected satiric fiction throughout Western Europe from as early as the 1530's. *The Praise of Folly* raises to the level of Christian type the anticlerical trickster of the Eulenspiegel tales and the fabliaux. *Colloquia familiaria*, originally intended as a speaking and writing manual for students of Latin, includes clever dialogues and realistic stories that continued to reappear in new garb throughout the century, in such works as those of William Shakespeare and Miguel de Cervantes. The French Humanist François Rabelais was influenced by Erasmus in his writing of the monumental *Gargantua et Pantagruel* (1532-1564; *Gargantua and Pantagruel*, 1653-1694, 1929), which was in turn disseminated widely by mid-century. Through the scatological and gluttonous acts, never subtle and frequently grotesque, of his Gargantua, Rabelais attacked the abuses of church, court, and marketplace, his rambling narrative in some ways a precursor of the picaresque novels that would flourish in Spain for close to a century.

A third Humanist and a friend of Erasmus, Sir Thomas More, made his mark on European fiction with *De Optimo Reipublicae Statu, deque Nova Insula Utopia* (1516; *Utopia*, 1551). Intended as criticism of the unregulated capitalism of English landowners, *Utopia* became a fully detailed picture of an ideal monarchy, related as a travel narrative by one Raphael Hythloday. Though an extended work of fiction, *Utopia* explores ideas rather than characters or events, and it may therefore be regarded as a model of what the novel is not, rather than what it usually has been. *Utopia* may perhaps be called an example of the pastoral novel, since it presents an idealized society (much nineteenth and twentieth century science fiction fits into this category as well), but it diverges from most pastoral literature, which sees its Arcadia as an escape from worldly affairs rather than an improvement in terms of social planning. True novels in every mode, even the heroic, tend to take a jaded view of human character and interaction. Perhaps part of the definition of the novel is that in it, society is never harmonious.

The novel in Spain: 1550-1630

Most historians see the Spain of the mid-sixteenth century as the birthplace of the novel, or at least of a form of fiction that they see leading clearly toward the eighteenth century novel of sensibility. The feature that sets these Spanish novels apart from their predecessors is their use of a first-person narrator who relates with unembarrassed candor the degradations of his life. Moreover, this character is a believably real Spaniard of the current time, who vividly depicts the sights, sounds, and, particularly, smells of the actual environment. One way to see this development of the novel is as a combining of the realistic/satiric mode with the confessional mode in Christian devotion, as exemplified by Augustine's *Confessions*. However this form is defined, the anonymous author of *Lazarillo de Tormes* (1554; English translation, 1576), which began this trend, hit upon a formula that changed European fiction and set it on a road it has followed ever since.

Why this phenomenon first occurred in Spain rather than elsewhere in Europe has been much debated. One reason frequently cited involves Spain's position in the sixteenth century as the most religiously and philosophically conservative nation in Europe, the country under the strongest domination by the Catholic Church and with the most rigid socioeconomic stratification. Whereas in England, for example, the satiric impulse produced visions of reform, such as *Utopia* and countless manuals for improvement in education and manners, in Spain the satiric eye looked inward and beneath the skins of other humans, to dwell on corruptions of the soul. In this climate, Renaissance Humanism merely deepened the cynicism, because it kept the observer focused on the imperfections of the here and now by denying the medieval choice of seeing this "vale of tears" as a mere steppingstone to eternal glory. Whereas Augustine's *Confessions* become a prayer of hope and thanksgiving, *Lazarillo de Tormes* and the works to follow—including the greatest, *Don Quixote de la Mancha* (1605, 1615)—end with the hero facing death or in a temporary lull before the next, and certain, disaster. What makes this literature comic and compelling is that the narrators are so resigned to the status quo that they can view the grotesque happenings they relate without anxiety; by contrast, the greedy and ambitious in these novels appear funny fools indeed, because they lack the hero's peace of mind.

In design, *Lazarillo de Tormes* and its followers retain the episodic structure of the medieval satires and the travel motif—the movement from adventure to adventure—of the Pentateuch, the *Odyssey*, and the tales of knighthood, but *Lazarillo de Tormes* departs from this tradition in its exact descriptions of the contemporary milieu and in the confessional candor of the title character. The portraits of Lázaro's masters, in particular the blind man, the squire, and the pardoner, are precisely drawn; one is convinced of the actuality of these men, even as one understands their function as representatives of several classes of Spanish society. Lázaro's self-portrait is the most convincing. He describes his experiences so minutely and accepts his sufferings so humbly that there can be no doubt that the reader is being addressed by the same man who has lived these adventures. One does not question, while reading, how the illiterate son of illiterate parents can so casually allude to the classics during his discourse; one merely enjoys his erudition, his practiced blending of formal address with the minutiae of the streets. The allusions, it is assumed, are convenient phrases he has picked up during a lifetime of surviving by his wits and his tongue. Yet herein lies the romantic illusion of the story and perhaps the essence of its charm, both in the sixteenth century and now: *Lazarillo de Tormes* simultaneously allows the reader to rub elbows with the oppressed, persevering child of poverty and to be comforted that Lázaro's life of pain does not lead to early death or to a career of villainy, but rather to mental serenity and the material reward of his clever tactics.

Lazarillo de Tormes spawned many imitations; what was fresh at the origins of the Spanish picaresque became, in a period of some seventy-five years, all too predictable. That one could work within the convention created by *Lazarillo de Tormes* and still produce a novel of stunning coherence and originality is shown, however, by the example of Miguel de Cervantes, whose *Don Quixote de la Mancha* was the popular rage of its time. To many modern critics, *Don Quixote de la Mancha* is the first work worthy of being called a true novel. This monumental book, published in two parts ten years apart, was intended by its aging author as a last attempt to gain popular success after a long, futile career as a playwright and pastoralist. He succeeded in fashioning a novel that realized an individual character more profoundly than had anyone since Augustine and that contained the best features of the heroic, pastoral, and realistic/satiric modes. Indeed, one explanation of the novel's power is that in *Don Quixote de la Mancha* the heroic, satiric, and pastoral stereotypes collide, destroying the illusions and pretenses of each mode and leaving their essences. This collision occurs because Cervantes sets the aged landowner Quixote, a man who loves and devoutly believes in the heroes of the medieval tales of knighthood, right in the middle of the same Spain—dry, poor, vicious, and self-deluded—through which Lázaro had been swept. Cervantes endows the old man with a crazy dream of becoming a knight-errant, riding off in search of adventures, chances for triumphs won on behalf of his virtuous lady, a creature of his imagination named Dulcinea del Toboso. The mission is heroic, but as a nostalgic dream its form is pastoral, an attempt to escape the sensible, dull, humiliating final years facing this childless, wifeless owner of a few dusty acres and some scrawny livestock. When these diverse modes come together in this way, an amazing thing occurs: Through nine hundred pages, the old man's dream proves so resilient that a kind of transformation begins to work in the hard-bitten, cynical minds of the other characters. It is not that they come to accept his heroically optimistic perspective on reality, but that they come to appreciate the beautiful alternative his faith and actions offer in an otherwise squalid world.

Indeed, it does not take Cervantes many pages to show the reader that each individual, no matter how he may scoff at the illusions of others, has his own comfortingly false views of the world. This is first demonstrated when the priest and the barber of La Mancha, in a parody of the Inquisition, ferret through Don Quixote's library to find and burn those books that have warped his mind. Like the local board of motion-picture censors, the more they search, the more excuses they find to save certain chivalric books because of particularly exciting stories or characters. As the novel proceeds, particularly in part 2, Don Quixote becomes a legend in his own time; even the nobility seek him out, supposedly as entertainment but really because they want to verify his faith in order to find something worth believing in themselves.

The sad countercurrent in the novel is that the absurdly cruel lengths to which characters go to test Quixote's beliefs eventually wear them out of him. On his deathbed, the old "knight," who now calls himself by his given name, Alonso Quixano, says that he "abominates" all the books of knight-errantry that once had guided him. Ironically, none of his hearers—who had so earnestly worked to "cure" him throughout the story—wants to hear this. They are all prepared to accompany him on a new adventure, going out to live like shepherds in idyllic pastoral fashion. They try to encourage him back into his delusion; his sudden sanity suggests that he is indeed about to die, and it is this that they cannot tolerate, for his death means the loss of an imaginative force that has dignified all of their lives.

Cervantes adhered to the framework, conventional in both the picaresque novels and the chivalric romances, of the hero's traveling from place to place, adventure to adventure. He used each episode in this format to refine further the reader's understanding of Quixote and his strange quest. Like the characters who surround the old man, these episodes test Quixote and define him for the reader. For example, the early episode with the windmills shows Quixote as a grave misinterpreter of reality, but later, when he rejects the attentions of a servant girl at an inn on the basis of his loyalty to Dulcinea, one sees the nobility of character that his new identity includes. Such use of the picaresque format is not primarily satiric, even though the contrast between gentle, fair-minded Quixote and the ignorant, equally self-deluded people he meets is clear enough. The satirist goes after more aggressive evils: thievery, seduction, malfeasance in office; Cervantes depicts primarily good-natured folk who sometimes hurt others unwittingly, or out of a sense of duty (as does Quixote himself), or out of fear, usually brought on by the narrowness of their views. *Don Quixote de la Mancha* continues to inspire readers because it is easy for them to see themselves in these people. Readers must admit that they would react to the old knight as do his niece, his housekeeper, the priest, and the barber.

The reader is particularly encouraged to identify with Sancho Panza, Quixote's "squire," an ever-present barometer of the typical reaction to Quixote of a person of good heart, some imagination, and little self-confidence—in short, an average person. Critics have argued about who is the more masterful creation, the knight or the squire. Undertaking Quixote's quest because he naïvely believes the old man's promise that he will one day receive an island as his reward, Sancho stays with him out of an ever-stronger loyalty and compassion, virtues put to painful test at every encounter, with every blow he receives from angry tradesmen and travelers. When, ironically, he eventually is given governorship of an island—if only as part of a large practical joke—he carries off the tasks of ruling with a clarity of judgment that does not surprise the reader but that could not have been predicted at the outset of the quest. Sancho consistently lets the reader judge how he himself has developed as an interpreter of Don Quixote; Sancho Panza's presence is a principal reason for the novel's remarkable coherence and momentum through its many diverse episodes.

The novel in France: 1600-1740

That the early histories of the novel in Spain, France, and England are largely independent phenomena is exemplified by the failure of *Don Quixote de la Mancha* to attract a wide readership in England and France for many decades. In England, *Don Quixote de la Mancha* was "discovered" in the eighteenth century and became an influential work. The most successful French writers of the period from 1600 to 1740, working in a very different fictional tradition in a very different social and philosophical climate, were not at all influenced by this book, though Cervantes and the other picaresque writers did have disciples among the few French satirists and realists of the age.

Aspects of the chivalric romances, particularly their aristocratic heroes and exotic settings, held the French imagination during much of this period. French writers of the late sixteenth and early seventeenth centuries modified the tradition in two important ways, however. First, the violence of the books of knight-errantry was subdued, replaced by greater emphasis on verbal combats conducted under strict rules of manners and decorum; second, the heroic ideal became more and more modified by the pastoral, with its focus on coy debates between lovers. Writers seized on the heroic/pastoral models provided by the rediscovered Greek romances and on more recent pastorals, such as those of the Spanish Jorge de Montemayor (*Los siete libros de la Diana*, 1559; *Diana*, 1598) and the Italians Jacopo Sannazaro and Giovanni Guarini. This literary movement in France was led by a powerful coterie of women within the court of Henry IV, its influence partly explained by a general desire throughout France for a literature of escape from the religious and political upheaval of the preceding half century.

One of the most popular works of this period, indeed throughout the seventeenth century, was Honoré d'Urfé's *L'Astrée* (1607-1628; *Astrea*, 1657-1658), its five volumes exploring countless varieties of love conflict and presenting for each a series of Platonic speeches by the impeccably mannered lovers. Set in the fifth century in a society of shepherds and nymphs, the novel is a thinly veiled portrait of an idealized seventeenth century French aristocracy. So popular was d'Urfé's work that members of the court, and many other aristocratic and bourgeois readers as well, strove to emulate the language and sentiments of Celadon, Astrea, and the many other characters. The course of the novel in France for the next fifty years was set by *Astrea*, as the Marquise de Rambouillet and the other members of literary high society cultivated imitators of d'Urfé.

If the French novel can be said to have developed in this period, it did so by gradually abandoning the pastoral idyll and returning to the more martial heroism of the chivalric tradition. The best-known exemplar of this shift is Madeleine de Scudéry, herself the leader of a literary salon and the author of *Artamène: Ou, Le Grand Cyrus* (1649-1653; *Artamenes: Or, The Grand Cyrus*, 1653-1655) and *Clélie* (1654-1660; *Clelia*, 1656-1661). Critics of the time applauded *Artamenes* for the greater verisimilitude of its pseudohistorical setting in ancient Greece and Persia, though her work was at an idealistic extreme from the earthy realism of the Spanish picaresque. The main concern of Scudéry's fiction is still the verbal intrigues of courtship, no longer of shepherds but of warlike heroes and elegant heroines. Within the episodic design of these novels, each encounter is an occasion for speeches and letters on the vagaries of passion. Another attraction of these novels for their readers was the similarity in description between the characters and actual members of the French court, with readers vying to unmask the "real" identities of Scudéry's figures.

The d'Urfé-Scudéry convention in France was not without its antagonists. Parallel to this trend, but beyond the pale, was a realistic/satiric school based on the medieval fabliaux, the gross satires of Rabelais, translations of the picaresques, and translations of violent tales of love intrigue written by the Italian Matteo Bandello in the sixteenth century. Actually, d'Urfé himself had contributed to this school by including within *Astrea* a cynical shepherd, Hylas, purportedly based on the author's view of himself. The first seventeenth century novelist to build a work around such a character was Prudent Gautier, whose *Mort d'Amour* (1616) mocked *Astrea* by making this same Hylas a seducer/hero; his love affair with Jeanneton, a real shepherdess, is grossly and realistically portrayed. Following Gautier in this satiric mode was Charles Sorel, an important critic as well as a boldly experimental novelist. His *Histoire comique de Francion* (1623, 1632; *The Comical History of Francion*, 1655) and *Le Berger extravagant: Ou, L'Antiroman* (1627; *The Extravagant Shepherd*, 1653) undercut the pretenses of the pastoral and no doubt hastened its downfall. *The Comical History of Francion* replaces the usual idealized setting with an actual countryside and also leads the reader, in picaresque fashion, through the French counterparts of the criminal districts described by Alemán. Instead of idealized aristocrats, Sorel peoples the book with accurately drawn bourgeois characters, petty nobility, and criminals. *The Extravagant Shepherd* attacks the pastoral by creating a Quixote-like figure, Lysis, a real shepherd, who fills his head with pastoral literature and wants his environment to conform to that of the books. The satire works by showing the impossibility of Lysis's task: Real life is simply not a pastoral. The flaw of Sorel's novel is that the contrivances of satire defeat the sympathetic intent, so the novel appears even more artificial than the convention Sorel is attacking. Ironically, this is the very flaw with which Sorel had charged Cervantes.

The most successful of the attacks on the mainstream French novel of this time was *Le Roman comique* (1651, 1657; English translation, 1651, 1657; also known as *The Comical Romance*, 1665), by the novelist and playwright Paul Scarron. His satire was more technical than thematic, directed against the ponderous descriptions of scenery and clothing in the pastorals and heroics, as well as their seemingly endless rhetorical displays. He practiced what he preached, for *The Comical Romance* is remarkably economical, but effective, in its descriptions and conversations. The book also succeeds as realistic fiction because, in the spirit of Cervantes, Scarron is not making fun of the provincial townspeople he presents but is merely trying to recount as accurately as possible their interactions, often ludicrous, with the troupe of actors who are the focus of the story. The book is so authentic, its comedy so natural, that historians have found it a trustworthy guide to the organization and ambience of actual troupes of the time of Molière. Scarron could achieve this because he was writing out of his experience, rather than out of his fantasies or to emulate a fashion. His dramatic background, particularly the demands of playwriting, also contributed to his ability to economize in prose, to suggest much about personality through salient rather than profuse description.

Where Scarron described people and places in the region surrounding Le Mans, another novelist, Antoine Furetière, contributed to the realistic movement by describing the manners and mores of Paris in his *Roman bourgeois* (1666; *City Romance*, 1671). A Parisian by birth, Furetière depicted a small segment of the capital's middle class, his plot centered on the love affairs of a young coquette, Lucrece, infatuated with the nobility, and of an ingenue, Javotte. Furetière's satire of the Scudéry school is implied in the contrast between Lucrece's expectations of noble behavior and what actually befalls her; nevertheless, as with Scarron, Furetière's intent is not really to attack mainstream fiction but to tell his story as accurately as he can. What keeps *City Romance* from reaching its novelistic potential is a somewhat disjointed second part, a series of Parisian anecdotes in which the unity of the Lucrece story is lost.

The pressure on the heroic novel exerted by Sorel and the realists produced a critical desire in the 1660's for a new kind of novel. The new form would abandon the exotic foreign settings and the rigidly Platonic love stories of the Scudéry novels, while staying clear of the merely entertaining, but morally uninstructive (it was thought), stories of the realists. French settings, recognizably French characters, and plots that would encourage the reader's respect for sound moral judgment were required. Such a novel appeared in 1678—Madame de La Fayette's *La Princesse de Clèves* (1678; *The Princess of Clèves*, 1679), which some critics see as not only the ideal novel for its time but also the first novel of sensibility—some sixty years before Richardson's. Its plot is extremely simple, especially in comparison to the involved tapestries of the heroics; its events are roughly based on French history, while its characters, particularly the heroine and her husband, exhibit believable psychologies, although some critics have been hard put to swallow their almost superhuman ability to reason and act logically.

In outline, the heroine, wife of a nobleman, confesses to her husband that she is in love with another man. Admirably, he sympathizes and thanks her for her candor, though his sympathy is greatly tested when the lover clearly shows himself to be a seducer, totally unworthy of the heroine's love. The tension of the novel lies in the struggle of the husband to overcome jealousy and of the wife to withstand her reckless passion. The ending is tragically ironic: The Prince of Clèves is dying, convinced that his wife has yielded to the seducer; gratefully, he hears the truth just before his death. The tragedy convinces the wife of her grave error and steels her to reject the lover.

Though this novel turned out to be exactly what the critical temper demanded, *The Princess of Clèves* was revolutionary in a number of ways. Unlike the heroic, pastoral, or satiric novels, it was not organized episodically on the resilient model of the chivalric romances. Instead, its focus on a single issue harked back to the short Italian *novelle* of Bandello and even further back to the fabliaux. The fabliaux also provided the stereotype of the adulterous wife, against which *The Princess of Clèves* works. This is actually the book's greatest coup; it asserted two unorthodox hypotheses: one, that a husband could realize that his wife did not love him yet could keep his reason and his dignity, and two, that a wife would dare confide her adulterous desires to her husband. These hypotheses were a strain under which no earlier French writer had dared place his or her characters; La Fayette both dared and succeeded, the spiritual and mental strength of her characters allowing them to perform these highly unorthodox moral feats.

The Princess of Clèves produced numerous imitators over the next few decades. A by-product of La Fayette's success was heightened interest in French history; native settings became the vogue. Imitators of La Fayette did not, however, satisfy the public's undying interest in the grand deeds and noble sentiments of heroes; thus, a new hybrid emerged, the autobiographical novel, which combined history (and quasi history), valorous deeds, a dose of satire from the realist school, and exciting heroes, blends of the Spanish picaro and the psychologically more interesting figures popularized by La Fayette. Noteworthy among these novels are *Les Mémoires de M. d'Artagnan* (1700), by Gatien de Courtilz de Sandras; *Les Mémoires du Comte de Grammont* (1713), by Anthony Hamilton; and the greatest of this type, *Histoire de Gil Blas de Santillane* (1715-1735; *The History of Gil Blas of Santillane*, 1716, 1735; better known as *Gil Blas*, 1749, 1962), by Alain-René Lesage.

Gil Blas, the work of a deliberate satirist and a fine novelist, accomplished what none of the picaresques or the works of the seventeenth century French realists had: a consistently comic novel of manners in every level of society, as well as a moving study of an individual. Though at times Lesage the satirist strives for comic effects at the expense of Gil's development, not since *Don Quixote de la Mancha* had a novel balanced so many characters and intercalated stories without losing sight of their purpose—to illuminate the central figure. That figure, Gil Blas, is the consummate rogue, and the succeeding stories, set in Spain, show how he learns from his mistakes to grow ever more adept at disguises and verbal ploys. Still, he is not a mere time waster; time and again he puts the interests of others before his own, sometimes leading to disasters for himself. Aware of this tendency in his character, Gil is puzzled because he judges himself a thoroughly worthless fellow. This paradox is one of the book's brightest attractions; frequently victimized, misunderstood, and punished for the evils of smoother hypocrites, Gil is a most sympathetic character.

A more somber, deterministic philosophy pervades the work of the next notable autobiographical writer to follow Lesage. Abbé Prévost, whose eminence spanned three decades beginning in 1730, brought to the French novel the dark foreboding of Jean Racine's tragic style and his own Calvinist theology. In his early *Le Philosophe anglois: Ou, Histoire de Monsieur Cleveland, fils naturel de Cromwell* (1732-1739; *The Life and Entertaining Adventures of Mr. Cleveland, Natural Son of Oliver Cromwell*, 1734, 1735; also known as *The English Philosopher: Or, History of Monsieur Cleveland*, 1742), Prévost's hero seems fated to be betrayed and well-nigh destroyed by his violent passions and those of others. The only hedge against passion in this system is reason, which means for Prévost a disciplined detachment and a universal acceptance of Calvinist social principles. The effect of this program on the novel is inevitable: Characterization and plot are manipulated to prove Prévost's thesis, and the pace of the story is painfully slowed by lengthy moralizing discourses. For the sake of his point, Prévost even transports Cleveland to America, so that his hero can make a rationalistic society out of a recalcitrant, but finally malleable, tribe of savages. Nevertheless, Prévost is a worthy successor to La Fayette and Lesage; his Cleveland is a forthcoming, personable narrator, intellectually interesting if not a man of real sensibility. In his post-1740 works, especially the novella-length *Histoire du chevalier des Grieux et de Manon Lescaut* (1731, 1733, 1753; *Manon Lescaut*, 1734, 1786), his masterpiece, Prévost develops his compelling characters according to the logic of their interactions rather than according to his philosophy; thus, they are characters of sensibility, not mere intellectuals.

In two regrettably unfinished novels of Prévost's contemporary Marivaux, the reader encounters an author's commitment to his character's integrity that equals that of Cervantes. The first, *La Vie de Marianne* (1731-1741; *The Life of Marianne*, 1736-1742; also known as *The Virtuous Orphan: Or, The Life of Marianne*, 1979), its initial part published nine years before Richardson's *Pamela*, is a collection of letters purportedly by an aging gentlewoman reflectively describing her adventurous life. The second novel, *Le Paysan parvenu* (1734-1735; *The Fortunate Peasant*, 1735), presents Jacob, a sharp-witted peasant, who rises to economic and social success not by roguish ruses but by the marvelous understanding of the desires and temperaments of others, especially women.

One of the ironies of the history of the novel is that *The Life of Marianne*, although it has influenced many novelists in France and England for two centuries, was not popular in its time. A major reason for this fact is that the qualities that make this novel great were not popularly or critically acceptable in the 1730's. Still tied to the status quo, the French would not accept the rise of an orphan girl (though an orphan, as it turns out, of noble birth) through her intelligence and self-assertion. Indeed, some critics have attributed Marivaux's failure to complete this voluminous novel to his fear of drawing it to its logical conclusion: Marianne's achievement of a secure place in the upper rank of society without having relied on her family connections. Another reason for Marivaux's unpopularity with both critics and the reader may have been that he was as experimental in style as he was in theme; he strained the patience of readers by having his characters exhaustively analyze events from every angle and by having them play with words, coining new ones and giving old ones unaccustomed shades of meaning. As a consequence of this practice, the somewhat pejorative term *marivaudage* entered the literary vocabulary.

Aside from the revolutionary conception of Marianne's character, what makes this book a landmark in the history of fiction is Marivaux's philosophy of the novel, as expressed in his preface.

> Marianne has no form of a work present in her thoughts. This is not an author, it is a woman who thinks. . . . It is neither, if you wish, the tone of the novel, nor that of history, but it is her own.

Marivaux warns the reader not to expect the typical chain of events, as if the novel were embodied in plot, but to be prepared to enter into the wonderful complex of Marianne's feelings, her analysis of those feelings, and her subsequent actions.

This emphasis on thought does not make the book a philosophical treatise, like Prévost's *The Life and Entertaining Adventures of Mr. Cleveland*; rather, it makes *The Life of Marianne* precisely what it says it is, the intimate letters of a thoughtful, sensitive woman trying to understand who she has been, who she is now, and how she relates to the worlds through which she has moved. This focus on thought, however, does not keep the novel from also being vividly precise in its descriptions of people and situations. It is a superb novel of manners, neither caricatured nor idealized. Marivaux thus became an important model for Honoré de Balzac and the other realists of the nineteenth century.

Christopher J. Thaiss
Updated by Laurence W. Mazzeno

BIBLIOGRAPHY

Bell, Michael. *The Sentiment of Reality: Truth of Feeling in the European Novel*. Boston: Allen & Unwin, 1983. Focuses on the emotional truth of European fiction. Includes useful bibliography and index.

Curtius, Ernst Robert. *European Literature and the Latin Middle Ages*. Translated by Willard R. Trask. New York: Pantheon Books, 1953. Focuses on works written in Latin from the fifth century until the blossoming of the Renaissance in Europe. Examines the rhetorical, stylistic, and metaphoric techniques used by poets, chroniclers, and romancers that influenced works traditionally considered the earliest novels and novellas.

Dunn, Peter N. *Spanish Picaresque Fiction: A New Literary History*. Ithaca, N.Y.: Cornell University Press, 1993. Traces the development of the picaresque novel in Spain, from sixteenth century versions such as *Lazarillo de Tormes* through seventeenth century tales written by Miguel de Cervantes and others. Explains distinctive qualities of the genre and demonstrates how these are continued in novels as the tradition of realistic fiction develops.

Gutiérrez, Helen Turner. *The Reception of the Picaresque in the French, English, and German Traditions*. New York: Peter Lang, 1995. Explores the ways in which a common tradition was adapted in various European countries to meet the needs of individual writers and the expectations of readers. Discusses the development of the picaresque in three countries, examining examples from the sixteenth through the twentieth centuries.

Jensen, Katherine Ann. *Writing Love: Letters, Women, and the Novel in France, 1605-1776*. Carbondale: Southern Illinois University Press, 1995. Examines how women novelists in seventeenth century France used the epistolary tradition as a strategy for constructing novels. Also shows how men adopted this technique, often using female pseudonyms to take advantage of the popularity of the genre.

Kay, Sarah, Terence Cave, and Malcolm Bowie. *A Short History of French Literature*. New York: Oxford University Press, 2003. Discussion of French literature is divided into sections chronologically, with the first of three parts covering the earliest works through the Middle Ages, the second discussing the period 1470-1789, and the third addressing the period 1789-2000. Includes informative introduction, illustrations, extensive bibliography, and index.

Mander, Jenny, ed. *Remapping the Rise of the European Novel*. Oxford, England: Voltaire Foundation, 2007. Collection of essays traces the history of the novel in Europe, beginning with an examination of the earliest English novel and of ancient long fiction. Analyzes English, Spanish, French, Greek, Russian, and German works. Supplemented with a helpful bibliography.

Moretti, Franco. *Atlas of the European Novel, 1800-1900*. New York: Verso, 1998. Takes an unusual and fascinating approach to the "geography of literature" in Europe, including chapters such as "Geography of Ideas," "Village, Provinces, Metropolis," and "The Three Europes." Includes maps, bibliographical references, and an index.

Turner, Harriet S., and Adelaida López de Martínez, eds. *The Cambridge Companion to the Spanish Novel: From 1600 to the Present*. New York: Cambridge University Press, 2003. Collection of critical essays addresses important subgenres of the Spanish novel, including the picaresque, the regional novel, and the realist novel, and themes in Spanish long fiction, including gender, culture, and modernity.

Williams, Ioan. *The Idea of the Novel in Europe, 1600-1800*. New York: New York University Press, 1979. Contradicts prevalent theories that the modern novel emerged in England in the eighteenth century. Argues instead that the development of the novel from 1600 to the nineteenth century was evolutionary and that writers from Spain, Germany, and France gradually developed an idea for a form of literature that would represent everyday life and provide realistic portraits of society.

French Long Fiction to the 1850's

The roots of French fiction run deep in France's history, from the medieval epic *chansons de geste* and *romans*, or "romances," of the late medieval period to the Renaissance and early modern periods, when the novel in its modern form began to emerge. Storytelling is fundamental to human life, and certainly the French are no exception to this rule. Stories can be told in verse, as in French epic poems and great tragedies and comedies for the stage; prose chronicles and histories also share a storytelling function, but they promise their readers "truth," not fiction, even when employing the technical devices of prose fiction writing. Long fiction in France, as in other Western societies, found its métier in the novel, and it is the story of the novel's rise to prominence and popularity among critics and the reading public alike that necessarily forms the central focus of this survey. While to modern readers the novel's place in literature is beyond dispute, the reasons for its emergence, development, and survival are varied and complex.

In English, the distinction between novel and novella is easier to grasp than in French; short fiction means the short story, and a novella represents some sort of halfway mark between a story and a full-fledged novel. The French word *roman* means simply "novel" to the modern reader, but its original usage conveyed instead the sense of "romance," a literary genre lacking what are now taken to be some of the novel's central features, even if certain conventions can be said to have survived. In the eighteenth century, when the novel was coming increasingly into its own, the philosophe Denis Diderot (1713-1784), in a glowing appreciation of the novels of Samuel Richardson, complained of the unfortunate connotations of *roman* and argued that a different word needed to be found for Richardson's novels.

As for "novella," the French *nouvelle*, which serves today as that word's equivalent, originally meant something other than a short novel. In the sixteenth and seventeenth centuries, *nouvelles* were more akin to short factual reports and were linked to what is now thought of as historical writing. This, in turn, points to a state of confusion concerning the relationship between novels and histories—*chroniques* or *histories*—confusion that occasionally resurfaces when contemporary historians debate the merits of employing novelistic techniques in their writing or perhaps express grudging envy for a best-selling "popular" historian whose books "read like novels."

In addition, both the English "novel" and the French *nouvelle* convey an obvious sense of something new—that is, novel. To eighteenth century French anglophiles, such as Diderot, who no doubt believed that they were witnessing the development of a unique new genre, the English word must have seemed more propitious than the French *roman*.

The novel, then, has evolved in France and elsewhere into a genre marked by certain conventions and formal characteristics. Yet even while pointing to the distinctiveness of the novel, one cannot lose sight of its kinship with earlier forms of storytelling and fictional narrative.

From *Chansons de geste* to *Romans comiques*

Today, fiction is associated with prose, but the earliest French tales appeared in verse, often in rhyming couplets. One notable thirteenth century exception to this rule was the anonymous *chante-fable* (song-fable) *Aucassin et Nicolette* (c. 1200; *Aucassin and Nicolette*, 1880), with its mixed prose and verse form. The earliest examples of the French verse epics were the tales of the great deeds of warriors and heroes known as the *chansons de geste*; the word *chansons* (songs) is a reminder of their beginnings in the oral tradition. The most famous of them, the *Chanson de Roland* (c. 1100; *The Song of Roland*, 1880), was set down by an anonymous author during the twelfth century, but it recounts deeds of the great French hero Roland from around the year 800. Despite its poetic form and its pretensions to historical accuracy, *The Song of Roland* established the idealized theme of the noble hero that would dominate French fiction until at least the seventeenth century.

The twelfth century was the period of high feudalism in France, characterized by the dominant role of the landholding aristocracy and the central importance of the Roman Catholic faith. The first works to be called *ro-*

mans were the *romans courtois* (courtly romances) of the twelfth century. The best-known author of such works was Chrétien de Troyes (c. 1135-c. 1183). His *romans courtois* featured idealized knights and aristocratic figures of court society, much like the personae of Arthurian legend. Similar to the songs of the Provençal troubadours, the *romans courtois* were composed of octosyllabic lines and rhyming couplets.

The most important romance of the thirteenth century was *Le Roman de la rose* (thirteenth century; *The Romance of the Rose*, 1846) of Guillaume de Lorris (c. 1215-c. 1278) and Jean de Meung (c. 1240-1305), a long epic poem that extolled modes of feminine conduct befitting the Cult of the Virgin, the increased preoccupation with the legend of the Virgin Mary in the popular religion of the day, a concern that complemented some of the themes of courtly love. As latter-day feminist scholars and others have been able to appreciate acutely, these idealized literary treatments of women not only masked the reality of their oppression but also participated directly in that oppression.

The late Middle Ages also saw the rise in importance of urban commercial centers on a limited scale. A bourgeois, or merchant, class played a vital cultural role in the towns and served as the audience for a newer form of literature, known as bourgeois or "realistic." *Fabliaux* (the word is of Breton or Norman origin), or "fables," were the chosen form of this new literature in the thirteenth and fourteenth centuries and, by featuring nonaristocratic characters, served to broaden the representational scope of French fiction. If the connotations of words such as "bourgeois" or "realistic" were far from positive, they nevertheless prefigured the later sense of those terms as applied to the novelistic treatment of recognizable figures placed within a familiar social landscape, even if such characters in the *fabliaux* are more often to be found in improbable situations.

Despite the popular trend, there was in the late Middle Ages at least one important aristocratic use of prose in the official chronicles of such beneficiaries of royal patronage as Jean Froissart (c. 1337-c. 1404), remembered for his *Chroniques de France, d'Engleterre, d'Éscose, de Bretaigne, d'Espaigne, d'Italie, de Flandres et d'Alemaigne* (1373-1410; *Chronicles*, 1523-1525) of the Hundred Years' War. This work serves as a reminder that, as far as the upper classes were concerned, the function of prose narrative was to supply historical chronicles, recording the deeds of actual historical personages in a favorable light. For many centuries to come, notions of "great literature" required the use of verse, as in the more valued genres of epic poetry and drama.

In the fifteenth and sixteenth centuries, French artistic and cultural life shared in the world of the Renaissance, deriving originally from the Humanism of Florence in the age of the Medicis. The aged Leonardo da Vinci spent his last years as the guest of the French king Francis I at the latter's château at Amboise, and this act of hospitality is symbolic of the interest taken in Italian Humanism by the arbiters of French cultural taste. The Renaissance in France was a great age for poetry and for both Neoplatonic and Neo-Aristotelian philosophy. Prose fiction realized a much smaller output. For that matter, the first of the two important French authors of fiction during this period derived her style and subject matter almost exclusively from Italian sources. That author was Marguerite d'Angoulême de Navarre (1492-1549), or Marguerite de Navarre, whose collection of seventy-two stories, known as *L'Heptaméron* (1559; *The Heptameron*, 1959), was heavily modeled on Giovanni Boccaccio's *Decameron: O, Prencipe Galetto* (1349-1351; *The Decameron*, 1620) and shared that work's tendencies toward the ribald. This similarity is worth mentioning, especially as a reminder that for centuries, salacious and erotic details and themes were thought to be the unavoidable tendencies of prose fiction, which thus by definition could never rise to the heights of eloquence and moral example to be gained from the more idealized genres of poetry and drama, especially great tragedy. The mimetic tendency of fiction to represent realities that aristocratic culture depended on literature to obscure was thus suspected early in the history of the novel, although it was not until the nineteenth century that this lifelikeness was to be celebrated as the ultimate goal of fiction.

This observation provides a fitting point at which to take up the achievement and significance of the second great French Renaissance author of fiction, one of the world's most entertaining and outrageous storytellers: François Rabelais (1490-1553). While the original sense of Humanism derived from the effort pioneered in Florence to cull from ancient writings exemplary models of moral and civic conduct to be applied to contemporary life, Rabelais represents the later expanded sense of Humanism as the appreciation of and even delight in all things human, including the coarsest details of bodily activity. It is this latter tendency by which most readers have known Rabelais over the centuries. In 1532, Rabelais, a Benedictine monk and physician, published *Pantagruel* (English translation 1653), following it two years later with *Gargantua* (English translation 1653). It was not until after Rabelais's death that the two were published together as *Gargantua et Pantagruel* (1532-1564; *Gargantua and Pantagruel*, 1653-1694, 1929). Ever since, Rabelais's masterwork has stood as one of the most ambitious, sprawling, and encyclopedic tales in Western literature, rivaling Dante's *La divina commedia* (c. 1320; *The Divine Comedy*, 1802) and James Joyce's *Ulysses* (1922) in its will to comprehensiveness. Fusing epochal synthesis with humor, *Gargantua and Pantagruel*, like Dante's and Joyce's works, encapsulates much of the cultural activity and controversy of its age.

"Tall tale" best captures for an American reader the sense of the surface narrative found in this book. Gargantua and Pantagruel are portrayed as giants, with character traits writ equally large. Indeed, the adjective "gargantuan" enshrines the Rabelaisian penchant for exaggeration. The giants, father and son respectively, are given grandiose characteristics, qualities, and appetites. Accordingly, they find themselves in outlandish situations that allow Rabelais to exploit their inherent excessiveness to rich comic effect. The result, for generations of critical readers, has been to rule this book out of bounds in discussions of the novel, one of whose chief characteristics is assumed to be believable characters of everyday proportions. Alternately, the book has been interpreted as a rich expression of the "carnivalesque" spirit of the folk culture of Rabelais's time. Erich Auerbach, author of perhaps the most authoritative study on the representation of reality in Western literature, treats *Gargantua and Pantagruel* in a manner more typical of a critical reading of a realist novel. In *Mimesis: The Representation of Reality in Western Literature* (1953), Auerbach focuses upon descriptive passages in which Rabelais presents a clearly recognizable world, once the fantastic premises introducing such episodes have been accepted by the reader. Such a reading differs from those that treat *Gargantua and Pantagruel* as an aberration in the French literary canon and places it instead more squarely in the novelistic tradition.

An important common characteristic of the texts mentioned thus far is that these works were not written in the modern French language, whose spelling and punctuation were not standardized until the seventeenth century. That was the achievement of the Académie Française, or French Academy, founded in 1635 by the powerful Cardinal Richelieu and charged with the immediate task of compiling a dictionary of the French language. Today, the French Academy functions more as a national honorary society for distinguished writers, yet it nevertheless retains something of its role as chief guardian of the treasure that is the national language. Its very existence might be taken as a symptom of the French compulsion toward centralization, a trend whose origins are located in the early seventeenth century period, during which the foundations of monarchical absolutism, of which Richelieu was a principal architect, were erected. Richelieu, regent to the boy king Louis XIII, undertook the establishment of more centralizing political and cultural policies. Analogous to the later national mercantilist projects of Louis XIV's finance minister, Jean-Baptiste Colbert, Richelieu's aim was not only to establish language itself, in an age in which "French" was still unknown in some regions of France, but also to establish a literary use of language on a truly national basis. For that, a learned body, or *académie*, was needed. By the end of the century—by which time Louis XIV had withdrawn, in the Revocation of the Edict of Nantes in 1685, royal toleration of religions other than Roman Catholicism—a parallel standardization that rigidly proscribed linguistic and aesthetic activity had been imposed.

If absolutism meant the vigorous assertion of hereditary monarchy and the imposition of rigid models of linguistic and literary expression, then it is not difficult to understand that the aristocracy would be in a position to dictate rules of literary composition, theme, and style. In Richelieu's day, "preciosity" held sway as the dominant literary aesthetic. Taking shape in the fashionable salons of upper-class aficionados, preciosity complemented the baroque spirit of the early seventeenth century in its emphasis on idealized love and heroism in literature, as well as in its affection for prolixity and highly embellished language. In prose, the most memorable example of a work embracing the aesthetic code of preciosity was the enormously long novel *L'Astrée* (1607-1628; *Astrea*, 1657-1658), written by Honoré d'Urfé (1568-1625).

Astrea was a tour de force within the novelistic genre of its day, but it was a genre for which even the French authors who worked within it felt the need to apologize; after all, "novels" were not really French but were instead derived from the literary traditions of Spain. French readers had been most impressed with Miguel de Cervantes' *Don Quixote de la Mancha* (1605, 1615)) and had developed some appreciation for the picaresque tradition in Spanish fiction; many of the French *romans* that followed in the decades after *Astrea* were based heavily on this imported style. They were adventure stories, often wildly comic and improbable—*romans comiques*, as they came to be known in France. Like the picaresque heroes of the Spanish novels from which they derived, such novels featured roguelike protagonists whose misadventures perhaps best qualified them as antiheroes. Leading examples include *Histoire comique de Francion* (1623, 1632; *The Comical History of Francion*, 1655), by Charles Sorel (1597-1674), and *Roman comique* (1651, 1657; English translation, 1651, 1657; also known as *The Comical Romance*, 1665), by Paul Scarron (1610-1660). Members of the French reading public, quite small and by definition elitist in this age, enjoyed these stories but were at the same time almost embarrassed to admit it. If one considers the apologies that intellectuals of today routinely offer for watching television, one can gain some sense of the mixture of bemusement and discomfort with which readers of the seventeenth century confronted this output that they were not quite willing to call "literary."

The legacy of this more or less imported tradition was that the word *roman*, like the word "bourgeois" in this aristocratic age, came to convey a sense of something low or debased, so that when Antoine Furetière (1619-1688) published his somewhat Swiftian parody of the heroic novel called *Le Roman bourgeois* (1666; *City Romance*, 1671), the title must have seemed redundant to his contemporaries. Those who clung to an older notion of *roman* as heroic romance, on the other hand, must have regarded the title as an oxymoron, by definition a contradiction in terms. In a country less prone to elevate questions of literary style and taste to a national focus, these trends might scarcely have been heeded. Yet this was France, and under Louis XIV, its most successful absolute monarch, leading cultural figures could flourish and influence the national aesthetic life only to the degree that the royal sun beamed down upon them.

By appointing the great tragedian Jean Racine (1639-1699) and the poet-critic Nicolas Boileau-Despréaux (1636-1711) to the newly created post of royal historiographer, Louis XIV vigorously reasserted the dominant positions of classical tragedy and poetry as the genres most capable of lending radiance to his royal splendor. Just as Jacques-Bénigne Bossuet (1627-1704), one of the leading prelates of the French Church, used his sermons and theological writings to unify the nation around its king and chief defender of the faith, so Boileau, steeped in the aesthetics of neoclassicism, joined forces with the French Academy to clearly spell out the acceptable forms and styles of literary creation, most vividly in his *L'Art poétique* of 1674. Prose fiction was banished from the fold; this cultural policy had the unintended effect, while codifying rules and criteria for the use of verse, of freeing the novel and other prose fiction for experimentation and innovation, constrained only by the threat, applied intermittently, of royal censorship.

The French novel in the twilight years of the ancien régime

During the hundred years or so that transpired before the great revolution of 1789, France experienced profound cultural, social, economic, and demographic changes. The realities of these changes can be obscured by excessive emphasis on narrowly defined political history or by a tendency to assume from the shock waves of 1789 that France was a dormant country prior to that time. From the artificially sheltered, and therefore distorted, point of view of the absolutist Bourbon monarchs, the social fabric lay largely undisturbed. This was the Age of Enlightenment, the *Siècle des lumières*, when a new class of writers and social critics called philosophes advanced progressive ideas to a rapidly expanding bourgeois readership critical of the Crown and anxious to be rid of the feudal obligations and restrictions that undergirded the edifice of French absolutism. Such philosophes as Voltaire (1694-1778), Charles de Montesquieu (1689-1755), and Denis Diderot also lashed out at the Roman Catholic Church for its legacy in France of persecution and bigotry. Here, too, they found ready assent from the middle-class readers to whom they appealed.

The philosophes could count on a burgeoning readership for their tracts and treatises and for the massive multivolume *Encyclopédie: Ou, Dictionnaire raisonné des sciences, des arts, et des métiers* (1751-1772; partial translation *Selected Essays from the Encyclopedy*, 1772; complete translation *Encyclopedia*, 1965) edited by Diderot and Jean le Rond d'Alembert (1717-1783); a steadily increasing literacy rate, an increasing number of outlets and vehicles for literary activity, and a general and dramatic population increase resulting largely from the growth of a middle, or bourgeois, class were perhaps the most significant trends shaping the literary culture of this period. Population growth was itself linked to a significant decline in pestilence and other natural disasters and to an impressive expansion of the food supply. Indeed, economic growth was steady throughout the eighteenth century, although England was as yet the only country in which manufacture rather than agriculture largely set the pace.

It is estimated that the percentage of literate (defined as those who could sign their names) French people at the end of the seventeenth century was 21 percent, increasing by the end of the eighteenth century to 37 percent. Unlike England, France had to wait until the revolution to experience a real proliferation in newspapers, but they were increasing, as were broadsides and pamphlets of various kinds. By the mid-eighteenth century, the institution of the café, modeled on the British coffeehouse, had taken hold as the social setting for reading and discussing new books, periodicals, and newspapers. Voltaire and the other philosophes all experienced censorship at one time or another, and several of them, including Voltaire, knew imprisonment and exile, yet they lived to see the ban lifted and experience the sense that their ideas circulated ever more widely. The growing body of readers to whom they appealed, however, were interested in more than political treatises and satires. They read novels eagerly, and occasionally the philosophes themselves accommodated them with *contes philosophiques* (philosophical tales) and didactic novels.

Though it would occupy a more central role in the publishing world of the nineteenth century, the novel's popularity was increasingly noted by French publishers of the ancien régime. On the face of it, the "frivolous" novel would seem to have been a safer venture for a publisher than the more overtly political writings of a Voltaire, but the latter were not always more vulnerable to censorship. The world of French publishing was far from standardized in the eighteenth century, and this lack of predictability and routine provided headaches for publisher and author alike. Surely one of the publisher's major headaches was the uneven and unpredictable exercise of royal censorship. In order to operate, a publisher needed a royal license, or *privilège*, which granted him, in some cases, a monopoly in certain types of publishing, but this could easily be withdrawn on a royal whim. Apart from that major uncertainty, publishers could not be sure when they might face censorship. By definition, broad powers of censorship were in the hands of royally sanctioned provincial courts called *parlements*, of which the most important and most active was the Parlement de Paris. The institution of *parlements* reflected the increasing tendency since the age of Louis XIV for publishing to be concentrated in and around Paris itself, whereas regional centers such as Rouen and Lyons had been prominent in earlier centuries. Even the Parlement de Paris, Voltaire's great nemesis, occasionally let a "scandalous" book pass. When censorship came, however, punishment was often harsh. This fact, coupled with the pessimistic tendencies of some publishers to expect the worst from the *parlements*, led to the creation of a thriving underground publishing industry. Diderot is the best-known name associated with this illegal publishing activity.

Authors, too, faced an uncertain existence—and not merely because of the more serious threats of censorship and imprisonment. Authors' relationships with their publishers were often severely strained. To begin with, nothing resembling a modern copyright law existed in the eighteenth century. An author's name would not necessarily appear on the book, and payment was not always guaranteed. Piracy was a common problem; unscrupulous publishers were known to seize manuscripts of authors whose names could be counted upon to sell copies. Royalties were unknown. Today, an author commonly receives a fixed percentage of the price of each copy that is sold. This practice was not, however, adopted until the nineteenth century.

In the age of the philosophes, it was possible for an author to enter into an agreement whereby he would receive a fixed sum for a certain number of copies to be printed, regardless of whether they were actually sold. If the book proved popular and additional printings were run, the author received nothing. Not until nearly the end of the eighteenth century was this practice modified so that the author was paid a fixed amount on a certain quantity of copies that were actually sold, and it was well into the nineteenth century before the per-copy royalty practice was adopted. As a result of these many uncertainties, most eighteenth century authors were forced to rely on some sort of patronage from wealthy admirers and benefactors. Diderot was one of the few examples of a truly professional writer who attempted to earn a living, albeit a modest one, by his pen, and even he benefited, at least temporarily, from the royal patronage of the Russian empress Catherine the Great.

Most critics and historians of French literature reserve the adjective "great" for the novels of the nineteenth century, but within the changing eighteenth century milieu, the French novel began to come into its own. To a great extent, this can be attributed to the very exclusion pronounced by Boileau and other guardians of tradition in the preceding century. Not that the sense of shame and apology held toward the novel, even by novelists themselves, was completely dispelled in the eighteenth century, but the novel and other fictional genres were free, in a sense, to develop in an undefined new literary space: a terra incognita unglimpsed by *académiciens* and other traditionalists. The novel's proven popularity with a steadily expanding readership further undermined whatever reservations authors might have.

It has become commonplace in French literary history to assign *La Princesse de Clèves* (1678; *The Princess of Clèves*, 1679), by Madame de La Fayette (1634-1693), the position of "first" in the development of the modern French *roman*, using the argument that it embodies the essential characteristics of the genre in its modern form: recognizable, believable characters; ordinary settings; and attention to the feelings, motivations, and psychological states of the principal characters. Set in the period of the French Renaissance, La Fayette's novel nevertheless offers descriptions of scenes much more recognizable to her late seventeenth century readers. In portraying privileged court society, she adhered to the aesthetic of the more established genres but broke radically with literary tradition by translating this milieu into the novelistic realm.

Much of the interest this novel has held for readers past and present has been its presentation of a woman as the central tragic figure, coupled with the fact of its feminine authorship. The Princess is a woman caught in an intolerable situation, for she is married to a man she does not love. Though she is pursued by a would-be lover, she resists temptation as she remembers the counsel of her beloved mother with regard to the crucial importance of wifely virtue. Even her virtue goes unrecognized and unacknowledged by her husband, who torments and eventually destroys himself through suspicious jealousy. At the end of the novel, the Princess has become widowed, and, shunning the attentions of the man she would then be free to marry, she retires to a convent, remaining true to the memory of the husband she never loved.

Certainly, in one sense, *The Princess of Clèves* reaffirmed the carefully circumscribed social role available to women, even women of the privileged class. Ending her days in the convent, the Princess recalls the much earlier, prototypically tragic, figure of Héloïse. Yet La Fayette was able to portray her protagonist in such a way as to encourage empathy with her on the part of readers both male and female. As an author herself, like her aristocratic predecessor, Marguerite d'Angoulême de Navarre, La Fayette provides a case study of the relatively greater degree of freedom enjoyed by an admittedly small group of women of her era. Not merely literate but an accomplished prose stylist, La Fayette has served to illustrate Virginia Woolf's well-known claim that, if women had been permitted incomes and "rooms of their own," they would have been the ones producing the world's literature. Still, the association between a well-to-do woman and a marginally acceptable literary genre would scarcely have posed a threat to the social and sexual order of the French classical age.

While few novels of the eighteenth century in France

matched *The Princess of Clèves* in attention to human psychology, most continued to examine central themes of social life, often exposing the contradictions and injustices of the social sphere to the harsh light of irony. This accords well with the project of the philosophes, and, not surprisingly, most leading philosophes tried their hand at the novel. More often, they showed little interest in extensive plot or character development, preferring to exploit the genre for didactic purposes. The typical novel or novella of the philosophes was what the French call a *roman à thèse*, or "thesis novel," like the *contes philosophiques* of Voltaire, of which *Candide* (1759; English translation, 1759) is the best-known example. In many such novels, the characters are extremely one-dimensional, mere mannequins over which the author has draped the extravagant clothing of his or her political opinions.

Occasionally, however, the philosophes made real contributions to the evolution of the novel as a genre. *Les Lettres persanes* (1721; *Persian Letters*, 1722), by Charles de Montesquieu (1689-1755), better known for his legal and juridical writings, was one such example. As a specious travel narrative, it was certainly typical of the writings of the philosophes. The text purports to be the discovered letters of a Persian sheikh, written to his homeland during a sojourn in France. He relentlessly dissects the baffling mores of the French people, much as an anthropologist might report on the customs of an isolated tribe. Naturally, this affords Montesquieu the opportunity to unleash his barbed criticism on his own society, under the ruse of claiming that this text is but a translation from the Persian. Suffice it to say that Montesquieu could avoid censorship best and perhaps register his criticism of France most effectively by these indirect means.

Philosophes occasionally availed themselves of the time-honored devices of adventure novels, with their improbable occurrences and their cliff-hanger episodes. It became clear that such novels could accomplish their goals of social criticism more effectively by including entertainment. Voltaire's *Candide* is once again the best-known such example. The earlier picaresque form remained somewhat in vogue during the eighteenth century and was recast most memorably in the novel *Histoire de Gil Blas de Santillane* (1715-1735; *The History of Gil Blas of Santillane*, 1716, 1735, better known as *Gil Blas*, 1749, 1962), by Alain-René Lesage (1668-1747), whose reputation in his own time was established more by his plays. Lesage's debt to Cervantes and the Spanish picaresque tradition was clear. Even though the adventures of Gil Blas might strain the reader's credulity, the settings had become recognizably French. Along with *The Princess of Clèves*, *The History of Gil Blas of Santillane* helped establish the novelistic practice of constructing the plot against a more recognizable backdrop.

Another playwright who, like Lesage, tried his hand at the writing of novels was Pierre Carlet de Chamblain de Marivaux (1688-1763). Despite the fact that he never completed his *La Vie de Marianne* (1731-1741; *The Life of Marianne*, 1736-1742; also known as *The Virtuous Orphan: Or, The Life of Marianne*, 1979) or *Le Paysan parvenu* (1734-1735; *The Fortunate Peasant*, 1735), these novels have not lacked for readers, as they provide rich and complex insights into the shifting, sometimes contradictory psychological states of their introspective characters. Marivaux's characters are continually expressing confusion and indecision, prompting some contemporary critics and literary historians to cite Marivaux as an example of the kind of eighteenth century novelist who, in this embryonic period of the novel's formation, prefigures the more difficult and ambiguous texts of literary modernism.

A particularly rich evocation of psychological torment is provided by *Histoire du chevalier des Grieux et de Manon Lescaut* (1731, 1733, 1753; *Manon Lescaut*, 1734, 1786), by the Abbé Prévost (1697-1763). *Manon Lescaut* is the story of the doomed love of des Grieux for the young Manon Lescaut, who, unlike the Princess of Clèves, is the embodiment of confusion and contradiction where sexual morality is concerned. Prévost depicts his characters' emotions more vividly and with much less ambiguity than does Marivaux.

Prévost also played a central role in discussions of novelistic form based on the examples being established in England. "Anglomania" was rife in French intellectual life in the eighteenth century. The English were admired for their freedom of the press and much greater religious and social toleration. For that matter, the expression of admiration for England was developed by the philosophes into an effective indirect means of criticizing France. The eighteenth century was the age of great achievement in the English novel; the names of Jonathan Swift, Daniel Defoe, Samuel Richardson, Henry Fielding, and Laurence Sterne spring immediately to mind. Prévost championed Richardson, one of the more complex, even daunting, English novelists, and translated his *Pamela* (1740-1741) in 1742, *Clarissa* (1747-1748) in 1751, and *Sir Charles Grandison* (1753-1754) between 1755 and 1758.

Prévost opened up a debate over the place of the novel in French letters, a debate joined by a novelist named Claude Crébillon (or Crébillon, *fils*, 1707-1777), who argued for an experimental approach as the one most befitting the genre itself, developing as it was in a sort of aesthetic limbo. Societies have a way of imposing limits on experimentation, however, and Crébillon, by publishing such novels as *Le Sopha* (1740; *The Sofa*, 1742) and *Les Égarements du cœur et de l'esprit* (1736; *The Wanderings of the Heart and Mind*, 1751), was judged by his society to have overstepped those boundaries. His books were condemned, and he served a sentence in that infamous prison of the ancien régime known as the Bastille. Crébillon was a member of the scandalous group of writers and wits known as "libertines." These libertines argued for the removal of all restrictions on the enjoyment of sexual pleasure, which they saw as indispensable to intellectual freedom. This "forbidden" tradition in French intellectual life resurfaced from time to time during the eighteenth century, most notably in the notorious Marquis de Sade (1740-1814) in the years of the great French Revolution.

The philosophe who contributed most to the ongoing discussion of the novel's aesthetic was Denis Diderot, the great encyclopedist who was himself the author of several works of fiction, including the novel *La Religieuse* (1796; *The Nun*, 1797) and the novella *Le Neveu de Rameau* (1821, 1891; *Rameau's Nephew*, 1897). The latter is thought to have been written around 1773 even though it was not published until 1821. With its frank discussion of sexual morality, including equality of the sexes and the toleration of homosexuality, Diderot judged it unsuitable for publication in his lifetime. Diderot's major intervention in the critical debate over the novel came in the form of a gushing expression of admiration for the novels of the English writer Samuel Richardson. This "Éloge de Richardson" (1762) was symptomatic of the anglomania to which many French writers were prey, yet Diderot went so far as to argue that Richardson's achievement constituted a radical break with earlier traditions in prose fiction. Richardson had ennobled the new genre, Diderot argued, but the connotations of the French word *roman* prevented people from realizing it. Diderot called for a search for a new word in the French language to designate the new "novel." Given Diderot's stature, this essay has had an unfortunate impact on later French criticism and literary history, creating a serious, though recently somewhat corrected, undervaluation of earlier works such as *The Princess of Clèves*.

If Diderot was perhaps the most representative of the philosophes, his contemporary Jean-Jacques Rousseau (1712-1778) was far less typical. While Rousseau joined with other philosophes in criticizing the monarchy and the injustices of the ancien régime and, like Diderot and Voltaire, produced a large body of writings of various types and genres, he sharply condemned the artificiality and aridity of the intellectual climate of his day. His one great novel, *Julie: Ou, La Nouvelle Héloïse* (1761; *Eloise: Or, A Series of Original Letters*, 1761; also known as *Julie: Or, The New Eloise*, 1968; better known as *The New Héloïse)*, exemplified his project of exhorting his contemporaries to abandon "polite" society to find true meaning and redemption in the natural world. *The New Héloïse* is suitably steeped in what would come to be called the Romantic attitude toward nature, and the story of Julie is extravagantly sentimental. Julie is presented to the reader as the paragon of feminine virtue, a "new Héloïse," recalling the devotion of Héloïse to Abélard. The source of her virtue, glimpsed through her unaffected personality, is her contact with nature. This heroine's "nature," however, turns out to be most typically expressed in her subservience toward her husband and serves as a reminder that Rousseau, who was widely and enthusiastically read by women as well as men, helped influence the strong reassertion of the patriarchal family put firmly in place by the later revolutionary and Napoleonic eras. It is one of the tragic ironies of this complicated genius that Rousseau, the "apostle of liberty," should have contributed so substantially to the tradition of modern misogyny.

Rousseau was a celebrated iconoclast, but other contemporary writers shared affinities with him, though his reputation has tended to relegate them to the shadows. One writer who should be mentioned in any survey of eighteenth century French fiction is Jacques-Henri Bernardin de Saint-Pierre (1737-1814). He was the author of a long and little-read work called *Études de la nature* (1784; *Studies of Nature*, 1796), which nevertheless contained the influential novella *Paul et Virginie* (1787; *Paul and Mary*, 1789; also known as *Paul and Virginia*, 1795). Rousseauesque in its natural settings and extreme sentimentality, *Paul and Virginia* became an important part of the stream of exoticism in modern French culture. One of the defining characteristics of Romanticism, this taste for the exotic was also manifested in the late nineteenth century novels of Pierre Loti (1850-1923) and paintings by Paul Gauguin (1848-1903) and Henri Rousseau (1844-1910).

The suppressed current of "libertinism" was to surface again in French fiction in the last years of the Bourbon monarchy and the heady early days of the French Revolution, before the austere Maximilien de Robespierre (1758-1794) imposed a Cromwellian "republic of virtue" on the infant French Republic in 1793. Thus, it is perhaps not surprising that one of the most notorious of the libertines, Nicolas Restif de la Bretonne (1734-1806), wrote both borderline pornographic novels and utopian political tracts. Restif de la Bretonne was a salacious fetishist whose most memorable novel is *Le Paysan perverti* (1776; *The Corrupted Ones*, 1967) and who, like the great utopian socialist Charles Fourier (1772-1837) whom he somewhat resembles, called for the establishment of a utopian community featuring, among other things, gratification of the most minutely specific forms of sexual pleasure.

Restif de la Bretonne's works are seldom read today, but one of the most famous libertine novels, *Les Liaisons dangereuses* (1782; *Dangerous Acquaintances*, 1784; also known as *Dangerous Liaisons*, 1962), by Pierre Choderlos de Laclos (1741-1803), has gained more and more readers in subsequent centuries. Laclos was a well-known libertine who later served under Napoleon Bonaparte. His contemporaries thought the book pornographic, but *Dangerous Liaisons* has been interpreted according to other criteria by later critics. An important example of the epistolary tradition in French fiction, *Dangerous Liaisons* consists entirely of letters circulated among four principal characters. Like Lovelace in Richardson's *Clarissa* (which may have served as a model for Laclos), the fictional authors of these letters attempt, successfully, to use them as vehicles for actual seduction. With a mixture of candor and dissimulation, they probe their shifting psychological states, attempting to register love's complicated emotional impact. The achievement of Laclos has been likened in this regard to the much later poems of Charles Baudelaire (1821-1867) and the great novel of Marcel Proust (1871-1922) in its contribution to the psychology of love. The aspects of *Dangerous Liaisons* that scandalized the late eighteenth century public would today be far from shocking.

The same cannot be said for the brutally sordid novels of the Marquis de Sade (1740-1814), whose books retain the ability to offend the modern reader. This author, who spent a significant portion of his life as a prisoner of King Louis XVI in the Bastille and, after the destruction of that hated symbol of royal oppression, in the asylum at Charenton (where he died), adhered to a philosophical outlook dominated by the central concept of evil. In such books as *Justine* (1791; English translation, 1889) and *Les 120 Journées de Sodome* (1904; *The 120 Days of Sodom*, 1954), he relentlessly and dispassionately cataloged the varieties of the human capacity for evil, including bestiality and the "sadism" that serves as a constant reminder of Sade's name. Perhaps these preoccupations can be likened to the taxonomic effort of eighteenth century biologists or, as Roland Barthes (1915-1980) suggested, to the massive effort evident in the theological writings of Saint Ignatius Loyola or the utopian writings of Fourier; less justifiable is the facile equation of some sort of Sadean "sexual revolution" with the political and social upheaval of the French Revolution.

Likewise, the relationship between Romanticism and the political events from 1789 through Napoleon's rule (1799-1814) has been exaggerated, at least with regard to French Romantic literature. This error is somewhat akin to the overestimation of the role played by the ideas of the philosophes in the revolutionary era. This is not to say that no link may be demonstrated. Certainly the spirit of Voltaire, Rousseau, and others was invoked by the revolutionaries themselves. Just as certainly, significant

Romantic poets, composers, and artists celebrated the coming of the revolution, even if its excesses later prompted some of them to repudiate it. At the time most of the events of the period from 1789 to 1814 took place, however, the Romantics who commented on them were for the most part not French. Romanticism in literature, music, and the visual arts was late in coming to France, partly because of the heroic classicism embraced by the Napoleonic regime and partly because the French identified Romanticism with Germany and England. Only after nearly running its course in those countries did Romanticism enter the main currents of French literature; once Romanticism arrived in France, however, it put down very deep roots.

Romanticism and early nineteenth century French novels

The seeds of Romanticism were sown to a great extent within the Enlightenment period that preceded the Romantic age, most obviously in the writings of Rousseau. Rousseau's influence on English and German Romantics was considerable, but the full-blown Romanticism that developed in those traditions reentered France by a circuitous route. Matters were complicated by the political and military upheaval of the quarter of a century, roughly, that transpired from the advent of the French Revolution to the defeat of Napoleon. European Romantics had been divided in their support for the French Revolution and likewise divided into groups expressing either admiration or contempt for Napoleon Bonaparte. Occasionally, this division became manifest within the same person, as in the example of the composer Ludwig van Beethoven (1770-1827), who moved sharply from adoration to hatred for the man he came to see as a tyrant. The story of the growing Romanticism in French literature during the last years of Napoleon's rule is further complicated by its mediation by writers such as Chateaubriand (1768-1848), who enjoyed official approval, as well as by Madame de Staël (1766-1817), denounced by the Bonapartist regime.

Be that as it may, clear distinctions can be made between Romanticism and the Enlightenment outlook that preceded it. The philosophes had stressed universal attributes and qualities, whereas Romantics savored the unique and the particular. Philosophes had championed the rational mind's capabilities, but Romantics asserted the claims of the heart and such alternatives to rational consciousness as dreams and the mysterious processes of the creative imagination. Romantics elevated the role of the suffering creative genius marked by his alienation from others—something of a repudiation of the philosophe's self-appointed role as crusader on behalf of his fellow human beings. The Enlightenment interpretation of history, inseparable from an ongoing propaganda war against the claims of the Church, had demanded the total discrediting of the Middle Ages as a backward age of superstition and hysteria, but many leading Romantics rehabilitated Christianity and celebrated the medieval period as a rich and poetic age of faith and imagination.

The lonely, questing spirit of the troubled Romantic protagonist emerges from the pages of two of the earliest French Romantic novels: *Obermann* (1804; English translation, 1910-1914), by Étienne de Senancour (1770-1846), and *Adolphe* (1816; English translation, 1816), by Benjamin Constant (1767-1830). Indeed, the title *Obermann* is certain to evoke for readers of today the "overman" (*Übermensch*) of Friedrich Nietzsche (1884-1900), a philosopher sometimes viewed as one whose work represents a late nineteenth century revival of Romantic themes. Senancour's novel seems more akin to an early, somewhat pre-Romantic style of German literature known as Sturm und Drang (storm and stress). The great Johann Wolfgang von Goethe (1749-1832) and Friedrich Schiller (1759-1805) had been the leading writers of this movement, and *Obermann* is strikingly similar to Goethe's *Die Leiden des jungen Werthers* (1774; *The Sorrows of Young Werther*, 1779).

Both *Obermann* and *The Sorrows of Young Werther* are notable examples of the epistolary novel. Senancour's work is a compilation of eighty-nine letters that, like the letters of Werther, portray their fictional author's turbulent emotional life. Like Goethe, Senancour presents a protagonist suffering from Romantic *Weltschmerz* combined with a sense of being isolated and overwhelmed by life; *mal du siècle* is the French phrase that was eventually adopted to denote this state of the soul. Constant's *Adolphe* continues this theme as well, and Adolphe's life unfolds in the novel along the lines of what Goethe and others have called a bildungsroman (a development novel, the story of the successive stages of a character's life through childhood, education, adolescence, and the entry into the adult world).

While these novelists made no particular issue of their debt to German literature, the French writer who campaigned most tirelessly on behalf of the examples set by German Romantics was perhaps the most famous European woman of the Napoleonic age: Madame de Staël (1766-1817). Acquainted with most of the leading writers of Continental Europe and especially partial to German writers (which is notable for the usually ethnocentric world of French letters), Madame de Staël became deeply interested in differences among national literatures. She avoided, however, the growing tendency in early nineteenth century culture to imagine some separate realm called "literature," divorced from specific historical and social contexts. Her great critical work, *De la littérature considérée dans ses rapports avec les institutions sociales* (1800; *A Treatise on Ancient and Modern Literature*, 1803; also known as *The Influence of Literature upon Society*, 1813), anticipated the day when twentieth century critics such as Lucien Goldmann (1913-1970) would call for the establishment of a sociology of literature. De Staël also argued vigorously for drastic improvement in the status of women, a stance that earned her the detestation of Napoleon Bonaparte, whose repressive *Code Napoléon* (1804) had legitimated a reactionary patriarchal sexual hierarchy. Her novels *Delphine* (1802; English translation, 1803) and *Corinne: Ou, L'Italie* (1807; *Corinne: Or, Italy*, 1807) feature strong, superior women who encounter the idiotic obstacles of sexual discrimination; the autobiographical element in them is pronounced.

If de Staël was the thorn in Bonaparte's side, Chateaubriand (1768-1848), devoutly Roman Catholic and Bonapartist, was almost the empire's poet laureate. Nobly handsome in a manner reminiscent of the English Romantic poet Lord Byron, with an ego of equally Byronic proportions, François-René de Chateaubriand nevertheless irked Bonaparte as something of a rival claimant to his mystique, or charisma. Chateaubriand made his mark with *Le Génie du Christianisme* (1799, 1800, 1802; *The Genius of Christianity*, 1802), the most substantial contribution to the Romantic project of restoring Christianity to its central cultural role. Themes of Christian faith and inspiration continued throughout Chateaubriand's long literary career, from *Les Martyres* (1809; *The Martyrs*, 1812) to *La Vie de Rancé* (1844; the life of Rancé). At the same time, the religious emphasis was worked in with the standard Romantic theme of the isolated creative genius who, by definition, cannot thrive in conventional human society. For example, *La Vie de Rancé* glorifies the extreme solitude of monastic life.

French Romanticism found one of its greatest champions in its most acclaimed writer of the nineteenth century, Victor Hugo (1802-1885), whose early plays and poetry exemplified the more dominant role Romanticism came to play in the years from 1815 to 1848. His celebrated novel *Notre-Dame de Paris* (1831; *The Hunchback of Notre Dame*, 1833) provides perhaps the best example outside the English novels of Sir Walter Scott of the Romantic fascination with the Middle Ages. However, Hugo was to live and write well beyond the limits of Romanticism in France, and his later novels owe more to realism and the increased stature realized by the French novel in the first half of the nineteenth century. Romantic attitudes continued to play a role in French literature but lost ground as the novel came more and more to eclipse other literary genres for the French reading public.

The golden age of the French novel: Balzac to Flaubert, 1829-1857

After the downfall of Napoleon, France attempted to reenter the ancien régime for a time. The Bourbon monarchy was revived, with Louis XVIII occupying the throne from 1814 to 1824 and Charles X, the last Bourbon king, reigning thereafter until 1830. Prerevolutionary France was a lost world that could not genuinely be revived. The bourgeoisie continued to expand and longed to reclaim the promise of property rights affirmed by the French Republic. France lagged behind England in the Industrial Revolution, but industrialization was under way, adding impetus to the bourgeois drive for recognition and enfranchisement. In 1830, the rebellion in Paris forced Charles X into exile, and Louis-Philippe, the Duc d'Orléans, formed a government that came to be known as the July Monarchy, in honor of the revolutionary events that ended the Bourbon monarchy.

Louis-Philippe originally enjoyed the support of the middle class but continually postponed real reforms and frustrated bourgeois hopes. A more decisive uprising followed in 1848, precipitating a general European rebellion in major capitals that Karl Marx (1818-1883) and Friedrich Engels (1820-1895) were briefly tempted to interpret as the opening chapter of the universal proletarian revolution they envisioned. France became a republic once again, but, after an interlude marked by constitutional wrangling and class division leading at one point to massacres in working-class neighborhoods of Paris, Louis Bonaparte, recapitulating his celebrated uncle's coup of 1799, seized control of the government in December, 1851. Not long afterward, he proclaimed the Second Empire, which lasted until 1870.

France thus experienced, during the first half of the nineteenth century, major episodes of revolution and rebellion, as well as the first wave of changes wrought by industrialization. These memorable and traumatic events, the stuff of heroic paintings by such artists as Eugène Delacroix (1798-1863), awakened the French people to an acute sense of history. Perhaps more than any other European nation, France entered into consciousness of what was to become one of the central preoccupations of nineteenth century culture: historical time and its transformations. The modern study of history was in fact a nineteenth century invention, and among its greatest practitioners was the great French historian Jules Michelet (1798-1874).

Novels, like works of history, depend on the accumulation of successive stages and episodes in the lives of their characters. Narrative has traditionally been seen as indispensable respectively to long fiction and historical writing. As far back as the seventeenth century, when it was possible for a poet to occupy the post of royal historiographer, confusion had been registered over the possible distinction between a *roman* and an *histoire*. The nineteenth century novel proved to be the literary genre most capable of nurturing, in the century of geology, morphology, and Darwinian evolution, this new consciousness of chronology, bringing to its readers the dramatic sweep of historical transformations.

The transformations visited upon French society by an emergent industrial capitalist economy, if not yet of the magnitude of those transformations observed in Britain in the same period, nevertheless increasingly became the focus of critical social commentary. As in England, the novel came to be regarded as the genre best suited to the demanding task of representing the complexities and contradictions of the society as a whole. The novel's mimetic capabilities were therefore assumed, and the longer the novel, the more comprehensive and supposedly more successful was the feat of representation. Readers demanded long novels, easily assimilable in their customary serialized form. The growth of a literate reading public favored the proliferation of a variety of newspapers (a variety that would astound a reader of today), and, through the practice of serialization, the novel's growth in popularity kept pace with expanded newspaper circulation. Because newspapers were usually willing to pay more for fiction than book publishers were, authors profited from this practice, as long as they were prolific.

Such a novelist was Honoré de Balzac (1799-1850), considered by many to have been the greatest realist of the nineteenth century (realism being defined as the literary or artistic effort to capture in detail the essence of everyday life). Balzac was an indefatigable writer, capable of writing for fifteen hours at a stretch. The demands of his publishers, to whom he continued to promise new books, kept him almost continually at his task. In all, he produced ninety-one novels and novellas. His first novel was a historical treatment of a chapter in the French Revolution. Then, in 1833, he conceived a plan for a comprehensive series of novels with the collective title *La Comédie humaine* (1829-1848; *The Comedy of Human Life*, 1885-1893, 1896; better known as *The Human Comedy*, 1895-1896, 1911).The echoes of Dante in this title were assuredly deliberate.

Balzac portrayed life as it was in postrevolutionary French society, particularly under the Bourbon Restoration. Out of sympathy with the spirit of the 1830 revolution, he preferred returning to the past in celebrating the promise of the future. In order to, in a sense, "repopulate" this lost world, he hoped to create ten thousand characters, a veritable universe. As it turned out, he managed to create "only" two thousand or so. These novels typically feature ambitious, often unscrupulous arrivistes, characters determined to take advantage of the new world of expanding opportunities afforded by nineteenth century Paris. The novels *Le Père Goriot* (1834-1835; *Daddy Goriot*, 1860; also known as *Père Goriot*,

1902) and *Illusions perdues* (1837-1843; *Lost Illusions*, 1893) provide especially memorable examples in the characters of Eugène de Rastignac and Lucien de Rubempré, respectively. The dialectic of the individual in society was thus central to Balzac's fictional project.

A monarchist at heart, Balzac was nevertheless able to portray peasants and urban laborers in a sympathetic light. Because his stated goal was to interject himself as little as possible into his narrative, for which he fashioned a neutral language that allowed him to hold a mirror up to the society of his day, he took pride in his ability to report dispassionately on the facts of life among the social orders he personally did not prefer. Many readers have argued that Balzac portrays the lower classes both more realistically and more sympathetically than those authors who profess much more egalitarian views. As for the other Balzacian boast, close reading of the novels will show that Balzac failed to live up to his credo of impersonal detachment from his narrative. Indeed, he intervenes vigorously and frequently with various rhetorical asides and digressions. Modern critics of fictional realism have grown increasingly distrustful of such claims.

Contemporary critical opinion assigns Marie-Henri Beyle, who is better known as Stendhal (1783-1842), a nearly equally distinguished position alongside Balzac in the history of the early nineteenth century novel. Yet, as Stendhal himself gloomily predicted, he was largely unnoticed and unread during his own time. In part, this fact may have resulted from the greater ambiguity of Stendhal's writing, particularly with regard to his characters' roles and motivations, though he shared with Balzac a fascination for the drama of the individual finding his way within a complex and often corrupt society. Stendhal painted, so to speak, with a softer brush, so that his novelistic canvases appear perhaps less vivid than those of Balzac. Moderately liberal, he was less pronounced in his political opinions and less imbued than the almost messianic Balzac with a grandiose sense of his artistic career. In his greatest novels, *Le Rouge et le noir* (1830; *The Red and the Black*, 1898) and *La Chartreuse de Parme* (1839; *The Charterhouse of Parma*, 1895), however, Stendhal was certainly capable of touching upon the conflicting and often confusing array of political, philosophical, and social trends at work in his time. The shadow of Napoleon haunts Stendhal's work, as does the legacy of the revolution. The novels of both Balzac and Stendhal illustrate the claim frequently made by literary historians that the novel flourishes during times of social or political turmoil.

The long literary career of Amandine-Aurore-Lucile Dupin, or George Sand (1804-1876), unfolded in such times. Known chiefly as a novelist, she moved from an early Romanticism to, after 1848, an increasingly pronounced avowal of a somewhat revolutionary socialism. Having taken by necessity a masculine nom de plume in order to publish her books, she organized her keen political sensibilities around the central theme of the oppression of women. This theme dominates such early novels as *Indiana* (1832; English translation, 1833) and *Lélia* (1833, 1839; English translation, 1978), while later novels, perhaps most notably *François le champi* (1850; *Francis the Waif*, 1889), embody themes of socialism and compassion for the lower classes. In enunciating humanitarian themes, Sand played a role similar to that of Victor Hugo in nineteenth century French culture. In her day, Sand's works were widely read in France and abroad. Even if she attracted more attention in her early years as the lover of Alfred de Musset (1810-1857) and Frédéric Chopin (1810-1849) and as one contemptuous of the opinions of conventional society than as a novelist, she came to be considered one of the most illustrious of French writers, and she received glowing tributes from foreign novelists. From her death until the resurgence of feminist literary scholarship, however, she was consigned to literary oblivion.

Prosper Mérimée (1803-1870) was one of the many fellow writers Sand befriended, and, like her, Mérimée cultivated his own circle of friends among foreign writers. Like Madame de Staël in her endorsement of German literature, Mérimée broke new ground in introducing nineteenth century French readers to the works of some of the greatest names in Russian literature. He befriended Nikolai Gogol and Leo Tolstoy and translated some of their writings. Mérimée was the author of a historical novel, *Chronique du règne de Charles IX* (1829; *A Chronicle of the Times of Charles the Ninth*, 1830; also known as *A Chronicle of the Reign of Charles IX*), and, in *Colomba* (1841; English translation, 1853), produced one of the notable examples in the novella genre.

James A. Winders

Bibliography

DeJean, Joan. *Tender Geographies: Women and the Origins of the Novel in France*. New York: Columbia University Press, 1991. Witty, highly readable study of the role of women in the development of the French novel includes analyses of salon life, social class, and the relationship between gender and authorship. Supplemented with a rich bibliography.

Gaunt, Simon, and Sarah Kay, eds. *The Cambridge Companion to Medieval French Literature*. New York: Cambridge University Press, 2008. Collection of seventeen critical essays includes several that analyze works of long fiction, including *Le Roman de la rose* and *Chanson de Roland.* Includes an essay by Keith Busby titled "Narrative Genres" and a bibliography.

Hollier, Denis, ed. *A New History of French Literature*. Cambridge, Mass.: Harvard University Press, 1989. Comprehensive and accessible history of French literature is arranged in a somewhat unusual fashion, approaching French literary history through selected landmark dates. Includes several valuable essays on the history of French fiction.

Jensen, Katherine Ann. *Writing Love: Letters, Women, and the Novel in France, 1605-1776*. Carbondale: Southern Illinois University Press, 1995. Examines the works of women novelists who used the epistolary tradition as a strategy for constructing novels and shows how men adopted this technique, often using female pseudonyms to take advantage of the popularity of this genre.

Kay, Sarah, Terence Cave, and Malcolm Bowie. *A Short History of French Literature*. New York: Oxford University Press, 2003. Discussion of French literature is divided into sections chronologically, with the first of three parts covering the earliest works through the Middle Ages, the second discussing the period 1470 to 1789, and the third addressing the period 1789 to 2000. Includes an informative introduction, illustrations, an extensive bibliography, and an index.

Showalter, English, Jr. *The Evolution of the French Novel, 1641-1782*. Princeton, N.J.: Princeton University Press, 1972. Classic work, with ambitious scope and clarity of presentation, is still a valuable source of information. Few critics cover such a wide range of novels, novelists, and themes.

Thiher, Allen. *Fiction Rivals Science: The French Novel from Balzac to Proust*. Columbia: University of Missouri Press, 2001. Presents analyses of the works of four important French novelists of the nineteenth century: Honoré de Balzac, Gustave Flaubert, Émile Zola, and Marcel Proust.

Unwin, Timothy, ed. *The Cambridge Companion to the French Novel: From 1800 to the Present*. New York: Cambridge University Press, 1997. Collection of critical essays provides an overview of the French novel of the nineteenth and twentieth centuries. Topics addressed include women and fiction, Romantic and realist fiction, and popular fiction of the nineteenth century.

Wolfgang, Aurora. *Gender and Voice in the French Novel, 1730-1782*. Burlington, Vt.: Ashgate, 2004. Analyzes four novels, including Marivaux's *The Life of Marianne* and Laclos's *Dangerous Liaisons*, and two lesser-known works by other authors, *Letters Written by a Peruvian Princess* and *Lettres de Mistriss Fanni Butlerd*.

French Long Fiction Since the 1850's

The ascendancy of the novel as the prime literary genre in France was established, by no means accidentally, during the reign of the so-called Bourgeois King, Louis-Philippe (r. 1830-1848). The shifting patterns of population and of economic status had made the middle class dominant, especially in that cradle of culture, Paris; it was perhaps no more than normal that the kind of reading the bourgeoisie preferred—the novel—should in that era have become what the nation as a whole preferred. The key factor in the novel's development to ascendancy, during the years 1830 to 1850, was that Honoré de Balzac, with his visionary ideal of the novel as society's true reflection and record, had imposed on the reading public, by his creative energy and example, his private conception of what a good novel should be: an accurate portrayal of some aspect of the contemporary world. By the start of Napoleon III's Second Empire in 1851, it could be said that, from an exercise in imagination, the serious French novel had become an exercise in observation. The novel had turned decisively realistic. Unhappily, however, the Second Empire, which owed its existence to the violent repression of revolt, was a sternly restrictive regime that alienated writers by its policy of censorship. After Napoleon seized dictatorial powers in the coup d'état of 1851, artists and intellectuals tended to withdraw into silence, concerning themselves with abstract theory rather than with the concrete, observable world around them.

Not surprisingly, the span of the Second Empire (1842-1870) was not a richly productive period for the French novel, or indeed for any of the literary arts. Accurate observation of reality was a risky business under such a regime, unless the reality being observed was inconsequential. On the basis of such reasoning, a literary school took shape in the 1850's that called itself Le Réalisme, publishing its own journal and offering readers novels exemplifying the aesthetic. Writers of this school avoided the attention of the state censor simply by defining realism as the art of depicting the ordinary, everyday life of humble citizens, arguing that literature had too long neglected the commonplace activities that were reality for the greatest number of French citizens. The novels produced by this school were, by and large, flat and pedestrian and did not sell; their authors had misunderstood the nature and purpose of Honoré de Balzac's insistence on the principle of realism in the novel.

Only one writer of that period really understood what Balzac meant—Gustave Flaubert (1821-1880), a brilliant recluse and a great admirer of Balzac's work, who managed to revolutionize the course of the modern novel with his first publication, the celebrated *Madame Bovary* (1857; English translation, 1886). Flaubert recognized that Balzac's ingenious notion of the novel as a record of what exists was focused on the need to be accurate, to avoid distorting reality, rather than on a specific definition of which aspect of reality merited attention from the novelist. Balzac was interested not only in the common person but also in all of society, which is why his novel *Le Père Goriot* (1834-1835; *Daddy Goriot*, 1860; also known as *Père Goriot*) offered a microcosm of Parisian society, from top to bottom, in the cast of characters associated with Madame Vauquer's boardinghouse. Flaubert's dismissive comment on the theories of the *réalistes* of the 1850's (Jules Champfleury, Louis-Émile-Edmond Duranty, and Ernest-Aimé Feydeau were the best known) was to note, dryly, that "Henri Monnier [author of a comic novel about a bourgeois who thinks and speaks in clichés] is not more real than Racine."

For Flaubert, the term "realism" as used by his contemporaries had no valid literary meaning, since it was restricted to but one corner of the observable world. Accordingly, he always rejected the label of "realist" whenever it was applied to him. Yet Flaubert fully embraced Balzac's insistence on fidelity to the real, for that was a matter of being true to the facts, which to Flaubert was not only a writer's obligation but also an aesthetic necessity; Flaubert was a firm believer in Plato's conception of beauty, according to which the preconditions for any object to be beautiful were that the object be true and good. Since the only worthy objective for a writer, Flaubert thought, was to create something beautiful, he argued that the writer's first task is to render the truth—*faire vrai* was his expression. If the writer's words faithfully render the truth, they will necessarily be morally good, for the truth cannot be evil, and if the words are both true and good, they meet the Platonic standard of beauty. From that reasoning, Flaubert derived the logic of his own practice as a novelist: Research the facts meticulously to be sure that what was written was true. Since the aesthetic value of what he produced depended wholly, according to his theory, on his fidelity to the truth, he took elaborate pains to get everything correct. Documentary research and recorded observations were indeed part of his method, as he readily acknowledged, but he refused to call that effort "realism," for that word distorted his literary purpose. The problem he saw with "reality" was that it can be whatever anyone decides it to be, whereas the truth is never merely a matter of opinion.

There was a good deal more to truth, as Flaubert saw it, than merely rendering the facts. To convey truth, words must be chosen and arranged properly, providing all the necessary nuances and distinctions and bearing the imprint of natural human speech. The mode of expression—which is to say, the style—is an implicit element in the truth of any assertion. A sentence or paragraph that is unnatural or artificial in its rhythm, sound, or vocabulary, Flaubert believed, was ipso facto false. For that reason, Flaubert devoted much of his time to rewriting, recasting his sentences over and over again, in search of the perfect arrangement that would "ring true" and pass the test of being read aloud. A sentence that could not be read aloud comfortably, without forcing the reader to breathe abnormally, was to Flaubert unacceptable and in need of revision. That kind of truth, both factual and stylistic, is a difficult standard to meet and explains why Flaubert took so long to complete each of his compositions and why his correspondence is filled with epic lamentations about the suffering he endured for the sake of his art—what he called *les affres du style*, or the tortures of style. There can indeed have been few writers for whom writing was a slower or more painful process than it was for Flaubert. Yet this strangely excruciating torture to which he subjected himself had a coherent rationale that points clearly to the nature of the revolution that Flaubert effected in the modern novel and that constitutes his most important contribution to its development.

While still an unpublished aspirant to the literary life, Flaubert meditated often on the art of composition and exchanged thoughts on the subject through letters with his friends. In response to a correspondent's question about his addiction to novel writing and his lack of interest in writing verse, Flaubert remarked that the art of poetry had been practiced for so long that every secret of meter, rhyme, rhythm, and sonority was known, and there were consequently no new discoveries to be made in that medium. The great attraction of novel writing for him, he declared, was that the art of prose was still relatively new and unstudied, and the most important discoveries about what makes a sentence artistic were yet to be made. From that observation, Flaubert elaborated a personal conception of the art of the novel that would make the novel as exacting to write as a poem, with each word weighed and selected for its perfect fit in its context, each sentence the perfect expression of its intended thought, and all parts of the novel carefully integrated into a harmonious and coherent whole. It became his ambition to raise the artistic level of the novel in his own lifetime and make it the equal of poetry in every respect. Much as he admired Balzac, he was pained by Balzac's frequent lapses of style and taste—which Flaubert knew to be the product of haste and a lack of concern for beauty. He set out to make his own first publication, *Madame Bovary*, a model of what a novel should be if it is an accomplished work of art. He succeeded, and the novel has never been the same since, anywhere in the Western world. Readers of *Madame Bovary* are still discovering new ways in which Flaubert's fanatic attention to detail gave that novel such a subtle, fine texture. Like a carefully wrought poem, *Madame Bovary* conceals its art beneath a seamless surface and gives up its secrets grudgingly.

It was not, however, *Madame Bovary*'s delicate art that attracted attention when the novel was published but rather what was perceived by the government censor to be its offenses against public morality. It was, after all, the story of sordid bourgeois adultery in a dull provincial town—shocking for the times. Because it did not concern heroic or noble people but rather scrutinized in minute detail the tawdry doings of commonplace characters, *Madame Bovary* was hailed—or denounced—for its daring realism, much to Flaubert's dismay. In spite of his many disclaimers, Flaubert was forced to watch helplessly as his suddenly notorious novel was avidly bought and read for what he considered to be the wrong reasons. His lovingly created masterpiece gave added impetus to the determinedly realist direction the French novel had taken since Balzac—an irony that Flaubert himself appreciated. Realism was what the age seemed to demand—or at least what the readers of novels in that age wanted—and Flaubert has been classified ever since as one of the masters of realism. Almost a generation passed before it was realized that the abiding importance of *Madame Bovary* was not that it was an example of realism but that it had transformed the novel, raising it to a high literary art and setting a new standard of excellence for the genre.

While the novel continued to be a popular form, published in profusion during the 1850's and 1860's, Flaubert now stands out as the only novelist of his generation to have made a lasting contribution to the genre. Only after the Franco-Prussian War did a new generation of young novelists begin to attract attention. The best of the new generation, it soon became apparent, were admirers and even disciples of Flaubert, who understood his artistic principles well enough to apply them to their own work and who had a clearly realistic bent. What set them apart was that their realism seemed more reasoned and more thoroughly grounded in theory and a sense of system. These novelists saw storytelling as both an art and a badly needed instrument of information gathering and analysis for a world grown too complex for the individual to grasp unaided. The special gift, and responsibility, of the artist, as they conceived it, was a superior sensibility that allowed a more profound perception of reality than most people commanded, as well as the ability to transmit that perception effectively through the power and attraction of art. Such ideas were repeatedly articulated by novelists in prefaces, manifestos, and journal articles during the 1870's and 1880's, presenting a concept of the novel's function that honored Flaubert's artistic idealism while simultaneously accepting a utilitarian role that served deeply felt public needs.

Authors in this new generation seemed to write not out of pure instinct or desire but rather as the result of a process of reasoning that justified their calling in practical terms; they were clearly influenced by their times, for it was an age of growing faith in the inevitability of progress based on the seemingly unlimited power of human reason to penetrate the secrets of nature and to understand—and therefore eventually control—the evolution of humanity's social institutions. It was an age that tended to place its hope for the future on the newly developed fields of sociology, psychology, and science. Science especially, with its well-advertised methods of investigation that guaranteed objectivity, had attained enormous public prestige by 1870, and writers found an irresistible logic in assimilating their own enterprise to that of the experimental scientists, seeing themselves as equally objective observers and investigators of the human animal.

The novelist who emerged as the clear leader of this new generation, Émile Zola (1840-1902), was also the one who undertook to codify and publicize its new artistic principles. The resulting action in the novel is not the product of the novelist's imagination, he argued, but the carefully observed consequence of the newly discovered laws of heredity, environment, and human physiology and psychology. In other words, Zola agreed with Balzac that the novel records and interprets social reality as it exists, but Zola insisted that the novel was able to be scientifically accurate and objective about many things not known in Balzac's day fifty years before. To underline the close relationship of the novelist's methods to those of the natural sciences, Zola gave the new form of realism the name "naturalism," and in a series of theoretical essays to which he did not hesitate to give the title *Le Roman expérimental* (1880; *The Experimental Novel*, 1894), he suggested that the novelist who chooses a milieu and a set of characters for a novel is actually setting up an experiment in much the same way as the laboratory scientist.

Whether Zola fully believed his published theories—and there is evidence that he did not, but was rather exercising his considerable gifts as a publicist—the concept proved popular and influential, and the great majority of the novels published in the 1880's were unmistakably in the naturalist vein. To be sure, not even Zola's own novels could be plausibly compared to a laboratory experiment in any literal sense, but the naturalist vein was readily identifiable by the tendency to write about a highly specific milieu, to provide the kind of detailed information about that milieu that could come only from direct observation or experience, and to govern all action in the novel by a consistently deterministic view of human nature.

In the heyday of naturalism, running from the mid-1870's to the mid-1880's, the major contributors, in addition to Zola himself, were Edmond de Goncourt and Jules de Goncourt, Joris-Karl Huysmans, Alphonse Daudet, and Guy de Maupassant, all of whom produced work of distinction that was widely read at the time. The novel was naturalism's ideal vehicle, but the movement extended, to an important degree, to the short story as well, and with less, but by no means negligible, impact on drama and even on poetry. Probably in no period in French cultural history has literature been more in consonance with the mood of the surrounding society than was the case during naturalism's hour of triumph, and for that reason, the greatest achievement of the naturalistic novel was that it provided for posterity an extensive, detailed, and quite reliable portrait of French society of the 1870's and 1880's. Zola alone delved into an impressive array of French social and economic institutions, each of which constituted a unique milieu: the world of banking, the atmosphere of the department store, the demimonde, squalid urban tenements, a coal-mining community, the artist's life, the railroad industry, and so on. One must add that, because the best of the naturalist novelists also wrote with skill and grace and imagination, striving to live up to the standards of form and style set by Flaubert, their works remain readable and worthy of study today, being both informative and aesthetically satisfying.

It was perhaps the very success of the movement, and the exceptional productivity of its members, that caused naturalism's dominance of the novel to wane toward the end of the nineteenth century. By 1890, the public seemed surfeited with solemnly presented information about themselves, and plainly longed for more inspiriting—or more frivolous—fare. A journalistic survey of 1891 confirmed that writers and readers agreed that naturalism's moment had passed. With historical hindsight, one can even recognize the telling symptoms of disaffection that had already appeared during the 1880's among some of naturalism's strongest partisans: the publication in 1884 of Huysmans's strange antinaturalist novel *À rebours* (*Against the Grain*, 1922); the violent antinaturalist manifesto of 1887 signed by five of Zola's young disciples; and the success of Paul Bourget's disturbing antirationalist novel *Le Disciple*, published in 1889 (*The Disciple*, 1898). Whatever the causes, there was no mistaking the fact that, in 1890, the French novel, its genius for realistic representation of society confirmed by a half century of outstanding achievement, had grown tired and was earnestly groping for new directions to take and new worlds to conquer.

New realities, new techniques: 1890-1940

If naturalism in literature had indeed run its course by 1890, it was surely because faith in science's role as the savior of French society had proved illusory. As it became clearer in the 1880's that there were many questions science could not answer, a wave of skepticism, sometimes turning to darkest pessimism, swept over intellectual circles, and it became fashionable to point to those phenomena of the natural order—including human nature—which the rationalism of the scientific method could never hope to explain. The irrational, the supernatural, the metaphysical, in all their variety of forms, once again fascinated those who had been most devastated by the discovery of the limits of science. By the 1890's, a religious revival and an intense curiosity about the human subconscious were in full bloom in France, and no time was lost in incorporating these new interests into the flow of fiction that continued unabated, inundating the reading public with what writers believed the public wanted to read.

Weary of the analysis of the observable data of their society, writers and readers now directed their attention to what was not observable, though just as real: the mysteries of belief and desire; the power over humans of the will to live and the consciousness of mortality; the exact nature of existence, time, and change—all the intangibles that define and distinguish the human spirit beyond its purely mechanistic components. Novelists began to pursue realities that were, by definition, missing in the naturalistic novel. Yet such is the power of custom that the analytical method, which had served the purposes of naturalism so effectively, continued to be the basic approach employed by the novelists of the 1890's and beyond. Though these were quite different realities with which they were now concerned, novelists instinctively recognized that the great strength of the novel was its representational or mimetic power, and they were content to use its analytical process to render these nonphysical realities as well.

A typical expression of this new mood among novelists can be found in the opening chapter of a novel about Satanism, *Là-bas* (1891; *Down There*, 1924; better known as *Là-Bas*, 1972), by Joris-Karl Huysmans (1848-1907), one of the original naturalist group. The protagonist is—what else?—a novelist who has been a practicing naturalist and an admirer of Zola. As the novel opens, the protagonist is discussing naturalism as a literary theory with a physician friend. They agree that Zola and company have served literature well but believe that the theory is now producing dull repetitions of its best work, because there is nowhere else for it to go, given the strict limits of material reality—the only reality naturalism recognizes. After the discussion, the protagonist (whose name is Durtal and who is clearly a surrogate for Huysmans himself) meditates regarding his next work and decides the naturalistic method itself must be adapted to the task of writing, not about the body exclusively but about the body and the soul, a duality that is far truer to the reality of human nature.

> It is necessary, he said to himself, to retain the veracity of the document, the precision of the detail, the substance and vitality of language in realism—but we must at the same time trace out a parallel path, another road, in order to get at what lies above and beyond the material realm, in a word, a spiritual naturalism.

With such arguments—or rationalizations, as some might say—Huysmans tried to bridge the gap between his past and present outlooks and to apply the methods of naturalism to the evocation of religious ideas, one of the new realities that naturalism had so far not touched.

Huysmans was articulating more than a private, personal mood with *Là-Bas*. By using a writer as a protagonist and by stressing the moral and spiritual realm as subject matter, he was forecasting the basic characteristics of the novel as it developed among the two generations of novelists whose work appeared between 1890 and World War II. The use of writers and other artists as fictional protagonists was a tradition that had begun with the Romantics and had been memorably represented in the work of Balzac, Flaubert, and Zola, to name only the most important French practitioners. In the original tradition, the focus of attention was on the troubled and often misunderstood personality of the artist, whereas after 1890 the focus tended to be much more on the nature of the art and of the creative process.

It should be noted that the novel about artists was not exclusively French; rather, it was European in scope, and because some of the earliest examples were in German, this type of novel has acquired the name *Künstlerroman*. What one may say of the European *Künstlerroman* generally—and it is entirely valid for the French tradition in particular—is that in the nineteenth century, its theme tended to be the sufferings of the artist as a human type. In the twentieth century, its theme shifted to the legitimacy of the art itself and the theoretical basis on which the art could claim to have a valid function in the world. Huysmans's novel *Là-Bas* was thus an early instance of what became a hallmark of twentieth century fiction: self-consciousness about the novel itself and a restless, self-scrutinizing investigation into its right to exist as an art. *Là-Bas* was equally the herald of a second hallmark of twentieth century fiction in France, the impulse to analyze and to probe into new realities not only more immaterial and more elusive than the realities that had preoccupied the naturalists but also more compelling and more urgent as topics of concern: the role of ideas in human conduct and the struggle with the moral and spiritual issues of existence. The twentieth century novel became, in short, a literature of thought and of moral anguish, characteristically centered on the dual themes of the legitimacy of art and of traditional values.

Nothing comparable to the naturalist movement took shape among French novelists as the nineteenth century turned into the twentieth century; no one theory or approach won enough adherents to become the focal center of a school or a movement. Novelists went their separate ways, each anxiously seeking new ground on which to stand as a replacement for the outworn naturalism. Between 1890 and 1914, the only coherent trends discernible in the torrent of novels being published were those suggested by *Là-Bas*: constant self-questioning about the nature of the novel and anxious exploration of ideas and moral problems. These two trends found a wide variety of modes of expression, however, leaving little in common to connect one novelist with another. Huysmans, for example, after *Là-Bas*, seemed to abandon the novel of invention, writing three barely disguised autobiographical narratives in which his novelist-character, Durtal, traverses the stages of Huysmans's own conversion to orthodox Catholicism and to acceptance of the monastic life. These narratives, though published as novels, have neither plot nor cast of characters nor structure; they simply record a writer's inward journey to salvation.

Meanwhile, Huysmans's contemporary, Anatole France (1844-1924), also wrote a novel with a writer as a protagonist, *Le Lys rouge* (1894; *The Red Lily*, 1898), but this novel treated the themes of love and jealousy and offered the ruefully ironic spectacle of a worldly and sensitive writer who could not understand a woman's desire for independence—in that way making an indirect comment on the limitations of the naturalistic novel. Thereafter, France turned to the theme of the past and tended to emphasize the inability of the historian to recover the past with any accuracy, suggesting the folly of claiming to represent reality exactly with the written word. Others of that same generation, such as Paul Bourget and Maurice Barrès, wrote in an increasingly dogmatic vein about moral and political ideas, to overcome the impasse into which they felt the naturalist novel had fallen by its presumed objectivity and determinism.

As for the younger generation of that period—those born around 1870, who began publishing in the 1890's and the early 1900's—they showed by their experiments with form and style, their introspective focus on artistic or intellectual protagonists, and their irresistible gravitation toward the world of ideas and of moral dilemmas that they, too, belonged fully to the postnaturalistic world. They worked in very different ways and had no discernible influence on one another. Among these distinctive voices were those of André Gide, Marcel Proust, Romain Rolland, and Colette. The period that the French call *la belle époque* (1890-1914) was, in the novel, a time of ferment, experimentation, and an uneasy search for new, viable directions, ways to renew and revitalize an art that had known great achievement but had lost its way when it narrowed its sights to the mere reporting of what can be readily observed.

Gide (1869-1951) and Proust (1871-1922), unquestionably the finest and most original novelists of their generation, succeeded in giving the novel new direction and new principles during the transitional era which preceded World War I, influencing profoundly not their own contemporaries but the next generation, those who came to prominence in the 1920's and 1930's. Nothing illustrates better, perhaps, the kind of privacy and isolation in which writers of that era seemed to work than the fact that these two innovators, although born only two years apart and schooled in the same Parisian literary milieu, should have had so little contact with each other and so little apparent appreciation for each other's work. It is even true that in 1913, Gide, acting as editor of *La Nouvelle Revue française*, the journal he helped to found, turned down for publication an early segment of Proust's great novel, *À la recherche du temps perdu* (1913-1927; *Remembrance of Things Past*, 1922-1931, 1981), because he failed to recognize its originality. It is also true, however, that Gide made a full and honorable admission of his error in judgment after World War I, when Proust was awarded the prestigious Prix Goncourt. The principal works of both authors were completed before the war, but it was only after the war that each became famous and truly influential, when a younger generation could appreciate the novelty of their separate yet similar concepts of what fiction could accomplish.

For Gide, fiction was always a personal, if not literally autobiographical, vehicle for expressing both the moral conflicts of private existence and the dilemmas of the novelist's craft. In two early specimens of the first-person confessional novel, *L'Immoraliste* (1902; *The Immoralist*, 1930) and *La Porte étroite* (1909; *Strait Is the Gate*, 1924), Gide examined both sides of the ethical problem created by the coexistence within the same individual of a reasoned rejection of traditional morality and a deeply ingrained puritan outlook. At the same time, both novels demonstrated, in a brilliant display of technique, the dangers of the first-person narrative style by presenting a text whose surface assures the narrator's absolute sincerity but whose subtle undercurrents alert the attentive reader to the narrator's bad faith. The two works, taken together, shake the reader's confidence both in the moral coherence of human behavior and in the truth of narrative discourse.

A few years later, Gide turned to the comic vein with *Les Caves du Vatican* (1914; *The Vatican Swindle*, 1925; better known as *Lafcadio's Adventures*, 1927) to tell a willfully improbable and convoluted story, featuring wildly unrealistic characters set in very real and carefully described surroundings. The central event of the novel brings together on a train, by pure chance, two of the main characters, who are strangers to each other; one character throws the other out a window of the speeding train, purely for the pleasure of performing a motiveless crime and observing the confusion of the authorities who try to decipher its meaning afterward. By such devices, Gide contrived to make his comic novel a disturbing challenge both to the reader's preconceptions about the rational basis of human conduct and, even more, to standard notions about order and coherence in the form and structure of novels. Life is never neat or orderly, Gide seems to be saying, and the traditional modes of fiction actually falsify reality, rather than represent it, by imposing an artificial order on events and presenting them as clear instances of cause and effect.

Gide's most daring and innovative challenge to the novel, however, came in 1925, with the publication of his longest and most complex narrative, *Les Faux-monnayeurs* (*The Counterfeiters*, 1927), the only one he chose to identify with the label "novel." There can be no doubt that *The Counterfeiters* is intended as a critique of the novel itself, since its central figure is a novelist who happens to be writing a novel called *The Counterfeiters* and who keeps a diary of his artistic dilemmas and decisions as he writes. The title ostensibly refers to the activities of a band of teenagers who defy society by making counterfeit coins and passing them off as real, but Gide is explicit about the title's more important symbolic value, suggesting not only that most individuals are "moral counterfeiters," passing themselves off as other than who they really are, but also that novelists are unwittingly the greatest counterfeiters of all, passing off as the true image of reality the sadly distorted products of their imaginations. What Gide did for the novel was to undermine previous assumptions about reality and about the fictional techniques appropriate for the rendering of that reality, and to offer models of narrative that could deal with the stubborn ambiguity and irrationality of the human world. Gide simply shattered the foundation upon which the naturalist novel of his predecessors had been constructed.

Proust chose a different approach, but he had approximately the same objective: to refute the validity of the traditional novel of realism and to demonstrate the techniques and concepts by which a novel can engage with a comprehensive view of reality and still be a work of art. These ideas he embodied in a single monumental novel, in excess of three thousand pages in length, composed over a period of more than a decade and bearing the evocative title *À la recherche du temps perdu*, rendered felicitously into English by C. K. Scott Moncrief with a phrase from Shakespeare as *Remembrance of Things Past*. The novel was so long that it had to be published in separate volumes, in spite of Proust's reluctance to distort his design in that way. Indeed, the first volume had to be published at the author's own expense in 1913, because no publisher would undertake the complete work, and its continuation was delayed until after the war. The final volumes appeared posthumously, for although Proust raced against a debilitating illness to complete his novel in 1922, he did not live to see all of it published.

Proust's one great novel may stand as the greatest single achievement of the twentieth century in the French novel and one of the most revolutionary works of fiction in the French canon. At the heart of the novel is a philosophical concept, the notion that time has a major role in shaping one's perception of reality and that traditional narrative modes have never given that role its due. Above all, Proust wanted to deal with the problem of the rapid passage of time and the consequent obliteration of the past, unless the memory of that past can somehow be recovered and preserved. Those ideas are implicit in his title. Two thematic strands make up the armature of that search for lost time that the title promises: One strand is the first-person account that the narrator, Marcel, is able to give of his own growing up, thanks to his involuntary memory, which brings back the past so vividly; the other strand is the careful dissection of the society in which Marcel grew up and the changes in it that he witnessed and finally learned to understand, as memory overcame the effects of time and enabled him to see the truth. When these two strands fuse at the end of the novel, Marcel realizes why he wants to be a writer: If the effects of involuntary memory can suddenly conjure up his own past so completely and in such exact detail, only the power of the written word can fix that past permanently and preserve it for future generations. For that reason, the calling of novelist seems to him both noble and worthy, and, having thus confirmed his vocation, Marcel decides to write the novel that the reader has just finished reading—a novel that demonstrates how art can recapture lost time.

As long, meandering, and formless as the novel can seem to readers making their way through it for the first time, there is a firm guiding hand in control at all times, for Proust planned his novel meticulously, like a piece of architecture, as he was fond of saying. Some have suggested that symphonic form is a better analogy for the way the novel is composed, because of Proust's use of themes that are stated, developed, interwoven with other themes, and returned to in a kind of grand recapitulation at the end. Characters appear and reappear, always as seen by Marcel at the different stages of his own development, so that they seem to have changed, sometimes startlingly. In this way, Proust is able to make readers aware of time and allows them to experience the effects of time's passing in the same way they experience it in real life. This was one of the ingenious devices Proust invented to make time a tangible presence in his novel and to convey the quality of one's encounter with it. Perhaps the novel's greatest success is that it really does recapture lost time for the reader: The world in which Proust grew up, and which he frequented during his formative years, springs to life in the witty and brilliant pages of the novel, and the reader comes away grateful that one corner of the past, at least, has been saved from oblivion. It is a pleasant paradox of Proust's work that, while the world he describes is, for the most part, snobbish and petty, utterly deserving of the scathing satire he heaps upon it, the reader is nevertheless gladdened by its resuscitation. Even a distasteful image can please when it represents, as does Proust's novel, human victory over time.

Proust's great masterpiece, which combines the values of the *Künstlerroman* with the grand-scale re-creative power of the naturalist novel at its best, proposes a new way to look at reality by adding the dimension of time, and demonstrates a new range of possibilities for giving a novel freedom to grow without losing the sense of form. These are capital enrichments of the novel's potential, but Proust's greatest contribution to the genre's development was surely the exalted function he imagined for the art of fiction: to reclaim the past for posterity from the dead hand of time. Proust's vision helped to give new dignity and prestige to the calling of novelist in the twentieth century.

Proust and Gide were not alone in laying the groundwork for influential new directions in the novel during the period before World War I. A significant, though lesser, role was also played by their contemporary Romain Rolland (1866-1944), who published a novel cycle almost as massive as Proust's masterpiece well before the first volume of *Remembrance of Things Past* appeared. This novel was a ten-volume saga of a musician's life called *Jean-Christophe* (*John-Christopher*, 1910-1913; better known as *Jean-Christophe*, 1913), published between 1904 and 1912. While there is no evidence that Rolland's multivolume novel had any direct influence on Proust's, the surface similarities at least are striking, since both works have an artist's consciousness at their center and both exhibit a looseness of structure aimed at breaking free of the nineteenth century tradition of the well-made novel. Rolland made no original contribution to the definition of reality or to the discovery of new novelistic techniques for the rendering of reality; he was, in fact, taking Balzac's novel sequence *La Comédie humaine* (1829-1848; *The Comedy of Human Life*, 1885-1893, 1896; also known as *The Human Comedy*, 1895-1896, 1911) and Zola's *Les Rougon-Macquart* (1871-1893, 20 volumes; *The Rougon-Macquarts*, 1896-1900) and modernizing the idea by giving it more unity.

Jean-Christophe is organized around a single central character rather than a family of characters or a society, and in relaxing the inclusive realism that would depict a milieu in depth (in order to concentrate on the psychological and moral development of the protagonist), Rolland can be credited with having renewed and modernized the concept of the novel cycle as developed by Balzac and Zola. That his creation proved a fruitful example for others can be seen in the successful cycles published in the 1920's and 1930's by Roger Martin du Gard, Georges Duhamel, and Jules Romains, to say nothing of the 1920's success of Proust's cyclic novel, which probably owed something, at least, to the fact that

Rolland had created an audience willing to give its attention to a multivolume composition.

The period between World War I and World War II was dominated, in the novel, by the influences of Gide and Proust and, to a degree, by that of Rolland. Insofar as that period produced fiction that broke with nineteenth century practices and pursued new forms and new themes, it was a vigorous continuation of the trends established during the belle époque. It cannot be said, however, that the interwar era changed the direction or the concept of the novel in any fundamental way, as Gide and Proust had done earlier.

Several writers carved out unique niches for themselves through their work in this period, mainly because of highly individual personal traits rather than because of new ideas about the genre. As a result, those authors generally had no influence on posterity. Each was one of a kind. Typical of the leading novelists of the between-wars generation was Colette (1873-1954), who perfected the small but delicate art of the novel of female sensuality. In her many novels, she made the depiction of all the pleasures of the senses her personal domain, evoking the sensations of smell and touch and taste as successfully in prose as Charles Baudelaire (1821-1867) had done in verse in the previous century. Wildly controversial and popular (as much for her open lesbian relationships and her three marriages as for her work), Colette became in 1945 the first woman admitted to the Académie Goncourt, and in 1948 she became its president. Her most popular novel, *Gigi* (1944; English translation, 1952), was made into a motion-picture musical, released in 1958, and subsequently was adapted as a Broadway musical. Colette was considered France's greatest writer during her lifetime, and she received a state funeral when she died in 1954.

The Catholic novelist François Mauriac (1885-1970) analyzed the sinful compulsions of the newly enriched provincial bourgeoisie with fine psychological insight and a remarkable flair for the dramas of the soul. Although he was also named a member of the Académie Goncourt and was awarded the Nobel Prize in Literature in 1952, his art and subject matter were too private to have inspired a trend.

The two outstanding novelists of the 1930's, Antoine de Saint-Exupéry (1900-1944) and André Malraux (1901-1976), are often compared because they are both associated with the novel of adventure and with writing about aviation as a new frontier. On inspection, however, their work, too, can be seen as highly individualized and only superficially similar. Saint-Exupéry romanticizes flying, presenting aviators most engagingly as the heroic pioneers of a new industry, venturing bravely and alone into an alien environment. Malraux, in contrast, writes obsessively about the adventurer as tragic hero, conscious of his doomed destiny as a mortal and determined to achieve some kind of dignity in his fated encounter with death. Malraux may be credited with inventing a modern technique of narration, eliminating the nineteenth century dependence on passages of physical description to set scenes and on sequential narrative to effect transitions from scene to scene. Instead, he plunges the reader abruptly and without preliminaries into each new scene, doing nothing to connect the scenes in terms of time or even cause and effect. The method forces the reader to participate in the "creation" of the novel as a coherent tale and, at the same time, imparts an extraordinary feeling of rapid action and high tension to the novel. In that technical aspect of his work, Malraux was an innovator and has apparently had some influence on subsequent generations, being one of the likely sources, for example, of the nervous, cinematographic style of rapid scene shifts employed in the novels of Alain Robbe-Grillet (1922-2008) and Michel Butor (born 1926) in the 1950's and 1960's. Malraux, however, is a solitary exception in his generation.

The conception of what a novel should be and how it should be composed, as exemplified by the novels published in France in the half-century from 1890 to 1940, was essentially the creation of Gide, Proust, and Rolland, insofar as that conception differed in significant degree from nineteenth century practices in the genre. The outbreak of World War II wrote a forcible end to that era, and what emerged after the war, in the domain of fiction, ushered in a new phase in the history of the novel in France.

The Age of Anxious Experiment: After 1940

Symptoms of the new phase could have been spotted by discerning readers even before the outbreak of war, in 1938, when Jean-Paul Sartre (1905-1980) published his first novel, *La Nausée* (*Nausea*, 1949), and in 1939, when Nathalie Sarraute (1900-1999) brought out her first work of fiction, *Tropismes* (*Tropisms*, 1963)—both works now recognized as belonging in spirit to the postwar era. In the late 1930's, however, those works passed almost unnoticed; they were not accorded serious attention until a decade later. The war years, mostly years of the Nazi Occupation in France, did not encourage much literary activity, and the production of novels slowed considerably, though one may note that the celebrated novel *L'Étranger* (*The Stranger*, 1946), by Albert Camus (1913-1960), also now associated with the postwar atmosphere, was published in 1942 without causing any stir.

With the bitter experience of World War II and the Occupation behind them, the French were suddenly receptive to philosophies of despair, because what they had witnessed of human nature and the value of life during the war proved to be profoundly demoralizing. The existentialist movement, led by Sartre, the Theater of the Absurd, which dominated the postwar Paris stage, and the first eyewitness accounts of the Holocaust, which began to find their way into print after 1945, all confirmed the postwar French public in their mood of pessimism, for all those phenomena proclaimed the same fundamental perception of life—namely, that it was random and meaningless, the product of pure chance and ungoverned instinct, and that such human-made concepts as virtue, morality, conscience, and belief in a just God had been revealed to be grotesque fantasies by the events the world had recently witnessed. In such an atmosphere, it was obviously difficult for both writers and readers to take the novel, as it had existed before the war, with any degree of seriousness or to believe very readily in the Proustian vision of the novel as the human instrument of victory over time. The urgently felt need in the late 1940's, and indeed throughout the 1950's and 1960's as well, was to devise a new kind of novel capable of giving adequate and truthful expression to this mood of despair and nihilistic outlook.

During the first postwar decade, it was chiefly those novels that reflected the philosophies of despair in their content that seemed to meet the public need best, while beginning in the late 1950's, public success went especially to those novels that dramatically shattered tradition in their form and technique. Both kinds of novel, however, were self-consciously experimental, for their authors were plainly responding to the anxious fear that the novel was a dying genre; they were motivated by the desperate hope that, with the right formula, the novel could be brought back to life and made relevant again. Indeed, since 1940, the French novel can be said to have been passing through an age of anxious experimentation, with both form and content, which has been giving to the genre a hesitant and tentative character suggestive of a period of transition, the outcome of which remains in doubt. Moreover, no durable trends have yet appeared, and few novels or novelists of this period seem likely candidates for lasting fame. There are, however, concepts and innovations associated with the philosophical novels of the 1940's and 1950's and with the New Novel group of the 1950's and 1960's that promise to have an ongoing influence on the way novels will be conceived and written in the future.

The leading innovators of the philosophical novel were Sartre and Camus, both of whom were trained in philosophy and could deal competently and naturally with philosophical ideas in their writing. Sartre's most important novel, *Nausea*, takes the form of an intellectual's diary and is therefore a novel of ideas—at the opposite extreme from a novel of action or adventure. Indeed, nothing happens in *Nausea* except that the diarist, Roquentin, who has been writing a biography of a minor historical figure, decides to abandon his project as pointless. The novel's focus is on the thought process by which Roquentin reaches his decision: He comes to realize that the past has no existence and that it is therefore an act of futility to try to recover it. Moreover, in a kind of strange, visionary experience, he discovers that the mere sight of what does exist, including himself, fills him with the sensation of nausea. His nausea is a symbolic reaction to his discovery that all existence is without inherent value and that no person or object has any significance beyond itself, even though people are constantly contriving specious arguments that would invest the world with transcendent meaning.

Although the novel offers a variety of examples of this incorrigible human need to find meaning in life—a philosophical idea that Sartre adapted from German philosopher Martin Heidegger (1889-1976)—the real originality of the book lies in the way that philosophical idea is communicated. Rendering the discovery of meaninglessness as a physical sensation, nausea, was a stroke of imaginative genius on Sartre's part. Moreover, he describes the sensation in elaborate clinical detail, including the stomach-turning alien ugliness that familiar objects such as a newspaper page, a tree's roots, or his own hand suddenly take on for Roquentin. The descriptions are as precise and as vivid as any to be found in a realistic novel of the nineteenth century, even though what is being described is an idea in Roquentin's mind rather than a tangible object. Sartre, in other words, had contrived a metaphoric means of rendering a new reality, the "feel" of an idea, thus fusing literature and philosophical thought. It was a device that Sartre himself would use again, effectively, in his plays, and that other writers of his generation would adapt to their own needs. The device added significantly to the expressive capabilities of the novel, once it was fully understood. Paradoxically enough, however, the philosophical idea that Sartre had discovered how to render in literature implied the pointlessness of all literature. It is perhaps because of that underlying contradiction that Sartre's fiction writing reached an impasse soon after the appearance of *Nausea*. During the 1940's he attempted a cyclic novel in four volumes as a portrait of his times, abandoning it after completing three undistinguished volumes.

The innovative contribution to the philosophical novel made by Camus was, like Sartre's, embedded in the first novel he published, *The Stranger*; it was also, as it happens, related to the same philosophical idea of the radical meaninglessness, or absurdity, of life. Camus invented not a metaphor but a character as the means of translating the idea into fictional terms. *The Stranger* is a monologue in written form, the account by a man named Meursault of his chance involvement in a crime and his subsequent trial and conviction. What fascinates the reader is that Meursault, by the indirect evidence of his own choice of words, has a disconcertingly detached and unemotional perception of the events he describes, not because he is pathological but because he is, in the most profound sense, a stranger to the beliefs and values of his society, as though he were a creature from another planet. Meursault's flat, matter-of-fact narrative style dramatizes for the reader the consequences of a confrontation between the philosophical idea that life has no meaning and a social order that attributes significance to life by all its laws, institutions, and customs. The confrontation shocks the reader into recognizing that it is Meursault who sees the world as it really is, while everyone around him invents fictions that give the illusion of meaning to their actions. Camus thus imagines an idea as a person in order to explore the full consequences of that idea when loosed upon the real world. It was a device he found fruitful, refining it with even more impressive results in his next two novels, *La Peste* (1947; *The Plague*, 1948) and *La Chute* (1956; *The Fall*, 1957). All three works constitute a major contribution to the novel of ideas, marrying the discipline of philosophy with the art of the novel.

The phenomenon known as *le nouveau roman* (the New Novel) can best be understood not as something really new in itself but as a systematic assault on the old. No two of the practitioners of that kind of novel actually apply the same principles in their work, so it is hardly accurate to speak of it as a coherent movement or school. Rather, it is a case of a generation of writers who concluded, each independently, that the novel was an outworn form whose conventional devices of plot, characterization, point of view, and time representation distorted the reality of the twentieth century world. Their analyses of the inadequacies of the conventional novel led them to experiment with novels that did without one or more of the devices they found to be so unsatisfactory.

Nathalie Sarraute, suspicious of the neat logic of human psychology as portrayed in the nineteenth century novel, depicted characters whose behavior is enigmatic, erratic, springing from inner impulses—and therefore more authentically human, from her point of view. Marguerite Duras (1914-1996) rejects both plot and psychological coherence in favor of depicting the effects of mood, atmosphere, and chance on events and of showing that people often tend to live their lives vicariously, in fantasy, rather than in coherently motivated actions. Her best-selling novel is the autobiographical *L'Amant* (1984; *The Lover,* 1985). Samuel Beckett (1906-1989) reduces plot, character, and time to the most primitive and elemental level conceivable, depicting derelicts who are little more than passive consciousnesses undergoing the brief but meaningless experience of existing in the mud and slime of the material world.

The most abstractly theoretical of the New Novelists, Alain Robbe-Grillet (1922-2008), conducted a series of novelistic experiments in which he gradually eliminated all the conventional devices of nineteenth century fiction, leaving only an incoherent sequence of images whose meaning never becomes certain for the reader. His best-known work, *La Jalousie* (1957; *Jealousy* 1959), evokes a suspected love triangle without employing any elements of plot or characterization and without supplying any clarifying circumstantial details of time or place. The narrator remains unidentified, unmotivated, and uninvolved, recording in cameralike fashion only what can be seen at a given time and from a given vantage point. So far as the reader can tell, the drama of the love triangle may be real or only imagined, a fact or the fevered fantasy of a jealous husband. The reader is deliberately given no way of knowing the truth. By implication, Robbe-Grillet has composed a scathing critique of a thousand conventional novels of jealousy, which analyze in subtle detail the motives of all the characters, describe intimately the actions of sin or folly committed, and so contrive to create the illusion of an eyewitness account of events that no person could know about or understand so completely. *Jealousy* illuminates brilliantly the artificialities of the conventional novel, but whether it succeeds as a novel as well as it succeeds as criticism is open to serious question.

In 2001, after twenty years without a new novel (having published only works of autobiographical fiction since 1981), Robbe-Grillet published the spy thriller *La Reprise* (*Repetition*, 2003). In this work, the protagonist, Henri Robin, is a spy who finds that his memory is unreliable and his account of a murder is contradictory and suspicious. As in *Jealousy,* the eyewitness account cannot be trusted, and the reader is tossed about between memory and the subconscious.

The most significant French novelists of the second half of the twentieth century are generally considered to be Marguerite Yourcenar (1903-1987), Michel Butor, and Claude Simon (1913-2005). They explored in highly creative ways the human effort to deal with the heavy weight of past events on present lives. Claude Simon received the Nobel Prize in Literature in 1985, and Yourcenar became, in 1981, the first woman elected to the French Academy since its creation in 1635. Although these novelists are highly original, their careers have been very different. Yourcenar was born into a wealthy French family. She emigrated to the United States in 1938 and became a U.S. citizen in 1947. Butor was born in France and taught literature for many years at the University of Geneva. Simon was born on Madagascar, an island off the southeastern coast of Africa, which was then a French colony. He was educated in France. During World War II he was a prisoner of war, and as a result of this traumatic experience he developed a tragic view of the world and came to understand the fragility of human life.

Yourcenar is especially famous for her historical novels, which frequently deal with classical antiquity. Her 1951 book, *Mémoires d'Hadrien* (*Memoirs of Hadrian*, 1954; also known as *Hadrian's Memoirs*), is her masterpiece. She presents this novel as autobiographical fiction written by the aging Roman emperor Hadrian to his friend Marcus. Yourcenar carefully recreates court intrigue and power struggles in Rome: Hadrian reflects on his long reign and his successful efforts to expand the boundaries of the Roman Empire. Although Hadrian considers himself a tolerant and peaceful emperor in comparison with such violent tyrants as Nero and Caligula, it soon becomes clear to the reader that the Roman peace of which Hadrian is so proud was achieved at a terrible human cost. Fear, terror, and exploitation were the foundations of Roman domination in its extensive colonies. Readers come to distrust the first-person narrator in this fictional autobiography. Hadrian is oblivious to the true suffering of the vast majority of his subjects, and he compliments himself on the many beautiful monuments that he constructed throughout the Roman Empire. Hadrian's love for the young man Antinous brought him a great deal of pleasure, but Hadrian fell into profound depression after the death of his lover. In his grief, Hadrian ordered coins, monuments, and statues to honor the memory of Antinous. His obsession with death makes it abundantly clear to readers that Hadrian is a self-centered individual who is indifferent to the real needs of his subjects.

Claude Simon also explores classical antiquity in his 1969 novel *La Bataille de Pharsale* (*The Battle of*

Pharsalus, 1971). The Battle of Pharsalus was the decisive battle in the Roman civil war. After the defeat of the republican forces, Julius Caesar succeeded in destroying the Roman Republic, and he established a dictatorship ruled by omnipotent emperors. As the narrator reflects on Caesar's description of this battle, he remembers his own difficulty in translating Caesar's Latin sentences into French and decides to visit the historical site where the battle took place. As he approaches Pharsalus, the narrator comes to realize that the use of military force by Caesar to overthrow an established and relatively democratic government is disturbingly reminiscent of the Nazis' use of military force to occupy countries and enslave citizens. This historical novel includes numerous references to the horrendous crimes against humanity committed by the Nazis and their collaborators. Memories of these traumatic events continue to haunt the narrator long after the liberation of Europe from Nazi domination. Both Simon and Yourcenar show in their novels that thinking about the past can enable people to understand more deeply the meaning of contemporary events.

Simon is known not just for his themes of war, history, time, and visual perception but also for his experimental style. His novels, which have been compared to those of Proust and of William Faulkner (1897-1962), frequently alternate passages of narration with passages of stream of consciousness, and it is not unusual for single sentences to run three pages or more. Punctuation is used rarely, with the exception of parentheses. Despite these manipulations, Simon's prose is readable and has attracted a large audience, although he once commented, "I am a difficult, boring, unreadable, confused writer." His autobiographical novel *Le Tramway* (2001; *The Trolley*, 2002) is representative: It is a collection of memories and anecdotes loosely connected through image or stream of consciousness, not chronologically arranged. Individual scenes focus on the visual but hint at the themes of aging (Simon was in his eighties when he wrote this work), the experience of war, and the pleasures of youth.

Michel Butor also eloquently described how the past continues to influence people; his finest novel is generally considered *La Modification* (1957; *Second Thoughts*, 1958; better known as *A Change of Heart*). In this second-person narrative, the narrator is speaking to a French businessman named Léon Delmont, who is traveling by train from Paris to Rome to join his mistress Cécile. For years Léon traveled regularly between these two cities; while in Paris, he stayed with his wife Henriette, and when in Rome he stayed with his mistress. He has a guilty conscience, and as the train slowly moves toward Rome, Léon thinks about his previous train trips between the French and Italian capitals. Readers come to understand Léon's hypocrisy and selfishness. By the end of the novel, readers no longer care whether Léon decides to live with Cécile or Henriette; just as in Yourcenar's *Memoirs of Hadrian*, readers of *A Change of Heart* are profoundly alienated from the major character.

New voices

At the close of the twentieth century and the beginning of the twenty-first, France, no less than other European countries, embraced the new voices that came with the era of globalization. After Simon won the Nobel Prize in 1985, the next French writer to win it was Gao Xingjian (born 1940), an immigrant from China, who won in 2000 for his novels and absurdist plays. Gao, who majored in French in college, writes in Chinese and has produced Chinese translations of the works of English and French absurdist playwrights. He settled near Paris in 1987 and became a French citizen in 1997. Gao's best-known novel is *Ling shan* (1990; *Soul Mountain*, 2000). The story, based on a trip the author took through rural China after he received a misdiagnosis of terminal cancer, is about a man's search for a mythical mountain and his exploration of what it means to be an individual self and a member of the human community.

Other important writers who illustrate the diversity of French novelists in this period include Christine Angot (born 1959), best known for her autobiographical and metafictional novel, *L'Inceste* (1999), about an incestuous affair with her father; Virginie Despentes (born 1969), whose novel and film, *Baise-moi* (1999), which is explicitly violent and sexual, has been referred to as an example of the "New French Extremity"; postmodernist Simonetta Greggio (born 1961 in Italy), whose first novel, *La Douceur des hommes* (2005; the softness of men), made her a critical and popular success; and Michel Houellebecq (born 1958), controversial for his explorations of the interchange between economics and sexuality, whose *La Possibilité d'une île* (2005; *The Possibility of an Island*, 2005) is set within a cloning cult. Other contemporary French writers have explored the experience of North African immigrants in France; novelists in this group include Nina Bouraoui (born 1967) and Farida Belghoul (born 1958).

In 2008, the Nobel Prize in Literature went to J. M. G. Le Clézio, author of novels as well as short stories, travel diaries, essays, and books for children. Over a long career, Le Clézio has worked in a variety of novel forms. His first novel, *Le Procès-Verbal* (1963; *The Interrogation*, 1964), is an experimental work exploring insanity and language. Later, he turned from experimentalism and began to write realist fiction about travel and the environment, and about childhood. By the time he won the Nobel Prize, he had become one of the most popular writers in France, although rather few Americans had heard of him. Among his best-known works are *Désert* (1980; *Desert*, 2009), about the conflict between desert tribes and the French colonialists in Morocco in the period 1910-1912; *Le Chercheur d'or* (1985; *The Prospector*, 1993), set on the island of Mauritius; and *Onitsha* (1991; English translation, 1997), about a European boy traveling through colonial Nigeria in the 1940's. By the end of the twentieth century, the French novel had moved beyond France's cities and countryside, and beyond the lives of the French middle class, to embrace the wider world.

Murray Sachs; Edmund J. Campion
Updated by Cynthia A. Bily

Bibliography

Baguley, David. *Naturalist Fiction*. New York: Cambridge University Press, 1990. Contains a thoughtful analysis of French naturalist novels written in the late nineteenth century and explains clearly the originality of Émile Zola as a novelist.

Best, Victoria. *An Introduction to Twentieth-Century French Literature*. London: Duckworth, 2002. Provides an overview of French literary movements and the major writers of the period, including Marcel Proust and Marguerite Duras.

Cardy, Michael, George Evans, and Gabriel Jacobs, eds. *Narrative Voices in Modern French Fiction*. Cardiff: University of Wales Press, 1997. Collection of essays includes excellent studies on important French novelists, including Nathalie Sarraute, Gustave Flaubert, and Albert Camus.

Fallaize, Elizabeth. *French Women's Writing: Recent Fiction*. New York: Macmillan, 1993. Presents insightful analyses of many important French women writers who were active in the second half of the twentieth century.

Frackman Becker, Lucille. *Twentieth-Century French Women Novelists*. Boston: Twayne, 1989. Provides good analyses of the contributions of several major twentieth century French women novelists. Includes a solid bibliography of primary and secondary works.

Kay, Sarah, Terence Cave, and Malcolm Bowie. *A Short History of French Literature*. New York: Oxford University Press, 2003. Discussion of French literature is divided into sections chronologically, with the first of three parts covering the earliest works through the Middle Ages, the second discussing the period 1470 to 1789, and the third addressing the period 1789 to 2000. Includes an informative introduction, illustrations, an extensive bibliography, and an index.

Motte, Warren. *Fables of the Novel: French Fiction Since 1990*. Normal, Ill.: Dalkey Archive Press, 2003. Focuses on the works of French avant-garde novelists since 1990. Includes a bibliography and an index.

Pasco, Allan H. *Novel Configurations: A Study of French Fiction*. Birmingham, Ala.: Summa, 1987. Good introduction to the French novel includes a series of well-written studies on such major novelists as Émile Zola, Marcel Proust, and Joris-Karl Huysmans.

Worth-Stylianou, Valerie, ed. *Cassell Guide to French Literature*. London: Cassell, 1996. Includes excellent studies on the general development in French novels. Each essay is supplemented with a solid bibliography.